COMPOST: PRODUCTION, QUALITY AND USE

Proceedings of a symposium organized by the Commission of the European Communities, Directorate-General Science, Research and Development, held in Udine, Italy, 17–19 April 1986

COMPOST: PRODUCTION, QUALITY AND USE

Edited by

M. DE BERTOLDI

Università di Pisa, Italy

M. P. FERRANTI, P. L'HERMITE

Commission of the European Communities, Brussels, Belgium

F. ZUCCONI

I.C.A. Università, Napoli, Italy

ELSEVIER APPLIED SCIENCE
LONDON and NEW YORK

ELSEVIER APPLIED SCIENCE PUBLISHERS LTD
Crown House, Linton Road, Barking, Essex IG11 8JU, England

Sole Distributor in the USA and Canada
ELSEVIER SCIENCE PUBLISHING CO., INC.
52 Vanderbilt Avenue, New York, NY 10017, USA

WITH 258 TABLES AND 269 ILLUSTRATIONS

British Library Cataloguing in Publication Data
Compost: production, quality and use.
1. Compost   2. Agricultural wastes
I. De Bertoldi, M.   II. Commission of the
European Communities. *Directorate-General
for Science, Research and Development*
631.8′75   S661

ISBN 1-85166-099-2

Library of Congress CIP data applied for

Publication arrangements by the Commission of the European Communities, Directorate-General Telecommunications, Information Industries and Innovation, Luxembourg

EUR 10636

LEGAL NOTICE
Neither the Commission of the European Communities nor any person acting on behalf of the Commission is responsible for the use which might be made of the following information.

Printed in Great Britain by Galliard (Printers) Ltd, Great Yarmouth

PREFACE

Composting is one of the topics studied in the framework of the research and development activities carried out by the Commission of the European Communities in areas of priority concern such as energy, raw materials, the environment, etc. and is part of the programme on the recycling of urban and industrial waste.

The programme was originally adopted by the Council of Ministers on 12 November 1979. Its aim is to coordinate, at Community level, national research projects being carried out in Member States and subsidised by public funds ; these coordinated activities also include the organisation of meetings between experts appointed by the Member States on specific and topical subjects of common interest, and the dissemination of scientific information at seminars, colloquia, symposia, and so on.

In fact, the potential for composting waste is enormous if one considers the quantities of agricultural waste which arise in the Member States of the Communities.

Therefore, it is obviously in the interest of Society as a whole to encourage the composting of agricultural waste so as to rationalise our use of resources and to improve protection of the environment.

In order to decide on those projects which, at Community level, could most effectively help to bring about the wider use of composting methods, it was decided to set up a committee of experts to coordinate composting research who were chosen by the Member States of the Community and appointed by the members of the Advisory Committee on the Management of the Programme on the Recycling of Industrial Waste. The committee of experts (the Contact Coordination Group on Composting) was given the task of indentifying priority research topics in respect of which specific regard to the length of the programme, lead to positive results.

The work done to date leads to the formulation of a number of working hypotheses regarding what still remains to be done at Community level. One of the difficulties recognised by all concerned is the current lack of specifications for different types of compost. These would guarantee users a specific product quality and properties which remain standard over time and which would be tailored to the different ways in which compost is used. Because there are no standard specifications, it is difficult to market compost and there is also a serious effect on the product image and on market development potential. This applies both to compost from urban waste an to compost from agricultural waste, because even though there are perhaps fewer problems with agricultural waste, there are still the same obstacles to marketing it more widely.

One of the priority tasks at Community levels is therefore felt to be any action which would encourage the wider use of compost. Alongside this, there is a need to provide information for potential users in order to help them decide on the product most suited to their particular needs (cultivation of vegetables, flowers, fruit trees, timber crops, etc.).

It is also important to ensure that products are absolutely harmless (i.e. phytotoxicity levels have to be checked) and to provide instructions for use and details on how to obtain the best results.

The need for action along these lines at Community levels was stressed repeatedly at the symposium on "Biological reclamation and land utilisation of urban wastes" held in Naples from 11 to 14 October 1983, and at the seminar on "Composting of agricultural and other wastes", held in

Oxford on 19 and 20 March 1984. Both meetings confirmed the degree of interest which the countries of the Community have in the composting of agricultural waste, and the gaps which still exist in this field showed that more research projects, more coordination, and more results are needed within the different research areas involved in this process.

CONTENTS

SESSION II : QUALITY OF THE PRODUCT

SESSION III : USE OF COMPOST

SESSION V : STRATEGIES, LEGISLATION AND MARKETING

OPENING SESSION

Present situation and future prospects of composting in Friuli-Venezia Giulia

Energy balance in compost production and use

Horticultural use of compost

Compost specifications for the production and characterization of compost from municipal solid waste

PRESENT SITUATION AND FUTURE PROSPECTS OF COMPOSTING IN FRIULI-VENEZIA GIULIA

PIERLUIGI NASSIMBENI
Centro regionale per la sperimentazione agraria per il Friuli-V. Giulia

Authorities, ladies and gentlemen, I am pleased and honoured to add to professor De Bertoldi's greetings and to the wishes of the authorities my own thanks to all of you for being here as speakers or simply to attend this meeting, which is very important for our region.

We insistently demanded this symposium to the EEC and, being the organizers of it, we have given all our care to a conference we believe is going to have an importance that goes beyond a merely scientific interest.

We are in fact going to learn from the General Reports that will be made during these three days, things of great importance for us, because of our situation and that will not be of purely theoretical interest, but will involve all that has been projected and proposed on the creation of new plants, on the characterization of the product, on the utilization of the product itself.

It will all be immediately faced with our administrative and territorial reality, since our region, Friuli-Venezia Giulia, is living in these last few years a period of great development and change.

For what concerns Compost, in fact, our present reality is the following : over a population of 1,250,000 inhabitants there are about 200,000 of them, living in 50 communes, who are served by composting plants. The production of Compost amounts to about 15/20,000 tons per year.

In other 30 communes the draining of the human solid waste of 400,000 people is carried out by incineration plants (the most important of which is in Trieste). The remaining 650,000 inhabitants get rid of their waste through sewers.

The only important remark that deserves to be made is that the Composts produced - coming from technologically different plants - are characterized by great differences. Moreover they have not a well-defined market in our region, even if they are known and used in areas near the plants.

Besides this situation it exists a trend, in our Administration, which, following a scheme aimed to get the maximum recovery of energy from raw materials and organic substance, has singled out some main lines to be followed and it is doing so together with the local bodies. This trend has been illustrated in a first hypothesis of a Regional Plan for the draining of urban solid waste of 1982 and in further modifications and integrations.

This line of action privileges the defence of the environment, which is the main and only objective to be pursued, but it also considers the draining methods depending on the different realities and taking into account the economic advantages and the resources available. Nevertheless in this project incineration, controlled discharge, composting and recycling must coexist. In fact a sole method of draining can present practical advantages together with risks and dangers, general or particular deficiencies.

Anyway, the main conclusion is that nowadays it is not possible to choose, without valid reasons, to destroy great quantities of energy, of raw materials, of organic substance rather than putting them into the production cycle again. This consideration lays at the basis of all our choices and our programme is always referring to it. For what particularly concerns agriculture, it is wrong to waste great quantities of organic substance and composts in areas like ours where the soil is facing a worrying and dangerous process of deterioration because of agricultural methods which have driven cattle-breeding away from our farms.

In accordance to these choices, therefore, during last year two composting plants were financed and are now being realized. One of them is situated in the district of Udine (S. Giorgio di Nogaro) and the other in the district of Pordenone (S. Quirino). They will serve a population of about 300,000 inhabitants.

In the next few years another important plant to be situated in Udine is going to be realized and put into activity. It will replace the old DANO, which was the first to be built in Italy about 30 years ago, and it will serve a population of about 300,000 inhabitants, that is all the Central Friuli area.

Therefore in not too long a time, possibly during the 90's, the composting plants in the region - 6 or 7 - will concern a population of more than 700,000 inhabitants, a percentage of about 60 % of the whole resident population.

Trieste and other towns - agriculturally less important - will carry on incinerating waste with a consequent recovery of heat.

The compost production of the above mentioned plants will amount to about 70,000 tons per year, a quite remarkable quantity, even if is not enormous, which could be risen if we could composting RSU with sewage sludge, thus solving also the problem of its draining and recycling.

Table 1 - Presumable situation in the 90's with a finanoial commitment of several thousands of millions.

	Plants per district	Pop.	Tons of compost per year
PORDENONE	1 or 2	150,000	15,000
UDINE	3 or 4	500,000	50,000
GORIZIA	1	50,000	5,000
		700,000	70,000

Therefore if on one hand our region could be quite safe, having faced and solved the problem of the draining of solid urban waste following the more advanced and universally accepted programmes (recycling and recovery), on the other hand it should find an adequate collocation for the growing production of compost into the agricultural sector.

As to this, I am sure we are going to face great difficulties, not only in our region Friuli-Venezia Giulia, but also in the whole nation, if adequate answers will not be found to these three major problems :
1) First of all that of plants, that should be aimed to obtaining a product which suits the needs of agriculture as well as those of the draining of urban solid waste.
2) Secondly, that of the production of a kind of compost, or better of a range of composts with physical-chemical and microbiological characteristics that should be easily fixed and singled out.
3) Third, the individualization of the sector, or sectors, which can be

most interested in this product on an agricultural level.

We must also remember that if an answer to these problems will not be found, many doubts could arise regarding the general choices that up to now have privileged, even if in a balanced way, programmes involving composting. In other words, if the present commercial disorder should continue — a disorder causing the presence on the market of too many kinds of compost with too wide a range of prices, some of them even too high, thus puzzling the consumer and leading him to avoid the product altogether — the great investments asked to the collectivity in order to realize these plants will not be justifiable any longer.

As to the first problem treated, much too often we can see that the designers engaged in the realization of sometimes complex plants are really only qualified to solve the engineering problems.

It should also be kept in mind that when a plant is aimed to obtaining a remarkable amount of compost, it must be built in order to accomplish this function.

Therefore the designer must project a structure able to give us a product devoid of inert substances (glass, plastics, metallic parts, etc.), with the highest possible contents of organic substance and, above all, a product which undergoes an adequate process of stabilization and that is not phytotoxic.

The last qualities could be considered unimportant, but one should remember that a farmer who has had negative experiences with phytotoxic or not stabilized products will hardly use compost a second time.

Because of this we ought to obtain precise settlements on what should be the characteristics of the product to be processed and an amelioration of the parameters for composting so that a plant could be easily operated also by not highly qualified personnel as can be found in most managements.

The best solution would be a complete automation in the control of the process, applying the new computerized technologies.

The second problem is that of the characterization of these materials. A non-defined product cannot find its place on the market. As regards this, when some time ago it was published on the "Gazzetta Ufficiale" an insert to the law n. 915 in which, besides other regulations, were fixed the physical, chemical and microbiological characteristics of compost, the maximum concentration of some elements into the soil and the maximum amounts of compost to be used in the different agricultural situations, we found them not realistic, restrictive and, in some parts, not appliable. Thus we prepared, with other colleagues, a proposal to modify the law and we sent it to the Minister of Ecology through the National Board of Research (CNR).

I therefore believe that out of this meeting we will be able to get valuable information to reach a better characterization of compost and precise indications on the experiences already made in the other countries.

The third aspect is that of the utilization of compost in agriculture. Compost is a product which is available in great quantities, but these are much more limited than the capabilities of absorption of the agricultural sector. In fact, if in our region we wanted to give in one year to the soils destined to grape-growing (23,000 ha) 10,000 kg per hectare (100 m^2) — certainly not a very great amount — we would need 230,000 tons as against the 70,000 tons that will be produced after the putting into activity of all the plants included in the programme. Consequently it proves necessary to single out the sector, or sectors, of our agriculture where compost can be more conveniently utilized.

It will be therefore important to value, from an agronomical as well as financial point of view, whether compost is to be used on all the cultures of an area situated around the plant itself, thus privileging the economy of distribution, or only in those areas where the soil will get more benefit from it because of its particular nature, or again just for specific and limited uses (i.e. floriculture, horticulture, or arboriculture, more specifically in our reality of viticulture).

This is therefore the situation in our region, a region which has found in composting a basic line to be followed in treating urban solid waste. In less than five years, that is from now to 1990, this will concern 700,000 inhabitants (60 % of the population), from the present 200,000. They will be served by these technologies and a financial effort that could be estimated today at 70 thousand million Lire.

To make this choice a winning one we must :
- as to plants : get at producing a compost that is perfect from a chemical, physical, microbiological and sanitary point of view — consistently with the characteristics of the organic substance we started from ;
- as to law and commerce : obtain laws defining better the characteristics of compost and attesting them so that we can offer the consumer a defined and possibly certified product ;
- as to utilization : single out the sectors of utilization with the best added value possible.

I believe that the meeting we are now opening is going to give precise answers to all those questions, since in the last few years we have greatly improved.

All the studies, research, experiences that each of you will present in this symposium will help everyone else to get to know the respective improvements but above all will help us, researchers and tecnicians of this region to put into practice and on a large scale what has been done best in the other Countries.

The programme described will lead our region to hold the first place in Italy as regards to the importance given to composting in relation to the number of inhabitants and the area concerned. This situation could allow the theoretical models hypotized to be verified in practice. We do hope this is going to happen and will provide in the future a datum-point also for other situations.

For all this we have to thank the EEC, the CNR (Italian National Board of Research), the International Society of Horticulture for choosing our region as seat of this meeting, the University of Udine for the financial support, its help and its collaboration.

We also want to thank the Minister of Agriculture and the Regione Veneto, F.A.O., E.N.E.A. (National Board for Atomic Energy) and to all the other associations for their help.

A warm thank you also to the speakers for their great commitment and to all the people attending this symposium for their presence. I thank you again wishing you all good work.

ENERGY BALANCE IN COMPOST PRODUCTION AND USE

L.F. DIAZ, C.G. GOLUEKE, and G.M. SAVAGE
Cal Recovery Systems, Inc.
Richmond, California, U.S.A.

Summary

An overview is presented of the processes involved and the energy
consumed in the preparation, production, and utilization of the compost produced in the composting of the organic fraction of municipal
solid wastes (MSW) and sewage sludge. The total energy required to
produce, transport, and apply compost is estimated to be on the order of 34.4 kWh/Mg of MSW for the case of a compost market located
10 km from the production facility. Energy expended in preparing
the MSW for the compost step amounts to about 16.0 kWh/Mg. Energy
consumed in the compost step averages about 5.1 kWh/Mg for the three
systems analyzed. Post-processing consumes about 6.1 kWh/Mg.
Transportation requires about 7 kWh/Mg; and landspreading the product, about 0.2 kWh/Mg. The paper closes with a brief survey of potential energy savings resulting from the utilization of compost in
agriculture.

1. INTRODUCTION

Prior to the latter part of the 1960's, composting was considered in
many developed and less developed countries to be an attractive means of
stabilizing the organic fraction of urban wastes. However, beginning
with the late 1960's, that favorable recognition began to wane and composting lost its popularity with respect to its use in urban waste management. Undoubtedly, a major factor in the loss in favor was the fact
that, as a whole, the urban waste stream was becoming increasingly unsuitable for composting. Other contributing factors were an absence of
markets for the finished product and the ready availability of low-cost
land for waste disposal. Recently, however, this unfavorable turn of
events has begun to change such that composting is regaining some of its
lost popularity.
Now that the role of composting in solid waste management seems to
have been delineated, at least to some extent, certain key factors remain
to be resolved before the role can be accepted and implemented on a broad
scale. In general, these factors involve economic and environmental considerations. A key economic consideration is the energy involved in composting and its practice. This consideration prompted an attempt on the
part of the authors of this paper to resolve basic questions regarding
the energetics involved in the production and utilization of compost from
urban solid wastes and municipal sludges. Progress made in pursuing this
attempt is described in the present paper.
A major problem encountered in the pursuit of the study was the nature and scarcity of information on the energetics of composting in all

of its aspects. The problem manifested itself in a multiplicity of variables and nebulous data. Despite this unfavorable combination, it was
possible to make a distinct advance in the knowledge and understanding of
the energetics involved.

Our presentation begins with an exploration of the energy expended
in all aspects of the compost process, i.e., feedstock preparation (pre-
processing), the composting process itself, and post-processing. The section on processing is followed by an exploration of the energetics involved in the disposition or application of the compost product, beginning with transport to the point of application or disposal and ending
with a survey of credits for energy saved through the use of compost. An
interesting point with regard to the latter is the fact that composting
is indirectly responsible for a net gain in energy by way of its promotion of growth of plants, thus making possible the fixation of solar
energy through photosynthesis.

2. PROCESS ENERGETICS

2.1. Characteristics of Feedstock

2.1.1. Municipal Solid Wastes

A search for an acceptable alternative means of final disposal soon
brings with it the realization that little or no reliable information is
to be had regarding the quantity and composition of the wastes to be disposed. To supply some of the missing information and to illustrate the
shortcomings of MSW as a substrate for composting, and at the same time
furnish clues as to the nature and amount of its energy, data on the composition of MSW generated in the U.S. and in communities in eight countries are assembled and tabulated in Table 1. The data in Table 1 are
especially useful in that they are based on actual measurements and not
simply on truck counts and visual observations. Truck counts and visual
observations unfortunately can and often do lead to the commission of
substantial and costly errors.

2.1.2. Municipal Sludges

A discussion of the energetics of municipal composting would be incomplete if sewage sludges were excluded from consideration, inasmuch as the
composting of sludges has gained much wider acceptance than that of MSW.
Because sludges are primarily organic in nature, they are more readily composted than is MSW, and hence the energetics involved are more favorable.

Inasmuch as quantities and characteristics of sludge generated are
functions of locale and type and extent of sewage treatment, they vary
widely. Depending upon stage and type of treatment, sludge production
can range from 530 m^3 to 20,000 m^3 per million m^3 of wastewater treated
[2,10,17]. These volumes do not include the sludges that result from
chemical precipitation (flocculation) in tertiary treatment. For purposes of estimation, primary sludge production commonly is considered to
be from 0.07 to 0.11 kg/capita/day.

2.2. Preparation of the Substrate (Pre-processing):

Because pre-processing accounts for a sizeable portion of the energy
consumed in the compost process as a whole, pre-processing is described
and discussed in some detail at this time. The pre-processing of raw MSW
involves three main groups of unit processes, namely, size reduction, recovery of desired components from the waste stream, and segregation of
the recovered components from each other.

By suitably arranging and operating these processes, a feedstock can
be produced that: 1) is free of "impurities" (glass, plastic, metallic

Table 1. Quantity and Composition of Municipal Solid Waste (percent wet weight)[a]

	Manila, Philippines [1]	La Paz, Bolivia [6]	Asuncion, Paraguay [7]	Lima, Peru [8]	Rio de Janeiro, Brazil [20]	Mexico City, Mexico [23]	Caracas, Venezuela [4]	Sasha Settlement, Ibadan, Nigeria [27]	Richmond, California U.S.A. [28]
Putrescibles	49.8[b]	53.5[b]	60.8[b]	34.3	47.7[b]	56.4[b]	40.4[b]	76.0	14.5
Paper	12.9	16.4	12.2	24.3	31.5	16.7	34.9	6.6	51.3
Metals	5.8	5.9	2.3	3.4	5.9	5.7	6.0	2.5	6.5
Glass	3.5	5.2	4.6	1.7	4.7	3.7	6.6	0.6	14.6
Plastics, rubber, leather	1.6	4.1	4.4	2.9	3.9	5.8	7.8	4.0	7.0
Textiles	1.8	3.8	2.5	1.7	4.1	6.0	2.0	1.4	3.2
Ceramics, dust, stones	17.7	11.1	13.2	31.7	2.1	5.7	2.3	8.9	2.9
Weight/capita/ day (kg)	0.42	0.50	0.64	0.96	0.54	0.68	0.94	0.17	--
Bulk Density (kg/m^3)	209	350	390	176	--	--	220	--	140

a) Based on actual measurements.
b) Includes small amounts of wood.

objects); 2) has a moisture content of 30 to 50 percent; and 3) has a particle size distribution such that the maximum dimension is within the range of 1.3 to 5 cm for paper and vegetable matter, and less than 1.3 cm for wood or comparable material.

2.2.1. Size Reduction

Size reduction is a relatively high-energy and maintenance-intensive operation. In the shredding process, energy consumption is a function of the particle size distribution of the incoming material and of that of the output. For example, it has been shown that the energy required to size reduce MSW to a characteristic particle of 2.44 cm is about 15 kWh/Mg [24]. (The characteristic particle size (X_0) is the size that corresponds to 63.2 percent of the cumulative particles passing through a screen of a certain dimension.) As shown in Figure 1, energy consumption increases with decrease in particle size. Other factors that influence energy consumption in size reduction are feed rate, moisture content, relative speed of the size reduction devices (hammers, rings, gears, etc.), and the clearance between hammers and grates [24]. A factor that should be added to the relatively high energy requirement is that of machine wear. Studies have demonstrated that the shredders evaluated in the field exhibited a hammer wear in the range of 0.02 to 0.1 kg/Mg of refuse processed [24].

2.2.2. Air Classification

Air classification usually follows size reduction. It is a unit process that has been used extensively in the waste processing industry

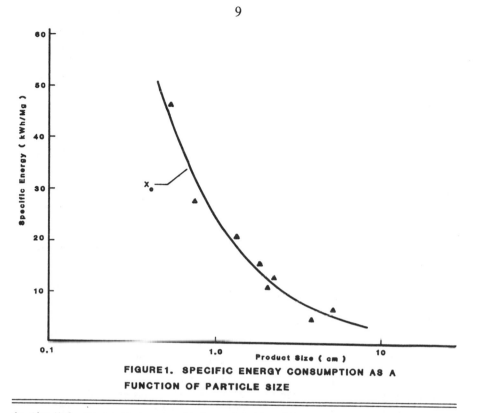

FIGURE 1. SPECIFIC ENERGY CONSUMPTION AS A FUNCTION OF PARTICLE SIZE

in the U.S. to separate shredded municipal solid waste into two fractions, commonly termed the "light" and "heavy" fractions. (Apparently, air classification was not used on a meaningful scale in Sweden as of 1984 [3].)

Several types of air classifiers are available on the U.S. market. The maximum capacity of classifiers currently available is approximately 70 Mg/h. Results obtained in reported studies [9] indicate that about 4.1 kWh/Mg were consumed in an air classifier system that processes roughly 30 Mg/h. Other reported results indicate a range of 3.4 to 4.2 kWh/Mg of throughput.

2.2.3. Magnetic Separation

Magnetic separation is perhaps the least complex of the methods used in the recovery of materials from the MSW stream. The two main types are the overhead belt and the drum magnets. The magnet in the overhead belt magnet is stationary, whereas the belt that surrounds it normally is set to travel in the same direction and faster than the conveyor belt. Typically, an overhead belt magnet is installed above the conveyor that is transporting shredded MSW. In some cases, the magnetic belt may be installed parallel to the conveyor and in other cases, perpendicular. With respect to a drum magnet, the drum rotates past a stationary magnet positioned within it. A drum magnet can be installed over a conveyor, over the end of a feeding mechanism, or above a conveyor head pulley.

Typically, magnetic separation is arranged to take place after some type of size reduction, because size reduction is thought to free ferrous metals from "contaminating" materials (e.g., labels and coatings). In other cases, the heavy fraction produced in air classification is subjected to magnetic separation. The reason for the latter arrangement is that air classification concentrates to some extent the feedstock to the magnetic separator. This is a result of the removal of much of the paper and plastics from the feedstock.

The average energy consumption by a magnetic belt is on the order of 0.4 kWh/Mg of material processed.

2.2.4. Screening

The basic function of screening is the separation of materials on the basis of differences in particle size. Normally, screening results in the separation of a mixture of particle sizes into two or more groups.

For the most part, three types of screens are used in the resource recovery industry -- the vibrating, the disk, and the trommel. Of the three types, the trommel screen has proven to be particularly well suited for processing refuse. Undoubtedly, the main reason for its suitability is the fact that the "tumbling" motion imparted to the particles prevents them from "blinding" the screen openings. In some cases, a trommel screen may be used to process raw refuse prior to size reduction ("pre-trommeling") and in others, to process various fractions of shredded refuse ("post-trommeling"). Trommeling may be successfully used for removing impurities (primarily plastics) from the compost product.

Trommel screens consume on the order of 0.8 to 1.1 kWh/Mg of material processed.

2.2.5. Miscellaneous Equipment

A typical refuse processing facility probably would require a few pieces of equipment in addition to those described in the preceding sections. Pieces of such equipment that collectively would have an impact on the overall energy budget are conveyors and mobile equipment such as front-end loaders. The energy consumption of each of these pieces of equipment varies with a number of factors, of which material density, flow rate, and size of motor are examples. Although precise numbers for energy consumption were not available, allowances were made for them in the development of the energy balances.

2.2.6. Manual Sorting

In situations in which labor is both abundant and inexpensive, manual sorting can be substituted for one or most of the unit processes without detriment to the quality of the final (processed) feedstock. The exception is size reduction. Reasons for the exception become readily apparent when one considers the nature of the material and the volumes involved.

2.3. Composting

For the purposes of this paper, the composting step includes the conveyance of the pre-processed refuse or refuse/sludge mixture to the composting area and then composting it in two stages, namely, primary composting and secondary composting. Alternatively, the two stages may be described as active composting and maturation or curing.

The entire collection of compost systems can be classified into two broad groups, "open" and "closed," albeit with some overlap between the two. A synonym for the "open" system is the "windrow system." Synonyms for the "closed" system are "mechanized" and "in-vessel."

2.3.1. Windrow Composting

Windrow composting can be subdivided into the "turned" and the "static pile" ("forced air") approaches. With the "turned-pile" approach, aeration is accomplished by periodically "turning" the piles. "Turning" is done by tearing down and reconstructing the pile or windrow. The operation brings about a renewal of air in the interstices of the pile, and therewith, a renewed supply of oxygen to the microbial populations in the pile. Several well-designed machines are now available with which turning can be accomplished rapidly and efficiently.

In a turned pile in which oxygen availability is the limiting factor and all other factors are at optimum levels, rate of composting becomes a function of frequency of turning. In a static pile system, the pile is underlain with air ducts through which air is forced up and through the piled material. The static pile system is well documented in the recent literature. Perhaps the most effective use of the static pile system is with materials that are granular in structure, relatively homogeneous in nature, and decidedly porous.

2.3.2. Mechanized Composting

Although the variations in the designs of mechanized systems are relatively numerous, they all are centered on the mode of providing aeration. Depending upon the design of the system, aeration may be accomplished either by agitating the composting mass or by forcing air through it, or by a combination of the two. Agitation may be done by tumbling and/or stirring the material. Most of the reactors presently on the market are but slightly altered versions of those available in the 1950's. The principal changes are in the claims made for reactor performance. Most claims have in common the following: 1) a transfer to sludge of the claims previously made for refuse; and 2) a magnification of prior claims (e.g., extremely short detention times).

2.3.3. Energy Requirements

For the purposes of this paper, a calculation was made of the energy required to produce a compost product from a mixture of MSW and digested sludge. The calculation or analysis is based upon a facility having the capacity to process 1200 Mg of MSW plus 300 Mg of sludge per day (i.e., a total capacity of 1500 Mg/d). A schematic diagram of the refuse processing plant (pre-processing) is presented in Figure 2. As the figure

FIGURE 2 - SCHEMATIC DIAGRAM OF PRE-PROCESSING STEP

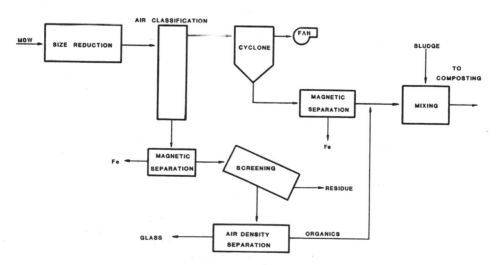

indicates, the basic unit processes are size reduction, air classification, screening, and magnetic separation. The design of the pre-processing plant is such that the major portion of the organic matter in refuse is recovered. Similarly, the refuse is processed in a manner such that objectionable materials are removed from the feedstock to the extent that an acceptable finished compost is produced.

As is indicated in Figure 2, the organic fraction of refuse is mixed with the sludge. The mixture is then composted. The analysis takes into account two types of composting systems or approaches, namely, the open (windrow) and the enclosed. After the composting step has been completed, the composted material is further processed (post-processing) to impart to it the desired quality. A schematic diagram of this stage of processing is presented in Figure 3.

A summary of the energy requirements involved in producing the compost product is given in Table 2. The data are divided in the table under the headings "windrow" and "enclosed." The data under "windrow" are further subdivided under the headings "turned" and "static." In addition, the data are presented for each major stage of the production process (pre-processing, composting, and post-processing). For purposes of comparison, pre- and post-processing designs common to all schemes are presented.

According to the data in Table 2, the preparation of the substrate (refuse) requires about 16 kWh/Mg or almost 50 to 70 percent of the total energy used in the entire compost process. The energy required for the composting step varies from 0.45 to 10.1 kWh/Mg, depending upon which system is used in the step. At this point, it is again emphasized that the amount of operational data on enclosed compost systems in the open literature is indeed sparse. On the other hand, data on open systems are more plentiful. Because of this disparity, values presented in Table 2 for enclosed systems are not as firm as those presented for open systems.

According to Table 2, the post-processing step involves the expenditure of 6.1 kWh/Mg. The expenditure for miscellaneous functions and activities amounts to about 1.0 kWh/Mg.

FIGURE 3
SCHEMATIC DIAGRAM OF POST PROCESSING STEP

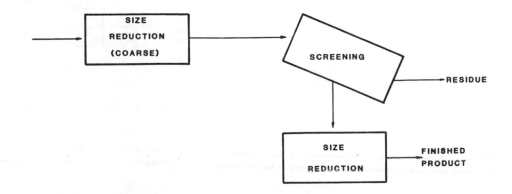

Table 2. Energy Requirements for Compost Production
(Based on 1200 Mg/d of MSW and 300 Mg/d Sludge)

Stage	Specific Energy Consumption (kWh/Mg MSW)		
	Windrow		Enclosed
	Turned	Static	Generic
Pre-Processing			
Mobile equipment	0.2	0.2	0.2
Size reduction	10.0	10.0	10.0
Segregation (air classifier, magnetic separator, trommel screen, stoner)	4.6	4.6	4.6
Conveying	0.5	0.5	0.5
Mixing (refuse/sludge)	0.7	0.7	0.7
Subtotal	16.0	16.0	16.0
Composting			
Turner	0.25	--	--
Blowers	--	4.5	--
Aerator, feed, discharge	--	--	10.0
Mobile equipment	0.2	0.1	0.1
Subtotal	0.45	4.6	10.1
Post-Processing			
Sizing	5.8	5.8	5.8
Conveying	0.1	0.1	0.1
Mobile equipment	0.2	0.2	0.2
Subtotal	6.1	6.1	6.1
Miscellaneous			
Ventilation, lighting	1.0	1.0	1.0
TOTAL	23.55	27.7	33.2

Finally, the energy expended in the three major stages, i.e. energy required to produce a Mg of finished compost amounts to about 24 kWh with the turned system to about 33 kWh with the enclosed system.

2.4. Post-Processing

The primary function of post-processing is to process the composted material such that it meets the specifications demanded by the use to which it is to be put. Hence, the degree of post-processing may range from minimal for compost destined to serve as landfill cover to extensive for compost intended for use in crop production. In practice, the specifications mostly pertain to particle size dimensions and freedom from impurities that lower the quality and utility of the product. Such being the case, post-processing is mostly a matter of screening and, in some instances, of size reduction. Screens and equipment used in post-processing are comparable to those used in pre-processing, and hence need not be described again in this section.

Pertinent not only to post-processing, but also to all steps in compost processing, is the important fact that different types and degrees of processing result in different qualities of compost products. Some of the major factors that influence the quality of the finished product include stability, concentration of contaminants, nutrient content, particle size, and appearance. There is a definite trade-off in waste processing between degree of processing and product quality and quantity. Typically, for a certain processing strategy, the quantity of the product decreases as the quality increases. Of course, as the "purity" of the product improves, the amount of reject materials increases. In addition, the cost of processing also increases as the concentration of impurities (i.e., the quality of the material) increases. Additional allusions to post-processing are made in Section 3, which deals with application energetics.

3. ENERGETICS OF COMPOST USE

3.1. Description of Compost Product
Aside from the merits of composting as a waste treatament device, an important reason behind most decisions to compost is the eminent utility of the compost product. Inasmuch as time and space do not permit a detailed exploration of all aspects of the utility of the compost product, this paper concentrates on the use of compost in agriculture. However, the discussion is preceded by a brief generic description of the material, inasmuch as the nature and extent of its utility are determined by its characteristics.
3.1.1. Generic
The term "generic" is used to make a distinction between the characteristics of compost in general and those specific to a given compost product. The latter vary from product to product and are functions of the nature of the raw waste and of the method of composting.

A suitable, and at the same time definitive, adjective for a properly and fully composted material is "humic," in that compost is an aggregate of amorphous substances that result from the complex of microbiological activities responsible for the breakdown of plant and animal residues. With respect to chemical nature, it is a heterogeneous mixture of substances, among which are the numerous compounds synthesized by the microbial complexes formed from decomposition and the materials that are resistant to further breakdown. As a humus, compost is not in a biochemically static condition.
3.1.2 Specific
As stated earlier, the chemical composition and appearance of a compost product directly after the completion of the composting phase and prior to any final processing of the product for purposes of marketing, etc., are largely functions of the chemical nature and physical characteristics of the waste that was composted. Because the eventual change in appearance is a reflection of a radical change in properties, all physical descriptions in this section pertain to the compost product directly after completion of the compost process.

The combined nitrogen, phosphorous, and potassium (NPK) content of compost is not at a level that would fit the legal definition of "fertilizer" prescribed in many countries. As is true with regard to appearance and other characteristics, the NPK content of the compost product is largely a function of that of the raw material. It follows then, that if the NPK content of the raw waste is appreciable, the NPK content of the product usually is also appreciable.

Because of the relation described in the preceding paragraph, the NPK content of compost varies widely. With respect to raw MSW, the nitrogen concentrations of refuse from three different countries in the two Americas can be taken as representative. They were found to be: U.S., 0.5 to 1 percent; Brazil (Sao Paulo), 2 to 4 percent; and Mexico (Mexico City), 2 to 4 percent. The nitrogen content of the composted refuse ranged from 0.4 to 1.6, 0.1 to 0.4, and 0.2 to 0.6 percent of the fresh weight, respectively. Generally, the phosphorus content (as P_2O_5) was only slightly less than that of the nitrogen content. The potassium content usually is much lower, unless wood ash is present. If the original carbon-to-nitrogen ratio (C/N) of the raw waste is not excessively high and the carbonaceous fraction is not unduly resistant to microbial attack, the C/N of the compost product will not exceed 20/1.

3.2. Agricultural Application
3.2.1. Advantages
The disparity between inorganic fertilizers and compost as a source of plant nutrients is apparent from the comparisons made in Table 3. Although the NPK content of compost may be relatively low, the major utility of compost in agriculture is not in its NPK content, but rather in the beneficial effect it exerts on the structure and other characteristics of the soil. Nevertheless, the fertilizer aspect should not be overlooked.

Because of the NPK in compost, the amount of the three elements added as a chemical fertilizer can be reduced in proportion to their concentration in the compost. Moreover, the addition of the compost brings with it an increase in efficiency of chemical NPK utilization, as was demonstrated by Krishnarajan and Balasubramaniyan [13] in their experiments. The increased efficiency comes from fixing into microbial protoplasm, the fraction of the chemical fertilizer loading that is not used by the crop. The bound NPK is slowly released as the microbes die off. In a soil devoid of or deficient in organic matter, from 30 to 35 percent of the nitrogen, 20 to 30 percent of the phosphorus, and a lesser percentage of the potassium added as a chemical fertilizer is leached beyond the root zone, and therefore is of no utility to crop production. Finally, compost is an important source of trace elements.

Table 3. Comparisons of NPK Contents of Compost with Those of Inorganic Fertilizers[a]

Fertilizer	Weight of Fertilizer Supplying Nutrient to Crops Equiv. to 1-Mg of Compost in Year of Application[b]		
	Nitrogen (kg)	Phosphorus (kg)	Potassium (kg)
Urea	3.8	--	--
Ammonium nitrate	5.1	--	--
Ammonium chloride	6.7	--	--
Ammonium sulphate	8.3	--	--
Di-ammonium phosphate	8.3	13.0	--
14:14:14 complex	12.5	21.4	--
Ammonium phosphate	15.9	14.3	--
Triple super phosphate	--	13.8-15.3	22.9
Muriate of potash	--	--	6.2-8.2

a) Adapted from Reference 5.
b) Composition of typical farm compost on a fresh weight basis and under tropical conditions: 0.7 percent N, 0.3 percent P, 0.4 percent K, 50 percent moisture. It is assumed that 25 percent of N will become available to the crop in the year of application. Availability in succeeding years is not involved.

The beneficial effect had on the structure of the soil is one of the major advantages that accrue from the use of compost, in that structure ranks with nutrient content in the determination of soil productivity. The tendency of compost to bring about soil aggregation makes the soil friable. Friability, in turn, is closely related to soil aeration and water-holding capacity [19] in that an increase in friability is accompanied by an increase in water retention and degree of aeration. Aeration and moisture are important factors in the development of root systems. An added advantage is the prevention of soil compaction and its attendant difficulty of cultivation.

Use as a mulch is another aspect of the water conservation potential of compost utilization. The utility of compost as a mulch is enhanced by the fact that eventually it can be incorporated in the soil and there exert its other beneficial effects.

Not the least of the many benefits that accrue from the metabolic activities of the bacteria in the compost are an increased chelating capacity and increased ability of the soil to absorb rapid changes in acidity and alkalinity (i.e., increased buffering capacity) [11,25].

With the rising concern about the introduction of heavy metals and toxic substances into the soil has come a recognition of the effectiveness of organic matter (and hence of compost) in the immobilization of the former and the destruction of the latter. In terms of immobilization capacity, the organic colloid is five times as effective as the clay (inorganic) colloid [15]. With respect to other toxic substances that may enter the soil, the application of compost is a very useful approach to lessening the severity of adverse environmental impacts resulting from their presence.

A final benefit to be mentioned is the increase in the resistance of crops to many plant diseases. Whether or not the increased resistance is simply a function of the more vigorous growth encouraged by the presence of compost, of an immunological response in the plant itself, or of the possession or development of a property toxic to plant pathogens, is immaterial. The result is beneficial.

3.2.2. Application Parameters

To fully obtain the many benefits that attend the use of compost in agriculture, it is essential that certain parameters, precautions, and constraints be observed. Among the more important parameters and constraints are those that pertain to the age of the compost, the C/N ratio, loading rate, and environmental and public health aspects. Of these parameters, loading is the one of most concern in this paper because of its direct influence on energy consumption.

The balance between the NPK consumption by the crop and the amount of the three elements added as compost is one of the principal factors that determine suitability of loading rate. The balance is important because nutrient elements not used by the crop will very likely be leached to the groundwater. Therefore, the maximum permissible loading is the one that results in the application of nitrogen (and other plant nutrients) in excess of that used by the crop during the growing season. Loadings that meet this specification can be determined from the information given in Table 3. In making the calculations, it should be remembered that only 25 to 35 percent of the nitrogen in the compost is available for plant growth during the year of application. The remainder is bound in the microbial populations. However most of it will become available in the second year, and probably all in the third year. Finally, it should be emphasized that the deciding factor in determining loadings is the presence or absence in the compost of substances toxic to man, animal, and plant.

Maturity of compost is a matter of concern because the use of an immature compost can be detrimental to crop yield. On the other hand, processing beyond that needed to sufficiently mature the compost results in an unnecessary expenditure of energy. If the C/N is much higher than 20/1, a strong possibility of a nitrogen shortage ("nitrogen-starvation") for the crop plants arises, and as a result, yield is adversely affected as well as efficiency of energy usage.

3.2.3. Transportation (Distribution)

A major constraint in the use of compost is the cost incurred in terms of energy and labor through the transportation of the compost product from the production facility to the point of utilization (the farm). The characteristics of composts produced from MSW, namely, low bulk density and relatively low concentrations of plant nutrients (fertilizer elements), render the transportation of it costly in terms of energy requirements. As a result, transportation over long distances becomes economically and energetically infeasible. It is estimated that transporting the product by truck would entail an energy expenditure on the order of 1.4 kWh/Mg compost/km. The expenditure in terms of Mg of raw refuse processed would be about 0.7 kWh/Mg/km. In the case of delivery of compost product to a market located 10 km from the composting facility, the energy requirement is about 7 kWh/Mg of MSW.

3.2.4. Energy Requirements for Landspreading

In the preparation of this paper, a calculation was made of the energy required to apply the compost product on agricultural land. In the calculation, it is assumed that the compost is applied through the use of a manure spreader presently on the market. Data are based on specifications supplied by the manufacturer. The spreader has a capacity of about 16 m^3 and is powered by a 108 kW motor. The energy requirement for landspreading compost is estimated to be on the order of 0.4 kWh/Mg of compost applied, or about 0.2 kWh/Mg of MSW processed.

3.2.5. Example of Energy Requirements

An example of the average energy consumed in the preparation and utilization of a compost produced from mixtures of MSW and sludge is presented in terms of kWh/Mg in Table 4. The data in the table indicate the following: 1) the total amount of energy required to produce, transport, and apply compost is on the order of 34.4 kWh/Mg of MSW; 2) the preparation of the refuse requires about 16.0 kWh/Mg, i.e., about one-half of the entire energy demand; 3) the composting step requires an average of

Table 4. Energy Requirements for the Production and Use of Compost

	Average Energy Consumption (kWh/Mg of MSW)
Pre-processing	16.0
Composting[a]	5.1
Post-processing	6.1
Transport[b]	7.0
Application	0.2
TOTAL	34.4

a) Average of the three processes.
b) Energy required to transport compost 10 km to market by truck.

5.1 kWh/Mg; 4) post-processing requires 6.1 kWh/Mg; 5) transportation of the finished product to a market located 10 km from the compost plant necessitates the expenditure of about 0.7 kWh/Mg/km; and 6) the material can be spread on the soil at 0.2 kWh/Mg.

3.3. Energy Conservation ("Credits") Due to Use of Compost

Among the many benefits attributed to the application of compost on agricultural land are erosion control, increase in soil organic matter, and enhancement of water retention.

Ranking high among the harmful effects of erosion are those on crop production, especially on yields. Although the negative effects are widely recognized, those on crop production are difficult to quantify and express in generalizations because of the wide range of variables involved (e.g., crop and soil types, availability of nutrients, temperature, moisture). Nevertheless, an estimate of energy savings attributable to the utilization of compost can be made by using a particular crop as an example and then making assumptions. In this paper, corn serves as the example.

It has been estimated that the production of corn in areas having a slope of 6 to 10 percent results in erosion rates on the order of 270 Mg/ha/yr when conventional agricultural practices are followed [16,18,22]. By applying organic matter (compost) to the soil at about 67 Mg/ha/yr, the erosion is reduced by about 20 percent or approximately 54 Mg/ha/yr [26]. The amount of plant nutrients contained in the 54 Mg of lost top soil is about 45.4 kg nitrogen and 5.1 kg phosphorus [14]. The savings in terms of energy that otherwise would have had to have been expended in producing chemical fertilizers to replace the lost nitrogen and phosphorus would be equal to about 61 kWh/ha-yr/Mg of compost applied.

It has also been estimated that the increase in topsoil loss brought about by erosion and subsequent degradation of soil quality and productivity over a 30-yr period results in a reduction of corn yields to the amount of about 1055 kg/ha/yr [21]. Using the amount of energy required to produce 1 kg of corn as 5071 kJ [22], it can be calculated that a reduction in yield of 1055 kg/ha/yr would require an additional 3682 kWh of energy input per hectare to replace the loss in yield.

Loss of topsoil means more than loss of plant nutrients and decrease in crop yield, it also entails an increase in energy required to till the soil. For example, it has been reported that erosion phase 1 soils require 22 percent more fuel for tillage when depleted to erosion phase 2 [1], and that another 17 percent increase in fuel was required when erosion phase 2 soils had been depleted to erosion phase 3.

REFERENCES

1. Agricultural Waste Recycling (1983). Prepared for the Asian Development Bank by Cal Recovery Systems, Inc. in association with Aquatic Farms, Maya Farms, and Seatec International
2. BABBITT, H.E. (1953). Sewerage and Sewage Treatment. 7th ed. John Wiley and Sons, New York
3. BERGVALI, G. and HULT, J. (1985). Technology, Economics and Environmental Effects of Solid Waste Treatment, Final Report from the DRAV Project. Statens naturvardsverk. Informationsenheten, Box 1302, S-17125 SOLNA (Sweden)
4. BRICENO, R. (1979). Quantitative and Qualitative Evaluation of Solid Wastes in Metropolitan Caracas and in Cua, Caracas
5. DALZELL, H.W., PHIL, M., GRAY, K.R., and BIDDLESTONE, A.J. (1979). Composting in Tropical Agriculture. Review Paper Series No. 2. The

19

International Institute of Biological Husbandry, Martello House,
Suffolk, England
6. DIAZ, L.F. (1985). El Manejo de Residuos Solidos Urbanos en La Paz y
Sus Areos Marjinales. Prepared for Foster Parents Plan International
7. DIAZ, L.F. (1984). Solid Waste Management Plan for Asuncion, Paraguay
8. DIAZ, L.F. and GOLUEKE, C.G. (1983). Findings of Mission to Lima,
Peru on Waste Management and Material Recovery. Report by Cal Recovery Systems, Inc. to The World Bank, Washington, D.C.
9. DIAZ, L.F., SAVAGE, G.M., and GOLUEKE, C.G. (1982). Resource Recovery from Municipal Solid Waste, Vol. I, Primary Processing. CRC
Press, Inc. Boca Raton, Florida
10. FAIR, G.M. and IMHOFF, K. (1965). Sewage Treatment, 2nd ed. John
Wiley and Sons, Inc. New York
11. GOLUEKE. C.G. (1977). Biological Reclamation of Solid Wastes. Rodale
Press
12. GOTAAS, H.B. (1956). Compost. World Health Organization Monograph
Series No. 31. World Health Organization. Palais des Nations, Geneva
13. KRISHNARAJAN, J. and BALASUBRAMANIAN, P. (1981). Management Trial
for Increasing Nitrogen Use Efficiency of Wetland Rice. International
Rice Research Newsletter, 6(4):21
14. LARSON, W.E., HOLT, R.F., and CARLSON, C.W. (1978). Residues for
Soil Conservation. In Crop Residue Management Systems. W.R. Oschwald,
ed. Am. Soc. Agron. Spec. Publ. No. 31. Madison, Wisconsin
15. LEEPER, G.W. (1978). Managing the Heavy Metals on the Land. Marcel
Dekker, Inc. New York and Basel
16. MANNERING, J.V., GRIFFITH, D.B., and JOHNSON, C.B. (1976). Conservation Tillage -- Effects on Crop Production and Sediment Yield. Am.
Soc. Agr. Eng. Winter Meeting. Paper 76-2551
17. McCABE, J. and ECKENFELDER, W.W. (1963). Advances in Biological
Waste Treatment. Pergamon Press, Inc. New York
18. MILLER, M.F. (1935). Cropping Systems in Relation to Erosion Control. Mo. Agr. Expt. Sta. Bull. 366
19. MONNIER, G. Les matieres organique du sol: etat et evolution, roles,
utilisation agronomique. Compost Information. Agence Nationale pour
la Recuperation et l Elimination des Dechats, France
20. PARAQUASSI DE SA, F. (1970). Solid Waste Management in Rio de
Janerio, Brazil. Unpublished report. West Virginia University
21. PIMENTEL, D., et al (1976). Land Degradation: Effects on Food and
Energy Sources. Science, 194:149-155
22. PIMENTEL, D. and PIMENTEL, M. (1979). Food, Energy, and Society. Ed-
ward Arnold. London
23. SAVAGE, G.M. (1979). Solid Waste Management in Mexico City. Report
to Pan American Health Organization
24. SAVAGE, G.M. et al (1982). Engineering Design Manual for Solid Waste
Size Reduction Equipment. Report by Cal Recovery Systems under U.S.
EPA contract no. 68-03-2972
25. SCHATZ, A., SCHATZ, V., SCHALSCHA, E.G., and MARTIN, J. (1964). Soil
Organic Matter as a Natural Chelating Agent, Part I: The Chemistry
of Chelation. Compost Science, 4(4):25-28
26. SCS (1977). Cropland Erosion. Soil Conservation Service. U.S.D.A.,
Washington D.C.
27. SNIDHAR, M.K.C., et al (1985). An Experimental Study of Composting
in a Nigerian Community. Univ. of Ibadan, Nigeria. Manuscript accepted for publication in BioCycle
28. TUCK, J.K., and SAVAGE, G.M. (1982). Investigations of Physical Sampling Methods for Raw and Processed Municipal Solid Wastes. Prepared
by Cal Recovery Systems for EGG Idaho, Inc.

HORTICULTURAL USE OF COMPOST

T. PUDELSKI
Department of Vegetable Crops. Agricultural University.
Poznan, Poland

Summary
The following report presents a survey of sources of organic waste
materials from different branches of industry, general life activity,
municipal economy as well as from horticulture, which can be used in
composting and as composts. Various conditions and up to date methods
of compost application in horticulture have been discussed.

1. INTRODUCTION
        Composting as a method of recycling all household refuse in order to
obtain new means of production which is organic fertilizer, or hortisoil,
is known to growers for a long time.
        Removal and neutralisation of organic waste materials appearing in
industrial, economical, and general life activity of a man if they can not
be used as secondary raw materials or as fodder, should not be carried out
by means of burning. However, this is often done so, particularly under
assumption that the burning energy can be used economically. However,
according to calculations even burning of wood wastes for heat energy often
has only apparent effect if we consider energy input necessary for
collecting, loading and preparing these materials for burning.
        Burning is almost always harmful for natural environment. By
utilizing different organic wastes in composting and by their horticultural
application in urbanized regions of the world we take into account
protection of natural environment of a man. Doing so we transform the
wastes into food (vegetables, fruit), or into plants of municipal forests,
cemeteries, parks, greeneries, flower beds, roof gardens, allotments and
home gardens, as well as all ornamental plants which in every place remind
us about our bonds with nature.

2. ORGANIC WASTES FROM INDUSTRIAL PLANTS
        The work done by Belgian scientists (11) casts some light on the
kinds of organic wastes that can be found in European countries. They sent
out over 2000 inquiry forms to Flemish industrial enterprises concerning
organic wastes being by-products of their production processes. The
percentage of returned questionnaires was rather high. From the commercial
viewpoint most of the organic wastes have found a more interesting outlet
than use in composting. Significant quantities, i.e. about 10 thousand tons
a year of compostable wastes can be found in some branches of chemical
industry, in the area of breweries, malt-houses and related activities, in
dairying industry, canning factories, and those producing special articles
of food (active coal loaded with organic material, soy scrap sludge, and
others). The remaining dumped wastes usually cannot be composted purely, so
to compost them they must be mixed with another structuring compostable
wastes. Only very few wastes have such characteristics. The best known is
bark, of which there is not too much in Flandres. The bark which is
accumulated in larger amounts in cellulose and paper mills is composted on
spot.

According to the author of this report in greater urban agglomerations such a structuring compost component could also be shredded twigs of trees and ornamental shrubs, woody stems of perennial plants obtained from pruning and cleaning greeneries, parks and municipal forests. We shall discuss their utilization elsewhere in this paper.

3. WASTES FROM WOOD INDUSTRY AND PAPER MILLS

During the last 15 years many scientists carried out broad investigation projects into application of the composts made from wood processing wastes, particularly from bark of both coniferous and deciduous trees.

Bark, sawdust and shavings of coniferous trees can be in many cases used without composting as materials building appropriate structure and improving physical parameters in the mixture, e.g. with better decomposed sphagnum peat or low moor peat, with clay or very heavy mineral soils (16). Bark composts after very short composting time, ranging from a few weeks to 3 months, can constitute a considerable part, up to 80 % by volume, in potting mixes, or substitute for peat substrates in growing many species of vegetables (16,17) and ornamental plants under protection, or in container media production of ornamental nursery stock. Short time composting of bark with addition of nitrogen fertilizer usually urea, or of another organic wastes rich in nitrogen compounds, e.g. soy scrap sludge, during which we should stimulate the course of hot fermentation processes is to :
- inactivate phytotoxic substances which can be present in the raw material,
- correct C:N ratio and thus counteract sorption of mineral N,
- and, initiate humification leading to increased sorption and water capacities.

Bark and other coniferous wood wastes composts before can be used as substrate require, just like sphagnum peat, deacidification and supplementing with mineral components. Optimal amounts of both macro and microelements considering nutritional needs of the plant species to be grown and their cultivation conditions, are introduced into bark substrates in the form of appropriate multicomponent fertilizer mixtures. Slow release fertilizers find increasing application in enriching substrates. These include those containing only microelements e.g. fritted trace elements, but also those with all necessary micro, and macro elements, e.g. Osmocote, Nutricote, Plantacote and others.

Bark, sawdust and wood shavings from hard wood species require longer composting times also with addition of mineral nitrogen or organic materials rich in nitrogen compounds. The hard wood wastes contain considerably greater amounts of phytotoxic components, generally phenolic compounds and longer, at least 6 to 9 months, composting time is necessary for their degradation. Inverting the compost piles and maintaining appropriate moisture level during composting are indispensable for securing intensive decomposition and humification processes in aerobic conditions.

The best recognized is application of common beech bark composts as substrates or mixture components in growing vegetables under protection and as organic fertilizer in vegetable production both in field and under protection (3, 14, 15). The beech bark compost is neutral to slightly alcalic and is richer in mineral components easily available for plants than the coniferous bark composts.

In numerous European countries coniferous bark composts, and in Poland also beech bark compost, are produced on industrial scale on basis of patented technologies by larger wood industry and paper mills using sewage-sludge or biologically active sediments from their purification plants. However, in some countries, e.g. GDR (1), Holland, Finland, the wood wastes and composts made of them constitute raw materials for specialized enterprises manufacturing substrates for production of seedlings, nursery stock for container medium method, for growing many species of vegetables and flowers under protection, and in different growing units, as well as the composts used in organic manuring in field and protected production for municipal greeneries, in allotments and home gardens, in recultivation of the land devastated by industry, building, or open pit mines.

Bark composts are particularly useful in establishing lawns and roof gardens due to their structure and since the substrates prepared from them show high resistance to trampling.

4. CITY REFUSE OF GREEN AREAS

Municipal green areas require systematic manuring both during establishment and maintenance. So far, mainly the so called gardening peat, i.e. processed sphagnum peat was used for this purpose. However, constantly increasing price of this product, and ecological considerations, that is relinquishment of peatbog exploitation, force us to use this material very cautiously also in horticulture.

During the maintenance work from green areas large quantities of organic material are removed, such as twigs of trees and shrubs, woody and green parts of perennial plants and annuals, leaves, and grass mown from lawns. Also in cemeteries are accumulated considerable amounts of organic material. According to Fischer (7) 400 ha of Hamburg cemetery yields 5300 m^3 of tree and shrub twigs a year. From the trees and shrubs growing in streets and green areas of Munich, municipal gardeners remove 23 000 m^3 of branches a year. Munich cemeteries accumulate about 45 000 m^3 of such materials as leaves, wraths, bunches, and ornamental annuals, which after proper composting give from 12 to 15 000 m^3 of compost soil.

In his large, 3 part paper, Rannertshauser (18) discusses :
1) the usefulness of different kinds of machinery in shredding twigs and branches,
2) the rules of application and composting shredded wood,
3) the utilization of shredded wood composts as substrates for production of annual flower seedlings and as organic manure in planting ornamental trees and shrubs in municipal green areas and on streets.

Fischer (7) reports that twigs volume after shredding decreases by about 20 %. He added 1 to 2 kg N per 1 m^3 of chopped twigs in the form of urea, watered them and composted in piles for 3 to 7 months. During this time the piles should be inverted once or twice and watered if necessary. After 6.5 months, larger pieces of wood found in the compost were shredded again. Then the composted material obtained the structure corresponding to weakly decomposed fibrous sphagnum peat. The author is of the opinion that by improving composting techniques of wood cuttings and by mineral fertilization of the composts according to the requirements of the plant species to be grown on it, it will be able to replace the gardening peat to a great extent. Plant tests on lettuce and barley have proved greater value of the composts of wood cuttings collected from few tree and shrub species than that of the compost of one deciduous species.

5. SEWAGE-SLUDGE AND CITY REFUSE

Sewage-sludge and its sediments accumulating in purification plants contain considerable amounts of very different organic materials.

Another source of sedimentary organic materials are household refuse. Already in mid 1970's in Holland there were about 300 kg = 1.5 m^3 of rubbish per head of population. In rich countries this phenomenon shows increasing tendency.

For dozens years authorities of almost all larger cities have dealt with the problem of utilization of all inorganic waste materials instead of destroying them by burning them with organic refuse. From many Dutch towns rubbish is removed in sealed carriages by government authorized firm N.V. Vuilafvoer Maatschappij VAM to central composting plants in Wijster and Mierlo region. In this totally mechanized plants the wastes from which metal and larger plastic or glass elements were removed, are piled in the open air. At 2 months intervals the piles are inverted and watered if necessary. After 6 to 8 months mature composts are sieved and bits of glass and other hard objects are separated and ground. Also the plastic foils which survived decomposition are removed. One ton of rubbish yields about 400 t of compost. The composting plant does not receive rubbish from hospitals, industrial plants and faeces.

In the second half of the 1970's the VAM enterprises produced two main kinds of composts. The "Superfein" compost contained fractions passed through the screens with 5 mm sieve mesh. The other compost was not sieved. The compost was mainly used as an organic fertilizer for recultivated areas, in municipal greenery farms, and, to a limited extent, in nurseries of ornamental trees and shrubs, and on farms producing some kinds of ornamental plants. About 15 % of the output with an addition of peat and mineral fertilizers was sold in plastic packages to individual growers for manuring home gardens. The composting plants returned their profits to the towns from which the rubbish was collected.

In many European towns, including Warsaw, and in Italy, Udine, there are Dano refuse composting plants in which, on basis of bio-thermal initial phase of composting, from the bio-stabilizer we obtain, so called fresh compost, and, after at least 3 months of composting in the open air, so called, mature compost. There were numerous research projects examining the organic substance content and manuring value of the urban composts produced by means of the Dano method.

Also the town refuse composts obtained after 6 to 9, and even 12 months of composting in piles in the open air were many times checked according to their usefulness in horticulture. Numerous papers were published concerning composting town refuse with addition of various organic waste materials, most often those which decompose quickly. These additives are to speed up humification processes, to increase organic substance content in the compost, to dilute, i.e. to decrease the concentration of phytotoxic compounds, first of all heavy metals and other components hazardous for people.

City refuse from towns or town districts which do not have centralized heating system for about 6 months a year contain substantial amounts of ashes from solid fuels.

Baumann and Schneider (2) investigated the value of composts originating from the experimental composting plant in Dresden during the four year vegetable crop rotation. The compost free from ashes as well as those with their 17 % contribution were tested. Favourable effect on crop yield after manuring with urban composts was similar to that obtained with farmyard manure. On the soils requiring liming during the first two years better results gave manuring with the composts containing ashes. In the second half of the investigation project better proved the refuse composts without ashes, i.e. richer in organic matter. During the whole 4 years period no significant differences between application of fresh and mature composts were observed. The possibility of utilizing the sewage-sediment composts, the composts made of the mixture of the sediments and refuse, and

in some cases, also the refuse itself are greatly limited due to the fact :
- that they carry into the soil the compounds harmful for people (mostly heavy metals) which are consequently taken up by vegetables and fruit,
- that when they are frequently applied as organic manures (the necessary condition in horticultural production) these compounds are accumulated in the soil up to phytotoxic concentrations.

Some countries have already issued bills forbidding application of sewage sediments in any form on the areas carrying food crops, for example in West Germany such a bill is valid since 1 April, 1983, and concerns the areas used both for vegetable production and orchards (7).

The composts produced from many different organic materials with changing in time concentrations and kinds of chemical compounds, and such composts include those made from town refuse, also have their manuring and utility value different in time.

Wider range of their application can be found in these branches of horticulture which do not deal with vegetable and fruit production. These composts can be admitted for commercial distribution in nurseries of ornamental trees and shrubs as well in municipal green areas after passing seedling tests. Quality testing of sewage - sludge compost is discussed in detail by Bidlingmaier (4) in A.H. No. 172.

6. COMPOSTS AS SUBSTRATES

In horticultural production under protection besides ornamental pot plants also the cultivation of cut flowers and vegetables is to an increasing degree carried out in all kinds of growing units or in isolation from the natural soil. The best environment for roots is no longer hortisoil composed mostly of humified organic substances but the substrates with precisely determined physical parameters.

Substrates differ from natural soil, with lower bulk density, larger pore space, and they are means of production so they can be used independently of the natural soil profile. The substrates are independent from the local soil fertility and can be adapted to the specific requirements of the cultivated species. When well composed, with their aid much better growing conditions can be realised than in soil. With substrates you can gain highest yields per m^2. The increased use of substrates by the grower is a good index for the intensity of utilization of the protected area.

For many years the substrate appropriate for practically all ornamental plants and vegetables was prepared from sphagnum peat. Diminishing supplies of this raw material in the countries of Middle Europe, increasing transport costs and hence prices, and last but not the least, ecological considerations contributed to prompt search for local substitutes.

Penningsfeld (12) in his survey of recognized and applied growing media presents characteristics of an universal substrate for the majority of ornamental plants (Table 1). According to the author, at least with respect to physical parameters the universality of such a substrate can be broadened onto all vegetables cultivated under protection.

The issue of utilizing wood waste composts as substrates has already been discussed here. Wood wastes occur in large quantities in all countries having developed wood and paper industry.

Also different kinds of fibrous or woody organic materials are accumulated locally which can be adapted by means of composting for further use as substrates.

Appropriate shredding of the materials supplementing the materials with high C:N ratio with mineral or organic nitrogen before composting, and differentiated length of composting according to the amount and the kind of phytotoxic compounds occurring in the raw material are the measures which lead to giving the composts the physical parameters characterizing the ideal substrate. The coarser fractions of the compost used as a substrate are more resistant to further humification processes, the longer the appropriate structure remains and hence better air-water relationship in the substrate for grown plants. Such substrates can be used repeatedly even for several years.

6.1. Vine canes

In Cretean vineyards about 160 thousand tons of vine canes are cut annually which usually were burned down.

Manios et al. (9) carried out experiments on composting this material using it as a substrate for production of tomato seedlings. Hammer milled canes with an addition of urea were composted for 6 months (fresh compost) and after further 5 months of maturation the mature compost were obtained. Mature compost yielded good results while the fresh one brought about worse results, probably due to remaining phytotoxicity and changes in NH_4-N and NO_3-N concentrations.

6.2. Sod and cuttings from moorland

New Dutch polders after draining are at first overgrown with purple moor grass (Molinia caerulea). Before starting agricultural utilization of these polders the moor grass is harvested and sod is removed.

Van der Boon and Niers (5) carried out investigations into moorland sod usefulness, composted and non-composted cuttings of moor grass and heather and their mixture as a potting soil for nursery stock. Testing these materials on several ornamental shrub species they found that both the composts from moorland cuttings and even non-composted material if shredded to a particle size suitable for use in a potting soil, and limed to the designed pH, and if the required amounts of major nutrient elements except nitrogen, were added, showed their full usefulness.

6.3. Seagrass (Posidonia oceanica L.)

In Tunesia successful investigations were carried out into the application of seagrass (Posidonia oceanica L.) compost as a substrate in growing tomatoes in grow-bags (21), and on using this compost for a few years in cultivating tomatoes (22). From the detailed analyses of physical parameters of the compost and the content of macro and microelements in the substrate and leaves, and of their mutual interreactions and the effect of these factors on the yield, the authors suggest the possibility of working out mathematical model explaining the yield with the most active parameters.

6.4. Olive marc

The Spaniards have lately worked hard on the utilization of olive marc (6, 10). The authors have found that after two months of composting of this by-product without any additives but water, the emergence of cucumber and lettuce seedlings was low due to large quantities of phytotoxic compounds. A gas chromatographic analysis gave 400 to 600 ppm of acetic and considerable amounts of their organic and fatty acids. After three months of composting, none of them was detectable and emergence increased in pure compost.

Nevertheless the composting process has reduced the particle diameter and as a result of it, the total pore space and the air volume percentage. Therefore, the use of those materials by themselves might cause problems of anaerobiosis in the rizosphere.

The use of physical conditioners in them is advisable in order to reach the physical properties of an ideal growing substrate.

6.5. Flax scutching dust

Almost half of the French flax cultivation area is concentrated in Normandy. Also flax scutching factories are numerous in that region.

This activity generates many by-products and wastes especially flax dusts, composed by vegetal and earthy dusts, causing a very large encumbrance for the factories. Le Nel (8) has found that by means of composting these wastes we can obtain a substrate with very good physical parameters which can be used in nursery stock and in horticultural production under protection.

6.6. Tropical organic waste products

In subtropical and tropical countries the organic waste materials may constitute the remains after processing coco – palm wood and nuts, dry palm leaves, rice hulls, tea wastes and others.

Verdonck et al. (19) after examining physical and chemical parameters of rice hulls, tea wastes, cocofibre dust and the composts made of them, and also from growing experiments have drawn the following conclusions :
- rice hulls can be composted with the addition of 1 % nitrogen and urea as nitrogen source,
- tea waste is very rich in nitrogen (3,5 %). Therefore mixtures with a carbon rich material as rice hulls and cocofibre dust are necessary,
- cocofibre dust is very high in carbon (45 %).

Despite adding 1 % nitrogen the decay process of this material and so the degradation of phytotoxic substances present was slow.

Four months long composting caused total disappearance of phytotoxic substances and facilitated growth even of these plants which are sensitive to them.

For having a good constant growing medium on the base of cocofibre dust a composting period with small amounts of urea is recommended of at least 2-3 months at an appropriate moisture content.

Recognition of chemical and physical parameters of the wastes discussed in this chapter which are generally constant in time and independent of their place of origin enables us to state generally valid rules of their composting and adaptation as a good growing medium for a given vegetable species or ornamental plants.

7. UTILIZATION OF THE EXOTHERMIC PHASE OF COMPOSTING

In some countries in cultivating stenothermal plants in hot beds and in greenhouses covered with glass or plastics for heating rizosphere, besides so called hot manures, are also used other organic materials such as straw or wastes from the organic fibre industry (cotton, wool, flax, hemp) (13), from wood industry and paper mills (bark, sawdust) (17). In order to prepare these materials for the initial phase of composting which is hot fermentation, they are appropriately watered and in many cases it is necessary to lower the C:N ratio by adding mineral nitrogen or the organic materials rich in easily decomposing nitrogenous compounds.

To materials rich in lignin and cellulose are added small amounts of stable manure, most often chicken manure or dried hen droppings (17).

In hot beds the materials are heated on spot whereas for use in glass or plastic greenhouses the start of hot fermentation takes place outside in piles and only when the material reaches the temperature of about 30°C it is moved to the buildings and covered with the substrate into which the plants are planted.

The same utilization can be found for the town refuse compost which was passed through the bio-stabilizer of the Dano refuse composting plants (13).

Biologically heating substrates :
- maintain the temperature of the substrate (rizosphere) from 28 to 20°C for 6 to 8 weeks,
- increase air temperature by 2-3°C also in places without artificial heating e.g. in plastic tunnels,
- affect the increase in CO_2 concentration in the air even to optimal concentrations, i.e. up to 800 - 1200 ppm, and during particularly intensive assimilation (the hours of highest insolation) they prevent CO_2 concentration from falling below the normal concentration.

This phenomenon is often observed while cultivating plants indoors by means of hydroponic methods. As the author's own investigations demonstrated, it takes place also during windless and sunny days in midday hours during cultivation in natural soil in plastic tunnels despite opening top vent-holes. The utilization of the hot fermentation phase occurring during decomposition of different waste materials in plant production also means saving artificially produced energy which is necessary for providing the plants growing under protection with optimal conditions for growth and development.

8. COMPOSTING AS MEANS OF INACTIVATING AGROCHEMICALS

Various organic materials used in horticulture are of agricultural origin, e.g. manures, straw and others, and they may be the carriers of such agrochemicals as herbicides, insecticides, fungicides and growth regulators to which numerous species of horticultural plants are much more sensitive, and on the other hand, when they are taken up by fast growing vegetables which in turn are eaten fresh by a man can be harmful for his health.

The composting of organic material is characterised by a very high biological activity so the composting conditions can be assumed to be very favourable for the break-down of agrochemicals. Vogtmann et al. (23) examined the degradability of various agrochemicals after 56 and 75 days of composting. The compost material varied within the series : it contained poultry manure as nitrogen source, pig manure, peat and straw as carbon source. The tested agents were - two herbicides (Bromofenoxin, 2, 4D), four insecticides (Lindane, Diazinon, Matasystox and Parathion), two fungicides (Benomyl, Propineb) and two growth regulators one for plants (CCC) and the other for animals (Tylosin). The degradability ranged from 100 % (Matasystox, Tylosin) down to 18 % (CCC) whereas most of the chemicals lay over 80 %. The degradation of investigated agrochemicals was caused by temperature and biochemical effects.

9. CONCLUSIONS

As results from the presented survey, the composts from very different organic waste materials, after different lengths of composting, with exception of the discussed limitations concerning sewage-sludge sediments and town refuse, are more and more widely used in horticulture. They are used in the initial composting phase, i.e. hot fermentation as heating agents and CO_2 producers, as a potting soil, as a component of potting mixes or the growing media themselves under protection, for mulching in orchard production, and as soil improver in field cultivation of vegetables and ornamental plants, in vineyards and orchards, in shaping and maintaining town green areas.

Table 1. - Universal substrate suitable for most ornamental plants
(Penningsfeld F.A.H. Nr 82, 1978)

Vol. % at container capacity water				Organic matter %	Absorption capacity me/dm^3
solid matter	air	water			
		total	easily available		
10-30	30-40	40-50	20-30	50	120

pH/CaCl$_2$	Available N	amount of nutrients P$_2$O$_5$	K$_2$O	/mg/dm^3/ Mg	
5.5	200	150	300	100	average
5.0-5.8	100-300	100-200	200-400	50-150	range

REFERENCES

1. BAUMANN, E., (1977) Organische Düngung und Erdwirtschaft bei der industriemässigen Produktion im Gartenbau und industrielle Düngestoffproduktion. IGA Ratgeber, Erfurt
2. BAUMANN, E., SCHNEIDER, E., (1980), Die Wirkung von Siedlungsabfallkomposten unterschiedlicher Zusammensetzung auf den Ertrag von Feldgemüse. Archiv Gartenbau, 5, 295-299
3. BAUMANN, E., SCHMIDT, R., (1981). Die Nutzung von Buchenrinden als organischen Düngestoff in der Gemüseproduktion unter Glas und Plasten. Archiv Gartenbau, 15-26
4. BIDLINGMAIER, W., (1985). Quality-testing of waste sewage-sludge composts. A.H. 172, 99-116
5. BOON VAN DER, J., NIERS, H., (1985). Use of bark, and of sod, and cuttings from moorland vegetation in potting mixtures. A.H. 172, 55-65
6. CALVET, C., PAGES, M., ESTAUN, V., (1985). Composting of olive marc. A.H. 172, 255-259
7. FISCHER, P., (1983). Alternativen zur Verwendung von Torf. Natur und Landschaft 58, 11, 412-415
8. LE NEL, D., (1982). Properties physiques du terreau de lin. A.H., 126, 123-129
9. MANIOS, V.I., TSIKALAS, P.E., (1985). Decomposition of vine-canes in heap and evaluation of the produced compost. A.H., 172, 39-53
10. PAGES, M., ESTAUN, V., CALVET, C., (1985). Physical and chemical properties of olive marc compost. A.H. 172, 271-276
11. PENNINCK, R., VERDONCK, O., DE BOODT, M., (1985). Different materials which can be used in compost. A.H. 172, 31-38
12. PENNINGSFELD, F., (1978). Substrates for protected cropping. A.H. 82, 13-18
13. PUDELSKI, T., (1977). Substancja organiczna w ogrodnictwie. Rozdzial w pracy zbiorowej pt. Nawozy organiczne. PWRiL Warszawa
14. PUDELSKI, T., (1978). Using waste products of wood industry and paper mills as substrates and organic fertilizer in growing vegetables under protection. A.H. 82, 67-77

15. PUDELSKI, T., (1980). Common beech bark compost as growing medium and soil improver in growing vegetables under protection. A.H. 99, 105-112
16. PUDELSKI, T., (1983). Composted and non composted wood-wastes in growing vegetables under protection in Poland. A.H. 133, 237-240
17. PUDELSKI, T., (1985). Woodwaste composts as growing media for vegetables under protection. A.H. 172, 67-74
18. RANNERTSHAUSER, J., (1982). Aufbereitung und Verwendung von Schnittholz. Das Gartenamt J. 31, 112-114, 309-315, 480-482
19. VERDONCK, O., DE VLEESCHAUWER, D., PENNINCK, R., (1983). Cocofibre dust, a new growing medium for plants in the tropics. A.H. 133, 215-226
20. VERDONCK, O., PENNINCK, R., (1985). The composting of bark with soy scrab sludge. A.H. 172, 183-189
21. VERLODT, H., KAMOUN, S., (1981). Influence du volume des sacs et de l'addition de fumier décomposé sur le comportement d'une culture de tomate en sac boudin à base d'une graminée marine (Posidonia oceanica L.) A.H. 126, 263-280
22. VERLODT, H., ZOUAOUI, M., HARBAOUI, Y., (1985). Relationship between physical and chemical properties of the substrate and foliar analysis with growth and yield results of a tomato crop cultivated in reutilized Posidonia oceanica L. seagrass substrates. A.H. 172, 231-249
23. VOGTMANN, H., FRAGSTEIN, P., DRAEGER, P., (1983). The degradation of agrochemicals during composting. Proceedings of the Second International Symposium Peat in Agriculture and Horticulture Bet Dagan, Israel.

COMPOST SPECIFICATIONS
FOR THE PRODUCTION AND CHARACTERIZATION
OF COMPOST FROM MUNICIPAL SOLID WASTE

Franco Zucconi   Marco de Bertoldi
Ist. Coltivazioni Arbore   Ist. Microbiologia Agraria
University of Naples   University of Pisa

INTRODUCTION

Promoting the recovery of organic wastes through composting requires a preliminary standard definition of process and product. Accordingly, the present document introduces a number of specifications regarding the composting process, stages, stabilization and hygienic standards as a prerequisite for ensuring quality products and fostering the agricultural use of reclaimed organic matter.

Indeed, the task of defining products and quality standards is far from simple considering the heterogeneity of situations existing today in terms of processes and plants, and the great diversity of materials that occur in city waste. The latter range from solid to liquid and vary greatly in composition (presence of inerts, elemental composition, dry matter, carbon/nitrogen ratio, etc.). Furthermore, existing specifications for organic soil conditioners are limited and not consistent, and definitions are conflicting or lack specificity. A standard nomenclature is necessary to discriminate compost from products of different origins (Section 4). This requires decisions on which definitions may contribute to a reduction of approximation and misunderstanding, and which guidelines may help to improve process performance and product quality (Paragraph 6.3).

This document introduces a number of standards generally related to minimum values of desirable constituents and to maximum tolerable loads for unwanted ones (Part I). It also discusses the state-of-the-art (Part II) as a necessary means to account for the specifications introduced (Sections 6-8), and for the existing limits in the identification of relevant parameters and setting of standards (Section 9). The advantage of establishing specifications becomes apparent when one considers: a) the need for promoting industrial management of organic wastes and the reclaiming of energy; b) the urgency for introducing some order into the existing array of processes and marketed products so that composts may be identified and compared; and c) the requirement for products that are compatible with different agricultural uses.

In debating definitions and specifications, the question often arises as to their restrictive nature and the tendency to exclude a number of

----

AKNOWLEDGEMENT
This study was proposed to the XII Directorate of the CEC and its analysis and advancement was included in the activities of the Specialized Group on Composting (R&D Progam - Recycling of Urban and Industrial Waste). The actual version is then the product of lengthy discussions,

confrontation with other normatives and legislations, and analyses of available scientific data. Active persons in the Group were: W. Bidlingmaier and R. Mach from Germany; P. Thostrup from Danemark;H. Naveau and I.O. Verdonck from Belgium; J. Oosthoek from the Netherlands; M. Daudin and P. Godin from France; E.I. Stentiford and J.K. Gasser from the United Kingdom; H. Tunney from Ireland; and J.K. Balis from Greece.

The contribution of critical analysis from people outside the Group is also recognized. These are: H. van Dijk and G.J. Bollen from the Netherlands; S. Baines and S.H.T. Harper from the United Kingdom; J.M. Merillot from France; R. Jodice and P. Sequi from Italy: R.C. Loehr from New York; C.G. Golueke and L. Diaz from California. At last, a special recognition must be given to J.K. Gasser, E.I. Stentiford and C. G. Golueke who, beyond providing a fundamental scientific support to the document, helped in achieving a simple and effective language, most necessary for a document wich aims to serve a wider international community.

existing situations. This is an important issue and conditions must be set in order to favour the disposal of organic matter in agriculture through composting. Two points, however, need to be focussed upon when debating the impact of specifications: 1) definitions and specifications in this document refer strictly to marketed products. Then, the use of terms like composting or compost in different contexts (e.g.: mushroom compost, etc.) does not necessarily interfere with this situation; and, 2), definitions and specifications should be consistent in promoting high quality standards.

Today's situation with respect to marketed "composts" is one of confusion and mistrust due to the heterogeneity of the products offered and the relative abundance of poor quality ones. The consequence is that the market for organic soil conditioner relies mostly on natural products (peat, natural humus), while declining to use composts from urban waste in spite of their lower cost. This justifies the repeated criticism that composting is not an effective way of recycling organic matter and that composting plants tend to be costly and inefficient.

To stretch specifications to include all existing situations in terms of processes and products would then appear unrealistic in as much as it would perpetuate today's failure to offer consistently good quality products. At the same time, specifications should promote higher standards and competiveness with marketed natural products.

Seen in this context, the importance of specifying a thermophilic stage during composting (Paragraphs 2.1 and 6.1) needs to be stressed as a means (effective and inexpensive) for sanitizing the organic mass. Such treatment is essential for a large scale use of compost in agriculture, because of the potential pathogen hazard (for animal and plants) and the difficulty of controlling hygienic standards or evaluating the product with other means (Paragraphs 3.5 and 9.2).

Analogous considerations apply in relation to promoting strictly controlled process conditions (Paragraphs 2.1 and 6.1). The advantage of restricting the term "composting" to controlled biooxidative processes is apparent when considering the impact on product quality and on improving the treatment of waste organic matter. Compared with other stabilization processes, controlled biooxidation promotes greater efficiency, better hygienic results, and a reduced time for stabilization. All of these conditions appear to be essential for the promotion of industrial management of organic wastes.

PART I

COMPOST SPECIFICATIONS

1 - FIELD OF APPLICATIONS

This document gives guidelines for the production and standard evaluation of compost originating from municipal solid waste (MSW), as well as from any mixture which contains MSW together with industrial or agricultural residues, and sludges from waste water treatment in proportion appropriate to the solid waste (Paragraph 2.3). These guidelines apply strictly to the industrial production of marketed compost to be used on agricultural crops. The classification of composts refers to products derived at different phases of the stabilization process. These products range from "fresh" to "cured" compost (Section 4).

2 - DEFINITIONS

2.1 - THE DEFINITION OF COMPOSTING

The term "composting" refers to processes that occur under strictly controlled biooxidative conditions (Paragraph 5.1), according to the definition: COMPOSTING IS A CONTROLLED BIOOXIDATIVE PROCESS THAT: 1) INVOLVES A HETEROGENEOUS ORGANIC SUBSTRATE IN THE SOLID STATE; 2) EVOLVES BY PASSING THROUGH A THERMOPHILIC PHASE AND A TEMPORARY RELEASE OF PHYTOTOXIN; AND 3) LEADS TO PRODUCTION OF CARBON DIOXIDE, WATER, MINERALS AND STABILIZED ORGANIC MATTER (COMPOST).

2.2 - THE DEFINITION OF COMPOST

The term "compost", when used on its own, specifically refers to products derived at a precise stage of evolution of the composting process (see Paragraph 6.2). It is consistent with the definition: COMPOST IS THE STABILIZED AND SANITIZED PRODUCT OF COMPOSTING WHICH IS BENEFICIAL TO PLANT GROWTH. IT HAS UNDERGONE AN INITIAL, RAPID STAGE OF DECOMPOSITION AND IS IN THE PROCESS OF HUMIFICATION.

2.3 - STARTING MATERIALS

This document refers to the composting of the organic fraction of municipal solid waste (from the city as a whole, individual neighborhoods, households, canteens, restaurants, etc.). In addition the following materials may be added to the municipal solid waste:
- wastewater sludges;
- industrial wastes and residues;
- food processing wastes;
- agricultural wastes.

Limitations on the use of a particular waste are the presence of hazardous materials and/or materials incompatible with composting (see Paragraphs 3.3 and 7).

3 - COMPOST SPECIFICATIONS

3.1 - COMPOST SPECIFICATIONS AND THE ORIGIN OF THE PRODUCT

The term "compost" without qualifyng adjectives must be restricted to the product of composting as defined in Paragraphs 2.1 and 2.2. Consequently, other names must be given to the products of fermentation or anaerobic digestion.

To be marketed for agricultural use, compost must be accompanied by specification relative to its origin, composition and degree of stabilization. If mixed substrates are used for composting, constituents (expressed in % dry weight) must be specified in order of decreasing concentration. When adding stabilized organic matter of different origin to compost for marketing, the mixture may not be designed "compost": i.e. it should be described as <u>organic soil conditioner</u> and the description be qualified by reference to specific components.

3.2 - PHYSICAL AND CHEMICAL PARAMETERS

The characteristics and composition of compost vary according to the type of starting material. The data listed in Table 1 refer to values compatible with compost from municipal solid waste.

Table 1 - Compost characteristics according to the grade of marketable product. Values listed under columns A represent today's situation; those of columns B represent target values at which to aim for the develpment of the process and product.

GRADE	SIEVE SIZE mm	MAXIMUM INERTS (% dry wt) GLASS		PLASTIC		MAXIMUM MOISTURE %	BIODEGRAD. ORG. MATTER (MINIMUM) % dry wt	
		A	B	A	B	A-B	A	B
Very fine	8	1	0.1	0.4	0.2	30	20	30
Fine	16	2	1	0.8	0.4	35	25	35
Medium	24	4	2	1.6	0.8	40	30	40
Coarse	40	6	3	3.5	1.6	50	35	45

Other required characteristics are:

a) - <u>Organic matter</u>: specifications should include % content of organic matter (see Table 1) and the degree of its stabilization (see Section 4). In relating organic matter to organic carbon (organic matter = K organic carbon), coefficients derived from soil analyses (K = 1,78) appear to be too small. Therefore a K value closer to 2.00 is suggested.

b) - <u>Moisture content</u>: lowering of the moisture content is one indication of progress in the composting process. Low moisture content avoids unnecessary transportation of water, and helps in sieving, storing or spreading operations. Moisture content may vary according to the climatic conditions in which the process is done. Yet, the moisture content must be stated on marketed compost to help in determining the commercial value of the product.

c) - <u>Inerts</u>: substantially inert-free compost is easier to market. The components which cause the greatest market resistence are normally glass and plastics. THe components need to be contained within the levels stated in Table 1. Ferrous metals are practically absent. Non ferrous metals are generally present at a low level and may be separated following composting together with glass and plastics. Separation of inerts is relatively straightforward in well stabilized and dried products thus providing an indication on the quality of the preceding process.

d) - Mineral content: admissible levels for certain nutrients in compost are summerized in Table 2.

-Nitrogen: total levels not less than 0.6% dry weight (dw.); organic nitrogen not less than 90%; inorganic nitrogen should mostly be in the nitrate form. The concentration of NH4+ in the finished compost should not exceed the level of 0.04% dw. (except for the "fresh compost"). The presence of NH4+ is an indication of unstabilized materials. It occurs most frequently when starting materials have a low C/N ratio.

- P and K: normal range for P2O5: 0.5 - 0.9% dw.; K2O: 0.2 - 0.8% dw.

- Micronutrients: micronutrient requirements are difficult to assess. Certain micronutrients are essential for plant growth. The presence of Fe, Cu or Zn chelates is advantageous to plants.

e) - Initial and final C/N values must be declared: C/N ratio must be below 22 in order to achieve the stabilization degree required for "compost" when the starting material has a C/N in the range of 35-40 or slightly above. When wastes contain nitrogen-rich products the final C/N values are expected to be proportionally lower.

f) - Salinity: an exceedingly high salinity may adversely affect plants and crops. Damage is proportionally greater in non-calcareous soils. Total salinity (conductivity) should not exceed 2 g salt/liter (expressed as NaCl) and the concentration of Na and Cl ions should be specified in marketed compost.

Table 2 - Total amounts of nutrients in compost (dry weight basis).

NUTRIENTS	ADMISSIBLE LEVELS (minimum)
N	0.6%
P2O5	0.5%
K2O	0.3%
CaO	2.0%
CaCO3	3.0%
MgO	0.3%

g) - pH: most common pH values range 6.5 to 8.0. Compatibility with plant growth is within the range of 5.5 to 8.0. If pH value are higher or lower, the reason for their departure from standards should be specified.

3.3 - HEAVY METALS

Limits of heavy metals in the use of compost in agricultural soils must be consistent with EC directives for sewage sludge disposal in soil.

In Table 3 maximum load/year and maximum concentration in agricultural soil reproduce proposed EC directives for the use of sludges in agriculture. However, maximum permissible levels of heavy metals in compost should be proportionally lower and a multiplication factor of 0.3-0.2 is suggested for adapting to the compost the EC levels set for sludge (Section 7). Values in Table 3 relating to separate garbage collection (de Bilt, Netherlands, VAM), are shown as an example of consistency with the proposed 0.3-0.2 multiplication factor.

Values included in Table 3 should not apply to pot cultivation of ornamental plants, for which higher values may be permitted.

Table 3 - Limiting values for heavy metals in relation to concentration in compost, annual addition and content in agricultural soils to which compost is applied. R and M values refer, respectively, to recommended and mandatory limits.

| | MAXIMUM IN COMPOST (mg/Kg dry wt) | | | MAXIMUM LOAD YEAR (3) | | MAXIMUM IN SOIL (3) | |
| | standard collection (1) | | separate collec. (2) | Kg/ha | | mg/Kg dry wt | |
	R	M		R	M	R	M
Zn	1000	1500	240	25.0	30.0	150	300
Pb	750	1000	160	10.0	15.0	50	100
Cu	300	500	40	10.0	12.0	50	100
Cr	150	200	30	10.0	-	50	-
Ni	50	100	10	2.0	3.0	30	50
As	-	-	-	0.35	-	20	-
Hg	5	5	0.5	0.40	-	2	-
Cd	5	5	1	0.10	0.15	1	3

1 - Flemish Public Waste Company limits for compost use in Agriculture: requested maximum levels relative to use on food crops (R in this table) or on ornamentals (M).
2 - Results of separate collection of degradable organic fraction of MSW in de Bilt, Netherlands (VAM).
3 - Proposal for the EEC Council Directive (25-5-1984) for the use of sludge in agriculture.

3.4 - STABILIZATION

To be compatible with agricultural uses, composts must be stabilized to a degree at which they do not hamper plant viability. The process of composting, mostly during the initial decomposition stage, is accompanied by the metabolic production of phytotoxins (see Paragraph 9.1). Toxin production progressively subsides as the stabilization progresses. This implies that different degrees of processing are required to match the various classes of marketed compost.

To assess the extent of stabilization appears to be a difficult task considering the present incomplete understanding of the parameters involved and related standards. An effort should be made to acquire more experience in a number of fields related to stabilization:

3.4.1 - Humification: the degree of humification (i.e. the ratio between total humic-like substances and total organic matter) may provide information on stabilization. The following parameters appear to be necessary:

- <u>Humified</u> <u>organic</u> <u>matter</u>: at least 10% of organic carbon. Specific research should clarify whether this value could be increased.
- <u>C/N</u>: this parameter is characterized by different dynamics depending on the initial substrate values (high or low). Therefore both initial and final C/N values must be shown to define stabilization (Paragraph 9.1.3). A final C/N ratio below 22 is recommended when starting with materials having values above 35-40.

3.4.2 - <u>Phytotoxicity</u>: Metabolic toxins are produced during decomposition, tending to subside during the stabilization stage. Toxicity measured with biological tests may indicate the degree of degradation and help in assessing plant compatibility. Direct toxicity analyses represent an imperfect gauge for stabilization (Paragraph 9.1). In spite of this limitation, toxicity evaluation fits in with the need for assessing physiological compatibility with plants and the best use of compost. The degree of maturation required may vary according to compost classification (see Section 4) and its specific uses.

A simple method which may be carried on in the factory is related to instantaneous toxicity (i.e. the toxicity which may be measured at any moment). The value of this test is bound to continuous monitoring of the composting process and understanding of the various phases through which it evolves.

3.4.3 - <u>Latent</u> <u>metabolism</u>: the stabilization of organic matter is accompanied by a number of metabolic changes. Incomplete stabilization leads to a latter resumption of metabolic process. Analyses of respiration, heat and toxin show a strict relationship between the metabolic phase already achieved and the complementary (latent) evolution occurring when condition again becomes favorable.

Laboratory analyses on latent metabolism then have the potential for providing objective information on the state of stabilization of organic matter, independent of material origin or our knowledge of the processes undergone. This allows the determination of how far the process was carried out, even on unknown products, and an assessment of the most appropriate agricultural uses.

3.5 - MICROBIOLOGICAL SPECIFICATIONS FOR SANITIZED COMPOST

Composts have to meet the requirements of epidemiology hygiene. This can be achieved if pathogenic organisms have been rendered harmless for man, animals and plants whether the germs originate from domestic wastes, sewage sludge or other components. There is need to take cognizance of the end use of compost. Since compost is principally used for ornamental plants, which are often kept in apartments, the absence of human pathogens should be ensured. Less severe requirements are needed for its use in open fields and forestry. Composts should be assessed in terms of hygiene by testing both the composting process and the end-product, the compost.

3.5.1 - <u>Processes</u>: Many microbiological investigations of composting plants have shown that the requirements of hygiene are met under proper operation of the decomposition process. These methods have to be used in the development and testing of composting processes in order to ensure that they are able to meet the hygienic requirements and allow data to be collected on performance. In this work, typical infectious germs of differing resistance are used as pilot organisms and their passage through the whole composting process is followed.

The chemical and physical parameters of the different processes have to be considered in the investigation, together with the differing types of processes. The sanitization effect depends on the duration and temperature of the decomposition process while temperature itself depends on chemical and physical parameters, such as water content, aeration, pH-value, particle size, available organic matter. To produce a hygienically safe compost, provisions have to be made that pathogenic organisms be rendered absolutely harmless for man, animals and plants through the composting process. The relevant methods of investigation are described in the literature.

3.5.2 - Of end-products: As well as controlling the process, testing of end-products can show them hygienically safe. Compost should not contain harmful contents of salmonellae, infectious parasites such as Ascaris and Tenia species. Germs infectious for plants, or nematodes should not be present in an amount greater than normally found in soils.

Other groups of organisms, e.g.: enterobacteria., coli-bacteria, fecal-steptococci, f2-phages, are being discussed as indicators of the hygenic safety of the end-product. In some experiments, fecal-streptococci and total coliforms appear to be the best candidates as indicators, and their limit values for hygenized compost should remain, respectively, below 5.10 3 and 5.10 2. However these limits may not be generalized at the moment, awaiting results of more comprehensive international experimental investigations.

4 - COMPOST CLASSIFICATION

Products to be used in agriculture may be taken at several stages of stabilization, preceding or following the completion of processes which lead to "mature" compost. Starting from the fresh material, products should be separated according to the following classification.

4.1 - FRESH ORGANIC MATTER (not to be called compost)
- Definition: Raw material before undergoing decomposition (or at the beginning of it).
- Agricultural uses: Unsuitable for agricultural use. However, it may serve as a substrate for composting, preparation of hot beds, preparation of mushroom compost, etc.
- Hygenic evaluation: Harzardous for man, animals and plants; the hazard persists if the organic matter is not properly composted.
- General evaluation: Useful as starting material for composting. Its direct use as a soil conditioner should be discouraged because of problems leading to the diffusion of animal and plant pathogens and parasites. In addition, the ongoing decomposition could endanger crops or standing plants (see: fresh compost). Special consideration should be given to the use of fresh organic matter for heat recovery (hot-bed preparation or similar uses).

4.2 - FRESH COMPOST
- Definition: Organic matter that has been through the thermophilic stage and achieved sanitization. It has undergone partial decomposition but it is not yet stabilized into mature compost. With the exception of moisture content (which may be higher) specifications for this product must satisfy those given for "coarse compost" (see Paragraph 3.2).

- <u>Agricultural</u> <u>uses</u>: This product may be used in a manner appropriate to the particular crop management (e.g. winter top dressings in orchards, soil preparation between crops, etc.). Further decomposition and stabilization normally takes place in the soil with benefits from the improvement of soil structure, organic matter mineralization and increased soil microbial activity. Maximum efficency of stabilization is obtained by turning-in the fresh compost to a depth of 5-10 cm, at which best oxygenation is achieved. Following this stage the material may be incorporated to full cultivation depth.

- <u>Hygenic</u> <u>evaluation</u>: The thermophilic stage having been completed, the product may be considered safe for the uses proposed.

- <u>General</u> <u>evaluation</u>: Use of fresh compost is possible only with proper care. Fresh compost is compatible with bulk supply and should not be packaged, as uncontrolled microbial transformations would occur.

4.3 - "COMPOST"

- <u>Definition</u>: The term "COMPOST" is a synonym of mature compost. To be thus designated, a compost must meet all of the specifications introduced in Chapter 3.

- <u>Agricultural</u> <u>uses</u>: The material is fully suitable for application on the land, even in the presence of standing crops. Nevertheless direct contact with the roots should be avoided (as in the preparation of potting mediums) because this may temporarily arrest growth.

- <u>Hygienic</u> <u>evaluations</u>: Safe as described.

- <u>General</u> <u>evaluation</u>: A valuable product for general purposes and as an organic soil conditioner on a large scale.

4.4 - CURED COMPOST

- <u>Definition</u>: A highly stabilized product which results from exposing "compost" to a prolonged period of humification and mineralization, beyond the stage of maturity. Minimum starting moisture content for curing should be above 35%, and should be raised to this value if necessary.

- <u>Agricultural</u> <u>uses</u>: Cured compost is a highly valuable material for the preparation of artificial substrates that have direct contact with root systems of transplanted crops. Its usefulness in the nursery, for flower cultivation, and for intensive cultivation may be matched only by that of natural humus.

- <u>Hygienic</u> <u>evaluation</u>: Safe for the agricultural uses given in this paper.

- <u>General</u> <u>evaluation</u>: Very valuable product especially for intensive cultivations, such as potting, flower production, nursery protected crops, etc.

5 - <u>METHODS</u> <u>OF</u> <u>ANALYSIS</u>

Methods described here are consistent with the "Proposal for the definition of parameters and analytical measurements applicable to composting experiments using urban waste (XII/MPS/34/83-EN) revised June 26, 1985.

5.1 - CHEMICAL AND PHYSICAL ANALYSES

Appropriate standard methods to be used for physical and chemical analyses of compost (listed in alphabetical order):

- <u>Ammoniacal nitrogen</u>: a) distillation b) direct measurement with ion selective electrode.
- <u>Calcium</u>: Acid solubilization and determination by spectrometric methods.
- <u>Carbon</u> (total organic carbon): a) a fraction (multiplied by 0.5) of the organic matter present; b) dichromate oxidation after careful homogenization of the sample; c) elemental analysis.
- <u>C/N ratio</u>: by calculation.
- <u>Conductivity</u>: conductivity meter.
- <u>Heavy metals</u>: acid solubilization and determination by spectrometric methods.
- <u>Inerts</u>: hand separation.
- <u>Magnesium</u>: acid solubilization and determination by spectrometric methods.
- <u>Moisture</u>: complement of total solids by calculation.
- <u>Nitrate nitrogen</u>: a) reduction to ammoniacal nitrogen and distillation; b) colorimetric determination; c) direct measurement with ion selective electrode.
- <u>Nitrogen</u>: a) Kjeldahl method; b) elemental analysis; c) dichromate oxidation.
- <u>Organic matter</u>: ignition at 450-600 C..
- <u>Particle size</u>: screening compost with sieves of different aperture.
- <u>pH</u>: standard electrochemical measurement.
- <u>Phosphorous</u>: acid solubilization and colorimetric determination.
- <u>Potassium</u>: acid solubilization and flame photometry.
- <u>Total solids</u>: drying at 105 C (or with microwaves) to constant weight.

5.2 - ANALYSES FOR STABILIZATION

No clear standard has yet been agreed upon to assess acceptable levels of compost stability. Yet methods are available and an effort should be made to evaluate their potentiality for assessing maturity. Most relevant methods may be related to:

- <u>Humus analyses</u>: the degree of humification (i.e. the ratio between total humic-like substances and total organic matter) may provide information on stabilization. Methods of extracting humus-like substances include: a) NaOH; b) Na4 P2O7; c) Na OH + Na4 P2O7. The quality of extracted humic substances may be evaluated: a) by standard separation of humic and fulvic acids (acid precipitation of fulvic acids); b) by fractionation (gel-cheomatography) of different molecular masses.

- <u>Respiration</u> activity: respiration is indicative of the amount of degradable matter still present and therefore it is inversely related to stabilization. Respiration activity needs to be measured on samples with 50% moisture. Results are expressed in mg O2/g of volatile solid, following 4 day incubation at 20 C. Respiration rate is expressed in mg O2/g of volatile solids/hr. Higher temperatures more representative of those existing during composting (e.g. 45 C.) should be explored in parallel to those at 20 C.

- <u>Spontaneous heat</u>: heat generated is directly related to the amount of readily degradable organic matter still present and inversely related to stabilization. Temperature evolution should be measured during 10 day incubation at 20 C. in open Dewar vessels. 500-1000 g of compost (particle size < 10 mm) are used and a thermometer inserted at two-thirds of the depth of the container.

- <u>Toxicity</u> (phytotoxicity): metabolic toxins are produced during decomposition, tending to decline during the stabilization stage. Toxicity measured with biological tests may help to reveal the ongoing degradation and in assessing plant compatibility. A fast reliable method may be provided by Cress (Lepidium sativum) seed germination analyses, following 24 hr. incubation at 28 C. Germination occurs in a Petri dish lined with filter paper saturated with the pressure extract solution (100 atm/cm2) from the material previously adjusted to 60% moisture.

5.3 - MICROBIOLOGICAL ANALYSES

<u>Isolation</u> of <u>Salmonellas</u>. Enrichment of samples in selenite (10g + 90g of selenite) for 18 hr at 37 C. Incubation in Petri dishes (37 C, 24 hr) using the following cultural media: SS, McConkey, Wilson Blair. Biochemical tests with TSI, Lysing, MIU, citrate. Sierological characterization.

<u>Isolation</u> of <u>Streptococci</u>. Kanomycin-asculin-azide-agar (KAAA). Bacto-M Enterococcus agar (EA).

<u>Isolation</u> of <u>total coliforms</u>. Desoxycolate-lactose agar (DLA). Bactobillant green bile agar (BGBA).

PART II

SCIENTIFIC AND TECHNICAL COMMENTS
ON COMPOSTING AND COMPOST

6 - SEPARATION OF STABILIZATION

The term compost, as most often used, refers to the uncertainly-defined product of waste organic matter decomposition. Such a usage is too vague, however, for separating processes or for recognizing dynamic sequences that lead to a specific product. A first consequence is that information related to controlled waste treatment appears to be inadequate or poorly conveyed. Also, current uncertainties regarding the evaluation of composting plants, processes, and the quality of end-products reflect the lack of standard definitions and of related parameters.

The problem is that the term "compost" is indiscriminately applied to a range of products embracing those derived from aerobic, anaerobic and fermentation processes, or those that are in varying stages of decomposition and stabilization. Specific definitions are needed to help in discriminating between processes and in recognizing stage sequnces. They are also a prerequisite for developing parameters that describe processes and products, and for arriving at analytical methods for quantifying such parameters.

6.1 - THE DEFINITION OF COMPOSTING

In the past decades, concerted attempts have been made to develop fast and efficient stabilization processes for dealing with the increasing amount of organic wastes. At this stage, attention has been concerted on aerobic biodegradation, because it is conducive to fast and simple operations. It also is attended by fewer objectionable odours and is characterized by a thermophilic stage that is beneficial in terms of destruction of animal and plant pathogens. Anaerobic (reducing) processes differ from aerobic processes in terms of metabolic pathways and microbial populations. Products of anaerobic processes will resume metabolic activity and further stabilizational changes (oxidative processes) when exposed to aerobic conditions.

Therefore, in order to avoid confusion and to keep abreast with development it is imperative to restrict the term "composting" to a specified type of process. Moreover, because controlled biooxidative processes appear to be by far the most interesting of the present developments in organic waste treatment, they should be specified as in the definition proposed: COMPOSTING IS A CONTROLLED BIOOXIDATIVE PROCESS THAT: 1) INVOLVES A HETEROGENEOUS ORGANIC SUBSTRATE IN THE SOLID STATE; 2) EVOLVES BY PASSING THROUGH A THERMOPHILIC STAGE AND A TEMPORARY RELEASE OF PHYTOTOXIN; AND 3) LEADS TO PRODUCTION OF CARBON DIOXIDE, WATER, MINERALS AND STABILIZED ORGANIC MATTER (COMPOST).

Key words and phrases:

a) Controlled...Process: This characteristic distinguishes "composting" from natural processes that occur in the absence of an imposed control. It implies a control of temperature, moisture, substratum composition, oxygenation, etc. (see Chapt. 8).

b) Biooxidative: The condition, "biological", distinguishes composting from physical and chemical treatments. Furthermore, the qualification "biooxidative" delineates composting with respect to other non-aerobic processes and operational conditions.

c) Organic Substrate: An organic substrate is consistent with the condition "biological stabilization", and with the production of an organic soil conditioner (see Paragraph 3.2).

d) Heterogeneous organic substrates: For the purpose of the definition, "heterogeneous" describes substrates containing a mixture of organic materials from different origins. MSW fits well in this category.

e) Solid state: A solid state is consistent with the practice of organic waste treatment, well established in industrial processes;

f) Thermophilic Stage: Biooxidative processes are exothermic. Substantial quantities of heat are produced in the initial part of the process which accounts for the temperature rise. The rate of heat production declines rapidly during the subsequent stabilization stage (generally associated with a temperature drop below 40-35 C). This dynamic quality of heat production may be considered a unique condition for characterizing composting. A slow or insufficient temperature rise, or a delayed drop, imply unfavorable process development and/or poor control of composting factors (see Paragraph 8.3). Special consideration should also be given to processes which use temperature feed-back control, where temperature rise is limited and the temperature drop anticipated.

g) Temporary Phytotoxin Release: The metabolic production of phytotoxins characterises the initial stage of fresh organic matter decomposition. Toxin production apparently is less intense and of shorter duration with heterogeneous substrates and under aerobic conditions. A persistent phytotoxicity indicates poor process development (most often insufficient oxygenation) or poorly balanced substrates (Paragraph 9.1).

h) Carbon dioxide, Water and Minerals: These terms refer to some of the products of biooxidative degradation processes.

i) Stabilized Organic Matter (Compost): Composting by definition leads to a stabilized (humified) product that is highly valuable for agricultural uses (organic soil conditioner). It may be easily handled or stored, or used directly on the land without giving rise to adverse environmental effects (Paragraph 6.2).

6.2 - THE DEFINITION OF COMPOST

Compost is the product of the composting process. As organic matter composts, it passes through a number of sequential changes. Accordingly, the composting process must be defined in terms of stages leading to a specific product. To be properly called compost the organic matter must have been stabilized to a humus-like product. It must have been degraded to fine particles, having lost its original identity. As a stable product it can be stored without further treatment, and can be applied on the land without damage to standing crops. If stabilization has not been achieved, phytotoxin production will continue in the soil until completion of the decomposition stage (see below).

The term "stabilization", although commonly attributed to the whole process, would be more appropriate for the second stage of composting (characterized by humification). This stage follows an initial decomposition stage where destabilization prevails. Heat and toxin production differ greatly between the two stages. They are at a maximum during the fast initial decomposition, tending to decline and subside as the process progresses toward stability (Paragraphs 6.1 and 9.1).

Consistent with the preceding discussion, a definition of compost may be given that links the product to a specific process and to a precise stage of its evolution. The definition is: COMPOST IS THE STABILIZED AND SANITIZED PRODUCT OF COMPOSTING WHICH IS BENEFICIAL TO PLANT GROWTH. IT HAS UNDERGONE AN INITIAL RAPID STAGE OF DECOMPOSITION AND IS IN THE PROCESS OF HUMIFICATION (STABILIZATION STAGE).

Key words and phrases in this definition are:

a) Stabilized: Stabilization is a prerequisite for storage, marketing and unrestricted use in agriculture. Stabilization must be achieved through the biological process itself. Stabilization must not be confused with or substituted by desiccation and sterilization. Although these may lead to an appearance of staization, the degradation (latent metabolism) would resume when conditions again become favorable.

b) Sanitized: To be of practical application, the composting must result in a self-sanitization, and thus allow a direct utilization of compost in agriculture. Pathogen destruction is accomplished through the combined effects of high temperature and competition with a non pathogenic microbial population "also favored by thermophilic condition (Paragraph 9.2). Self-sanitation must not be confused with or substituted by artificial pasteurization or sterilization.

c) Product of Composting: It associates the product with the process, and excludes products from other processes.

d) Beneficial to plants: It is essential that the product does not adversely affect plant viability (i.e. phytotoxicity).

e) Initial Rapid Stage of Decomposition: Defines "decomposition" as being the first of two stages of organic matter degradation. The second stage (stabilization) implies that the first stage must be terminated and presence of soluble organic residues and catabolites should be at a very low level.

f) Process of Humification: Defines the stabilization stage as being characterized by a relatively slow process of humification and mineralization.

6.3 - IMPLICATIONS OF PROCESS AND PRODUCT DEFINITION

The above definitions tie "compost" and "composting" to the controlled biooxidative treatment of organic wastes. To be consistent, the use of terms such as "fermentation" or "aerobic fermentation", in reference to biooxidation should be eliminated as not being appropriate or pertinent. Also, in view of the definition of composting, adding the adjective "aerobic" to the process (i.e. "aerobic composting") would become redundant and must be dropped.

For the same reason unfinished products (not yet humified, or still phytotoxic) may not be called "compost" although they may be qualified for special uses (e.g. fresh compost: see Paragraph 4.2), even when drived from a composting process. Finally, products of different origin or processes should be named differently. This also holds for products from biooxidative stabilization under conditions different from composting.

The preceding specifications help to exclude prolonged metabolisms and extended heat or phytotoxin production that characterize processes different from composting and interfering with it (Paragraphs 7, 8.2, and 8.3). They would also exclude unmanaged or poorly controlled processes euphemistically termed "composting".

The advantage of restricting the term "composting" to controlled biooxidative processes is apparent when the impact on product quality and the improvement of the treatment of waste organic matter are considered. Compared with other processes, controlled biooxidation ensures greater efficiency, is more effective hygenically, eliminates objectionable odours, and shortens the time needed for stabilization. All of these conditions are essential to the promotion of sound industrial management of organic wastes.

7 - SUBSTRATES

All organic matter of biological origin and many synthetic products are biodegradable and may serve as starting material for composting.
Examples of wastes that can be used are:
- the organic fraction of municipal solid waste (from the city as a whole, individual neighbourhoods, households, canteens, restaurants, etc.);
   - wastewater sludges (from aerobic or anaerobic sewage treatment plants);
   - industrial wastes and residues (fermentation industries, paperwaste and cellulosic residues, wood bark and cork residues, vegetal tannery sludges, etc.);
   - food processing wastes (canning industries, fish and shell-fish wastes, slaughter house effluents and residues, etc.);
   - agricultural wastes (plant and product residues, animal wastes and slurries).

Wastes contaminated with hazardous materials should not be used for composting. Hazardous materials of importance in this context are heavy metals and slowly degradable toxic organic compounds. The latter pose a health risk either directly or through their metabolic (breakdown) products.

At present, the content of heavy metals in compost is increasing. The use of sludges in composting can add to the problem. Therefore, starting materials should be selected that will not contaminate the compost produced and pollute the soil. Pretreatments should be geared in order to restrict composting to the organic fraction of MSW thus limiting the transfer of heavy metals into the organic matter. To achieve this, inerts should be removed, where possible, prior to composting.

The concentrations of heavy metals in compost should not exceed those given in the EC Directive for sewage sludge disposal to agricultural land. However, considering the relatively high amount of organic matter annually requested for soil conditioning (5-25 t dry matter/ha) maximum permissible levels of heavy metals in compost should be proportionally lower. A totally different problem characterizes sludge disposal. This is essentially a water-disposal operation which reduces the need for expensive water separation procedures.

A multiplication factor of about 0.3-0.2 is therefore suggested for adapting to the compost specifications the EC levels on heavy metals set for sludge. This suggestion is consistent with the heavy metal content which may be achieved by early separation of the organic fraction from wastes or, better by the separate collection of organic wastes to be composted.

Table 3 gives data on heavy metal content in compost, relative to conventional and separate collection of wastes. Compared to values of heavy metals in compost in Tab. 3, values of minimum load/year would appear rather high. However, the EEC proposal for sludge takes into account the reduced impact of heavy metals in soil due to insolubilization effects and to the relatively smaller assimilation by the plants.

Values included in Table 3 should not apply in pot cultivation of ornamental plants, for which higher values may be permitted.

As with the heavy metals, hazardous organic compounds (detergents, pesticides, phenols, hydrocarbons, products of pharmaceutical industries, etc.) must be dealt with according to existing legislation on hazardous waste disposal. They must not be allowed to be present in the compost produced for agricultural use. Again, less vigorous conditions may be permitted for the pot cultivation of ornamental plants.

8 - FACTORS IN THE CONTROL OF COMPOSTING

Factors that determine the course of composting are those that are related to optimium biological activity. Those which may be technically controlled are:

8.1 - MOISTURE CONTENT

Moisture content varies greatly with different starting materials. The addition of liquids and sludges also affects moisture content. Composting is compatible with a high moisture content provided that this does not restrict porosity and oxygen exchange.

Moisture requirements vary with the changing composition of the microbial populations. Most water is required during the initial decomposition stage, in which bacteria prevail. If the moisture content is less than 35-40% during this stage, microbial activity is slower or inhibited, and the completion of the entire process is proportionally delayed. Moisture content requirement is lower during the stabilization stage when actinomycetes and fungi prevail.

The organic fraction from municipal solid refuse is often characterized by less than optimal moisture levels. Raising the initial content by adding water or sludge (i.e. to a limit of 60-65%) appears to be favourable and should be encouraged.

8.2 - OXYGENATION

Oxygen supply appears to be the factor that most frequently limits composting in poorly controlled plants. Oxygen demand is very high during the initial decomposition stage, because of a rapid expansion of the microbial population, a temperature rise, and a high rate of biochemical activity. It is recommended that at this stage the oxygen concentration be maintained at a minimum value compatible with aerobic conditions in the particular composting system being used. Oxygen demand decreases somewhat during the stabilization stage and even more during the curing stage. Excess oxygen during the last stage would lead to humus consumption and fast mineralization.

8.3 - TEMPERATURE

The thermophilic stage results from the intense metabolic activity of a rapidly expanding microbial population which develops on the most readily available fractions of the substrate (e.g. simple molecules, soluble organic components). Consequently, if the substrate was previously stabilized or is lacking in a readily available fraction, the temperature rise will not be sufficient for hygienizing the mass (Paragraph 9.2).

During the initial stage, the heat must be retained within the mass of compost to permit the necessary temperature rise and the resulting sanitization (Paragraph 9.2). For open composting the latter condition is favoured by suitably turning the pile, so that all material eventually is exposed to the high temperature. With forced aeration in static pile systems, covering with a blanket of mature compost will ensure a uniform distribution of heat.

Following sanitization, a temperature above 60-65 C. should be prevented. Decomposition is slowed at a high temperature and the more sensitive microorganisms may be killed. The mesophilic population (i.e. the one most responsible for the succeeding stabilization) may also be adversely affected. A continuing high temperature, lasting beyond 5-6 weeks, indicates an abnormally prolonged decomposition and a delayed transition to the stabilization stage. A delayed temperature drop most often is a function of poor process control (inadequate aeration). On the other hand, the temperature drop must occur naturally and not be artificially induced (e.g. by dehydration, excess ventilation).

8.4 - pH

Although organic substrates having a wide range of pH levels (pH 3 to 11) can be composted, optimum levels are within the range of pH 5.5-8.0. Whereas bacteria thrive at a nearly neutral pH, fungi are favoured by an environment that is fairly acid.

In practice, the pH level is not easily changed. Generally, the pH level drops at the beginning of the composting process due to the activity of acid-forming bacteria, which break down complex carbonaceous material. Protein degradation and liberation of ammonia from aminoacids account for the subsequent pH rise.

An alkaline pH in the decomposing stage combined with a high temperature leads to a loss of nitrogen volatilization of ammonia. This loss occurs mostly when the composting materials have a low C/N ratio.

8.5 - THE CARBON-NITROGEN RATIO (C/N)

If the initial C/N ratio is higher than 35, the microorganisms must oxidize the excess carbon before reaching a more favourable C/N. The C/N ratio of the microbial cell is about 10. However, due to the energy requirement, initial C/N values of 28-30 favour the maximum rate of process development. This ratio is generally lower than that of the organic fraction of MSW. Hence, the addition of N-rich materials, such as sludges from wastewater treatment, is beneficial. A C/N lower than 20 may retard decomposition, and increases nitrogen loss. As stated in Paragraph 8.4, loss of nitrogen during composting may also be related to pH and temperature.

9 - COMPOST SPECIFICATIONS

The specifications for marketed compost given in Chapter 3, are intended to provide minimum physical and chemical standards for product quality. However, they appear inadequate in relation to stabilization and hygienic standards. This chapter debates advances in this field and provides suggestions relative to steps to be taken to reduce the existing uncertainty.

9.1 - STABILIZATION

The control of the decomposition process in commercial plants appears to be mostly empirical. This results from a lack of standard procedures for evaluating process performance and product stabilization (maturation, etc.). The latter deficiency reflects the existing lack of suitable methodologies. Existing methods remain confined to a few laboratories or are limited to processes that occur with specific substrates or under specific conditions. The problem with such methods is that their performance with changing conditions remains unknown. Also, their utility in discriminating between stabilization processes must be better clarified before they can be applied.

9.1.1 - The value of analyzing latent metabolism. The stabilization of organic matter is accompanied by a number of metabolic changes. Interruption of composting leads to the resumption of metabolic processes, when favourable conditions are restored. Analyses of respiration, or of heat and toxin production show a close relationship between the metabolic phase already achieved, and the complementary (latent) evolution which may be observed when conditions again become favourable. Laboratory analyses of latent metabolism offers the potential for providing objective information on the stabilization of organic matter, independent of the origin of the materials or of our knowledge of the processing they have had.

Available methods for latent metabolism are based on the evaluation of oxygen uptake, self-heating capacity (i.e. production of heat in controlled conditions), or toxin evolution (latent toxicity). The latter method has shown a great adaptability to products coming from different materials and processes. They include municipal solid waste, maure, plant residues and sludges from aerobic or anaerobic processes.

9.1.2 - The value of analyzing degree of humification. The stabilization stage (Paragraph 6.2) is one of progressive anabolic synthesis and polymerization in which "humic" components are prevalent. Disappearance of soluble catabolites or substrate residues (present during the decomposition stage) and especially the appearance of new humus-like polymers may provide a valuable measure for stabilization. The value of the analyses of humic components introduced in Paragraph 3.4 should be clarified particularly when applied to products of different origins and processes, or when stabilized organic matter from other sources (root, natural humus, etc.) is added to the marketed compost.

9.1.3 - The value of other parameters.
- C/N ratio: C/N ratio undergoes changes during composting and

yet its dynamics strongly varies with different substrates. A decline from an initial C/N of 35-40 or higher to a final level of 18-20 would imply an advanced degree of stabilization. However, care must be taken in interpreting the significance of the C/N level in composts of unknown origin. When products rich in nitrogen serve as starting substrates (e.g.: animal wastes, sludges from water treatment, etc.). The initial C/N ratio may be low (even below 10) and tends to rise during the process of stabilization. Therefore, it is necessary that both initial and final C/N values be indicated for a correct evaluation of stabilization. Also, a concerted effort should be made to acquire more experience in this field and to assess changes which may help in assessing stabilization.

- Chemical or biological oxygen demand: A number of suggestions have been made that BOD or COD values should be introduced. Before such values are made a part of specifications, however, the manner must be defined in which COD and BOD are related to the process evolution and stabilization .

9.2 - MICROBIOLOGICAL SPECIFICATIONS FOR SANITIZED COMPOST

At the time of delivery by the treatment plant to the customer the compost should meet the following requirements:
- the compost should not contain salmonellae (pre-enrichment) in 100 g (fresh compost);
- the compost should not contain infective parasite ova;
- the compost should not contain more than 5.10^2 faecal coliforms per g;
- the compost should not contain more than 5.10^3 faecal streptococci per g.

For efficient disinfection of compost, the technologies used should meet the following requirements;
a) Windrow composting. To ensure a hygienically safe product the composting process must be operated for at least three to four weeks. During this time the temperature should exceed 65 C for at least one week. It is most important that all of the compost mass in the windrow reaches this temperature for the recommended period of time. These requirements can be met by operating a program of regular turning of the piles or by covering static piles with a layer of composted material. Thus a more uniform temperature profile in the composting material can be achieved. To further improve the hygienic quality of the compost, the composting process should be followed by curing the material in stacks for another three or more weeks.
b) Aerated static pile composting. The rate of aeration must be controlled so that the appropriate temperature/time profile required for sanitization is maintained (this can be achieved using temperature feedback control). Covering the piles with compost (mature compost) will permit the required temperatures to be attained throughout the composting material.
c) Bioreactor-Composting. In bioreactors more uniform temperature profiles in the composting material can be attained and the temperature can be influenced by the aeration rate and the technique of feeding. For a hygienically safe product the thermophilic treatment may be of shorter duration than in the open, due to a more uniform temperature distribution. The flow time of the material through the reactor(s) should be in the range of two weeks or more to avoid problems of regrowth. A subsequent curing time of at least three weeks will help to improve the technical and hygienic quality of the compost.

In bioreactors the temperature must be closely monitored and in case of disturbances immediate countermeasures by the operator are necessary. That material which has not reached the required temperature must be used as reflux material for another passage through the reactor.

This discussion also applies to plant pathogens, especially so when composting plant residues. An exposure to 55-60 for a few days is sufficient for the elimination of plant pathogens and nematodes. Few viruses would escape. Most plant viruses, including heat resistant ones, are destroyed by passing through the thermophilic stage of composting.

PART III

GLOSSARY

AERATION: the bringing about of contact of air and of composting solid organic matter by means of turning or ventilating to allow microbial aerobic metabolism (biooxidation).

AEROBIC FERMENTATION: improper, to be rejected.

AEROBIC RESPIRATION: the energy yielding chemical reaction in which the final electron acceptor is oxygen.

ANAEROBIC DIGESTION: the energy yielding chemical reaction in which the final electron acceptor is an inorganic molecule.

ARTIFICIAL SOIL: growth medium for plants obtained by mixing soil, or inert soil substitutes, with stabilized organic matter.

BIOASSAY: a laboratory assay using a biological test organism.

BIODEGRADABILITY: the potential which an organic component has for being converted into simpler structures by enzymatic activity.

BIOOXIDATION: aerobic microbial metabolism which involves the oxidation of organic or inorganic compounds, for the purpose of supplying energy and precursors for the biosynthesis of cell material.

BOD (biochemical oxygen demand): the amount of oxygen used in the biochemical oxidation of organic matter.

C/N RATIO (carbon-nitrogen ratio): ratio of organic-carbon/organic-nitrogen in compost or in the organic matter of origin.

COMPOST (synonym of mature compost): the stabilized and sanitized product of composting which is beneficial to plant growth. It has undergone an initial stage of decomposition and is in the process of humification (stabilization).

COMPOST CLASSIFICATION: division into fresh, mature and cured compost, according to the degree of stabilization.

COMPOST GRADE: division into very fine, fine, medium and coarse compost according to its physical and chemical characteristics.

COMPOSTING: controlled biooxidative process that: involves an heterogeneous organic substrate in the solid state; 2) evolves by passing through a thermophilic stage and a temporary release of phytotoxins; and 3) leads to the production of carbon dioxide, water, minerals and stabilized organic matter (compost).

CONTROLLED COMPOSTING: a process in which most important operating factors are controlled for the purpose of achieving maximum efficiency, reducing process time and sanitizing the organic mass.

CURED COMPOST: a highly stabilized product which results from exposing compost to a prolonged period of humification and mineralization beyond the stage of maturity.

DECOMPOSITION: the initial stage in the degradation of an organic substrate. It is characterized by processes of destabilization of the preexisting structure. In properly controlled composting, decomposition is conducive to a subsequent stage of stabiliza= tion (humification and mineralization).

FERMENTATION: the energy yielding chemical reaction in which the final electron acceptor is an organic compound.

FRESH COMPOST: organic matter that has gone through the thermophilic stage of composting and achieved sanitization. It has undergone a partial decomposition but it has not yet stabilized.

FRESH ORGANIC MATTER: raw organic substrate for composting before undergoing decomposition (or at the beginning of it).

HAZARDOUS COMPOUNDS: any organic or inorganic compound that may endanger life or health. Poisons, heavy metals, pesticides, etc. which may be found in waste belong to this group.

HOT-BED: cultivation or rooting bed in which a layer of decomposing (heat producing) organic matter underlies a layer of cultivated soil or artificial substrate.

HUMIFICATION: the microbial synthesis of three-dimensional polymers of saccharides and phenols resembling gums and lignin. It is a process of storing organic energy into compounds of high molecular weight which are slowly degradable.

INERTS: non-biodegradable products contained in wastes (glass, plastic, metals, etc.). They are permitted only at low levels in marketed compost.

LATENT METABOLISM: metabolic processes that remain to be completed before achieving stabilization. Latent metabolism may be measured by the evolution of respiration, heat production, toxicity, etc. in appropriately set conditions.

MATURE COMPOST: synonym of "Compost".

MESOPHILIC PHASE: phase of composting during which the temperature of the organic mass is between 30 and 45 C.

MUNICIPAL SOLID WASTE (MSW): residential and commercial solid waste generated within a community.

MUSHROOM COMPOST: cellulose-rich organic matter that has undergone the initial (decomposition) stage of a controlled composting process. The fungi bring about cellulolysis and humification of the substrate (stabilization stage).

ORGANIC MATTER: includes synthetic organic matter and matter having a biological origin. Biodegradability is mostly confined to the second group.

ORGANIC SOIL CONDITIONER: stabilized organic matter marketed for conditioning soil structure. It also improves other (chemical and biological) properties of the soil.

PATHOGEN: any disease producing microorganism.

PHYTOTOXINS: toxins which may endanger plant viability or funtionality.

SANITIZATION: the reduction of disease-producing organisms below the level of health risk.

SLUDGE: waste material deriving from the treatment of sewage.

STABILIZATION: second stage of composting (following decomposition). It is characterized by slow metabolic processes, lower heat production and the formation of humus.

50

THERMOPHILIC PHASE: phase of composting during which the temperature of the mass exceeds 45 C.

TOXICITY: reversable adverse biological effect due to toxins and other compounds.

TOXIN: unstable poison-like compounds of biological origin which may cause a reduction of viability or functionality in living organisms.

REFERENCES

Isolation of Salmonellas and Streptococci

(1) STANDARD METHODS FOR THE EXAMINATION OF WATER AND SEWAGE. A.P.H.A. 13th Edition 1971
(2) RECOMMENDED METHODS FOR MICROBIOLOGICAL EXAMINATION OF FOOD. A.P.H.A. 2nd Edition
(3) IDENTIFICATION OF ENTEROBACTERIACEAE. 3rd Edition Burgess Publ. Co.

Isolation of total coliforms
(4) STANDARD METHODS FOR THE EXAMINATION OF WATER AND SEWAGE. A.P.H.A. 13th Edition 1971
(5) Noble and Tonney - J. Am. Water Works Association; 27: 108, 1933
(6) Mossel et al 1978 - Streptokokken der Lancefield Crop in Lebensmitteln und Trinkwasser. Arch. S. Lebensmittelhyg. 29: 121-127
(7) Reuter 1978 - Selective Kultivierung von Enterokokken aus Lebensmitteln Tierisher. Arch. S. Lebensmittelhyg. . 29: 128-131

SESSION I : PRODUCTION OF COMPOST

Recent developments in composting

Compost options in integrated waste management systems

Composting and use of agricultural wastes in container media

Experimentation of three curing and maturing processes of fine urban fresh compost on open areas. Study carried out and financed on the initiative of the county council of Cotes-du-Nord - France

Can biomethanation be included in the processing of compost-like materials ?

Transformation of urban sludges mixed with grape stalks into organic fertilizers

Recycling of industrial waste : use of coco, jute, cotton and wool residues in vermicomposting

Thermophilic dry anaerobic fermentation process for the stabilization of household refuse

Vermicomposting of rabbit manure : modifications of microflora

Microorganisms and environmental factors in composting of agricultural waste of the Canary Islands

Municipal organic solid waste composting. An integrated component of recycling centers that process solid waste

Composting within an integrated system for processing agricultural waste

REPORT BY L. DIAZ

RECENT DEVELOPMENTS IN COMPOSTING

E.I. STENTIFORD
Department of Civil Engineering, The University of Leeds, U.K.

Summary

Composting using reactor based systems has seen few major changes over the past 10 years. In this time forced aeration static piles have come from research units to large scale fully operational plants. Pile systems have been used extensively on sewage sludge and are now being considered for full scale refuse composting operations. The control in terms of odour, temperature, process time and pathogen inactivation can now be compared favourably with reactor systems. The micro computer offers control and process monitoring possibilities even to low cost pile systems.

1. INTRODUCTION

One thing which those involved in composting agree on is that the process itself has been carried out in many forms for thousands of years. Some of the earliest records we have of a windrow type of operation date back over 2000 years to China. It was not really until the work of Sir Albert Howard in India in the 1920's, from which the Indore process emerged, that a systematic approach to composting commenced(1).

The Indore process was very much labour intensive, which was suitable for relatively small communities but the expansion of towns and cities required a more intensive type of operation. In the 1930's several mechanical devices were built to improve or speed up the composting operation. Many of these devices formed the basis of a variety of commercial composting systems. New commercial systems kept coming onto the market until about the mid-1960's when a succession of financial failures produced a distinct lack of interest in composting. The concern since that time with the quality of health and the environment has led to a revival of interest in composting, particularly related to sewage sludge and domestic refuse.

In recent times commercial reactor-based systems of composting have shown very little in the way of exterior changes. Changes have taken place, however, as our knowledge improves, with respect to items such as process control. In contrast to the reactor systems composting in piles has made dramatic advances over the past 10 years. This is largely as a result of the work carried out on forced aeration static piles at Beltsville, Maryland, USA in the mid-1970's(2). A recent survey in the USA showed that of a total of 79 operational plants on sewage sludge, 49 were aerated static piles(3). It should be noted however, that reactor based systems are also very much involved with future plans, with more than 50% of the planned, designed or in-construction plants in the USA being reactor types.

2.   COMPOSTING SYSTEMS

Despite the appearance of the many different types of composting plants
the process taking place within is very similar in all systems. In some
areas of composting the term has been used to describe both aerobic and
anaerobic processes. There is a strong school of thought, certainly prevalent within the EEC, which proposes that the term "composting" is restricted
solely to aerobic processes. It is to these processes that the remainder of
this paper is directed.

There are many ways of differentiating between system groups related to:
level of complexity, degree of control, method of aeration, open or enclosed,
and so on. In chemical engineering terms it is more realistic to think in
terms of reactor and non-reactor systems. Examples of both of these groups,
indicating some of their key features are given in Table 1. (It should be
noted that these are intended only as representative examples and the list
is by no means exhaustive). This table is based on the work of Gray et al.
which was published in 1973 (3).

If we are looking to recent developments in composting, which for
arguments sake I will take as the last ten years, then the developments can
maybe be highlighted by examining Table 1. The only system type in this
table which did not appear in the earlier work of Gray was the aerated static
pile.   It is not proposed to give any more detailed descriptions of these
commercial systems since many writers have examined them more fully (4,5,6).

A large part of recent compost research and development has been in the
field of aerated static piles. In 1975 work commenced at Beltsville(2) on
the use of forced aeration composting for sewage sludge. This followed
earlier work using windrows which proved to be inadequate when the capacity
had to be increased to handle more raw sludge. Concern over increase odour
and the greater likelihood of significant pathogen survival lead to the
development of the aerated static pile.

Both the windrow and the aerated static pile are, in most circumstances,
a lower cost option than reactor based systems. In addition the technology
involved is at a significantly lower level than with reactors which becomes
more important the smaller the installation. In respect of small installatons
most reactor systems are not economically viable due to their high capital
baseline costs. Almost all full scale aerated static pile installations
are working on sewage sludge cake although extensive research, at pilot scale,
has been carried out on refuse/sludge mixtures(7).

The remainder of this paper concentrates on the aerated static pile
making general comparisons with reactor systems.

3.   FORCED AERATION STATIC PILES
3.1 General

Sewage sludge cake, as produced, is not amenable to proper aeration,due
to its structure some physical processing is required prior to composting.
This takes the form of mixing and incorporation of bulking agent to give an
open structure suited to maintaining aerobic conditions within the composting
mass. Many mixing methods have been used depending on site, plant throughput and budget implications(8).

In sludge cake systems woodchips are the preferred bulking agent but
in the United States demand associated with the opening of more composting
installations has greatly increased the cost of woodchips. The situation
now existing is such that many municipalities are no longer in the compost
business but more in the woodchip business. Some research work has been
successful in using recycled compost on a bulking agent(9). However, some
attention might be needed in the area of long term carbon requirements for
process optimisation. Sewage sludge has a relatively low carbon/nitrogen

ratio (8-12) and woodchips act as a source of carbon to bring the initial C/N ratio to around 25, which appears to be optimum for this mixture. Low initial C/N ratios could lead to excessive losses of nitrogen in the form of ammonia.

The air required for the process is provided by a fan connected to a length (or lengths) of perforated pipe laid on a slightly sloping concrete base slab. This pipe is covered to a depth of approximately 150 mm with straw, or similar material, to improve air distribution and prevent blocking of the holes in the pipe. The mixed material is then placed over the pipe to form a pile which is either triangular in cross-section (for a single pile) or constitutes part of a multipile system (Figure 1.). The outer part of the pile is then covered with a layer of mature compost (100-150 mm) which both insulates the pile and assists in odour control. Fuller details of the sludge woodchip system can be found in many publications (2,10,11).

Recent research on a pilot scale has extended the use of aerated static piles to refuse/sludge mixtures(7). Findings have been very similar to those for sludge/woodchip piles. The additional variable which exists in the refuse/sludge piles is   the refuse bulking agent, which also constitutes a substantial part of the substrate. The system has the advantage however, that the bulking agent does not need to be recovered which is a primary economic concern with sludge/woodchip mixtures.

3.2 Land requirement

Many claims are made for the relatively short composting times which are possible in reactor type systems but it is unlikely, even under the most beneficial conditions, that the rapid biooxidative stage can be completed in less than 7-10 days. In the best run aerated static pile systems, working with sewage sludge, a period of at least 15 days is necessary. This additional process time together with the low profile nature of the static pile system means a much larger land requirement for this process stage.

This, however, does not complete the land use picture since this is very much dependent upon the compost market. Previous work with domestic refuse has identified the need for a period of maturation, of up to 4 months, to produce a general purpose material(7). If this is linked to a seasonal demand for compost then periods of storage of 6-8 months might be necessary. In this case, the saving of one or two weeks process time in the initial stage becomes relatively insignificant when viewed in the context of the subsequent storage requirement.

3.3 Odour

Reactor systems, for the most part, are either themselves closed vessels or are installed within a structure. In consequence malodours which might be produced at different stages of the process are contained and present a low nuisance risk to the surrounding community. This gives the reactor system an apparent immediate advantage over any pile system, which for economic reasons is generally established in the open air.

A major preoccupation in most of the early aerated static pile work in the United States was that of odour. It is easier to control potential odour problems if they have a single discrete source and are not emanating from many diffuse sites. It is possibly for this reason that the early work seemed primarily concerned with maintaining negative pressure aeration with its accompanying single source of exhaust air. This exhaust was directed into a small pile of mature compost which acted, very effectively, as an odour filter(2).

The unfortunate side-effect of this preoccupation was a yielding up of the ability to control pile temperature, and hence biochemical reaction rates. Subsequent research work in the United States examined positive pressure aeration and demonstrated its superiority in terms of temperature control and obtaining substantial moisture reductions in the final product(11).

However, this was not thought to be sufficient justification to implement the concept on a large scale.

In most aerated static pile systems a covering layer of mature compost, 100-150 mm thick is used for insulation purposes. The same material is used in the secondary odour control piles employed with negative pressure aeration. If we consider the pile configuarations illustrated in Figure 1. In the case of sludge/woodchip piles a height of approximately 2 metres and a width of 4 metres is used. A one metre length of pile with a 100 mm thick insulating layer has a volume of mature compost per metre of approximately 0.55 m³ for the single pile, and 0.2 m³ for the multipile system. At a bulk density of 400 kg.m⁻³ the weight of compost per unit length is approximately 1.45 tonnes for the single pile, and 1.50 tonnes for the multipile. Thus the volume of mature compost per tonne is 0.38 m³ for the single pile and 0.13 m³ for the multipile. If we consider a 50 tonne pile then the cover material used is approximately 19 m³ for the single pile and 6.5 m³ for the multipile. In a Beltsville type aerated static pile system the recommended quantity of material for an odour scrubber pile is approximately 1 m³ per 10 wet tonne of material(2). On this basis a 50 tonne pile of compost would require 5 m³ of dry screened compost which is less than that used in the positive pressure system. Provided our process is such that the air flow is relatively uniformly distributed, it seems likely that odour control under positive pressure aeration should be at least as good as negative pressure aeration if it is solely a function of the odour filter.

It has been argued that improving the process control, as might be possible using positive pressure aeration, could of itself bring substantial reductions in offensive odours(12). However, odour is a very difficult parameter to quantify and over certain concentration ranges "offensiveness" is highly subjective which suggests it will be sometime before quantitative proof exists of improved odour emmission resulting from closer process control.

3.4 Temperature

The temperature generated within a composting mass is important for two main reasons:

  (i)   to maximise decomposition rates; and
  (ii) to produce a material which is microbiologically
        'safe' for use.

It has been known for some time that compost temperatures greater than 60-65°C will significantly reduce the rate of biooxidation in bench scale composters(13). Recent work using samples from a full scale composting plant showed the optimal temperature for composting, as measured by microbial activity (incorporation of [¹⁴C] acetate) was consistently below 55°C(14).

However, earlier work which demonstrated a logarithmic increase in oxygen consumption(which was related to breakdown rates)over the 20-70°C temperature range still seems to find wide acceptance in many composting plants(15). This has produced a preoccupation with achieving high temperatures, justified by the need to produce a safe product. Temperatures in excess of 70°C are routinely obtained with many systems, both reactors and piles. This severely reduces overall activity and can produce false indications of process completion.

3.5 Pathogen Inactivation

Reactor systems, which include significant mechanical agitation, can be run such that relatively constant temperature profiles exist throughout the composting mass. If these temperatures are matched to retention times within reactors then overall elimination of pathogens, during the rapid biooxidative phase, should be routinely better than any pile system. The long accepted minimum temperature / time profile for achieving this in many installations is 55°C for 3 days (16). In any pile system this standard is practically impossible to attain throughout the pile mass. Figure 2. shows simultaneous temperature profiles at two cross-sections of an aerated static pile using refuse and sewage sludge. The fan end of the pile shows a more even temperature distribution than the tailend but with more material at slightly lower temperatures. This profile differs not only with position along the pile as shown (small variation) but also with the fan operating cycle and the degree of degradation which has taken place. Each segment of the pile will have its own unique temperature/time profile for the rapid biooxidative phase, where sanitisation should ideally be accomplished.

Concern over the extent of pathogen elimination in cooler regions of the pile has led to substantial research on a variety of indicator organisms. Some of this work has shown that even in these cool areas, just beneath the insulating layer, significant reductions are obtained(17). The mechanism for this inactivation is not fully understood but it is almost certain that it is not just a temperature/time effect. Some other mechanisms, related to competition and the general antagonistic nature of the composting mass, are involved. Figure 3. shows the reduction in Escherichia coli from various sampling sites within a refuse/sewage sludge pile, using positive pressure forced aeration.

In any composting system, reactor or pile, it would be unrealistic to be expected to guarantee that a compost was pathogen free, especially where end use makes direct ingestion an unrealistic possibility. What is needed is a guarantee of a significant reduction or inactivation of indicator organisms such that the use of the compost constitutes an acceptable risk.

3.6 Control

The conditions which are established at the initial mixing stage of a process eg. C/N ratio, moisture content, and porosity affect the behaviour of the compost mass during composting. The external controls exerted during the process over this behaviour either take the form of mechanical agitation, forced aeration or materials addition. The latter of these is really only a possibility with reactor systems and generally the additon, if required, is that of water.

During the process itself the primary concern should be to control temperature in such a way to optimise both the breakdown of organic material and pathogen inactivation (approximately 55°C). In the aerated static pile system the external factor which is used to exert control is the rate of aeration. The early pile systems used negative pressure aeration (sucking air through the pile) and were unable to keep operating temperatures at the optimum(10). Subsequent work in the United States used positive pressure aeration (blowing through the pile) on a pilot scale(11). This latter method of operation, linked with temperature feedback control, has been shown to be very effective in controlling temperature. However, caution is necessary when using this system on new combinations of materials since there are high evaporative moisture losses. Provided the moisture content is maintained above approximately 40% of wet weight then microbial activity is not impaired.

The developments seen in microcomputers over the past 10 years have now made their use a viable control proposition even on low cost static pile schemes. Rather than just having simple temperature feedback control which can look after aeration during the thermophilic phase we can now control piles as follows:

Phase 1 - Temperature increasing from ambient to the operating point. The aeration rate is matched to satisfy the requirements of the aerobic process whilst maximising the rate of temperature increase.

Phase 2 - Thermophilic phase. The aeration rate is controlled by
temperature feedback to maintain the optimal process
set point.

Phase 3 - Substrate depletion. The heat ouput has decreased
and the set point temperature can no longer be maintained
but air is supplied at a rate necessary to ensure aerobic
conditions within the pile, whilst maintaining elevated
temperatures.

Pilot scale work with refuse/sludge mixtures has examined and compared
various methods of control which can be grouped as follows:

(i)   fixed rate aeration;

(ii)   simple variable rate timers;

(iii)   temperature feedback which includes a low rate
        aeration facility; and

(iv)   microcomputer control(17).

This work showed that the more sophisticated the control system then the
more closely the process was controlled. However, it was demonstrated
that with all systems (apart from those which maintain an unchanging
fixed rate of aeration) good control was possible. In the case of the
simpler systems the good control developed as a result of detailed
knowledge of the material. This confirmed once again the importance of
experience when using any control system.

It is important to stress that sophisticated control systems are not
essential to establish good process control. On the other hand as the price
of microcomputer control systems continues to fall their cost related, for
instance, to that of the concrete compost pad, is minimal. An additional
advantage with the microcomputer is its data storage potential which means
we can not only examine current operating conditions but also the process
history of each pile.

4. CONCLUSIONS

Recent developments in composting have largely taken place in the area
of aerated static piles. Reactor based systems, although continually being
improved have not shown any dramatic changes over the last ten years.

The use of temperature feedback control, in many cases utilising microcomputers, has developed the control of aerated static piles to a stage where
it is comparable with most reactor systems. This control produces rapid
breakdown of organic matter and ensures substantial reductions or elimination
of pathogen indication organisms. This has been possible with no great cost
penalty on what is essentially a low cost system.

REFERENCES

1. GRAY, K.R., A.J. BIDDLESTONE and R. CLARK. (1973). "Review of Composting
    Part 3: Processes and Products". Process Biochem. October, pp 11-15 & 30
    1973.
2. WILSON, G.B., J.F.PARR, E. EPSTEIN, P.B. MARSH, R.L.CHANEY, D. COLACICCO,
    W.D. BURGE, L.J. SIKORA, C.F. TESTER and S. HORNICK. (1980) "Manual for
    Composting Sewage Sludge by the Beltsville Aerated - Pile Method". USEPA
    Report No EPA-600/8-80-022. May 1980.
3. GOLDSTEIN, N., (1985). Sewage Sludge Composting Facilities on the Rise.
    Biocycle, Vol. 26, No 8, pp 19-24, 1985.
4. HAUG, R.T., (1980). "Compost Engineering - Principles and Practice".
    Published by Ann Arbor Science, Michigan, USA, 1980.

5. RABBANI, K.R., R. JINDAL, H. KUBOTA and L. OBENG. (1983). Composting of Domestic Refuse. Environmental Sanitation REviews, No. 10/11, Oct 83, published by Environmental Sanitation Information Centre, Thailand.

6. WORLD HEALTH ORGANISATION, (1985), Solid Waste Management - Selected Topics, Ed by M.J. Suess, publ by WHO Regional office Europe, Copenhagen, Denmark.

7. STENTIFORD, E.I., D.D. MARA and P.L. TAYLOR, (1985), "Forced Aeration Co-Composting of Domestic Refuse and Sewage Sludge in Static Piles". In Composting of Agricultural and Other Wastes ed by J.K.R Gasser, Elsevier Applied Science, pp 42-54, 1985.

8. HIGGINS, A.J., V. KASPER Jr, D.A. DERR, M.E. SINGLEY and A. SINGH, (1981). "Mixing Systems for Sludge Composting", Biocycle, 22, No 5, 18-22, Sept/Oct 1981.

9. MILLER, F.C., S.T. MacGREGOR, K.M. PSARIANOS, and M.S. FINSTEIN, "Static Pile Sludge Composting with Recycled Compost as the Bulking Agent". Proc 14th Mid-Atlantic Conf. Indust. Waste Trmt. pp34-44, Ann Arbor Science, Michigan.

10. EPSTEIN, E., G.B. WILLSON, W.D. BURGE, D.C. MULLEN and N.K. ENKIRI, (1976) "A Forced Aeration System for Composting Wastewater Sludge" Jour Water Pollut Cont. Fed., Vol. 48, No 4. p 688-694, 1976.

11. FINSTEIN, M.S, J. CIRELLO, S.T. MacGREGOR, F.C. MILLER and K.M. PSARIANOS (1980). "Sludge Composting and Utilization: Rational Approach to Process Control". USEPA report No. C-340-678-01-1.

12. FINSEIN, M.S. and F.C. MILLER (1985) Principles of Composting Leading to Maximization of Decomposition Rate, Odour Control, and Cost Effectiveness. In Composting of Agricultural and Other Wastes, ed by J.K.R. Gasser, Elsevier Applied Science, pp13-26, 1985.

13. JERIS, J.S., and R.W. REAGAN. (1973). Controlling Environmental Parameters for Optimum Composting. 1 Experimental Procedures and Temperature. Compost Science, 14, pp10-15, 1973.

14. McKINLEY, V.L., VESTAL, J.R., and ERALP, A.E. (1985). Microbial Activity in Composting. Biocycle, Vol.26, No 7, Oct 85, pp 47-50.

15. SCHULZE, K.L. (1962). Continuous Thermophilic Composting, Applied Microbiology, 10, pp 108-122, 1962.

16. GOLUEKE,C G. (1983). "Epidemiological Aspects of Sludge Handling and Management". Biocycle, July-August, 24(4), p50-59, 1983.

17. PEREIRA-NETO, J.T., E.I STENTIFORD and D.D. MARA (1986). Low Cost Controlled Composting of Refuse and Sewage Sludge. Paper to be presented at 13th Int. Conf. of IAWPRC, Rio de Janeiro, Aug. 1986.

TABLE I - COMPOSTING SYSTEMS (after Gray et al 1973)

System Type	Configuration	Aeration	Agitation
REACTOR			
Dano	Horizontal Flow	F	C
Earp-Thomas	Vertical Flow	F	C
Eweson	Horizontal Flow	F	C
Fairfield	Mixed Flow	F	C
Paygro	Walled container	F	I
Peabody	Vertical Flow	F	I
Tollemache	Walled container	N + F	I
NON-REACTOR			
Aerated Static Pile	Batch pile	F	U
Indore	In trench	N	I
Windrow	Batch pile	N	I

Aeration: N - natural   Agitation: C - continuous

F - forced   I - intermittent

U - undisturbed

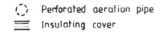

◌ Perforated aeration pipe
☰ Insulating cover

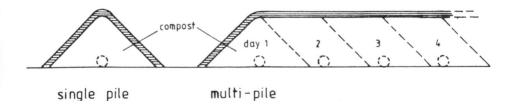

single pile   multi-pile

Figure 1 - Diagrammatic representation of a single and multi-pile aerated
static pile systems.

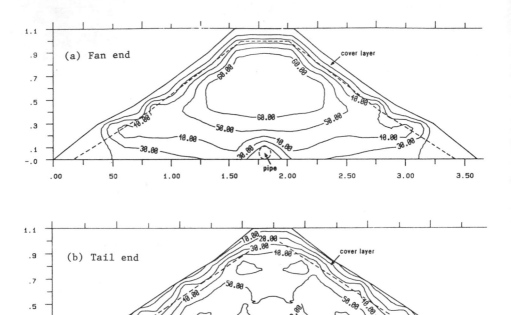

Figure 2 - Temperature distribution at different cross sections of an aerated static pile, fan not operating. (a) fan end; and (b) tail end of the pile. (temperatures in °C, dimensions in metres)

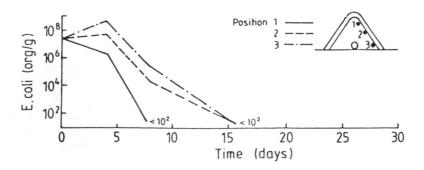

Figure 3 - <u>E.coli</u> reductions at 3 positions within an aerated static pile, just beneath the cover layer.

COMPOST OPTIONS IN INTEGRATED WASTE MANAGEMENT SYSTEMS

C.G. GOLUEKE, L.F. DIAZ, and G.M. SAVAGE
Cal Recovery Systems, Inc.
Richmond, California, U.S.A.

Summary

Three major compost options and the basic option, to compost or not
to compost, are discussed and evaluated. The three major options
pertain to the position or role assigned to composting in an overall
treatment program. They are: 1) composting as the sole or major
treatment; 2) composting as one of two or more major treatments; and
3) composting as an adjunct introduced for a special waste or purpose. The descriptions and discussions take into account the relative size and nature of the compostable fraction to be processed,
the preparation of the wastes, appropriate compost methods, disposition of the product, constraints on the exercise of each option, and
integration of the option into the overall waste treatment system.
Examples cited for the third option are the composting of yard and
garden debris and the composting of hazardous wastes.

1. INTRODUCTION

Because of its broad connotation, the term "option" may be interpreted in many ways. Aside from its broadest implication with respect to
composting itself, namely, "to compost or not to compost", "compost option" usually refers in common practice to a compost system and its attendant technologies. However, the term may be applied with equal validity to the assignment of a hierarchical position to composting in an
overall treatment system. In this paper the term is used both in its
broadest sense and in its hierarchical sense.

2. COMPOSTING AS A SOLID WASTE MANAGEMENT OPTION

A discussion of composting as an option should begin with a consideration of the viability of composting in a given situation. It is viable if the waste to be treated is compostable under reasonable conditions
and if the amount of wastes is sufficiently large. Size limitation in
terms of viability is one of minimum size permitted by compost technology
(threshold size) and that of the waste input commensurate with that size.
Fortunately, the technology of composting is sufficiently broad to accom-
modate almost any magnitude of input. The main technological variable
dependent upon size is degree of sophistication or complexity of the indicated technology. The bottom line is justification of the cost of the
minimum equipment required by the compost option. At present, justification for even the smallest and simplest equipment necessitates a relatively substantial operation, unless a dual use is found for the
equipment.

Whereas threshold size is a major consideration regarding viability, it is only one of the factors to be considered when determining optimum size. Here, amount of incoming wastes and the benefits and penalties associated with scale come into consideration. It does not require much effort to reach the conclusion that maximum potential size and optimum size are by no means necessarily identical.

The third logical step in considering the compost option is to investigate and decide upon the technology required to put a selected compost option into practice. Finally, there is the exceedingly important consideration of economic feasibility. Economic feasibility represents an extreme, in that it provides a monetary cost point beyond which an undertaking becomes impractical, if not impossible.

In its broadest sense, "viability" could be expanded to encompass advisability and preferability in that both promote viability. A wealth of literature, too voluminous to cite in a single paper, attests to the superiority of composting over even its closest competitor in terms of desirability. With due allowance made for inflated claims and for the biases of proponents, it nevertheless can be said without serious contradiction, that composting surpasses other waste management and disposal options not only in terms of superiority of the process, but also of its product. Perhaps the weightiest point in its favor is the utility of the compost product in food production and soil conservation.

3. HIERARCHICAL OPTIONS

The three hierarchical compost options of concern in the present paper pertain to the position or role assigned to composting in an overall solid waste management program. They are: 1) composting as the sole or major treatment; 2) composting as one of two or more major treatments (e.g., integrated with incineration); and 3) composting as an adjunct introduced for a special substrate and purpose. Co-composting would fit in either option-1 or option-2.

In the sections that follow, the three options are described, and each option is discussed in terms of the limitations resulting from the constraints associated with it. The descriptions and discussions take into account: 1) the relative size and nature of the compostable fraction (substrate) destined for composting; 2) applicable waste preparation and brief mention of compost methods; 3) the disposition of the compost product (i.e., product quality); 4) the situation (constraints) to which each option is best suited; and 5) the integration of the options into the overall waste treatment system.

4. COMPOSTING AS THE MAJOR TREATMENT (OPTION-1)

4.1. Substrate and Its Preparation

This option is especially applicable in situations in which biologically decomposable wastes constitute the greater part of the waste stream. It is even more appropriate if the biodegradable wastes are highly putrescible in nature and consist of food preparation and market wastes, and in some cases, of animal manures and human body wastes. Their high moisture content and relatively low calorific value due to the usual presence of inert fines combine to render such wastes poorly suitable for incineration or other thermal process.

Substrate preparation for option-1 is the same as that described in some detail in section 5.3 ("Preprocessing"). However, the expensive machinery and energy expenditure involved undoubtedly would entail considerable adaptations for lesser industrialized regions or for those in which the economic situation is poor.

4.2. Compost Methods

The range of suitable compost methods for option-1 is quite broad, in that it extends from the very simple to the relatively highly mechanized. The simpler methods include the turned windrow and the forced aeration windrow, either of which may be carried out under a shelter or in the open. The turning may be done manually or mechanically. The more complex compost systems involve the use of reactors more or less sophisticatedly designed to provide close control of environmental conditions. Between the two extremes are methods that involve composting within a shelter in which the ambient temperature can be regulated and from which rain and snow can be excluded. Within the shelter, either the turned windrow or forced aeration or a combination of the two may be used. If turning is used, it usually is done mechanically. Curing generally takes place in the open.

Obviously, choice of method depends upon economic and technological feasibility. Again, it should be emphasized that where time and space are not critical, and especially where economics are severely limiting, the simpler approaches are the appropriate approaches. A factor that does have an influence on choice of method and which might suggest the adoption of a more highly technological method is the projected disposition of the compost product. Generally, the higher the quality desired for the product, the more complex should be the method of composting. However, as is shown in the section that follows, lack of complexity of method can be compensated to a great extent by the treatment accorded the compost product.

4.3. Treatment and Disposition of the Compost Product

If the product is to be used for fill cover, for land reclamation, or for some non-critical use, it would require little if any treatment, provided of course, that it has been satisfactorily composted. At the most, a rudimentary screening may be sufficient. Conversely, a fair amount of treatment may be required for the more critical uses. Obviously, general agricultural applications require fewer and less stringent qualities than would food crop applications. Usage in orchards would entail an intermediate quality.

If the compost process has been satisfactorily conducted and completed, the only product treatment required is physical in nature, and usually involves the attainment of a more uniform and smaller particle size. That being true, most processing can be done by way of screening.

4.4. Applicability

Option-1 is suitable for almost any waste treatment program. It differs from option-2 in that its range of applicability is from the least developed regions to the highly industrialized -- i.e., to any region that produces a biodegradable waste. It is especially suited to the needs of less developed nations in that if needs be, the technology can be very simple. On the other hand, if conditions are such that not only environmental and health safeguards but also aesthetic standards must be strictly applied, the compost process can be carried out in a carefully manipulated reactor from which all emissions can be rendered innocuous.

5. COMPOSTING AS ONE OF TWO OR MORE MAJOR TREATMENTS (OPTION-2)

5.1. Substrate

With option-2, composting is but one of two or more major treatments to which the organic (biodegradable) fraction of the incoming municipal waste stream is subjected. Hence, the compost option must be designed in terms of integration with the other system or systems in the overall treatment complex. Among the non-compost options more likely to be used for treating biodegradable wastes are incineration, refuse-derived fuel (RDF) production, gasification (thermal or biological), and of course, sanitary landfill. (It should be noted that landfill is an essential element, major or minor, in all municipal solid waste disposal complexes.)

5.2. Integration into the Overall Disposal Complex

Integration with the other elements of an overall system consists mainly in: 1) deciding which of the waste stream components are to be composted and then separating and diverting those components from the stream; and 2) conducting the compost operation such that it fits without detracting from the efficiency of the overall treatment program.

The decision as to which of the waste stream components are to be composted is a complex one and rests in large part upon the perceived local, regional, and national priorities with respect to energy and to conservation of the soil and food production. If energy is the major interest or need, then components having a high and recoverable energy content would be diverted to the energy recovery systems -- incineration, RDF production, or gasification. Biodegradable wastes that fit into this category are highly carbonaceous, relatively easily manipulated, not excessively moist, and neither intimately nor tenaciously contaminated with inert fines. Biodegradable wastes little suited to energy recovery would be directed to the compost system. Thus, in an industrialized setting, the result could well be an emphasis on the energy recovery element, and composting would be relegated to a relatively minor role. This outcome would be reversed in "under-developed" regions.

If soil conservation and food production have top priority, then composting has the first consideration in terms of sharing the waste stream regardless of whether the setting is an industrial ("developed") or non-industrial ("undeveloped") country. However, in an industrial setting, the biodegradable waste stream would have an appreciable fraction that would be difficult to biodegrade, but which would be readily susceptible to thermal processing. Moreover, in such a setting, the carbonaceous fraction might be so large as to raise the carbon-to-nitrogen ratio of the organic waste stream to a level exceeding that for successful composting. In both cases, integrating a compost subsystem with an energy subsystem would be a satisfactory solution. Therefore, in most situations in industrialized regions, energy recovery and composting existing side-by-side can be important elements in an overall waste treatment complex.

Another decisive factor that has been gaining more attention in the past decade is the use of processed refuse as a bulking agent for composting sewage sludge ("co-composting"). With such a use, composting the refuse fraction is secondary to that of the sewage sludge in terms of design and decision making. However, a trend is developing in which composting the refuse fraction ranks in importance with that of the sludge.

5.3. Preprocessing

The procedures used for separating compostable wastes from the municipal waste stream are in essence those used in the front-end processing ("preprocessing") conventionally applied in resource recovery from municipal wastes. The major unit processes in preprocessing are size reduction, air classification, screening, and magnetic separation. The sequence of these unit processes is flexible in that it should best fit a given situation.

5.3.1. Size Reduction

Whereas several types of shredders are on the market, those sufficiently rugged to size reduce municipal solid waste (MSW) on a continuous basis are but few in number. The necessarily sizeable capital and operating costs of such machines impose a substantial financial burden on the composting of MSW. Furthermore, there are the additional costs that arise from special demands regarding particle size imposed by unit processes downstream. Attaining the demanded size distribution involves a considerable consumption of energy and a serious imposition of wear-and-tear on the machine.

Energy requirements and the consequent cost of size reduction increase nonlinearly and vary sharply with decrease in product particle size [5,13,14]. For example, in one study [12], it was found that the specific energy requirement increased from about 5 kWh/ton to produce a 6-cm particle size to about 45 kWh/ton for a product having a particle size of 0.6 cm. Machine wear accelerates in proportion to the reduction in particle size of the product. In the study cited, increasing the degree of size reduction from about 0.6 to 0.9 brought about an almost six-fold increase in hammer wear regardless of hardness of the hammer facing. Hardness may slow rate and lessen extent of wear, but it did not alter the basic relation between wear and product particle size.

Needless to say, the drastic increase in energy and wear and the consequent elevation of costs entailed in lowering the particle size of the product renders it impractical to counter the problem of glass and plastic contaminants in the compost product by size reducing particle dimensions to those of grains of sand [5].

5.3.2. Air Classification

Air classification probably is preferable to manual separation in operations in which RDF is one of the products. The reason is the tendency of inert fines to cling to or be entrapped in the RDF particles. The processing required during and after passage through an air classifier and the nature of air classification combine to remove a significant fraction of such fines [5].

Essentially, air classification is based upon the interaction between a moving air stream and shredded refuse within a column such that resultant drag forces exerted upon the particles are simultaneously opposed by gravitational force. The important and ultimate outcome of the interaction is that the "light" (large drag-to-weight ratio) components are separated from the "heavy" (small drag-to-weight ratio) components. Examples of the former are paper and plastic film; of the latter, glass, rock, metals, rubber, and dense plastic. The greater part of the heavy fraction generally is inorganic and therefore, not compostable. On the other hand, most of the light fraction is organic and hence, compostable. One of the shortcomings of air classification is the occasional loss of readily compostable yard waste, food waste, and wet paper that almost invariably ends with the heavy fraction.

5.3.3. Screening

With a suitably designed and operated screening system, it is possible: 1) to remove particles of a size large enough to interfere with operational and process efficiency or lower product quality; and 2) to separate certain types of organic materials from particular varieties of inorganic substances (e.g., fines from paper). For the first function, screening is positioned either before or after air classification. Separation is accomplished in the second function by designing and operating the screen to take advantage of characteristic differences between sizes and types of materials.

Three basic types of screens are used in processing refuse, namely, trommel, disc, and flatbed. Although valid arguments can be offered for and against each of the three, generally, the experience has been more successful with the trommel and disc screens than with the flatbed.

5.3.4. Magnetic Separation

Needless to say, the reason for introducing magnetic separation into preprocessing is to remove ferrous objects and thereby attain the following three important benefits: 1) reclamation of an important resource and the economic benefits therefrom; 2) removal of items that might interfere with the compost operation; and 3) removal of items that by virtue of their physical presence would lower the quality of the compost product.

Magnets used in ferrous recovery may be either of the permanent or of the electromagnetic type. One or more of the following three configurations are applied in refuse processing: the drum, the magnetic head pulley, and the magnetic belt.

The efficiency of magnetic metal recovery (weight of metal recovered per unit weight of magnetic metal in the in-feed stream) usually is about 80 percent [1]. With respect to positioning magnetic separation, the general experience has been that the quality of ferrous scrap recovered by a magnetic separator placed directly downstream of primary size reduction equipment is inferior to that of ferrous scrap removed by a separator positioned in an air-classified heavies stream.

5.4. Integration of Preprocessing

Several factors determine the course to be followed in the integration of the unit processes in preprocessing, whether it be for composting, for RDF production, or for purposes associated with energy recovery (e.g., biogasification). They also determine the required complexity and equipment needs of the integration. The factors of major importance can be classified into four groups: 1) those that pertain to the nature of the wastes to be processed; 2) those that are related to the recovered product specifications; 3) those concerned with the budgetary situation; and 4) those that arise from the waste management goals of the community or country. The interrelation between the four groups is exemplified by the relation between budget and product quality, in that the cost of processing is proportional to the degree of the enhancement of the quality of the preprocessing product.

The beneficial effect had by preprocessing on product quality is especially pronounced in composting, particularly with respect to particle size and incidence of contaminants. A less desirable but inevitable parallel effect is the decline in quantity of product because of the increase in amount of reject material needed to bring about the improvement in quality.

A brief illustration of the costs of preprocessing, composting, and postprocessing is made by comparing the overall costs of low technology with those of high technology composting [12]. The "low technology"

composting used in the comparison involves windrow composting in the open
and aeration by means of a mechanical turner. The "high technology" system involves the use of a silo in which aeration is done mostly by forcing air into the composting mass, and to a lesser extent by agitation
(stirring). The respective total costs per ton composted are roughly $18
with the windrow system as contrasted to $27 with the silo system (in-
cludes amortization of capital and cost of operation and maintenance).
On the other hand, the pre- and post-processing costs and miscellaneous
costs for the windrow system are roughly similar to those for the silo
system. Therefore, the major difference between the high and the low
technology systems is in the costs of the composting step, which in the
silo system is a little more than twice that in the windrow system, i.e.,
approximately $16/ton vs $7/ton municipal solid wastes processed (400
tons/day). Although the dollar values given in the comparison are functions of a variety of local and universal factors and hence will vary
from situation to situation in terms of actual values, the comparative
differences between system costs will remain roughly the same.

5.5. MSW as a Bulking Agent

While on the subject of preprocessing and its costs, a few words on
the use of refuse as a substitute for woodchips as a bulking agent for
the composting of sewage sludge are in order. At the outset, it should
be emphasized that raw refuse is inferior to woodchips as a bulking agent
for a number of reasons. Nevertheless, undesirable effects of the shortcomings of raw refuse can be satisfactorily ameliorated or even avoided
through a combination of careful preprocessing, avoidance of high moisture content, and use of a suitable aeration procedure. In terms of relative economics, at the time of this writing and in the San Francisco Bay
area, the cost of preprocessing the amount of refuse needed per ton of
sludge was only about one-third that of the woodchips for which it would
be substituted. However, more study is needed to determine the costs of
the other measures that would have to be instituted to upgrade the utility of MSW as a bulking agent.

In a comparison between the economics of using woodchips as a bulking agent with those of using processed MSW, it would be a mistake not to
take into account the appreciable monetary credits that would accrue from
the use of MSW. Also not to be overlooked is the possible sale of the
co-compost product, and the utility of the product in soil reclamation
and agriculture.

On the basis of this cursory comparison, one might tentatively conclude that the substitution of processed refuse for woodchips could be
economically justified [12].

6. COMPOSTING AS AN ADJUNCT (OPTION-3)

As stated earlier, composting in option-3 is an adjunct introduced
to handle a special residue or waste. It is an "adjunct", because it is
neither the major nor one of the major elements of the overall waste
treatment-disposal complex. In option-3, composting is introduced because it is the simplest satisfactory means of disposing of a particular
type of waste and of thereby reducing the burden on the major treatment
setup. Depending upon the particular waste, a secondary reason may be to
produce a useful product. Excepting under particular circumstances, volumes involved are but a relatively small fraction of that of the main
waste loading. Unless the nature of the waste dictates otherwise, the

simpler of the composting methods are followed and the open windrow
method has become the preferred approach.

Applications are widely diverse in terms of the wastes to be treated,
of the compost methods to be applied, and of the amounts involved. Two
applications that receive attention in this paper are the composting of
yard wastes and park debris to prolong sanitary landfill life and the
composting of certain hazardous wastes to render them safe for landfilling or other disposal. The first application could be adapted to handle
the organic fines (residue) in the production of some types of RDF.

6.1. Yard Wastes and Park Debris

The most commonly encountered examples of option-3 are the composting of yard and park debris in conjunction with a sanitary landfill or as
part of a resource recovery project. In both cases, the major reasons
are the increase of the lifespan of a sanitary landfill and the production of a material that could be used to augment available cover material.

The attractive features of composting park and garden debris and
other landscaping wastes are: 1) the ease with which they can be composted; and 2) the utility of the resulting product as a substitute for
soil commercial amendments and as a source of fertilizer elements that
would otherwise have to be purchased by a community for its landscaping
needs. More immediately, the product can be used to augment and enhance
material that must be brought in to serve as cover material for the sanitary landfill [2].

6.1.1. Systems

The open or minimally sheltered windrow system is the system of
choice. Aeration can be accomplished by mechanical turning, by forced
aeration, or by a combination of the two. Our experience with forced
aeration for this particular type of application has been less than desirable. We find that it leads to an excessive drying and cooling of the
composting mass, especially when tree trimmings and dried vegetation
(leaves, straw) constitute a large fraction of the wastes. The reason
for the drying and cooling probably is ultimately the very porous nature
of the wastes. The porosity not only permits relatively unimpeded movement of air but also diminishes the moisture holding capacity of the
windrowed mass. The latter is due to the rapid percolation of water to
the bottom and out of the windrow.

6.1.2. Equipment

A shredder is essential. Moreover, the shredder must have the capacity to process the input intended for it. Despite the fact that this
requirement seems so obvious as to render its mention superfluous, inade-
quacy of the shredder has been and is one of the more commonly encountered
problems in projects involving the composting of park and garden debris.
The grinder must be able to size reduce fairly large-sized branches and
brush, as well as twigs, tree clippings, and other woody material to a
particle size small enough to permit easy manipulation and to encourage
biological breakdown. In addition, the size reduction equipment should
be sufficiently strong to deal with the occasional contaminants such as
rocks, bricks, or pieces of metal. If the shredder is inadequate, the
almost invariable outcome is an accumulation of branches and other woody
debris that eventually becomes so great as to be unmanageable, and in
some cases constitutes a serious fire hazard.

For small operations, turning can be satisfactorily done with the
use of a front-end loader or even of a bulldozer equipped with a standard
blade. For larger operations, a mechanical turner specifically designed
for the task would be indicated.

6.1.3. Moisture Content

The need to maintain the moisture content of the composting mass often is overlooked. Usually, the oversight has its origin in the absence of a conveniently accessible water source. Extending a water line to the composting site to remedy the lack often is economically prohibitive. Nevertheless, for effective composting, water is necessary. A possible but doubtfully acceptable solution that might be tried if sufficient space is available, is to allow the piles to remain undisturbed until the rainy season comes. At that time the compost program could be begun.

6.1.4. Product

Unless undesirable elements have been allowed to contaminate the input wastes, the compost product is an excellent soil amendment and partial source of fertilizer elements. With proper screening it would be suitable for the more critical of landscaping activities.

6.2. Hazardous Wastes

The recent surge of interest in the treatment of certain biologically degradable hazardous wastes by composting is by no means a novel concept [11]. Moreover, investigations and work on the disposal of petroleum wastes by way of incorporation and treatment in the soil through disking and aeration of the soil have been in progress over the past decade [6,7,9]. The reason for the revival of interest is the discovery that a sizeable number of organic substances (i.e., synthetic, and those of biological origin whether present or fossil) are susceptible to attack by microbes capable of using them as nutrient sources [4,8,10]. The inclusion of synthetic organics is important because most pesticides are synthetic organics. Moreover, some organic substances although not subject to biological attack may be chemically or physically unstable in the environmental conditions brought about by microbes decomposing (composting) susceptible materials [8]. For example, carbamates rapidly break down at the high temperatures and pH levels encountered in an actively composting mass.

Despite the many seeming advantages of composting hazardous wastes, the option has many and severe constraints with respect to its implementation. For instance, the entire compost process (i.e., from storage of the raw waste through preparation for composting and the composting process itself) must be carefully monitored and controlled so as not to allow the escape of toxic materials into the environment. Some hazardous substances, although biologically degradable, may be so resistant to microbial attack as to require an impractically long treatment period in the reactor. Moreover, there is the strong possibility of intermediates being produced that may be more toxic and resistant than the raw substance. Other problems may arise from the physical state of the raw waste. Unless the compost product can be unequivocally demonstrated as being harmless, it should be regarded as if it were a toxic waste.

Apparently, some hazardous substances are species specific with respect to susceptibility to microbial attack. However, our experience gives reason for wondering whether or not it may be that the isolation and enrichment techniques used may lead to one particular species of microbe instead of another. The fact could well be that if another enrichment and isolation procedure had been used, a different and yet equally efficacious species of microbe might have been found. If the latter were true, then there is the likelihood that many types of hazardous substances may be vulnerable to attack by a variety of microbial species.

Thus far, the most promising application for composting in hazardous waste disposal is for the treatment of oily (refinery) wastes. Although reports dealing with composting oily wastes are extremely few in number, those dealing with its destruction through land cultivation are numerous [6,7,9].

REFERENCES

1. ALTER, H. and CRAWFORD, B. (1976). Materials Recovery Processing Research -- A Summary of Investigations. Report prepared for U.S. EPA under Contract No. 67-11-2944
2. Anonymous. (1985) Composting Saves Landfill Space. World Wastes. 28(12):29,31
3. BUMPUS, J.A., MING TIEN, WRIGHT, D., and AUST, S.D. (1985). Oxidation of Persistent Environmental Pollutants by a White Rot Fungus. Science. 228:1434-1436
4. Decomposition of Toxic and Nontoxic Organic Compounds in Soils. OVERCASH, M.D. Editor (1981). Ann Arbor Science Publishers, Inc.
5. DIAZ, L.F., SAVAGE, G.M., and GOLUEKE, C.G. (1982). Resource Recovery from Municipal Solid Wastes, Vol. I and II. CRC Press, Boca Raton, Florida
6. Land Treatment Practices in the Petroleum Industry (1983). Environmental Research and Technology, Inc. Prepared for the American Petroleum Institute
7. MEYERS, J.D. and HUDDLESTON, R.L. (1981). Treatment of Oily Refinery Wastes by Landfarming. Proceedings 34th Industrial Waste Conference. Purdue University, Lafayette, Indiana. Ann Arbor Science Publishers, Inc., Ann Arbor, Michigan
8. MOUNT, M.E. (1981). Carbaryl: A Literature Review: Residue Reviews, Vol. 20. Springer Verlag, New York
9. NORRIS, D.J. (1983). Landspreading of Oily and Biological Sludges in Canada. Proceedings of the 35th Industrial Waste Conference. Purdue University, Lafayette, Indiana. Ann Arbor Science Publishers, Inc. Ann Arbor, Michigan
10. PITTER, P. (1976). Determination of Biological Degradability of Organic Substances. Water Research. 10:231-235
11. ROSE, W.W. and MERCER, W.A. (1968). Fate of Insecticides in Composted Agricultural Wastes. National Canners Association. Washington, D.C.
12. SAVAGE, G.M. and GOLUEKE, C.G. (1986). Major Cost Elements in Co-Composting. BioCycle. in press
13. SAVAGE, G.M. and SHIFLETT, G.R. (1981). Processing Equipment for Resource Recovery Systems, Vol. III, Field Test Evaluation of Shredders. EPA-611/2-81-117c, U.S. EPA, Cincinnati, Ohio
14. SAVAGE, G.M. and TREZEK, G.J. (1981). Significance of Size Reduction in Solid Waste Management, Vol. 2, EPA-611/2-81-115, U.S. EPA, Cincinnati, Ohio

COMPOSTING AND USE OF AGRICULTURAL WASTES IN CONTAINER MEDIA

Y. CHEN[1] and Y. HADAR[2]
[1]The Seagram Center for Soil and Water Sciences
[2]Department of Plant Pathology and Microbiology
Faculty of Agriculture, The Hebrew University of Jerusalem
Rehovot 76100, Israel

Summary
Composted agricultural wastes were tested as substitutes for peat in container media. The wastes reported in this review, all composted prior to their use as media, were: (1) the solid fraction of slurried cattle manure separated either as raw material or after anaerobic digestion, (2) grape marc. The physical, chemical and biological properties of the composts were determined. The composts were tested as growth media for the production of vegetables' seedlings and for growing ornamentals up to an age of 8 months. Plant growth response was either equal or better as compared to peat. Mixtures of 1:1 of the composts with peat seemed to provide a recommended growth medium. Mechanisms for the improvement of growth in the compost are proposed. The composts were found suppressive to soil-borne plant pathogens such as Pythium, Rhizoctonia and Sclerotium rolfsii.

1. INTRODUCTION

The concept of growing plants in containers is markedly different than growing plants in a field. When pots are used the volume of medium from which the plant can absorb water and minerals is limited and is usually smaller than that available for plants growing in open soil. Moreover, under intensive culture with controlled temperatures and high nutritional levels, the stomata commonly stay open for longer periods of time enhancing water uptake and loss. In order to exploit these conditions an adequate amount of easily available water must exist within the root zone. Whenever such a water regime is being maintained the problem of aeration arises. Since artificial growth media are usually very porous and relatively homogeneous, strict control of water and air contents is attainable. In contrast, many soils have relatively low air porosity and their profile is heterongeneous. Therefore a proper simultaneous control of both water and air regimes is difficult to achieve (13).

The production of healthy, uniform plants is a basic requirement of modern agriculture. The growth media used must be homogeneous, aerated, reproducible and pathogen-free. In order to meet the need for a medium with proper air and water capacities, growers use many types of organic and inorganic materials.

The most common organic component is peatmoss which also serves as a sole component in growth media (22, 24). The use of peat is, however, accompanied by some problems: (i) The price of horticultural peat is high and its shipping to long distances considerably increases its price. (ii) Peat resources throughout the world are limited and non-renewable in short-term periods (24). (iii) In some cases, sterilized peat serves as an enrichment medium for various phytopathogenic fungi species such as Pythium sp. (22). (iv) Peat bogs act as an important site for atmospheric CO_2 fixation (10). Digging peat from these bogs prevents CO_2 fixation for a long period. Atmospheric CO_2 enrichment has some implications which are as yet poorly understood (1). Nevertheless, the most widely accepted assumption is that the actual rise in CO_2 level (about 1 ppm per year) can lead to earth warming, ice melting in the poles and some other disastrous consequences. It seems, therefore, that finding substitutes for peat is an important task for soil scientists and horticulturists.

In the last decades the demand for peat as a substrate in horticulture had increased continuously while its availability is decreasing. A number of organic wastes such as bark, leaf mould, town refuse, sawdust, spent mushroom compost, treated animal excreta and many other organic materials were introduced as peat substitute in container media after proper composting (2,6,19,23,28). Both cattle manure and grape marc (the residue of wine processing) are agricultural wastes which are produced in many countries over the world. By proper treatment, these wastes can be converted into container substrates.

This paper summarizes some research conducted on the recycling of these agricultural wastes to container media.

THE USE OF CATTLE MANURE AS RAW MATERIAL FOR GROWTH MEDIA PRODUCTION

The traditional way of treating cattle manure is to spread it on the soil as source of nutritional elements or as a conditioner, either raw or after omposting. The solid fraction of cattle manure is a potential raw material for composts produced as container media. Two strategies were studied: (i) anaerobic digestion followed by solid-liquid separation, (ii) solid-liquid separation of raw slurried manure. In both cases, composting of the solid fraction prior to its utilization as growth media is required and was therefore applied and studied.

The anaerobic digestion of organic matter is a well known technology which is used to produce biogas from wastes, especially manures. The digested slurry is usually used for direct application in the field. Chen et al. (4) found that by sieving and leaching the digested slurry on a vibrating screen, two major products are obtained: (1) a fibrous fraction that may serve as a growth substrate; (2) an effluent which is similar in its composition to liquid fertilizers. The fibrous fraction has been tested for its physical and chemical properties and was found to maintain high hydraulic conductivity and air capacity as well as an adequate water and nutrients retention. As a result of the high temperature in the digesters (55°C), plant disease problems were not observed in any of our experiments. The particle size of the material ranges from 1-5 mm, which is slightly larger than sphagnum peatmoss from Finland. The bulk density is 0.08-0.12 g/cm^3 and the porosity reaches 93-95%. Water and air capacity are 62% and 31-33%, respectively. Hydraulic conductivity at saturation is as high as 150 cm/h. Similar values were measured on peatmoss. Chemical properties are related to leaching intensity and duration. Electrical conductivity ranges from 0.5-3.0 mmhos/cm or less (if required), pH range is 7.0-7.6 and nutrient contents resemble that of enriched sphagnum peatmoss from Finland (4,5).

In another study (Inbar et al., 1985), the fibrous fraction was composted in windrows for 100 days. Temperatures rose to 55°C within a week. Chemical analysis of samples taken during composting revealed that the total contents of macroelements (N, P, K), minor elements (Fe, Mn, Cu, Zn) and ash increased about two-fold, while the C/N ratio decreased from 40 to 15. The pH dropped from 7.5 to 6.6, and the amount of soluble salts rose from 15 to 37 meq/100 g. Growth experiments were conducted under greenhouse conditions. Germination and seedling development of peppers, cucumbers and tomatoes were compared in growth media consisting of raw material, compost and peat. The raw material had a strong inhibitory effect on tomatoes. This inhibition was not removed by fertilization. For all plants, the mature compost appeared to be as good or superior as compared to peat. Fertilization with inorganic fertilizers or slurry effluent increased both plant dry weight and height (8,15). This compost can be used as a sole medium or as a component in a mixture at levels similar to those known for peat.

Huijsmans and Lindley (14) investigated solid-liquid separation systems for pre-processing dairy cattle manure prior to anaerobic digestion. They suggested that the main product is the liquid fraction which may be used either for irrigation or for biogas production. In their system, the solids fraction is a by-product which can be applied to land as soil conditioner and if composted, as a mulch for nurseries and landscape use. Cull (6) stated that animal fibers appear to be promising substrates but composting and distribution could introduce problems.

In our studies, cattle manure is separated to liquid and solids. The liquid is used after dilution as an organic liquid fertilizer, while the fibrous solids are composted in windrows and later used as growth medium (16). Composted separated manure (CSM) was successfully tested as peat substitute or peat complementary medium for vegetables seedling production. Development of pepper, cucumber and tomato seedlings was faster in compost containing media in comparison to peat+vermiculite media.

In recent experiments, CSM was found to support cucumbers growth. Cucumber yields were 50% higher in CSM:tuff (scoria) mixture (1:1) than in tuff alone which is the most commonly used medium in Israel. Peat:CSM mixture (1:1) was also found optimal for growth of foliage plants such as Ficus benyamina.

THE USE OF GRAPE MARC AS A RAW MATERIAL FOR GROWTH MEDIA PRODUCTION

In wine producing industry, the which accumulates in relatively large quantities is usually considered a waste and its disposal seems expensive. Grape marc is not suitable for direct soil application since during its degradation, materials that are highly incompatible with plant root systems are released. As a result, it was not previously considered to utilize grape marc as an organic fertilizer. Graefe (7) and Streichsbier et al., (27) investigated the biological process in which marc material was decomposed by microbes. They propose to use the composted grape marc as a high grade organic fertilizer, while recovering heat and CO_2 which are produced during the process.

Because of their high sugar content grapes belong to the class of fruits which are highest in calories. Grape pressing residues which contain more than 50% moisture contain a sufficient amount of easily degradable carbohydrates in solution to provide the micro-organisms with easily available nutrients. Thus, in 3-4 days temperatures higher than 50°C are reached during the aerobic decay. If adequate supply of moisture and oxygen is available, skins and stalks can be converted after only a few weeks at the high decaying temperature prevailing in the compost pile to a fine friable humus. Only the grape seeds can stand the action of the micro-organisms and maintain their external structure and shape. Two to four years in a compost heap or in soils are required to achieve decomposition (7) of the seeds.

Grape marc which consisted of grape skins, seeds and stalks was

composted in windrows for 6 months.   The composted material was tested   as
growth media (16).   The composted grape marc   (CGM) was found   to be   a
promising organic component in growth media.   It was tested for   several
vegetable crops as well as for ornamentals such as carnations   and   ficus.
CGM was compared to peat and CSM in the experiment described above and was
usually found to resemble CSM in its effects on plant growth and yield.

PHYSICAL AND CHEMICAL CHARACTERISTICS OF CSM AND CGM SUBSTRATES

The composting process of both separated cattle manure and grape   marc
resulted in homogeneous friable material.   Some physical properties of the
composts and their mixture with peat (1:1) are: bulk densities of CSM   and
CGM are   0.20 and 0.30 g/cm^3, respectively.   These values seem   to be
superior to the extremely light weight of peat (0.08 g/cm^3) when plant
anchorage is to be considered.   Ash content in the composts is high   (25–
30%) as a result of organic matter decomposition.   Total porosity is   high
in manure based composts and their mixtures with peat (above 87%).   In the
case of CGM, the value was slightly lower (82%).   Air content in a 10 cm
column in manure based composts was around the optimum (20–26%) while
CGM contained more air (35%).   As a result, water content in manure based
composts was 60–70% while for for CGM only 46%.   From these properties, it
was concluded that all the substrates are adequately aerated.   Attention
has to be paid to the lower water content in substrates containing CGM   as
sole component and very high values of hydraulic conductivity   at
saturation.

Some chemical properties of the substrates were measured.   The pH was
around neutral.   Electrical conductivity was high in CSM containing
treatments, thus, they were leached prior to planting.   CGM had an EC
level below 2.00 dS/m.   Nitrate levels in CSM were very high (25 meq/l) and
much lower in CGM (1.2 meq/l).   P and K levels of both CSM and CGM were 89
and 59 ppm P and 31 and 15 meq/l K, respectively.

Cation exchange capacity (CEC) is higher in peat when calculated on   a
weight basis.   However, when the CEC data were expressed on a volumetric
basis, higher levels were found for CGM (210 meq/l) and CSM (282 meq/l) as
a result of their higher bulk densities.   Thus, the composts provide
higher CEC to substrates in containers.

COMPOSTS SUPPRESSIVE TO SOIL–BORNE PLANT PATHOGENS

Pythium, Rhizoctonia and Fusarium are soil–borne plant pathogens
causing severe diseases and yield losses.   These diseases are of major
importance to plants grown in soilless systems containing peat as an
organic component.   Growers commonly control the diseases by applying soil
fungicides after the disease is evident or by steaming the growth mixture
before planting (26).   However, the growth media can be rapidly recolonized
by pathogens from soil particles which may be transported by tools or as
dust (18,26).   Another approach for suppressing the activity of pathogens
is by using composts as the organic component in the potting soil mix.
(11,12).   Hardwood bark compost was found to be suppressive to the
following plant pathogens: Phytophthora cinnamomi, P. cactorum, Rhizoctonia
solani, Fusarium oxysporum and Pythium (3,11,20,25).

Hadar and Mandelbaum (9) tested composted Licorice roots (CLR) for the
ability to suppress Pythium spp.   Compost and peat media were inoculated
with the pathogen.   Inoculum was prepared by growing cucumbers in infested
peat which showed above 90% disease incidence.   The peat was· mixed to
levels of 1–10% in the medium.   After inoculation cucumbers were planted in
plastic boxes (9x9x10 cm) each containing 500 ml medium, and were incubated

in the greenhouse at temperatures of 25–28°C. Disease development in the peat medium was faster than in CLR. At the end of the experiment 85% diseased plants were recorded in peat, while only 10% were found in the compost medium.

This experiment was repeated several times with different inoculum levels and in the same media containing vermiculite (one third by volume). In all cases the results were similar, indicating that CLR is suppressive to Pythium. In another experiment (17,21) container media were inoculated with Pythium oospores produced in culture. This inoculum did not cause any diseases both in peat and in CLR. The plants were uprooted and cucumber seeds were planted in the same media. Damping-off was recorded in the peat medium during the second and third growth cycles but not in the CLR medium. It seems that the compost was effective in preventing disease build-up.

Apparently the suppression of plant pathogens in compost is due to biological mechanism developing during the final stage of composting.

Indeed, CLR taken from a heap during the thermophilic stage was not suppressive. When mature CLR was either heated (60°C for 4 hrs) or autoclaved (121°C for 60 min) it lost its ability to suppress Pythium damping-off. Disease incidence observed in sterile CLR was higher than in non-sterilized peat. The fungal population of the CLR consists mainly of members of the Genus Penicullium and Aspergillus and total fungal count was $5 \cdot 10^4$ CFU/g CLR.

Peat and CLR were mixed in different ratios and were inoculated with Pythium. It was observed that when the mixture contained above 60% by volume CLR, disease incidence was low, similar to a medium containing CLR only. However, at lower CLR rates disease incidence was higher (40–60%) but not as high as in peat alone (80–90% diseased plants).

Composted separated cattle manure (CSM) and composted grape marc (CGM) were tested for suppressiveness to Rhizoctonia solani and Sclerotium rolfsii. The media were inoculated with these pathogens at several concentrations and were planted with beans. Severe disease was observed when peat was inoculated while at inoculum levels 100 times higher plants grown in CSM or CGM were still healthy. Reduction of R. solani damping-off in CGM and CSM were also observed with radish as test plants. In another experiment, Phothos transplants were grown in peat, CGM or CSM mixes infested with R. solani. Root-rot was firstly observed two weeks after planting in the peat mix and at the end of the experiment 90% of the plants were dead, whereas in CGM only 10% dead plants were observed. Similar results were obtained when a CGM:peat mixture (1:1 by volume) was used.

Germination of S. rolfsii sclerotia was tested in Petri dishes containing composts. Sclerotia were placed on the medium and incubated at 30°C. In the peat treatment 100% germination took place after 48 hrs of incubation, colonies were formed and new sclerotia were produced. However, on CGM media only 10% of the sclerotia germinated and attack by compost microflora was observed. This was followed by a collapse of the sclerotial rind evident in scanning electron microscope micrographs. Penicillum spp. isolated from the sclerotia was found to produce inhibitory compounds to S. rolfsii. This compound is fluorescent and its production is inhibited by addition of iron to the culture medium.

The results presented here demonstrate that CLR, CGM and CSM have the potential to suppress soil-borne plant pathogens when used in container media. The suppression results from biological mechanisms, developing during the final stages of composting (maturation).

CONCLUSIONS

Compost produced from readily available agricultural wastes such as cattle manure and winery wastes were found to be suitable materials for container media, thus, solving environmental problems and upgrading waste material while providing high quality peat substitutes.

The positive effects of the composts on plant growth can be explained by their physical, chemical and biological properties. The physical properties fit well with optimal requirements. In greenhouse setups, where fertigation is continuously applied, the nutrient content may not be as important. However, slow release of nutrients in periods between irrigations, high contents of humic substances and bio-activity of the medium, may improve plant growth. Mature composts are also suppressive to several soil-borne plant pathogens such as Pythium, Rhizoctonia and Sclerotium rolfsii. As a result application rates of hazardous pesticides can be reduced or eliminated.

ACKNOWLEDGMENTS

This research was supported by a grant from the National Council for Research and Development, Israel, the European Economic Community, and by a grant from the Binational U.S.A.-Israel Agricultural Research and Development (BARD).

REFERENCES

(1) BACH, W. (1980). Climatic effects of increasing atmospheric CO_2 level. Experientia 36:796-806.

(2) BIK, A.R. (1983). Substrates in floriculture. Proc. XXI Intern. Hortic. Congr. 1982, Hamburg, II:811-822.

(3) CHEF, D.G., HOITINK, H.A.J. and MADDEN, L.V. (1983). Effect of organic components in container media on suppression of Fusarium wilt of chrysanthemum and flax. Phytopathology 73:279-281.

(4) CHEN, Y., INBAR, Y., RAVIV, M. and DOVRAT, A. (1984a). The use of slurry produced by methanogenic fermentation of cow manure as a peat substitute in horticulture - physical and chemical properties. Acta Hort. 150:553-561.

(5) CHEN, Y., INBAR, Y. and RAVIV, M. (1984b). Slurry produced by methanogenic fermentation of cow manure as a peat substitute in horticulture. Proc. 2nd Intern. Symp. Peat in Agriculture and Horticulture, pp. 297-317, Bet-Dagan, Israel.

(6) CULL, D.C. (1981). Alternatives to peat as container media. Organic resources in the U.K. Acta Hort. 126:69-81.

(7) GRAEFE, G. (1980). Methods and apparatus for preparing high grade fertilizer. United States Patent 4,211,545, July 8, 1980.

(8) HADAR, Y., INBAR, Y. and CHEN, Y. (1985). Effect of compost maturity on tomato seedling growth. Scientia Horticultae 27:199-208.

(9) HADAR, Y. and MANDELBAUM, R. (1986). Suppression of P. aphanidermatum damping-off in container media containing composted Licorice roots. Crop Protection (in press).

(10) HAMPICKE, U. (1980). The effect of the atmosphere - biosphere exchange on the global carbon cycle. Experientia 36:776-781.

(11) HOITINK, H.A.J. (1980). Composted bark, a lightweight growth medium with fungicidal properties. Plant Disease 64:142-147.

(12) HOITINK, H.A.J. and FAHY, P.C. (1986). Basis for the control of soil borne plant pathogens with composts. Ann. Rev. Phytopathol. 24:93–114.

(13) HOLLEY, W.D. (1967). Inert media to replace soil. Colo. Flo. Gro. Ass. Bull. 205:12.

(14) HUIJSMANS, J. and LINDLEY, J.A. (1984). Evaluation of a solid-liquid separator. Transactions of the ASAE:1854–1858.

(15) INBAR, Y., CHEN, Y. and HADAR, Y. (1985). The use of composted slurry produced by methanogenic fermentation of cow manure as a growth media. Acta Hort. 172:75–82.

(16) INBAR, Y., CHEN, Y. and HADAR, Y. (1986). The use of composted separated cattle manure and grape marc as peat substitute in horticulture. Acta Hort. (in press).

(17) KUTER, G.A., NELSON, E.B., HOITINK, H.A.J. and MADDEN, L.V. (1983). Fungal populations in container media amended with composted hardwood bark suppressive and conducive to Rhizoctonia damping-off. Phytopathology 73:1450–1456.

✗(18) LOUVET, J. (1982). The relationship between substrates and plant diseases. Acta Hort. 126:147–152.

(19) LOHR, V.I., O'BRIEN, R.G., and COFFEY, D.L. (1984). Spent mushroom compost in soilless media and its effects on the yield and quality of transplants. J. Amer. Soc. Hort. Sci. 109:693–697.

(20) NELSON, E.B. and HOITINK, H.A.J. (1982). Factors affecting suppression of Rhizoctonia solani in container media. Phytopathology 72:275–279.

(21) NELSON, E.B. and HOITINK, H.A.J. (1983). The role of microorganisms in the suppression of Rhizoctonia solani in container media amended with composted hardwood bark. Phytopathology 73:274–278.

(22) PUUSTJARVI, V. (1977). Peat and its use in horticulture Publ. 3, Torveteollisuusliittory, Helsinki, Finland.

(23) RAVIV, M., CHEN, Y. and INBAR, Y. (1986). Peat and peat substitutes as growth media for container-growth plants. In: Chen, Y. and Avnimelech Y. (eds.): The Role of Organic Matter in Modern Agriculture. Martinus Nijhof/Dr. W. Junk Publ., The Hague (in press).

(24) ROBINSON, D.W. and LAMB, J.G.D. (1975). Peat in horticulture. Academic Press, London, England.

(25) SPRING, D.E., ELLIS, M.A., SPOTTS, R.A., HOITINK, H.A.J. and SCHMITLHENNER, A.F. (1980). Suppression of the apple collar rot pathogen in composted hardwood bark. Phytopathology 70:1209–1212.

(26) STEPHENS, C.T., HERR, L.J., SCHMITLHENNER, A.F. and POWELL, C.C. (1983). Sources of Rhizoctonia and Pythium spp. in a bedding plant greenhouse. Plant Disease 67:272–275.

(27) STREICHSBIER, F., MESSNER, K., WESSELEY, M. and ROHR, M. (1982). The microbiological aspects of grape marc humification. European J. Appl. Microbiol. Biotechnol. 14:182–186.

(28) VERDONCK, O. (1984). Reviewing and evaluation of new materials used as substrates. Acta Hort. 150:467–473.

EXPERIMENTATION OF THREE CURING AND MATURING PROCESSES
OF FINE URBAN FRESH COMPOST ON OPEN AREAS. STUDY CARRIED OUT AND FINANCED
ON THE INITIATIVE OF THE COUNTY COUNCIL OF COTES-DU-NORD - FRANCE +

A. LE BOZEC - A. RESSE
CEMAGREF - RENNES (FRANCE)
Division Génie Rural

Summary

The analysis process of inerts in urban composts recently
developped by the CEMAGREF and ANRED is presented first, then the
results of the experimentation of three methods for curing and
maturing a fine urban fresh compost carried out on a real scale
during periods of four months, the one in Summer, the other one
in Winter : static composting, without any intervention, dynamic
composting with turnings, controlled dynamic composting with turnings and waterings. The evolution of the components (water,
organic matter and inerts) has been studied each week, and temperatures have been recorded, too.
Static composting keeps compost in a dormant state (final C/N:22)
with low temperature zones. Turnings contribute to the dehydration
of compost in Summer (25 % water) and to its humidification in
Winter (45 % water). Early waterings with turnings, bringing moisture up to 50-55 %, accelerate maturation (C/N : 20).
In fact, turning the windrows, together with waterings in Summer,
twice during the first six to eight weeks then, four weeks later,
the reshaping of compost for storage should ensure and accelerate
the maturation and sanitizing of the compost.

1. Introduction

In 1984, thanks to 87 composting plants, France produced
650,000 t of urban compost including Brittany's 70,000 t. That
compost is produced by the eight urban waste composting plants
thanks to the SOBEA process, without any beforehand waste grinding.
At the output of the BRS biostabilizer, fresh compost must be
matured on an open area, after refining and grinding, before marketing it and using it for cauliflower, artichoke and vegetable market
gardening in open-field.
The study carried out compares the controllable operation
factors with the climate factors so as to define the stabilization
process to obtain mature compost in the shortest possible time.

2. Method of analysis of inerts in urban compost

2.1 Interest of the method

Urban compost is composed of three basic elements : water,
organic matter and inerts, which are defined as physical components
which are biodegradable in the soil. A method of analysis and
quantitative determination of such inerts was perfected in 1982
by the CEMAGREF and ANRED. The interest of the method consists in
the knowledge of the total amount of inerts present in the compost,
taking into account all the components over 2 mm and heavy fines
under 2 mm. This method is applicable according to the efficiency
of the devices and refining of the compost.

2.2 Method of analysis

The analysis is carried out in two stages, with a phase of
destruction of the organic matters first, then separation of the
inerts thanks to a densimetric sorting in a solution.

+ Study carried out and financed on the initiative of the County Council of
  Côtes-du-Nord, France.

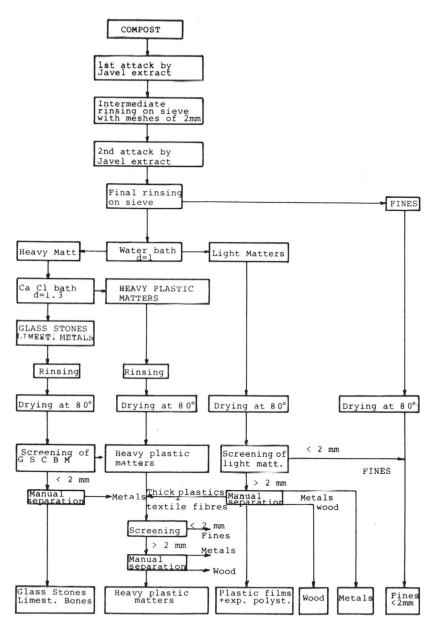

Fig. I - Method of analysis of the inerts of compost.
(CEMAGREF-ANRED)

. Destruction of organic matter : immerse 1 kg compost in sodium hypochlorite and allow to act until complete destruction of organic matter. Rince then abundantly with water, the product being placed on a sieve with round meshes of 2 mm in diameter, so as to trap fines. Do it again if necessary.

. Separation of the components of inerts : a densimetric sorting by water enables to separate "light" elements which float and heavy elements which settle. A fraction of "heavy" elements remaining afloat are separated in a bath of calcium chlorid; they are composed of "heavy plastics", and a residual portion of "glass, stones, limest.,bones". The sorting of "light" elements only leaves in that category : plastic films and expanded polystyrene (PSE); thick plastics and textile fibres are grouped with "heavy plastic matters".Limest.- bones" are determined by an acid attack. After drying, screening, magnetic and manual separation, the 6 following categories of inerts components are defined : "Glass-Stones-Chalk -Bones"; "Light Matters : Polystyrene films - PSE"; "Heavy Matters: PVC, PS, various plastics"; "Wood"; "Metals" and "Fines < 2mm". The results are presented in an analysis report (see fig. II).

After more than 1,500 analyses on 40 plants, the analysis methodology is operational. A mechanization of the organic matter destruction is being developped in order to reduce the necessary delays, and treat up to 5 samples simultaneously.

ANALYSIS OF INDESIRABLE INERTS AND INERTS

PLANT OF   : ETABLES   Sampling ref.: COMPOST 5 months PILE 1
Sampled by   : CEMAGREF   Humid weight : 726 g
Date of sampling : 12/12/84   Moisture   : 43.3 %
Date of receipt :   Dry weight   : 412 g
Date of analysis : 13/12 to 16/12/84

WEIGHT OF DRY ELEMENTS (in g)

Meshes (mm)	Metals	Glass Stones Limestone	PVC,PS Various Plastics	Polyst. Films PSE	Totals Weight	Totals %dry w.
>40 square	0.00	0.00	0.00	0.00	0.00	0.00
25 to 40 square	0.00	0.00	0.00	0.00	0.00	0.00
12.5 to 25 square	0.00	0.00	0.78	1.58	2.36	0.6
6.3 to 12.5 square	0.90	6.96	1.59	3.11	12.56	3.0
5 round to 6.3 sq.	0.16	10.97	1.88	1.49	14.50	3.5
2 to 5 round	0.15	44.38	<----- 7.35 ----->		51.88	12.6
<2 round		85.35			85.35	20.7

INDESIRABLE INERTS >5 round

Designation	Metals	Glass Stones Limestone	PVC,PS Various Plastics	Polyst. Films PSE	Total Indesirable Inerts
Weight (in g)	1.06	17.93	4.25	6.18	29.42
% dry weight	0.3	4.4	1.0	1.5	7.1

INERTS

Designation	Metals	Glass Stones Limestone	Plastics Matters	Total Inerts
Weight (in g)	1.21	147.66	17.78	166.65
% dry weight	0.3	35.8	4.3	40.4

Fig. II - Example of an analysis of inerts.

3. Experimentation of three maturation modes

3.1 Composting process

The study has been carried out in the household waste treatment plant of the "Syndicat mixte intercommunal" (Union belonging to several "communes") of the area of Etables sur Mer, Lanvollon, Chatelaudren and Plouagat, in the Department of "Côtes du Nord" in Brittany. The compost plant was built in 1980 and, thanks to the SOBEA process, treats 7,000 t/year of household waste produced by 25,000 sedentary inhabitants, of a coast zone with an agricultural orientation which receives a crowd of tourists in Summer (see Fig. III). Maturation is realized on concrete areas by turnings with loaders.

Composting plant of
Etables sur Mer

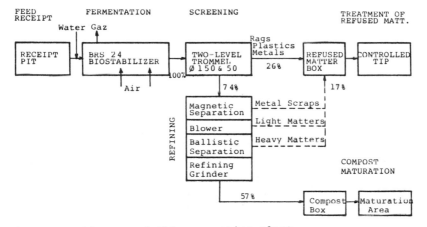

Fig. III - Diagram of the composting plant.

3.2 Experimental protocol

. Characteristics of fresh compost : the rotary biostabilizer,the first function of which is to ensure a biologic treatment by aerobic fermentation (2 to 4 days) of raw waste, realizes a differential mechanical treatment by fragmenting the fermentable fraction, while preserving the inert fraction. The proportion of fresh compost going through at 12.5 mm is 80 % at the biostabilizer output and 95 % after grinding and refining. The fresh compost used for the Winter experiment has a higher moisture content (49 to 53 % whereas it is 42 to 44 % in Summer). It is richer as far as organic matter is concerned, 62 to 64 % (% dry weight) whereas it contains 30 to 32 % in Summer.
Total inerts include :
- more than 45 % fines inferior ot 2 mm in size
- more than 35 % glass-stones-limestone
- less than 20 % plastics ranging from 2 to 25 mm

Fig. IV - Development of the experimentation.

. Experimentation : the experimentation was carried out during two distinct climatic periods of 20 weeks (140 days): one in Summer period from July to November 1984 and one in Winter period from January to June 1985. For each experiment, three windrows have been formed with fresh compost from the refining box, three metre high with at least 50 t per windrow.

The first windrow is submitted to static composting, it undergoes external weather conditions only.

The second windrow is submitted to dynamic composting with turnings by loader.

The third windrow is submitted to controlled dynamic composting with turnings and waterings.

. Follow up and analysis: temperature records are made every 50 cm over the pile cross section. Every week compost is sampled 1 m deep under the mycelian layer thanks to an auger. During turnings, a section is realized through the median axis of the windrow.

The analyses deal with :
- Moisture: drying at 80°C up to constant weight of 1kg raw product.
- Total Organic Matter (MOT): calcination of 30g dry weight at 545°C for 2 hours.
- Total nitrogen: Kjedahl process with bucci on 2g dry weight.
- Inerts: CEMAGREF ANRED process on 1kg raw product.
- Carbon Anne calculated by the formula :
C=0.3834.MOT-0.5405 determined on products of different ages and origins.

3.3 Results
. Windrow temperature : the thermophase does take place in each windrow, despite the fineness of the product, in Summer as well as in Winter. Temperature varies a lot according to the location in the pile the differential recahing 30 to 40°C between the lower part-which is colder- which is colder and the upper part-which is warmer. The maximum temperatures are observed in tne 1.50-2.00m section. The temperature rise phase is linear and of the form T=at+b. The daily variation of temperature rapidly increases according to the vertical section of the pile in accordance with the equation:
Δ T=0.32x4.16^h . Temperatures do not vary very much after reaching the steady phase. The windrow inertia surely explains that difference with the experimental tests carried out on small quantities of product.

* Static composting (Fig. V)

In Summer, the temperature of 60°C is not reached in the lower part of the windrow (0-80 cm), and in almost the whole windrow (0-190 cm) in Winter. After a twenty-day period, the maximum temperatures are reached and are near steady temperatures. After a forty-day period, the temperatures are steady, and after a four-month period, (110 days), they range from 62 to 68°C in Summer and 50 to 58°C in Winter in the zone between 1 m and 2 m.

* Dynamic composting (Fig. VI)

The temperature of 60° C is reached beyond 1.00 m in Summer and beyond 1.60 m in Winter. The maximum temperatures are higher at the end of the first turning and then decrease after further turnings. In Winter, after 2nd turning (3 months), they are under 60° C. Between Summer and Winter, the temperature differential gets near 30° C in the core of the pile. Generally, the temperatures of piles 2E and 2H are superior to those of piles 3E and 3H as far as controlled dynamic composting is concerned.

* Controlled dynamic composting (Fig. VII)

The temperature of 60°C is reached beyond 1.00 m in Summer and beyond 1.40 m in Winter. The maximum temperatures are higher after the 1st turning in Summer and at the end of the first fifteen days (before the 1st turning) in Winter. After the 3rd turning (3 months) in Winter, the temperature differential gets near 10°C in the core of the pile.

84

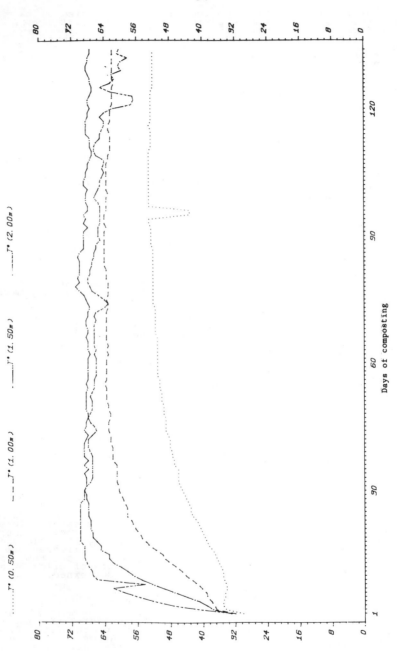

Fig. V - Temperatures pile 1E

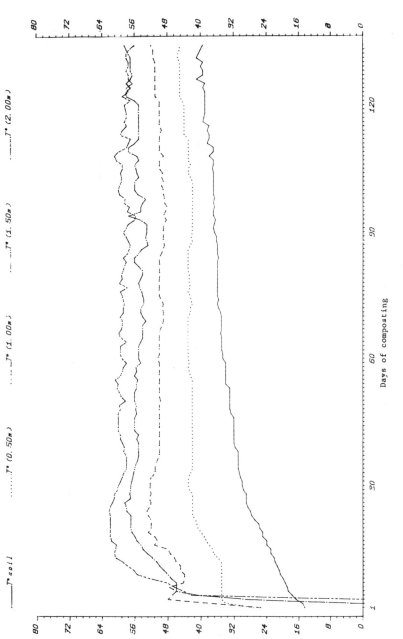

Fig. V - Temperatures pile 1H

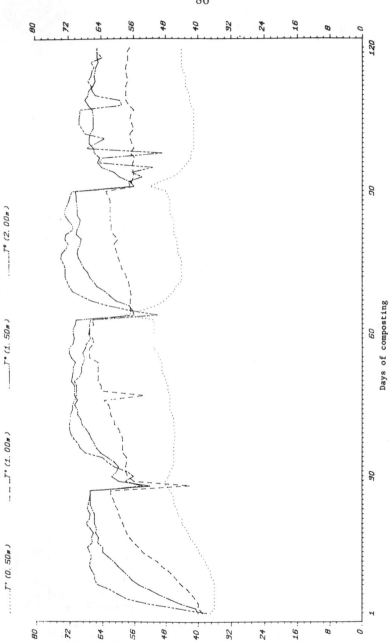

Fig. VI – Temperatures pile 2E

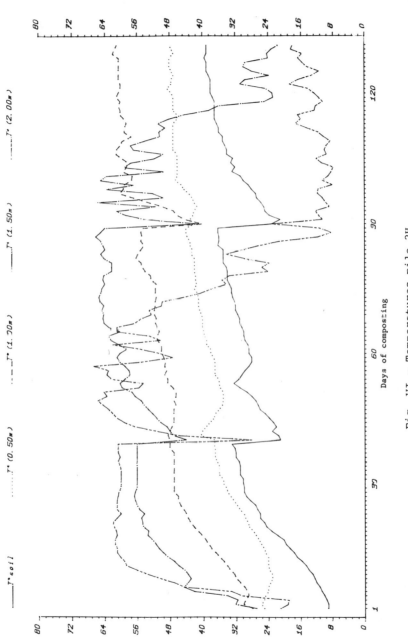

Fig. VI - Temperatures pile 2H

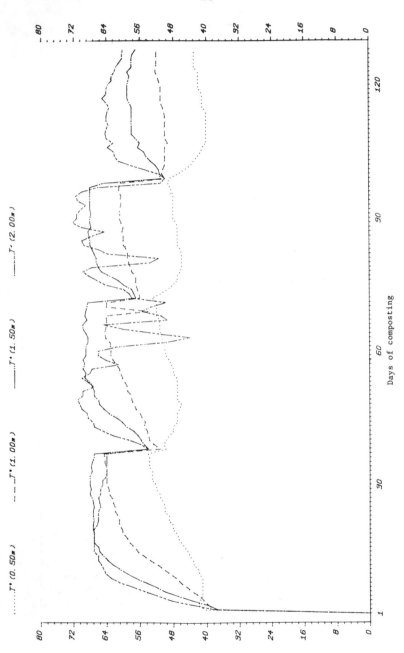

Fig. VII - Temperatures pile 3E

Days of composting

......T° (0. 50m)   — - —T° (1. 00m)   ....T° (1. 50m)   ——T° (2. 00m)

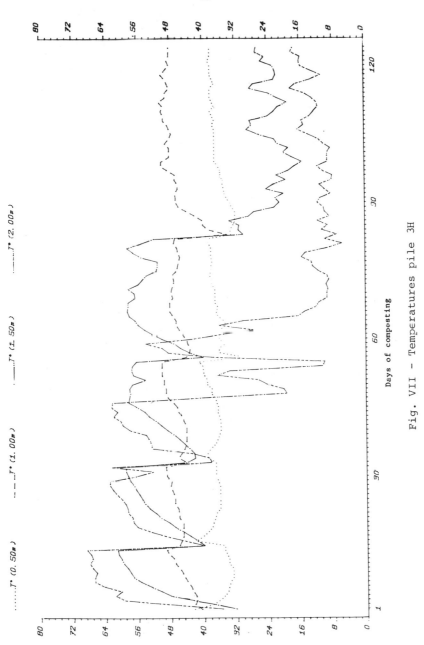

Fig. VII – Temperatures pile 3H

. Evolution of the compost physical components
  * Water

COMPOSTING METHOD	STATIC		DYNAMIC		CONTROLLED DYNAMIC	
Pile	1E	1H	2E	2H	3E	3H
Start	42.6	46.0	43.8	50.9	42.6	48.7
Week 10	35.6	48.9	36.6	48.6	33.2	58.7
Week 18	33.2	36.4	27.5	45.3	45.0	55.6

Fig. VIII - Moisture evolution (% humid weight'

In case of static composting, windrows have a tendency to self-regulate and become insensitive to weather conditions because of the protective effect of the mycelian layer. Pile 1H gets drier and its final moisture content reaches that of pile 1E : about 35% after 20 weeks.

After an evolution which is similar to that of the piles undergoing static composting during the first 10 weeks, the moisture rate of pile 2E gets to 25% after 5 months on area and the moisture rate of pile 2H holds constant, over 45%.

When in controlled dynamic composting, the moisture rate is maintained over 40% as for pile 3E and over 55% as for pile 3H.

  * Organic matter

COMPOSTING METHOD	Pile	MONS* at start	Regression straight line MONS=a-b.t		Correlation coefficient	MONS after week 18
			a	b		
Static	1E	55.4	50.0	0.41	0.665	50.8
	1H	58.6	58.3	0.56	0.709	46.7
Dynamic	2E	61.0	57.9	0.60	0.672	46.2
	2H	59.2	63.5	1.17	0.758	47.1
Controlled Dynamic	3E	62.2	59.5	0.90	0.879	42.2
	3H	58.0	60.3	1.84	0.962	32.5

Fig. IX - Evolution of the MONS (% dry weight)
  *MONS = Non Synthetic Organic Matter

The MOT (Total Organic Matter) includes Plastics. The MONS (Non Synthetic Organic Matter) is obtained by deducting all the titrated plastics content : MONS = MOT - Plastics.

In case of static composting, the compost evolutions meet one another (1E-1H).

In case of dynamic composting, the Winter windrow (2H) evolution is more rapid and reaches that of the Summer windrow in case of controlled dynamic composting (3E).

91

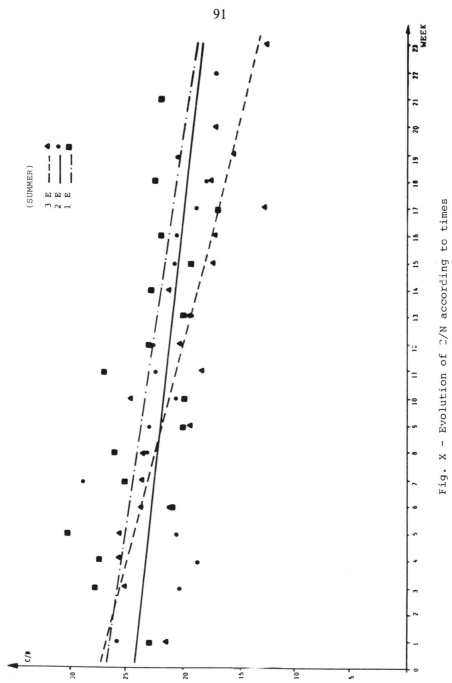

Fig. X - Evolution of C/N according to times

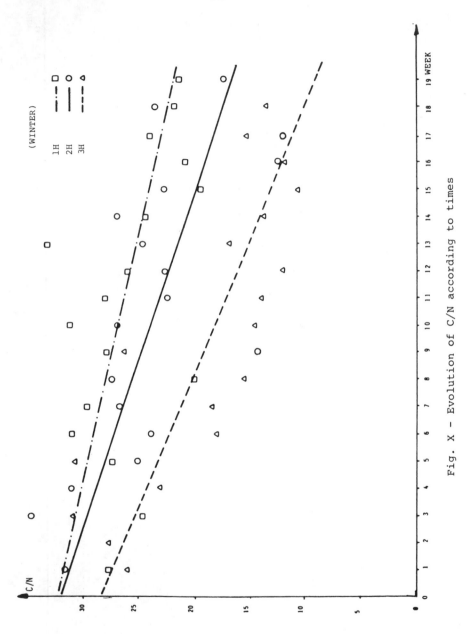

Fig. X - Evolution of C/N according to times

The controlled dynamic composting makes the evolution of windrows more rapid, particularly for the Winter one (3H) which reaches a stand-steady degree on the tenth week. Turnings accelerate the organic matter degradation, in Winter particularly.

* Carbon Nitrogen Ratio (C/N)

The compost maturity evolution of the various piles, expressed through the Carbon/N trogen ratio is shown in Fig.X with the corresponding regression straight lines.

The fresh compost C/N ratio, at the start and after it has stayed in biostabilizer is 27 in Summer and 32 in Winter, after compost has been on area for 20 weeks that ratio becomes :

- Static composting : Pile 1E : 20   Pile 1H : 22
- Dynamic composting: Pile 2E : 19   Pile 2H : 16
- Controlled dynamic composting : Pile 3E : 15   Pile 3H : 10

Compost is considered as mature when its C/N ratio gets inferior to 20, the duration of the required composting according to the method used would then be :

	SUMMER	WINTER
Static composting :	20 weeks (4.5 months)	22 weeks (5 months)
Dynamic composting:	17 weeks (4 months)	15 weeks (3.5 months)
Controlled dynamic composting :	12 weeks (3 months)	8 weeks (2 months)

Turnings associated to waterings favour the compost evolution towards maturation and make it more rapid. Particularly, it seems, if waterings are parctised during the first month. Piles 2H and 3E have a rather similar evolution, pile 2H is advantaged though, it is more humid even if not watered. Maturation then really seems to depend on humidity which can be obtained by waterings or favoured by turnings.

It must be noted that mature compost may reach temperatures as high as 40 to 60°C.

The pH, which shows a tendency to acidity during the first month, becomes markedly basic at 8-8.5.

*Total inerts (Fig. XI)

COMPOSTING METHOD	Pile	Fines <2mm	Glass Stones Limest.	Various plastics	PE PSE	Wood	Metals	Total Inerts
Static	1E start	17.1	11.2	2.7	-	0.18	0.08	31.3
	end	14.5	13.7	1.1	2.6	0.46	0.44	32.8
	1H start	12.7	7.1	1.5	2.5	0.18	0.99	24.9
	End	14.1	9.1	2.9	2.4	0.04	0.12	28.6
Dynamic	2E start	14.2	12.7	3.0	0.0	0.10	0.34	30.3
	end	16.1	15.5	1.0	1.9	0.51	0.17	35.2
	2H start	11.8	7.0	2.3	2.6	0.14	0.25	23.9
	end	14.3	10.4	2.5	2.4	1.90	0.87	32.4
Controlled dynamic	3E start	14.6	11.9	4.2	0.0	0.24	0.15	31.6
	end	17.7	15.8	1.4	2.6	0.58	1.30	39.4
	3H start	12.4	7.3	1.0	3.9	0.08	0.31	25.1
	end	22.9	12.4	3.3	3.2	0.03	1.20	43.1

Fig. XI - Evolution of Inerts -(% dry weight)

Total inerts obviously have no evolution. They hold constant as for quantity and their contents increase all the more rapidly as the contents of organic matter decrease. Consequently, an enrichment of compost in total inerts can be observed, from 20 to 25% in Summer and from 30 to 45% in Winter.

. Distribution of the compost physical components inside windrows :
The moisture rate decreases from the bottom to the top of windrow (-5 to -10 points) in a rather evenly distributed way. Despite a slow temperature rise in the lower part, the organic matter evolution suffers no slow down. Thus the interest of windrow turnings is emphasized as regards to the mass homogenization.

. Mycelian layer and weather conditions
During all the observation time the presence of a mycelian layer could be noticed which coated the whole windrow.

That mycelian layer has the following characteristics :

     - compact consistancy on 10 to 20 cm
     - white colour
     -dryness (moisture : 20 to 30%)
     - low organic matter content (40 to 50%)
     - high total inerts content (40 to 45%)

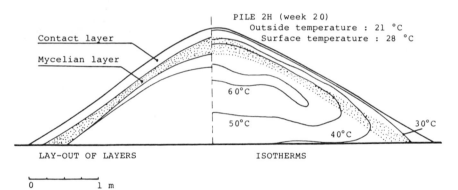

Fig. XII

That layer acts as a barrier between the outside part - the contact layer which is exposed to weather conditions - and the inside part - the pile inner part, the evolution of which is almost independant from the exterior weather conditions -. So that the thermal evolution of windrows is dissociated from exterior thermal variations. Moreover, only important rainfalls, superior to 15mm, generate a slight cooling of 0 to 3°C which is followed by micro thermophases of 0.5 to 5°C from the bottom to the top of piles. An exterior temperature of -15°C, 5 days after the 1st turning of pile 3H, caused no disturbance on the thermophase and had no other impact than a 2°C drop of temperature 20cm under the surface of the pile.
That layer first is close to the surface and then moves towards the inside of the pile down to 40-50cm deep. After each turning, that layer regenerates itself and progresses deeper and more rapidly. When compost reaches a high degree of maturity (C/N ≤ 15), that layer gets fragile and looses its structure.

. Chemical characteristics of final composts :

After the experiments, the compost piles have been weighed again and composts analysed. The losses of humid weight of windrows prove to be considerable, an average 25 to 30% in Summer and 40 to 50% in Winter. The volumal masses of final compost are 800 to 900kg/m3 for specific compost on area and 600 to 750kg/m3 for compost which has been reshaped and compressed.

The seaside proximity has originated the production of a compost which is calcium and magnesium enriched. Composts which are obtained in Winter appear to have a higher content of various elements (Fig. XIII), particularly of limestone (+26%), phosphorus (+27%), magnesium (+84%)and potassium (+72%). The heavy metals contents are rather constant from one season to another (Fig. XIV).

COMPOSTING METHOD	STATIC	DYNAMIC		CONTROLLED DYNAMIC	
Pile	1H	2E	2H	3E	3H
N	1.01	1.07	1.15	1.17	1.21
P2O5	0.561	0.562	0.719	0.566	0.775
K2O	0.53	0.40	0.74	0.43	0.63
CaO	6.05	4.98	6.03	0.67	6.46
MgO	0.75	0.51	1.05	0.57	0.94
Na2O	0.765	0.604	0.973	0.710	0.839

Fig. XIII - Final compost nutrients (% dry weight)

COMPOSTING METHOD	STATIC	DYNAMIC		CONTROLLED DYNAMIC	
Pile	1H	2E	2H	3E	3H
Pb	401.6	447.9	802.6	769.6	701.2
Cr	48.6	50.9	48.6	52.7	52.7
Ni	33.5	40.7	33.4	40.6	35.1
Hg	1.20	4.2	1.85	2.0	2.20
Cd	3.1	3.7	3.5	3.2	3.5

Fig. XIV - Heavy metals content of final compost (mg/kg dry weight)

One ton of final compost, moisture rate 50%, supplies : 230kg organic matter (humus 57kg), 5.8kg nitrogen, 3.6kg P_2O_5, 3.7kg K_2O, 30.2kg C_aO and 7.5kg MgO.

The visual aspects of composts which have been obtained through dynamic composting and through controlled dynamic composting are quite different. The first one has a rather powdery and dry aspect, a brown colour and a fugitive and sourish odor. The second one is lumpy and humid, it has a black colour and a persistent odor.

4. Conclusions

When no turning is practised, the mycelian layer keeps compost inside the pile in a thermal stationary phase which might prove to be insufficient for the compost pasteurization in the lower part of windrows (0-0.50 m in Summer and 0-1.00 m in Winter).

When no watering is operated, turnings indirectly contribute to dry the compost in Summer and humidify it in Winter.

In Winter, the turning frequency has been lowered in controlled dynamic composting : three turnings in ten weeks instead of two in Winter. Waterings have been practised at the same intervals in Winter and only after the tenth week in Summer. That sole factor of moisture seems to play a determining part during the first two thermophases of composting as for the maturation rapidity.

5. Arguments

The main practical guidelines which could be given to operators of composting plants are the following ones : stack fresh compost in windrows about 3 m high on a concrete area and turn it over twice during the first six to eight weeks. Between the tenth and twelfth week, compost should be reshaped and stocked in piles 3 to 4 m high.

In ummer, compost should be watered when being stacked up and during the two turnings in order to bring its moisture rate between 50 and 55%. In Winter, it will not be necessary to water or to cover windrows.

Those general recommendations will have to be adapted to the site specific data of a given plant. They concern a fine compost which have undergone pre-fermentation inside a bio-stabilizer.

Finally, an extraordinary thermal inertia has to be noted as for static windrows, the upper part of which remains at about 65°C after 6 months on area. That thermal bed can be of great interest for users of low temperature heat, though it is hardly possible to predict the behaviour of windrows during a calorific extraction.

References :

   - "Les Indésirables dans les Composts Urbains" - CEMAGREF RENNES - ANRED - December 1982

   - "Etude de l'Amélioration de la Qualité du Compost" - CEMAGREF RENNES - Department of "Côtes du Nord" November 1985

CAN BIOMETHANATION BE INCLUDED IN THE PROCESSING OF COMPOST-LIKE MATERIALS ?

E.-J. NYNS

Unit of Bioengineering, University of Louvain,
B-1348 Louvain-la-Neuve, Belgium

Summary

The process by which a given biomass is transformed into a product called "compost", and which is refered to as "composting" is not only looked at from the scientific or technological standpoint but also from a legal standpoint. There is a tendency to legally define the process of "composting" rather than to define the product "compost". The purpose of this paper is to call to attention that there are alternative processes to "composting" which may well yield a product with properties similar to a "compost" and which could prove not only more reliable from a scientific and technological standpoint but also more profitable from an economic standpoint. The energy-yielding process of biomethanation which processes the biomass anaerobically instead of aerobically can be typically quoted in this respect (Dahiya and Vasudevan, 1986). Indeed, it should be recalled that biomethanation is a stabilizing process, i.a. for solid and semi-solid biomasses, which yields a biogas containing methane, CH_4, and carbon dioxide, CO_2, leaving in the digested residue all nitrogen, N, phosphorus, P, and potassium, K.

1. INTRODUCTION

Most wastes and residues which are destined to be used as a fertilizer and/or soil conditioner on agricultural lands, need some sort of stabilization for proper use. One can simply store these substrate biomasses untill use. This is often the case for animal manure. But one should recall that spontaneous fermentation of these substrate biomasses will occur not only during storage but also after being spread on land. "Composting" is a technology which combines this stabilization necessity with the control of the necessarily-occuring fermentation, which is conducted in the aerobic mode. Biomethanation is a technology which could result in the required stabilization but controls the necessarily-occuring fermentation in the anaerobic mode.

2. QUESTIONS WITH BIOMETHANATION AS ALTERNATIVE TO COMPOSTING

The question which arises then is : "What is the fertilizing value of the biomethanized biomass ?". Looking through the literature seems to indicate that there are no particular problems (Lannoye, 1984, Demuynck, 1984), but a thourough scrutiny indicates that the presently available experiments are not yet conclusive. Indeed, often one kg of biomass substrate is compared to one kg of biomethanized substrate for its fertilizing value. However, through biomethanation, one kg of biomass substrate (as dry organic matter) may yield as much as 400 g of biogas and leave only 0.6 kg of digested residue. Assays should compare the fertilizing value of one kg of biomass feedstock with whatever is left after the stabilizing fermentation process, namely 0.6 kg of biomethanized product in the example quoted (see also Mehta and Daftardar, 1984).

Furthermore, strictly comparative assays need to be performed as well in cultivation jars as on land, namely a control, a set of experiments with the stabilized-fermented product through "composting" and a set of experiments with the stabilized-fermented product through biomethanation.

One of the arguments against biomethanation as stabilizing fermentation process has often been that biomethanation mineralizes the organic nitrogen and, in this way, modifies the nitrogen availability and its rate. It is true that when a biomass substrate has a low carbon to nitrogen (C/N) content ratio, one observes during biomethanation that excess organic nitrogenous compounds generate methane, CH_4, thereby mineralizing organic nitrogen to ammonia, NH_4^+ /NH_3. However, when the substrate biomass has a high C/N ratio (and this can be achieved in proper mixtures of wastes, namely by mixing low N-containing agricultural wastes with high N-containing animal manures), one observes, on the contrary, the mobilization of inorganic nitrogen, NH_4^+ /NH_3 into organic nitrogen, i.a. as a result of microbial growth (Melchior et al., 1982, 1984).

The real question is : "What is the chemical composition of a biomass substrate stabilized by biomethanation as compared to the same biomass substrate stabilized by composting ?". Few data have been published which would allow to answer this question. Higgins et al. (1982) analyzed composted and biomethanized sewage sludge. Table 1 summarizes their results.

Table 1. Comparison of composted and biomethanized sewage sludge

Parameter	Composted	Biomethanized
	sewage sludge	
Volatile solids (VS, as % of dry weight)	49	60
Ratio COD/VS (dimentionless)	0.71	0.83
Oxidised state	Higher	Lower

According to Higgins et al., 1982.

2. CONCLUSIONS : THE WAY AHEAD

The way ahead should then be to model possible scenarios of processes which will lead to a final product acceptable as a compost-like product, taken in a broader sense. One of these scenarios may consist in a first fermentation step in the anaerobic mode (thus possibly a biomethanation step) followed by an aerobic finition composting step.

Technologies are evolving fast. These evolutions should not be neglected. In this respect, it will help if, legally, the "compost" is mainly defined by the properties of the end-product. It will help if, legally, some flexibility is allowed in the stabilizing fermentation processes. It will also help if public authorities such as the CEC sponsor comparative assays of compost-like end-products, namely obtained with and without a biomethanation step.

4. LITERATURE

Dahiya, A.K. and Vasudeva, P. (1986). Biogas plant slurry as an alternative to chemical fertilizers. Biomass, 9, 67-74.

Demuynck, M. (1984). Utilization in agriculture of anerobically digested effluents. Rept. (62 pp., 43 ref.) of Contract n° ECI-1012-B7210-83-B by Unit Bioengin., Univ. Louvain, Belgium to CEC, DGXII.

Higgins, A.J., Kaplovsky, A.J., and Hunter, J.V. (1982). Organic composition of aerobic, anaerobic, and compost-stabilized sludges. J. Water Pollut. Control Fed. 54, 466-473.

Lannoye, M. (1984). La valorisation agronomique des effluents de digesteur. Symp. "Quel Avenir pour la Biométhanisation en Région Wallonne ?" Charleroi, Belgium, Dec., Proc. 25 pp.

Mehta, S.A. and Daftardar, S.Y. (1984). Effect of anaerobically prepared wheat straw composts and city garbage composts on yield and N and P uptake by wheat. Agric. Wastes, 10, 37-46.

Melchior, J.-L., Binot, R., Perez Aguilar, I., Naveau H.P., and Nyns E.-J. (1982). Influence in the years to come of the knowledge in the physiology of methanogenesis on the technology of biomethanation. J. Chem. Technol. Biotechnol. 32, 189-197.

Melchior, J.-L, Naveau, H.P., and Nyns, E.-J. (1984). Disposal of liquid and solid effluents from a methane digester. In "Biomethane, Production and Uses", R. Buvet, M.F. Fox, and D.J. Picken, eds., Bowskill, R., Ltd., Exeter, UK, pp. 209-214.

The author is consultant for the CEC-DGXVII for their Demonstration Programme "Biomass and Energy from Wastes".

TRANSFORMATION OF URBAN SLUDGES MIXED WITH GRAPE STALKS INTO ORGANIC FERTILIZERS

G.C. SPAGGIARI and G.L. SPIGONI
Azienda Gas Acqua Consorziale
Reggio Emilia
R. JODICE and M. CONSIGLIO
Istituto per le Piante da Legno e l'Ambiente
Turin

Summary

Urban sludges undergoing a stabilization treatment during the anaerobic phase with 80% moisture content were mixed with grape stalks and underwent thermophil transformation for 120 days.

Sludges and grape stalks intermixed at different volume rations were heaped into piles.

Airing of the piles where the composting process took place was obtained by periodically overturning them at planned intervals. On the whole, four overturning operations were carried out.

Periodical analytical checks of the chemio-physical, chemical and microbiological parameters were made both during the process and on the final product.

High temperatures reached during the process, especially in the initial phase (over 70°C) caused Salmonellae to disappear and microorganisms to be reduced.

During the first transformation phase, organic matter mineralization prevailed while the C/N ratio became sensibly lowered. During the second phase, the formation of more stable humic substances had greater importance.

The product showed balanced ratios between mineral nutrients and high levels of humic substances with high molecular weight.

1) Introduction

In 1982, AGAC of Reggio Emilia and IPLA of Turin started experiments concerning the microbiological transformation of sludges mixed with poplar bark into organic fertilizer. The positive results obtained during this experimentation phase (8) and other similar phases (2, 3), encouraged researchers to continue their studies according to the following two considerations:

a) that of identifying other lignocellulose residuals to be mixed with sludges and able to ensure correct microbiological transformation in view of the fact that the quantities of sludge produced in Italy are notably higher than the availability of poplar bark.

b) That of modifying the trandformation times in order to diminish the process period which, in the previous experience with poplar bark, amounted to 210 days.

Wine-producing activities in the province of Reggio Emilia and neighbouring areas with the consequent production of grape stalks, a little used by-product, facilitated the choice of material to mix with the sludges.

Experimentation thus started with the drafting of a study program characterized by the following research subjects:

a) study of the microbiological transformation of piles of sludge mixed with grape stalks;

b) checks on the products obtained at the end of the fermentation process according to their fertilizing value and their hygienic-sanitary reliability.

2. Materials and methods

2.1 Raw materials

2.1.1 Sludges

The utilized sludges (1) are supplied by the urban waste water depuration system belonging to AGAC (Mancasale, Reggio Emilia); these are thickened by a belt filter and have a humidity of about 80%. The ash content exceeds 50% (tab. 1).

Humidity	%	79	Iron	%	1.3
pH		7.1	Manganese	ppm	580
Ashes	%	55	Zinc	ppm	2300
Carbon	%	25	Copper	ppm	320
Total nitrogen	%	4.1	Nickel	ppm	150
C/N		6.1	Lead	ppm	300
Total phosphorous	%	2.2	Chromium	ppm	120
Total potassium	%	0.15	Cadmium	ppm	6
Calcium	%	4.2	Fecal choliforms	MPN/g	2.5×10^6
Magnesium	%	0.66	Fecal strepto-		
Sodium	%	0.11	coccus	MPN/g	1.3×10^7
			Salmonellae	MPN/g	1.2×10^3

Tab. 1 : Analytical characteristics of the Mancasale sludges. With the exception of humidity, all results are expressed on the dry substance.

2.1.2 Grape stalks

The utilized grape stalks are obtained from grape stripping operations and account for about 3-4% of the weight of the processed grapes. They tend to ferment spontaneously in piles since their C/N ratio is around 50 and they have a sufficiently porous structure to enable the mass to be aired. However, the high relative humidity (70%) and the acid reaction (pH 3.5-4), encourage transformations which inhibit the decomposition and synthesis of the organic substances. They have a high degree of fibers (lignin and cellulose) and a high degree of nutritive mineral elements, especially nitrogen (0.9%) and potassium (0.4%).

2.2 Experimental program

The sludges were mixed with grape stalks in three different ratios, according to the following scheme:

EXPERIMENT No.	SLUDGES weight	GRAPE STALKS weight	SLUDGES volume	GRAPE STALKS volume
1	1	0.4	1	1
2	1	0.8	1	2
3	1	1.2	1	3

The sludge-grape stalk mixing ratios were chosen by taking into account the initial value of the C/N ratio of the two materials in order to check which ratios guarantee a better fermentative process in view of the priority aspects of the research: elimination and destruction of pathogens and fecal indicators; agronomical quality of the final products; diminution of process times.

Thus mixed, the materials were piled in heaps having the following average dimensions: width 4 - 5m height 1.5-2 m, length 50-70 m.

The piles were prepared by mixing the two components with a shredder having a horizontal axis (TRITER) while the piles were periodically overturned by the same machine in order to encourage aeration and to prevent anaerobic fermentation activities.

Overturning was effected at programmed intervals according to the degree of oxygen in the pile itself.

A total of four overturning operations were effected excluding initial mixing, and these were accomplished according to the following frequencies:

Overturning No.	1	2	3	4
Overturning period (days)	15	45	80	120

The experiments were considered to have terminated on the 120th day.

2.3 Analytical checks

The research program included analytical checks on the materials during the various transformation process phases and on the final products. The following analytical checks were effected:

- Chemio-physical parameters: temperature,   humidity, pH;
- Chemical parameters: ashes, carbon, total nitrogen, total phosphorous, total potassium, total humus, humic acids and fulvic acis;
- microbiological parameters: Salmonellae, fecal Choliforms, fecal Streptococcus.

Furthermore, the humic extracts were tested to establish fractions having a different molecular mass. The determinations were effected on chromatographic columns by allowing the sample to flow over various types of Sephadex gel (6, 7). Lastly, the percentages of heavy metals in the sludges and final products were determined.

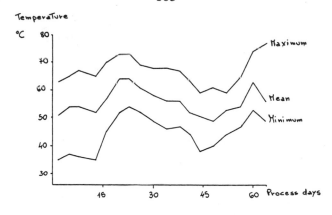

Fig. 1 : Temperature trend during first two month of process

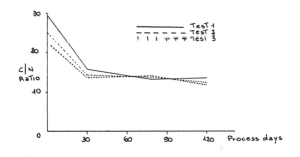

Fig. 2 : C/N ratio development of materials during the process

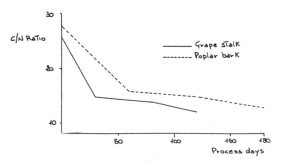

Fig. 3 : C/N ratio trend for grape stalk and poplar bark

3. Results

3.1 Chemical, physical and microbiological modifications of the materials during the transformation process in piles

The transformation process was optimum in all experiments. Humidity, which was normally above 70% at the start of transformation, was a limiting factor for the start of the process. However, the high degree of easily degradable organic substances in the grape stalks (sugars, fats, starches, etc.) enables microbic activity to start even when humidity conditions are not optimum and this consequently quickly increases the temperature which favourably conditions the humidity level itself.

After only a few days of transformation, the temperature becomes about 65% (fig. 1) while the addition of grape stalks ensures the start of microbic activity owing to their easily degradable organic content but above all because they guarantee a better oxygenation of the mass since they effect an amendment function. Anaerobiosis activities never, in fact, occurred throughout the entire cycle.

The analytical results (tab. 2) show that during the first transformation phase, there is an intense biological activity owing to the effects of the high temperature and the presence of organic substances which are easily able to ferment. Ashes are, in fact, subjected to the greatest increase during the first 30 days of composting while they successively tend to become stabilized at values of around 50%. The same trend in the C/N ratio (fig. 2) shows the intense initial mineralization of the organic substance; the values quickly decrease during the first 30 days to become established at around 12-13.

Figure 3 shows the average trend of the C/N values pertaining to the experiments with grape stalks and sludges compared to the experiments with poplar bark and sludge conducted in a similar manner during previous research

The humis acid-fulvic acid ratio passes from initial values of 0.4-0.7 to greater final values of 2 (tab. 3).

Meanwhile, the humification index (humic acids/organic substance x 100) is subjected to notable increases especially in the experiments with greater quantities of grape stalks (fig. 4). The analytical results (tab. 3) of tests on the humic substances extracted by means of chromatographic gel confirm a percentage increase of the humic fractions to a higher molecular mass: on average, the initial values for the fractions with a molecular mass of > 10,000 are around 21% while they exceed values of 50% at the end of fermentation.

Lastly, as regards the hygiene-sanitary aspects, the analytical results confirmed the results obtained during previous experiments (2, 3, 8). The high temperatures which are reached within the mass starting from the first days of composting, guarantee the disappearance of Salmonellae and a consistent diminution in the considered fecal indicators (Choliforms and Streptococcus), figure 5 .

3.2 Obtained products

The analytical results pertaining to the products thus show that the products obtained from the three experiments do not differ from each other: table 4 shows the final average values of the chemical and physical parameters.

The pH values are near neutrality (6.5–7.0) and the humidity values are between 55 and 60%. The organic carbon percentages are fairly high (27.4–28.6%) and the total nitrogen values are particularly important, exceeding 2% in all experiments.

The C/N ratio is normally around 12. The quantity of heavy metals (especially cadmium, chromium and lead) is very much below the limits proposed by the EEC (1982) and CNR (1982)(4, 5, 9).

Furthermore, regarding the quality of the organic substances, analytical determinations (tab. 4) pertaining to the quantity and quality of the humus, show a fair percentage of total humus (4–4.3%) and above all, a clear prevalence of humic fractions with a higher structural complexity; the humic acid values are very near 70% and the values of the fractions with PM > 10,000 are near 50%.

For comparison purposes, table 4 shows the values of the humus and humic fractions determined on Sephadex and pertaining to mature vaccine manure and a product obtained by composting sludge and poplar bark (8); the data show that there are no significant differences between the different materials. The Salmonellae are absent while the presence of fecal indicators is very low.

4. Discussion

The results obtained during these experiments show that sludge mixed with grape stalks and allowed to transform in piles, are subjected to a composting process very similar to that described in previous experiences (1, 2). Transformation occurs in thermophil phase and in microaerobiosis conditions. As for the experiments using poplar bark, it is possible to divide the process into two distinct phases: the first phase (0–30 days) mainly involves the mineralization processes to which the organic substances are subjected while there is an important elimination of fecal microorganisms and pathogens owing to the high temperatures which are reached; during the second phase (30–120 days), the organic substance is transformed into humus, especially of high molecular mass (humic acids).

The heavy metal content is very low especially considering the type of sludge used. The composting process also showed that when grape stalks are used, the transformation times are lower than those pertaining to poplar bark without jeopardizing experimentation objectives concerning hygiene safeguards and the fertilizing value of the final products.

Tab. 2 : Analytical characteristics of the materials during the process (with the exception of humidity, all results are expressed on the dry matter)

TESTS	PROCESS DAYS	HUMIDITY %	pH	ASHES %	O.M. %	C %	N %	C/N
1	0	73	7.0	25.0	75.0	38.5	1.3	29.6
	30	65	6.8	43.0	60.0	31.6	2.0	15.8
	80	55	6.8	51.0	49.0	26.5	2.0	13.2
	120	55	7.0	50.0	50.0	28.6	2.1	13.6
2	0	75	6.9	27.0	73.0	37.4	1.5	24.9
	30	64	7.1	40.0	60.0	31.6	2.2	14.3
	80	60	6.5	49.0	51.0	27.6	2.0	13.8
	120	55	6.4	52.0	48.0	27.4	2.2	12.4
3	0	78	7.1	30.0	70.0	35.9	1.5	22.4
	30	69	7.0	39.0	61.0	32.1	2.3	13.9
	80	65	6.8	45.0	55.0	29.7	2.1	14.1
	120	60	6.5	52	48.0	27.4	2.3	11.9

Tab. 3 : Analytical characteristics of humic substances during the process. (The results are expressed on the dry matter).

TESTS	PROCESS DAYS	TOTAL HUMUS	HUMIC ACIDS	FULVIC ACIDS	AU/AF	HUMUS TRANSFORMATION INDEX	MOLECOLAR MASS < 10.000 % OF TOTAL HUMUS	> 10.000
1	0	6.2	29.3	70.7	0.4	2.4	78.2	21.8
	30	4.8	51.2	48.8	1.0	4.1	61.2	38.8
	80	4.5	65.6	34.4	1.9	6.0		
	120	4.3	74.5	25.5	2.9	6.4	45.3	54.7
2	0	6.5	31.4	68.6	0.4	2.8	75.4	24.6
	30	5.1	47.1	52.9	0.9	4.0	59.7	41.3
	80	4.7	64.9	35.1	1.8	6.0		
	120	4.3	68.3	31.7	2.2	6.1	48.6	51.4
3	0	6.6	41.7	58.3	0.7	3.9	68.4	31.6
	30	4.9	50.5	49.5	1.0	4.1	64.4	35.6
	80	4.2	63.3	36.7	1.7	4.8		
	120	4.0	66.5	33.5	2.0	5.5	51.3	48.7

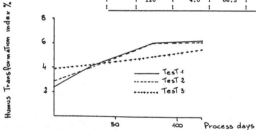

Fig. 4 : Humus transformation index trend during the process

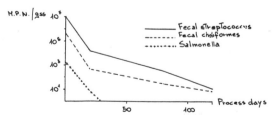

Fig. 5 : Fecal streptococcus, fecal choliformes and Salmonella development during the process

In short, besides confirming the concrete possibility of recovering urban sludges for productive use, the results of the experiments showed that grape stalks, by-products of the wine-making industry, can be perfectly mixed with urban sludges and transformed into organic fertilizer.

Tab. 4 : Analytical characteristics of the products obtained with grape stalks and bark, compared to those obtained with vaccine manure (with the exception of humidity, all results are expressed on the dry matter).

PARAMETERS		BARK FERTILIZER	GRAPE STALK FERTILIZER	VACCINE MANURE
HUMIDITY	%	55.0	55.0	75.0
pH		6.9	6.5	8.0
ASHES	%	50.0	52.0	44.0
ORGANIC MATERIAL	%	50.0	48.0	56.0
TOTAL NITROGEN	%	2.2	2.0	2.0
C/N		12.5	12.2	15.0
TOTAL PHOSPHOROUS	%	0.45	0.69	0.70
TOTAL POTASSIUM	%	0.40	1.4	0.8
TOTAL HUMUS	%	7.3	4.2	8.0
HUMIC ACIDS % OF THE HUMUS	%	73.3	70.7	77.0
FULVIC ACIDS % " "	%	26.7	29.3	23.0
AU/AF		2.8	2.3	3.3
HUMUS TRANSFORMATION INDEX	%	10.4	6.0	13.9
MOLECULAR MASS > 10.000	%	61.1	51.4	57.0
MOLECULAR MASS < 10.000	%	38.9	48.4	43.0
IRON	%	1.5	1.4	1.4
CALCIUM	%	7.0	5.4	4.0
MAGNESIUM	%	0.7	0.8	0.3
CADMIUM	ppm	4.4	4.2	N.D.
NICKEL	ppm	29.4	59	128
ZINC	ppm	900	855	8,250
LEAD	ppm	90	127	66
CHROMIUM	ppm	75	94	265

Bibliography

1. AGAC, 1982. Report and synthesis on the activity and prospects of depuration sludge treatment. Reggio Emilia.
2. Fassi, B., Breesy, G., Jodice, R., 1976-77. Organic fertilizers from poplar bark and other paper-mill residuals. Industrial system and agronomical use. Annals of the Academy of Agriculture of Turin; 119.
3. Jodice, R., Consiglio, M., Roletto, E., 1982. Organic fertilizers from bark and woody residuals: industrial production and agronomical use. L'Italia Agricola; 119, (3): 147-160.
4. EEC, 1982. Provision proposal of the Council concerning the use in agriculture of sludges from depuration processes. Official Gazzette of the European Common Market; N.C.: 264: 3-7.
5. CNR, 1982. Guide for the use in agriculture of sludges from the biological treatments to which urban waste waters are subjected. AQ/2/13.
6. Pharmacia Fine Chemicals, 1979. Gel Filtration, theory and practice. Uppsala, Sweden.
7. Roletto, E., Barberis, R., Zelano, V., 1982. Gel filtration and absorption spectroscopic investigations on humic substances from organic fertilizers. Plant and Soil; 66, 383-390.
8. Jodice, R., Spaggiari, G.C., 1983. Transformation of sludges muxed with poplar bark into organic fertilizer. Annals of the International Symposium of Naples.
9. D.P.R. 915 of 10th Sept. 1982 and deliberation of 27/7/84 No. 52.

RECYCLING OF INDUSTRIAL WASTE :
USE OF COCO, JUTE, COTTON AND WOOL RESIDUES IN VERMICOMPOSTING

V.C. DEL MAZO SUAREZ, O.J.F. LANTIERI and O.H.A. LANTIERI
Sao Paulo, Brazil

It is becoming more and more common in the industrialized nations to find industry concentrated in cities with a high population density. The problem of the waste produced by industry is immense, not only because no one knows where to put it but also on account of the pollution it can cause if it is burned or left in the open on refuse tips. The cost of transporting the waste to the tips is also fairly high, because as cities grow the tips are located farther and farther from industrial centres.

The purpose of our research was to carry out an analysis and find a solution to the exploitation of animal and vegetable waste, not only in the manufacturing industries but also in the processing industries and in those based on fibre extraction.

The first and the best results were obtained with dust and fibre waste from jute, a raw material commonly used by the textile industry. Good results were also obtained with coco dust and fibres and with cacao waste. In the case of jute, the greatest production of waste is found in factories where jute cloth and sacking is recycled for the manufacture of industrial felt. When the sacks and the material are shredded in high-power machines, vast amounts of dust and short fibres are produced. This waste has no industrial use and can be regarded simply as rubbish. Most of the dust is caught in the air filters of dust removers. A rough calculation suggests that about 60 tonnes of jute waste are produced every month in Sao Paulo alone.

The problem is more complex in the industries based on the coconut palm and starts on the vast plantations where the coconuts are cultivated commercially. When the coconuts are harvested, the husks become a serious problem because mountains of them accumulate. They are not put to any use, they are difficult to dispose of and they contaminate the areas where the coconuts are husked by providing breeding grounds for insects which attack the plants and also for snakes, lizards and other nasty things.

A certain amount of the husks is used to produce fibre for industrial use, for doormats and for other products. When the husks are shredded, 70 % of what is produced is in the form of dust and small fibres and the rest is fibre suitable for industrial use. The consumption of coco fibre in Brazil is approximately 300 tonnes per month, which leaves another 600 tonnes or so of waste which is difficult to get rid of. Great heaps of waste dust are produced and the waste cannot be burned since a wet process is used in shredding the husks. The waste cannot be dumped in rivers or the sea either, since it would be a cause of pollution, particularly on account of the high level of tannin which is a problem in the waste. Small lakes and hollows close to fibre-manufacturing factories are quickly filled by the dust which is dumped in them. A significant amount of dust is also found inside the factories ; the fibre contains a certain amount of dust which is caught in the dust removers.

On cacao plantations where the fruit is opened so that the cacao beans can be removed and then dried, the discarded pods pose a serious problem of contamination because as they pile up they create an environment which is ideal for the growth of bacteria which then spread disease - known in Brazil as <u>podição parda</u>, a kind of grey rot - and attack the trees in the plantation.

We looked into ways of recycling these wastes. We wanted to find a simple and practical solution which could be easily used on any farm or plantation regardless of size and the skills of its workers. The most practical solution proved to be composting as humus for use on the farm or plantation or, in the case of waste produced near cities, for use in gardens and orchards, etc.

The advantages of the system which was conceived are that it does not require a lot of space, generate unpleasant smells or encourage insects such as flies and mosquitoes, and for these reasons it can be used in the open and in densely-populated areas.

We considered the factory-produced wastes of coco fibre (<u>cocos nucifera</u>), jute (<u>corchorus capsularis</u>) and cotton (<u>gossypium barbadense</u>).

We decided on a "humus heap" method - to be described later - for the production of humus for agricultural use as fertilizer and for the subsequent process of vermicomposting. Our study did not involve detailed research but verification of fertility by practical means on the same farm where composting took place. We also set out to check initially that aerobic fermentation occurred with the definite help of the worms which were used.

Five compost heaps were prepared with an initial volume of 3 m^3, which in the end became 1.5 m^3. The first heap contained a mixture of cotton, jute, coco and wool fibres in equal amounts. This experiment did not work, however, and was abandoned.

The compost heap consisting solely of jute was the first to give indications of success when it was turned for the first time after 30 days. The temperature was 65°C, the maximum humidiy was 35 % and the pH had risen from 4.5 to 6.8. After another 30 days the temperature had stabilized at 30-40°C with a neutral pH and was tending to fall as a result of aeration when the heap was turned a second time. At this point we did not hesitate to introduce the worms bred on the farm, using native species such as <u>pherentina sp</u>. and imported species such as <u>eisenia fetida</u>, and humus production was boosted considerably by their introduction. It is estimated that vermicomposting from jute produced 60-70 % of humus and 30-40 % of organic matter. Humidification would continue in the soil, thus continuing its microbiological improvement.

Our slides show the results of jute vermicomposting when used on elephant grass (<u>pennisetum purpureum</u>).

The compost heap using wool waste did not give satisfactory results, as the waste had to be mechanically ground to a fine powder to facilitate fermentation.

The initial results from the compost heap using cotton waste were satisfactory, but we are now about to modify the process and shall shortly be able to provide definite data.

Similarly, we have not yet finished work on the compost heap using coco fibre waste, but the initial field experiments indicate that the short-term results are more than satisfactory. The processing of coco waste is of tremendous importance for the north of Brazil and other tropical countries. The local economy could benefit if this waste could be recycled where it is produced to provide organic fertilizer for sandy soil.

We are convinced that further work needs to be done in this area of industrial recycling, not only by us but also by other countries, so that we can work together to produce a fund of knowledge. Our future lies in combatting waste and making full use of recycling opportunities.

THERMOPHILIC DRY ANAEROBIC FERMENTATION
PROCESS FOR THE STABILIZATION OF HOUSEHOLD REFUSE

L.DE BAERE[*] and O. VERDONCK[+]

[*] ACEC-Noord, Dok Noord 5, B-9000 GENT, Belgium
[+] State University of Gent, Lab Soil Microbiology, Coupure L 653,
B-9000 GENT, Belgium

Summary

The organic fraction of household refuse can be stabilized through a
new process, called DRANCO, which recovers both energy in the form of
biogas and a stabilized organic end-product. The process is a thermophilic anaerobic fermentation, which takes place at solid state or
"dry" conditions. This results in the production of roughly 180 m^3 of
biogas (55 % methane) per ton of raw organic waste within a period of
2 to 3 weeks. The process can be compared with biogas recovery in a
landfill, but sped up by a factor of about 1000 through process
control. A pilot plant has been operating successfully for more than
15 months, while a full-scale plant for 150,000 ton of household
refuse is being designed.

1. Introduction

The stabilization of the biodegradable fraction of household
refuse is normally accomplished through aerobic bacterial decomposition. The aerobic organisms responsible for the degradation convert
the organic matter into CO_2, water and fairly large amounts of heat,
with a compost as residual product. Organic matter can also be
stabilized through the activity of microorganisms if oxygen is absent.
During anaerobic decomposition, however, only a minor amount of heat
is produced. Most of the energy is released in the form of methane
gas. In comparison with aerobic decomposition, only about 15 % as much
heat is produced during the anaerobic conversion of glucose to final
products. About 85 % of the energy is released as methane. The
potential gas production from 1 ton of household refuse through
anaerobic degradation is about 100 m^3 of methane, equivalent to 90 l
of light fuel oil.

2. Process description

A new process, called DRANCO[R], has been developed for the
anaerobic stabilization of the organic fraction from household waste
(1,2). The DRANCO process combines production of a humus-like endproduct and intensive biogas production.

Prior to the anaerobic fermentation phase, raw household refuse
is pretreated through shredding, iron removal and selection of a
fraction of paper and plastics in the case of RDF production. The
remaining substrate is further homogenized and glass, stones and large

items are removed. The remaining fraction is mostly organic and highly amenable to biological conversion.

A very limited amount of water is added to the organic fraction before pumping into the dry fermentors. The water can be replaced by recycled sludge coming from the press after the anaerobic fermentation or by sewage sludge for co-digestion. The anaerobic fermentation takes place at 35°C or 55°C and at a total solids concentration between 30 and 40 %. This is about 6 to 10 times more concentrated than currently existing completely mixed anaerobic digestion processes for biogas recovery from refuse. The system is designed so that there is no decrease in microbial activity in comparison with completely mixed digestion, so that specific gas productivity is roughly 6 to 10 times higher than conventional digesters. The DRANCO process can also be compared with biogas production in landfills, where gas production takes place spontaneously over a period of 40 to 50 years under "dry" or solid state conditions. The process taking place in a landfill is optimized in the controlled fermentation by a factor of roughly 1000, so that only 2 to 3 weeks are necessary to obtain the same amount of biogas per ton of waste. Due to the high solids content in the fermentors, separation of solids and liquids does not occur so that no crust is formed. Crust or scum formation frequently cause considerable mixing problems in completely mixed digestors.

The digested residue, about 30 to 35 % solids, is dewatered by means of a press. The resulting sludge can be completely recycled if the total solids content of the incoming organic fraction is sufficiently high, or the sludge must be partially purged. The cake is broken up and dried using the waste heat of the gas engines to 75 % solids. The dry product is further refined so that it is virtually free of plastics, stones and glass. The final residue is a humus-like product, called Humotex, which can be applied for landscaping or used for horticultural purposes.

The biogas produced can be converted into electricity or purified to make a pipe-line quality gas.

3. Post-fermentation

The digested residue after a solid state fermentation during 16 to 18 days is still relatively active. In order to obtain a very stable end-product, a post-fermentation was deemed advantageous. A postfermentation means that the residue coming from the first step reactors is digested in a second step for a short period without any additional feeding.

A series of lab-scale tests were set up to determine the feasibility of a post-fermentation. Digested residue was obtained from continuous reactors operating at the same loading rate but at different temperatures. The digester operating at mesophilic (35°C) and at thermophilic (55°C) temperatures produced 90.3 and 98.4 l CH_4 of kg of incoming organic fraction. This is consistent with normally obtained results as thermophilic digestion produced 5 to 10 % more biogas per kg of waste added than mesophilic digestion. The residues from the first step were in turn fermented at their respective operating temperature in a post-fermentor.

The results indicate that fermentation under thermophilic conditions still yields more extra gas during the first 3 days of postfermentation than mesophilic fermentation. The rate of production for both cases, however, is about 5 times lower than during the first step, and activity drops down even more drastically after 5 days of postfermentation.

Table 1. Effect of post-fermentation

Operating temperature	Production 1st step (l CH_4/kg)	Extra production (l CH_4/kg)		
		after 3 days	after 5 days	after 7 days
Mesophilic (35°C)	90.3	2.3	3.5	4.0
Thermophilic (55°C)	98.4	2.8	3.3	3.8

A post-fermentation of maximum 2 to 3 days is considered useful, not only because of extra energy production, but because the post-fermentor also serves as a buffer between the fermentation and the press and drying process. The digested residue after thermophilic fermentation in two steps yields a highly stabilized humus-like product with a C/N ratio of 12 to 15 and a cumulative oxygen consumption of 50 to 60 mg of O_2/g of volatile solids. This can be compared with a compost after about 4 months in windrows. The hygienic aspects, in relation to the presence of fecal coli, fecal streptococci and salmonella are very positive. Analyses for these microorganisms indicated that the anaerobic fermentation process causes a complete kill-off which is in contrast to other composting techniques (3).

4. Pilot plant results

A continuous pilot plant installation was started up in November 1984 and has been performing highly satisfactorily during more than 1 year. The pilot plant has a total volume of 57 m^3 and a capacity to handle 3 ton per day of organic fraction coming from the solid waste treatment plant. Two main modes of operation have been investigated, namely mesophilic and thermophilic operation, over a period of at least 22 weeks each. The results (Figures 1 and 2) clearly indicate that thermophilic fermentation outperforms mesophilic fermentation. Gas production rates of 2 to 3 m^3/m^3reactor.day were obtained at 35°C, with daily peaks of 4 to 5 m^3/m^3 reactor.day. Thermophilic digestion yielded rates of 6 to 8 m^3/m^3reactor.day. A minimum retention time of 12 days was attained during week 19, corresponding to a volumetric loading rate of 25 kg of COD/m^3reactor.day. The average production per ton of organic fraction amounted to circa 180 m^3 of biogas over the course of the first year of operation.

5. Full scale application

Design of a full scale plant is currently under way for a refuse treatment plant which ll handle 150,000 ton of household refuse per year. About 60 % of the wastestream will be treated through the DRANCO process. The biogas will be converted into electricity and will yield about 1.8 megawatt of power, significantly reducing treatment costs. About 40 % of the electricity will be used in the treatment plant itself while the remainder will be sold to the public utility. The plant will yield 20,000 ton of Humotex at 70 to 75 % dry solids annually. Even though the capital investment and maintenance costs are considerably higher for the DRANCO process than for the aerobic windrow composting process that was originally planned, the total treatment cost per ton of organic fraction is the same. This full-scale plant should be operational by mid 1988.

REFERENCES

1. DE BAERE, L. and VERSTRAETE, W. (1984). High-rate anaerobic composting with recovery of biogas. Biocycle 25(2), 30-31
2. DE BAERE, L., VAN MEENEN, P. and VERSTRAETE, W. (1986). Anaerobic fermentation of refuse. 3rd International Symposium Materials and Energy from Refuse, MER-III, March 18-20, Antwerp, Belgium
3. DE BERTOLDI, M., FRASSINETTI, S., BIANCHIN, L. and PERA, A. (1984). Inactivation of microorganisms in sewage sludge by stabilisation processes. Ed. by Strauch, D., Havelaar, A.M., L'Hermite, P. Elsevier Applied Science Publishers, 64-76

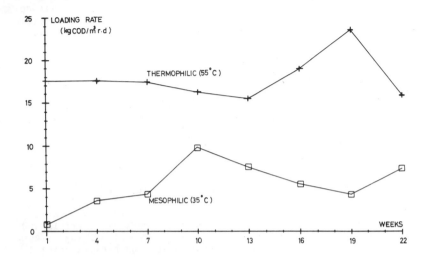

Fig. 1 : Loading rate for thermophilic and mesophilic operation over a
period of 22 weeks on a pilot-scale

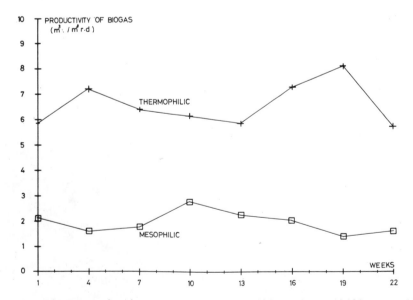

Fig. 2 : Biogas production rate for thermophilic and mesophilic operation
over a period of 22 weeks on a pilot-scale

VERMICOMPOSTING OF RABBIT MANURE: MODIFICATIONS OF MICROFLORA

L. ALLIEVI, B. CITTERIO and A. FERRARI
Dipartimento di Scienze e Tecnologie Alimentari e Microbiologiche
Università di Milano - Via Celoria 2, I 20133 Milan (Italy)

Summary

In the last few years Italy has seen a veritable boom in the production of vermicompost, this being obtained from the action of earthworms on various types of manure. Vermicomposting is being studied in
many countries since it is a process which offers the possibility of
treating organic waste substances and converting them into fertilizer
(i.e. sewage sludge, municipal solid waste etc.). In order to study
the modification of microflora during vermicomposting we first determined the number of microorganisms of the various groups, during and
after the process carried out on rabbit manure, on full-scale, in a
small earthworm farm, comparing it with those resulting from a parallel spontaneous maturation process of the same material. During the
preliminary maturation process, before vermicomposting in order to ren
der the material tolerable for earthworms, important changes, such as
decrease in counts, were observed. The substantial decrease of fecal
bacteria almost totally limited to this stage is particularly important. Actual vermicomposting brought about less changes in microbial
counts, analogously to that which comes about during a prolonged spontaneous maturation of the manure in question.

1.1 Introduction: a short review of research on vermicomposting

In the last few years there has been a notable development of vermiculture in Italy. The objects of this are to breed earthworms for various
uses and to produce organic fertilizer usually from various manure bases.
Vermicomposting is also considered as an alternative to the usual methods
of treatment and disposal of organic waste.

The aspects of vermicomposting has been taken into consideration by
various researchers, usually referring to the "red worm" Eisenia foetida
(66). The most interesting aspects taken into consideration and the results
obtained may be synthesized as follows:

- Materials suitable for earthworm feeding and the production of vermicompost, and the consequent possibility of using earthworms for the treatment of waste material: it has been verified that growth can come about,
creating suitable conditions, in municipal solid waste, various types of an
imal manure, in solid fraction pig slurry, human excrement, various vegetable wastes, food wastes, domestic wastes, microbial biomass as such or en-

riched with cellulose, many types of sewage sludge especially aerobic biological type and mixtures of some of these materials. Earthworm action can
also be used to further improve the characteristics of a compost. The following materials proved to be practically unutilizable: freshly-voided human or animal excrement, some anaerobic sludges, if not previously exposed
to the open air, some primary or industrial sludges, high salt content
sludge, newspaper, sawdust, simple organic substances such as starch, sac-
charose or proteins, alone or mixed, pure cellulose or with added mineral
salts and vitamins (1,5,13,16,17,20,21,22,28,32,34,36,38,41,42,43,53,54,55,
61,63,64,80,85). The positive action of the earthworm has already been verified in some wastewater treatment plants, such as "trickling filters" (44,
78).

- Economic validity in the treatment of waste materials: in some cases
vermicomposting is equally if not more advantageous than traditional methods, especially if there is a market for the products (4,5,21,29,31,34,55,
56,60,73). Waste treatment plants have therefore been constructed in many
countries (4,13,21,22,34,37,63,73).

- Importance and quality of the chemical and physical transformation of
materials subjected to vermicomposting: vermicompost as a finished product
is crumbly and well fragmented (33,61). There is no doubt that there is an
accelerated decomposition and transformation of organic matter, even if the
various Authors do not agree on the real advancement of the humification
process (5,20,22,33,35,39,54,61,65,72,74,75,80). According to some this remains limited and anyway similar to that found in the case of other organic
fertilizers, whilst others maintain that humification is better. Plant hormones found appear to be substantially present in the material before treatment (33,38,80). The earthworm can accumulate heavy metals and various toxic substances which means a decrease in the concentration of these in the
treated materials. It has been verified that this accumulation comes about
in the case of DDT, TCDD, PCBs, cadmium, chromium, copper, lead, mercury,
nickel and zinc but not iron and manganese. This is also in relation to factors such as pH, concentration of the substance considered, earthworm species (6,7,11,12,15,25,45,46,47,53,57,58,59,68,71,76,84).

- Modifications in the microbial population present, regarding generic
and physiological groups as well as indicators of fecal contamination: the
microorganisms present in the gut of the earthworm proved to be practically
the same as those in the material ingested, but these tend to increase or
decrease in the vermicompost according to the microbial group considered,
the type of organic material utilized, the vermicomposting technique (8,10,
22,24,26,27,39,50,62,65,67,77,83). With regard to fecal microorganisms
there was a net inhibition of Salmonella (18,21,22,29,61), which according
to some is due to the secretion of anti-microbial substances by the earthworm (51,81). With regard to the whole fecal bacteria group however whilst
it has sometimes been absent in vermicompost as a finished product (30) on
other occasions fecal bacteria proved to be present even in elevated numbers (10^5- 10^6/g) (14,15,52).

- Fertilizing value of vermicompost: available data differs. Whilst some
research workers have found that it's action is equal to or more positive

than other organic fertilizers, others exclude differences even between
land treated with vermicompost and that not treated (19,29,33,34,35,69,79,
80,82).

The object of our research was to determine the variations in the numbers of microorganisms of the various groups (generic, physiological and in
dicators of fecal contamination) found in rabbit manure during the necessar
y preliminary maturation process and during the actual vermicomposting. Var
ious earthworm breeding techniques were taken into consideration, applied
in a small farm on full-scale. The vermicompost was moreover compared with
a product obtained by a parallel spontaneous maturation process by the same
manure.

1.2 Materials and Methods

1.2.1 Breeding method used

A small vermicomposting farm near Milan in Italy was taken into consideration. The compost beds occupied a total area of 100 m^2 approximately
and were placed in a plastic covered tunnel giving a greenhouse effect. The
material subjected to vermicomposting was a mixture of straw and semi-solid
rabbit droppings. These droppings came from a rabbit farm, and were removed
from underneath the grid every month. In order to render the manure suitable for the earthworms, this was allowed to mature spontaneously for about
three months in a covered heap before using it as earthworm feed. The earth
worms had been bought a few years before from another farm and had been
kept on the same type of manure used for the experiment.

Three experimental compost beds were used of approximately 100 x 130
cm. The height of the initial layer of manure of which the compost bed was
made was 20-25 cm when the earthworms were added. During the vermicomposting process this height varied between 20-35 cm. In order to maintain the
correct humidity level it was watered with drinking water when necessary.
The process was conducted according to the following methods:
- Compost bed n°1: a layer of a few centimeters of manure was added to
the bed every fifteen days; the top ten centimeters were turned before this
was added.
- Compost bed n°2: no periodic addition to the original layer; the top
ten centimeters were turned every fifteen days.
- Compost bed n°3: no periodic addition to the original layer of manure,
all the material was turned every fifteen days.

1.2.2 Sampling

Sampling was carried out corresponding to the various treatment stages,
on:
- Fresh manure: rabbit droppings mixed with straw on arrival at the vermi
composting farm, sampling carried out in March.
- Manure matured for three months: manure allowed to mature spontaneously
for three months before using it for vermicomposting; sampling carried out
in June; a part of this matured manure was used for vermicomposting, whilst
another part was left to mature spontaneously (see following points).

- Vermicompost: in the number 1 and 2 compost beds the superficial layers
were sampled separately (0–10 cm) and the deeper one, in compost bed n°3
the entire mass was sampled; these samples were taken after three months of
vermicomposting (September) and repeated after six months (December).

- Manure matured for nine months: manure matured for three months left to
mature spontaneously for another six months in the same period during which
vermicomposting was carried out; sampled in December.

Every sample was taken choosing material from various parts of the
heap or compost bed then placing the samples in sterile plastic bags. Sample storage was at +4°C.

1.2.3 Microbiological analyses

A 10 g suspension of the sample in 90 ml of quarter-strength Ringer's
solution (40) was homogenized sterile in a Omni Mixer (Sorvall). The initial suspension was serially diluted in ten-fold steps in the same solution.
Suitable aliquots of the various dilutions were then inoculated into liquid
culture media into test tubes (multiple tube technique for the determination of the Most Probable Number, MPN; quintuple set test tubes) or in agar
ized media (double set pour-plates). Incubation in anaerobiosis was carried
out with the Gas-Pak System (BBL) where necessary.

The microbial groups sought, the media and incubation conditions used
were:
- Total aerobic bacteria: plate count agar (7 days/28°C).
- Total anaerobic bacteria: Todd Hewitt broth + 1.4% agar (10 days/28°C
in anaerobiosis).
- Fungi: malt agar with the addition of rose bengal 33 mg/l and tetracy-
cline 100 mg/l (7 days/28°C).
- Aerobic nitrogen-fixing bacteria (Azotobacter): liquid medium according
to Pochon (70) (15 days/33°C); microscopic verification of the growth of
Azotobacter.
- Anaerobic nitrogen-fixing bacteria: liquid medium according to Augier
(9) (30 days/28°C in anaerobiosis); findings on gas production and lowering
of rH.
- Ammonifiers: asparagine liquid medium according to Pochon (70) (15 days
/28°C); ammonium detection with Nessler reagent.
- Nitrifiers: ammonium liquid medium according to Pochon (70) (40 days/
28°C); nitrite and/or nitrate detection using diphenylamine-H_2SO_4 reagent.
- Aerobic and anaerobic cellulolytic microorganisms: liquid media using
paper smear according to Pochon (70) (20 days/28°C for aerobes, 20 days/33°
in anaerobiosis for anaerobes).
- Fecal coliforms (E. coli): according to IRSA Italian standard methods
(48,49): presumptive test in lactose broth (24 and 48 h/37°C), confirmatory
test in brilliant green lactose bile broth and in tryptone water (24 h/44°);
final confirmation by streaking Levine-EMB agar plates.
- Fecal streptococci: according to IRSA Italian standard methods (48,49):
presumptive test in azide dextrose broth (24 and 48 h/37°C), confirmatory
test in ethyl violet azide broth (48 h/37°C); microscopic verification of
the growth of streptococci.

Dry weights were determined drying aliquots of the samples at 105°C.
95% confidence limits were calculated through standard deviation for
plate counts and according to Cochran (23) for the MPNs.

1.3 Results and Conclusions

Figure 1 shows the results of the microbiological analyses giving quan
tity modifications of the microflora in the material used for vermicomposting, during the maturation stage before vermicomposting, during the actual
vermicomposting itself and during the spontaneous maturation process as an
alternative to the earthworm action.

Taking into consideration the various factors which could have influenced the variations in microbial numbers during vermicomposting itself and
the results obtained, the following can be affirmed.

- Methods used for vermicomposting process: in compost beds numbers 1, 2
and 3 respectively the process was carried out using three different methods. These differed, as described in chapter 1.2.1, for the entity of the
mass of manure being vermicomposted the periodic turning (therefore the introduction of air) and either adding or not adding more manure during the
process. These differences do not seem to have influenced the microbiological characteristics of the vermicompost as a finished product.

- Depths of the compost beds: in the case where the turning of the manure
periodically in the beds only regarded the top 10 cm (as in beds n°1 and n°
2) this superficial layer was analysed separately from that underneath it,
in order to discover if with time differences may have arisen with regard
to the microflora as a result of greater or lesser exposition to air in the
treated material. No great differences were detected, however the superior
layer understandably tended to be richer in aerobes and poorer in anaerobes.
This effect was more evident in compost bed number 2, which had not been
subjected to periodical addition of manure.

- Time of vermicomposting: data obtained after six months treatment was
similar to that after three months. It must be kept in mind however that
the second half of the period coincided with months (October-December)
which are much colder than those of the first half.

By generally taking into consideration the various successive stages
of the treatment carried out, it can be noted that the greatest variations
in microbial numbers were verified during the maturation stage before the
actual vermicomposting itself. In fact the following was detected:

- decreases which can be evaluated in approximately one order of magnitude in the numbers relative to generic groups (total aerobic and anaerobic
bacteria, fungi);

- more marked decrease in the case of fecal bacteria: approximately six
orders of magnitude (from 10^7 to 10^1) in the coliforms, and four (from 10^7
to 10^3) for the streptococci;

- increases estimable in three orders of magnitude in the cellulolytic
aerobes and in almost five for the nitrifiers, coming from relatively low
numbers (10^2). These increases could be due to the fact that during this
stage conditions favourable to development were established (above all with
regard to oxygenation).

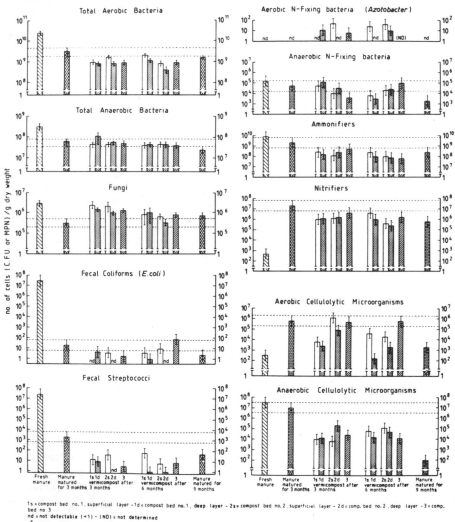

Fig. 1 – Microbial numbers in the treated matter.

Only the <u>Azotobacter</u> proved to be under the minimum detection level.

The changes which came about after the successive stage of vermicomposting appear to be much more modest. A slight decrease in the numbers rel ative to total aerobic bacteria was noted, whilst the fungi seemed to increase slightly, at least during the first months. The numbers relative to total anaerobic bacteria remained almost constant. The presence of <u>Azoto-bacter</u> was sporadic. With regard to the other physiological groups, it was found that there was a tendency towards decrease in numbers, this was particularly evident in the case of the cellulolytic anaerobes (from 10^7 to 10^4- 10^5). The behaviour of the fecal bacteria at this stage is certainly to be noted: only the streptococci underwent a definite further reduction, evaluated at 1-3 orders of magnitude.

It can be observed therefore that this process of prolonged spontaneous maturation of the manure carried out alongside that of the vermicompost ing, did not generally have an effect much different from that of the vermi composting itself on the microbial numbers.

To conclude, the vermicomposting seems to have provoked very limited numeric modifications in the microflora, which proved similar to those brought about by the spontaneous maturation of the tested manure without earthworms. The greatest variation found was in the preliminary maturation stage deemed necessary to render the feed tolerable for earthworms. This stage moreover, appears to be the most important one as regards improving the sanitary quality of the material treated. Our results therefore appear to confirm the findings of some Authors (14,15,52) i.e. the possibility of survival of fecal microorganisms in the vermicompost. On the other hand, it must be kept in mind that in our experiment the vermicompost was analysed immediately after treatment, whilst that in commerce undergoes a drying process and a fairly prolonged period of warehousing.

It must also be considered that the environmental temperature could have influenced the microbial numbers, even if the structure of the system used tends to attenuate the influence of climatic factors.

REFERENCES

1. —— (1981). Abstr. of the "Int. Conf. on Earthworms in Waste and Environmental Management", Cambridge (GB), 23-27 July.
2. —— (1983). Proc. of the conference of the "1° Assemblea Nazionale sull'Allevamento del Lombrico", Verona, 15th March. Published by Ass.It.A.L., Milan.
3. —— (1983). Study Day on "Aspetti Biologici, Chimici, Agronomici e Igie nico-sanitari della Lombrico-coltura", Roma, 13th January. (Proceedings being printed).
4. —— (1980). Vermicomposting for Sludge Management. Compost Science, 21 (3), 42.
5. —— (1984). Waste Management Using Earthworms. BioCycle, 25(4), 56.
6. ANDERSEN, C. (1979). Cadmium, Lead and Calcium Content, Number and Biomass, in Earthworms (Lumbricidae) from Sewage Sludge Treated Soil. Pedo biologia, 19, 309.

7. ASH, C.P.J. and LEE, D.L. (1980). Lead, Cadmium, Copper and Iron in Earthworms from Roadside Sites. Environ. Pollut.- Ser.A, 22 (1), 59.

8. ATLAVINYTE, O. and POCIENE, C. (1973). The Effects of Earthworms and their Activity on the Amount of Algae in the Soil. Pedobiologia, 13, 445.

9. AUGIER, J. (1957). A propos de la fixation biologique de l'azote atmospherique et de la numeration des Clostridium fixateurs dans les sols. Ann. Inst. Pasteur, 92, 817.

10. BASSALIK, K. (1913). Uber Silikatersetzung durch Bodenbakterien. Z. GärPhysiol., 2, 1.

11. BEYER, W.N., CHANEY, R.L. and MULHERN, B.M. (1982). Heavy Metal Concentrations in Earthworms from Soil Amended with Sewage Sludge. J. Environ. Qual., 11 (3), 381.

12. BEYER, W.N., CROMARTIE, E. and MOMENT, G.B. (1985). Accumulation of Methylmercury in the Earthworm, Eisenia foetida, and its Effect on Regeneration. Bull. Environ. Contam. Toxicol., 35, 157.

13. BLICKWEDEL, P. and MACH, R. (1983). Treatment of Wastes Using Earthworms. BioCycle, 24 (1), 24.

14. BOCCIA, A. (1983). Aspetti igienico sanitari dell'allevamento dei lombrichi (Proposta di una guida igienica per l'allevatore). (See ref. n° 2), page 21.

15. BOCCIA, A. and STRONGOLI, M. (1983). Conversione dei materiali di scarto nella lombricoltura: problemi igienico-sanitari. (See ref. n°3).

16. BOUCHE, M.B. The Processing of Organic Industrial Waste. In: Research Project of the I.N.R.A., Dijon, France.

17. BRENNAN, J. and HARTENSTEIN, R. (1984). Use of Earthworms in Sludge Management. J. Wat. Pollut. Control Fed., 56 (10), 1136.

18. BROWN, P.A. and MITCHELL, M.J. (1981). Role of the Earthworm E. foetida in Affecting Survival of Salmonella typhimurium. Pedobiologia, 21.

19. BURROWS, I. (1984). The Potential of Earthworm Composts for Growing Plants. (See ref. n°1), page 44.

20. BUSINELLI, M., PERUCCI, P., PATUMI, M. and GIUSQUIANI, P.L. (1984). Chemical Composition and Enzymic Activity of some Worm Casts. Plant & Soil, 80, 417.

21. CARMODY, F. (1979). Earthworm Composting - A Growing Technology. Compost Science, 20 (5), 30.

22. CARPI COUNTY COUNCIL, Assessorato alle Gestioni Speciali (1982). Note informative su: trasformazione e recupero dei rifiuti solidi con la tecnica del vermicomposting. Obiettivi e primi risultati della sperimentazione realizzata a Carpi con impianto pilota. (Printed by Carpi County Council, Italy).

23. COCHRAN, W.G. (1950). Estimation of Bacterial Densities by Means of the "Most Probable Number". Biometrics, 6, 105.

24. DAY, G.M. (1950). Influence of Earthworms on Soil Microorganisms. Soil Sci., 69, 175.

25. DIERCXSENS, P., DE WECK, D., BORSINGER, N., ROSSET, B. and TARRADELLAS, J. (1985). Earthworm Contamination by PCBs and Heavy Metals. Chemosphere, 14 (5), 511.

26. DOMSCH, K.H. and BANSE, H.J. (1972). Mykologische Untersuchungen am Regenwurm Exkrementen. Soil Biol. Biochem., 4, 31.

27. EDWARDS, C.A. and LOFTY, J.R. (1977). Biology of Earthworms.(2nd edn.), Chapman & Hall, London.

28. FEROCI, S. (1981). Concimare con i lombrichi. Terra e Vita, 22 (17),67.

29. FERRARI, A. and BONAZZI, G. (1983). Il fenomeno lombrico tra realtà, fantasia e compiacenza. L'Informatore Agrario, 39 (9), 24751.

30. FERRARI, G. and MESSINA, M. (1984). Aspetti microbiologici di alcuni fertilizzanti organici maggiormente utilizzati in agricoltura. Biologi Italiani (Official Magazine of the Italian National Order of Biologists), 14 (5), 18.

31. FIELDSON, R.S. (1984). The Economic Viability of Earthworm Culture on Animal Wastes. (See ref. n°1), page 31.

32. FLACK, F.M. and HARTENSTEIN, R. (1984). Growth of the Earthworm Eisenia foetida on Microorganisms and Cellulose. Soil Biol. Biochem., 16 (5), 491.

33. FONTANESI, C.A. (1984). Smaltimento dei rifiuti. (See ref. n°2), p.59.

34. FRANZ, M.F. (1978). The Economic Future of the Earthworm in Recycling. Compost Science, 19 (6), 20.

35. GENEVINI, P.L., GIGLIOTTI, C., GARBARINO, A., ZACCHEO, P. and MOR, P. (1983). Vermicomposte: caratterizzazione chimica e valore fertilizzante. L'Informatore Agrario, 39 (44), 28109.

36. GRAFF, O. (1974). Gewinnung von Biomasse aus Abfallstoffen durch Kultur des Kompostregenwurm Eisenia foetida (Savigny 1826). Landbauforsch. Völkenrode, 24 (2), 137.

37. GRAFF, O. (1984). Vermiculture in West Germany. (See ref. n°1).

38. GRAPPELLI, A., TOMATI, U. and GALLI, E. (1983). Fattori di fertilità biologica della vermicomposta. (See ref. n°3).

39. HAND, P., HAYES, W.A., SATCHELL, J.E. and FRANKLAND, J.C. (1984). The Vermicomposting of Cow Slurry. (See ref. n°1), page 22.

40. HARRIGAN, W.F. and McCANCE, M.E. (1966). Laboratory Methods in Microbiology. Academic Press, London and New York.

41. HARTENSTEIN, R. (1979). A Progress Report on the Potential Use of Earthworms in Sludge Management. Proc. of the 8th Nat. Sludge Conf., Info. Transfer Inc., Silver Spring, Md.

42. HARTENSTEIN, R. and AMICO, L. (1983). Production and Carrying Capacity for the Earthworm Lumbricus terrestris in Culture. Soil Biol. Biochem., 15 (1), 51.

43. HARTENSTEIN, R., HARTENSTEIN, E. and HARTENSTEIN, F. (1981). Goat Load and Transit Time in the Earthworm E.foetida. Pedobiologia, 22.

44. HARTENSTEIN, R., KAPLAN, D.L. and NEUHAUSER, E.F. (1984). Use of the Earthworms Eisenia foetida and Eudrilus eugeniae in Trickling Filters. J. Wat. Pollut. Control. Fed., 56 (3), 294.

45. HARTENSTEIN, R., NEUHAUSER, E.F. and COLLIER, J. (1980). Accumulation of Heavy Metals in the Earthworm Eisenia foetida. J. Environ. Qual., 9, 23.

46. HELMKE, P.A., ROBARGE, W.P., KOROTEV, R.L. and Schomberg, P.J. (1979). Effects of Soil-applied Sewage Sludge on Concentrations of Elements in

Earthworms. J. Environ. Qual., 8, 322.

47. IRELAND, M.P. (1979). Metal Accumulation by the Earthworms Lumbricus rubellus, Dendrobaena veneta and Eiseniella tetraedra living in Heavy Metal Polluted Sites. Environ. Pollut., 19 (3), 201.

48. ISTITUTO DI RICERCA SULLE ACQUE (Consiglio Nazionale delle Ricerche, Rome) (1972). Metodi analitici per le acque. Quaderni I.R.S.A., 11 (3).

49. ISTITUTO DI RICERCA SULLE ACQUE (Consiglio Nazionale delle Ricerche, Rome) (1983). Metodi analitici per i fanghi. Parametri biochimici e biologici. Quaderni I.R.S.A., 64 (1).

50. KHAMBATA, S.R. and BHATT, J.V. (1957). A Contribution to the Study of the Intestinal Microflora of Indian Earthworms. Archives Mikrobiology, 28, 69.

51. KOBATAKE, M. (1954). The Antibacterial Substance Extracted from Lower Animal. I.The Earthworm. Kekkaku, 29, 60.

52. LEGNANI, P.P. (1983). Alcune considerazioni sull'evoluzione microbiolo gica del worm-casting proveniente dalla trasformazione dei rifiuti solidi urbani. (See ref. n°2), page 69.

53. LIBERTI, A. and CANTUTI, V. (1983). La lombricoltura ed i suoi problemi ecologici e chimici. (See ref. n°2), page 37.

54. LIBERTI, A., CANTUTI, V., CECCHINI, F. and MURA, S. (1983). Problemi chimici connessi alla conversione di materiali di scarto nella lombricoltura. (See ref. n°3).

55. LOEHR, R.C., MARTIN, J.H., Jr. and NEUHAUSER, E.F. (1985). Liquid Sludge Stabilization Using Vermistabilization. J. Wat. Pollut. Control Fed., 57 (7), 817.

56. LOEHR, R.C., MARTIN, J.H.,Jr., NEUHAUSER, E.F. and MALECKI, M.R. (1984). (See ref. n°1), page 27.

57. MA, W. (1982). The Influence of Soil Properties and Worm-related Factors on the Concentration of Heavy Metals in Earthworms. Pedobiologia, 24 (2), 109.

58. MA, W., EDELMAN, T., VAN BEERSUM, I. and JANS, T. (1983). Uptake of Cadmium, Zinc, Lead, and Copper by Earthworms near a Zinc-smelting Complex: Influence of Soil pH and Organic Matter. Bull. Environ. Contam. Toxicol., 30, 424.

59. MANELLI, E., MASTROLIA, L. and MILANO, E. (1983). Morfologia e biologia del lombrico in condizioni normali e sperimentali. (See ref. n°3).

60. MILHAU, C. and VIGNOLES, M. (1984). Treatment of Fats and Other Floating Wastes: One Solution: Vermicomposting. (See ref. n°1), page 15.

61. MITCHELL, M.J., MULLIGAN, R.M., HARTENSTEIN, R. and NEUHAUSER E.F. (1977). Conversion of Sludges into "Topsoils" by Earthworms. Compost Science, 18 (4), 28.

62. NARDI, S., NUTI, M.P. and DELL'AGNOLA, G. (1983). Evoluzione della biomassa microbica e della sostanza organica durante il vermicomposting. (See ref. n°3).

63. NEUHAUSER, E.F. and MALECKI, M.R. (1984). Earthworms and Waste Management. BioCycle, 25 (3), 26.

64. NEUHAUSER, E.F., KAPLAN, D.L., MALECKI, M.R. and HARTENSTEIN, R.(1980). Materials Supporting Weight Gain by the Earthworm Eisenia foetida in

Waste Conversion Systems. Agricultural Wastes, 2, 43.

65. NUTI, M.P. (1983). Aspetti chimico-microbiologici del vermicompostaggio. (See ref. n°2), page 31.

66. OMODEO, P. (1983). Il cosiddetto "Lombrico rosso" è una Eisenia foetida. (See ref. n°2), page 15.

67. PARLE, J.N. (1963). Micro-organisms in the Intestines of Earthworms. J. Gen. Microbiol., 31, 1.

68. PIETZ, R.I., PETERSON, J.R., PRATER, J.E. and ZENZ, D.R. (1984). Metal Concentrations in Earthworms from Sewage Sludge-amended Soils at a Strip Mine Reclamation Site. J. Environ. Qual., 13 (4), 651.

69. PIMPINI, F. (1983). Primi risultati di una ricerca preliminare sull'impiego di casting su Poinsezia (Euphorbia pulcherrima,Willd). (See ref. n°2), page 43.

70. POCHON, J. and TARDIEUX, P. (1962). Techniques d'analyse en microbiologie du sol. Editions De la Tourelle, St.Mandé (Seine).

71. REINECKE, A.J. and NASH, R.G. (1984). Toxicity of 2,3,7,8-TCDD and Short-term Bioaccumulation by Earthworms (Oligochaeta). Soil Biol. Biochem., 16 (1), 45.

72. ROLETTO, E., ABOLLINO, O., DE LUCA, I. and VOLANTE, M. (1985). Letame bovino e vermicomposta: studio comparato di alcune caratteristiche analitiche. L'Informatore Agrario, 41 (8), 89.

73. ROSSI, B.A. (1983). Vermicomposting in the Philippines. In: Zucconi F., De Bertoldi M., Coppola S.: Proc. of the Int. Symp. on "Biological Roclamation and Land Utilization of Urban Wastes, Naples,11-14 Oct., p.621.

74. SATCHELL, J.E. and MARTIN, K. (1984). Phosphatase Activity in Earthworm Faeces. Soil. Biol. Biochem., 16 (2), 191.

75. SATCHELL, J.E., MARTIN, K. and KRISHNAMOORTHY, R.V. (1984). Stimulation of Microbial Phosphatase Production by Earthworm Activity. Ibid.,p.195.

76. SIEGEL, S.M., SIEGEL, B.Z., PUERNER, N. and SPEITEL, T. (1975). Water and Soil Biotic Relations in Mercury Distribution. Water Air Soil Pollut., 4, 9.

77. STOCKLI, A. (1928). Studien über den Einfluss der Regenwürmer auf die Beschaffenheit des Bodens. Landw. Jb. Schweiz, 42 (1).

78. TERRY, R.J. (1951). The Behaviour and Distribution of the Larger Worms in Trickling Filters. J. Proc. Inst. Sew. Purif., 16.

79. TESI, R. and TALLARICO, R. (1985). Impiego di un vermicompost nelle colture in vaso di ciclamino e poinsettia. Colture Protette, 14 (4), 102.

80. TOMATI, U., GRAPPELLI, A. and GALLI, E. (1983). Lombrichi, fertilità del suolo e sviluppo delle piante. Il vermicompostaggio come alternativa nel riciclo dei rifiuti organici. (See ref. n°2), page 45.

81. VAN DER BRUEL, W.E. (1964). Le sol, la pedofauna et les applications de pesticides. Ann. Gembl., 70, 81.

82. VIKRAM REDDY, M. (1984). Effects of Casts of Pheretima alexandri on the Growth of Vinca rosea and Oryza sativa. (See ref. n°1), page 46.

83. VON AICHBERGER, R. (1914). Untersuchungen über die Ernährung des Regenwürmes. Kleinwelt, 6, 53.

84. WADE, S.E., BACHE, C.A. and LISK, D.J. (1982). Cadmium Accumulation by Earthworms Inhabiting Municipal Sludge-amended Soil. Bull. Environ. Contam. Toxicol., 28, 557.

85. WATANABE, H. and TSUKAMOTO, J. (1976). Seasonal Change in Size Class and Stage Structure of Lumbricid <u>Eisenia foetida</u> Population in a Field Compost and its Practical Application as the Decomposer of Organic Waste. Rev. Ecol. Biol. Sol., <u>13</u> (1), 141.

MICROORGANISMS AND ENVIRONMENTAL FACTORS IN COMPOSTING OF AGRICULTURAL WASTE OF THE CANARY ISLANDS.

E. Corominas; F. Perestelo; M.L. Pérez and M.A. Falcón
Departamento de Microbiología, Facultad de Biología, Universidad de La Laguna. Tenerife. Islas Canarias. Spain.
Departamento de Ornamentales Equipo de Microbiología. I.C.I.A.
Tenerife. Islas Canarias. Spain.

Sumary

The composting process in piles containing agricultural – and forestal residues of the Canary Islands was monitored for 200 days, in which maturity of the piles was completed Changes in ambiental factors (pH, temperature, moisture, aeration) were followed as well as the evolution of micro bial populations. In the mesophilic phases of the composting, several bacterial strains were identified as species belonging to the gena Bacillus, Pseudomonas, Arthrobacter, Alcaligenes. Their activity in the phenol-oxidases produc tion and their ability for degrade various phenolics compounds were assayed in order to elucidate their roles in the lignin breackdown in natural conditions.

1. INTRODUCTION

The formation of compost from agricultural and forestal – residues in the Canary Islands can be of great importance for Canarian agriculture. In different experiments with horticultu ral and ornamental plants, it has been shown that the efficien cy of these crops improves significantly with the use of the above mentioned compost, as a ground conditioner and/or sustrat. Also, due to the peculiarities of this region, compost made out of these waste products, is one of the few organic fertilizers available on the Islands. This fertilizer would substitute – other imported ones of rather inferior quality, in order to – improve agricultural efficiency. We have effected an investiga tion as regards the evolution of a series of parameters in the compost piles built up from the mentioned waste products, up – to their maturation in which the compost achieves a certain – degree of stability. In thes sense, we have observed the condi tions of the environment, mainly temperature, pH, moisture and aeration, which affect the compost process significantly (Poin celot, 1975, Deschamps et al., 1979). We have also studied the development of microbian population during this process.

On other hand, if we analyze the composition of the waste products used to make the compost piles, we can see that a high percentage is made up of gymnosperm lignin, due to which it is potencially degradable. The microorganisms involved in the lig nin degradation, and in the different population in the lignolytic process, have not been totally identified. At present, it is not clear as to the role played by bacteria in this process

(Janshekar and Fiechter, 1982; Janshekar and Fiechterm 1983), thus being subjet to strong controversy at present.

Technical data about the maturity process of the compost pile, and about the possible implication of the isolated bacteria as regards the lignin degradation, will be shown in the — present study.

2. MATERIALS AND METHODS

Construction of the compost pile. The material used for a pile of 1000 Kg (dry weight) has been the following:

Pine needles (Pinus canariensis) .... 700 Kg.
Banana plantation waste (Musa acuminata colla) ... 105 "
Chicken droppings .... 100 "
Hops .... 55 "
Calcium sulphate (agricultural plaster) .... 40 "

This material is distributed in alternate layers of pine needles, and banana leaves, until 5 levels are made up. On the third turning of the pile (towards the thirdweek of its cons-—truction) the chicken droppings are added, later, the piles to tal nitrogen is adjusted with urea until a proportion of 30 — (C/N=1/30) is achieved with respect to the total carbon. The — total nitrogen was analyzed by Kjendahll's method, and the total carbon was calculated by the expression: $\%C = \dfrac{100 - \%ash}{1,8}$

The optimal dimensions of the compost pile, in order to achieved ideal temperature, moisture and aeration, was 1.8 m. hogh and 2 m. wide.

Control of Environmental Factors. The temperature of the pile was controled every week, and measurement took place in — the surface and inside. The pH was measured dissolving 1 gr. of compost in 99 ml. of sterilized destilled water, being observed weekly. The aeration was achieved by successive turnings — which became increasingly frequent as the temperature of the — pile rose. This turning process also prevented the pile from becoming compact. The moisture was calculated by weight difference of a sample of humid material from the pile and its later dry weight (10ºC during 24 h.). As before, in this case observations were also undertaken weekly.

Compost Maturity. Spohn's method (1977) was used to deter mine maturity of the pile.

Isolation and cultivation of Microorganisms. On the different techniques for the isolation of compost microorganisms (Casida Jr et al, 1968; Odier and Monties, 1978; Crawford, 1978 Deschamps, 1980) we chose Casida Jr's, having substituted the soil extract for a compost extract. Among the methods used for microorganisms count are: Saboureau Agar with addition of ampiciline (0.25 mg/l) for the total fungus count; yeast. Extract (Difco) and Nutrient Agar (Difco) with addition of actidione — (0.06 mg/ml.) for the specific count of bacteria. In every case the incubation was effected in duplicate at 25º and at 40ºC.

Identification of microorganisms. Many of the strains –
isolated were identified by the usual identification techniques
(API 20E system and other biochemical trials)following Bergey's
manual of determinative bacteriology (1974).

Test used to detect lignin degradation and phenoloxidases
production. The bacterial strains were tested for their abili–
ty to degrade the lignin on plates by Sundman test, described
initialy for fungi (Sundman and Näse, 1971).

To detect the production of bacterial phenoloxidases,two
method were employed. One of them, to test the laccase produc–
tion (Law and Timberlake, 1980) and the other test the tyrosi–
ne production (Brisou et Menantaud, 1971).

Substrates Employed in the Auxanograms. Different phenols
with structural relationship to the lignin building blocks was
employed for selection, and degradation studies of lignin decom
posing bacteria. The substrates employed were: benzoic acid, –
p-OH benzoic acid, veratric acid (3,4-dimethoxi-benzoic), feru
lic acid (4-hydroxy-3methoxi-cinnamic), vanillin (4-hydroxy-3-
methoxi benzaldehyde), protocatechuic acid (3,4-dihydroxy-ben-
zoic), catechol (1,2-benzenediol), syringaldehyde (4-hydroxy-
3,5-dimethoxi-benzaldehyde), cinnamic acid (3-phenylpropenoic)
and pyrogallol (1,2,3-trihydroxy-benzene).

3. RESULTS

Development of Environmental Factors in the Compost Pile.
As mentioned above, the standard pile comprised 1000 Kg of agri
cultural and forestal residues If we study the temperature du–
ring the compost process, we observe its maximum value at 70ºC
(thermophilic stage). This temperature is achieved three weeks
after the beginning. At first, the pile is at 15.5ºC and this
temperature is found again after 80 days of maturation, remai–
ning constant after that until 200 days have passed. In every
case, the measurements were effected at 60 cm depth. The pH va
lue was initially 6, and dropped to 5.5 by the second week of
the process. During the thermophilic phase a maximum value of
8.5 was found. Later, it dropped to 7.5 and remained stable –
there as of the 80 th day until the end of the process. Fig. 1
(A and B) describe the environmental factors development through
out the process. Moisture was maintained around 60% during –
the whole period. To this effect the pile was irrigated on each
turning (with water), and during the thermophilic stage, this
occurred more frequently. This way temperatures above 70ºC we–
re prevented. The turnings also prevented the pile from ente––
ring anaerobic stages.

Development of the Microbial Populations During the Matu–
ration of the Compost. We have approached our study on the evo
lution of the fungi and the bacteria population. The fungicount
maximum was achieved during the thermophilic phase, and a total

of 2.1 x 10^6 v.u./gr. of compost was found. Later a gradual de
crease in the fungi population was observed, until the maturity of the pile was reached, with a total of 2 x 10^3 v.u./gr.of
compost. On other hand, the bacterial population envolved presenting two maxima stages, coinciding with the mesophilic phase (up to 2 weeks from the construction of the pile) and the -
final mesophilic phase. The number of bacteria in these phases
was respectively 10^6 v.u./gr. of compost and 1.85 x 10^5 v.u./gr
of compost. fig. 2 show this evolution.

Tests Effected with the Different Strains. The results -
of these tests at 25ºC show that 12 of the strains gave positive results jointly, in the Sundman and laccase test. Only 2 of
the strains studies under these conditions gave positive results
in all tests effected. They are 4P-2 and the 4P-3 strains. -
Futhermore, 4 of the strains gaven negative results on all -
tests, affected. On the other hand, the strains isolated and
incubated at 40ºC, gave the following results: 3 of them gave
positive result on all tests: 2P'3, 4P'4 and 4P'9 strains. -
Futhermore, 16 of them gaven positive results jointly, in the
Sundman and the laccase test, and 6 of the strains gave negative results in all tests (table 1 and 2).

Assimilation of the Different Phenolic Compounds. All -
those strains which have given positive results in table 1, at
least in the Sundman test and which showed high activity of the
laccasa enzyme (data not shown), were screened with different
phenolic compunds related to the polymeric structure of the lig
nin (table 3). Some of them have grown using all and every one
of the substrate tried out in the auxanograms. Such is the case with strains 4P'8 and 6P'8 and 6P'3. Out of the 10 strains
experimented upon, we observed that 8 of them assimilate as -
their only source of carbon the simple aromatic compounds like
benzoic acid. Another 8 strains, 7 of which coincide with those
that use benzoic acid, are capable of assimilating p-OH-benzoic.
Futhermore, another 6 strains, 5 of which coincide with those
that used the before mentioned substrate used another simple -
aromatic compound like veratric acid. 5 of the strains were capable of assimilating ferulic acid. The vanillin was assimilated by 6 of the strains experimented upon. The protocatechuic
acid was assimilated by 9 of the strains, and catechol was -
assimilated by all strains studied. Syringaldehyde was assimilated by 6 of the samples studied. Cinnamic acid and pyrogallol
were assimilated by 7 and 8 strains, respectively.

The results of these auxanograms was read ten days after
the beginning of incubation, which was effected at 25º and at
40ºC according to the isolation temperature of each of the -
strains.

4. DISCUSSION
Evolution of the Ecological Factors During the Compost -
Process. Until the stage of maturity (pile stability) is rea--
ched, the different ecological factors which we have studied,
present a series of fluctuations in their values. The stability in the composition of the pile is achieved, when only traces

of NH3 and NO2 are found, together with an abundance of NO3 -
(as indicate by Spohn, 1977). Temperature, must reach 70ºC during the thermophilic phase in oder to give a stable compost.
Jeries and Regan (1973), propose the same value as this phase,
in order to archived a mature compost. Nevertheless, in others
studies (Jeris and Regan, 1973), establish that the piles made
from urban residues containing 60 of 70% paper, only need 59ºC
for the pile to achieve stability. Also, when the compost is -
basically newspaper waste, the temperature does not rise above
48ºC during the thermophilic phase, giving however, a pile of
marked stability. In our case, if we surpassed 70ºC for 12 h,
the result was a slowing down in the process due to the death
of the bacterial and fungi populations. This implies a difini
tive inhibition toward the pile maturity. We avoided surpassing
these temperature by means of successive turnings, with which
at the same time, aeration of the pile was assured, preventing
anaerobiosis. During these turnings. Which were done at a rate
of 4 or 5 during the thermophilic phase, the whole material was
humidified. Thus it was possible to avoid surpassing 70ºC. for
more than 12 h. and to control the moisture, which had to be -
kept at 60% during the different stages of the process.

Other studied like the pH factor, presented a development
common to that described in other compost piles, (Kochtitzky -
and col, 1969). At first, a slight decrease is observed at the
beginning of the process, going from 6 to 5.5, which is the mi
nimum value reached during the inicial mesophilic phase. Later
this value increases to 8,5. If the value increases to 8,5. If
the value reached is well below 8.5 it is not possible to achie
ve a total maturation of the pile, and the result is a incomple
te compost. Thus the optimal conditions which in our case are
of vital importance was obtained, and the product can be used
as ground conditioner in horticultural and ornamental crops. -
In this sense, we observe that Allison (1973) shows that a sig
nificant change in the environmental conditions, especially pH
and temperature, affect the nature of the humic substance formed. In this sense, it was indicated that the availability of
micronutrients can be expected to depend upon the humidifica--
tion of the organic material (Pavanasasivam, 1973; Courpron -
and Just, 1975). Due to this , it is logical that alterations
in the values of these parameters should cause an incorrect -
humus, and consequently the efficiency as a ground conditioner
or a fertilizer would be inferior, as expressed beforehand.

Evolution and Characteristics of the Microbial Populations
Given the objective of this study, the characteristics of mainly the bacterial populations were studied although we have only
effected a profile where only the evolution of fungi are indicate.

Different types of bacterial populations in relation with
the thermophilic and the mesophilic phases have been studied -

(De Bertoldi and Citemesi, 1981). Thus during the mesophilic -
phase, bacteria of the gena Azomonas, Klebsiella and Enterobacter are found, related to the fixation of nitrogen. These popu
lations are substituted by other sporogenous, facultative anae
robic bacteria of the genus Bacillus which predominate during
the thermophilic phase. This last date of information coincides
with our findings. The majority of strains which we have isola
ted up to the moment, (during the thermophilic phase) are morphologically sporogenous bacilli and facultative anaerobic of
which we have identified 4P'2 as Bacillus megaterium. However,
we have also observed an abundance of these bacilli during the
initial mesophilic phase in which we identified strains 4P-3,
4P-8, 4P-7 and 6P-1, as being respectively Bacillus cereus, Ba
cillus pumilus, Bacillus sphaericus and Bacillus subtilis. Futhermore, we have also seen other genus, exclusively identified
during this phase, like for example, Alcaligenes, strain 4P-2
having been identified as A. faecalis.

On the other hand, lignin is the residual component present in greatest proportion in our compost pile. Some types of
lignin can be degraded and assimilated by bacteria (Deschamps
et al, 1980; Janshekar and Fiechterm 1982). In this sense, we
have effected a series of tests in order to establish the possibility that some of the bacterial strains isolated can be re
lated to the lignilytic process. To this effect, we have stu--
died the production of phenoloxidases in various strains of -
the ones we isolated. These enzymes, mainly laccase and tyrosi
nase, are involved in the degradation of lignin (Kaplan, 1978).
As the polymer can be decomposed by other means (Sundman and -
Näse, 1971), we have used other tests which manifest exclusive
ly the degradation of lignin. These tests have been used, traditionally, for the identification of lignolytic fungi. In this
study, we have observed that at least 5 of the analyzed strains
give positive results to all effected tests. Of these, 2 have
been identified as Alcaligenes faecalis (4P-2) and Bacillus megaterium (4P'2).

On the other hand, the structural units of lignin are aro
matic compounds of the type coniferyl, sinapyl and siringyl al
cohols (Higuchi, 1980). It is logical that many authors have -
used differents phenols, of a structure related to the subunits
of the polymer, for the isolation and selection of microorga--
nisms that would degrade that substrate (Fukuzumi and Katayama
1977; Ohta et al, 1979). Under this point of view, we have used
the substrates expressed in table 3, and we have checked its -
assimilations by the different strains tested. Some of them, -
like Bacillus pumilus (4P-8) used all the substrate experimented.
Others, like Bacillus megaterium (4P'2), used all substrates -
except siringaldehyde. Due to this, we believed that some the
isolated strains from our compost pile like B. pumilus, B. megaterium and that unidentified strain 3P-2, possess enough of
the requisites to be considered as potential degraders of lignin.

REFERENCES

(1) Allison FE (1973) Soil organic matter and its role in crop production. Elsevier Scientific Publishing Company. Amster dam London New York.

(2) Bergey's Manual of Determinative Bacteriology (1974) In: - Buchanan RE; Gibbons NE (eds) 8th edn. The Williams and - Wilkins Company, Baltimore.

(3) Brisou J. Menantaud J. (1971) Metabolisme des produits cycliques et aromatiques. In: Masson et Cie (eds) Techniques d'enzimologie bacterienne. Masson et Cie, Paris, p 241.

(4) Casida Jr LE (1968) Methods for the isolation and estima-- tion of activity of soil bacteria. Liverpool University - Press, Liverpool, pp. 97 - 122.

(5) Courpron C. Just C. (1975) The effect of incorporation of certains forms of organic matter of incorporation of cer-- tains forms of organic matter on the development of chloro sis on plants on a calcareus soil. Ann Agronomiques 26 (2) 215-227.

(6) Crawford DL (1978) Lignocellulose decomposition by selec-- ted Streptomyces strain. Appl Environ Microbiol 35: 1041-1045.

(7) De Bertoldi M, Citemesi U. (1981) Microbial population in compost process. In: The staff of compost science/land uti lization (eds) Composting theory and practice for city, in dustry and farm. The JG Press, Emmaus. pp. 26-33.

(8) Deschamps AM. Henno P. Pernelle C. Caignault L, Lebeault JM (1979) Bench-scale reactors for composting research. Bio technol lett 1: 239-244.

(9) Deschamps AM (1980) Identification et caractères biochimiques des bacteries hemicellulolytiques d'un compost de bois et d'ecorce. CR Acad. Sci. Paris 291: 485-487.

(10) Fukuzumi T, Katayama Y (1977) Bacterial degradation dimer relating to structure of lignin. Mokuzai Gakkaishi 23:214 215.

(11) Higuchi T. (1982) Biodegradation of lignin: Biochemistry - and potential application. Experiencia 38: 159-166.

(12) Janshekar H, Fiechter A. (1982) On the bacterial degrada-- tion of lignin. Eur J. Appl. Microbiol Biotechnol 14: 47-50. Janshekar H, Fiechter A. (1983) Lignin: Biosynthesis, appli cation, and biodegradation. Adv. Biochem. Eng. Biotechnol 27: 119-177.

(13) Jeris JS, Regan RW (1973) a Controlling environmental para meters for optimal composting. Compost Sci. 14 (1): 10-15. Jeris JS, Regan RW (1973)b Controlling environmental parameters for optimal composting. Compost Sci. 14 (3): 16-22.

(14) Kaplan DL (1979) Reactivity of different oxidases with - lignins and lignin model compounds. Phytochemistry 18:1917 1919.

(15) Odier E, Monties B (1978)Biodegradation de la lignine de -
16)blé par <u>Xanthomonas</u> 23. Ann Microbiol 129A: 361 - 377.
  Ohta M, Higuchi T, Iwahara S. (1979) Microbial degradation of -
  dehydrodiconiferyl alcohol a lignin substrate model. Arch Micro
  biol 121: 23-28.
17)Pavanasasivam V, (1973) Manfanese studies in some soils with a
  high organic matter content. Plant soil 38: 245-255.
18)Poincelot RP. (1975) The biochemistry and methodology of compos
  ting. Bulletin 754, The Connecticut agricultural experiment sta
  tion, New Haven, pp. 1-17.
19)Spohn E (1978) Determination of compost maturity. Compost land/
  Science utilization 19:26-28.
20)Sundman V, Näse L. (1971) A simple plate test for direct visua-
  lization of biological lignin degradation. Papper och trä 2:67-
  71.

Table 1. Tests results obtained of the strains isolated from compost pile, at different maturity levels and at 25ºC.

Strains	Tests			Strains	Tests		
	S	B	L		S	B	L
2P-1	+	−	+	3P-7	+	−	−
2P-2	+	−	+	4P-1	−	−	+
2P-3	+	−	+	4P-2	+	+	+
2P-4	+	−	+	4P-3	+	+	+
2P-5	+	−	+	4P-4	−	−	−
2P-6	+	−	+	4P-5	−	−	+
2P-7	+	−	+	4P-6	−	−	+
2P-8	+	−	−	4P-7	−	+	+
2P-9	−	−	+	4P-8	+	−	+
2P-10	+	−	−	5P-1	−	−	+
3P-1	−	−	−	5P-2	−	+	+
3P-2	+	−	+	5P-3	−	−	−
3P-3	+	−	+	6P-1	−	+	+
3P-4	+	−	−	6P-2	−	+	+
3P-5	−	−	+	6P-3	−	−	−
3P-6	+	−	−				

Symbols: S= Sundman tests; B= Brisou test; L= laccase test; P= pile designation; first number = week turning operation (after the pile was constructed) in which i-solation was made; last number = different strains iso-lated from each sampling.

Table 2. Tests results obtained of the strains isolated
from compost pile at different maturity levels and at
40ºC.

Strains	Tests			Strains	Tests		
	S	B	L		S	B	L
2P'1	+	+	-	4P'2	+	+	+
2P'2	-	-	+	4P'3	+	+	-
2P'3	+	+	+	4P'4	+	+	+
2P'4	+	-	+	4P'5	-	-	+
2P'5	+	-	+	4P'6	-	-	+
2P'6	+	-	+	4P'7	-	+	+
2P'7	+	-	+	4P'8	+	-	+
2P'8	+	-	+	4P'9	+	+	+
2P'9	+	-	+	5P'1	-	-	+
2P'10	-	-	-	5P'2	-	-	+
2P'11	+	-	-	5P'3	+	-	+
3P'1	-	-	+	5P'4	-	-	+
3P'2	-	-	-	5P'5	+	-	+
3P'3	-	-	+	5P'6	+	-	+
3P'4	+	-	+	6P'1	-	-	-
3P'5	-	-	+	6P'2	+	+	-
3P'6	-	-	-	6P'3	+	-	-
3P'7	-	-	+	6P'4	-	-	-
3P'8	-	-	+	6P'5	+	-	+
3P'9	-	-	-	6P'6	-	+	+
4P'1	-	-	+	6P'7	+	-	-

Symbols: S= Sundman test; B= Brisou test; L= laccase test; P'= pile designation; first number = week turning o-
peration (after the pile was constructed) in which isolation was made; last number = different strains isolated from each sampling.

Table 3. Assimilation of phenolic compounds.

Strains	2P-3	4P-3	4P'4	3P-2	4P-8	6P'3	4P'2	4P-7	6P'2	6P-1
p-OH-benzoic	−	−	+	+	+	+	+	+	+	+
Pyrogallol	−	+	+	+	+	+	+	+	−	+
Catechol	+	+	+	+	+	+	+	+	+	+
Protocatechuic	−	+	+	+	+	+	+	+	+	+
Vanillin	−	−	−	+	+	+	+	+	−	+
Ferulic	−	−	−	+	+	+	+	+	−	−
Veratric	−	−	+	+	+	+	+	+	+	−
Cinnamic	−	−	+	−	+	+	+	+	+	+
Syringaldehyde	+	+	−	−	+	+	−	−	+	+
Benzoic	−	+	−	−	+	+	+	+	+	+

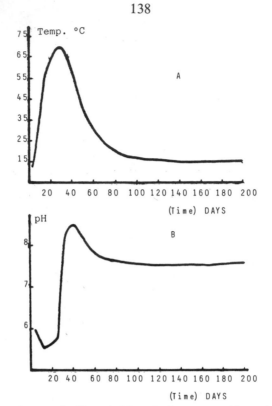

Fig. 1 : Temperature and pH variation during composting at 50 cm inside the pile. A) Temperature. B) pH

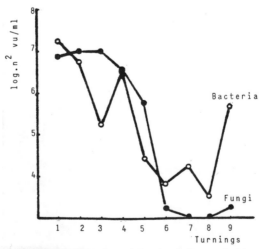

Fig. 2 : Development of fungal and bacterial populations during composting. (-o-o-) bacteria; (-•-•-) fungi.

MUNICIPAL ORGANIC SOLID WASTE COMPOSTING

AN INTEGRATED COMPONENT OF RECYCLING CENTERS THAT PROCESS SOLID WASTE

C. J. CASSARINO
President, Cassarino Environmental Services

Summary

Northeastern United States cities and towns generate thousands of tons of solid waste per day, a high percentage of which goes to landfills which have a life expectancy of five years or less. Furthermore, new land fill sites which meet state and federal requirements are becoming scarce and expensive. Thus many municipalities are searching for ways to extend existing landfill life or eliminate the need for landfill altogether. The composting of the organic portion of the solid waste stream (i.e. food waste, yard waste, brush, etc.) is a process which both reduces the volume of solid waste and increases its value. The organic waste fraction becomes a compost which can be safely applied locally to build soil. The remaining fraction of waste is both lower in volume and moisture content and higher in B.T.U.s should it be burned for energy production.

The following study took place at the Wilton, New Hampshire Recycling Center. The Wilton Center and its participating six towns are required to source separate their solid waste. Because of the cold climate and source separated organics it was an ideal site for the development and testing of an intermediate scale composting system which could be integrated into municipal waste recycling programs.

Introduction

The study had two major goals. The first was a technical evaluation to determine if the organic waste stream generated by the 8,000-10,000 people using the Wilton facility could be safely composed, (biologically stabilized).

The second goal was to evaluate this intermediate scale composting on an economic basis and to refine the present Wilton system. So the product of the evaluation could be a design other municipalities could use in the event they decided organic solid waste (i.e. food waste, yard waste, brush, etc.) composting be deemed desirable.

Effect of Cold Weather on Composting

Regression analysis was used to determine whether compost temperatures in the 5.9 cubic yard bins were affected by ambient air temperatures. Regressions were run both using the full range of recorded temperatures and using only those cases in which ambient temperatures were below freezing (0° C). The results of these analyses indicated that there was no statistically significant relationship between the compost and ambient air temperatures. Even when only days with below freezing ambient air temperatures were considered, the coefficient of determination was very small (R^2= .06), indicating no significant influence of air temperature on compost temperature, even in cold weather.

Capacity and Time Requirements for Biological Stabilization

Capacity requirements at the Wilton center required that garbage be biologically stabilized within nine months in order for composting to be a practical alternative. In fact, the time required for biological stabilization was found to be far less. Aerobic stabilization was achieved in about two months (nine weeks) as indicated by oxygen readings above 5 percent, lack of garbage smell, lower moisture level, and stable lower temperatures. Furthermore, when, after nine weeks, the composted garbage was moved to the storage area, it remained aerobic in spite of the fact that it was no longer being aerated. As a safety check, three fresh (nine week old) batches were analyzed chemically for nitrogen, phosphorus, potassium, calcium, magnesium, chromium, and zinc. The pH and percent solids by weight were also determined. Extractable ammonia nitrogen (NH_3) levels were found to be low (0.0095 - 0.0648%), and all metal concentrations measured, including zinc and chromium, were found to be well below safety limits set by the state of New Hampshire. Furthermore, the pH was found to be quite high (7.1 - 7.9) indicating that the compost would be excellent for buffering as well as conditioning New Hampshire's acidic soils. During the study period, the compost did in fact have a market value and was sold at the center by the truck load for about $4 per cubic yard.

Least Cost Processing: Grinding of Garbage and Addition of Bulking Agent

One aspect of the technical evaluation was determining the least level of processing (and hence the least expensive process) which still would result in satisfactory biological stabilization. The two processing steps which were thought possibly unnecessary were the grinding of the garbage and the addition of yard waste as a bulking agent.

The grinder purchased for the town for use in the study was a Royer Model 120 grinder-shredder. However, it was determined during the first winter of the study that *grinding was not a necessary requirement* for biological stabilization and that bins with unground garbage quickly reached pasteurizing temperatures. In fact, it was found that grinding tended to produce a slurry that did not compost well because of insufficient aeration.

The addition of yard waste as a *bulking agent* was found to be a *necessary step* for two reasons. First, when yard waste was not added periodically to the self-dumping hoppers during the day, odors and fly concentrations made the receptacle unattractive for both citizens and attendants. And second, without the yard waste as a bulking agent, aeration in the composting bins was insufficient to permit aerobic decomposition and timely biological stabilization.

To control flies and odors and to permit adequate aeration, yard waste was added periodically to cover garbage in the hoppers and then again to produce a cover of about one half foot in the bins each time hoppers were emptied into the binds. The resulting final ratio of yard waste to garbage was about one to one.

Wood chips and sawdust were both yard waste types found to make good bulking agents. But both are slow to break down, and both have the potential for higher value as energy sources and may therefore not always be affordable or even available. However, leaves and grass clippings will most likely be available for use in most communities. This yard waste provded also to be a good bulking agent particularly when allowed to partially decompose into leaf mold, over 8 to 12 months, prior to use. (Fresh leaves tended to mat and hence not allow for adequate aeration.) For several months in the fall of 1981, waste from a cider mill consisting of apple pomice and rice hulls was tried as the bulking agent. This material also worked well except that the rice hulls were slow to break down.

Finally, and perhaps the most important discovery made regarding bulking agents, was the fact that curing compost can be "recycled" and used in place of yard waste as the cover material and bulking agent. This material was first tried in January and February of 1982 when extremely cold ambient air temperatures caused other piles of yard waste to become frozen solid and hence unavailable for use. The two to five month old curing compost did not freeze solid and furthermore acted as an innoculate for starting new compost batches.

Verimicomposting

As supplement to microbial composting, vermicomposting using red wiggler worms (*Eisenia foetida*) was tried but found not to be practical. Feeding raw garbage to the worms proved to be costly in that it required the use of a grinder and consequent man hours which otherwise were both unnecessary. Furthermore, the worms did not become active until the garbage became warm, and even then, worm activity did not appreciably reduce volumes.

However, it was found that the worms would thrive and reproduce well in the curing compost piles even through mid-winter conditions. In the fall of 1982 approximately 10,000 worms were innoculated into a curing pile and by spring their numbers had increased many times. A local spot market (a bait store) was found which offered a penny apiece for the worms. Thus in the Wilton area worms could possibly be raised as a profitable crop to be harvested for the fishing season.

The Wilton System Refined with Economic Analysis

Refined System Design

The design lends itself to a variety of sizes depending on the volume of material to be processed by the system, but the basic unit is a two-bin module. The bins consist of a concrete slab and three 4' high concrete walls constructed in an H-shaped configuration so that the two bins share a common end wall. The module is covered by a tin roof supported by a post and beam structure. Cleats are attached to the posts at the open end of each bin; so the bins can be closed by dropping wood planking between the cleats.

The bins are aerated by the forced aeration method using 4" diameter flexible plastic tubing and a 1/3 h.p. blower. Sections of perforated tubing spaced at two foot intervals run the width of each bin's floor. At one end, the perforated sections are connected to solid tubing which extends vertically and interconnects with other solid tubing that runs along the top of the wall to the blower.

A total facility consists of a series of two-bin modules constructed at right angles to each other with the concrete slab extending beyond the modules as illustrated in Figure 1 which depicts a 3 module system. The Vs formed by the side walls of adjoining modules provide convenient bins for curing and storing compost immediately adjacent to the processing bins. The piles of stored compost can extend beyond the opening of the V's as indicated by the dash lines. Storage areas for yard waste are provided immediately adjacent to the outer walls at the end modules and along the sides of the facility. An access road encircles the facility. The sharing of side walls with compost and yard waste storage areas tends to insulate the processing bins as well as making temperature moderation more practical. Storing of compost on a concrete slab is an added cost not incurred with the original Wilton design, but it allows all of the compost to be removed without danger of picking up stones with the bottom layer, and provides a solid working surface during wet periods.

In the refined design's aeration system, a single blower can serve up to two modules by being located at the point of the V formed by those modules. The air blown into the processing bins can be ambient air, or in periods when the injection of extremely cold ambient air might inhibit the composting process, its temperature can be moderated by being drawn through the stored compost. Perforated tubing runs along the floor of the storage bins next to the wall and connects to a vertical section of solid tubing at the corner. When temperature moderation is desired, the solid tubing can be connected to the blower's air intake port. This aeration design differs from the original Wilton facility in both materials and layout.

It may be useful in extremely cold periods, and the option of drawing air through stored compost adds little to the system's cost. Also in the refined system, the aeration tubing runs widthwise within the processing bins instead of lengthwise (as in the Wilton facility). When the tubing runs widthwise (i.e., parallel to the entrance of the bin), each section of tubing is put in place (and covered with yard waste) just before the garbage reaches that portion of the bin, and it is easily removed when that portion of the bin is emptied. The front of the bin is therefore always unobstructed from the entrance up to the point where garbage is being added or compost is being removed.

The materials handling equipment used in this system consists of two 2-cubic yard dumpsters and a skid loader. The dumpsters, which have built-in dumping mechanisms, are the receiving containers for incoming garbage. They are placed at the edge of the road in front of the bins being filled at the particular time. Yard waste is piled next to the dumpsters and periodically added to their contents as a cover material and bulking agent. The loader is used: to move the dumpster between the receiving and processing areas; to cover the aeration tubing in the processing bins with yard waste; to cover each dumpster load emptied into a processing bin with a six-inch layer of yard waste; to trasnfer compost from the processing bins to the curing/storage areas; and to bulk load the compost into trucks when it is used or sold. It has a forklift attachment, a 1/4 cubic yard bucket, and a "quick-change" mechanism which allows the operator to switch from one attachment to the other without getting off the loader.

Economic Analysis

The economic viability of the system will depend on its costs compared to the sum of the product value (market or use) and the appropriate disposal credit. Both the product value and the credit must be determined within the context of the specific community. For that reason, the analysis here is strictly in terms of costs.

The program examined processing modules with widths varying from 8' to 32' in 4' increments, and lengths varying from 16' to 64' in 4' increments. Total annual costs (annual capital costs plus annual operating costs) were examined for annual volumes up to 10,000 cubic yards with the computer program determining the number of modules of a given size required to process each annual volume. The physical input-output relationships, specifications, and constraints used in the determination of the least-cost solutions are presented in Appendix I. Appendix II presents the unit prices and amortization periods assumed in the analysis.

All cost estimates are dependent, of course, on both the physical parameters of the system and the assumed unit prices, amortization periods and the interest rate. In different communities and at different times, unit prices, amortization periods and the interest rate may differ from those used in the analysis. For that reason, the analysis was extended to determine how sensitive the average cost estimates are to changes in these factors. The interest rate, each unit price, and each amortization period was varied one at a time by an amount equal to 50% of their value in the original analysis. In each case, the percentage change in average costs was determined for annual volumes ranging from 1000 to 10,000 in increments of 100 cubic yards. These percentages were divided by 50 to get an *elasticity coefficient*, i.e., the percentage change in average cost for each one percent change in the value being examined.

The coefficients for all 21 variables at volumes of 1000 and 10,000 are included in Appendix II.

The elasticity coefficients should be useful in adjusting the costs estimates to fit the unit prices, interest rates, and amortization periods appropriate for a given community. The wage rate and loader elasticities should also be useful for some additional adjustments.

The labor cost component of the average cost estimates have been computed on the basis of the labor hours needed to perform the work required at each volume. The amount of labor required per cubic yard is relatively small, and at low volumes the weekly labor requirement may be substantially less than the number of hours the community will want the facility to be open to its residents. If the compost system is not integrated with a recycling or other waste management system in which the labor can be gainfully employed, the compost system labor cost is understated by an amount equal to the additional labor required to keep the facility open the desired number of hours per week. Since an increase in labor hours will have the same effect on average costs as a proportionate increase in the wage rate, the wage rate elasticity of 0.1 can be used to increase the average cost estimate accordingly.

It seems more likely that a compost system of this type will, in fact, be operated in conjunction with a recycling or other waste disposal system. Since such systems are also likely to employ labor for more hours than actually needed to perform the required work, some, if not all, of the compost work may be performed without purchasing additional labor-hours. In such cases, the wage rate coefficient can be used to make the appropriate reduction in the average cost estimate. For instance, if all of the compost labor-hours were provided by labor available from the accompanying system, average costs for the compost system are *10% less* than the original estimate. (A 100% reduction in labor-hours purchased x the elasticity coefficient of 0.1.)

A skid loader is also usually required in a recycling system even if there is no composting. In many cases, it will be sitting idle a good portion of the time. If it is idle enough of the time that the loader-hours required for the compost operation can be met without purchasing an additional loader, the average cost estimate for the compost operation can be reduced using the loader price elasticity which ranges from 0.2 at an annual volume of 1000 cubic yards to 0.1 at an annual volume of 10,000 cubic yards.

As noted above, a full economic analysis must include the product value and disposal credits appropriate for the specific community. However, the cost estimates and adjustment elasticities provided here should provide planners with a sound basis for arriving at cost figures which can be compared to those values for their particular community.

TABLE 1

Annual Costs Per Cubic Yard
With 20' x 60' Modules

# of Modules	Annual Volume Range* For Which Module # is Required:	Annual Cost Per Cubic Yard + At Range:		
		Beginning	Midpoint	End
	(cubic yards)		(dollars)	
1	– 400	–	57	43
2	400–1400	60	30	20
3	1400–2300	23	18	15
4	2300–3300	18	15	13
5	3300–4200	15	13	12
6	4200–5200	14	13	12
7	5200–6100	13	12	11
8	6100–7100	13	12	11
9	7100–8000	12	11	11
10	8000–9000	12	11	11
11	9000–9900	11	11	11

*rounded to next lowest even multiple of 100 cubic yards
+rounded to nearest whole dollar

It is estimated that a capacity of 1000 cubic yards would be required for every 2,300 persons assuming that half of that capacity would be filled by yard waste as a bulking agent.

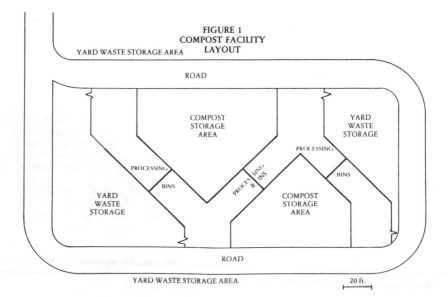

FIGURE 1
COMPOST FACILITY LAYOUT

Appendix I: Physical Characteristic

1. Input is 1/2 food waste; 1/2 yard waste.

2. Volume of finished compost is equal to 2/3 the volume of the input.

3. Once a bin is full, it is not filled again for nine weeks. (The Wilton experience indicates eight weeks is an adequate processing period.)

4. The blowers run for 5 minutes of every 30 minutes.

5. Finished compost if piled 8 feet high and the pile has a 45° slope.

6. Storage area for finished compost is sized to hold one full year's production and still have 12 feet of concrete slab between the compost and the road.

7. Storage area for yard waste is sized to be adequate for a full year's requirement of yard waste (calculated on the simplifying assumption that yard waste will be piled only four feet high.)

8. Concrete walls are 8" thick on a 12" footing; the slab is a 6" slab on a 6" ground base; all concrete is reinforced; the road is a 12" base gravel road.

9. Labor and loader requirements are, respectively, .16 and .12 hours per cubic yard of input (based on timings at Wilton) plus an additional term that depends on the bin size.

10. The land requirement is calculated to provide a minimum of a 50' border between the compost and all sides of the site.

Appendix II

Unit Prices, Amortization Periods,
Interest Rate, and Elasticities

| | Unit Price | Elasticity Coefficients[1] At Annual Volumes Of | |
		1,000 cubic yards	10,000 cubic yards
Operating Cost:			
Wage Rate	$ 6.00/hr.	0.1	0.1
Loader Operating Cost	3.00/hr.	<0.1	<0.1
Electrical Rate	.08/kwh	<0.1	<0.1
Capital Cost:			
Structure:			
Concrete Slab	$ 2.30/sq.ft.	0.1	0.2
Concrete Walls	7.00/lin.ft.	<0.1	<0.1
Post and Beam			
Structure	10.00/sq.ft.	0.1	0.2
Site:	$1,000/acre	<0.1	<0.1
Land	.70/sq.ft.	0.2	0.1
Site Prep	.70/sq.ft.	0.1	0.1
Road			
Equipment:			
Loader	$20,000	0.2	0.1
Dumpsters	1,000 ea.	<0.1	<0.1
Blowers	250 ea.	<0.1	<0.1
Tubing	1.34/lin.ft.	<0.1	<0.1
Tubing Fittings	2.45/T	<0.1	<0.1
	1.85/cap	<0.1	<0.1
		0.5	0.5
Interest Rate: 12%			
Amortizations Periods For:	Years		
Structure, Land &			
Site Preparation	20	0.3	0.4
Road	3	0.5	0.3
Loader	5	0.6	0.1
Dumpsters	5	0.1	<0.1
Blowers	5	<0.1	<0.1
Tubing (including T's and caps)[2]	2	<0.1	<0.1

[1] percentage change in average cost resulting from a 1% change in indicated variable.

[2] all tubing inside the processing bins is assumed to be replaced annually and is treated as an annual operating cost.

COMPOSTING WITHIN AN INTEGRATED SYSTEM FOR PROCESSING AGRICULTURAL WASTE

P. THOSTRUP, L.M. JESPERSEN and P.E.B. JENSEN
Crone & Koch, Consulting Engineers
Jernbanegade 22, 8800 Viborg, Denmark

Summary

The Danish Parliament has recently tightened up the law concerning storage and handling of slurry, solid manure, silage and straw in order to reduce pollution of the environment. Consequently a great demand for new methods of utilization and handling of agricultural waste has arisen.

In the near future an integrated agricultural waste treatment system for a village area will be set up by 4 Danish firms: Crone & Koch, Bigadan A/S, Mullerup A/S and Samson. The Danish National Agency of Technology has supported a feasibility study on such systems. The system involves a separation of slurry into a liquid and a solid fraction. The liquid part will be gasified and afterwards purified in water-hyacinth ponds while the solid fraction will be composted in a composting heat plant together with solid manure, available plant residues and straw.

By integrating composting in such a system, the feed material will be more homogeneous and consequently the compost produced will have a more uniform composition, which is a condition of selling compost in Denmark.

As the integrated system is going to be placed in an intensive green-house cropping area it should be possible to sell methane gas and heat from the composting plant for green-house heating, CO_2 for enrichment of green-house atmosphere and compost as a growth medium.

Preliminary analyses show that in such a case it should be possible to sell high grade compost for a minimum of 0.5 D.kr./kg (50% DM content).

Furthermore a village plant with an input of 100 tonnes of organic material per day will produce about 960 m^3 of methane gas, 950 m^3 of CO_2 and 7,000 kg of compost per day. A feasibility study of this system shows a direct pay-back time of about 3 years.

1.   Introduction

In the last two decades specialization and intensivation as a means for optimizing production has caused a concentration of livestock production in bigger units in Denmark, as probably in most of the other European countries. This situation has led to increased problems concerning disposal of animal manure since many individual farmers do not have sufficient land for disposal.

The present handling of manure and slurry is mostly done in the traditional way: storing and landspreading. However, this method has a lot of disadvantages:

-       sedimentation and formation of top layer in slurry tanks.

- slurry cannot be spread on growing crops.
- danger of hydrogen sulphide (H_2S) poisoning of man and animals.
- manure gives problems with flies
- loss of nitrogen. Normally only 1/3 of the nitrogen in animal waste is available to the crop.
- parasite and pathogen problems. Animal diseases are often transmitted via slurry and manure.
- odour problems.

As a consequence of increased pollution of ground and surface waters with nitrate, phosphorus and organic matter from agricultural fertilizers, a new Danish legislation concerning storage and handling of slurry, solid manure, silage and straw has come into force per 1. February 1986.

The main items of the legislation are:

- Animal farms must have a storage capacity of at least six month manure/slurry production.
- The amount of slurry and manure which is allowed to be disposed per hectare is restricted to: 1.7 animal units of swine or 2.3 animal units of cows.
- Slurry must not be spread from harvest to November, and never on frozen soil.

These demands shall be fullfilled by the end of 1989.

For many farmers the new legislation will cause large investments in slurry tanks and other equipment, and furthermore it will give a lot of practical problems. In Denmark the total investments will be in the order of 3 billions D.kr. (0.4 billion ECU) for improvement and enlargement of existing storage capacity.

From a resource point of view animal waste contain large amounts of energy and nutrients. For Denmark the economical value of energy and nutrient resources in animal manure is estimated to 5 billions D.kr. (0.6 billion ECU) per year.

The mentioned facts and the new legislation indicate that there is a great need for improved treatment and handling systems.

In the light of the above presented situation a group of firms has started a cooporation in order to give alternative solutions to the described problems. The following four firms are representing the group:

Bigadan A/S
Industrivej 9, 5850 Nørre Åby, Fyn, Denmark
(Experts on anaerobic digesters)

Mullerup Machine Factory
5540 Ullerslev, Denmark
(Producers of composting heat plants)

Samson Machine Factory
Bjerringbrovej 10, 8850 Bjerringbro, Denmark
(Producers of equipment for transportation and spreading of manure and slurry)

Crone & Koch, Consulting Engineers
Jernbanegade 22, 8800 Viborg, Denmark
(Experts on utilization of bio-energy and environmental management)

149

At the moment (April 1986) the group is preparing a feasibility study on "integrated agricultural waste processing" supported by the National Danish Agency of Technology (Teknologistyrelsen).

Furthermore a number of such integrated farm waste processing and management plants are under projection for groups of farmers who have set up cooperatives to own the facilities.

In the following an overall description of such facilities will be given.

2.   General description of the integrated system

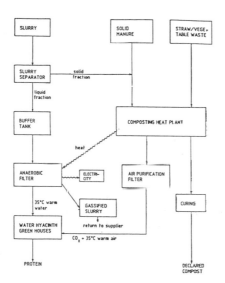

Fig. 1. Flow-Diagram of an integrated agricultural waste processing facility

The main elements of the system are shown in fig. 1. The innovatory aspects of the system are particularly the separation of slurry into a solid and a liquid fraction. The advantage of this separation is the production of substrates, which separately are more suitable for energy utilization than raw slurry. The low DM content (about 3%) of the liquid fraction makes it possible to apply this fraction for biogas production in an anaerobic filter with the achievement of high energy production relative to organic loading ratio. The high DM content (about 22%) of the solid fraction makes this fraction convenient for heat production in a composting plant, with an additional production of valuable compost.

Waste heat and CO_2 from the two energy producing facilities and gasified slurry from the anaerobic filter are utilized for growing water-hyacinths in green-houses. It should be emphasized that this element is not planned to be built in full scale in the first step of the project, as the effluent from the anaerobic filter is returned to the farmers as fertilizer for growing crops. This means that almost all

effluent must be stored until springtime and therefore a storage capacity of 9 months is necessesary for the facilities.

The composting process does not produce a fully stabilized product, therefore the process must be followed by a simple curing in
order to achieve a high grade compost of an accurate and uniform specification. By doing this it is possible to sell the compost for a high
price and to ensure a constant demand.

2.1 The separator

This is an important element of the system because it produces the
suitable substrates for the biofilter and the composting plant.

The separator shall be able to produce a solid fraction of 22% DM
and liquid fraction of 2-3% DM at a capacity of 100 tonnes/day. Several
types of separators can meet the demands (Pos. et. al, 1984): the
centrifugal separator (fig. 2), the brushed screen/roller press separator (fig. 3) and the auger type of separator (fig. 4). The problem is
the reliability and further investigations have to be made before
choosing separator type.

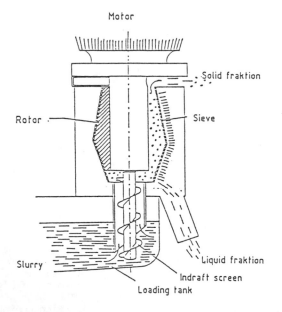

Fig. 2 Centrifugal separator

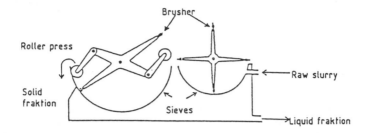

Fig. 3 Auger separator

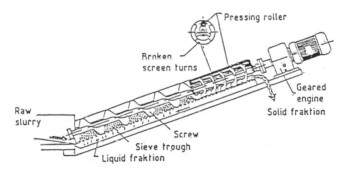

Fig. 4 Brush screen/roller press separator

2.2 Anaerobic biofilter

The anaerobic biofilter is suitable for treatment of low loaded agricultural wastes, e.g. separated slurry (Marique et. al, 1984). It presents several advantages as opposed to conventional biogas digester types, and the features of these reactors are:

- shorter hydraulic retention time
- higher volumetric gas production
- higher methane content in the biogas

The anaerobic filter is characterized by a packing material within the reactor which provides a large surface area on which anaerobic organisms can grow and be retained within the system and therefore have a high volumetric gas production of 4 m^3 biogas/m^3 reactor volume/day, with a methane content of 70-90% (Roy and Baumann, 1984). A short hydraulic retention time of 3-5 days allows reduction of the digester volume about 4 to 8 times compared to a conventional continous flow biogas reactor. The initial investment cost per m^3 slurry treated are thus reduced.

2.3 Water-hyacinth production

The aim of applying green-houses with water-hyacinth ponds in connection to these integrated facilities are:

1) to utilize the gasified slurry and its inorganic nutrient content as a growth substrate

2) to use the waste-heat in the effluent from the biofilter and the heat and CO_2 in the heat composting exhaust air to create an optimal growth environment in green-houses

3) to take advantage of the high transpiration rate from a water-hyacinth crop.

The consequences of these points are versatile, firstly inorganic nutrients of the gasified slurry are efficiently converted into valuable vegetable protein, secondly the need for storage capacity is reduced or even eliminated and last but not least the large amount of waste heat from the biofilter is utilized in stead of being lost due to infeasibility of utilizing it through traditional heat exchanging systems.

Water-hyacinth is well known as a very productive tropical and subtropical water weed. Unfortunately the plant is unable to grow in temperate areas, except for a few warm summer-months. However, grown and harvested under favourable growth conditions in green-houses the production potential far exceeds production in its natural environment. In large scale green-house experiments dry matter productions of about 200 t/ha with a protein content of 35-40% of DM (Vanrenterghem, J, 1985). CO_2 enrichment of green-house atmosphere has a positive effect on production (Larigauderie et. al, 1985) so it is likely that the production of biomass can be further increased in the future.

If it is possible to prevent accumulation of water and nutrients by balancing hydraulic loading with transpiration and inorganic nutrient loading with plant nutrient uptake, this field has great opportunities in solving slurry storage problems. Transpiration rates of 225 ml/plant/day and nitrogen uptake of plants of 13-32 kg/ha/day have been demonstrated by Rogers & Davies (1972) and Reddy & DeBusk (1985), respectively. These values of 250-350 m^3 water/ha/day and 10-15 t N removal/ha/year are likely to fullfill the balance conditions.

2.4 Composting heat plant

The composting heat plant is the type previously descriped in Thostrup (1985). The plant is developed in Denmark during the last six years and is now developed to a commercial stage. A more comprehensive explanation of the advantages is given below under point 3.

As mentioned earlier the product from the composting heat plant is not stabilised enough to be called compost. Therefore it needs to be further cured. This can be done either by ordinary windrow-composting or by vermicomposting. By using vermicomposting the substrate from the composting plant is converted into highly valuable products: Wermicompost and worms (Edwards et. al, 1985). The choise of system will depend very much on the prices of the different composts.

At the moment curing in windrows is the cheapest solution but how the situation will be in the long term is difficult to predict.

2.5 Transport of slurry and manure

To feed the treatment facility it is economically feasible to transport slurry and manure from farms within a distance of 10 kilometers and to return treated slurry to the farmers.

Most of the equipment for transport of slurry exists already so it is more a question of optimization of the transport system. The present investigations indicate that a 20 tonnes truck mounted vacuum tank with crane will give the most optimal solution.

Transport of manure without odour problems is more difficult to solve so investigations are still going on at the moment, but a container system is most likely to be the best solution.

3. Composting heat plant as an element in an integrated processing system

The composting heat plant discussed in details in Thostrup (1985) is characterized by the following features:

- Many different sources of organic material can be fed to the plant, because an efficient mixing unit is built into the system.
- The composting process if fully controlled resulting in a very high composting rate. For agricultural waste a minimum of 30% of the DM content is converted within 5 days, which is the mean retention time of the biomass in the plant.
- Since the plant is a completely closed system exposing the biomass to a temperature of $60^{\circ}C$ for 5 days, this treatment process is a very efficient way of killing plant and animal pathogens as well as parasites and weed seeds.
- Odour from the plant is very limited.
- Nitrogen loss during the composting process is limited, due to process regulation and because volatile ammonia is trapped in an airwasher in connection with the heat exchanger system.
- The biologically produced heat can be recovered with an efficiency of 70%. The remaining 30% is lost with the exhaust air, in the hot compost and by transmission.
- The exhaust air is rich on CO_2, which profitably can be applied for CO_2 enrichment of green-house atmosphere.

The hot water $(60^{\circ}C)$ produced in the composting plant can be used to heat the anaerobic filter to process temperature. CO_2 and hot exhaust air $(30-35^{\circ}C)$ can improve and heat water-hyacinth green-house environment or other green-house cultures.

4. Mass and Energy budget for a slurry and manure system

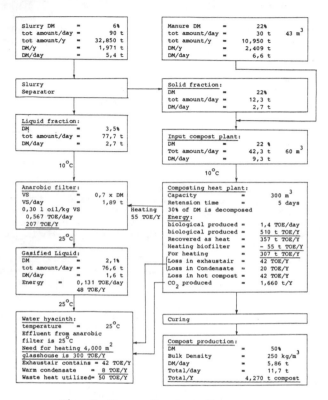

Fig. 5. Mass and energy flow

Based on a capacity of 100 t slurry/day and the previous mentioned data for the single elements it is possible to set up the mass and energy flow of the system shown in fig. 5. In table 1 the annual energy budget of the system has been calculated as follows:

Anaerobic filter:	207 TOE
Heat composting plant:	357 TOE
Process heating of anaerobic filter:	−55 TOE
Net energy for heating	509 TOE
Recovery of waste heat in water hyacinth green house	50 TOE
Net energy used/year	559 TOE

TABLE 1.Annual energy balance for a 100 tonnes slurry/day facility.

5. Discussion

A highly integrated system as the one described in this paper has still a lot of uncertainties which cannot be fully highlighted until there are units operating.

National money support will be given to such systems, mainly because of the following.

5.1 Feasibility for the farmer

The advantages for the single farmer as a member of the co-operative facility are as follows:

- There is no need for investments in increased storage capacity.
- It is easier to handle and spread seperated gasified slurry than raw slurry.
- The digested slurry can be brought out when the crop needs it, not when the tank is full.
- The fertilizer effect of the nutrients in the slurry is improved.
- Odour in the farm surrounding is less.
- Risc of infection is less.
- It is possible to have more than two animal units per hectar.

5.2 Feasibility for the society

The advantages for the society are as follows:

- Reduced pollution of surface waters and groundwater.
  No odour problems from animal farms.
- Improved utilization of energy and nutrient content in the farm waste which gives a positive effect on balance of trade.
- Easier administration of approvals for industrial animal production units.

5.3 Aspects for the future

This paper only describes the beginning of a technology which all countries with animal production sooner or later must adapt in one or another way.

But of course much is still to be done before such systems will be common and therefore it is important to set up demonstration facilities in order to face and solve the problems - technically as well as economically.

REFERENCES

(1) EDWARDS, C.A; BURROWS, I; FLETCHER, R.E. and JONES, B.A., 1985. The use of earthworms for composting farm waste. In: J.K.R. Gasser (ed). Composting of agricultural and other wastes, pp. 221-241. Elsevier, London.

(2) KROODSMA, W. and POELMA, H.R., 1985. Mest scheiding. Instituut voor mechanisatie, Arbeid en gebouven, Publikatie 209, IMAG, Wageningen.

(3) LARIGAUDERIE, A.; ROY, J.; BERGER, A., 1985. Photosynthetic basis of biomass production by water hyacinth grown under high CO_2 level. In: Palz, W., Coombs, J. and Hall, D.O. (eds). Energy from Biomass, 3rd E.C. conference. Elsevier, London.

(4) MARIQUE, Ph.; GILES, A. and JOASSIN, L., 1985. Anaerobic fixed bed down-flow reactor: efficiency and performances in treating low

loaded piggery waste. In: Egneus, H. and Ellegård, A. (eds.).
Bioenergy 84, vol. III: 392–396. Elsevier, London.

(5) POS, I.; TRAPP, R.; HARVEY, M., 1984. Performance of a brushed
screen roller press manure separator. Trans. ASAE, 27: 1102–1108.

(6) REDDY, K.R. and DEBUSK, W.F., 1985. Nutrient removal potential of
selected aquatic macrophytes. J. Environ. Qual., 14: 459–462.

(7) ROGERS, H.H. and DAVIES, D.E., 1972. Nutrient removal by water-
hyacinth. Weed Science, 20: 423–428.

(8) ROY, D. and BAUMANN, R.H., 1985. Attached growth anaerobic conversion process. In: Egneus, H. and Ellegård, A. (Eds.). Bioenergy
84, vol. III: 397–400. Elsevier, London.

(9) THOSTRUP, P., BERTHELSEN, L., 1985. Komposteringsvarme fra fast
staldgødning. Jordbrugs Teknisk Institut Meddelse no. 43.

(10) VANRENTERGHEM, J., 1985. Forædling af Biomasse gennem energigen-
vinding. SPIE-BATIGNOLLES Frankrig. Paper at M.E.I. konference
Paris 21. Nov. 1984.

(11) VEMMELUND, N., BERTHELSEN, L. (1977). Udnyttelse af komposteringsvarme fra staldgødning. Jordbrugsteknisk Institut Meddelelse No.
28.

SESSION 1

PRODUCTION OF COMPOST

Rapporteur: DIAZ L.

This session covered a wide range of topics in the area of biological stabilization of organic residues. These topics can be classified into four general areas: 1) composting methods and options; 2) vermicomposting; 3) uses of the compost, and 4) anaerobic digestion.

The presentations involving composting methods and options dealt with a review of recent developments in composting process in a waste management system (for both municipal and agricultural wastes), the evaluation of methods of maturing urban compost, and the use of agricultural residues for composting urban sludges.

The presentation in the area of vermicomposting covered the application of the process for dealing with certain industrial wastes as well as the measurement of microbial activities in the process.

The single presentation regarding the use of compost involved the evaluation of utilizing composts produced from some agricultural wastes as growing media.

Finally, the papers dealing with biological stabilization through anaerobic digestion discussed: 1) the appropriateness of including biomethanization as part of a composting system, and 2) the results of work carried-out on dry anaerobic digestion of solid wastes.

These presentations demonstrated that:
- substantial advances have been made in the area of windrow composting particularly with the application of forced aeration for treating urban sludges;
- composting can be incorporated in a waste management system either as a single process or in conjunction with other processes, such as incineration, RDF production and recycling;
- proper control of aeration and moisture content of a compost pile accelerates the maturation process;
- grape stalks can be successfully used as a bulking agent for composting urban sludges;
- vermicomposting can be utilized for stabilizing certain industrial residues;
- tests using some animal manures showed that vermicomposting brings about less changes in microbial counts than prolonged maturation.
- Biomethanization may be incorporated in an overall waste management strategy. The process would result in the production of energy (biogas) and a residue suitable for composting.
- Controlled, dry anaerobic digestion of the organic matter of urban wastes resembles the decomposition of organic matter in a landfill. The major difference is that the controlled process takes place at rates
- Composting of certain agricultural residues can result in the production of a high-quality growth medium which can control soil-born pathogens.

SESSION II : QUALITY OF THE PRODUCT

Experience gained in the composting of the solid wastes obtained during the separate reclamation of valuable materials

Lignocellulolysis in composts

Lignin metabolism in the soils amended with compost

Health and safety aspects of compost preparation and use

Microbiological specifications of disinfected compost

Optimisation of agricultural industrial wastes management through in-vessel composting

Biochemistry of manure composting : lignin biotransformation and humification

The decomposition, humification and fate of nitrogen during the composting of some plant residues

Heavy metals in compost from municipal refuse strategies to reduce their content to acceptable levels

Bacterial and fungal atmospheric contamination at refuse composting plants : a preliminary study

Comparative survival of pathogenic indicators in windrow and static pile

Phytotoxicity of olive tree leaf compost

Cation exchange capacity variation during the composting of different materials

Criteria of quality of city refuse compost based on the stability of its organic fraction

The priming effect and the respiratory rate/compost dose ratio as compost ripeness index

Application of a new method for C.E.C. determination as a compost maturity index

Stabilization process of sewage sludge compost in soil

Monitoring the composting process using parameters of compost stability

Compost maturity by water extract analyses

Quality of urban waste compost related to the various composting processes

Changes in the chemical and horticultural properties during composting of slurry produced by methanogenic fermentation of dairy cow manure

REPORT BY P. BOUTIN

EXPERIENCE GAINED IN THE COMPOSTING OF WET SOLID WASTES OBTAINED DURING THE SEPARATE RECLAMATION OF VALUABLE MATERIALS

Dr. W. Bidlingmaier, J. Folmer, G. Frank
Universität Stuttgart

1. Introduction

Developments in the area of the separate collection of waste materials have revived interest in composting as a method of treatment. This is because natural organic substances are isolated in a distinct fraction during the separation process in the households. At the present, one can distinguish between two modes of procedure:

    1. the collection of valuable materials

    2. the collection of "bio-wastes"

The difference lies in the objectives. In the first case emphasis is placed on obtaining a mixture of valuable substances that is free of undefined matter in order to facilitate the reclamation of reusable materials. The remainder consists of natural organic substances, mingled with all the other substances that also cannot be marketed as reusable materials. Examples for such materials are fine trash, disposable diapers, vacuum cleaner bags etc.

In the second case the ultimate goal is obtaining a mixture of substances that is as "pure" suitable as possible. This mixture can consist of natural organic substances, such as wastes from the preparation of meals and gardening wastes, and as some model experiments have shown, also of paper wastes.

The separate collection of wastes represents a challenge for composting in two aspects. If "bio-wastes" are collected, then the collection method is tailored to the subsequent rotting process; the basic concept is the production of compost with little or no harmful substance and ballast contents.

The collection of valuable materials leaves behind a residual fraction with an enticingly high proportion of natural organic substances, that are most desirable when attempting to produce high-quality composts.

In the following, the behaviour of differently treated wet wastes during the processing and rotting procedures is discussed.

2. The Composting of Wet Wastes

2.1 The Method of Composting

2.1.1 Composting in Mounds with Forced Aeration

The experiments were carried out in mounds with triangular cross-sections
(Please see Fig. 1):

```
Height             : approx.  1.5 m
Width at the base: approx.  2.9 m
Length             : approx. 10.0 m
```

Figure 1 also shows how the existing aeration channels in the Wieslocher
rotting bed-plate were used. In order to evaluate the influence of
precipitation on the course of the rotting process, the mounds were
protected longitudinally only up to half of their lengths and the half-
sections of the mounds equipped separately with inner and outer measuring
devices. The roofs were constructed by anchoring common greenhouse arches
to the bed-plate and then covering them with transparent plastic foils.

```
Dimensions of the roofs:     Height                : 2.0 m
                             Width at the base     : 3.3 m
                             Distance between arches: 2.5 m
```

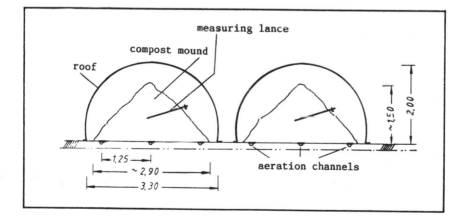

Figure 1: Composting mounds

2.1.2 Composting with the Brikollare Procedure

The briquettes were pressed in an experimental plant (courtesy of the EAWAG) and placed loosely by hand onto a wooden frame.

Dimensions of the briquettes: Length: approx. 25 cm
                               Width : approx. 15 cm
                               Height: approx. 15 cm

Dimensions of the Brikollare composting mound: Height: approx. 1.0 m
                                                Width : approx. 1.5 m
                                                Length: approx. 1.5 m

During the experiment the composting mound was situated in the testing laboratory of the Department of Waste Technology of the Institut für Siedlungswasserbau in Stuttgart-Büsnau.

2.2   Processing Methods

2.2.1 Composting Plant in Wiesloch

When delivered, the solid wastes are weighed and then dumped into a low bunker. The bunker has two functions. On the one hand it serves as buffer storage between delivery and further processing of the wastes, and on the other hand as a mixing station. From there the refuse is transported by means of a semi-automatic crane to the feed hopper of the shredderscreener unit.

The screen overflow from the shredder is carried by a conveyor belt to the intermediate storage area for such residues. The screen underflow is passed by means of a conveyor belt under a suspended magnet and then diverted to the rotting area.

2.2.2 AVEG Experimental Unit

The mode of operation and the mechanical equipment of the AVEG experimental unit can be seen in the following figure (Fig. 2).

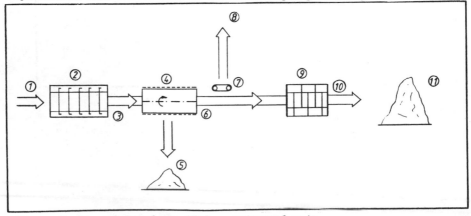

Figure 2: Flow-sheet of the AVEG experimental unit

Legend:

NUMBER	PROCESS OPERATION	MECHANICAL EQUIPMENT
1	Feeding	Shovel loader
2	Metering	Chain conveyor
3	Transport	Conveyor belt
4	Screening, Mixing	Screening trommel (12/8 mm)
5	Discharge of screen underflow	Conveyor belt
6	Transport	Conveyor belt
7	Fe-separation	Suspended magnet
8	Fe-discharge	Conveyor belt
9	Size reduction,Mixing	Duplex-rotor,cutting aggregate, slow speed
10	Discharge of processed material	Conveyor belt
11	Piling of the composting mounds	

Variations in the processing mode were possible and were exploited, as follows, in the course of the experimental program:

1. Variation of the screen mesh size:
   - 12 mm: Mound 2, Mound 3, Mound 5, Mound 6, Mound 8
   - 8 mm: Mound 7

2. Processing without size reduction:
   Mound 3

2.3 Post-treatment Operational Procedure

In order to obtain comparable results in respect to the degree of rotting achieved and the heavy metal contents of the compost, all experimental composting-mounds were subjected to a uniform post-processing treatment. It was of foremost importance to obtain a homogeneous compost material that would allow representative sampling. For this purpose it was convenient to use the existing equipment of the composting plant in Wiesloch (screen and air classifier). A size reduction stage was installed ahead of these aggregates, in order to mechanically break down and homogenize the material. A single-rotor hammer mill, manufactured by the Herbold Company was used for this purpose.

2.4 Heavy Metal Contents in the Composts

Analyses of the composts yielded values for the heavy metal contents, based on the dry substance (DS) contents of the composts. These figures are listed in Table 1 . It is only possible to compare composting mounds on the basis of values independent of the degree of degradation and thus also the ignition loss; therefore the concentrations were related to the corresponding mineral contents (DS_{min}). Table 2 gives the values obtained in this way. It can be seen that the samples taken from the core and the shell of a mound agree quite well with each other, a fact evidencing the representative character of the samples analyzed. Additionally, the highest concentrations of each heavy metal determined in the composts (based on DS_{min}) was related to the values for compost from composting mound 1 (See Table 3).

Moreover, the concentration values (based on DS) were subjected to a normalization in respect to limit values, in order to facilitate the evaluation of the usability of the composts. As limit values, those outlined in Directive M 10 and also the more stringent ones of the presidial authorities in Tübingen, as given in Table 4, were chosen. Figures 8 and 9 show the resulting diagrams, from which the normalized heavy metal contents and the standardized limit value resulting from the normalization procedure for all metals can be ascertained. Finally the minimum intervals of application under the presumption of the normal practice of applying 40 t/ha of DS were calculated according to the KVO (Regulations for the Application of Clarifier Sludge) and are listed in Table 5.

In view of the post-processing treatment chosen, the following results can be protocolled:

1.
By processing the wastes in the AVEG experimental unit, all heavy metal contents in the household waste composting mounds, with the exception of copper, could be reduced in comparison to the treatment in the composting plant. Obviously the "accumulation effect" of the intensive size reduction with the screening-shredding unit makes itself noticeable, whereas during treatment in the AVEG unit a decrease in the heavy metal contents is achieved by drawing off the screen underflow.

2.
The heavy metal contents based on DS as well as on DS_{min} tend to be higher in all wet waste composting mounds than in the household wastes composting mounds that undergo the same treatment. This is especially true for the concentrations in mound 5. This is due to an enrichment of the heavy metals in the compost as a consequence of the separation procedure for valuable materials.

3.
Within the wet waste group (M4 – M8) the concentrations of Cd, Cr, ·Ni and Zn in mound 6 are distinctly lower than in the other mounds processed. This agrees with the findings during the treatment procedure, where a significantly higher removal of the heavy metals could be observed. Furthermore the values in the unprocessed mound were lower than in all other wet composting mounds, with the exception of copper.

In mound 7 the heavy metal concentrations are lower than those in mound 5, with the exception of zinc and copper. This is probably due to the lower cut size during the screening stage of the processing procedure, which resulted in a higher proportion of fines and above all more mineral substances in the raw compost.

In mound 8 (Brikollare) the concentrations for all heavy metals, without exception, are of almost the same order of magnitude as those in mound 5.

4.
After normalization in accordance with current limit values (Figs. 3 and 4) the heavy metal contents determined in all of the composts are by far lower than the upper limit values delineated in Directive M 10. With the exception of mound 1 the zinc contents are decisive for the value of the compost. Presuming a practice-related application of 40 t/ha of dry substance, then (according to Table 5) application intervals of 4.3 to 7.5 years for composts from household wastes and 5.2 to 8.2 years for composts from wet wastes would be possible. In contrast to this, the much more stringent values set up by the presidial authorities in Tübingen are not adhered to by any of the composts. For all composts the critical concentrations are, without exception, those of the metals nickel, lead and zinc.

Composting experiments in Wiesloch 1985

Heavy metal analyses

Digestion procedure : $HNO_3 + H_2O_2$

Analytical method : AAS (flame; graphite furnace)

Dimension : ppm; based on DS

Metal		Mound 1 HM Composting Plant Wiesloch	Mound 2 HM pro- cessed AVEG 12 mm	Mound 3 HM only screened AVEG 12 mm	Mound 4 WM unpro- cessed	Mound 5 WM pro- cessed AVEG 12 mm	Mound 6 WM Pre- rotting AVEG 12 mm	Mound 7 WM pro- cessed AVEG 8 mm	Mound 8 WM Bri- kollare
Cd	i	2,4	2,3	1,4	1,3	3,0	2,7	2,5	3,2
	a	2,3	2,0	1,5	1,4	3,3		2,3	
Cr	i	21	18	17	25	28	27	26	29
	a	26	16	18	26	30		29	
Cu	i	86	130	151	161	99	130	125	122
	a	99	125	141	150	126		119	
Ni	i	43	37	17	28	44	43	38	48
	a	44	30	21	26	49		42	
Pb	i	391	164	143	183	207	270	177	247
	a	326	131	135	182	219		234	
Zn	i	740	700	530	670	897	920	920	948
	a	640	580	540	730	1.040		920	

Table 1 : Results of the heavy metal analyses; contents based on DS

Composting experiments in Wiesloch 1985

Heavy metal analyses

Digestion procedure: $HNO_3 + H_2O_2$

Analytical method : AAS (flame; graphite furnace)

Dimension: ppm   **based on DS min**

Metal	Mound 1 HM Composting Plant Wiesloch	Mound 2 HM pro-cessed AVEG 12 mm	Mound 3 HM only screened AVEG 12 mm	Mound 4 WM unpro-cessed	Mound 5 WM pro-cessed AVEG 12 mm	Mound 6 WM Pre-rotting AVEG 12 mm	Mound 7 WM pro-cessed AVEG 8 mm	Mound 8 WM Bri-kollare
Cd i	4,6	4,3	3,4	2,8	6,8	5,4	5,6	6,5
a	4,8	5,0	3,6	3,2	6,3		4,6	
Cr i	40	33	41	55	62	54	58	58
a	54	40	43	58	57		58	
Cu i	165	241	361	351	227	260	281	248
a	205	310	341	336	239		236	
Ni i	82	68	41	61	99	86	86	97
a	91	75	51	58	93		83	
Pb i	749	304	343	400	466	540	399	502
a	676	325	327	407	416		465	
Zn i	1.430	1.300	1.271	1.460	2.020	1.840	2.072	1.927
a	1.328	1.440	1.302	1.633	1.973		1.825	

Table 2: Results of the heavy metal analyses;
contents based on DSmin

Composting experiments in Wiesloch 1985

Heavy metal analyses

Digestion procedure: $HNO_3 + H_2O_2$

Analytical method : AAS (flame; graphite furnace)

Dimension: -----

relative to the concentrations in mound 1 (= 100)

Metal	Mound 1 HM Composting Plant Wiesloch	Mound 2 HM pro- cessed AVEG 12 mm	Mound 3 HM only screened AVEG 12 mm	Mound 4 WM unpro- cessed	Mound 5 WM pro- cessed AVEG 12 mm	Mound 6 WM Pre- rotting AVEG 12 mm	Mound 7 WM pro- cessed AVEG 8 mm	Mound 8 WM Bri- kollare
Cd	100	104	75	67	142	113	117	135
Cr	100	74	80	107	115	100	107	107
Cu	100	151	176	171	117	127	137	121
Ni	100	82	56	67	109	95	94	107
Pb	100	48	51	60	69	80	69	74
Zn	100	101	91	114	141	129	145	135

Table 3 : Heavy metal concentrations in the composts,
relative to the concentrations in the compost from mound 1

Limit values in ppm DS		
metal	KVO	Pre.Auth. Tü
Cd	20	3
Cr	1200	150
Cu	1200	150
Ni	200	25
Pb	1200	150
Zn	3000	375

Table 4: Heavy metal limit values
for composts

Mound	Decisive heavy metal concentration ppm DS		Minimum application interval years
M1	Pb	391	7,5
M2	Zn	700	5,5
M3	Zn	540	4,3
M4	Zn	730	5,2
M5	Zn	1040	8,2
M6	Zn	920	7,2
M7	Zn	920	7,2
M8	Zn	948	7,4

Table 5: Minimum application intervals
for applications of 40 t/ha DS

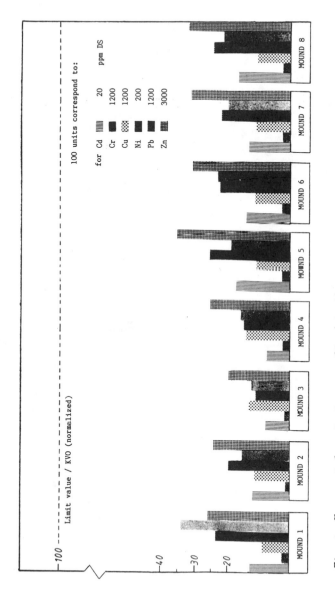

Fig. 3: Heavy metal contents, normalized to the
limit value according to KVO

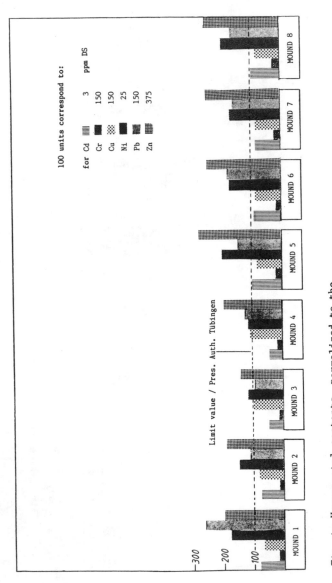

Fig. 4: Heavy metal contents, normalized to the
limit value of the presidial authorities in Tübingen

3. Composting of Bio-wastes

In order to obtain comparable results, both of the experimental composting mounds were subjected to the same processing procedure. For this purpose the facilities already in existence at the composting plant in Wiesloch were used.

The individual processing steps consisted of the following operations:

	Processing Step	Equipment
1	Size reduction	Shredder
2	Transporting and loading	Shovel loader
3	Intermediate storage	Manure silo
4	Transporting of coarse material	Conveyor belt
5	Screening	Screen (mesh size: 10 mm)
6	Transport of the screen overflow to the residue bunker	Conveyor belt
7	Discharge of the screen underflow	Conveyor belt
8	Separation of hard substances	Air classifier
9	Discharge of hard substances	Conveyor belt
10	Discharge of light materials	Pneumatic conveyor
11	Separation of light materials	Cyclone separator
12	Transport of light materials	Conveyor belt

Composite samples of the compost material were taken and subjected to the following laboratory analyses:

- Thermo-generation profile
- Water content
- Ignition loss
- Heavy metal analyses

3.1 Composting Mound No. 1

The processing of composting mound no. 1 was unproblematic; there was absolutely no trouble with obstructions or with adhesive behavior of the material. The water contents of the whole composting mound as well as of the separate fractions differ only slightly from each other. According to the experience gained at the composting plant in Wiesloch, the limit value for the water content, at which processing can take place without problems, lies at about 35 %. A lower, experimental value of 33 % was found.

Losses due to the adherence of fine material to the conveyor belts were a minimal 2.2 %; the mass balance is presented in Table 5.1 The proportion of compost material in the discharged hard substances was minimal, as confirmed by the thermo-generation curve shown in Figure 4.2. If the thermo-generation curve of vessel no. 2 from the compost sample is not taken into consideration, then the maximum temperature of 45° C is characteristical for a finished compost (Rotting grade III) in accordance with Directive M 10 (Figure 4.1.

3.2 Composting Mound No. 2

The bio-wastes underwent rotting for 7-13 weeks.

The results of the processing of compost mound no. 2 are definitely worse than those obtained with mound no. 1. Proportionally, only one-third of the compost quantity was produced (based on the quantity of compost material processed; see Table 5.2).

The processing took place without any major problems; for a short period of time the feed hopper of the screen was obstructed. The bad results can be traced back to the high water content of the processed material

The moist fine materials adhered to the conveyor belt, so that the losses of 8.9 % were considerable. In the air classifier hard substance particles stuck to the fines from the screening process and formed larger lumps of material that were then separated off because of their higher weight.

The thermo-generation curves of the compost sample (Fig. 4.3) show a maximum temperature of 74.5° C. This is indicative of a (continuing) high activity of the compost.

This compost must therefore be classified as still being fresh or raw compost, that still must undergo a post-rotting process.

The sample from the hard substance fraction shows a higher generation of heat than the sample from composting mound no. 1 (Fig. 4.4). This is caused by the higher proportion of fresher, organic material (see also Table 5.2: Ignition loss).

3.3 Heavy Metal Analyses

The samples were dried and then ground to a smaller particle size using a knife mill and a ball mill. Thereafter the samples were sieved through a screen with a mesh size of 0.25 mm. If the amount of screen residue (over-flow) was large, then it was once again subjected to the fine grinding process.

The samples prepared in this way were digested with HNO_3 and H_2O_2. There-after the atomic emission spectra, with inductively-coupled plasma as stimulating source (ICP), were measured. The following samples were examined:

- compost samples from mounds nos. 1 and 2
- hard substance samples from mounds nos. 1 and 2.

The hard substance samples were examined for purposes of comparison with the analyses of the compost samples. Because of the low contamination of bio-wastes with foreign matter, it was interesting to determine the amount of heavy metals that were removed with the hard substance fraction. Analyses were carried out for the following heavy metals:

- Cd   Cadmium
- Cr   Chromium
- Cu   Copper
- Ni   Nickel
- Pb   Lead
- Zn   Zinc

The results are summarized in Table 5.3.

The following analytical results were used as a basis for comparison:

- average values of the compost analyses from composting plants;
  Directive M 10, January 1984 (Table 2)
- Limit values for composts;
  Presidial government authorities in Tübingen
- "Green Box Action", Witzenhausen;
  2. Intermediate Report (Analysis of a combined sample of a
  finished compost).

It can be seen that all three of the composts – even the compost from
mound no. 3 without separation of the hard substances – show results below
the stringent limit values of the presidial government authorities in
Tübingen and also below the results from the "Green Box Action", Witzenhausen, with the exception of cadmium and chromium.

In comparison with the average values given in the Directive M 10, the
values found were distinctly lower.

The hard substances also lie, with the exception of lead (Mound 1) and
copper and zinc (Mound 2), within the limits set by the presidial
government authoritiies in Tübingen.

Therefore it can be presumed that the process of separating-off the hard
substances can reduce the proportion of heavy metals in compost. The
values for the compost from a third mound without hard substance removal
are significantly higher than those of the other two composts.

Date   : 15/11/85

Sample   : Composting mound 1

Initial quantity   : 7.740 kg of bio-wastes

Processed compost quantity: 2.270 kg = 29,3 %

Compost   < 10 mm   681 kg = 30,0 % *

Hard substances < 10 mm   233 kg = 10,3 %

Residues   > 10 mm   1.306 kg = 57,5 %

Loss   50 kg = 2,2 %

----

* based on the quantity of processed compost

Table 5.1 : Mass balance for composting mound 1

Date   : 29/11/85

Sample   : Composting mound 2

Initial quantity   : 14.060 kg of bio-wastes

Processed compost quantity: 5.610 kg = 39,9 %

Compost   < 10 mm   591 kg = 10,5 % *

Hard substances < 10 mm   895 kg = 16,0 %

Residues   > 10 mm   3.624 kg = 64,6 %

Loss   500 kg = 8,9 %

----

* based on the quantity of processed compost

Table 5.2 : Mass balance for composting mound 2

Table 5.3 : Heavy metal analyses

Digestion procedure : $HNO_3 + H_2O_2$
Analysis : ICP
Dimension : mg/kg based on DS (dry substances)

Heavy metal	Compost Mound 1	Compost Mound 2	Hard substances Mound 1	Hard substances Mound 2	Averages M 10	Pres. gov.auth. Tübingen	Witzenhausen 1984
Cd Cadmium	1,2	2,4	1,4	1,7	5,5	3,0	0,7
Cr Chromium	32	28	43	40	71,4	150	74
Cu Copper	60	68	92	192	274	150	51
Ni Nickel	16	15	20	22	44,9	25	36
Pb Lead	136	126	184	140	513	150	189
Zn Zinc	331	363	366	489	1.570	375	367

PROJECT LEIMEN   DATE : 16/11/85
Sample : M 1 Compost   Thermo-generation

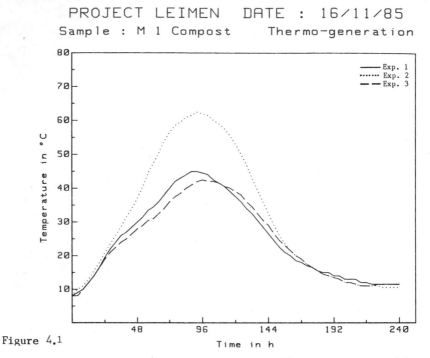

Figure 4.1

Sample : M 1 Hard subst.   Thermo-generation

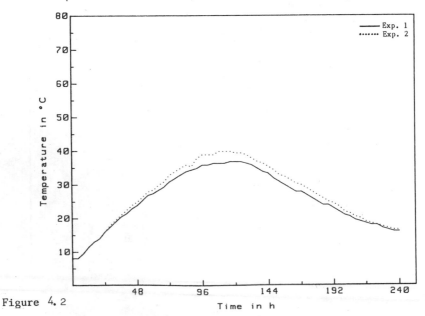

Figure 4.2

PROJECT LEIMEN   DATE : 30/11/85

Sample : M 2 Compost   Thermo-generation

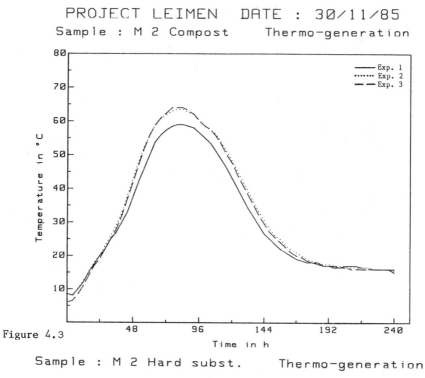

Figure 4.3

Sample : M 2 Hard subst.   Thermo-generation

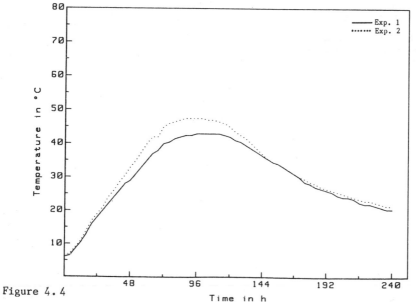

Figure 4.4

LIGNOCELLULOLYSIS IN COMPOSTS

J.M. LYNCH

GCRI, Worthing Road, Littlehampton, West Sussex, BN17 6LP, UK

Summary

Lignocellulolysis occurs in composts undergoing stabilization but also occurs in stabilized composts which have been subject to primary degradation, such as those in which edible fungi are inoculated. The chemical composition of various lignocellulosic materials which might be used for composts is given. Biochemical pathways of cellulose, hemicellulose and lignin metabolism are outlined. The effects of some additives and supplements containing proteins which may affect lignocellulolysis are discussed.

Nitrogen may also be provided to composts by atmospheric fixation using the co-operative associations of bacteria and fungi. Other potentially beneficial effects during ligno-cellulolysis are the formation of secondary products such as polysaccharides and humic acids to assist in soil structural stabilization, and the production of antibiotics to control plant pathogens. Harmful effects of lignocellulolysis during fermentative metabolism include the production of phytotoxic organic acids. Inoculants might promote beneficial effects against harmful ones and, for example, produce a plant growth medium resistant to disease.

1. CHEMICAL COMPOSITION OF POTENTIAL COMPOST SUBSTRATES

Most composts which are of plant origin can be regarded as ligno-cellulosic. The cellulosic components are collectively referred to as holocellulose and consist of cellulose and hemicellulose. Cellulose is a polymer of glucose (Fig. I) and hemicellulose is a heterogenous polymer of

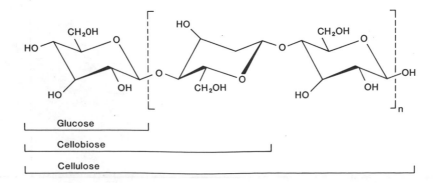

Fig. I Structure of cellulose

hexoses (glucose, mannose and galactose) and pentoses (xylose and arabinose). The hemicelluloses include a D-xylans with a backbone of poly-β-1,4-xylan linked laterally to arabinose, glucuronic and arabino-glucuronic acid, mannans and galactans (Fig. II).

Lignin is a polymer based on three phenolic acids (p-comaryl alcohol, coniferyl alcohol and sinapyl alcohol) (Fig. III).

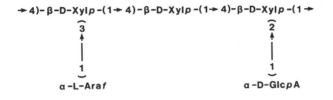

Fig. II. L-Arabino-D-glucurono-D-xylan. Araf = arabinofuranose; Xylp = xylopyranoside; GlcpA = glucopyronosyluronide

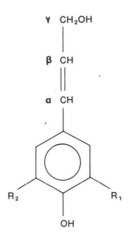

Fig. III. Basic molecular structure of lignin. p-coumaryl alcohol - R_1 and R_2 = H; sinapyl alcohol - R_1 and R_2 = OCH_3; coniferyl alcohol - R_1 = OCH_3, R_2 = H.

The three groups of lignins are coniferous (formed mainly from coniferyl alcohol units), hardwood (coniferyl and sinapyl alcohol units) and grass (formed mainly from coniferyl, sinapyl and p-coumaryl alcohol units). The structure of spruce lignin has been characterised in detail (11) but no other lignins have been fully characterised.

On a weight basis, the minor components of lignocellulosics are proteins, pectins, lipids and minerals. The chemical compositions of several lignocellulosics which might serve as compost substrates are given in Table I. Generally they can be divided into woods and plant residues, woods usually having larger proportions of lignins than those found in straw. The use of these raw materials is geographically variable. In parts of Europe where straw is not burnt in the field after harvest, the decomposition of straw can lead to the production of phytotoxic metabolites by microbial fermentation (22). Straw is used widely for the production of composts for the growth of the cultivated mushroom Agaricus bisporus. In England and Wales this use accounts for about 5% of the total wheat straw produced in the United Kingdom (38). Composting for mushroom production represents proven technology and novel approaches to composting of waste should benefit from the extensive literature on mushroom production (10, 28).

Table I. Typical composition of lignocellulosic materials

Raw material	Cellulose (%)	Hemi-cell. (%)	Lignin (%)	Extract-ives (%)	Ash (%)	Reference
Spruce wood	43.0	27.0	28.6	1.8	0.4	Rydholm (32)
Pine wood	44.0	26.0	27.8	5.3	0.4	" (32)
Birch wood	40.0	39.0	19.5	3.1	0.3	" (32)
Pine kraft pulp	77.0	18.0	5.0	0.2	0.4	" (32)
Bagasse	33.4	30.0	18.9	6.0	2.4	Clark (4)
Wheat straw	30.5	28.4	18.0	3.5	11.0	" (4)
Rice straw	32.1	24.0	12.5	4.6	17.5	" (4)
Bamboo	nd	19.6	20.1	1.2	3.3	" (4)
Cotton	80-95	5-20	nd	nd	nd	Cowling & Kirk (6)
Municipal refuse	76	nd	nd	nd	nd	Dunlop (8)

nd = no data given

Lignin from hard- and softwoods is much more available where there is forestry close to agriculture and there has been much interest in lignin biodegradation in the USA where there is much hardwood and softwood bark available.

2. LIGNOCELLULOLYSIS

At least three types of enzymes are involved in the biodegradation of cellulose in fungi.

Cellulose

Exo-β-1,4-glucanase (EC 3.2.1.91)   Endo-β-1,4-glucanase (EC 3.2.1.4)
(also known as cellobiohydrolase   (also known as carboxymethyl-
and C_1 component)   cellulase) and C_x component)
- Hydrolyses amorphous and   - Hydrolyses soluble cellulose
  microcrystalline cellulose)   derivatives

Cellobiose

β-glucosidase (EC 3.2.1.21)
(also known as cellobiase)
- Hydrolyses cellobiose and
cellodextrins

Glucose

It has been demonstrated by Wood (39) that the various enzyme components of the complex can act synergistically. The nature and properties of these enzymes vary between the various cellulolytic organisms, which include aerobic and anaerobic fungi and bacteria (5, 21).

Xylan forms a large part of the hemicellulose in plants and therefore much attention has been focussed on endo-xylanases (β-1,4-D-xylan xylanohydrolase, EC 3.2.1.8). Far less is known about exo-xylanases. β-xylosidases (β-D-xyloside xylohydrolase, EC 3.2.1.37) have been characterised; these hydrolyse $\beta(1-4)$ links at the non-reducing ends of xylooligosaccharides and $\beta(1-4)$-aryl xylopyranosides to produce xylose.

The complexity of the lignin polymer has made studies on bio-degradation difficult. Two prominent theories have been put forward as mechanisms for lignin metabolism: (1) degradation by enzymes such as ligninases (37) and (2) oxidation by a non-specific 'active-oxygen' species such as singlet oxygen (13). These options are not necessarily exclusive. Many of the studies have concerned the biodegradation of wood and accordingly wood-rotting fungi, particularly Phanerochaete chrysosporium, have been the organisms of choice for study. However, there has also been an interest in actinomycetes (7), which are major components in mushroom (19) and presumably other composts.

There has been much excitement recently in the ligninase route of degradation because the identification of such a gene product opens the possibility of cloning suitable genes with elevated enzyme activity (30). This assumes that degradation of lignin is a rate-limiting step in ligno-cellulose biodegradation, which is not necessarily the case. Certainly in straw, there is degradation of a primary cellulosic fraction, without any ligninolytic activity (14). The secondary cellulosic fraction appears to be bound to lignin and it is here that elevated ligninolytic might be useful in hastening breakdown. However, in the production of a compost this is really only useful if disposal of waste is the main objective. Preliminary observations (D.M. Gaunt, A.P.J. Trinci and J.M. Lynch, unpublished) have shown no accelerated substrate breakdown in adding a ligninolytic actinomycete, Thermomonospora mesophila, to the strongly cellulolytic Trichoderma reesei on sterilized straw. Environmental, chemical, physical and temporal factors could be responsible for this lack of increased activity. In any event, acceleration of substrate decomposition would only be useful if composting is being used as a means of disposal.

Evidence that there can be synergistic enzyme activity, within the cellulase enzyme complex (39) suggests that a mixture of cellulolytic micro-organisms might be more effective in enhancing cellulolysis. However, studies using a mixture of cellulolytic species (Aspergillus fumigatus, 3 strains of Fusarium oxysporum, Gliocladium roseum, Penicillium lilacinus, P. nigricans, and P. simplicissium isolated as members of a cellulolytic community showed no enhanced cellulase activity compared with A. fumigatus and P. simplicissium alone (15). This lack of synergism could result from competition between members of the community for available nutrients such that the most active members gained less substrate than they did in pure culture. It could also be a consequence of antagonism between members of the community, for example by antibiotic production. There may also simply be a lack of co-operation in the degradation.

Positive co-operation would be likely to result if members of the community utilized glucose or cellobiose to prevent end-product inhibition of cellulases, thus increasing the rate of cellulolysis. Possibly bacteria or yeasts would achieve this more likely than fungi. However, when a cellobiose-utilizing yeast, Hansenula californica, was isolated and added to T. reesei in a defined model system with straw as substrate, no enhanced cellulolysis was evident (D.M. Gaunt, A.P.J. Trinci and J.M. Lynch, unpublished).

Another route to positive co-operation would be the provision of growth factors to the primary cellulose degraders. A positive interaction which has been identified is the co-operative action of Trichoderma harzianum with the anaerobic N_2-fixing bacterium Clostridium butyricum (27). The fungus provides simple sugars to the non-cellulolytic bacterium and the bacterium makes available the N_1 which fixes to the fungus, an observation confirmed using the tracer ^{15}N. In an N-limited environment, common in composts, the bacterium thus supports increased fungal biomass to generate more cellulase and hasten substrate decomposition. However the process, in the model system, is promoted by the addition of primer N at very low concentration (0.1 mg ml^{-1} $(NH_4)_2SO_4$) which could be responsible for the initial cellulase generation. It seems likely that this effect could also be obtained in practical composts, although it would be very difficult to achieve budgets of the nitrogen cycling because it would be almost impossible to apply an isotopic label and in a non-labelled state gaseous losses of N are difficult to measure.

Having identified a positive co-operation during lignocellulolysis, it should be recognized that a single species might have the necessary enzyme profile to deal with all the components of a substrate to be composted and that the objective would then be to achieve a non-axenic or selective state where that organism takes the major part of the available substrate. This is the objective in the production of mushroom composts where Agaricus bisporus forms a major part of the decomposer biomass after the composting stage. This organism is dependent on the initial decomposition by other organisms generating a suitable secondary substrate which is relatively stable and satisfactory for 'spawning' with A. bisporus (9, 10).

3. COMPOST ADDITIVES AND SUPPLEMENTS

Whereas there have been some attempts to generate horticultural composts by stabilizing lignocelluloses with chemical treatment, the normal objective is to biologically treat the materials to reduce the bulk. It is evident from Table I, that lignocelluloses themselves are very deficient in N and therefore do not provide a very favourable substrate for micro-organisms. A cheap source of N is usually required and animal wastes not only provide this but the process provides a satisfactory means for the disposal of these waste-products of agriculture. Table II gives some typical nutrient compositions of animal wastes. Most of the N is in the amino-form and conditions of composting must be controlled to avoid the rapid loss of this in ammonification. It should also be noted that ammonia can be fungistatic (18) and the risk would be in depressing the activity of the cellulolytic decomposers. The animal wastes contribute more lignocellulose to the existing pool and also contribute useful amounts of minerals to favour microbial growth in the compost.

The amino acids of the animal wastes may be a useful source of growth factors for the decomposer micro-organisms. However the amino acids are usually present as proteins. A selection of other proteinaceous materials has been used to supplement mushroom composts; the supplements also provide a source of carbohydrates and fats (oils) (31). This is particularly relevant to the utilization of the stabilised compost where productivity of the inoculated lignocellulolytic edible fungus will depend in part on its production of proteases and lipases. A relatively recent innovation to mushroom supplements is the introduction of delayed-release nutrients. The scientific evidence was published by Carrol and Schisler (1) and has been the subject of a patent (U.S. Patent No. 3,942,969). In the primary application, a derivative of cotton-seed meal was blended with peanut oil, spray-dried and then treated with 10% formaldehyde to denature the protein. It was assumed the denaturation inhibited the utilization of the protein by 'weed' moulds (fungi other than A. bisporus), so that when the mushroom mycelium became dominant in the compost two weeks after spawning, it could utilize the slowly-available lipo-protein supplement throughout the cropping period. Stoller (35) however has indicated that the suppression of the weed moulds could be due to residual formaldehyde. Other forms of denatured protein can generate similar effects and a cost-benefit analysis is usually positive in terms of yield increase of mushrooms, which is a high-value product relative to any other compost products. However, the cost of the supplementation is quite high because the denaturation process is covered by the patent. Thus whereas such delayed-release supplements might be useful in other composts, at the present prices, it seems unlikely that supplementation of this kind would be economic.

184

Table II. Typical nutrient composition of animal wastes
(after Shuler (33). All figures are percentages except those asterisked which are mg kg^{-1}

Component	Cattle manure	Swine waste	Broiler litter
Total dry matter	91.6		84
Crude protein	13.5	20	30
True protein		15.6	15
Crude fibre	31	14.8	17
Lignin	9.4		
Cellulose	30.3		
Hemicellulose	26.1		
Ether extract	2.8	7.0	3.4
Ash	6	18	17
Ca	0.95	3.1	2.4
P	0.8	2.4	1.9
Na			0.54
K	0.5	1.3	1.78
Mg	0.4	0.8	0.45
S		0.3	
Cu*	31	220	98
Fe*	1340	1940	451
Mn*	147	342	225
Zn*	242	530	235
Al*		544	284
Bo*			38
Cd*		1.0	
Mo*		0.3	
Pb*		12.1	
Amino acids			
Aspartic acid	0.71	1.68	1.22
Threonine	0.29	0.78	0.57
Serine	0.24	0.69	0.57
Glutamic acid	0.62	2.18	2.19
Proline	0.29	0.81	0.93
Glycine	0.44	0.97	2.14
Alanine	0.65	1.51	0.88
Valine	0.38	0.85	0.82
Cystine		0.30	0.09
Methionine	0.09	0.38	0.13
Isoleucine	0.21	0.73	0.64
Leucine	0.03	1.48	1.0
Tyrosine		0.65	0.33
Phenylalanine	0.00	0.83	0.54
Lysine	0.47	1.02	0.57
Histidine	0.12	0.29	0.24
Arginine	0.18	0.58	0.51

4. PRODUCTS OF LIGNOCELLULOLYSIS

Efficient aerobic lignocellulolysis would result in complete conversion of the substrates to carbon dioxide, usually through sugar intermediates. However, this total catabolism never occurs in composts, in part due to the recalcitrant nature of some of the components. In much simplified pathways, the following biochemical processes during the fermentation (anaerobic breakdown) of cellulose and hemicellulose.

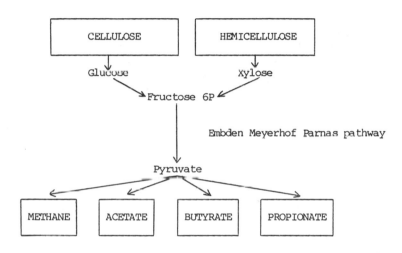

These pathways have been well-characterised for rumen bacteria (20) which is an ecological niche that has received more attention from biochemists than any other niche where lignocellulolysis is occurring. However, the pathway appears to be the same in other ecological niches; these include sewage digestor, silage, plant residue decomposition in wet soils as well as composts. The problem in composts to be used in agriculture or horticulture is if organic acids result from the fermentation of pyruvate because these acids are phytotoxic (22, 36). Much is now known about the mechanism and field significance of these toxins which arise when straw degrades in the soil (24). Of particular significance for composts is that the acids are only formed at redox potentials around zero and they are usually responsible for the sweet smell of composts, a 'danger signal' for a poorly prepared compost which will likely have an adverse effect on plants. The appearance of these steam-volatile fatty acids is a different problem in sewage digestors where methane is a product and used to fuel the plant because it is indicative of the fermentation 'sticking' and not reaching a sufficiently low redox potential for the generation of methane. Thus one major reason for aeration of composts is to elevate the redox potential above that which is conducive to organic acid formation. The redox potential can also be elevated by the addition of nitrate as an alternative electron acceptor to oxygen, but this is unlikely to be economic in a compost. Simultaneous with the formation of the organic acid and the lowered redox potential, iron and manganese enter their reduced state and are solubilized. Thus whereas the availability of these minerals is increased, the reduced state may be toxic to some plants, a point worthy of attention.

When straw decomposes in soil, acetic acid production continues until only 21.5 percent of the straw remains as polysaccharides but in practice, phytotoxic concentrations of the acid (5 mM at pH 6.5, equivalent to 0.1 m moles g^{-1} straw (22)) do not accumulate after approximately 50 percent of these components have been decomposed (14). There is thus a temporal factor governing phytotoxin production which will be relevant to the stabilization of a compost satisfactory as a plant growth medium.

In the breakdown of lignin, there is the potential for phenolic acids to form and these, on a molar basis, are more phytotoxic than the aliphatic acids (23). However, as the lignin is present in lower concentrations than the celluloses in lignocellulose and as its decomposition rate constant (0.0005 d^{-1}) is very low compared with cellulose and hemicellulose (0.007 d^{-1}) (14), only low concentrations of soluble phenolics accumulate and their contribution to the phytotoxicity from straw is small by comparison with the aliphatic acids (22). With other lignocelluloses, such as wood, they may play a more important role.

Although some of the primary products of lignocellulolysis may be phytotoxic, some of the secondary products may be indirectly beneficial to plant growth. It has been recognized that straw and other substrates are useful for the production of the antibiotic, patulin (anhydro-3-hydroxymethylene tetrahydro-1:4-pyrone-2-carboxylic acid) by Penicillium patulum, Aspergillus clavatus and A. terreus respectively (12) and that this antibiotic has the potential to control damping-off diseases of plants. Trichoderma harzianum has a very powerful cellulase enzyme complement to utilise available substrates as a saprophyte, produces the volatile antibiotic, 6-pentyl- γ -pyrone (N. Claydon and J. Hanson, unpublished) and work in my Department (J.M. Lynch, M.H. Ebben, J.M. Whipps, P. Hand, N. Magan and C. Ridout, unpublished) has shown that T. harzianum can be grown on straw and is a broad spectrum biocontrol agent; this is consistent with studies elsewhere (29).

One of the major attributes of composts which is claimed to be of benefit in agriculture and horticulture is the ability to provide a suitable physical medium for plant growth. In this respect however it should be recognized that most horticultural 'composts' do not contain composted material but refer to media containing suitable mixtures of mineral materials with peat. It is now generally considered that microbial polysaccharides are major agents in generating stable soil structure (25). Growth of bacteria, yeasts and fungi on straw can generate these agents from the cellulose and hemicellulose substrates (2, 3). The monomer composition of the polysaccharides, their molecular weights and intrinsic viscosity and ability to aggregate soils depends on the micro-organism or groups of organisms inoculated onto the straw. The metabolism of lignin might lead to the formation of the similarly complex polymers of humic and fulvic acids. These can also be important in soil structure formation because clays have affinity for humic substances (16).

5. CONCLUSION: THE POTENTIAL OF COMPOST INOCULANTS

The idea of inoculating composts with micro-organisms to direct the pathways of lignocellulolysis in favourable directions is appealing. For example the rate of phytotoxin production from straw can be hastened and length of production period reduced by inoculation in non-axenic model systems (26) but this has not been tested on a practical scale. In principle the challenge may seem immense because the size of the microbial biomass in the compost is large in relation to the inoculant. However, even though the biomass of mushroom compost was found to be c. 2% w/w of the established compost prior to spawning (34) the subsequent inoculation with A. bisporus yields about 250 kg fresh fruit bodies per tonne of fresh compost, indicating the dominance of A. bisporus in substrate utilization and in degrading the biomass of the compost (9, 10). There is thus scope for this approach with other types of composts, particularly for the introduction of biocontrol agents. Bark composts have already shown great potential in the suppression of disease (17) even without inoculants and the scope for developments in this direction appears to be very great. It seems that inoculation of a stabilised compost after the primary composting has occurred may offer greater scope for the inoculant to dominate the total biomass than inoculation into non-degraded materials. However, for this potential to be realised much more investigation is necessary at both the fundamental and more practical levels.

Acknowledgements. Part of this work was funded under the CEC contract RUW-033-UK. Helpful comments by Dr D.A. Wood are appreciated.

REFERENCES

(1)   CARROLL, A.D. and SCHISLER, L.C. (1976). A delayed release nutrient for mushroom culture. Applied and Environmental Microbiology 31, 499-503.
(2)   CHAPMAN, S.J. and LYNCH, J.M. (1985). Some properties of micro-organisms from degraded straw. Enzyme & Microbial Technology 7, 161-163.
(3)   CHAPMAN, S.J. and LYNCH, J.M. (1985). Polysaccharide synthesis by capsular micro-organisms in co-culture with cellulolytic fungi on straw and stabilization of soil aggregates. Biology & Fertility of Soils 1, 161-166.
(4)   CLARK, T.F. (1969). Cited by Brown, D.E. (1983). Lignocellulose hydrolysis. Philosophical Transactions of the Royal Society of London B300, 305-322.
(5)   COUGHLAN, M.P. (1985). The properties of fungal and bacterial cellulases with comment on their production and application. Biotechnology and Genetic Engineering Reviews 3, 39-109.
(6)   COWLING, E.B. and KIRK, T.K. (1976). Properties of cellulose and lignocellulosic materials as substrates for enzymatic conversion processes. Biotechnology and Bioengineering Symposium 6, 95-123.
(7)   CRAWFORD, R.L. and CRAWFORD, D.L. (1984). Recent advances in studies of the mechanisms of microbial degradation of lignins. Enzyme and Microbial Technology 6, 433-480.
(8)   DUNLAP, C.E. (1981). Comparative evaluation of cellulose resources. In: Proceedings of the Bioconversion and Bioengineering Symposium pp. 397-412. I.I.T., Delhi.
(9)   FERMOR, T.R. and WOOD, D.A. (1981). Degradation of bacteria by Agaricus bisporus and other fungi. Journal of General Microbiology 126, 377-387.
(10)   FLEGG, P.B., SPENCER, D.M. and WOOD, D.A. (ed.) (1985). The Biology and Technology of the Cultivated Mushroom. John Wiley, Chichester.

(11) FREUDENBERG, K. (1965). Lignin: its constitution and formation from p-hydroxycinnamyl alcohols. Science 148, 595–600.

(12) GROSSBARD, E. (1952). Antibiotic production by fungi on organic manures in soil. Journal of General Microbiology 6, 295–310.

(13) HALL, P.L. (1980). Enzymatic transformation of lignin. Enzyme and Microbial Technology 2, 170–176.

(14) HARPER, S.H.T. and LYNCH, J.M. (1981). The kinetics of straw decomposition in relation to its potential to produce the phytotoxin acetic acid. Journal of Soil Science 32, 627–637.

(15) HARRISON, L.A. (1985). The characterisation of a microbial cellulolytic community isolated from soil. PhD Thesis, University of Warwick.

(16) HAYES, M.H.B. (1980). The role of natural and synthetic polymers in stabilizing soil aggregates. In: Microbial Adhesion to Surfaces, pp. 263–296. Ed. R.C.W. Berkeley, J.M. Lynch, J. Melling, P.R. Rutter and B. Vincent. Ellis Horwood, Chichester.

(17) HOITINCK, H.A.J. (1980). Composted bark, a lightweight growth medium with fungicidal properties. Plant Disease 64, 142–147.

(18) KO, W.H., HORA, F.K. and HERLICKSA, E. (1974). Isolation and identification of a volatile fungistatic substance from alkaline soil. Phytopathology 64, 1398–1400.

(19) LACEY, J. (1973). Actinomycetes in soils, composts and fodders. In: Actinomycetales: Characteristics and Practical Importance, pp. 231–251. Eds. G. Sykes and F.A. Skinner. Academic Press, London.

(20) LATHAM, M.J. (1979). The animal as an environment. In: Microbial Ecology. A Conceptual Approach, pp. 115–137. Blackwell Scientific Publications, Oxford.

(21) LJUNGDAHL, L.G. and ERIKKSON, K.-E. (1985). Ecology of microbial cellulose degradation. Advances in Microbial Ecology 8, 237–299.

(22) LYNCH, J.M. (1977). Phytotoxicity of acetic acid produced in the anaerobic decomposition of wheat straw. Journal of Applied Bacteriology 42, 81–87.

(23) LYNCH, J.M. (1980). Effects of organic acids on the germination of seeds and growth of seedlings. Plant Cell & Environment 3, 255–259.

(24) LYNCH, J.M. (1983). Soil Biotechnology. Microbiological Factors in Crop Productivity. Blackwell Scientific Publications, Oxford.

(25) LYNCH, J.M. and BRAGG, E. (1984). Micro-organisms and soil aggregate stability. Advances in Soil Science 2, 133–172.

(26) LYNCH, J.M. and ELLIOTT, L.F. (1983). Minimizing the potential phytotoxicity of wheat straw by microbial degradation. Soil Biology & Biochemistry 15, 221–222.

(27) LYNCH, J.M. and HARPER, S.H.T. (1985). The microbial upgrading of straw for agricultural use. Philosophical Transactions of the Royal Society of London B310, 221–226.

(28) LYNCH, J.M. and WOOD, D.A. (1984). Controlled microbial degradation of lignocellulose: the basis for existing and novel approaches to composting. In: Composting Agricultural and Other Wastes, pp. 183–193. Ed. J.K.R. Gasser. London, Elsevier.

(29) PAPAVIZAS, G.C. (1985). Trichoderma and Gliocladium: Biology, ecology and potential for biocontrol. Annual Review of Phytopathology 23, 23–54.

(30) PATTERSON, A. McCARTHY, A.J. and BRODA, P. (1984). The application of molecular biology to lignin degradation. In: Microbiological Methods for Environmental Biotechnology, pp. 33–68. Eds. J.M. Grainger and J.M. Lynch. Academic Press, London.

(31) RANDLE, P.E. (1983). Supplementation of mushroom composts – a review. Crop Research 23, 51–69.

(32) RYDHOLM, S.A. (1965). Cited by Brown, D.E. (1983). Lignocellulose hydrolysis. Philosophical Transactions of the Royal Society of London B300, 305–322.

(33) SHULER, M.L. (1980). Utilization of farm wastes for food. In: Utilization and Recycle of Agricultural Wastes and Residues, pp. 67–133. Ed. M.L. Shuler. CRC Press, Boca Raton.

(34) SPARLING, G.P., FERMOR. T.R. and WOOD, D.A. (1982). Measurement of the microbial biomass in composted wheat straw, and the possible contribution of the biomass to the nutrition of Agaricus bisporus. Soil Biology & Biochemistry 14, 609–611.

(35) STOLLER, B.B. (1979). Synthetic casing for mushroom beds. Mushroom Science 10, 187–216.

(36) TANG, C.S. and WAISS, A.C. (1978). Short-chain fatty acids as growth inhibitors in decomposing wheat straw. Journal of Chemical Ecology 4, 225–232.

(37) TIEN, M. and KIRK, T.K. (1984). Lignin degrading enzyme from the hymenomycete Phanerochaete chrysosporium Burds. Science 221, 661–663.

(38) WHITE, D.J. (ed.) (1984). Straw Disposal and Utilisation. A Review of Knowledge. Ministry of Agriculture, Fisheries and Food, London.

(39) WOOD, T.M. and McCRAE, S.I. (1978). The mechanism of cellulase action with particular reference to the C_1 Component. In: Bioconversion of Cellulosic Substances in Energy, Chemicals and Microbial Protein, pp. 111–141. Ed. T.K. Ghose. ITT, Delhi.

LIGNIN METABOLISM IN THE SOILS AMENDED WITH COMPOST

G.Giovannozzi-Sermanni

Agric. Chem. Institute of the University of Tuscia. Viterbo
(Italy).

Summary

In the present paper few details are given on the metabolism
of the lignins during the degradation of the plant materials
in the soils or during the composting.
The referred data, most of them obtained in the author's
Institute, suggest the fondamental importance of studying the
ligninolysis since it is the slowest process of degradation
of plant matter (lignins, cellulose, hemicellulose, proteins,
nucleic acids) whereas the lignin is the most abundant
macromolecule for the humus biosynthesis.

1.Introduction

The fertility of the soils, seen as capacity to support the
growth of the plants, is due to few their fondamental
characteristics: presence of the water, well-balanced
concentration of the elements, right porosity.
In the soils the oxygen tension, pH, temperature and water
content vary from microsite to microsite both in space and
time so that the rate of the recycling of the organic matter
can change considerably from quantitative and qualitative
points of view.
Since the porosity is due to the relationships among solid
particles like sand, lime, humic substances and clays, their
mixture determine the oxygen availability and the water
content, necessary for the biological activities.
As consequence the fertility of the soils depends on the
quality of the components and in turn of the quality of
organic matter.
By focusing the attention on the humic substances, the
difficulty to study their chemical and biochemical
characteristics is well-known, since the humic substances are
compounds having different chemical structure and largely
different molecular weigths, as described by many
reviews(1,2,3,). Nevertheless one characteristic seems to be
present always, namely an aromatic core.
Because the plant materials are transformed into humus,
lignins, aromatic aminoacids, nucleic acids can be considered
as the main molecules utilized for the humus biosynthesis.
However many fungi are able to synthetize phenolic lydroxy
aromatic acids from non aromatic C-sources and the dark
colored substances show resistence to microbial
decomposition, exchange capacity, total acidity, elemental
analysis and molecular weights, properties of soil humic
acids.

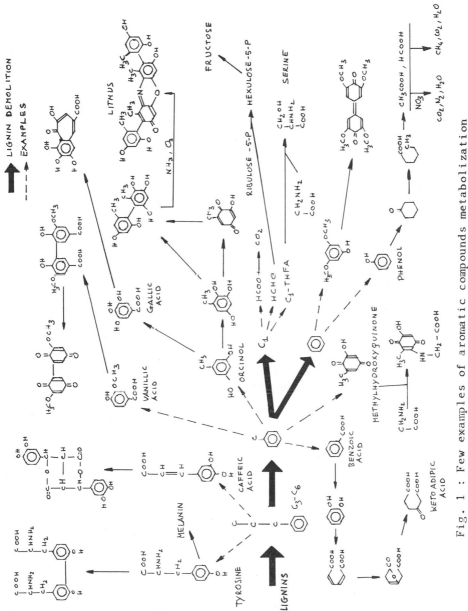

Fig. 1 : Few examples of aromatic compounds metabolization

2. Ligninolysis

The lignin is the most abundant macromolecule in the world and therefore it seems that the comprehension of the lignin degradation will give important details on the first steps of the humus biosynthesis and its good quality for the soil fertility.

The lignin is a net of propanoid-phenolic units linked by means of C-C and C-O bonds. The propanoid-phenolic units are relatively few, namely the cinnamic acids. Their percentage in the lignins can vary so that different kinds of lignins are present in different plants: the lignins of the conifers contain relatively high amounts of synapyl alcohol, those of herbaceus plants contain p-coumaric units as well as conyferyl and sinapyl alcohols. The % of different monomers gives different resistance to the biodegradation.

The lignins, freed of their linkages with cellulose during the decomposition of plant residues, are subjected in presence of oxygen to a slow oxidative splitting with the formation of structural units, derivatives of phenylpropane, whereas it is biologically inert in anaerobic environments. During the lignin decomposition in soils vanillic, p-hydroxy benzoic, ferulic acids, conyferylaldheide and other phenols are released.

The side chains of lignin-building units are demethylated, oxidized and the phenol groups are converted to quinones. Quinones react with N-containing compounds to form dark-colored polymers.

Brown nitrogenous polymers are produced also by condensation of reducing sugars with aminoacids or amines. After the formation of a Schiff base, the subsequent glycosylammine undergoes rearrangements to form molecules highly reactive which polymerize readily in presence of amino compounds to form brown colored compounds, e.g. humic and fulvic acids.

The number of molecules and the possible combinations of reactions give an astronomic number of possibilities, thereby accounting for the heterogeneous nature of the natural humus. In the fig 1 only few reactions are reported, choosen among the enormous amount of literature data concerning chemical and biochemical reactions, to point out few main points:

-the structural units of the lignins can be utilized for dimeric or polimeric reactions and degraded, giving structures of interest for humus formation.

-the C_6-C_1 units like vanillic, gallic and benzoic acids can give polymeric compounds or be oxydized to alifatic compounds, which will be easily respired,

-aromatic nucleus can polymerize or give aliphatic compounds.

-the formation of alifatic molecules, like acetic and formic acids may enter in well-known biochemical pathways for a great variety of biosynthesis.

-in presence of nitrate as oxygen donor the acids are oxydized, giving carbon dioxide, nitrogen and water, but in anaerobic conditions methane formation occurs.

-the C_1 units can be utilized for sugars and aminoacids biosynthesis through THFA mechanism.

-the importance of the nitrogen compounds is shown by the

formation of typical nitrogen and oxygen bridges found in humic substances. Howewer until now no clear evidence for ligases catalyzing the bonds formation has been obtained.
The ligninolysis seems to be dependent, besides by oxygen pressure, also by water content of the humifying system: modified lignin biosynthesis may predominate in poorly drained soils and wet sediments (swamps), whereas synthesis from poliphenols in leachates from leaf litter may be of considerable importance in certain forest soils.
Among the most important humifying organisms of the soils and capable to utilize lignins and cellulose, the fungy have been more extensively studied since they are of interest also as food-producers (mushrooms).
Their growth on solid substrates is dependent by water content as shown by Agaricus hyphae, which have their optimum growth at the 75% of water content, roughly.
The importance of water content may be due to the changes of porosity of the compost, i.e. the oxygen content and carbon dioxide exchanges and to CO_2 dissolution which affects the pH value, to which the mycelia are rather sensitive.
The straw humification, studied by changing the nutritive and ecological conditions for the mycelia growth appears as an interesting tool to understand the humus biochemistry.

3.Apparatus for the degradation studies

Fig 2 presents an home-made device with which is possible to follow the straw degradation in sterile conditions (4). The device has the possibility to take samples under sterile conditions, to analyze the atmosphere composition and to control the fermentation temperature.

Fig. 2 : Home-made solid-state fermentor

4.Fungal physiology.

During the first week of fermentation, the oxygen and carbon dioxide concentrations change heavily as an index of very active metabolism, probably due to the necessity to prepare soluble substrate for the cell biosynthesis (fig 3).

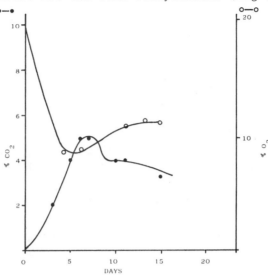

Fig. 3 : Atmosphere composition during PLEUROTUS growth on straw

Infact soluble lignins are formed during the fermentation and can be obtained from clear liquid extracts by means of HCl pH=1 as brown precipitate. Its fractioning on Sephadex G 100 column shows fractions of different molecular weights, ranging from 9000 to over 100000. (fig 4).

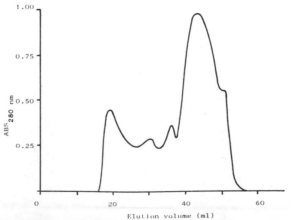

Fig. 4 : SEPHADEX G 100 filtration of soluble lignin.
The peaks show the following molecular weights :
> 100000; 50000; 30000; 9000; 3000

At the same time laccase, a main enzyme for the lignin degradation (6), and cellulase reach the maximum of activity (fig 5).

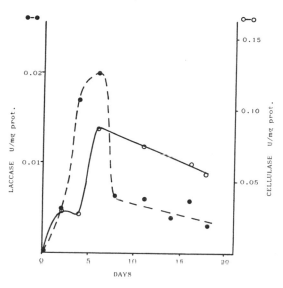

Fig. 5 : Laccase and cellulase activities during Pleurotus growth

The humic compounds seem to have importance as components of humic acids and as metabolites of fungy. Infact a greasy brown humus-like compost, suitable for the growth of Agaricus mycelium is obtained by fermentation of the straw by wild microflora, since it has been ascertained that the formation of N-rich humus complex is essential for its growth. (12), and a condensed ring aromatic compounds formed by microbes serve as structural units for soil humus formation and are present in the ascomycetes of Aspergillus niger or in the fruiting bodies of Daldinia concentrica (7,8,9).
Therefore it is difficult to consider the humus in the soils simply as a by-product of biological activities and not also as a way to mantain a given organic matter turnover.
5.The beginning of the lignin degradation
It is evident that different degradation rate can be related to the possibility of the enzymes to attach the chemical structure of the lignins.
The polyphenoloxidases are enzymes present in the plant cell with scarce substrate specificity. Few of them, the esocellular laccases, are very important for the metabolism of the lignin.
The laccases are oxyreductases which use the oxygen as acceptor of electrons, extracted from phenolic structures.
The flux of the electrons is due to the possibility of the Cu

atoms contained in the laccase protein, to be in divalent or monovalent forms.

In such way a phenoxy radical is produced which can give quinons, dimers, olygomers and formation or breakage of chemical bonds.

Therefore the initial degradation of the lignins appear to be strictely O_2-dependent.

The species able to attack the lignins -over 2000 species - can produce also peroxydases (ligninases) and super-oxyde dismutase (SOD) which are related to the oxygen metabolism i.e. to the lignin degradation, since literature data show that superoxide anion and hydrogen peroxide are involved in lignin degradation (11).

The peroxydases are, like the catalase, heme proteins which use hydrogen peroxyde as oxygen donor: the catalase produces water and oxygen, meanwhile the peroxydases oxydase organic matter.

The superoxide dismutases are Cu-Zn proteins, which catch the superoxide anion, normally present in the cells, produced during the reduction of the oxygen to water and very dangerous for the cells because destroys the membranes integrity with lost of the compartimentation.

SOD activity could be involved in the control of the lignin degradation in two ways: by producing hydrogen peroxide or by lowering the superoxide anion, both chemical species very active on the lignin attach.

By following our trials, laccase and SOD appear inversely related.

6.Conclusions

This lecture would not be a review of the trmendous amount of researches on the phenolic compounds biochemistry, but has the aim to stress that the straw degradation for mycelial growth and humus fermentation have many similarities as: oxygen needs, water content, the formation of brown compounds, the production of soluble lignins so that the straw/mycelia system appears to be a good model to study the humus formation.

A controlled straw degradation by means solid-state fermentation gives informations on the role of environmental parameters (oxygen, carbon dioxide, temperature, water, nutrients etc.) on the characteristics of biosynthetic humic compounds.

Our solide state fermentor permits to follow fairly well such changes in different environmental conditions.

It has been confirmed the role of oxygen pressure and related enzymes (poliphenol oxydase, peroxydases, superoxide dismutase) for the lignin solubilization, which occurs chiefly during the first week of the fermentation.

The increment of carbon dioxide concentration blocks the lignin degradation and enhances the cellulose hydrolysis since the cellulase degradation occurs at high CO_2 levels (10). Laccase and cellulase activities confirms this behaviour.

The increment of the SOD activity could be explained as an additional control of the ligninolysis.

As consequence of the above presented data, we can believe that the lignin metabolism in the soils amended with compost is strictly dependent by soil porosity and humidity, being

oxygen abundance necessary for the lignin degradation, whereas carbon dioxide favorites the cellulose utilization. Different exchanges between soil and atmosphere could give different degradation pathways not only for the changes of the microflora but, more simply, for the enzymatic activities.
Therefore CO_2 /O_2 ratio appear of fondamental interest for efficient plant material transformation and for the humus characteristics, even if the data on this matter are still scarce.

ACKNOWLEDGEMENTS
The A. wishes to express his gratitude to drs. M. Luna and M. Colognola for their help in the drawings and manuscripts preparation

REFERENCES

1. K. Haider, J.P. Martin, Z. Filip - Humus biochem. in: Soil Biochem. 4,195-245 - Ed E.A. Paul, A.D. McLarry, Marcel Dekker (1975).
2. D.S. Jenkinson - The fate of plant and animal residues in soils in: The Chemistry of Soil Processes 504-555 Ed. D.J. Greenland, H.B. Hayes.John Wiley & Son (1981).
3. F.S. Stevenson - Humus Chem. Jolu Wiley (1981).
4. G. Giovannozzi, M. Luna, M. Felici, F. Artemi, M. Badiani - Symp. on Mycelial Proteins - Waterloo-Canada (1985).
5. D.L. Crawford, A.L. Pometto, R.C. Crowford. Appl. Envir. Microb. 45, 898-904 (1983).
6. T. Jshihara - The role of laccase in lignin biodegradation. 2, 17-30, Ed. T.K. Kirk, T. Higuchi, H. Chany. CRC press (1980).
7. K. Kumada, O. Sato - Soil Sc. Pl. Nutr. 8,31 (1962).
8. K. Kumada   Soil Sc. Pl. Nutr. 11,181 (1965).
9. K. Kumada, O. Sato: J. Soc. Soil Manure (Japan) 36,373 (1965).
10. M.W. Platt, Y. Hadar, I. Chet - Appl. Microb. Biotecl. 20,150-154 (1984).
11. B.D. Faison, T. Kent Kirk - Appl. Environ. Microb. 46,1140-1145 (1983).
12. J.P.G., Gerrits, H.C. Bels-Koning: Mush. Sci. 7,112-126 Hamburg (1969).

HEALTH AND SAFETY ASPECTS OF COMPOST PREPARATION AND USE

by P. BOUTIN* and J. MOLINE**
(* CEMAGREF, B.P. 3, F 33610 CESTAS
** C.H.R., F 37044 TOURS, FRANCE)

Summary
A sanitary threat appears for people involved in compost processing and use, and for consumers of vegetables grown on compost enriched soils. This hazard arises from three sources of contamination :
- primary pathogens of intestinal origin,
- secondary pathogenic forms, mainly moulds, developed during processing and stocking, at first rank **A. fumigatus,**
- bacterial and fungal allergens and toxins.
Even recent studies bring insufficient data : it remains difficult to estimate the importance of contamination; processing specificities (pathogens natural decay, temperature x time relations), technical variants have to be taken into account. Concerned populations include consumers and compost users, and in the first place compost workers. At each stage of compost processing, mainly through the respiratory route, they are exposed to different associated hazards :
- bacterial, as in wastewater treatment plants,
- secondary fungal : the literature mentions an observation of **A. fumigatus** alveolitis followed by a probable invasive aspergillosis,
- immunological and toxinical mechanisms.
Infectious syndromes were described : besides a "sewage worker's syndrome", mainly linked to liquid materials, it seems now possible to distinguish a "compost worker's syndrome".
Risk prevention has to be undertaken with technical measures and particular occupational medical survey. Further long-term investigations are necessary for a better appreciation of risk extent.

IDENTIFICATION OF RISKS
        A potential sanitary threat appears for people involved in compost processing and use and for consumers of vegetables grown on compost enriched soils. This hazard arises from three possible sources of contamination (4) :
- primary pathogens of intestinal origin (bacteria, viruses, intestinal parasites cysts or eggs),
- secondary pathogenic forms, mainly moulds, developed during compost processing and stocking,
- bacterial and fungal allergens and toxins.
        The first source is linked to the faecal pollution of raw materials. This contamination is maximum for products incorporating high amounts of urban wastewater sludges or farm wastes, lower for household refuse composts, which are however soiled by human (baby disposable nappies) or animal (domestic pets litters) faeces. It is reduced for industrially processed composts of vegetable wastes (bark, sawdust, straw, etc.). Although applied treatments are generally able to reduce the initial load

of faecal microorganisms, the final contamination level of processed composts is usually related to it. Some enterobacteria are however supposed to be able to multiply in composts and so to behave partially as secondary pathogens.

The resultant nature of risk is similar to the hazard from handling and agricultural reuse of wastewater and sludges. Public health specialists first attended this classical form of risk, for it concerns also consumers and is not only a problem of occupational hygiene.

More specific is the second hazard, which results of the development of meso- and thermophilic fungi (and actinomycetes), which play a major role in compost preparation and maturation (2). Large amounts of spores and mycelian fragments are emitted as often garbage or compost is dumped or mechanically stirred (grinding, screening, pile turning, etc.). Some thermophilic forms are well-known as pathogens, **Aspergillus fumigatus** first, so common in dry sludges and compost.

The allergic hazard is not fully independent from the former : a number of thermophilic and some mesophilic fungi and actinomycetes from fermenting compost are renowned as antigen producing agents. Mycotoxin-producing species can equally induce a potential toxic hazard (1). Gram-negative bacteria are another source of antigenic substances (bacterial endotoxins), as first recognized more than ten years ago from sludge composts by Swedish researchers (30, 35).

AVAILABLE DATA

Development of studies
       Since these early studies, much work was done, more often as a development of waste water treatment plant studies (dried sludge handling, sludge composting), with the same scientific teams involved in. On the whole, data on refuse composting without admission of sludge are by far rarer than on water treatment sludges (3, 25). Exlusive garbage composting appears as a less widespread technique, with a yet limited production, a low number of involved workers and less evident hazards. Nevertheless, it is the common practice in several countries where sludge composting plants are exceptions. In this field, our global information appears still deficient, although Clark **et al.** point on that subject that the effects they have observed "may be due to the nature of the process itself and therefore may not be related to the use of waste water sludge in the composting operation" (12).
       The many planned plants are a sufficient justification to sum up the present situation and for further studies when necessary.

Epidemiological studies
       Positive epidemiological evidence is the best argument to conclude from potential hazard to actual risk. Consequently, several surveys on compost workers were started these last years. However, emphasis must be placed on possible biases, which may lead to some underestimation of long-term effects. In fact, many compost plant employees consider their job as temporarily accepted (for 2 or 3 years), while they look for a less hard, better paid and better regarded work. Executives are usually stabler in their employment. Such an unsteadiness makes long-term surveys difficult, many people vanishing before the end of the study. In addition, as soon as some possibly compost-related clinical symptoms are observed, doctors in charge of occupational medecine for the plant immediately request and obtain the employee to change his work for an unexposed environment.

CONTAMINATION INTENSITY

A methodological preamble

A preliminary problem results from difficulties to search for pathogens and indicator organisms, to identify and number them in such an heterogeneous (at the bacterial scale) solid material as garbage or compost. Standardized procedures are not defined or universally recognized, neither for sampling nor for sample preparation before microbiological analysis. The efficiency of usual methods for desaggregation of bacterial clusters from inert supports and individualization of cells is probably poor. So we certainly underestimate bacterial populations in composts, by an almost unknown amount. The same can be told for all pathogens.

The difficulty is similar for aerocontamination studies. With the classical Andersen impactor, viable dusts are counted, but not actual bacterial numbers, for each particle may bear several bacteria, about one hundred by mean in waste water aerosols according to Lundholm (26). Sampling efficiency is poor for large size particles.

Technically, the search for bacteria is worsened by the occurence of moulds which quickly invade plates, even with fungal growth limiting additives. In such conditions, the tube MPN technique is often preferable, but does not free from the hindrance of bacterial clustering.

All this makes difficult every comparison of processing results (and jeopardizes every standardization policy).

Intestinal pathogens in refuse and compost

There is probably no major difference between pathogens species present in sewage sludges and in faecally contaminated composts. So detailed and rather impressive lists drawn up for sludges (5, 18, 21) can be transported to composts. Corrections for contamination intensity must then be applied according to :
- sludge mixing with uncontaminated matters,
- temperature reached through thermophilic fermentation,
- natural decay during long time stocking.

The effects of temperature on pathogens were recently extensively reviewed (19). They give some security, as far as every particle is brought at the effecient temperature during enough time.

These phenomena, combined with analytical problems, lead usually to zero counts for most pathogens in industrially processed composts, what does not mean necessarily their total absence. Let us say that isolation of pathogens in well fermented composts is a technical success and a matter of chance as well. Knowledge on parasites occurrence is especially insufficient, in spite of their interest for public health.

That's why the notion of "indicator bacteria" was unanimously and successfully translated to composts, with the usual (and questionable) joint significances for faecal contamination and treatment efficiency. Specific adaptations are however studied to consider other germs than enterobacteria.

Fungi and actinomycetes in composts

Many moulds of health interest develop during garbage householding, compost processing and maturation. A dense mycelian layer develops 20-40 cm inside compost piles. Each conidial head can liberate hundreds of spores. Fungi were present in raw garbage too, but with lower densities. Sewage sludge mycoflora was studied by Diener, Morgan-Jones et al. (17), sludge and compost moulds by de Bertoldi (1). Very high counts of thermophilic filamentous fungi were obtained, with large dominance of **Aspergillus**

fumigatus. Less attention was paid to actinomycetes, although they are present in large amounts too (**2, 41**).

EVALUATION OF THE SANITARY RISK

Potential for occurrence of sanitary hazards

Compost may constitute a sanitary hazard at three stages (**4**) :
- processing, for compost workers, people around composting plants,
- use as an enriching agent for agriculture, horticulture, etc.,
- consumption of vegetables grown on compost enriched fields.

The demonstrated presence of pathogens equals a potential risk. The eventual occurrence of pathogens, when it may be suspected from abundance of faecal indicator bacteria, indicates a potential risk too, the actuality of which needs however to be evaluated.

Risk for consumers

Intensity of the actual risk from faecal pathogens must be estimated through several factors, in first the initial microbial density of compost, natural decay on the field, waiting period between compost spreading and crop harvesting, consumed part of the vegetable, preparation of produces (peeling, cooking, etc.), minimal and mean infective doses, seriousness of disease, etc.

In the absence of detailed studies in this area, comparisons with wastewater affords useful information. During years, the tendency was to severe standards for agricultural landspreading of urban wastewater. In 1971, proposals from a group of W.H.O. experts (less than 100 coliform organisms/100 ml) were not among the more restrictive regulations. Considerations upon infective doses (of the order of 10^4-10^6 for salmonellas, of 10^2 for viruses, but of 1 for intestinal worms) and "epidemiological evidence", the further implementation of a finalized epidemiological model led last year to the more permissive rules suggested by the "Engelberg Report" (less than 1000 faecal coliforms/100 ml as geometrical mean ; less than 1 viable nematode egg/1) (**43**). In fact this is a drastic revision, for bacterial limits are thus multiplied by a factor 50 in respect with the formerly accepted W.H.O. proposals. Even if these new rules may (and must) be discussed and adapted, such an evolution indicates that the faecal risk from waste reuse by agriculture must not be overestimated and that it was probably exaggerated during years by specialists.

Transposition to compost of models elaborated for evaluation of the actual risk from waste water agricultural reuse has not been yet tempted. Meanwhile it may be estimated that the risk level is low, according to pathogen density in compost and features of use : usually, compost is spread on field in autumn or spring, months before crop harvesting, then often superficially buried.

From our knowledge, no incident from this origin was described. As far as epidemiological evidence may be invoked (though, Oliver points, "negative epidemiological evidence is even less persuasive than most other kinds of negative evidence"), the corresponding level of risk is surely low, almost not detectable.

However, attention must be paid to compost use in greenhouses and mushroom caves. For hotbeds however, compost often replaces unstabilized farm manure, by far faecally more contaminated.

Risk for compost users

In open field, with occasional contacts only, risks from compost handling and spreading are probably low, except for predisposed or sensibilizated (atopic) people. Once more, it would be interesting and more revealing to study confined surroundings with intensive cultivation, as greenhouses and mushroom caves.

Although minor according to quantities involved, domestic utilizations of compost have to be examined. Compost is regularly used to fill pots for ornamental plants. A too common practice is to bring these pots into the kitchen and to water them on the sink. By this way, opportunity is offered to bacteria to contaminate food and then to multiplicate till to reach their infective dose. The hypothesis of sensibilization accidents has been evoked too, but the actuality of such a hazard lacks any demonstration.

Risk for compost workers

Workers are submitted to all classes of sanitary hazard, from pathogenic faecal germs, secondary fungal and bacterial pathogens and emitted antigens and toxins. Direct contact when handling raw or elaborated material is an unquestionably possible way, but we can probably consider it as secondary if we compare it to airborne contamination. Just a glance at a compost plant is enough to realize how dusty are the main work places, and what a kind of atmosphere workers breath 8 hours a day. Throughout compost processing, every mechanical operation emits dust, as well as wind erosion of dry piles.

Primary pathogens

That's why rather little attention has been given to consequences for compost workers from direct contact with microbially contaminated garbage, sludge or compost. Is this sufficient to indicate a factually minor or non existing problem ? As far as we can invocate current experiences from compost and waste water treatment plants, the answer is probably yes. Waste water workers, who are in close contact with faecally more contaminated matters, show only rare indices for a specific pathology from intestinal pathogens, in spite of large surveys (**6, 7** to **10, 29**).

Airborne bacterial contamination must be considered as a potential hazard too. The large-size part of bacterial dusts is stopped by the upper respiratory tract, and then eliminated by nose blowing and expectoration or swallowed. Many others reach the bronchial tubes, from which they are lifted by ciliated epithelia up to the throat. A third part may deposit into alveolae, where they are neutralized by physiological processes. Non stopped particles are reemitted by breathing. Inhaled bacteria (and viruses as well) can thus originate both a digestive risk through swallowing and a respiratory risk from particles reaching the deepest part of the pulmonary tree.

The risk is shared by wastewater workers, specially by activated sludge plants employees, to whom an important and well-documented literature was recently devoted (**6**). The pulmonary route for infective bacterial and viral agents was reviewed and discussed by Cliver (**15**), who concluded that "sewage aerosols are probably a relatively inefficient means of transmitting enteric infections".

For compost plants, a similar opinion is conforted by observed faecal bacteria densities. If high levels of bacterial contamination are noted, with for instance total counts as high as 18000 BVP/m3 at Beltsville for sludge compost (**15**), or even up to 10^5 BVP/m3 at some sites of french garbage processing plants (3), faecal bacteria amounts are by far lower : 724 and 1783 faecal coliforms and streptococci (BVP/m3) near the garbage dumping hopper at Joué-lès-Tours, 13 and 225 respectively at the top of the fermentation tower (with forced aeration), 10-30 elsewhere. American sources (11, 12) give comparable amounts, at which the presence of bacterial or viral pathogens is unlikely, even for resistant germs, unless abnormal contamination of raw material.

Secondary pathogens

The fungal respiratory threat originates from high densities of thermophilic ascomycetes (33). Direct pathogenicity of **Aspergillus fumigatus** and some other related forms is well known, and may lead to rather dramatic manifestations : saprophytic aspergillosis (fungal growth confined to bronchi) with expectoration of mucus and blood, even of fungus balls, or invasive aspergillosis (invasion of the pulmonary tissue, eventually dissemination **via** the circulatory system and colonization of other organs). **A. Fumigatus** is most often encountered in human pathology : 97 % of recorded cases, according to Perdrix et al. (34).

The respiratory tract usually clears rapidly from **Aspergillus** spores, alterated and phagocyted by alveolar macrophages. By this way, 90 % of inhalated conidia would be eliminated in 24 hours. Aspergillary attack depends on infectious power of moulds, linked to elastase production (24) and often too on the subject's general health status and immunity level. Preexisting bronchial, pulmonary or pleural lesions favour infestation.

Only one case of suspected pulmonary invasion by **A. Fumigatus** was reported, and accurately published by Vincken and Roels (42). A 20-year old compost plant worker, who started working two months before, ailed suddenly dispnoea, dry cough and fever. X-ray chest examination revealed a bilateral reticulonodular shadowing. Bacteriological examinations were negative. The patient received some corticotherapy and could leave hospital after a 10-day stay only. Three weeks later, he was visited at home by mates in their work clothes. Six hours after they left, the symptoms and signs he previously presented recurred and he had to be readmitted. Respiratory exploration showed very restricted functions. A test for serum precipitines against **A. fumigatus** was strongly positive, while precipitines against thermophilic actinomycetes, **Micropolyspora faeni** and other fungi were absent. The patient apparently recovered over 10 days but, a few later, he developped purulent sputum and haemoptysis, with high fever, diopnoea and respiratory failure again ; bronchial washing revealed **A. fumigatus**. This precise diagnosis allowed the patient to be intensively and successfully cured by antifungal antibiotics. On discharge from hospital, he evidently changed his job. He associated an evident allergic reaction (pulmonary extrinsic allergic alveolitis = PEAA) and a probable beginning invasive aspergillosis, favoured by the inflammatory reaction of lung tissue to previous PEAA. No immunodeficiency was detected, neither natural nor corticotherapy-induced by the earlier treatment. Incidentally, this case evidences the vector role of work clothes, formerly evoqued by Strauch (40).

Clark et al. report less serious cases : chronic otitis with **A. niger** isolated from purulent discharge from the ear, and some shadows in both lungs (11), three skin rashes related to fungal infections (12).

Allergens

Indices are available of antigenic troubles from bacterial and fungal antibodies and allergens, produced by Gram-negative bacteria, actinomycetes and fungi present in composted matters.

The allergenic aspergillary syndrome is well-known from other occupational situations :

- for sensibilizated (atopic) subjects, broncho-pulmonary aspergillosis, with asthma, lung infiltration, eosinophily, immunitary reactions ; it may be induced by low amounts of **Aspergillus** spores,
- for non-atopic subjects, extrinsic allergic alveolitis, following a heavy breathing of **Aspergillus** conidia as antigen source, and possibly developing as fibrosis if repeated ; both may predispose to invasive aspergillosis.

In Swedish composting plants, Clark et al. found astonishing concentrations of **A. fumigatus** spores, commonly larger than 10^6 FVP/m3 (**13**). Lower counts are given at work locations, inside and outside, by Kothary et al. (**23**), Millner et al. (**32**), Clark et al. (**12**), Boutin et al. (**3**), with maximums less than 10^5 FVP/m3.

In spite of rather impressive figures for fungal aerocontamination and positive cultures for **A. fumigatus** from the nares and throat of compost workers, Clark et al. quote from their survey : "a pool of antigens prepared from **A. fumigatus, A. flavus, A. carneus** and **A. niger** was not detected in the sera obtained from any of the study participants. These results suggest that serologically-detectable infections caused by these fungi were uncommon among the workers studied" (**12**). With such a lack of evidenced cases, it may be of interest to mention an isolated positive test for precipitines against **A. fumigatus,** without clinical signs, for a worker in charge of dry sludge handling and loading at waste water plants (**16**).

An actinomycetes-induced potential hazard may be infered from both presence of many pathogenic species in sludges (**1**), and in compost (**40**), and actual pathology observed at other jobs which implicate fermenting matters handling (farmer's lung, mushroom worker's lung, bagassosis, etc.). Nothing clear was yet mentioned for compost workers. In the same way, the threat for a toxic hazard was hypothesized, following the identification of mycotoxin-producing fungi. The common **A. flavus** secretes volatile aflatoxins, possibly liable to be inhalated by workers or to reach the food-chain through compost-grown vegetables or fodders (**1**). All this deserves further confirmation.

We are on a more certain ground with the pathogenic role of common gram-negative bacteria. More than ten years ago, Mattsby and Rylander (**30**) first observed (1975) and then described (1978) a series of ailments (diarrhoea, eye inflammation, asthenia, etc.) commonly affecting employees involved in sludge drying, powdering and handling. High levels of dusts were observed at work places (0,5-4 mg/m3, sometimes more). Among the 10^4-10^7 BVP/m3 of air, gram-negative bacteria widely predominated. During intense dust episodes, 30 to 50 % of workers suffer fever, shivering, purulent eye inflammation, 13 % occasional diarrhoea. Symptoms seem dose-related. They disappear rapidly, generally the next day, but they give way to persistent asthenia. Immunologic marks are noted (IgA, IgC, **E. coli** endotoxin antibodies, etc.). The authors attribute these phenomena to gram-negative bacteria endotoxins liberated by cell destruction.

A few later, Rylander et al. describe first the "sewage worker's syndrome" (**35**), designation which became rapidly popular (**8**). Their hypothesis was strengthened by an oriented review of previous literature on this field (**29**). Above all, large scale studies by Clark et al. concerning waste water workers confirmed soon the factuality and general occurrence of the ailments (**7, 9, 10**). Other epidemiological studies of interest were performed in Sweden by Rylander and Lundholm (**37**).

Probably even more related to our purpose are surveys of sludge composting plants employees. In 1978, Lundholm and Rylander (**27**) examined eleven workers of an experimental plant where sludges and refuse were fermented together. They evidenced large amounts of gram-negative bacteria in the air near the piles, which they connected to the typical symptoms (nausea, head-ache, fever, shivering, diarrhea) presented by four of the workers. The suspected agent is bacterial endotoxin. The immunitary response of laboratory animals after breathing air suspended lipopolysaccharids was assessed by Rylander and Snella (38), who demonstrated high levels of specific IgG, IgM and IgA in the sera of exposed rats. A broncho-pulmonary washing revealed high levels of IgA and IgG against **E. coli** endotoxins. The actuality of reaction to inhaled endotoxins was thus experimentally confirmed, with the form of an acute inflammatory response. If persisting, it may result in an attack of the lung parenchyma, as observed in cotton mill workers.

Rylander et al. observe elsewhere (39) that "fever and influenza-like symptoms observed are typical of those which would be expected after inhalation of airborne endotoxin". They also point that, with common levels of dust and exposure (0,5 mg dust/m3, 8 hours, 50 % pulmonary deposition), the estimated inhalated dose for endotoxins is "10 times higher than the threshold for fever after an intravenous injection".

From the important survey conducted on sludge handling workers by Clark et al. (**11, 12, 14**), it is drawn that levels of specific IgG antibodies against lipopolysaccharids prepared from compost were significantly higher in compost workers from two plants out of three. Abnormal rates of skin disease, ear and nose conditions were found among compost workers and intermediate-exposed subjects.

The Swedish and American authors synthesized their observations by identifying a major group of clinical signs for compost workers, associating more or less regularly fever, influenza-like symptoms, upper respiratory airways irritation, eye inflammation otitis, asthenia. Waste water and liquid sludge workers present a different set, more related to the gastro-intestinal tract (diarrhea) ; skin and eye irritation are commonly found, as well as weariness (39).

From these findings, is it now possible to distinguish a "compost worker's syndrome" from a revised "sewage worker's syndrome", restricted to people in close contact with liquid matters ?

RISK PREVENTION

Concerned populations

From this review, it is clear that compost workers are actually exposed to some hazard. It is rather risky to suggest an evaluation of concerned employees numbers, now and in the future.

In France, where less than 100 refuse composting plants are effectively working (and some sludge composting systems), we can estimate that 1,000 people at most are presently involved. At a rough guess, this leads to numbers about 3,000-4,000 at equilibrium for refuse treatment, 5,000 if sludges are usually admitted (less than 1/10,000 of the general population). If we feel authorized to extrapolate such figures to the whole E.E.C., the result is high enough to justify complementary research and development of occupational risk prevention. We can add that every people working on refuse facilities (sanitary landfills, incineration plants) are equally concerned, for the sanitary hazard to which they are currently exposed differs only by degree, not by nature to what happens on compost plants.

Risk prevention passes through technical and health actions, to be simultaneously undertaken.

Technical measures

 It would be unrealistic to claim compost preparation to become dustless. It is equally fanciful to require workers to continuously wear uncomfortable equipment, as goggles or respiratory masks : dust deposits on glasses, irritation of skin by sweat-mixed dust, breathing and moving discomfort lead quickly the employees to take them off. Instruction edicters must be aware of actual work conditions on plants...

 The same obligation is required from process designers. Avoidable technical unsuitabilities result in an increased sanitary hazard. It is truly difficult to limit dust emission, but some practical corrective measures may be proposed, among many others :
- to prohibit hand sorting of refuse (although some workers think they find occasionally advantage in this operation),
- to enclose the main dust emitting devices (grinders, trommels, screens, hoppers, conveyors, etc.), and in the same time to succeed them not to stuff repeatedly, and thus to limit the number of manual interventions to put them in working order again,
- to equip as often as possible refuse and compost handling places with superpressured cabins supplied with fresh filtered air,
- to favour dust dilution by easy air circulation (sheds instead of closed premises),
- to avoid confusion between process premises and technical or hygiene rooms (office, mechanical workshop, changing room, etc), preferably to be isolated, etc.

 Discipline is necessary for personal hygiene, work clothes changing and cleaning, etc. Corresponding facilities must be easily and liberally accessible.

Medical survey

 Occupational medecine specialists in charge of the survey of compost workers must be conscious of the specificities of such a job. Classical preventive measures (personal hygiene, vaccination) are evident, but some other precautions have to be taken.

 Before taking on, because of the main nature of risk from compost, the examination of applicants must be oriented to detect subjects :
- with a previous pulmonary affection or surgical operation,
- presenting an atopic ground (asthma, allergic disorders),
- submitted to a long-term corticotherapy or other immunodepressing treatments,
- naturally immunodepressed (diabetic patients).

 Heavy smoking, at most when associated with high alcohol consumption, is a significant factor to consider too. It is of the responsability of occupational physicians to decide if such precedents are, by nature and degree, compatible with recruitment.

 Subsequent periodical examination must be oriented according to possible detection of occupational diseases. Statements by Gellin and Zavon (20) on solid waste collectors illustrate clearly at once the consequences of unoriented, all-purpose medical tests and the attitude of many workers considering their common minor occupational diseases. After they examined 97 subjects, the authors contacted the two physicians whose industrial medical practice included them. "One had no recall for occupational diseases among the solid waste workers. The other doctor had not noted 'significant skin problems'. It is presumed that their nonrecognition (...) is due to a lack of dermatologic expertise. It should be stressed that the workers who visited them did so almost solely for traumatic conditions. The triviality, despite the high frequency, of the occupational dermatoses identified probably also accounts for a lack of attention or interest in them. The stigmata or occupational marks noted among solid waste workers usually were not sources of complaint but, as with occupational injuries and diseases in other types of work, they were accepted by them as 'badges of the trade'".

Then, to have an effective preventive attitude in the connected fields of compost preparation and wastewater treatment, the occupational practician has to systematically search for :
- dermatological or oto-rhino-laryngological diseases,
- infectious digestive troubles,
- a pulmonary pathology, extrinsic allergic alveolitis oriented or aspergillary, even asthma.

Beyond the clinical and radiological examination, it will be necessary to add immunological investigations, also a spirometry and a carbon monoxyde transfer, finally a search of precipitines (**A. fumigatus** and thermophilic actionomycetes).

BY WAY OF A CONCLUSION

The previous citation from Gellin and Zavon's paper deserves to be meditated. It still reflects accurately the comportement of many workers. It must not reflect longer the attitude of responsibles and executives. Since ten years, much research time and money was devoted to the evaluation of actual risk through compost processing and use. Many additional knowledge was acquired in this field. Refuse and sludge composting first appeared as an annex to the more common waste water treatment problem, but we have now to consider it according to its own specificities. If we know now where a possible occupational pathology lies, we are still unaware of its actual extension. Current developments of composting justify further efforts for a better measurement of long-term effects of exposition to potentially pathogenic agents and, meanwhile, for a preventive health policy.

BIBLIOGRAPHY

(1) de BERTOLDI M. - Pathogenic fungi associated with land application of sludge, **Sewage sludge to land, health implications of the microbial content,** Proc. of a W.H.O. meet., Wat. Res. Center, Stevenage, Jan. 6-9, 1981, 12 p.
(2) de BERTOLDI M., VALLINI G., PERA A. - The biology of composting, a review, **Waste Mgmt Res.,** 1983, **1,** 157-176
(3) BOUTIN P., TORRE M., MOLINE J. - Bacterial and fungal atmospheric contamination at refuse composting plants (to be presented to this symposium)
(4) BURGE W.D., MILLNER P.D. - Health hazards of composting : primary and secondary pathogens, in **Sludge - health risks of land application** (BITTON G. et al., eds), AnnArbor Science, AnnArbor, 1980, 245-263
(5) CARRINGTON E.G. - The contribution of sewage sludges to the dissemination of pathogenic microorganisms in the environment, Wat. Res. Center, Stevenage Lab., **Techn. Rep. n° 71,** 1978, 32 p.
(6) C.E.M.A.G.R.E.F. - Risques sanitaires susceptibles d'être encourus par les personnels travaillant sur les stations de traitement d'eaux résiduaires - étude bibliographique, CEMAGREF, Group. de Bordeaux, Section "Qualité des Eaux", **Etude n° 16,** Nov. 1983, 45 p.
(7) CLARK C.S., CLEARY E.J. et al. - Disease risk of occupational exposure to sewage, **J. Environ. Div. (Am. Soc. Civ. Engnrs),** 1976, **102,** EE2,

375–388

(8) CLARK C.S., BJORNSON A.B. et al. – Sewage workers' syndrome, **Lancet,** 1977, 1009

(9) CLARK C.S., SCHIFF G.M. et al. – A seroepidemiological study of workers engaged in waste water collection and treatment, in **State of knowledge in land treatment of waste water** (McKIM H.L., ed.), 1978, U.S. Corps of Engineers, C.R.R.E.F., Hanover, N.-H., vol. 2, 263–271

(10) CLARK C.S., VAN MEER G.L. et al. – Health effects of occupational exposure to wastewater, in **Waste water aerosols and disease** (PAHREN H., JAKUBOWSKI W., eds) EPA-600/9-80-028, Dec. 1980, Cincinnati, US EPA, 239–264

(11) CLARK C.S., BJORNSON H.S. et al. – Occupational hazards associated with sludge handling, in **Sludge – health risks of land application** (BITTON G. **et al.,** eds), AnnArbor Science, AnnArbor, 1980, 215–244

(12) CLARK C.S., BJORNSON H.S. et al. – Biological risks associated with the composting of wastewater treatment plant sludges, in **Biological risks of sludge disposal to land in cold climates** (WALLIS P.M., LEHMANN D.L., eds), Un. of Calgary Press, Calgary, 1983, 79–93

(13) CLARK C.S., RYLANDER R., LARSSON L. – Levels of Gram-negative bacteria, **Aspergillus fumigatus,** dust and endotoxins at compost plants, **Appl. Environ. Microbiol.,** 1983, **45,** 5, 1501–1505

(14) CLARK C.S., BJORNSON H.S. et al. – Biological health risks associated with the composting of wastewater treatment plant sludges, **J. Wat. Poll. Control Fed.,** 1984, **56,** 12, 1269–1276

(15) CLIVER D.O. – Infection with minimal quantities of pathogens from waste water aerosols, in **Waste water aerosols and disease** (PAHREN H., JAKUBOWSKI W., eds), EPA-600/9-80-028, Dec. 1980, Cincinnati, US EPA, 78–87

(16) COURSEAU A. – Stations d'épuration et pathologies infectieuses : l'exemple du risque aspergillaire à travers une enquête prospective à Tours, **Thèse Doct. Méd.,** Fac. Méd. Tours, 1984, 84 p.

(17) DIENER V.L., MORGAN-JONES G. et al. – Mycoflora of activated sludge, **Mycopathologia,** 1976, **58,** 2, 115–116

(18) DUDLEY D.J., GUENTZEL M.N. et al. – Enumeration of potentially pathogenic bacteria from sewage sludges, **Appl. Environ. Microbiol.,** 1980, **39,** 1, 118–126

(19) FEACHEM R.G., BRADLEY D.J. et al. – Sanitation and disease : health aspects of excreta and wastewater management, Chichester & New York, J. Wiley & Sons, 1983, 501 p.

(20) GELLIN G.A., ZAVON M.R. – Occupational dermatoses of solid waste workers, **Arch. Environ. Health,** 1970, **20,** 510–515

(21) GOLUEKE C.G. – Epidemiological aspects of sewage sludge handling and management, **Biocycle,** 1983, **24,** 3, 52–58 – 4, 50–58

(22) HICKEY J.L.S., REIST P.C. – Health significance of airborne microorganisms from waste water treatment processes, **J. Wat. Poll. Control Fed.,** 1975, **47,** 12, 2741–2773

(23) KOTHARY M.H., CHASE T., McMILLAN J.D. – Levels of **Aspergillus fumigatus** in air and in compost at a sewage sludge composting site, **Environ. Pollut. (Ser. A),** 1984, **34,** 1–11

(24) KOTHARY M.H., CHASE T., McMILLAN J.D. – Correlation of elastase production by some strains of **Aspergillus fumigatus** with ability to cause pulmonary invasive aspergillosis in mice, **J. Infect. Immun.,** 1984, **34,** 1–14

(25) LEMBKE L.L., KNISELEY R.N. – Coliforms in aerosols generated by a municipal solid waste recovery system, **Appl. Environ. Microbiol.,** 1980, **40,** 5, 888–891

(26) LUNDHOLM M. - Comparison of methods for quantitative determination of airborne bacteria and evaluation of total viable counts, **Appl. Environ. Microbiol.**, 1982, **44**, 1, 179-183

(27) LUNDHOLM M., RYLANDER R. - Exposure to sewage sludge : a new occupational hazard, Dpt of Environm. Hyg., Un. of Gothenborg, presented at the **XIXth Congress on occup. health**, Sept. 25-30, 1979, Dubrownik (Yu.), 12 p.

(28) LUNDHOLM M., RYLANDER R. - Occupational symptoms among compost workers, **J. Occup. Med.**, 1980, **22**, 4, 256-257

(29) MAJETI V.A., CLARK C.S. - Potential health effects from viable emissions and toxins associated with wastewater treatment plants and land application sites, EPA-600/1-81-006, Jan. 1981, Cincinnati, US EPA, 74 p.

(30) MATTSBY I., RYLANDER R. - Clinical and immunological findings in workers exposed to sewage dust, **J. Occup. Med.**, 1978, **20**, 10, 690-692

(31) MILLNER P.D., MARSH P.B. et al. - Occurrence of **Aspergillus fumigatus** during composting of sewage sludge, **Appl. Environ. Microbiol.**, 1977, **34**, 6, 765-772

(32) MILLNER P.D., BASSET D.A., MARSH P.B. - Dispersal of **Aspergillus fumigatus** from sewage sludge compost piles subjected to mechanical agitation in open air, **Appl. Environ. Microbiol.**, 1980, **39**, 5, 1000-1009

(33) MOLINE J., BOUTIN P., BOISSINOT E. - Un risque respiratoire nouveau : les stations d'épuration et les installations de compostage, **Bull. Soc. Mycol. Méd.**, 1982, **XI**, 2, 375-380

(34) PERDRIX A., PARAMELLE B., COULOMB M. - Agression fongique et pathologie bronchopulmonaire, **Cahiers Méd. Lyonn.**, 1975, **51**, 15, 811-819

(35) RYLANDER R., ANDERSSON K. et al. - Sewage worker's syndrome, **Lancet**, 1976, 7983, 478-479

(36) RYLANDER R., ANDERSSON A. et al. - Studies of humans exposed to airborne sewage sludge, **Schweiz. Med. Wschr.**, 1978, **107**, 6, 182-184

(37) RYLANDER R., LUNDHOLM M. - Responses to wastewater exposure with reference to endotoxin, in **Waste water aerosols and disease** (PAHREN H., JAKUBOWSKI W., eds), EPA-600/9-80-028, Dec. 1981, Cincinnati, US EPA, 90-96

(38) RYLANDER R., SNELLA M.C. - Endotoxins and the lung-cellular reactions and risk for disease, **Progress in Allergy**, 1983, 33, 332-344

(39) RYLANDER R., LUNDHOLM M., CLARK C.S. - Exposure to aerosols and toxins during handling of sewage sludge, in **Biological health risks of sludge disposal to land in cold climates** (WALLIS P.M., LEHMANN D.L., eds), Calgary, 1983, Un. of Calgary Press, 69-78

(40) STRAUCH D. - Zur Frage der Reinigung von Schützkleidung für das Personal von Kläranlagen, **Korr. Abwasser**, 1978, **25**, 44-47

(41) STROM P.F. - Identification of thermophilic bacteria in solid waste composting, **Appl. Environ. Microbiol.**, 1985, **50**, 4, 906-913

(42) VINCKEN W., ROELS P. - Hypersensivity pneumonitis due to **Aspergillus fumigatus** in compost, **Thorax**, 1984, **39**, 1, 74-75

(43) WORLD BANK, U.N.D.P., W.H.O., I.R.C.W.D. - Health aspects of wastewater and excreta use in agriculture and aquaculture : the Engelberg report, **IRCWD News**, n° 23, EAWAG, Dec. 1985, 11-18

MICROBIOLOGICAL SPECIFICATIONS OF DISINFECTED COMPOST

D. STRAUCH

Institute of Animal Medicine and Animal Hygiene,
University of Hohenheim, Stuttgart, Fed. Rep. of Germany

Summary

Some selected literature dealing with indicator organisms for control
of disinfection measures for compost is discussed. The question whether bacteria or bacteriophages can be used as indicators for pathogenic viruses is still undecided and must be further investigated.
Also still uncertain is the suitability of certain groups of bacteria
as reliable indicators for other pathogenic bacteria. Enterobacteriaceae and fecal streptococci seem to be suitable to a certain extent.
Further comparative investigations are still necessary.
Since no standardized microbiological methods in this field are available internationally a pragmatic proposal of the requirements for an
efficient disinfection of compost with various methods is presented
for discussion. This seems necessary because in several countries the
authorities are in need of such definitions to prepare legal regulations for public health reasons.

1. INTRODUCTION

The Working Party (WP) 3 of the CEC-Concerted Action "Treatment and
Use of Sewage Sludge" (COST Project 68ter) is dealing with "Hygienic
Aspects Related to Treatment and Use of Sewage Sludge". Within the framework of that definition the WP has also commented on the question of indicator organisms and the following conclusions have been drawn for the Final Report (Part II) of COST 68ter "Treatment and Use of Sewage Sludge"
(1).

Indicator bacteria have only a limited use in the field of sewage
sludge hygiene. In many cases it is advisable to analyse for or seed with
pathogens directly. Two possible uses of indicator organisms have been
identified: monitoring disinfection processes and checking for regrowth
after disinfection. Fecal streptococci appear to be most useful for critical monitoring of disinfection processes. E. coli or other related counts
(coliforms, enterobacteriaceae) have a general low resistance and would
only detect gross underprocessing. Bacteriophages (especially male-speci-
fic) and mycobacteria are potentially useful, but there is too little data
to further define their use. To check for regrowth in disinfected sludge,
enterobacteriaceae and most probably also total coliforms can be used.

In the following paper we do not intend to repeat all the discussions
on indicator organisms with pro and contra. We rather would like to discuss
the problem on the basis of some recent developments in that field and
finally present a pragmatic proposal for the hygienic evaluation of some
disinfection methods as in some countries it may be needed for political
decisions.

2. BACTERIA AND BACTERIOPHAGES AS INDICATORS FOR VIRUSES

Scarpino has recently discussed indicator systems for monitoring the virological quality of potable water, wastewater, solid waste, shellfish, fish and crops (2). For drinking water he directed concern at the bacterial indicator system that is routinely used to approve its safety. Based on reported viral isolations, the coliform standard used may itself be inherently defective or the bacterial sample quantity and timing may be the difficulty. In addition, consideration must be given to the wide range of susceptibility to chlorine disinfection displayed by different viruses and the more recent disclosure that there may be disinfection rate differences between stock virus strains commonly used in laboratory disinfection studies and the apparently more resistant indigenous viruses. Studies have shown how low levels of viruses may pass through the water treatment procedure and be later isolated from drinking water samples while the coliform indicators apparently do not survive the rigors of water treatment.

It has also been established that fecal coliforms, fecal streptococci and total coliforms are not always adequate indicators of viruses in disinfected primary sewage effluents. Viruses were found to survive in all the effluents even though the fecal coliform counts were within the limits permitted in USA for recreational waters and for approved shell-fish-growing waters. It was emphasized that even if the total coliform counts had been used instead of the fecal coliforms, the bacterial counts would still have been within the acceptable limits of safety – with pathogenic viruses still present.

Concerning bacteriophages as an indicator of water contamination the author expresses guarded optimism that under certain circumstances bacteriophage indicators can be used to detect viral presence and inactivation but not in all situations.

Studies with solid wastes suggest that _Salmonella_ are rather stable microorganisms which could be a better indicator for the potential presence of viruses in sewage than currently used fecal streptococci or fecal coliforms. Studies of viruses and bacteria under identical conditions show that viruses survive longer than bacteria under most conditions. This of course would cast doubt on using bacteria as indicators of virus presence. Scarpino draws the conclusion in his study that in the solid waste environment it would appear that the only reliable indicator of virus presence is finding the virus itself.

For the indication of viruses on or in crops he thinks that although fecal coliforms have been used to evaluate public health risk in regard to crops, the indicators for virus presence seem justifiable at present. Also in this case there does not appear to be a substitute for direct evaluation of pathogenic viral presence.

Scarpino has drawn these conclusions: "Certainly we should continue to strive to develop a surrogate system or model that would enable us to replace the direct determination of pathogenic viruses. However, this has not always been possible, but the vision does not need to fade; the same and other candidates need to be re-examined or discovered. Perhaps we should accept the fact that indicators need not to be 100 % successful in every case – and that direct pathogenic virus determination is the best way to safeguard public health. The indicators could provide us with assistance in reducing public risk, but should never replace direct observation. Again, perhaps the best indicator for pathogenic virus presence is the virus itself" (2).

3. INDICATOR ORGANISMS FOR PATHOGENS OTHER THAN VIRUSES

3.1 The US-Environmental Protection Agency has initiated a literature review on density levels of indicator and pathogenic organisms in municipal wastewater sludge (3). This report is based on the assumption that "sludges originating from municipal wastewater treatment plants harbor a multitude of microorganisms, many of which present a potential health hazard. Risk of public exposure to these organisms is possible when sludges are applied to land as a means of disposal. In recognition of this problem, and as required by Section 405 of the Clean Water Act of 1977 8PL 95-217), criteria for the control of infectious disease in the land application of sewage sludge and septic tank pumpings were issued by the U.S. Environmental Protection Agency (EPA) in 40 CFR Part 257 (Federal Register Vol. 44, No. 179, September 13, 1979).

The "Part 257 criteria" specify what minimum treatment of municipal wastewater treatment plant sludges is required prior to land application of the residue. Acceptable treatment methods, termed "Processes to Significantly Reduce Pathogens", are as follows:
- Composting – Using the withinvessel, static aerated pile or windrow composting methods, the sludge is maintained at minimum operating conditions of 40°C for five days. For four hours during this period, the temperature exceeds 55°C.
- Anaerobic digestion – Maintenance of sludge in the absence of air at residence times ranging from 60 days at 20°C to 15 days at 35°C to 55°C, with a volatile solids reduction of at least 38 %.
- Aerobic digestion – Agitation of sludge in aerobic conditions at residence times ranging from 60 days at 15°C to 40 days at 20°C, with a volatile solids reduction of at least 38 %.
- Lime stabilization – Application of lime to sludge in quantities sufficient to produce a pH of 12 after two hours of contact.
- Air drying – Draining and/or drying of liquid sludge on underdrained sand beds, or on paved or unpaved basins in which the sludge is at a depth of 9 inches (22.9 cm). A minimum of three months is needed, two months of which temperature average on a daily basis is above 0°C.
- Techniques demonstrated to be the equivalent of the above on the basis of pathogen removals and volatile solids reduction.

An additional category of treatment processes, termed "Processes to Further Reduce Pathogens", was designated in Appendix II of 40 CFR Part 257 as required if (1) affected land is to be used within 18 months of sludge application for the cultivation of food crops and (2) the edible portion of the crop is likely to be exposed to the sludge. These additional processes are:
- High temperature composting
- Thermophilic aerobic digestion
- Heat drying
- Heat treatment
- Irradiation.

For the review the following organisms, categorized into four groupings, were emphasized:
- Indicators – Total coliform, fecal coliform, and fecal streptococcus bacteria; Clostridium perfringens (welchii); bacteriophage
- Pathogenic bacteria – Salmonellae, Shigellae, Pseudomonas sp., Mycobacterium spp., Candida albicans, Aspergillus fumigatus
- Enteric viruses – Enterovirus and its subgroups (polioviruses, echoviruses and coxsackieviruses), reovirus and adenovirus

- Parasites - <u>Entamoeba</u> <u>histolytica</u>, <u>Ascaris</u> <u>lumbricoides</u>, <u>Taenia</u> <u>spp.</u>,
<u>Schistosoma</u> <u>spp.</u>, and others.

In addition to reporting density levels in raw sludge and septage,
and the effectiveness of conventional sludge treatment processes in redu-
sing density levels, this review also identified design and operating variables that affect process efficiency, compared results of laboratory
pilot-scale studies to those of full-scale plants, and contrasted survival
of indicator organisms to that of pathogens. Methods used by each resear-
cher to enumerate organisms were also described, and brief summaries were
provided of related citations that were encountered but were not actually
used in this report.

Density levels in raw sludge

Levels of bacteria, viruses and parasites in raw sludge are presented
in Table 1. Note that the densities of pathogenic organisms are several
logs less than indicator organisms. Also, there is a noticeable lack of
information on the densities of select pathogenic organisms in raw sludges
and septages (i.e., lack of parasite organisms data in septages).

The following sludge treatment methods were evaluated in their effect
to reduce the numbers of indicator organisms and of pathogens: anaerobic
digestion, mesophilic aerobic digestion, "mesophilic" composting (45°-65°C
or higher), lime stabilization, drying beds, sludge storage/lagooning,
sludge conditioning/mechanical dewatering.

The review results in the following conclusions and recommendations:
"Because a large body of literature containing comparable data is not available, it is recommended that additional research be conducted on the effectiveness of sludge treatment processes in reducing density levels of
organisms. It is recommended, further that researchers document carefully
all pertinent aspects of their experimental design.

The following conclusions appear to be valid based on the literature
reviewed.

Anaerobic digestion and lime stabilization consistently produce reductions of about 1 to 2 logs in densities of indicator and pathogenic bacteria and, in the case of anaerobic digestion, in densities of viruses as
well.At a minimum, effectiveness depends on the processes being carried
out under the conditions specified in 40 CFR Part 257. Neither sludge stabilization process appears to be particularly effective for inactivating parasite organisms.

Conditions of **mesophilic composting** may inactivate common indicator
and pathogenic bacteria and viruses, provided that specified temperatures
are attained uniformly throughout the compost mass for over the specified
time period. The pathogenic fungus <u>Aspergillus</u> <u>fumigatus</u> thrives under conditions of **mesophilic composting**, however, and parasite ova appear to survive this process.

Density reductions of bacteria by aerobic digestion are variable and
of relatively small magnitude. However, there is a lack of data on the performance of this process and also of air drying in reducing densities of
microorganisms.

Sludge lagoons can achieve 1-log reductions in densities of bacteria
and viable parasite ova, but, depending on conditions, storage of one month
to more than three years may be required.

Mechanical dewatering of sludge, with or without the use of chemical
conditioners, has little reliable effect on densities of pathogens.

Few of the laboratory-scale studies reviewed could be related to results obtained at full-scale treatment plants. Operating parameters used

Table 1 : Density levels of organisms in raw sludge and septage
(Average geometric mean of organisms per gram dry weight) (3)

Organism	Primary	Secondary	Mixed	Septage
Total coliform bacteria	1.2×10^8	7.1×10^8	1.1×10^9	1.4×10^8
Fecal coliform bacteria	2.0×10^7	8.3×10^6	1.9×10^5	1.2×10^6
Fecal streptococci	8.9×10^5	1.7×10^6	3.7×10^6	6.6×10^5
Bacteriophage	1.3×10^5	NR	NR	NR
Salmonella sp.	4.1×10^2	8.8×10^2	2.9×10^2	5.1×10^{-1}
Shigella sp.	NR	NR	ND	NR
Pseudomonas aeruginosa	2.8×10^3	1.1×10^4	3.3×10^3	2.6×10^1
Parasite ova/cysts (total)	2.1×10^2	NR	$<5.0 \times 10^1$	NR
Ascaris sp.	7.2×10^2	1.4×10^3	2.9×10^2	NR
Trichuris trichura	1.0×10^1	$<1.0 \times 10^1$	o	NR
Trichuris vulpis	1.1×10^2	$<1.0 \times 10^1$	1.4×10^2	NR
Toxocara sp.	2.4×10^2	2.8×10^2	1.3×10^3	NR
Hymenolepis diminuta	$6. \times 10^0$	2.0×10^1	o	NR
Enteric viruses*	3.9×10^2	3.2×10^2	3.6×10^{2}**	NR

NR = No data available

ND = None detected

* = Plaque forming units per gram dry weight (PFU/gdw)

** = $TCID_{50}$ = 50 percent tissue culture infectious dose

in laboratory experiments differed radically from those at full-scale plants. For this reason, comparing density levels was seldom possible. In addition, laboratory studies often used seeded bacteria, viruses, or parasites and it is doubtful whether their behavior mimics that of naturally occurring organisms.

No single indicator organism (either bacteria or bacteriophage) was found to maintain a density level of a constant relative value to that of pathogenic organisms. The data available made it impossible to determine whether this inconsistency is due to the inability of current techniques to enumerate pathogenic bacteria and enteroviruses accurately, or to the fact that densities actually vary.

Of the traditional indicators, fecal streptococci appear to be the most conservative indicator of both the density levels of pathogenic bacteria and enterovirus in raw sludge and of their inactivation during sludge treatments. Additional research is required to identify other indicator systems, both bacterial and viral, whose numbers better reflect both density and reduction of density levels of pathogenic organisms.

A wide variety of methods were used to enumerate all of the organisms considered in this review. Although standard methods are available for quantifying the coliform and streptococcus bacteria and for Salmonella sp., there are no standard techniques for other pathogens, enteroviruses, or parasites. It is recommended that this area be addressed so that comparable data can be produced in future studies."

3.2 In extensive **microbiological studies a variety of composting systems** were investigated by de Bertoldi et al. (4, 5) and the isolated numbers of Salmonella spp., fecal coliforms and fecal streptococci compared (Table 2 and 3).

Based on their results in Table 2 and 3 as well as on results published elsewhere and on unpublished data de Bertoldi et al. (5) did evaluate the composting methods tested. Their conclusion are:

"Several factors affect pathogen survival during treatment. In composting, heat is one of the primary factors contributing to pathogen inactivation. Most pathogenic microbes are destroyed by heating for several hours to temperatures above 50°C. Microbial competition is another important factor in controlling pathogen diffusion during composting. A variety of saprophytic microorganisms participates in the composting process; these microorganisms might be considered the indigenous or natural microflora of the compost system. Municipal sludge contains a second microbial population, the pathogens, which represent a numerically insignificant fraction of the total microbial population. Hence competition comes into play when the community is heterogeneous and the population density is high relative to the supply of any limiting feature of the environment. The indigenous saprophytic population has a highly distinct competitive advantage over the other population; composting material is not the natural environment for pathogenic microorganisms, therefore in this ecosystem competition will tend to result in the elimination of the less fit rival.

The choice of the most suitable composting process depends on differing local situations and conditions; nevertheless only processes which guarantee good quality and sanitized end-products should be chosen.

All the experimental data reported in this paper indicate that static composting systems provide a better control over pathogens than does turning.

In the closed systems, horizontal reactors seem to guarantee better control over pathogens than vertical continuous reactors. This may be mainly due to the fact that masses over three meters high are difficult to con-

Table 2 : Effect of sludge composting on the recovery of salmonellas, fecal coliforms and fecal streptococci (5)

MICROORGANISMS	SLUDGE + SUW		SLUDGE + RICE HULL				
	sludge	compost	sludge	compost			
Salmonella sp	$2.4x10^1$	absent	absent	absent			
Fecal coliforms	$4.8x10^5$	$5.6x10^4$	$5\ x10^6$	$3\ x10^5$			A
Fecal streptococci	$2.4x10^5$	$2.0x10^5$	$1.8x10^5$	$3\ x10^4$			
	SLUDGE + SUW		SLUDGE+WOOD CHIPS		SLUDGE+INERTS		
	sludge	compost	sludge	compost	sludge	compost	
Salmonella sp	$2.4x10^1$	absent	$1.0x10^5$	absent	$5.0x10^4$	absent	
F. coliforms	$4.8x10^5$	$4.1x10^2$	$2.0x10^7$	$5.0x10^1$	$7.0x10^7$	$1.0x10^1$	B
F. streptococci	$2.4x10^5$	$7.0x10^2$	$7.0x10^6$	$3.5x10^1$	$7.0x10^5$	$1.0x10^1$	
	SLUDGE + SUW		SLUDGE + CORK		SLUDGE + STRAW		
	sludge	compost	sludge	compost	sludge	compost	
Salmonella sp	$2.4x10^1$	absent	$3.1x10^2$	absent	$1.2x10^2$	absent	
F. coliforms	$4.8x10^5$	$1.2x10^3$	$9.3x10^5$	$5.9x10^2$	$8.5x10^6$	$7.8x10^2$	C
F. streptococci	$2.4x10^5$	$8.2x10^2$	$6.0x10^6$	$8.1x10^2$	$4.8x10^6$	$3.0x10^3$	

A = Composting in turned piles (30 d)

B = Composting in static pile aerated by vacuum induced pressure (suction)

C = Composting in static pile aerated by forced pressure ventilation (blowing)

SUW = Solid urban waste

Table 3 : Effect of sludge composting in different types of bioreactors on the recovery of salmonellas, fecal coliforms and fecal streptococci (5)

MICROORGANISMS	STARTING MATERIAL	AFTER REACTOR PASSAGE	
Salmonella sp.	absent	absent	
F. coliforms	1.4×10^7	2.5×10^6	A
F. streptococci	3.4×10^5	9.0×10^6	
Salmonella sp	absent	absent	
F. coliforms	2.2×10^8	7.8×10^3	B
F. streptococci	8.5×10^6	1.9×10^9	
Salmonella sp	absent	absent	
F. coliforms	3.1×10^8	2.5×10^5	C
F. streptococci	4.7×10^7	7.6×10^6	
Salmonella sp	1.3×10^2	absent	
F. coliforms	5.7×10^7	2.5×10^2	D
F. streptococci	8.0×10^6	1.7×10^2	
Salmonella sp	8.1×10^2	absent	
F. coliforms	7.9×10^8	9.2×10^1	E
F. streptococci	4.5×10^6	1.9×10^2	

A = Vertical reactor (Weiss). Mixture sludge + organic fraction of SUW (14 d)
B = Vertical reactor (Weiss). Mixture sludge + organic fraction of SUW (21 d)
C = Vertical reactor (BAV). Mixture sludge + organic fraction of SUW (15 d)
D = Horizontal reactor (Yokohama/Japan). Mixture sludge + composted sludge (10)
E = Horizontal reactor (Paygro/USA). Mixture sludge + sawdust + composted sludge (14 d)

trol during the composting process. In particular oxygenation of the mass is not homogeneous, resulting in anaerobic zones with lower temperatures.

Since the term "composting" encompasses numerous processes which may create physiologically disparate physico-chemical environments for pathogens in the sludge being composted, it can not be tacitly assumed that composting renders municipal sludge pathogen-free. However, well-conducted processes with prolonged periods of high temperatures do seem to provide a sanitized product.

Finally, there is a need for a better definition of the term "sanitized compost". At present, there is no legal specification of what should be a disinfected sludge compost.

For this reason, and because it is essential for compost to have specifications for pathogens, too, it is of primary importance to lay down not only which microorganisms are to be monitored, but also their maximum permitted level in a sanitized product."

It is therefore suggested to use as indicators enterobacteriaceae with a limit of $5x10^2/g$ and fecal streptococci with a limit of $5x10^3$. These figures derive from numerous experiments which were carried out by de Bertoldi and co-workers in Pisa on many different composting processes. When these indicators are lower in number than the limits given above, Salmonella spp. is always absent according to the authors opinion.

For parasites the eggs of Ascaris suum are usually considered as the representative indicator or test organism. Their thermosensitivity is in the range between 50° - 55°C so that they are covered by tests performed with microorganisms like fecal streptococci or f2-phages with a higher thermostability.

The figures for fecal streptococci mentioned above present a contradiction to a statement of Havelaar (6) who proposed for the hygienic evaluation of the aerobic-thermophilic stabilization (ATS; this treatment method is also sometimes known as "liquid composting") of liquid sludge the fecal streptococci as indicators with an upper limit of $10^1/g$. Further investigations under practical conditions are necessary to disentagle this difference in opinion.

There is a further contradiction in the opinions as far as the hygienic evaluation of ATS is concerned. The evaluation of ATS is based on the assumption that ATS is performed in only one reactor (6). Recent investigations in practice have shown that ATS in one reactor may result in a hygienically safe product when all necessary parameters for pathogen kill are favorable, which never can be guaranteed under the hard conditions of sewage works practice (7). Therefore a prerequisite for the production of a hygienically reliable product is the two or three stage operation of such ATS plants combined with a continuous registration of the temperatures in the reactors with liquid sludge (8, 9, 10). Under these conditions the proposed continuous monitoring of each batch of the end-product of ATS plants based on indicator organisms like fecal streptococci (6) is superfluous. Moreover a batch-wise control of the end-product of a single-stage ATS plant is practically not possible because none of the ATS plants to date is operated as batch system for economic reasons; all of them are continuous or semi-continuous systems.

3.3 In a very thorough study in three German plants where municipal refuse is composted in different systems:
- Prat-system: refuse + refluxcompost + water + ammonium compounds
- DANO-system: refuse + sludge
- Hazemag-system (aerated static pile): refuse + sludge,
the authors inoculated the raw material directly with liquid cultures of

Staphylococcus aureus	ATCC 6538
Klebsiella pneumoniae	ATCC 4532
Streptococcus faecalis	ATCC 6057
Candida albicans	ATCC 10231

These bacterial strains are the same which are used in the Federal Republic of Germany as test strains for testing the antibacterial effect of chemical disinfectants (11).

The results of this study are very important for the evaluation of composts from municipal refuse. In none of the composts investigated the outer compost layers were considered to be hygienically safe. Even if the material of these layers was put into the inner core of the windrows by mechanical means the authors did not always succed in destroying all of their test microbes. But also in these experiments Streptococcus faecalis proved to be a reliable indicator organism.

Based on their results the authors doubt that the results of studies in other composting systems which are published in the literature and indicate that these other systems are producing composts free of pathogens, are appropriate. They ask the question whether it is really necessary to make such rigid demands on the hygienic quality of refuse composts and tried to answer it by other investigations.

They made microbiological analyses of composts of the three plants tested which were sold to the public and compared the results to analyses of organic fertilizers, garten molds, peat which were bought in ships and soils of private gardens, sand from children play grounds and top-soil of forests. Three typical results are shown in Figures 1-3. From the results of this study the authors draw the conclusion that the refuse composts usually had higher densities of germs than the fertilizers or soils. This seems to be very natural since the composts are produced by microbiological conversion processes and are used from bacteria and fungi as substrates for nutrition. They consider all 18 of the detected bacterial species as pathogenic or facultative pathogenic. From these they found in compost and in the other materials investigated: Citrobacter, Enterobacter, E. coli, Klebsiella, Pseudomonas, Aspergillus, Salmonella. Only from compost were isolated: Achromobacter, Proteus, Serratia, Enterococcus, Streptomyces, Mucor, Rhodotorula, Penicillium, Geotrichum candidum.

Since these microbes may become pathogenic only under certain conditions they do not raise the hygienic risk of the compost so that no aggravating differences between the composts on the one hand and the sum of the other substrates analyzed could be seen. The question of the real risk of the utilization of refuse or refuse/sludge composts in agriculture, landscape gardening or private gardening can only be answered by a thorough analysis of risk which could not be done within this study. As long as the utilization of the substrates like organic fertilizers, garden molds, peat, soils etc. is not regularized the authors do not have objections against the utilization of refuse composts for the purposes for which they are destined (11).

3.4 Another approach to the problem of indicator organisms and monitoring pathogen destruction was made by a research group in the USA (12, 13). Although several studies showed the potential for **destruction of pathogens by composting,** the authors thought a method for determining the capability of a particular system was needed.

"A straightforward method of determining the success of a process in destroying pathogens would be, of course, monitoring for the pathogens themselves or for an indicator organisms. The utilization of pathogens is

Figure 1 : Qualitative microbiological analysis of refuse compost samples

Sample	Water content %	pH-value	Total germ count/g (Gelatin)	Total germ count/g (Agar)	"Coliforms"/g	"E. coli"/g	Achromobacter	Citrobacter	Enterobacter	E.coli	Klebsiella	Proteus mirabilis	Proteus vulgaris	Serratia	Salmonellen	Enterokokken	Gaebrand-Gruppe	Pseudomonaden	Streptomyces	Mucor	Rhodotrula	Aspergillus	Penicillium	Geotrichum candidum	kein Wachstum
Special grade compost I	25	8,4	40.000.000	70.000.000	23.000	92.000			X	X								X							
" II	30	7,9	6.000.000	30.000.000	300.000	280.000				X										X					
" III	29	8,2	3.000.000	25.000.000	25.000	11.000			X	X									X	X					
" IV	35	7,9	30.000.000	35.000.000	10.000	10.000			X	X	X		X	X				X							
Cured compost I	40	8,6	7.000.000	100.000.000	13.000	16.000			X	X			X	X				X		X	X				
" II	38	7,9	1.000.000	90.000.000	12.000	9.000																			
" III	29	7,7	22.000.000	45.000.000	300.000	50.000										X		X							
" IV	25	7,8	2.400.000	6.000.000	7.000	4.000														X					
" V	31	8,0	2.400.000	1.900.000	20.000	1.000																			
Bagged compost I	29	7,2	10.000.000	20.000.000	300	300															X				
" II	41	8,1	450.000	55.000.000	70	130		X	X					X				X		X	X				

Figure 2 : Qualitative microbiological analysis of organic fertilizers

Sample	Water Content %	pH-value	Total germ count/g (Gelatin)	Total germ count/g (Agar)	"Coliforms"/g	"E. coli"/g	Achromobacter	Citrobacter	Enterobacter	E.coli	Klebsiella	Proteus mirabilis	Proteus vulgaris	Serratia	Salmonellen	Enterokokken	Gasbrand-Gruppe	Pseudomonaden	Streptomyces	Mucor	Rhodotroula	Aspergillus	Penicillium	Geotrichum candidum	kein Wachstum
Cow manure, dried I	52	8,2	4.000.000	160.000.000	0	0												■							
" II	49	8,5	2.000.000	3.000.000	0	0												■							
Guano I	12	8,8	140	0	0	0																			
Guano II	12	8,9	10	0	0	0																			■
Organic flower fertilizer I	7	8,3	550	7.000	10	0			■							■	■								
" II	10	7,9	1.000	2.000	150	0																			
Organic vegetable fertilizer I	14	8,5	6.700	15.000	20	0			■	■					■		■								
" II	n.b.	8,5	27.000	30.000	10	10																			
Horn powder and chips I	7	6,2	180.000	40.000	0	0											■	■							
" II	8	6,5	8.000	4.000	0	0											■	■							
Biokomposter	n.b.	8,0	10	<1	10	10			■																

222

Figure 3 : Qualitative microbiological analysis of soils, sand and garden compost

Sample	Water content %	pH-value	Total germ count/g (Gelatin)	Total germ count/g (Agar)	"Coliforms"/g	"E. coli"/g	Achromobacter	Citrobacter	Enterobacter	E.coli	Klebsiella	Proteus mirabilis	Proteus vulgaris	Serratia	Salmonellen	Enterokokken	Gasbrand-Gruppe	Pseudomonaden	Streptomyces	Mucor	Rhodotorula	Aspergillus	Penicillium	Geotrichum candidum	kein Wachstum
Garden soil I	15	7,9	250.000	9.000	12	10		■		■															
" II	10	8,1	100.000	10.000	0	0			■								■	■							
" III	20	8,0	900.000	15.000	950	0			■																
" IV	12	8,4	900.000	230.000	0	0				■							■	■							
Garden soil + org. fertil. I	10	8,4	570.000	550.000	300	200				■								■							
" II	15	7,9	160.000	126.000	7	0				■							■	■							
Garden compost 1 year old	20	7,4	2.100.000	1.800.000	390	11			■																
Garden compost 2 years old	15	7,9	200.000	300.000	39	10																			
Garden compost 3 years old	21	7,9	100.000	79.000	34	0																			
Garden compost 1 years old	14	7,8	100.000	350.000	31	0				■	■						■	■							
Garden compost 2 years old	17	8,0	250.000	1.400.000	0	0																			

not practical because, for most, the procedures are too difficult for routine application. The use of a specific pathogen is ruled out not only because of the difficulty, but to be effective one would have to know the concentration of the pathogen at the initiation of composting. A specific pathogen could be low enough in numbers or sensitive enough to destruction by heat so that its absence would not guarantee that all others had been destroyed.

The use of the indicator organisms (fecal coliforms) were ruled out because although these organisms may be destroyed during the composting process, they are capable of repopulating the compost if they are reinoculated and reinoculation is impossible to prevent in most composting processes as they are presently conducted.

To overcome these problems it was decided to use a temperature-by-time monitoring system with the relatively heat-resistant bacterial virus f2 as a standard. A search of the literature showed that the resistance of f2 to heat was high enough so that if it was destroyed all enteric pathogens would be also. The D values of a number of enteric pathogens as compared with f2 are shown in Table 4. A D value is the amount of time required to cause a ten-fold (one log) reduction in population numbers. The temperature must be specified. A plot showing the number of logs of f2 killed for different temperatures with time is shown in Figure 4. As a reasonable goal for a composting operation it was decided to use 15 logs of f2 inactivation. At 55°C this could be achieved in 2.5 days. In the canning industry, the time at a particular temperature to inactivate 11 logs of bacillus spores is considered adequate, but even with the control realizable in the canning process for uniform heating the theoretical spore reduction often is not obtained. Therefore, in a much less controllable composting system, the use of a 15 log criterium did not seem to be an unreasonable value to insure safety.

To determine the applicability of the approach to the Beltsville procedure and to determine the most suitable monitoring sites, 15 composting piles were monitored taking random probings associated with three pile regions: the center, the lateral portions, and the lower portions at the pile end (pile toes). Consistently the latter area was found to be at the lowest temperatures. Nevertheless it was found that one could expect to achieve at least 55°C in this portion of the pile and therefore in all portions of the pile for 10.6 days of the 21 day composting period with a confidence level of 95 percent. Therefore it appeared reasonable to monitor the pile in this zone.

Studies have shown that salmonellae are capable to some degree of repopulating sludge and compost. In sterilized compost growth can be extensive, but in sludge and compost that has not been sterilized, the population increase over the inoculation levels is usually only a log or so with a reduction to undetectable levels in a few days. The experience at Beltsville has been that during periods when windrow composting of raw sludge was interrupted by heavy rains and cold, one was able to find salmonellae in stored compost and on the site pad. But monitoring monthly for one and one-half years while composting by the aerated-pile method, one was unable to detect salmonellae on the pad or in stored compost. As a result of this experience it is recommended that in addition to temperature monitoring the finished compost be monitored monthly at the site for salmonellae by an agency independent of the organization operating the site and doing the temperature monitoring.

As of March 18, 1982, the Dickerson sewage sludge composting site in Montgomery Country, Maryland had been in operation for 15 months and had been using the temperature-by-time criteria and salmonella monitoring since

224

Table 4 : Time required for a 10-fold reduction of enteric pathogens by heat as compared with that for f2 bacteriophage (13)

Organism	D Value (Minutes)	
	55°C	60°C
Adenovirus, 12 NIAID	11	0.17
Poliovirus, type 1	32	19
Ascaris ova	-	1.3
Histolytica cysts	44	25
Salmonella*	80	7.5
Bacteriophage, f2	267	47

* Serotype senftenberg 775 W

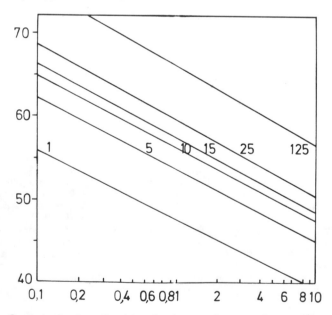

Figure 4 : Curves showing the time-by-temperature regimes necessary for the inactivation of a desired number of logs of f2 bacteriophage (12)

starting. Once the six monitoring points have maintained a minimum temperature of 55°C for at least three consecutive days then only biweekly temperature monitoring is required. In addition to temperature monitoring, a monthly sampling of the 21 day old aerated piles, screened compost storage piles, and unscreened compost storage piles was conducted. Samples were taken at a point one-foot below the pile surface and analyzed for salmonellae. As yet no samples positive for salmonellae have been found."

All the above quoted results show that until now no reliable indicator system is available, not even for salmonellas not to mention for other pathogenic microorganisms in composts made from sewage sludge, municipal refuse or a mixture of both. Therefore we were assigned a research project from the Federal Office for Environmental Protection into this direction. Very first and only few results (Table 5) do not show a definite correlation between the numbers of enterobacteriaceae and the occurrence of salmonellas (samples No. 1, 4a-c). As well it cannot be concluded from the values proposed for fecal streptococci by de Bertoldi et al. (4, 5) that salmonellas are absent (samples No. 2d, 5a). Possibly the complete absence of fecal streptococci could give the security for salmonella-negative results (samples No. 2c, 3c, 5b). Whether these observations are really sound can only be proved by as many further investigations as possible.

Certain contradictions emerge from our investigations also with respect to the Swiss method for evaluation of disinfected sludge, based on the numbers of enterobacteriaceae (max. value 100/g of substrate). In the vertical column 4 of Table 5 these figures are given. According to the Swiss regulations the samples 3a and 3b were considered as being sanitized Despite that fact salmonellas were isolated from that material. Also for a final evaluation of this method one cannot do without many more comparing investigations, preferably in international scale.

We also could confirm the statement of Scarpino (2) that there may be differences in disinfection rate when using laboratory stock virus strains versus indigenous virus. We found certain differences in the temperature sensitivity between laboratory strains of Salmonella spp. when seeded into the sludge and indigenous Salmonella spp. strains isolated from the same sludge. The same was also true for strains of Streptococcus faecium (ATCC 6057) and strains indigenous of the same sludge.

In other own experiments it could be proved that indigenous fecal streptococci (FS) have a considerably lower pH-sensitivity than Salmonella spp. thus indicating that it may become necessary to choose different indicators for the hygienic control or evaluation of different sludge treatment systems.

3.6 In summarizing the literature quoted and other literature as well as own experiences it must be concluded that the problem of monitoring methods to render sewage sludge free of pathogens by looking for indicator organisms is not solved for a long time yet. Several approaches were described but all of them still have to prove their efficacy under practical conditions and for more than only one system of sludge treatment. The concerns of Scarpino (2) and others about the use of bacteria or bacteriophages as indicators for pathogenic viruses have to be considered as well as the conclusions and recommendations of Pederson (3) and the demands of de Bertoldi et al. (5) to better define the term "sanitized compost" and to lay down not only which microorganisms are to be monitored, but also their maximum permitted level in a sanitized product. For this evaluation also the results of Schrammeck and Sauerwald (11), which are of practical importance, have to be drawn into consideration.

Table 5 : Preliminary results of bacteriological investigations with wastewater and sewage sludge for the evaluation of different bacteria or groups of bacteria as indicator organisms

Material	Total Germ Germ 1	Enterobacteriaceae 2	3	4 (Swiss Meth.)	Coliforms 5	Fecal Strept. 6	Phages	Salmonellas
1. Digested SS	2.4×10^7	2.0×10^6	2.4×10^5	2.4×10^3	3.4×10^4	5.6×10^4	2.5×10^3	-
2a. Influent STP	3.2×10^6	1.0×10^5	5.0×10^4	2.1×10^5	1.4×10^5	6.0×10^4	7.0×10^3	+
2b. Chemic. condit. SS	5.8×10^8	1.2×10^8	5.0×10^7	7.3×10^7	8.4×10^7	4.0×10^6	3.1×10^6	+
2c. Thermic. condit. SS	3.4×10^4	4.2×10^2	1.3×10^2	2.0×10^2	-	-	-	-
2d. Effluent STP	1.0×10^4	3.2×10^3	5.0×10^2	2.1×10^2	2.8×10^3	3.0×10^2	1.1×10^3	+
3a. Influent STP	1.6×10^8	4.8×10^7	4.5×10^7	-	3.3×10^4	5.0×10^4	6.0×10^3	+
3b. Digested SS	2.4×10^9	3.0×10^8	3.2×10^8	-	4.0×10^3	2.3×10^4	1.5×10^4	+
3c. Effluent STP	8.0×10^4	7.9×10^3	1.2×10^4	-	-	-	5.0×10^3	-
4a. Influent STP	2.2×10^7	8.5×10^5	1.0×10^5	2.0×10^6	3.2×10^5	8.4×10^5	1.7×10^4	-
4b. Dewatered SS	4.8×10^6	1.6×10^6	6.4×10^5	5.3×10^5	5.0×10^4	3.1×10^4	1.1×10^5	-
4c. Effluent STP	5.6×10^4	1.5×10^4	8.4×10^3	2.5×10^3	1.4×10^4	4.0×10^2	1.9×10^3	-
4d. 218 kg CaO/m³ SS	4.5×10^3	-	-	-	-	6.0×10^2	4.5×10^3	-
4e. 48 kg CaO/m³ SS	4.8×10^4	3.0×10^4	1.0×10^2	3.5×10^2	-	2.1×10^4	6.0×10^2	+
5a. Digested SS	1.0×10^6	-	n.d.	n.d.	1.0×10^2	7.0×10^2	n.d.	-
5b. 150 kg CaO/m³ SS	2.0×10^3	-	n.d.	n.d.	-	-	n.d.	-

1 = Standard 1-Agar;   2 = McConkey-Agar;   3 = Violet Red Bile-Agar;   4 = Violet Red Bile-Agar, Submers-method acc. to Swiss regulations;   5 = Endo C-Agar;   6 = Slanetz-Bartley-Agar;   SS = Sewage Sludge;   STP = Sewage Treatment Plant;   n.d. = not done

In following the conclusions of Working Party 3 that it is in many
cases advisable to analyse composts for pathogens directly and use them
for seeding to test the efficacy of treatment systems. The described observations have to be considered that under certain circumstances differences
in sensitivity of indigenous pathogens and the seeded laboratory strains
may exist which can distort the results of such studies. This question has
especially to be investigated in connection with the recommendation of f2-
phages as indicator organisms (12, 13).

Much more practical work is to be done in this respect before final
decisions can be made and standardized methods are internationally available.
To achieve this easier the recommendation of Pederson (3) should be better
observed in the future that researchers document carefully all pertinent
aspects of their experimental design.

Since the authorities in several countries are preparing regulations
for the safe utilization of composts in agriculture, gardening and possibly
in forestry the politicians need definitions of parameters for hygienically
safe composts which are relating to practice, which can be controlled by
the authorities and which can easily be changed when new scientific results
indicate that there is a need for revision. Therefore in the following
chapter we are presenting for discussion a proposal of the requirements for
efficient disinfection of composts.

4. PROPOSAL FOR REQUIREMENTS OF DISINFECTING SLUDGE

I. At the time of delivery of hygienically safe compost by the producer
to the customer the compost should meet the following requirements:
- it should not contain more than 5×10^2 Enterobacteriaceae and
5×10^3 Fecal Streptococci per gram
- it should not contain salmonellas (pre-enrichment) in 100 g,
- it should not contain infective parasite ova.

II. For efficient disinfection of compost the technologies used should
meet the following requirements:

1. Composting

a) Windrow (Stack)-Composting

To ensure a hygienically safe product the composting process must be
operated for at least three to four weeks. During this time the temperature
should exceed 65°C for at least one week.

It is most important that all of the compost mass in the windrow must
reach this temperature for the recommended period of time. These requirements
can be met by operating a program of regular turning of the piles or by covering them with a layer of composted material. Thus a more uniform temperature profile in the composting material can be achieved. To further improve
the hygienic quality of the compost the composting process should be followed by curing the material in stacks for another three or more weeks.

b) Bioreactor-Composting

In bioreactors more uniform temperature profiles in the composting
material can be attained and the temperature can be influenced by the aeration rate and the technique of feeding. For a hygienically safe product the
temperature of the compost in the reactor should reach 65° - 70°C and the
material should not pass this temperature range faster than in 48 hours.
The flow time of the material through the reactor(s) should be in the range
of two weeks or above. A subsequent curing time of at least three weeks

will help to improve the technical and hygienic quality of the compost.

In bioreactors the temperature must closely be monitored and in case of disturbances immediate counteractions by the operator are necessary. That material which has not reached the required temperature either must be used as reflux material for another passage through the reactor or must be stored in a.windrow for at least three weeks with at least one turning.

2. Aerobic-thermophilic stabilization

Aerobic-thermophilic treatment of liquid raw sludge as the sole stabilization process, combined with the aim to disinfect the sludge, should, as a rule, always be operated at least as a two-stage system with two reactors. The mean hydraulic detention time in the system should at least be five days and the minimum detention time in each of the reactors one day.

Disinfection under these technical conditions can be achieved if in the course of the whole process a minimum temperature of 55°C for at least 48 hours with a pH about 8 or 60°C for at least 24 hours with a pH distinctly above 8 can be ensured.

With single stage aerobic-thermophilic stabilization an inactivation of pathogens in sewage sludge can be achieved under certain conditions and observance of certain parameters. But it is nearly impossible in the daily practical operation to constantly maintain these necessary parameters and control them. Moreover hydraulic short-circuits resulting in still infectious effluent cannot be excluded.

Even in the two-stage aerobic-thermophilic stabilization process one has to reckon with a breakthrough of pathogens in reactor I for similar reasons as in the single-stage process which can be counterbalanced by the thermical and biochemical activities in reactor II. Therefore aerobic-thermophilic stabilization of raw sludge with the purpose of eliminating pathogens basically should only be operated as a two or more stage system.

III. Newly developed technologies for the disinfection of compost should be tested before they are introduced into practice and, according to the results, be approved by national or local authorities. For these tests the system should be controlled for its efficacy by using known and representative pathogens like salmonellas, parvovirus and Ascaris eggs. If this is not feasible for certain reasons also fecal streptococci can be introduced as bacterial test organisms. For testing the disinfecting efficacy on viruses instead of parvovirus also the f2-phage should be used to add more practical experience to the results described by Burge et al. (12, 13).

Disinfection processes should result in a complete inactivation of salmonellas and infective ascaris eggs, a reduction of 4 logs of parvovirus or a reduction of 4 logs of fecal streptococci (that not more than 5×10^3 g/ml can be isolated) and 15 logs of f2-phages. All the results obtained in following these recommendations of part III should be subject to international discussions and be tesserae for a final international standardization of monitoring methods.

5. LITERATURE

(1) Concerted action treatment and use of sewage sludge. COST 68 ter; Final report of the Community - Cost Concertation Comittee; TT. Scientific Report; CEC SL/94/83 - XII/ENV/44/83, Brussels 1983

(2) SCARPINO, P.V. (1982). Selection of practical indicator systems for
     monitoring the virological quality of potable water, wastewater, solid
     waste, shellfish, fish and crops. 11th Conference of the International
     Association on Water Pollution Research, Post-Conference Seminar 2:
     Water Virology, Pretoria/SA, 5./6. April 1982.
(3) PEDERSON, D.C. (1981). Density levels of pathogenic organisms in muni-
     cipal wastewater sludge - a literature review. Natl. Techn. Inform.
     Service, 5285 Port Royal Rd., Springfield, VA 221 61, USA. Order No.
     PB 82-102 286
(4) DE BERTOLDI, M., COPPOLA, S. and SPINOSA, L. (1983). Health implica-
     tions in sewage sludge composting. In: Bruce, A.M., Havelaar, A.H.,
     L'Hermite, P. (Eds.), Disinfection of sewage sludge-technical, economic
     and microbiological aspects, 165-178. D. Reidel Publ. Comp., Dordrecht/
     Holland
(5) DE BERTOLDI, M., FRASSINETTI, S., BIANCHIN, L. and PERA, A. (1985).
     Sludge hygienization with different compost systems. Joint Seminar CEC-
     German Veterinary Medical Society: Inactivation of microorganisms in
     sewage sludge by stabilization processes, Hohenheim, 8-10 Oct. 1984.
     Strauch, D., Havelaar, A.H. and L'Hermite, P. (Eds.), Elsevier Applied
     Science Publ., London-New York
(6) HAVELAAR, A.H. (1985). Mikrobiologische Spezifikationen für die Desin-
     fektion von Klärschlamm (Microbiological specifications for the disin-
     fection of sewage sludge). Paper to be presented at 119. Seminar of
     FGU Berlin 'Umwelthygiene in der Abfallwirtschaft - Stand und Beurtei-
     lung (Environmental hygiene in waste management - state and assessment).
     Berlin 29-30 April 1985, (canceled).
(7) HAMMEL, H.-E. (1983). Hygienische Untersuchungen über die Wirkung von
     Verfahren zur Kompostierung von entwässertem Klärschlamm und zur aerob-
     thermophilen Stabilisierung von Flüssigschlamm (Hygienic investigations
     on the efficacy of methods for composting dewatered sludge and for
     aerobic-thermophilic stabilization of liquid sewage sludge). Veteri-
     nary Medical Thesis, Univ. Giessen/Germany.
(8) STRAUCH, D., HAMMEL, H.-E. and PHILIPP, W. (1985). Investigations on
     the hygienic effect of single stage and two-stage aerobic-thermophilic
     stabilization of liquid raw sludge. Loc. cit. No. 5, pp. 48-63.
(9) RÜPRICH, W. and STRAUCH, D. (1984). Technologische und hygienische
     Aspekte der aerob-thermophilen Schlammstabilisierung - System Fuchs
     (Technological and hygienic aspects of aerobic-thermophilic sludge
     stabilization - system Fuchs). Korrespondenz Abwasser, 31(11) 946-952.
(10) LANGELAND, G. and PAULSRUD, B. (1985). Aerobic thermophilic stabili-
     zation. Loc. cit. No. 5, pp. 38-47.
(11) SCHRAMMECK, E. and SAUERWALD, M. (1984). Gutachten über die hygieni-
     sche Beschaffenheit von Müll- bzw. Müll-Klärschlammkomposten aus den
     Werken in Ennepetal, Duisburg und Lemgo (Expertise on the hygienic
     quality of compost from municipal refuse or refuse/sludge produced
     in the plants of Ennepetal, Duisburg and Lemgo/Germany). Hygiene-In-
     stitut des Ruhrgebietes, Rotthauser Straße 19, D-4650 Gelsenkirchen.
(12) BURGE, W.D., COLACICCO, D. and CRAMER, W.N. (1981). Criteria for
     achieving pathogen destruction during composting. J. Water Poll.
     Contr. Feder. 53(12) 1683-1690.
(13) BURGE, W.D. (1983). Monitoring pathogen destruction. BioCycle March/
     April, 48-50.

OPTIMISATION OF AGRICULTURAL INDUSTRIAL WASTES MANAGEMENT THROUGH IN-VESSEL COMPOSTING

Maurice VIEL, Daniel SAYAG and Louis ANDRE
Laboratoire de Pédologie : Physicochimie du Sol
Ecole Nationale Supérieure Agronomique
145 avenue de Muret, F-31076 Toulouse Cédex,France

Summary
The insulated and unheated 100 1 reactor developed for the high-rate composting of agricultural wastes under adiabatic conditions affords a satisfactory control of the physical and chemical parameters involved in the process rate and yield : temperature, aeration and various substrate requirements (free air space, particle size, water-holding capacity, pH, C/N ratio). The available N K nutrient content of sewage sludges or cattle slurry could be valorised by the incorporation of suitable agricultural wastes promoting aerobic fermentation. The following mixtures were thus investigated : M 1 (30 % sewage sludge + 60 % sawdust + 10 % fats), M2 (49 % cattle slurry + 51 % ground straw), and M 3 (20 % sewage sludge + 20 % mushroom wastes + 25.5 % sawdust + 25.5 % ground straw + 6.5 % slaughterhouse wastes + 2.5 % fats). In every case, the residual oxygen rate in the exit air was ca. 2 % and the oneweek single composting runs were characterized by a peak temperature of ca. 75°C. The quality of the end product could be improved by removing some of the excess heat which could be used for other purposes. The most significant points are a marked decrease in the C/N ratio, reflecting the organic matter degradation (50 %), and more particularly the fast and nearly complete (> 80 %) disappearance of fats and the breakdown of ligno-celluloses to humic matter characterized by a high ion-exange capacity and an increased water-holding capacity. The equipment and the procedure developed are being applied successfully to the full-scale operational composting of various agricultural industrial wastes. This rational and efficient approach to solid waste disposal provides valuable organic fertilizers and soil conditioners for market-garden crops.

INTRODUCTION

Composting is increasingly used as a means of waste disposal, providing a rational approach to the bulk treatment of organic wastes. Composting is an exothermal biological oxidation of organic matter carried out by different groups of aerobic microorganisms (bacteria, fungi, actinomycetes). The heterogeneous organic matter present in the starting material is transformed into a stabilized end product through partial mineralization and humification. The mesophilic (25-45°C) and the thermophilic (45-75°C) stages are characterized by a rise in temperature corresponding, successively, to the depletoire of the more readily soluble and available constituents of the substrate and to the attack of the lipid, protein, hemicellulose, cellulose and even lignin fractions. The ripening stage then results in a fairly homogeneous and stable end product after a few months. Composts can be used agriculture and horticulture to improve a soil tilth often impaired by low levels or depletion of organic matter.

The main advantages of closed systems (i.e. of in-vessel or high-rate composting) over open systems (windrows,aerated static piles) are the shortening of the mesophilic and thermophilic stages, together with a higher process efficiency and a decreased number of pathogens, resulting in a safer and more valuable end product.

The laboratory investigations reported here, a preliminary step in the industrial development of the procedure and to the assessment of the quality of the composts, are a follow-up to the earlier determination of the optimum conditions promoting aerobic fermentations, using 2 l bench-scale composters (1, 2).

IN-VESSEL CO-COMPOSTING

Many detailed analyses of the main parameters involved in composting have been reported in the literature (3,4,5). The biological activity of the microorganisms is conditioned by various environmental factors, particularly oxygen availability, moisture and temperature. The high-rate composting of urban, agricultural and industrial wastes under optimum conditions is aimed at producing a good quality compost in a short time.

1. COMPOSITION OF THE MIXTURES

The selection of suitable agricultural wastes for successful composting took into account their local availability in large amounts. The factors to be optimized were particle size, porosity, moisture, pH and the C/N ratio.

The most highly polluting wastes, such as sewage sludges, cattle slurries, slaughterhouse wastes or mushroom canning wastes, contain finely divided, nitrogen-rich (2-4 %) biodegradable organic matter and large amounts of water (> 80 %). Composting could also benefit from the input of fats from sausage manufacturing effluents of flotation foams of wastewater purification plants.

Bulking agents, such as shredded wheat straw or poplar sawdust, have a very low nitrogen content and can absorb the excess moisture of sludges while increasing the porosity of the mixtures. Their high cellulose-lignin content may promote the formation of humic matter.

Mixtures M1, M2 and M3, were prepared so as to comply with the following requirements : C/N 25-35, pH 6.5-7.5, porosity (free air space) ca. 30 %, moisture 60-70 %. The composition of the mixtures and the physicochemical characteristics of their constituents are listed in Table I. Mixture M3 corresponds to the optimum utilization of the municipal, agricultural and industrial wastes from Thouars, a small French town in the Limoges area.

MIXTURE	% CONSTITUENTS	pH	% DRY MATTER	% ASH	% N	% C	C/N	% P
M_1	anaerobically digested sewage sludges (32)	6.9	22	42.5	2.7	33	12	0.13
	flotation fats (8)	5.4	47.5	4.5	1	77	77	0.24
	poplar sawdust (60)	8.9	73	2.5	0.15	48	$\approx$ 300	0.013
M_2	Feedlot slurry (35)	7.6	13	12.3	3.9	43	10	1
	wheat straw (65)	7.8	78	8.7	0.5	45	90	0.07
M_3	stabilized sewage sludges (20)	6.8	28.5	45	2	30	15	0.13
	mushroom wastes (20)	5.7	34	12	3.6	27	7.5	0.33
	pork wastes (2)	6.1	24.5	8	1.5	77	51	0.52
	slaughterhouse wastes (6)	7.5	14	5	3	50	16	0.60
	ground wheat straw (29)	7.8	94	6	0.5	48	96	0.07
	poplar sawdust (23)	8.9	73	2.5	0.15	48	$\approx$ 300	0.013

Table 1 : Physicochemical characteristics of the constituents of the mixtures used in composting trials (% on a dry matter basis).

2. COMPOSTING RUNS

Single composting runs were carried out, under adiabatic conditions, in a 100 l insulated and unheated cylindrical stainless steel reactor. Minimization of heat losses was achieved by an adequate selection of the active to insulating volume ratio so that a sufficient rise in temperature could occur. Water could be circulated within the reactor double wall and act as a thermal exchanger.

The load was fractionated : the constituents were first introduced separately into the reactor, then mixed for 15-20 minutes. The initial volume of the mixture was ca. 65 l, corresponding to ca. 32 kg of starting material with a moisture content of ca. 65 %.

Water-saturated air was forced through the system by means of a small pressure gradient. The air flow rates selected and the substrate moisture were such that the effluent gas was saturated permanently. Water was trapped at the outlet of the reactor and the effluent gas was sent to a sampling chamber and analyzed for O_2 and CO_2. The value of the oxygen content of the effluent gas was maintained in the range 2-5 % and used for the automated control of the aeration of the substrate. The initial air flow rate of 30 1/h was gradually increased to a maximum value of 160 1/h when the microbiological activity was optimum. Stirring for 3 minutes every 3 hours was adequate for the maintenance of aerobic conditions within the composting mass and for its homogenization.

At the end of the composting run, i.e. when the oxygen consumption rate fell below 0.4 l/h.kg dry matter (in other words, after a retention time of 7-9 days), the reactor was unloaded and the "stabilized" product was transferred into perforated plastic bags where the ripening stage could proceed for 2-6 months.

RESULTS

Microbial activity can be assessed by measuring oxygen consumption, carbon dioxide production, or chemical and physical changes in the composting mass. Temperature is also a parameter frequently used to rate the efficiency of composting processes.

1. OXYGEN CONSUMPTION AND TEMPERATURE

Figure 1, 2 and 3 show the temperature and the oxygen consumption rate profiles obtained for mixtures M1, M2 and M3, respectively, during the first week. These profiles are characterized, over the first two days, by a bimodal pattern, i.e. by the occurrence of two optima in relation to differing microbiological activities. The oxygen consumption rate profiles exhibit sharp peaks ; the temperature profiles follow the same general pattern of change although the peak overlap and the time lag are a result of thermal inertia.

Initially, the material was at the same temperature as the surrounding air. As soon as the mixture was prepared, microorganisms started to multiply within the composting mass and a rapid warming occurred. The temperature rose from 20 to ca 50°C during the first 16 hours. The values observed for the first peak of the oxygen profile - 1.7 l/h.kg dry matter at 45°C (M1) and 53°C (M3) against 2.4 l/h.kg dry matter at 57°C (M2) - reflect the higher fermentescibility of mixture M2 since the sewage sludges of M1 and M3 had been previously digested anaerobically.

The transition between the mesophilic and thermophilic stages was characterized by a marked decrease in oxygen consumption and a much slower increase in temperature for the next 5-10 hours.

The temperature then rapidly increased further to stabilize above 70°C before cooling down gradually and slowly. As the temperature rose above 65°C, the oxygen consumption decreased markedly (1.6 l/h.kg dry matter at

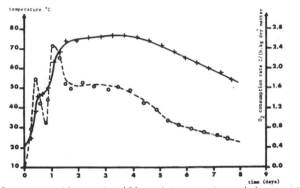

Figure 1 : O_2 consumption rate (O) and temperature (+) vs. time for mixture M_1

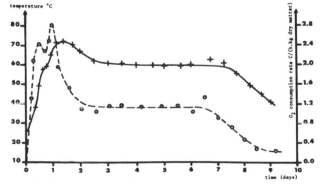

Figure 2 : O_2 consumption rate (O) and temperature (+) vs. time for mixture M_2

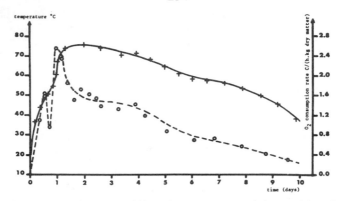

Figure 3 : O_2 consumption rate (O) and temperature (+) vs. time for mixture M_3

75°C for M1 and 1.4 l/h.kg dry matter at 70°C for M3) : the decrease in metabolic activity is a result of the change in microflora and of the thermal inhibition of microbiological activity. High temperatures are highly selective towards the microflora ; they have however a positive effect in destroying thermosensitive pathogens. Some of the excess heat could be removed by the water circulating within the thermal exchanger, using a temperature control unit responding to a temperature sensor. The main advantage of thermoregulation is improved efficiency, i.e. increased yields and faster composting (6).

At the end of the thermophilic stage, the oxygen consumption rate was below 0.4 l/h.kg d.m. and the temperature below 40°C.The duration of the stabilization phase (i.e. mesophilic and thermophilic stages) was 7-9 days.

A major advantage of in vessel co-composting, contrary to the gradients observed in windrow or static pile composting, is the fairly homogeneous microbial activity within the whole composting mass. Chanter and Spencer (7) could show that homogeneous temperature conditions promote the development of thermophilic bacteria and the disappearance of mesophilic fungi that release antibiotics.

2. pH

Figure 4 shows the pH vs time plots obtained for mixtures M1, M2 and M3. The pH drop observed at the initiation of the composting process results from the activity of the mesophilic microorganisms which break down complex carbonaceous material to organic acid intermediates. The thermophilic stage was characterized by a sharp increase in pH, followed by a stabilization around pH 8.5 (M1, M3) or even pH 8.9 (M2), in relation to ammonia release through protein hydrolysis. During the ripening stage, as ammonia was used by microorganisms, the pH values gradually got closer to neutrality.

3. MOISTURE

The dry matter values listed in Table II show that the moisture content of the composting medium at the end of the thermophilic stage was higher than the initial value : water release through microbiological activity then outweighed evaporation. On the contrary, during the ripening stage, evaporation prevailed over metabolic activity, and the contents of the bags were homogenized and watered twice a month so as to maintain adequate moisture.

4. ORGANIC MATTER

Table III and Figure 5 clearly show that the breakdown of the organic matter proceeds much more slowly during the ripening stage (especially after 50 days) than during the stabilization. The higher breakdown rates observed for M2 (50 % against 36 and 38 % for M1 and M3, respectively) are to be ascribed to the higher fermentescibility of cattle slurries.

MIXTURES		pH	% DRY MATTER	% ASH	% N	% C	C/N	'/..P	'/..Ca	'/..K	'/..Mg	'/..Na
M_1	s	7.5	37.4	15.9	1.27	42.9	34	0.49	16.7	1.35	1.0	0.24
	f	8.5	36.9	18.7	1.31	40.5	31	0.55	17.0	1.40	1.8	0.28
M_2	s	8.4	30.0	10	1.6	44	28	2.8	4.0	4.6	0.98	0.85
	f	8.9	25.2	13	1.8	39	23.6	4.1	5.8	5.4	0.60	0.58
M_3	s	6.2	41.6	20	1.14	40.5	35	5.3	20.6	3.3	1.3	0.5
	f	8.4	37.7	24	1.19	35.0	31.6	6.2	22.6	4.3	1.6	0.6

Table 2 : Physicochemical characteristics of the mixtures used in composting trials (s = starting material; f = after stabilization (7-9 days)).

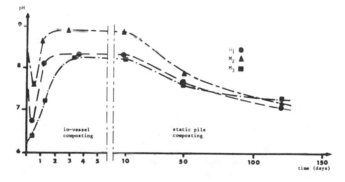

Figure 4 : pH vs time for mixtures M_1, M_2 and M_3

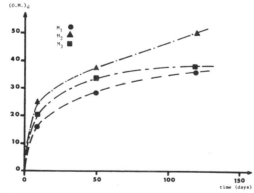

Figure 5 : Organic matter degraded (%) vs time for mixtures M_1, M_2 and M_3 :

$$(O.M.)_d = 100-100[a_i(100-a_f)] / a_f(100-a_i)$$

with a_i = initial % ash and a_f = final % ash.

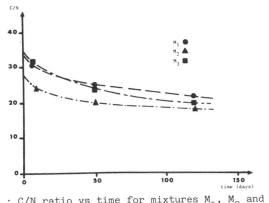

Figure 6 : C/N ratio vs time for mixtures M_1, M_2 and M_3

5. C/N RATIO

Table III and Figure 6 show that, in spite of markedly differing initial values, a C/N ratio value of ca 20 was obtained at the end of the ripening stage. The differences observed are likely to originate from higher nitrogen losses through volatilization of ammonia as a result of the higher pH value (8.9) during the thermophilic stage in the case of M2. A higher initial C/N value or pH adjustment to 8.5 could have minimized nitrogen losses.

6. FATS

Table III shows that, during the stabilization phase, the lipid content of Ml was decreased by ca 80 % : the high temperatures of the thermophilic stage promote the microbial attack of the fats. The breakdown proceeds further during the ripening stage and results in the nearly complete disappearance of fats. In-vessel co-composting can therefore be a safe means of disposal of agricultural wastes containing fats.

Parameters	Mixture	Start.	After stabilization (7-9 days)	After 50 days	After 120 days
Organic matter	M_1	84.1	81.3	79	77
	M_2	90	87	84	82
	M_3	80	76	72.5	70
Lipids	M_1	9.3	1.4	0.8	0.5
Organic carbon	M_1	42.9	41	39	38
	M_2	44	42.5	42.5	40
	M_3	40.5	38	36.5	36
Total nitrogen	M_1	1.27	1.31	1.56	1.7
	M_2	1.6	1.8	2.1	2.2
	M_3	1.14	1.29	1.5	1.8
C/N ratio	M_1	34	31	25	22
	M_2	28	23.6	20	18
	M_3	35	31.6	24	20
pH	M_1	7.5	8.5	7.7	7.1
	M_2	8.4	8.9	7.9	7.2
	M_3	6.2	8.4	7.6	7.3

Table 3 : Physicochemical characteristics of the mixtures used in composting trials at various stages (% on a dry matter basis).

CONCLUSION

The results of these laboratory investigations can readily be used for the development of operational composting procedures on a full scale. The most significant points are the high rate of organic matter degradation (40-50 %), and more particularly the fast and nearly complete (> 80 %) disappearance of fats and the breadown of lignocelluloses to humic matter characterized by a high ion-exchange capacity and an increased water-holding capacity. The ion-exchange, buffering and water-holding capacities as well as the mechanical properties of the composts thus prepared compare favourably with those of commercial peats. The land application of these organic fertilizers and soil conditioners would therefore be highly beneficial to market garden-crops.

REFERENCES

(1) PLAT J.Y., SAYAG D. and ANDRE L. (1984). Effect of some physical parameters on composting rate and yield. Studies in Environmental Science, vol. 23, 553-558. Elsevier, Amsterdam (Chemistry for Protection of the Environment, Proceedings of an International Conference, Toulouse, 19-25 September 1983).

(2) PLAT J.Y., SAYAG D. and ANDRE L. (1984). High-rate composting of wool industry wastes, BioCycle, 25 (2), 39-42.

(3) a. WILEY J.S. (1956). I. Progress report on high rate composting studies. Proceedings of the 11th Industrial Waste Conference, Purdue University, 334-341.
b. WILEY J.S. (1957). II. Progress report on high rate composting studies. Proceedings of the 12th Industrial Waste Conference, 596-603.

(4) a. SCHULZE K.L. (1958). Rate of oxygen consumption and respiratory quotients during the aerobic decomposition of a synthetic garbage. Proceedings of the 13th Industrial Waste Conference, Purdue University, 541-554.
b. SCHULZE K.L. (1962). Continuous thermophilic composting. Appl. Microbiol., 10, 108-122.
c. SCHULZE K.L. (1962). Automatic temperature and air control in composting. Compost Sci., 2 (1), 31-34.

(5) a. POINCELOT R.P. (1974). A scientific examination of the principles and practices of composting. Compost Sci., 15 (3), 24-31.
b. POINCELOT R.P. (1975). The biochemistry and methodology of composting. Conn. Agr. Exp. Stat. Bull. n° 754, 18 p.

(6) VIEL M., SAYAG D., PEYRE A. and ANDRE L. (1986). Optimization of invessel co-composting through heat recovery. Trans. A.S.A.E. (submitted for publication).

(7) CHANTER D.P. and SPENCER D.M. (1974). The importance of thermophilic bacteria in mushroom compost fermentation. Scientia horticulturae, 2, 249-256.

BIOCHEMISTRY OF MANURE COMPOSTING :

LIGNIN BIOTRANSFORMATION AND HUMIFICATION

B. GODDEN and M. PENNINCKX.

Laboratoire de Microbiologie de
l'Université Libre de Bruxelles.

Summary.

It was shown that lignin was degraded to a limited extent
(15%) but only in the early stage of cattle manure compos-
ting.Lignin was purified by a gentle procedure and further
characterized by IR, UV Spectroscopy and HPLC. About 50 percent of lignin was found under the form of a lower MW and
oxidised fraction after five weeks of composting. After 8
weeks of composting the lower MW fraction decreased subsequently. This pattern could be related to humification of
the material.

1. Introduction.

Lignin is one of the most resistant fraction in composting
materials (5). Indeed, lignin is a very elaborate and non-recuring
polymer of phenylpropane units, joined by C-C and C-O-C linkages
(5, 2). This polymer is closely associate to cellulose fibres and
hampers the microbial degradation of the polysaccharide fraction
of lignocellulosic materials (5, 2).

In previous investigations (4 ,3), we have shown that cellulose degradation, during composting of cattle manure, occurred
mainly in the mesophilic phases, including the initial stage of the
process.

In the present work we have studied cellulose degradation in
relation with lignin alteration and humic compounds genesis.

2. Experimental.

2.1 Starting material and composting procedure.

Pile composting of 5 tons of fresh cattle manure was carried
out during two months with appropriate mixing of the heap in order
to ensure aerobic conditions. The material was protected with a
straw cover.

2.2 Analytical and Preparative procedures.

Lignin evolution during composting was estimated by the standard ASTM procedure (1). Lignin samples for physicochemical analyses, were prepared by the dioxane - HCl procedure (10). Cellulose was estimated by the KURSCHNER method (8). Resins were estimated by the proximate analysis procedure (13). Humic substances were extracted by 0.1M sodium pyrophosphate (pH 9.0) under a nitrogen stream (11). Humic carbon was determined by a dry combustion method. All enzymatic determinations were performed on extracts obtained after treatment under agitation (160 strokes/min.) of fresh compost with 0.5% Triton ^{R} x 100 during 10 min. at room temperature. Laccases activities were assayed with syringaldazine (9) and guaïacol (12). Cellulase activity was estimated by determining reducing sugars released from insoluble CF1 WATHMAN cellulose. Molecular weights distribution of lignin and humic substances was estimated by HPLC using a ZORBAX ^{R} GF-250 Column (DUPONT) eluted with dimethylformamide. Lignin IR spectra (KBr) were performed with a UNICAM SP 1100 apparatus. Lignin UV spectra in dioxan were performed according to KIRK and CHANG (7) with a CARY 15 apparatus.

3. Results and discussion.

The data collected during pile composting of cattle manure are summarized in Fig I. The starting material contained 33 percent (dry weight) of cellulose of which more than the half disappeared during composting. Cellulose degradation was faster during mesophilic phases where cellulase activity was more important (Fig I).

Lignin was only degraded to a very limited extent (15 %) but only in the early stage of composting (Fig Ib). We did not observe any significative increasing in the resins fraction during this stage (not illustrated). In fact, resins may include monomers derived from lignin. In the course of this investigation, we also estimated the levels of laccases, that could play some role in lignin degradation (2). Guaïacol oxidising activity was higher than the activity with syringaldazine (Fig I), wich peaked during the apparent lignin degradation step.

The apparent very weak degradation of lignin prompted us to investigate the polymer alteration by physicochemical methods. Analysis of molecular weight distribution by HPLC (Fig II) showed a sequence of depolymerization-repolymerization steps during the composting process. Depolymerization of lignin seems to occur just after the thermophilic phases of composting. UV and IR spectra of lignin prepared at different stages of composting have shown similarities between the altered samples of lignin. The UV spectra of these samples had increased absorbance centered around 260 nm and 300 nm (Fig III). These differences reflect most probably oxidative changes relative to the aromatic carboxyl content (6, 7). This was supported by UV titration experiments which have shown a lower content of phenolic OH groups in altered lignin. IR spectra were more difficult to interpretate but, at firt glance, seems to confirm the above-mentionned observations. Humic acids content depended on the stage of composting (Fig IV).

Humic carbon increased during the whole process but was more marked
between the tenth and the eighteen days of composting. On the other
hand, humic acids were invariably excluded from the HPLC column
that we used during this investigations (see Material and Methods).
This corresponds to molecular entities of MW   250,000.

It must be noted that a humic acid carbon fraction was already obtained at the starting of the composting process. This experimental observation could serve as basis for a discussion centered
around the concepts of humic compounds (14).

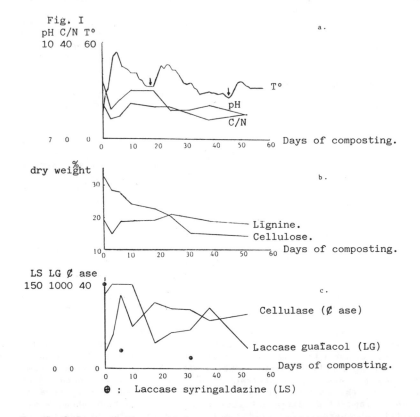

Figure I : Evolution of lignocellulose and enzyme activities during a pile
composting of cattle manure. All data were obtained according to the
methods described in the text. Additional data (pH, T°, C/N ratio) are
included for the purpose of establishing the general physico chemical
environment where composting took place. Enzyme units Cellulase is expressed
as g of reducing sugar released /h per g dry compost. Laccases (guaïacol and
synringaldazine) are respectively expressed as the variation of optical
density units at 460 nm and 525 nm/h per g dry compost.

(↓) : Turning over of the compost heap.

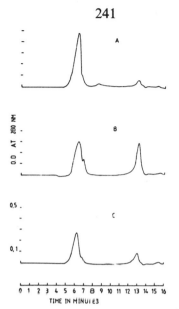

Figure II : HPLC of lignin samples obtained at different composting times.
Molecular weights distribution of lignin was estimated by using a ZORBAX^R
GF-250 Column eluted at 1.2 mL/min with dimethylforacide.

(A) : Starting of composting; (B) : 10 days of composting;
(C) : 51 days of composting.

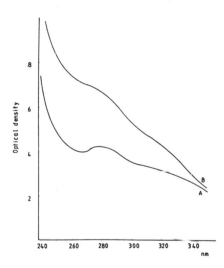

Figure III : UV Spectra of lignin samples obtained at different composting
times.

(A) : lignin at the starting of composting;
(B) : lignin at 10 days of composting.

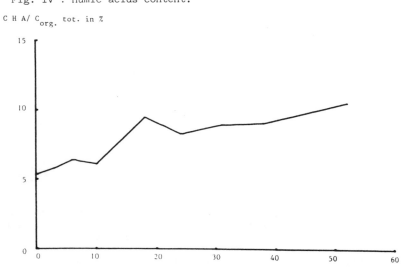

Fig. IV : Humic acids content.

C H A/ C$_{org.}$ tot. in %

Figure IV : Evolution of the ratio between the humic carbon and total carbon during composting. The data were obtained as described in the Experimental section.

References.

1. ASTM ;
    "Standard test method for Lignin in Wood."
    ANSI/ASTM D 1106-56 (Reapproved 1977);
    Annual Book of ASTM Standards part 22 (1977) pp. 367-369.

2. CRAWFORD R.D. & CRAWFORD D.L.;
    "Recent advances in studies of the mechanisms of microbial
    degradation of Lignins."
    Enzyme Microb. Technol., vol.6, (october 1984), 434-442.

3. GODDEN B., PENNINCKX M., PIERARD A. & LANNOYE R.;
    "Evolution of enzyme activities and microbial populations
    during composting of cattle manure."
    Eur. J. Appl. Microbiol. Biotechnol. (1983),
    vol. 17, 306-310.

4. GODDEN B. & PENNINCKX M.;
    "Identification and evolution of the cellulolytic microflora
    present during composting of cattle manure: on the role of
    actinomycetes sp."
    Ann. Microbiol. (Inst. Pasteur) (1984), vol. 135B, 69-78.

5. HALL P.;
    "Enzymatic transformations of lignin: 2."
    Enzyme Microb. Technol., (1980), vol. 2, july, 170-176.

6. KIRCK T.K. & CHANG H.M.;
    "Decomposition of Lignin by white-rot fungi. 1. Isolation of
    heavily degraded lignins from decayed Spruce."
    Holzforschung (1974), vol. 28, 217-222.

7. KIRCK T.K. & CHANG H.M.;
    "Decomposition of Lignin by white-rot fungi. 2. Characteriza-
    tion of heavily degraded lignins from decayed Spruce."
    Holzforschung (1975), vol. 29, 56-64.

8. KURSCHNER K & HANKE A.;
    "A new method for the determination of cellulose in cacao."
    Zeitschrift für Untersuchung und Lebensmittel (1930),
    vol. 59, 484-494.

9. LEONOWICZ A. & GRZYWNOWICZ;
    "Quantitative estimation of laccase forms in some white-rot
    fungi using syringaldozine as a substrate."
    Enzyme Microb. Technol., (1981), vol. 3, 55-58.

10. ODIER E. & MONTIES B.;
    "Biodégradation de la lignine de blé par Xanthomonas 23."
    Ann. Microbiol. (Inst. Pasteur) (1978), vol. 129A, 361-377.

11. ROLETTO E., BARBERIS R. & ZELANO V.;
    "Gel filtration and absorbtion spectroscopic investigations
    on humic substances from organic fertilizers."
    Plant and Soil, (1982), vol. 66, 383-390.

12. G. G. SERMANNI, G. BASILE & M. LUNA;
    "Biochemical changes occurring in the compost during growth
    and production of Pleurotus ostreatus and Agaricus bisporus."
    Mushroom Science, (1978), vol. 10, part 2, 37-53.

13. STEVENSON F.J.;
    "Gross Chemical Fractionation of Organic Matter"
    In:"Methods of Soil Analysis.";
    C.A.BLACKE et al Eds.;
    American Society of Agronomy, Madison, Wisc. (1965),
    1409-1421.

14. WAKSMAN S.A.;
    "Humus"
    WILLIAMS & WILKINS, Baltimore (1932).

THE DECOMPOSITION, HUMIFICATION AND FATE OF NITROGEN DURING THE COMPOSTING OF SOME PLANT RESIDUES

G.H.H. HAMMOUDA and W.A. ADAMS

Soil Science Unit, Department of Biochemistry and Agricultural
Biochemistry, The University College of Wales,
Aberystwyth, U.K.

Summary

Three plant residues, grass, hay and straw, differing widely
in nitrogen content and C/N ratio were each composted over
a period of 180 days. Straw was composted alone and with
sufficient $(NH_4)_2HPO_4$ to lower its C/N ratio to that of hay.
Over the composting period the plant materials showed different
patterns and extents of carbon and nitrogen loss. Losses of
carbon ranged from around 70% for grass to 30% for unamended
straw and losses of nitrogen from 60% to zero respectively.
Grass compost contained the greatest amount of extractable humic
substances from a fixed initial weight of plant material.
Composting produced a fall in water soluble protein but, apart
from the grass compost, a marked rise in acid-hydrolysable
protein. Amendment of straw with $(NH_4)_2 HPO_4$ caused increases
in the extent of decomposition, organic nitrogen content and
the nitrogen content of extracted humic acid. However, there
was no increase in the quantity of humic substances produced.
The humic acids produced from the plant materials differed
substantially in nitrogen content and there were smaller
differences in active acidic group content. The E4/E6 ratios
suggested that the humic acid in the grass compost was of greater
molecular size than humic acids in the other composts.

1. Introduction

Heterotrophic microorganisms exhibit such a wide diversity in
catabolic capability that no natural carbon containing product of
plant or animal metabolism accumulates indefinitely in the terrestrial
environment. Nevertheless natural products differ in the difficulty
which their heterotrophic utilisation presents. Furthermore the
physical and non-carbon nutritional environment moderates potential
heterotrophic attack.

Plants in general contain a similar array of structural and
metabolically functional constituents but there are substantial
differences in the concentration of constituents both between species
and within species in relation to physiological age. The main
differences in plant material composition affecting quality as a
microbial substrate in composts are nitrogen content and degree of
lignification. For most plant materials a nitrogen content of not

less than 1.0-1.5% is required to ensure unrestricted heterotrophic attack. A nitrogen content of this order represents a C/N ratio near 30 (1,3,16).

In the case of highly lignified tissues much lower nitrogen contents are required because the rate of microbial attack on both lignin itself and the structural polysaccharides it protects is low (11). When plant residues with nitrogen contents greater than around 1.5% are composted then the nitrogen extra to microbial requirement may be lost in gaseous forms (8,16).

Whilst these general principles are well established there is little information on the yield and quality of humus produced when different types of plant material are composted. Thus experiments were set up in order to examine the pattern of decomposition and humification of three widely differing plant residues, the fate of endogenous and added mineral nitrogen and the yield and character of humus products.

2.   Materials and Methods

Three plant materials were used for the study. These were (1) young growth of Lolium perenne "Barlenna", nitrogen content 3.7% and C/N ratio 12,; (2) mature growth of a Lolium perenne dominant permanent pasture, nitrogen content 1.5% and C/N ratio 29 and (3) straw of Triticum aestivum, nitrogen content 0.52% and C/N ratio 85. These materials were termed grass, hay and straw. The plant materials dried at 80°C were milled to pass a 1mm aperture sieve.

Samples of each of the three plant materials were composted at 60% of their water holding capacities for 180 days at 20°C ± 3°C. Straw was also composted with the addition of diammonium phosphate applied in solution sufficient to reduce the C/N ratio to that of hay.

A soil inoculum was added to the distilled water used to moisten the plant material at the rate of 50ml per litre. The inoculum was prepared by shaking in a reciprocal shaker approximately 200ml of moist garden soil with 500ml of distilled water for 30min in the presence of 2 drops of a surfactant. The suspension was then centrifuged at 1000g for 30 min and the supernatant filtered through a glass wool plug.

Two sets of samples of each plant material were composted. In order to permit eight harvests during the composting period 24 replicates were composted as 15g samples in 300ml polystyrene pots. Larger samples of some 500g were composted under the same conditions in polythene bowls to provide sufficient material for comprehensive analyses at the end of the 180 day composting period. Containers were covered with polythene permitting gas exchange but reducing moisture loss. The composting materials were thoroughly mixed at weekly intervals.

Three of the smaller samples were harvested at 0, 7, 15, 30, 60, 90, 120 and 180 days in order to determine changes in mineral nitrogen, total nitrogen and carbon and pH. The larger samples were used to determine, in addition to these, composition by proximate analysis at the beginning and end of the composting period and the amount and character of humic substances at the end of the composting period.

Organic carbon was determined by the method of Allison (2) and total nitrogen by the method of Bremner (4). Mineral nitrogen was extracted with 2M KCl and determined by distillation in the presence of MgO and Devarda's alloy (5). A compost:water ratio of 1:1 (v/v) was used to measure pH.

The proximate chemical analysis was based on the method described by Stevenson (15). Modifications included the use of a 1:1 alcohol:benzene mixture to obtain the fats, oils, waxes and resin fraction, and the use of the anthrone method (10) for the determination of hemicellulose and cellulose hydrolysis products. Total protein was determined as total nitrogen minus inorganic nitrogen multiplied by the factor 6.25. Total protein was fractionated into water soluble protein, 80% H_2SO_4 hydrolysable protein and non-hydrolysable protein from total nitrogen determinations on the water soluble and non-hydrolysable fractions. The non-hydrolysable protein was subtracted from the non-hydrolysable residue to give a lignin fraction.

Samples at the end of the composting period were extracted with NaOH solution or sodium pyrophosphate to assess relative degrees of humification. The sodium pyrophosphate extraction was carried out by the method of Schnitzer and Desjardins (12). Sodium hydroxide extraction was carried out by shaking with a 0.1M solution for 18hr under nitrogen with a sample:solution ratio of 1:20. Absorbance of the supernatants was measured at 550nm and expressed in terms of 1g of ash-free compost extracted into 250ml of solution.

Larger, 10g samples of composted materials were extracted with 0.1M NaOH as described earlier to determine the amounts of humic and fulvic acids and the functional groups of the humic acids. Following extraction with NaOH the insoluble material was sedimented by centrifugation at 10000g for 30 min. The supernatant was then acidified to pH 2 with M HCl and the humic acid sedimented by centrifugation at 1000g for 30 min. Humic and fulvic acids were determined gravimetrically as ash-free material by igniting the dried samples at 550°C.

The humic acids used for functional group determination were further purified using HCl-HF as described by Schnitzer and Desjardins (12). Following this humic acids were further cleaned by dialysis against distilled water in the presence of anion and cation exchange resins in OH and H forms respectively. Purified humic acids were freeze dried. Total acidity of the humic acids was determined by baryta absorption under nitrogen and carboxyl groups by the calcium acetate method (13).

The E4/E6 ratios of the humic acids were determined by dissolving 5mg samples in 10ml of 0.05M $NaHCO_3$. Absorbances of the solutions, which fell in the pH range 8.5-8.8 were measured at 465nm and 665nm diluting as necessary.

3. Results and Discussion

Changes in carbon and total nitrogen during composting are shown in Fig. 1. Both the pattern and extent of loss of carbon differed between the three materials. Loss of carbon from the composted grass was rapid with more than 50% lost in 15 days. The rate of loss decreased markedly after about 30 days but less than 30% of the original carbon remained at the end of the composting period. The early reduction in the rate of carbon loss from composted grass probably resulted from the increasing importance of secondary, more chemically resistant products of composting to the loss of carbon from the residual material. This contrasts with the composted straw where, apart from an initial rapid loss of carbon, common to each material but differing in amount, the rate of loss of carbon remained reasonably constant over the period. This probably reflects the continuing importance, as oxidizable substrates, of the primary constituents within the straw. Addition of $(NH_4)_2$ HPO_4 to the straw resulted in an increase in the loss of carbon but the pattern of loss of carbon was similar in both amended and unamended straw.

<u>Fig. 1.</u> Changes in total nitrogen and carbon in composts of grass, hay and straw over a 180 day period.

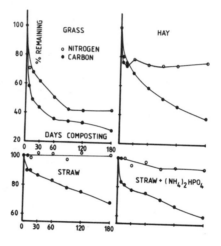

There was a substantial loss of nitrogen from the grass compost over the first 15 days which resulted in a fall in the C/N ratio from 12 to around 9. From this point the loss of nitrogen matched the loss of carbon and the C/N ratio remained almost constant. Most, if not all, of the nitrogen was lost by volatilisation rather than denitrification. The total loss of nitrogen over the composting period amounted to over 55% and the extent of this loss was similar to that found by Floate (8) when composting grass material of similar nitrogen content.

There was an initial loss of nitrogen from the composted hay but after approximately 15 days no further loss occurred. There was a minor loss of nitrogen from the amended straw amounting to between 5 and 10 percent but no loss from the straw alone. The relatively minor losses of nitrogen compared with carbon from the hay and straw composts resulted in major reductions in C/N ratios. At the end of the 180 day period the C/N ratios of the hay and straw composts expressed as total carbon over organic nitrogen were as follows:

hay, 15; amended straw, 36; straw, 48.

The hay and amended straw composts differed in loss of nitrogen even though initially both had the same ratio of total carbon:total nitrogen. In the amended straw inorganic nitrogen accounted for 65% of the total nitrogen compared with 5% in the hay. Since more nitrogen was lost from the hay compost it is evident that NH_4^+-N status was not the main factor determining loss. Both pH and temperature differences within the composts were probably of importance. Unfortunately internally generated increases in temperature were not measured, however, it is reasonable to assume that higher temperatures would have occurred within the hay compost during the early stages because of a higher content of easily fermented constituents. There were differences in pH and the pH of the hay compost rose from 6.6 to 8.8 over the first seven days whereas the pH of the amended straw compost did not exceed 7.2 over this period.

The differences in nitrogen loss between these two composts implies that there is likely to be a conflict between efficient nitrogen retention and the development of thermal conditions within composts conducive to rapid humification and the destruction of weed seeds and pathogens.

Table I shows the change in constituents within the plant materials when composted for 180 days. The data must be treated with caution because of the somewhat non-specific character of proximate analysis. For example it would be unwise to assume that the non-hydrolysable fraction at the end of the period was unaltered lignin. The nitrogen fractions were expressed as protein to facilitate comparisons.

TABLE I

Proportion of original constituents in plant materials composted for 180 days (initial = 100).

Plant materials	Fat, oils waxes, resins	Water soluble protein	Acid hydrolysable protein	Non-hydrolysable protein	Hemicellulose	Cellulose	Lignin
Grass	35	11	6	20	9	8	47
Hay	33	18	161	34	16	9	48
Straw*	32	26	224	180	39	21	73
Straw	38	74	147	66	47	54	87

*with added $(NH_4)_2$ HPO_4

There was a substantial reduction in both hemicellulose and cellulose in each compost with the suggestion that the attack on cellulose was rather more extensive. The amendment of straw with $(NH_4)_2$ HPO_4 resulted in a marked increase in the attack on cellulose so it is clear that nutrient status, presumably nitrogen, restricted the decomposition of straw. Apart from the grass compost where total nitrogen losses were very large, each compost showed a marked increase in the acid-hydrolysable protein fraction. Conversely each compost showed a fall in the labile, water-soluble protein fraction. In the amended straw compost the entry of mineral nitrogen into the hydrolysable and non-hydrolysable protein fractions resulted in an overall increase of 63% in total protein. The observation that the main increases in protein occurred in the acid hydrolysable fraction is of interest since it suggests that at the end of the period much nitrogen still occurred in forms reasonably accessible to microorganisms. This supports the concept of 'young' soil organic matter as a predominant source of mineralizable nitrogen (9).

Assessments of the degree of humification are given in Table II. Both 0.1M NaOH and 0.025M $Na_4P_2O_7$ extractions indicate a similar pattern with major differences between the composts in the sequence grass > hay >> straw. Rather more organic matter was extracted with NaOH. The amendment of straw with $(NH_4)_2 HPO_4$ did not result in a greater degree of humification even though decomposition was affected.

Table II

Degree of humification expressed as absorbance of an extract produced from 1g of dry ash-free compost in 250ml extractant.

Plant Material	0.025M $Na_4P_2O_7$	0.1M NaOH
Grass	0.84	1.10
Hay	0.47	0.67
Straw*	0.11	0.15
Straw	0.13	0.18

*with added $(NH_4)_2 HPO_4$

Table III

Organic matter remaining and humic substances produced from 1kg of organic matter in different plant materials composted for 180 days.

Plant material	Residual organic matter (g)	Humic acid (g)	Fulvic acid (g)
Grass	360	97	61
Hay	420	92	63
Straw*	660	31	65
Straw	720	58	41

*with added $(NH_4)_2 HPO_4$

The humic and fulvic acids extracted from the composts are given in Table III. These are presented in a manner which shows the quantity produced from a fixed initial amount of plant material. The data show that the greatest amounts were produced in the grass and hay composts despite the fact that much more of these materials was decomposed during the composting than was straw. Thus the concentration of extractable humic substances in the grass and hay composted residues was much higher than in the straw compost. The humic substances formed from equal weights of grass and hay were similar in amount and in distribution between humic acid and fulvic acid. There was no evidence that addition of $(NH_4)_2$ HPO_4 to straw increased the amount of humic substances produced from a given amount of straw supporting earlier data on degree of humification.

Witt (17) has suggested that alkaline soluble humus in relation to total organic matter may be useful as an index of maturity. In the composts produced, humic plus fulvic acids ranged from 137mg g^{-1} for the straw compost to 440mg g^{-1} for the grass compost. All of these are greater than the recommended minimum of 110mg g^{-1} for finished composts.

It is recognised that degradation products of plant derived aromatic compounds and lignin in particular constitute important precursors of humic substances in soils, nevertheless compounds synthesized by microorganisms also contribute to the complex chemistry of humic substances (14). It is of interest that in both the grass and hay composts the quantity of humic substances extracted could not have been derived from plant lignin. Indeed in the grass compost more than half of the humic substances extracted must have been formed from products of microbial synthesis and/or products of microbial alteration of plant constituents other than lignin.

Some properties of the humic acids extracted from the composts are given in Table IV. The nitrogen content of the humic substances was greater the greater the nitrogen status of the plant material and the more easily it was decomposed. The nitrogen content of the humic acid in the grass compost was very high and at least 1% greater than soil humic acids. In contrast the humic acid from the straw compost was below the normal range for soil humic acids (14). Although the yield of humic acid was rather low in the straw composts the nitrogen content of the humic acid from amended straw was almost double that in the unamended straw. The pH of the amended straw compost never exceeded 7.5 and experiments with model systems have indicated that phenols do not react with NH_4^+-N in the presence of oxidizing enzymes below pH 8 (7). It seems therefore that NH_4^+-N incorporation into either α amino or heterocyclic nitrogen compounds preceded its incorporation into the humic acid fraction of amended straw compost.

Table IV

Some properties of humic acids extracted from residues resulting from the composting of different plant residues for 180 days.

Plant material	Ash %	Total nitrogen	Active acidic groups eq kg^{-1} ash-free humic acid total	carboxyl	E_4/E_6 ratio
Grass	0.46	6.7	4.6	2.5	4.6
Hay	0.29	4.5	4.4	2.5	7.1
Straw*	–	3.4	3.8	1.4	6.3
Straw	0.28	1.8	3.3	1.7	6.4

*with added $(NH_4)_2$ HPO_4

The total acidity of the humic acids ranged from 3.3 eq kg^{-1} for the unamended straw to 4.6 eq kg^{-1} for the grass compost. These values are around half to two-thirds of those commonly found in soil humic acids although the proportion of the total acidity in carboxyl groups was similar (14). The data show a much greater range in the nitrogen concentrations between the humic acids than in acidic group content.

The grass compost humic acid had a markedly lower E4/E6 ratio than the others. Chen et al., (6) found that E4/E6 ratio was negatively correlated with molecular size and positively correlated with both total acidity and carboxyl group content. Since both of the latter were rather low in all compost humic acids it would appear that the molecular size of the humic acid from grass compost was distinctly greater than the rest.

4. Practical Conclusions

For many home owners lawn clippings contribute a major source of plant material for composting. Composting such material produces quite rapidly, high yields of high quality humus. Nevertheless nitrogen retention is poor. Mature, lignified plant tissues are humified at a slower rate but nitrogen losses are negligible. The humus may be of lower nitrogen status but this can be increased substantially by nitrogen supply to the compost even though the total yield of humic substances may not be increased. Lawn clippings may be used to enrich up to four times their own bulk of nitrogen deficient compost materials.

REFERENCES

1. ALEXANDER, M. (1961). Introduction to Soil Microbiology. John Wiley and Sons Inc., London.
2. ALLISON, F.E. (1965). Total Carbon. In Methods of Soil Analysis, Pt. 2, ed. C.A. Black. Agron. 9, 1346-66. Amer. Soc. Agron., Madison, Wisc.
3. ALLISON, F.E. (1973). Soil Organic Matter and its Role in Crop Production. Elsevier Scient. Publ. Co., Amsterdam, London, New York.
4. BREMNER, J.M. (1965). Total nitrogen. In Methods of Soil Analysis, ed. C.A. Black. Pt. 2, Agron. 9, 1149-78. Amer. Soc. Agron., Madison, Wis.
5. BREMNER, J.M. (1965). Inorganic forms of nitrogen. In Methods of Soil Analysis, ed. C.A. Black. Pt. 2. Agron. 9, 1179-1237. Amer. Soc. Agron., Madison, Wis.
6. CHEN, Y., SENESI, N. and SCHNITZER, M. (1977). Information provided on humic substances by E4/E6 ratios. Soil Sci. Soc. Amer. J. 41, 352-358.
7. FLAIG, W., BEUTELSPACHER, H. and RIETZ, E. (1975). Chemical composition and physical properties of humic substances. In Soil Components, ed. J.E. Gieseking, Vol. 1. Organic Components, Chapter 1, Springer-Verlag, New York.
8. FLOATE, M.J.S. (1970). Decomposition of organic materials from hill soils and pastures 11. Comparative studies on the mineralization of carbon, nitrogen and phosphorus from plant materials and sheep faeces. Soil Biol. Biochem. 2, 173-85.

9. JANSSEN, B.H. (1984). A simple method for calculating decomposition and accumulation of 'young' soil organic matter. Plant and Soil 76, 297-304.
10. OADES, J.M. (1967). Carbohydrates in some Australian soils. Aust. J. Soil Res. 5, 103-15.
11. SARKANEN, K.V. (1963). Wood lignins. In The Chemistry of Wood, 249-311. ed. B.L. Browning. John Wiley and sons, New York, London.
12. SCHNITZER, M. and DESJARDINS, J.G. (1965). Carboxyl and phenolic hydroxyl groups in some organic soils and their relation to the degree of humification. Can. J. Soil Sci. 45, 257-64.
13. SCHNITZER, M. and GUPTA, U.C. (1965). Determination of acidity in organic matter. Soil Sci. Soc. Amer. J. 29, 274-277.
14. SCHNITZER, M. (1978). Humic substances: Chemistry and Reactions in Soil Organic Matter, eds. M. Schnitzer and S.U. Khan 1-58, Elsevier Publ. Co.
15. STEVENSON, F.J. (1965). Gross chemical fractionation of organic matter. In Methods of Soil Analysis, ed. C.A. Black. Agron. 9, 1409-21. Amer. Soc. Agron., Madison, Wis.
16. THORSTENSEN, A.L. (1967). Refuse composting with sewage sludge. Water Pollut. Control 66, 525-35.
17. WITT, J. (1982). Die humusstoffbestimmung als Grundlage fur die Erkennung des Reifegrades von Siedlungsabfallkompost. Landwirtschaftliche Forschung Sonderheft 38, 297-304.

HEAVY METALS IN COMPOST FROM MUNICIPAL REFUSE
STRATEGIES TO REDUCE THEIR CONTENT TO ACCEPTABLE LEVELS

P. Krauss, R. Blessing, U. Korherr
University of Tuebingen
Institute of Organic Chemistry

Summary

Methods of reducing the heavy metal content of compost from municipal refuse such as discarding sreening fractions, collection of refuse in two separate bins, public collection of heavy metals by truck and by distributed bags are discussed. An example for a new attempt to purify the refuse by technical means is presented.

1 Introduction

Methods for composting municipal refuse with and without addition of sewage sluge are well developed. The advantages of static and dynamic processes have been well investigated and composting plants have generally few problems concerning the biological process. The optical problems (glass, plastics) which reduce the retail value of compost, have been solved in most plants.

Only recently pollutants have been recognized as being the limiting factor for the use of compost from municipal refuse. Organic pollutants such as polycyclic aromatic hydrocarbons (PAHs), polychlorinated biphenyls (PCBs), pesticides and phthalate esters have been investigated and their potential environmental hazard has been discussed <1-5, Table I>. Their maximum content in compost is not regulated in most countries. High amounts of inorganic salts and of heavy metals seem to be the main problems related to inorganic pollutants. This paper covers the heavy metal content of refuse, the nature of these heavy metals and strategies to reduce their content in compost products.

2 Heavy metal content of refuse and compost

In Germany, the heavy metal content of refuse has been estimated for several small areas and for the country as a whole <4,6,7, Table II>. There are marked regional, sociological and seasonal differences. As far as values from other European countries are known, they show the same distribution.

The values reported for the heavy metal content of compost from municipal refuse in different european countries cover a wide range (Table III). This can be due to numerous factors:
* Different extent of industrialisation
* Seasonal changes have not been taken into consideration
* Different methods of preparing the raw material from refuse
* Different methods of compost processing
* Different analytical methods

It is evident however that the values for nearly all metals exceed acceptable levels for normal soils. This becomes quite clear if they are

compared with either the "Kloke-values", being a measure for soil tolerance, or with German limiting values for compost itself (Table IV).

Strong seasonal dependence for lead, copper and zinc has been shown
as well as sociologial influences . In winter, lead values for example are
twice as high as in summer and refuse (and thus compost) from houses with
one to three families shows higher values than from large apartment buildings <4,7,14,15>.

3 The nature of the heavy metals in municipal refuse

It has been suggested by some authors, that fine fractions of refuse
(<10 mm) are responsible for most of the heavy metal burden. In addition,
batteries (mercury, cadmium and zinc), leather (chromium), paint (chromium, lead, cadmium), plastics (cadmium) and paper (lead) have fallen
under suspicion <10>.

In a thirteen months study <4> we analyzed municipal refuse separately collected in Baienfurt, a small town in Southern Germany. Two dustbins
were distributed to every houshold. One of them was intended for "valuable" matter (paper, plastics, glass, metal), the other one for the wet remainder. The latter one, containing the major part of the organics, was
investigated in detail according to the heavy metal content and the heavy
metal freight in three sieving fractions: <8 mm, 8-40 mm and > 40 mm.
Though the content of Pb, Zn, and Hg was 50 percent higher in the <8mm
fraction than in the others it became clear on a freight basis, that
neither these metals nor Cu, Ni, Cr and Cd can be significantly eliminated
by only eliminating the fines (Figure 1 and 2).

It was very surprising, that the even the "native organic fraction"
>40 mm, purified manually from remaining paper, plastics, glass, visible
metal pieces and other nonorganics was characterized by high concentrations of Pb, Zn, Cu and Cd. Seasonal variations of the heavy metal content
with a maximum in December/January could be observed. The piece of bread,
the sausage or the leaf of lettuce we found couldn't be the reason. More
information could only be obtained, when we changed our system for sample
preparation. Normally samples for chemical analysis are prepared by grinding an aliquot of the original sample as a whole down to a particle size
of 0.1mm. This grinding procedure was cut into two steps. In the first
step, a maximum particle size of about 3 mm was reached. At this stage,
the material was separated into two fractions by horizontal air classification. The resulting light and dense fractions were treated separately.

High metal contents in the whole sample are always paralelled by
extremely high values in the dense fraction. To illustrate this, an example for the lead content of two organic fractions shall be given. In the
organic matter with particle size 8-40 mm and a lead content of 3144
mg/kg, 78.5 percent of the total lead content is fixed in the dense
fraction, whereas in the corresponding organic matter with particle size
> 40 mm and a lead content of 36 mg/kg, only 9.5 percent of the total lead
content is found in the dense fraction. This effect is very marked for the
metals lead, zinc, copper and mercury.

Further information concerning the nature of the heavy metals in the
dense fraction was obtained by microscopic examination: metallic particles
and particles of metallic oxides were found in the dense fraction of < 8
mm, 8-40 mm and > 40 mm organic material as well as in the corresponding
fraction of paper and plastics. It was possible to pinpoint the original
products principally responsible for heavy metal input to municipal refuse.

Potential lead sources are: pieces of lead-foil (e.g. from caps of wine bottles or from Polaroid-films), silver tinsel, bullets of air-guns, solder. Copper was mainly found as wire and as particles of brass (small cog-wheels, snap-fasteners, zip fasteners, refills of ball pens). Zinc was found as foil-pieces and as brass. It is important to note, that small particles as a piece of copper wire was found in the < 8 mm material as well as in the > 40 mm material <20>.

4 Strategies to reduce the heavy metal content of compost

4.1 Traditional methods

The efforts of composting plants to reduce the heavy metal burden are concentrated on the following steps:
* separation of magnetic material
* separation of sieve fractions
    - e.g. rejection of > 40 mm-material by forced sieving
    - e.g. rejection of the < 10 mm-material
* processing of matured compost (e.g. stoner or air table)
* public battery-collections
* public collection of hazardous wastes
In addition there are some attempts to separately collect the non-polluted organic fraction (wastes from kitchen and garden).

The success of the methods marked with an asterisk is dubious. The data from table III collected from plants practising one or more of these methods and nevertheless producing compost enriched in heavy metals demonstrates this clearly. Evidently, efforts to produce compost from municipal refuse poor in heavy metals by mechanical means only has hitherto been largely unsuccessful. The related landfill preserving rate is about 50 percent.

4.2 Two bins with organics optimized

With this conclusion in mind, many German counties responsible for collection and disposal or utilization of municipal refuse are now favouring the method called "Biotonne". This is a two bins system covering the biological waste in one bin (blue or green coloured) and the residual waste in the second one (normally grey).

According to pilot runs with this system, about 35 percent of total municipal waste is found in the organic bin. After composting another 5 percent go to the landfill after refining of the compost. This means, that about 30 percent of total refuse can be recycled. The heavy metal content of the corresponding compost e.g. from Witzenhausen and Bad Dürkheim in Germany and Murimoos in Switzerland lies rather low in summer (see table V), the range being close to that of tree- and shrub-wastes, agricultural wastes and pure garden wastes (see table VI). In winter however a significant increase has been reported indicating that some of the problems related with total municipal refuse are specific for the "Biotonne" too. Further investigations to specify the winter maxima are in progress in our laboratory.

4.3 Two bins with valuable matter optimized

When the first experiment of collecting "valuable" matter in a separate bin (Baienfurt, see above) was initiated, it was suggested that the second bin, containing the wet remainder, could be a good starting material for composting. It was shown however, that the heavy metal content of

the resulting compost was as high as that obtained from "traditional" material.
With this method, the amount of material requiring landfill disposal is reduced by 25 percent <4,19>.

4.4 Public collection of hazardous wastes

In the last years, numerous attempts have been made in Germany to reduce the hazardous content of municipal refuse, often in connection with the production of compost as a final product. Although heavy metals were known at that time to be a limiting factor for compost, the only sources of heavy metals collected were batteries (lead and mercury). Emphasis was placed on the collection of waste oil, solvents, acids, bases, paints, pharmaceuticals and plant-protective agents.
We therefore changed in two experiments the mode of collection in such a way that the requirements for composting be better fulfilled.
First, we attempted to simply include lead, zinc, copper, cadmium and nickel in the collection list by explaining to the population via the local press, which articles were to be sorted out (e.g. lead caps of wine bottles etc., see above). The experiment was run in the counties of Reutlingen and Tübingen in Southern Germany (400 000 inhabitants). A truck was sent to every settlement and stayed there for half an hour to collect the hazardous waste delivered by the residents. The result was disillusioning. Although the percentage of heavy metal products (27.9 %) was high (figure 3), the relative quantity (per resident and year) was lower than expected. Only 0.01 grams of lead in small particles (excluding lead accumulators) and 0.6 grams of copper, zinc and brass have been found, the quantity normally found in refuse being 30 grams/resident and year for lead and 70 grams for the copper/zinc-group.
For this reason, closer contact with the population was attempted by distributing small plastic bags designed to be filled with heavy metals (and aluminium to stimulate the collecting ambition). The result was surprising. Despite moderate publicity, the average citizen filled 0.3 bags per year containing 87 grams of aluminium, 1.5 grams of lead and 12 grams of the copper/zinc-group, all materials being small in size and therefore of potential relevance for composting. Further improvement by the factor of 10 or more is possible.

4.5 "New" technical methods to produce compost poor in heavy metals

All methods mentioned above have only landfill preserving rates between 25 and 50 percent. Most of them still have severe problems with heavy metal contamination of compost. In addition, the two-bins-systems need continuous support by the population. Thus new attempts have been made to solve the problem by sophisticated technical means.
One of these attempts shall be presented since with this example, the essential requirements can be demonstrated. The process has been developed by ORFA-AG (Switzerland), the pilot plant being in Leibstadt.
In the ORFA-plant (for the basis flowsheet see figure 4 and 4a) the total refuse is treated by the following steps: Pregrinding, magnetic separation, grinding in two separate streams "H" hammermill and "C" cutting mill, followed by drying of the reunited streams ("total"), screening in four fractions "S1", S2", S3" and "S4" (< 0.5 mm, 0.5-1 mm, 1-2 mm and > 1 mm), air classification to the corresponding light fractions "L1", "L2", "L3", "L4" and dense fractions "D1", D2", "D3", "D4" <19>.
With the exception of the magnetic fraction, the total refuse is processed by the plant.

The material balance is shown in figure 5. The results of chemical analysis (see Table VII for characteristic lead data) point out significant heavy metal freight reduction of the refuse by the dense fraction. In these fractions of different particle size, the metals lead, copper, zinc, nickel, cadmium and chromium were found in their metallic form or as alloys.

Figure 6 shows lead concentrations along the whole plant (see sampling positions in figure 3) during a typical run.

This method bases upon the supposition that the heavy metals are present in metallic form (i.e. not as metal compounds). The only feasable method of separating heavy metals from the remaining waste is to take advantage of their high density using air classification. In order to permit an effective classification, the particles must be homogeneous in size, this being effected by a combination of grinding and screening. Effective screening on the other hand requires that the material be dry.

5 Conclusions

Compost from municipal refuse poor in heavy metals can be obtained by different attempts. The most promising are separate collection of biomass and sophisticated technology for waste treatment using the physical properties of metals (such as their high density). Intensive public heavy metal collection (e.g. by small plastic bags) is useful in addition to "traditional" composting plants.

Literature:
<1> K. Wagner, Die toxischen Inhaltsstoffe in Siedlungsabfällen und deren Aufbereitungsprodukten - Müll, Müllkompost, Müllklärschlammkompost und Klärschlamm, Fortschr.-Ber.VDI-Z.15, 10 (1977)
<2> H. Hagenmaier, H. Kaut, P. Krauß, Analysis of polycyclic aromatic hydrocarbons in sediments, sewage sludges and composts from municipal refuse by HPLC, Int.J.Environ.Anal. Chem. (in press)
<3> W. Müller, H. Rohleder, W. Klein, F. Korte, Modellstudie zur Abfallbeseitigung. Verhalten xenobiotischer Substanzen bei der Müllkompostierung. GSF-Bericht Ö104 (1974)
<4> H. Hagenmaier, P. Krauß, Schadstoffuntersuchungen im Rahmen des F+E-Vorhabens "Getrennte Sammlung von Wertstoffen und Sonderabfällen dargestellt am Beispiel Ravensburg". Bericht erstellt im Auftrag des Ministeriums für Landwirtschaft, Umwelt und Forsten, Baden-Württemberg und des Umweltbundesamts (1984)
<5> K. Fricke, H. Vogtmann, Th. Turk, Projekt "Grüne Tonne Witzenhausen" - Kompostierung getrennt gesammelter organischer Siedlungsabfälle, in ANS-INFO-Band Heft 7, Berlin (1985)
<6> O. Tabasaran, Schwermetalle in kommunalen Abfällen und Konsequenzen für die Kompostierung, Müll und Abfall 13 (1981) 208
<7> Bundesweite Hausmüllanalyse 1979/1980, Argus - Arbeitsgruppe Umweltstatistik TU Berlin (1981), Forschungsbericht 10303502
<8> A.N.R.E.D, Compost Information No. 16 (1984)
<9> Merkblatt M10, Qualitätskriterien und Anwendungsempfehlungen für -Kompost aus Müll und Müll/Klärschlamm, Müllhandbuch 6856 (1985) Erich Schmidt Verlag (Berlin)
<10> O. Tabasaran, Separierung schwermetallhaltiger Hausmüllkomponenten durch Absieben, Müll und Abfall 16 (1984) S. 15-22
<11> Injunctions of the ministry of agriculture of Baden-Wuerttemberg (FRG) concerning the composting plants "Rems-Murr-Kreis" and "Reutlingen-Tübingen"

<12> O. Furrer, Abfallverwertung - ein Beitrag der Landwirtschaft zur Lösung von Umweltproblemen, Schweiz.Landwirtsch.Forschung 23 (1984) 269

<13> J. Buchner, Die Ö-NORM S 2022 "Kompost, Gütekriterien", in: Institut für Wassergüte und Landschaftswasserbau, TU Wien (Hrsg.): Gütekriterien für Müllkompost - Die Ö-NORM S 2022, Wien (1983)

<14> P. Krauß, H. Hagenmaier, Bestimmung des Schwermetallgehalts von Hausmüllproben, Fresenius Z. Anal. Chem. 317 (1984) 407.

<15> P. Krauß, Gibt es die Strategie zur Erzeugung schwermetallarmen Komposts aus Siedlungsabfällen?, Müll und Abfall 17 (1985) 227

<16> J. Jager, 2. Fachtagung Abfallwirtschaft, Heidenheim (1985)

<17> A. Pfirter, MIGROS Sano (Switzerland), personal communication

<18> Communication of the Saar-Pfalz county

<19> K. Scheffold, Getrennte Sammlung und Kompostierung, EF-Verlag Berlin (1985)

<20> P. Krauß, H. Hagenmaier, Zur Bindungsform von Blei, Kupfer, Zink, Cadmium und Quecksilber in Hausmüll und Hausmüllkomposten. Ein Schlüssel zur Schwermetallreduktion, in "Sonderstoffproblematik in der Abfallwirtschaft, 4. Abfallwirtschaftliches Fachkolloquium, Saarbrücken", Saarbrücken 1984.

			B a l e n f u r t <4>			Witzen-
	compost		refuse fractions (avg.)			hausen
	avg.	max.	< 8mm	8-40mm	> 40mm	compost<5>
	(n=21)		(n=36)	(n=36)	(n=36)	
HCB	5	13	3	3	2	<1
Gamma-HCH	31	85	70	51	30	4
DDT-group	44	701	37*	28*	17	32
Clophen A60	520	1765	420*	378	290	50
PAHs(selec.)	21340*	173380	16070*	5730	2550	201

* one extreme value omitted

Table I : Organic pollutants in refuse and compost pesticides, PCBs, PAHs (ug/kg dry matter)

| | B a l e n f u r t 82/83 <4> | | | F R G 79/80 <7> | |
| | one to three fam.houses | | app.build. | | |
	avg.82/83	June 82	Jan. 83	Jan. 83	winter	summer
Lead	416	128	945	295	868	279
Copper	376	140	365	225	377	308
Zinc	578	446	619	324	839	663
Nickel	27	20	37	21	–	–
Chromium	67	46	68	42	–	–
Cadmium	3.8	1.8	3.5	1.0	4.1	6.0
Mercury	0.2	0.1	0.2	0.1	0.6	1.2

Table II : Heavy metal content of municipal refuse (mg/kg dry matter)

	Heidenh. 82/83 (n=64)	Rome 82 (n=12)	Perugia 82 (n=12)	France 84 <8> (n=61)	FRG 76/81 <9> (n=207)
Lead	673	324	530	447	513
Copper	291	475	150	322	274
Zinc	1369	964	427	1054	1570
Nickel	75	33	38	71	45
Chromium	90	108	109	109	71
Cadmium	6.5	4.2	2.5	3.9	5.5
Mercury	4.1	3.1	2.4	3.9	2.4

Table III : Heavy metal content of European composts (mg/kg dry matter)

	FRG <9> (40to/ha*3a)	Rems-Murr <11>	RT/TUE <11>	Switzer-land <12>	Austria <13>
Lead	150	200	150	100	900
Copper	150	200	150	100	100-1000
Zinc	375	500	375	300	300-1500
Nickel	25	50	50	-	200
Chromium	150	200	150	-	-
Cadmium	2.5	5	3	3	6
Mercury	3.2	4	3	1	4

Table IV : Limiting values for compost from municipal refuse
(mg/kg dry matter)

	Witzenhausen <5>			B.Duerkh. <16>	Murimoos
	avg.	summer	winter	summer	summer <17>
Lead	133	~ 70	~ 220	82	69
Copper	33	-	-	59	41
Zinc	408	~ 200	~ 600	224	241
Nickel	29	-	-	10	14
Chromium	36	-	-	78	30
Cadmium	1	-	-	0.6	< 1
Mercury	-	-	-	0.7	-

Table V : Heavy metal content of compost from separate organ.
collect. (mg/kg dry matter)

	tree- and shrub-w. FDS (n=12)	tree- and shrub-w. Saar-Pfalz<18>	agricult. wastes RT (n=9)	garden- wastes RT (n=9)
Lead	23	28	31	57
Copper	17	14	35	38
Zinc	70	87	83	171
Nickel	7	34	21	12
Chromium	17	9	23	26
Cadmium	< 1	0.8	1.0	0.9
Mercury	< 1	< 1	< 1	< 1

Table VI : Heavy metal content of compost from tree- and shrub-wastes (mg/kg dry matter)

Metall	mun.refuse (mg/kg)	coarse light fraction (mg/kg)	reduction (%)	compost X/84-V/85 (mg/kg)
Lead	423	135	68	120
Copper	803	113	86	114
Zinc	798	386	52	580
Nickel	71	16	77	29
Chromium	126	67	47	28
Cadmium	6.5	3.1	52	5.3
Mercury	0.5	0.3	40	1.8

Table VII : Heavy metal reduction of refuse in the ORFA-plant XII/84 - X/85

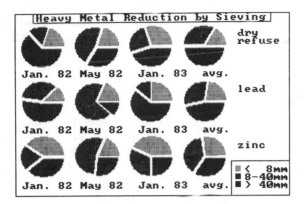

Figure 1

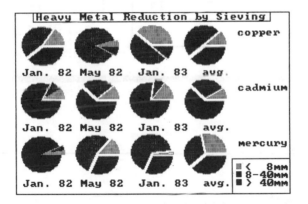

Figure 2

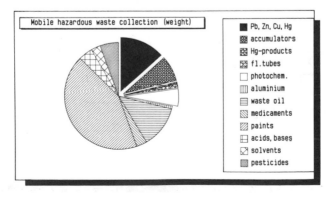

Figure 3

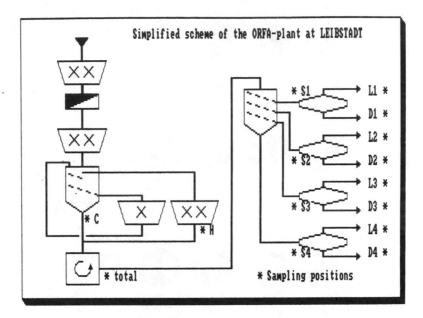

Figure 4

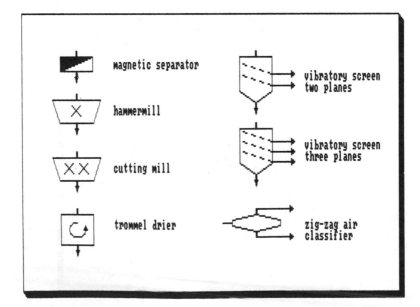

Figure 4a

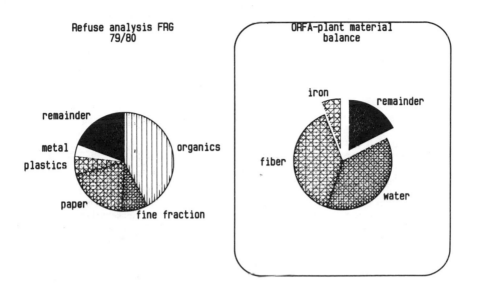

Figure 5

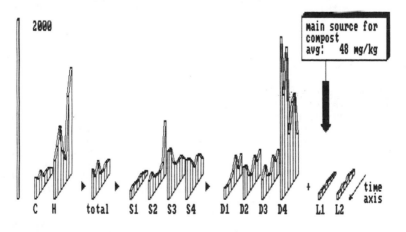

Figure 6

BACTERIAL AND FUNGAL ATMOSPHERIC CONTAMINATION
AT REFUSE COMPOSTING PLANTS : A PRELIMINARY STUDY

P. BOUTIN*, M. TORRE*, J. MOLINE**
(* CEMAGREF, B.P. 3, F 33610 CESTAS,
** C.H.R., F 37044 TOURS, FRANCE)

Summary

Four refuse composting plants and one pinewood rubbish fermenting plant were monitored for a preliminary study of airborne bacterial and fungal contamination.

At the main working stations, the number and the granulometry of viable particles were followed by means of Andersen impactors for "total" mesophilic bacteria, mesophilic and thermophilic moulds, incidentally for faecal indicator bacteria and thermophilic actinomycetes. High densities were measured near the dumping hoopers, in the closed-in premises sheltering refuse or compost loading, grinding, milling and screening, and outside while piles are turned or when mature compost is loaded.

The observed numbers fall in the range of previous data for aerocontamination at sludge composting plants. The sanitary interpretation of results is improved through application of a respiratory model. High amounts of bacteria and fungal conidia are able to reach the pulmonary alveolae.

While these last years several **sludge** composting plants were carefully studied for airborne contamination, equivalent information was lacking for domestic **refuse** fermenting systems. Consequently four garbage composting plants were recently monitored for bacterial and fungal aerocontamination around the main dust emitting devices. Another process, preparing enriching agents from pinewood sawdust and bark, was examined for comparison.

1. DESCRIPTION OF PLANTS

* Forced aeration plant (Joué-lès-Tours, **JT**).
     This 12-year old system converts 22000 t/y of household solid waste. Garbage from collecting hoppers is roughly sorted, grinded and sent through a conveyor belt to the 5-stage fermentation tower with forced aeration. At ground level, fermented compost is carried out by shovels, then screened and temporarily stocked in open air piles before final loading and dispatching to horticulture and mushroom cultivation caves. The plant is located in the middle of a wood clearing and sheltered from moderate winds.
* Turned pile plants (Massugas, **MA**; Saint-Léon, **SL**; Saint-Denis-de-P., **SD**).

     In these new or recently renovated plants, the compost is fermented on open air areas and periodically turned for aeration by man driven engines. Closed premises shelter mechanical treatments. Process for plant **MA** is : grinding, screening, fermentation, refining, and for plants **SL** and

SD : grinding, sorting and screening, fermentation. Their wide fermentation areas are situated in rather exposed surroundings.
* Bark and sawdust composting plant (Landiras, LA).
 This private installation ferments by-products of pinewood-industry (branches and twigs, barks, sawdust) as a material to prepare enriching agents for ornamental gardens. Raw material is first grinded, then fermented, screened and fertilizer-added before packing into bags and dispatching. Production is repeatedly adjusted to meet demand.

FORCED AERATION PLANT JT	1rst run	2nd run	TURNED PILE PLANT MA
JT0 – Upwind	MA0a		– Upwind
JT1 – Picking up garbage (2nd floor)	MA1a		– Garbage collecting hopper (ground level, outside)
JT2 – Fermentation tower, top (5th floor, inside)	MA2a	MA2b	– Grinding and screening (inside)
JT3 – Fermentation tower, ground level (compost shoveling)		MA3b	– Grinding (inside)
JT4 – Fermented compost screening	MA4a	MA4b	– Compost hopper(to fermentation area)
JT5 – Stocking area, between compost and refuse piles	MA5a	MA5b	– Composting area, near pile turning
JT6 – Workshop	MA6a		– On compost piles
		MA7b	– Composting area, 30 m from pile turning

TURNED PILE PLANT SL	TURNED PILE PLANT SD	VEGETABLE WASTE COM-POSTING SYSTEM LA (under sheds)
SL0 – Upwind	SD0 – Upwind	LA0 – Upwind
SL1 – Garbage dumping	SD1 – Garbage dumping	LA1 – Grinder
SL2 – Manual sorting, screening (ins.)	SD2 – Garbage grinding (inside)	LA2 – Unrefined compost pile
SL3 – Conveyor to fermentation area	SD3 – Grinded refuse screening (ins.)	LA3 – Refined compost heap
SL4 – Composting area, non working	SD4 – Compost tipping to ferm. area (outside)	LA4 – Compost bagging
SL5 – Composting area, loading a lorry	SD5 – Composting area a just after lorry loading b 10 mn after	
SL6 – Mature comp. shed		

TABLE I – Sampling sites

2. SAMPLING SITES

Garbage sampling

Some samples were taken from garbage and compost piles for microbial evaluation of the dust emitting materials.

Air sampling sites

They were chosen according to the process, as representative as possible of contamination intensity at commonly frequented work places. Four to seven indoor and outdoor sampling sites were elected at each plant, as summarized by Table I, with one more upwind site for comparison and meteorological recordings.

3. EXPERIMENTAL PROCEDURE

Sampling device

The only apparatus for this study were 3 6-stage Andersen impactors (**1**). At constant air-flow, Andersen impactor sorts airborne particles according to their size. Aerosol granulometry is thus segmented in 6 classes of "aerodynamical equivalent diameters", i.e. from stage 1 to stage 6 : > 9.2 um, 5.6-9.2 um, 3.2-5.6 um, 2.0-3.2 um, 1.0-2.0 um, 1.0 um. These limits follow approximatively a geometrical progression. Equivalent diameters differ from the actual size as soon as the particle deviates from spherical shape and density one. Impactor stages receive Petri dishes with appropriated growth media, on which particles impact and then eventually develop bacterial or fungal colonies. Incubated plates reveal viable particles for the considered medium. Positive holes counts are statistically corrected to give final stage by stage and total counts (bacterial viable particles = BVP, fungal viable particles = FVP). Large-size particles (> 18-20 um) are poorly captured (**9**).

Investigated microorganisms. Growth media

From previous studies on wastewater treatment plants and spraying devices, the mesophilic bacterial flora appears as a good tracer for aerocontamination. It develops quickly on trypticase-soya agar (TSA) after a 24-hour incubation at 30°C.

For enterobacteria, the modified Drigalski lactose medium (Pasteur 64667 - **DRI**) was used for turned pile plants, the usual Chapman TTC and tergitol agar (Merck 5471 - **TTC**) at other plants. "Faecal" streptococci were grown on Slanetz & Bartley agar (Merck 5262 - **SLB**), moulds and yeasts on modified Czapek & Dox agar (Merck 5460 - **CZD**) and on acidified malt extract agar (Merck 5398 - **MAL**). At **JT**, the actinomycetes agar (Difco 0957.01.2 - **ACT**) was precociously invaded by filamentous fungi, and Littman ox-gall agar (**LOA**) was substituted at **LA**. Table II summarizes growth media, incubation temperatures and times.

In this preliminary study, identification of moulds was not pursued, except for some characteristic colonies at **JT** and **MA** (Dr de Closets).

Sampling procedure and plates reading

Most media allow mould growth. To obtain readable bacterial counts in spite of the proliferation of many quick-growing fungi, compromises were to be sought. Agar invasion by filamentous forms, even with addition of fungal growth inhibiting agents, awkwardly limitated both exposure and incubation times. In dusty sites, this leads to sampling times as short as 2 mn, which the representativity of samples certainly suffers from. Incubation had to be cautiously monitored, with successive repeated numberings. After

Investigated germs	Growth medium	JT	MAa	MAb	SL	SD	LA
Mesophilic fl.	TSA	30°/24h	30°/24h	30°/24h	30°/24h	30°/24h	30°/24h
Enterobacteria	TTC	37°/48h					
	DRI		37°/24h		37°/24h	37°/24h	
Faecal colif.	TTC	44°/48h					
Faecal strept.	SLA	37°/48h					
Mesoph. moulds	MAL	30°/48h	30°/48h				30°/5j
	CZA	30°/5j	30°/48h		30°/48h		30°/3j
	ACT	30°/5j					
	LOA						30°/5j
Thermo. moulds	MAL	44°/48h		43°/48h	44°/48h	48°/48h	44°/48h
	CZA	44°/48h		43°/72h		48°/72h	44°/72h
	ACT	44°/48h					
	LOA						44°/48h

TABLE II - GROWTH MEDIA AND INCUBATION CONDITIONS

Andersen impactor stage n°	Equivalent aerodyn. diam. (um)	At rest (RCV = 450ml)				Mod. act. (RCV = 900 ml)			
		RP	TB	DL	EX	RP	TB	DL	EX
1	> 9.2	15	63	16	6	13	67	14	6
2	5.6-9.2	2	48	37	13	3	54	37	6
3	3.2-5.6	0	30	39	31	2	35	45	20
4	2.0-3.2	0	16	32	52	1	17	54	28
5	1.0-2.0	0	8	25	67	0	9	49	42
6	< 1.0	0	6	12	82	0	6	29	65

TABLE III - RESPIRATORY MODEL

Plant	Material	"Total" mes. fl.	"Total" coliforms	"Faecal" coliforms	"Faecal" streptoc.
MA	Refuse	$5.8.10^8$	$1.5.10^7$	$1.7.10^6$	$3.0.10^7$
	Compost	$1.5.10^8$	$5.3.10^6$	$4.0.10^6$	$4.7.10^7$
JT	Compost	$2.1.10^7$	$1.5.10^5$	$1.0.10^5$	$1.2.10^6$
LA	Compost	$1.6.10^8$	$4.0.10^6$	$1.1.10^5$	$1.7.10^6$

TABLE IV - BACTERIAL CONTENT OF GARBAGE AND COMPOST (CFU/g)

incubation, a number of plates appear however nearly saturated (almost 400 impacts), what leads to uncertainties in corrected counts. Some saturated plates were obtained in highly contaminated atmospheres, even with short exposition times. Inhibition may also occur.

4. METHODS FOR INTERPRETATION OF RESULTS

Granulometry of aerosols

Considering that wastewater and compost aerosols usually tend to fit a log-normal pattern, a simplified digest-notation is proposed here for a rapid approach of aerosol granulometry. The percentages of the total count of viable particles are first calculated for each stage from n° 6 to n° 1 and then cumulated. The numbers (n1, n2, n3) of the stages on which are totalized respectively 17 %, 50 % and 83 % of the total count (N/6, N/2, 5N/6) are noted. If more than 33 % of the total count is numbered on stage 6, 7 is marked instead of 6, and symetrically 0 instead of 1 if more than 33 % of particles impact on stage 1.

The triplet (n1, n2, n3) affords an elementary information on the shape of the corresponding granulometric curve, usually sufficient for comparisons. The average fineness of the aerosol can be estimated through F = (n1 + n2 + n3)/3. The direction of the cumulative curve concavity and some idea on its curvature may be deduced from f = n2 - (n1 + n3)/2. A symmetrical distribution leads to f = 0, a relative overrepresentation of fine particles to positive values of f.

Respiratory model

Some help in the sanitary interpretation of dust granulometry is given by recourse to a respiratory model, which allows to determine the deposition sites in the respiratory tract. The model we use here was deduced from figures furnished by Chrétien (3), by interpolation to adjust the limits of each stage of the Andersen impactor (Table III). It recognizes three levels for retained inhalated particles : rhinopharyngeal (RP), broncho-pulmonary (BP), deep lung (DL) (exhalated particles = EX).

5. EXPERIMENTAL RESULTS

Garbage and compost

Table IV affords some characteristic results.

Airborne contamination

Table V delivers calculated total densities/m3 for all sites and media, except at **JT** for actinomycetes (**ACT** agar non selective, with extensive growth of moulds and bacteria). In all plants, upwind sites give 30-35 BVP/m3 for mesophilic "total" flora (on TSA).

6. INTERPRETATION

Garbage and compost

Grossly, garbage and garbage composts appear rather heavily contaminated by faecal bacteria. Comparisons are not possible about single samples in such coarse and heterogeneous materials. Composted sawdust and bark is also polluted by faecal indicators, what may indicate a rapid growth from some inoculated germs.

Viable particles densities

In spite of some irregularities, probably depending on circumstances

Site	Mesophilic "tot." flora	Enterobacteria		Mesoph. fungi			Thermoph. fungi		
	TSA	TTC	DRI	MAL	CZA	LOA	MAL	CZA	LOA
JT1	47000	2800		---	40000		3100	1400	
JT2	13000	550		2000	2800		100	1400	
JT3	2100	44		480	1300		17	440	
JT4	260	38		190	280		550	51	
JT5	300	---		31000	>73000		61000	17000	
JT6	26000	---		5800	3300		200	400	
MA1	1700/---		160/---	950/---	580/---		---/---	46000/---	
MA2	10000/57000		2200/---	6800/---	4200/---		3300/---	28000/---	
MA3	---/>140000		---/---	---/---	---/---		---/1500	---/18000	
MA4	16000/85000		780/---	11000/---	18000/---		---/470	---/1900	
MA5	3300/860		230/---	11000/---	1800/---		---/1100	---/---	
MA6	3100/---		150/---	7700/---	---/---		---/---	---/---	
MA7	---/1600		---/---	---/---	24000/---		---/350	---/3100	
SL1	>33000		4100		5500		5400		
SL2	>32000		8700		>21000		520		
SL3	8400		1000		3400		36		
SL4	2900		28		570		78		
SL5	4500		15		5600		320		
SD1	2700		7800		1600		1300		
SD2	>110000		36000		21000		520		
SD3	18000		2800		7400		7300		
SD4	34000		720		20000		18000		
SD5	1400		4		310		65		
SD6	5600		80		500		330		
LA1	1700			23000	27000	17000	17000	830	4300
LA2	490			---	19000	2600	410	4700	1000
LA3	5600			---	2200	10000	>36000	1100	15000
LA4	250			340	460	---	1200	25	520

TABLE V – EXPERIMENTAL RESULTS – TOTAL COUNTS

(At MA, 1rst run/2nd run ; --- = no measurement for this run)

for short times of sampling (<5 mn), VP countings are coherent for the various studied types of microorganisms at most sites. However discrepancies for thermophilic moulds on malt agar and Czapek & Dox agar respectively are observed at **MA** and at **LA**, but in an inversed sense here and there : this unexplained difference is about one order of magnitude. At **JT**, both media give more comparable counts.

High bacterial counts (TSA) are observed :
- irregularly, at raw garbage reception (dumping hopper),
- near garbage grinders and near screening devices (for garbage and fermented compost as well),
- wherever fermented compost is tipped down.

Dust density depends on intensity of compost crumbling. The worsening action of confinement is clear. Higher densities were observed in sheltered or closed-in situations than at more exposed sites. Although bacteria and mesophilic or thermophilic moulds numbers are usually positively correlated, compost maturation is marked by a relative enrichment in fungal particles.

Of particular interest are the high figures for bacteria concerning the workshop at **JT6**. These premises are on the groundfloor of the building which shelters refuse dumping and grinding, and compost screening. In spite of doors and airlocks, dust reaches easily and abundantly this busy workplace; medium-size particles predominate, with the granulometric triplet (5, 4, 3). In contrast, the fungal contamination is low here, nearby unfermented refuse processing devices.

If such calculations may be tempted in spite of a probable representation bias, for 27 sampling sites on 4 composting plants the distribution of numbers of mesophilic bacterial particles (TSA growing) adjusts conveniently a log-normal pattern, with a median about 10^4 and an estimated mean value of 4.10^4 BVP/m3. By the same way, malt-agar growing thermophilic organisms may be evaluated about 10^3 (median) and 4.10^3 (average) FVP/m3 (22 available sites). Higher values would be given by Czapek & Dox agar (6.10^3 and 2.10^4 for 11 samples only).

For hazard evaluation, the upper values of airborne contamination must be also considered, for workers may stay for rather long times at very dusty places. 3 indoor sites were monitored for more than 10^5 (TSA) BVP/m3. One indoor and one outdoor (pile turning) site was counted for more than 3.10^4 FVP/m3, respectively on malt-agar and on Czapek agar. At **LA** (vegetable compost), bacterial numbers are comparatively low (< 6,000 BVP/m3), but we observe more than 3.10^4 FVP/m3 near compost milling.

Dust granulometry

On 22 sampling sites, data are available for TSA growing bacteria (non saturated plates). Most viable particles aerosols are of medium size (3 < F < 4), two only of large and six of fine size. Fine or rough aerosols do not seem characteristic of any device or situation. The typical triplet is (5, 3, 1) ; it indicates a rather staggered distribution of equivalent diameters. The mean value for f, f < 0.1, confirms the overall symetrical aspect of distributions, which usually do not get off a log-normal model. Particles larger than 10 um are frequently encountered.

For malt-agar growing microorganisms, where fungi predominate (21 sampling sites), the average triplet is (5, 4, 3), revealing a finer (F = 4) and above all more restricted granulometry, with an overrepresentation of fine viable particles (f = 0.33). Most particles range around 3 um, what may indicate a wide predominance of isolated fungal conidia, and yeasts when they are present. Large particles (aggregated conidia, mycelium fragments) are not so common.

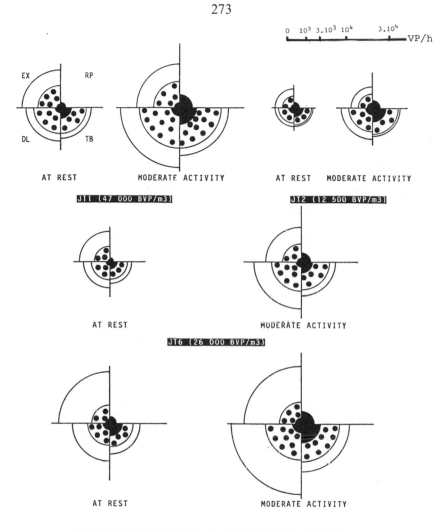

Figure 1 : Inhalated viable particles (per hour) and respiratory deposition site according to activity at some working places on the **JT** plant. Each quadrant gives clockwise :
    — rhinopharyngeal stop (RP)   — tracheobronchial deposition (TB)
    — deep lung deposition (DL)   — exhalated particles (EX),
and, for TB, DL, and EX only, from the center, large (black = Andersen impactor stages 1 and 2), medium (stippled = stages 3 and 4) and fine (stages 5 and 6) particles. For sites JT1, JT2, JT6, bacterial (TSA growing) particles; for site JT5, fungal (malt-agar growing) particles.

Identified organisms
Airborne faecal indicator bacteria were looked for at **JT**. Coliforms, both total and thermotolerant, and "faecal" streptococci are abundantly found above the refuse dumping hopper, just nearby the grab-handler's cabin, and also total coliforms (but not "faecal") and streptococci at the loading level of the fermentation tower. In these two places, garbage is not yet fermented. Lower concentrations are encountered when compost is shovelled, in spite of rather high bacterial numbers in the fermented matter. At **MA**, **Klebsiella pneumoniae** and **Enterobacter cloacae**. **Pseudomonas aeruginosa**, **Staphylococcus aureus** were also observed in rather large numbers.

At **JT**, **Penicillium sp**. is very abundant in raw garbage (36 on 37 identified colonies on **CZA** near the dumping hopper). **Aspergillus fumigatus**, **Cladosporium sp.**, **Monilia sitophila** are present. **Cephalosporum sp.**, **M. sitophila**, **Mucor sp.**, **Penicillium sp.** widely dominate **A. fumigatus** at the top of the fermentation tower, where very numerous **Rhodotorula rubra** are also observed ; here is their only recognized appearance on this plant. Further in the processing chain, **A. fumigatus** widely gains, but **Monilia, Mucor, Penicillium** are still present. Exceptional is this plate (loading of refined compost, impactor stage 5 - malt-agar, 30°C) on which were counted 154 FVP of **A. fumigatus** exclusively.

At **LA, A. fumigatus** is widely represented among thermophilic fungal forms. An actinomycetes, a very probable **Nocardia sp.**, was also identified in high numbers. Most of these moulds were formerly identified in composts **(2, 6)**.

Sanitary interpretation
According to the observed levels of airborne faecal indicator bacteria, it may be deduced that inhalation of primary pathogens of intestinal origin at numbers in the same order of magnitude than infective doses is unlikely.

From epidemiological surveys, it was recognized that a sanitary hazard for workers may be due to germs inhaled in high numbers, i.e. gram-negative bacteria, thermophilic moulds and actinomycetes. This hazard is mainly correlated to the number of microorganisms which are able to reach the deepest parts of the lung.

TSA counts may be considered representative for the bacterial (in fact gram-negative bacteria associated) hazard. By application of the previously considered respiratory model, it may be deduced that, at rest or moderate activity, dust stop at the upper levels (rhinopharyngeal = RP and tracheobronchial = TB) remains stable about 25-30 %, but the balance is inversed for exhalation : while RP and TB stop predominates at rest, deep lung deposition appears more important both by number and percentage for an active subject (fig. 1).

With finer fungal aerosols, the upper respiratory stop is lowered (about 20 % only), but the same inversion is still observed : 30 % of deep lung penetration at rest, 45 % during activity. This leads to figures of 25-30,000 FVP/hour for alveolary deposition at highly contaminated sites as **JT6**, where mature compost is shovelled without any respiratory protection.

7. CONCLUSION
This preliminary survey of five household garbage composting plants indicates that the bacterial and fungal contamination encountered by workers is in the same order of magnitude than previously monitored at wastewater sludge composting systems **(5, 7, 8, 10, 11)**. These findings

legitimate the extrapolation to refuse compost workers of the previous conclusions from epidemiological studies on sludge compost workers, as formerly suggested by Clark et al. **(4)**. These employees are exposed to breath large numbers of bacterial and fungal dusts, with an important alveolary deposition. The pathogenic role of these viable dusts was abundantly demonstrated, even if disease extension needs to be clarified (**BOUTIN, MOLINE,** this symposium). Such data are a complementary justification for technical and medical preventive measures for an exposed, still poorly recognized class of workers.

ACKNOWLEDGEMENTS
We appreciated a kind welcome on visited plants : thanks to everybody we sollicitated. As a trainee, Miss N. Sabourin provided us an efficient help. Our gratefulness to Dr de Closets (C.H.R., Tours) for her valuable and unreserved contribution to this study (identification of fungi).

BIBLIOGRAPHY

(1) ANDERSEN A.A. - New sampler for the collection, sizing and enumeration of viable airborne particles, **J. Bact.**, 1958, **76**, 5, 471-484

(2) de BERTOLDI M., VALLINI G., PERA A. - The biology of composting, a review, **Waste Mgmt Res.**, 1983, **1**, 157-176

(3) CHRETIEN J. - Abrégé de Pneumologie, Masson, Paris, 1976

(4) CLARK C.S., BJORNSON H.S. et al. - Biological risks associated with the composting of wastewater treatment plant sludges, in **Biological risks of sludge disposal to land in cold climates** (WALLIS P.M., LEHMANN D.L., eds), Un. of Calgary Press, Calgary, 1983, 79-93

(5) CLARK C.S., RYLANDER R., LARSSON L. - Levels of Gram-negative bacteria, **Aspergillus fumigatus**, dust and endotoxins at compost plants, **Appl. Environ. Microbiol.**, 1983, **45**, 5, 1501-1505

(6) KANE B.E., MULLINS J.T. - Thermophilic fungi in a municipal waste compost system, **Mycologia,** 1973, **65**, 1087-1100

(7) KOTHARY M.H., CHASE T., McMILLAN J.D. - Levels of **Aspergillus fumigatus** in air and in compost at a sewage sludge composting site, **Environ. Pollut. (Ser. A),** 1984, **34**, 1-11

(8) LEMBKE L.L., KNISELEY R.N. - Coliforms in aerosols generated by a municipal solid waste recovery system, **Appl. Environ. Microbiol.,** 1980, **40**, 5, 888-891

(9) LUNDHOLM M. - Comparison of methods for quantitative determination of airborne bacteria and evaluation of the total viable counts, **Appl. Environ. Microbiol.**, 1982, **44**, 1, 179-183

(10) MILLNER P.D., MARSH P.B. et al. - Occurrence of **Aspergillus fumigatus** during compostage of sewage sludge, **Appl. Environ. Microbiol.**, 1977, **34**, 6, 765-772

(11) MILLNER P.D., BASSET D.A., MARSH P.B. - Dispersal of **Aspergillus fumigatus** from sewage sludge compost piles subjected to mechanical agitation in open air, **Appl. Environ. Microbiol.**, 1980, **39**, 5, 1000-1009

COMPARATIVE SURVIVAL OF PATHOGENIC INDICATORS IN WINDROW AND STATIC PILE

J.T. PEREIRA NETO, E.I. STENTIFORD and D.D. MARA
Department of Civil Engineering, The University of Leeds, U.K.

Summary

The work reported compares the performance of windrows and aerated static pile composting systems with respect to certain physical, chemical and microbiological parameters. Four piles were studied, two windrow and two static piles, comprising approximately 120 tonnes of material. The systems performed in a similar manner with regard to temperature, pH, moisture changes, volatile solids, carbon, nitrogen, ammonia nitrate and COD. The inactivation of pathogen indicator organisms was more effective with the aerated static pile over the composting period.

1. INTRODUCTION

The most important reasons for composting organic wastes are: the conservation of the nutrient and fertiliser value of the wastes, the sanitary treatment and disposal to prevent the spread of disease, and the preservation or improvement of the quality of the environment (1,2).

Following the development of the well known Indore Process in the early 1920's, research has led to the establishment of at least 30 different process systems. However, the literature leaves the impression that the most used system has been the windrow (wind-row) loosely based on the Indore Process. Research has been directed at both reactor and non-reactor systems depending on whether the overriding concern was well-controlled or low-cost operations. In most systems these two criteria appear not to have been compatible. In the 1970's, with the arrival of the forced aeration static pile it seemed that these two concerns could be addressed in one process. It is in this area that most composting research has probably been directed over the past 10 years.

The windrow is mainly characterized by the method of aeration, accomplished by turning the pile periodically. The static pile system (or forced aeration static pile system) does not employ turning and aeration is accomplished by means of blowers forcing air through the composting mass.

The basic mechanism in both pile systems, as in any other composting process, is the decomposition of the organic matter by continuous microbial mass transformation. This complex mechanism is characterized in its various phases by many properties which can interfere in the whole process performance. In order to determine how far some external factors could be used to improve control of the whole process in terms of: energy cost; reduced process time, improved nutrient conservation, and pathogen inactivation, the Unversity of Leeds has been studying many aspects of pile operation. The greatest part of the previous work concentrated on the forced aeration static pile which involved more than 45 piles (20-40 tonnes each), using a mixture of domestic refuse and sewage sludge. Several aeration control regimes have been evaluated from a simple low cost fixed rate of aeration to microcomputer based systems (3,4,5). During this period three alternative methods of aeration were employed, i.e. positive pressure (blowing into the pile), negative pressure (sucking through the pile) and a hybrid system ("suck" followed by "blow") (3,6,7,14). These investigations included: physical, physico-chemical and chemical changes in the compost piles (4,8); changes occurring during the maturation phase (9,10); and pathogen survival studies (4,6,11,12).

Over this period a total of 8 windrows have been built (using similar tonnage and materials as in the aerated piles) in order to compare the relative merits of the two pile systems. This paper concentrates on some of the findings arising from part of the study.

The piles selected for this paper were from:

    Run 16 - pile 1 - windrow
            pile 2 - aerated static pile
    Run 17 - pile 1 - aerated static pile
    Run 19   - windrow.

2. MATERIALS AND METHODS
2.1 Raw Materials

The domestic refuse used in the reported work was the "fines" material taken from the end of a Dano drum (50mm mesh), run by the Greater Manchester Council (Manchester, U.K.). The sludge used was from Sandall Sewage Treatment Works (Doncaster, U.K.), and consisted of mixed primary and secondary sludge. Typically it was used with 4-6% solids content and no further treatment was given prior to composting. The materials were mixed using a rubber-tyred front end loader, similar to the arrangement described elsewhere (13). The moisture content and the carbon/nitrogen ratio were adjusted (using dried sludge) to the initial values of 55 to 65% (depending on the material characteristics) and 30-40:1 respectively. Tables 1 and 2 show the typical analyses for the raw materials used.

2.2 Aerated Static Pile Construction and Operational Control

After thoroughly mixing the components, the mixture was piled over a single perforated plastic aeration pipe (100mm diameter) as shown in Figure 1. The layer of straw (150-200mm) which provided a pile base material also facilitated better air distribution throughout the composting mass. This prevented the compost material from blocking the aeration pipe. Finally, the whole pile was covered with a layer of mature compost (100-150mm thick), to provide the insulation needed to hold thermophilic temperatures in as much of the pile material as possible. In addition it acted as a filter layer against odour emission.

The piles were built using approximately 20-40 tonnes of material in each pile. Typical pile dimensions were approximately 4m wide at the base, 1.8m high and 15m long. Air was supplied by means of a 350 watt blower, which was adequate to ensure aerobic conditions throughout the composting mass. In order to maintain the pile temperature below the desired set point temperature (55-60°C), by regulating the fan-on time, two different controllers were used. In run 16 Pile 2, a variable rate, simple timer was used (3-10 mins. on every 15-20 mins.). In run 17 the pile was operated using temperature feedback control.

The pile temperature profile was recorded by means of a series (6 to 12) of thermocouples, placed in different positions within the pile mass connected to a digital thermometer (made by Leeds University).

During the first composting phase the piles were usually aerated for a period of about 28 days. At the end of this phase, lower temperatures (15-35°C) were recorded, piles were dismantled and put to maturation for 3 to 4 months. This type of compost system has also been described elsewhere (14,15).

2.3 The Windrow Pile Operation

The windrow pile was built using the same mixture of materials and with a similar physical configuration as the aerated static pile.

In order to avoid high core temperature (>65°C) and also to provide the aeration needed to support microbiological activity, the pile was turned (using a front end-loader), every 3 days during the more active bio-oxidative phase (first 40 days). As the available substrate was used and the pile temperature reduced, it was turned every 5 to 6 days. At the stage when thermophilic temperatures were no longer achieved after the pile had been turned (40-60 days), it was put to maturation (10). In the case of the windrow piles, water was added, after the first 30 days, to bring the moisture content to 50-55%. This was done to prevent low moisture inhibiting microbial activity, which could give a false result during the pathogen survival study. Six thermocouple probes were used to record the pile temperatures to determine the correct turning period and observe the temperature profile during the composting period. The pile shape was usually changed during the composting period, to adjust the pile surface area and thereby achieve a balance between the heat produced and heat lost and thus maintain the desired pile core temperature (55-65°C). This long established system of composting has been described by many workers (1,2). The piles reported on in this paper are: Run 16 - pile 1, and Run 19.

2.4 Sampling Technique

Samples were taken from the composting pile at specific sites and these depended on the type of investigation. This particular study was more directed towards microbiological distribution and survival in the pile, and organic breakdown. Three replicate samples were taken from many different positions within the compost mass e.g. surface, apex, core, bottom, corners etc. A conventional soil post auger holding about 1 Kg of sample was used to collect the material for analysis. Samples were bulked, mixed, sieved (through 6mm) and then used as the stock sample for analysis. During the first oxidative phase of the composting period samples were taken from the aerated piles on days: 0 (mixing), 4, 8, 16 and 28-32 when the aeration phase was finished. Windrow pile samples were taken on day 0, 8, 16, 32 and 55-60, when pile temperature was usually lower than 35°C.

2.5 Analytical Methods

To evaluate the relative effectiveness of both composting systems, a number of physical, chemical and bacteriological parameters were monitored during the composting period.

pH was determined as described by Cannes et al.(16). Moisture content, volatile solids and carbon were determined as reported in the standard methods literature (17,18).

The nitrogen balance was monitored by three methods: total kjeldahl nitrogen and ammonia, determined as reported by Havilah et al. (19), and nitrate determined by evaporating with sulphuric acid and glacial acetic acid followed by the calorimetric measurement using EDTA-NaOH solution (20).

The measurement of chemical oxygen demand (COD) was carried out using a microdigestion sealed tub method (17).

Ammonia, nitrate and COD analyses were carried out on a sample which was obtained by blending 100g of dried material (70°C/18-20 hrs), in a litre of deionised water followed by centrifuging and filtration using a Whatman 54 filter paper. /The pathogenic organisms were monitored using so-called indicator organisms. The indicator organisms used were: faecal coliforms (E. coli), streptococci and salmonella   These organisms were chosen because of their high concentrations in the raw materials, urban refuse and domestic sludge (21), and also because they have been used for many years in public health engineering (4). The basic philosophy behind using indicator organims in composting is discussed elsewhere (13).

The bacteriological analyses used serial dilutions of the emulsified sample (1-20g of the stock sample 99-100ml of Ringer solution), and then either membrane filtration, MPN and/or surface spreading for enumeration (22,23). Faecal coliforms were enumerated using membrane filtration, with sodium lauryl sulphate broth (SLB) as the growing median according to the procedure described by Stainfield et al.(24). The identification test followed the technique reported by Cowans (25). API-20E was also used as recommended in the manufacturer's profile index. Faecal streptococci were enumerated using membrane filtration and incubation on the KF streptococci agar of Kenner et al.(26), following the procedure described by Oragui et al.(22). Salmonella analysis was carried out using the modified Rappaport-Vassiliadis (R.V.) media, as described by Vassiliadis (27). The confirmation test was performed using serological testing (17) or the API test.

3. RESULTS AND DISCUSSION
3.1 Temperature
The information on the effects of temperature on composting indicates that optimum decomposition takes place between 55 and 60°C (14,15,28). Numerous other research workers report that destruction of pathogenic organisms in composting (FAC system) occurs provided the temperature reaches 55-60°C for a minimum of 3 consecutive days (2,29). In a well-controlled composting system temperature constitutes the main mechanism for bringing about pathogen inactivation (13).

The temperature/time profile, operating with a fixed rate of aeration (Run 16 - pile 2) and with a temperature feedback control (Run 17 - pile 1) showed high core temperatures (55-60°C) which remained for a period of about 15 days (Figure 2). The temperature profile recorded from the separate piles showed that both means of control used achieved their objective in maintaining a high temperature in a large proportion of the pile mass (albeit < 65°C) even though relatively low ambient temperatures prevailed (max. of 10°C). The windrow piles were characterized more by high core temperatures. This was due to the less effective means of heat dissipation and removal. The high temperature was concentrated in the core of the pile whilst the outer layers remained cool under direct influence of the ambient conditions. However, a better temperature distribution was produced during Run 19, where a better balance between heat produced and lost was achieved, by increasing the pile surface area.

3.2 pH
The pH variation ranged from 5.8 to 8.6, nevertheless no reduction in pH was registered at the start of the compost process. This initial drop in pH has been reported by other workers (1,28,29,30) and is a consequence of the activity of acid-forming bacteria which break down complex carbonaceous material to organic acid intermediates. However, the products formed are readily used and simultaneous protein degradation starts releasing basic compounds which increase the pH.

In all piles analysed the pH showed a progressive increase (with slightly higher values in the windrow systems) with similar behaviour in both systems (Figure 3). Generally, the pH levels remained for most of the compost time at alkaline values. This fact associated with high temperatures can cause nitrogen loss through volatilization of ammonia (1,2,14, 19). This is indicated by the change in total nitrogen shown in Figure 7

3.3 Moisture Content
The change in moisture content is closely related to aeration and other parameters such as: porosity; pile configuration; mode and rate of aeration; temperature; heat generation; and weather. Extreme values of

moisture affect the rate of composting. High values cause anaerobiosis, with all its deleterious effects, and low levels inhibit microbial activity preventing true completion of the initial composting stage. Initial moisture value of 55 to 65% has been suggested by many investigators (31, 30) for optimal composting conditions. It seems that the more absorbent the raw material then generally the higher should be the initial moisture content.

In the first 32 days of composting there was little difference in moisture loss between the two systems. It was necessary to add moisture to the windrows on day 32 to prevent the possible inhibition of microbial activity during the subsequent composting period. In the aerated static piles it is important to control the initial moisture content and the process operation such that at no time is moisture a limiting factor. Generally it should be greater than 40% throughout the process. (Figure 4).

3.4 Volatile Solids

As a result of the organic matter degradation, the volatile solids concentration decreased during the composting period. The greatest reduction was recorded during the thermophilic phase, as is shown in Figure 5. The windrows showed similar volatile solids reduction, as the aerated static piles for the same period of composting (32 days). If we consider the total composting period used for the windrows (60 days) then the volatile solid's reduction was more than in the aerated static piles. Run 19, for example, showed an overall reduction of 47% over this 60 day period. However, it should be noted that the composting times in the two systems are considerably different.

3.5 Carbon and Nitrogen

The organic carbonaceous material is the major nutrient required by micro-organisms during the degradation of organic compounds. Moreover, the cooling of the compost piles is most often caused by depletion of the carbonaceous energy supply (28) (Figure 6). The micro-organisms use carbon for cell synthesis and as a source of energy to build up protoplasm and this synthesis depends on the availability of nitrogen. Thus the quantities of these two elements present in the composting mass greatly affects microbial activity. The carbon/nitrogen ratio can affect the composting process diminishing the rate of decomposition (at high C/N ratios) or causing nitrogen loss, by leaching or volatilization (at low C/N ratios). Extensive work has been carried out on this particular subject and there seems to be general agreement that a good initial value for the C/N ratio is 30/1. However, it is important to note that composting most often involves heterogeneous raw materials where some carbon, recorded in the analysis, could be present in a form so resistant to biological attack that its presence is not significant in the first phase of the process. In such cases, a higher starting value could be used, without adversely affecting the process. The initial C/N ratio for the piles used in this reported work averaged 34/1. At the end of the composting period the aerated pile (Run 16, pile 2) registered a lower value (22/1) than the windrow (27/1: Run 19). This difference was largely due to the loss of nitrogen in the windrow between days 32 and 60 since the percentage reduction in carbon was similar for both piles.

Nitrogen constitutes the second most important major element after carbon, in the composting process.

The mechanisms which affect gains, losses and changes in form are very complex and depend upon the compost pile environmental conditions. The total nitrogen recorded (Figure 7) showed a decrease in concentration over the composting period. This was expected due to degradation of the amino groups which released nitrogen as amines and ammonia etc. Other investigators attribute much of this loss of nitrogen to ammonia volatilization (29,30,32,33,34) and also to chemical decomposition of nitrate (34). Ammonia can be lost by evaporation due to high pH associated with high temperatures (1,2,14,15,30,31,32,35).

The main sources of nitrogen in refuse/sludge composting are: vegetable trimmings, food waste, lawn and garden cuttings, animal and human waste products. Nitrogen is present in a variety of forms in organic compounds, the breakdown of which involves complex interactions between several species of micro-organisms. Nitrogen is constantly transformed by microbial assimilation, denitrification, nitrification, fixation, leaching, volatilization etc., which makes it extremely difficult to quantify the nitrogen balance throughout the composting process.

Small nitrogen increases during composting have been attributed to fixing bacteria (30,33). However, the loss in volatile nitrogen solids can mask the real nitrogen changes.

A correction can be made, for this loss, by modifying the nitrogen concentration relative to ash, since ash is non-compostible and thus the total amount present throughout the process will remain constant (11). A nitrogen reduction of 7.3% was recorded for the aerated static pile (Run 16, pile 2) against a reduction of 34.5% for the windrow (Run 19). Many workers have reported better results, as far as nitrogen fixation is concerned, with static piles system than with windrow system (29,32,35). The windrow pile demonstrated similar behaviour in terms of pH and temperature and yet the windrow showed a reduction in nitrogen 27% greater than the aerated static pile. This suggests that the nitrogen loss is very much process dependent.

Figure 7 shows that nitrogen decreased during composting, whilst ammoniacal nitrogen initially increased sharply until a peak was reached (Figure 8). Subsequently ammoniacal nitrogen concentration decreased. The increase in ammonia during the first days of the composting process can probably be explained by two main mechanisms:

i) as previously mentioned, by the degradation of amino groups, releasing ammonia (34); and

ii) the influence of ammonia-producing bacteria, these have been isolated from composting systems with a population as great as 10^6 cells/g.d.w. (32). Despite the high temperature at this time (Figure 2) and the high pH (Figure 3) (the main factors affecting ammonia volatilization), the total ammonia produced was greater than the ammonia lost by volatilization. The subsequent decrease in the ammoniacal nitrogen level can probably be explained by nitrification (Figure 8) (35,36,37) and the volatilization processes being superior to the ammonia production from the amino group degradation, and the ammonia-producing bacteria. Both pile systems showed similar results throughout the process which confirms the observations of other workers (35).

Nitrate concentration typically showed a decrease at the beginning of the composting process followed generally by a progressive increase towards the end (Figure 9). Many investigators have reported in their work an increase in nitrate levels (35) and suggested nitrate changes for estimating the stability of the organic matter (10,11,34,37). The initial nitrate decrease can be explained by the action of denitrifying bacteria. The subsequent increase can be attributed to the action of autotrophic nitrifying organisms but should be viewed in the light of the continuous loss of organic matter. Once the ammonia levels fall the environmental conditions become more biologically favourable because of ammonia's toxic characteristics. The nitrogen loss, through volatilization of ammonia, might then be partially recovered due to the activity of nitrogen-fixing bacteria.

Many species of such bacteria have been isolated from similar composting systems (29,32) and also have been shown to be sensitive to high temperatures (34), and to presence of ammonia (38). These factors would account for the observed increases in nitrate concentration towards the end of the aeration period, as temperature and ammonia decrease.

3.6 Chemical Oxygen Demand (COD)

A decrease in COD was expected as the waste material was stabilised by microbial degradation of the organic matter. The method of determination is relatively straightforward and was thought to have potential as a process indicator (11). In this work the COD reduction was greater than 50% in all piles studied. This confirms previous work at Leeds on the same material.

Over the composting periods used the windrows showed greater reduction at the end of 60 days but on day 32 (end of static pile aeration) the reductions were very similar for both systems. (Figure 10).

3.7 Pathogen Indicator Organisms

The main mechanisms that bring about the destruction of pathogenic organisms during the composting process are: temperature/time profiles, competition, depletion of nutrient and antibiotic factors. These agents are usually present in a composting process as a consequence of the complex microbial population involved and the ecological behaviour of the whole system (13). However the pathogen population represents numerically an insignificant fraction of the total microbial population which puts them at a distinct competitive disadvantage, compared to the total population, this is thought to assist in their elimination (29,32,33). The competition and predation effects are more accentuated when the readily available substrate has been consumed. At this point there is a considerable increase in the population of fungi and actinomycetes, these initiate the major breakdown of cellulose, lignin etc. A consequence of this fungal actinomycete activity is the production of diversified antimicrobial agents (antibiotics). Some researchers have demonstrated the effectiveness of these antibiotic substances in inhibiting the growth, or causing the elimination of populations of: bacteria, yeasts, and fungi of many toxomic categories (34). However, competition and antibiosis are very difficult parameters to monitor and/or control on a daily basis (13). Consequently, temperature/time becomes a most important parameter, because it can be readily measured and related to pathogen destruction. The available literature states that pathogens, present in the solid urban waste and sewage sludge (39,40,41), can be destroyed in properly operated composting plants (2,7,12,13,30,31).

The effectiveness of the aerated static pile and the windrow in terms of pathogen elimination was determined by the use of indicator organisms, i.e. Escherichia coli, faecal streptococci and salmonella. The results for the aerated static piles showed overall a more effective performance in terms of indicator organism reduction than the windrows (Figure 11). Salmonellae and E. coli were reduced below detection limits in the static piles by day 16. Faecal streptococci, by the end of the process (32 days), were reduced to <10^2 colony forming units/g.w.w. Elimination of salmonella during similar composting operations has been reported by other workers (13,14,32,44). Other research has recorded the growth of micro-organism populations (13,14,39,40,41 and 42) in particular salmonella this phenomenom was recorded in Run 17. Research work with other species of indicator organisms, eg. virus, bacillus and the very resistant Ascaris lumbricoides ova, has concluded that those indicators would be destroyed in the aerated static pile composting system (31,40,43).

The same analysis procedures and indicator organisms were used to

evaluate pathogen survival performance in the windrow system and the results are presented in Figure 11. Even with the high temperature/time
profile (65-70°C for more than 10 days) recorded, this compost system was
unable to reduce the indicators to the same extent as the static pile. A
significant reduction was found but, 10^3 cfu/gww of streptococci, for
example, were still present at the end of the process. Evidence for re-
invasion of organisms was also found when salmonella were monitored at a
particular position within the pile core. Samples taken just before the
pile was turned showed no salmonella present but, for all samples taken
24 hours later (after turning and rebuilding) a positive result was found
indicating re-invasion of salmonella . Similar results have been reported
and show the relative ineffectiveness of the windrow system in reducing
pathogenic indicator organisms (32,46,45). There seems to be agreement
that the inability of the windrow system to inactivate pathogens occurs
because of recontamination when the pile is turned.

The method of operation of a windrow means that no insulating layer of
mature compost is used as a cover, and initially raw material exists at
the surface at ambient conditions. On mixing this surface material, which
is still contaminated with potential pathogens, is incorporated into the
main body of the pile. Following mixing the new surface layer consists of
material which has not been subjected to adequate temperature/time treatment to effectively sanitise it. At ambient temperature this surface
layer now acts as a pathogen reservoir. In time this reservoir of pathogens will be reduced to an acceptable level but the time involved is
greater than that allowed in most windrow composting processes.

4. CONCLUSIONS

In both pile systems it was possible to maintain the temperature
within the optimal range, 50-65°C, by means of either controlling the
aeration rate or, in the case of the windrow, changing the pile configuration or turning interval. Both the variable rate aeration timer and the
temperature feedback system were equally effective in terms of optimising
organic breakdown and pathogen inactivation with the aerated static piles.

In terms of pathogen inactivation the aerated static pile was more
effective than the windrow with all the indicator organisms used. This
probably is due to the surface layers of the windrow which, being at or
near ambient temperature, act as reservoirs for these organisms. On mixing
these organisms reinfected the materials which had already been subjected
to a period at elevated temperatures.

The nitrogen loss in the windrow system was greater than with the
aerated static pile but the complexity of nitrogen transformations is such
that a specific reason was not obvious. It was probably a result of the
system itself since similar high pH and temperature were also present in
the aerated static piles.

Despite the relative ineffectiveness of the windrow with respect to
pathogen inactivation its organic breakdown rate was high and it gave an
excellent end product. Its low cost and ease of operation could make it
an attractive process proposition for poor areas in developing countries
where the substantial reductions in pathogen numbers achieved would be an
improvement on existing practices.

5. ACKNOWLEDGEMENTS

Funds for this research were in part made available by the Science
and Engineering Research Council, U.K. The day to day running of the
experimental work would not have been possible without the co-operation
and support of the Yorkshire Water Authority.

6. REFERENCES

1. GOTAAS, H. B. (1956). Composting – Sanitary Disposal and Reclamation of Organic Wastes. W.H.O., Geneva, Switzerland. 205 p.
2. GOLUEKE, C. G. (1977). A Biological Reclamation of Solid Wastes. Rodale Press. 249 p.
3. STENTIFORD, E. I., MARA, D. D. and TAYLOR, P. L. (1985). Forced Aeration Co-Composting of Domestic Refuse and Sewage Sludge in Static Piles. Paper in Composting of Agricultural and Other Wastes. Edited by J. K. R. Gasser, Elsevier Applied Science Publishers. pp. 42–54.
4. PEREIRA-NETO, J. T., STENTIFORD, E. I. and MARA, D. D. (1985). The Aerated Static Pile Composting System: A Process for Sludge/Urban Refuse Treatment. ABES Conference – Maceio, Al. Brazil. 26 p.
5. LETON, T. G., TAYLOR, P. L., MARA, D. D. and STENTIFORD, E. I. (1983). Temperature and Oxygen Control of Refuse/Sludge Aerated Static Pile Systems. Proceedings of an International Conference on Composting of Solid Wastes and Slurries, University of Leeds, 1983.
6. STENTIFORD, E. I., TAYLOR, P. L., LETON, T. G. and MARA, D. D. (1985). Forced Aeration Composting of Domestic Refuse and Sewage Sludge. Journal of the Institute of Water Pollution Control, Volume 84, No. 1, pp. 23–32.
7. STENTIFORD, E. I., PEREIRA-NETO, J. T., TAYLOR, P. L., MARA, D. D., LOPEZ REAL, J., and WITTER, E. (1985). Sanitisation Potential of Composting for Sewage Sludge and Refuse in a Static Pile System. Advances in Water Engineering, edited by T. H. Y. Tebbutt. Elsevier Applied Science Publishers. pp. 269–277.
8. MARA, D. D. and STENTIFORD, E. I. (1983). Forced Aeration Composting of Domestic Refuse and Sewage Sludge. Leeds University Internal Report.
9. STENTIFORD, E. I. and PEREIRA-NETO, J. T. (1985). Simplified Systems for Refuse/Sludge Composts. Biocycle, Volume 26, No. 5, pp. 46–49. July/August 1985.
10. See reference 9.
11. PEREIRA-NETO, J. T., STENTIFORD, E. I., MARA, D. D. and SMITH, D. V. (1986). Survival of Faecal Indicator Micro-Organisms in Refuse/Sludge Composting Using the Aerated Static Pile System. Internal Report (to be published).
12. PEREIRA-NETO, J. T., STENTIFORD, E. I. and MARA, D. D. (1986). Pathogen Survival in a Refuse/Sludge Forced Aerated Compost System. Institution of Chemical Engineers – Conference on Effluent Treatment and Disposal. Bradford, U.K., 1986.
13. See reference 3
14. EPSTEIN, E., WILLSON, G. B., BURGE, W. D., MULLEN, D. C. and ENKIRI, N. K. (1976). A forced aeration system for composting wastewater sludge. Journal of Water Pollution Control Federation. 48:688–694.
15. FINSTEIN, M. S., CIRELLO, J., MACGREGOR, S. T., MILLER, F. C. and PSARIANOS, K. M. (1980). Sludge Composting and Utilization: Rational Approach to Process Control. Final report to USEPA, NJDEP, CCMUA. Rutgers University. New Brunswick, N.J.
16. CARNES, R. A. and LOSSIN, R. D. (1970). An Investigation of the pH Characteristics of Compost. Compost Science: 11 (5), pp. 18–21.
17. YORKSHIRE WATER AUTHORITY (1981). Methods of Analysis. Leeds, U.K.
18. SOLYOM, P. (1977). Inter-calibration of Methods for Chemical Analysis of Sludge. Vatteu, 33 (1). pp. 21–26.
19. AVILAH, E. J., WALLIS, D. H., MORRIS and WOOLNAUGH, J. A. (1977). A micro-clorimetric method for determination of ammonia in Kjeldahl digests with a manual spectrophotometer. Lab. Report 26 (7). pp. 545–547.

20. HMSO (1984). The Bacteriological Examination of Drinking Water Supplies. Report No. 71, 122 p. London.
21. NELL, J. H. (1983). Hygienic Quality of Sewage Sludge Compost. Water Science Technology, Volume 15, pp. 181-194, G.B.
22. ORAGUI, J. I. (1982) Bacteriologial Methods for the Distinction between Human and Animal Faecal Pollution. Ph.D. Thesis, University of Leeds, Leeds, England.
23. Standard Methods for the Examination of Water and Wastewater, 13th edition. APHA, New York, N.Y., 1971.
24. STANFIELD, G. and IRVING, T. E. (1981). A Suitable Replacement for Teepel 610 in the Selective Isolation of Coliforms from Marine Waters and Sewage. Water Research 15: pp. 469-474.
25. COWAN, S. T. (1974) Manual for the Identification of Medical Bacteria. 2nd Edition, Cambridge University Press, Cambridge, U.K.
26. KENNER, B. A., CLARK, H. F. and KABLER, P. W. (1961). Faecal Streptococci: Cultivation and Enumeration of Streptococci in Surface Water. Applied Microbiology 9, pp. 15-20.
27. VASSILIADIS, P. (1983). The Rappaport-Vasiliadis (RV) enrichment medium for the isolation of salmonella: An overview. Journal of App. Bact., 1983, 54, 69-76.
28. SIKORA, L. J., and SOWERS, M. A. (1983). Factors Affecting the Composting Process in Proceedings of the International Conference on Composting of Solid Wastes and Slurries. September 1983. Leeds, U.K.
29. BERTOLDI, M., VALLINI, G. and PERA, A. (1983). The Biology of Composting: A Review. Waste management and Research (1983) 1, 157-176.
30. POINCELOT, R. P. (1975). The biochemistry and methodology of composting. Comm. Agr. Exp. Sta. Bull. 754. 38 p.
31. WILLSON, G. B., PARR, J. F. and CASEY, D. C. (1978). Criteria for Effective Composting of Sewage Sludge in Aerated Piles and for Maximum Efficiency of Site Utilsation. In the National Conference on Design of Municipal Sludge Compost Facilities, Chicago.
32. BERTOLDI, M. de., VALLINI, G., PERA, A. and ZUCCONI, F. (1982). Comparison of Three Windrow Compost Sysems. Biocycle, 23 (2). pp. 45-50.
33. BERTOLDI, M. de., CITERNESI, V. E. and GRISELLI, M. (1982). Microbial populations in compost process. In Composting (The Staff of Compost Science and Land Utilisation, Eds). p. 26. The JG Press, Emmaus, PA., U.S.A.
34. ALEXANDER, M. (1977). Introduction to Soil Microbiology. J. Wiley and Sons, New York, U.S.A.
35. BISHOP, P. L. and GODFREY, C. (1983) Nitrogen Transformation During Sludge Composting. Bio-Cycle, July/August, 24 (4), pp. 34-39, G.B.
36. GRAY, K. R., SHERMAN, K. and BIDDLESTONE, A. J. (1971). A review of compost - Part I. Process Biochem 6: 32-36.
37. SPOHN, E. (1979). Composting by Artificial Aeration. Comp. Sci. 11(3) 22-23.
38. FOTCH, D. D. and CHANG, A. C. (1975). Nitrification and Dentrification Processes related to Waste Water Treatment. Advances in Applied Microbiology, 19, 153-186.
39. SHUVAL, H. I. GUNNERSON, C. G. and JULIUS, D. S. (1981). Night-soil Composting. World Bank, Volume 10, December 1981.
40. BURGE, W. D., MARSH, P. B. and MILLNER, P. D. (1978). Occurrence of pathogens and microbial allergents. In Composting of Municipal Residues and Sludges, p. 128. Information Transfer Inc. and Hazardous Material Control Research Institute. Rockville, M.D., U.S.A.
41. WILEY, J. S. (1962). Pathogen survival in composting municipal wastes. Jour. Water Poll. Contr. Fed. 34: 80-90.

42. RUSS, C. F. and YANKO, W. A. (1981). Factors Affecting Salmonellae Repopulation in Composted Sludges. Appl. and Environ. Microbial., 41 (3), pp. 597-602.

43. WILEY, B. B. and WESTERBERG, S. C. (1969) Survival of Human Pathogens in Composted Sewage. Appl. Microb. 18, No. 6., 994-1001.

44. BURGE, W. D. (1983). Monitoring Pathogen Destruction. Biocycle, March-April, 24 (2), pp. 48-50.

45. EPSTEIN, E. et al. (1983). Composting: Engineering practices and economic analysis. Wat. Sci. Tech., Vol 15, pp. 157-167, G.B.

46. EPSTEIN, E., WILLSON, G. B. and PARR, J. F. (1978). The Beltsville Aerated Pile Method for Composting Sewage Sludge. New Processes of Waste Water Treatment and Recovery. Editors G. Nattock and E. Marwood. Chapter 12, 201-213.

COMPONENT	VALUE
< 20 mm	15*
Vegetables & Putrecibles	22*
Papers	35*
Metals	8*
Textiles	3*
Glass	10*
Plastic	4*
Unclassified	3*
pH	6.5
Moisture content (%w.w)	40.0
Dry solids (%w.w)	60.0
Volatile solids (%d.w)	68.0
Ash (%d.w)	32.0
Carbon (%d.w)	38.0
Total nitrogen (%d.w)	0.5
Total phosphorus (%d.w)	0.06
F. coliforms (cells/ g w.w)	10^7
F. streptococci (cells/g w.w)	8×10^5
C. perfringens (cells/g w.w)	5×10^4

*percentage of wet weight

Table I : Typical analysis for Manchester refuse

PARAMETER	LIQUID SLUDGE
pH	5.7
Moisture content (%w.w)	96.0
Total solids (%w.w)	4.0
Volatile solids (%d.w)	75.0
Ash (%d.w)	25.0
Total Kjeldahl Nitrogen (%d.w)	4.0
Total Organic Carbon (%d/w)	41.4
Iron (Fe) (%d.w)	0.69
Calcium (Ca) (%d.w)	2.73
Potassium (K) (%d.w)	0.17
Total Phosphorus (%d.w)	1.17
Zinc equivalent mg/kg	1250
F. coliforms (cells/gm w.w)	4×10^6
F. streptococci (cells/gm w.w)	6×10^6
C. perfringens (cells/gm w.w)	2.5×10^6

Table II : Typical analysis for Doncaster sewage sludge

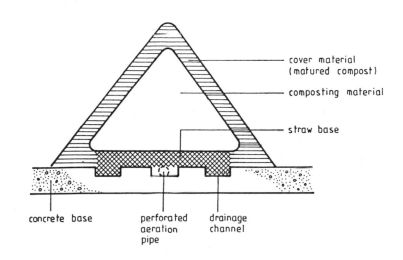

cover material (matured compost)

composting material

straw base

concrete base   perforated aeration pipe   drainage channel

Figure 1 – Cross section of a Typical Aerated Static Pile

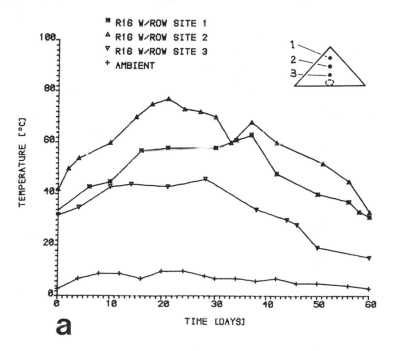

Figure 2(a) – Run 16 – windrow

288

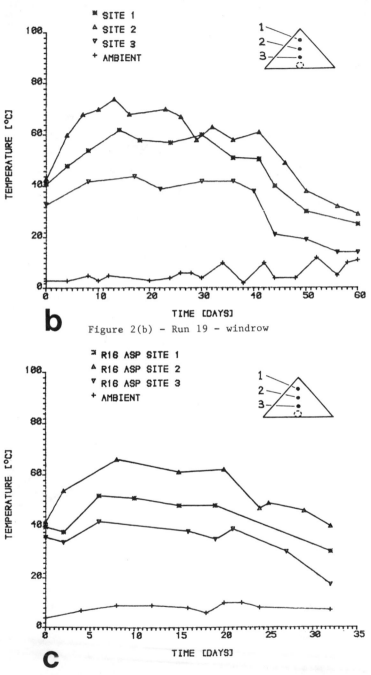

b Figure 2(b) - Run 19 - windrow

c Figure 2(c) - Run 16 - aerated static pile

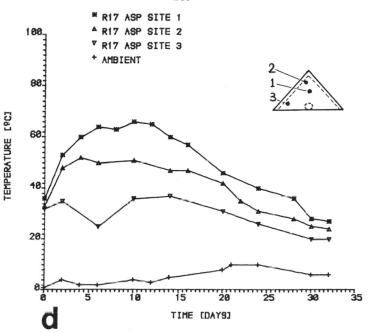

Figure 2(d) – Run 17 – aerated static pile

Figure 2 – Temperature profiles for

       (a) Run 16 – windrow;
       (b) Run 19 – windrow;
       (c) Run 16 – aerated static pile; and
       (d) Run 17 – aerated static pile

     Note: The temperatures for the windrows were recorded just prior to turning.

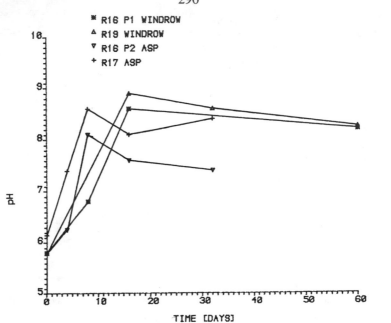

Figure 3 - pH Variation with Time for Windrows and Aerated Static Piles (ASP)

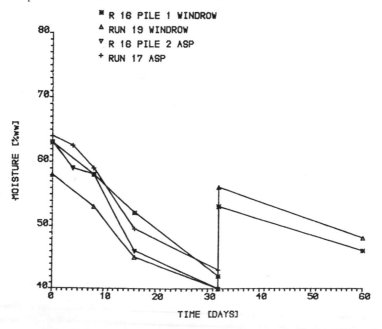

Figure 4 - Moisture Content Variation with Time for Windrows and Aerated Static Piles (ASP)

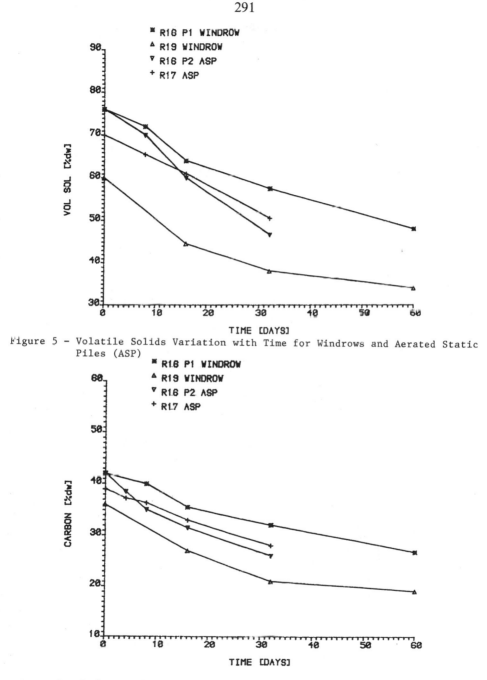

Figure 5 - Volatile Solids Variation with Time for Windrows and Aerated Static
Piles (ASP)

Figure 6 - Carbon Variation with Time for Windrows and Aerated Static Piles
(ASP)

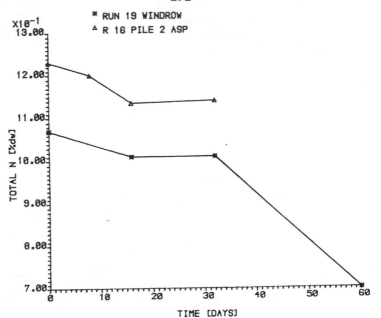

Figure 7 - Total (kjeldahl) Nitrogen Variation with Time for Run 19 (windrow) and Run 16, pile 2 (aerated static pile)

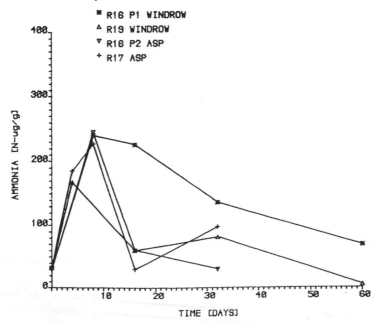

Figure 8 - Ammoniacal Nitrogen Variation with Time for Windrows and Aerated Static Piles (ASP)

293

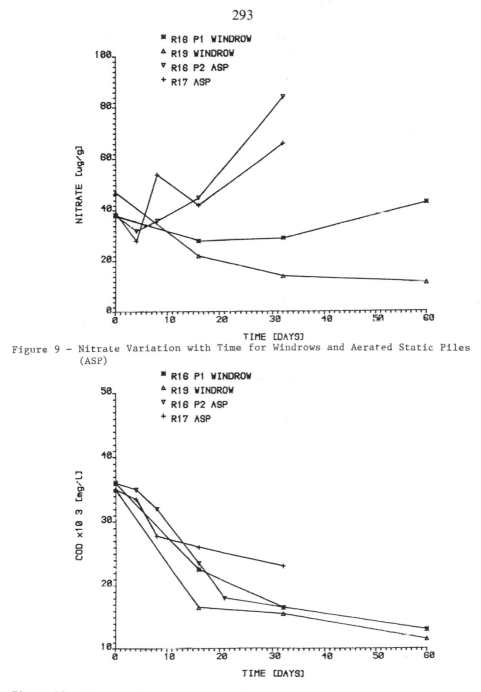

Figure 9 - Nitrate Variation with Time for Windrows and Aerated Static Piles
(ASP)

Figure 10 - Chemical Oxygen Demand Variation with Time for Windrows and
Aerated Static Piles

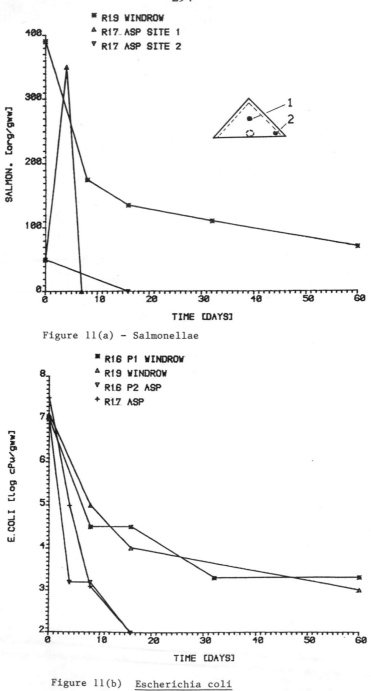

Figure 11(a) - Salmonellae

Figure 11(b) <u>Escherichia coli</u>

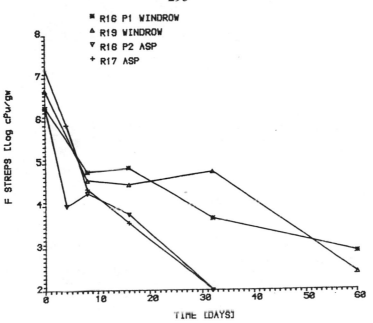

Figure 11(c) Faecal streptococci

Figure 11 - Pathogen Indicator Organism Survival with Time:

      (a)   Salmonellae;
      (b)   Escherichia coli; and
      (c)   Faecal streptococci

PHYTOTOXICITY OF OLIVE TREE LEAF COMPOST

V.I.MANIOS,P.E.TSIKALAS and H.I.SIMINIS
Institute of Viticulture,Vegetable Crops and Floriculture
Heraklion,Crete,Greese

O.VERDONCK
Laboratory of Soil Physics,Faculty of Agricultural Science
State University of Ghent,Belgium

Summary

Olive tree leaves are one of the most abundant organic residues on the island of Crete. The objective of this study was
to investigate the changes of phytotoxicity of olive tree
leaves during the composting process in piles, in relation
to the changes of organic acid concentration. For this purpose four piles were established with urea or ammonium nitrate as nitrogen sources. They were turned and sampled every
8 or 10 days. The organic compounds were extracted by ether
from water extracts of the olive tree leaf samples and redi-
solved in water. To test phytotoxicity of the above organic
compounds, lettuce seeds germinated in these water solutions.
Pure organic acids (formic,acetic,benzoic,salicylic and tannic) in several concentrations (200-1600 ppm) and sterile
water were also used as controls. All these solutions were
adjusted to EC 1.8 mmhos/cm at 25° C and pH=5. The results
indicated that the organic acid concentration increases for
about two weeks during the composting process and then decrease progressively. Phytotoxicity is positively related to organic acid concentration. Nevertheless the lower phytotoxic
concentration of organic acids tested indicated that, not
these but probably other organic acids, or even other ether
soluble organic compounds, are the main phytotoxic agents.

1. Introduction

Numerous studies related to the phytotoxicity of various
organic residues and their biodegradation products have been
carried out. It is known that some tissues and residues of several plants contain organic compounds which, in low or high concentrations, may increase or decrease plant and especially root
growth (Gartner,1973; Still et al., 1976; and Solbraa,1979).
Also it is known that in the decomposition process of organic
residues some changes in the nature and the concentration of the
phytotoxic compounds have been observed. The concentration of
the phytotoxic compounds usually increases during the first period of biodegradation following a progressive decrease, as the
decomposition period increases (Patrick et all.,1963; Still et
al., 1976; De Vleeschauwer et al.,1981). On the other hand several works have been carried out on the nature of phytotoxic or-

ganic compounds. Toussoun et al.(1968) reported that benzoic acid and phenylacetic acid were the major components of the ether-soluble phytotoxins present in samples from barley decomposing in the field and from cotton and soybean decomposing in soil in the laboratory. Solbraa (1979) found that fresh and insufficiently composted bark, when used as a growth medium, reduced plant growth because of its content of phenols and phenolic compounds. De Vleeschauwer et al.(1981) demonstrated that the phytotoxic effects of fresh town refuse compost can be mainly attributed to the presence of large amounts of acetic acid. Other organic acids, such as propionic and butyric acid could also account for the phytotoxicity effects.

Olive tree leaves (OTL) are one of the most abundant organic residues on the island of Crete. These are accumulated as a waste at olive oil factories (OOF) from November to February of each year. OTL have two advantages as organic residues for compost production: (a) the high quantities which can be found accumulated outside the OOF and (b) the availability, which is free of charge, for the users.

Earlier work (Manios et al.,1985) showed that two to three months are required for the digestion of OTL in composting piles. The resulting compost however had phytotoxic effects. The objective of this study was to investigate the changes of phytotoxicity of OTL, during the composting process in piles, in relation to the changes of organic acid concentration.

2. Materials and methods

To study phytotoxicity of OTL (Olea europea var. microcarpa) compost, four composting piles were established. OTL used in the first and second pile (No.74 and 75 respectively) were accumulated during January - February 1984 and then remained at the OOF for about two months. Consequently they were dried in the sun, their aggregates were smashed by hand and stored until September 1984 when the piles were established. OTL used in the third pile (No 76) were accumulated from January - February 1985 and also remained at the OOF for about two months. The pile was established at the beginning of March without drying and smashing the OTL aggregates. OTL used in the fourth pile (No.77) were accumulated in early December 1985. They were fresh and had no aggregates. This pile was established as soon as OTL had been collected.

For each pile 2.5 m^3 of OTL (about 250 Kg dry matter) were used and the C/N ratio was adjusted to 28.5, which has been found to be the optimum for OTL composting (Kritsotakis and Manios, 1984) using urea as nitrogen source in piles No.74,76 and 77 and ammonium nitrate in pile No.75. The piles No.74,75 and 76 were established outdoors and were covered with a black perforated plastic sheet to avoid drying due to the high temperature which prevailed during fall and spring. Pile No.77 was established under a plastic shelter to protect it from the winter rainfall. The temperature of the piles was daily taken. Composting material was turned over manually at 10 day intervals for piles No.74,75 and 76 and 8 day intervals for pile No.77.One sample from each pile was taken after each turning. All samples from

piles No.74 and 75 were dried at 60° C for 24 hours, immediately a-
fter sampling. The samples from piles No.76 and 77 were divided
into two parts. One of them was put at - 20° C immediately after
sampling and the other one was dried as previously.

The following measurements and analyses were carried out
for each sample:
- pH and EC in water extracts (1:10,w/v) of samples taken
  from the pile No.77.
- Organic acids, by the method of silicic acid (McLean et al.,
  1980), in water extracts of samples and ether extracts. (Patrick et al., 1963). For the preparation of ether extracts,
  50 ml of water solution was extracted three times, by 100
  ml ether at each extraction. The ether solution, floated
  on 30 ml of distilled water was removed by evaporation in
  a water bath at 45° C under nitrogen. The remained water
  solution was transferred to a volumetric flask and completed with water up to 50 ml.
- Phytotoxicity, measuring the germination of lettuce seeds
  in water solutions of ether extracts (Patrick et al.,1963).
  The solutions were adjusted to give EC 1.8 mmhos/cm at 25°C
  by solution (0.02 M) of $NaCl,CaCl_2,MgSO_4$ and Na_2SO_4 and pH
  5, by 0.1 N solution of NaOH or concentrated H_2SO_4. Sterile
  water adjusted to the same EC and pH was used as a control.
  In the bioassay tests, 6.5 ml portions of the adjusted water solutions or control solution were added to each Petri
  dish (9 cm) layed with two layers of Whatman No.1 paper.
  Each dish was seeded with 25 lettuce seeds (var.Romana).
  To test phytotoxicity of pure organic acids (formic, acetic,
  benzoic,salicylic and tannic) four concentrations (200,400,
  800 and 1600 ppm) of each of them were used with the same
  way. Each test was repeated three times with four replicates per treatment.

3. Results

In pile No.74 with urea, the temperature declined more rapidly than in pile No.75 with ammonium nitrate (Fig.1). In pile
No.76, also with urea, but without smashing the OTL aggregates
the temperature declined even more rapidly than in the previous
piles (Fig.1). In the last pile, No.77, also with urea, but with
fresh OTL, the temperature rose higher than in the other piles.
A reheating of pile No.77 was noticed after the seventh and
eighth turning when the OTL aggregates were smashed and watered
respectively (Fig.2).

The highest concentration of organic acids (560.5 ppm) was
found about 15 days after the establishment of pile No.77 and
was about double that found in the fresh OTL (259.2 ppm)(Table
3). Thereafter they decreased progressively until the 43rd day
of composting (seventh turning). A new increase in organic acid
concentration was noticed again after the seventh turning in
parallel with a new rise in temperature (Fig.3). Similar changes
were recorded in pile No.74 with urea except that the organic
acid concentration in OTL from OOF was already considerably
higher than in the fresh OTL, when the pile was established
(Table 1). In pile No.75, with ammonium nitrate, the decline in

organic acid concentration was slower than in the previous pile with urea (Table 1). In pile No.76, with old OTL, without
smashing the aggregates of OTL and with urea, the decline in
organic acid concentration was considerably slower compared
with that in the other piles (Table 3).

The data presented in Tables 1,2 and 3 and Figs.3 and 7
indicated that the ether extracts of fresh OTL from OOF in pile
No.77, had no inhibitory effect on lettuce seed germination.
It started progressively to increase after the initiation of
the composting process as the organic acid concentration increases. Thereafter the changes in phytotoxicity were closely related to the organic acid concentration.

With an exception of tannic acid, the biossay experiments
with defferent pure organic acids, indicated an inhibitory effect on lettuce seed germination at concentration higher than
400 ppm. Tannic acid concentration were not related to the inhibition of lettuce seed germination (Figs.4 and 5).

The inhibitory effect of fresh OTL ether extracts and acetic acid, on root-hairs growth of lettuce seedlings are shown
in Fig.6 and 8. On the other hand, the dry and frozen samples
of OTL had about the same organic acid concentration and phytotoxicity (Table 2).

4. Discussion

The lower temperature of piles No.74,75 and 76, compared
with pile No.77, was probably due to the partial decomposition
of the OTL used while they were at the OOF (Figs.1 and 2). In
fact, their temperature was quite high at the collection time.
The more rapid decline in temperature in pile No.76, compared
with the other piles with OTL of nearly the same age, was probably due to the limited decomposition of OTL, because of the
large aggregates of OTL which were not smashed during the composting process (Fig.1). The more rapid decline in temperature
in pile No.74 (with urea), than in pile No.75 (with ammonium
nitrate), indicates that urea accelerates decomposition of OTL
in piles more than ammonium nitrate does (Fig.1). Similar results, for hardwood bark, have also been reported by Yates and
Rogers (1981).

The changes in moisture, pH and EC of OTL during the composting process in pile No.77 are very similar to those reported
by several other workers for different materials (Golueke et al.,
1954 and Finstein and Morris, 1975).

The increase in organic acid concentration of OTL, about
two weeks after the initiation of the composting process and
the folowing progressively decrease, as indicated in Table 1,2
and 3 and Fig.3, are in close agreement with the data of De
Vleeschauwer et al. (1981). They reported that during the first
month of town refuse composting, a high content of acetic acid
was detected, and two months later its concentration strongly
decreased. Also, Golueke et al.(1954) have reported an increase,
mainly in acetic acid concentration and less that of lactic and
butyric acid, in the composting of garbage and mixed municipal
refuse. The above data support the idea that the decomposition
of OTL used in piles No.74,75 and 76 started before the esta-

blishment of the experimental piles, since their organic acid concentration was higher than the fresh OTL (Table 1 and 2). A more rapid decrease in organic acid concentration with urea, than with ammonium nitrate, was probably due to more rapid decomposition of OTL with the first nitrogen source (Table 1).In addition, the slow decrease in organic acid concentration in pile No. 76 (Table 2) was probably due to the limited decomposition of OTL and the anaerobic conditions into the OTL aggregates. Harper and Lynch (1982) reported that acetic acid is primarily produced from anaerobic fermentation of straw.

The total organic acids transferred to ether extracts were 30-50% of water soluble organic acids (Table 1,2 and 3). Toussoun et al.(1968) also reported that the ether-soluble fraction of phytotoxicity was approximately 60% of that of the crude water extracts.

The changes in the inhibitory effect of ether extracts,on lettuce seed germination, while related to the changes of organic acid concentration, they were probably other than pure organic acids tested or even other ether-soluble organic compounds, since their concentration in phytotoxic ether extracts were lower than the minimum phytotoxic concentration of pure organic acids tested (Tables 1,2 and 3 and Figs.3,4 and 5). De Vleeschauwer et al.(1981), also found that the inhibition of acetic acid starts at 300 ppm. On the other hand, the phenols and phenolic compounds are responsible for inhibition exerted by different Kinds of barks (Still et al.,1976 and Solbraa,1979). However, while the ether extracts of fresh OTL and the 400 ppm concentration of pure acetic acid tested had no inhibitory effect on lettuce seed germination, they inhibited the growth of root-hairs of lettuce seedling (Figs.6 and 8).

It is concluded that the concentration of organic acids increases for about two weeks during the composting process of OTL in piles and then decreases progressively. Phytotoxicity is positively related to organic acid concentration. Nevertheless the lower phytotoxic concentration of organic acids tested indicated that, not these but probably other organic acids, or even other ether soluble organic compounds, are the main phytotoxic agents. The present data as well as those of a previous work, indicate that the fresh olive tree leaves after aproximately three months composting, followed by two months maturity, gives a compost with very low phytotoxicity.

Acknowledgments

We thank Mrs E. Sphakianaki and Mr D. Karalis for their technical assistance.

REFERENCES

1. DE VLEESCHAUWER, D.,VERDONCK,O. and VAN ASSCHE,P.(1981).Phytotoxicity of refuse compost. BioCycle.January/February:44-46.
2. FINSTEIN,M.S. and MORRIS,M.L.(1975). Microbiology of mynicipal solid waste composting. Advan.in Appl. Microbiol.19:131-151.

3. GARTNER, J.B.,STILL,S.M. and KLETT,J.E.(1973).The use of hard-wood bark as a growth medium. Int.Plant.Prop.Society Proc. 23:222-231.
4. GOLUEKE,C.G.,CARD,B.J. and McGAUHEY,P.H.(1954). A critical evaluation of inoculums in composting.Appl.Microb.(2):45-53.
5. HARPER,S.H.T. and LYNCH.J.M.(1982). The role of water-soluble components in phytotoxicity from decomposing straw. Plant and Soil 65:11-17.
6. KRITSOTAKIS,I. and MANIOS,V.(1984). Effect of ventilation and C/N ratio on the biodegradation of olive tree leaves in rotary composters. Agricultural Research,8:249-262.
7. MANIOS,V.,VERDONCK,O. and KRITSOTAKIS,I.(1984). The relation between phytotoxicity and maturation of olive tree leaves compost. Proceedings of the 3rd Conference on Protected Vegetables and Flowers (Abstracts).
8. McLEAN,D.A.(1980). Organic acids and volatile acids,pp. 467-471. In GREENBERG,A.E.,CONNORS,J.J. and JENKINS,D. standard methods. American Public Health Association 1015 Fifteenth Street NW, Washington, DC 20005.
9. PATRICK,Z.A., TOUSSOUN,T.A. and SNYDER,W.C. (1963). Phytotoxic substances in arable soils associated with decomposition of plant residues. Phytopathology 53:152-161.
10.SOLBRAA,K.(1979).Composting of bark.IV.Potential growth reducing compounds and elements in bark. Medd. Norsk inst.Skogforsk.34:443-508.
11.STILL,S.M.,DIRR,M.A. and GARTNER,J.B.(1976). Phytotoxic effect of several bark extracts on mung bean and cucumber growth.J.Amer.Soc.Hort.Sci.101 (1):34-37.
12.TOUSSOUN,T.A.,WEINHOLD,A.R.,LINDERMAN,R.G. and PATRICK,Z.A. (1968). Nature of phytotoxic substances produced during plant residues decomposition in soil. Phytopathology 58:41-45.
13.YATES,N.L. and PROGERS,M.N.(1981). Effects of time, temperature and nitrogen source on the composting of hardwood bark for use as a plant growing medium.J.Amer.Soc.Hort.Sci.106 (5):584-593.

Table 1. Organic acid concentration in water and ether extracts and lettuce seed germination in ether extracts of olive tree leaves (OTL),composted in pile with urea (No.74) and ammonium nitrate (No.75).

Days from initiation of composting process	Organic acid concentration(ppm)		Lettuce seed germination in ether extracts[2]
	In water extracts (1:10,w/v)	In ether extracts[1]	
Control[3]	-	-	22.90[4] a
Fresh OTL	259.2	78.0	23.50 a
OTL from factory	508.8	252.0	0.25 d
Pile 74			
10	528.0	-	-
20	292.8	-	-
30	223.2	-	-
40	183.6	60.0	2.25 d
80	126.0	55.0	22.00 ab
180	111.6	19.6	23.50 a
Pile 75			
10	513.6	-	-
20	405.0	-	-
30	355.2	-	-
40	325.2	136.8	1.00 d
80	192.0	64.8	13.25 c
180	222.0	69.6	20.00 b

1. Water solution of ether extracts compounds,from water extracts.
2. Average number of germinated seeds from 25 seeds,after 36 h, at 27°C.
3. Sterile water adjusted to give the same pH and EC as the ether extracts (5 and 1.8 mS).
4. Means followed by the same letter are not different at the 5% level by Duncan's multiple range test.

Table 2. Organic acid concentration in water and ether extracts and lettuce seed germination in ether extracts of olive tree leaves (OTL),composted in pile No.76 with urea.

Days from initiation of composting process	Organic acid concentration(ppm)		Lettuce seed germination in ether extracts[2]
	In water extracts (1:10,w/v)	In ether extracts[1]	
Control[3]	-	-	22.90[4] a
Fresh OTL	259.2	78.0	23.50 a
OTL from factory	444.0	-	-
10 (Dry sample)	492.0	-	-
10 (Frozen sample)	485.0	-	-
20 (Dry sample)	439.2	216.0	0.00 d
20 (Frozen sample)	388.8	151.2	0.00 d
60 (Dry sample)	261.6	132.0	9.00 b
60 (Frozen sample)	256.8	98.0	4.75 c
100 (Dry sample)	202.8	98.4	9.75 b
100 (Frozen sample)	109.8	72.0	11.25 b

1. Water solution of ether extracts compounds,from water extracts
2. Average number of germinated seeds from 25 seeds,after 36 h, at 27°C.
3. Sterile water adjusted to give the same pH and EC as the ether extracts (5 and 1.8 mS).
4. Means followed by the same letter are not different at the 5% level by Duncan's multiple range test.

Table 3. Organic acid concentration in water and ether extracts and lettuce seed germination in ether extracts of olive tree leaves (OTL), composted in pile No.77 with urea.

Days from initiation of composting process	Organic acid concentration (ppm)		Lettuce seed germination in ether extracts after[2]:	
	In water extracts (1:10,w/v)	In ether extracts[1]	36 h	84 h
Control[3]	-	-	24.00[4] a	24.50 a
Fresh OTL	259.2	78.0	23.50 a	24.50 a
OTL from factory	251.3	69.1	24.25 a	25.00 a
8	445.2	157.6	4.00 c	10.25 c
15	560.5	233.0	0.25 d	2.00 ef
22	406.7	162.9	0.25 d	1.00 ef
29	416.7	183.0	0.00 d	0.00 f
36	228.7	87.6	1.25 d	10.00 c
43	194.6	58.8	3.25 c	10.75 c
50	242.6	94.1	1.50 d	8.50 c
57	274.8	121.9	0.00 d	2.50 de
64	260.4	109.9	1.50 d	4.75 d
71	223.0	92.1	6.25 b	15.75 b

1. Water solution of ether extracts compounds ,from water extracts.
2. Average number of germinated seeds from 25 seeds,at 27°C.
3. Sterile water adjusted to give the same pH and EC as the ether extracts (5 and 1.8 mS).
4. Means followed by the same letter are not different at the 5% level by Duncan's multiple range test.

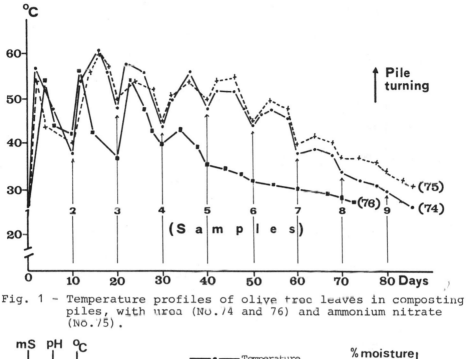

Fig. 1 - Temperature profiles of olive tree leaves in composting piles, with urea (No. 74 and 76) and ammonium nitrate (No. 75).

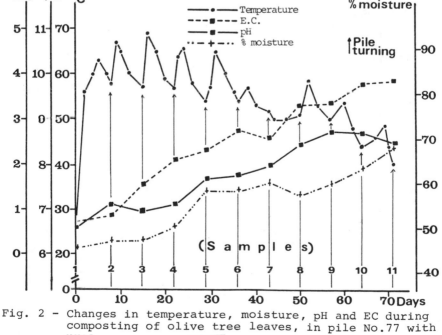

Fig. 2 - Changes in temperature, moisture, pH and EC during composting of olive tree leaves, in pile No. 77 with urea.

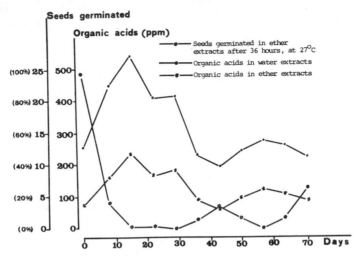

Fig. 3 - Changes in organic acid concentration in water and
ether extracts of olive tree leaves, composted in pile
No.77 with urea and the effect of ether extracts on lettuce seed germination.

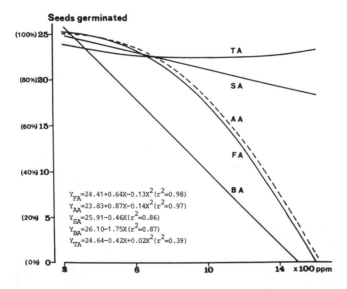

Fig. 4 - Lettuce seed germination in different concentrations
of formic acid (FA), acetic acid (AA), benzoic acid
(BA), salicylic acid (SA) and tannic acid (TA) after
36 h at 27°C.

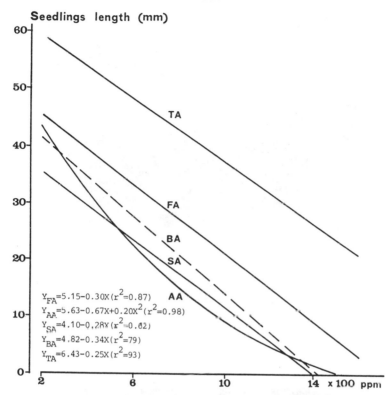

Seedlings length (mm)

TA

FA

BA

SA

$Y_{FA}=5.15-0.30X(r^2=0.87)$
AA
$Y_{AA}=5.63-0.67X+0.20X^2(r^2=0.98)$
$Y_{SA}=4.10-0.28X(r^2=0.82)$
$Y_{BA}=4.82-0.34X(r^2=79)$
$Y_{TA}=6.43-0.25X(r^2=93)$

2   6   10   14   x 100 ppm

Fig. 5 - Lettuce seedling length (mm) in different concentrations
of formic acid (FA), acetic acid (AA), benzoic acid (BA),
salicylic acid (SA) and tannic acid (TA) after 36 h at
27°C.

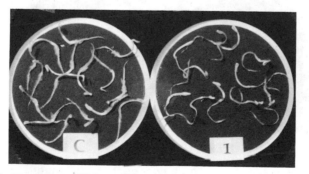

Fig. 6 - Lettuce seedlings in control solution (c) and ether
extracts (1) of olive tree leaves of pile No.77, immediately after their collection from olive oil factories, after 60 h at 27°C.

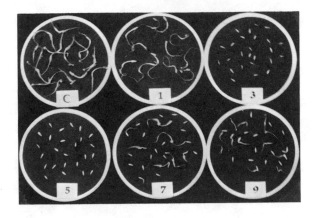

Fig. 7 - Lettuce seedlings and non germinated seeds in control
solution (c) and in ether extracts of olive tree leaves
of pile No.77 (1) and after 15 (3), 29 (5), 43 (7) and
57 (9) composting days, after 60 h at 27°C.

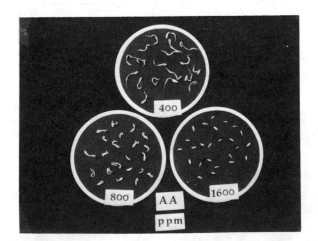

Fig. 8 - Lettuce seedlings and non germinated seeds in three
concentrations of acetic acid (AA), after 36 h at 27°C.

CATION EXCHANGE CAPACITY VARIATION DURING THE COMPOSTING OF DIFFERENT
MATERIALS

J.JACAS, J.MARZA, P.FLORENSA and M.SOLIVA

Departament de Química. Escola d'Agricultura de Barcelona

Summary

The variation of the CEC in different composting assays carried out
in our Departament was determined as proposed by Dr. Y. Harada and
A. Inoko in their simplified method. A high correlation was found
between ripeness and CEC even though the raw materials used in these
composting assays were very different.
This determination has thus been considered a good yardstick for the
estimation of compost maturity as a routine method because of its
precision, simplicity, cheapness and speed.

1.1 Introduction

Detection of the end point of the composting process has been recognized as one of the main problems. It is important for producers and for
users too and at present there is no absolute indicator of compost maturity.
A great many chemical, biochemical, toxicologic and physical changes
take place in the composting process and parametres reflecting all of these
changes have appeared; most of them give us only a relative information and
in order to obtain a fair indication of compost maturity some of them must
be taken together. Only the respirometric techniques are classed as good
indicators of maturity; the rest are just fair and their information increases its value when they are taken together.
The CEC is a physico-chemical determination unusual in compost because
of the poor relation between the CEC values of compost before its application
and once applied to the soil. But recently some authors (1,2,3) have demos-
trated that it is a good determination for the estimation of compost maturity; this is the reason for this study.

1.2 Materials

The compost samples we worked with were taken from the following com-
posting assays:
A.- Pine bark composted alone (4).
B.- Milled domestic refuse mixed with liquid sewage sludge (5).
C.- Residual sludge of paper industries mixed with pine bark and
liquid sewage sludge (6).
D.- Pine bark composted with $CaO-FeCl_3$ precipited and filtered sewage(4).
E.- Pine bark composted with digested and open-air dried sewage(4).
F.- Compost D and E were used as a potting medium; Scindapsus aureus
was the plant tested. Samples from this growing assay were also
analyzed (7).

G,H.- Commercial compost obtained from urban garbage applying the Dano process. The compost is commercialized after one month of matu- in open-air windrows. Two different garbage-composts were analyzed, from two different compost-plants(8) located in Vilafranca del Penedés (G) and in Mataró (H).

Except for the samples of commercial compost, the other processes were carried out in our department.

The samples considered came from different periods in the composting process. So the values obtained show us the evolution of different parametres during the process. All those samples have been studied before, and the results of this study has already been published (5,6,7,8).

The samples of commercial compost were taken from different steps of industrial processes: first, inmediatly after digester; second, fortnight later; and third, from the commercial product.

All the characteristics of the samples studied are shown in tables I, II and III.

1.3 Methods

The method used in the determination of the CEC is that of Drs. Y. Harada and A. Inoko (2). The authors recognized that this method requires a special apparatus, the potentiometre, and takes too much time to be used as a normal composting plant test, so they propose some simplifications. Their simplified method was tried.

The recipe of the simplified method says: "Put 200mg. milled compost sample into a sintered-glass filter (3G3) fitted with a rubber tube with pinchhock. Add 25 ml of 0.05 N HCl solution, stir intermittently with a glass rod, and stand for 20 min. Then , open the pinchcock an filter using an aspirator. Add another 25 ml of 0.05 N solution and filter again. Wash the sample with distilled water until the washing is free of chloride (150 ml is generally adequated). Close the pinchcock, add 25 ml of 1 N $Ba(OAc)_2$ solution (adjusted to pH 7.0), and stand one hour. After filtration,add another 25 ml of 1 N $Ba(OAc)_2$ solution, filter again and wash the sample with destilled water throughly about 150 ml). Combine filtrates and washing, and titrate this solution up to an inflexion point with standar 0.05 N NaOH solution, using a Potentiometre or Tymol Blue indicator. Carry out the blank titration with the same quantity of the 1 N $Ba(OAc)_2$ solution. The difference between two titration values is equated with the proton release from the sample, which gives the CEC".

The main simplification is to reduce the saturation time of $Ba(OAc)_2$. In one hour the $Ba(OAc)_2$ has almost completly saturated the sample; so even though there is a loss accuracy with this simplication advisable in order to make this determination simple and fast.

The precision of this method was evaluated, the results of this evalua- tion are shown in table IV. According to these results and the precision given by Y. Harada and A. Inoko this method can be classed as reproducible and only in very heterogeneous samples the variation coeficient was slightly greater, but this problem is common in all compost determination because of its low homogeneity.

Before the application of the method, another assay was made. The CEC of different samples was determined on an unmilled sample, kitchen-grindrer milled sample, 0.75 mm pulverized sample and 0.12 mm pulverized sample. The results are shown in table V. It is obvious, looking at the results, that CEC increases in all four treatments, so it could be concluded that working with unmilled compost is the best because no alteration is produced in the sample, but that is so, unmilled an kitchen-grinder milled compost are so heterogeneous that dispersion of results is greater than in the other cases. It is not necessary to mill the sample to 0.12 mm because it takes too much time (it is necessary to pulverise the sample to 0.75 mm previously). So the conclusion was that 0.75 mm was enough.

1.4. Results

Results are expressed as me/100 g ash-free sample (CEC/TOM). This expression is recommended because of the negligible contribution of inorganic constituents of compost to the CEC. So, even though CEC in soils is expressed as me/100 g of dried soil, in this case the proposed method seems more suitable. An extra advantage in expressing the results on ash free material is that it shows more clearly the CEC increases during the composting processes. (Fig. 1)

Values of CEC obtained from our samples are shown in table VI, VII and VIII and the regresion lines between time of composting and CEC are represented in figure 2.

Comparing our results to those obtained by the Harada and Inoko (2) using a similar compost, similar values are also obtained but the most important item is the similar patterns offered by the figures where CEC and composting time are represented; composts can be grouped according to similarity of slope as follows:

-Slope of aproximately 0.40.   Pine bark and composts of pine bark with sewage sludge.

-Slope of aproximately 0.26   Domestic refuse and paper residual sludge with sewage sludge.

-Slope of aproximately 10^{-3} Ripe composts used as potting medium. It's also remarkable that composts with the same basic product reach similar CEC final values. So products with bark reach 150 me/100 g and products with city refuse reach 80 me/100 g.

The commercial compost samples don't reach maturity values obtained by Harada and Inoko and ourselves in similar products. Although G14 and H14 samples reach these values.

The results of composts used as a potting medium, with a slope of about 10^{-3}, can surprise, but it is absolutely normal in a mature compost and the evolution of this parametre is the same as observed in the other parametres considered in these samples, there was almost no change; the compost were very stabilized and their initial properties were practically the same at the end of the growing assay.

1.5 Conclusions

From the results obtained we consider the method for determination of CEC as proposed by Inoko and Harada to be a useful and routine plant-composting test and we would underline the following points:

-Simplicity of the material used; no sofisticated apparatus is required.

-Speed; the determination takes about five hours and many results may be obtained simultaneously. These is very important in a method qualified as routine.

-Precision and highly reproducible results; although accuracy is loss because of the simplification of the method and milling, this handicap is Known and assumed inasmuch as precision, rapidity and economy but not exactitude is demanded.

Although, the CEC is a relative parametre, the information about compost maturity is only reached if initial values of CEC are known. So it is not valid for isolated samples with no "pedigree".

But it is absolutely advisable in qualification of compost as a routine-test or in comparing samples of compost obtained similarly (the same process or the same raw materials). These occurs in commercial compost samples. So it seems reasonable to think that in a more extensive study of this parametre, it would be possible to standardize the CEC values of different composts and then the CEC could be used as an absolute indicator of compost maturity by comparison with these standard values.

REFERENCES

1. CEQUIEL, R.Mª and CRUAÑAS, R. (1984). Determinación de la capacidad de iuntercambio catiónico en residuos orgánicos de origen diverso: posible aplicación de la metodología utilizada en suelos. I Congreso Nacional de la Ciencia del Suelo. Madrid. Vol. 1º: 465.
2. HARADA, Y. and INOKO, A. (1979). The measurement of the cation-exchange-capacity of compost for the estimatuion of the degree of maturity. Soil Sci. Plant Nutr., 26 (1).
3. HARADA, Y. and al. (1981). Maturing process of city refuse compost during piling. Soil Sci. Plant Nutr., 27 (3).
4. BURES,O. and SOLIVA, M. (1984). Composting sewage sludge-pine bark. Acta Horticulturae 150.
5. SOLIVA, M. and al. (1984). Composting combined city refuse and sewage sludge. Acta Horticulturae 150.
6. SOLIVA, M. and al. (1984). Possible use of residual sludges from paper industry as a substrate . Acta Horticulturae 150.
7. ARNO, J. and SOLIVA, M. (1984). Behaviour of two different compost used as sustrates. International Symposium on Composting. Gent.
8. FLORENSA, P. (1986). Results not published.

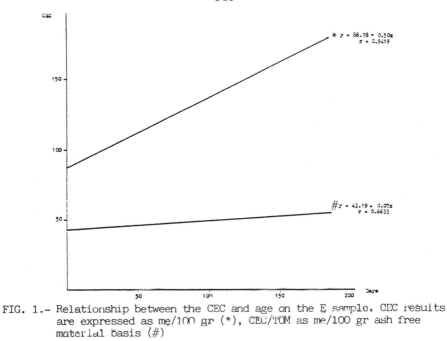

FIG. 1.- Relationship between the CEC and age on the E sample. CEC results are expressed as me/100 gr (*), CEC/TOM as me/100 gr ash free material basis (#)

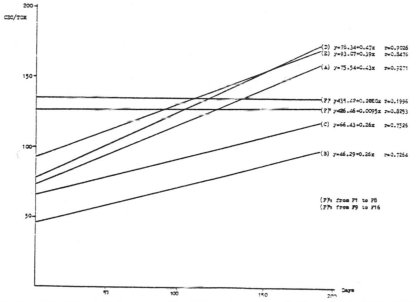

FIG. 2.- Relationship between the CEC and age on different studied compost.

SAMPLES	AGE (days)	% TOM	% Cox	%N	D.D.	C/N
A1	0	65.70	29.90	0.58	57.38	65.61
A2	15	59.00	26.82	0.53	–	65.14
A3	36	62.12	–	–	–	–
A4	50	58.38	26.54	0.54	–	62.29
A5	85	58.34	26.38	0.58	58.31	57.87
A6	116	53.43	24.29	0.57	–	54.35
A7	155	53.18	25.15	0.54	70.22	57.32
B1	5	36.66	16.74	1.13	–	18.76
B2	15	31.35	–	0.87	–	20.94
B3	49	19.15	17.60	0.97	–	11.45
B4	69	16.10	12.61	0.86	–	10.85
B5	126	16.96	14.36	0.99	–	9.90
B6	187	14.58	11.40	0.95	–	8.94
C1	1	47.41	27.50	0.47	23.70	58.50
C2	50	41.62	24.14	0.43	37.80	56.10
C3	70	28.10	16.30	0.58	46.00	28.10
C4	97	33.41	19.38	0.55	49.00	35.20
C5	122	38.86	22.54	0.51	46.00	44.20
C6	127	34.18	19.83	0.41	48.20	27.90
D1	0	70.36	31.98	1.31	51.34	31.11
D2	12	65.06	29.57	1.24	–	30.49
D3	18	73.06	33.21	1.22	–	34.65
D4	33	74.35	–	–	–	–
D5	47	70.99	32.27	1.18	–	34.89
D6	57	62.59	28.45	1.18	51.98	30.83
D7	68	64.31	–	–	–	–
D8	78	65.26	29.66	1.33	–	28.43
D9	89	63.75	28.98	1.48	–	25.01
D10	117	57.71	26.23	1.33	64.71	25.25

TABLE I.- Some chemical characteristics of A, B, C, D samples.

SAMPLES	AGE (days)	% TOM	% Cox	%N	D.D.	C/N
E1	3	46.30	20.48	1.26	50.09	21.34
E2	15	44.05	20.02	1.53	-	16.76
E3	30	39.25	17.84	1.57	-	14.55
E4	36	43.46	-	-	-	-
E5	39	43.06	19.57	1.29	-	19.32
E6	50	45.29	20.58	1.42	-	18.59
E7	66	47.39	21.54	1.37	-	20.01
E8	71	39.20	-	-	-	-
E9	85	39.85	18.11	1.10	68.52	20.99
E10	95	34.82	15.83	1.07	-	18.83
E11	106	40.92	-	-	-	-
E12	116	36.81	16.73	0.84	-	25.61
E13	127	36.73	16.69	1.28	-	16.66
E14	155	33.56	15.29	1.02	61.14	19.07
E15	176	36.73	16.70	-	-	-
F1	0	35.64	18.76	1.24	80.60	16.70
F2	26	29.68	17.80	1.17	80.25	14.66
F3	58	38.25	-	1.37	-	16.20
F4	83	32.76	17.06	1.20	90.36	15.84
F5	114	35.28	-	1.02	-	20.04
F6	134	38.26	18.00	0.94	-	23.56
F7	157	37.26	-	1.39	-	15.57
F8	192	35.29	20.70	0.98	65.19	20.83
F9	0	61.28	35.55	1.46	56.66	24.43
F10	26	51.90	27.14	1.28	61.34	23.59
F11	58	50.73	-	1.44	-	20.41
F12	83	51.62	24.98	1.36	63.58	21.93
F13	114	55.12	-	1.36	-	23.41
F14	134	60.64	27.60	1.18	-	29.68
F15	157	56.42	-	1.42	-	23.10
F16	192	51.98	25.03	1.54	61.94	19.53

TABLE II.- Some chemical characteristics of E,F samples.

SAMPLES	AGE (days)	% TOM	% Cox	%N	D.D.	C/N
G11	0	72.04	36.20	1.59	23.30	22.77
G12	15	74.66	34.68	1.53	9.40	22.67
G13	30	60.52	26.98	1.72	24.70	15.69
G14	150	49.47	22.92	1.97	-	11.63
G21	0	73.43	35.71	1.62	10.70	22.04
G22	15	64.86	29.69	1.79	25.25	16.55
G23	30	64.85	29.73	2.22	25.70	13.39
G31	0	75.51	31.44	1.83	23.56	17.18
G32	15	64.61	29.52	2.32	26.90	12.72
G33	30	67.07	33.89	1.87	27.51	18.12
G41	0	72.15	33.01	1.99	24.70	16.59
G42	15	68.37	34.40	1.85	23.93	18.59
G43	30	58.97	27.68	1.64	25.66	16.88
G51	0	73.74	35.15	1.97	20.63	17.84
G52	15	68.06	33.08	1.85	24.31	17.88
G53	30	60.61	30.56	1.89	32.58	16.17
G61	0	72.26	33.36	1.59	23.10	20.98
G62	15	66.14	31.61	1.84	30.09	17.34
C63	30	63.29	31.97	1.34	19.88	23.86
H11	0	65.03	33.31	1.51	27.30	22.06
H12	15	63.28	33.63	1.57	35.90	21.42
H13	30	50.49	25.40	1.43	29.54	17.76
H14	100	30.37	14.61	1.13	-	-
H21	0	70.29	30.87	1.64	25.40	18.82
H22	15	54.19	24.65	2.04	30.66	12.08
H23	30	47.08	22.37	1.46	36.00	15.32
H31	0	68.96	31.02	2.12	25.15	14.63
H32	15	69.37	33.93	2.53	21.10	13.41
H33	30	50.13	24.78	1.43	30.43	17.45
H41	0	57.42	30.01	1.76	25.88	17.05
H42	15	59.79	31.46	1.91	27.50	16.47
H43	30	46.40	24.26	1.28	19.15	18.95
H51	0	66.44	32.99	1.80	25.63	18.33
H52	15	58.51	32.70	1.56	27.99	20.96
H53	30	42.76	24.75	1.10	27.52	22.50
H61	0	64.38	34.24	1.91	23.82	17.93
H62	15	68.58	34.76	1.90	30.84	18.29
H63	30	49.57	22.61	1.32	27.29	17.32

TABLE III.- Some chemical characteristics of G,H samples.

COMPLETE METHOD	SIMPLIFIED METHOD	
CEC/TOM	CEC/TOM	
	59.8570	
62.6334	60.1705	
62.0098	58.0715	
60.6432	60.6846	
61.7621	59.8534	$\overline{X}$
1.65	1.90	V.C.%

TABLE IV.- Evaluation of the method precision. All the results are refered to sample E11.

SAMPLES	CEC/TOM			
	I´	II´	III´	IV´
A1	54.00	68.58	79.62	87.41
A3	72.64	73.51	106.84	101.82
A5	66.42	87.85	103.64	120.07
A7	92.05	102.69	129.17	134.95

TABLE V.- The particle size influence on CEC/TOM values.

I´: unmilled sample.
II´: kitchen-grinder milled sample.
III´: 0.75 mm pulverized sample.
IV´: 0.12 mm pulverized sample.

SAMPLES	AGE (days)	CEC	% TOM	CEC/TOM
A1	0	52.31	65.70	70.62
A2	15	48.35	59.00	81.95
A3	36	66.38	62.12	106.84
A4	50	52.54	58.38	89.99
A5	85	60.15	58.04	103.64
A6	116	62.90	53.43	117.72
A7	155	68.69	53.18	129.17
B1	5	27.25	80.65	33.79
B2	15	24.59	69.41	35.42
B3	49	28.38	42.13	67.36
B4	69	33.50	35.38	94.69
B5	126	26.70	37.29	71.61
B6	187	27.70	32.08	86.36
C1	1	33.49	47.41	70.64
C2	50	29.29	38.41	76.25
C3	70	28.89	41.61	69.43
C4	97	23.65	28.10	84.16
C5	122	40.77	33.41	122.03
C6	127	37.94	34.18	110.99
C7	188	34.29	33.12	103.54
D1	0	58.12	70.36	82.60
D2	12	62.62	65.06	96.25
D3	28	61.89	73.06	84.71
D4	33	65.85	74.35	88.57
D5	47	63.07	70.99	88.85
D6	57	67.98	62.59	108.60
D7	68	67.62	64.31	105.15
D8	78	76.10	65.26	116.61
D9	89	72.71	63.75	114.06
D10	117	83.04	57.71	143.89

TABLE VI.- Age, % TOM, CEC and CEC/TOM values of A, B, C, D samples. CEC as me/100 gr, and CEC/TOM as me/100 gr of ash-free compost.

SAMPLES	AGE (days)	CEC	% TOM	CEC/TOM
E1	3	40.68	46.30	87.86
E2	15	48.00	44.05	108.97
E3	30	43.40	39.25	110.56
E4	36	42.90	43.46	98.71
E5	39	45.36	43.06	107.66
E6	50	48.80	45.29	107.14
E7	66	50.72	47.39	107.02
E8	71	41.69	39.20	106.34
E9	85	52.72	39.85	132.29
E10	95	46.44	34.82	133.38
E11	106	58.42	40.92	142.76
E12	116	55.38	36.81	150.46
E13	127	56.07	36.73	152.65
E14	155	56.67	33.56	168.85
E15	176	48.29	36.73	131.48
F1	0	70.03	61.28	114.28
F2	26	72.46	57.90	125.14
F3	58	62.07	50.73	122.36
F4	83	60.54	51.62	132.77
F5	114	71.83	55.12	130.31
F6	134	75.18	56.90	132.12
F7	157	71.90	56.01	128.37
F8	192	68.53	50.55	135.58
F9	0	45.85	35.64	128.64
F10	26	43.54	29.68	146.69
F11	58	50.36	38.25	131.66
F12	83	46.37	32.76	141.56
F13	114	44.53	35.28	126.22
F14	134	52.16	38.39	135.86
F15	157	51.05	37.36	136.63
F16	192	48.59	35.29	137.69

TABLE VII.- Age, % TOM, CEC and CEC/TOM values of E,F samples.

SAMPLES	AGE (days)	CEC	% TOM	CEC/TOM
G11	0	15.86	72.04	22.02
G12	15	19.36	74.66	26.29
G13	30	22.39	60.52	37.00
G14	110	37.06	49.47	74.92
G21	0	15.95	73.43	21.72
G22	15	17.79	64.86	27.50
G23	30	22.11	64.85	34.10
G31	0	16.05	75.51	21.26
G32	15	21.73	64.61	33.62
G33	30	27.28	67.07	40.67
G41	0	15.17	72.15	21.02
G42	15	23.28	68.35	34.04
G43	30	24.24	58.97	41.10
G51	0	20.28	73.74	27.50
G52	15	24.33	68.06	35.75
G53	30	30.34	60.61	50.05
G61	0	20.38	72.26	28.21
G62	15	23.26	66.14	35.17
G63	30	24.74	63.29	39.08
H11	0	16.19	65.03	24.90
H12	15	23.25	63.28	36.74
H13	30	22.43	50.49	44.42
H14	100	22.34	30.37	73.55
H21	0	17.71	70.29	25.19
H22	15	22.21	54.19	40.99
H23	30	26.18	47.08	55.60
H31	0	15.16	68.96	22.07
H32	15	27.50	69.37	39.64
H33	30	21.56	50.13	42.96
H41	0	22.74	57.42	39.59
H42	15	25.88	59.79	43.29
H43	30	21.45	46.40	46.23
H51	0	20.64	66.44	31.06
H52	15	27.37	58.51	48.85
H53	30	23.03	42.76	53.85
H61	0	25.27	64.38	39.25
H62	15	33.20	68.58	48.42
H63	30	28.00	49.57	56.49

TABLE VIII.- Age, % TOM, CEC andCEC/TOM values of G,H samples.

CRITERIA OF QUALITY OF CITY REFUSE COMPOST BASED ON THE STABILITY

OF IT ORGANIC FRACTION

J.C.Moré and J.Saña

Area de Química. Escola d'Agricultura de Barcelona

Summary

On a total of 43 compost samples of different origin and state of maduration, three different analytical techniques were developed: (1) a fractionization of the organic matter, (2) decomposition degree and (3) total organic matter.

These analytical techniques are subject to well defined protocoles, are relatively simples and garantee their reproductibility.

These analytical techniques yield a serie of parameters and relation ships which bring out information of the organic matter.

Dealing with these parameters as quantitative variables within a discriminant factorial analysis, a procedure is established in order to delimit three qualitatively different compost groups as a function of their organic fraction characteristics.

1.Introduction and Objetives

To dispose of criteria of quality -ripeness- for Composts is a basic question for its correct comercialization, as well for the possibility of improving the thecnical management of its production, as to prevent the nocive effects of its application to the soils.

The problems derived from the application of an immature compost are well known (15). The germination or the young plants development can be inhibited by increasing the temperature or by producing anaerobic conditions into the soil, by slowing down the respiration and the mineral elements' absortion and lowering the synthesis and the transport of gibberellins and cytokinins (1), or by providing phitotoxic substances with the compost, like Acetic, Propionic or Butiric Acids or Ammonia.

The Priming effect, that is the more energic mineralization of the own soil Organic Matter caused by the easily decomposable organic matter addition by an unripe compost (6) can also appear.

In particular cases, the composts that had not passed a good thermophilia stage can provide vegetal Parasites and Pathogens. In other cases the composts with high C/N ratios can produce the temporal Nitrogen blockade.

Compost Maturity Degree evaluation is usually determined by respirometrical and chemical techniques. "A priori" the last ones seem the most suitable. In theses techniques the respiratory activity of the microorganisms of a soil, to wich a compost has been added, is mesured, approximately reproducing the real compost behaviour as a manure. An index of this respiratory activity is the Complementary Mineralization Rate (CMR) defined by (10) as the percentual expression of the CO_2-C emission attributed to the Compost in relation to the Compost-C introduced into the soil, in a given incubation conditions. The CO_2-C emission measurements are taken at specific periods, usually of 7,15 or 21 days. Its interpretation is very simple: the ripest a compost will be, the lowest its CMR.

But the respirometrical techniques has the inconvenient of its low reproductibility, making it unusable as an inter-laboratory method: a same compost presents different CMR according to the soil used as reference.

The Chemical Techniques indirectely determine the microbial activity consequences during the Composting process, measuring the Organic Matter or the total Organic Carbon or some organic fraction levels (for exemple: humic fractions, non hydrolyzable fractions, sugar types, etc.). Any one of these chemical parameters holds useful but partial information about Compost Organic Matter maturity condition, so that individually considered they are not usefull to establish the different stages in the composting evolution (8).

These parameters present the advantage of being much more reproducible than Respirometrical techniques, but also the disadvantage of its more laborious interpretation, and sometimes, even impossible if the origin and features of the composted material are unknown.

In this work, an analytical system is proposed to characterize the Compost maturity, based on interpretative potencial of the CMR and developed on chemical techniques with good reproductibility, by means of the statiscal system called Discriminant Factorial Analysis (2).

2.Method and Materials

We have been working with a collection of 43 compost samples from very different origins. In some cases, samples with the same origin but taken in different composting stages have been available.

The codes used in the samples denomination (table-I) are formed with the following criteria:

a- In all the cases, the first letter is related to the different origins.

b- When it exists, the second letter determines, in the samples from the same origin, outstanding differences by direct recognition or individualized reception.

c- The three digith that appear in certain samples coincide with the composting time in days, when this is known.

In the Compost samples, a respirometrical (7 days-CMR) and different chemical parameters (Total Organic Matter-TOM; Oxidable Carbon-Cox; Humic Fractionation; Colorimetric Index of Humic extract- E_4/E_6; Decomposition Degree-DD; and non-hydrolyzable Nitrogen-Nnh)are determined.

The 7 days-CMR has been determined by a simplification of the method described by (9), and it has been used as a previous ripeness criterion on basis to the considerations detailed in the Introduction. A superficial sample from a Calcixerollic Xerochrept soil has been used as a incubation base. The characteristics of this sample appear in Table-II.

The Composting process always involves an Organic Matter loss in CO_2 form, due to microbial activity (4). The extent and speed of the decline depens on the material origin and the composting system. So, the Organic Matter percentage cannot be used, by itself, as a general naturity index, but further on we will see how it can be usefull.

The total Organic Matter (TOM) has been determined by sample calcination (11).

The called Decomposition Degree (DD) is defined as the percentage of Organic Matter resisting two consecutive hydrolysis with H_2SO_4 concentrated (72%) and subsequently diluted (7).

The N present in the residuum resisting these hydrolysis can be determined, and it is called Non-Hydrolyzable Nitrogen (N-nh). It can be related to the Total Organic Matter (% N-nh/TOM), expecting an increase of this index during the composting process. This way of relation combines the interpretative potencial of both parameters, with clear dynamics, into a single expression relativizing the absolute differences due to the origin of the material and the composting process.

(4) determine, in their composts, a similar parameter to the DD, hydrolyzing the samples with 80 H_2SO_4, finding a significant negative correlation not only between non-hydrolyzable Organic Matter and the C/N ratio (the most classic maturity criterion), but also between non-hydrolyzable Nitrogen and the C/N ratio.

In addition to its interpretative value, the N-nh level has the advantage no to be affected by the drying process, contrarily to the total-N (5), and so it can be determined on the 110ºC dried compost sample, which is more easily made homogeneous than the moist one, on which the total N has to be determined to avoid losses.

The coloured substances, classically called Humic Substances, are separated from the Compost by extraction using basic solutions. They can be classified in Humic (HA) or Fulvic Acids (FA), depending on its precipation or unprecipitation in an acid medium. Really, most of theses compost Humic Substances are not equivalent to the soil Humic Substances (probably the Fulvic fraction is mostly made up by sugars (8)). In this sense we have to take into account the differences in the organic-mineral medium and in the time scale, both considered between the Organic Matter Humification process into the soil and into the Composting.

During the Composting process (5, 10 and 14), irregular fluctuations on the levels of Humic fractions are observed, which show deep qualitative changes. Futhermore, the positive correlation found in composts (8) between C_{HA}/Cox and C_{FA}/Cox, indicates, at least, that the distintion between the two fractions are inadequate in the composting case. Therefore we are going to work with the called Extraction Rate (100 x C_{HA+FA}/Cox), quantifying the content of the basic extract by oxidation with $K_2Cr_2O_7/H_2SO_4$ mixture and by colorimetric measure of the formed $Cr(III)$ (12).

The oxydable Carbon (Cox), used in the previous panameter as a reference for the extractable Carbon, has been measured with the same oxydant mixture, and the $K_2Cr_2O_7$ excess titrated with a Ferrous salt (3).

It can be noticed visually that the coulour of the Humic Substances solution changes during the composting process (13) from yellow to darker coulours. (10) suggest that the quantification of this event can be used as ripeness index. (14) do it measuring the differences on the absorptions, at 400 and 600 nm., of the Humic Substances solution, observing in most cases an increase of these differences, when the compost maturity advances, and they attribute the absorption increase at lower wave lenght to oxidation processes, characteristic of the composting, which cause an increase of the aromatic and insaturated electrons. We have employed a similar index, the E_4/E_6 ratio, that is the quotient between the absorption at 472 and 665 nm. of the Humic solution.

3.Resultats and Discussion

In broad outline, the Discriminant Factorial Analysis can show the relation between a group of quantitative variables (in this case, the compost chemical parametres) towards a qualitative variable, which takes discreet categories (Groups or Classes in our case, Ripeness stages).

To develop a Discriminant Factorial Analysis it is essential to have a sample collection (a Standars' battery), perfectly known, that is to say, without the slightest doubt about the qualitative classification of their elements. This standards' collection has been formed evaluating the following characteristics of the 43 studied samples:

- Its physical aspect, and, in the known cases, its history (composting days, kind and quality of industrial composting process, etc.).
- Its 7 -days- CMR (Table III).This parameter was the most definitive one. It could be observed that composts with 7d - CMR lower than 1.55 -in our working conditions- were clearly ripe composts, while the ones with a 7d-CMR higher than 2.40 were clearly fresh ones.

Following this criteria we classified with certainty a subcollection of 26 samples: 9 Fresh Composts, 8 Semi-ripe ones and 9 Ripe-ones. The Discriminant Factorial Analysis confirms these classification in the basis of the Chemical Parameters DD, % Nnh/TOM, Extraction Rate and E_4/E_6 index, and so the Standars' Battery took form.

It was not be possible to fix the quality of the remaining 17 Composts, either history, or because of its 7d-CMR was in contradiction with its history, on any other particular analytical problem.

Table III shows the analytical results of all 43 samples which have taken part in the study, separating the ones in the standards' battery from the others, classified only by calculation. Table III also shows the averages and standard deviations of the chemical parameters, for every stablished class.

4.Conclusions

The proposed method for the qualification of problem composts consist on:

a- The methodology of the analytical thecniques, which generate 4 parameters: DD, % Nnh/TOM, Ext. R. and E_4/E_6 index.

b- The standards' battery.

c- The calculus mechanism of Discriminant Factorial Analysis which working with the analytical data of a problem sample attributes it to a given class.

The method is characterized by a great simplicity in the inputs/outputs and a relative intern complexity. It works with Chemical Paramethers of easy determination and very reproducible (inputs), from which ne get a clear classification without ambiguity (output), thanks to the overall participation of different chemical information. This avoids or compensates the interpretation mistakes caused by the treatment of the information, about an unknown compost, generated by a single chemical parameter.

On its present stage, the method allows the individual classification of any compost sample in one of the three categories (Fresh, Semi-ripe and Ripe) just from the considered analitycal parameters. It can also be useful in the starting of the composting plants, and their later quality control.

The most interesting condition of this system may be its open nature:

a- It is open to new chemical parameters. It can include the ones that, adding complementary information, are determined in the samples of the standards battery. In this sense, the own system works like a test to evaluate the opportunity of this new variables.

b- It is open to changes into the standard-samples battery.This collection can extend to new items provided that its qualification is beyond doubt.

We notice that the three present established groups of maturity are built in a relative way and they could be reconsidered and modified according to the real behaviour of this kind of compost, when applied as manure.

c- Its own discriminant capacity is open to change. The system structure allows considering a different number of maturity stages if the samples of the standards' battery and the selected quantitative variables give enough basis.

5.Bibliography

1- BONNEAU M.AND SOUCHIER B. (1.979). Constituants et Propietés du Sol. p.459. Ed. Masson

2- FOUCANT T. (1.982). Analyse Factorielle, Programation sur Micro-ordinateurs.Ed. Masson

3- GUITIAN F. AND CARBALLAS T. (1.976). Técnicas de Análisis de Suelos. Ed.Pico Sacro

4- INOKO A.,MIYAMATSU K.,SUGAHARA K.AND HARADA Y. (1.979). On some constituents of city refuse Compost produced in Japan. Soil Sci.Plant Nutri. 25(2) p.225-234

5- JORDA U. (1.982). Estudi de les Característiques Agronòmiques dels Composts d'Escombraries fabricats a Catalunya. Treball Final de Carrera. Escola d'Agricultura de Barcelona.

6- KUNC F. (1.974). Stimulatory effect of Glucose on the microbial decomposition of native Soil Organic Matter. Rostlinnà Vyroba 20(47) p.853-860.

7- MINISTERE DE L'AGRICULTURE DE BELGIQUE (1.971). Mtde. Convention pour l'Analyses des Engrais et des Amendements du Sol. Part II p.202-203 Div.B. Ad. Services Economiques d'Inspection de Matières Premières.

8- MORE JC. (1.983). Control Analític de la qualitat del Compost i Estudi de la seva maduració. Treball Final de Carrera. Escola d'Agricultura de Barcelona.

9- MOREL JL. (1.977). Contribution a l'étude de l'evolution des Bones Résiduaires dans le Sol. Thesis Doctoral. Université de Nancy.

10- MOREL JL.JACQUIN F. AND GUCKERT A. (1.979). Test de la détermination de la Maturité de Compost Urbain. Compte Rendu de Fin de Contract. Convention nº 75124-77137.

11- PRIMO E.AND CARRASCO J.M.(1.973). Química Agrícola I: Suelos y Fertilizantes. p.454-455. Ed. Alhambra.

12- SAÑA J. (1.985). La Utilització dels Fangs de Depuradores urbanes com adobs: caracterització de la seva fracció orgànica. Tesi Doctoral. Fac. Ciències Químiques. Univ. Central Barcelona.

13- SUGAHARA K.,HARADA Y. AND INOKO A. (1.979). Colour change of city refuse during composting process.Soil Sci. Plant Nutr. 25(2) p.197-208

14- SUGAHARA K.AND INOKO A.(1.981). Composition Analysis of Humus and - Characterization of Humic Acid obtained from city refuse compost. Soil Sci. Plant Nutr. 27(2).p.213-224.

15- ZUCCONI F., FORTE M. MONACO A. AND BERTOLDI M. (1.981). Biological Evaluation of Compost Maturity. Biocycle (Jul.-Aug.).p.27-29.

TABLE I. COMPOST SAMPLES ORIGIN

CODE	ORIGIN
A-031 A-038 A-045	Samples from an experimental pile constituted by a mixture of urban refuse and solid aerobic sewage sludge
B-043	Sample from an experimental pile constituted by a mixture of urban refuse and liquid aerobic sewage sludge
C-A C-B C-C C-D C-E C-F	Commercial samples from Lorca (Spain)
D-006 D-120 D-240	DANO composting system samples
E-120 E-240	CASEL-FOUCHET composting system samples
F-006 F-060 F-120 F-240	Samples from an experimental pile constituted by a mixture of urban refuse and anaerobic sewage sludge
G-006 G-060 G-120 G-240	Samples from an experimental pile constituted by a mixture of urban refuse and undigested sewage sludge
H-006 H-060 H-240	Samples from an experimental pile constituted by a mixture of urban refuse and aerobic sewage sludge
I-060 I-120 I-240	Samples from an experimental pile constituted by a mixture of urban refuse cesspool material
J-006 J-060 J-120	Samples from an experimental pile constituted by a mixture of urban refuse and liquid manure
K-A K-B K-C K-D	Commercial samples from Tarragona (Spain)
L	Commercial sample from Alicante (Spain)
M	Commercial sample from Madrid (Spain)
N-A N-B	Commercial samples from Crevillente (Spain)
O	Commercial sample from Jaén (Spain)
P	Commercial sample from Castellón (Spain)
Q	Comercial sample from Alcázar de San Juan (Spain)

TABLE II. INCUBATION SOIL CHARACTERISTICS*

% Cox.	%N	C/N	Salinity mmhos/cm	pH	%CaCO$_3$	%Sand	%Silt	%Clay
1.05	0.17	6.3	1.00	7.5	11	68	12	20

*20 upper cm. of a Calcixerollic Xerochrept

TABLE III. ANALYTICAL RESULTS AND RIPENESS CLASSIFICATION OF COMPOST

CODE	7d-CMR	Expected Ripeness*	E4/E6	D.D.	%Nnh/TOM	Ext.R.	Calculated Ripeness*
SAMPLES FROM STANDARDS BATTERY							
C-A	3.50	3	5.6	24.6	0.29	31.63	3
C-B	6.90	3	3.5	26.3	0.18	29.92	3
C-C	2.70	3	4.3	27.7	0.27	28.54	3
C-D	9.55	3	4.0	20.2	0.30	26.89	3
C-E	3.27	3	4.1	25.3	0.40	33.19	3
C-F	5.80	3	3.4	22.0	0.12	32.78	3
H-006	3.00	3	3.4	36.5	0.42	22.52	3
k-A	5.48	3	5.5	33.1	0.80	34.01	3
L	3.73	3	3.0	30.7	0.22	30.91	3
			$\bar{X}$=4.1	$\bar{X}$=27.4	$\bar{X}$=0.33	$\bar{X}$=30.04	
			s=0.9	s=4.9	s=0.19	s=3.42	
D-006	2.30	2	4.5	33.0	0.17	19.08	2
E-120	1.90	2	5.0	35.4	0.49	18.73	2
F-060	1.70	2	5.8	41.6	0.24	17.05	2
G-120	2.36	2	7.4	36.6	0.47	13.87	2
H-060	2.27	2	4.5	43.1	0.35	13.74	2
I-060	1.80	2	6.1	24.3	0.21	14.83	2
I-120	1.77	2	5.8	44.8	0.52	13.78	2
J-120	1.73	2	7.9	38.5	0.37	14.31	2
			$\bar{X}$=5.9	$\bar{X}$=37.2	$\bar{X}$=0.35	$\bar{X}$=15.67	
			s=1.2	s=6.1	s=0.13	s=2.12	
D-120	1.05	1	6.9	38.1	1.33	23.57	1
D-240	0.97	1	7.2	48.6	1.05	18.85	1
E-240	1.57	1	6.6	48.7	0.35	19.10	1
F-120	1.17	1	6.4	51.1	0.32	19.21	1
F-240	0.73	1	6.8	57.4	0.40	17.62	1
H-240	0.75	1	7.3	52.3	1.02	14.22	1
K-B	1.10	1	6.6	45.9	0.92	32.67	1
K-C	0.78	1	6.4	46.6	1.70	33.24	1
K-D	1.30	1	6.6	35.8	0.95	36.10	1
			$\bar{X}$=6.8	$\bar{X}$=47.2	$\bar{X}$=0.89	$\bar{X}$-23.84	
			s=0.3	s-6.4	s=0.44	s=7.58	
SAMPLES CLASSIFIED ONLY BY CALCULATION							
A-031	3.55		3.2	32.6	0.39	32.79	3
A-038	2.05		3.6	30.6	0.42	21.82	3
A-045	2.23		3.3	41.3	0.31	25.51	3
B-043	3.40		2.8	32.3	0.38	36.53	3
F-006	1.80		4.0	32.3	0.32	14.21	2
G-006	3.10		4.7	28.9	0.34	18.62	2
G-060	3.86		6.6	30.0	0.32	11.55	2
G-240	1.57		7.7	52.3	0.73	13.05	1
I-240	0.60		6.9	45.3	0.78	16.87	2
J-006	2.77		4.4	23.8	0.20	14.77	2
J-060	2.93		7.4	24.2	0.32	13.83	2
M	3.50		6.9	39.2	0.33	46.10	1
N-A	2.53		4.7	30.1	0.28	26.14	3
N-B	3.20		3.3	27.9	0.23	27.93	3
O	0.83		6.7	38.0	1.10	33.66	1
P	2.93		6.0	33.3	0.45	33.37	3
Q	4.50		4.5	52.7	0.44	30.14	1

*1:RIPE; 2:SEMI-RIPE; 3:FRESH

THE PRIMING EFFECT AND THE RESPIRATORY RATE / COMPOST DOSE RATIO
AS COMPOST RIPENESS INDEX

R. Ribalta, JC Moré and J. Saña
Area de Química. Escola d'Agricultura de Barcelona

Summary

The priming effect has been measured when different compost samples
were added to different soils. The presence of this effect has been
attributed to a low ripeness in the assayed product.
The priming effect has been indirectly quantified from the respiratory rate of the soil with increasing compost doses.
The respiratory rate/compost dose ratio has also resulted in a fine
index for the maturity of compost.

1. Introduction and objectives

In a previous work (4) the advantages and disadvantages of the Respirometrical thecniques have been discussed as a compost maturity qualification system. The more evident advantage is its simplicity, and the main
disadvantage is its bad reproductibility, because the results depend on the
reference soil where the compost has been incubated.
In this work, it has been attempted to overcome the problem of the Respirometrical Thecniques, expressing the results in different ways from the
usual (removed CO_2-C by a specific soil - compost mixture, in determined
conditions), studying to see if this ways are insensitive to the referentcial soil used.
This attempt has been made in two different directions: on one hand
using the so called Priming effect and on the other, studying the increase on the soil-compost mixture respiration with reference to the of the
Compost dose added to this soil.
The Priming effect is the increase of the own soil organic matter mineralization caused by an organic substratum addition, the compost in this
case. That is to say, the soil respires more, only by the manure presence.
(3) justifies the existence of this matter at two levels: The presence of
a decomposable substratum on the one hand increases the general microbial
population (and then the mineralization) and on the other, the energy source that the manure means, activates the transport mechanisms through the ce-
llular membrane, facilitating the contact between the organic compounds and
the decomposant endoenzimes in the Bacteria.(1) considers that the Priming
effect is also caused by an increase of the exocellular microbial enzimes,
produced as an answer to the decomposable organic matter addition. (6) using
a synthetic labelled carbon sewage sludge, evaluate the Priming effect of
the average three soils in 2.20 times the soil basal respiration during the
first 28 incubation days and in 1.63 times during a longer period (nearly
one year) . It is evident that this Priming effect evaluation method can't
be used for common manure. However, (5) suggest and check -working with rice straw- a simple system of this effect determination. This system consists

on representing the manure-soil mixtures respiration versus increasing added manures, in a specified time. In these plots the intersection of the regression line on the y-axis is a measure of soil Carbon loss in straw a-mended samples without the use of isotopically labelled straw. To compare this Carbon loss with the without straw soil loss, we have an estimation of the Priming effect produced by the straw. The Priming effect determined with this system on any soil allows to consider the following hypothesis: a ripe compost will not produce a detectable priming effect, in opposition to a fresh compost. In this work we will attempt to test this hypothesis, that´s to say, we will attempt to verify the Priming effect utility as a maturity index. We have worked with a short soil-compost incubation time (7 days) for considerations about the practical and routine utility of the method as well as the better priming effect appreciation, what (5) remark with short incu-bation periods.

On the other hand, the slopes of this regression lines will show the soil-compost mixture respiration increase caused by the manure Carbon unity added to this soil, which we will name Respiratory Rate-Compost Dose Ratio (RR/CD). It is to be expected that fresh compost cause remarkable RR/CD in-creases, in opposition to a ripe Compost.

This study is the second part of this paper.

We will check if the Priming effect and the RR/CD ratio are not sensi-tive to the reference soil used. In the opposite case, these parameters will be unsuitable for the interlaboratory qualification of the Compost maturity.

2. Method and materials

We have worked with three different soil samples as referentcial soils, that are described at Table I, and with nine Compost simples. Its origin and its chemical and respirometrical characteristics are shown in a previous work (4). The Compost samples belong to three categories, ripe (D-120, D-240 and K-C), semi-ripe (D-006, E-120 and I-120) and fresh-Compost (C-D, E-F and N-B), defined according to the criteria described in this work, especially its Res-pirometrical Rate, its history and its physic aspect.

For the determination of the Priming effect and the RR/CD ratio, nine different Compost-soil mixtures increasing in dose (5, 7.5, 10, 12.5, 15, 17.5, 20, 22.5 and 25 g. Compost-C / 100 g. soil-C) have been used. The mix-tures, once moistened to 75% soil water holding capacity, have been incubated into hermetic pots at 27-28°C, collecting the evolved CO_2 on a 0,5N NaOH solu-tion. After 7 days, an aliquot is titrated with 0.05N HCl using phenolphta-lein as indicator, with previous precipitation with $BaCl_2$ 10% of the Na_2CO_3 present. (Winkler method for the NaOH titration in the presence of carbonate) Also plain soil samples have been incubated, to the soil basal respiration (BR). Every determination has been made in triplicate.

3. Results and Discussion

For every Compost and Soil, the mg. of evolved C as CO_2 (Y-axis) are plotted versus the doses (X-axis). The corresponding regression lines are calculated and they all result significant at 0.01 level. (Figures I, II and III).

The Priming effect, according to (5) must be reflected in the diffe-rence between the ordinate origin of the regression line (Evolved C at zero dose) and the soil basal respiration (BR).

The Respirometrical Rate-Compost Dose Ratio (RR/CD) will be shown by the regression line slope.

As it can be observed in the Figures I, II and III, the Priming effect determinated with this method is not clearly manifested in any of the Compost categories. This fact can be explain either because the (5) hypothesis with rice straw can not extrapolate to another manures like the Compost or, with more chances, as some low and anomalous origin ordinates suggest, because the relatively important variability shown by the discontinuous respirometrical thecnique used by us.

However the RR/CD ratio results follow a behaviour much more conformed to the hypothesis suggested for this parameter on the introduction. In the Figures I, II and III it can observed the tendency shown by the fresh compost to produce sharper slopes than the ripe ones, while the semi-ripe compost regression lines adopt, consistently, intermediate slopes. This behaviour is reproduced into the three tested soils.

To determine the described tendency in a useful way, it must be cheked that the soil used as incubation support does not affect the RR/CD mean values on the three defined maturity classes. The ANOVA of the slopes shown on the Table II has been carried out. From the F contrast it can be said:
1- There are significant differences at 0.05 level between the generated slope by ripe, semi-ripe and fresh Compost.
2- There are not significant differences to consider the different incubation supports used.
3- There is not a significant interaction between the considered variation sources.

To confirm, on our experimental conditions, the discriminant capacity of the RR/CD values associated to the three Compost groups, the Newman-Keuls average separation test has-been carried out, and, at 0.05 level, significant differences have appeared between all the three studied groups (Table II).

Working with a more extensive group of known Compost samples, it could be considered the establishment of an intervals collection, where the RR/CD calculated values could be contrasted, obtaining that way a discred qualitative classification.

We would like to observe the restrictions that the used reference soil could inpose in certain circunstances. The RR is a measure of evolved CO_2-C from a mixture of two components (Compost-soil), sensitive to the mineralization processes. More over, it is known that in specific circunstances, the compost presence can modify the expected mineralization of the own soil organic matter (priming effect). So, it´s important not forget that it will only be possible to draw out valid conclusions on one of the two factors (the compost) which take part on the RR/CD ratio, when the effect of the other factor (the soil) are not detectable (and this is our case).

As a precaution, it is be advisable to use for the incubations, as we have done, soils with the characteristics recommended by (2) for this kind of techniques: a not too high organic matter content, a pH close to neutrality, and a small amount of carbonates.

4. Conclusions

Just one of the hypothesis originally proposed to make good use of the interpretative content of the respirometrical techniques showns encouraging perspectives.

The disagreement between our results and these obtained by (5) are attributed to a real weak priming effect on the tested materials, that is not detectable by our simple respirometrical technique.

The discriminant capacity of the RR/CD parameters is confirmed in the experimental conditions, taking into account the explained limitations about the incubation soil. This methodology represents and alternative to the characterization of Compost organic fraction: using a quite short and very sample metrical technique, that keeps all its interpretative value, and avoids the reproductibility inconvenients common in other respirometrical parameters.

5. Bibliography

(1) Jenkinson D S 1966. The Priming Action. Use of Isotopes in Soil Organic Matter Studies. pp 199-208 FAO-IREA Technical Meeting 1963. Pergamon Press. Oxford.
(2) Jenkinson D S, Powlson D S 1976. The effects of biocidal treatments on metabolism in Soil. V-A method for measuring soil Biomass. Soil. Biochem.8.
(3) Kunk F 1974. Stimulatory effect of Glucose on the microbial decomposition of native Soil Organic Matter. Rostlinnà Vyroba 20 (47) p. 853-860.
(4) Moré J C, Saña J. 1986.   Criteria of Quality of City Refuse Compost based on the Stability of it Organic Fraction. International Symposium on Compost. Udena (Italia).
(5) Pal D, Broadvent F E 1975. Kinetics of Rice Straw Decomposition in Soils. J. Environ Qual. 4 (2) p 256-260.
(6) Terry R E, Nelson D W i Sommers L E 1979. Carbon Cyding during Sewage Sludge Decomposition in Soils. Soil Sci. Soc. Am. J. 43 (3) p 494-499.

TABLE I

CHARACTERISTICS OF INCUBATION SOILS

Soil	CALDES	TORDERA	LLOBREGAT
Texture	Sandy-clay	Sandy	Silty
pH (H_2O)	7.93	6.58	7.60
E.C.(mS)	.28	.06	1.19
% C	1.20	.92	.99
% N	.756	.107	.131
P(Bray ppm)	66	17	64
K(ppm)	231	88	267
$CaCO_3$ %	10.7	0	29.7
C/N	7.69	8.60	7.56

TABLE II

THE RESPIRATORY RATE / COMPOST DOSE RATIO

Soil		CALDES	TORDERA	LLOBREGAT	
RIPENESS	COMPOST				
Ripe	K–C	0.726	0.795	0.519	$\bar{X}$=0.804 A
	D–240	0.796	1.355	0.516	s=0.302
	D–120	0.978	1.102	0.423	
Semi-ripe	E–120	1.896	1.459	2.411	$\bar{X}$=1.693 B
	I–120	0.983	1.754	0.740	s=0.573
	D–006	2.181	2.276	1.536	
Fresh	C–D	2.766	3.420	2.494	$\bar{X}$=2.376 C
	C–F	2.442	2.295	2.302	s=0.512
	N–B	2.132	1.908	1.639	
		$\bar{X}$=1.656 A	$\bar{X}$=1.818 A	$\bar{X}$=1.398 A	
		s=0.785	s=0.784	s=0.870	

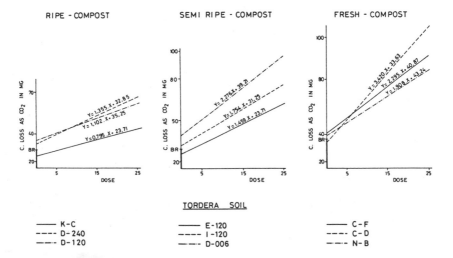

Figure I

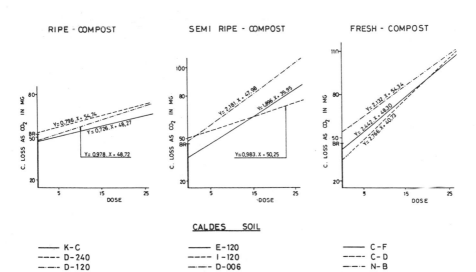

Figure II

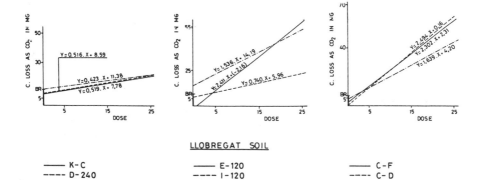

Figure III

APPLICATION OF A NEW METHOD FOR CEC DETERMINATION AS A COMPOST MATURITY INDEX

J. ESTRADA*, J. SAÑA*, R.M. CEQUIEL** and R. CRUAÑAS**

* Departamento de Química Agrícola. Escuela Universitaria de Ingeniería Técnica Agrícola de Barcelona.
** Departamento de Edafología. Facultad de Farmacia. Universidad de Barcelona.

SUMMARY

A new method for CEC determination has been applied to different compost samples. It is based on saturation of a sample with a strong acid resin (Amberlite IR-120) followed by removal of H^+ ions with 1N $BaCl_2$ solution. The values obtained from the application of this method, by itself or with other chemical parameters of organic fraction, were assayed as a simple and routine index for the determination of the degree of maturity (calculated by the Complementary Mineralization Rate or CMR). The results were satisfactory.

KEY WORDS: Cation Exchange Capacity (CEC), Composts, Degree of Maturity.

INTRODUCTION

Harada and Inoko (1980a) proposed a simple method for the determination of Cation Exchange Capacity (CEC) of composts. Afterwards, Harada and Inoko (1980b), found a high correlation between the CEC and the C/N ratio in several types of composts, suggesting a possible use of the CEC as a maturity index, as opposed to the C/N ratio, considered unsatisfactory. Based on this work, the CEC was taken into consideration to establish compost maturity index.

The methodology used for CEC determination in organic wastes is generally the same as that wich is applied to soils. Cequiel and Cruañas (1984) compared the results obtained from appling the four most common methods used for CEC determination of soils to organic wastes, concluding that, for practical considerations as well as reproductibility, the Bascomb method (1964) is the most suitable to use for these samples.

At any rate, nowadays the use of the CEC as a compost maturity index, in our opinion, presents two important problems:
- On the one hand, there is little information about the effectiveness of the methods used for CEC determination with organic wastes, and they tend to be laborious and poorly reproducible.
- On the other hand, an inherent problem in all chemical parameters used as a maturity index (Moré and Saña 1986) is the difficulty of interpreting the results if the nature of the compost is unknown.
  For these reasons, the aims of this work are the following:
- To apply a simple and effective method to CEC determination proposed first for soils by Cruañas and Cardús (1984),and later extended to different organic wastes by Cequiel (1986),to an extensive group of composts.

-To study the possible use of the CEC obtained by this method as a maturity index, with or without other parameters of the organic fraction, and to compare the results with the CMR (Morel, Jacquin and Guckert,1979) an easily interpreted but poorly reproductible biological index of maturity.

MATERIALS AND METHODS

We worked with a group of 25 samples, whose characteristics and res-pirometric and chemical parameters have been described in a previous article (Moré and Saña, 1986) and are supplemented in Table I, according to the methodology used by Moré (1983). The samples underwent an appropiate process consisting of grinding and milling in order to obtain uniform particle size of < 200 μm $\emptyset$.

For the CEC determination we used the method previously mentioned, consisting of acid saturation of the samples with a strongly cationic ex-change resin in acid form, followed by potentiometric titrarion at a pre-viously selected costant pH to displacement of H^+ ions retained by the exchange complex with 1N $BaCl_2$ solution (Fig.1).

This methodology permits greater efficacy of acid saturation without altering the samples, and the removal of carbonates, gypsum, and other so-luble salts which may interfere with the CEC determination.

100 mg of sample were treated with 1g of exchange acid resin (Am-berlite IR-120) and 75 ml distilled water and mixed together for 12 hours in a rotary shaker. Then the resin was removed from the sample suspension by sieving (size of 200 μm $\emptyset$), and subsequently, the sample was obtained in acid-saturated form by centrifugation and decantation. The excess of free acidity retained by the sample, coming from the H–resin dissociation and the soluble salts, was removed by washing with 20 ml of 96% etanol. After centrifugation and decantation, the sample was suspended again in 20 ml of distilled water.

2 ml aliquots of homogeneized sample suspension were used for po-tentiometric titration of the displaced H^+ with 25 ml of 1N $BaCl_2$ at pH 8.1 (or other previously selected conditions), the pH was kept at 8.1 by continuous, automatic addition of 0.025N $Ba(OH)_2$.

A Radiometer RTS-822 automatic recording titration system was emplo-yed using pH stat modality in an inert atmosphere (N_2), and time elapsed was approximately 20 minutes.

The CEC expressed in meq /100g of treated sample, was obtained from the number of meq of $Ba(OH)_2$ used for titration and the weight of dry samples contained in the aliquots at 105ºC.

RESULTS AND DISCUSSION

The CEC data (meq /100g compost) obtained from the samples studied, are described in Table II, which also contains, as sugested by Harada and Inoko (1980b),the CEC in 100g of ash-free compost (CEC/TOM). In this way the CEC evolution during the compost maturity process is clearly shown, as will be noted in samples sequences F,G,H and J.

The main reasons to justify these facts are based on the following:
-In these samples it is the organic fraction which has the highest CEC va-lue (50-150 meq /100 g), greater than the mineral fraction (10 meq/100g). On the other hand ,while the former may undergo considerable change during the composting process, the latter remains practically invariable.
-Throughout the entire composting process, the total organic content in the samples decreases, and this weight loss may counteract, or at least make less evident, the possible CEC increase in the organic fraction and there-by, in the compost; this is what happens in sequence J, expressed as to-

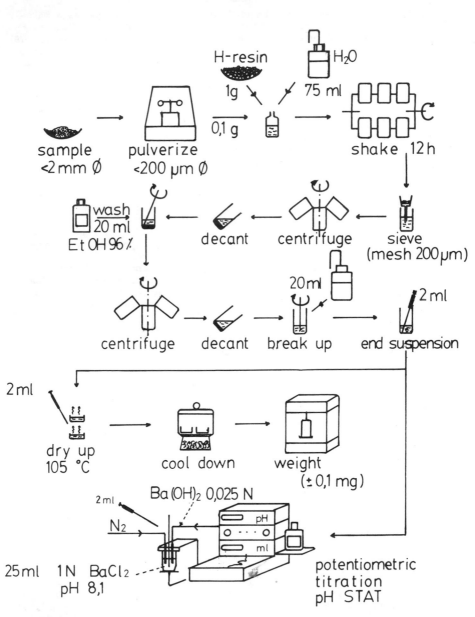

H-resin 1g

H₂O 75 ml

0,1 g

sample <2 mm Ø

pulverize <200 μm Ø

shake 12 h

wash 20 ml EtOH 96%

decant

centrifuge

sieve (mesh 200 μm)

centrifuge

decant

break up 20ml

end suspension 2 ml

2 ml

dry up 105 °C

cool down

weight (± 0,1 mg)

2 ml

N₂

Ba(OH)₂ 0,025 N

pH

ml

25 ml 1N BaCl₂ pH 8,1

potentiometric titration pH STAT

FIG.1 – BASIC SCHEME OF THE METHOD USED TO CEC DETERMINATION

SAMPLES	% TOM	EXTRACTION RATE*	POLYMERIZATION RATE**
A-031	50.94	32.79	0.87
B-043	69.38	36.53	0.51
C-B	48.89	29.92	0.99
C-C	48.41	28.54	1.19
D-240	28.75	18.85	3.94
F-006	34.01	14.21	1.50
F-060	37-27	17.05	1.12
F-120	28.15	19.21	0.77
F-240	30.12	17.62	0.78
G-006	47.60	18.62	1.35
G-060	43.73	11.55	0.88
G-120	40.42	13.87	0.71
H-006	38.63	22.52	1.07
H-060	43.50	13.74	1.00
H-240	28.30	14.22	0.66
I-060	56.39	14.83	0.89
J-006	59.82	14.77	1.36
J-060	34.67	13.83	1.16
J-120	26.81	14.31	0.84
K-D	31.47	36.10	1.31
L	50.81	30.91	1.06
M	39.21	46.10	1.49
N-A	42.65	26.14	1.27
O	29.18	33.66	1.23
P	40.44	33.37	1.62

TABLE I- Some chemical characteristics of the samples.
*Extraction rate= (Humic + Fulvic Carbon/Total Carbon) x 100
**Polymerization rate= Fulvic Carbon/Humic Carbon

SAMPLES	CEC	CEC/TOM	CEC MM	CEC TOM
A-031	37.2	73.03	7.6	65.71
B-043	47.3	68.2	9.89	63.81
C-B	34.3	70.2		
C-C	39.6	81.8		
D-240	27.1	94.3		
F-006	20.7	60.9		
F-060	25.8	69.9		
F-120	35.0	124.3		
F-240	38.1	126.5	7.77	108.43
G-006	23.5	49.4		
G-060	24.0	54.9		
G-120	28.2	143.3	7.08	59.30
H-006	29.0	75.1		
H-060	29.0	66.7		
H-240	49.6	175.3	8.75	152.97
I-060	30.1	53.4	8.95	46.42
J-006	22.1	36.9		
J-060	22.7	65.5		
J-120	19.7	73.5	5.26	59.01
K-D	39.7	126.2		
L	34.7	68.3		
M	32.0	81.6		
N-A	36.4	85.3		
O	66.7	228.6		
P	45.2	111.8		

TABLE II- CEC values as meq /100 g , and meq /100 g of ash-free compost (CEC/TOM) .

tal compost weight and as organic fraction weight.

In order to consider the usefulness of CEC as a maturity index, we calculated the simple correlation coefficients between the CMR (expressed on a naperian logarithmic scale) and the CEC , as well as the CMR and the CEC/TOM ratio. The results show a significant correlation with the CEC/TOM ratio (r=-0.670), whereas it is not so with the CEC (r=-0.130); this can be explained because of the considerable differences in organic matter levels of the composted samples, during the composting process.

In spite of these questions, the CEC/TOM ratio, is not enough to explain the observed variations (determination coefficient r^2=0.449).Thus we have taken into consideration the information on CMR, and consequently maturity, given by other chemical parameters previously discussed amply and studied by Moré and Saña (1986), such as Decomposition Degree (DD), Humic and Fulvic acids (given as extraction rate and polymerization rate) and colorimetric index E_4/E_6 of the humic extract.

The relationship of all these chemical parameters with the CMR was obtained throgh the following multivariant regression equation:

$$
\begin{aligned}
\text{Ln CMR} = \quad & -0.007 \times \text{CEC/TOM} \\
& -0.025 \times \text{DD} \\
& +0.017 \times \text{Extr. rate } (C_{HA+FA}/C \times 100) \\
& -0.148 \times \text{Pol. rate } (C_{FA}/C_{HA}) \\
& -0.027 \times E_4/E_6 \\
& +2.148
\end{aligned}
$$

this equation explains remarkably well the degree of CMR variations (determination coefficient r^2= 0.755). When the CEC/TOM ratio is eliminated from this multivariant regression, the determination coefficient (r^2= 0.644) decreases considerably, showing a good participation of this parameter in the interpretation of the maturity index.

$$
\begin{aligned}
\text{Ln CMR} = \quad & -0.037 \text{ DD} \\
& +0.007 \text{ Extr. rate} \\
& -0.070 \text{ Pol. rate} \\
& -0.099 \; E_4/E_6 \\
& +2.571
\end{aligned}
$$

From the analytical point of view, it is relatively easy to obtain the calculated CMR data because only three kinds of techniques are needed: extraction and fractionation, with the colorimetric index measurement E_4/E_6, and DD and CEC determinations.

Using this CMR calculated from chemical parameters,with its good reproductibility, and an empirical scale of maturity like the one proposed by Moré in 1985 (giving mature with Ln CMR calculated at < 0.45; semi-mature between 0.45 and 0.88, and fresh > 0.88), the quality of any compost can be determinated.

CONCLUSIONS

The method used for CEC determination, has been shown suitable to achieve our previously mentioned aims.

The CEC/TOM ratio obtained in this manner, has been shown to be a chemical parameter correlated with the maturity index (CMR).

The incorporation of the CEC into a multivariant regression where other chemical parameters (the ones of the equation) are taken in consideration, succeeds in expressing the degree of maturity of the composts studied in a reliable fashion and with good reproductibility.

REFERENCES

1.-BASCOMB C.L.,1984. Rapid method for the determination of cation-exchange capacity of calcareous and non-calcareous soils. J. Sci. Fd. Agric. 12:821.

2.-CEQUIEL R.M.,1986. Estudio de la capacidad de intercambio catiónico en resíduos orgánicos de origen diverso. Tesis Doctoral. Facultad de Farmacia. Universidad de Barcelona. (composition stage)

3.-CEQUIEL R.M.and CRUAÑAS R.,1984. Determinación de la capacidad de intercambio catiónico en resíduos orgánicos de origen diverso: posible aplicación de la metodología utilizada en suelos. I Congreso Nacional de la Ciencia del Suelo. Madrid. Vol. 1º:465.

4.-CRUAÑAS R. and CARDUS J.,1984. Aspectos fundamentales de un nuevo método potenciométrico para la determinación de la Capacidad de Intercambio Catiónico en suelos. I Congreso Nacional de la Ciencia del Suelo. Madrid. Vol. 1º:125.

5.-HARADA Y. and INOKO A.,1980a. The measurement of the cation-exchange capacity of composts for the estimation of the degree of maturity. Soil Sci. Plant Nutr. 26 (1):127.

6.-HARADA Y. and INOKO A.,1980b. Relationship between cation-exchange capacity and degree of maturity of city refuse compost. Soil Sci. Plant Nutr. 26 (3): 353.

7.-MORE J.C.,1983. Control analític de la qualitat del Compost i estudi de la seva maduració. Trabajo fin de carrera.Escuela Universitaria de Ingeniería Técnica Agrícola de Barcelona.

8.-MORE J.C.,1985. Caracterització del Compost d'escombraries. Quaderns Agraris. nº 6: 61.

9.-MORE J.C. and SAÑA J.,1986. A criteria of quality of city refuse compost based on the stability of it organic fraction. International Symposium on Compost. Udine. Italy.

1Q-MOREL J.L., JACQUIN F. and GUCKERT A.,1979. Test de la determination de la maturité de compost urbain. Compte rendu de fin de contact. Convention nº 75124-77137.

STABILIZATION PROCESS OF SEWAGE SLUDGE COMPOST IN SOIL

A. KATAYAMA, K.C. KER, M. HIRAI, M. SHODA and H. KUBOTA
Research Laboratory of Resources Utilization
Tokyo Institute of Technology
4259, Nagatsuta, Midori-ku, Yokohama, 227. Japan

Summary

The stabilization process of sewage sludge composts with different degrees of maturity, which were incorporated into a coarse sandy loam soil, was investigated during their incubation at 25°C. In the immature compost-soil mixtures, ammonification, the decrease of nitrate concentration and/or the accumulation of nitrite were observed in the early stages of incubation and followed by nitrification. In the mature compost-soil mixtures, only nitrification was observed during incubation. These nitrogen transformations were well correlated with the transitions of characteristic patterns; I, II, and III of gel chromatograms of the water extracts. The redox potential decreased appreciably in the immature compost-soil mixtures in the early stages of incubation and increased in the later stages, when pattern III of the chromatogram was observed. When sludge composts became stable in soil, shown by the chromatographic pattern III, the values of pH and NH_4^+/NO_3^- ratios in the mixtures were about the same regardless of the degree of compost maturity. The time required for the stabilization in soil shortened as the degree of maturity increased. It was suggested that the sludge compost in which ammonification has completed during composting has enough stability for practical land application.

1. Introduction

Although land application of sewage sludge, as one of the most economical way of sludge disposal (3), is an attractive proposition, plant growth inhibition had been observed when sludge was directly applied to land (8). Composting of sewage sludge is therefore recommended as a method to avoid the plant growth inhibition. Besides, the composting can solve other problems such as pathogens and odors of the sludge (7).

When the composted sludge is appled to land, the primary concern is whether the compost is mature or not. The authors (9) reported that the main inhibitory factor of immature sludge compost on plant growth was ammonia gas liberation, and the maturity of sewage sludge compost can be judged both by the measurements of ammonia gas evolved from the compost-amended soil and by the ratio of organic carbon to organic nitrogen ratio in the water extract from the compost. The gel chromatography of the water extract was also proposed to be an effective method for monitoring both the progress of composting reaction (4) and the decomposition process of sewage sludge in soil (10).

In this study, the stabilization process of sewage sludge composts with different degrees of maturity in soil was investigated and the effect of the compost maturity on the stabilization process in soil was evaluated by applying the gel chromatographic method.

2. Materials and Methods

2.1 Soil and sewage sludge compost used in the experiment

Soil was collected from the surface horizon of a coarse sandy loam soil at Hiratsuka, Kanagawa Prefecture. Properties of the soil were described in the previous paper (10).

Two kinds of sewage sludge were used as raw materials of composts. One sludge, which contained polyamine and polyacrylamide derivatives as dewatering agents, was obtained from Tsurukawa Wastewater Treatment Plant, Tokyo. The sludge was mixed with rice husk as bulking agent and the compost product as seed, and was composted at constant temperature (60°C) by means of air-flow control in our laboratory (denoted as polymer sludge compost). Details of the composting digester system have been described previously (2). The other compost was made from the raw sludge which contained slaked lime and ferric chloride as dewatering agents in Minamitama City Composting Plant, Tokyo (denoted as lime sludge compost). The composting reactor was a bin-type digester with forced bottom aeration coupled with mechanical stirring.

The inventory of the two kinds of compost samples with different degrees of maturity is shown in Table I. Some chemical properties of them are shown in Table II. Details of the analytical procedures were described in the previous paper (9).

2.2 Incubation and chemical analysis of compost-soil mixture

Each sewage sludge compost was mixed with the soil at a loading rate

Table I. Compost samples used in the experiment

Compost	Symbol	Specifications
	PRS	Mixed raw material
Polymer sludge	P5D	5 day compost
compost	P10D	10 day compost
	P2M	2 month compost
	LRS	Dewatered sludge cake
Lime sludge	L5D	5 day compost
compost	L10D	10 day compost
	L6M	6 month compost

Table II. Chemical properties of the compost samples

Properties	Polymer sludge compost				Lime sludge compost			
	PRS	P5D	P10D	P2M	LRS	L5D	L10D	L6M
Solid sample								
pH (-)	5.5	8.5	8.4	7.6	12.5	7.7	7.5	8.0
Carbon (%)*	42.48	40.05	37.67	36.68	26.46	19.61	18.65	14.62
Total Nitrogen (%)*	3.19	3.04	2.47	2.67	3.08	2.06	1.96	1.62
Organic-N (%)*	3.05	2.42	1.92	2.15	3.05	1.49	1.64	1.51
NH_4^+-N (%)*	0.13	0.61	0.54	0.51	0.03	0.56	0.31	0.11
$NO_3^-+NO_2^-$-N (%)*	0.005	0.010	0.007	0.008	0.005	0.009	0.006	0.004
C/N ratio (-)	13.3	13.2	15.2	13.8	8.59	9.52	9.51	9.02
Water extract								
Org.-C/org.-N ratio (-)	7.74	6.70	6.62	6.70	4.96	11.69	5.94	5.69

* On a dry weight basis.

of 5% on a dry weight basis. The loading rate is equivalent to 75 dry tons per hectare. The compost-soil mixtures were placed in Neubauer's pots and incubated at 25°C in the dark for 8 weeks. The moisture content was maintained at 55 to 60 % of the maximum water holding capacity of the soil during incubation. Duplicate pots for each mixture were sacrificed periodically for the following experiments: gel chromatography with Sephadex G-15 of water extract from the mixture and the measurements of pH, the inorganic nitrogen content and the redox potential of the mixture. Details of the analytical procedures were described in the previous paper (10).

3. Results and Discussion

3.1 Change of gel chromatogram of water extract

Fig. 1 shows the change of gel chromatogram of the water extract during polymer sludge composting. With the progress of composting, the peaks showing low molecular weight compounds decreased and the peak at Kd=0 showing high molecular weight compounds increased as described previously (2,4). In particular, the increase of the peak at Kd=0 was drastic during 5

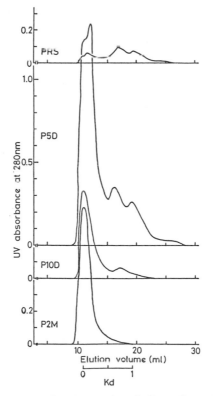

Fig. 1 Gel chromatograms of water extract from the polymer sludge composts with different maturities.

days of composting. This suggests that the water-soluble humic substances was produced during the composting process. After 10 days of composting, the peak at Kd=0 was prominent, and no change of the chromatographic pattern was observed. In the lime sludge composting, the same trend of gel chromatographic pattern was observed (data not shown). These patterns were similar to patterns I and II appeared during the decomposition of sludge in soil as described below.

Fig. 2 shows changes of gel chromatograms of the water extracts during incubation after mixed raw material of polymer sludge compost (PRS) and its 2-month compost (P2M) were incorporated into the soil. In the PRS-soil mixture, the transition of the gel chromatographic pattern was the same as

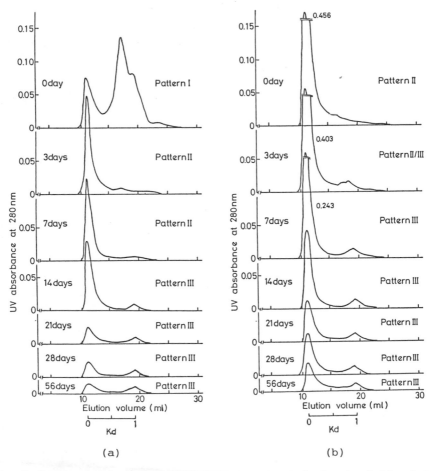

(a)   (b)

Fig. 2 Change of gel chromatogram of water extract during incubation (a) in the polymer raw sludge (PRS)-soil mixture and (b) in the polymer 2 month compost (P2M)-soil mixture.

345

Table III. Gel chromatographic patterns appeared during incubation of
        compost-soil mixtures*

Compost added to soil	Incubation period (day)						
	0	3	7	14	21	28	56
Polymer sludge compost							
PRS	I	II	II	III	III	III	III
P5D	I/II**	II	II	III	III	III	III
P10D	II	II	II	III	III	III	III
P2M	II	II/III**	III	III	III	III	III
Lime sludge compost							
LRS	I/II	I/II	II	II/III	III	III	III
L5D	II	II	II	II/III	III	III	III
L10D	II	II	II	III	III	III	III
L6M	II	II	III	III	III	III	III

* For definition of gel chromatographic patterns I, II and III, refer to
  the text.
** I/II and II/III mean the intermediate pattern between patterns I and II
   and that between patterns II and III, respectively.

that in dewatered sludge-soil mixture reported previously (10). This
indicates that the addition of bulking agent and seed did not affect the
change of chromatographic pattern. The pattern changed from pattern I to
pattern II and then to pattern III, with patterns I, II and III defined as
follows(10):
   Pattern I : A peak at Kd=0 and two peaks at Kd ranging from 0.5 to 1.0.
   Pattern II : A prominent peak at Kd=0.
   Pattern III: A low peak at Kd=0 and a peak at Kd near 1.
In the P2M-soil mixture, pattern I was not observed and patterns II and III
as shown in Fig. 2(b) were seen. After pattern III appeared, no further
appreciable change was observed throughout incubation. In the incorporation
of the other polymer composts, P5D and P10D, with different degrees of
maturity into the soil, the chromatographic pattern transition was similar
to that in the P2M-soil mixture. The time required for the appearance of
pattern II and pattern III after the composts were incorporated into the
soil shortened as composting progressed as shown in Table III. The
comparison between Figs. 2(a) and 2(b) shows that the peak intensity at
Kd=0 of the chromatogram in the P2M-soil mixture was stronger than that in
the PRS-soil mixture throughout incubation. This may reflect that the
water-soluble humic compounds of the P2M compost were less degradable.
   In the lime sludge compost-soil mixtures, the trend of the
chromatographic pattern transition was the same as that in the polymer
sludge compost-soil mixtures (Table III).

3.2 Nitrogen transformation
   In the composting process of sewage sludge, total nitrogen
concentration decreased drastically, especially during the first 10 days of
composting (Table II). The decrease of organic nitrogen concentration was
remarkable. Ammonium nitrogen concentration increased during 5 days of
composting, but decreased later. The decrease of organic nitrogen and
ammonium nitrogen concentrations was associated with the evolution of
ammonia gas from the compost with high pH above 7.5. The sum of nitrate and
nitrite concentrations was very low even after several months of curing.
This might be due to high pH combined with high concentration of ammonium
nitrogen, which inhibit nitrification (1).

Figs. 3 and 4 show changes of inorganic nitrogen concentrations in the polymer sludge compost- and the lime sludge compost-soil mixtures, respectively. The trend of nitrogen transformation was little different between the two groups of sludge compost-soil mixtures. In the raw sludge-soil mixtures, the ammonium nitrogen concentration increased during the first 7 days of incubation and then decreased (PRS in Fig. 3 and LRS in Fig. 4). While, in the compost-soil mixtures, ammonium nitrogen concentration decreased from 0 day of incubation regardless of the different degree of compost maturity. This indicates that ammonification was almost complete during the first 5 days of composting.

Little nitrite nitrogen was detected throughout incubation of the

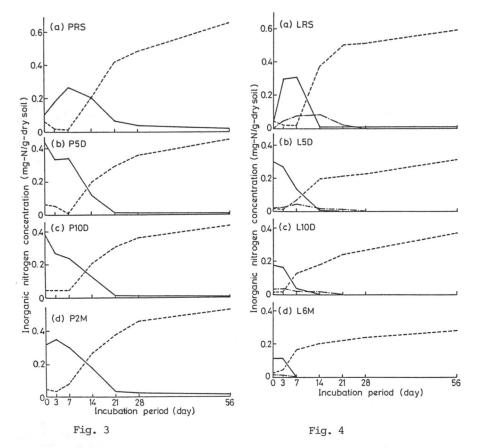

Fig. 3   Fig. 4

Fig. 3 Changes of inorganic nitrogen concentrations in the polymer sludge compost-soil mixtures with different maturities (refer to Table I) during incubation. —— ;NH_4^+-N, ----;NO_3^--N.

Fig. 4 Changes of inorganic nitrogen concentrations in the lime sludge compost-soil mixtures with different maturities (refer to Table I) during incubation. —— ; NH_4^+-N, ----;NO_3^--N, ---- ; NO_2^--N.

polymer sludge compost-soil mixtures, but in the lime sludge compost-soil mixtures, nitrite accumulated in the early stages of incubation. Since Nitrobacter spp., i.e. nitrite oxidizing bacteria, were reported to be moresensitive to high pH than Nitrosomonas spp. which are ammonia oxidizing bacteria (1), the inhibition of nitrite oxidation at pH above 7 of the mixtures can be a main reason for the nitrite accumlation. As the compost maturity increased, the nitrite concentration decreased and disappeared quickly.

The nitrate nitrogen concentration decreased in PRS-, P5D- and LRS-soil mixtures at the early stages of incubation. This means that when the raw sludge or the immature compost was incorporated into the soil, nitrogen immobilization and/or denitrification occurred. The findings were supported by those of EPSTEIN et al. (6) that nitrogen immobilization and denitrification were observed during the decomposition process of raw sewage sludge or its compost in soil by using $K^{15}NO_3$. In the later stages of incubation, the nitrate nitrogen concentration increased in all the mixtures. When the composts which were composted for more than 10 days were incorporated into the soil, the decrease of nitrate nitrogen and/or the inhibition of nitrification were seldom observed and nitrification proceeded easily.

The nitrogen transformation was well correlated with the transition of the chromatographic patterns both in the composting process of sludge and

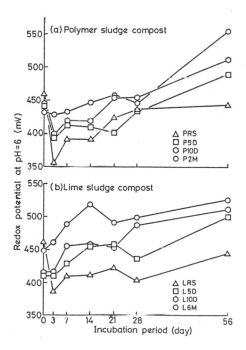

Fig. 5 Change of redox potential of the compost-soil mixtures during incubation

in the decomposition process of sludge compost in soil. In the decomposition process of the raw sludge in soil, when ammonification occurred, the chromatographic pattern changed from I to II (Fig. 2(a)). In the composting process, similar results were obtained as shown in Fig. 1. When nitrification occurred, the pattern changed from II to III in each compost-soil mixture used.

3.3 Change of redox potential of the mixtures during incubation
Fig. 5 shows change of redox potential of the compost-soil mixtures. The redox potential decreased significantly in the less matured compost-soil mixtures after 3 days of incubation, though the chromatographic patterns at 3 days were almost the same regardless of compost maturity (Table III). The decrease reflects the anaerobic environment in the mixture, which indicates the possibility of the adverse effect on plant growth (11). The redox potential increased gradually in all the mixtures in the later stages of incubation, when pattern III of gel chromatogram was observed and nitrification occurred under the aerobic environment.

3.4 Stabilized condition of compost-soil mixtures
In Fig. 6, gel chromatographic patterns are shown in relation to pH and the ratio of ammonium nitrogen concentration to nitrate nitrogen concentration (NH_4^+/NO_3^- ratio) in each mixture. In the polymer compost-soil mixtures, pattern I or II was categorized in the region where pH was in the range from 6 to 7, and NH_4^+/NO_3^- ratio was more than 2. When pattern III appeared, pH decreased to the range from 5 to 6 and NH_4^+/NO_3^- ratio decreased to less than 1. In the lime compost-soil mixtures, pH was almost constant in the range from 7 to 7.5 during incubation, while NH_4^+/NO_3^- ratio decreased drastically during the transition of the gel chromatographic pattern. In each compost-soil mixture, the region where pattern III was observed was almost the same regardless of the degree of compost maturity. In the region of pattern III which was the left side of broken line (Fig. 6), free ammonia concentration in soil was less than 0.1 μg-N/g-dry soil, which was the critical concentration to give inhibitory effect on seedling growth of komatsuna (Brassica campestris L. var. rapiferafroug) (10). Thus, when pattern III of gel chromatogram was observed, the sludge compost had become stable in soil, and no inhibitory effect of the compost on plant growth would be expected. Previous result (9) showed that the inhibitory factor of the immature sewage sludge compost was ammonia gas, which was observed on the surface of the compost-amended soil. In the compost-soil mixtures, the ammonia gas evolution period became short as the compost increased in maturity.

3.5 Maturity of sewage sludge compost
As described above, it is clear that when the compost is incorporated into soil, the stabilized state can be achieved after most of ammonia remained in the compost has been nitrified in the soil. Therefore, the compost can be judged as a matured compost, after ammonification has been completed followed by nitrification during the composting process. In fact, SUZUKI and KUMADA (12) claimed that the rice straw compost in which nitrification has ocurred during composting is mature.

In the case of sewage sludge composting, nitrification proceeded little even after several months of the curing stage of composting. After the sewage sludge compost in which ammonification had been mostly completed was incorporated into soil, however, the nitrification proceeded within 7 days. The inhibitory effect on the growth of komatsuna (Brassica campestris L. var. rapiferafroug) was little observed in the soil amended with such a sludge compost (9). The ratio of organic carbon to organic nitrogen of the water extract from the compost was in the range from 5 to 6 (Table II), which was the value postulated as the required condition of the matured compost (5).

It can be concluded that it is possible to apply sewage sludge compost to land when ammonification during composting is not detected any more. Thus, nitrification is not necessarily an essential condition for practical land application.

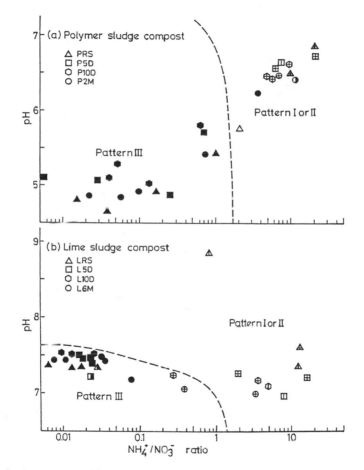

Fig. 6 Gel chromatographic patterns of water extract in relation to ratio of ammonium nitrogen concentration to nitrate nitrogen concentration and pH of the compost-soil mixtures. White symbols show pattern I of gel chromatogram, symbols with vertical line show pattern I/II, symbols with cross show pattern II, half-black symbols show pattern II/III and black symbols show pattern III. Broken lines show the boundary, in left of which pattern III of gel chromatogram was observed.

REFERENCES

1. ALEXANDER, M. (1977). Introduction to soil microbiology, Second edition, 223-304, John Wiley and Sons, New York.
2. BACH, P.D., SHODA, M. and KUBOTA, H. (1985). Composting reaction rate of sewage sludge in an autothermal packed bed reactor, J. Ferment. Technol., 63, 271-278.
3. BRUCE, A.M. and DAVIS, R.D. (1983). Utilisation of sewage sludge in agriculture - maximising benefits and minimising risks -, Proceedings of International Symposium on Biological Reclamation and Land Utilisation of Urban Wastes, Naples-Italy, 121-143.
4. CHANYASAK, V., YOSHIDA, T. and KUBOTA, H. (1980). Chemical components in gel chromatographic fractionation of water extract from sewage sludge compost, J. Ferment. Technol., 58, 533-539.
5. CHANYASAK, V. and KUBOTA, H. (1981). Carbon/organic nitrogen ratio in water extract as measure of composting degradation, J. Ferment. Technol., 59,215-219.
6. EPSTEIN, E., KEANE, D. B., MEISINGER, J. J. and LEGG, J. O. (1978). Mineralization of nitrogen from sewage sludge and sludge compost, J. Environ. Qual., 7, 217-221.
7. GOLUEKE, C.G. (1977). Biological reclamation of solid wastes, 137-142, Rodale Press, Emmaus, PA.
8. HINESLY, T.D. and SOSEWITZ, B. (1969). Digested sludge disposal on crop land, J. Water Pollut. Control Fed., 41, 822-830.
9. KATAYAMA, A., HIRAI, M., SHODA, M., KUBOTA, H. and MORI, S. (1985). Inhibitory factor of sewage sludge compost for growth of komatsuna Brassica campestris L. var. rapiferafroug, Environ. Pollut. (ser.A), 38, 45-62.
10. KATAYAMA, A., HAYASAKA, N., HIRAI, M. SHODA, M. and KUBOTA, H. (1986). Application of gel chromatography to monitor the decomposition process of sewage sludge in soil, Soil Sci. Plant Nutr., 32, in press.
11. LYNCH, J.M. (1983). Soil biotechnology, Microbiological facters in crop productivity, 15-17, Blackwell Scientific Publications, Oxford.
12. SUZUKI, M. and KUMADA, K. (1977). Nitrogen transformation during the rotting process of rice straw compost, Soil Sci. Plant Nutr., 23, 163-174.

MONITORING THE COMPOSTING PROCESS USING PARAMETERS OF COMPOST STABILITY

E. Witter and J. M. Lopez-Real

Department of Biological Sciences, Wye College (University of London)
Ashford, Kent, United Kingdom

Summary

Raw, dewatered sewage sludge, bulked with straw was composted on a pilot scale (4-6 ton piles) and on a bench-scale composting simulator.

The pilot scale and the bench-scale composting trials illustrated that both the rate of water loss and aeration demand accurately reflected changes in microbial activity. Trials with the bench-scale composter indicated that the measured ratio of water to dry solids is only slightly lower than would be expected from theoretical considerations (7.2 compared with 8-9, respectively), and is affected by the aeration strategy.

The composting process in the pilot scale trial was monitored over a one year period using several parameters of compost stability. Cumulative dry solids losses reached more than 60% after one year, with 50% of the loss taking place in the first month. Dry solids losses were double logarithmically related to the reduction in volatile solids content (r=0.999).

There was no change in the humic acid content of the material, but the E_4/E_6 ratio of the humic fraction increased in a similar pattern to dry solids losses during the composting period, indicating qualitative changes in that fraction.

Other parameters of compost stability studied were carbon content, and the C/N ratio.

1. Introduction

The composting process is essentially a stabilization process similar to the decomposition of organic residues in soil. The early phases of composting (active phase) are characterized by high metabolic activity typically resulting in an increase in temperature of the decomposing material which acts itself as insulation. The second (maturing) stage of composting is characterized by much lower rates of metabolic activity, but the material is transformed into a stable, dark, amorphous, humus-like material, with an earthy smell. The maturation phase is generally believed to be characterized by the formation of humic compounds (eg. Gray & Biddlestone, 1971a, 1971b; Zucconi & DeBertoldi, 1984). The main reaction in the formation of humic compounds is the condensation of phenolic compounds derived from lignin degradation or from microbial synthesis, with proteins and their degradation products into complex polymers with a high molecular weight.

The aim of the treatment process is to maximize sludge stability and weight losses, to mimimize phytotoxicity, and to destroy both plant and animal pathogens. The latter two aspects of composting were not investigated in this study, but have been discussed in detail elsewhere (Phytoxicity: Vleeschauwer et al, 1982; Zucconi et al, 1981a, 1981b. Animal/human pathogen inactivation: Burge et al, 1981; Finstein et al, 1982; Savage et al, 1973: Plant pathogens: Bollen, 1985).

Finstein et al (1986) proposed the use of ventilation demand and rate of water removal as comparative indicators of decomposition during the active phase of composting when ventilation demand via temperature feedback is employed. The concept of water removal as a measure of decomposition was further expanded by Miller & Finstein (1985), who calculated weight losses during composting from measurements of initial and final moisture content of the material, and initial mass of the material by employing a constant for the ratio of water loss to dry solids loss, for a given aeration strategy. The value of this constant was calculated from the energy required per unit of water lost and the energy released per unit of organic matter oxidized to CO_2 and H_2O. Thus a value of 10.2 gram water lost per gram of volatile matter decomposed was arrived at (Finstein et al, 1983), a figure similar to that calculated by Haug (1980). When taking into account metabolic water, heat loss through dry air convection and the energy required to raise the temperature of the vaporized water a figure of 8.07 was arrived at under a regime of aeration by temperature demand, and 8.33 under a regime of aeration by oxygen demand (Miller & Finstein, 1985). The relationship is only valid when evaporation represents the bulk of the energy demand, which is the case in static aerated pile composting of materials with a high moisture content (Haug, 1980) under a regime of temperature demand aeration (Finstein et al, 1980).

There is generally a lack of standard analytical procedures to monitor process performance during the maturing phase of composting. Progress has been made to evaluate phytoxicity using empirical tests (eg. Zucconi et al, 1981a, 1981b; Vleeschauwer et al, 1982; Stentiford & Pereira Neto, 1985), but characterization of the compost in relation to its content of humic compounds appears to be less successful. Roletto et al (1985) reported a continuous increase in the humic acid content during the composting of poplar bark waste over an 84 month period. Of various bark composts and farmyard manure, the more stbilized (older) materials had a higher humic acid content (Roletto et al, 1982). Almendros et al (1983) and Elserafy et al (1980), however, reported no change in the humic acid content during the composting of straw-manure mixtures, and water hyacinth straw, respectively. Indeed a whole range of relatively unstabilized manures and sewage sludges revealed a humic acid content ranging from 2.3% to 25.2% (Riffaldi et al, 1982, 1983).

In this study dry solids losses, changes in the volatile solids, organic carbon, and humic acid content, and in the E_4/E_6 ratio of the humic fraction were monitored over a one year composting period of a sewage sludge-straw mixture. The relationship between dry solids and water loss was studied from data obtained in trials with a bench-scale composting simulator.

2. Materials and Methods

The pilot scale composting trials were carried out at the Southern Water Authority Bybrook sewage treatment works at Ashford, Kent. Raw sludge consisting of primary and secondary settled sludge, dewatered on a beltpress with polymers to a moisture content of 75-80%, was used in the trials. The sludge originated from Lenham sewage works a small, rural treatment plant in the Ashford area. Unchopped wheat and barley straw was used as the bulking agent.

In the trials 4-6 tons of sludge was mixed with the straw at a 1:1 volume or 10:1 wet weight ratio. The mixing was carried out manually and with the help of a front end loader. The mixture was placed on a single perforated polyvinyl chloride pipe (17 cm diameter) connected to a squirrel-cage type blower with a 1/2 hp capacity. The pile was covered in a 15 cm thick layer of straw to act as insulation.

Dry solids losses were monitored by placing nylon mesh bags containing a precisely weighed amount of the sludge-straw mixture, in the compost pile. The bags were recovered after 1,2,3,4,8,12,22,35, and 52 weeks of composting. Five bags were taken at each sampling. Chemical analysis was carried out on the freeze-dried samples.

Volatile solids content was determined by weight loss on ignition (550 °C). Organic carbon was determined by the Walkley-Black method (Nelson & Sommers, 1982); a factor of 1.3 was used to correct for unoxidised carbon. Humic acid was extracted as described by Schnitzer et al (1981). This method has been proposed as a standard technique for composts (Zucconi & DeBertoldi, 1984). Extraction of the humic material was carried out using 0.1 N NaOH/0.1 M $Na_4P_2O_7$ as extractant under an atmosphere of nitrogen. The humic acid fraction was separated from the alkaline soluble fraction by centrifugation (1/2 hour at 6000 rpm) after acidification to pH 1-2. The humic acid was rinsed in distilled water and re-centrifuged before freeze-drying. The E_4/E_6 ratio of the humic acid was determined by dissolving the humic acid in 0.05 N $NaHCO_3$ (pH 8.3) at a concentration of 250-500 ppm, as described by Chen et al[3] (1977), and reading the absorbance at 465 and 665 nm.

The bench-scale composting simulator used in this study is based on systems built by Sikora et al (1983) and Mote & Griffis (1979), which use a heated waterbath as insulator for the composting material, by maintaing a water temperature fractionally below that of the compost. In this study no attempt was made to pre-heat or humidify the in-going air, and the air was passed through, rather than around the composting mass. The temperature difference between the waterbath and the compost was maintained at 0.5 ± 0.2 °C. The system is described in detail in Witter (1986) and will also be described in a further paper.

3. Results and Discussion

The pilot scale and the bench-scale composting trials illustrated that both the rate of water loss and aeration demand accurately reflected changes in microbial activity (Figure 1). Peak activity ocurred in the first heating phase of composting, after which microbial activity decreased asymptotically.

Aeration demand does, however, only give a comparative measure of microbial activity (Finstein et al, 1986), whilst water loss may be used as an indirect measure of organic matter losses as suggested by

Miller & Finstein (1985). In the bench-scale composting trials the ratio of water to dry solids loss was 7.2 $\pm$ 0.4 under a regime of temperature demand aeration (TDA) (Table 1). This figure is slightly lower than the figure (8.07) calculated by Miller & Finstein (1985) from theoretical considerations. Their calculations were based on the observation that more than 90% of heat loss is through evaporative cooling in pilot scale composting trials (6-18 tons) (MacGregor et al, 1981). Assuming that 25 kJ (6000 cal) is released per gram of organic matter oxidised (Haug, 1980; Finstein et al, 1983) it can be calculated that in the bench-scale composting trials 81% of the heat generated could be accounted for by evaporation, and 9% of the heat was used to heat the water in the compost from 10 °C to 55 °C. When aeration was at a fixed low rate (FixedA) of 36 cc/min.kg (3% of the peak aeration requirement under temperature demand aeration) both organic matter and water losses were reduced so that the ratio of loss was 7.2, similar to that under a regime of temperature demand aeration. Under a regime of oxygen demand aeration (ODA; maintaining 10-15% oxygen in the compost) dry solids were, however, reduced to a far less extent than water losses and the ratio was reduced to 5.5. This would indicate that the heat balance is to a greater extent affected by the aeration regime than suggested by Miller & Finstein (1985). The studies on the bench-scale composter were not originally intended to evaluate the ratio of water to organic matter loss, but these prelimanary results illustrate that there is a need to study this relationship, and the heat balance during comosting as affected by the aeration strategy in general, in more detail.

TRIAL	Dry Solids	Volatile Solids	Water	Water to dry solids loss
	---------- % initial content ----------			--- ratio ---
TDA[*]	27.7 ± 0.9	35.2 ± 3.4	63.0 ± 0.9	7.2 ± 0.4
ODA[+]	22.1	26.4	28.0	5.5
FixedA[+]	12.3	20.4	25.9	7.2

[*]: Mean of three independent trials.
[+]: Results from single trials.

Table 1: Studies on a bench-scale composter: Dry solids, volatile solids, and water losses; and ratio of water to dry solids loss as affected by the aeration regime.

Cumulative dry solids losses during the active phase of composting (four weeks) in the pilot scale trials accounted for 50% of total losses over a one year period (Figure 2). Reduction in volatile solids content followed much the same pattern, but closer analysis showed that in this trial both measures were not linearly related, but double logarithmically (r=0.999). Bearing this in mind, reduction in volatile solids content which uses the initial volatile solids content on day 0 as reference point, and which can easily be routinely measured, appears to be an accurate measure of dry solids losses during composting. Stentiford & Pereira Neto (1985) monitored the reduction in volatile solids content during the maturation phase (after acration) for up to seven months, but concluded that the variability was too great for the measure to be reliable. Higher variability may be expected when refuse rather than a more homegenous material such as sewage sludge is used, and is also likely to be higher when decomposition, and hence changes in the volatile solids content are relativley small, such as during the maturation phase.

The organic carbon content of the compost showed the same pattern as the volatile solids content (Table 2) and both measures were linearly related (r=0.97). As the volatile solids content is generally easier to measure than the organic carbon content, the former may be a more appropiate measure to estimate composting performance during the active phase of composting.

The C/N ratio (organic carbon to organic nitrogen) showed an initial increase in the first week of composting as more nitrogen than carbon was lost. Thereafter the C/N ratio steadily decreased, but not in line with dry solids losses. Changes in the C/N ratio therefore do not accurately reflect the decomposition process, although the measure is an important characteristic of organic matter in relation to its agricultural use.

Time (weeks)	Organic Carbon	Volatile Solids	Humic Acid	Humic Acid E_4/E_6	C/N
	----- content (% dry solids) ------				
0	61.2 ± 0.9	81.3 ± 1.7	16.0 ± 0.9	1.3 ± 0.2	27.5 ± 1.4
1	61.6 ± 2.1	80.7 ± 2.9	12.0 ± 0.7	3.4 ± 0.4	35.3 ± 3.4
2	59.4 ± 3.3	78.7 ± 2.3	11.7 ± 0.7	4.2 ± 0.6	31.9 ± 4.2
3	58.8 ± 2.9	78.8 ± 1.6	12.4 ± 1.3	4.1 ± 1.2	29.3 ± 4.8
4	56.2 ± 2.8	75.6 ± 3.2	11.8 ± 0.8	4.4 ± 0.4	23.6 ± 5.3
8	48.6 ± 1.9	68.7 ± 1.1	12.2 ± 2.4	5.7 ± 0.6	17.7 ± 2.4
12	39.6 ± 2.7	65.2 ± 2.6	-	-	11.7 ± 0.7
?1	40.1 ± 2.3	62.5 ± 1.7	15.6 ± 1.1	6.8 ± 0.5	11.7 ± 0.7
33.7	37.6 ± 1.6	57.7 ± 1.8	12.4 ± 2.4	7.1 ± 0.9	11.5 ± 1.0
51.9	40.1 ± 2.3	61.8 ± 3.4	14.3 ± 3.4	7.5 ± 1.3	12.4 ± 2.3
L.S.D. (0.05)	2.8	2.9	2.3	1.0	4.1

Table 2: Change in sludge characteristics over a one year composting period in a pilot scale (5 ton) trial. Change in sludge characteristics significant (F) at 99.9%.

The maturation phase was characterized by reduced levels of microbial activity as indicated by dry solids losses, and changes in organic carbon and volatile solids content. The maturation phase is thought to be characterized by the formation of humic compounds. In this study, however, there was no change in the humic acid content during the entire maturation phase of 11 months, and only a small reduction after the first week of composting (Table 2). The E_4/E_6 ratio of the humic acid increased, however, during composting, in a pattern very similar to that of dry solids losses (Figure 2). This indicates that significant qualitative changes occur in the humic fraction during composting. The subject of qualitative changes in the humic acid fraction during composting will be discussed in a further paper.

4.0 References

1. **Almendros, G.; Polo, A.; Dorado, E. (1983):** Studies of humic compounds in various types of composts prepared with wheat straw. II. Physico-chemical characterization of the humic compounds. (In Spanish). Agrochemica: 27 310-325.

2. **Bollen, G. J. (1985):** The fate of plant pathogens during composting of crop residues. In: Gasser, J. K. R. (Ed.): Composting of agricultural and other wastes, p. 282-290. Elsevier Applied Science Publishers, London.

3. **Burge, W. D.; Colacicco, D.; Cramer, W. M. (1981):** Criteria for achieving pathogen destruction during composting. J. Water Poll. Cont. Fed.: 53 683-689.

4. **Chen, Y.; Senesi, N.; Schnitzer, M. (1977):** Information provided on humic substances by E_4/E_6 ratios. J. Soil Sci. Soc. Am.: 41 352-358.

5. **Elserafy, Z. M.; Sonbol, H. A.; Eltanwy, I. M. (1980):** The problem of water hyacinth (Eichornia crassipes) in rivers and canals. II. Physic-chemical properties of humic substances occurring at various degrees of humification of the composted weed. Soil Sci. Pl. Nutr.: 26 399-404.

6. **Finstein, M. S.; Cirello, J.; MacGregor, S. T.; Miller, F. C.; Psarianos, K. M.** (1980): Sludge composting and utilization: Rational approach to process control. Final Report Project No. C. 340-678-01-1, Department of Environmental Science; Rutgers, State University of New Jersey, Cook College, New Brunswick, New Jersey.

7. **Finstein, M. S.; Wei-Ru Lim, K.; Fischer, G. E. (1982):** Sludge composting and utilization: Review of the literature on temperature inactivation of pathogens. N.J.A.E.S.; Department of Environmetal Science; Rutgers, State University of New Jersey, Cook College, New Brunswick, New Jersey.

8. **Finstein, M. S.; Miller, F. C.; Strom, P. F.; MacGregor, S. T.; Psarianos, K. M.** (1983): Composting ecosystem management for waste treatment. Bio/Technology: 1 347-353.

9. **Finstein, M. S.; Miller, F. C.; Strom, P. F. (1986):** Evaluation of composting process performance. Composting of Solid Wastes and Slurries. Proceedings of a conference held at Leeds University (UK) (1983). Leeds University Press. In press.

10. **Gray, K. R.; Biddlestone, A. J. (1971a):** Review of composting. Part 1. Process Biochemistry: 6 22-28.

11. **Gray, K. R.; Biddlestone, A. J. (1971b):** Review of composting. Part 2. Process Biochemistry: 6 32-36.

12. **Haug, R. T. (1980):** Compost Engineering - Principles and Practise. Ann Arbor Science, Michigan.

357

13. **MacGregor, S. T.; Miller, F. C.; Psarianos, K. M.; Finstein, M. S.** (1981): Composting process control based on interaction of microbial heat output and temperature. Appl. Env. Microbiol.: 41 1321-1330.

14. **Miller, F. C.; Finstein, M. S.** (1985): Materials balnce in the composting of waste water sludge as affected by process control strategy. J. Water Poll. Cont. Fed.: 57 122-127.

15. **Mote, C. R.; Griffis, C. L.** (1979): A system for studying the composting process. Agric. Wastes: 1 191-203.

16. **Nelson, D. W.; Sommers, L. E.** (1982): Total carbon, organic carbon, and organic matter. In: Page, A. L.; Miller, R. H.; Keeney, D. R. (Eds.): Soil Analysis Part 2: Chemical and Microbiological Properties. Second Edition. Agronomy: 9 539-580. Madison, Wisconsin.

17. **Riffaldi, R.; Sartori, F.; Levi-minzi, R.** (1982): Humic substances in sewage sludges. Env. Poll. (B): 3 139-146.

18. **Riffaldi, R.; Levi-minzi, R.; Saviozzi, A.** (1983): Humic fractions of organic wastes. Agric. Ecosystems Env.: 10 353-359.

19. **Roletto, E.; Barberis, R.; Zelano, V.** (1982): Gel filtration and absorption spectroscopic investigations on humic substances from organic fertilizers. Pl. Soil: 66 383-390.

20. **Roletto, E.; Chinono, R.; Barberis, E.** (1985): Investigation on humic matter from decomposing poplar bark. Agric. Wastes: 12 261-272.

21. **Savage, J.; Chase, T., Jr.; MacMillan, J. D.** (1973): Population changes in enteric bacteria and other microorganisms during aerobic thermophilic windrow composting. Appl. Env. Microbiol.: 49 42-45.

22. **Schnitzer, M.; Lowe, L. E.; Dormaar, J. F.; Martol, Y.** (1981): A procedure for the characterization of soil organic matter. Can. J. Soil Sci.: 61 517-519.

23. **Sikora, L. J.; Ramirez, M. A.; Troeschel, T. A.** (1983): Laboratory composter for simulation studies. J. Env. Qual.: 12 219-224.

24. **Stentiford, E. I.; Pereira Neto, T. J.** (1985): Simplified systems for refuse/sludge composts. Biocycle: 26 46-49.

25. **Vleeschauwer, D., de; Verdonck, O.; Assche, P., van** (1982): Phyttoxicity of refuse compost. Biocycle: 23 44-46.

26. **Witter, E.** (1986): The fate of nitrogen during high temperature composting of sewage sludge - straw mixtures. Ph.D. thesis, Wye College, University of London.

27. **Zucconi, F.; DeBertoldi, M.** (1984): Compost specifications (Second draft proposal). (Unpublished).

28. **Zucconi, F.; Forte, M.; Monaco, A.; DeBertoldi, M.** (1981a): Biological evaluation of compost maturity. Biocycle: 22 27-29.

29. **Zucconi, F.; Pera, A.; Forte, M.; DeBertoldi, M.** (1981b): Evaluating toxicity of immature compost. Biocycle: 22 54-57.

Acknowledgements

The authors would like to thank the Southern Water Authority (Kent Division) for their assistance with the pilot scale composting trials, and supply of the material.

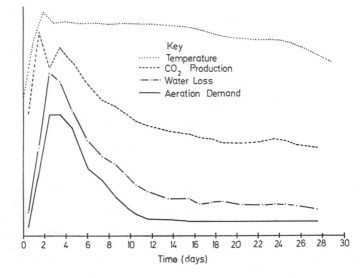

Figure 1: Temperature profile, and patterns of carbon dioxide
production, water loss, and aeration demand under a regime
of temperature demand aeration (limit 55 °C) in a bench-
scale composting trial.

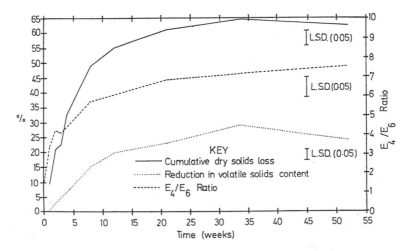

Figure 2: Cumulative dry solids losses, reduction in volatile
solids content, and change in the E_4/E_6 ratio of the
humic acid fraction over a one year composting period
in a pilot-scale trial.

COMPOST MATURITY BY WATER EXTRACT ANALYSES

A. SAVIOZZI, R. RIFFALDI, R. LEVI-MINZI

Institute of Agricultural Chemistry, University of Pisa (Italy)

Summary

Water extracts of a paper processing waste-water composted with straw
were analyzed in order to investigate the stabilization process. During the composting period, the following findings were obtained: dry
matter, carbon, nitrogen, volatile acid and amino acid contents decreased after an initial increase, whereas phenol content decreased only
after thirty days; C/N and E_4/E_6 ratios as well as $\Delta \log K$ values in
creased clearly. All the above parameters did not reach the equilibrium. After about twenty days removal of phyto toxicity was practically achieved and the relatively low molecular weight components (M.
W. < 1500) were disappeared.

1. Introduction

Recently, interest has increased in land application of organic wastes as a means of recovery organic matter for soils and of reducing disposal costs in comparison with other procedures. However, the organic materials should not be applied to the soil until well stabilized, to avoid
adverse effects on plants. Therefore, evaluation of the maturity of compost products has long been recognized as one of the more important problems
encountered in a composting operation and in the utilization of the product, especially for crop production. For this reason it becomes essential
to formulate methods useful to provide information about waste maturity.

There are many proposals for indicators of compost degradation (Harada and Inoko, 1980; Harada et al., 1981; C.N.R., 1983; Morel et al.,1984;
Levi-Minzi et al., 1986; Riffaldi et al., 1986) but none has been widely
accepted. A recent review of the evaluation of the maturity of municipal
refuse compost has been published by Morel et al. (1984). Most of the suggested methods concern the solid phase, whereas a few of these concern the
water soluble extract (Fuller et al., 1979; Chanyasak and Kubota, 1981;
Chanyasak et al., 1982; Hirai et al., 1983), that can be considered a representative phase of biochemical transformations, since the microorganisms' metabolism occurs mainly in the water soluble fraction.

In a recent work (Riffaldi et al., 1986) several chemical and biologi
cal parameters were tested to characterize the stabilization process of a
paper processing waste-water composted with straw. Some parameters indicated two months a suitable period for the establishment of an equilibrium in
the decay process, although other parameters show that compost reaches an
acceptable level of stability in 30 days.

Bearing in mind that the composting reaction is a biochemical decomposition of organic matter, during the which insoluble substances are decomposed into water soluble components, subsequently metabolized into the microorganism cells, we have now attempted to evaluate the contribution that
the changes of the water soluble components can give as a measure for assessing the degree of compost maturity.

2. Materials and methods

A mixture of waste-water sludge from a paper processing factory and
chopped wheat straw was used as raw material. Composting process, sampling
and chemical characteristics of materials are reported elsewhere (Riffaldi
et al., 1986). The aqueous extract was obtained by refluxing of 1 g of ma
terial with 75 ml of distilled water for 1 hour. On the soluble fraction
the following analyses were performed: organic carbon by $Cr_2O_7^{2-}$ oxidation;
total nitrogen by Kjeldhal method; volatile acid content by direct titration, according to the method described by Di Lallo and Albertson (1961);
total phenols, expressed as coumaric acid, by a modification of the method
of Folin, according to Kuwatsuka and Shindo (1973); free-amino acid content,
after drying and dissolving in O.2 M sodium citrate buffer at pH 2.2, by
means of a LKB amino acid analyzer.

The evaluation of the germination index was tested on the aqueous extract obtained refluxing 1 g of material with 25 ml of water, according to
the method described by Zucconi et al. (1981) for assessing product quality
of city refuse compost.

Gel chromatographic fractionation was carried out on Sephadex G 15 column of 2.5 x 58 cm, on a water extract optained shaking 4 g dry weight of
sample with 30 ml of distilled water at 60°C for 30 minutes, according to
Hirai et al. (1983). The 0.1 M NH_4OH solution was used as the eluent, fed
through the column at a rate of 20 ml/hr. The effluent from the column was
continously monitored by absorption at 280 nm with a LKB ultraviolet spectrometer.

3. Results and discussion

Figure 1 reports the trends of dry matter, organic carbon and nitrogen content of the water extract from samples tested during a 140 day period of composting process. As it can be seen the values for all the analytical characteristics follow the same trend: after and initial period of
increase for up to five days, they fall during the course of the experiment
and by the end of the period account for approximately 15, 20 and 40 % of
the initial amount for dry matter, organic carbon and nitrogen content, respectively,without practically attaining constant values. As consequence
of the different decreasing rates of the above mentioned parameters, the
C/N ratio continues to increase as time proceeds.

From the results it can be hypothized that the increase of the water
solubles components during the first days of the composting period can be
due to the increasing of the rate of   decomposition by microorganisms; during this stage, apparently, hydrolysis and solubilization of the complex
substances predominate over the mineralization or immobilization process.

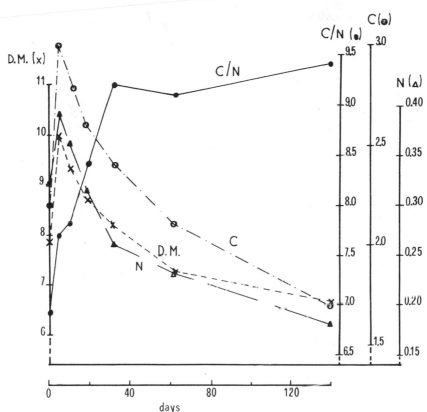

<u>Figure</u> 1 - Dry matter, carbon and nitrogen contents of compost water
extracts (% D.M. of compost).

After about a week the microbial activity induces a gradual constant decrease of soluble organic matter components that are mineralized and metabolized to more biologically stable components.

The results of phenol and volatile acid contents as well as germination index of compost water extracts are reported in Fig. 2. As can be
seen, the soluble phenol content does no show a definite tendency during
composting, except that in the last sample in which comes down of the 20%
of the initial amount. Since low molecular weight phenolic substances,
particularly phenolic acids are extracted by water, the results suggest
that over the first two months of composting time, an equilibrium is attained between decomposition or polymerization of these phenolics and their
production from substances such as lignin. As the composting advances, the
oxidative degradation or polymerization of the secondary derived phenolic
acids exceeds their formation under aerobic conditions, so the water solu-

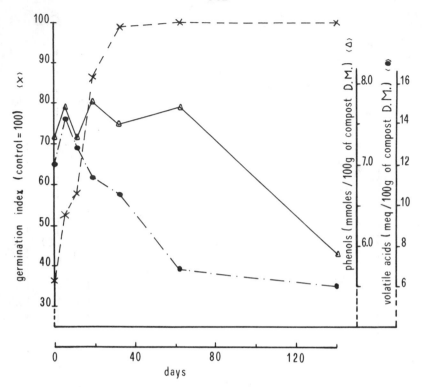

Figure 2 - Germination index, phenol and volatile acid contents
of compost water extracts.

ble phenol content decreases significantly after 140 day period.

Volatile acids, the toxic end products of hydrolizing fats, proteins,
and carbohydrates (Di Lallo and Albertson, 1961), accumulate increasingly
during the first days of decomposition process. This in turn decelerates
decomposition and thus protects labile components, such amino acids (see
Fig. 3), from destruction. However, after the first week, the volatile a-
cid content decreases almost linearly for two months and thereafter the
decrease continues but at a greatly reduced rate up to about 50%of the ini
tial content. These findings are basically comparable to the findings on
the decomposition of city refuse compost reported by Fuller et al. (1979)
and Hirai et al. (1983), who found that during the course of composting water soluble low fatty acids decrease significantly.

In Fig. 2 is also shown the evolution of phytotoxicity during composting, tested in vitro with Lepidium sativum and expressed by germination
index (Zucconi et al., 1981), that combines germination and root growth.
It appears that germination index increases considerably as composting con
tinues; it results also negatively related with the volatile acids
(r = - 0.813; P = 0.05) that represent transitory phytotoxic substances.

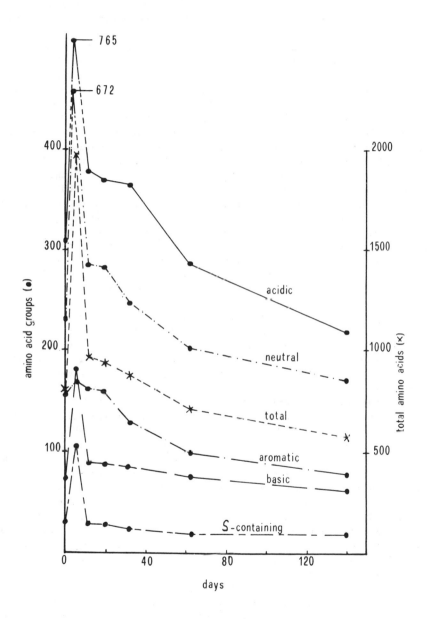

Figure 3 - Water soluble free amino acids
(µg/g of compost D.M.).

Disappearance of toxicity, evaluated on the basis of the above mentioned
method was practically achieved after twenty days, whereas no evidence of
inhibition was found after approximately one month.

In Fig. 3 are represented patterns of the water soluble amino acids,
qualitatively and quantitatively determined during the composting experiment. The amino acids are grouped in acidic, neutral, aromatic, basic, sul
phur-containing, and are expressed as µg/g D.M. of compost. The variations
are quantitative rather than qualitative, with glutamic acid, representing
about one third of total content, as the dominant amino acid (value not re
ported). The acidic , neutral, aromatic, basic and S-containing amino a-
cids represent approximately 40, 30, 15, 10 and 5% of the amino acid total content, respectively. As can be observed, all the amino acid groups
present the same trend during the experiment period. Also in this case a
rapid increase is observed during the initial period, followed, as the
composting process advances, by a decreasing of amino acids in water extracts, probably because of the synthesis of higher molecular weight nitrogen compounds in the solid phase, according to the findings reported by
Hirai et al. (1983) concerning the decomposition of city refuse compost.
A measurement of amino acid total content, expressed as the percentage of
compost proteins, shows that the percent varies from 0.93 to 2.15 in the
first five days, then falls by the end of the experiment period to 0.49
µg/g D.M..

An approach to characterize water soluble organic matter by spectroscopic measurements in regions of visible was attempted. In particular, the
optical densities were tested at the following wavelenghts:465 and 665 nm,
whose ratio was object of an exhaustive study on humification process by
Chen et al. (1977); 400 and 600 nm, from that Δlog K values were evaluated
as differences in logarithmic absorbances at the two wavelenghts and used
as indicators of humification (Tsutsuki and Kuwatsuka, 1984). In Fig. 4 are
reported the values of the above mentioned measured parameters. As is
shown, after the initial period of composting, during the which Δlog K fol
lows an opposite trend, the curves of E_4/E_6 and Δlog K plotted against
composting time, constantly increase throughout the experiment.These trends,
analogous to the trend of the C/N ratio, increasing as composting advances
(Fig. 1), would seem to reflect a progressive relatively smaller molecular
size or low weight particles (Chen et al., 1977) and lower degree of humification (Tsutsuki and Kawatsuka, 1984) of the water soluble organic matter. Neverthless, the classic analysis of humified organic matter, accomplished by spectroscopic measurements for characterization purposes, is
not likely to be satisfactory in this context and the progressive increases
of the optical densities are principally a reflection of the decreasing
carbon content of the solutions (Chen et al., 1977).

Gel chromatograms of water extracts from compost at various stages of
maturity are reported in Fig. 5, limitately to samples from 1 to 4, since
the following samples show the same pattern of the sample 4.

During the first five days of composting (sample 2), the relatively
low molecular weight component (M.W. < 1500) increases considerably, from

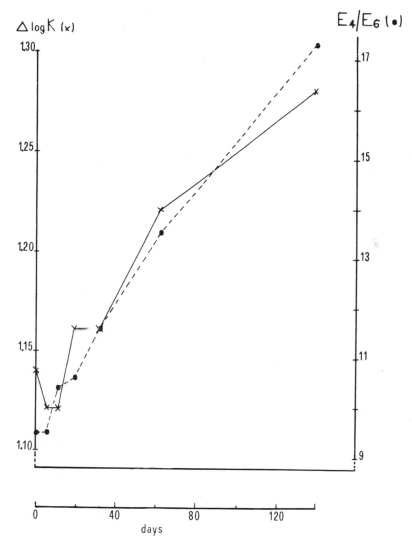

Figure 4 - Optical values of compost water extracts.

about 9 to 18% of the total elution volume of water soluble organic matter, decreases to traces at the eleventh day, and then disappears as decomposition of the material progresses further. These findings are in agreement with those obtained for C, N, volatile acid and amino acid contents (Figg. 1, 2, 3) and with the findings of Chanyasak and Kubota (1981), Chanyasak et al. (1982), and Hirai et al. (1983) on the aqueous extracts of city refuse compost, all showing that as composting progresses water soluble organic substances, after an initial increase, tend to decrease with a parallel decrement of low molecular weight components.

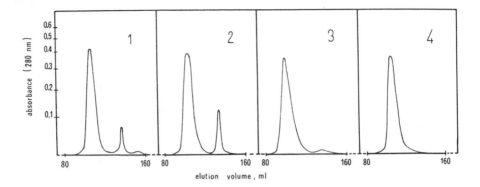

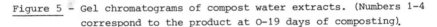

<u>Figure 5</u> – Gel chromatograms of compost water extracts. (Numbers 1-4
correspond to the product at 0-19 days of composting).

4. Conclusions

The results of the present study, carried out to valuate the maturity
of a paper processing waste-water composted with straw by analyses of water
extracts, show that evaluation of chemical stability of the product is qui
te impossible to be determined with only one analysis. The water soluble
components do not represent a chemically distinct group of compounds, but
they include degradation products of many components of the compost, so
the significance of any changes in aqueous extracts is not easily assessed.
However, among the parameters investigated, those indicating that the compost reaches an acceptable level of stability are: germination index, that
shows disappearance of toxicity within thirty days and the relatively low
molecular weight component (M.W. < 1500) that disappears in the aqueous extract after about twenty days. The other tested parameters do not reach
the equilibrium, so the duration of composting of the product remains mostly undefined.

A definition of the stabilization degree of the material can be reached by taking into account the parameters tested both on the solid (Riffaldi et al.,1986) and on the water soluble phase of the compost.

Acknowledgements

This research was supported by C.N.R., Italy, special grant I.P.R.A.,
sub project 1, paper n.819 and by Commission of the European Communities,
Contract ENV/810/I (S).

The authors whish to thank Mr. B. Bernardini for technical assistance.

References

CHANYASAK V., HIRAI M., and KUBOTA H. (1982). Changes of chemical components and nitrogen transformation in water extract during composting of
garbage. J. Ferment. Technol., 60, 439-446.

CHANYASAK V., and KUBOTA H. (1981). Carbon/organic nitrogen ratio in water
extract as measure of composting degradation. J. Ferment. Technol., 59,
215-219.

CHEN Y., SENESI N., and SCHNITZER M. (1977). Information provided on humic
substances by E_4/E_6 ratios. J. Soil Sci. Soc. Am., 41, 352-358.

C.N.R. (1983). Analisi della fitotossicità della sostanza organica in de-
composizione mediante bioassaggio con Lepidium sativum. In: "Metodi analitici per i fanghi". Quad. I.R.S.A., n. 64, Roma.

DI LALLO R. and ALBERTSON O.E. (1961). Volatile acids by direct titration.
J. W.P.F.C., 14, 356-365.

FULLER W.H., ALESII B.A., and CARTER G.E. (1979). Behavior of municipal so
lid waste leachate. I. Composition variations. J. Environ. Sci. Health.,
A14, 461-485.

HARADA Y., and INOKO A. (1980). The measurement of cation-exchange capacity
of compost for the estimation of degree of maturity. Soil Sci. and Plant
Nutr., 26, 127-134.

HARADA Y., INOKO A., TADAKI M., and IZAWA T. (1981). Maturing process of
city refuse compost during piling. Soil Sci. and Plant Nutr., 27, 357-
-364.

HIRAI M., CHANYASAK V., and KUBOTA H. (1983). A standard measurement for
compost maturity. BioCycle, 24, 54-56.

KUWATSUKA S., and SHINDO H. (1973). Behavior of phenolic substances in the
decaying process of plants. Identification and quantitative determination of phenolic acids in rice straw and its decayed product by gas
chromatography. Soil Sci. and Plant Nutr., 19, 219-227.

LEVI-MINZI R., RIFFALDI R., and SAVIOZZI A. (1986). Organic matter and nu
trients in fresh and mature farmyard manure. Agric. Wastes, (in press).

MOREL J.L., COLIN F., GERMON J.C., GODIN P., JUSTE C. (1984). Methods for
the evaluation of the maturity of municipal refuse compost. In: K.R.
Gasser (ed), "Composting of agricultural and other wastes"., Elsevier,
London.

RIFFALDI R., LEVI-MINZI R., PERA A., and DE BERTOLDI M. (1986) Evaluation
of compost maturity by means of chemical and microbial analyses, (submitted).

TSUTSUKI K., and KUWATSUKA S. (1984). Molecular size distribution of humic acids as affected by the ionic strenght and the degree of humification. Soil Sci. and Plant Nutr., 30, 151-162.

ZUCCONI F., FORTE M., PERA A., and DE BERTOLDI M. (1981). Evaluating toxicity of immature compost. BioCycle, 22, 54-57.

QUALITY OF URBAN WASTE COMPOST
RELATED TO THE VARIOUS COMPOSTING PROCESSES

François-Xavier de BLIGNIERES
Ingénieur d'Affaires
A.N.R.E.D. (National Agency for Recovery and Disposal of Waste)

Summary

The efficiency of a composting plant which aim is to recycle biodegradable organic matters into a good quality agricultural fertilizer depends on the way of combining together the various stages of the process. The most important difficulty is to separate the waste biodegradable part from impurities (plastics, glass, stones, metals).

A.N.R.E.D. and precisely its S.A.T.U.C. (Technical Assistance Team for Composting Plants) who has studied 70 % of french plants, mainly works on compost quality related to the various units of treatment line.

Those are :

1° - the primary mechanical treatment (milling or dilaceration) ;
2° - ageing phase with or without mechanical trituration ;
3° - final refining line.

The first stage determines the inert size as plastic and glass, which sorting efficiency depends of. Then a wellmanaged ageing phase is required for a wellmatured and suitable compost ; but a simultaneous operation of trituration decreases the length of ageing phase and consequently areas size and operation costs ; moreover trituration makes sorting between organic matter and impurities easier.

At last, some various sorting processes have been studied, their efficiency and performance have been tested. Those results make possible to choose the appropriated sorting process for a given composting line, considering the impurities characteristics. Such an approach is necessary for the conception of a rational plant able to produce good quality fertilizers.

1. INTRODUCTION

The undermentioned results are taken out from two studies led in 1984 by the SATUC (Technical Assistance Team for Composting Plants) from the ANRED (National Agency for Recovery and Disposal Waste) :

- the first one is about the impact of different grinding means of raw domestic refuse on the impurities granulometry such as glass and plastic matters ;
- the second one concerns the evolution of non synthetic organic matter —MONS— (that is to say biodegradable or fermentescible organic matter used in agriculture) during composting according to different means of turning over.

Indeed, it appeared during the seventy visits of the SATUC that the organic matter's final content of an urban compost depends on the separation's efficiency between the fermentescible organic components of the domestic refuse and the inert particles or impurities such as glass, stones, limestones, metals, plastic matters, textiles and so on.

The efficiency of this separation is as such closely bound to the results of different mechanical operations made over refuse (grinding, dilaceration) and the conditions in which the biological stage of the treatment took place, that is to say the composting stage.

2. IMPACT OF DIFFERENT MECHANICAL TREATMENTS ON THE GRANULOMETRY OF DOMESTIC REFUSE IMPURITIES (GLASS, STONES, PLASTICS)

2.1. Presentation of the tests

The study consisted in comparing the granulometries of heavy inert wastes (glass, pebbles) and plastic matters from urban wastes obtained from two completely different mechanical treatments as for the working principle:

- a test was made from a "DILACERATOR" ; its principle is to shred refuse between two axes equipped with knives, when they turn at a low speed in the opposite direction, they carry along in only one time the wastes between these knives.
- a series of tests was led on a "HAMMER MILL" ; a rotor equipped with articulated hammers and which turns at a high speed carries along the refuse which must go through a grate, after as many revolutions of the rotor as necessary. The grate space determines the granulometry of the ending milled matter. During this series of tests, four different grate spaces were chosen : 250 mm, 200 mm, 150 mm and 80 mm.

2.2. Results and interpretations

The results of the granulometric analyses are presented in the figures 1 a.b.c. The granulometric curves resulting from the different mechanical treatments are superposed for a same type of product (glass, pebbles, plastics and organic matter).

The proportioning of impurities and the determination of their granulometry were made according to the method "CEMAGREF-ANRED".

2.2.1. Heavy inert particles : glass - pebbles (figure 1 a.)

There is a fundamental difference of glass granulometry between product coming from a "DILACERATOR" and product coming from a "HAMMER MILL", whatever the dimension of the grates may be. It is interesting to notice that the utilization on the hammer mill of different grates which spacing ranges between 1 and 3 (80 to 250 mm) do not modify in a significant way the granulometry of heavy inert waste (glass, pebbles). We may think that the high speed revolution of the rotors is the reason why the first contact or impact between the hammers and the heavy inert particle (glass bottle for example) determines almost definitely the ending granulometry of the mentioned product. Indeed 90 % of these heavy inert particles measure less than 8.5 mm on the average for grates with spacing from 80 to 250 mm.

On the other hand it is possible to obtain with the "dilacerator" a much rougher granulometry of glass and pebbles since with the same mesh of 8.5 mm only 42 % of the product go through. Since very thin heavy inert particles are difficult to sort and to eliminate mechanically, it is desirable to keep the much rougher granulometry as possible : a material such as a "DILACERATOR" will also allow to obtain such a result. The hammer mill especially gives a thin granulometry whatever the size of the grate may be.

1 a : Lights (Glass-Stones)		1 b : Plastic		1 c : Organic Matters	
90% of product retained at a mesh of :	% of product retained at 12.5 mm square mesh	90% of product retained at a mesh of :	% of product retained at 50 mm square mesh	50% of product passing at a mesh of :	% of product retained at a 50 mm square mesh
1	1		38	10.4 mm	8.5
2	2.5	8 mm	53	13 mm	16.5
3 0.5 mm	4	9 mm	67.5	16 mm	22.5
4	7	13.4 mm	78.5	20 mm	38.0
5 2.3 mm	43.5	19 mm	79.5	–	65.5

1 : 80 mm GRINDED WASTE
2 : 150 mm GRINDED WASTE
3 : 200 mm GRINDED WASTE
4 : 250 mm GRINDED WASTE
5 : DILACERATED WASTE

Table 1 : Granulometric analyses

		T 0		T + 30 days 0 after 1 turning over		T + 90 j 0	
		<25	>25	<25	>25	<25	>25
TRIAL B 150 mm, SHOVEL DREDGER	ORGANIC MATTER	64	36	67	33	74	26
	PLASTIQUES	31	69	30	70	30	70
TRIAL C 150 mm, SPREADER	ORGANIC MATTER	70	30	86	14	90	10
	PLASTIQUES	29	71	38	62	38	62
TRIAL D 80 mm, SHOVEL DREDGER	ORGANIC MATTER	72	28	73	27	78	22
	PLASTIQUES	35	65	35	65	35	65

Table 2 : Simulation for a 25 mm. Square mesh screening

The table 1 a. simulates the efficiency's difference that a 12.5 mm screening, generally used in a composting plant to produce a thin compost, could have on glass disposal according to the primary treatment of domestic refuse.

2.2.2. Plastics (figure 1 b.)

Concerning plastics, the granulometry obtained from a shredder is different from the one of thin grinded matters because of the lowest quantity of thin plastic particles. So a 19 mm mesh holds back 90 % of plastics after having passed through the shredder whereas a 8 mm mesh is used in the case of a 80 mm milled matter.

Generally plastics granulometry depends on grate space. The rougher it is the larger the screening space is. The shredded matter produces the thicker granulometry for plastics.

The 80 and 150 mm grinded matters give similar results for plastics under 25 mm ; beyond this size, a 150 mm grinding with a less important shredding is very different from the 80 mm grinding. The 200 mm and 250 mm milled matters and the shredded matters obtain similar results and distinguish themselves from other products by a rougher granulometry (see table 1 b.).

2.2.3. The organic matter

Concerning the granulometry of organic matter, there is a difference between the "shredding machine" and "grinding machine" which is nearer to the one observed for heavy inert waste than the one of plastics.

Concerning shredded refuse the granulometry curve of plastics is very near the one of organic matter. On the other hand concerning milled matters, the granulometry of organic matter is in all cases inferior to the one of plastics with an important part inferior to 12.5 mm for 80 mm milled matters. This granulometry increases with spacing between the grates (table 1 c.)

The organic matters appear then more sensitive to the dividing up through milling than plastic matters.

2.3. Commentary

None of the above mechanical treatments allow to make a clear difference between organic matter and impurities or inert particles of waste. However they allow a preparation of the refuse for subsequent phases, especially biologic such as composting :
- the shredding preserves a large granulometry of glasses, stones and plastics but also of a part of the organic matter ;
- the grinding produces in all cases a very thin granulometry of glasses and heavy particles. The granulometry of plastic matters grows with grinding grate space and the organic matter presents an intermediary granulometry.

It is then obvious that a primary mechanical treatment connected with a dimensional sorting (screening) cannot separate on his own the organic matter from inert waste.

3. EVOLUTION OF THE ORGANIC MATTER ACCORDING TO THE WAY OF COMPOSTING

3.1. Experimental protocol

This second study consisted in following precisely the evolution of physico-chemical characteristics of the organic matter and especially the granulometric aspect according to the initial characteristics of refuse

after treatment and of different ways of composting.
Among the different tests made, we will present the following ones :

| TRIAL | GRINDED MATTER GRANULOMETRY (Grate spacing) | OVERTURNING | |
		WAY	FREQUENCY
B	150 mm	SHOVEL DREDGER	1 day / 15
C	150 mm	MANURE MUCK SPREADER	1 day / 15
D	80 mm	SHOVEL DREDGER	1 day / 15

We will only examine the evolution of following parameters :
- the granulometry of the M.O.N.S. (Non Synthetic Organic Matter), that is to say the fermentescible or biodegradable parts ;
- the C/N ratio.

3.2. Results interpretations

3.2.1. Organic matter's granulometry
The role of the turning over way influences clearly and rapidly the granulometry of the organic matter. The 80 mm and 150 mm grinded matters turned over by a shovel dredger move very little from this point of view. The granulometry of the organic matter from the test B at 150 mm links up the one of the test C at 80 mm after 90 days (figure 2).
On the contrary organic matter of 150 mm milled waste which are turned over with a manure muck spreader split up very fast : after 30 days and only one passing through the spreader, only 14 % of this organic matter above 25 mm remains (table 2 and figure 2), whereas this value reaches on the average 25 % after 90 days in the tests B and D and 5 turning over with a shovel dredger.
This different evolution of the organic matter's granulometry between milled matters turned over by a muck speader and a shovel dredger is bigger if considering the product passing through at 12.5 mm : after 60 days, 77.5 % of the organic matter is inferior to this mesh for test C against 57 % for test B.

3.2.2. Plastic's granulometry
The turning over with a shovel dredger does not modify the plastic matter's granulometry, whatever their initial size may be. On the other hand, the manure muck spreader turning over reduces obviously plastic's granulometry : this phenomenon only happens during the first passing through. Afterwards the size of plastics does not evolve any more, despite the succesive passing through the muck spreader (table 2).

3.2.3. Evolution of the C/N ratio
The "trituration's" mechanical action of the manure muck spreader during successive turning over entails a faster fall of the product's C/N ratio than in the case of a classical turning over (loader machine or shovel dredger). This phenomenon is more especially important as this same mechanical action increases at the same time and at each turning over the

quantity of cellulosic matters with a high C/N ratio (papers - cardboard) in the fraction submitted to the agronomic analysis of C and N, that is to say the milled matter's fraction inferior to 50 mm.

So it is possible to obtain from grinded domestic refuse at 150 mm after 75 days of slow composting a mature product with a C/N ratio inferior to 20 whereas grinded matters composted in the same way but without any "trituration" do not reach a C/N ratio inferior to 20.

3.2.4. Evaluation of tests

The manure muck spreader used during this study is not directly adjustable to industrial stage in composting plants. However, its mechanical part on the grinded domestic refuse during slow composting is very interesting from different points of view.

First, it allows a fast reduction of organic matter's granulometry without changing a lot the one of inerts and impurities. From this point of view, a dimensional sorting (screening) can then be taken into consideration in order to separate efficiently the organic matter from inert waste (plastics, glass ...).

The table 2 shows that a theoretical sham screening at 25 mm allows to recover from grinded domestic refuse at 150 mm. 86 % of refuse's organic matters and to eliminate 62 % of plastics after only 30 days. In the case of a usual turning over, only 74 % of this organic matter is recovered in a 3 time longer delay (90 days) and 70 % of plastics are eliminated. This observation has a fundamental advantage for the scale of composting areas.

On the other hand, the mechanical action due to the muck spreader allows a faster maturation of products and should also allow a gain concerning maturation areas.

4. CONCLUSION

These two studies allowed to understand which parameters influence the physical characteristics of domestic refuse components intended to be composted and to know the factors which determine the organic matter's evolution during this composting.

These results allow to define more precisely the principles to be used in a process treatment according results to be obtained : optimal recovery of urban waste's organic matter to be treated, production of inert composting's over sizes on the organic level.

Figure 4 illustrates clearly the performance difference that two divergent composting processes can reach : "process A" corresponds to a treatment with screening, after a fermentation-trituration stage without any previous grinding and allows to recover in compost 80 % of the organic matter contained in raw refuse ; "process B" corresponds to a screening immediately after grinding and only allows to recover 26 % of this organic matter in the compost.

Finally, in order to well know the working of different composting's stages, efficiency of different principles for impurities sorting are to be determined (ballistic, densimetric, pneumatic sorting) according to their size ; it will then be possible to establish a complete treatment's logic from mechanical preparation of refuse to refining of composted product. This study is being realised.

FIGURE 1 : Granulometric curves

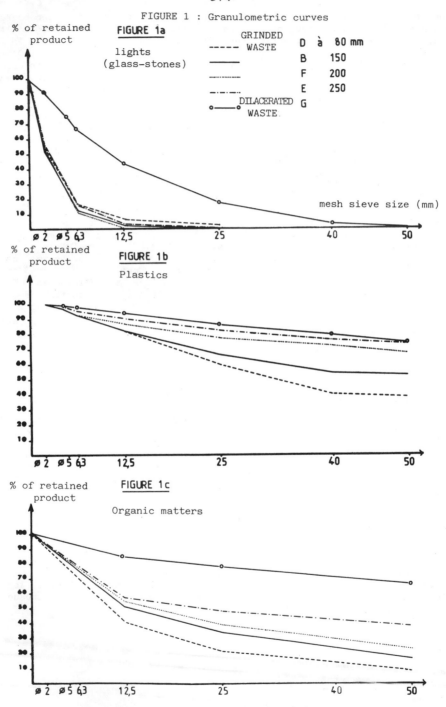

FIGURE 1a

% of retained product

lights (glass-stones)

GRINDED WASTE — D à 80 mm
B 150
F 200
E 250
DILACERATED WASTE G

mesh sieve size (mm)

FIGURE 1b

% of retained product

Plastics

FIGURE 1c

% of retained product

Organic matters

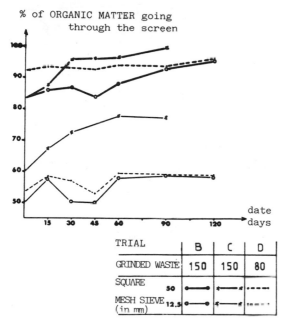

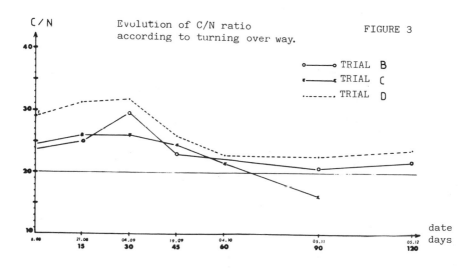

Evolution of organic matter's granulometry
according to turning over way.

FIGURE 2

Evolution of C/N ratio
according to turning over way.

FIGURE 3

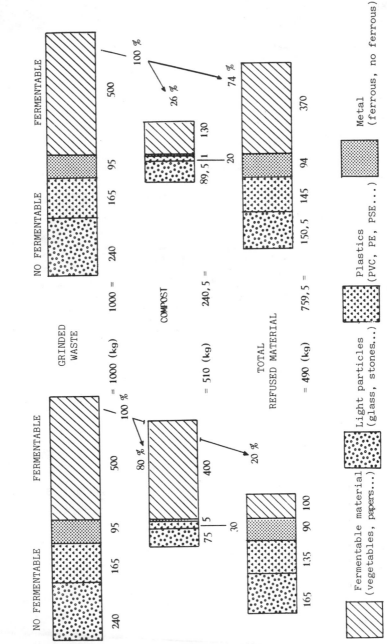

Figure 4 : Comparison of two different composting process' performance
– Results in DRY MATTER –

CHANGES IN THE CHEMICAL AND HORTICULTURAL PROPERTIES DURING COMPOSTING OF SLURRY PRODUCED BY METHANOGENIC FERMENTATION OF DAIRY COW MANURE

M. RAVIV and S. MEDINA
Agr. Res. Org. Newe-Ya'ar
Exp. Stn. P.O. Haifa
ISRAEL

Y. CHEN and Y. INBAR
The Hebrew Univ. of
Jerusalem. Faculty of
Agriculture. Rehovot
ISRAEL

Z. GELER
Kibbutz Industry
Assoc. Tel Aviv.
ISRAEL

Abstract
Screened and leached slurry produced by methanogenic fermentation of dairy cow manure is now being served as a peat substitute in Israeli horticulture for some years. For some growing systems its use as a stabilized material is preferred and attempts were made so as to characterize and optimize the stabilization process.
Fresh screened and leached anaerobically digested slurry was composted till temperatures lower than 40°C were permanently achieved.
During the 80 days composting period the heap was turned 7 times using front-loader tractor. Moisture content was monitored and kept at the level of 74 % $\pm$ 2 %. Ash content increased from 14 % in the raw material to 36 % in the mature compost.
Bulk density increased from 0.085 to 0.215 gr. cm^{-3}.
Air Space increased and water holding capacity decreased along the process probably due to aggregation of tiny particles.
Mineral levels in the water extracts were relatively low during the whole period.
Biologically active materials in the water extracts (as were tested using the mung bean rooting bioassay) were not damaged by the composting process.
The end-product after curing, is a friable, easy to mix, odorless, pathogen-free and without weed seeds material and was found to be superior as compared to sphagnum peat for the soilless culture of many plants.

1. INTRODUCTION

The biological stabilization of organic materials which serve as plant growth media is of utmost importance when prolonged growing periods are considered (Hoitink and Kuter, 1986). As opposed to sphagnum peat, most of the peat substitutes are relatively unstable and subjected to slow biodegradation (Raviv et al. 1986).

Previous studies have shown that composted fibrous fraction of methanogenic slurry of cow manure (composted "Cabutz") is usually superior to the raw material (Inbar et al. 1985).

The aims of the present study were to determine the physical, chemical and biological properties of the raw material and to characterize their changes during the composting process.

2. MATERIALS AND METHODS

2.1. Compost preparation

Fresh "cabutz" which obtained from a biogas plant at kibbutz Yagur, Israel, was composted for 80 days in a concrete cell measuring about 2x2x2m.

The methanogenic processing included both thermophyllic (10 days) and mesophyllic (20 days) stages.

Eight m^3 raw material were composted. The heap was turned over with a front loader seven times during composting : the first five turnings were performed whenever the temperature in the center of the heap reached 55°C ; the last 2 turnings, during temperature decline - at two weeks intervals. Moisture content was maintained constant at 72–76 % by a single water addition after 33 days. Temperature and moisture content were monitored daily and twice a week, respectively.

2.2. Physical and chemical properties

2.2.1. Bulk density, total porosity, air space (0–10 cm tension) and water holding capacity (> 10 cm tension) were measured by the following procedure: The materials were water saturated for 48 hours, then packed in a 350 ml glass column at 10 cm height. The material was resaturated and allowed to drain for 2 hours, weighed, and placed in a 105°C oven until oven dry, and weighed again. The physical parameters were calculated from the weights and volume.

2.2.2. Chemical analyses were performed on a 1:10 (w/w) solid water extract as previously described (Inbar et al. 1985). pH, electrical conductivity (EC), $NO_3^- NH_4^+$, K^+ and P were determined in the extract.

2.2.3. Ash content was determined by oven heating of the materials for 6 hours at 550°C.

2.3. Biological properties

2.3.1. Rooting bioassay

Active biological fractions were separated and tested in the mung bean rooting bioassay as described by Hess (1965) and modified by Raviv and Reuveni (1984). Preliminary tests showed that rooting promoters migrate in the paper chromatography system to a distinct region which was subsequently used throughout.

2.3.2. Growing experiment

Peperomia caperata rooted cuttings were grown in either fresh or fully composted "cabutz" for 2 months. Growing media were composed of equal parts of organic component and perlite nr. 4.

Plants were grown in 450 cm containers, watered daily and fertilized with Osmocote 14:14:14, 4 grams per liter medium. At the end of the growing period the shoots were cut and weighed.

Results and discussion

The heap temperature firstly reached 55°C at the sixth day. Fluctuations of temperature and moisture content are presented in Fig. 1. In the first period the temperature build up rate was high. About 6–7 days were required to reach optimal temperatures of 53°–57°C (Mac Gregor et al.

1981) after each turning.

The fast heating rate is probably due to the insulating nature of the coarse, fibrous fresh material and the high content of easily biodegradable components. After the fifth turning the heating rate slowed down somewhat and the temperature remained steady for about 10 days. Lower temperatures were recorded during the last 25 days. Water content decreased slightly from 76 % to 71 % during the first 32 days when water added to restore the original level. Subsequently water content remained practically steady (Fig. 1).

Ash content (Fig. 2) increased at a steady rate from 14 % to 36 % during composting. The final ash content value is significantly higher than the 22 % reported by Inbar et al. (1985). This difference may result from the additional mesophilic stage which was applied to this material at the anaerobic stage. Another possible reason is the higher decomposition intensity related to the difference in composting conditions : more frequent turnings, better insulation achieved by performing the composting under roof and in a concrete cell rather than a windrow in the open.

The physical properties of the compost samples and their variation with time are presented in Table 1. The bulk density increases in the course of composting from 0.085 to 0.215 g/cm^3. The particle density increases as well from 1.69 to 1.95 g/cm^3. This is probably due to the increase in ash content which usually consists of minerals of 2.4-2.7 g/cm particle density. Subsequently to the changes in the bulk and particle density the porosity decreases with composting time from 95 to 89 %. These changes are expected in composts and basically result from a decrease in particle size of the organic components and an increase in the ash content. In contrast to these results are the air space and water holding capacity results.

An increase in air space and decrease in water holding capacity with composting time were measured. This effect may result from aggregation of particles due to the formation of humic substances during composting. The high value of air space is probably explained by oven drying of the samples prior to testing. Although oven drying was applied we believe that whenever possible samples should be stored at the same moisture content as sampled and oven drying avoided.

The chemical properties are presented in Table 2. The electrical conductivity, (EC) of the compost decreased in the first stages due to nitrate and other minerals uptake by microorganisms acting extensively during this period. At a later stage the EC and nitrate concentration increase in relation to decomposition of microbial entities. A similar trend is observed for phosphorus, although less prominent. Potassium concentrations are practically constant whereas those of NH are in accord with observations by other investigators (Pages at al. 1985).

The effect of the composting process on the content of rooting promoters is presented in Table 3. It can be seen that there is no net destruction of rooting promoters along the composting process and that their levels are comparable to that of sphagnum peat.

Peperomia caperata plants grown in raw "Cabutz" + perlite (1:1, v:v) reached after 2 months of growth an average fresh weight of 5.56 gr $\pm$ 0.78 gr. When fully composted "Cabutz" was used instead of raw material the final average fresh weight was 8.05 gr $\pm$ 0.65 and the plants were more uniform and had a better bushy appearance.

CONCLUSIONS

The slurry of methanogenic fermentation of cow manure undergoes some physical and chemical changes while achieving biological stability.

The use of the mature compost as plant growth medium is preferable to the fresh screened and leached slurry which was previously described (Putievski et al. 1983, Chen et al. 1984, Raviv et al. 1984). These results are in agreement with those presented by Inbar et al. (1985) for tomato and pepper seedlings.

LITERATURE CITED

Chen, Y., Inbar, Y., Raviv, M. and Dovrat, A. 1984. The use of slurry produced by methanogenic fermentation of cow manure as a peat substitute in horticulture - physical and chemical characteristics. Acta Hort. 150 : 553-561.

Hess, C.E. 1967. Rooting co-factors, identification and functions. Proc. Intl. Plant Prop. Sci. 15 : 181-186.

Hoitink H.A.J. and Kuter, G.A. 1986. Organic residues and composts as growth media for plants. In : Chen, Y. and Avnimelech, Y. (eds.) : Organic matter in modern agriculture. Martinus-Nijhof/Dr. W. Junk Publ. The Hague. In Press.

Inbar, Y., Chen, Y. and Hadar Y., 1985. The use of composted slurry produced by methanogenic fermentation of cow manure as a growth media. Acta Hort. 172 : 75-82.

MacGregor, S.T., Miller F.C., Psarianos, K.M. and Finstein, M.S. 1981. Composting process control based on interaction between microbial heat out-put and temperature. App. & Env. Microbiol. 41 : 1321-1330.

Pages, M., Estaun, V. and Calvet, C. 1985. Physical and chemical properties of olive marc compost. Acta Hort. 172 : 271-276.

Putievski, E., Raviv, M. and Chen Y. 1983. Development and regeneration ability of lemon balm and marjoram on various media. Biol. Agr. and Hort. 1: 327-333.

Raviv, M., Chen, Y., Geler, Z., Medina, S., Putievski, E. and Inbar, Y. 1984. Slurry produced by methanogenic fermentation of cow manure as a growth medium for some horticultural crops. Acta. Hort. 150 : 563-573.

Raviv, M., Chen, Y. and Inbar, Y. 1986. Peat and peat substitutes as growth media for container grown plants. In : Chen, Y. and Avnimelech Y. (eds.) : Organic matter in modern agriculture. Martinus-Nijhof/Dr. W. Junk Publ. The Hague. In press.

Raviv, M. and Reuveni, O. 1984. Endogenous content of a leaf substance(s) associated with rooting ability of avocado cuttings. J. Amer. Soc. Hort. Sci. 109 : 284-287.

ACKNOWLEDGMENT

This research was supported by a grant from the National Council for Research and Development, Israel and the European Economic Community.

Compost's age (days)	Particle density gr/cm^3	Bulk density gr/cm^3	Porosity %	Air pace %	Water holding capacity	
					(% of volume)	(% of weight)
0	1.60	0.085	95.0	44.1	50.9	583.3
7	1.70	0.087	94.9	44.3	50.6	580.9
13	1.73	0.090	94.8	44.8	50.0	555.5
20	1.75	0.098	94.4	45.4	49.1	502.4
27	1.78	0.110	93.8	41.8	52.1	473.9
35	1.80	0.120	93.3	44.3	49.0	407.8
51	1.86	0.136	92.7	49.7	43.0	316.4
64	1.93	0.143	92.6	48.0	44.6	311.9
80	1.95	0.215	89.0	50.0	38.5	179.5

Table 1 : Changes in some physical properties during the composting process of "Cabutz"

Compost's age (days)	EC 25 (mmnos/cm)	pH	NO$_3^-$ meq/l	K$^+$ meq/l	NH$^+$ meq/l	P (ppm)
0	1.47	7.50	0.63	5.1	1.50	35.0
7	1.33	7.40	0.34	4.9	1.35	33.8
13	1.33	7.35	0.32	4.8	1.15	36.9
20	1.21	7.34	0.27	4.0	0.85	22.5
27	1.23	7.16	0.25	4.3	1.33	21.3
35	1.28	7.05	0.30	4.4	1.28	20.6
51	1.54	7.28	0.46	4.4	1.20	25.3
64	1.62	7.18	0.58	4.8	0.90	26.9
80	1.60	6.80	0.58	4.7	0.60	21.6

Table 2 : Changes in some chemical properties during the composting of "Cabutz"

Material	time of composting (days)	Roots $\bar{x}$	/ $\pm$	Cutting SE
Wather control	—	6.6		0.5
Sphagnum peat	—	18.0		2.9
Fresh "Cabutz"	0	18.8		2.8
Composted Cabutz	7	20.3		4.3
Composted Cabutz	13	17.8		3.5
Composted Cabutz	20	19.1		2.8
Composted Cabutz	27	21.6		3.9
Composted Cabutz	35	24.6		4.6
Composted Cabutz	51	23.1		3.2
Composted Cabutz	64	18.8		3.1
Composted Cabutz	80	22.9		3.8

Table 3 : Rooting response of mung bean cuttings to partially purified rooting promoters extracted from sphagnum peat, fresh and composted "Cabutz"

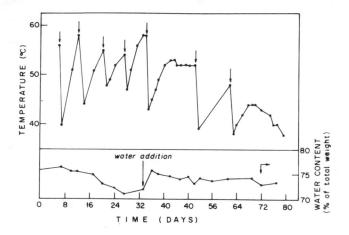

Figure 1 : Temperature and moisture content of "Cabutz" during composting

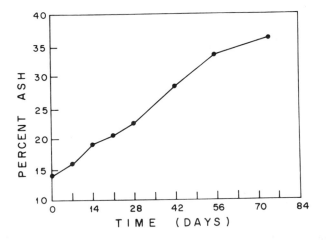

Figure 2 : Ash content of "Cabutz" during composting

SESSION: 2

QUALITY OF THE COMPOST

Rapporteur: BOUTIN P.

The papers dealing with the quality of the product fall in 3 main areas: a) decomposition of the substrate; b) heavy metals in compost; and c) health and safety aspects.

The number of papers presented in each area was variable, and probably reflects the current scientific and agricultural interest, and not necessarily the overall importance of the subject matter.

For convenience, the area will be reported in the order given above.

Decomposition of substrate

The information presented may be divided into a number of topics. Some of the papers dealt with more than one topic but, for convenience, the information has been collected under the following subheadings:

- The first one is basic processes;
- the second is changes in the substrate during composting;
- the 3rd one will be methods of assessing stability;
- the 4th one will be phytotoxicity and value of compost as a growing media.

Some of the patterns of decomposition are now fairly well understood, based upon a knowledge of attack by bacteria and other organisms and decomposition by enzymes. However, degradation of lignin is much less understood than that of the other components, as cellulose. This is a topic which deserves further attention from research scientists. One particular line of investigation which was mentioned was the effect of mixed communities compared with simple populations. Genetic manipulations appear to offer a means of modifying organisms, including the production of enzymes to increase the breakdown of lignin.

The next subheading is substrate changes during composting, with a large number of papers presented on the changes in the carbon and nitrogen compounds in the composted material. There was a general trend to measure the optical extinction of water extracts and E4/E6, this ratio being an evaluation of the degree of humification. This appears to be a potentially useful empirical measurement. An other property which has received much attention has been the CEC of the organic part of the composted materials, which normally increases during composting.

Stability: many authors consider a stabilized compost as a good product. There appears to be some confusion between definitions of stability and quality. Several speakers stressed that compost is a biologically achieved material and therefore may be described as "stable" when the biological activity has decreased to a particular level, typically shown by a reduced respiratory rate. In this state, the compost is usually called "mature" and is considered to be suitable for the normal uses. Biological measurements are time-consuming to make, and therefore identification of simple chemical parameters which would indicate the status of maturity is highly desirable. A number of speakers described various approaches to solve their problem.

Within the definition of composting, there is a recognition that phytotoxic compounds are normally reduced during the early stages and are realized by the biomass during the last stages. A number of plant toxins have been shown to be produced during the early decomposition of lignocellulosic materials and among them acetic acid. Under adverse conditions, sulphydric acid and ethylene can be produced too. Therefore, partly decomposed materials should not be used if there is a risk of growing plants. Mature compost has been shown to be a valuable substrate for plant growth and as a manure.

Less attention from the participants was devoted to the two remaining areas, however they are main interest centers and discussion matters in Brussels consulting groups.

Heavy metals

For heavy metals, a major preliminary point was objected: have we to consider total heavy metals content, or only plant available metals, with the subsequent problems of availability determination? The total content apparently shows important seasonal variations, which have to be confirmed and taken into consideration.

For heavy metals reduction in compost, two ways were evocated:

- Separate collection of organic fermentescible wastes, a particular attention being given in some cases to vegetal residues from gardening;
- reduction of metal contents of garbage and compared by mechanical, magnetic and aerodynamical sorting of the heavy fraction.

The first policy, if correctly applied, gives a compost with low levels of undesirable metals, but it supposes a faultless cooperation of everybody. Some are convinced it is an actually possible purpose for domestic refuse. Other distrust it is a realistic solution. So they propose sophisticated technical devices for heavy fraction separation and component lowering of amounts of heavy metals in compost.

Sanitary aspects

The sanitary aspects are another important concern for compost quality. Much work is still needed in pathogenic forms numbers and fate in garbage and compost and after compost use; information is particularly lacking on viruses and parasites. The opportunities of common treatment of wastewater sludges and garbage must be discussed according to local circumstances.

An extensive review on current literature on the topic reveals fundamental discrepancies in the approach toward microbiological standards for composts, with two main problems. The first of them is the level of pathogens which can be tolerated in compost. The present trend is surely to zero or very low numbers for the main pathogens and is often considered as an evidency. However, it must be discussed with the help of quantitative methods of modern epidemiology, with reference to recent research on treated wastewater agricultural reuse. We can presume it would conclude to different recommendations for open field spreading of compost and more intensive uses, as in greenhouses. The second point under discussion is the quest for indicator organisms, and the definition of their actual role, as indicators of the eventual presence of pathogens and of treatment sanitary efficiency. Entrobacteriae and faecal streptococci appear to be suitable candidates, but it is unanimously admitted that further research is still needed before standardization on a subject with so much practical implications for compost preparation and use.

Working conditions on compost plants have not attracted a sufficient attention till now. Security has to be improved. Observed high densities of potentially pathogenic organisms (gram negative rods and fungi) in the air everywhere compost is handled, reveal a potential risk. This risk is confirmed by observations of an aspergillosis pathology and the recent definition of a "compost worker's syndrome".

Epidemiological studies on compost workers are expected to precise the actual extent of such elements. Meanwhile, an adapted, prevention-oriented medical survey is necessary for workers in such particular surroundings. Technical measures must be taken to reduce dust levels as far as reasonably possible.

Globally, the contributors delivered during this session confirmed the necessity for an integrated approach to produce "good" composts, after a clear and precise definition of the objectives, with a better knowledge of compost processing, upon which comparative studies afford the most valuable information, as it was demonstrated here, too.

SESSION III : USE OF COMPOST

Factors influencing the agronomic value of city refuse composts

Compost as a growing medium for horticultural plants

End product of composting process for use as horticultural substrate

Compost for control of plant diseases

Microbial aspects of compost application in relation to mycorrhizae and nitrogen fixing microorganisms

Compost for mushroom production and its subsequent use for soil improvement

New ways for design, construction and operation of compost filters for special purposes

Organic wastes as soil amendments for the reclamation of Egyptian sandy soils
I. Effects of different combinations of organic wastes
II. The effect of different rates of organic wastes

Effects of manure compost on soil microbiological properties

Agronomic characterization and evaluation of two new municipal waste composts

The influence of different cultural media on tomato growth

Comparison of the physical and chemical properties of humic acids extrated from a podzolic soil and a mature city refuse compost

Odour investigations at two composting plants in Sweden

Utilization of farm animal manure for humus substrate production

Oxygen, water and temperature in the decomposition process of an organic substance during composting

Use of composted urban wastes in viticulture

REPORT BY O. VERDONCK

FACTORS INFLUENCING THE AGRONOMIC VALUE OF CITY REFUSE COMPOSTS

C. JUSTE, P. SOLDÂ, M. LINERES
Station d'Agronomie, I.N.R.A.
Centre de Recherches de Bordeaux
33140 PONT DE LA MAYE (FRANCE)

Summary

Nearly 800 000 t of city refuse composts are yearly used in France for several crop productions. Excessive salt content, induced nitrogen deficiency and absence of maturity bringing harmful effects on plant germination and growth, are the most hazardous factors sometimes involved in city refuse compost use as soil amendment.

In the present report, we examine the possibility to utilize a bag experiment method to evaluate quickly the degree of maturity and the phytotoxicity of various city refuse composts. Severals examples of applications of this method are also presented. This paper reports besides the magnitude of some modes of compost treatments in improving their agronomic values for instance : removal of salt excess by leaching, increase of aeration rate of insufficiently mature compost by coarse material addition, general decrease of potentially toxic effects mediated by long term composting and peat dilution.

1. INTRODUCTION

About 800 000 t of city refuse composts are yearly used in France for several crop productions as vine, mushroom, fruit-trees and, at minor extent, for arable crops. In the Bordeaux area, three town refuse composting plants are recently constructed in the vicinity of the famous vineyard. The annual production of these plants (20 000 t) are chiefly used by vine or mushroom growers.

The agronomic value of this particular organic fertilizer is the result of both favourable (nutrients, organic matter and lime content) and unfavourable factors (salinity, high content of glasses, gravels, plastics and toxic elements, unmaturity). The rapid assessment of the agronomic value of compost, before land application, is very important because the use of toxic products must be avoided.

The methods for the evaluation of compost maturity presented by MOREL et al. in the last symposium held in Oxford in 1984 (7) are not sufficient to assess the global agronomic value of a growing medium : for this purpose, a biological test, involving effective plant growth like in the field, seems the most appropriate method (2).

In the present paper, we describe a biological test (3) based on the measure of the growth of two test plants (Maize and Bean) seeded directly on the compost to assess quickly the agronomic value of the organic waste. The purpose of this study is also, using the proposed test, to determine the effect of several treatments applied to various city refuse composts on their agronomic value.

I. BIOLOGICAL TEST DESCRIPTION

The test plants (Maize and Bean) were grown in plastic bags (45 x 30 x 7 cm) filed by a volume of the experimented compost equivalent to 2 kg of dry matter. Each bag was sown with 15 maize and 15 bean seeds put in 3 lines of 5 seeds for each specie. The seed were sown into a thin layer (0,8 cm) of peat in order to avoid a direct contact between the seed and the city refuse composts.

Plants were raised for 4 weeks in a growth chamber (16 h light at 22° C temperature and 8 h darkness at 16° C). The bags (2 replicates for each treatment) were daily watered using distilled water pulverizations.

Fresh and dry weight of harvested plants were measured individually ; the oven-dried tissue samples were ground and mineralized for chemical analysis.

For the study reported here, the control compost was an unfertilized peat mixed with 50 g of $CaCO_3$ (for 1 kg dry matter) in order to bring the pH at the same level (about 7,5) for all growing mediums. Each city refuse compost was experimented alone or diluted with the unfertilized peat at both 75 and 90 % rates.

After bean and maize harvest, pH, conductivity and $N-NO_3$ content of the composts were determined.

II. STUDY OF SEVERAL FACTORS INFLUENCING THE AGRONOMIC VALUE OF CITY REFUSE COMPOSTS

- a/ Fermentation period of the compost

Composts from six french cities were subjected to the biological test. The composts were obtained from the same raw material in the course of the following periods of fermentation : 6, 60, 120, 240 days.

Fig. 1 did not indicate an effect of the period of the fermentation on the agronomic value of the town refuse when this latter was experimented without peat addition. In contrast, when the compost was mixed with peat, a strong increase of the agronomic value was observed as the fermentation increased.

The composts originating from screening very old cities raw materials without controled fermentation process are sometimes used in France as organic fertilizer or growth medium, specially for home gardening, parks...

Table 1

Agronomic value of old screened town refuse
as influenced by their organic matter content

N° of sample	Organic matter content (% / dry matter)	Dry matter yields (as % of yield from peat bag)	
		Bean	Maize
1	36,6	57	104
2	27,0	47	119
3	21,8	76	108
4	13,4	90	96
5	8,4	105	112

Despite its low content in organic matter (less than 15 %/dry matter), the agronomic value of the old screened town refuse is often higher than the agronomic value of 4 or 6 month old composts (Table 1). However the use of old screened refuse may be hazardous because the raw material is not subjected to a fermentation process involving a thermophilic phase : accordingly, the resulting organic materials have sometimes a high content of weeds and pathogens (8).

- b/ Salinity
Fig. 2 shows that the experimented compost resistivity (1/salinity) :
. decreased as the period of fermentation increased ;
. increased when the compost was diluted by peat.

Besides leaching a 10 cm layer of compost by a simulated 100 mm rainfall induced opposite effects depending on the compost maturity (Table 2): the 120 day old compost value was greatly increased while the leaching treatment was deleterious for a 12 day old compost ; in this case, the organic material was quickly invaded by numerous fungi and mouldiness and, as a result, plant growth was severely inhibited. The strong increase in fungal activity resulting from the leaching treatment was probably due to the removal of unidentified toxic substances limiting the microorganism development.

Table 2

Influence of compost leaching on mean yields of bean and maize plants

| Experimented substrates | Maize | | Bean | | Resistivity* of the aqueous extract |
	Fresh weight g/plant	% of peat	Fresh weight g/plant	% of peat	
Peat	2,51	100	3,11	100	1 952
Compost 120 d. : . unleached . . .	0,72	29	0,74	24	300
. leached (100 mm water)	1,20	48	2,27	73	1 952
Peat	5,44	100	4,36	100	2 157
Compost 12 d. : . unleached . . .	4,87	90	2,99	69	268
. leached (100 mm water)	3,87	71	3,10	71	573

* Resistivity : $\Omega /cm^2/cm^{-1}$

- c/ Nitrogen availability and degree of maturity
The low agronomic value and sometimes the phytotoxicity of unmature composts are often related to a strong immobilization of mineral nitrogen in the growth medium.
Fig. 3 demontrates a continuous increase of the mineral nitrogen content in the $CuSO_4$ extract as the composting period increased. However, at the rate of compost dilution by peat corresponding to the highest agronomic value of the organic fertilizer, the nitrogen content in the growth medium was lower.

As expected, the increasing availability of the mineral nitrogen originating from the 180 or 240 day old composts resulted in an enhancement of the N uptake by test plants (Table 3).

Table 3

Influence of the compost fermentation period and the dilution rate by peat on the nitrogen content of Maize and Bean plants (% dry matter)

	Fermentation period (days) :				Dilution effect (mean)
	6	60	120	180 or 240	
Maize :					
Undiluted compost	1,90	1,85	2,53	3,37	**2,41**
Rate of dilution by peat :					
- 90 %	1,60	1 74	1,72	2,65	**1,93**
- 75 %	1,53	1,67	1,43	2,23	**1,72**
Fermentation period effect (mean)	**1,68**	**1,75**	**1,89**	**2,75**	
Bean :					
Undiluted compost	2,71	3,83	4,61	4,28	**3,86**
Rate of dilution by peat :					
- 90 %	2,10	2,97	2,99	4,34	**3,10**
- 75 %	2,18	2,75	2,60	3,88	**2,85**
Fermentation period effect (mean)	**2,33**	**3,18**	**3,40**	**4,17**	

The phytotoxic effect brought by an unmature compost may be counteracted incorporating a slow release N fertilizer as nitroform at rates pH 0,5 or 1 p. 1 000. In contrast, addition of other nitrogen fertilizers as $Ca(NO_3)_2$ or urea was ineffective to alleviate the harmful influence of the compost despite the strong increase of the mineral nitrogen content observed in the growth medium (Table 4).

Table 4

Effect of several nitrogen fertilizer addition on the agronomic value of 12 day-old city refuse compost

Nitrogen fertilizer	p. cent of plant yield from compost alone	Total N of plant % D.M.	N (NO_3) aqueous extract (mg/l)
$Ca(NO_3)_2$, 0,5 p. 1 000	101	1,56	85,2
Urea . . " "	105	1,63	86,0
Nitroform " "	111	1,83	66,0
Nitroform 1 p. 1 000	117	2,61	58,5
Compost alone	100	1,40	49,7

- d/ Aeration
Composts subjected to the biological test were previously sieved through a 25 mm sieve and then mixed with polystyrene chips or pine bark

pieces at rate of 2 kg compost (dry matter) for 2,5 l of the experimented coarse dilutants which size varied from 20 to 40 mm.

As demonstrated in Table 5, the agronomic value of compost was increased as a result of bark pieces or polystyrene chips addition. According to the observed data, this beneficial effect on plant growth might have occured as a consequence of a mineral nitrogen content increase in the growth medium.

Table 5

Effect of coarse polystyrene or pine bark chip addition
on the agronomic value of compost

Treatment		Yield (as % of yield from peat bag)	Nitrogen in plant (% dry matter)	N (NO_3) aqueous extract (mg/l)
Com-post	Age (days)			
A	60 alone	100	2,91	35,0
A	60 + polystyrene	129	3,30	58,8
A	120 alone	100	1,35	67,0
A	120 + polystyrene	185	1,55	114,2
B	120 alone	100	4,60	10,9
B	120 + pine bark	274	3,55	13,0

- e/ Heavy metal content

From the various experimented composts only zinc, manganese and, at minor extent, copper were accumulated on test plants (Tables 6 and 7). The heavy metal bioavailability increased as the composting period and the rate of dilution by peat increased. The enhanced uptake of metal by plants growing in the diluted peat compost was probably due to the growth medium acidification resulting from peat addition, as testified by the decreasing pH from 7,6 to 6,4 when the compost was diluted by 25 % of peat.

Table 6

Effect of compost fermentation period
on sodium and heavy metal content in maize and bean plants
(ppm/dry matter)

Fermentation period (days)	Na		Zn		Mn	
	Maize	Bean	Maize	Bean	Maize	Bean
Control (peat)	25	45	52	27	26	44
6 days . . .	224	436	71	145	50	145
60 days . . .	380	359	116	183	65	137
120 days . . .	783	1 311	159	173	73	172
240 days . . .	1 287	1 216	214	164	66	170

Table 7

Effect of the dilution rate of compost by peat
on heavy metal accumulation in maize plants
(ppm/dry matter)

	Mn	Zn	Cu
Undiluted compost	57	69	3,3
Rate of dilution by peat 90 %	86	89	4,1
" " " 75 %	130	95	5,1

Contrasting with the low maize and bean heavy metal uptake, the use of city refuse compost to prepare mushroom growth medium may be, in some cases, very hazardous. Indeed, and as evidenced on table 8, addition of increasing rates of city refuse compost up to 75 % in a mushroom growth medium resulted in a noticeable **Agaricus bisporus, Agaricus edulis, Lepiota naucina** uptake of mercury, cadmium and lead (4).

Table 8

Differential uptake of heavy metals by three species of mushroom
growing on town refuse enriched compost
(ppm dry matter)

Town refuse addition rate	Mushroom	Hg	Cd	Pb
Control	Agaricus bisporus	0,67	0,23	traces
	Agaricus edulis	3,85	0,29	"
	Lepiota naucina	1,20	1,06	"
Town refuse 25 %	Agaricus bisporus	2,65	0,54	4,23
	Agaricus edulis	3,47	0,87	4,82
	Lepiota naucina	0,90	5,45	traces
Town refuse 75 %	Agaricus bisporus	3,82	1,18	18,52
	Agaricus edulis	9,10	3,63	25,10
	Lepiota naucina	2,70	14,80	12,28

- f/ Persistent toxic organic chemicals
    Phytotoxicity of unmature city refuse compost results sometimes of their high content in some unstable organic compounds as aliphatic acids : for instance de VLEESEHAUWER et al. (1981) (1) have demonstrated that acetic acid might be involved in the toxicity resulting from too unmature compost utilization.
    However, besides labile toxic organic compounds, very toxic remaining substances resulting from occasional city deposit pollution may be encountered in composts. In our laboratory, a very strong toxicity was observed on experimental dicotyledon crops growing on a city refuse compost highly polluted by the pichloram herbicid.
- g/ Vermicomposting
    The use of earthworm cultures (**Eisenia fetida**), in order to hasten or

perhaps to improve the composting process of various wastes, is often experimented in several countries. In France, some attempts were made recently to evaluate the town refuse vermicomposting as compared to the classical composting scheme (5)(6).

During experiments conducted in our laboratory from 1981 to 1984, the agronomic value of several vermicomposts or classical composts produced from the same raw city material was measured and compared with the agronomic value of an animal manure sample. The composts were experimented after 6 or 8 weeks of vermicomposting or single composting process.

As compared to the classical composts, the agronomic value of the 6 week old compost was not affected, while a small increase (10 to 15 %) in the agronomic value was observed for the 10 week old compost. This beneficial effect was likely the result of a nitrogen availability increase in the growth medium (Fig. 4).

III. CONCLUSION

The above described biological test was useful for a rapid screening of various city refuse composts.

The test was also very effective to evaluate the validity of several treatments able to alleviate the potential harmful factors characterizing some compost.

Although the proposed test required more time than other tests, as the cress (**Lepidium sativum**) test (9) it was undoubtely more representative of the agricultural practices.

REFERENCES

(1) de VLEESCHAUWER D., VERDONCK O., Van ASSCHE P., 1981. Phytotoxicity of refuse compost. Biocycle, 43-47.

(2) JUSTE C., SOLDÂ P., DUREAU P., 1980. Mise au point de tests agronomiques légers permettant de déterminer simultanément la phytotoxicité globale des composts d'ordures ménagères et leur degré de maturation. Convention n° 77-147 INRA/Ministère Environnement, oct. 1980, 42 p.

(3) JUSTE C., 1983. Méthodes d'estimation de la toxicité éventuelle des boues, des composts et des sols. Symposium "Protection des sols et devenir des déchets", La Rochelle (France), 22-24/11/1983, 409-420.

(4) LINERES M., 1982. Présence de métaux lourds (mercure, cadmium, plomb) dans les champignons comestibles produits sur ordures ménagères. Convention n° 77-82 INRA/Ministère Environnement, 45 p.

(5) LINERES M., FAYOLLE L., SOLDÂ P., TAUZIN J., JUSTE C., 1983. Lombricompostage sur ordures ménagères : valeur agronomique globale du compost obtenu. Teneur en métaux lourds d'Eisenia fetida. Convention code 65/9064 INRA/EMC/DGRST, déc. 1983, 44 p.

(6) LINERES M., FAYOLLE L., TAUZIN J., JUSTE C., 1985. Accumulation des métaux lourds dans Eisenia fetida Andrei (Oligochaeta Lumbricidae) élevé sur ordures ménagères. Agronomie, 5, 779-784.

(7) MOREL J.L., COLIN F., GERMON J.C., GODIN P., JUSTE C., 1984. Methods for the evaluation of the maturity of municipal refuse compost. Proc. Symposium of Oxford (UK), 10-20 March 1984, 56-72.

(8) SOLDÂ P., JUSTE C., DUREAU P., 1982. Appréciation de la valeur agronomique globale des criblés de décharge d'origines différentes. Rapport fin de contrat INRA/ANRED (Angers, France), 11 p.

(9) ZUCCONI F., PERA A., FORTE M., de BERTOLDI M., 1981. Evaluating toxicity of immature compost. Biocycle, 54-57.

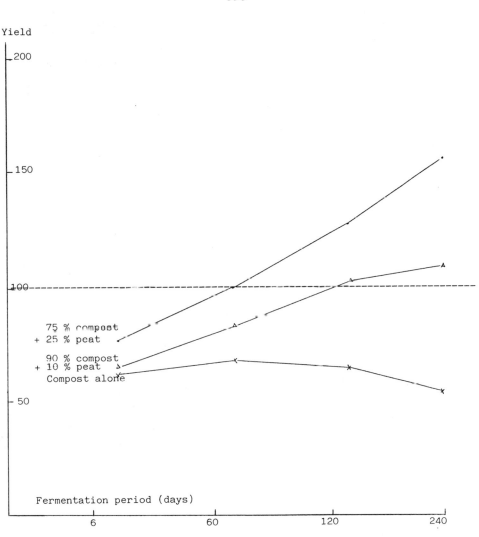

Figure 1 : Effect of the fermentation and the dilution rate of city refuse
compost by peat on the yield of bean (100 = yield measured on
the peat control bag)

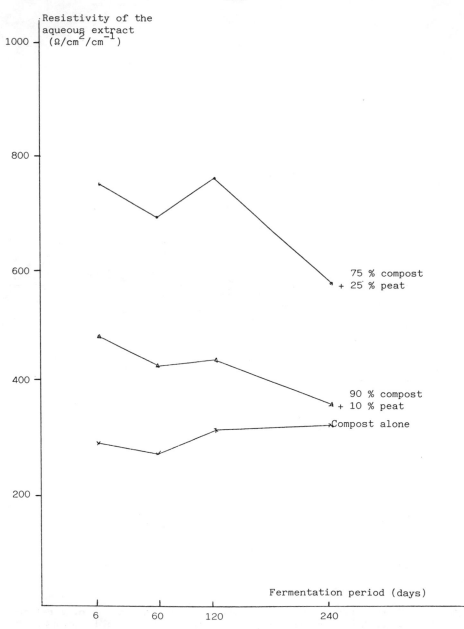

Figure 2 : Effect of the fermentation period and the dilution rate of city refuse compost by peat on the aqueous extract resistivity

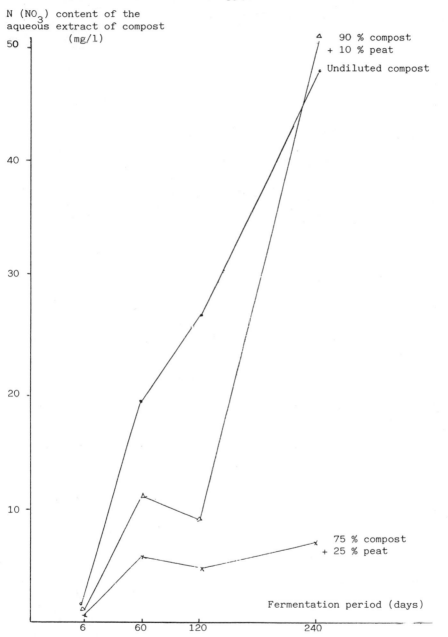

Figure 3 : Effect of the fermentation period and the dilution rate by peat
on the N (NO_3) content of the compost aqueous extract

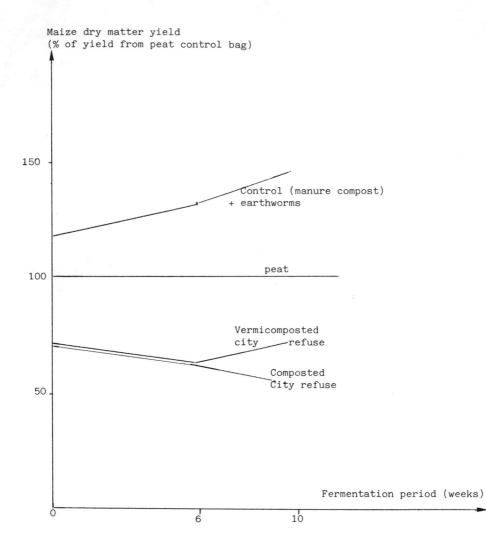

Figure 4 : Effect of the composting or vermicomposting period on the agronomic value of city refuse compost (expressed as maize yield)

COMPOST AS A GROWING MEDIUM FOR HORTICULTURAL PLANTS

O. VERDONCK (*), M. DE BOODT (*) and R. GABRIELS (**)
(*) Laboratory of Soil Physics, Soil conditioning
and Horticultural Soil Science
Faculty of Agricultural Sciences, State University Ghent, Belgium.
(**) Research Station for Ornamental Plants
Ministry of Agriculture, Melle, Belgium

Summary

More and more importance is given to composts of different organic
waste materials because they are becoming one of primary ressources of
potting soils. Potting soils are normally made of pine litter, peat
and anorganic materials such as perlite, rockwool, expanded clay,
polystyreen etc...
The last decenia we have carried out many research projects for the
optimalisation of compost as horticultural substrates. In most cases
the organic waste materials cannot be used as such because of different
disadvantges such as: phytotoxicity, nitrogen immobilisation, salt
damage, structure etc... Therefore composting is a possibility to
solve many of the disadvantages and together with an exact mixture
we can make an excellent growing medium for horticultural plants.
Good results have been obtained with composted bark, stabilised
townrefuse compost, sludge from waterpurification mixed with bark,
soyscrap mixed with bark, hop residues mixed with different barks etc..
as growing medium.

1. INTRODUCTION
    In Belgium we are using about 500,000 m^3 of growing media in horti-
culture which mainly exist out of peat and pine litter.
    Peat is imported for more than 80 % from Germany and small amounts
from Russia and Finland. Pine litter is mainly taken in our Belgian forests
but also imported from France and Germany.
    The reason why we started to valorize organic waste materials was that
we are depended from import for our growing media's and that very big amounts
of bark, sludge, townrefuse compost and other materials are available in
our country.
    In table 1 we indicate the amount of townrefuse compost available in
Belgium.
    In table 2 we give a list of possible waste materials on which we have
done research for the use in compost.
    Most of these materials indicated in table 2 have been composted and
tested as horticultural substrate or organic soil conditioner.
    Next to these materials we also work together with research institutes
from other countries as Greece, Sri Lanka, Spain, Portugal, Egypt, Tunesia,
Indonesia etc... in order to make good composts of their products as cork,
rice hulls and straw, olive leaves and cake, vine branches, cocofibre dust
and sea grasses.

Table 1. Composting plants in Belgium.

Plant	Maximum capacity of compost in ton/year	Composting system
Ghent	15,000 – 20,000	Dano
Dendermonde (Verko)	20,000 – 25,000	Triga
Hoeselt-Bilzen (Intercompost)	15,000 – 20,000	Vickers
Habay (Idelux)	12,000 – 15,000	Buhler
Tenneville (Idelux)	12,000 – 15,000	Buhler
Mons	± 10,000	Windrows
Total:	84,000 – 105,000	

Table 2. List of organic wastes which can be used in compost.

Industries	Products
Wood industry	bark
	sawdust
Town wastes	leaves of the trees during autumn
	sludge waterpurification
	wood ships
	nicht soil
	garden waste
	garbage
Textile industry	flax residues
	wool residues
	cotton residues
Bioindustry	chicken manure
	piggery manure
	straw
Food industry	soy scrap
	carbon black waste
	fruit residues
	coffee waste
	hop waste
	chaff
Tobacco-industry	tobacco nerves
	tobacco dust
Natural resources	brown coal
Paper industry	bark
	sludge waterpurification

2. MATERIALS, METHODS AND RESULTS

The valorisation of the different waste materials are carried in 4 steps.

2.1. Chemical and physical properties:

Before starting composting experiments with organic materials we will analyse following chemical parameters:

- pH H_2O
- conductivity of 1/5 extract in volume
- total and watersoluble nitrogen in mg/l
- extractable P, K, Ca and Mg (in NH_4Ac)
- total heavy metal content in ppm

401

In table 3 we give the guidelines for optimal conditions in horticultural substrates..

Table 3. Chemical optimal conditions in growing media for ornamental plants.

Level (*)		1	2	3
pH H$_2$O		4.0 - 5.5	4.3 - 5.8	4.5 - 6.0
EC (µS)		400 - 750	400 - 750	400 - 850
N		25 - 40	25 - 70	30 - 100
P		> 30	> 30	> 30
K	in mg/l	90 - 175	120 - 250	150 - 360
Ca		> 400	> 400	> 400
Mg		125 - 200	150 - 300	150 - 300

(*) Level 1: salt sensitive plants
    Level 2: normal cultivation in peat and composts for moderately
             growing plants
    Level 3: intensive cultivation, salt tolerant plants

Organic wastes or mixtures with it must more or less correspond with the optimal data.
The maximum levels of heavy metals are indicated in table 4.

Table 4. Maximum levels of heavy metals in materials used for growing media.

Element	Maximum content in ppm				
	All crops (1)	Food crops (2)	(3)	Ornamental plants (2)	(3)
Zn	100	300	1000	1500	1500
Cu	50	50	100	500	500
Pb	50	300	600	500	1000
Cr	-	25	150	200	200
Ni	10	50	50	100	100
Co	-	50	-	50	-
Hg	2	5	5	5	5
Cd	2	5	5	5	5

(1) proposal Ministry of Agriculture
(2) (3) proposals Public Waste Company

Organic waste materials can be used in growing media when the total amount of heavy metals doesn't increase the maximum proposed levels in table 4.

Not only the chemical parameters are important, but also physical properties. Following soil physical properties are important for quality determinations: - volume weight
- total pore space and pore size distribution
- volume % easily available water
- volume % air
- maximum watercapacity in g water/100 g dry material
- shrinkage in volume %

Because of many difficulties of structure in potting soils we have developped quality criteria together with the inspection service of the Ministry of Agriculture. The quality of growing media is divided in 6 classes which are given in table 5.

Table 5. Quality classes of substrates.

Quality classes	Volume % air	Volume % easily available water
I	> 40	> 5
II	30 – 40	> 10
III	20 – 30	> 15
IV	10 – 20	> 15
V	5 – 10	> 20
VI	< 5	> 20

This quality classes give the advantage for the nurseries that any time the same quality can be ordered. The potting soil factory must often control his mixtures on this physical properties so that a standard product can be delivered.

2.2. The optimisation of the parameters of composting.

With our laboratory composting simulator we will determine the optimal parameters and the best mixtures for composting. The laboratory composting experiments are followed up by composting trials on an industrial scale in order to determine the minimum time of composting and maturing.

Following parameters are followed:

1. Before the composting process: - pH H_2O
   - conductivity
   - % organic matter
   - total, NH_4- and NO_3-N
   - % moisture content
   - macro- and micro-elements

2. During the composting process: - temperature
   - oxygen consumption
   - respiration coefficient
   - maximum oxygen consumption
   - CO_2-production

3. After the composting process: - pH H_2O
   - conductivity
   - C/N ratio
   - total, NH_4-, NO_3-nitrogen
   - % organic matter
   - low fatty acids
   - volume weight
   - pore size distribution
   - volume % easily available water
   - volume % air
   - watercapacity

As moisture content and nitrogen level are the most important parameters, we give an example of:

1. Influence of moisture on the oxygen consumption of town refuse (table 6)
2. Influence of nitrogen level on the oxygen consumption of bark (table 7)

From tabel 6 and 7 we can conclude that for any organic material we must determine the optimal parameters for composting.

The optimalization of the different parameters takes about 3 months of research in the laboratory and the composting on industrial scale about 6 months.

403

Table 6. Influence of the moisture content on the oxygen consumption of
        townrefuse.

Moisture content in %	Maximum oxygen consumption in mg O_2/g org. mat./h	Total oxygen consumption in mg O_2/g org. mat.
43	2,23	332,6
48	2,64	387,6
53	2,48	390,0
58	2,84	417,5
63	2,37	417,5
68	2,36	393,2

Table 7. Influence of the nitrogen level on the oxygen consumption of
        pine bark.

Added nitrogen in %	Maximum oxygen consumption in mg O_2/g org. mat./h	Total oxygen consumption in mg O_2/g org. mat.
0	0,190	35,1
0,5	0,696	99,5
0,75	0,797	114,3
1	0,642	115,2
1,5	0,727	125,2

2.3. Growing experiments with ornamental plants.

After composting on an industrial scale we can use these compost for testing with ornamental plants. The first tests are carried out on small plots in greenhouses or fields from research institutes or universities. When these tests are positive, bigger trials were carried out together with commercial nurseries. As example we give some results with townrefuse compost in comparison with composted bark and peat (table 8).

Table 8. Growth experiments in compost.

Substrates	number of leaves		height of the plant	
	Fatshedera			
1. composted bark	19.0	a	71.9	a
2. peat	19.7	a	81.0	a
3. barkcompost/townrefuse compost 3/1	19.9	a	76.3	a
4. barkcompost/townrefuse compost 1/1	17.7	b	62.1	b
	Dieffenbachia exotica			
1. composted bark	20.6	a	42.0	a
2. peat	21.3	a	42.3	a
3. barkcompost/townrefuse compost 3/1	19.3	a	41.5	a
4. barkcompost/townrefuse compost 1/1	18.0	a	43.6	a
	Cordyline celeste			
1. composted bark	32.9	a	59.1	a
2. peat	34.9	a	62.4	a
3. barkcompost/townrefuse compost 3/1	34.0	a	60.4	a
4. barkcompost/townrefuse compost 1/1	34.3	a	61.5	a

The results from table 8 indicate that composted bark and mixtures from townwaste compost with barkwaste can be used as substitute for the normal peat substrates.

Another example we like to give is the use of composted organic wastes as organic soil conditioner in comparison with manure. Following composts are used:
1. manure 80 ton/ha
2. tobacco waste 25 ton/ha
3. tobacco waste 50 ton/ha
4. papersludge 75 ton/ha
5. papersludge 150 ton/ha
6. filtercake (foodindustry) 40 ton/ha
7. filtercake (foodindustry) 80 ton/ha

As testplant we grow Picea amorica during 2 years on a loamy sandy soil where the different composts are added to the soil. The results are given in table 9.

Table 9. Growth results of Picea amorica.

Used compost	Height of the plant		
1. manure 80 T/ha	48.50	a b	
2. tobacco waste 25 T/ha	49.16	a	
3. tobacco waste 50 T/ha	47.60	b	
4. papersludge 75 T/ha	49.36	a	
5. papersludge 150 t/ha	47.67	b	
6. filtercake 40 T/ha	49.42	a	
7. filtercake 80 T/ha	45.97		c

These results also indicate that different composts from organic wastes of different origin can be used with the same results as with manure.

3. CONCLUSION

From our research of recycling organic wastes we can conclude the following:
- each material must be analysed chemically and physically before we can say that it can be used in agriculture or horticulture
- for the composting of these materials we must optimise the different parameters (nitrogen level, moisture content, mixtures with other products, structure and particle size, etc...) in order to become a stabilised and mature product
- the use of the mature compost is depended on the chemical and physical parameters of the endproduct therefore growing experiments must be carried out before we can say that these composts can be used as horticultural substrate or as organic soil conditioner

4. LITERATURE

- CAPPAERT, I., VERDONCK, O. and DE BOODT, M. (1976). A respiratory appararus for the behaviour of organic materials. Proceedings International symposium on soil organic matter studies, 6-10 September, 1976, Braunswick, IAEA-SM-211/62, pp. 131-167.
- PENNINCK, R., VERDONCK, O. and DE BOODT, M. (1984). Different materials which can be used on compost. Acta Horticulturae "Symposium Compost", nr 72, June 1985, pp. 31-38.

405

- VERDONCK, O., DE VLEESCHAUWER, D., PENNINCK, R. and DE BOODT, M. (1982).
  The determination of optimal parameters for the composting of solid
  organic wastes. Seminar "Composting of organic wastes", Denmark,
  pp. 1-25.
- VERDONCK, O. and PENNINCK, R. (1984). The composting of bark with soy
  scrap sludge. Acta Horticulturae "Symposium Compost", nr 72, June 1985,
  pp. 183-190.
- VERDONCK, O., DE BOODT, M., STRADIOT, P. and PENNINCK, R. (1984).
  The use of tree bark and tobacco waste in agriculture and horticulture.
  Composting of agricultural wastes, Elsevier Applied Science Publishers,
  pp. 203-215.

END PRODUCT OF COMPOSTING PROCESS FOR USE AS HORTICULTURAL SUBS-
TRATE

E. Corominas; F. Perestelo; M.L. Pérez and E. M.A. Falcón
Departamento de Microbiología, Facultad de Biología, Universidad
de La Laguna. Tenerife. Islas Canarias. Spain.
Departamento de Ornamentales Equipo de Microbiología. I.C.I.A.
Tenerife. Islas Canarias. Spain.

Sumary
Compost was made using agricultural and forest wastes commonly found in considerable quantities in the Canary Islands,
thus a cheap substitute for the usual organic substrates –
used in composting, which are expensive and need to be imported.
The expensive were decomposed during 80 days, in static pi
les. Airing was done turning the piles, and weekly irrigation of the piles was done using liters of water.
The end product was of correct physical and chemical charac
teristics for use as a substrate, and was subsequently stu
died with several of the ornamental plants normally grown
in greenhouse for the Islands export market, which constitute a reliable comparative base for our trials.

1.1. Introduction
      One of the major problems of ornamental plant culture in –
the high cost of substrates, which has lead to the development
of processes which result in cheaper organic substrates of equal,
if not better, quality.
      We have used forest residues, chiefly needles, and banana
leaves – both abundant in the Canary Islands – as basic compo--
nents in our composting process. Both materials were laid down
in alternating layers of 40 cms. depth, until a compost pile of
2x2x2 meters, with a pH of 7 and 2% N/dry matter content, was –
obtained.
      Temperature was the decisive factor for a correct fermenta
tion of the plant material. In order to maintain a maximum of –
70%C, the pile was turned weekly. Humidity was maintained between 55 and 65% by weekly sprinkling, and the pH which was initially 6, was brought up to 7.5 at the end of the process.
      The homogenous, porous compost obtained is being used for
potted ornamentals such as Peperomia obtusifolia, Scindapsus –
aureus, Asplenium nidus, and Noeregelia coraline tricolor. Trials
using four types of substrate mixtures varying percentages of –
composts and soil – are used to study their influence on produc
tion and size, using controls grown in enriched peat and perlite. Results are analysed according to the sum square of errors
method.

1.2. Description
      Peperomia obtusifolia (fig. 1) 100 plants were divides into
5 equal groups, one for each compost mixture and one for the con
trol. Data on the number of cuttings and knots per plant was   –

taken five times during the 11 months of the trials.

Statistical analysis showed that substrate 4-40% compost and 60% soil - was ideal for this ornamental, giving a larger and more homogeneus production of cuttings.

Comparison of mean values obtained from the 5 data recor dings with those of the control group also showed that the - number of cuttings obtained from the substrate 4 group was the most similar to that of the control.

Noeregelia carolinae tricolor (fig. 2). As plant size was the main interest of this trial, 3 data recordings were taken during the trial period. The desing was one plant/pot with 10 pots per substrate group. The trial leasted 2 years.

Data analysis showed that substrate 3 - 50% compost and 50% soil - produced the largest plants on the most regular ba sis. Graphed plotting was more homogeneus with none of the os cilations obtained from the other substrate groups. Scindapsus aureus (fig. 3).

This is another plant that is produced through cuttings. Its production was studied during 19 months, using the same - desing as for Peperomia obtusifolia.

Data analysis showed that substrate 3 - 50% compost and 50% soil, gave the greatest quantity of cuttings, wich our - goal in this test substrate 1 - 70% compost and 30% soil - was the closest to that of the control group.

Asplenium nidus (fig. 4) leaf size is the determining fac tor for this ornamental, using a standard scale giving nine - sizes, with 1 = smallest and 5 = largest.

Our goal was 3 the production of large and homogenous - fronds; substrate 4 - 40% compost and 60% soil - gave the best results.

REFERENCES
1. Alvey, N.G. 1965. Adapting John Innes composts to grow Eri cas. J. Roy. Hort. Soc. 80, 376-81.
2. Arnold Bik, R. 1970. Nitrogen salinity, substrates and growth of Gloxinia and Chrysanthemum. Mededeling nº. 3 Overdruk - Van: Verslagen landbouwkundige Onderzoeking 739.
3. 1972. Influence of nitrogen. phosphorus and potassium rates on the mineral composition of the leaves of the Azalea varie ty Ambrosius. Colloquium Proceedings nº 2, 99-102 Potassium Institute.
4. Asen, S. and C.E. Wildon 1953. Nutritional requirements of greenhouse chrysanthemums growing in peat and sand. Quart. Bull. Mich. Agric. Exp. Sta. 36, 24-9.
5. Baker, K.F., ed 1957. The UC system for production healthy container-grown plants. Calif. Agric. Exp. Sta. Manual 23.
6. Barry, T.A. 1969. Origins and distribution of peat types in the bogs of ireland. Irish Forestry, 26 (2), 1-14.

7. Bollen, W.B. 1953. Mulches and soil conditions, carbon and nitrogen in farm and forest products. J. Agric. Food. Chem. 1, 379–81.

8. Branson, R.L., R.H. Sciaroni and J.M. Rible 1968. Magnesium deficiency in cut-flower chrysanthemums. Calif. Agric. 22 nº 8, 13–14

9. 1961. Some physical properties of pot plant composts and their effect on plant growth, II: Air capacity of substrates. Plant and Soil 15, 13–24.

10. 1971. The use of peat-sand substrates for pot chrysanthemum culture. Acta Horticulturae 18, 66–74.

11. 1973b. Factors contributing to the delay in the flowering of pot chrysanthemums grown in peat-sand substrates. Acta – Horticulturae 31, 163–72.

12. 1974a. Physical and chemical characteristics of loamless pot plant substrates and their relation to plant growth. Proc. Symposium Artificial Media in Horticulture, 1973, 1954–65 Ghent: Int. Soc. Hort. Sci.

13. De Boodt, M. and O. Verdonck 1971. Physical properties of – peat and peat-moulds improved by perlite and foam plastics in relation to ornamental plant-growth. Acta Horticulturae 18, 9–27.

14. Eaton, F.M. 1941. Water uptake and growth as influenced by inequalities in the concentration of the substrate. Plant – Physiol 61, 545–64.

15. Fruhstorfer, A. 1952. Soil mixture for horticulture. Complete specification, Pat. Spec. 670–907. London: Brit. Patent Office.

16. Gartner, J.B., S.M. Still and J.E. Klett 1973. The use of – hardwood bark as a growth medium. The Int. Plant. Prop. Society, Combined Proc. 23, 222–31.

17. Green, J.L. 1968. Perlite-advantages and limitations as a growth medium. Colo. Flo. Gro. Ass. Bull. 214, 4–8.

18. Holden, E.R., N.R. Page and J.I. Wear 1962. Properties and use of micro-nutrient glasses in crop production. J. Agric. Food Chem. 10, 188–92.

19. Homes, M. V. 1963. The method of systematic variations, Soil Sci. 96, 380–6.

20. Johnson, J. 1919. The influence of heated on seed germination and plant growth. Soil Sci. 7, 1–104.

21. Joiner. J.N. and C.A. Conover 1965. Characteristics affecting desirability of various media components for production of container-grown plants. Proc. Soil. and Crop Sci. Soc. Florida 25, 320–8.

22. Joiner, J.N. and W.E. Waters 1973. The influence of cultural conditions on the chemical composition of six tropical foliage Grower, 10, nº 8 1–2.

23. Kohk, G.C., A.M. Kofranek and O.R. Lunt, 1955. Effect of various ions and total salt concentrations on Saintpaulia. – Proc. Amer. Soc. Hort. Sci. 68, 545–50.

24. Laurie, A. 1931. The use of washed sand as a substitute for soil in greenhouse culture. Proc. Amer. Soc. Hort. Sci. 28, 427–31.
25. Lawrence, W.J.C. and J. Newell 1939. Seed and Potting Composts. London: George Allen&Unwin.
26. Nelson, P.V. and K.H. Hsiek 1971. Ammonium toxicity in chrysanthemum: critical level and symptoms. Comm. in Soil Science and Plant Analysis 2, 439–48.
27. North, C.P. and A. Wallace 1959. Nitrogen effects on chlorosis in macadamia. Calif. Macadamia. Soc. Yearbook 5, 54–67.
28. Owen, O. 1948. The occurence and correction of magnesium deficiency in solanum capsicastrum under commercial conditions Rep. Exp. Res. Sta. Cheshunt, 80–1.

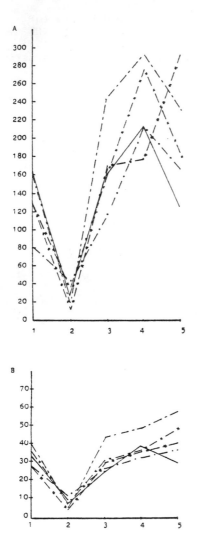

SUBSTRATE 1 — • — • — • —
SUBSTRATE 2 — x — x — x —
SUBSTRATE 3 — - — - — - —
SUBSTRATE 4 — * — * — * —
SUBSTRATE 5 ——————

$$S = \min \sum_{j=1}^{5} \sum_{i=1}^{4} (x_{ij} - x_j)^2$$

x_i = Substrate in study
       i=1,...., 4
x = Pattern substrate
j = Sample
       j=1,.....,5

CASE A		CASE B	
S_{2-5} =	6.384	S_{1-5} =	129
S_{1-5} =	10.627	S_{4-5} =	216
S_{3-5} =	23.305	S_{2-5} =	458
S_{4-5} =	33.037	S_{3-5} =	1.297

CASE A = Number of the knots
CASE B = Number of the cuttings

Scindapsus aureus : This is another plant that is produced through cuttings. Its production was studied during 19 months, using the same design as for Peperomia obtusifolia.

Data analysis showed that Substrate 3 - 50 % compost and 50 % soil - gave the greatest quantity of cuttings, which was our goal in this test.

Substrate 1 - 70 % compost and 30 % soil - was the closest to that of the control group.

Figure 1 : Scindapsus aureus

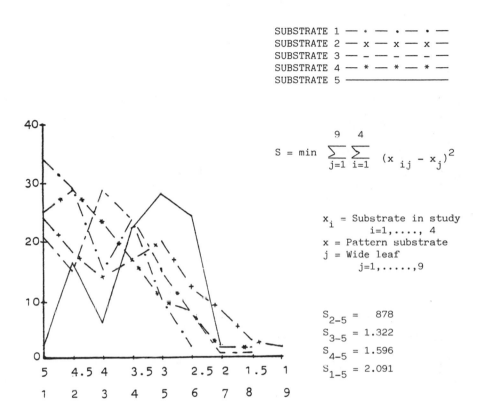

SUBSTRATE 1 — . — . — . —
SUBSTRATE 2 — x — x — x —
SUBSTRATE 3 — - — - — - —
SUBSTRATE 4 — * — * — * —
SUBSTRATE 5 ————————

$$S = \min \sum_{j=1}^{9} \sum_{i=1}^{4} (x_{ij} - x_j)^2$$

x_i = Substrate in study
          i=1,...., 4
x = Pattern substrate
j = Wide leaf
          j=1,.....,9

S_{2-5} =   878
S_{3-5} = 1.322
S_{4-5} = 1.596
S_{1-5} = 2.091

Asplenium nidus : Leaf size is the determining factor for this ornamental using a standard scale giving nine sizes, with 1 = smallest and 5 = largest. Our goal was the production of large and homogeneous fronds; Substrate 4 - 40 % compost and 60 % soil - gave the best results.

Figure 2 : Asplenium nidus

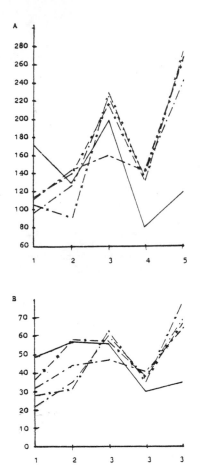

SUBSTRATE 1 — · — · — · —
SUBSTRATE 2 — x — x — x —
SUBSTRATE 3 — - — - — - —
SUBSTRATE 4 — * — * — * —
SUBSTRATE 5 ─────────────

$$S = \min \sum_{j=1}^{5} \sum_{i=1}^{4} (x_{ij} - x_j)^2$$

x_i = Substrate in study
$\quad i=1,\ldots, 4$
x = Pattern substrate
j = Sample
$\quad j=1,\ldots,5$

CASE A	CASE B
$S_{1-5} = 23.827$	$S_{4-5} = 1.251$
$S_{4-5} = 27.099$	$S_{3-5} = 2.016$
$S_{3-5} = 29.801$	$S_{1-5} = 2.416$
$S_{2-5} = 32.019$	$S_{2-5} = 3.290$

CASE A = Number of the knots
CASE B = Number of the cuttings

Peperomia obtusifolia : 100 plants were divided into 5 equal groups, one for each compost mixture and one for the control. Data on the number of cuttings and knots per plant was taken five times during the 11 months of the trial.

Statistical analysis showed that Substrate 4 – 40 % compost and 60 % soil – was ideal for this ornamental, giving a larger and more homogeneous production of cuttings.

Comparison of mean values obtained from the 5 data recordings with those of the control group also showed that the number of cuttings obtained from the Substrate 4 group was the most similar to that of the control.

Figure 3 : Peperomia obtusifolia "variegata"

$$S = \min \sum_{j=1}^{10} \sum_{i=1}^{4} (x_{ij} - x_j)^2$$

x_i = Substrate in study; i=1,...., 4
x^i = Pattern subtrate

j = Flowerpots; j=1,.....,10

S_{1-5} = 496.94

S_{3-5} = 502.21

S_{2-5} = 1,105.10

S_{4-5} = 1,247.69

SUBSTRATE 1 — . — . — . —

SUBSTRATE 2 — x — x — x —

SUBSTRATE 3 — - — - — - —

SUBSTRATE 4 — * — * — * —

SUBSTRATE 5 ——————

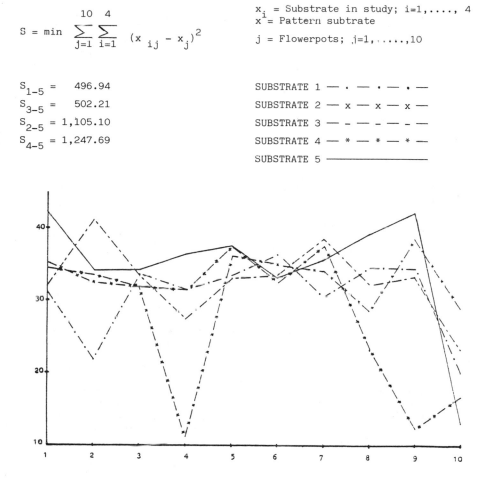

<u>Neoregelia coralinae tricolor</u> : As plant size was the main interest of this trial, 3 data recordings were taken during the trial period. The design was one plant/pot, with 10 pots per substrate group. The trial lasted 2 years.

Data analysis showed that Substrate 3 - 50 % compost and 50 % soil - produced the largest plants on the most regular basis. Graphed plotting was more homogeneous, with none of the oscillations obtained from the other substrate groups.

Figure 4 : Neoregelia carolinae tricolor

COMPOST FOR CONTROL OF PLANT DISEASES

H.A.J. HOITINK, W. CHEN, M.I. TRILLAS-GAY and Y.R. CHUNG
Department of Plant Pathology
The Ohio State University
Ohio Agricultural Research and Development Center
Wooster, OH 44691 USA

Summary

Addition of composts to soils or plant substrates may affect disease
incidence in several ways. Their physical, chemical, as well as
biological properties play a role. For example, large particles
typically present in bark composts, improve physical properties
related to drainage and, therefore, reduce diseases caused by water
molds. Composts that release nitrogen after incorporation, i.e.
composted municipal sludges, may increase severity of Phytophthora
diseases of both roots and aerial plant parts, unless the amount of
mineral N applied to the crop is reduced. On the other hand,
composts prepared from wood residues that immobilize N, may decrease
diseases that are most severe on plant tissues with high N
concentrations. Composts prepared from tree barks also may release
inhibitors of Phytophthora spp. This activity varies with the tree
species from which the bark was removed and can have a significant
effect on incidence of Phytophthora root rots.

   The best appreciated, but perhaps least understood, effect of
composts on disease incidence is that caused by microbial
antagonists. The type and source of raw product, the composting and
curing processes used and the environment in which composts are
utilized during plant growth, determine the spectrum of antagonists
of plant pathogens present. Compost-amended substrates may be
suppressive to one pathogen but conducive to another. Only
preliminary information is available on this subject. The fate of
antagonists of plant pathogens in composts warrants additional
research.

1.1 Introduction
    Composts have been used with beneficial effects in various parts of
the Orient for years (8). But in the West their utilization is a
relatively recent phenomenon. Most of the Western literature on this
subject is on ornamental crops. Only a few diseases of vegetable and
field crops have been controlled with composts (reviewed in 4 and 5).
    Composts may control plant diseases by one or more of several
mechanisms. First of all, plant pathogens, generally, are killed during
composting. Proper management, through turning of windrows so that all
parts are exposed to high temperatures (> 55 C) results in kill of all

but the most heat resistant pathogens. Tobacco mosaic virus is an
example of a heat tolerant pathogen. In small piles, where high
temperatures frequently do not develop, pathogens may be killed through
the activity of antagonists. Bollen (1985) reviewed the fate of plant
pathogens during composting and it is not discussed further here.

Various chemical, physical and biological properties of composts
affect plant pathogens during their utilization. Container media amended
with tree bark have better physical properties related to drainage than
media that contain peat as the only organic component. Therefore,
bark-amended media suppress root rots caused by water molds such as
Phytophthora spp. (reviewed in 4 and 5). Tree barks also release
inhibitors of Phytophthora spp. for some time after potting (3). Even
after these inhibitors are no longer released in adequate concentrations,
Trichoderma and Pseudomonas antagonists, as well as other unidentified
biological control agents of Phytophthora spp., suppress these diseases
(4, 5). These bark-amended container media therefore remain suppressive
to Phytophthora cinnamomi, based on one or more mechanisms, for at least
2 years after potting. However, container media amended with hardwood
tree bark, that has decomposed for years in landfills, are not
consistently suppressive to this pathogen. In the late 1960's and early
1970's nurserymen learned to avoid this variability by preparing composts
from fresh bark only or by using fresh pine bark that does not have to be
composted before utilization. This development was reviewed recently (5)
and is not presented in detail here.

In this article we discuss factors affecting incidence and activity
of biological control agents (antagonists of plant pathogens) in
composts. Much of this information was developed during the past 3 years
and is presently being submitted for publication. Composts may not only
affect diseases caused by soilborne plant pathogens, but also those of
aerial plant parts. The scant information available on this subject is
discussed below.

1.2 Occurrence of Antagonists in Composts
Examples of antagonists isolated from suppressive composts are
isolates of Trichoderma and Gliocladium spp. (13, 14), various bacteria
including Bacillus spp., Pseudomonas spp., and others (G. A. Kuter, P. C.
Fahy and H. A. J. Hoitink, unpublished information), as well as various
unidentified actinomycetes. Most have been isolated from container media
amended with various types of composted tree barks. These microorganisms
are almost ubiquitous. They are typically associated with decaying
organic matter in soils.

Recently, composted municipal sewage sludge (CMS) has become more
widely available for utilization in container media in the U.S.
Composting plants in the eastern U.S. use whole-chipped trees (woodchips)
and/or bark as bulking agents (18). During the tree harvesting process,
logs are dragged over the forest floor and as much as 10% of the weight
of tree bark removed from such logs consists of clay and organic matter
that was scraped up from the forest floor and embedded in crevices in the
bark. This high biomass-content material is mixed as a component of
woodchips and bark into sludges before composting. It is thought that
much of the suppressive microflora occurring in composted tree bark
originates from this forest floor litter.

During composting, the beneficial microflora survives in the outer
most low temperature layer of windrows only. For example, areas in

hardwood tree bark compost piles, after 4 months of composting, with temperatures >40 C, do not harbor antagonists that suppress Rhizoctonia damping-off. Parts of these compost piles >60 C do not harbor microbial antagonists of any diseases, examined so far (Fusarium wilts, Rhizoctonia and Pythium damping-off or Phytophthora diseases). During composting of bark in windrows antagonists recolonize low temperature edges after each turn.

During municipal sludge composting, high temperatures are maintained throughout the mass to ensure kill of fecal pathogens and parasites and guarantee safety of the product. This process could also affect beneficial microorganisms, therefore. During the past 3 years we have examined effects of this treatment process on their survival.

Container media prepared with compost collected from CMS piles cured 4 months, typically are conducive to Rhizoctonia and Pythium damping-off immediately after their formulation. Laboratory assays have shown that these media become suppressive to Pythium damping-off within 4 days but they had to be incubated up to 4 weeks before they were suppressive to Rhizoctonia damping-off.

Surveys and bioassays of CMS media samples collected from nurseries and greenhouses demonstrated that Pythium root rots are suppressed consistently in media amended with CMS (Pythium diseases caused by P. ultimum, P. irregulare and P. aphanidermatum) and losses were not observed. However, none of CMS media samples collected from growers suppressed Rhizoctonia damping-off, unless such media had been stored 4 weeks or more before utilization. On cyclamen, in one greenhouse location where high levels of sanitation were practiced, both Rhizoctonia crown rot and Fusarium wilt developed in epidemic proportions in a CMS medium that was utilized immediately after its formulation. On the other hand, in three nursery locations, where diseases did not develop, the CMS media became suppressive to Rhizoctonia damping-off within 2 months after potting into freshly prepared media. The foregoing suggests that CMS media should be prepared well ahead of utilization. Also, it is now known that specific antagonists can be added to CMS media to render them suppressive to these diseases. The Ohio State University has a U.S. patent pending for this process.

Variability in effects of CMS media on suppression of Rhizoctonia diseases may not be limited to plants produced in container media. Lumsden et al. (1983) found that field soil amended with CMS, did not consistently suppress Rhizoctonia damping-off. However, the treated soil did become more suppressive to R. solani with time.

The foregoing observations and measurements on suppressive effects of CMS media suggest that not only detrimental fecal pathogens but also beneficial microorganisms, such as antagonists of plant pathogens, may not survive the composting process for municipal sludges. This may become more critical as more efficient, enclosed composting plants are built in which both heating and rates of decomposition can be controlled (9). Controlled inoculation with antagonists, therefore, may become a necessity in the future.

1.3   Effect of Compost Maturity on Activity of Antagonists

Composts become more suppressive to Rhizoctonia solani with age. This applies to both the disease and the pathogen (10, 12, 13, 14). Even though the population levels of specific Trichoderma antagonists typically decreases with age of CHB used in container media, the suppressive effect increases. Addition of cellulose to mature CHB that is low in cellulose content increases the Trichoderma population. In spite of this, the disease was increased. Therefore, cellulose content appears to affect Rhizoctonia damping-off severity. This may explain why composts prepared from sawdusts (high C/N ratio) are not or only mildly suppressive to particular diseases (7, 16, 17). It may also explain why media prepared with compost prepared from hardwood tree bark that was excessively high in cellulose content did not suppress Phytophthora root rot of Rhododendron (3).

It is widely recognized that biological control agents are most active over a narrow range of concentrations of available carbohydrates and other nutrients in soils. Mixing of high temperature compost (>60 C) with peat and neutral aggregates during formulation of media, results in stress for the high temperature compost microbiota now incubated at 20-25 C. The stressed microflora may undergo lysis and therefore, release nutrients, thus creating a biological vacuum. Infestation of such container media with an opportunistic pathogen such as a Pythium spp., results in infections and can lead to a rapid increase in inoculum density, in the absence of competing antagonists. To avoid losses caused by Pythium ultimum, media must be stored at least 4 days after their formulation (W. Chen and H. A. J. Hoitink, unpublished information). In summary, container media amended with composts should be stored for several weeks to allow adequate levels of suppressiveness to develop.

1.4 Effects of Composts on Diseases of Above Ground Plant Parts

Soil fertility affects severity of many plant diseases. Some diseases are more severe under high levels of fertility but others are enhanced by chronically deficient nutrient conditions. Phytophthora leaf blight and stem dieback diseases, generally, are enhanced by high levels of available nitrogen in soils (15). Phytophthora dieback of Rhododendron, for example, is severe on plants with nitrogen concentrations of 1.8-2.5% in juvenile foliage (6). Plants with low N concentrations (<1.2%) are more resistant. The disease, typically, is not severe in nurseries on Rhododendrons produced in container media amended with composted hardwood bark (CHB). CHB media immobilize N during plant growth (reviewed in 5). During a survey of Rhododendron plant fertility in Ohio nurseries in 1983, it was found that the mean N concentration maintained in juvenile foliage of such plants as well as in field-produced rhododendrons, where the disease also was sporadic, was 1.2-1.4%. In other nurseries, where predominantly pine bark was used in the container medium for the first time, the disease was severe and the mean N concentration in juvenile foliage ranged from 1.8-2.1%. Pine bark does not immobilize significant amounts of N (2). CMS, from which significant amounts of nutrients are mineralized for 6-8 weeks after potting, including N, also has been used in nurseries for experimental production of rhododendrons. N concentrations established in leaves were >2% and Phytophthora dieback losses were severe.

The effect of compost-type on incidence of Phytophthora dieback of rhododendron is due to differences in rates of immobilization and mineralization of N in media. These fertility problems can be avoided once a case history has been established for each type of compost and after corrective fertility treatments are put into effect by growers. Undoubtedly, other examples of effects of compost applications on disease incidence will appear in the literature as compost utilization in the highly intensive ornamentals industry increases.

REFERENCES

1. BOLLEN, G. J. (1985). The fate of plant pathogens during compost-in of crop residues. Pages 282-289 in: Composting Agricultural and Other Wastes. J. K. R. Gasser, ed. Elsevier Appol. Sci., London/New York. 320 pp

2. COBLE, G. S., and KEEVER, G. J. (1984). Effects of supplemental N on plant growth in fresh and aged pine bark. HortScience 19:127-129

3. HOITINK, H. A. J. (1980). Composted bark, a lightweight growth medium with fungicidal properties. Plant Dis. 64:142-147

4. HOITINK, H. A. J., and FAHY, P. C. (1986). Basis for the control of soilborne plant pathogens with composts. Ann. Rev. Phytopathol. 24:000-000

5. HOITINK, H. A. J., and KUTER, G. A. (1985). Effects of compost in growth media on soil-borne plant pathogens. Pages 000-000 in: The Role of Organic Matter in Modern Agriculture. Y. Chen and Y. Avnimelech, eds. Martinus Nyhof/Dr. W. Junk, publishers. Kluwer Academic Publishers Group, Dordrecht, The Netherlands. 000 p.

6. HOITINK, H. A. J., WATSON, M. E., and FABER, W. R. (1986). Effect of nitrogen concentration in juvenile foliage of rhododendron on Phytophthora dieback severity. Plant Disease 70:000-000

7. KATO, K., FUKAYA, M., and TOMITA, I. (1981). Effect of successive applications of various soil amendments on tomato Fusarium wilt. Res. Bull. Aichi Agric. Res. Cent. 13:199-208

8. KELMAN, A., and COOK, R. J. (1977). Plant pathology in the People's Republic of China. Ann. Rev. Phytopathol. 17:409-429

9. KUTER, G. A., HOITINK, H. A. J., and ROSSMAN, L. A. (1985). Effects of aeration and temperature on composting of municipal sludge in a full-scale vessel system. Journal WPCF 57:309-315

10. KUTER, G. A., NELSON, E. B., HOITINK, H. A. J., and MADDEN, L. V. (1983). Fungal populations in container media amended with composted hardwood bark suppressive and conducive to Rhizoctonia damping-off. Phytopathology 73:1450-1456

11. LUMSDEN, R. D., LEWIS, J. A., and MILLNER, P. D. (1983). Effect of composted sewage sludge on several soilborne pathogens and diseases. Phytopathology 73:1543-1548.

12. NELSON, E. B., and HOITINK, H. A. J. (1982). Factors affecting suppression of Rhizoctonia solani in container media. Phytopathology 72:275-279

13. NELSON, E. B., and HOITINK, H. A. J. (1983). The role of microorganisms in the suppression of Rhizoctonia solani in container media amended with composted hardwood bark. Phytopathology 73:274-278

14. NELSON, E. B., KUTER, G. A., and HOITINK, H. A. J. (1983). Effects of fungal antagonists and compost age on suppression of Rhizoctonia damping-off in container media amended with composted hardwood bark. Phytopathology 73:1457-1462

15. SCHMITTHENNER, A. F., and CANADAY, C. H. (1983). Role of chemical factors in the development of Phytophthora diseases. Pages 186-196 in: Phytophthora: Its Biology, Taxonomy, Ecology and Pathology.

D.C. Erwin, S. Bartnicki-Garcia, and P. H. Tsao, eds. Amer. Phytopathol. Soc., St. Paul, MN. 329 p

16. TAMURA, M., and TAKETANI, K. (1977). Biology and control of clubroot of Chinese cabbage in the Ishikawa Prefecture. Ishikawa Pref. Agric. Exp. Stn. Bull. 9:1-26

17. VAUGHN, E. K., ROBERTS, A. N., and MELLENTHIN, W. M. (1954). The influence of Douglas fir sawdust and certain fertilizer elements on the incidence of red stele disease of strawberry. Phytopathology 44:601-603

18. WILLSON, G. B., and DALMAT, D. (1983). Sewage sludge composting in the USA. BioCycle 24:20-24.

MICROBIAL ASPECTS OF COMPOST APPLICATION IN RELATION TO MYCORRHIZAE AND

NITROGEN FIXING MICROORGANISMS

R. JODICE and P. NAPPI

Istituto per la Piante da Legno e l'Ambiente
(IPLA) Torino

Summary

Some modifications of the biological characteristics of soils due to
the application of composts obtained from different organic raw materials are here discussed. Compost and other organic materials such as
crops residues, straw, farmayard manure increase asymbiontic nitrogen
fixation in the soil. Chemical characteristics of organic materials
deeply influence the process : low C/N ratio, with high NH_4-N level
and heavy metals induce negative effects.Compost application influences directly and indirectly the presence of endomycorrhizal fungi in
the soil and in the plants. Endomycorrhiza presence positively influences plant physiology, especially mineral nutrients absorption. The
repeated applications of composts obtained from lignocellulosic wastes
and sludges on fruit-trees (apple-tree, vine) or on horticultural
crops have pointed out the existence of a tight correlation in the soil
between organic matter and endophyte spore number as well as between
organic matter and the quantity of highly mycorrhized plants'absorbing
rootlets. Several experiences of fertilization using compost are here
stated compared with other cultivation techniques (mechanical and chemical weeding, permanent grass cover) with respect to endomycorrhiza
presence.

1.1. Introduction

The agronomic use of composts is responsible for great changes in the
soil microbial population. The factors leading to such changes are of various kinds, and may depend on the characteristics of either the soil or
the compost. As far as the latter is concerned, great importance attaches
to its chemical compostition, physical characteristics, application doses
and techniques, etc.

This paper examines the influence of some types of compost on the presence and function of two large groups of soil microorganisms that are of
extreme importance in the nutrition of the higher plants : non-symbiotic
nitrogen fixers, and the fungal endophytes involved in vesicular-arbuscular

mycorrhizal symbiosis. It must be stated at the outset that our knowledge
of this sector is far from complete, indeed most of the experimental results have been obtained in research work relating the organic substance
of the soil, sometimes in general terms, to these two groups of microbes,
whereas only a few studies have used composts. The overall picture of the-
oc relations is thus very far from being clear. Attention is devoted here
to what is at present known with regard to the effect of compost on free
nitrogen fixers (diazotrophic heterotrophic) and vesicular-arbuscular mycorrhizae. In addition, some general observations will be derived from
what is known about the organic substance in the soil.

1.2. Influence of the organic substance on non-symbiotic nitrogen fixation in the soil

There has been a considerable development of studies of non-symbiotic
nitroge fixation in the soil over the last few years. In the first place,
it will be recalled that methods for analytical determination of the process have been worked out, and the factors influencing it have been made
clearer. During the last ten years, too, a great boost has been given to
studies of nitrogen bacteria of the Azospirillum genus. Their physiology
and the morphological and functional interaction they set up with higher
plant rootlets have gradually revealed the existence of a powerful effect
of potential benefit to agriculture. An important monograph on these questions has recently been published. (26).

Attention has long been devoted to the role of the organic substance
in the overall process of non-symbiotic fixation. Even so, it is still not
wholly clear. It has been known for many decade that the inclusion of cultivation residues in the soil leads to an increase in free nitrogen fixation. Its intensity however, has been the subject of numerous contradictions, since the process is a function of numerous ambient factors, such
as temperature, humidity, soil pH, the amount of total and mineral nitrogen, etc. In general terms, it can be said that the rate of fixation is
universally agreed to be much higher during the first days of uptake, followed by a gradual decline, as shown in fig. 1.

In effect, the fixing microorganisms, which belong to the heterotro-
trophic diazotrophic group, require organic carbon as a source of energy
and the basic material for protoplasmic synthesis. It has been shown in
vitro that Azotobacter, Azospirilla, Clostridia, etc. can make use of a
great variety of simple carbon compounds, such as glucides (glucose, sac-
charose, etc.), organic acids, alcohols, etc. In unsupplemented cultures,
these nitrogen fixers are unable to metabolise cellulose, hemicellulose
and humic substances with a high degree of molecular weight (5). Addition
to the soil of "fresh" organic matter boosts the number of heterotrophic
microorganisms, leading to the formation of intermediate products that can
be used by the nitrogen fixers, whose population also increases to a considerable extent. The intensity of the process subsequently diminishes as
the carbon source is gradually metabolise. Remacle and Vanderhoven (24)

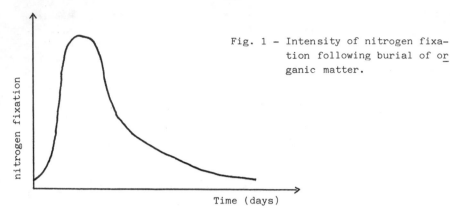

Fig. 1 - Intensity of nitrogen fixation following burial of organic matter.

Time (days)

(24) have worked out the formula relating in a long period the quantity of
nitrogen fixated to the organic carbon consumed shown in fig. 2.

Fig. 2 - Relation between nitrogen fixation and mineralisation of the organic substance.

$$N_2 = N_1 \frac{100 - C_2}{100 - C_1}$$

where

N_2 = theoretical nitrogen content at the end of the process

N_1 = nitrogen content at the beginning of the process

C_2 = Organic carbon content at the end of the process

C_1 = Organic carbon content at the start of the process.

Interesting studies have been carried with the burial of wheat and rice straw, manure, compost obtained from solid municipal waste, etc. (11-16
-3). Experiments under controlled conditions in which cellulosic materials
were inoculated with mixed populations of cellulolytic and heterotrophic
nitrogen fixers have shown nitrogen increases of the order of 6-14 mg per
gramme of substrate consumed. (20) (Table 1).

Table 1 - Fixation yield and nitrogen contribution obtained with cereal
straw.

Fixation yield (range)	6-14	mg N/g
mean fixation yield	5	mg N/g
mean straw production	7	t/ha y
nitrogen fixed	35	kg/ha/y
straw nitrogen content	3	mg N/g
straw nitrogen contribution	21	kg/ha/y
total nitrogen contribution	56	kg/ha/y

If cereal growing results in a mean production of straw of the order
of 7 tonnes per hectare, the microorganisms already mentioned, when inoculated on this straw, can fix a mean 5 mg of N per gramme of dry matter,
that's to say 35 kg N/ha. As straw itself contains about 3 mg/g N, the to-

tal direct and indirect addition to the soil will be 56 kg/hectare, which is about half the mean annual contribution of nitrogen fertiliser. In this connection, it is interesting to note that the Authors find that the fixed nitrogen can be assimilated by the plant to an extent comparable with that of mineral nitrogen. Work is now going on to devise an efficient method for inoculating the straw provided by farming where much use is made of machinery. In addition, Dart (4) is of the opinion that inoculation can be put to wider use in the final stages of composting, when the temperature on heap is relatively low and suitable for the growth of nitrogen fixers. here it will be recalled that some workers have already demonstrated that nitrogen fixers are "spontaneously" present, both in composts and in sludges obtained from the purification of urban waste water (Table 2).

Table 2 - Nitrogen fixers in composts and sludges.

	Nitrogen fixers	
	aerobes	anaerobes
Compost (urban wastes)	$10^2 - 10^3$/g.	$-$ (1)
Compost (urban wastes)	$10^2 - 10^3$/g.	$10^1 - 10^3$ (2)
Sewage sludge	$10^2 - 10^6$/g.	$10^5 - 10^6$ (2)

(1) de Bertoldi et al., - 1980 - Compost Science.
(2) Istituto di Microbiologia Agraria, Torino. (in press)

Evidence that the organic substance influences nitrogen fixation has also been obtained with other substrates, such as manure and composts. Ishac et al. (17),for example, found that application of a solid municipal waste compost with a nitrogen content of 0.5% and a C/N ratio of 21.4 to a wheat crop stimulated the nitrogenasic activity of both the rhizosphere and the soil. Some of their findings are set out in Table 3.

Table 3 - Nitrogenasic activity of the soil and the wheat rhizosphere in relation to amending with fertiliser and inoculation with nitrogen fixers after 30 days of culture (nmol C_2H_4/h/g of soil) (from Ishac et al.).

Soil	Not amended	Fertilised with compost
Control	3,71	4,33
Azotobacter	4,39	4,73
Azospirillum	3,86	4,28
Rhizosphere		
Control	31,43	46,22
Azotobacter	50,00	85,26
Azospirillum	73,58	52,70

This table also illustrates the positive effect of the compost in the presence of the nitrogen fixer inoculum on wheat seeds prior to sowing.

Other studies have made it clear that the amount of nitrogen in the organic substrate is important to the process. In other words: - fixation is stimulated by small concentrations of organic and mineral N (17-28), - fixation is inhibited in the presence of higher N concentrations (or do-

ses) in the substrate. This means that an organic substrate with a low me-
tabolisable carbon: mineral nitrogen (nitric and ammoniacal) ratio is not
a good promoter of nitrogen fixation (5). This inhibition is a general phe
nomenon that is also observed in the case of symbiotic fixation.

Lastly, with regard to the qualitative aspects of the organic substance, attention must be paid to the presence of toxic minerals. A symbiontic
nitrogen fixation is impeded by high soil concentrations of the heavy metals, aluminium and iron salts (5). No evidnece is available with respect
to composts, though it may be supposed that the position is the same.

1.3. Influence of the organic substance on the vesicular-arbuscular mycorrhi- zae (VAM)

This part of our paper stresses certain essential functions of the VAM,
and then comments on their effects on organic substance in general and composts in particular. The VAM are anatomical and functional symbioses between primary plant roots and a group of fungi (class Phycomycetes). They
are found in an overwhelming majority of higher plants, or, to be specific,
the Angiosperms. In this type of symbiosis, the fungus penetrates the cells
of the root cortical parenchyma. This results in an endomycorrhizia, as opposed to the ectomycorrhizia typical of forest plants, where the hyphae always remain outside the cells.

Both partners draw benefits from this association. The plant releases
its metabolic products to the fungus. It has been calculated, indeed, that
about 10% of the products of photosynthesis (mainly sugars) pass to the
fungus endophyte. Factors promoting photosynthesis, therefore, such as light,
temperature and humus, also encourage the symbiosis. The fungus in its turn
enhances absorption of nutrient elements from the soil. This greater efficiency is the result of two factors. The increased length provided by the
hyphae compared with the root hairs alone enables the plant to go beyond
the depletion area that forms about its roots and thus explore a larger
volume of soil. In addition, the smaller diameter of the hyphae permits
better penetration of the soil and its organic substance.

Absorption, indeed, is particularly important in poor soils and with
regard to poorly mobile ions present in soluble form and relatively low
concentrations, such as phosphorus. It has been shown that infested roots
absorb decidedly larger amounts of phosphorus, and the same is true of
magnesium andcalcium (7-25).

Moreover, Tinker (29) has demonstrated that the rate of P absorption
by infested roots is 18×10^{-14} mol/cm/sec. as opposed to only 4×10^{-14}
mol/cm/sec when the mycorrhiza is not present.

When it is recalled that 1 mg of hypha with a diameter of 10 u has the
same length as 1600 mg of roots with a mean diameter of400 u, it becomes im
mediately clear that this great ion and water absorption efficiency is al-
lied cith a considerable saving of energy.

As to trace elements, recent work has equally shown that mycorrhizae
are significantly involved in the absorption of zinc, manganese and boron

(19-13), particularly in soils that are very poor in these elements.

In addition, infected plants are less sensitive to soil water shortage (27). Mycorrhizae improve water absorption by reducing the resistance to its transport, as a consequence of an improvement in the plant's nutrition.

Lastly, Barea and Azcon (2) have shown that G. mosseae, an endomycorrhizal fungus, forms hormones of the gibellerin and cytokinin type. Allen and Moore (1) have reported enhanced activity of gibellerin-like substance in the leaves of mycorrhizised plants, together with smaller amounts of abscissic acid.

It may thus be considered that the mycorrhizae and their symbionts are true integrated biological fertilisers. They share in the establishment of a state of plant nutrition that is definitely more balanced and lead to longer vegetation, thus enabling the plant to remain "younger" and preventing ageing phenomena.

Many factors have a beneficial effect on this symbiosis : light, temperature, organic substance, dampness of the soil, etc. Many others, however, depress it : the excessive use of mineral fertilisers, the presence of toxic metals, the application of some fungicides and weedkillers, and poor aeration of the soil. There have been many demonstrations of the adverse effect of some heavy metals on endophyte growth. Gamin et al. (6) report that the mycorrhizal infection of Glomus caledonicus in fescue was greatly inhibited by a solution of aluminium, whereas manganese was five times less inhibitory.

Gildon et al. (8) found that infection was greatly reduced when onion plants were treated with cadmium, and copper while high doses of zinc and nickel completely suppressed symbiosis and also depressed plant growth.

Salinity, too, has an adverse effect on symbiosis (La Bounty) (18).

The organic substance, on the other hand, can encourage mycorrhizia. As long ago as 1940, Peyronel (23) showed that humus offsets the adverse effect of low light intensity on the endomycorrhizae of some Alpine plants. Other workers have reported that the formation of symbiotic fungus spores and sporocarps is associated, among other things, with the presence of organic substance (14-15). Hayman (10) observed greater development of the arbuscules (the organelles responsible for the mycorrhiza's food exchange) and hence more "efficient" symbiosis in soils with a relatively high concentration of organic substance. Other reports describe more intense mycorrhization in soils with high concentrations of organic substance (12), or supplemented with turf (9).

At this point, one must seek to determine the direct influence of composts on VAM. Nappi and Jodice (21) collected a series of specimens from South Tyrol vineyards in a comparison of three different ways of working the soil, namely permanent grass cover, mulching with poplar bark composts, and mechanical and chemical weeding. The specimens covered an entire year. Consideration was given to both the presence of endomycorrhizal spores in the soil and the degree of root infection (Fig. 2-3).

The results showed that spore were present in higher numbers in composted soils, than in grass-covered soils. and much more so than in weeded

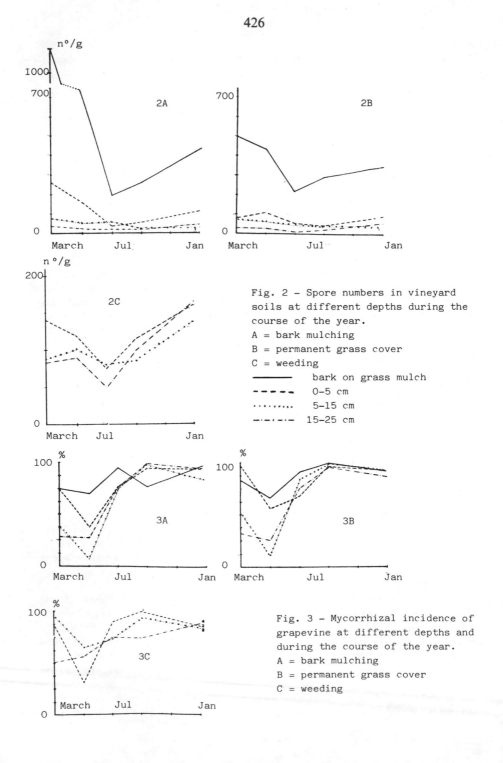

Fig. 2 – Spore numbers in vineyard soils at different depths during the course of the year.
A = bark mulching
B = permanent grass cover
C = weeding
—————— bark on grass mulch
‒ ‒ ‒ ‒ 0-5 cm
·········· 5-15 cm
–·–·–·– 15-25 cm

Fig. 3 – Mycorrhizal incidence of grapevine at different depths and during the course of the year.
A = bark mulching
B = permanent grass cover
C = weeding

soils. It was also found that this increase was primarily confined to the
compost layer. There was a close relation between the number of spores and
the presence of organic substance.

No substantial difference between the three methods of cultivation
were noticed with regard to the degree of mycorrhization. It may be pointed
out, however, that more plant rootlets were found in compost-treated soils,
with the result that the total number of enophytes on the root apparatus
was correspondingly higher. These results were corroborated by a similar
study on South Tyrol apple orchards. Once again, there were more spores in
soils strewn with poplar bark compost (22) (Fig. 3).

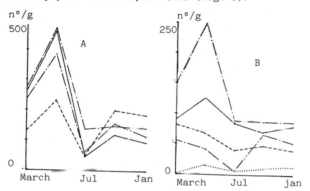

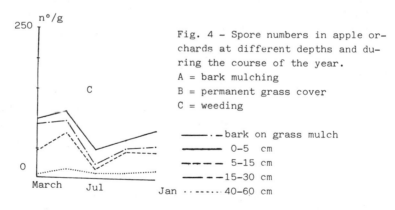

Fig. 4 - Spore numbers in apple or-
chards at different depths and du-
ring the course of the year.
A = bark mulching
B = permanent grass cover
C = weeding

————·—bark on grass mulch
————— 0-5 cm
—·—·— 5-15 cm
— — —15-30 cm
········· 40-60 cm

In a further unpublished study, a layer of compost from grape stalk
and municipal sewage sludges was applied to 2-year-old apple trees. One
year later, there was a marked increase in root growth and fine ramifica-
tion into the humus layer. Examination of these roots also showed a marked
degreenof fungal infection (over 70%). Statistical analysis showed a positive correlation betaxeen the amount of organic substance and the presence
of spores in the soil.

1.4. Conclusions

The organic substance of composts has a beneficial influence on the number and functions of heterotrophic nitrogen fixers and vesicular-arbuscular mycorrhizae. As stated in the introduction, the overall picture of these relations has not yet been drawn. In the light of what has been discovered so far, however, the"quality" of a compost is evidently of importance. By this we mean that set of chemical and biological characteristics which appear to have a more specific influence on the soil microorganism functions discussed in this paper.

Of these, the following deserve particular mention:
- the high amount of organic substance as a source of energy and the basic material for the growth of nitrogen fixers;
- the high amount of humic substances, which promote the establishement of an endomycorrhizal symbiosis;
- the balanced organic C / organic N ratio
- the limited amount of mineral nitrogen (especially NH_4-N); if this is not so, the activity of nitrogen fixers is restricted
- the limited concentration of potentially toxic minerals, especially the heavy metals and aluminium. These have an adverse effect on the function of nitrogen fixers and the mycorrhizia;
- the presence of active and efficient microbe populations, introduced, if necessary, in the form of inocula, such as the heterotrophic nitrogen fixers. In agreement with other workers, we feel that this field must be further explored in the future, since it is one that represents an important objective for soil biotechnology.

REFERENCES

1. ALLEN, M.F., MOORE, T.S. and CHRISTESEN, M. (1982). Phythormone changes in Bouteloua gracilis infected by VA mycorrhizae. II. Altered levels of gibberellin-like substances and abscisic acid in the host plant. Can. J. Bot. 60, 468-471

2. BAREA, J.M. and AZCON-AGUILAR, C. (1982). Production of plant growth-regulating substances by the vesicular-arbuscular mycorrhizal fungus Glomus mosseae. Applied and Environ. Microbiol. 43, 810-813.

3. CHISTYAKOVA, I.K. and KALIRISKAYA, T.A. (1984). Nitrogen fixation in Takir like soils under rice. Mikrobiologya, 53, 123-128.

4. DART, P.J. (1986). Nitrogen fixation associated with non legumes in agriculture. Plant and soil, 90, 303-334.

5. DOMMERGUES, Y. and MANGENOT, F. (1970). Ecológie Micróbienne du sol. Masson et Cie Ed., Paris.

6. GAMIN WANG, D.P. , STRIBLEY, P.B., TINKER, P.B. and WALKER, C. (1984). Soil pH and vesicular-arbuscolar mycorrhiza. In "6th North American Conference on Mycorrhizae". Bend, Oregon, U.S.A.

7. GEDDEYA, Y.I. (1983). Apple mycorrhizae and their effects on growth and nutrient concentration in apple seedlings grown in two soils with va-

ried levels of P. Thesis Ph. D. Oregon Univ.

8. GILDON, A. and TINKER, P.B. (1983). Interactions of vesicular-arbuscolar mycorrhizal infection and hevy metals in plants. I. New Phytol., 95, 247-261.

9. GIOVANNETTI, M. and AVIO, L. (1984). VAM infection and reproduction as influenced by different organic and inorganic substances. In "6th North American Conference on Mycorrhizae" Bend, Oregon U.S.A.

10. HAYMAN, D.S. (1975). The occurrence of mycorrhiza in crops as affected by soil fertility. In "Endomycorrhyzas"Ed. by Sanders, F.E., Mosse, B. and Tinker, P.B.

11. HAGARI, N.A., KHAWAS, H.M., FARAG, R.S. and MONIR, M. (1986). Effect of incorporation of crop residues on development of diazotrophs and pattern of acetylene reducing activity in Nile Valley soils. Plant and Soil, 90, 383-389.

12. HEPPER, C.M. and WARNER, A. (1983). Role of organic matter in growth of a vesicular-arbuscular mycorrhizal fungus in soil. Trans. Br. Mycol. Soc., 81, 155-156.

13. JODICE, R., NAPPI, P. and LUZZATI, A. (1980-81). Influenza delle micorrize vescicolo-arbuscolari e della sostanza organica sulla nutrizione borica del girasole. Allionia, 24, 43-47.

14. KOSKE, R.E., SUTTON, J.C. and SHEPPARD, B.R. (1975). Ecology of Endogone in Lake Huron sand dunes. Can. J. Bot., 53, 87-93.

15. KRUCKELMANN, H.W. (1975). Effects of ferilizers, soils, soil tillage, and plant species on the frequency of Endogone Chlamidospores and mycorrhizal infection in arable soils. In "Endomycorrhizas" Ed. by Sanders F.E., Mosse B. and Tinker P.B.

16. ICRISAT. (1983). International Crops Research Institut for the Semi-Arid Tropics Annual Report. 1982. Patancheru India, 247-257.

17. ISHAC, Y.Z., EL HADDAD, M.E., DAFT, M.J., RAMADAN, E.M. and EL DELERDASH, M.E. (1986). Plant and soil, 90, 373-382.

18. LA BOUNTY, K.L. and MENGE, J.A. (1904). Interspecific competition between Glomus mosseae and Cigaspora margarita. In "6th North American Conference on Mycorrhizae". Bend, Oregon U.S.A.

19. LAMBERT, D.H., BAKER, D.E. and COLE, H. (1979). The role of mycorrhizae in the interaction of phosphorus with zinc, copper, and other elements. Soil Sci. Soc. Am. J. 43, 976-980.

20. LINCH, J.M. (1984). Interactions between biological processes, cultivation and soil structure. Plant and soil, 76, 307-318.

21. NAPPI, P., JODICE; R. and KOFLER, A. (1980-81). Micorrize vescicolo-arbuscolari in vigneti dell'Alto Adige sottoposti a differenti tecniche di lavorazione del suolo. Allionia 24, 27.

22. NAPPI, P. (1983). Influenza delle tecniche di lavorazione del suolo e delle stagioni sulle micorrize VA del melo. Mic. Ital. 3, 39-46.

23. PEYRONEL, B. (1940). Prime osservazioni sui rapporti tra luce e simbiosi micorrizica. Annuario n. 4 Lab. della Chanousia, Giardino Botanico Alpino dell'Ordine Mauriziano al Piccolo San Bernardo 4; 1-19.

24. REMACLE, J. and VANDERHAVEN, C. (1973). Evolution of the carbon and nitrogen contents in incubated litter. Plant and Soil 39, 201-203.

25. RHODES L.H., GERDEMAN, J.W. (1978). Traslocation of calcium and phosphate by external hypae of vesicular-arbuscular mycorrhizae. Soil Science 126, 125-126.

26. SKINNER, F.A. and VOMALA, P. (1986). Nitrogen fixation with non legumes. Plant and soil, vol. 90, n° 1-3.

27. SIEVERDING, E. (1981). Influence of soil water regime on VA mycorrhiza. I. Effect on plant growth, water utilization and development of mycorrhiza. Zeitschrift für Acker und Pflanzenbau 150, 400-411.

28. TCHAN, Y.T. and JENSEN, H.L. (1963). Proc. Linn. Soc., N.S.W. 80, 97-104.

29. TINKER, P.B. (1975). Effects of vesicular-arbuscular mycorrhizas on higher plants. Symp. Soc. Exp. Biol. 29, 325-350.

COMPOST FOR MUSHROOM PRODUCTION AND ITS SUBSEQUENT USE FOR SOIL IMPROVEMENT.

J.P.G. GERRITS
Mushroom Experimental Station
Horst, the Netherlands

SUMMARY

In mushroom growing composting is used as the fundamental process in the preparation of the substrate. The procedures in mushroom growing and composting are described in this paper. Straw, horse manure, chicken manure and gypsum are the basic materials most often used. The main objective of composting is to obtain a substrate homogeneous in physical and chemical respects and which is selective for the mushroom.
The intensity of the composting process is emphasized as well as its relatively short duration.
At the end of cropping a mixture of compost and casing soil remains, known as spent mushroom compost. Its composition, its value as a fertilizer and possible applications are discussed.

1. CULTIVATION

Mushrooms (Agaricus bisporus and A. bitorquis) are heterotrophic organisms. For their nutrition and metabolism C-sources are necessary which have already been produced by green plants by means of photosynthesis. For this purpose straw is used, enriched with N-sources like horse manure or chicken manure. This mixture is submitted to a heating process in two phases. Phase I takes place in the open air or under a roof in large heaps (windrows). Phase II is carried out in a mushroom house (in layers either in shelves or trays) or in bulk in a tunnel. During this second phase the conditions (temperature and aeration) can be controlled.

When the compost is "ready", it is mixed with spawn (monoculture of mushroom mycelium on cooked and sterilized grain). After about 2 weeks the compost is completely colonized by the mycelium and is next covered or "cased" with a layer of casing soil normally consisting of peat and calcium carbonate (in cave growing, for example in France, often only calcium carbonate is used). The mycelium grows upwards in a vertical direction and after about 2 weeks the temperature and CO_2 concentration are decreased by ventilation.

This induces the formation of pinheads which develop into mushrooms. Three weeks after casing the first mushrooms can be harvested. Mushrooms appear in weekly peaks, called flushes. Harvesting lasts for 3-8 weeks. Then the compost is sterilized (preferably using steam) during 12 hours at 70°C. The sterilized mixture of compost and casing soil is further available for agriculture or horticulture as spent mushroom compost.

2. THE COMPOST

In general two types of compost are distinguished (7): horse manure compost and synthetic compost. The main difference is that the straw in horse manure has, in a sense, already been pretreated by the horses in the stable. The preparation of synthetic compost takes more time because the straw used for it first has to be pretreated. In both cases the N content has to be increased to a certain value. This normally happens by the addition of chicken manure. First of all water is added to horse manure during a pretreatment of about one week until the desired moisture content has been obtained. Then the manure is put in long piles (windrows) 2 m wide and 2 m high. This time is called day 0. The windrows are turned mechanically on day 0, 3, 6 and 8. On day 0, 100 kg of chicken manure and 25 kg of gypsum are added per metric tonne of horse manure. In the piles maximum temperatures between 75 and 80°C are achieved. On day 8 the compost is delivered to the growers. One tonne of horse manure yields over one tonne of compost. The surplus mainly depends on the moisture content of the fresh manure.

In case not enough horse manure is available, straw is used (4). To one tonne of straw 700-900 kg of chicken manure, 70 kg of gypsum and more than 5000 litres of water are added. Eventually this yields about 3 tonnes of so-called synthetic compost. In the Netherlands there is less horse manure in summer than in winter, because horses are then kept outside. Up to 50% of the compost produced in summer is synthetic compost. Before the proper composting process the straw is pretreated for 7-10 days, i.e. part of the chicken manure is added and the mixture is watered. The product is mixed with horse manure on day -7 and treated in the same way. It is also possible to work with 100% synthetic compost. This is practised on several farms in France, Italy and the UK. Phase I composting is only practised by large mushroom farms. Smaller farms normally use custom compost produced by large composting enterprises. In the Netherlands all the compost for 850 growers is produced by two composting operations.

3. BASIC MATERIALS

For the production of compost either wheat, rye, barley or oat straw can be used. However, wheat and rye are preferred because they are firmer, maintaining a better structure during the composting process. In the Far East rice straw is generally used. In the USA hay and corn cobs are also used. Several factors affect the utility of the straw such as the year of production, age and the use of chemicals during field production.

In horse manure this variable straw also contains urine and horse droppings. These three components can be present in various proportions. Also, the composition of horse manure depends on the horses' feed, stable system, frequency of mucking, etc. In this respect in mushroom growing a distinction is made between poor manure (with much straw) and heavy manure (with little straw). It is important that manure is fresh and not mouldy. This can only be realized when the manure is regularly removed from the stables.

Other sorts of manure like pig manure can also be used successfully, if they contain sufficient straw. In practice pig manure is hardly even used, because almost all pigs are kept on slurry systems.

In the Netherlands the average composition of horse manure is: moisture content 63% (55-75%), N content 1.3% in dry matter (1.0-1.5%), NH_4 content 0.2-0.3% in dry matter and the bulk density is 375 kg per m3 (200-500). On a dry matter basis this manure contains 54% straw and 46% droppings. This average ratio is derived from the following data. The daily manure production of an adult horse (600 kg) is 6.4 kg of dry matter. Per horse on average 7.5 kg of straw (dry matter) is used daily.

A compost which is optimum for mushroom production is obtained by ad-

ding 100 kg of chicken manure to one tonne of horse manure of the previously mentioned average composition. If less straw is present, less
chicken manure has to be added and if more straw is present, more. The
chicken manure originates from broilers, contains wood shavings and has an
average moisture content of 38%. On a dry weight basis it contains 4.0% N,
3.9% P2O5 and 19% ash. Depending on the composition of the horse manure
the addition of chicken manure can vary between 0 and 200 kg/tonne.

Instead of chicken manure a variety of N sources have been used to
stimulate heating and to obtain a better production. These include materials like malt sprouts, brewers' grains, cotton seed meal, blood meal,
urea, ammonium sulphate, ammonium nitrate and special activators. Some of
these materials are still used. For mushroom production the nature of the
supplements is not so important, as long as sufficient C is available.
However, the quantity of N is of decisive importance, mainly because this
effects the C/N ratio directly.

The mushroom consists of 7-10% dry matter of which only one-tenth is
inorganic. Therefore, the amount of minerals the mushrooms withdraw from
the compost is in fact limited. The numerous minerals in the compost originate either from straw, horse manure or chicken manure. Because of the
decomposition of organic matter the inorganic matter in the compost
increases relatively. Therefore, most minerals in the compost are present
in sufficient quantity and most probably are not limiting factors for
yield. There will also be a reasonable balance between the minerals. As a
matter of fact, animals from which the manure originates also have a certain need for minerals. In case these are not present in their foodstuffs
in sufficient amounts or in the right proportions, they are added.
However, all minerals are excreted again to a great extent and are found
again in the manure. Because the mushroom absorbs more organic than
inorganic substances, the compost contains relatively more minerals at the
end of cropping than at the beginning. There is no experimental evidence
that in a normal compost minerals are a limiting factor to yield.

Although the mushroom contains very little calcium, this element
plays an important role in the compost especially in the form of gypsum.
Gypsum improves the structure and decreases the pH (5).

4. OBJECTIVES

The production of mushroom compost has some special features. Heating
is very intense with high temperatures which are mainly obtained by boos-
ting the nitrogen content. The process is completed within a relatively
short period of time. Ammonia which is still present is removed during
phase II at about 50°C. This is also the optimum temperature for most
thermophilic microorganisms. The objective is to obtain a substrate homogeneous from a physical and chemical point of view and selective for the
growth of mushroom mycelium. This selectivity has microbiological and
chemical aspects (6):

a. During the breakdown of readily available components, heat is released. The mesophilic microflora is replaced by a thermophilic one. If
the temperature is decreased (such as at spawning) a large mesophilic
microflora can no longer develop because the readily available components
have disappeared and the inoculum of mesophilic organisms is limited. The
thermophilic microflora has been inactivated. At spawning a large amount
of (mesophilic) mushroom mycelium is mixed into the compost. This is competitive with regard to the greatly reduced mesophilic microflora and uses
the inactive thermophiles as food.

b. Because readily available carbohydrates like cellulose and hemicellulose disappear there is a relative accumulation of lignin. The methoxyl content of the lignin decreases and at the same time nitrogen is incorporated into the lignin which changes into what is called a nitrogen-rich lignin-humus complex or lignoprotein. During this process the colour of the substrate turns dark brown. This is a kind of humification involving phenolic compounds. Many of these substances have an inhibiting influence on various microorganisms. Once formed, this complex is of low availability, but it is accessible to representatives of the group of the Basidiomycetes, which have phenoloxidases at their disposal. The cultivated mushroom is especially rich in this enzyme. After spawning, this lignin-humus complex is attacked first, the substrate becoming lighter in colour. This is why the cultivated mushroom belongs to the white rot fungi. Later on cellulose and hemicellulose are used as well.

Under sterile conditions mushroom mycelium can be grown in a non-composted substrate as well, but it is expensive to keep large amounts of substrate sterile. It is not necessary to keep compost sterile because it is selective. The desired selectivity, however, can only be obtained by sacrificing part of the dry matter. Breakdown by the microflora has to be restricted because otherwise insufficient cellulose and hemicellulose would remain for the mushroom. Furthermore, an excessive breakdown of cellulose is injurious for the structure of the compost and limits aeration. So it is important to achieve the highest possible selectivity with a minimum breakdown of dry matter.

Table 1 shows some information on quantitative aspects of breakdown during composting and cropping.

Table 1. Losses during various phases of mushroom growing.

	Compost (kg)	Moisture (%)	Water (1)	D. M. (kg)	(Ash + Org.M.)
Start Phase I	1,600	75	1,200	400	(84 + 316)
End Phase I (filling)	1,000	72	720	280	(84 + 196)
End Phase II (spawning)	712	67	477	235	(84 + 151)
Casing	625	64	400	225	(84 + 141)
End of cropping	458	60	276	182	(82 + 100)

This data is an approximation based on 1000 kg mushroom compost with a moisture content of 72% and 30% ash in the dry matter. From the original organic matter, over 50% is decomposed during phases I and II by the compost microflora and nearly 20% during cropping (by the mushroom). About 70% of the original organic matter will therefore be broken down, reason why a compost cannot be used for a second time. On a fresh weight basis half of the compost present at the end of Phase I remains at the end of cropping.

5. CASING SOIL

In general a mixture of peat and calcium carbonate is used as casing soil. If no peat is available loamy top soil or ground vulcanic rock can be used. The water holding capacity must be high. In the Netherlands, casing soil consists of peat (80%v/v) and sugar beet factory waste lime (20% v/v). The latter is a by-product of sugar production consisting mainly of calcium carbonate. The weight by volume is 1,500 kg/m3. Peat is light, so that in fact on a dry weight basis casing soil is 60% ash. The majority of the ash is calcium carbonate. The casing soil is not decomposed during cropping. However, some material can disappear with the harvested mushrooms. The majority of it can be found again with the spent mushroom compost. The proportions between compost and casing soil are 0.4 m3 of casing soil for every tonne of fresh compost. The weight of 1 m3 of casing soil with a moisture content of 60% is about 600 kg.

6. SPENT MUSHROOM COMPOST

The basic materials used in the mushroom industry in the Netherlands are known in detail (Table 2).

Table 2. Use of basic materials for the production of mushroom compost and casing soil in 1984 in the Netherlands.

	Fresh weight (Tonnes)	Moisture (%)	Dry weight (Tonnes)
horse manure	334,000	60	134,000
chicken manure	64,000	40	38,000
straw	42,000	15	36,000
gypsum	13,000	20	10,000
total	453,000	-	218,000
resulting compost	535,000	72	150,000

peat	175,000 m3
sugar beet factory waste lime	45,000 m3
resulting casing soil	190,000 m3

From the 535,000 tonnes of compost produced in 1984, 20,000 tonnes were exported and 515,000 tonnes were used by Dutch growers. After cropping about half of the weight of the compost remains (Table 1) i.e. about 260,000 tonnes. The casing soil represents on additional 115,000 tonnes. Thus in 1984, the total production of spent mushroom compost (SMC) in the Netherlands amounted to 375,000 tonnes. This represents a volume of about 750,000 m3. The production of SMC is closely associated with the production of mushrooms. With this in mind, I have estimated the production of SMC in the other EC countries in 1984 based on their mushroom production levels. Table 3 shows the data concerned.

Table 3. Estimation of spent mushroom compost (SMC) production in the EC in 1984.

Country	mushroom production (x 1000 tonnes)	SMC (x 1000 tonnes)	SMC (x 1000 m3)
France	201*	802	1,600
the Netherlands	94	375	750
UK	84	335	670
Italy	46*	184	370
W. Germany	35	140	280
Belgium	14	56	110
Ireland	14	56	110
Denmark	8	32	65
Luxemburg	-	-	-
Total	496	1,980	3,955

(*including stumps)

Lemaire mentioned a quantity of 500,000 tonnes of SMC in the Loire Valley as being 60% of the total French production (11). This agrees well with the data in Table 3. The total production of SMC in 1984 in the EC can thus be estimated at 2 million tonnes. This quantity will gradually increase in the future.

7. COMPOSITION OF SMC

Most SMC is used in agriculture and horticulture. However, some of the material is dumped locally or used for landfill. For users it is important to know the composition of SMC. For this purpose it is regularly analysed in the Netherlands. Table 4 shows data collected prior to 1983. Some data on heavy metals is shown as well. These were not determined using SMC but earlier, for compost without casing soil during the first flush (1). Thereafter additional organic matter disappears, causing a relative increase in minor elements. In SMC this is partly compensated by the presence of casing soil which contains few heavy metals. Therefore the data concerned can be considered as a good approximation of the occurrence of heavy metals in SMC.

Table 4. Composition of spent mushroom compost (SMC) in the Netherlands (data collected prior to 1983)

	Average	Minimum	Maximum	Number of samples
	(kg/1000 kg fresh weight)			(n)
dry matter	391	285	547	36
ash	188	106	262	36
organic matter	203	127	337	36
N	7.0	4.0	9.0	36
P205	7.8	2.9	11.2	36
K20	9.6	3.3	18.2	36
CaO	51.1	34.3	83.4	18
MgO	2.9	2.3	3.8	16
Na20	2.6	1.4	4.1	8
Cl	2.8	1.5	7.5	13
SO3	13.8	–	–	2
	(g/1000 kg fresh weight)			(n)
Cu	15	–	–	8
dry matter (%) *	37.7	31.5	43.6	22
As*	0.77	0.36	1.40	22
Cd*	0.29	0.15	0.47	22
Hg*	0.030	0.018	0.100	22
Pb*	6.9	4.0	18.5	22
Zn*	64	44	97	22

* data derived from Amsing (1).

SMC is also analysed regularly in France. A survey of the data has been given by Lemaire(11). In this country, compost is either cased with pure marl or with a mixture of marl and some peat. Therefore the calcium content of SMC is even higher than in the Netherlands. In comparison with town waste composts, SMC is a very clean product with few components injurious to the environment.

8. VALUE OF SMC AS A FERTILIZER

Relatively little data is available about the effect of SMC on various agricultural and horticultural crops. Some results have been published (8, 8a, 9, 12, 16, 17), some are only available in internal reports or as personal communications. Lemaire has studied the physical properties of substrates prepared using SMC (11).

It has been generally accepted that SMC is an attractive material for improving soil structure. It has a high organic matter content, few heavy metals and no disease germs or weed seeds injurious to agricultural and horticultural crops.

However, depending upon the nature of the soil and the crop, high calcium and salt contents have to be taken into account. Calcium is present as $CaCO3$ (nearly 70%, from the casing soil), and as $CaSO4$ (nearly 20%, from the compost). The remainder originates from the straw and manure. Calcium may become a problem if SMC is used in crops that need a soil with a low pH. Soluble salts may be a problem in soils that already have a high salt content and in salt sensitive crops. Generally problems with salt in glasshouse crops or potting soils far exceed those in outdoor crops. One of the reasons is that the application rate in outdoor crops is lower and there is more leaching. I will not go into the working coefficients of N, P and K because little is known about them and because they may vary depending on their respective application rates, so that no general directives can be given.

Sometimes ammonium toxicity has been observed after the application of fresh SMC, especially if seedlings or young plants are concerned. This problem can be solved by aging the material. Soluble salts are removed by leaching and some leaching takes place during aging. However, during aging heating starts again, involving the loss of organic matter and thus resulting in a relative increase in minerals including soluble salts. To remove soluble salts small quantities of SMC can be washed. Large quantities can be piled outside in thin layers and leached during a lengthy period of time.

9. MISCELLANEOUS

a. Pasteurisation of the compost with steam at the end of cropping (cooking-out) is recommended to mushroom growers in connection with hygiene. The temperature of the compost has to be kept at $70^{\circ}C$ for 12 hours. This results in a 70-76% reduction in microbial numbers (10). In my opinion cooking-out is not only important for farm hygiene but also for users of SMC.

b. In 1976 SMC was experimentally used in the Netherlands as litter in chicken coops. The results were slightly inferior to those obtained using wood shavings. The variation in moisture content of SMC was particularly experienced as a disadvantage.

c. The potential production of biogas from SMC has been shown to be limited to only 2.7 - 44 litres of methane gas per kg dry matter (2,15). The first figure is about 1.5% of the methane production of chopped straw. This is probably a consequence of the chemical composition of SMC. Only 10% of the dry matter can be converted to methane gas. Furthermore much water has to be added which seriously hampers the final disposal of the residue. In conclusion: there is hardly any perspective for the production of biogas from SMC.

d. Sometimes combustion is proposed for the generation of energy. The potential heat production of SMC has been estimated at 1556 KJ/kg (13). Unpublished Dutch results show slightly higher data. However, SMC contains 60% moisture and about 50% of the dry matter is ash. This means that it has to be dried first and therefore the net production of energy is limited. Moreover, a considerable amount of ash remains and the combustion process is not clean, requiring special action to prevent air pollution. In conclusion: the combustion of SMC for energy production or as a means of disposal offers no perspectives as yet.

e. Once in 1978 a very large heap of stored SMC started to produce H2S. The heap originally measuring 60,000 m3, had been piled to over 10 m high and pressed firmly by the dragline used. H2S production started a year later. In the meantime the volume of the heap had decreased to 30,000 m3 and the height had become 9 m. Neighbours complained and therefore it was necessary to remove the heap. The maximum H2S concentration measured during digging was 4 mg/m3. After disposal of the heap it was decided to prevent large heaps and lengthy storage times in the future. I think it is worth mentioning this incident because the same could possibly happen anywhere where SMC is dumped in large quantities or used for landfill.

f. SMC is often used in glasshouse tomato production. During 1982 winter production several Dutch growers noticed hormone-like malformations in their tomato plants. These were supposed to be related to the use of SMC. Samples of SMC were analysed, but no growth hormones could be detected. As another possible cause residues of glyphosate (Roundup) were considered. In Germany, Roundup had recently been permitted for use in cereal crops just before harvesting. A great deal of our straw originates from Germany. If Roundup is not broken down during composting and not injurious to the mushroom, residues in SMC could still affect plants when SMC is used as a fertilizer. In an extensive trial, straw was treated with Roundup and composted (14). In one treatment a high dose of Roundup was added after composting. Roundup proved to be broken down easily. Table 5 shows some average data.

Table 5. Breakdown of glyphosate during composting and cropping (data in ppm on fresh weight basis).

	Straw	After Phase I	After Phase II	End of cropping
Non-treated	0.2	0.2	0.1	< 0.05
treated	16	1.6	0.7	0.2
extra (after crop)	-	210	97	3.3

Even during cropping, breakdown continued. Tomato plants were grown on the SMC of the various treatments. No malformations showed up, not even on SMC with the highest Roundup residues. It is therefore very unlikely that Roundup was the cause of the malformations. The real origin of the problem has not yet been discovered.

The use of fungicides, insecticides and herbicides in agriculture has to be watched carefully however in relation to possible residues in straw or manure. This is not only important for mushroom growers but for users of SMC as well. I can illustrate this with an example.

In 1965 straw treated with the herbicide TBA was used for the preparation of mushroom compost (3). The mushrooms were not effected at all, not even at doses up to seven times the maximum possible residue following the use of TBA at the recommended rate. However, severe growth malformation was produced in cucumbers planted into the SMC and in tomatoes grown in a mixture of one part SMC to three parts potting soil. The existence of persistent residues is one of the reasons that TBA is no longer used.

REFERENCES

(1) AMSING, J.G.M. (1983). Inventarisatie van lood, cadmium, kwik, arseen

en zink in geteelde champignons (Agaricus bisporus) en compost. De Champignoncultuur 27, 275-285.

(2) BAADER, W., F. SCHUCHARDT & K. GRABBE (1981). Gewinnung von Biogas aus organischen Rückständen. Der Champignon 236, 26-32.

(3) COCK, L.J. & R.E. TAYLOR (1965). The effect of TBA residues in compost on the growth of mushrooms and subsequently on tomatoes and cucumbers. Plant. Pathology 14, 105-108.

(4) GERRITS, J.P.G. (1974). Development of a synthetic compost for mushroom growing based on wheat straw and chicken manure. Neth. J. agric. Sci 22, 175-194.

(5) GERRITS, J.P.G. (1978). The significance of gypsum applied to mushroom compost, in particular in relation to the ammonia content. Neth. J. agric. Sci 25, 288-302

(6) GERRITS, J.P.G. (1981). Main points of a rational compost preparation. Mushr. J. 106, 329-333.

(7) GERRITS, J.P.G. (1985). Developments in composting in the Netherlands. Mushr. J. 146, 45-53.

(8) GRABBE, K. (1984). Die Verwertung von abgetragenen Pilzkultursubstraten als Düngemittel und für die Bodenverbesserung im Gartenbau. Proc. Int. Symposium on Substrates for Mushroom Growing and Cultivation of Pleurotus Species. Budapest 1984, 104-114.

(8a) GUNTHER, J. (1986). Praktische Einsatzmöglichkeiten von Champignonkompost. Der Champignon 294, 29-37.

(9) HENNY, B.K. (1979). Production of six foliage crops in spent mushroom compost potting mixes. Proc. Fla State Hort. Soc. 92, 330-332.

(10) KLEYN, J.G. & T.F. WETZLER (1981). The microbiology of spent mushroom compost and its dust. Can J. Microbiol. 27, 748-753.

(11) LEMAIRE, F. (1985). Properties of substrate made with spent mushroom compost. Acta Hort. 172, 13-29.

(12) LOHR, V.I., R.G. O'BRIEN & D.L. COFFEY (1984). Spent mushroom compost in soilless media and effects on the yield and quality of transplants. J. american Soc. for Hort. Sci. 109, 693-697.

(13) MUSIL, V. (1981). Unter welchen Voraussetzungen kann Kompost Brennstoff erzetzen? Der Champignon 235, 5-14.

(14) NABER, H. & J.P.G. GERRITS (1985). Schade aan tomaten door champost? De Champignoncultuur 29, 51-57.

(15) SCHÄFER, R., K.H. KROMER & J. DALLINGER (1980). Methangewinnung durch Vergärung abgetragenen Champignonkompostes. Der Champignon 231, 5-10.

(16) WANG, S.H., V.I. LOHR & D.L. COFFEY (1984). Growth response of selected vegetable crops to spent mushroom compost application in a controlled environment. Plant & Soil 82, 31-40.

(17) WANG, S.H., V.I. LOHR & D.L. COFFEY (1984). Spent mushroom compost as a soil amendment for vegetables. J.Am. Soc. Hort. Sci. 109, 698-702.

NEW WAYS FOR DESIGN, CONSTRUCTION AND OPERATION OF
COMPOST FILTERS FOR SPECIAL PURPOSES

by Dipl. agr. A. A. ERNST, G + E Design Joint Venture, Aachen and
Dr. Ing. D. EITNER, City of Duisburg, Refuse Compost Plant Huckingen
(Germany)

Summary

The construction and operation of compost filter installations was so far mainly restricted to the classical areas of use in sewage plants, compost plants, rendering plants etc. New investigations carried out by the City of Duisburg in cooperation with the G + E Design Joint Venture group have opened up the field for compost filter application in industry to as far as the treatment of flue gas. New ways of dimensioning have optimized the effectivity and reduced the space requirements simultaneously. The improved design facilitates the construction and operation of large technical installations. Prefabricated systems permit fast establishment of filter installations at low costs.

The possibilities of load dependent dimensioning are demonstrated on examples. To investigate the feasability of the method in special fields, so far not yet covered, a procedure is described that enables a safe and optimized design approach for the installation.

1. INTRODUCTION

The application of compost filters for the decomposition of the contents of waste air, mainly odours, has proved successful in many fields. So far these "classical" areas were places of emission, where organic material is naturally set free (for instance sewage plants, compost generating plants, rendering plants etc.). Meanwhile the compost filter process has been applied successfully in special areas of use, were synthetic organic matter is set free, that is, substances developed during production processes (for instance chemical industry, rubber and plastic processing).

Dimensioning of the installations has so far always been carried out "hydraulically" by computing filter area respectively the load on the filter volume (for instance m^3 waste air per m^2 filter area per hour). Orientation was by out-dated literature and "experience" which of course by todays standards for example due to improved filter material (special compost for filter purposes) is not valid any longer. Waste air composition, existing concentrations or intensities have not been considered. However it appears obvious that with systems based mainly on biological reaction (compost filters) the elimination effect depends not only on the throughput of air volume but to a much greater degree on the concentration of waste air. The dimensioning has to consider the input waste air load. Here a comparison with the technique of sewage clarification seems appropriate : The dimensioning of a sewage plant is not done in relation to the amount of water flowing in, but in relation to its loading (for instance kg BOD_5/d).

2. SURVEY OF THE POSSIBILITIES FOR FILTER INSTALLATION DESIGNS

Future dimensionings of compost filter installations should differentiate between two objectives :
1. the "classical" application (for instance sewage plants, compost generating plants)
2. "special" applications (for instance chemical industry, food producing industry).

The means of application named under point 1 normally require for an experienced planner only knowledge of the waste air composition and of the volume to be exhausted. Then he can design an efficient and economical waste air treatment installation. The most influential parameters of the waste air have to be established for every individual case. Sometimes statutory restrictions have to be considered.

For those means of application as named under point 2. first of all the waste air to be treated has preliminarily to be analysed with respect to its composition and its concentration. Thus first clues about possibilities of biological treatment in compost filter installations may be gained. In case of a positive decision the following procedure is recommended :
- initiating a test programme for pilot trials (establishing of boundary conditions, composting of the filter material, preliminary measures for providing a waste air "suitable for biofilters") ;
- pilot trials (parallel tests under different trial conditions) ;
- to derive dimensioning and operating data from the trial results ;
- prepare design (preliminary and construction design) ,
- completion of the installation according to the requirements (slabs suitable for heavy vehicles, valve controlled sections, operating installations) ;

For unknown application purposes, always pilot trials should be carried out, to provide dimensioning data for large installations. The costs necessary for it are many times less, than those caused through faulty planning. To interpret test results to cases of similar application is not to be recommended in the interest of a safe and economical dimensioning.

After this detour to dimensioning now proposals of proceedings for "classical" and "special" applications demonstrated on practical examples.

3. METHODS FOR THE ANALYSIS OF WASTE AIR

The following methods may generally be applied for the analysis of odour active substances in the air (see figure 1).

Olfactometry is a method to measure sensitively the odour coefficient of waste air in odour units (OU). Chemical/physical measuring methods differentiate between the "wet chemical" method for analysing specifically a certain clearly defined substance and those methods that make use of gas chromatography. Since odour loaded waste air normally contains a mixture of many complex substances the "wet chemical" method has only minor importance. Capillary gas chromatography with a very high solving capacity can be used to separate mixtures of complex substances and identify groups of chemical combinations and even unique substances if the samples are sufficiently concentrated.

The instrument used mostly in this field is the so called flame ionization detector (FID). It enables the continuous recorded measuring of organically bound carbon contained in waste air. If waste air contains a mixture of organic compositions as it is the case in sewerage plants this measuring method is not odour specific nor is it clearly volume proportional. For example, will strong smelling sulfur or nitrogene

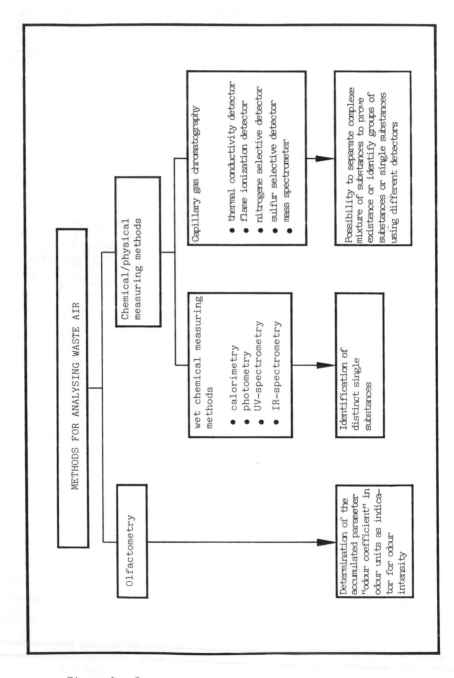

Figure 1 : Summary of methods for waste air analysis

combinations not be registered with the method of measuring the total carbon content, on the other hand will the odour free methane (CH_4) be registered. This fact shows that a direct correlation between odour perceptibility and carbon content is not generally permissible.

Quantification of the remaining concentration in the clean air output of waste air treatment installations enables an estimation of the unpleasantness effect of the odour of a certain single substance. However it seems uncertain how even very small odour concentrations of different waste air constituents remaining in the cleaned air will effect possible odour emissions.

The development in the detector field tends towards selective detectors. Here to be mentioned have for example sulfur selective detectors (SSD) or nitrogene selective detectors (NSD) which enable, as compared to FID, a better evaluation of air, concerning its odour emissions. The identification of single substances is carried out by gas chromatography (GC) combined with a mass spectrometer (MS).

The major difference between those methods described is, that olfactometry investigates odours and the analysing methods describe substances that cause odours including their concentration.

For the following examples have olfactometrically determined odour units (OU) as well as analytically accumulated parameters (for instance total carbon) been used as basis for dimensioning.

4. PRACTICAL EXAMPLES

4.1. Sewage plant with flotation hall for primary sludge thickening

This example belongs to the "classical" applications. The main aim was the achievement of an odour emission reduction by installing a waste air treatment arrangement. Therefore the basis of dimensioning was the olfactometrically determined odour coefficient (OU) of the waste air to be treated.

This sewerage plant worked on primary sludge thickening by flotation. To avoid odour emissions the plant was roofed and cased in by a $1,000\,m^3$ hall construction. A source of main emission within this building was the sump for the floor sludge extraction (approximately a volume of $7\,m^3$). During pumping extremely with odour substances loaded waste air streams were intermittently set free and reached possibly untreated the sewerage plant surroundings via the installed roof fans or through open windows and doors, causing odour molestations.

As is known for all cleaning methods, bumperloadings have negative effects. In this case the suggestion was, to dampen the intermittently occurring waste air out of the pumping sump by extracting and treating the entire waste air of the hall together, meaning that during pumping periods a diluting effect is achieved. The continuous air extraction from the hall offers in addition safety against uncontrolled escape of odour substances from the pumping sump, since the whole hall is due to the extraction subject to a certain underpressure. Furthermore will the working conditions in the hall improve due to the waste air extraction, so that it becomes improbable that someone might carelessly open windows or doors for ventilation purposes.

The following figure N° 2 shows the waste air parameters measured in the emission areas of the flotation hall and the pumping sump.

The osmotic loading of the crude air was measured in the flotation hall to be 437 OU and for the pumping sump to be 5,438 OU. The odour intensity of waste air with such high odour unit values are noticed by the individuum as to be "very strong".

The compost filter has to be dimensioned for maximum load, meaning hall and sump ventilation to operate. The mean odour value for operating is approximately 500 OU.

	Odour unit (OU)			Exterior tempera-ture	waste air tempera-ture	relative humidity
	Z_{50}	s	Z bot lim	Z top lim	(°C)	(°C)	(%)
Flotation hall	437	2	701	272	8.4	9.2	28
pumping sump	5,438	2	9,323	3,239	8.4	11.0	75

Z_{50} : Odour in treshold concentration for half the test persons

s : Standard deviation

$Z_{bot\ lim}$ $Z_{top\ lim}$: Bottom and top limit of the 95 % confidence fraction

Figure 2 : waste air parameters of the flotation hall

For a crude air loading of approximately 500 OU, according to the dimensioning method developed by G + E planning joint venture, the permissible area load should not exceed q_A = 40 m^3 waste air/ (m^2 filter area x h) for a clean air quality of 30 OU. The necessary filter area is 180 m^2.

Unlike the conventional method of pure hydraulic dimensioning of an installation over the area load (volume throughput per m^2 filter area per hour) the preceding case demonstrates a design based on a load determination by considering the odour substance volume. The differences between the two methods and their consequences will be explained in short in a practical example.

4.2. Sewerage pumping station

A sewerage pumping station (spindle drag pump) was supposed to be covered up for exhausting, the compost filter for treating the waste air had to be dimensioned and the following variants had to be investigated.
- completely to cover the pumping station : a large waste air volume, containing a high percentage of less odourous, diluted air, has to be treated.
- partly to cover the pumping station especially the spindles : a smaller waste air volume with a considerably higher content of odour substances has to be treated.

	Dimensioning on the basis of			
	odour loading		air volume	
	cover		cover	
	completely	partly	completely	partly
Odour coefficients of crude air	285 OU	445 OU		
clean air	25 OU	25	25 OU	(25 OU) ?
Throughput air volume (m^3/h)	6,000	3,800	6,000	3,800
Load on filter area $(m^3/m^2 \times h)$	50	30	40	40
filter area required	120	127	150	95

Figure 3 : Comparison of dimensioning

Figure N° 3 shows that with a load dependent dimensioning for both examples the filter area required is almost equal. Using a hydraulic dimensioning substantial differences become obvious. A filter installation for a part cover of the pumping station would be under dimensioned and not able to achieve the required value of 25 OU in clean air, on the other hand would the installation for the completely covered station be overdimensioned, what again could lead to operation disturbances.

4.3. Chemical industry
The chemical industry is doubtless a case of a "special" application. Those plants investigated showed in spite of a similar production range very different emission spectra (see figure 4).

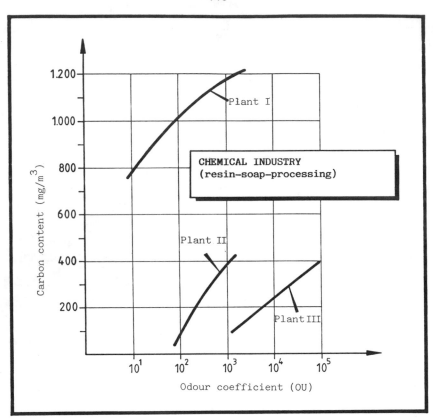

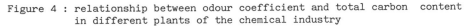

Figure 4 : relationship between odour coefficient and total carbon content
in different plants of the chemical industry

  For example was the total carbon content in plant N° I 1,000 mg/m^3
with an odour coefficient of 100 OU, with this same value plant n° II
showed only 100 mg/m^3 total carbon content, whereas plant N° III has a
similar total carbon content in its waste air as plant n° II but is much
more odour intensive. Values of odour coefficients of over 25,000 OU were
measured with total carbon concentration of 300 mg/m^3.
  The danger of assuming investigation results for similar scopes of
emission to be equal is here especially pointed out, to gain measured proof
is indispensable.
  In the following example the authorities demanded treatment for the
odour loaded waste air developing during the production process at various
places. A large amount of this waste air generated from batch reactions
each of very different constituents and odour loading. For a qualified
design and dimensioning of a major installation first of all half scale
technical tests were carried out.

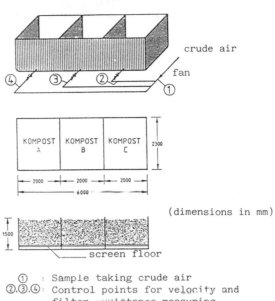

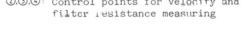

(dimensions in mm)

screen floor

① : Sample taking crude air
②,③,④: Control points for velocity and
filter resistance measuring

Figure 5 : Test set up for biological waste air cleaning in the chemical
industry

Figure N° 5 shows a mobile pilot plant in container scale.

The plant consisted of 3 filter chambers of equal size of 4.60 m^2 each. The intake crude air was distributed in the respective filter chamber by a high performance radial fan through a screen bottom. The design of those filter chambers minimized the uncontrolled leakage of the waste air in peripheric zones. The volume of every chamber can separately be regulated by valves. This test setup enables parallel different experimental arrangements and/or filter materials. In this case the filter material was a "special compost for filter purposes" from Kompostwerk Duisburg-Huckingen.

The effectivity of the setup was documented with different experimental arrangements through crude and clean air analyses in every filter chamber.

The efficiency coefficient (η) is computed according to the following formula

$$\eta C = \frac{Ccr - Ccl}{Ccr}$$

meaning :
 C = waste air concentration (for instance OU, mg carbon/m^3)
 cr = crude
 cl = clean
 η = rate of decomposition or elimination

The samples for the olfactometry were taken by vacuum trap and collected on the site in special receptacles, then they were analysed on the company premises at a more or less odour free place using a dynamic olfactometer (type 1158).

The total carbon content analysis was conducted with an on-line gas chromatograph as well by adsorption to active charcoal and follow-up analysis in a laboratory.

The samples of the crude air could directly be taken out of the pressure pipe leading into the filter. For the clean air sample taking a vacuum trap was fixed to the respective filter chamber, to provide samples out of the clean air current for olfactometric measurements and total carbon content analyses. The flowing direction of the clean air during sample taking was controlled by a thermical anemometer, making sure that intake of atmospheric fresh air could be recognized and thus excluded.

The loading at clean air sample taking is established by a measuring setup with a thermic anemometer out of the flowing clean air current. Only thus assurance is given that the loading, intended for the experiment, does in fact exist at the sample taking vicinity.

Since the effectivity of elimination depends to a large degree on the environmental conditions prevailing in the filter substrate, the filter material has been analysed to its humidity and its organic content (ignition loss), existing at the time of the measuring. According to the task have additional parameters to be checked (for instance pH-value, respiration activity etc.).

The check of these "exterior" conditions of all types of compost to be used is especially important when carrying out parallel tests, because a comparison of the decomposition effect is only possible if the basic conditons were comparable.

loading on filter area	25 m³/(m²·h)		50 m³/(m²·h)		100 m³/(m²·h)	
measuring series	I	II	I	II	I	II
Olfactometric measuring results Explanations : ☐ decomposition effectivity % ▨ Odour units in clean air	99,6 95	98,7 91	99,5 117	98,4 109	99,4 139	97,9 138
Odour units in crude air	25.873	6.654	25.873	6.654	25.873	6.654
water content %	58	59	52	63	57	59
Organic content (ignition loss) %	42	45	40	49	43	45
temperature	16,4	18,3	16,9	17,1	15,3	16,9
filter resistance compost filling depth approximately 90 cm (mbar)	1,0	2,1	2,1	3,4	2,7	7,2

Figure N° 6 shows in accumulated presentation the olfactometric results of the analyses of the compost material in the measuring series I and II. The measuring series were carried out at different times in different currents of waste air.

The substance analyses in hand of the applied compost materials illustrate that due to the minute range of variation of all parameters the decomposition effects of all measuring series are comparable.

The calculated efficiency coefficients stated, were in relation to the crude air loading fed in, found to be very high in all loading concentrations, namely between 97.9 % to 99.6 %. The odour coefficients achieved for clean air too looked quite favourable, depending on the filter area load and the value of the odour coefficients of the crude air fed in, they read between 91 OU and 139 OU. These results are the more notable if one considers the odour coefficients of the crude air fed in, which were between 25,873 OU and 6,654 OU.

The odour coefficients of the clean air mentioned were measured directly at the filter surface. With increasing distance from the filter they will decrease further.

The total carbon content was eleminated to a degree of 50 % to 70 %.

The pilot tests were carried out on the plant premises. The intended waste air treatment is planned to cover finally the whole plant area. Since the other emission areas use the same raw materials, similarly composed waste air as in the test area was to be expected. The carbon concentration was ascertained and the volume to be exhausted determined. The dimensioning of the filter installation now was carried out as follows :
- determination of the permissible carbon content for the biofilter material according to the results of the pilot tests ;
- determination of the maximum carbon loading from all emission areas ;
- estimation of the biofilter material volume necessary ;
- determination of the fill depth for the material ;
- determination of the filter area ;
- estimation of the filter area loading and review of the cleaning effectivity achievable according to the test results with concern to the odour intensity.

Accordingly for the described example a filter area of 170 m^2 was required for a total air current of approximately 4,500 m^3/h.

The example shows a feasible combination of the two dimensioning possibilities :
- pilot tests
- measuring of the waste air concentration as basis for loading related dimensioning.

5. REFERENCES FOR THE CONSTRUCTION AND OPERATION OF COMPOST FILTER INSTALLATIONS

With the original design, the so called "gravel bed filters" the air intake was effected through perforated pipes, which for a better air distribution were covered by a gravel layer. The filter material was placed on top of the gravel layer with 1.0 m filling depth. This design has the following disadvantages :
- non rideability of the installations substructure ;
- costly maintenance ;
- insufficient air distribution ;
- development of reduction zones ;
- missing possibility for visual control of the air distribution system ;
- danger of blockages ;
- drainage of the installation runs separately ;
- high aero-dynamic resistances.

The non existent rideability of the installation substructure considerably obstructs a proper placing and removal of the material. At large installations for this purpose excavators, conveyors or similar have to be provided, whilst in cases of rideable slab floors the employment of a frontloader is sufficient.

The necessary distance between pipe axes and the pointlike cone-shaped spreading of the air favour an insufficient air distribution and thus the development of reduction zones, as is demonstrated in the following figure N° 7.

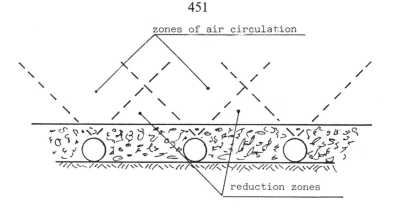

zones of air circulation

reduction zones

Figure 7 : Developments of reduction zones in conventional gravel bed filter installations

The new developments in the sector of filter installation constructions does not only allow for pretreatment measures of the waste air (for instance dust separation, correction of the temperature, moistening of the waste air) but also for the treatment of seepage water. A respective system will in the following be described in short, namely the SIEBO-Stein system (precast concrete block). It shows the following advantages :
- standardized system programme that is sufficiently flexible in cases of topographical defiles ;
- synchronized construction material of all system modules (purpose made blocks, connection pieces etc.) ;
- integrated drainage and irrigation systems of precast blocks ;
- simple and fast installation due to easy to handle system precast blocks;
- high standard of quality of the precast blocks due to continuous quality control at the manufacturers ;
- adaptation of the construction materials to the waste air composition.
The floor slab of the installation consists of ventilating blocks, especially designed for the biofilter construction (see figure N° 8).
Due to the arrangement of multiple slots in a staggered order has been made certain, that an area covering air intake is possible. No reduction zones develop. The slabs are rideable so material placing and removing may be carried out by mechanized means. The air-hydraulic layout of the installation is designed and controlled to enable the shutdown of certain slab sections for necessary maintenance work, whilst the remaining sections are operated. The whole air distribution system may simultaneously be used as drainage system. Installations of this type are already in use for the waste air treatment in sewage plants, refuse utilization plants, refuse incineration plants and in the chemical industry.

6. FUTURE PROSPECTS
The method of using compost filters for the biological treatment of waste air is compared to other possibilities a very cost saving solution. Its possible application should therefore be envisaged for cases so fare not under discussion. The execution of pilot tests in half scale is

recommended. The pilot tests will provide for the individual case the basic parameters for dimensioning and designing the installation.

The dimensioning has always to be load related. For the construction of compost filter installations always the newest state of the art should be considered. Here it is recommended to install rideable floor slabs for example according to the SIEBO-STEIN system, which provides the advantages of an integrated
- pretreatment of the waste air,
- irrigation and drainage of the installation,
- measuring and control technique.

Using prefabricated system elements that kind of installation can be realized fast and to favourable expenditures.

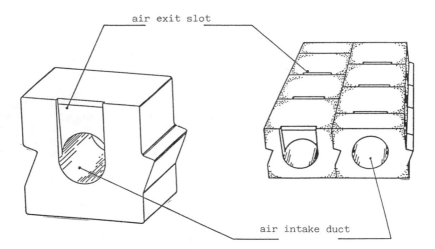

air exit slot

air intake duct

Figure 8 : Compost filter installation, system SIEBO-Stein

ORGANIC WASTES AS SOIL AMENDEMENTS FOR THE RECLAMATION OF EGYPTIAN SANDY SOILS

(I)- EFFECTS OF DIFFERENT COMBINATIONS OF ORGANIC WASTES.

N. SALEM*   M.VERLOO   &   M. DE BOODT

Faculty of agriculture, State Univ. Ghent, Ghent, Belgium

A greenhouse pot experiment was conducted using an Egytian sandy soil to study the effect of Farmyard manure (FYM), Sewage sludge (S.S), Rice straw (R.S) and a combination of FYM + R.S & S.S + R.S on dry matter yield and nutrient element uptake of corn maize.

Application of FYM at a rate of 2% with or without mineral fertilization decreased the dry matter yield, due to excessive salinity. In the contrary application of S.S and /or R.S combined with mineral fertilization increased the dry matter yield, while in absence of mineral fertilizers, application of S.S at a rate of 2% reduced the dry matter yield. A yellowish colouration of the leaves was observed at rate of 2% R.S, indicating a nitrogen deficiency.

The dry matter yield was increased with application of the following combinations FYM 1.5% + R.S 0.5%, FYM 1% + R.S 1% and FYM 0.5% + R.S 1.5%. The maximum yield was observed within application of S.S 1% + R.S 1% and S.S 0.5% + R.S 1.5%.

FYM had a greater influence on the electrical conductivity (Ece) than S.S. The relation between dry matter yield,N,P,K,Fe,Zn,Mn, and Cu concentration in the plant varies strongly with the chemical composition of different organic materials.

1. INTRODUCTION

Sandy soils cover vast areas in Egypt. These soils are generally poor in respect to their physical properties, soil-plant-relationship and their nutrient economy. The nutrient applied to these soils are subject to loss with irrigation water.

Fertilization of these soils is a necessary practice. Responses to organic and inorganic fertilizer is usually obtained. Organic matter is very important for the structure of soils, water properties and retention and release of nutrient elements. Soils rich in organic matter are recognized as fertile, because of the constantly release of the nutrients during the time of decompositions (ref.3).

The aim of this study is to investigate the effect of FYM, S.S, R.S and different combination of FYM + R.S and S.S + R.S on some physico-chemical properties in relation to the nutrient element uptake by plants.

----

* The perminant address: Soils & Water uses, National Research Centre(NRC) Dokki, Cairo, Egypt.

2. MATERIALS and METHODS

2.1. Materials

A. The soil sample

An Egyptian sandy soil was collected from the Southeren Sector of Tahrir. It has the following characteristics:$CaCO_3$ content 0.73%, organic matter 0.16 %, and pH (1/5) 8.8. The soil was throughly mixed, air dried, and passed through 2 mm sieve. The chemical analysis is presented in table (I).

B. The organic materials

Farmyard manure (FYM), Sewage Sludge (S.S) and Rice Straw (R.S) are used. The chemical analysis and some characterization of these organic materials are presented in tables (I) and (II).

C. Soil treatments

The soil treatments can be presented as follows:

- Control
- Soil + FYM or SS at a rate of 2% + R.S at a rate of 0.00 %   (1)
-    "   "   "   "   1.50% + "   "   0.50 %   (2)
-    "   "   "   "   1.00% + "   "   1.00 %   (3)
-    "   "   "   "   0.50% + "   "   1.50 %   (4)
-    "   "   "   "   0.00% + "   "   2.00 %   (5)

2.2. Experimental details

A green house pot experiment was conducted in three replicates for each treatment. Corn maize (Zea mays L) is chosen as indicator plant. Approximately one and half kg of soil sample was mixed throughly with the different combinations of the organic materials, as explained above. Each pot received half doses of the nutrient elements before cultivation and was equilibrated for 15 days at 50 % of its water holding capacity. After equilibration, 5 grains of corn maize were placed in each pots, and after emergence, thinned to 3 per pot. At the end of experiment each pot recieved as total the following amounts of nutrients:
875 mg NH_4NO_3, 375 mg KH_2PO_4 and 115.8 mg K_2SO_4. After 6 weeks the plants were harvested by cutting the stem just above the soil level. The plant samples were placed in paper bags dried at 60°C for at least 48 hours, dry weights were taken. The dried plants were ground in a stainless steal mill to pass through a 1 mm sieve and kept in plastic containers for analysis. The rest of the soil in the pots were collected to determine the electrical conductivity.

2.3. Method of analysis:

Sample preparation, plant analysis, and methodology used are described by (Cottenie et al ref. 4)

3. RESULTS AND DISCUSSION

The effect of different combinations of FYM + R.S and S.S + R.S on dry matter yield (DMY) bulk density (BD and Electrical Conductivity (Ece) are presented in fig 1 and 2, where as the net effect of these combinations on nutrient elements concentration and uptake by plant are given in tables   III, IV, V and VI.

3.1. Dry matter Yields

As general results, the dry matter yields increased in all treatments recieving rice straw with or without farmyard manure or/sewage sludge. These increases were higher than in the pots with the application of farmyard manure or sewage sludge at a rate of 2 %.

Another intresting point is that the application of farmyard manure at a rate of 2 % besides the nutrient elements solution decreased the dry matter yield by 56.8 % relative to the control. Whereas application of sewage sludge at a rate of 2 % besides the nutrient solution insignificantly increased the dry matter yield by 9.06 % over the control. These results can be explained as follows:

- Decrease of the dry matter yield in the cas of 2 % farmyard manure beside the nutrient element solution is mainly due to the higher salinity occurring in this treatment (see fig 1). The electrical conductivity is upto 6.6 mS.cm^{-1} , which is enough to decrease the yield of corn maize by 64 % (ref.2). The results are in agreement with the observation of many authors (ref 5, 6, 8 and 1?).

The electrical conductivity increased upto 1.65 mS.cm^{-1} with the application of both sewage sludge beside the nutrient element solution. This is enough to decrease the dry matter yield by 4 % (ref 2), the dry matter yield in this test increased by 9.06 % over the control. This could be due to the lower bulk densit of the treated soil. The bulk density decreased from 1.75 g cm^{-3} in the control to 1.639 g.cm^{-3} in this treatment. Similar results were obtained by many investigators (ref 7,10, 13 and 14).

- Addition of rice straw with FYM/or S.S, increased the dry matter yield owing to serveral reasons:

1- decreasing the bulk density relative to control. The figs (1) and (2) are ronocquently showing a structure improvement (ref 1)

2- presence of rice straw needed more water to enhance the biological activity necessary for decomposition (60 % moisture content).Each gram of rice straw needs 1.5 g of water (ref.11), it was found that O_2-consumption and CO_2-production increased with increasing moisture content from 10 % upto 17 % by weight. This means an adequate amount of water was supplied which was needed to leach part of the salts from the root zone specially in the begining of germination.

3- more potassium has been added through addition of rice straw. (see table I).

3.2. The concentration and uptake of nutrient elements

The concentration of an element in the plant tissues decreased or increased due to a change in environmental conditions, which could

456

be addition of inorganic and organic materials and water to soil, as well
as temperature, light etc., (ref 9).

From the data obtained (figures 1 to 16), it is evident that organic
matter applications decreased the bulk density, changed the electrical
conductivity and improved the nutritional status of the soil. As a result
of this, dry matter yield, nutrient element concentrations and uptake by
plants are changed.

In case of farmyard manure & rice straw treatments,it is observed that:
- P, Fe and Cu showed a decrease in concentration, this could be due to
  the fact that, the relative rate of dry matter accumulation increases
  more rapidly than the rate of nutrient accumulation (dilution effect)
  as a consequence of organic matter application.

- Application of FYM + R.S increased both the dry matter yield and the
  K and Mn concentration(Synergism effect ref.9) see table (VII). However
  with the application of FYM at rate of 2 %, the dry matter yield was
  decreased but the concentration of the elements increased (concentration
  effect ref.9).

- N and Zn showed a dilution effect when rice straw was applied,this
  could be due in the case of nitrogen to the immobilization of this
  element and in the case of Zn due to the increasing of dry matter yield.

In case of sewage sludge & rice straw treatments:
- N, P, Fe and Cu showed a decrease in concentration in the tissue of the
  plant with increasing dry matter yield as a result of organic matter
  application (dilution effect), see table (VII).
- K, Zn and Mn show a synergism effects due to the increasing of both dry
  matter yield and uptake of the plant as a consequence of the higher K
  content (rice straw) and zinc & manganese (sewage sludge), see table
  (VII).

The different behaviour of the elements in the plant can be summerized
in table (VII), using the symboles methods described by Jarrel and Baverly
(ref.9)

4. REFERENCES

1. BISWASS,T.D. JAIN, B.L., and MANDAL S.C (1971). Cumulative effect of
    different levels of manures on the physical properties of soil
    J. Ind.Soc. Soil Sci., 19: (31-37)
2. CARTER D.L. , (1981) Saline and sodic soils, Principles-Dynamic-
    Modeling Bresler et al., Ed. 1982, PP (175)
3. CHENG, B.T. (1976) Soil organic matter as a plant nutrient. IAEA-SM-
    211/59: (31-39)
4. COTTENIE,A., VERLOO, M.,KIEKENS,L., VELGHE,G.and CAMERLYNCK,R.(1982)
    Chemical analysis of plant and soils.
5. EPESTIEN,E., TAYLOR,J.M., CHANEY, R.L.(1976) Effect of sewage sludge
    and sludge compost applied to soil on some physical and chemical
    properties.J. Environ.Qal.5:(422-426)
6. GUIDI G.,PAGLIAI,M. and GIACHETTI,M. (1981) Modification of some
    physical and chemical soil properties following sludge and compost
    applications. Proc.,Seminar: The influence of sewage sludge applica-
    tion on physical and biological properties of soils. Catroux et al.

Ed.,PP(122-133). D.Reidal publishing Co.
7. HALL,J.E. and COKER E.C. (1981) Some effects of sewage sludge on soil physical conditions and plant growth. Proc. Seminar: The influence of sewage-sludge application on physical and biological properties of soils. Catroux et al.,PP(43-61). D.Reidal publishing Co.
8. HENRICHS,D.C., MAZURAK A.P and SWANSON N.P(1974).Effect of effluent from beef feedlots on the physical and chemical properties of soil. Soil Sci.Soc.Amer.Proc., 38:(661-663)
9. JARRELL W.M. and BEVERLY R.B.(1981) The dilution effect in plant nutrition studies Adv.Agron.,34:(197-224)
10. PAGLIAI M., GUIDI G., LAMARCA M., GIACHETII M., and LUCKMANTE(1981) Effect of sewage sludge and compost on soil porosity and aggregation J.Environ.,Qual.,10:(556-561)
11. SALEM N.,VERDONCK O.,and DE BOODT M.,(1985)Comparative studies on the effect of soil conditioners on the biological activity of organic wastes
12. TIARKS A.E., MAZURAK A.P. and CHESNIN L. (1974). Physical and chemical properties of soil associated with heavy applications of manure from cattel feedlots Soil Sci.Soc.Amer.Proc. 38:(826-830)
13. WEI Q.F.,LOWERY B.,and PETERSON A.E.(1985)Effect of sludge application on physical properties of a silty clay loam soil.J.Environ.Qual.14:(178-180)
14. ZWARICH M.A., and MILLS J.G.(1979) Effects of sewage sludge application on the heavy metal content of wheat and forage crops. Cand J. Soil Sci. 59:(231-239)

Table (I). Total chemical analysis of Egyptian soil and the organic materials

	N	P	Na	K	Ca	Mg	Fe	Zn	Mn	Cu
	mg/100 g						µg/g			
Sandy soil	6.65	85.70	6.68	14.56	197.62	94.07	2342	7.05	72.8	2.53
F.Y.M.	1358	481.4	538	2668	1779	744.4	3965	241.4	176.4	50.0
S.S.	2366	394.5	83.3	149	5393.2	504.8	10905	1397	211.6	367.2
R.S.	435	76.1	512	1947	3106.1	410.5	263	323	279.8	1.87

Table (II) Some chemical characteristics of organic materials

	Ece 1/20	pH 1/20	O.C %	N %	C/N
F.Y.M.	3.43	8.50	20.48	1.358	15.08
S.S	1.20	7.70	31.66	2.366	13.38
R.S	2.45	7.70	44.78	0.435	102.94

Table (III) Effect of combined FYM & R.S on nutrient elements concentration

	N	P	K	Fe	Zn	Mn	Cu
	mg/100 g			μg/g			
Control	2994.48	458.43	2304.94	122.46	53.32	41.01	29.76
Soil+FYM 2%+R.S 0.0%	3888.21	449.16	6837.43	85.32	54.96	94.66	11.67
" "1.5% " 0.05%	3149.94	421.25	5994.47	118.76	57.12	92.17	20.23
" 1.0% " 1.00%	2258.59	432.86	5675.24	86.59	39.64	81.53	17.61
" 0.5% " 1.50%	1503.97	376.08	4845.78	81.59	36.41	61.68	18.59
" 0.0% " 2.00%	1269.84	372.65	4849.26	78.05	25.52	70.09	17.50

Table (IV) Effect of combined FYM & R.S on nutrient element uptake by plant

	N	P	K	Fe	Zn	Mn	Cu
	mg/pot			μg/ pot			
Control	245.64	38.91	195.10	1042.52	436.89	356.47	263.04
Soil+FYM 2%+R.S 0.0%	142.37	16.33	250.70	306.49	200.90	364.67	42.37
" "1.5% " 0.5%	279.95	37.64	538.30	1066.3	505.47	821.30	179.32
" "1.0% " 1.0%	217.69	41.90	548.31	834.96	382.71	787.74	170.82
" "0.5% " 1.5%	180.56	45.29	582.94	979.50	438.37	741.85	224.08
" "0.0% " 2.0%	137.72	40.47	523.96	849.85	287.27	760.71	189.72

Table (V) Effect of combined S.S &R.S on nutrient elements concentration

	N	P	K	Fe	Zn	Mn	Cu
	mg/100 g			μg/g			
Control	2994.18	458.43	2304.94	122.46	53.32	41.01	29.76
Soil+S.S 2%+R.S 0.0%	2770.89	252.93	2193.48	92.41	84.89	39.65	25.14
" "1.5% " 0.5%	2843.82	294.44	3002.08	94.59	80.30	59.98	20.45
" "1.0% " 1.0%	2222.90	349.58	3527.27	117.56	68.52	58.52	22.82
" "0.5% " 1.5%	1710.93	352.32	4212.91	109.21	55.09	54.76	19.71
" "0.0% " 2.0%	1269.84	272.63	4849.26	78.05	25.52	70.09	17.50

Table(VI) Effect of combined S.S & R.S on nutrient element uptake by plant

	N	P	K	Fe	Zn	Mn	Cu
	mg/pot			μg/pot			
Control	245.64	38.9	195.10	1042.52	436.89	356.47	263.04
Soil+S.S 2.0%+R.S 0.0%	255.00	23.31	201.59	853.30	784.04	365.26	203.75
" " 1.5% " 0.5%	275.94	28.54	290.67	917.05	778.96	581.49	199.37
" " 1.0% " 1.0%	305.09	48.39	489.40	1621.91	957.15	806.08	317.38
" " 0.5% " 1.5%	273.91	56.59	676.30	1745.78	882.87	875.85	316.09
" " 0.0% " 2.0%	137.7	40.47	523.81	849.85	287.27	760.71	189.72

	N	P	K	Fe	Zn	Mn	Cu
	U Y C̄ R	U Y C̄ R	U Y C̄ R	U Y C̄ R	U Y C̄ R	U Y C̄ R	U Y C̄ R
Soil +FYM 2.0%+R.S 0.0%	↓↓↑c	↓↓↑a	↓↓↑c	↓↓↓a	↓↓↑c	↓↓↑c	↓↓↓a
" ,, 1.5% ,, 0.5%	↑↑↑s	↑↓↓d	↑↑↑s	↑↑↑d	↑↑↑s	↑↑↑s	↓↑↓d
" ,, 1.0% ,, 1.0%	↑↑↑d	↓↑↑d	↑↑↑s	↓↑↓d	↓↑↓d	↑↑↑s	↓↑↓d
" ,, 0.5% ,, 1.5%	↓↑↓d	↑↑↓d	↑↑↑s	↑↑↑d	O↑↑d	↑↑↑s	↓↑↓d
" ,, 0.0% ,, 2.0%	↓↑↓d	↓↑↓d	↑↑↑s	↓↑↓d	↓↑↓d	↑↑↑s	↓↑↓d
Soil+S.S 2.0%+R.S 0.0%	↑↑↑d	↓↑↓d	↑↑↑d	↓↑↓d	↑↑↑s	↑↑↑d	↓↑↓d
" ,, 1.5% ,, 0.5%	↑↑↑d	↓↑↓d	↑↑↑s	↑↑↑d	↑↑↑s	↑↑↑s	↓↑↓d
" ,, 1.0% ,, 1.0%	↑↑↑d	↓↑↓d	↑↑↑s	↑↑↑d	↑↑↑s	↑↑↑s	↑↑↑d
" ,, 0.5% ,, 1.5%	↑↑↑d	↓↑↓d	↑↑↑s	↑↑↑d	↑↑↑s	↑↑↑s	↑↑↑d
" ,, 0.0% ,, 2.0%	↓↑↓d	↓↑↓d	↑↑↑s	↓↑↓d	↓↑↓d	↑↑↑s	↓↑↓d

Table (VII) General representation of changes in total elemental accumulation (U), dry matter yield (Y) and concentration (C⁻) as affected by different combinations of organic wastes.

↑ : significantly increased
↓ : significantly decreased
O: no change
⊥ : insignificantly increased
⊤ : insignificantly decreased

a : antagonism effect
s : synergism effect.
d : dilution effect
c : concentration effect
R : response

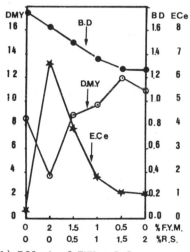

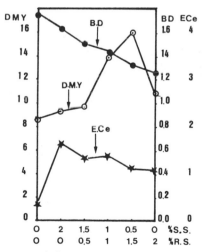

Fig (1) Effect of FYM + R.S on dry matter yield (DMY g/pot), electrical conductivity (Ece mS.cm⁻¹) and bulk density (B.D g.cm⁻³).

Fig (2) Effect of S.S + R.S on dry matter yield (DMY g/pot), electrical conductivity (Ece mS.cm⁻¹) and bulk density (B.D g.cm⁻³).

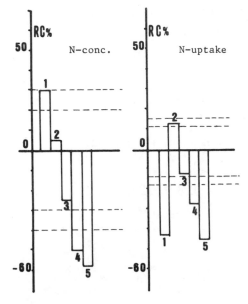

Fig (3) Effect of FYM + R.S on N-concentration and uptake by plant.

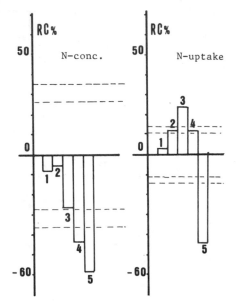

Fig (4) Effect of S.S + R.S on nitrogen concentration and uptake by plant.

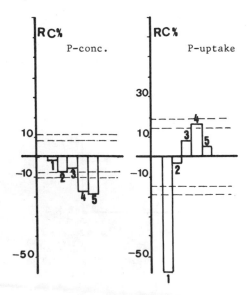

Fig (5) Effect of FYM + R.S on P-concentration and uptake by plant.

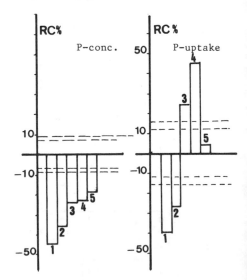

Fig (6) Effect of S.S + R.S on P-concentration and uptake by plant.

461

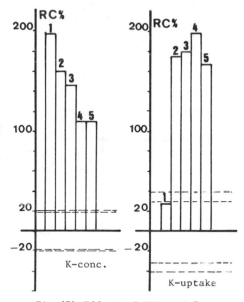

Fig (7) Effect of FYM + R.S on
K-concentration and uptake by
plant.

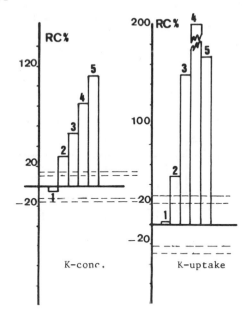

Fig (8) Effect of S.S + R.S on
K-concentration and uptake
by plant.

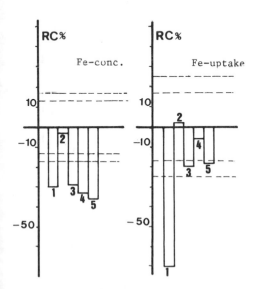

Fig (9) Effect of FYM + R.S on
Fe-concentration and uptake
by plant.

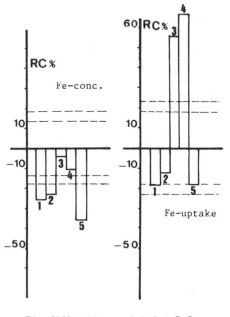

Fig (10) Effect of S.S + R.S
on Fe-concentration and uptake
by plant.

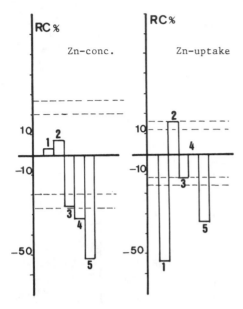

Fig (11) Effect of FYM + R.S
on Zn-concentration and uptake
by plant.

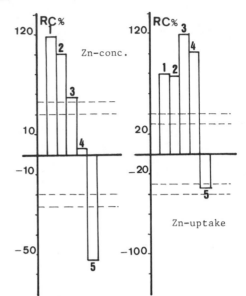

Fig (12) Effect of S.S + R.S
on Zn-concentration and uptake
by plant.

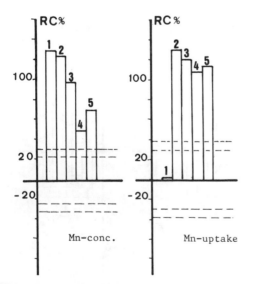

Fig (13) Effect of FYM + R.S
on Mn-concentration and uptake
by plant.

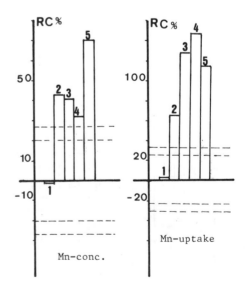

Fig(14) Effect of S.S. + R.S
on Mn-concentration and uptake
by plant.

463

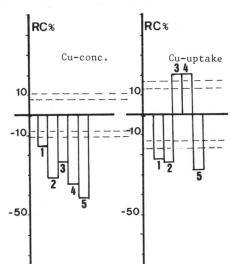

Fig (15) Effect of FYM + R.S on
Cu-concentration and uptake
by plant.

Fig (16) Effect of S.S + R.S on
Cu-concentration and uptake
by plant.

LEGEND figs(3-16)

(1)	Soil + O.M (FYM OR S.S) 2 % + R.S 0.0 %
(2)	" " " " 1.5 % + " 0.5 %
(3)	" " " " 1.0 % + " 1.0 %
(4)	" " " " 0.5 % + " 1.5 %
(5)	" " " " 0.0 % + " 2.0 %

- R.C % = the value is calculated in % relative to control-100 %
- The internal doted lines: are the limits of significant at 0.05
  level of probability.
- The external doted lines: are the limits of signifcant at 0.01
  level of probability

ORGANIC WASTES AS SOIL AMENDMENTS FOR THE RECLAMATION OF EGYPTION SANDY SOILS

II - THE EFFECT OF DIFFERENT RATES OF ORGANIC WASTES

N. SALEM, O. VERDONCK, M. VERLOO and M. DE BOODT
Faculty of Agricultural Sciences, State University Gent, Belgium

Summary

A pot culture experiment was conducted in Egyptian sandy soil to study the effect of different levels of farmyard manure (FYM) and sewage sludge (S.S) on dry matter yield and nutrient elements uptake by corn maize. The bulk density of the sandy soil decreases with the application of different levels of both organic wastes, whereas the electrical conductivity increases. The dry matter yield decreased with increasing amounts of farmyard manure in conjuction with mineral fertilization. Whileas insignificant changes were observed with application of different amounts of sewage sludge combined with mineral fertilization.
Application of FYM at a rate of 2 % combined with or without mineral fertilization, decreased the dry matter yield. Whereas application of S.S at a rate of 2 % without mineral fertilization decreased significantly the dry matter yield, which is increased insignificantly when it is combined with mineral fertilization.
At a rate of 4 % of FYM application combined with mineral fertilization, the electrical conductivity reached upto 14 mS.cm-1 which was enough for a complete wilting of the plant. While at the same rate of sewage sludge application, the dry matter yield showed a slight decrease.
A different plant responses in terms of changes in total elemental accumulation, dry matter yield and concentration were observed when different organic wastes with or without mineral fertilization were used.

1. INTRODUCTION

The Egyptian sandy soils suffer from a low cation exchange capacity and high permeability. These problems can be solved by applying some clay or organic materials.

Nutrient availability is governed by a large number of soil and crop factors. Among the most limiting factors are soil pH, $CaCO_3$, organic matter, inherent soil fertility, physical conditions and biological activities of soils (ref. 7).

The addition of farmyard manure in conjunction with mineral fertilization may help in increasing nutrients availability both applied and native source.

Sewage sludge application to agricultural land has long been practiced. It has been employed to improve soil physical conditions and as a source of plant nutrients. In recent years, one potential problem that has been recognized, in connection with application of sewage sludge to agriculture land, is the accumulation of heavy metals in the soil and their uptake by plants.

2. MATERIALS AND METHODS

A sandy Egyptian soil having pH 8.8, O.C. 0.08 %, CaCO$_3$ 0.73 % and clay content less than 1 %, was used for a pot culture experiment. Different lots of soil were treated with 0, 0.25, 0.5, 1.0, 2.0 and 4 % farmyard manure and/or sewage sludge. Extra treatments were added to compare the dry matter yields and nutrient elements uptake by plant in the presence and absence of mineral fertilization, at a rate of 2 % FYM or S.S.

More details concerned, total chemical analysis of the soil and the organic material, experimental details and methodology are given in the first article (ref. 5).

3. RESULTS AND DISCUSSIONS

3.1. Dry matter yields

It is evident from the data (Fig. 1) that dry matter yield (DMY) increased significantly with application of 0.25 and 0.5 percent of FYM in the presence of mineral fertilization. The dry matter yield significantly decreased with application of 2.0 percent FYM with or without mineral fertilization. At a rate of 4 % FYM a complete wilting of the plant was observed. This could be due to the higher salinity. The relation between dry matter yield and both electrical conductivity (Ece) and bulk density (B.D) is given in Fig. 1. The electrical conductivity of the soil treatments after harvesting the plants were 0.355, 0.425, 0.6, 1.3, 6.6 and 14 mS.cm^{-1} at the rate of 0.0, 0.25, 0.5, 1.0, 2.0 and 4.0 percent of FYM respectively. These results are in agreement with the observations of many authors (ref. 1 and 8). At the rate of 2 % of FYM without mineral fertilization, the Ece was 3.2 mS.cm^{-1} compared with 6.6 mS.cm^{-1} in the presence of mineral fertilizers. In the case of sewage sludge treatments the Ece of the soil after harvesting were 0.355, 0.49, 0.5, 0.9, 1.65 and 2.41 mS.cm^{-1} at a rate of 0.0, 0.25, 0.5, 1.0, 2.0 and 4.0 percent respectively (Fig. 2). Therefore, insignificant differences between the control (received only mineral fertilization) and sewage sludge treatments (received both S.S and mineral fertilization) were observed. At a rate of 2 % of S.S application, the absence of mineral fertilization shows a very high significant reduction, in dry matter yield, this is due to the less available forms of the nutrient elements present in the sludge (ref. 4 and 6).

3.2. The concentration and uptake of nutrient elements

The results of the effects of different rates of FYM and S.S on nutrient elements concentration and uptake by plants are presented in Fig. 3 to Fig. 16. These results are expressed in percent relative to control.

Generally, addition of FYM and/or S.S decreased the bulk density and increased the Ece, consequently the dry matter yield changed with application of these materials. As a result of different accumulation rate of dry matter yield and nutrient elements inside the plant, different phenomena were observed.

1. Dilution effect - The phenomenon occurs when the accumulation rate of dry matter is more higher than the absorption rate of the nutrient element

in the plant (ref. 3). This was observed in case of N, at a rate of 0.25 and 0.5 % of FYM and 0.25, 0.5 and 1.0 % of FYM in case of P, Fe, Zn and Cu. Whereas in the case of S.S the phenomenon was observed with all elements except Zn, show some synergism effect.

2. Concentration effect - The phenomenon occurs if the rate of nutrient uptake does not decrease more rapidly than the growth rate drops, its concentration in the tissue increases. However, in most instances when the growth of plant is stunted, nutrients may continue to accumulate in tissue and reach higher concentrations than in control plants. The reduction in plant size may accelerate the toxic effect because the toxic ion will accumulate to higher levels because of a (concentration effect) and have an increasingly detrimental effect on growth (ref. 3). The concentration effect phenomenon was observed at higher rate of FYM (2 %) and S.S (4 %) application where the dry matter yield decreased in relation to control. In the case of FYM treatment this phenomenon occurred with N, K and Mg and slightly with Zn, while in S.S treatments it is observed with K and Zn and slightly with N and Mn (see Table I).

3. Synergism effect - The synergism effect occurs when the concentration of any element in plants has increased as plants respond to another applied element (ref. 2). This response has been variously attributed to increasing growth, improved energy supply to the roots, and generally better health of the plant (ref. 3). This phenomenon has been observed with K and Mn when FYM is used at a rate of 0.25, 0.5 and 1 %. Whereas it is observed with Zn when S.S is used at a rate of 1.0 and 2 % (see Table I).

4. Antagonism effect - This phenomenon is occuring when both accumulation rate of dry matter and element inside the plant are dropped down in relation to control plant (ref. 3) as a result of changing in the environmental plant such as soil solution salinity, addition of ions causes a concentration effect only for themselves, and tended to substantially restrict the uptake rates of other nutrients etc. This phenomenon was observed with P, K, Fe and Cu at a rate of 4 % of sewage sludge.
   The antagonism effect was observed with all nutrient elements except K and Mn showed a (concentration effect) when FYM was added at a rate of 2 % without mineral fertilization. After addition of mineral fertilization only P, Cu and Fe show an antagonism effect while N, P, Zn and Mn show a concentration effect (see Table I).
   In the case of using sewage sludge at a rate of 2 % without mineral fertilization all elements have shown an antagonism effect except Mn has shown a concentration effect. After addition of mineral fertilization all elements showed a dilution effect as a result of increasing dry matter yield.
   The different patterns of nutrient elements responses under different organic matter treatments are shown in Table I.

4. REFERENCES

1. EVANS, S.S., GOODRICH, P.R., MUNTER, R.C. and SMITH, R.E.C. (1979) Effects of solid and liquid beef manure and liquid hog manure on soil characteristics and on growth, yield and composition of corn. J. Environ. Qual. 6, 361-368.

2. GRUNES, D.L. (1959) Effect of nitrogen on the availability of soil and fertilizer phosphorous to plants. Adv. Agron. II, 369-396.
3. JARRELL, W.M. and BEVERLY, R.B. (1981) The dilution effect in plant nutrition studies. Adv. Agron. 34, 198-224.
4. MAYS, D.A., TERMAN, G.L. and DUGGAN, J.C. (1973) Municipal compost : effects on crop yields and soil properties. J. Environ. Qual. 2, 89-92.
5. SALEM, N., VERLOO, M. and DE BOODT, M. (1986) Organic wastes as soil amendments for the reclamation of Egyptian sandy soil. I - Effect of different combinations of organic wastes. Accepted in International Symposium on compost, production, quality and use, Udine (Italy), 17-19 April 1986.
6. SIMS, J.T. and BOSWELL, F.C. (1980) The influence of organic wastes and inorganic nitrogen sources on soil nitrogen, yield, and elemental composition of corn. J. Environ. Qual. 9, 512-518.
7. SINGH, R. and DAHIYA, S.S. (1980) Effect of farmyard manure and iron on dry matter yield and nutrients uptake by oats (Avina Sativa). Plant and Soil 56, 403-412.
8. TIARKS, A.E., MAZURA, K.A.P. and CHESNIN, L. (1974) Physical and chemical properties of soil associated with heavy applications of manure from cattle feedloots. Soil Sci. Soc. Amer. Proc. 38, 826-830.
9. ZWARICH, M.A. and MILLS, J.G. (1979) Effects of sewage sludge application on the heavy metals content of wheat and forage crops. Canad. J. Soil Sci. 59, 231-233.

	N	P	K	Fe	Zn	Mn	Cu
	u y c̄ r	u y c̄ r	u y c̄ r	u y c̄ r	u y c̄ r	u y c̄ r	u y c̄ r
Soil + FYM 0.25 % N P K	↑↑↑̄d	↓↑↓d	↑↑↑s	↑↑↑̄d	↓↑↓d	↑↑↑s	↑↑↓d
, , 0.50 % ,	↓↑↑̄d	↓↑↑̄d	↑↑↑s	0↑↓d	↓↑↓d	↑↑↑s	↓↑↓d
, , 1.00 % ,	↓↑↑s	↑↓↑̄d	↑↑↑s	↑↓↑↓d	↑↓↑̄d	↑↑↑s	↓↓↓d
, , 2 00 % ,	↓↓↑c	↓↓↑̄a	↑↓↑c	↓↓↓a	↓↓↓c	↓↓↑c	↓↓↓a
, , 4.00 % ,	—	—	—	—	—	—	—
Soil+FYM 2.00% N P K	↓↓↑c	↓↓↑̄a	↓↑↑c	↓↓↓a	↓↓↑c	↓↓↑c	↓↓↓a
, , 2.00% – – –	↓↓↓a	↓↓↓a	↑↓↑c	↓↓↓a	↓↓↓a	↑↓↓c	↓↓↓a
Soil+S.S 0.25 % N P K	↓↓↑̄d	↓↑↓d	↑↓↑̄d	↑↓↑̄d	↑↓↑̄d	↓↑↓d	↓↑↓d
, , 0.50 % ,	↓↓↑̄d	↓↑↓d	↑↓↑̄d	↑↓↑̄d	↓↓↓s	↑↓↑̄d	↓↑↓d
, , 1.00 % ,	↑↓↑̄d	↓↑↓d	↑↓↑̄d	↑↓↑̄d	↑↓↓s	↑↓↑̄d	↑↓↑̄d
, , 2.00 % ,	↓↓↑̄d	↓↑↓d	↓↓↑̄d	↑↓↑̄d	↑↓↓s	↓↓↑̄d	↓↑↓d
, , 4.00 % ,	↑↑↓c	↓↑↓a	↑↑↓c	↓↑↓a	↑↑↓c	↑↑↓c	↓↑↓a
Soil+S.S 2.00 % N P K	↑↓↑̄d	↓↑↓d	↓↓↑̄d	↓↑↓d	↑↑↑s	↓↓↑̄d	↓↑↓d
, , 2.00 % – – –	↓↓↓a	↓↓↓a	↓↓↓a	↓↓↓a	↓↓↑c	↓↓↓a	↓↓↓a

Table I. General representation of changes in total elemental accumulation (u), dry matter yield (y) and concentration (c) as affected by different rates of organic wastes

a : antagonism   ↑: significantly increased
s : synergism   ↓: significantly decreased
d : dilution effect   0: no change
c : concentration effect   ↑: insignificantly increased
n : no change in concentration   ↓: insignificantly decreased
r : response

Legend of Figures 3 to 16

1 : soil + FYM or S.S   0.25 %
2 : soil + FYM or S.S   0.50 %
3 : soil + FYM or S.S   1.00 %
4 : soil + FYM or S.S   2.00 %
5 : soil + FYM or S.S   4.00 %
6 : soil + FYM or S.S   2.00 % without N.P.K.

469

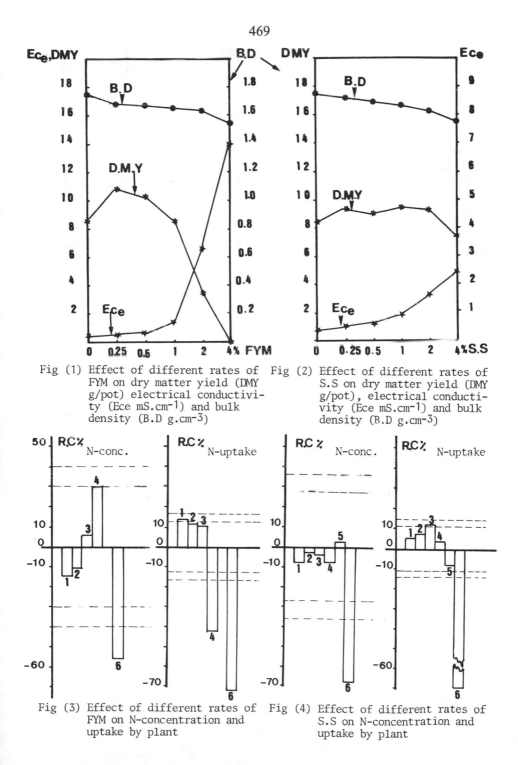

Fig (1) Effect of different rates of FYM on dry matter yield (DMY g/pot) electrical conductivity (Ece mS.cm-1) and bulk density (B.D g.cm-3)

Fig (2) Effect of different rates of S.S on dry matter yield (DMY g/pot), electrical conductivity (Ece mS.cm-1) and bulk density (B.D g.cm-3)

Fig (3) Effect of different rates of FYM on N-concentration and uptake by plant

Fig (4) Effect of different rates of S.S on N-concentration and uptake by plant

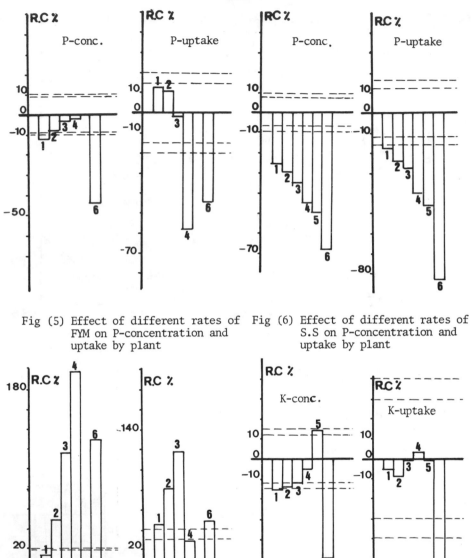

Fig (5) Effect of different rates of FYM on P-concentration and uptake by plant

Fig (6) Effect of different rates of S.S on P-concentration and uptake by plant

Fig (7) Effect of different rates of FYM on K-concentration and uptake by plant

Fig (8) Effect of different rates of S.S on K-concentration and uptake by plant

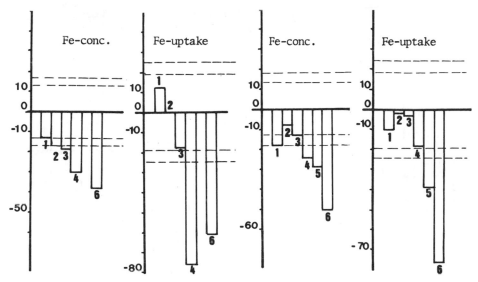

Fig. (9) Effect of different rates
of FYM on Fe-concentration
and uptake by plant

Fig (10) Effect of different rates
of S.S on Fe-concentra-
tion and uptake by plant

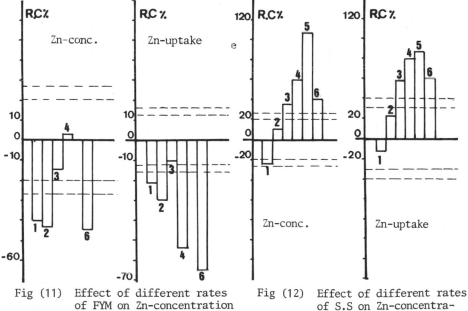

Fig (11) Effect of different rates
of FYM on Zn-concentration
and uptake by plant

Fig (12) Effect of different rates
of S.S on Zn-concentra-
tion and uptake by plant

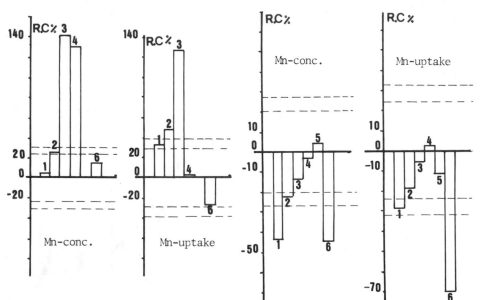

Fig (13) Effect of different rates of
FYM on Mn-concentration and
uptake by plant

Fig (14) Effect of different rates
of S.S on Mn-concentration
and uptake by plant

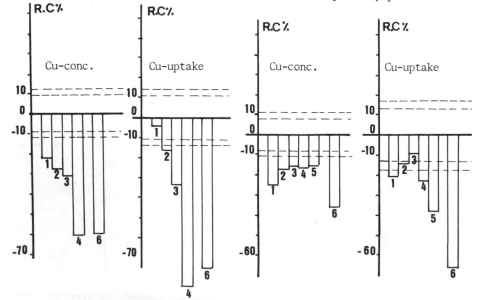

Fig (15) Effect of different rates of
FYM on Cu-concentration and
uptake by plant

Fig (16) Effect of different rates
of S.S on Cu-concentration
and uptake by plant

EFFECTS OF MANURE COMPOST
ON SOIL MICROBIOLOGICAL PROPERTIES.

by

B. GODDEN, M. MARESCHAL, X. VEKEMANS & M. PENNINCKX.
Laboratoire de Microbiologie de
l'Université Libre de Bruxelles.
1, Avenue E. Gryson,
B1070   Brussels.
BELGIUM.

Summary.

Addition of cattle manure compost ($\pm$ 30 tons/ha) to a loamy acidic soil has a stimulating effect on microbial counts and enzyme activities after several weeks. In contrast, cationic exchange capacity and pH increased rapidly after compost incorporation. Studies with ^{15}N labeled compost have shown a rapid nitrogen immobilization step followed by mineralization.

1. Introduction.

Cattle manure has been commonly used as a soil conditionner, but, in the last years, the practice of spreading previously composted manure has gained some popularity (2).

In this paper we report a preliminary three months field-scale study for estimating the effects of this practice on some microbiological and other properties of soils.

2. Results.

2.1 Microbial counts.

Plate counts on TAYLOR medium (8) have shown that the addition to soil of cattle manure compost (30 tons/ ha), seems to have a long-term stimulating effect on the soil microflora (Fig Ia), as compared to the addition of a NPK fertilizer. The peak in the microbial count, observed for the second sample, could be attributed to a climatic fluctuation (high temperature and soil moisture).

2.2 Enzyme activities.

Alkaline phosphatase and urease were estimated as described elsewhere (3,4). The evolution of the first enzyme activity paralleled the evolution of microbial count but only for the compost-amended parcel (Fig 1b). No significative activity was detected in the NPK amended parcel. At first glance, this result might not be ascribable to an effect of inorganic phosphate. Indeed we have observed that the respective inorganic phosphate content of compost and NPK amended soils were very similar.

Except for the first day after the treatment, no significative differences were recorded between the parcels for urease activity (**Fig Ic**).

Figure Ia : Microbial counts.

log N/gr

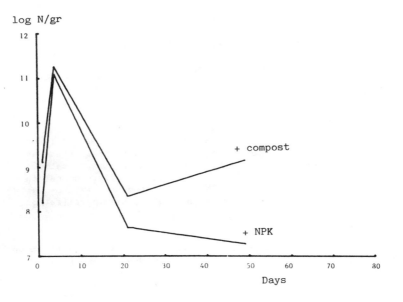

Figure Ib : Phophatase activity.

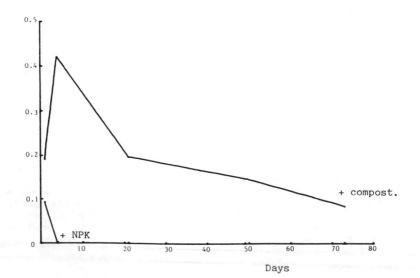

Figure Ic : Urease activity.

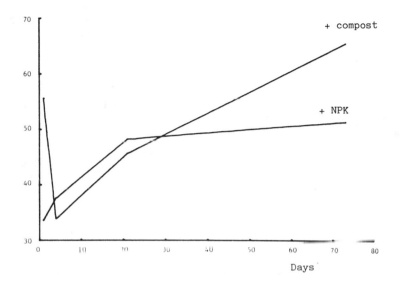

Fig I: Evolution of microbial counts and enzyme activities in soils amended respectively with cattle manure compost and NPK fertilizer. Experimental parcels (1 x 1.50 m) of a loamy soil (73.3% total loam:; 13.9% clay; 12.8% sand) were respectively amended with cattle manure compost (1.73% nitrogen) and a NPK (10N (4 NO_3^-; 6NH_4^+): 8 P_2O_5; 5K_2O) fertilizer ($\pm$ 1 ton/ha).
(A): microbial counts;
(B): Alkalinophosphatase units (mg phenol released/h per g dried soil);
(C): Urease unit (μg N-NH_3 released/h per g dried soil).

2.3 Chemical properties.

The initial pH of the experimental loamy soil was low: (pH(H_2O)= 5.0; pH(KCl)= 4.1). A slight alkalinizing effect was observed with compost addition (Table I) whereas mineral fertilization resulted in a small acidification. It was shown that the cationic exchange capacity (1) of the soil was strongly influenced by organic matter of compost (Table I).

Table I:

Evolution of chemical properties of soils respectively amended with compost and NPK fertilizer. See legend of Fig I for experimental conditions.

		date	21/05	24/05	10/06	08/07	01/08
pH	H_2O	Compost	5.25	5.5	5.5	5.3	5.7
	KCl		4.10	4.4	4.3	4.2	4.1
	H_2O	NPK	4.5	4.9	4.9	4.6	4.7
	KCl		4.10	4.2	4.2	3.8	3.8
CEC mcq/ 100gr dry soil		Compost	8.83	8.61	8.36	–	7.85
		NPK	7.75	7.12	7.51	–	7.27
O.M. Organic matter in % dry weight		Compost	2.2	2.0	2.0	1.9	1.9
		NPK	1.3	1.4	1.60	1.8	1.4

2.4 Experiments with ^{15}N.

Soils were respectively enriched with $^{15}NH_4NO_3$ labeled compost ($^{15}N/N$ total = 0.85%) and NH_4 $^{15}NO_3$ labeled mineral fertilizer ($^{15}N/N$ total = 4.85%). The results were difficult to interpretate. But, in the case of compost, we observed an initial enrichment of the organic nitrogen fraction. This could result from nitrogen immobilization whereas the further decrease could arise from mineralization (Table II). No significative immobilization was recorded with the NPK fertilizer but the decrease in the $N-NO_3^-$ enrichment could however result from lixivation or (and) denitrification

Table II:

Evolution of the ^{15}N isotopic exces in nitrogen fractions of amended soils.

	N-	21/05	24/05	10/06	08.07
Compost	N total	0.49	0.16	0.28	0.09
	N org	0.0	0.16	0.04	0.06
NPK	N total	4.49	3.46	0.46	0.58
	N org	0.6	0.08	0.15	0.14
	$N-NH_4^+$	0.0	0.0	0.0	0.0
	$N-NO_3^-$	22.24	19.34	18.14	N.D.

N.D.: not determined.

3. Conclusions.

Notable modifications of soils are only expected after several years of treatment (5). Nevertheless it was of interest to characterize initial changes. The effects of compost addition on soil microbiological properties seem to appear only at the end of this investigation period. In contrast, chemical properties are rapidly modified. As far as we are aware, very few studies were published on the effects of compost on soil properties (6,7). Our results may constitute a basis for further extensive studies.

Experiments are also currently engaged for evaluating the long-term effects of respective additions of compost and fresh manure to soil

References.

1. COTTENIE A.;
    "F.A.O. Soil and plant testing as a basis of fertilizer recommendations."
    F.A.O. Roma (1978).

2. GASSER J.K.R.;
    "Composting of agricultural and other wastes."
    Elsevier Applied Science publ. (1985).

3. GODDEN B. & PENNINCKX M.;
    "Biochemistry of manure composting: humification and lignin biotransformation."
    Accompanying paper.

4. GODDEN B., PENNINCKX M., PIERARD A. & LANNOYE R.;
    "Evolution of enzyme activities and microbial populations du-
    ring composting of cattle manure."
    Eur. J. Appl. Microbiol. Biotechnol. (1983), vol. 17, 306-310.

5. JHONSTON A.E.;
    "The effect of forming systems on the amount of soil organic
    matter and its effect on yield at Rothamsted and Wolburn."
    In: "Soil degradation"; D. BOELS, D.B. DAVIES & A.E. JHONSTON;
    A.A. BALKEMA / ROTTERDAM (1982), 187-202.

6. NISHIO M.;
    "Direct-count estimation of microbial biomass in soil applied
    with compost."
    Biological Agr. and Hort., vol. 1, (1983), 109-125.

7. NISHIO M. & KUSANO S.;
    "Fluctuation patterns of microbial numbers in soil applied
    with compost."
    Soil Science-Plant Nutrition (1981), vol. 26, nber 4, 556-561.

8. TAYLOR in HARRIGAN W.E. & M.E. Mc CHANCE;
    "Laboratory methods in Microbiology"
    Academic Press, London (1966).

AGRONOMIC CHARACTERIZATION AND EVALUATION OF TWO NEW MUNICIPAL WASTE COMPOSTS.

M. BAUDUIN, E. DELCARTE and R. IMPENS
Faculté des Sciences Agronomiques de l'Etat
Département de Biologie végétale
théorique et appliquée
5800 GEMBLOUX - BELGIQUE

Summary

As municipal waste composts are more and more widely used in agriculture, it is very important to determine their agronomic value and the heavy metal contamination risks of soils and crops. Therefore we tested two composts quite different : the Idelux's compost (well humified) and the Intradel's one (non-humified). These composts are organic amendments which have a fertilizing action. Considering their heavy metal concentrations and our experimental results, we have to limit their agricultural using at the dosis of 25 t/ha.

1. Introduction

The household refuses production of the South of Belgium raised in 1983 about 926.000 tons (1) and it is still increasing. About one eighth of these wastes were treated by composting at Cuesmes (ISPH[x]), Tenneville and Habay-la-Neuve (Idelux[x]). Nowadays, two new more composting factories are working at Thumaide (Sideho) and Herstal (Intradel[x]).

As municipal waste composts are widely used in agriculture and horticulture, it is necessary to characterize them. Also, with a grant of the Wallonia Region's Ministry, our laboratory was devoted to assume quality controls of these products.

We are mainly testing the Idelux's compost and the Intradel's one in field and pot trials. The work goals we are carrying on are :
- the definition of the agronomic value of the tested composts (fertilization, soil amendments, horticultural substrates);
- the research of their utilization limits : rates of application, heavy metals contents and risks of accumulation of these contaminants in soils and crops.

2. Material and methods.

The two tested composts are quite different. The Idelux's one is a traditional compost well humified obtained by a low fermentation in piles (Buhler's process). The second one is prepared by a new technology : it is obtained uniquely by mechanical treatments (heating and pulverizing of the organic matter) (2). Thus it is not a true compost. It consists in a

---

x : Intercommunales Associations.

mixture of organic particles and fibres.

We namely studied the effects of various amounts of each compost on quantitative (field trials) and qualitative yields of rye-grass (Lolium multiflorum Lam. var. Lemtal cv. Optima). Table I gives details on various trials.

Outside, trials 1 and 2 were performed in four replicated small parcells (4 m2). Rye-grass was also grown in plastic pots (five replicates) containing a loamy soil (trial 3) or a sand-vermiculite mixture (trial 4).

This latter was performed under controlled climatic conditions (temperature : 25°C day – 15°C night; day length : 12 hours) and all pots received weekly 200 ml of a complete nutrient solution (3).

For every treatments, several rye-grass harvests were made and sampled. Moreover all compost-substrate mixtures were sampled at the final harvest.

Soils, plants, compost-substrate mixtures samples were analysed according to methods described elsewhere (4, 5).

Table I. Details of various trials on rye-grass.

Trials	Kinds of trials	Origin of compost added	Amounts of compost added (t/ha)
1	Field trial	Idelux	0-12,5-25-50
2	Field trial	Intradel	0-12,5-25-50
3	Pots trial	Idelux	0-12,5-25-50-125-250-625
4	Pots trial	Intradel	0-22-45-90-122

3. Results.

3.1. Composts used : chemical characteristics.

Results of tables II and III show us that :
- there are large variations between observed contents of a same element in the different Intradel's samples. This must be related to the process itself which is new and thus must be improved.
- the two used composts are quite different about the :
  1. humification degree (Idelux's compost has a low C on N ratio, high C on N ratio for Intradel's product);
  2. heavy metals and nutrient elements contents. It seems it is related to the origins of the wastes and not to the processes itselves.

Moreover, for each compost we observed :
- high extractible contents in K, Zn, Pb and Cd;
- according to proposed Belgian guidelines for urban composts applied on food crops (6), total contents in Zn and Cu are too high.

3.2. Effects of composts on soils fertility.

It is generally considered that municipal waste composts have positive effects on soils fertility : they improve physical and chemical soils properties (7, 8).

As for us, we mainly studied effects of composts on major elements con-

Table II. pH, humidity, C/N ratio, contents in organic matter, in C, and total and extractible major elements contents in the Idelux and Intradel's composts (results are expressed in % on dried matter).

Elements \ Composts	Idelux		Intradel	
pH	7,5		6,3-7,4	
H_2O	22,8		3,4-68,2	
Organic matter	33,6		32,4-58,2	
C	17,4		18,0-36,6	
N	1,20		0,40-0,97	
C/N	14,5		29,1-84,8	
	Total	Extractible	Total	Extractible
P_2O_5	0,05	0,01	0,03 0,22	0,04-0,17
K_2O	0,83	0,85	0,34-0,74	0,25-0,47
CaO	6,30	2,63	1,61-4,20	1,16-2,80
MgO	0,68	0,28	0,46-1,00	0,08-0,20

Table III. Total and extractible heavy metals contents in the Idelux and Intradel's composts (results are expressed in ppm on dried matter).

Elements \ Composts	Idelux		Intradel	
	Total	Extractible	Total	Extractible
Pb	216	345	77-408	72-360
Cd	3,3	2,6	0,87-2,30	0,32-0,70
Cu	548	73	33-178	12-33
Ni	48	9	4,1 -12,4	2,9 -3,8
Zn	1.308	860	250-725	250-725
Cr	109	5	5,0 -14,5	0,9-2,9

tents of soils. Urban composts are relatively poor in nutrients. Nevertheless, due to their high dried matter content, they have a fertilizing effect
when applied at sufficient dosis. Following their chemical analysis, we
estimated the nutrient elements quantities brought by a 25 t/ha applying of
Idelux and Intradel's compost at :

− ± 250 units N   for the Idelux's compost
    50 units P_2O_5

   150 units K_2O

−   125 units N   for the Intradel's product
    50 units P_2O_5

  125 units K_2O

The availability of these major elements is dependant upon the humification degree of the compost : 15-20 % of N, 50-60 % of P_2O_5 and 80-100 % of
K_2O in the first year of compost applying (9).

By means of chemical analysis, it is very difficult to distinguish effects of low dosis of compost on soils fertility (table IV) and higher is
this fertility level more it is difficult (10).

3.3. Effects of composts on heavy metal contamination of soils.

The effects of compost application on the concentrations of heavy metals
in the soils were dependant upon the amounts of compost applied and the initial concentration of the individual metal in the compost (11). At low
applying dosis (until 50 t/ha), only the concentrations in total and extractible Zn and in total Cu and Pb increased (table IV). Similar results for
Zn were previously observed (12). Uniquely for a 25 t/ha applying dosis,
EEC's guidelines on tolerated annual heavy metals deposits on soils were
respected (table V).

Table V. Assessment of heavy metals brought by a 25 t/ha applying dosis of
Idelux's compost and tolerated annual deposits (EEC's guidelines).

Elements	Quantities brought by a 25 t/ha applying dosis		Tolerated annual quantities kg/ha/year	
	kg/ha	mg/kg dried earth	recommended values	limited values
Pb	5,1	1,9	10	15
Cd	0,03	0,01	0,10	0,15
Cu	6,9	2,3	10	12
Ni	0,7	0,2	2	3
Zn	23,1	7,7	25	30
Cr	0,9	0,3	10	−

Table IV. Effects of various amounts of Idelux's compost (t/ha) on soil
fertility and heavy metal contamination (results are expressed on
dried matter).

Elements	Dosis of compost	0	12,5	25	50	125	250	625
N		0,11	0,11	0,12	0,11	0,14	0,15	0,53
P_2O_5	tot.	0,03	0,04	0,05	0,03	0,03	0,03	0,04
	ext.	<0,01	<0,01	<0,01	<0,01	<0,01	<0,01	0,01
K_2O	tot.	0,50	0,46	0,45	0,41	0,59	0,41	0,66
	ext.	0,02	0,02	0,02	0,04	0,05	0,05	0,30
CaO	tot.	0,60	0,57	0,61	0,59	0,87	0,88	3,05
	ext.	0,39	0,36	0,38	0,41	0,52	0,60	1,58
MgO	tot.	0,53	0,61	0,55	0,53	0,62	0,55	0,73
	ext.	0,01	0,01	0,01	0,01	0,02	0,03	0,13
Pb	tot.	13	14	19	19	35	54	189
	ext.	12,4	10,0	13,9	16,4	32,8	50,5	169
Cd	tot.	0,26	0,27	0,29	0,27	0,42	0,38	1,5
	ext.	0,21	0,14	0,17	0,20	0,32	0,34	1,2
Cu	tot.	24	25	26	21	40	45	300
	ext.	4,3	3,5	5,3	5,0	8,5	9,5	37,0
Ni	tot.	15	19	18	18	21	20	29
	ext.	1,1	1,2	1,3	1,4	1,6	1,8	3,8
Zn	tot.	54	56	75	72	123	132	621
	ext.	10	8	15	19	41	68	385
Cr	tot.	8	8	10	11	9	17	22
	ext.	0,15	0,14	0,21	0,22	0,49	0,62	1,62

tot. : total.

ext. : extractible.

3.4. Effects of composts on rye-grass yields.

Municipal waste composts had benefical effects on rye-grass crops (table VI). These results confirmed others one previously obtained (5, 13) on a wide range of crops.

Table VI. Effects of various dosis of Idelux and Intradel's composts (t/ha) on yields of rye-grass crops grown in 1983 and in 1984 (results are expressed in % of untreated parcells yields).

Dosis of composts	Yields		
	Idelux's compost		Intradel's compost
	1983	1984	1984
0	100	100	100
12,5	101	103	-
25	119	105	116
50	105	113	112

3.5. Heavy metal contamination risks of crops.

All the rye-grass harvests of pots and field trials were analysed for determining heavy metal contamination levels. Results obtained (tables VII and VIII) show that :
- heavy metal contamination levels were dependant upon the rate of compost application;
- transfer rates were greater at the first harvest than at the second one;
- high amounts of compost deppressed heavy metals uptakes by plants;
- Zn and Cu seemed to be the most mobile.

4. Conclusions.

Municipal waste composts are organic amendments which have a fertilizing action particularly important in poor soils.

About heavy metal contamination risks of soils and crops, our experimentations showed that :
- risks were limited when they were used at the dosis of 25 t/ha;
- the most contaminants were Zn, Cu and at a lower degree Pb. These results were related to their initial concentration in the compost.

REFERENCES.

1. FONTAINE, R. (1984). Les déchets ménagers en Wallonie. Beswa Rev., 84 (4) : 12-26.
2. MICHAUX, J. (1984). Etude de mise au point d'une nouvelle technologie de valorisation de fractions organiques d'origine urbaine. Rapport final de convention entre la Région wallonne et Intradel.
3. AVRIL, C. (1985). Qualification d'une matière organique micronisée pour sa valorisation en agronomie. Trav. fin d'étud., Fac. Sc. Agro., Gembloux 90 p.

4. DELCARTE, E., ANID, P., IMPENS, R. (1982). Présence de métaux lourds dans les composts. Ann. de Gembloux, 88 : 133-144.
5. DEPARTEMENT DE BIOLOGIE VEGETALE THEORIQUE ET APPLIQUEE (1985). Valeur agronomique des composts urbains : synthèse des résultats de deux années d'étude : avril 1983-avril 1985. Fac. Sc. Agro., Gembloux : 30 p.
6. ANONYME (1983). Propositions de normes pour les composts urbains belges, 8 décembre 1983 : 2 p.
7. SEGURA, J. (1980). Intérêt des composts formés à partir des déchets domestiques en agriculture. Diplôme d'étude approfondie, Univ. Paris-Sud, Centre d'Orsay : 8 p.
8. S.U.A.D. (1979). Etude comparée de la valeur agronomique de déchets organiques urbains sur différents types de sols de Seine-et-Marne. Chambre d'agriculture de Seine-et-Marne, 77350 Le Mee-sur-Seine : 64 p.
9. JUSTE, C. (1982). La valeur fertilisante du compost urbain. Compost Inf., 9 : 8-11.
10. DEPARTEMENT DE BIOLOGIE VEGETALE THEORIQUE ET APPLIQUEE (1985). Valeur agronomique de composts urbains : état d'avancement au 1er octobre 1985. Fac. Sc. Agro., Gembloux : 8 p.
11. ANID, P., DELCARTE, E., IMPENS, R. (1983). Heavy metals transfer from town refuse compost to plants. International Conference on Heavy metals in the environment, Heidelberg, sept. 1983 : 653-656.
12. JACQUIN, F., VONG, P.C. (1984). Incidence de divers déchets organiques sur les propriétés physico-chimiques du sol et sur le devenir de certains métaux réputés toxiques. Compost Inf., 16 : 2-5.
13. KJENTZLER, L., GUCKERT, A. (1983). Etude de l'effet de divers déchets organiques utilisés comme amendements sur cultures de maïs. E.N.S.A.I.A., Nancy : 17 p.

Table VIII:

Dosis of compost / Elements	0	12,5	25	50	125
Harvest 1					
Pb	4,6	6,0	7,1	4,1	0,8
Cd	2,0	1,9	2,0	1,6	2,5
Cu	21	23	23	22	5,5
Ni	6,4	6,9	6,7	6,6	6,6
Zn	77	75	88	95	330
Cr	2,9	4,2	2,3	2,3	0,5
Harvest 2					
Pb	8,0	8,2	8,9	8,4	8,0
Cd	0,48	0,65	0,48	0,35	0,68
Cu	10,0	9,4	10,0	8,7	8,7
Ni	0,40	0,45	0,80	0,70	0,50
Zn	31	33	33	29	45
Cr	2,2	3,2	2,6	2,4	2,6

Table VIII : Effects of various amounts of Idelux's compost (t/ha) on heavy metal contamination of ryegrass grown in pots (results are expressed in ppm on dried matter)

Table VII:

Dosis of compost / Elements	0	12,5	25	50
Harvest 1				
Pb	2,2	1,9	3,7	2,6
Cd	0,32	0,20	0,35	0,42
Cu	6,0	8,7	9,2	9,5
Ni	2,8	2,6	3,8	3,2
Zn	31	29	34	32
Cr	0,6	1,0	1,2	1,9
Harvest 2				
Pb	5,7	6,9	5,7	6,8
Cd	0,56	0,50	0,38	0,53
Cu	13,2	14,6	11,6	10,6
Ni	3,6	3,6	3,5	3,2
Zn	48	47	46	41
Cr	1,0	0,9	0,7	1,0

Table VII : Effects of various amounts of Idelux's compost (t/ha) on heavy metal contamination of ryegrass grown in field (results are expressed in ppm on dried matter)

THE INFLUENCE OF DIFFERENT CULTURAL MEDIA ON TOMATO GROWTH

P. Nappi*   C. Di Vaio**   R. Barberis*
* Istituto per le Piante da Legno e l'Ambiente (IPLA) - Torino
**CNR scholarship holder at the Istituto di Coltivazioni Arboree - Facoltà
  di Agraria - Portici

Summary

Three different cultural media were tested. Compost obtained from grape stalks and sewage sludge, compost obtained from RSU, sewage sludge.
The media were tested in pots at two different doses (1 and 3%) with
two soils (ST and SE) on Tomato. Yields obtained and media modification
after 2 productive cycles of 40 days each, have been measured. The experiment pointed out a different productive yield for the tested media.
In fact during the first productive cycle in both soils compost obtained from stalks and sludges gave the maximum productive yield while
RSU compost showed phytotoxic effects. During the second productive
cycle differences between the soils were noticed. While in SE the maximum yield was obtained with the highest RSU dose, in ST the maximum
yield was noticed with the highest sludge dose. In the different tested substrata N mineralization was noticed: it was more evident in the
sludge and in the compost at the highest dose. Nitrification instead
is higher in the sludge test and in the RSU compost. These two proces
ses were more evident in the structurally lighter SE soil.

1.1. Introduction

The problems associated with the employment in agriculture of products
derived from agricultural, urban and industrial residues and wastes are of
varying origin.

Apart from the question of hygiene, in fact, consideration must be
given to the features that render waste disposal compatible with the equilibrium of the soil and the environment (e.g. the presence of heavy metals).
The conditions under which such products can be applied to the advantage of
growing crops must also be known (1,5,6).

The stabilisation of organic wastes is a question of particular interest. The presence in products for use in agriculture of incompletely decomposed fractions of organic matter may give rise to phytotoxic substances and cause damage of various kinds and extent to numerous factors, among
which the soil plays a very important role.

IPLA has a series of ongoing studies designed to work out methods for determining the possible phytotoxicity of sludges (4) and the investigation of their employment in agriculture (3).

This paper describes the preliminary results of a test in which three types of organic matter were applied to two soils with different texture. The evolution of these substances was followed through the examination of two growing cycles of tomato platlets in pots.

1.2. Material and method

The three organic substances were a sewage sludge from the Collegno (Turin) water treatment plant (SS), a 5-month compost produced from solid urban wastes by the Pistoia plant (UC), and a 6-month compost produced from grape stalks and sewage sludge produced by Reggio Emilia(GC).Their analytical characteristics are illustrated in Table 1. The doses employed for the organic materials corresponded to 1% and 3% of dry matter. They were mixed with two types of soil collected near Turin: soil 1 from Settimo (SE),a sandy loam soil (sand 70%, silt 27%, clay 3%, pH 6,9, OM 1.5%); soil 2 from Stupinigi (ST) was predominantly silty (sand 39,6%, silt 45,7%, clay 14,7%, pH 7,6, OM 3,4).

Tab. 1 - Analytical characteristics of the organic substances utilised.
(values, but for moisture, are expressed on the dry matter)

	Moisture %	pH	Conductivity mS/cm	Ntot. %	NH_4-N ppm	NO_2-NO_3 ppm	C %	C/N
Sewage sludge	76,5	8,08	0,946	3,42	3645	35	29.76	8,70
Compost (GC)	54,1	7,83	0,520	2,17	1432	27	30,20	13,9
Compost (UC)	60,0	7,10	1,669	1,32	1555	40	25,00	18,9

The test was carried out in 1-litre pots containing two 10-cm high tomato plantlets ("round" variety). Three repetitions were prepared for each thesis at the same time as for the controls. The plants were cultivated under a PVC tunnel.

The scope of the experiment was to evaluate the changes in the organic matter over the course of time and its influence on the growing plants. Two cycles were examined. The end of each cycle was fixed as the moment when the plants presented the phenological "full flowering" stage.

At the end of the first cycle, the epigeal parts of the plantlets were mixed together and evenly buried in the pots for the second cycle.

Controls with fresh soil were prepared for the second cycle, along with those supplemented with the cultivation residue.

The following parameters were examined at the time of flowering: production of dry matter and wet matter per pot and the height of each plantlet.

The main physical and chemical substrate parameters were checked for each specimen before and after the two cycles: total nitrogen, ammoniacal nitrogen, nitric nitrogen, organic carbon percentage and C/N ratio.

Analysis of variance was used for statistical assessment of the plant growth data. Their significance was determined by using Duncan's test.

1.3. Results

First cycle

Fig. 1 sets out dry matter yield from the tomato) plantlets for the first cycle (40 days). Its histograms show that soil SE gave a significantly higher yield than ST. In addition, the specimens treated with SS and GC gave higher yields than UC.

The production of dry matter increased with the amount of organic matter applied.

The better production obtained with soil SE is particularly evident in case of compost UC: 2.84 g dry matter per pot, as opposed to only 1.77 when applied to soil ST.

This negative interaction between soil and organic matter is more marked at the higher dose, when only 1.10 g/pot are obtained.

The results relating to the production of wet matter and plant height follow the same pattern as those for the dry matter.

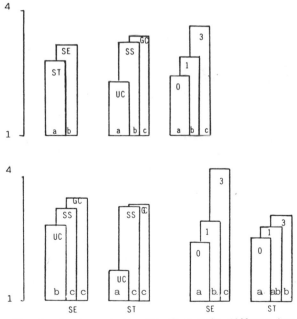

Fig. 1 - Tomato production at the first cycle. Different letters correspond to significative differences for p = 0,05.

Second cycle

The main results for the dry matter at the end of the second cycle (30 days) are illustrated in fig. 2. On this occasions, the means for the two soils were much the same : SE 3.46 g/pot, ST 3.57 g/pot.

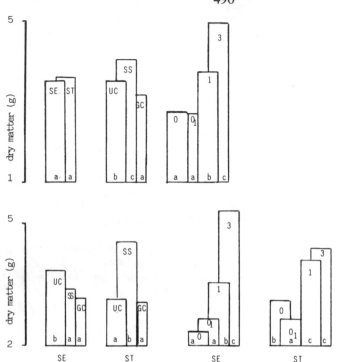

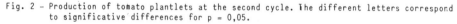

Fig. 2 - Production of tomato plantlets at the second cycle. The different letters correspond to significative differences for p = 0,05.

Compost GC, which gave the highest production in the first cycle, was now significantly less productive than both UC (3.10 versus 3.18 g/pot) and SS (3.96 g/pot).

A marked increase in production was obtained with the 3% dose : 4.85 g/pot compared with 3.82 at 1%. Both values were higher than in the controls with and without the addition of cultivation residue : 2.66 and 2.72 g/pot respectively (not significant). Soil SE produced best with UC (3.83 g/pot), whereas SS gave the best result on ST (4.53 g/pot).

There was no significant between the two doses in the case of soil ST. This was because the amount obtained with UC at 3% (2.70 g/pot) was less than with 1% (4.05 g/pot). The two controls supplied statistically different yields. That supplemented with cultivation residues (0_1) gave a lower value than that consisting of soil only (0) : 2.67 vs 3.12 g/pot.

Once again, the wet matter and plantlet height data followed the same pattern as those for the dry matter.

Chemical analysis

The amount of ammoniacal and nitric nitrogen in the substrates when the pots were prepared and at the end of the two cycles is shown in fig. 3. Both soils display the same analytical pattern. Analytical data of the substrates are exposed in table 2.

Treatment		Time 0 N tot %	NH$_4$-N ppm	NO$_3$-N ppm	C org. %	C/N	Time 1 N tot %	NH$_4$-N ppm	NO$_3$-N ppm	C org. %	C/N	Time 2 N tot %	NH$_4$-N ppm	NO$_3$-N ppm	C org. %	C/N
Sludge	1%	0.20	52	4	1.40	7.0	0.19	23	15	1.50	7.9	0.19	4	21	1.71	9.0
Sludge	3%	0.29	96	11	1.91	6.6	0.20	24	48	2.20	11.0	0.10	11	14	2.01	10.0
Compost UC	1%	0.17	27	14	1.44	8.5	0.15	12	12	2.00	13.3	0.17	18	29	1.55	9.1
Compost UC	3%	0.27	102	14	1.90	7.0	0.23	16	28	2.10	9.1	0.19	14	18	1.84	9.7
Compost GC	1%	0.18	13	40	1.39	7.7	0.17	10	16	2.00	11.8	0.14	11	15	1.63	11.6
Compost GC	3%	0.24	31	86	1.31	5.4	0.19	20	23	1.90	10.0	0.18	15	18	1.89	10.5
Control		0.16	20	26	0.90	5.6	0.16	19	11	1.40	8.7	0.11	13	10	0.69	6.2
Sludge	1%	0.24	31	7	1.79	7.4	0.22	20	16	2.00	9.1	0.21	14	18	1.99	9.5
Sludge	3%	0.31	125	29	2.39	7.7	0.26	25	38	2.00	7.7	0.22	14	18	2.19	9.9
Compost UC	1%	0.20	41	20	1.40	7.0	0.20	17	13	1.90	9.5	0.22	11	19	1.95	8.9
Compost UC	3%	0.22	63	17	1.95	8.8	0.24	23	18	1.80	7.5	0.25	15	31	2.52	10.1
Compost GC	1%	0.22	17	49	1.79	8.1	0.18	18	18	2.10	11.7	0.21	12	20	1.93	9.2
Compost GC	3%	0.26	17	48	2.03	7.8	0.22	16	20	2.10	9.5	0.25	14	18	2.17	8.7
Control		0.20	12	20	1.60	8.0	0.19	11	19	1.90	10.0	0.18	19	22	0.98	5.4

Table 2 - Analytical characteristics of the soil. Time 0 = beginning of the trial; Time 1 = end of first cycle; Time 2 = end of second cycle.

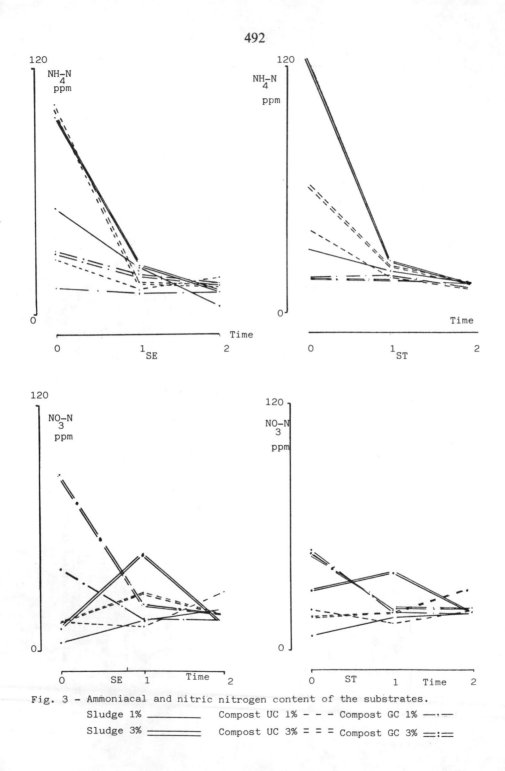

Fig. 3 - Ammoniacal and nitric nitrogen content of the substrates.

Sludge 1% _____   Compost UC 1% - - -   Compost GC 1% —·—

Sludge 3% =========   Compost UC 3% = = =   Compost GC 3% ==:==

The ammoniacal nitrogen values at time 0 were rather different in the various specimens. By the end of the second cycle, however, they were much the same.

When substance GC was used, the ammoniacal nitrogen content did not change to any great extent. By contrast, the nitric nitrogen content started from relatively high levels and then was virtually exhausted during the first cycle, whereas at the end of the second cycle it was very close to the levels in the other substrates.

With sludge SS, on the other hand, the level of ammoniacal nitrogen fell, mainly during the first cycle, whereas the amount of nitric nitrogen rose after the first cycle and was at the same level as the other substrates by the end of the second. Ammoniacal nitrogen also fell more markedly during the first cycle in soils supplemented with UC. In addition, they displayed a slight increase in nitric nitrogen during the second cycle. There were slight fluctuations in both nitrogen parameters in the controls in each cycle.

1.4. Discussion

Agronomic interpretation of these results involves several factors. The varying dry matter yields supplied by the three organic substances can nevertheless be examined in the light of the differences between the soils and between the two cycles.

The following points are worthy of note.

The relatively high yield provided by GC during the first cycle can be related to the presence of readily assimilable nitrogen, i.e. nitrate, which was available for use by the plantlets when the substrates were prepared. Coupled with the low level of ammoniacal nitrogen, this shows that the substance in question did not need to mature further to achieve its fertilising power. Indirect confirmation of this can be seen in the fact that during the second cycle the nitrate content was reduced following its utilisation during the first, with the result that the yield with GC was much less than with the other substrates.

Sewage sludge on the other hand, had a relatively high NH_4-N content, which fell during trial, whereas its nitrate content increased. This points to a modification, the benefits of which can be seen in the higher production compared with the other specimens during the second cycle.

The position with regard to UC is more complicated. Its low initial yields can be attributed to its insufficient ripening probably characterised by the presence of phytotoxic substances. Moreover, the presence of a relatively low total nitrogen value suggests that this element is primarily used by the microorganism to decompose the wet organic matter, so that there is a shortage of nitrogen for the plant.

The recovery observed in the looser soil (SE) treated with UC in the second cycle can probably be ascribed to conversion, as can also be deduced from the dynamics of the forms of nitrogen. An experiment using UC by Wong (7) showed that as the composting process continued there was a fall in

NH_4-N parallel to greater plant growth when UC was used.

Cecconi et al. (2) also found that decomposition was faster in looser soil when a UC from the same establishment was tested in different soils.

When soil ST was used, on the other hand, the yields given by UC were lower, even in the second cycle. This may be explained as the results of the difficulty encountered by this substance in conversion in a silty soil that was more compact, and probably less aerated, than the sandy loam soil SE.

The pattern displayed by the controls also incates that UC has difficulty in progressing in soil ST. In the second cycle, in fact, controls supplemented with residues from the first cycle gave lower yields than those prepared with soil only.

It may thus be concluded that a substance such as sewage sludge,though potentially toxic at first, can evolve and be of benefit to growing plants. Urban compost requires a longer composting period. During the first cycle, in fact, it retained a high toxic potential, which was partially removed in the second. Grape compost, on the other hand, gave the best yields in the first cycle. This, however, exhausted its fertilising power. Wehn used for a second cycle, therefore, it requires mineralsupplementation to be able to keep up its fertility levels.

REFERENCES

1.   BLACK, S.A. and KRONIS H. (1973). Fertility and toxicity of chemical sewage sludges. International Conference on land for waste management. Ottawa, October.
2.   CECCONI,C.A., VIDRICH, V., SERRITELLA, G. and FUSI P. (1980). Alcuni aspetti della dinamica dei rifiuti solidi urbani precomposti nel suolo. Atti dei georgofili 257-276.
3.   CONSIGLIO, M., BARBERIS, R., PICCONE, G., DE LUCA, G. and TROMBETTA, A. (1985). Productivity and quality of cereal crops grown on sludge-treated soils. 4° Simposio Internazionale Roma 8-11 ottobre '85. "Trattamento ed utilizzazione di fanghi organici e da scarichi liquidi agricoli".
4.   NAPPI, P., BARBERIS, R., CONSIGLIO, M., JODICE, R. and TROMBETTA, A. Biological evaluation of sludge phytotoxicity. Roma 8-11 ottobre 1985.
5.   PARIS, P. (1977).Possibilità e limiti agronomici dell'utilizzazione a-gricola dei fanghi da impianti di depurazione. Rivista di agronomia, 11 133-145.
6.   RIFFALDI, R., LEVI-MINZI, R., SARTORI, F. and CONTI, B. (1979). Elementi di fertilità e metalli pesanti nei fanghi provenienti da impiantidi depurazione. Agric. Ital. 108.
7.   WONG, M.H. (1985) Phytotoxicity of refuse compost during the process of maturation. Environmental Pollution (serie A) 37, 159-174.

COMPARISON OF THE PHYSICAL AND CHEMICAL PROPERTIES OF HUMIC ACIDS EXTRATED FROM A PODZOLIC SOIL AND A MATURE CITY REFUSE COMPOST

A. GOMEZ and C. LEJEUNE
Station d'Agronomie, I.N.R.A.
Centre de Recherches de Bordeaux
33140 Pont-de-la-Maye (France)

Summary

The present report, by characterizing the humic acids obtained from a four month old city refuse compost and from an organic sandy podzolic soil, reveals strong differences between the two classes of compounds The compost humic acids are less rich in ashes, have a higher level of nitrogen and sulfur than the soils ones. Beside, the cation exchange capacity of soil humic acids is twice the C.E.C. of the compost humic acids. The data concerning electrophoretical mobility, infrared spectra and respirometric studies corroborates the large difference between the two kinds of compounds and shows that compost humic acids have an important proteinic content, related to their biological lability.

1. INTRODUCTION

City refuse composts, after elimination of glasses, gravels and plastics, are of great interest to increase soil fertility in agricultural utilization. The high level of organic (1) matter of these materials is the main factor of interest for this purpose.

However, it is important to know the value of this organic matter in comparison to the native organic matter of soil.

Because of their stability and chemical activity, humic acids are a good model of the organic matter involved in the fertility of soils. For this reason, we have compared the physical and chemical properties of humic acids extracted from a podzolic soil and from mature city refuse compost.

2. MATERIALS AND METHODS

The soil used in this experimentation was collected in the "Landes de Gascogne" area. This soil was chosen because of its low clay content (90 % of coarse sand) and its high level of organic matter (5,4 %) (Table 1).

The city refuse compost was collected in a treatment plant after four months of composting of a row material. This row material was ground and screened at 20 mm after elimination of inert parts. The characteristics of the compost are given in Table 1.

In the case of the soil, the sample was suspended in a 0,5 N solution of sodium hydroxide using a soil/solution ratio of 1 to 2, shaken for 2 hours and centrifugated at 4 00 RPM for ten minutes. The supernatant was filtered and acidified to pH 1, using a diluted solution of nitric acid. The suspension was allowed to settle for 24 hours and then centrifuged in order to separate the precipited humic acids from the fulvic acids remaining in the solution. The humic acids were suspended in deionized water and centrifuged once again. This operation was repeated 3 times in order to remove the nitrate and sodium excess ions. The humic acids suspended in deionized water are dialized for 24 hours. The pH of the suspension was adjusted to 6 with the help of 0,1 N sodium hydroxide. The purified suspension was dried at 50° C. The final product was ground and screened at 300 μm.

The same preparation procedure was used for the compost sample, after decationization through a chlorhydric acid treatment and water leaching.

The following chemical characteristics of the humic acids were determinated : dry matter content at 105° C, ash and organic matter content at 800° C, carbon and sulfur content measured by the mean of a coulometric apparatus (Eraly), nitrogen content by the Kjeldahl procedure, phosphorus content using a colorimetric method, and several metals (Ca, Mg, Fe, Zn, Pb) using A.A.S.

By an other way, physical and biological properties were determined : cation exchange capacity, electrophoretic mobility, infrared spectra (Beckman Acculab 8), biodegradability using a respirometric method (Gilson respirometer).

3. RESULTS AND DISCUSSION

The chemical composition of the soil and the compost is given in the following table 1.

Table 1

Organic and mineral composition of soil and compost

		S o i l	Compost
H_2O	%	0,82	1,77
Ashes	%	93,9	62,3
C	%	2,82	19,22
N	%	0,13	1,01
C/N . . .		22,6	19,0
P_2O_5	ppm	322	3 250
Ca	ppm	69	39 977
Mg	ppm	99	2 983
Na	ppm	31	2 520
Fe	ppm	2 620	6 207
Zn	ppm	5,5	5 984
Pb	ppm	5,8	344

Table 2 presents the composition of humic acids extracted from soil and compost.

By the mean of a densitometer, the electrophoregrams were studied by reflection. Measuring the integrated surface of the mobile humic acids and the surface of unmoved humic acids, it was established a mobility index which is the ratio of surface of mobile to unmoved humic acids.

The electrophoregrams and the densitograms are shown in Figure 1 and the mobility index is given in the following table 3.

Table 2
Organic and mineral composition of humic acids
extracted from soil and compost

		S o i l	Compost
Ashes	%	24,8	10,1
C	%	40,65	48,2
N	%	2,15	5,41
C/N		18,6	8,9
S	%	0,51	1,07
P_2O_5	ppm	4 134	5 348
Ca	ppm	116	109
Mg	ppm	224	
Na	ppm	27 975	21 500
Fe	ppm	23 969	2 026
Zn	ppm	48	207
Pb	ppm	31	152
C.E.C. (at pH 6)		332	160

Table 3
Mobility index of humic acids

Humic acids	S o i l	Compost
Mobile integrated surface	46	19,7
Unmoved " "	26	2,3
Index	1,8	8,6

Infrared spectra are presented in Figure 2 and the results of respirometric study are shown in Figure 3.

The composition of humic acids extracted from soil or compost seems
to be quite different (Table 2). If we examine the carbon content, we can
see that the ratio carbon to extracted organic matter is similar (0,54),
but the nitrogen and sulfur content of humic acids extracted from compost
are higher than those of soil. The increased content of N and S indicate
that a large part of organic matter of compost is a proteinic material.
The lower ash content of humic acid originating from compost shows that
organic matter of compost is less bounded to the mineral part than the
soils organic matter, especially by iron. The heavy metal content of humic
acids extracted for compost indicates a higher pollution of compost by
these metals. The very high content of sodium is the result of the humic
acids extraction procedure.
An additional important result is the great difference of cation
exchange capacity. This point is related with the difference of organic
matter origin in soil and compost.
The electrophoregram (Fig. 1) of humic acids extracted from soil is
characterized by an important part of unmoved humic acids, this explains
the low mobility index in comparison to the higher index observed in the
case of compost humic acids. The greater content of unmoved soil humic
acids appears to be a result of the strong bounding of soil organic matter

with the mineral part.

The infrared spectra (Fig. 2) of the compost humic acids is quite different of that of the soils ones (3) : in the case of soil, the 3 400 cm^{-1} band is attribuable to the OH stretching indissociated carboxylic group ; this band is shiffed at 3 300 cm^{-1} region as a consequence of the presence of N-H stretching associated to the OH stretching by H bounds (this indicates the proteinic nature of this compound).

The band at 1 600 cm^{-1} observed in the case of soil humic acids is probably due to -COO^{-} group. this band is not observed for compost humic acids but in this region a strong band at 1 650 cm^{-1} attribuable to stretching of C=O from amine amide and proteins is observed. The bands observed between 1 000 and 1 100 cm^{-1} for soil humic acids results of silicate compounds inclusion (Si-O stretching vibrations) in the extracted organic material.

A strong reduction of these band intensities occurs for compost humic acid as a result of the weak bounding of the compost organic material with the mineral part of the waste.

As evidenced in Figure 3, the biological stability expressed by a respirometric method is considerably lower for the compost humic acids than for the soils one. It is very important to observe that these humic acids are extracted from 4 months old compost. This point shows that a longer period of composting could be necessary to obtain a strong increase in biological stability of compost organic matter.

4. CONCLUSION

The present work, by characterizing the humic acids obtained from city refuse compost and soil, reveals quite very important differences between the two materials. Even after several months of composting, the organic matter of city refuse compost remains unstable from the biological point of view. This unstability is probably related to the organic matter composition of the raw materials of the compost, as evidenced by comparison to the soil organic matter composition.

This points out the problem of the long term pattern of compost organic matter, indeed city refuse compost applied to soils must be of stabilized organic constituents (4), this implies a very long time of composting inducing a very strong decrease of organic matter content.

5. BIBLIOGRAPHY

(1) JUSTE C., 1980. Avantages et inconvénients de l'utilisation des composts d'ordures ménagères comme amendement organique des sols ou supports de culture.
     J. intern. sur le Compost, Madrid, 22-26/01/1986, 16 p. + annexes.
(2) GOMEZ A., LINERES M., TAUZIN J., SOLDA P., JUSTE C., 1984. Etude de l'incidence de l'apport de boues de station d'épuration à des sols sableux sur l'évolution qualitative et quantitative de la matière organique de ces sols.
     Conv. ét. INRA/Secr. Etat Environ., n° 81-285, 37 p. + Annexes.
(3) SUGAHARA K., INOKO A., 1981. Composition analysis of humus and characterization of humic acid obtained from city refuse compost.
     Soil Sci. Pl. Nutr., 27 (2), 213-224.
(4) JUSTE C., SOLDA P., DUREAU P., 1980. Mise au point de tests agronomiques légers permettant de déterminer simultanément la phytotoxicité globale des composts d'ordures ménagères et leur degré de maturation.
     Conv. ét. INRA/Min. Environ.& Cadre de Vie, n° 77-147, 19 p.+ annexes.

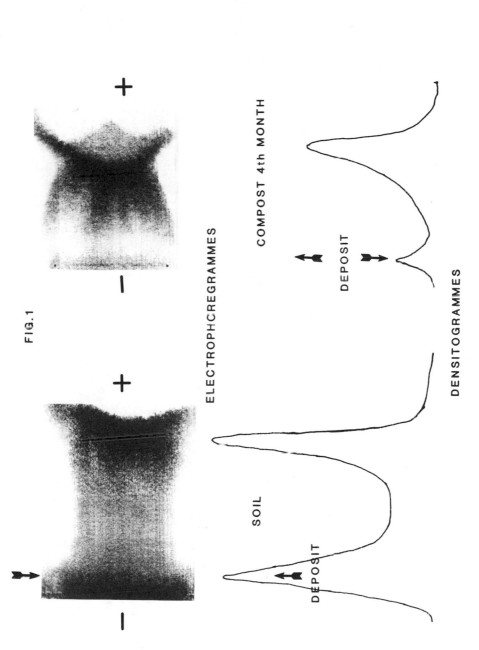

FIG. 1

ELECTROPHCREGRAMMES

COMPOST 4th MONTH

DEPOSIT

SOIL

DEPOSIT

DENSITOGRAMMES

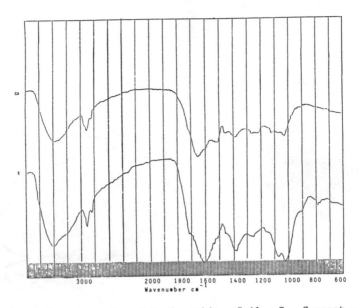

Figure 2 : Infrared spectra of humic acids - Soil = S - Compost = C4

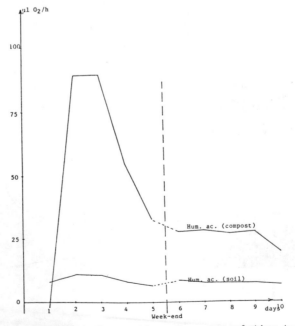

Figure 3 : Respirometry - Consumption of oxygen relative to 20 mg of humic
acid carbon

ODOUR INVESTIGATIONS AT TWO COMPOSTING PLANTS IN SWEDEN

Gunnar Hovsenius
Gunnar Hovsenius AB

Summary

At several forced aerated and open composting plants in Sweden, problems
in the form of odour disturbances have occured. The reasons have in some
cases their explanations both in the design and in the operation of the
plants.

Among the technical reasons at one plant in this investigation are the
design of and faults in a complicated system for forced aeration and
to that an unsufficient negative pressure for sucking the air through
the composting mass. It is also worth to mention that there was no equipment for turning and conditioning the composting mass.

Among reasons, which have their background in the operation of the plant,
are a high moisture content and substantial variations in the raw compost.
This resulted in press water in the bottom zone of the composting mass.
It also worth to mention that the moisture content in the soil filters
was unsufficient.

Most of the above mentioned faults have been clarified during the study.
An important step to decrease the odour nuisances was to spray the exhaust
air with water before its entrance in the compost filters.

1.   Background

The market for compost in Sweden is concentrated to the establishment
of parks and leisure grounds. Among the demands on compost, those connected
to the maturity, are of specific relevance to this study. As a matter
of fact they result in longer decomposition periods than those applied
in central and southern Europe. Thus the volume of composting material
of the plants (relative to the received waste volume) becomes greater.
From economics and process reasons this has lead to other technical solutions of the composting process being developed in Sweden - compared
with those used in for instance southern Europe.

The primary characteristic of the Swedish composting plants is the fact
that the composting is carried out out-doors and under forced aeration.
In some plants the intention was to blow the air through the composting

mass, while others intended to supply sucking. In some, like the plants at Borlänge and at Karlshamn, the aeration system was designed in such a way that both blowing and sucking could be used. It also worth mentioning that only a few plants have equipment to turn the composting mass. Instead the nature of composting has been static and turning has usually been made only when compost has been moved from one part of the composting area to another.

Several of the composting plants established in Sweden have had problems with embarrassing odour from the composting process. For this reason the National Environmental Protection Board (NEPB) took initiatives in order to find a solution to this problem. In co-operation with NEPB the composting plant at Borlänge was chosen as a test plant. Later the ideas from the investigation at Borlänge were confirmed at the composting plant at Karlshamn.

2.   Project idea and project plan

The olfactory organs in the nose are covered with a watery layer of phlegm. In this layer the substances that we percive have a smell must be disolved. This means for example that the evil-smelling substances created during composting are soluble in water. This fact was the idea on which this study is based. The idea was supported by certain observations made at composting plants.

The reason that evil-smelling substances are formed is commonly considered to be due to insufficient aeration in certain parts of the composting mass.

As long as the composting mass has a moisture content of 35 % or more, the exhaust air at forced aerated systems will in practice be saturated. If the aeration is made through sucking a condensate is formed in the exhaust air channels. In this condensate as well as in the water droplets in the exhaust air, the smelly substances can dissolve. If aeration is made through blowing, condensation is created instead in the upper part of the composting bed as a result of heat emission by radiation. At blowing as well as at sucking it is accordingly possible that evil-smelling substances are partly distributed by water droplets in the exhaust air from the compost. A consequence of this would be that the odour is noticeable only at a certain distance from the plant, and that the odour experiences depend on i.a. the humidity of the ambient air. Complaints made earlier in the vicinity of the plants in Borlänge and Karlshamn support this theory.

The project plan consisted of the following parts:

1. To locate sections with a risk of anaerobic conditions and to investigate the reasons behind the insufficient aeration. It was assumed that variations in moisture content and density were the main reasons for maldistribution of air.

2. To separate water droplets from the exhaust air of the process, when sucking is used as aeration method.
3. To wash out the evil-smelling substances from the exhaust air, when sucking is used as aeration method.
4. To decrease the quantity of remaining evil-smelling substances, by treating the exhaust air in compost filters.

As the project plan had to be adapted to existing condition at the test plant, certain characteristics of the composting plant at Borlänge are described below.

3.   Specific characteristics of the composting plant at Borlänge

The waste treatment plant at Borlänge is made upp of a pretreatment part consisting of shredding and separation, and a composting part consisting of a Dano drum to which sludge is added and of pre- and post-composting concrete tiles aerated by force. The equipment to compensate for moisture during progressing composting was lacking, for which reason maximum moisture was aimed at he preparation of raw compost. Accordingly, the risk of anaerobic conditions was greatest during the pre-composting. Therefore the investigations were concentrated to this phase.

Experience had earlier shown that the inconveniences caused by odour were less at sucking, when the air passed through compost filters than they were at blowing. It was therefore assumed that the composting mass should be aerated by sucking.

The pre-composting concrete tile consists of ten parallel-functioning sections of 30 m lenght and 12 m width. The aeration was made in intervals of 45 minutes of operation and 45 minutes'pause. During the aeration periods the aeration capacity correspond to 10 cu.m./h, sq.m. at a negative pressure of about 150 mm water column. The air was sucked off through grids somewhat sunken into the concrete tile, and with a c-c distance of about 1.5 m. To each row of grids belongs a pipe cast in the concrete tile, which ends in a junction channel common to each section. These channels were in their turn connected to a common exhaust channel.

In the junctions between, the junction channels and the pipes cast in the concrete tile on the one hand, and the junctions channels and the common exhaust channel on the other, butterfly valves had been mounted. The function of these, however, was so inadequate that aeration of one section could not be started until it had been completely filled with raw compost.

The spreading of raw compost was made with the help of a scraper the lower edge of which was situated 2.6 m above the concrete tile. Through this method the composting mass was exposed in its upper part to a bigger compression where the spreading had started, compared to where it ended.

The identification of suspected anaerobic spots was made through gas samples and measurement of the temperature around and directly above 11 aeration grids. At each grid samples were taken within a triangular aera of 1.8 x 0.9 m. The gas samples were analyzed for carbon dioxide and in some cases also for organic carbon, which is considered to be the measure of the content of evil-smelling substances. The measurement of the moisture in the composting mass and the density was carried out by radiation probes. These were released down through 6 permanent steel tubes per aeration grid.

The condensate droplets of the exhaust air were separated by the placing of droplet separators in the exhaust channel. The separators consisted of PVC rods with a diameter of 30 mm, placed in a uniform partition of about 120 mm. Their depth in the flow direction was some 1.5 m. Below the rods a tray was placed to collect and drain off condensate.

The washing of the exhaust air was made by spraying water into the channel system with nozzles of full-cone model. The nozzles were mounted on tubular frames so adjusted that the whole flow cross section was covered by water droplets. Up to four spray zones could be connected in series.

The ability of the compost filters to separate organic carbon was studied by periodical sampling of the emitted air directly under or on the upper surface of the filters.

4.   The experimental realization of the project at Borlänge

The starting point for this work was that it should be carried out in applying the operational practice achieved at the plant.However, it was evident that certain modifications needed to be done before a more comprehensive study was made.

4.1   Process changes before the main trial

According to achieved operational practice the moisture content of the raw compost was to be 58-60 %. In connection with the first sampling, which took place about a week after the conveyeing of raw compost was finished, it was observed that there was free water in large parts of the bottom zone of the composting bed. The pressure drop needed to bubble air through such parts amounted to 1.5 to 1.7 m water column; that is more than 10 times the sucking capacity of the fans. This meant that anaerobic conditions dominated, which could be observed when examining a dug-out part of the bed, where particularly evil-smelling substances were set free to the environment.

After about 5 weeks enough press water had drained off via the aeration grids for the composting bed to be aerated in some parts. It can be assumed that malodorous gases were ventilated off.

To avoid the presence of a non-aerated bottom zone, the moisture content of the raw compost was decreased to about 55 %. Furthermore, the composting concrete tile was covered with a layer 25 cm thick of compost with a moisture content of about 35 %. These measures resulted in a well-aerated compost bed. In connection with the so-called main experiment it was discovered that brief but substantial variations in the moisture content of the raw compost took place. The reason for this was that sludge was pumped into the Dano drum at intervals. After the sludge dosing apparatus had been adjusted to almost continuous dosing the raw compost became more homogenous in its moisture content.

In connection with the start of meaningful carbon dioxide measurements, it was established that the carbon dioxide content of the exhaust air was considerably lower than the contents found in the compost bed. A systematical analysis of the reasons showed that:

1. the arrangement made around the fans to allow blowing as well as sucking lead to a leakage of air. For this reason the system was changed so that only sucking was possible.
2. the assembly channels to the sections which were shut off due to no compost, were swept through by air. For this reason all valves were cleaned and the air pipes belonging to non-utilized sections were shut off with plastic plugs.
3. the outer air pipes in each section emitted a greater amount of air than the others. The reason was that the height of the compost bed was lower in the outer parts.

When the measuring programme for the exhaust air was started, a considerably uneven distribution of the flow through the compost filters was noted. The reason for this was that the outer parts were dried up while the inner parts were damp. On these grounds the material in the compost filters was changed. In that way they became homogenous.

4.2   The realization of the main study

Eleven measuring stations were located in the test section to determine carbon dioxide, temperature, moisture content and density round and above 11 aeration grids. The stations were placed in three rows. Two of these contained four stations each. Along the two outer rows the moisture content of the raw compost was 55-56 %, while it was 58-60 % along the middle row.

The carbon dioxide content was determined in the bottom layer of the compost bed, in junction channels and so on through in situ measurements.

Organic carbon, sulphur and nitrogen in the exhaust air were determined through absorption in water. Up to four washing bottles were connected in series. From the content changes discovered between the bottles the equilibrium constant between gas and liquid phase can be determined and thus also the quantity of water needed to wash away a certain quantity of the evil-smelling gaseous components.

The quantity of condensate, collected from the droplet separators, was collected periodically for quantity determination and analysis.

5.   Variations in the dry matter content and density of the composting material

At discontinuing sludge charging to the Dano drum the dry matter content of the raw compost could deviate with 3-4 % units from the daily mean value during one hour; i.e. variations of up to 8 % units occured. After the sludge adding had become more continous the differences decreased between various hourly mean values, but there were isolated samples with notably high dry matter contents. The probable reason for this was that the commercial and industrial wastes, which are drier than domestic waste, at times were the dominating types of wastes.

After about 3 weeks of aeration it was observed that a considerable dessication of the compost bed had taken place. In the upper one-third of
the bed moisture contents of 40 % or less were very frequent. In the lower
two-thirds moisture contents of between 42 % and 60 % had occurred. The
distribution of fields between 58 and 60 % was however very limited in
height and concentrated to the lower one-third. The density of the composting material varied between some 720 and 800 kg per cu.m., and no
connection with moisture could be found. The highest density (780 - 800 kg
per cu.m.) occurred closest to the surface and down to about 0.4 m below
it. This is probably a manifestation of the compression created by the
scraping conveyor. A proportioanlly high density was also found close
to the bottom tile, while the lowest ones (720 - 740 kg per cu.m.) occurred
from 0.3 m to about 1.0 m above the concrete tile.

To prevent continued dessication of the compost bed, which among other
things could lead to a retardation of the composting process, the test
section was sprinkled with 200 to 250 mm of water during two days and
nights. Directly after the sprinkling it was noted that:

1. the added water hade been unevenly distributed
2. at half of the investigated stations the water had accumulated both
    in a surface and in a bottom layer. At about one-third of the measuring
    stations water had accumuᴌated in its intended place; i.e. in the upper
    one-third of the compost bed. At about 20 % of the stations the water
    had primarily found its way down to the bottom layer and accumulated
    within limited but non-connected volumes. Within these the moisture
    content was as high as 60 % or thereabouts.

As a consequence of moisture accumulation in the bottom layer the aeration
was obstructed and in some cases stopped. In the beginning the latter
was the case at some 25 - 30 % of the sampling points. After about 2 weeks,
however, so much water had drained off that the aeration worked again
at the channels that were blocked earlier.

During a period of about 5 weeks after the sprinkling a considerable
dessication of the composting material took place. Up to a height of 1 m
above the concrete tile the moisture content decreased by 2 - 4 % units. At
the top of the compost bed the dessication was greatest, as expected.
Within the top 50 cm the moisture content changed from 50 - 54 % to
40 - 46 %.

The conclusin which can be drawn from the above observations is that
the material repeatedly has to be turned during simultaneous addition
of water. In this way the compact top layer would be broken up, which
would facilitate an even aeration of the composting material.

6.   The dependence of the aeration on the local pressure drop
        across the composting material

The activity of the microorganisms at aerobic composting leads i.a. to
the formation of carbon dioxide and the development of heat. The object
of aerating the composting material is on the one hand to provide the
microorganisms with the required oxygen, and on the other hand to carry
off the carbon dioxide and the heat.

In order for the forced aeration to succed it is necessary that the composting material has a number of free pores. By way of these pores a
gas exchange can take place, both by the added air flow and by "molecular
migration", so-called diffussion. Owing to the latter process certain
parts can be supplied with oxygen, as long as the pores are not filled
with water - even if the forced aeration is blocked.

The aeration took place, as mentioned earlier, in periods of 45 minutes
of sucking and a pause of 45 minutes. During the first three weeks of
aeration (that is before sprinkling) it was observed that:
1. at the transition from pause to sucking the carbon dioxide content
   varied between 2 and 17 % with a mean value of 9 %. At the end of the
   sucking period the content had been reduced to an average of 5 - 6 %.
2. at certain points with carbon dioxide contents of over 15 % the reduction was only 1 - 2 % units, while the content at other points was
   reduced to about one-third of the original value.
3. for test points in the range of 6 - 10 % carbon dioxide changes occurred
   of the same kind mentioned in 2. However, the content could at certain
   points be reduced to less than 1 %.

After sprinkling the carbone dioxide content in the bottom layer was
about 13 % at the end of the rest period. The distribution between contents
at different points was great, however. In no less than about 45 % of these
the content was as high as 15 - 21 %. A share almost as big was found in
the interval 6 - 15 %. The content reductions observed during the sucking
phase had the same pattern as before the sprinkling.

In connection with gas sampling the pressure drop,which was needed to make
a small gas stream pass through the sampling pipes, was measured. At test
points with a well-functioning exchange of air the pressure drop amounted
to only 25 - 30 mm water column, while it at points where smaller quantities of free water had been noted, was as high as 150 - 175 mm water
column. To increase the negative pressure and by this create a better
distribution of air, was considered very difficult, as the mentioned
type of imbalance would be reinforced, if anything. This is an additional
argument for the fact that the composting material needs to be mixed
during the decomposition phase.

During the sucking periods the carbondioxide content was measured in the
junction channel to the test section and compared with the contents in
this. It turned out that the content in the junction channel was lower
throughout, which may depend on the following:
1. a big share of the air passed through very easily ventilated parts of
   the compost bed.
2. air is added to the junction channel from other sections through the
   complex aeration system.

By this comparison it may be deduced that the sucking and the rest periods
were too long. By shortening the rest periods the carbon dioxide content
would be lower at the end of the rest period as well as at the end of
the sucking period.

The median temperature in the bottom zone of the investigated compost bed
was as high as 74° C. In nearly 10 % of the measuring points the temperature was lower than 55° C. In spite of this a temperature of 51 - 52° C was

measured in the junction channel. Within the group of measuring points, where the temperature was 55° C at the most, the aeration was so good that the carbon dioxide content was reduced to 2 - 3 % during the sucking period.

With the data arising from the experiment it can be shown that diffusion probably was responsible for a significant portion of the gas exchange in the investigated compost bed. In its nature the activity radius of the diffusion was probably not more than 1 m. This means that a total oxygen deficiency aries at aeration grids which are blocked for aeration. The test material supports this view. It would also be characteristic of the diffusion that badly ventilated parts get a higher temperature than others. The observations made support also this view.

7.   The possibilities of separating evil-smelling substances from the exhaust air at composting

The parameters chosen as indicators of evil-smelling substances were:
    * total organic carbon (TOC)
    * nitrogen, expressed as N-Kjeld and $N-NH_4$
    * total sulphur (S)

In the concept N-Kjeld also $N-NH_4$ is included. Since the latter nitrogen form in this case turned out to be dominating (>95 %), the difference between N-Kjeld and $N-NH_4$ was regarded as an uncertain indicator of the presence of the other nitrogen compounds. For this reason not as many nitrogen analyses were carried out as TOC analyses. For sulphur it was a rule that the contents were very low, bordering those which could be established with the method used. For this reason the number of analyses for sulphur was reduced.

Gas samples were taken in the test section, partly at a point where the carbon dioxide content reached about 20 % shortly before the sucking period was begun, partly at a point where 8 % carbon dioxide at the most was noted. Furthermore, gas samples were taken in the junction channel to the test section. The results are:

* at the test point with high carbon dioxide content the contents of TOC reached 800 - 2700 mg C/cu.m. of gas, $N-NH_4$ was 25 - 150 mg/cu.m. of gas and total sulphur was about 15 mg/cu.m. of gas or less.
* at the test point with low carbon dioxid content the contents of TOC was 80 - 230 mg/cu.m. of gas $N-NH_4$ was about 15 mg/cu.m. of gas and total sulphur was about 15 mg/cu.m. of gas or less.
* in the junction channel the content of TOC was about 470 mg/cu.m. of gas, $N-NH_4$ about 4 mg/cu.m. of gas and finally total sulphur < 8 mg/cu.m. of gas.

After the droplet separators gas was sampled during five days of operation. Contents of TOC were notet that were between 230 and 440 mg/cu.m. of gas. For $N-NH_4$ the content was lower than 2 mg/cu.m. of gas. For sulphur the contents of were so low that the reliability of the analytical method can be questioned.

From the data, on which the above results are based, the equilibrium constant was calculated at 25° C between TOC content in gas and aqueos phase to about 0.002 mg TOC/l of gas per mg TOC/l of water. The spray zone was designed

on the mentioned value of the equilibrium constant. The intention was
that the injection capacity with all four steps connected should be about
300 l/minute. Due to pressure drops in the pipes no more than half of
this capacity was reached. The gas samples which were taken after the
spray zone showed TOC contents of 35 - 45 mg/cu.m. of gas, independet
of wether 2, 3 or 4 washing steps were operational. In comparison with
TOC contents before the wash the result means that somewhat more than
80 % of the TOC content had been removed. This is more than the theo-
retically calculated result. The deviation is probably due to the fact
that the washing water was as cold as about 7° C, while the equilibrium
constant was determined for 25° C. No difference was noted for various
numbers of washing steps. This may be due to the fact that the available
water quantity had been the same and that it was controled by the pressure
drop in the flow pipe.

After the material in the compost filters had been changed samples were
taken of exhaust gas, partly before the spray zone had been taken into
operation, and also when the spray had been operational for 2 weeks.
In both cases two parallel filters were connected. The test results indicate that:

* the content of TOC in exhaust gas is considerably lower after the spray
  had been taken into operation. This may be due to the fact that the
  bed under the filter, which consists of pebbles, functioned as an additional wet contact step.
* the outer edges of the filter give a somewhat poorer adsorption of
  TOC compared with the central parts.
* the filters take care of some 70 % - 80 % of the TOC content left in
  the gas after the washing step.

Together the washing steps and the compost filters would thus separate
90 - 95 % of the TOC content in the air after the droplet separators.

The condensate quantity which was collected at the droplet separators
amounted only to about 0.15 mg/cu.m. exhaust air, which constituted
20 - 25 % of the total quantity of liquid droplets present in the exhaust
air.

The content of TOC in the preserved liquid amounted to 7900 - 8300 mg/l.
The content of N-Kjeld was 2000 - 3800 mg/l, of which $N-NH_4$ constituted
more then 95 %. The total content of sulphur was in one of the samples
as low as 4 mg/l, while it was 55 mg/l in another. Of the exhaust air's
TOC content the share which was caught in the droplet separated constituted less than 0.5 %. The situation is almost the same for nitrogen
content - however some 3 % was separated. Even if the efficiency of the
droplet separators should have increased considerably this would not
have meant any significant improvement in the TOC reduction.

8.   Hypothesis-controlling final tests

By the account made in earlier parts it is evident that certain adjustments
were made during the course of the tests. In order to check what the
results would have been if the measurements had been taken from the
beginning, a final test was carried out at Borlänge, in which all the
adjustments were included.

The conclusions which can be drawn from the final test are:

1. that the aeration is not sufficiently even despite the fact that the moisture content was decreased from 60 to 55 % in the raw compost. For this reason the composting process was not sufficiently controlled. For this reason the plant has afterwards been supplied with equipment for turning, mixing and redampening of the composting material.

2. washing of the exhaust gases with water will reduce the TOC content in the gases, but will also improve the separating ability of the compost filters. This is demonstrated be the following data for TOC.

         junction channel at test section   700 - 750 mg TOC/cu.m.
         at fan inlet   about 250   - " -
         after water wash   148 - 180   - " -
         after compost filters   10 - 25   - " -

Subjectively, the reduction of evil-smelling substances, seems to be greater than the TOC reduction.

The experiences from this investigation were during 1985 applied to the composting plant at Karlshamn, Sweden, which also had problems with embarrassing odour from the process. In this case the raw compost is put on the pre-composting area by means of afront loaded tractor. The layer of the raw compost is about 1.8 m deep.

The moisture content of the raw compost was about 60 %. By the first inspection it was observed that the bottom layer was very wet. In spite of a negative pressure of 1500 mm water coloumn - the plant was operating by sucking air through the composting mass - no air penetration occured in reality. This resulted in temperatures from 70° to over 80° C and a content of carbon dioxide from 18 % to more than 21 %.

By decreasing the moisture content from 60 % to less than 55 % and by turning the material at intervals of three weeks the process changed from anaerobic to aerobic and the temperature could be controlled to the range of 50° to 60° C. It was also noticed that this change allowed the negative pressure to be only about 250 mm of water coloumn.

In spite of the above mentioned improvement the plant was considered as a risk for emission of odour compounds. Therefore it was also in this case decided to let the exhaust air pass through very wet soil filters. For this reason a water spray system was installed between the fans and the filters. This resulted in an excellent reduction of the odour around the plant.

The conclusions from the two Swedish studies are consequently:

1) the primary risk for odours is involved in the preparation of the raw compost. A moisture content exceeding 55 % can not be recommended.
2) to avoid mal-distribution of air at open forced aerated systems it is necessary to turn the composting material
3) spraying the exhaust gases with water in combination with very wet soil filters is an effective method to eliminate odours.

UTILIZATION OF FARM ANIMAL MANURE FOR HUMUS SUBSTRATE PRODUCTION

Dr. Svatopluk MACKRLE, Dr. Vladimir MACKRLE
Slovak technical University, Bratislava

Summary
Two concepts of animal manure utilization are analyzed in the present
contribution : BIOGAS system and HUMUS system.
For the purpose of their comparison the criterion of efficiency of
the cyclic compensation feedback between vegetal and animal
production has been used, in particular from the viewpoint of
returning the fertilizing components of manure back to soil, in
optimum form for the production of plants.
Upon this basis the conclusion may be drawn that the HUMUS technology
with direct transfer of fertilizing matter from the manure in its
original form, into the solid phase achieved by mechanical and
chemical processing, with following compostation, is more efficient
and at the same time more economical than the BIOGAS system where the
fertilizing matter is transfered into applicable fertilizer only
after anaerobic fermentation ; the production of biogas being used
for fermentation and separation purposes.

INTRODUCTION
The production of stall manure in classical animal farms and its
application for soil fertilization used to represent an efficient cyclic
compensation feedback between vegetal and animal production. It is often
left out of consideration that the decisive component of this system was
the dung hill that performed the function of a fermentor contributing to
the bioconversion of organic residua of vegetal and animal production to
form high-molecular humine matter. This original feedback, allowing perfect
utilization of fertilizing matter contained in the excrements, represents
an ideal state sui generis with which any substituting solution should be
compared.
The concentrations of livestock in large animal farms implementing
industrial technologies replaces very frequently a former cyclic motion of
nutrients by a linear one, resulting in the loss of these nutrients on the
account of deteriorating, and even devastating the environment.
In numerous production units, liquid manure from industrial animal
farms represents rather scrap than highly valuable organic material. This
is due to the lack of appropriate procedures for its treatment that would
allow efficient, economical, lossfree utilization of valuable material
contained in it, while returning the latter to the soil in the form of
high-molecular humines. This, however, cannot be achieved without including
a thermophilic bioconversion stage into the cyclic compensation feedback
for the transformation of organic matter.
In this way the importance of composting for agricultural processes
appears to be well explained. It is also obvious that a come-back to the
original cyclic compensation linkage between vegetal and animal production,
such as existed on the technical level of small family farms, would not be
efficient for large industrial livestock plants ; therefore novel technical
solutions should be sought allowing to reach the specified objective with

economic means.

In the framework of introduction to the present discussion relating to liquid manure from large animal farms, it seems appropriate to mention the fact that all aspects of this problem have not yet found perfectly satisfactory solutions world wide.

However, two most important concepts for the utilization of organic matter from manure have gradually crystallized out of the considerable numbers of various technical and technological possibilities of approach :
- the first concept is the BIOGAS system
- the second concept is the HUMUS system, offering re-usage of liquid manure in the form of humus substrate.

It is not uninteresting to realize that the concept of energetic revaluation of liquid manure in the form of BIOGAS appeared as a reaction to the shock from the energetic crisis after the dramatic rise of crude oil prices. Under this influence also big companies with world renown, such as FIAT in Italy, orientated their efforts in the direction of energetic revaluation of liquid manure. This tendency was clearly felt all over Europe. As an example the organizing of international congresses covering this topic may be mentioned, such as Congresso internationale sul tema "Trattamento ed utilizzazione delle deiezioni zootechniche" in Mantova in 1980.

The outcome of that congress was in favour of the energetic utilization trend that was full "en vogue" at those days. The contribution of the Czechoslovak participant of the above congress, published later (1), however, offered as early as at that time a rough energetic and economic estimate in comparing the system BIOGAS and HUMUS, pointing to some disadvantages of the energetic revaluation of the organic mass of manure.

Since the Mantova congress 6 years have elapsed that have been filled with intensive development of both competing concepts. The object of this contribution consists in the evaluation of the mentioned development over the given time interval, i.e. from the Mantova congress down to the present day, and in drawing some conclusions for the actual solution of this problem attracting attention world-wide.

DETERMINATION OF CRITERIA FOR THE EVALUATION OF THE EFFICIENCY OF LIQUID MANURE UTILIZATION

The original reasoning in favour of the BIOGAS system was based solely upon acquiring a local source of primary energy. The majority of published technical and economical studies of manure utilization under the form of BIOGAS introduce, as their principal criterion, the profitability of the production of energy within a narrow, and often an incomplete subsystem, the production of BIOGAS as such, without an essential interconnection with the overall system of agricultural production.

An example of such approach is offered by the technical and economical analysis of the BIOGAS system (2) evaluating the BIOGAS system, but without any consideration of sludge water produced in the process of manure fermentation.

The incorrectness, and unsupportability of such approach will become obvious from the evaluation of the subsystem of processing and usage of liquid manure in the framework of the whole system of agricultural primary production.

One of the decisive factors for agricultural production in general terms is the fertility of soil. With respect to soil fertility a global notion may be introduced under the name of "bioenergetical potential of soil" covering the capacity of soil to produce plants in connection with energetic inputs into soil working, fertilizing, irrigation etc.

The bioenergetical potential of soil depends, to a great extent, upon the structure and the sorbtion capacity of soil that are affected, in the first instance, by the contents of stable high-molecular humine material.

A fundamental source of stable humus for soil used to be the dung hill where stable humus with a high ratio of high-molecular humine material used to be produced by way of thermophilic fermentation under increased temperatures.

The molecular bond of humine chains during the bioconversion of organic matter through microbiological processes of humification depends directly on the temperature under which these processes are going on. For this reason it cannot be sufficient to return residual organic materials to soil just as they are. Low temperatures under which the bioconversion of organic matter in soil takes place are enough for rottening processes resulting into products of low stability, enriching soil solely by an easily degradable organic component that is indispensable as a source of energy for soil microorganisms.

However, no stable humus needed for maintaining desirable soil structure can be produced in this way. Thus the importance of original dung fertilizer can be explained in the framework of the system of the cyclic compensation feedback between animal and vegetal production. Any approach to the problem of liquid manure that does not contribute to the support of stable humus in soil is fundamentally incorrect. In this respect attention should be drawn to the fact that the process of decrease of stable humus in soil, in connection with its stability, is a long term one, and the disastrous effects can become obvious as late as after dozens of years.

A research of humus contents in soil in Czechoslovakia, under conditions of decreasing renovation of stable humus due to extensive manure management in connection with the transition to industrial farming, without solving the final stage of manure handling, has brought evidence as to deteriorated quality of humus in soil, in particular the diminution of its high-molecular component.

Consequently, the solution of the cyclic compensation feed-back of vegetal and animal production under conditions of high concentrations of animals in industrial farm halls appears to be of vital importance.

The synthesis of high-molecular humine matter from organic material is a microbiological process with high energetical demands ; no surrogate has been found as yet by way of chemical synthesis and, consequently, it is irretrievable. From this standpoint of view the concept of energetic utilization of the organic matter in manure has no foundation at all.

When trying to substantiate in favour of the BIOGAS concept, there are frequent arguments as to only a smaller part of the organic matter in manure being subject to biodegradation, yet the fact is omitted that this is just the part that is most easily accessible also for the humification procedures of the bioconversion, for the production of high-molecular humine material, and that the energy absorbed in the process of anaerobic fermentation for the production of BIOGAS is necessarily lacking for the synthesis of stable humus.

In the long run the bioenergetic potential of soil is deprived of values, which corresponds with energetic losses in the agricultural production due to required higher energetic inputs that are necessary to improve the poorer fertility of soil by other means, e.g. by way of artificial fertilizers, by more exacting soil working, by higher requirements relating to humidity, etc., the sum of which exceed by far the value of energy acquired in the form of BIOGAS.

For this reason also the BIOGAS system has had to shift its target priorities quite substantially ; namely from the priority of energetic utilization to the priority of maximum revaluation of matter contained in manure in the form of fertilizer.

The changed approach has become apparent in particular in the orientation towards the treatment of sludge water after anaerobic fermentation. In this respect, the sludge water as such with some contents of fertilizing matter in diluted form has again presented a certain form of difficult waste, however, in a modified form, as compared with raw manure.

Without an efficient and economical solution of the problem of sludge water the BIOGAS system represents an incomplete technology that does not treat liquid waste satisfactorily, while being a real abuse to environment in the cases of big farms. It can be even said that the problem of sludge water was among the main reasons that cooled down the first enthusiasm towards this technology.

MODIFIED BIOGAS SYSTEM WITH SLUDGE WATER TREATMENT (TO TURN IT TO FERTILIZER)

Methods of processing sludge water so as to obtain fertilizing matter contained in it have been drawn attention to all over the world. In Czechoslovakia further development of the method mentioned in lit. (1) has been carried on, i.e. the chemical and physical process of separating ammonia from sludge water under increased temperature, ammonia being transformed into free form in heavily alkaline environment, with following after-treatment of sludge water by aerobic activation. This integrated technology will be briefly designated as Integrated System Biogas (ISB). Such technological process represents an analogy to an existing purification technique of coke waste that has been introduced quite some time ago. A modified method of such chemical and physical separation of ammonia is described in lit (4).

DESCRIPTION OF THE TECHNOLOGY OF THE INTEGRATED SYSTEM BIOGAS (ISB), INCLUDING REMOVAL OF AMMONIA FROM SLUDGE WATER AFTER ANAEROBIC FERMENTATION OF MANURE

A diagram covering the integrated system Biogas including the processing of sludge water, as worked out by CSAV (Czechoslovak Academy of Sciences), is in Fig. 1.

Sludge water after methane fermentation and after the separation of the solid phase of manure is alkalified by adding calcium oxide for expelling ammonia and for precipitating phosphoric salts. The resulting precipitate is separated and the removed ammonia is boiled at the following stage. The separation of ammonia is achieved by way of a rectification column ; the condensation heat extracted from the vapours in the condensing unit is made use of to heat the manure in the anaerobic fermentor, applying the fermented manure as a cooling liquid in the condensing unit. The amount of heat needed for maintaining the required temperature of about 35°C in the fermentor corresponds roughly with the amount of heat that should be taken away from the vapours in the condensing unit.

Thus the heat is utilized twice ; at first, at a higher temperature level, it is supplied to the boiler of the rectification column for the removal of ammonia and obtaining concentrated ammonia water and, in the second instance, heat at a lower temperature level is used to heat up the fermentor. Under conditions of good heat management only a small amount of heat is consumed for ammonia removal (25 to 45 MJ/t of water free from ammonia).

Through rectification more than 90 % of ammonia contained in waste water are obtained in the form of ammonia water having about 8 - 10 mass percent of ammonia.

Ammonia water is not suitable for direct fertilization. The drafted technology suggests ammonia to be bound by an acid component at the following stage, in particular by carbon oxide that is present in biogas and, consequently, can be used for the process.

During the absorption of carbon oxide from biogas into ammonia water the biogas is simultaneously freed from sulphur (to about 95 - 98 %) and its caloric value is improved. This is favourable from the viewpoint of the following combustion process.

As liquid phase, diluted technical ammonium carbonate leaves the absorber. Ammonia removal is followed by aerobic biological after-purification of sludge water.

PROCESSING OF FARM ANIMAL MANURE TO PRODUCE HUMUS SUBSTRATE - THE HUMUS SYSTEM

By analogy with the BIOGAS system, having achieved a certain shift related to the technical solution level, the HUMUS system has not stagnated, either, the development having been concentrated upon improved efficiency of utilization of various matter contained in manure, as well as upon cutting the humus production cost.

In this direction an integrated technology for producing humus substrate from manure has been finalized that will be further referred to briefly as ISH (Integrated System Humus). Its diagram with respective mass balance is in Fig. 2.

DESCRIPTION OF THE INTEGRATED SYSTEM HUMUS (ISH) FOR PROCESSING MANURE TO HUMUS SUBSTRATE

The ISH technology consists of three interrelated technological procedures, namely :
- tranforming of matter contained in manure into solid phase, using a coagulation-absorption process with following filtration,
- after-purification of the liquid phase of manure in applying the integrated biological purification system, with simultaneous nitrification and denitrification serving for the removal of residual carbonaceous and nitrogenous matter from the effluent,
- biotechnological conversion of the separated solid phase of sludge in a continuous bioreactor, resulting in humus substrate.

First of all raw manure is coagulated by calcium hydroxide under very high pH values over 11,5, with following absorption upon humus substrate that is produced by composting of the separated solid phase of manure. The effect of the coagulation - absorption process is seen in a marked improvement of filtrability of treated sludge as compared with raw manure, which allows an advantageous application of mechanical filtration for these purposes, modified in accordance with the high concentrations of dry matter with some specific features. For this purpose a special mechanical separator upon the basis of a filter press has been developed, and is in the stage of experimental testing, its essential features being high separation ratio and acceptable cost.

Then the liquid phase of manure is after-purified in an integrated biotechnological process comprising, along with the biodegradation of residual organic matter, also the nitrification and denitrification of residual contents of nitrogenous matter. In this case the coagulation - absorption process is controlled so as to achieve the required ratio between the residual concentration of biodegradable organic matter in the form of BOD_5 and the contents of residual nitrogenous matter in the liquid phase of manure, as necessary for the denitrification processes. Excessive sludge is then returned back to the on-flow to the system, subjected to the coagulation - absorption process, and finally separated by filtration.

The homogenous separated solid sludge has about 25 % of dry matter, and the overall efficiency of the conversion of various matter contained in the manure into solid phase suitable for further treatment by composting amounts to about 90 % for total solids, as well as 90 % for total organic matter, up to 45 % for nitrogenous matter expressed in values of TKN, to about 98 % of phosphorus and about 12 % of potassium.

For composting the raw organic substrate separated from manure, by a continuous biotechnological process, the aerobic bioreactor has been used for the ISH technology. The reasons for the choice of a continuous production process of humus substrate are, on the one hand, a marked intensification of the process and, on the other hand, the possibility to control the operation. The reliability of the process of organic material humification depends on ensuring optimum conditions, in particular temperature, humidity and regular distribution of oxygen in the whole charge of the bioreactor, as well as suitable mechanical structure and chemical composition of the charge.

From the viewpoint of energy, the humification of organic matter represents, as has been already mentioned, a process of synthetising high-molecular humines with high energetical demands. The energy required for the course of these reactions is obtained by way of the microbiological oxidation processes of the transformation of the biodegradable components of the organic mass charge of the bioreactor.

The loss of organic material during the bioconversion in the bioreactor amounts to about 20 %, and further 5 to 10 % get lost in the course of ripening of fresh humus substrate on piles. For this reason the biotechnology of continuous humification of organic material in bioreactors requires the charge to have sufficient proportions of organic mass that is easily accessible to microbial processes, in particular during their first bacterial stage characterized by high temperature.

Organic mass without appropriate biodegradable share can not be effectively processed by way of intensive bioconversion processes in continuous bioreactors.

In addition to the microbiologically accessible energetic potential of organic mass also a well balanced ratio C : N : P of the charge is of considerable importance.

In the light of the above criteria relating to organic material for continuous humification in the bioreactors the separated solid phase of manure is seen to fulfil all these conditions. In addition to that it contains practically all calcium used for the coagulation of sludge. Thus the favourable effect of the Ca contents is doubled ; on the one hand, calcium takes directly part in the humification processes and, on the other hand, it has a certain buffer function within the charge, positively contributing to the preferable alkaline reaction of the charge during the humification process of the organic charge mass. The high energetic contents accessible to the bioconversion processes, as well as the contents of N and P in the solid phase of animal manure allow to process simultaneously with it further complementary organic mass in the bioreactors, such as vegetal production waste, secondary wood mass (such as sawdust, rind, waste paper) and further organic material, such as municipal solid waste, biological sludge from purification plants etc. that cannot be processed all alone by intensive humification processes in bioreactors. Together with the solid phase of the animal sludge, however, such secondary organic raw material can be well composted allowing, as carbon carrier, not only to compensate for the loss of organic mass during the humification processes, but in addition to that also to increase the production of humus substrate from animal sludge. This fact has a substantial effect from the viewpoint of the economy of the whole process.

APPROXIMATIVE TECHNICAL AND ECONOMICAL EFFECTS OF THE ISB AND ISH TECHNOLOGIES

The objective of the suggested solutions and the function of both compared technologies consists in purposeful treatment and utilization of farm animal manure for better efficiency of the cyclic compensation feed-back of vegetal and animal production, and at the same time also for essential improvements of the environment protection.

In this stage the technical and economical effects can be expressed solely in a generalized way, serving orientation purposes. The integrated, yet appropriately modified approach is based upon the following principles:

1. The principle of integrity of the supposed achievable positive results and the claims of all participants of the innovation process ; in other words not only the requirements of the farmers, but also those of the following branches of national economy.

2. The principle of dynamics and of relativity of individual factors encountered in the development of the social and economic efficiency of environment protection, a notion that has not yet been adequately quantified down to the present day ; on the one hand, the retarding influence of traditional subjective opinions and, on the other hand, the vital necessity of accounting for the time factor for the restoration of impaired environment balance, both are factors the extent of which does not appear to be considered to the full.

3. The principle of seeking the optimum variant both for agricultural practice and for the whole society, minimizing the cost and maximizing the effects. Consequently, instead of assessing definitive routine processes, this study offers an analysis based upon the present day knowledge, trying to support the correct choice and the reasoning in favour of further progressive methods leading to the fulfilment of the set out objectives.

4. The principle of objectivity, without any influencing a priori due to tendencies ensuing from partial, one-sided over-estimation of certain features (e.g. under the effect of the shock caused by the outbreak of the energetic crisis).

The technical and economical analysis is concentrated upon the evaluation of two selected variants of a progressive solution based upon a practical example of a pig farm for 5000 animals, namely :

1) full implementation of ISB (Integrated System Biogas)
2) full implementation of ISH (Integrated System Humus)

The ISB variant has been complemented by a biological purification plant, in order to ensure comparability of effluent quality. The operation of the ISH variant has been considered, for calculation purposes, equiped to ensure composting with two bioreactors, 400 m^3 each, from the company Gebrüder Weiss KG (German Federal Republic).

In order to assess the internal cost structure related to the individual operations of both systems, diagramatical representations are given in Figs. 3 and 4. Whereas the most essential cost items of ISB are the coagulation with sedimentation and recuperation including rectification, representing 72 % of overall cost, in ISH the continuous composting operation is seen to require 65 % of overall cost.

Whereas the BIOGAS system, in view of the technical requirements related to the first two operations, does not allow us to expect any reduction of the share of these operations within the overall cost, rather admitting a certain risk of their possible rise (according to experimental model data), the HUMUS system has objective prerequisites for cutting down both investment and operation cost of the continuous composting operation, this being also an indispensable claim as concerns successful implementation in agriculture production and in environmental protection.

Fig. 5 offers a cost analysis related to composting in bioreactors of Weiss.

The cost dependance on the capacity of the bioreactors appears to be all too pronounced, narrowing down their profitable application in smaller farms. The investment cost of composting represents 84 % of the overall investment cost of the HUMUS system. For this reason further research and development are carried on with the orientation towards lower investment cost that should be reduced by some 40 - 50 %, which would induce also some operation cost cut. Naturally, the technical and economical considerations are based upon present day data. The results of the positive effects of both ISH and ISB, as well as the conditions for achieving them, are reviewed in Fig. 6 for a 5000 pig farm having daily manure production amounting to 80 m^3, i.e. 29 200 m^3 per year.

Some brief comments as concerns the introduced characteristics :

1. At present the investment cost of ISH, in absolute representation, is about 58 %. However, as calculated for 1 m^3 of the final product, it is by 24 % lower than in the case of ISB. Of course the ISH humus has about 40 % dry matter, whereas the ISB humus only 25 %. After the implementation of an innovated solution of continuous compostation the absolute value of investment cost will be equal for both systems ; however, if calculated in terms of 1 m^3 of substrate (ISH offering double fertilizing value, as compared with ISB), ISH will require only 54 % of investment cost needed for ISB.

2. The production cost of 1 m humus is by 57 % lower in the case of ISH, against ISB, further cost reductions appearing to be viable in near future.

3. The BIOGAS system used to be favoured as a certain partial way out of an urgent shortage of energy in cases of limited resources. Its advertizing, however, appears to have been based upon erroneous partial approach. If ammonia is to be eliminated (by boiling of ammonia water), a considerable part of produced biogas is consumed for this process, the rest representing no particular energetic asset. From the viewpoint of energetic requirements related to 1 m^3 of final product, ISH lies by 7 % lower than ISB.

4. If viewing the energetical claims from the platform of the whole society, using an integral approach, the consumption of energy in chemical industries should not be left out of consideration : the production of 1 kg N requires 80 MJ, 1 kg P 40 MJ and 1 kg K 25 MJ, respectively. In humus produced by both systems the above elements are present, in the ratio given under paragraphs 7 - 9. The economy of energy, as viewed from the standpoint of the whole nation, favours quite unambiguously and most objectively the ISH way, registering savings of energy by 127 % higher than those of ISB. Thus a myth is done away with that used to be spread relating to the reputed advantages of BIOGAS thanks to energetic savings, disregarding further disadvantages in terms of fertilizing effect etc.

5. The number of operators needed for ISH is by one third lower than for ISB.

6. The final product of ISH is most valuable humus sustrate, enriched by nitrogen, phosphorus and potassium in organically bonded form, the fertilizing effect of which doubles its value, as compared with the resulting product of ISB. It can be compared with a mixture of soil blended with peat and enriched with mineral fertilizers the price of which amounts to 210,- DM per 1 m^3 in the Federal Republic of Germany. For the composting process ISH makes use, in addition to the solid phase of manure, also of C-carriers and further admixtures (poultry dung, sawdust, waste, straw, etc.) and, accordingly, if the amount of

raw manure at the on-flow equals that of ISB, the production of enriched humus substrate is by 173 % higher. However, if considering the fertilizing effect, the production exceeds that of ISB by 346 %.

7. The phosphorus contents of the final product of ISH is by 62 % higher.

8. Nitrogen in organically bounded form (equivalent with double the amount in form of inorganic fertilizer) has by 363 % higher contents in ISH as opposed to ISB.

9. Practically the same proportion is seen concerning the richness in potassium of the ISH humus substrate : by 367 % more than of the ISB.

10. The data quoted under points 7 - 9 make it obvious that ISH helps to save about 25 % of mineral fertilizer cost, resulting in further positive outcome as concerns social and economic aspects of the environment.

11. The fertilizing effect of the resulting final product, in maintaining a 4-year organic fertilizing cycle, corresponds with the acreage of 1300 ha of fertilized fields for an ISH plant, and only 350 ha for comparable ISB one.

12. Due to the technology of the ISH system the seeds of weed, unwanted germs and bacteria are destroyed, thus yielding better hygiene of the environment and savings of about 70 % of herbicide cost. Neither hygienization nor herbicide cost cuts are achieved by ISB.

13. The ISH system contributes markedly to improvements of the bioenergetic potential of soil, allowing the vegetal production to rise by as much as 12 %, whereas the ISB system can offer about 3 % (through intensification, using the same acreage).

14. In accordance with increasing vegetal production also animal production can be raised ; by about 6 % in the case of ISH and by about 1,5 % in that of ISB.

An approximative technical and economical analysis can evaluate, predominatingly, qualifiable features. Nevertheless, also further social and economic aspects should be drawn attention to, such as : improved capacity of humidity retention in soil, as well as preserving nutrients, better workability of soil, creation of living conditions for useful soil organisms, improvement of environment, applications not only in agricultural production, but also in forestry, gardening, and recultivation deals.

The present technical and economical comparison of the HUMUS and the BIOGAS systems for orientation purposes has not been motived by any subjective efforts based upon one-sided preference of prejudice with respect to the one or the other system of purposeful treatment and utilization of raw pig manure. The objective resides in stressing the necessity of integrated many-sided approach for any assessment and decision making in this region. It is natural that the quoted example can not cover all specific conditions that may affect the results and modify the solutions. At any rate, the integrated system HUMUS makes full use of all progressive knowledge related to the solution of the problem, representing one of the viable variants.

REFERENCES
(1) MACKRLE, S. : Technologie speciali negli impianti di depurazione a fanghi attivi. Acqua-Aria, 5, 1980
(2) DI PINTO, A.C., et all : Indagine technico-economica sul trattamento anaerobico di scarici liquidi con redupero di energia. Ingegneria sanitaria 6, 1984
(3) Information bulletin of the Company Gebr. WEISS K.G. BIO-Reaktor-Bau
(4) CERVENKA, J. et all. New technology for complex manure treatment. Report UTZCHT-CSAV, Praha (1986)

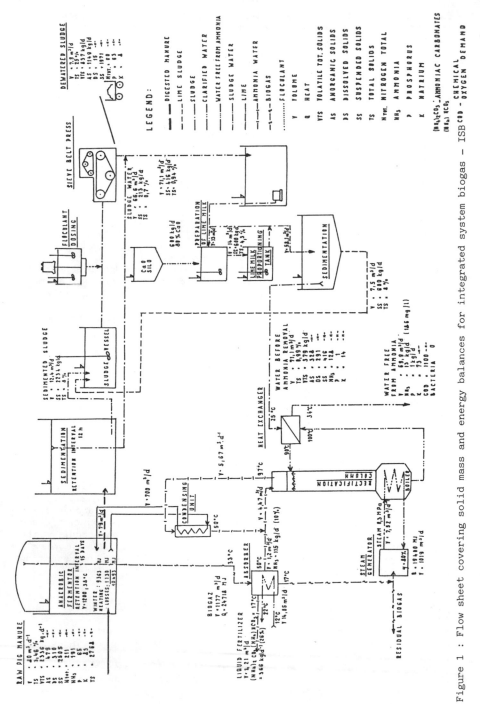

Figure 1 : Flow sheet covering solid mass and energy balances for integrated system biogas – ISBCOD – CHEMICAL OXYGEN DEMAND

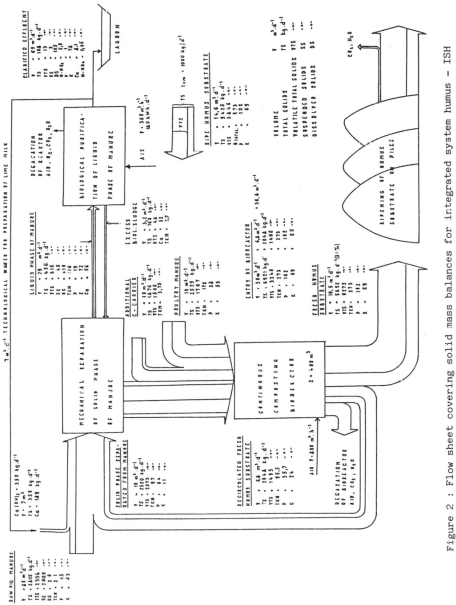

Figure 2 : Flow sheet covering solid mass balances for integrated system humus – ISH

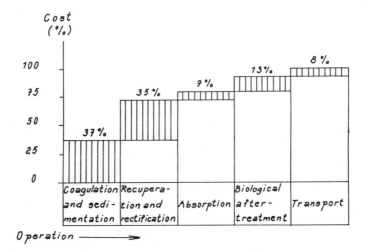

Figure 3 : Cost structure of an integrated BIOGAS system

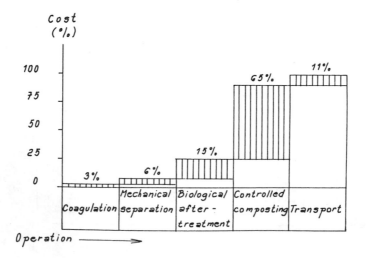

Figure 4 : Cost structure of an integrated HUMUS system

523

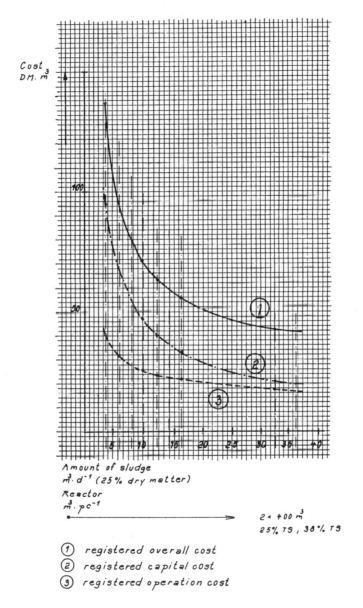

Figure 5 : Cost analysis of composting bioreactor (Weiss)
Cost required for m³ of sludge having 25 % dry matter

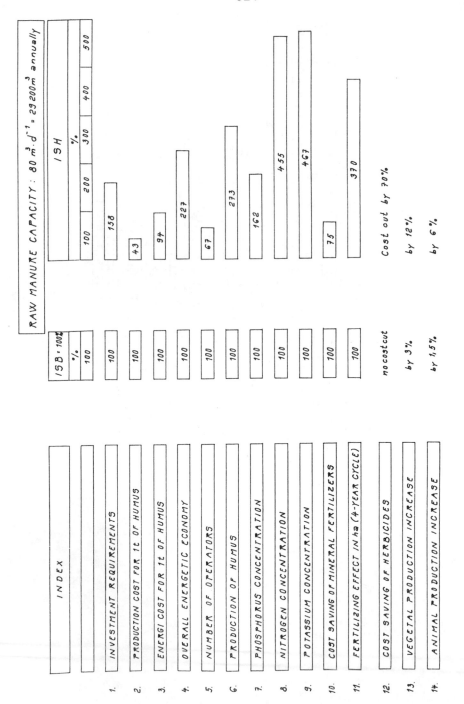

Figure 6

OXYGEN, WATER AND TEMPERATURE
IN THE DECOMPOSITION PROCESS OF AN ORGANIC SUBSTANCE DURING COMPOSTING

Giulio FERRARI
Ecobancatecnologica Bologna, Italy

Summary

A careful evaluation of the water and oxygen content and the temperature balance during the decomposition process of organic material
is necessary if one is to optimise the composting process. The main
parameters governing the maturation of compost were measured during
composting tests using forced aeration. Comparison of experimental
values with theoretical values (stoichiometric and thermodynamic)
for the same sample of solid municipal waste showed that these values were nearly identical. For this reason it is important therefore
that during the planning phase of a recycling plant, the chemical/
physical process parameters should also be considered in addition
to the usual data necessary for establishing the dimensions of mechanical plant (i.e. quantity of refuse, capacity, number of shifts,
type of refuse, etc.). Calculation of the theoretical values for
the oxygen requirement, the quantity of water produced and evaporated during the microbiological reactions and the heat developed in
the synthesising process by the unused kcal.s, provide the inputs
necessary to establish the optimal characteristics (also from an
economic point of view) of a composting line. In the case of plant
which has already been planned, it is possible to use this methodology to evaluate the precise characteristics of the proposed system. To draw up this theoretical balance sheet the parameters taken
into consideration are as follows:
- composition of Solid Urban Refuse expressed in tonnes
- quantity of material for composting (expressed as %)
- water content
- dry content
- organic material content (dry)
- ash content (dry)
- cellulose content (dry)
- organic carbon content.
The fixed parameters are:
- energy available in the form of heat
- total amount of water produced
- total amount of water evaporated
- CO_2 production
- quantity of O_2 required
- average amount of O_2 required per ton/hour of dry material
- amount of air required per ton of organic material.

1. Introduction

The disposal of solid urban wastes using recycling methods which may easily be inserted in the production cycle, most probably provides the best response to current social needs.

For some years recycling plants have operated in the urban waste (refuse) disposal sector, both recycling some of the material contained in refuse and at the same time hygenically disposing of wastes in accordance with strict ecological criteria. Composting forms part of a wider field covered by the recycling and re-utilisation of the organic part of waste material.

Composting involves the exothermic dioxidising of organic material by microorganisms known as schizomycetes, actinomycetes and eumycetes. In the course of this process an organic substance undergoes a fundamental chemical/physical change (composting) to then arrive at biological stability (maturation) (Picci et al. 1978). Biodegradable organic material is physically separated from solid urban wastes using suitable machinery (employing rudimentary physical principles) and then undergoes this process of dioxidation.

During the planning/design of a recycling plant it is therefore important to take into account not only data referring to the mechanical characteristics of the plant (quantity of refuse, capacity, number of work shifts, characterstics of waste, etc.) but also the chemical/physical parameters which are typical to the composting process.

In this phase the design engineer thus requires a thorough stoichiometric and thermodynamic knowledge of the reactions which take place during the transformation of an organic substance into compost.

Further useful indications for the planning of a plant are provided by two laws: Law No. 915 (and its subsequent application) governing refuse disposal, and Law No. 748 which governs the sale of fertilisers and defines the characteristics that compost should have.

Using data from various experiences in the composting sector and applying stoichiometric and thermodynamic techniques, this paper sets forth a theoretical/experimental analysis of the composting process and a balance sheet of the materials involved. Consequently, the correlation between experimental and theoretical values enables a reliable theoretical prediction to be made if the composition of the urban wastes in question are known.

The design engineer will thus have useful information enabling a correct proportioning of the maturation line for the organic substances to be composted.

Some basic considerations about composting are an integral part of this introduction.

The composting process consists of two phases: a thermofile phase followed by a phase of thermal stability.

In the first phase there is a sudden increase in temperature (which can reach 70°C) and an increase in pH due to an augmented production of ammonium caused by deamination of ammino-acids in proteolysis (breakdown of proteic molecules). The subsequent stabilisation phase, on the other hand, is characterised by a gradual reduction in both temperature and pH.

Composting is a process which takes place spontaneously in nature. We only have to think of the decompostion of a forest floor or of animal manure. In nature however the maturation process is very long and not at all suited for industrial application where it is necessary to control such a process and reduce the time necessary to within economically acceptable limits.

It is in fact necessary to optimise certain environmental factors which play a key role in the process in order to guarantee the quality of compost destined for agricultural use. These factors are: oxygenation, temperature, humidity and the C/N ratio.

2. Study of the composting process through theoretical/experimental analysis

The parameters needed in order to draw up the theoretical balance of materials are as follows:

a) The composition of Solid Urban Wastes (percentage by weight)
b) Chemical/physical characterstics of sludges
c) Quantity of material sent for composting
d) Water content of material to be composted
e) Content in terms of organic substances
f) Ash content
g) Biodegradable organic carbon content.

The analyses were carried out on various samples of urban refuse which had been mixed with biological sludges in constant proportions. These materials were subject to numerous standardised experimental studies in order to arrive at standard values. The average values of the individual parameters were used in the calculation of the material balance.

The average percentage composition of urban refuse following manual separation of the individual main components was as follows.

Organic substances from canteens	34	%
Paper and similar cellulose waste papers	30	%
Light plastic	10	%
Heavy plastic	4	%
Ferrous metals	4	%
Glass and heavy inert materials	12	%
Non-ferrous metals	1.5	%
Rags	3	%
Rubber, leather etc.	1.5	%
TOTAL	100	%

The organic substances used for the tests were obtained by sifting on a screening line in readiness for further preparation where the organic component of total refuse was ground and reduced in size. Heavy inert materials were then separated from organic material by means of an aeroballistic separator.

The various samples of material obtained in this way were then mixed with 30% biological sludges with 85% humidity. Tests were then carried out to determine: humidity, ash and inert material content, biodegradable organic carbon content, non-biodegradable organic carbon content, content of organic substances and organic nitrogen. The values are shown in the table below:

Humidity	55	%
Ashes and inert materials	20	% when dry
Organic substances	80	% when dry
Biodegradable organic carbon	45.25	% when dry
Non-biodegradable organic carbon	3.45	% when dry
Organic nitrogen	1.2	% when dry

2.1 Stoichiometry of the process and the oxygen balance

Analysis of Solid Urban Wastes mixed with sludge showed the presence of the main elements in the percentages shown below:

Carbon	51	%
Oxygen	28	%
Hydrogen	9	%
Nitrogen	1.5	%
Others (P, K, Mg, Ca, etc.)	10.5	%

If we now consider the composting process as a typically aerobic process, and given that we know that the final products of the respiration reaction are H_2O and CO_2, we can on the basis of the previous analysis establish the oxygen requirement; in other words, it is possible to establish the amount of air required by the compost. It should be remembered here that in this elementary analysis of waste we can only consider the four basic elements, i.e. hydrogen, oxygen, nitrogen and carbon.

Taking a base of 100%, the percentages of the four elements are:

$$C = 57\% \qquad O = 31.3\% \qquad H = 10\% \qquad N = 1.7\%$$

which when expressed in moles, becomes:

$$C = 4.75 \qquad O = 1.96 \qquad H = 10 \qquad N = 0.12$$

The oxygen requirement in grammes is therefore:

O_2 for the formation of CO_2	152	+
O_2 for the formation of H_2O	80	−
O_2 present in the initial substrata	31.3	=
TOTAL O_2 REQUIREMENT	200.7	g/100 of S.V.

The quantity of oxygen to be supplied through the aeration equipment is therefore 2 kg. per kg. of S.V. for each ton of volatile material. This amount is certainly an overestimation since material mineralisation is not total; this value is therefore only indicative.

At sea level, with an mean temperature of 20°C and with a relative air humidity of 50%, the absolute gravity of air is: 1.119 kg/cu.m.

By weight, oxygen is 23.15% and therefore for each cubic metre of air we have: 0.277 kg. of oxygen.

If we take the organic ratio: Oxygen 1:2 and if we estimate that, on the basis of experimental tests, the process time is 24 days, then the quantity of O_2 and therefore of air which needs to be supplied each hour for every ton of volatile material will be:

$$\frac{2 \quad x \quad 10}{24 \quad x \quad 24} = 3.472 \text{ g. of } O_2 \text{ hr/t. S.V.}$$

which could be supplied by:

$$\frac{3.472}{0277} = 12.6 \text{ cu.m. of air hr/t. S.V.}$$

3. Energy and water balance

In order to establish the energy balance, we experimentally measured the low heat value of numerous samples of material being sent for composting. The average value obtained in this way was: 3315 kcal/kg.

We obtained the rough formula from the percentages of the main elements contained in the organic part of the solid urban waste. When this undergoes combustion and/or typical metabolic dioxidising, then we have the following chemical equation:

$$C_{38} H_{80} O_{16} N + 50O_2 \rightleftharpoons 38CO_2 + 40 H_2O + N + 3315 \text{ Kcal.}$$

which in the case of cumulate composting for 24 days has a mineralisation coefficient of 0.54 (see appendix). It will be noted that also according to this equation, the amount of oxygen required for total oxidation of the compost is again 2 kg. per kg. of organic material.

Given that the kcal.s not utilised in the synthesising processes are half of the total for the water balance, then for the purposes of calculating water loss by evaporation, we have 3315/2 = 1657.5 kcal/moles available. From this we have to subtract 652 kcal/mole or 29345.7 kcal/t selected (see appendix) which are the calories lost due to convection.

The evaporation heat of water when calculated at the average composting process temperature is about 550 kcal/kg. and therefore from a ton of selected intial material it is possible to evaporate:

$$\frac{(1657.5 - 65.2) \text{ x } 450* \text{ x } 0.54}{550} = 703.5 \text{ litres of water}$$

(* Where 450 represents the moles of the compost contained in one ton of selected organic refuse).

To this we can add the water removed by air unsaturation which is 5% of the total lost through the heat caused by the composting process (Finstain et. al.). Thus the total amount of water lost for every ton of selected organic waste is 738.7 kg.

From the stoichiometric equation, which represents the total oxidation of organic waste undergoing composting, we can estimate the quantity of water formed:

$$18 \times 40 \times 450 \times 0.45 = 175 \text{ kg. } H_2O/t. \text{ of selected organic refuse}$$

For the water balance therefore, the amount of water lost for each ton of material in a complete composting cycle is:

$$738.7 - 175 = 563.7 \text{ kg. of selected refuse}$$

From an analysis of fresh organic material mixed with sludges (see above) it is possible to estimate the final humidity that the compost will have after the evaporation of water as previously calculated. Thus if we take material with 55% humidity, 20% ashes (when dry) and 80% volatile solids (when dry), with the evaporation of 563.7 litres of water we obtain an organic fertiliser with a humidity of 38%.

Conclusion

On the basis of experimental data and by a theoretical analysis of the composting process, we determined the basic chemical/physical parameters governing the composting of organic substances.

The composting system under examination was of the cumulate type with forced aeration, where the initial material material consisted of 70% selected organic material and 30% sludge, the latter having 85% humidity. In this case the process parameters are as follows:

Oxygen requirement	3.472 kg. hr/t S.V.
Amount of air required	12.5 cu.m.t/ S.V.
Energy which can be used for the water balance	386929 kcal/t selected
Water removed during the process	563.7 kg./t selected
Maturation period	24 days
Mineralisation coefficient	0.54
Final humidity of matured material	38%

Appendix
Calculation to determine the calories lost through convection

We used the formula $Q = cO \times A/s \ (t_1 - t_2)$
where
c = convection coefficient 2.2
O = duration of process in hours
A = exchange surface in square metres
s = cumulate theoretic thickness in metres
t_1 = exchange surface temperature
t_2 = temperature of surrounding environment
In our example involving the cumulate composting of 38 tonnes, the formula gives the following result:

$$Q = \frac{2.2 \times 576 \times 70.4 \times (30 - 20)}{0.8 \times 38} = 29345.7 \text{ kcal/t}$$

which is equal to

$$\frac{29345.7}{450} = 65.2 \text{ kcal/mole}$$

Test to determine mineralisation coefficient

Analyses carried out during a maturation cycle of 4 weeks

	Start	1st Week	2nd Week	3rd Week	4th Week
Water	60%	52%	47%	42%	38%
Dry	40%	48%	53%	58%	62%
Ashes*	22%	28%	35%	39%	38%
Organic*	78%	72%	65%	61%	62%

* when dry

Mineralisation coefficient = 0.54

BIBLIOGRAFIA

1) Berglund S.: "Compost from sludge and refuse application and quality requirements" - Elmia Avfal 79 Jonkoping Sweden. Settembre 1979.

2) Chrometzka P.: "Determination of the oxygen requirements of maturing compost" - International research group on refuse disposal information bulletin 33 (1968).

3) De Bertoldi M., Zucconi F.: "Microbiologia della trasformazione dei rifiuti solidi urbani in compost e loro utilizzazione in agricoltura" - Ing. Ambientale Vol. 9 n. 3 Giugno 1980 Ed. Ist. Ing. San. Politecno Milano (I.S.W.A.)

4) De Bertoldi M., Vallini G., Pera A.: "The biology of composting a riwiew" - Waste management research Vol. 1 Ed. C.E.E. (1983).

5) De Renzo D.J.: "Sources of waste materiales for reconversion. Energy from reconversion of waste materials" - Noyes data corporation USA (1977).

6) Dietz A.: "Biotechnology, Microbial fondamentals" - Ed. by H.J. Rhem and G. Reed Verlag Chemie - Wheinheim - Deerfield beach Florida - Basel Vol. 1 Chapter 6 B.

7) Epstan E., G.B. Willson, W.D. Burge, D.C. Mullen, N. Enkiri: "A forced aeration system for composting wastewater sludge" J. Water pollution control fed. 48: 4/1976.

8) Ferrari G.: "Il recupero della frazione organica dai rifiuti urbani; aspetti economici ed ambientali " - Atti convegno Il compost è risorsa multiuso: metodi condizioni, prospettive. Ed. Ecobancatecnologica ed Edilter Bologna Ottobre 1985.

9) Ferrari G.: "Lo smaltimento dei rifiuti urbani in piccole comunità montane; un ipotesi di soluzione con produzione di Biogas" - Atti del convegno intern. Il disinquinamento degli ambienti di alta montagna - Riva del Garda Giugno 1983 Ed. Provincia Autonoma di Trento.

10) Ferrari G.: "Energia recuperata in un impianto di rifiuti solidi urbani; il progetto Agripoils. Rifiuti urbani ed industriali trattamento, smaltimento nuovi aspetti tecnologici e normativi A. Frigerio Ed. BI e GI Verona (1985).

11) Ferrari G.: "La valorizzazione dei prodotti del trattamento di rifiuti solidi". Ambiente risorse e salute N. 28 Ed. Centro studi l'Uomo e l'Ambiente - Padova (1984).

12) Ferrari G.: "Controllo sul processo di maturazione della sostanza organica in compost".
Atti del Simposio Internazionale "Recupero come?" Napoli Ed. Zucconi - De Bertoldi - Coppola (1983).

13) Finstain M.S., Cirello J., Macgregor St. Miller F.C.: "Engineering principles of sludge composing"
I. Water pollution control federation USA 52, 2037 (1980).

14) Haug R.T.: "Compost engineering principles and pratice" Ed. Ann Arbor Science Michigan 48106 (1980).

15) Kuchova Kratachilova A.: "Biotechnology, microbial fondamental" Ed. by Rhem and G. Reed, Verlag Chemie - Wheinheim - Deerfield Beach Florida - Basel Vol. 1 Chapter 1 (1981).

16) Moore W.: "Chimica fisica" Ed. Piccin Padova (1979).

17) Pelzclar M. I., Reid R.D., Chan E.C.: "Microbiologia" Ed. Zanichelli (1982).

18) Picci G.: "Microbiologia del compostaggio considerazioni generali e implicazioni di carattere sanitario" - Atti del convegno Il compost è risorsa multiuso metodi, condizioni, prospettive. Ed. Ecobancatecnologica ed Edilter Bologna Ottobre 1985.

19) Picci G.: Intervento microbiologico nel riciclaggio della sostanza organica da R.S.U." - Atti del Simposio Internazionele "Recupero come?" Ed. Zucconi De Bertoldi, Coppola Napoli Ottobre 1983.

20) Stainer R.Y. Doudoroff M., Adelberg E.A.: "Il mondo dei microrganismi" Ed. Zanichelli (1978)

21) Zucconi F., Forte M., Monaco A., De Bertoldi M.: "Biological evalvation of compost maturity" - Compost science Giugno Agosto 1981 Ed. The I.G. Press, Inc. Emmaus PA USA

USE OF COMPOSTED URBAN WASTES IN VITICULTURE.

SCIENZA A. (1)(2) - FORTI D.(2) - ZORZI G.(2) - CARGNELLO G.(3)

INTRODUCTION

One of the most alarming aspects of modern society is environmental pollution and that is mainly due to the constant development of conurbation.
Among the many agents of pollution, we find urban waste, which constitute the most striking example.
The disposal of the latter from densely-populated areas, using "ecological" methods, is the aim that Public Administrations must have, also because it is becoming harder and harder to find new areas to use as dumps.
The pressure of pollution of such residues has increased at the same rate as technological progress which has allowed the introduction, in the reality of today, of new materials with often difficult or improbable chemical-physical-microbiological assimilation or bearers of highly toxic substances.
The transformation into compost from the organic biodegradable part of urban waste can be quite interesting especially when the production system of composts is set in an agricultural area able to absorb the final product. What's more the compost represents an interesting recovery of energy which can be assigned to an agriculture greatly dependent, in this case, on other productive sectors.
The agronomical interest for the compost is due to the presence in it of titres of organic sustances, that makes it suitable to replace the traditional organic fertilizers (manure) today almost impossible to find in areas with arboreal monoculture (vine).

INTEREST OF COMPOST IN VITICULTURE

The high needs of humus in vineyard soils, increased by the poverty of the organic restitutions of the cultivation (limited to the leaves and, not always, to the shoots) and the abandonment, for many years, of the traditional soil improvement, makes the field of viticulture particularly receptive to the use of composts from urban waste.
Many experiences confirm the efficacy of contributions of

----

(1) ISTITUTO COLTIVAZIONI ARBOREE DELL'UNIVERSITA' DI MILANO
(2) ISTITUTO AGRARIO SAN MICHELE ALL'ADIGE (TN)
(3) ISTITUTO SPERIMENTALE PER LA VITICOLTURA - S.O.P. ASTI

composts from urban waste for the improvement of the humus content in the soil.

Annual applications of 37,5 - 75 and 150 t/ha have led to an annual increase of the O.M. (Organic Matter.) rate, respectively of 0,2% - 0,4% and 0,9% (Enkelmann, Völkel - 1982).

Bosse (1967) notices that in quinquennal experiments made with 50-100 t/ha year the content of humus varied from 1,7% to 3% in clayey soils and from 0,8% to 1,7% in sandy soils.

In consequence of contributions of compost from urban waste equal to 35 t/ha year, the content of O.M. increased from 1,8 to a maximum of 6,5% (Walter - 1980).

The effects of humus derived from urban wastes composts, possibly together with urban sludges, extend in time.

Contributions limited in amounts of 80-100 t/ha/every three years are anyway sufficient (Bosse 1967, Buchmann 1972, Dieter 1977).

A further factor to underline is the content in the composts of mineral elements. They make themselves available during the year of utilization in measure of 10-20%; then up to a maximum of 40-60% for azote and phosphorus and of 100% for potassium and other elements.

On the basis of these considerations, a contribution of 800 q./ha of composts from urban waste every three years, makes annually available: 55-80 Kg of azote; 40-65 Kg of P_2O_5; 110 Kg of K_2O; 1100 Kg of CaO and 130 Kg of MgO (Gysi - Koblet - 1975).

The amount of mineral elements released are able to cover a good part of the nutritive needs of the vine.

According to Kick (1972) the nourishing value of 100 q of garbage-sewage sludge-composts is approsimatively equal to 0,5 of ammonic nitrate; 0,7 q of basic slag; 1 q of potassic manure at 40%; 18 q of carbonate of Ca and 60-65 Kg of borax.

Medium composition of composts from urban waste (various authors)

PARAMETERS	CONTENT IN %		
	minimum	medium	maximum
Water	20	40	70
O.M.	15	18	30
N	0,3	0,5	0,9
P_2O_5	0,2	0,4	0,7
K_2O	0,3	0,4	0,8
CaO	2	4	8
MgO	0,3	0,5	0,6

USE OF URBAN WASTE IN VITICULTURE

The most frequent use is composts from urban waste alone or added
to depuration sludge. The spheres of use of such products depends
more on their stage of maturity, than on their amount of O.M.
The fresh composts, with high content of organic substances
sligtly decomposed, applied to the topsoil, constitute a source
of nourishing humus, essential for the development of all the
vital phenomena of the soil.
Applications in nurseries or with trenching are excluded.
The mature composts, well combined with humus, can be instead
applied without harm, to the subsoil in amounts of 80-100
t/ha every three years (Bosse 1967, Buchmann 1972, Walter 1972-
1980).
Some authors refer to the direct use of depuration sludges which
have undergone an assimilative treatment and which presents a
water content equal to 78-82%.
They are applied to the soil with a light cultivator in amounts
of 200 m3/ha every three years.

EFFECTS   ON QUANTITY AND QUALITY OF THE PRODUCTIONS

The influence of composts from urban waste on the productive
yield mostly depends on the environmental conditions. An increase
attributed to contributions of composts are referred to by many
authors. Schrader (1968) verified, in the region of Nahe, an
average hield increase of 14%, compared with mineral manuring, in
consequence of composts manuring of 100 t/ha; Enkelmann and
Völkel (1982), in the course of six years of experiments,
noticed a production increase of up to 10% (in one case 50%) in
vines of Müller Thurgau on loess with a distribution of 225-450
t/ha of composts, while in acid soils the yield increase was
only obtained with amount of 900 t distributed in the course of
the six years of experiments.

Influence on productive yield and quality

AUTHORS	THESIS	PRODUCTIONS q/ha	SUGARS °Oe	ACIDITY ‰
ENKELMANN	CONTROL	158,6	74	7,64
VÖLKEL	225 t/ha 6 yrs	171,6	74,6	7,32
(1974-79)	450 t/ha 6 yrs	178,6	74,6	7,34
ALLEWELDT	CONTROL	178	72	7,8
(1974-77)	37 t/ha year	184	73	7,4
	75 t/ha year	193	72	7,5
WALTER	CONTROL	139	74	12,75
(1970-75)	35 t/ha year	151,4	72	13,05
	75 t/ha year	155,4	74,5	12,55

Alleweldt (1980) reports the results of experiments carried out at the Experimental Station for Viticulture of Freiburg on Müller Thurgau (1974-1977). Analogous researches were carried out by Walter (1977) on Riesling. Other authors, however, do not find any yield increase in consequence of the use of composts in viticulture.

Peyer-Zwicky (1972) in 10-years experiments on Pinot nero, using different organic sources, do not find any quantitative and qualitative differences. Walter (1980), Bastgen (1976) and Dieter (1977) arrive at the same conclusions.

With regard to the influence of composts on the degree of sugar and on must acidity, we must notice that no significative differences are determined. Any variations on such parameters are only due to environmental conditions.

The taste of wine is never, even slightly, influenced by manuring with a basis of composts from urban waste.

RESTRICTIONS ON USE OF COMPOSTS IN VITICULTURE WITH REGARD TO THE CONTENT OF HEAVY METALS.

In the soil, the heavy metals are above all absorbed by clay and humus of the topsoil.

We can notice enrichments of Cu-Pb-Cr-Zn and Cd that are in

relation with the utilized amounts of garbage-sewage-sludge-composts. That's not the case of Ni and Co (Walter 1980, Mohr 1980).

Content of heavy metals in the soil (0-20 cm):

AUTHORS	THESIS	CONTENT IN ppm						
	/	Cu	Pb	Cd	Zn	Ni	Cr	Co
Walter (1980)	35 t/ha year	178	349	1,1	470	70	157	25
	70 t/ha year	140	249	1,5	392	66	124	25
	200 t/ha 3 yrs	237	364	1,7	230	64	223	25
	control	237	60	0,7	157	67	45	25
Mohr (1980)	35 t/ha year	124	130	1,0	297	100	192	30
	70 t/ha year	200	171	1,2	437	100	234	31
	200 t/ha 3 yrs	202	171	1,1	441	92	195	28
	control (manure)	82	40	0,2	151	98	126	36

Also Enkelmann and Völkel (1982) refer to substantial increases of Cu - Pb - Cr - Zn-Cd and Ni in acid soils in consequence of contributions of 450-900 t/ha of composts distributed in six years of experiments.

Disposal of 450 t/ha in alkaline soils mantained the levels of heavy metals considerably under the limit of tolerance fixed by Kloke.

The top parts of the roots, which are in direct contact with the compost, show an increase in the rate of heavy metals considerably higher than that of the shoots.

The degree of radical assumption observed by Mohr (1980) is the following: Cu, Cd > Zn >> Pb-Co-Ni-Cr.

Walter (1980) reports that the accumulation of heavy metals in the roots, as a consequence of contribution of garbage-sewage-sludge-composts, concerns Cu-Ni-Zn and Cr and not Co, Cd and Pb.

Analogous results were also reached by Foroughi and others (1975-1976) and Suchodoller (1967).

Greenhouse-experiments, in container with 200-400 g of compost Kg of soil

in highly acid soil indicate a different degree of heavy metals
mobility inside the plant, in the following order: Zn > Cu > Cd
and Pb. The result is that the amount of Cd carried to the
leaves, to the shoots and to the bunches is hardly appreciable
(Mohr, 1980).

Experiments carried out with 35-70 t/ha year and with 200
t/ha every three years of garbage-sewage-sludge-compost did not
indicate any substantial variations of heavy metals in vegetative
organs of vines, cv Riesling (Mohr 1980). Walter (1980),
Enkelmann and Völkel (1982) and Mohr (1980), as result of high
 a m o u n t of composts, did not notice in must any significant
variations of them or such to cause concern.

The content of heavy metals, already reduced in must, is further
lowered during the fermentation with the precipitation of them as
sulphides (Mohr 1980).

It is been noticed a reduction of 75%-90% for Cu, up to 10% for
Zn, 35% for Pb and 30% for Cd (Enkelmann, Völkel 1982).

Some researches carried out in Freiburg (1974-77), in different
places, point out insignificant variations of Cu, Zn, Mn, Pb, Cd
and Hg in must.

Increases in must as a consequence of big of amount
composts (150 m^3 and 300 m^3/ha/every 2 years) are indicated, as
far as Cd and Zn are concerned, by Bergner-Lang (1971); however,
after the alcoholic fermentation, the presence in the wine is
reduced to such percentuages that cannot cause concern. Also
Buchmann (1974) notices a slight increase of Cd in must but not
in wine.

Content of heavy metals in leaves, grapes, must and wines:

AUTHOR	VARIANT	PRODUCED ORGANS	ELEMENTS IN ppm			
			Zn	Cu	Pb	Cd
	test (manure) every 3 years	leaves	25,0	3,3	2,5	0,04
		berries	10,0	3,3	< 0,7	< 0,04
		must	1,0	< 0,09	< 0,1	< 0,005
	35t/ha year	leaves	30,8	3,2	2,6	0,04
		berries	10,7	3,5	< 0,7	< 0,04
		must	1,1	0,14	< 0,1	< 0,005
MOHR (1980)	70t/ha year	leaves	22,7	3,5	2,6	0,05
		berries	12,1	4,6	< 0,7	< 0,04
		must	0,8	< 0,09	< 0,1	< 0,005
	200t/ha every 3 year	leaves	25,6	3,9	2,6	0,04
		berries	12,2	4,7	< 0,7	< 0,04
		must	0,6	< 0,09	< 0,1	< 0,005
	test	must	1,36			0,0046
		wine	1,16			0,0013
	150 m^3/ha every 2 years	must	1,82			---
		wine	1,62			---
BERGNER LANG (1971)	300 m^3/ha every 2 years	must	3,44			0,007
		wine	3,40			0,0029

Content of heavy metals allowed in wines by the german law (Enkelmann, Völkel 1982) Pb=0,3 mg/l; Cd=0,1 mg/l; Cu=5,0 mg/l; Zn=5,0 mg/l.

CONCLUSION

The experiments on agricultural field with the use of composts lead to these considerations.
- Composts have a manuring and soil improvement value which justifies their use in viticulture, above all for the

conspicuous contribution of humus, for the positive effects on the soil's texture and for the absorption potential of water and manuring principles.

- The interest for the urban waste, employed as a substitute for manure is limited to those areas placed near the production system (transport cost).

- The dangerous enrichment of heavy metals in soil and plants as a result of the disposal of composts from urban waste can be avoided through the right agronomical use, the analytical control of the produced compost and of the soils which are subject to the treatment.

SUMMARY

The authors report the results of cognitive researches which aims to point out the side-effects of manurings based on composts from urban waste in viticulture.
These products, so long as of high quality standards, can find an effective employment as a substitutive for manure, for their fertilizing and soil conditioning value.

BIBLIOGRAPHY

1. **ALLEWELDT G.**: Die Verwendung von Siedlungsabfällen im Weinbau. Die Weinwirtschaft, 9 (1980), 261-264.

2. **BADOUR C.** : Sur un Essai de Fumure organique de la Vigne en Champagne - Vigneron Champenois, 3 (1963), 80-89

3. **BANSE H. J., BUCHMANN I., GRAFF. O.**:Biologische und physikalische Untersuchungen an Weinbergsböden des Kreuznacher Kronenberges. Landwirtsch. Forsch, 25 (4) 1972, 355-365

4.**BERGNER K.G., LANG B.**: Einflüsse der Müllkompostdüngung auf die Spurenelemente.
Rebe und Wein, 24 (1971), 307-308

541

5. **BOSSE I.** : Ein Versuch zur Bekämpfung der Bodenerosion in Hanglagen des Weinbaus durch Müllkompost.Weinberg und Keller, 15 (1968), 385-397

6. **BRANAS J.** : Emploi des déchets urbains en viticulture. Le Progrés Agricole et Viticole, 84 (19) 1967, 503-510

7. **BRUGGER G.** : Die Aufbereitung von städtischen Siedlungsabfällen und ihre Verwendung im Weinbau.Rebe und Wein, ottobre (1966), 344-348

8.**BUCHMANN I.**: Zur Frage von Benzpyren und Schwermetallen bei der Anwendung von Müllkompost. Der deutsche Weinbau, 26 (1974), 894-895

9.**DELAS J.** : Entretien du taux de matiere organique des sols viticoles - Vignes et Vins, 231, 1974, 17-20

10.**DIETER A.**: Untersuchungen zur Verbesserung der Bodenstruktur und des Wasserhaushaltes in Weinbergen.Weinberg und Keller, 24 (6) 1977, 237-284

11.**ENKELMANN R.** : Mangangehalte in Rebblättern, Most und Wein. Z.Lebensm. Unters. Forsch., 167 (1070), 171-175

12. **ENKELMANN R., VÖLKEL R.** : Einsatz von Müllklärschlammkompost und Müllkompost in Weinbau.Landwirtsch. Forschung 35 (1-2) 1982, 77-89

13. **D'ERSU Ph., KROEPFLI J., ROD Ph.**: Les boues d'épuration en agriculture.Revue suisse Agric, 11 (4) 1979, 191-199

14. **GYSI CH., KOBLET W.**: Anwendung von Müllkompost im Weinbau. Schweizerische Zeitschrift für Obst und Weinbau, 111 (20) 1975, 514-519

15. **GYSI CH., NEUKOMM H.**: Müllkompost im Rebbau. Schweizerische Zeitschrift für Obst und Weinbau, 117 (5) 1981, 138-141

16. **MANIÉRE G.**: Manutention et epandage des engrais organiques dans le vignoble. Le Progrés Agricole et Viticole, 82 (15) 1965, 65-70

17. **MOHR H.D.**: Einfluß von Müll-Klärschlammkompost auf den Schwermetallgehalt von Weinbergsböden, Reborganen und Most. Weinberg und Keller, 26 (8) 1979, 333-344

18. **MOHR H.D.**: Schwermetallgehalt von Wurzel und Sproßporganen der Rebe (Vitis vinifera L.) nach Düngung mit Müll-Klärschlammkompost.
Zeitschrift für Pflanzenernährung und Bodenkunde, 143 (2) 1980, 129-139

19. **PEYER E.**: Abschwemmverhütung durch Kompost im Rebbau.
Schweizerische Zeitschrift für Obst und Weinbau, 69 (1960), 109-111

20. **PEYER E., ZWICKY P.**: Versuch in Malans mit verschiedenen Humusdüngern im Rebbau.
Schweizerische Zeitschrift für Obst und Weinbau, 108 (23) 1972, 597-601

21. **ROD Ph.** : Le point de vue de La Station fédérale de Changins sur les boues d'épuration.
Revue suisse Agric. 13 (2) 1981, 81-82

22. **SCHRADER Th.**: Utilisation dans les vignobles des composts d'ordures méenagéres des villes.
Bulletin de l'O.I.V., 44 (444), 1968, 159-171

23. **SCHRADER Th.** : Organische Stoffe zur Verbesserung der Weinbergböden.
Rebe und Wein 24, 1971, giugno, luglio, agosto

24.**WALTER B.**: Erfahrungen bei der Anwendung von Müllklärschlammkompost im Rebenanbau.
Landwirtsch. Forsch., 25 (3), 1972, 118-119

25. **WALTER B.**: Erfahrungen bei der Anwendung von Klärschlamm im Rebenanbau.
Landwirtsch. Forsch., 25 (3), 1972 120-121

26. **WALTER B.** : Untersuchungen über die Wirkung von Müllklärschlammkompost auf Boden und Rebenertrag.
Landwirtsch. Forsch., 30 (2) 1977, 119-124

27. **WALTER B.** :Possibilités et limites d'utilisation des déchetes urbains en viticulture.
Bulletin de l'O.I.V., 53 (590), 1980, 273-284

- o O o -

SESSION:3

USE OF COMPOST

Rapporteur: VERDONCK O.

During this session we can say that the following main topics are discussed:

1) The use of compost as growing media for ornamental plants. Compost can be used as a substitute for the normal used growing media as peat and pine litter but we must follow restrictions before one or the other organic waste can be used:
- Analyzing the raw materials chemically and physically as well;
- the optimization of the composting parameters;
- test-out with growing trials during several seasons.
Experiments have shown that it will be possible to substitute up to 50% of the imported peat in several countries.

2) The use of compost as a soil amendment in viticulture. Viticulture needs a high demand of organic matter which helps to solve problems of soil structure, water retention, erosion and it helps to increase the chemical fertility of the soil. It doesn't effect the quality and quantity of the grapes and also no effect is found on the taste of wine but analytical control of the soils on which we use the compost must be carried-out.

3) The increasing fertility of agricultural soils with the use of compost. Several contributions were made on the great influence of the use of compost in agriculture.
It helps to solve problems of structure on a long-run basis and also it increases many times the yield of the crops.
In special cases, as discussed here in Egypt, it will increase tremendously the fertility of those very coarse, sandy soils in decreasing the leaching of the fertilizers and it helps to have a more stable structure.

4) The use of mushroom compost. Mushroom compost is mainly made of horse manure but also synthetic compost is mainly made of but also synthetic compost as mentioned by Gerrits which is made of straw and chicken manure can be used for mushroom compost.
In France also a part of town waste compost (+ 10-15%) is used in the mushroom compost.

As there are a lot of mushroom growers there is in the European Community about 3.955.000 m3 spent mushroom available. This is normally an excellent product for the use as organic soil conditioners. Sometimes we will have difficulties for sensitive plants with high salt content and high acidity. In most cases it is recommended to sterilize the compost at 70 C during 12 hours.

5) The use of compost in a biological filter. There were two

presentations about the necessity of odour control with the use of compost.

Town waste compost as well as composted bark are used. The main problems are:
- avoid the use of compost with very high moisture content (preferable <55%);
- use coarse materials in order to minimize the resistance (maximum 100 mm WS);
- sometimes it is necessary to turn the compost above the filter and if possible exhaust gases must be washed;

6) Microbiological activity of compost. In this topic we have three main points:

6.1) The effect of suppressiveness of soil borne plant pathogens. This is very complicated because compost in potting mixtures can react in a different way depending on the primary starting material. The age of the compost and the temperature can affect the success of the suppressiveness. Not only in potting soils can compost be effective but also an addition of 5-15% to mineral soils (specially against Rhizotonia for Lactuca sativa).

6.2) The nitrogen fixing effect and the mycorrhizae symbiose the organic substances in soil that have at the beginning a high nitrogen fixation which disappears rapidly.

Compost amended soil has higher nitrogen-fixation which is related to the mineralization rate of the organic matter content.

Mycorrhiza involves higher absorption of different chemical elements as P, Cu, Mg, etc.

6.3) Adding compost to the soil which increases the microbiological activity which is expressed with the increase of phosphatase content. This can be easily measured. There was no difference in measuring the urease in treated and non treated soils.

7) Energy balance of composting. Through elementary analysis we could determine an empirical formula (C38, H80, O16, N) which hekps us to calculate the exact need of oxygen and nitrogen during composting.

8) Economical difference between aerobic and anaerobic systems. Because of increase of livestock in Czechoslovakia they have made economical calculations of aerobic and anaerobic systems.

The anaerobic systems were very complicated and much more expensive than the aerobic composting which was much easier to realize.

SESSION IV : C.N.R. AND ENEA PANEL

Manuring a maize crop with composts obtained from different technological processes : short-term effects on soil-plant system

Aerobic stabilization in the solid state of partially dewatered sewage sludge. Microbiological and technological aspects

Agronomic valorization of municipal solid waste compost. Results of a comparative trial

Some effects of compost on soil physical properties

Effects of composted agricultural residues on apple trees and of urban wastes on peach trees

Extraction and dosage of heavy metals from compost-amended soils

Microbial variations in compost amended soils

Control of a composting process in bioreactor by monitoring chemical and microbial parameters

Fertilizing value and heavy metal load of some composts from urban refuse

Evaluation of heavy metals bioavailability in compost treated soils

Optimization of composting process utilizing urban and agricultural wastes

Compost production in a long-retention-time horizontal reactor : technical sides

REPORT BY L. CAVAZZA

MANURING A MAIZE CROP WITH COMPOSTS OBTAINED FROM DIFFERENT TECHNOLOGICAL PROCESSES: SHORT-TERM EFFECTS ON SOIL-PLANT SYSTEM

F. DEL ZAN, L. BARUZZINI, M. CANDOTTI, I. TONETTI and G. MURGUT
Centro Regionale per la Sperimentazione Agraria
per il Friuli - Venezia Giulia
Pozzuolo del Friuli (Italy)

Summary

Short-term results from a fertilization trial are presented in wich composts of different origin, at various rates of application, in comparison with mineral fertilizers and farmyard manure have been applied annually to a maize crop on the same site for three years. Compost application increases the C,N,P and K content of the soil and allows to obtain higher yields than the untreated test, but lower with respect to the application of only mineral fertilizers. Combined applications of the two forms give the best results. Among the composts, the best was that obtained by mixing municipal solid wastes with sewage sludge. Lower results were achieved with immature or refined composts.

1. Introduction

Compost production from the organic fraction of municipal wastes is becoming increasingly important. It represents, in fact, the only practical means of recovery with respect to systems of mere discharge, because it supplies agriculture with organic fertilizers, more and more necessary where livestock production has been displaced by new farming systems.

Many scientific papers have been published about this subject, with special regard to composting technologies as well as hazards and cautions connected with the use of these products: experiments about the agricultural value of compost have been seldom carried out. The subsequent shortage of information heavily influences compost utilization: the farmer mistrusts it, because he doesn't fully know crop responses to compost application.

For these reasons we started a study about the influence of compost distribution on the soil-plant system. Four crops, of different botanical species and edible parts (corn, potato, dry bean and leaf beet) were tested on two different soil types. In this paper we are presenting only a small part of the results obtained with one crop on one soil type,

Contribution from C.N.R. - Project I.P.R.A. - Subproject 1.

after three years of experimentation. Although this represents a period too small to allow a complete evaluation of the effects of organic dressings, we believe in the practical usefulness of a first appraisment, because of the increasing importance of short-term conclusions even in the agricultural practice.

Microbiological (6) and physical (3) patterns of the soil, as well as heavy metals (1) behaviour were studied by other research workers.

2. Materials and methods

The experiment started in 1983 at Aiello del Friuli, in the Northeast of Italy, on a alluvional, loamy, calcareous, basic soil (Calcic Cambisols FAO/UNESCO). Barley was grown in the last year, and previously various hort crops in rotation, without any addition of organic matter from outside.

Twelve treatments (see table I) were selected for use in a randomized complete block design, with four replications. The application rates of treatment 3 corresponds to the current agronomical practice; the comparison among the different types of organic materials was carried out on the common base of N supply, arbitrarly fixed at 1000 Kg ha^{-1} year^{-1} of total N (table II). Plot dimensions were m 3 x 10; the observations were made only in the central strips (m 1.5 x 9).

Fertilizers were distributed every year on the same plots during spring before plowing (35 - 40 cm depth). Inorganic nitrogen was supplied half before plowing and half with cover application. Corn (Solar, 1983; Roberta, 1984 and 1985) was sown at the beginning of May at a distance of 75 cm between the rows and 22 cm on each row, and regularly irrigated; crop residues were always removed.

During the growing season, plant development, flowering precocity, deficiency symptoms and grain yield were observed. On a sample of two plants per plot, collected at the silage stage, the following patterns were determined: N (Kjeldahl), K, Na, Mg, Ca (A.A. spectrophotometry on nitroperchloric solution), P (colorimetry on nitroperchloric solution) and B (colorimetry on burning residues). Soil was sampled before the annual distribution of fertilizers, at two different depths (0-20 and 20-40 cm); the following analyses were performed: pH in H$_2$O and KCl (1:2.5), C.E.C. (S.I.S.S.), organic C (Walkley-Black), total N (Kjeldahl), available P (Olsen) and available K (ammonium acetate N, pH 7). Total P and K content will be determined at the end of the experiment. The water retention curve was determined by the Richards apparatus.

The statistical analysis of soil composition data was carried out by separating the effect of the annual application of fertilizers from that of the previous years' dressings. Therefore, multiple linear regression techniques were adopted, using the models shown in table III. Both separate regressions (treatments 1, 2, 3 and 4 - 10) and common ones (treatment 1 - 10) were computed, testing the hypothesis of using common regression coefficients, in order to find differences due to the type of material employed (2). The same techniques were employed in the analysis of yields, for continuous factors (treatment levels); for discrete factors (type of organic materials) the statistical analysis was carried out according to a randomized block design, combined in the years, by a mixed ANOVA model, in wich the treatments' effects were considered fixed and those of the years random (4). Apparent recoveries were

Treatment	Description	Quantities q x ha^{-1} x yr^{-1} supplied		
		1983	1984	1985
1	Control	-	-	-
2	Ammonium nitrate (26-27)	3.84	3.84	3.84
	Superphosphate (19-21)	3.74	3.74	3.74
	Potassium sulphate (50-52)	3.00	3.00	3.00
3	Ammonium nitrate (26-27)	7.69	7.69	7.69
	Superphosphate (19-21)	7.48	7.48	7.48
	Potassium sulphate (50-52)	6.00	6.00	6.00
4	m.s.w. compost	1483	1480	1639
5	Immature m.s.w. compost	1607	1111	1742
6	Refined m.s.w. compost	1481	1222	1404
7	Fym	1754	1296	1373
8	m.s.w. + s.s. compost	816	1037	1077
9	m.s.w. + s.s. compost	1633	2074	2155
10	m.s.w. + s.s. compost	2450	3111	3233
11	Treatment 8 + 2	816+(3.84+3.74+3.00)	1037+(3.84+3.74+3.00)	1077+(3.84+3.74+3.00)
12	Treatment 8 + 3	816+(7.69+7.48+6.00)	1037+(7.69+7.48+6.00)	1077+(7.69+7.48+6.00)

(m.s.w. = municipal solid wastes; s.s. = sewage sludge; fym = farmyard manure).

Table I : Fertilizers employed in the experimentation : description and quantities applied

Material	Year	C%	N%	C/N	P%	K%	Na%	Ca%	Mg%	B ppm	pH	Volatile solids %	Moisture %	Treatment
m.s.w. compost	1983	13.06	0.89	14.67	0.27	0.29	0.39	9.42	1.78	27.74	7.23	34.12	29.00	
	1984	15.14	0.95	15.94	0.31	0.51	0.37	3.92	1.00	23.97	7.80	48.27	33.40	4
	1985	13.29	0.70	18.96	0.42	0.73	0.44	8.29	1.07	51.27	7.45	37.70	32.70	
m.s.w. + s.s. compost	1983	11.32	0.81	13.98	0.24	0.26	0.39	9.55	2.11	29.14	7.32	29.35	33.00	8,9,10,
	1984	11.22	0.94	11.94	0.33	0.62	0.44	4.51	1.22	25.99	7.90	43.83	35.80	11,12
	1985	8.86	0.75	11.81	0.31	0.38	0.32	11.13	2.24	34.60	7.45	36.10	38.80	
Refined m.s.w. compost	1983	10.84	0.80	13.55	0.28	0.28	0.44	10.22	2.04	28.33	7.00	31.01	26.00	
	1984	15.05	0.90	16.72	0.30	0.53	0.38	4.61	1.50	23.89	7.70	45.36	32.20	6
	1985	25.81	1.27	20.32	0.27	0.88	0.55	5.51	0.61	56.76	7.20	71.50	46.30	
Immature m.s.w. compost	1983	14.17	0.81	17.49	0.30	0.26	0.34	8.97	2.11	28.52	6.74	35.98	26.00	
	1984	16.22	0.78	20.79	0.18	0.38	0.30	4.39	1.35	20.50	7.50	51.43	34.20	5
	1985	24.10	1.09	22.11	0.28	0.61	0.61	6.01	0.89	45.79	7.15	76.60	49.30	
Fym	1983	23.93	2.33	10.27	0.43	2.09	0.11	2.92	0.73	13.74	7.52	89.04	82.10	
	1984	28.93	2.49	11.62	1.96	3.51	0.47	1.94	0.80	20.95	7.30	74.67	80.80	7
	1985	26.62	2.38	11.18	1.69	4.08	0.98	3.56	0.72	34.18	7.20	74.00	74.90	

(Composts were supplied by Daneco S.p.A. - S. Giovanni al Natisone - Udine - Italy)

Table II : Composition of organic materials employed in the experimentation. (Values on dry Weight basis)

calculated as:

$$\frac{\text{Uptake by fertilized plots - Uptake by untreated test}}{\text{Annual supply}} \times 100$$

3. Results and Discussion

3.1 Effects on the soil

During the first three years of trial, significative differences were found for organic C and total N and for available P and K contents in the soil; measures of pH (H_2O and KCl), C.E.C. and water retention capacity didn't show appreciable variations.

a. Carbon. The carbon content increased only in the plots that received organic manure; this increase depended upon the annual carbon supply and, for a greater extent, upon the cumulative supply of the previous years (fig. Ia and table III). In correspondence with the maximum dressings, equivalent to 585 q/ha of carbon over a period of three years, the C content of the soil raised by 66 per cent, from an average value of 0.75 (untreated test) to a maximum of 1.25 per cent (treatment 10): this remained, however, under the optimum agronomic value correspondent to this soil type (5).

b. Nitrogen. Total N content significatively increased only with the annual dressings of organic manure (fig. Ib and table III). Nitrogen raised from an average rate of 0.12 to 0.15 per cent, with a difference of more than 25 per cent. The maximum increase (41 per cent) was obtained with treatment 10.

The C/N ratio didn't give significative variations, because of the similar trends shown by C and N increases: its value varied between 6 and 7, widely lower than the optimum ratio of 10.

c. Available Phosphorous. Both inorganic and organic fertilizers increased the available P content of the soil, although a proportionally greater effect was performed by the former ones. This could indicate a different solubility of P for the various materials. In both cases, however, a significative effect was observed only in correspondence with the annual application rates, particularly with the highest ones (linear term negative, quadratic term positive). Organic dressings applied in the previous years had a negative influence on availability of phosphorous; non significative, in this case, was the effect exerted by inorganic fertilizers. For these last, a significative and negative interaction was found between annual and previous years' applications (fig. Ic, Id and table III). Available P content showed an average variation of more than 100 per cent for the organic fertilizers, raising from low (11.5 ppm) to medium-hight levels (24 ppm).

d. Available Potassium. Available K content increased with both inorganic and organic fertilizers. This effect was highly correlated with the annual dressings as well as with the cumulative applications of the previous years. A significative and positive interaction was found between the effect of annual and previous years' dressings (fig. Ie and table III). Available K raised from 83 (untreated test) to 142 ppm (plots treated with organic fertilizers), reaching a maximum of 209 ppm after three years of farmyard manure applications. Even in this case availability increased from low to medium-hight levels.

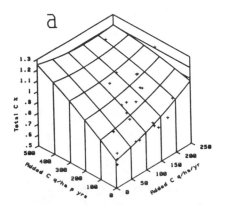

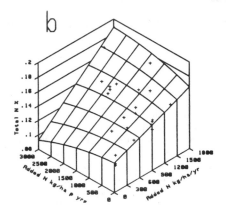

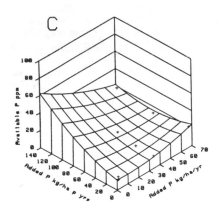

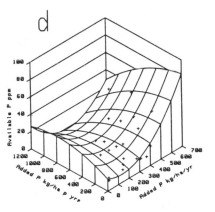

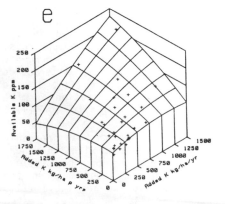

Fig. I - Effects of annual and previous years' dressings of different elements on their content in the soil.
(Figures c and d are referred to P added with mineral and organic fertilizers, respectively).

Figure	Regression equations	R^2
1a	$Y = .75 + 7.05 \times 10^{-4**} C1 + 1.16 \times 10^{-3**} C2 + 2.36 \times 10^{-6} C1^2 - 3.11 \times 10^{-7} C2^2 - 2.96 \times 10^{-6} C1 \times C2$	.71
1b	$Y = .12 + 2.40 \times 10^{-5**} N1 - 2.62 \times 10^{-6} N2 + 5.33 \times 10^{-10} N1^2 - 2.21 \times 10^{-9} N2^2 + 9.44 \times 10^{-9} N1 \times N2$	.81
1c	$Y = 11.52 - 7.54 \times 10^{-2**} P1 + 1.48 \times 10^{-1} P2 + 3.74 \times 10^{-3} P1^2 + 1.55 \times 10^{-3} P2^2 - 5.51 \times 10^{-3**} P1 \times P2$	.96
1d	$Y = 13.62 - 6.37 \times 10^{-2**} P1 + 4.31 \times 10^{-2} P2 + 2.34 \times 10^{-4*} P1^2 - 2.73 \times 10^{-5**} P2^2 - 8.06 \times 10^{-5} P1 \times P2$	.81
1e	$Y = 80.02 + 5.11 \times 10^{-2**} K1 + 9.40 \times 10^{-3**} K2 - 2.45 \times 10^{-5} K1^2 - 1.67 \times 10^{-5} K2^2 + 6.13 \times 10^{-5*} K1 \times K2$	.90
2a	$Y = 38.20 + 38.39^{**} M - 6.91^{**} M^2 - 9.01^{**} Z1 + 23.93^{**} Z2$	.95
2b	$Y = 39.97 + 27.43^{**} W - 5.25^{**} W^2 - 8.22^{**} Z1 + 17.13^{**} Z2 + .08^{**} W \times Z1 + 18.72^{**} W \times Z2 - 1.18 W^2 \times Z1 - 3.09 W^2 \times Z2$	.93
2c	$Y = 37.95 + 38.53^{**} M + 24.03^{**} W - 6.84^{**} M^2 - 12.45^{**} M \times W + 2.10 M^2 \times W - 4.95^* Z1 + 20.64^{**} Z2 - 6.68^* M \times Z1 + 6.26 M \times Z2 - 2.46^* W \times Z1 + 8.47^* W \times Z2 + 1.57 M^2 \times Z1 - 1.78 M^2 \times Z2$	.96

M = mineral dressing levels; W = m.s.w. + s.s. compost levels;
$Z1$ and $Z2$ = dummy variables referred to the years (1983: $Z1 = 1$, $Z2 = 0$;
         1984: $Z1 = 0$, $Z2 = 1$; 1985: $Z1 = Z2 = 0$)
$C1, N1, P1, K1$ = C,N,P,K/year;
$C2, N2, P2, K2$ = C,N,P,K/previous years;
* significative at $p = 0.05$, ** significative at $p = 0.01$

Table III : Regression equations and R^2 : relationships illustrated in the correspondent figures

3.2. Effects on Plants

3.2.1 Grain Yield

Statistical analysis of production data was performed assembling the treatments in four groups, in order to evaluate: a) the effect of increasing rates of inorganic fertilizers (treatments 1,2,3); b) the effect of increasing rates of compost (treatment 1,8,9,10); c) the effect of mixed dressings of inorganic and organic fertilizers (treatments 1,2,3,8,11,12); d) finally, the efficiency of different organic materials (treatments 4,5,6,7,9).

a. Curves describing yield response to inorganic fertilizers in the single years are equally shaped, although the intercept on the ordinate is significatively different. This indicates that the effect of inorganic fertilizers isn't related to seasonal variations, that actually influence the yield potential of the crop. From these curves we realize that the different rates of fertilizers didn't provide maximum yield response. (fig. IIa and table III).

b. Curves describing yield response over three years of compost applications show significatively different trends: the agronomic effect of increasing quantities of compost depends upon seasonal variations. Over all the years these functions showed a maximum in correspondence with about 1750, 3000 and 2800 q/ha of compost in 1983, 1984 and 1985 respectively. Grain yield was in both 1983 and 1985 lower than the maximun obtained with only inorganic fertilizers (fig. IIb and table III).

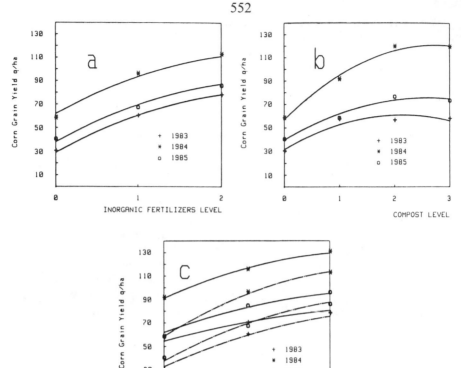

Fig. II - Effects of increasing rates of fertilizers on corn grain yield
(15.5% moisture content).
(Inorganic fertilizers level: 0 = treatment 1, 1 = treatment 2,
2 = treatment 3; m.s.w. + s.s. compost levels: 0 = treatment 1,
1 = treatment 8, 2 = treatment 9, 3 = treatment 10).

c. Also in this case, functions describing grain yield are significatively
different over the years. The addition of compost allowed to obtain higher
yields than only mineral fertilizers: these last show, however, a
decreasing efficiency, as can be drawn from negative interaction between
compost and mineral fertilizers (fig. IIc and table III).

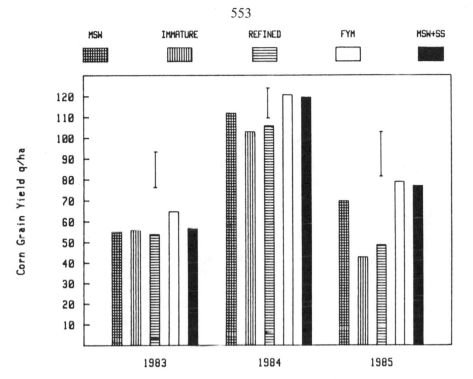

Fig. III - Corn grain yield attained with different types of organic
materials (15.5% moisture content).
(I LSD at p = 0.05; effect of the year significative at p = 0.01;
effect of treatments significative at p = 0.05; interaction treat‐
ments x year not significative).

d.   The different types of organic materials showed significative
differences only in some years. Their overall influence, however, was
constant (material x year interaction = n.s.). Higher yields were obtained
with farmyard manure and compost from sewage sludge and solid wastes,
lower with immature or refined composts. In 1985, yield obtained with
immature compost was equal to that of the untreated test. Compost from
only municipal solid wastes gave intermediate yields (fig. III).

3.2.2. Effects on plant composition

Only N, P and K contents showed significative variations within
the different treatments. These effects are not correlated with the element
concentration in the soil, with the exception of K, which shows quite
low coefficients of regression (table IV).
Apparent N and P recoveries for organic treatments were always lower
than those relative to the inorganic treatments. Apparent K recoveries
were similar for all the materials but farmyard manure, which showed
a lower efficiency over the first two years (table V).

Element	Treat. Year	1	2	3	4	5	6	7	8	9	10	11	12	L.S.D. p=0.05	r (1)
N%	1983	0.85	0.98	1.14	0.87	0.93	0.85	0.97	0.88	0.92	0.93	0.99	1.07	0.1109	0.05
	1984	0.66	0.83	0.96	0.89	0.84	0.85	1.06	0.87	0.89	0.97	0.89	1.03	0.0944	0.33
	1985	0.95	0.83	0.96	1.02	0.98	1.07	0.95	0.98	0.93	0.98	0.92	1.16	0.1300	0.18
P%	1983	0.15	0.15	0.17	0.19	0.21	0.19	0.19	0.20	0.18	0.20	0.17	0.15	0.0299	0.02
	1984	0.23	0.17	0.17	0.25	0.26	0.24	0.20	0.23	0.23	0.20	0.19	0.19	0.0425	0.16
	1985	0.26	0.23	0.21	0.28	0.30	0.26	0.20	0.26	0.25	0.26	0.20	0.17	n.s.	0.16
K%	1983	0.89	0.95	0.96	1.18	1.17	1.21	1.15	1.09	1.14	1.17	1.05	,1.08	0.1290	0.34
	1984	0.60	0.58	0.68	1.00	0.85	0.95	0.94	0.81	0.89	1.05	0.84	0.86	0.1850	0.56
	1985	0.57	0.50	0.65	0.78	0.78	0.72	0.81	0.78	0.68	0.80	0.70	0.65	0.1300	0.55

(1) r = Linear regression coefficient between soil content and percentage in plant tissues.

Table IV : N,P,K contents in maize plants collected at silage stage (values on dry weight basis)

Element	Treat. Year	1	2	3	4	5	6	7	8	9	10	11	12
N%	1983	-	52	45	2	6	2	5	8	0	5	11	13
	1984	-	57	60	7	12	8	16	11	10	8	16	18
	1985	-	21	37	2	0	- 2	6	2	5	4	9	18
P%	1983	-	16	14	2	4	3	7	9	3	4	6	4
	1984	-	6	16	7	19	8	4	5	5	5	.7	6
	1985	-	20	17	1	0	- 4	1	1	3	2	3	3
K%	1983	-	35	22	18	26	20	10	43	23	23	24	20
	1984	-	20	29	24	35	25	16	15	14	12	21	18
	1985	-	8	22	3	2	- 1	5	9	9	9	14	12

Table V : Apparent % recoveries, calculated on the basis of annual supplies (corn plants at silage stage)

4. Conclusions

Compost application increased organic C and total N as well as available P and K contents of the soil, attaining levels that can be considered medium from an agronomic point of view. As a consequence of the high application rates, these values are generally superior than those relative to only inorganic fertilizers. These last, however, gave higher average yields than organic dressings themselves.

The highest performances were reached with the combined application of the two forms, though with the application of very high quantities of compost.

Both the nature of wastes and kind of process influenced the agronomic value of composts. Among these, the best, equivalent to farmyard manure, was that obtained by composting municipal solid wastes and sewage sludge toghether. Refined compost always gave lower results than not refined one; refining process, therefore, gives a better appearance to the product, but reduces its productive efficiency.

Extreme importance must be attributed to the stabilization phase: not sufficiently stabilized compost showed inhibitory effects on maize plants.

In order to obtain positive short-term effects, it's preferable the use of composts derived from municipal solid wastes and sewage sludge, well stabilized and distributed together with mineral fertilizers. Besides this, it appears as a necessity to distribute high quantities of materials, exceeding the limits imposed by the present italian law (DPR 915/1982).

Results presented can provide useful elements in order to attribute a commercial value to the compost, according to the attainable yield's increases.

More indications about the fertilizing value of compost will be given only when final long-term results of this experimentation will be available.

Aknowledgements. The authors wish to thank Mr. Franco Tasca and Adriano Rasera for the chemical analyses and Mr. Alfredo Gallas for his contribution to the field trials.

REFERENCES

1. BARBERA, A. (1986). Extraction and dosage of heavy metals from compost-amended soils. Proceedings of International Symposium on Compost production, Quality and Use. Udine, April 1986 (in press).
2. DRAPER, N., SMITH, H. (1981). Applied Regression Analysis. J. Wiley & Sons, N.Y.
3. GUIDI, G. (1986). Some effects of compost on soil physical properties. Proceedings of International Symposium on Compost Production, Quality and Use. Udine, April 1986 (in press).
4. MCINTOSH, M.S. (1983). Analysis of combined experiments. Agron. Journal, 75, 153-155.
5. REMY, J.C., MARIN-LAFLECHE, A. (1974). L'analise de terre: réalisation d'un programme d'interpretation automatique. Ann. Agron., 25, 607-632.
6. RUTILI, A., CIVILINI, M., CITTERIO, B., DE BERTOLDI, M. (1986). Microbial variations in compost-amended soils. Proceedings of International Symposium on Compost Production, Quality and Use. Udine, April 1986 (in press).

AEROBIC STABILIZATION IN THE SOLID STATE OF PARTIALLY
DEWATERED SEWAGE SLUDGE.
MICROBIOLOGICAL AND TECHNOLOGICAL ASPECTS

S. COPPOLA, F. VILLANI
Istituto di Microbiologia agraria e Stazione di Microbiologia industriale
F. ROMANO
Istituto di Meccanica agraria
Universita' degli Studi di Napoli
I-80055 Portici, Italia

Summary
Partially dewatered sewage sludge in the form of filter-cake pieces,
treated with pure oxygen in a closed system, quickly reaches 60°C or
more by self-heating, following a typical temperature ascent
corresponding to microbial successions occurring during the process.
Mineralization activities are promoted at a maximal extent and
sanitization is easily achieved. Sludge stabilization can then be
completed by ripening through conventional windrow system.
Preliminary microbiological study of the sludge during the
thermophilic stage of the treatment allowed to isolate 164 biotypes
of bacteria, whose identification is still in progress. The variety
of the microbial strains resulted in relation to the isolation media
utilized. Microbial diversity resulted to decrease increasing the
temperature : spore-formers and Gram-positive bacteria increase :
coccal shaped bacteria are far inhibited at 55°C. Anyway a
metabolically versatile microbial population is always present.

INTRODUCTION
        A previous paper (Coppola et al., 1985) described the conditions
necessary for the composting of sewage sludge in the absence of other solid
support materials. The advantage of this method of stabilization is that,
like other composting techniques, it produces a solid which is genuinely
stable and preservable and, moreover, it opens up the way to making other
solid wastes available. It also yields a product which is richer in
nitrogen and which is therefore of greater use for agricultural purposes.
        By using an adiabatic experimental system, it has been shown that it
is possible to cope with the problems normally presented by raw sludge with
regard to self-heating and explained by Sikora and Sowers (1983) as being
caused by a too low C/N ratio and by Haugh (1983) as having thermodynamic
causes resulting from excess humidity. Sludge dewatered by filtration (with
27-28 % of total solids) could reach a temperature of 62-63°C in 11-12
hours if treated in a closed system with pure oxygen at a slight
overpressure (0.025 atm). This shows that self-heating which is quite
adequate for hygienic sanitization is possible if the necessary aerobiotic
conditions are provided.
        Treatment of this kind naturally leads to a marked promotion of
genuinely mineralizing activities. In ideal operating conditions the
mineralization of organic carbon occurred in fact in accordance with a

kinetic process which can be expressed (with R = 0.991) in the following equation :

$$C = 0.6338 \ t + 0.0382$$

where t is the time in hours and C is the carbon produced in the form of carbon dioxide in grammes per kg of dry matter. This typically exoergic process must be considered of interest for the purpose of achieving the temperature required to eliminate the pathogenic microorganisms, viruses, helminths and seeds which infest the sludge, but it is not so useful for composting, as compost has to contain a suitable amount of more or less humified organic material which can condition the soil when it is applied. The treatment has therefore been considered suitable solely for the hygienic sanitization of sludge. For this purpose the duration of the process can be kept to the minimum required, and stabilization can be completed by means of ripening through the conventional windrow system.

Transformation is effected in this second phase by the microorganisms which have survived the self-heating or for which self-heating provides suitable conditions for activity and development. These thermoresistant and/or thermophilic microorganims are in fact very often assumed to be present in some composts obtained from other organic materials. These have recently been partially described but not yet properly identified in the case of composting of sludge alone (Duvoort-van Engers and Coppola, 1985).

A speciographic microbiological survey has therefore been carried out to study the successive microbial populations occuring during the treatment of sludge by the process indicated earlier. This paper gives the findings which are still at a very preliminary stage - and describes the construction of a modular test installation which can treat sludge in sufficient amounts for large-scale testing of the process which has been evolved and also for an agronomic evaluation of the product.

EQUIPMENT AND METHODS

The test equipment and the sludge have been described in an earlier paper (Coppola et al., 1985). Stabilization was achieved by reproducing the conditions which had proved best during the earlier research : sludge partially dewatered by means of a Diemme filter press after conditioning with Zetag 51, up to 72 % humidity, reduced to particles less than 8.5 mm in diameter, with an oxygen flow of 0.5 l/min. The oxygen was sterilized by filtering through a Sartorius membrane 113 038 (diameter of pores : 0.15µ). On the basis of the typical temperature curve during the treatment (see Figure 1), it was decided to carry out a microbiological analysis of the sludge at each of the most typical phases of the process, which were assumed to be related to the successive occurrence of various microbial populations. The three phases were in fact : 1) the first change in the temperature curve when, at around 45°C, the increases in the sludge temperature began to level out ; 2) the moment when the temperature started to rise again, probably as a result of the microbial groups which were left ; 3) after reaching the maximum temperature, above 60°C, which is definitely a very selective and restrictive level. It was of course necessary to conduct the experiment at the various stages of the process in different ways. At the required moment the Dewar vessel containing the sludge was removed in sterile conditions from the equipment, transferred and opened under a cover with a laminar flow of sterile air for the sample to be extracted. The sample was suspended in a physiologically sterile solution, homogenized in a stomacher, subjected to graduated dilution and suspension and then transferred to plates. The following substrates were used :

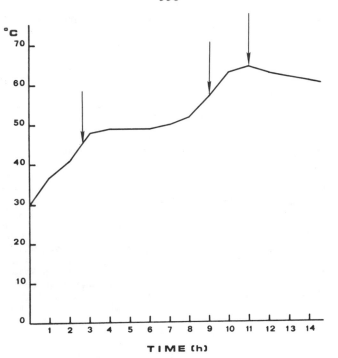

Figure 1

- plate count agar (oxoid CM 325), indicated by PCA ;
- extract of agar-treated sludge, indicated by EFA, prepared by treating 1 kg of raw sludge with 3 litres of spring water in an autoclave at 1.5 atm for 30 minutes, centrifuging, filtering through paper, adding 1.8 % of agar and then sterilizing at 120°C for 20 minutes ;
- plate count agar + sludge extract, indicated by PCA + EF, prepared in the same way as PCA but using 250 ml/l of sludge extract ;
- agar-amido-casein for actinomycetes (Williams and Davies, 1965) ;
- agar malt (oxoid CM 59).

After seeding, the plates were incubated aerobiotically at the same temperature recorded for the sludge at the time the sample was taken. All the morphologically different colonies were isolated, purified and retained on the same substrate before being subjected to morpho-biochemical identification. The presence of cilia was then determined using an electron microscope after colouring with uranyl acetate. The fermentative metabolism (OF/F) was calculated in accordance with Hugh and Leifson (1953) and biochemical activities were determined with the aid of the API 20 B system.

RESULTS AND COMMENTARY

The findings which are given here relate to the microbial strains in the sludge undergoing transformation during the first two typical phases of the process, which were described in the previous section.

Isolation of the strains was not random but aimed at identifying all the morphologically different colonies. As a result of this approach,

together with the use of different   culture substrates, it was possible   to
study no less than 211   strains. These may be considered   without doubt   as
being those which are most prevalent in the   sludge when it reaches 45   and
55°C respectively, but   they are   not the only   strains present,   since   of
course any microbial strain which numbered less than 100 units in a   colony
per gramme of material was disregarded.

The following tables indicate, with   regard to groups and   conditions
of isolation,   some of   the   phenotypical characteristics of   the   various
strains. The strains of the group   are numbered progressively in the   first
column. Under the asterisk is listed the number of isolated strains showing
the same characteristics and the exponent   of dilution of the sample   which
permitted isolation,   and the   thermoresistance at 70, 80 and 90°C.   The
letters indicating biochemical characteristics must be read vertically,   as
follows : CAT = catalase   ; OFF = fermentative metabolism   ; GEL = gelatin
liquefaction ; NIT = nitrate reduction ;   ONP = beta-galactosidase ; SAC   =
sucrose acid production ; ARA = same from arabinose ; MAN = from mannose   ;
FRU = from fructose ; GLU = from glucose ; MAL = from maltose ; AMD =   from
amygdalin ;   RHA =   from rhamnose ; GAL =   from galactose ; MNE =   from
mannite ; SOR = from sorbitol ; GLY = from glycerol ; URE = urease ; IND   =
indole production ;   H2S =   hydrogen sulphide production   ; VP   =
Voges-Proskauer (acetoin production) ; CIT = citrate attack ; OX = oxidase.

N.	*	Dil. lim.	Resist. 70	80	90	C A T	O F F	G E L	N I T	O N P	S A G	A R A	M A N	F R U	G L U	M A L	A M D	R H A	G A L	M N E	S O R	G L Y	U R E	I N D	H 2 S	V P	C I T	O X
1	2	-8	+	+	+	+	+	+	−	+	+	+	+	+	+	+	+	−	+	−	+	−	−	−	+	+	+
2	2	-3	+	+	+	+	+	+	−	+	+	+	+	+	+	+	+	+	+	+	+	−	+	−	+	+	+
3	9	-3	+	+	+	+	+	+	−	+	+	+	+	+	+	+	+	+	+	+	+	−	−	−	+	+	+
4	1	-3	+	+	+	+	+	+	−	+	+	+	+	+	+	+	+	+	+	+	+	+	+	+	+	+	+
5	1	-4	+	+	+	+	+	+	−	+	+	+	+	+	+	+	+	+	+	+	+	−	−	+	+	+	+
6	1	-5	+	+	−	+	+	+	−	+	+	+	+	+	+	+	+	+	+	+	+	+	−	+	−	+	+
7	4	-4	+	+	+	+	+	+	−	+	+	+	+	+	+	+	+	+	+	+	+	−	−	−	+	+	+
8	1	-6	+	+	+	+	+	+	−	+	+	+	+	+	+	+	+	−	+	+	−	−	−	+	+	+	+
9	1	-7	+	+	+	+	+	+	−	+	+	+	+	+	+	+	+	+	+	+	+	−	−	−	+	+	+
10	2	-4	+	+	+	+	+	+	−	+	+	+	+	+	+	+	+	+	+	−	+	−	−	−	+	+	+
11	1	-7	+	+	+	+	+	+	−	+	+	+	+	+	+	+	+	+	+	−	+	+	+	−	−	+	+
12	1	-8	+	+	+	+	+	+	−	+	+	+	+	+	+	+	−	−	+	−	+	−	+	−	+	+	+
13	1	-3	+	+	−	+	+	+	−	+	+	+	+	+	+	+	+	+	+	+	+	−	+	−	+	−	+
14	1	-4	+	+	+	+	+	+	−	+	+	+	+	+	+	−	−	+	+	−	+	−	−	+	+	+
15	1	-3	+	+	+	−	+	+	+	−	+	−	+	+	+	+	+	+	+	+	−	−	−	+	+	+	+
16	1	-4	+	+	+	+	−	+	−	−	−	−	−	−	−	−	−	−	−	−	+	−	−	+	+	+
17	1	-8	+	+	−	+	−	−	+	−	−	−	−	−	−	−	−	−	−	+	−	−	+	+	+
18	2	-8	+	−	−	+	−	+	−	−	−	−	−	−	−	−	−	−	−	−	+	−	−	+	−	+
19	1	-7	+	+	+	+	−	+	−	−	−	−	−	−	−	−	−	−	−	+	−	−	+	+	+
20	1	-3	+	+	+	+	−	+	−	−	−	−	−	−	−	−	−	−	−	−	−	−	+	−	+
21	1	-3	+	+	+	+	+	+	−	+	+	−	−	+	+	+	+	+	+	−	+	+	+	−	+	−	+
22	1	-7	+	+	−	+	+	−	−	+	+	−	+	+	+	−	+	+	−	+	+	+	+	+	+	−	+
23	1	-5	+	+	+	+	+	−	+	−	+	−	+	−	−	−	−	−	−	+	−	−	+	+	+
24	1	-5	+	−	+	−	−	−	−	+	−	+	−	−	−	−	−	−	+	−	−	−	+	−	+
25	1	-6	+	+	+	+	+	+	+	+	+	+	+	+	+	+	+	+	+	−	−	−	−	−	+	−
26	1	-8	+	+	+	+	−	−	+	+	+	+	+	+	+	+	+	+	+	+	−	−	−	+	+	+

Table 1 : Spore-forming gram-positive bacteria isolated on PCA plates   from
stabilizing sludge at 45°C

```
N.   *   Dil.  Resist.   C O G N O S A M F G M A R G M S G U I H V C O
         lim. 70    90   A F E I N A R A R L A M H A N O L T N 2 P I X
                   80    T F L T P C A N U U L D A L E R Y E D S     T

1    1   -3    + + +     + - + - + + + + + + + + + + + + + + + - + + +
2    1   -6    - - -     - + + - - - - - - - - - - - - - - - - - + - +

1    1   -6    - - -     + + + - + + + + + + + + + + + + - - - + - +
2    1   -8    - - -     + + + - - - - - - - - - - - - - - - - - + - +
3    1   -7    - - -     + + + - + + - + + + + + + + + - - - - + + +

1    1   -4    - - -     - + + - - + + + + + + + + + + + + - - - + - -
2    3   -6    - - -     - + + - + + + + + + + + + + + + + - - - + - +
```

Table 2 : Non-spore-forming gram-positive (first group), gram-negative (second group) and coccal-shaped gram-positive (third group) bacteria isolated on PCA plates from stabilizing sludge at 45°C

```
N.   *   Dil.  Resist.   C O G N O S A M F G M A R G M S G U I H V C O
         lim. 70    90   A F E I N A R A R L A M H A N O L R N 2 P I X
                   80    T F L T P C A N U U L D A L E R Y E D S     T

1    2   -8    + + +     + + + - - - - - - - - - - - - - + - - - + - +
2    1   -3    + - -     - - + - - - - - - - - - - - - - + - - - + - -
3    1   -5    + + +     + - + - - - - - - - - - - - - + - - + - +
4    1   -6    + + +     + + + - - - - - - - - - - - - - + - - + - +
5    1   -6    + + +     + - + - - - - - - - - - - - - - - - - - - +
6    1   -6    + + -     + - + - - - - - - - - - - - + - + - - - +
7    1   -7    + + +     + - + - - - - - - - - - - - + - - + - +
8    1   -7    + + +     + + + - - - - - - - - - + - + - - + - +
9    1   -3    + + +     + + + - + + + + + + - - - - + - + - +
10   1   -4    + - -     + + + - + + + + + + - + + + + + - - + - +
11   1   -7    + + +     + - + - + + + + + + - + + + + + - - + - +
12   1   -8    + + +     + + + - + + + + + + + + + - + - + - + + +
13   1   -8    + + +     + + + - + + + + + + + + + + + - + - + - +
14   1   -8    + + +     + + + - + + + + + + + + + + + - - - + - +
15   1   -3    + + +     + - + - - - - - - - - - - - + - + - + - +
16   1   -4    + - -     + - + - + - - - - - - - - - + - + - + - +
17   1   -6    + + +     - + + - - - - - - - - - - - + - - + - +
18   1   -7    + + +     + + + - + - - - - - + - - - + - + - +
19   1   -3    + - -     + + + - + - - + + - + - - - + - + - +
20   1   -3    + + -     + - + - + - + - - - - - - - + - - - +
21   1   -4    + + +     + + + - - - - - + + + - + + + + - - + - +
22   1   -4    + + -     + - + - - + - + - - - - - - - - - + - +
23   1   -7    + + +     + + + + + + + + + + + - + + + + - - + - +
24   1   -8    + + -     + - + - + + + + + + + + + + + - - + - +
25   1   -8    + + +     + + + + + + + + + + + - + + + + - + - +
26   1   -8    + + +     + + + + + + + + + + + + + + + + - + - +
27   1   -4    + + -     + + + - - - - - + - - - - - - + - +
28   1   -6    + + +     + + + - - - - - - + - - - - - + - +
29   1   -5    + - -     + + + - + + + - - + - - + - + - +
30   1   -5    + + +     + - + - + - - + + + + - + + + + + - +
31   1   -6    + + +     - - + - + - + - - - + - - - + - +
32   1   -8    + + -     + - + - - - - + - - - - - + - + - +
33   2   -6    + + +     + + + - + - - - + - - - - + - + - +
34   1   -7    + + +     - + + - + - - + - - + - - - + - +
35   1   -6    + + +     + - + - - + + + + + + + + + - + - + - +
```

Table 3 : Spore-forming gram-positive bacteria isolated on PCA + EF plates from stabilizing sludge at 45° C

N.	*	Dil. lim.	70	80	90	CAT	OFF	GEL	NIT	ONP	SAC	ARA	MAN	FRU	GLU	MAL	AMD	RHA	GAL	MNE	SOR	GLY	URE	IND	H2S	VP	CI	OXT
1	1	-7	-	-	-	+	+	+	+	+	+	+	+	+	+	+	+	+	+	+	+	+	-	+	-	+	-	+
2	1	-7	-	-	-	+	-	+	-	-	-	-	-	+	-	-	-	-	-	-	-	+	-	-	-	+	-	-
1	1	-8	+	-	-	+	-	+	-	-	-	-	-	-	-	-	-	-	-	-	-	+	-	-	-	+	-	-
2	1	-3	+	-	-	+	+	+	-	+	+	+	+	+	+	+	+	+	+	+	-	+	-	-	-	+	-	+
3	1	-7	+	+	+	+	+	+	-	+	-	-	-	-	-	-	-	-	-	-	-	+	-	-	-	+	-	+
4	1	-7	-	-	-	+	+	+	-	+	-	-	-	+	-	+	-	-	-	-	-	+	-	-	-	-	-	+
5	2	-4	+	-	-	+	+	+	+	+	+	+	+	+	+	+	+	+	+	+	-	+	-	+	-	-	-	+
6	1	-5	-	-	-	-	+	+	+	+	+	+	+	+	+	+	+	+	+	+	+	+	-	+	-	+	-	+
7	2	-8	-	-	-	+	-	+	-	+	-	-	-	-	-	-	-	-	-	-	-	+	-	-	-	+	-	-
8	1	-8	+	-	-	+	+	+	-	-	+	+	+	+	+	-	+	-	-	-	+	+	-	-	-	-	-	-
9	1	-8	+	-	-	+	+	+	-	-	+	+	+	+	+	-	-	-	-	-	-	+	-	-	-	-	-	-
1	2	-8	-	-	-	-	+	+	-	+	+	+	+	+	+	+	+	+	+	+	+	+	-	-	-	+	-	+
2	1	-5	-	-	-	-	+	+	-	+	+	+	+	+	+	+	+	+	+	+	+	+	-	-	-	+	+	+
1	1	-5	-	-	-	-	+	+	+	+	+	+	+	+	+	+	+	+	+	+	+	+	-	+	-	-	-	+
1	1	-3	+	+	+	+	+	+	-	-	+	+	+	+	+	+	-	+	+	+	+	+	-	-	-	+	+	+
2	1	-3	+	+	+	+	+	+	-	+	+	+	+	+	+	+	+	-	-	-	-	-	-	-	-	-	-	+
3	1	-3	+	+	-	+	-	+	-	+	+	+	+	+	+	+	-	+	+	+	-	+	-						
4	3	-4	+	+	+	+	+	+	-	+	+	+	+	+	+	-	-	+	+	+	+	+	-	-	-	+	-	+
5	1	-4	+	+	+	+	+	+	-	+	+	+	+	+	+	+	+	+	+	+	+	-	-	-	+	-	+
6	1	-5	+	+	-	+	+	+	-	+	+	+	+	+	+	-	-	-	-	-	+	-	-	-	+	-	+
7	2	-5	+	+	-	+	-	+	-	+	-	-	-	-	-	-	-	-	-	-	+	-	-	-	+	-	+
8	1	-4	+	+	+	+	-	+	-	+	-	-	-	-	-	-	-	-	+	-	-	-	+	-	+
9	3	-7	+	+	+	+	-	+	-	+	-	-	-	-	-	-	-	-	+	-	-	-	+	-	+
10	1	-4	+	+	+	+	-	+	-	+	-	-	-	-	-	-	-	-	+	-	-	-	+	-	+
11	1	-6	+	+	-	+	-	+	-	-	+	+	-	+	+	+	-	-	+	+	-	+	-	+
12	1	-3	-	-	-	-	+	+	-	+	+	+	+	+	-	+	+	+	-	+	+	-	+	-	+
13	1	-5	+	+	-	+	+	+	-	+	+	+	+	+	-	-	+	-	+	-	+	-	-	-	+
14	1	-5	+	+	+	+	-	+	-	+	+	+	+	-	-	-	+	-	-	+	-	-	+	-	+
15	1	-5	+	+	+	+	-	+	-	-	-	-	-	-	-	-	+	-	-	-	+	-	-	-	+
16	1	-6	+	+	+	+	+	+	-	-	+	+	-	+	+	-	-	-	-	+	-	-	-	-	+	+
1	2	-6	-	-	-	+	+	+	-	-	+	+	+	+	+	-	+	+	+	+	+	-	-	+	-	+
2	2	-8	-	-	-	+	+	+	-	-	+	+	+	+	+	-	+	+	+	+	+	-	-	-	-	+
3	1	-7	-	-	-	+	+	+	-	-	+	+	+	+	+	+	+	+	-	+	-	+	-	-	-	-
4	1	-8	-	-	-	+	+	+	-	+	+	+	+	+	-	+	+	-	-	+	-	-	+	-	-
5	1	-7	-	-	-	+	+	+	-	+	+	+	+	+	-	+	-	-	+	+	-	-	-	-	-
6	1	-7	-	-	-	+	+	+	-	+	+	+	+	+	-	+	+	+	-	-	-	-	-	-	-
7	1	-7	-	-	-	+	+	+	-	+	+	+	+	+	+	+	+	-	-	+	-	-	-	+	-
8	1	-4	-	-	-	-	+	+	+	-	+	+	+	+	+	+	+	+	+	-	-	-	+	-	+

Table 4 : Non-spore-forming gram positive (first group), gram-negative (second group), coccal-shaped gram-positive (third group) and gram-negative (fourth group) bacteria isolated on PCA + EF plates ; spore-forming gram-positive (fifth group) and gram-negative (sixth group) bacteria isolated on EFA plates from stabilizing sludge at 45°C

N	*	Dil. lim.	Resist. 70	80	90	CAT	OFF	GEL	NIT	ONP	SAC	ARA	MAN	FRU	GLU	MAL	AMD	RHA	GAL	MNE	SOR	GLY	URE	IND	H2S	VP	CIT	OX
1	1	-6	+	-	-	-	+	+	+	+	+	+	+	+	+	+	+	+	+	+	+	+	-	-	-	+	-	+
2	1	-2	+	+	+	+	+	+	-	+	+	+	+	+	+	+	+	+	+	+	+	+	-	-	-	-	-	+
3	3	-7	+	+	+	+	+	+	+	+	+	+	+	+	+	+	+	+	+	+	+	+	-	-	-	+	-	+
4	1	-2	+	+	+	+	+	+	-	+	+	+	+	+	+	+	+	+	+	+	+	+	-	-	-	+	+	+
5	1	-4	+	+	-	+	+	+	-	+	+	+	+	+	+	+	+	+	+	+	+	+	-	-	-	+	-	+
6	1	-4	+	+	+	+	+	+	+	+	+	+	+	+	+	+	+	+	+	+	+	+	-	+	-	+	-	+
7	1	-4	+	+	+	-	+	+	-	+	+	+	+	+	+	+	+	+	+	+	+	+	-	-	-	-	-	+
8	1	-3	+	+	+	+	+	+	-	-	+	+	+	+	+	+	+	+	+	+	+	+	-	-	-	-	-	+
9	2	-5	+	+	+	-	+	+	+	+	+	+	+	+	+	+	+	+	+	+	+	+	-	-	-	+	-	-
10	1	-7	+	+	+	+	+	+	+	+	+	+	+	+	+	+	+	+	+	+	+	+	-	-	-	-	+	-
11	1	-2	+	+	-	+	+	+	-	+	+	+	+	+	+	+	-	+	-	+	-	-	-	-	-	-	-	-
12	1	-6	+	+	+	-	+	+	+	+	+	+	+	+	+	+	+	+	+	+	+	+	-	-	-	-	-	-
13	1	-5	+	+	-	-	+	+	+	+	+	+	+	+	+	+	+	+	+	+	+	+	-	-	-	-	-	+
14	1	-3	+	+	+	+	-	+	-	+	+	+	+	+	+	+	+	+	+	+	-	-	-	-	-	-	-	+
15	1	-3	+	+	+	+	+	+	-	-	+	+	+	+	+	+	+	+	+	+	+	+	-	-	-	-	-	-

N	*	Dil. lim.	Resist. 70	80	90	CAT	OFF	GEL	NIT	ONP	SAC	ARA	MAN	FRU	GLU	MAL	AMD	RHA	GAL	MNE	SOR	GLY	URE	IND	H2S	VP	CIT	OX
1	1	-4	-	-	-	-	+	+	-	+	+	+	+	+	+	+	+	+	+	+	+	+	-	-	-	-	-	-

N	*	Dil. lim.	Resist. 70	80	90	CAT	OFF	GEL	NIT	ONP	SAC	ARA	MAN	FRU	GLU	MAL	AMD	RHA	GAL	MNE	SOR	GLY	URE	IND	H2S	VP	CIT	OX
1	1	-2	+	-	-	+	+	+	-	-	+	+	+	+	+	+	-	+	+	+	+	-	-	-	+	-	+
2	1	-5	+	-	-	+	+	+	+	+	+	+	+	+	+	+	+	+	+	+	+	-	-	-	+	-	+

Table 5 : Gram-positive spore-forming (first group) and non-spore-forming (second group) bacteria and gram-negative bacteria isolated on PCA plates from stabilizing sludge at 55°C

N.	*	Dil. lim.	Resist. 70	80	90	CAT	OFF	GEL	NIT	ONP	SAC	ARA	MAN	FRU	GLU	MAL	AMD	RHA	GAL	MNE	SOR	GLY	URE	IND	H2S	VP	CIT	OX
1	2	-4	+	+	+	+	-	+	-	-	+	+	+	+	+	+	+	+	+	+	+	-	-	-	-	-	+
2	1	-3	+	+	-	+	+	+	-	+	+	+	+	+	+	+	+	+	+	-	-	-	-	-	-	-	+
3	2	-5	+	+	+	-	+	+	-	+	+	+	+	+	+	+	+	+	+	+	+	-	-	-	+	-	+
4	1	-5	+	+	-	-	+	+	+	+	+	+	+	+	+	+	+	+	+	+	+	-	-	-	+	-	+
5	2	-6	+	+	+	+	+	+	-	-	+	+	+	+	+	+	+	+	+	+	+	-	-	-	+	-	+
6	2	-4	+	+	+	-	+	+	-	-	+	+	+	+	+	+	+	+	+	+	+	-	-	-	+	-	+
7	1	-4	+	+	+	+	+	+	+	+	+	+	+	+	+	+	+	+	+	+	+	-	-	-	+	-	-
8	1	-4	+	+	+	+	+	+	+	+	+	+	+	+	+	+	+	+	+	+	+	-	-	-	-	-	+
9	1	-2	+	+	+	+	+	+	-	+	+	+	+	+	+	+	+	+	+	+	+	-	-	-	+	-	+
10	1	-2	+	+	+	+	-	+	-	-	+	+	+	+	+	+	+	+	+	+	+	-	-	-	+	-	+
11	1	-5	+	+	+	-	-	+	+	+	+	+	+	+	+	+	+	+	+	+	+	-	-	-	+	-	-
12	5	-6	+	+	+	+	+	+	-	+	+	+	+	+	+	+	+	+	+	+	+	-	-	-	+	-	+
13	1	-6	+	+	-	+	+	+	+	+	+	+	+	+	+	+	+	+	+	+	+	-	-	-	-	-	-
14	1	-6	+	+	-	-	+	+	-	+	+	+	+	+	+	+	+	+	+	+	+	-	-	-	-	-	+
15	1	-6	+	+	+	+	+	+	-	+	+	+	+	+	+	+	+	+	-	-	-	-	-	-	-	-	-
16	2	-6	+	+	+	+	+	+	-	+	+	+	+	+	+	+	+	+	+	-	-	-	-	-	-	-	+
17	1	-8	+	+	+	+	+	+	-	-	+	+	+	+	-	-	-	-	-	-	-	-	-	-	-	-	+
18	2	-6	+	+	+	+	+	+	-	-	+	+	+	+	-	+	+	+	+	+	-	-	-	+	-	+
19	1	-7	+	+	+	-	+	+	-	-	+	+	+	+	+	+	+	+	+	+	-	-	-	-	-	+
20	1	-3	+	+	+	+	+	+	+	+	+	+	+	+	+	+	+	+	+	+	+	-	-	-	+	-	+

Table 6 : Spore-forming gram-positive bacteria isolated on PCA + EF plates from stabilizing sludge at 55°C

N	*	Dil. lim.	70	80	90	C A T	O F F	G E L	N I T	O N P	S A C	A R A	M A N	F R U	G L U	M A L	A M D	R H A	G A L	M N E	S O R	G L Y	U R E	I N D	H 2 S	V P	C I	O X T
1	2	−5	+	+	−	−	+	+	−	+	+	+	+	+	+	+	+	+	+	+	+	+	−	−	−	+	−	−
2	1	−4	+	+	−	−	+	+	+	+	+	+	+	+	+	+	+	+	+	+	+	+	−	−	−	+	−	+
3	1	−4	+	+	+	+	+	+	−	+	+	+	+	+	+	+	+	+	+	+	+	+	−	−	−	+	−	−
4	3	−7	+	+	+	+	+	+	−	+	+	+	+	+	+	+	+	+	+	+	+	+	−	−	−	+	−	+
5	1	−3	+	+	+	+	+	+	−	−	−	−	−	−	−	−	−	−	−	−	−	−	−	−	−	+	−	+
6	1	−2	+	+	−	+	−	+	−	−	−	−	+	+	+	+	+	+	+	−	−	−	−	−	−	+	−	+
7	2	−5	+	+	−	−	+	+	−	−	+	+	+	+	+	+	+	+	+	+	−	−	−	−	−	+	−	+
8	2	−7	+	+	+	+	+	+	+	+	+	+	+	+	+	+	+	+	+	+	+	−	−	−	+	−	+
9	1	−7	+	+	+	+	+	+	+	+	+	+	+	+	+	I	I	+	+	+	+	−	−	−	+	−	+
10	1	−8	+	+	+	+	+	+	−	−	+	+	+	+	+	+	+	+	+	+	−	−	−	−	−	+
1	1	−6	−	−	−	−	+	+	+	+	+	+	+	+	+	+	+	+	+	+	+	+	−	−	−	+	−	+
2	1	−3	−	−	−	+	+	+	−	+	−	+	−	−	+	+	−	−	+	−	−	−	+	−	−	+	−	+
3	1	−2	−	−	−	+	+	+	−	+	−	−	−	+	+	−	−	+	−	−	−	−	−	+	−	+
4	1	−2	+	−	−	+	+	+	−	+	+	+	+	+	+	−	+	+	−	−	+	−	−	+	−	+
5	1	−5	+	−	−	+	+	+	+	+	+	−	−	−	−	+	−	−	+	+	−	−	+	−	+
6	1	−6	−	−	−	+	+	+	−	+	−	−	−	+	+	+	−	−	−	−	−	−	+	−	+
7	1	−6	−	−	−	+	+	+	−	−	+	+	+	+	+	−	+	I	−	−	+	−	−	+	−	+
1	1	−3	+	−	−	+	−	+	−	−	+	+	+	+	+	−	+	+	+	+	+	−	−	+	−	+
2	1	−5	−	−	−	+	−	+	−	−	−	−	−	−	−	■	■	■	■					I	+
0	1	−5	+	−	−	+	−	+	−	+	−	−	−	−	−	−	+	I	I	+	+	−	−	+	+	−	+

Table 7 : Gram-positive spore-forming (first group) and non-spore forming (second group) bacteria and gram-negative bacteria (third group) isolated on EFA plates from stabilizing sludge at 55°C

The substrates which were used did not lead to the isolation of actinomycetes and eumycetes. These groups were present in large numbers in the composting of sewage sludge mixed with other organic waste materials, particularly when the final mixture has a particularly high C/N ratio and dewatering of the medium is fostered (Coppola et al., 1983 ; De Bertoldi et al., 1983). Nakasaki et al. (1985a) found that there was a negligible level of mesophilic actinomycetes in the composting of dewatered sewage sludge after conditioning with lime, while a significant presence of thermophilic actinomycetes occurred only later (in the system designed by the present authors, this occurred approximately 48 hours after the start of the process and after about 20 hours (at 60°C).

The authors' explanation for these results is that actinomycetes develop more slowly than bacteria and that they are rather ineffective rivals where there are large amounts of nutrients ; as a result, they are able to benefit from their thermo-resistance only at a later stage. With regard to the isolation stage referred to in this paper, the fact that actinomycetes were not isolated would be consistent with these calculations. Further efforts are being made, however, to determine the presence of these microorganisms in the system under study using different culture methods. It nevertheless seems that the conditions of the material and the treatment are not at all favourable during the stabilization phase which is being considered here. The schizomycete strains which were isolated - and which have not yet been finally identified and classified -

cover a vast range of biochemical activities and would appear to form, even at the higher temperature, a fairly composite microflora. Table 8 summarizes the results of isolation.

	45°C			55°C		
	PCA	PCA+EF	EFA	PCA	PCA+EF	EFA
TOTAL OF ISOLATED STRAINS	50	54	31	21	30	25
NUMBER OF DIFFERENT STRAINS	33	49	24	18	20	20
DIFFERENT STRAINS (%)	66.0	90.7	70.6	85.7	66.7	80.0
SPORE-FORMING (%)	82.0	68.5	67.7	85.7	100.0	60.0
GRAM-POSITIVE (%)	94.0	77.8	67.7	90.5	100.0	88.0
BACTERIAL FORMS (%)	92.0	92.6	100.0	100.0	100.0	100.0

Table 8 : Distribution of isolation for three different substrates of culture, carried out in stabilizing sludge self-heated to two different temperatures

A total of 164 biotypes can be identified. There are not yet enough data available to indicate the number of species into which all the strains presenting different "profiles" may be divided, but various taxa can already be identified on the basis of spore formation, gram-reaction and morphology.

They include strains with particular characteristics, such as strain N° 1 in Table 2, N° 3 and others in Table 4, thermo-resistant but non-spore-forming, and strain N° 12 in Table 4, not resistant at 70°C but capable of showing, with all the usual colouring methods, the ability to produce spores. Complete identification must bear in mind the problems mentioned by Strom (1985b) on the difficulties pointed out by various writers on thermophilic microorganisms and linked both to the effect of the incubation temperature on nutritive requirements and to the loss of particular biochemical functions during the rise to temperatures close to those tolerated as maximum.

The variety of strains collected seemed linked to the isolation substrates which were used. It was particularly from hotter material that the sludge extract allowed a greater variety of strains to be isolated, contrary to the findings of other researchers (Nakasaki et al., 1985a).

From the number of different strains isolated at the various stages of the treatment, it would appear confirmed that variety is reduced as the temperature increases, bearing out the findings long ago of Waksman et al. (1939) on the ripening of manure and the more recent findings of Strom (1985a) on the composting of solid urban waste.

Even at 55°C, depending on the isolation substrate, the microflora in the stabilizing sludge may comprise only 60 % of spore-forming bacteria. This confirms the findings of Nakasaki et al. (1985b), who applied the inactivation technique using UV radiation to sludge at the thermophilic stage of composting and found that the spores can be in relation to vegetative cells up to a maximum of 60 %.

Similarly, the percentage of gram-positive bacteria increases with the temperature, but even at 55°C they would seem to be accompanied consistently by the gram-negative bacteria.

The coccal forms are completely inhibited at 55°C.

In his study of solid-waste composting, Strom (1985b) isolated on tryptic soy agar 652 colonies from material at 49-69°C. Using aspergillus fumigatus, he was able to identify strains of streptomyces and thermoactinomyces, two non-spore forming schizomycetes and ten forms of bacillus : B. licheniformis, B. subtilis, B. coagulans types A and B, B. circulans, B. stearothermophilis, B. brevis, B. sphaericus and two types of the same genus which could not be attributed to any of the known species. These species represent the microorganisms which, on the basis of available literature, may be considered present in the thermophilic stages of the composting of organic material. It will probably be possible to extend this knowledge as a result of findings based on efforts at specific isolation on various nutritive substrates.

Temperature is currently considered without question to be the most important factor in the control of composting ; it has a decisive influence both on microbial activity and on the variations in the successive microbial populations occurring during componting (McKinley and Vestal, 1984-1985). The sludge stabilization process referred to in this paper includes an initial phase designed to create the conditions whereby high temperatures can be rapidly achieved. In order to move from the experimental stage in the laboratory to large-scale use of the process, the equipment illustrated in Figure 2 has been designed. It is a mechanical unit which can handle two loads of sludge of approximately 100 kg in each cylinder (1). The number (2) and size (1 = 2 m ; useful diameter = 0.4 m) of the cylinders are not fixed but allow for possible enlargement of the installation for industrial-scale use.

The need to facilitate the oxidation of the sludge as much as possible prompted the design of a system which can rotate on a longitudinal axis at varying speeds but generally within 2 rmp by means of a TKD 15 2-hp adjustable speed motor (2). The transmission is by means of flat belts (3). The cylinders are made of PVC with an isolation chamber in expanded polyurethane. They are equipped at the front and back with removable covers to which are fitted rotating pressure intakes (5) for the entry and exit of reactive gases.

During the loading and unloading phases the cylinders may be tilted by means of the screw jacks (4) attached to the base of the metal mounting (6) which holds the equipment. Oxygen tanks (7) are fitted to the mounting and attached to the reactors by flexible pipes.

The study of the microbiological phenomena occurring during the treatment of sludge in this closed system - as illustrated in this paper - should determine the microbiological characteristics of the sludge at the moment of unloading. These characteristics will affect subsequent stabilization.

A metabolically varied and versatile microbial population, such as has been determined hitherto, may be considered definitely favourable.

ACKNOWLEDGMENT

This research was carried out with the aid of a contribution from the National Research Council (IPRA programme), Rome.

566

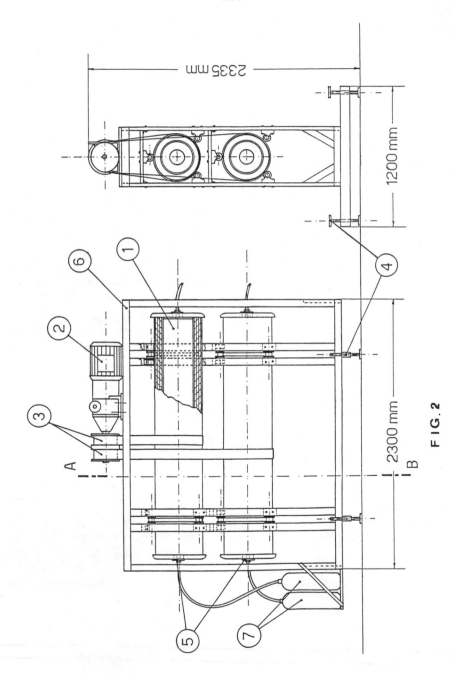

FIG. 2

BIBIOGRAPHY

1) COPPOLA, S., DUMONTET, S. and P. MARINO (1983). Composting raw sewage sludge in mixture with organic or inert bulking agents. International Conference on "Composting of solid wastes and slurries", Department of Civil Engineering, Univeristy of Leeds (UK), 28-30 September.

2) COPPOLA, S., VILLANI, F. and F. ROMANO (1985). Aerobic stabilization in the solid state of partially dewatered sewage sludge. EEC 4th Int. Symp. on "Processing and use of organic sludge and liquid agricultural wastes", Rome, 8-11 October.

3) DE BERTOLDI, M., COPPOLA, S. and L. SPINOSA (1983). Health implication in sewage sludge composting. In : Disinfection of sewage sludge : technical, economic and microbiological aspects (Bruce, A.M., Havelaar, A.H. and P. L'Hermite eds., Commission of the European Communities), D. Reidel Publ. Co., Dordrecht, 165-178.

4) DUVOORT-VAN ENGERS, L.E. and S. COPPOLA (1985). "State of the art" on sludge composting. EEC 4th Int. Symp. on "Processing and use of organic sludge and liquid agricultural wastes", Rome, 8-11 October.

5) HAUGH, R.T. (1983). Thermodynamic and kinetic constraints in compost system design. In : Biological reclamation and land utilization of urban wastes (F. Zucconi, M. De Bertoldi and S. Coppola Eds.), Proc of the Int. Symp. held in Naples, 11-14 October.

6) HUGH, R. and E. LEIFSON (1953). The taxonomic significance of fermentative versus oxidative metabolism of carbohydrates by various Gram negative bacteria. J. Bacteriol., 66, 24-26.

7) McKINLEY, V.L. and J.R. VESTAL (1984). Biokinetic analyses of adaptation and succession : Microbial activity in composting municipal sewage sludge. Appl. Env. Microbiol., 47, 933-941.

8) McKINLEY, V.L. and J.R. VESTAL (1985). Physical and chemical correlates of microbial activity and biomass in composting municipal sewage sludge. Appl. Env. Microbiol., 50, 1395-1403.

9) NAKASAKI, K., SASAKI, M., SHODA, M. and H. KUBOTA (1985a). Change in microbial numbers during thermophilic composting of sewage sludge with reference to CO2 evolution rate. Appl. Env. Microbiol., 49, 37-41.

10) NAKASAKI, K., SASAKI, M., SHODA, M. and H. KUBOTA (1985b). Characteristics of mesophilic bacteria isolated during thermophilic composting of sewage sludge. Appl. Env. Microbiol., 49, 42-45.

11) SIKORA, L.J. and M.A. SOWERS (1983). Factors affecting the composting process. International Conference on "Composting of solid wastes and slurries", Department of Civil Engineering, University of Leeds (UK), 28-30 September.

12) STROM, P.F. (1985a). Effect of temperature on bacterial species diversity in thermophilic solid-waste composting. Appl. Env. Microbiol., 50, 899-905.

13) STROM, P.F. (1985b). Identification of thermophilic bacteria in solid-waste composting. Appl. Env. Microbiol., 50, 906-913.

14) WAKSMAN, S.A., CORDON, T.C. and N. HULPOI (1939). Influence of temperature upon the microbiological population and decomposition processes in composts of stable manure. Soil Sci., 47, 83-98.

15) WILLIAMS, S.T. and F.L. DAVIES (1965). Use of antibiotics for selective isolation and enumeration of actinomycetes in soil. J. Gen. Microbiol., 38, 251-261.

AGRONOMIC VALORIZATION OF MUNICIPAL SOLID WASTE COMPOST - RESULTS OF A
COMPARATIVE TRIAL   (*)

P.L. GENEVINI
Istituto di
Chimica Agraria
Università degli
Studi di Milano

V. MEZZANOTTE
Istituto di
Ingegneria Sa-
nitaria - Poli-
tecnico di Mi-
lano

C. ZAMBON
Istituto di Chimi-
ca Agraria - Uni-
versità degli Stu-
di di Milano

(*) Research works supported by CNR, Italy. Special IPRA. Sub. project 1,
Paper n. 880

Summary

Five different products, deriving from municipal solid wastes, barks
mushroom litter and various mixtures of such substrata with peat, have been analyzed for fertilizing elements, metals, pH, ash, HCl insoluble residue, organic carbon, humic acid carbon, fulvic acid carbon
and then tested in greenhouse on ryegrass (Lolium multiflorum).
The plants have been cropped and analyzed for metals at fixed time
intervals.
Statistical analysis has shown thet metal uptake and translocation
take chiefly place during the early groth stages of plants, thus de-
monstrating no immobilization in soil of the metals applied compost.
However, metal availability, as percentage value is quite low for com
post. The total metal amount applied with compost is anyway significantly higher than that relating to farmyard manure treatment.
The fertilizing value of compost is rather low and a certain inhibiting effect can be observed on plant growth, not explainable by C/N
ratio.

1. Introduction

As a complex system, soil can receive and metabolize organic matter of various origin with positive effects on its physical structure as well as on
its chemical properties. That's why the possibility of agricultural disposal of wastes, of industrial by-products and of sewage sludges is taken into account whenever the properties of such materials allow their use as fertilizers and/or amendants, without inducing negative effects on the agrarian
ecosystem.
          The composting of various kinds of residues is yet apccepted
to produce a potentially usefull recycled material: besides allowing reso-

urce recovery, organic matter enrichment of soil and a reduction of the
amount of waste to be disposed of by other means, composting acts as a
hygienizing treatment on the original material. Under the agronomic and environmental points of view, however, composting can have a real future only if any effort is make to obtain a truely good product. In this sense,
an important consideration must be drawn about the agronomic value of compost, expecially of MSW compost, which cannot be defined as a fertilizer,
but rather as an organic amendant. Hence, the final goal of composting
should be the obtainment of a product whose effects on soil and plants are
comparable to those of farmyard manure. Such a goal cannot be achieved
but by means of a severe selection on the kind and fraction of wastes to
be processed, leaving, in the case of MSW, more than 50 % of the total waste amount to be disposed of. That's why composting cannot be regarded as
a solution to the disposal problem, but only as an integrative way,which
could thus be to expensive with respect to the benefit obtainable. To overcome the problem, exploiting at best the available technology, municipal
solid waste could be jointly composted with other organic wastes. When the
finding of adequate materials is not a limiting aspect, the mixing of different substrata would allow the production of a desired quality amendant,
and the combined elimination of wastes of various kinds and origin at low
cost. An evident result of such a process is the dilution effect on metals
in MSW compost, due to the mixing with materials characterized by lower
metal concentrations. Analogous considerations apply to sludge composting
with straw or sawdust or other low metal matrices. However, a great margin
of doubt still exists on the metal availability in the final product and
on the effects of mixing and composting on metal speciation (1), so as on
the availability of fertilizing elements in mixed substrata compost.

Besides agronomic and environmental considerations, it is worth
reminding that in Italy as in most interested countries, composting is no
more held experimental, but standard qualities are set by law, and no product can thus be sold if not responding to the desired conditions. That's
an important constraint for compost producers, who cannot grant in advance
for the composition of the processed waste, expecially for municipal solid
waste, and for the properties of the final product.

Several applicative examples of the waste mixing conception
exist in various countries, concerning both sewage sludge and municipal
solid waste compost.

The present report deals with the results of a comparative
trial carried out on different products from the same plant, derived from
the joint composting of various kinds of wastes (MSW, Picea excelsa barks,
mushroom litter and peats), or from the mixing of compost with other organic wastes, or simply from the mixing of uncomposted organic materials.

2. Materials and methods

Tested materials

The tested samples derived from five different products :

1 - Municipal solid waste compost
2 - Mixture of black peat , mushroom litter and municipal solid waste compost (50% , 35% and 15% respectively)
3 - Mixture of black peat , bark compost and blond peat (70% , 20% and 10%
   respectively)
4 - Mixture of municipal solid waste compost , black peat and mushroom
   litter (33% , 33% and 33% respectively)
5 - Mixture of municipal solid waste compost and bark compost (80% and
   20% respectively) .

All products derived from one plant , exploiting the same substrata and
recycling municipal solid waste from the same source .

Analyses

Samples were analyzed for pH , electric conductivity , ashes and HCl insoluble residue , nitrogen , phosphorus , potassium , calcium , magnesium ,
sodium , organic carbon , humic acid carbon , fulvic acid carbon and
heavy metals (Zn , Pb ,Cu , Ni , Cr , Cd) , according to IPLA methods for
composts (2) .

Pot trial

To test the above mentioned materials , a comparison was made among them ,
farmyard manure and sand as plant growth substrata . Sand was the basis
matrix used for all treatments . 7 g of amendant was added to 450 g of
sand to simulate a field application rate of 600 q/ha , double to the total amount of compost allowed in Italy for the whole of three year application . All pots received   additional nitrogen , phosphorus (P_2O_5) and
potassium (K_2O) , corresponding to 30 kg/ha for each nutrient .
        The tested plant species was <u>Lolium multiflorum</u> , cropped for
a global period of 160 dd and cut at pre-set intervals.
        The experimental design consisted of three series of plants
(five replicates for each series) , on which the first and second cut were
effected at 80 and 80 days , at 100 and 60 days , and at 120 and 40 days
respectively . The different cut intervals were chosen in order to get
comprehensive information about time related effects of the tested materials over the vegetative cycle .
        All cut plants were weighted , dried and then analyzed for me-
tal concentrations .

3. Results and discussion

The results of the chemical analyses performed on the tested materials are
reported in Tab.I . As it can be observed , municipal solid waste compost
(n.1) shows median values for nutrient concentrations , but a high electric
conductivity (corresponding to high salinity) , high percentages of both
ashes and HCl insoluble residue , and a relatively low organic carbon content , with respect to the other tested materials . Such a comparison also

Tab.I - Chemical properties of the tested organic amendants

Parameters	samples					
	1	2	3	4	5	FYM
pH (1:10)	6.5	7.2	5.4	7.5	7.6	8.6
EC (μS)	1670.0	1560.0	780.0	1010.0	590.0	-
% d. w.						
Ash	56.8	46.4	17.0	45.9	44.0	-
HCl ins. res.	43.3	24.1	3.6	30.2	31.5	-
TKN	1.0	1.2	1.3	1.1	1.2	2.1
P	0.7	1.2	0.4	1.0	0.7	0.6
K	0.3	0.7	0.3	0.5	0.4	1.8
Ca	3.4	6.4	1.9	3.9	3.0	-
Mg	0.2	0.3	0.4	0.3	0.2	-
Na	0.3	0.2	0.4	0.3	0.4	-
Org. C	22.7	26.0	37.5	23.4	27.0	27.4
Humic Ac. C	4.6	3.9	3.9	3.6	1.8	-
Fulvic Ac. C	3.1	1.3	1.0	1.2	1.0	-
mg/kg d.w.						
Cu	128	60	23	106	129	47.8
Pb	317	86	34	151	267	43.7
Ni	36	23	9	31	85	15.3
Zn	1217	349	123	559	1070	545.0
Cr	57	17	8	38	172	9.3
Cd	.... from 0.004 to 0.006....					

shows a relatively low value for humic acids / fulvic acids ratio and high
heavy metal concentrations , which keep anyway within the standards set ,
for instance , by Italian law .

Metal concentrations in compost n.5 (80% MSW compost , 20% bark
compost) are , on average , comparable to those of compost n.1 , being
lower for zinc and lead , nearly the same for copper and higher for nickel
and chromium . Nutrient concentrations are comparable too,while organic
carbon is significantly higher . Both humic acid carbon and fulvic acid
carbon fractions are lower than in MSW compost , but the ratio between
them is similar . Both electric conductivity and ash content are lower .

A significant drop in metal concentrations can be observed in
compost n.4 , where MSW compost is mixed with equal amounts of black peat
and mushroom litter (33% for each component) . For nutrients , compost n.4
is comparable to n.1 and n.5 , however being richer than n.1 in nitrogen
and than both in P and K. Its conductivity is higher than n.5's, while orga
nic carbon, humic acid carbon and fulvic acid carbon are included between
n. 1's and n. 5's (n. 1 representing the minimum for organic carbon and
the maximum for humic acid carbon and fulvic acid carbon).

Analogous values for humic acid carbon and fulvic acid carbon
concentrations characterize samples n.2 and n.3 . The latter , however ,
is richer in organic carbon but quite poor in both phosphorus and potassium , and has low pH , while the former has high salinity and ash content,
and a great fraction of ashes represented by HCl insoluble residue .

The highest values of electric conductivity relate to n.1 , n.
2 and n.4 , all containing municipal solid waste compost , while n.5 ,
still containing 80% MSW compost , shows a lower value , probably due to
the the the effect of bark compost , characterized by very low salinity . As
to conductivity , it is worth pointing out that levels exceeding 1500 uS
(n.1 and n.2) can prevent compost use on horticultural crops (3) and that
products whose conductivity is over 1800 uS should not even be used for
tolerant plant species (4) .

As to pot trials , ANOVA was performed on the obtained results
and the average values were compared by Tukey test .

Two main aspects were taken into account : the cut time intervals (80 - 100 - 120 days and 80 - 60 - 40 days for the first and second
cut respectively) and the relative yield and metal concentrations in plants,
and the tested compost or organic amendant with respect to the same parameters .

Yield

Tab.II - Yield of ryegrass (fresh weight g / pot) as mean values for each
cut for all three series .

	1	2	3	4	5	FYM	Sand
1st cut	2.1 a	3.46 c	4.3 d	4.3 d	3.25 bc	3.41 c	2.75 b
2nd cut	1.28 a	1.44 a	1.78 ab	1.85 ab	1.82 ab	2.29 b	1.7 ab

As reported in Tab.II , farmyard manure shows better effects than other

products on fresh weight yield , clearly observable in the second cut ,
while comparable to n.4 in the first one . The better results obtained
with farmyard manure can easily be explained by either the amount of nutrients applied (greater than those related to other treatments) and by
their gradual availability in time . As to composts, n.3 and n.4 (containing no MSW compost and 33% MSW compost respectively) appears to induce good
level yield . Products containing up to 80% MSW compost (n.5),anyway, can
still grant ,at least for the first cut , yields comparable to those due
to farmyard manure application .The fertilizing properties of MSW compost
(n.1) appears , on the contrary , comparable to those of blank (sand only).
        Dry weight data (Tab.III) confirm the trend observed for fresh
weight .

Tab.III - Yield of ryegrass (dry weight g / pot) as mean values for each
cut for all three series .

	1	2	3	4	5	FYM	Sand
1st cut	0.33 a	0.61 bc	0.82 d	0.77 d	0.55 b	0.65 c	0.60 bc
2nd cut	0.42 ab	0.44 bc	0.44 abc	0.51 c	0.45 bc	0.73 d	0.37 a

Copper
Both cut values show the highest copper concentrations in plants treated
by MSW compost . For the second cut , compost n.2 and 3 also induce a certain increase in copper concentration , with respect to farmyard manure
treatment (Tab.IV) .

Tab.IV - Copper concentrations in ryegrass plants(mg / kg d.w.) as mean
values for each cut for all three series.

	1	2	3	4	5	FYM	Sand
1st cut	46 b	42 ab	38 ab	38 a	37 a	39 a	37 a
2nd cut	45 d	42 cd	40 bcd	36 abc	35 ab	31 a	38 abc

As to uptake and translocation, ANOVA shows a direct proportionality between
the plant development and its metal content, meaning that translocation
keeps proportional to dry matter increase in plants.
Lead
The first cut values confirm the tendency of MSW compost to induce the highest metal concentrations and the lowest metal content of manure treated
plants. No correlation exists between total lead concentration in composts
and lead concentration in plants. Among the second cut values, the only remarkable data relates to the lowest copper concentration in manure treated
plants, while the levels reached by plants undergone to other treatments
are substantially analogous (Tab.V).
For both cuts, ANOVA shows that translocation takes place essentially in
the early stages of plant growth, being successively reduced.
Nickel
For the first cut, nickel concentration corresponding to FYM treatment is
significantly lower than those observed in MSW compost treated plants, but
comparable to those induced by all other treatments. In the second cut, FYM

Tab.V - Lead concentrations in ryegrass plants (mg/kg d.w.) as mean values for each cut for all three series.

	1	2	3	4	5	FYM	Sand
1st cut	14 b	9 ab	10 bc	7 ab	7 ab	6 a	7.5 ab
2nd cut	17 b	17 b	16 ab	17 b	15 ab	11 a	19 b

keeps inducing the lowest nickel concentrations in plants, wich are however comparable to those deriving from compost n. 4 and 5 treatments.

Tab.VI - Nickel concentrations in ryegrass plants (mg/kg d.w.) as mean values for each cut for all three series.

	1	2	3	4	5	FYM	Sand
1st cut	27 b	9 a	9 a	6.7 a	8 a	7.3 a	7.1 a
2nd cut	10 d	9 bcd	9 cd	7.5 ab	8 abc	7 a	9 cd

For both cuts MSW compost is confirmed to induce the highest concentrations for nickel as for other metals. Translocation takes place during the early growth stages, in the first cut, while in the second no significant difference can be observed for time.

Zinc

Tab.VII - Zinc concentrations in ryegrass plants (mg/kg d.w.) as mean values for each cut for all three series.

	1	2	3	4	5	FYM	Sand
1st cut	91 bc	66 ab	68 ab	80 bc	96 c	64 ab	41 a
2nd cut	100 c	76 abc	67 ab	77 abc	77 abc	59 a	87 bc

The highest zinc concentration in the first cut can be observed for compost n. 5 (80 % MSW compost), while an analogous but blunter tendency to zinc increase in plants, with respect to those grown on sand only is attributable to all treatments.
In the second cut the highest zinc concentrations correspond on the contrary, to compost n. 1 and to sand, while no significant difference is found among the zinc levels induced by the other treatments. Uptake takes chiefly place in the early growth stages for the first cut, while no significant difference among series as been detected for time in the second cut.

Conclusions

The main conclusions drawn from the experimental trial carried out can be summarized as follows.
As it can be seen in Tabb. II, III and VIII, the fertilizing value of MSW compost appears to be low. With respect to crop yield, the availability of nitrogen, phosphorus and potassium in MSW compost is comparable to that of

sand, equally treated by 30:30:30 enrichment. Moreover, a certain inhibiting effect can be observed in MSW compost treated plants, not explained by C/N ratio, but probably due to other, still unknown, causes.

Metal concentrations keep always on higher levels in MSW compost treated plants than in the others. This could relate eitheir to the greater amount of applied metals or to the reduced plant development, and thus to the lacking of diluting effect inside the plant itself. Statistical analysis seems to confirm the second hypothesis, clearly showing that metal uptake and translocation take chiefly place in the early growth stages. Metal availability is anyway low especially if compared to the high metal amounts applied and considering the absence of significant relations between these and metal concentrations in plants (Tab. IX).

Tab.VIII - Fertilizing elements applied with the various tested organic amendants (mg/pot)

	1	2	3	4	5	FYM
N	71.4	84.0	89.6	74.2	87.5	186.9
P_2O_5	49.0	84.0	25.2	70.0	47.6	98.0
K_2O	46.9	117.6	51.8	71.7	73.5	152.0

Tab.IX - Ratios metals uptaken/metals applied in pot trials (%)

	1	2	3	4	5	FYM
Cu	3.8	10.5	30.3	6.4	4.0	14.3
Ni	5.2	5.9	18.1	4.1	1.3	9.3
Zn	0.8	3.0	9.9	2.6	1.2	2.2
Pb	0.5	2.2	6.4	1.3	0.6	4.2

Compost n. 3, not containing MSW, shows the highest values for the ratio metal uptaken/metal applied, followed by FYM. A certain tendency can be observed for such ratio to decrease with increasing levels of MSW compost in the tested amendants, confirmed by the minima reached by compost n. 1 (MSW compost) for three metals out of four. These results would support the hypothesis of an immobilizing action of the composting process on metals.

In all cropped plants, chromium, however present in all tested amendants, never reached levels over detectable limit.

Each compost anyway, represents a single problem, and its agronomic value cannot be predicted by chemical analysis.

The mixture of various compostable substrata carries on remarkable advantages with respect to both fertilizing value and metal dilution. Thus, the hypothesis of enriching a "poor" substratum as MSW compost by other organic matrices finds serious basis, while it is worth pointing out the need for further research.

REFERENCES

1. REGAMEY, P. et al. (1985). Recherche interdisciplinaire sur la préparation des composts de boues d'épuration et sur leur utilisation en agriculture. Published by EPFL, Lausanne, Juin 1985.

2. IPLA (Istitutoper le Piante da Legno e l'Ambiente) (1984). Metodi analitici: Fertilizzanti organici, Compost, Fanghi degli impianti di depurazione, Rifiuti organici, Substrati in fermentazione metanica, Biogas. Published by IPLA, Torino.

3. VERDONCK, O., DE VLEESCHAUWER, D. (1981). La recherche des matières premières susceptibles d'être compostées. In : Rapport du colloque international "Composts, amendements humiques et organiques", 16-17 Novembre 1981, Paris ISG-A.v.en.i.r.

4. RYSER, J.P., GYSY, C. (1983). Analyse des sols pour les cultures maraîchères et les plantes ornamentales. Le maraîcher, 17/1983

SOME EFFECTS OF COMPOST ON SOIL PHYSICAL PROPERTIES

G. GUIDI and G. POGGIO

C.N.R. Institute for Soil Chemistry, Pisa, Italy

Summary

Different rates of composts were compared with farmyard manure in two field experiments on different soils and the effects on some soil physical properties evaluated. In both experimental sites variations of soil parameters were observed during the growing season of the cultures. After three years from the beginning of the experiment any treatment with organic materials was still ineffective in increasing the water stability index (WSI) with respect to the control in the first soil rich in calcium carbonate (36.3%). In the other soil, at the second year of treatment, the effect of the composts was similar to the manure and WSI's were significantly higher than the control in June. In September only the higher rate of compost differed from all other treatments. For both soils no differences were found in the determination of total porosity and pore size distribution between treated and untreated samples. However the decrease of total porosity was always accompanied by a loss of larger pores.

1. Introduction

The agricultural use of the organic fraction of urban refuse composted alone or with sewage sludge has been investigated in Italy since the late 70's when the National Research Council (C.N.R.) provided funds within some special research projects with the aim of keeping the environmental impact of waste disposal as low as possible.

Italian arable soils are generally low in organic matter (less than 2%) and therefore any addition of organic materials should be encouraged especially wherever the monoculture is associated with a shortage or lack of farmyard manure. Relationships between the addition of organic wastes and the modifications of soil structure already found (1,2,3) need to be further clarified and this paper deals with the effects of composts on some physical properties related to soil structure in two longer term experiments under natural field conditions.

2. Materials and Methods

Results from two field experiments are reported herein. The first field study, based on the nitrogen effect of compost, was established in Friuli in 1983 in a randomized complete block design with four replications and plots of 9x1.5 m. The soil is a Calcic Cambisol (FAO classification) and some selected characteristics are reported in Table 1. Plots were seeded with continuous maize and received yearly in early spring the following treatments: mineral fertilizer (M), farmyard manure (FYM), and three rates of a compost (UC1, UC2 and UC3). Control plots (C) were also present. UC1, UC2 and UC3 added to the soil 100 Kg/ha, 200 Kg/ha and 300 Kg/ha of available nitrogen, respectively. The available nitrogen added to the soil with FYM and M was 200 Kg/ha. The available nitrogen was considered to be 20% of the total nitrogen present in organic materials.

The second field study, based on the organic matter effect of compost, was established in Emilia in 1984 in a randomized complete block design with four replications and plots of 4x60 m. The soil is a Eutric Fluvisol (FAO classification) and some selected characteristics are reported in Table 1. Plots were seeded with Italian ray-grass in the spring after they had received the organic dressings in late autumn the year before. The following treatments were compared: control (C), farmyard manure (FYM), an experimental compost at two rates (PC1 and PC2), and another compost which was the same compost utilized in the experiment described before (PCU). The rates of all the organic materials except PC2 added to the soil 15 metric tons of organic matter per year. The organic matter added with PC2 was 40 metric tons per year.

Table 1 - Some characteristics of the soils.

	Udine	Piacenza
Clay (%)	28.7	21.1
Silt (%)	24.5	30.6
Sand (%)	46.8	48.3
Organic C (%)	0.79	0.85
Total N (%)	0.13	0.09
pH (H_2O)	7.8	6.5
C.E.C. (meq/100 g)	10.3	17.0
$CaCO_3$ (%)	36.3	n.d.

Some characteristics of the composts used in this study
are listed in Table 2.

The procedures followed for the sampling and the
preparation of soil samples are described in detail elsewhere
(1,4).

A wet-sieving method (1,5) was used to determine the
stability of air-dried soil aggregates (1-2 mm) in water. The
water stability index (WSI) is defined as: WSI = 100 (1-A/B)
where A and B are the weights of aggregates passing through
the sieve after 5 and 60 min, respectively. Each determination was made at least in triplicate. Porosity and pore-size
distribution (p.s.d.) were measured on the outgassed aggregates by means of the mercury intrusion porosimetry using a
porosimeter Carlo Erba 200 equipped with a macropore unit
Carlo Erba 120. Measurements were made on aggregates of about
1 g air-dry weight (4).

3. Results and Discussion

3.1 Water stability of soil aggregates. WSI's of soil
aggregates taken at the two experimental sites are reported
in Table 3.

At the Udine fields the stabilising effect of the
different organic treatments was negligible in June. The FYM
resulted even lower than C and M and the only significant
difference was found between FYM and the lowest rate of
compost (UC1). A similar behaviour was also found in
September when the FYM treatment gave again the lowest figure
and the three rates of compost did not differ from the
control and from the treatment with mineral fertilizer.

Table 2 - Some characteristics of the composts and manures
utilized in the two experiments.

	UDINE		PIACENZA		
	FYM	UC	FYM	PCU	PC
pH (H$_2$O)	7.3	7.9	8.3	7.9	7.6
Water (%)	80.8	35.8	75.2	35.8	18.3
Organic C (% d.m.)	28.9	11.2	40.1	11.2	20.3
Total N (% d.m.)	2.49	0.94	2.23	0.94	1.35
Total P (% d.m.)	1.96	0.33	0.65	0.33	0.30
Total K (% d.m.)	3.51	0.62	1.42	0.62	0.67

The effect of the organic amendments was clearly shown
in the experimental site of Piacenza where, in June, the WSI
of the control plots was significantly lower than WSI's found

in plots treated with FYM and composts. The stabilising effect of the higher rate of compost (PC2) was still measurable in September while all other organic treatments did not differ from the control.

Table 3 - Water stability index of soil aggregates taken at the two experimental sites in 1985.

WATER STABILITY INDEX

UDINE			PIACENZA		
Treatments	Sampling time		Treatments	Sampling time	
	June	September		June	September
C	10.5 ab*	16.2 ab	C	8.0 a	4.9 a
M	11.6 ab	19.2 b	FYM	13.0 b	7.0 a
FYM	8.5 a	11.8 a	PC1	12.8 b	7.3 a
UC1	14.8 b	19.0 b	PC2	16.6 b	11.6 b
UC2	11.8 ab	19.8 b	PCU	15.2 b	4.1 a
UC3	10.1 ab	14.4 ab			

* Values followed by the same letter in the same column are not significantly different at the 5% probably level.

In previous experiments the WSI of soil aggregates has been found not to be constant throughout the growing season of maize (1,3). The results reported in this study show a similar pattern, especially those referring to the Udine trials, where the WSI increased over the period June-September. The decrease observed in samples taken near Piacenza was probably caused by local meteorological conditions which could have speeded up the normal decrease of the WSI already observed in autumn (3) in coincidence with the beginning of the rainy season.

Another important point of discussion arises from the question of why such huge amounts of organic matter applied yearly for three years were not able to improve the stability of the Udine soil aggregates while in the Piacenza soil smaller amounts of FYM and composts achieved such an improvement. Since we have no analytical data about the main binding agents acting in the two studied soils we can only speculate about this phenomenon. It is well known that organic matter is not the only aggregating agent present in soils. Moreover when the inorganic binding agents are

dominant in a given soil the presence of organic binding
agents may be of extra little benefit (6) and this is likely
in the case we are dealing with. In the Udine soil the large
amount of calcium carbonate present in the soil may act both
by cementing particles or aggregates together, when it is
present in a precipitated solid state, and by maintaining
calcium ions in the soil solution at a level sufficiently
high to inhibit dispersion of clay particles (7). The other
soil which behaves in a "normal" way after the addition of
organic materials does not possess any calcium carbonate.

3.2 Porosity

The addition of organic materials had very little effect
on the porosity and the p.s.d. of soil samples taken in both
experimental field trials. In any case, due to the high
variability found between replicates at each sampling time,
the differences between the means were not significant and
for this reason individual figures were not reported. If we
consider the means of total porosity of all treatments at
each sampling time (Table 4) significant differences ($P=0.05$)
were found between samples taken in June and September.
However for both experimental sites, Udine and Piacenza, a
reduced total porosity was accompanied by a loss of pores
larger than 3 um (Fig. 1).

Table 4 - Mean total porosity of soil aggregates taken at the
two experimental sites in 1985.

Soil	Sampling time	Total porosity (cm^3/g)
Udine	June	0.181 a*
	September	0.153 b
Piacenza	June	0.154 a
	September	0.181 b

* For each soil values followed by the same letter are not
  significantly different at the 5% probability level.

The behaviour just described for total porosity is
different from that observed previously, i.e. a general
contemporaneous increase or decrease of total porosity and
W.S.I. (2), and this fact seems to indicate that at least in
particular situations, where probably the climatic conditions
play an essential role, the mechanisms which regulate the

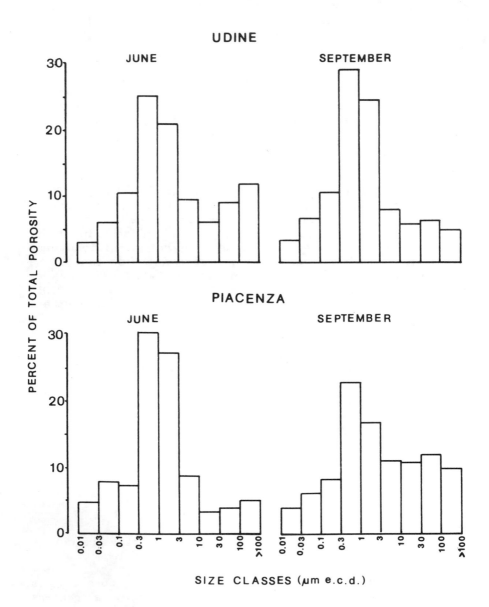

Fig. 1 Mean pore size distributions of soil aggregates taken at the two experimental fields in 1985.

583

formation of soil pores and those which stabilize their walls against water stresses do not reach their respective maxima of activity at the same time.

Acknowlegments. Authors thank R. Palazzetti for his helpful assistance. This research work was supported by the C.N.R., Italy. Special grant IPRA Sub-project 1. Paper n.

REFERENCES

1) M. PAGLIAI, G. GUIDI, M. LA MARCA, M. GIACHETTI and C. LUCAMANTE - Effects of sewage sludges and composts on soil porosity and aggregation. J. Environ. Qual., 10, 556 (1981).

2) M. PAGLIAI and G. GUIDI - Porosity and pore size distribution in a field test following sludge and compost application. In: L'Hermite P. e Ott H. eds. "Characterization, treatment and use of sewage sludge". D. Reidel Publ. Co., p. 545 (1981).

3) G. GUIDI, M. PAGLIAI and M. GIACHETTI - Modifications of some physical and chemical soil properties following sludge and compost applications. In: G. Catroux, P. L'Hermite e E. Suess eds. "The influence of sewage sludge application on physical and biological properties of soil". D. Reidel Publ. Co., p. 122 (1983).

4) G. GUIDI, G. POGGIO and G. PETRUZZELLI - The porosity of soil aggregates from bulk soil and from soil adhering to roots. Plant and Soil, 87, 311 (1985).

5) A. MALQUORI and S. CECCONI - Determinazione seriale dell'indice di struttura nel terreno. Agrochimica, 6, 199 (1981).

6) J.M. TISDALL and J.M. OADES - Organic matter and water-stable aggregates in soils. J. Soil Sci., 33, 141 (1982).

7) D.L. RIMMER and D.J. GREENLAND - Effect of calcium carbonate on the swelling behaviour of a clay soil. J. Soil Sci. 27, 129 (1976).

EFFECTS OF COMPOSTED AGRICULTURAL RESIDUES ON APPLE TREES AND OF URBAN WASTES ON PEACH TREES.

G. Strabbioli and A. Angeloni
Istituto Sperimentale per la Frutticoltura
Roma - Italy

Abstract

The results obtained in the first five years of tests on apple trees, and the first two years on peach trees, grown in pots are referred.

The apple trees, treated with mineral fertilizers supplemented with compost obtained from olive residue, showed less growth and production than those trees treated exclusively with mineral fertilizers. This may be explained by the nutritional competition of nitrogen and phosphorus that occurs between the trees and the micro-organisms introduced into the soil together with the compost. In fact, microbiological analyses showed that soil treated by adding organic substances have a greater microbic load and an increase in ammonizing micro-organisms, that leads to a possible loss of ammonia through volatilization. The results obtained on peach trees, planted in three different types of soil with three fertilizations (manure, compost from solid urban waste, control), although they are only indicative, since they have been obtained only during the first two years of tests, have shown that yield is less in the clay soil, irrespective of the fetilization; while there has been no difference noted in the fertilization treatments.

Effects of soil-fertilization interaction on yield have only been seen in sandy soil, where the two fertilized treatments cropped better than control.

1. Introduction

Within the framework of IPRA[(*)], Sub-project 1, Area Problem 1, Test 6, is carrying out a research into the effects of the use of organic compost obtained from bioconversion on apple and peach trees.

The fertilization of the soil with organic matter is essential for maintaining the biological, physical and chemical fertility at optimum levels. Up to a few years ago, the supply of organic substances was provided almost exclusively by dung.

More recently, owing to the gradual reduction of the livestock in Italy, the need of substitute organic fertilizers has become important. The method followed has been that of using refluent by-products from various sources. These substances cannot be used directly, but must pre-

---

(*) IPRA: Research Project of the National Research Council (CNR).

viously be transformed into compost, by means of bio-oxidation processes, with humification of the organic substance itself and a partial mineralization of the components (De Bertoldi, 1983). Otherwise, the organic substances introduced into the soil without having undergone humification beforehand are degraded by microflora with the development of intermediate acid metabolites incompatible with a normal growing of the trees (Zucconi, 1981; Zucconi, De Bertoldi, 1982).

The use of compost, furthermore, also proves useful as a means of disposing and re-cycling the enormous quantities of waste matter produced by the present-day society.

The validity of agricultural use of fertilizers derived from organic waste products has not yet, however, been sufficiently assessed, as far as its effects on trees are concerned, above all. In fact, in spite of the previuos "composting" process, the trees could come into contact with possible substances that are toxic to their metabolism.

Bearing this in mind, it has thus been thought interesting to study the effectiveness of both a commercial compost obtained from by-products of olive-processing, enriched with micro-organisms, and one obtained from the bioconversion of solid urban waste. The agronomic effects of the first type of compost on apple trees have been evaluated, and those of the second type on peach trees.

2. Materials and methods

2.1. Apple trees

In Spring, 1981, apple trees of the cultivar "Lutz Golden" grafted on to M9, were planted in 30 pots. Bearing in mind the fact that the fertilization program considered most suitable for apple cultivation, in soils that are well supplied with nutritional elements, is indicated by Lalatta (1981 and 1983) as 120–150 kg of nitrogen (N), 50–70 of phosphorus (P_2O_5), 120–150 of potassium (K_2O) per hectare, and also taking the volcanic nature of the Latium soil into account, which was used in the pots (relatively lacking in N and P_2O_5, but rich in K_2O), the following treatments were carried out, each one of them having six plants (dosage per hectare):

- "A": Mineral fertilization with 200 units of N, 100 of P_2O_5, and 100 of K_2O;
- "B": Mineral fertilization with doses double those of "A";
- "C": Mineral fertilization as in treatment "A", plus compost, in doses corresponding to 1 ton per hectare, as the producers advised;
- "D": fertilizer and compost in doses double those of treatment "C";
- "E": control.

The following fertilizers were used: urea, mineral superphosphate, potassium sulphate. The chemico-biological composition of the compost is given in Table 1.

Phosphorus and potassium were distributed in late Autumn, nitrogen during Spring, and the organic substance in Winter.

The trees were drip irrigated, by means of a dropper in each pot able to supply 4 l/h.

During the five-years test period, the following surveys were taken:
- annual measuring of the circumference of the tree trunks at 10 cm from the grafting point, to calculate the cross-section area;
- leaf analysis on a sample of 60 leaves per treatment (10 leaves per tree) analysed according to the usual method (Cobianchi, 1976);
- yield and number of fruits to calculate the average weight;
- chemical and microbiological analyses of the soil. The following methods were adopted for the chemical analysis: total nitrogen (Kjeldahl method); assimilable phosphorus (Olsen method); assimilable potassium (International method).

The technique of progressively dissolving different soil samples and their subsequent inoculation in suitable growth media was adopted for the microbiological testing; this shows the different micro-organisms (total microflora, fungi, nitrogen fixers, ammonifiers, nitrosators, nitrifiers, and cellulosolytics) (Pochon, Tardieux, 1966).

The data were statistically analyzed according to the randomized block experimental design.

2.2. Peach trees

In Spring 1984, 108 peach trees of the cultivar Cresthaven grafted onto seedling and trained as central leader were planted out in pots of about half a cubic metre volume.

The nine treatments compared, were formed of three types of soil and three different fertilizations.

The three types of soil that we shall call "sandy", "clay" and "intermediate" for the sake of convenience (the latter was obtained from a mixture of the two former), actually turned out to be sandy loam, clay and sandy-clay respectively, as may be seen from Table 6.

The three fertilizations were manure, compost prepared by a Working Unit involved in the same test 1.1.6 (as reported in the introduction at page 1), and a control that was not manured.

The nitrogen content present in the two fertilizers was taken as the basis for calculating their quantities; thus, taking the supply of 160 fertilizing units of nitrogen per hectare as optimum, 7.5 kg of compost and 15 kg of manure were administered for each pot respectively.

The trees were drip irrigated, by means of two self-regulating droppers in each pot, able to supply 4 l/h each.

The vegeto-productive surveys were carried out with regard to the following parameters: trunk diameter; canopy volume (the canopy shape has been assimilated to a cone); weight of pruning wood, average weight of the fruit and production per tree.

The data were statistically analyzed according to the split-plot design.

3. Results and discussion

3.1. Apple trees

Analysing the data on the increase in trunk section, over the five-year period (Table 2), it may be seen that the growth of treatment "C" is significantly less than that of both "A" and "E" (control).

Concerning the cumulative production (Table 2), "A" has given a significantly larger yield than the other treatment, except for "B".

The average weight of the fruit, over 4 year period, has shown no significant differences between the various treatments (Table 2).

The lack of effects, or sometimes, the negative effects of the organic manuring on both the growing and the yielding, over these first five years, may be justified by an analysis of the results of the microbiological tests on the soil performed in the pots (Table 3).

The quantitative increase in the microflora (especially fungi and cellulosolytics), recorded in "D" in particular, may have provoked competition between micro-organisms and the trees for the nitrogen. The importance of nitrogen in growing is, in fact, well known.

The rather notable presence of ammonizing micro-organisms with respect to nitrosators (chemio-lytotrophic bacteria that oxidize ammonia into nitrate), which took place in "C" particularly, may have brought about a further imbalance in the nitrogen cycle, through the initial accumulation of ammonia in the soil, and the subsequent dispersion in the atmosphere with the resulting loss of this element of the micro-organism-tree cycle (Florenzano, 1983).

These assumptions tend to be confirmed by chemical analysis of the soil (Table 4) that, in the case of nitrogen, shows the greatest loss occurring in "C" and "D", compared to the corresponding samples "A" and "B". As far as phosphorus and potassium are concerned, the progressive loss of these in the soil proved to be more homogeneous in all the treatments, except for the control, where a more accentuated fall occurred, especially as far as phosphorus is concerned (from 17 to only 3 ppm).

The chemical analysis of the leaves, carried out during the various years (Table 5), has shown up mineral contents that are, in general, falling within the limits taken as optimum (Lalatta, 1978): the exceptions include potassium, whose level in 1983 and 1984 may be considered high (probably as a result of the rather large initial presence of K in the soil) (Table 4), and phosphorus, which recorded a reduction in the control and "C" and "D", especially in 1984. This latter circumstance would seem to confirm the existence of competitive processes between tree and micro-organisms in this element too.

Furthermore, the fact that the trunks of the control trees grew over 5 years to a degree similar to that of the "A" treatment, may be explained if we think of their lesser degree of fructification, resulting in a reduced consumption of nutritional elements, to the advantage of the vegetative development.

Nitrogen in the soil has served to allow the growth of the trees, in the absence of competitive phenomena occurring in the treatment with compost; while the gradual reduction of phosphorus in the control, on the other hand, explains its reduced fructification.

It is well-known, in fact, that the lack of phosphorus in the soil has a negative influence on the flower bud formation, as it is proved by the increase of phosphorus in the flower buds during the Winter shows (Branzanti, Ricci, 1977).

3.2. Peach trees

The following points may be noted from the vegeto-productive results given in Table 7: the less trunk diameter growth occurs in the samples growing in clay soil; however, there are no significant differences between sandy and clay soils.

As far as the fertilized treatments are concerned, the lesser growth occurred in those not fertilized. The two fertilized samples do not show any significant differences.

As far as the soil fertilization interaction is concerned, the trees growing in sandy soil with added manure have a diameter statistically greater, followed by those using compost and those without manure. In the intermediate soil, the two samples fertilized with caw manure and compost do not show any significant differences from one another, but prove to be statistically greater than the control. In clay soil, no significant differences were found between the three methods of fertilization being compared.

The canopy volume is significantly less in the samples growing in clay, compared with the ones growing in sandy soil, which proved to be the same as those growing in the intermediate soil.

The gowth of the canopy volume of the two samples that were manured proved to be practically identical and greater than those of the control.

As regards the soil fertilizers interaction, the values of the samples being manured proved to be greater in the sandy and intermediate soils. In the clay soil, on the other hand, the three fertilized treatments being compared proved to be statistically equal.

Significantly different amounts of pruning wood were removed from the three soil types; most in the sandy soil, followed by the intermediate, then the clay.

The pruning wood is statistically greater in the samples manured with caw manure, compared with that using compost, followed by the control.

As far as the soil-fertilization interaction is concerned, it may be noted that a significantly greater amount of wood was removed from the trees that were manured, growing in sandy or intermediate soil, than from the control. Differences were also noted between manure and compost, in fact, more wood was pruned in the sandy and intermediate soils where dung was used. In the clay soil, there was a significant difference only between manure and control, where the least quantity of wood was pruned away.

The average fruit weight compared over the three types of soil proved to be significantly higher in the sandy and clay soils.

Significant differences may also be noted among the fertilization treatment; the control produced highest average fruits weight compared to the manure using the compost shows intermediate values.

As far as interaction is concerned, the bigger fruits were found in the sandy soil without fertilization.

Yield proved to be the same in the sandy and intermediate soils, that produced more compared with the clay soil.

Significant differences were not noted as far as the three types of fertilization were concerned.

The treatments "sandy soil plus manure" and "sandy soil plus compost" turned out to be the same as far as interactions are concerned, but they are significantly greater than "sandy soil without manure". In intermediate and clay soil, on the contrary, there are no significant differences between manure, compost and control.

4. Conclusions

4.1. Apple trees

In the conditions under which the trial was carried on tests, adding to the soil organic substances derived from reffluent by-products, has not brought about any positive effects on the control, at least during the first five years. The possible immobilization of nitrogen in the microflora and the subsequent reduction in yield and growth of the trees has also been proved (Paris, Gavazzi, 1982).

This can happen when the compost has not reached a high enough degree of maturity; that is, when the humification processes are still in the initial stage. For this reason, the C/N ratio tends to be rather high, and this favours the competition phenomena (Paris, Gavazzi; 1982).

Under test conditions, however, it is necessary to bear in mind the fact that the microbic load of the compost was already rather high in the beginning (12,000 x 10^6 micr.), and thus, independent of the degree of maturity, this may be the factor causing the micro-organism-tree competition with regard to the nitrogen. It is possible, therefore, that the quantity used, suggested furthermore by the firm producing it, was excessive in relation to the mineral fertilizers, as the use of more limited quantities of this compost may have a better result. Besides this, it might be necessary to bring forward the date for administering the compost to the Autumn, so as to allow a greater availability of nutritive elements when, in spring the trees growth begins.

On the other hand a more balanced microbic load in the compost could induce, either from a quantitative or a qualitative point of view (increasing in nitrosators and reduction of heterotrophic flora) a better utilization of this organic waste from fruit trees.

4.2. Peach trees

The results refer to the first two years of trial and are thus only indicative of the trees' first response to the different tests. For now, it may be said that the growth of the trees and their yield depends first of all upon the physical nature of the soil. In clay soil, in fact, lower rates of growing and yielding have been noted compared with intermediate and sandy soils, that have given statistically equal responses.

Crop has not been influenced by the different types of fertilization. In the sandy soils, fertilizers play a positive role compared with the control. In fact, in the sandy soil, manure has given rise to greater growth, compared to the compost, while the yield of the two fertilized treatments has turned out to be statistically the same. There are no differences between the trees in clay soil that were fertilized and not, neither for growth yield.

Our thanks are due to p.c. E. Turci, of the Forlì section of the Istituto Sperimentale per la Frutticoltura, for kindly performing the chemical analyses of the soil.

Our thanks are also due to Dr. R. Pirazzi of the Società Agricola Forestale - Rome, for his kind cooperation on the microbiological analyses.

References

Branzanti, C.E., Ricci, A., 1977. Manuale di frutticoltura. Edagricole Bologna.

Casalicchio, G., 1982. Notiziario tecnico E.R.S.O., N°8.

Cobianchi, D., 1976. Frutticoltura, X/XI.

De Bertoldi, M., 1983. Atti del Simposio Internazionale sul recupero biologico ed utilizzazione agricola dei rifiuti urbani. Napoli 11-14 ottobre.

Florenzano, G., 1983. Fondamenti di microbiologia del terreno. R.E.D.A. Roma.

Lalatta, F., 1978. La fertilizzazione nell'arboricoltura da frutto. Edagricole, Bologna.

Lalatta, F., 1981. Il melo. R.E.D.A., Roma.

Paris, P., Gavazzi, C., 1982. Prove agronomiche di "compost" da rifiuti solidi urbani. Programma Finalizzato Energetica. C.N.R.

Pochon, J., Tardieux, P., 1966. Techniques d'analyse en microbiologie du sol. Editions de la Tourrelle, St. Mandè (Seine).

Zucconi F., 1981. Biocycle, 22 (4).

Zucconi, F., De Bertoldi, M., 1982. Ingegneria ambientale, 11 (2).

Tab. 1 - Chemical and biological composition of the compost used

MOISTURE	28%
pH	6,8
ORGANIC MATTER	64%
MICROBIAL NUMBER (CELLS/g DRY SOLID OF COMPOST)	12.000×10^6
NITROGEN FIXERS	2.500
AEROBIC BACTERIA	8.500×10^6
MICROMYCETES	900×10^6
ACTINOMYCETES	4.600×10^6
AUXINS	PRESENTS
NUCLEIC ACIDS - TOTALS (% organic matter)	2,2%
ORGANIC NITROGEN	1,4%
AVAILABLE PHOSPHORUS	0,15%
TOTAL POTASSIUM	0,2%
C/N RATIO	22,8

Analysis provided by: Centro di Studio per la Microbiologia del Suolo del C.N.R. (Pisa)

Tab. 2 - Trunk cross-section increase, average yield per tree, average fruit weight.

YEARS TREAT-MENTS	TRUNK CROSS SECTION INCREASE (cm²)*					AVERAGE YIELD PER PLANT (kg)					AVERAGE FRUIT WEIGHT (g)				
	1982	1983	1984	1985	TOT.	1982	1983	1984	1985	CUMU-LATED	1982	1983	1984	1985	M
A	3.78 a	1.80 ab	2.58 a	2.38 ab	12.13 a	1.987 ab	7.868 a	8.537 ab	16.183 a	34.575 a	197.1 a	146.5 b	182.5 a	133.3 b	164.8 a
B	2.55 ab	2.20 ab	1.63 abc	1.91 b	9.94 ab	1.948 ab	6.885 a	8.623 ab	13.858 a	31.314 ab	173.0 ab	161.7 ab	182.8 a	152.5 ab	167.5 a
C	1.77 b	1.53 b	1.37 b	2.09 b	8.47 b	1.975 ab	5.442 a	8.113 ab	11.717 ab	27.247 b	156.2 b	163.0 ab	157.0 b	159.0 ab	158.8 a
D	1.85 b	2.55 a	1.15 c	2.28 ab	9.41 ab	2.673 a	5.123 a	8.987 a	8.983 b	25.766 b	165.0 b	177.3 a	162.6 ab	167.5 b	168.1 a
E (TEST)	2.77 ab	2.09 ab	2.17 ab	3.28 a	11.88 a	1.280 b	5.563 a	6.395 b	11.833 ab	25.071 b	179.7 ab	162.3 ab	172.8 ab	160.2 ab	168.8 a

* Initial average trunk cross-section area (spring 1981) for the five treatments was (cmq): "A" = 0.95; "B" = 0.99; "C" = 1.05; "D" = 0.98; "E" (Test) = 0.96.

Data marked with the same letters are not significantly different at P = 0;05 level.

Tab. 3 - Microbiological analysis of soils in the pots (1983) (N°of Microorganisms x g of dry matter)

MICRORGA-NISMS TREATMENTS	TOTAL MICROFLORA	FUNGI	NITROGEN FIXERS	AMMONI-FIERS	NITROSA-TORS	NITRIFIERS	CELLULO-SOLYTICS
A	1500.10^6	--	450	45.10^6	4500	4500	950
B	2000.10^6	1500	450	250.10^6	4500	2500	9500
C	2000.10^6	700	450	950.10^6	3	2500	30000
D	4500.10^6	20000	950	95.10^6	250	2500	30000
E (TEST)	750.10^6	--	450	$4,5.10^5$	--	250	1500

Tab. 4 – Trend of total N, assimilable P and K in the soil.

YEARS	1 9 8 2			1 9 8 3			1 9 8 4		
ELEMENTS	N	P	K	N	P	K	N	P	K
TREATMENTS	(%)	(ppm)	(ppm)	(%)	(ppm)	(ppm)	(%)	(ppm)	(ppm)
A	1,31	34	2362	0,70	44	1902	0,50	19	1350
B	1,40	76	2786	0,75	84	1982	0,40	18	1120
C	0,65	61	2859	0,75	33	1942	0,30	15	1250
D	1,03	75	2363	0,84	42	2190	0,30	16	1800
E (TEST)	0,65	19	2252	0,47	23	2149	0,30	3	1450

Initial values (1981): N = 0,70% ;   P = 17 ppm;   K = 2432 ppm
Standard contents (Casalicchio, 1982) For loam Soil: N = 1,0–1,6% ;   P = 18–22 ppm;   K = 100–150 ppm

Tab. 5 - Foliar analysis (g of mineral elements/100 g of dry matter)

ELEMENTS % TREATMENTS	1 9 8 2					1 9 8 3					1 9 8 4				
	N	P	K	Ca	Mg	N	P	K	Ca	Mg	N	P	K	Ca	Mg
A	2,49	0,24	1,99	1,50	0,34	2,48	0,19	2,34	2,01	0,34	2,23	0,22	2,50	1,64	0,33
B	2,64	0,24	1,85	1,74	0,37	2,51	0,18	2,32	1,99	0,34	2,35	0,23	2,37	1,73	0,37
C	2,57	0,22	1,89	1,78	0,36	2,44	0,17	2,34	1,82	0,33	2,26	0,15	2,29	1,75	0,36
D	2,69	0,23	1,83	1,73	0,33	2,39	0,17	2,45	1,96	0,33	2,35	0,15	2,25	1,84	0,36
E (TEST)	2,46	0,22	2,02	1,66	0,37	2,41	0,16	2,42	1,86	0,33	2,23	0,14	2,45	1,59	0,32

Optimal values (Lalatta, 1981): N = 2,40-2,60%; P = 0,18-0,20%; K = 1,60-1,90%;
Ca = 1,50-1,80%; Mg = 0,30-0,40%.

Tab. 6 – Fisical and chemical analysis of the three types of soil at planting.

SOIL CHARACTERISTICS	MEASUREMENT UNITS	SANDY	INTERMEDIATE	CLAY
SAND	%	75	49	23
LOAM	%	7	11	19
CLAY	%	18	40	58
pH		6.5	7.9	8.0
TOTAL CARBONATE	% $CaCO_3$	-	8.8	14.4
FREE CALCIUM CARBONATE	% $CaCO_3$	-	6.6	7.7
TOTAL NITROGEN	% N	0.07	0.12	0.15
C/N RATIO		7.1	8.7	9.3
ORGANIC MATTER	%	0.86	1.55	2.32
PHOSPHORUS AVAILABLE	ppm P	18	14	14
EXCHANGEABLE POTASSIUM	ppm K	189	290	388
EXCHANGEABLE MAGNESIUM	ppm Mg	197	262	346
CATION EXCHANGE CAPACITY	meq % g	7.47	26.39	36.08

Tab. 7 - Yield on growth performances

DESCRIPTION		VEGETATIVE RESULTS			PRODUCTION RESULTS	
		TRUNK DIAMETER mm	CANOPY VOLUME dm c	PRUNING WOOD WEIGHT g	AVERAGE FRUIT WEIGHT g	AVERAGE YIELD PER PLANT g
SOIL TYPE	SANDY	33.5 a	750.3 e	426 a	153.0 a	3578 a
	INTERMEDIATE	33.0 a	715.4 a	319 b	140.6 b	3203 a
	CLAY	29.8 b	648.0 b	225 c	152.3 a	2780 b
FERTILIZING TYPE	MANURE	33.6 a	780.6 a	411 a	143.6 b	3237 a
	URBAN WASTES	32.6 a	724.4 a	316 b	147.4 ab	3298 a
	CONTROL	30.0 a	608.8 b	242 c	154.9 a	3027 a
INTERACTION SOIL/FERTILIZERS	S A N D Y MANURE	36.4 a	852.4 a	592 a	149.1 bcd	3780 a
	URBAN WAS.	33.7 b	789.1 ab	404 b	147.0 cd	3845 a
	CONTROL	30.3 c	609.5 c	282 cd	163.0 a	3110 bc
	I N T E R MANURE	33.9 b	853.5 a	380 b	142.9 cd	3085 bc
	URBAN WAS.	34.3 b	698.9 bc	317 c	138.7 d	3320 ab
	CONTROL	30.7 c	593.9 c	260 d	140.1 d	3205 abc
	C L A Y MANURE	3C.6 c	635.9 c	262 cd	138.9 d	2845 bc
	URBAN WAS.	29.7 c	685.1 bc	227 de	156.4 abc	2730 c
	CONTROL	29.1 c	623.0 c	185 e	161.7 ab	2765 c

Data marked with the same letters are not significantly different at P = 0.05 level.

EXTRACTION AND DOSAGE OF HEAVY METALS FROM COMPOST-AMENDED SOILS

A. BARBERA
Fertimont - s.p.a.
Centro Ricerche Fertilizzanti

Summary

Short term results of the behaviour of heavy metals in compost-amended soils are presented in comparison with manure
and mineral fertilization. The application of compost in
agriculture increases in the soil both total levels and a-
vailable fraction levels of some metals. Significative li
near relationships hold among the different types of analy
sis performed on metals: total, EDTA and DTPA extractable.
Significant uptakes of metals in Corn Silage and Leaf Beet
have been noticed. Generally the uptake variations of metals in plant tissues are related to variations of their a-
vailable fraction in the soil. In particular a strict line
ar relationship was found for Zn between its available fraction in the soil and the metal uptake in corn silage.
Mineral fertilizers have no effect on the levels of total
and available metals in the soil or on the uptake of meta
ls in plant tissues.

1. Introduction

The agricultural use of M.S.W. (municipal solid wastes)and
s.s. (sewage sludges) is extensively investigated all over the
world, especially for the aspects concerning the conservation
of natural resources and energy saving.
There are a lot of problems however, principally connected
with Agronomy, Chemistry, Health and material handling. To over
come at least a part of them, M.S.W. and S.S. can be processed
by composting techniques, with the aim of destroying viruses and
other dangerous agents, increasing the organic matter concentra
tion level, lowering the inert material content and improving
the quality.
However, the generally high content of heavy metals in compost is still a problem for their use in agriculture.
Annual application of composts on the land can increase its
total content of heavy metals, which depends on initial le-

vels in raw materials.

The availability of metals to crops depends on the nature
of the soil, the type of metal compounds and the type of crop

Several authors have referred to the accumulation of metals
in plant tissues of crops grown in sludge - amended soils and,
on the other hand a lot of authors have undervalued the same
problem.

It has been however demonstrated that, if metals like Cd,
Cr, Ni and Pb are present at critical levels in the consumable
part of plant tissues, they can be introduced into the food cha
in with serious damage to animal and human health (1,2,3,4).

In order to investigate the behaviour of metals applied to
the land by composts, the evolution of total and available ele
ments (Fe,Mn,Zn,Cu,Cd,Pb,Ni and Cr) has been evaluated in compost amended soils.Composts have been compared with manure and
mineral fertilizers.

Possible metal accumulations in the epigeal part of Corn Si
lage and Leaf Beet have also been evaluated.

This paper refers to the results obtained during the first
3 years of a five year trial and simply gives a " picture "
of the situation, the way it has evolved in that period. A more
accurate evaluation of the research will be possible at the
end of the total trial period when all the necessary data will
be at our disposal.

2. Materials and Methods

In the trial being carried out by C.R.S.A. of Udine (5),
Fertimont S.p.a. has preliminarily investigated the mobility of
heavy metals in the soil and plant tissue uptakes only in treat
ments N°1 (Control), N°3 (mineral fertilizers), N°4 (compost a-
mended), N°7 (manure amended) and N°10 (M.S.W.and S.S. compost
amended), taking into account the possibility of wider research
in the other treatments, if necessary.

Metals in the soils have been analyzed only in the Corn Silage treatments. This paper shows however metal evolution in
the Leaf Beet treatments fertilized and amended with materials
equivalent to the ones applied to Corn Silage both in quality
and quantity.

At the moment only average samples of Leaf Beet plots have
been analyzed. A certain behaviour pattern has been suggested,
the significativity of which will be fully tested when all the
data is available.

The trials have been carried out on a sandy-silt calcareous
soil, having a pH of 8.3.

The concentration ranges of the total metals present in the
raw materials applied in each treatment for the 3 years are listed in Table 1.

Total metals in the different samples have been quantitati
vely analyzed via Atomic Absorption after their solubilization
with a mixture of $\overline{H}Cl$, HNO_3 and H_2O_2.

Available metals have been analyzed via Atomic Absorption
after their extraction with EDTA (6) and DTPA (7) chelating so
lutions.

3. Results

The prevision of the concentration of total metals in the
soil, derived from the amounts of elements applied with the raw ma
terials used (Table 2), has shown higher values than those sup
plied by analysis. This can be explained (8,9) by sampling or
analysis errors, depth changes during preparation of plots,ap
parent density changes and,not insignificant in our opinion,by metal
migrations down to the subsoil.

As expected, Me-EDTA levels, are always higher than corresponding Me-DTPA levels.

The treatment fertilized with inorganic salts and the one
amended with manure do not show increases either of total or
extractable metals.

Me-Total (analytically determined), Me-EDTA and Me-DTPA le
vels significatively increase in the compost-amended treatments,
apart from some cases which will be further discussed.

Significative correlations have been found among the vario
us combinations of Me-A (Metal applied to soil),Me-Total,Me-
EDTA and Me-DTPA.

Also metal accumulation in plant tissues of Corn Silage and
Leaf Beet has been observed.

3.1 Iron (Figures 1 a, 1 b, 1 c, 1 d,)

Significative variations of total iron levels in soils have
not been observed either in treatments or in the period, due
to the high concentration of this metal in the soil selected
for the trials

The Level of Fe-EDTA (about 200 p.p.m. in the control treat
ment) has significatively increased since 1984 in treatment 10,
reaching the maximum of concentration (395 p.p.m.) in 1985, the
year in which occurred a significative increase also in treatme
nt 4 (320 p.p.m.).

The level of Fe-DTPA (about 20 p.p.m. in the control) signi
ficatively increased in 1985 in treatments 4 and 10 reaching
the value of 48 p.p.m.

A significative linear regression has been found between the
Fe- EDTA and the Fe-DTPA values given by the relationship.

$$Fe\text{-}DTPA = 0.14 \times Fe\text{-}EDTA - 10.96 \quad (r^2 = 0,82)$$

No iron accumulation in corn silage has been observed. In
1985 the iron level of Leaf Beet in treatment 4 was 4500 ppm
against a control of 1400 ppm.

3.2 Manganese (Figures 2 a, 2 b, 2 c, 2 d,)

For the Mn-Tot. level in soil the same explanation holds as above expressed for iron.

The Mn-EDTA concentration does not show significative diffe rences either in treatments or in the period.

That holds also for Mn-DTPA level in 1983 and 1984. In 1985 all the treatments showed a decrease of the Mn-DTPA values.

No satisfactory explanation for this behaviour, observed also by other authors (10), is readily available.

Plant tissues did not show any metal accumulation phenomena.

3.3 Zinc (Figures 3 a, 3 b, 3 c, 3 d)

Compost application to soil (treatments 4 and 10) has caused a significative increase of the Zn-Tot. level since 1984.

A significative linear regression has been found betwen Zn-A and Zn-Tot. given by the relationship:

$$Zn\text{-}Tot. = 0.11 \times Zn\text{-}A + 60.29 \ (r^2 = 0,80)$$

The Zn-EDTA level (3,5 p.p.m. in the control) shows significative increases each year, particularly in treatments 4 and 10. Between 1983 and 1985 the Zn - EDTA concentration rose from 10 p.p.m. to 35 p.p.m. in treatment 4 and from 24 p.p.m. to 60 p.p.m. in treatment 10.

Also the increase of Zn-DTPA concentrations is significative, and the levels reached the maximum value of 17 p.p.m. in treatment 4 and 25 p.p.m. in treatment 10 in 1985.

The following significative linear regressions have been found.

$$Zn\text{-}EDTA = 0.75 \times Zn\text{-}Tot. - 42,09 \ (r^2 = 0,91)$$

$$Zn\text{-}DTPA = 0,33 \times Zn\text{-}Tot. - 18,49 \ (r^2 = 0,93)$$

$$Zn\text{-}DTPA = 0,47 \times Zn\text{-}EDTA - 0,24 \ (r^2 = 0,97)$$

Zn has had a tendency to accumulate in treatments 4 and 10 in corn silage since 1984. This trend was confirmed in 1985 when the Zn level reached 50 p.p.m. in both treatments (25 ppm in the control).

Leaf Beet has shown a strong tendency to accumulate Zn in treatments 4 and 10 since 1983.

3.4 Copper (Figures 4 a, 4 b, 4 c, 4 d,)

Treatment 10 showed a significative increase of total Cu le vel in 1984.- Cu-Total level also significatively increased in 1985 in treatment 4.

Even if manure is added to the soil with an amount of Cu equi valent to that of compost, this application does not affect total Cu level. We made the hypothesis that Cu chemical compounds in manure are easily leacheable.

The same considerations made for Zn hold for the Cu-EDTA and Cu-DTPA levels both in the treatments and in the period.

The following significative linear regression has been found.

$$Cu\text{-}DTPA = 0.47 \times Cu\text{-}EDTA - 0.20 \quad (r^2 = 0,97)$$

Corn silage shows a significative trend to uptake Cu in treatments 7, 4, 10, each year apart from treatment 4 in 1984.

The Cu level in Leaf Beet reached the value of 24 p.p.m. in 1985 in treatment 4 (control 18 p.p.m.).

3.5 Cadmium (Figures 5 a, 5 b, 5 c, 5 d,)

Significative increases of Cd-Total, both in the treatments and in the period, compared with the control, are shown by treatments 4 and 10 in 1984 and in treatment 10 in 1985.

No significative variation of the Cd-EDTA and Cd-DTPA levels has been shown.

The Cd-DTPA values in 1985 tended to decrease with the same behaviour shown by Mn-DTPA in the same year.

No uptakes of Cd by plant tissues have been noticed.

3.6 Lead (Figures 6 a, 6 b, 6 c, 6 d)

The Pb-Total level in soil has shown in treatment 10 significatively higher values than the control since 1983 and this holds also for treatment 4 in 1985.

The Pb-Total level had a value of 28 p.p.m. in treatment 10 in 1983 and 45 p.p.m. in 1985. Treatment 4 in 1985 showed a Pb-Tot. level of 31 p.p.m.

The following significative linear regression has been found.

$$Pb\text{-}Tot. = 0.10 \times Pb\text{-}A + 19.01 \quad (r^2 = 0,96)$$

The Pb-EDTA level, the value of which was 6 p.p.m. in the control, increased in treatment 4 from 8 p.p.m. to 22 p.p.m. betwen 1983 and 1985, while it increased in treatment 10 from 12 ppm to 26 ppm.

The Pb-DTPA level, the value of which was 1 ppm in the control, increased in treatment 4 from 3 ppm to 14 ppm between 1983 and 1985, while it increased in treatment 10 from 2 ppm to 8 ppm.

The following significative linear regressions have been found.

$$Pb\text{-}EDTA = 0.79 \times Pb\text{-}Tot. - 8.15 \quad (r^2 = 0,88)$$
$$Pb\text{-}DTPA = 0.33 \times Pb\text{-}Tot. - 5,59 \quad (r^2 = 0,91)$$
$$Pb\text{-}DTPA = 0.51 \times Pb\text{-}EDTA - 2,39 \quad (r^2 = 0,81)$$

Corn silage showed significative uptakes of Pb at a level of 4,5 ppm in 1985 in treatment 4 (control 3 ppm).
The Leaf Beet shows heavy uptakes of Pb in treatment 4 (11 ppm) against a control of 4 ppm.

3.7 Nickel (Figures 7 a, 7 b, 7 c, 7 d)

No significative increases of Ni-Tot. have been noticed.
The Ni-EDTA level significatively increased during 1983 (control 3,8 ppm) in treatments 7 and 10, reaching in both cases a value of about 5,8 ppm which did not significatively change in 1984 or 1985.
Treatment 4, even if the application of Ni was higher than in treatment 7, shows a Ni-EDTA level lower than treatment 7 and the control.
The Ni-DTPA concentration in treatment 4 has reached a significatively higher value than the control since 1983. In 1985 also treatment 10 showed a significative increase of Ni-DTPA level.
Corn silage does not show a significative uptake of Ni.
The Leaf Beet showed a heavy uptake of Ni in 1985 in treatment 4 reaching a value of 13,3 ppm against a control of 5,5 ppm.

3.8 Chromium (Figures 8 a, 8 b, 8 c, 8 d,)

The total Cr level in soil shows no significative variation either in the treatments or in the period.
The Cr-EDTA level has shown significative increase against the control (0,35 ppm) since 1983 only in treatment 10 (0,54 ppm), and in treatment 4 in 1985.
Corn silage shows no significative accumulation of Cr.
The Cr level in Leaf Beet during 1985 reached a level of 16 ppm in treatment 4 showing higher values than the control (8 ppm).

4. Conclusions

The application of composts in agriculture increases both total and available fraction levels in the soil. The amount of Zn and Pb applied to the soils shows significative linear regressions against the total elements determined by analysis.
The increase of available Zn and Pb, extracted with EDTA and DTPA chelating solutions, shows significative linear regression against the total elements determined by analysis. Significative linear relationships have been found for Fe, Zn, Cu, and Pb between Me-EDTA and Me-DTPA values.
Significative uptakes of metals in Corn Silage have been observed. The Leaf Beet has shown a very high tendency to ac-

cumulate metals in 1985.

Nevertheless after 3 years of experimentation, we found only for Corn Silage and Zn a significative linear regression between available fraction of the metal and metal uptake by the plant (r^2 = 0,75).

Generally we have however observed that uptake variations of metals by plant tissues quite often are related to variations of their available fractions in the soil.

Mineral fertilizer treatments do not show increases of total and available metals in the soil neither do they induce significative metal uptakes in Corn Silage and Leaf Beet. The same considerations, except for Ni, are valid for manure.

Considering the observed trends for soils and plant tissues we intend to extend the research to all the treatments carried out by C.R.S.A. of Udine, in order to confirm and/or better define the obtained results.

The residual effects of composts applied to the soil will not be neglected.

Acknowledgements

The author wishes to thank Mr. Diego Canepa and Riccardo Bellin for the chemical analysis, Mr. Franco Franzin and Miss Stefania Facco for their contribution in data processing.

REFERENCES

1. Council for Agricultural Science and Tecnology (CAST).(1980)
   Effect of sewage sludge on the cadmium and zinc contents of crops.
   Rep. 83, Ames I A
2. CHANEY, R.L.(1973). Crop and food chain effects of toxic in sludges and effluents. In proceeding of the joint conference on recycling municipal sludges and effluents on land EPA/USDA/Nat'l. Assoc.of State Universities and Land Grant Colleges, Champoign, III, July 9-13, 129-141.
3. U . S Environmental Protection Agency (1976)
   Application of sewage sludge to cropland.
   Appraisal of potential hazards of the Heavy Metals to plants and animals. Published by USEPA office of water program operations I.S. n° EPA - 430/9 - 76 - 013, p.63.
4. NATIONAL ACADEMY of SCIENCES(1974)
   Geochemistry and Envitonement I. The relation of selected trace elements to health and disease.
   Nat'l Accad. of. Sci. Washington, D.C.

5. DEL ZAN, F., BARUZZINI, L., CANDOTTI, M., IONETTI, I, and MARGUT G. (1986). Manuring a maize crop with composts obtained from different technological processes: short term effects on soil plant system. Proceeding of International Symposium on Compost Production, Quality and Use - Udine, April 1986

6. LAKANEN, E. and ERVIO, R. (1971) A comparison of eight extractants for the determination of plant available micronutrients in soils. Acta Agr. Fehn., 123, 223 - 232.

7. LINDSAY, W.L. and NORWELL, W.A. (1969). Development of DTPA micronutrient soil test. Agron. Abstr., 69, 84.

8. MOREL, J.L., GUCKART, A., SIBOUT, V. and JACQUIN, F. (1978). Possibilites de valorization agricole de boues residuaires urbaines. I.Etude de variations de la composition des boues. E.N.S.A. IA. Nancy, 20, 21, 29.

9. ROBERTSON, W.K. LUTRICK, M.C. AND YUANT, L. (1982). Heavy applications of liquid digested sludge on three ultisols. I. Effects on soil chemistry. J. Environ. Qual., 11, 278-282.

10. WILLIAMS, D.E., VLAMIS, J., PUKITE, A.H. and COREY, J.E. (1980). Trace element accumulation, movement, and distribution in the soil profile from massive applications of sewage sludge. Soil Sci., 129, 119-131.

RICERCA SVOLTA NELL'AMBITO DEL PROGETTO FINALIZZATO C.N.R./ I.P.R.A.

Table 1 : Heavy metal concentration ranges in fertilizers employed in the experimentation

Treatment	Fe %	Mn ppm	Zn ppm	Cu ppm	Cd ppm	Pb ppm	Ni ppm	Cr ppm
3	0.14	12	155	12	2.2	1	23	72
7	0.14-0.27	93-320	92-800	20-375	0.5-2.5	2-18.5	5-16	8-23
4	0.90-1.06	408-725	565-1000	115-653	2.3-4.0	186-375	16-37	26-65
10	1.00-2.35	417-637	700-860	147-320	1.2-5.0	220-365	21-54	32-57

Table 2 : Cumulative amounts of metal (Kg/ha) distributed to soils with the different treatments

Treatment	Fe 83	Fe 83-84	Fe 83-85	Mn 83	Mn 83-84	Mn 83-85	Zn 83	Zn 83-84	Zn 83-85	Cu 83	Cu 83-84	Cu 83-85
1	0	0	0	0	0	0	0	0	0	0	0	0
3	0.45	0.9	1.35	0.05	0.1	0.15	0.05	0.1	0.15	0.01	0.02	0.03
7	228	578	949	17	52	96	96	120	213	4	53	91
4	1578	2910	4483	67	133	252	84	180	344	25	42	93
10	5758	9211	15224	141	286	492	211	429	667	49	105	153

Treatment	Cd 83	Cd 83-84	Cd 83-85	Pb 83	Pb 83-84	Pb 83-85	Ni 83	Ni 83-84	Ni 83-85	Cr 83	Cr 83-84	Cr 83-85
1	0	0	0	0	0	0	0	0	0	0	0	0
3	0.09	0.39	0.64	0	0	0	0.01	0.02	0.03	0.02	0.04	0.06
7	0.4	1.0	1.4	0.5	2.8	5.5	1.2	3.3	4.5	1.6	4.5	7.5
4	1.2	1.7	2.1	48	78	139	6	9	12	6	15	19
10				60	157	255	10	20	27	12	33	43

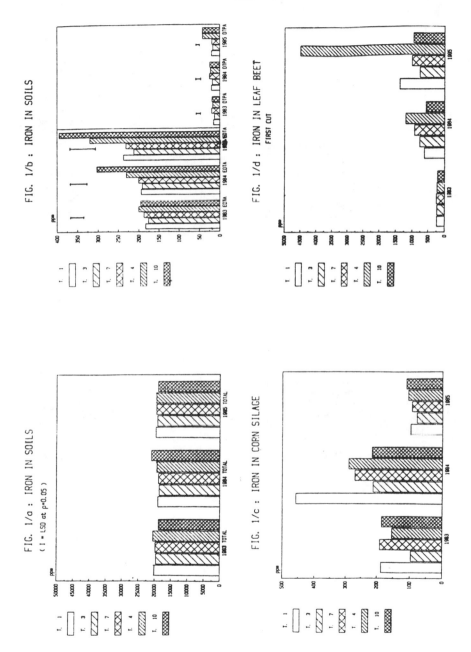

FIG. 1/b : IRON IN SOILS

FIG. 1/d : IRON IN LEAF BEET
FIRST CUT

FIG. 1/a : IRON IN SOILS
(I = LSD at p=0.05)

FIG. 1/c : IRON IN CORN SILAGE

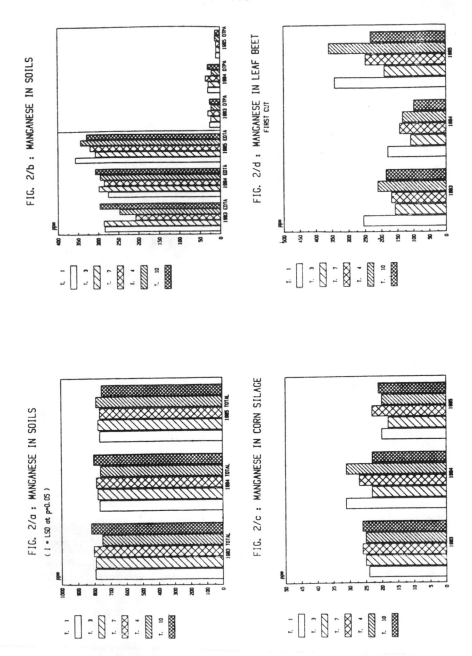

FIG. 2/b : MANGANESE IN SOILS

FIG. 2/d : MANGANESE IN LEAF BEET
FIRST CUT

FIG. 2/a : MANGANESE IN SOILS
(I = LSD at p=0.05)

FIG. 2/c : MANGANESE IN CORN SILAGE

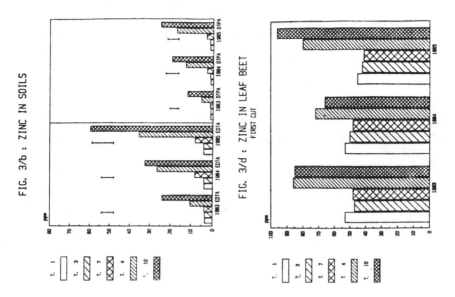

FIG. 3/b : ZINC IN SOILS

FIG. 3/a : ZINC IN SOILS
(I = LSD at p=0.05)

FIG. 3/d : ZINC IN LEAF BEET
FIRST CUT

FIG. 3/c : ZINC IN CORN SILAGE

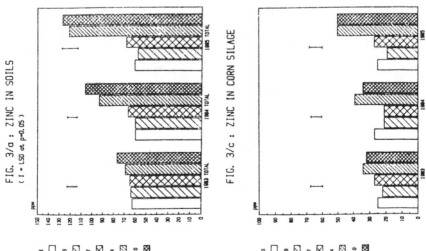

610

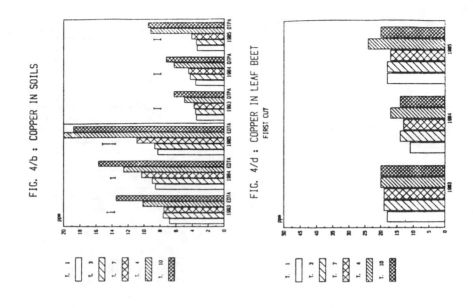

FIG. 4/a : COPPER IN SOILS
(I = LSD at p=0.05)

FIG. 4/b : COPPER IN SOILS

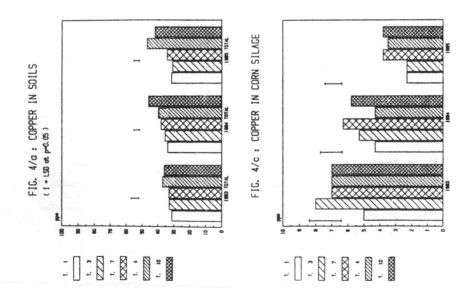

FIG. 4/c : COPPER IN CORN SILAGE

FIG. 4/d : COPPER IN LEAF BEET
FIRST CUT

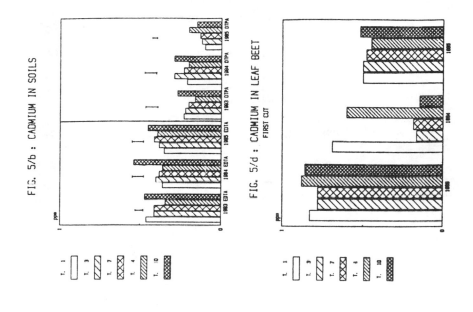

FIG. 5/b : CADMIUM IN SOILS

FIG. 5/a : CADMIUM IN SOILS

(I = LSD at p<0.05)

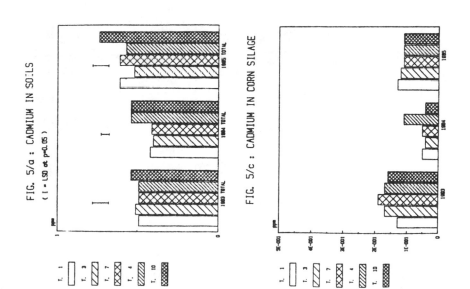

FIG. 5/d : CADMIUM IN LEAF BEET

FIRST CUT

FIG. 5/c : CADMIUM IN CORN SILAGE

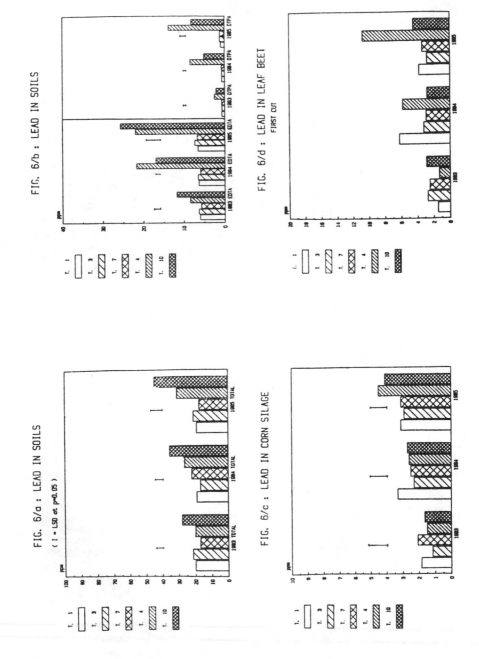

FIG. 6/b : LEAD IN SOILS

FIG. 6/d : LEAD IN LEAF BEET
FIRST CUT

FIG. 6/a : LEAD IN SOILS

(I = LSD at p=0.05)

FIG. 6/c : LEAD IN CORN SILAGE

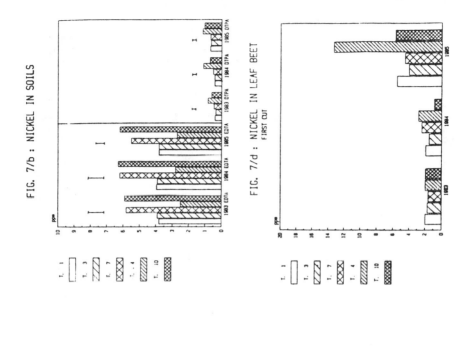

FIG. 7/a : NICKEL IN SOILS
(I = LSD at p=0.05)

FIG. 7/b : NICKEL IN SOILS

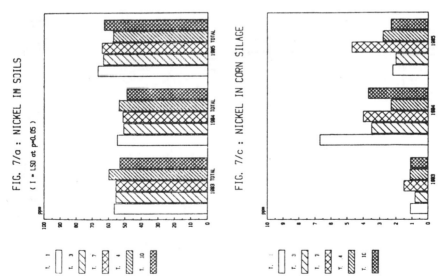

FIG. 7/c : NICKEL IN CORN SILAGE

FIG. 7/d : NICKEL IN LEAF BEET
FIRST CUT

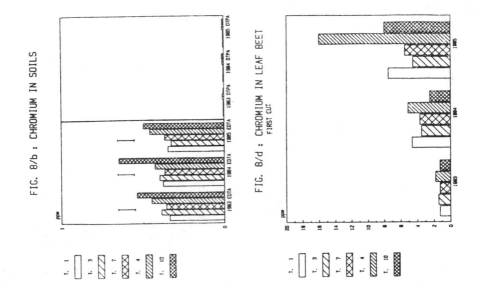

FIG. 8/b : CHROMIUM IN SOILS

FIG. 8/a : CHROMIUM IN SOILS

(I = LSD at p<0.05)

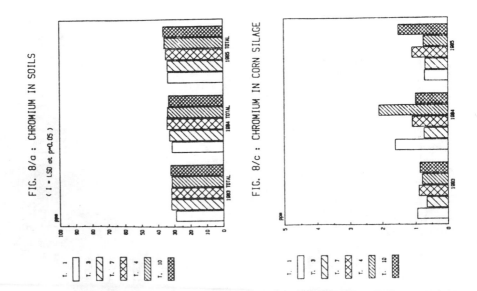

FIG. 8/d : CHROMIUM IN LEAF BEET
FIRST CUT

FIG. 8/c : CHROMIUM IN CORN SILAGE

MICROBIAL VARIATIONS IN COMPOST AMENDED SOILS

A. RUTILI, M. CIVILINI, B. CITTERIO, S. FRASSINETTI
and M. DE BERTOLDI
Istituto di Microbiologia Agraria, Università di Pisa and Centro Studio per la Microbiologia del Suolo, C.N.R., Pisa, Italy.

Summary

The aim of this research was to study the effect of compost amending over several years on the biological fertility of soil cultivated with maize. The parameter used for measuring the effect of compost on soil fertility was the evolution of some physiological groups of microorganisms from the maize rhyzosphere, during the vegetative cycle of this crop. Three different dosages of compost (the end-product obtained from sludge and the organic fraction of solid urban waste) were comparated with a control with plots treated with mineral fertilizer and with soil fertilized with manure.
Work, planned to cover a five year period, began in 1900.

1.1 Introduction

Frequent topics of discussion nowadays are the terms "ecological agriculture" and "renewable energy in agriculture". This is a reflection of the need felt to change and improve agricultural methods by lowering energy consumption and reducing pollution, since our environment is endangered by methods at present in use.

This means reducing the massive doses of fertilizers, pesticides and other chemical products at present used to increase yields. This is the only way of reducing environmental pollution to benefit health and to restore a biological-ecological equilibrium.

For the above reasons the study of all recycling processes of, and energy recovery from, waste became of paramount importance particularly when concerning the use of the products in agriculture. It is essential, however, to acquire definite knowledge of the effects of incorporating recycled material in agricultural soil, particularly when concerning qualitative and quantitative aspects of yields, the risk of disturbing soil biological equilibrium and the influence on the dynamics of the chief macroelements.

This research is a contribution to the research project "Progetto finalizzato: Incremento Produttività-Risorse Agricole (I.P.R.A.), Tematica 1.1.6., Riciclaggio di Sottoprodotti e Reflui Agroalimentari ed Urbani come Intervento Disinquinante e Produttivo di Fertilizzanti Organici" (Recycling Agricultural-Industrial and Urban Wastes for Depollution and Organic Fertilizers Production).

Composting is a biological oxidation process the end-product of which is highly stabilized organic matter suitable for direct use in amending agricultural land and for improving its fertility (9,12,13). It disposes of organic wastes (solid urban waste, agricultural and industrial wastes, etc.) and as such it answers the need for reducing and minimizing environmental pollution while allowing much of the energy in the wastes to be recovered which means a saving (16,20). Finally, it is a valuable source of organic matter, sorely needed by agricultural land particularly in Italy, where the difficulty of obtaining manure and other traditional sources of organic matter continues to worsen (9,10).

The aim of work reported here was to study the effects of repeated use of compost over several years on the biological fertility of agricultural land.

The parameters used to evaluate the influence of compost on fertility were based on variations undergone by physiological groups of cellulolytic microorganisms, autotrophic nitrifying bacteria and vesicular-arbuscular mycorhizal fungi following repeated fertilizing with compost produced from sludge + the organic fraction of solid urban waste (S.U.W.), when applied over a five-year period.

These microorganisms were chosen because they have a fundamental role in recycling nutrients and are therefore essential to the biological fertility of the same.

It must not be forgotten, with reference to cellulolytic microorganisms, that the use of compost on agricultural land involves the application of organic matter only partially humified with a cellulose content varying on average between 20 and 40%, depending on the starting material (8,16).

Matter containing cellulose, once in the soil, is subjected to intense biological activity producing glucose, through hydrolysis. This is an important source of energy for many microorganisms.

Humus is obtained from the products of microbial transformation, re-arrangement and re-synthesis of ligno-cellulose complexes.

It is a result of the activity of heterogeneous microflora, comprising eubacteria, mixobacteria, fungi and actinomycetes through strictly aerobic activity (9,13).

Efficient cellulolysis therefore is an active contribution to the dynamics of humified organic matter in soil.

Autotrophic nitrifying bacteria take part in the nitrogen cycle by oxidising the ammonium ion to nitric which is the chief form of nitrogen that plants can take up.

Obviously then, good nitrifying activity is a basic premise for supplying sufficient nitrogen to the crop. Moreover, the formation of nitric acid lowers soil pH which increases the availability of certain ions usually difficult for plants to absorb. Nitrification therefore is involved in changing the concentrations of soluble K, P, Mg, Fe, Mn and Ca (2).

The classical studies by Winogradsky and Omeliansky placed nitrifying bacteria among the exclusively chemiolithotrophics (39,40,41,42). This definition meant that they were thought to be inhibited by the presence of organic matter, particularly water-soluble, in the soil. Recent studies, however, have suggested that this opinion should be modified; new light has been cast on the relationship between autotrophic nitrifying bacteria and organic matter (5,15,21,23,33,34).

This induced us to include an investigation in our research of the effect of organic matter in compost added to the soil on the dynamics of nitrifying microorganisms.

Finally vesicular-arbuscular mycorhizal fungi play a fundamental part in plant nutrition by stimulating phosphorus absorbtion. This gives rise to a chain of anatomical and physiological changes in the plant which generally improves available nutrients. A high concentration of phosphorus within cells does, in fact, promote root development, allowing plants to explore a larger volume of soil and therefore have a greater quantity of nutrients at their disposal (38).

It is highly important to examine and measure the influence of organic matter on mycorhizal infection and evaluate its effect on the dynamics of the indispensable macroelemnt of phosphorus in the soil, together with carbon and nitrogen, for plant life.

Research, planned to cover a five-year period, began in 1983. This length of time was chosen in order to have time for any deleterious effects through accumulation of organic matter due to repeated applications of compost to be discerned on the soil microbial populations discussed above, of our experimental plots.

The biodegradable organic fraction of solid urban waste contains a wide variety of pathogens for man and animals. The use of these substances in agriculture might increase the possibility of transmitting dangerous microorganisms (14). The thermophilic stage of composting has the effect of reducing the number and variety of pathogens present. Such sanitizing is essential for health reasons, particularly for products used in agriculture (11)

The laboriousness of testing for pathogens present makes it unsuitable for routine analyses (29). It was decided therefore to use indicators, for example Faecal Streptococchi and Bacteria Coli, whose reduction in numbers below a certain limit can be considered a good indication of sanitization (14,35,36). Indicator organisms can be used in two ways:
1. to check the level of sanitization;
2. to look for re-infection after sanitization.
Faecal Streptococchi are more suitable in the former case and Enterobacteria in the latter. Probably total coliforms are useful too in the latter case (36).

Furthermore it was decided to investigate for Salmonella sp (one of the chief pathogens for man) in case the elimination of indicator bacteria did not tally with that of pathogens.

1.2 Materials and methods

Field tests

Experiments were carried out at Aiello del Friuli on clay soil on a farm belonging to the Centro Regionale per la Sperimentazione Agraria di Pozzuolo del Friuli. The crop used was spring maize seeded in early May and harvested in October-November.

The crop was grown on a split-plot system with the systematic distribution of the units. Each plot had the following dimensions:
- overall: 9 x 3 m;
- excluding borders: 9 x 1.5 m

The effects of different dosages of compost, with a nitrogen-assimilable content of 100, 200 and 300 units were compared with: a) the control (no fertilization); b) manure fertilization (assimilable-nitrogen 200 units); c) mineral fertilization with NH_4NO_3 (assimilable-nitrogen 200 units). Table I shows the plan of the fertilizations investigated. Each type of fertilization was carried out with four replications.

Characteristics of organic matter employed

The composts used in this research were the end products obtained from sludge and the organic fraction of solid urban waste, produced by "DANECO", Udine, Italy. These composts have proved to be almost standardised in their chemical composition over many years. The same may be said for the manure used. All fertilizers were applied immediately before spring seeding.

Microbiological analyses

A) SOIL
The physiological groups of cellulolytics and autotrophic nitrifiers were detected by Pochon's et al methods (31).
The percentage of vesicular-arbuscular mycorhizal infections in maize roots were measured according to Phillips' et al methods for root staining and Giovannetti's et al for the measurement of the degree of infection (30,18).
Samples were taken periodically for microbiological analyses throughout the cultivation cycle until harvest.

Sampling

One soil sample was taken from each of the four replications of each fertilizer. Samples were taken at 20 cm depth in the region of the maize rhyzosphere. All figures in the graphs represent the logarithm of the number of microorganisms per g of soil dry matter.

B) COMPOST
The indicated microorganisms and pathogens were isolated and identified in random samples of the compost procured for our experiments using standard methods (3,7,17,25,32).
All figures in the table represent the number of unit-forming colonies per g of compost dry matter.

1.3 Results and Discussion

Figures 1, 2 and 3 represent changes in total cellulolytic microorganisms during the cultivation cycle of maize over the three years of research.
During the first year the plots amended with compost and manure showed the highest counts in cellulolytic microorganisms, although there were no statistically significant differences among the various types of fertilizers (Table II). However, in 1984 notable differences were detected in the chosen microbial populations between plots dosed with compost from sludge and S.U.W. and the others (Fig. 2).
The plots treated with compost showed a statistically significant increase in microbial counts of cellulolytic microorganisms (Table III).

The 1985 tests too, show a trend towards an increase in the number of microorganisms in the plots treated with compost in comparison to the others (Fig. 3, Table IV).

It is interesting to note that the graphs for the three years of testing show analogous behaviour in cellulolytic microorganisms.

Highest counts are found in late summer during the plant growth phase.

Microbial growth declines and stops more or less when the season grows colder and plant development ceases. This behaviour is also shown by the other two physiological groups investigated (autotrophic nitrifying bacteria and vesicular-arbuscular mycorhizal fungi).

Autotrophic nitrifying bacteria, like the cellulolytic microorganisms, gave highest counts in 1983 in those plots amended with manure and even higher in those with compost (Fig. 4), although statistically significant differences were not detected among the fertilizers (Table V).

In 1984, however, the differences in microbial counts between plots with high doses of compost from sludge and S.U.W. and the others were statistically significant (Fig. 5, Table VI). One important observation to be made at this point, after two years of microbial analysis, is that the application of partially humified organic matter to soil as manure or compost does definitely not have an inhibiting effect on nitrification.

This confirms what has already been pointed out in the literature concerning the effect of organic matter on the growth and metabolism of autotrophic nitrifying bacteria (28).

Our results obtained to date strongly suggest quite the opposite. In other words the amendment of soil with organic matter, particularly compost, has a more pronounced stimulating effect on the development of these microorganisms than that of chemical fertilizers.

Trends in the autotrophic nitrifying microorganism population for 1985 are difficult to interpret (Fig. 6, Table VII) because there was no numerical increase in the counts from plots treated with compost, in comparison to the others in 1985.

Moreover, the shape of the curves representing trends in microbial populations were different in comparison to the previous two years, there being no numerical increase in September.

This anomalous behaviour might be explained by the already mentioned close relationship between soil microbial populations and the weather, in particular the sensitivity of nitrifying bacteria to all those parameters which have an influence on the partial pressure of oxygen in the soil, particularly temperature and moisture variations (4,6).

These variations were more marked in 1985 with an unusual weather pattern of heavy rain in June and a pronounced drought in early Autumn.

Under these conditions, soil amended with organic matter, because of its greater water retentivity, withheld more moisture after the violent rainfalls reducing air and oxygen in the soil interstitial spaces.

This might explain the lower microbial counts in plots fertilized with compost and manure in comparison to those fertilized with ammonium-nitrate.

All the plots dosed with compost of high assimilable-nitrogen content revealed a higher content in autotrophic nitrifying bacteria with values close to those for plots treated with manure, which perhaps indicates a partial compensation of the effect suggested above.

The vesicular-arbuscular mycorhizal fungi are also highly sensitive to variations in the weather; highest infection values are found in late summer exactly as observed for cellulolytic and nitrifying microorganisms (Fig. 7 and 8, Table VIII and IX).

Higher infection percentages in September may be caused either by the weather or by the state of plant development, but it is impossible to determine the exact cause for variations in field tests (19).

Seasonal variations in mycorhizal infections found to date over the experimental period are quite frequent although highest infection percentages are not found to be simultaneous all over the world because of climatic and pedological differences (19,26,37). An examination of the graphs yields some interesting information.

Firstly mycorhizal infection is strongly inhibited in the plots treated with manure. This confirms similar variations found by Pera et al, Mosse et al, in vesicular-arbuscular mycorhizal fungi, caused by treatment with manure (24,27).

On the other hand, other authors have found that organic matter increases the number of spores from this fungi (22).

In our opinion this divergence over the effects of organic matter added to soil depends on what type of organic matter is added and its level of humification.

The graphs and the tables show that infection in plots treated with compost always reaches higher levels than in those treated with mineral fertilizers as well as being higher than in those treated with manure.

Throughout the three years of experiments indicator microorganisms were always below the limits shown in Table X. Maximum indicator levels permissible in sanitized compost have been indicated by De Bertoldi et al (11,14). These are;
- total Enterobacteriaceae: 5×10^2/g d.m.
- Faecal Streptococchi: 5×10^3/g d.m.

When indicators are found in fewer numbers than those quoted above, Salmonella sp is invariably absent.

It can therefore be affirmed that material used in these trials as organic fertilizer was sufficiently sanitized at all times.

1.4 Conclusions

Three years are too short a period considering the strong homeostatic properties of soil (1). Only after many repeated applications and trials can the possibility of an agent changing soil properties be truly determined and investigations give reliable results.

The influence of experimental practices is more clearly evident if other variables are reduced to a minimum; for this reason trials in greenhouses or other controlled environments are usually carried out. However, given the essential feature of compost as being an amendant for use in open field, which is natural environment subject to climatic, metereological and pedological variations, it was considered more suitable to carry out our trials in open field, although this required us to investigate more parameters over a longer period of time.

It is too early yet to consider results obtained so far over only three years testing as being definitive. Nevertheless data gathered does show a trend towards higher numbers in the microorganisms in question in soil amended with high dosages of compost, which presumably has a higher microbial activity.

This brings about a more effective recycling of nutrients in the soil with positive chemical, physical and biological consequences on the soil and should reflect favourably on yield.

Livelier microbial activity obtained by using compost instead of manure is probably due to a greater content in the former of nutrients with respect to the latter, when compared by dry weight.

It is definitely unfounded to believe, as some do, that repeated amendment with organic matter from compost adversely affects plant growth and the rhyzosphere.

Such ill-effects are the result of using very low quality, inadequately stabilized organic matter (43,44,45).

BIBLIOGRAPHY

1. ALEXANDER M. (1971). Microbial Ecology. J. Wiley & Sons Inc., New York.
2. ALEXANDER M. (1977). Introduction to Soil Microbiology. J. Wiley & Sons Inc., New York.
3. APHA, AWWA, WPCF (1971). Standard methods for the examination of water and wastewater. Ed. Am. Pub. Heal. Ass., Washington D.C., U.S.A.
4. BELSER L.W. (1979). Population ecology of nitrifying bacteria. Ann. Rev. Microbiol. 33, 309-333.
5. BOCK E. (1976). Growth of Nitrobacter in presence of organic matter. II Chemoorganotrophic growth of Nitrobacter agilis. Arch. Microbiol. 108, 305-312.
6. CAMPBELL N.E.R., LEES H. (1971), The Nitrogen Cycle. In Soil Biochemistry. Eds. A.D. McLaren and G.H. Peterson, Marcel Dekker Inc., New York, 194 p.
7. CARRINGTON E.G. (1980). The isolation and identification of Salmonella sp. in sewage sludges: a comparison of methods and recommendations for a standard technique. WRC, Technical report TR129, Stevenage, U.K.
8. CNR (1977). Utilizzazione energetica dei Rifiuti Solidi Urbani. Progetto finalizzato energetica.
9. DE BERTOLDI M., ZUCCONI F. (1980). Microbiologia della trasformazione dei rifiuti solidi urbani in compost e loro utilizzazione in agricoltura. Ingegneria Ambientale, 9, (3), 209-216.
10. DE BERTOLDI M., GIOVANNETTI M., PERA A., VALLINI G. (1981). Utilizzazione dei fanghi e compost in agricoltura: impatto con la microflora del suolo. In "Collana del progetto finalizzato: Promozione della qualità dell'ambiente", CNR AR/2/20-27, Rome, 127 p.
11. DE BERTOLDI M., COPPOLA S., SPINOSA L. (1982). Health implications in sewage sludge composting. CEC Workshop, Zurich, May 11-13. Ed. D. Riedel Co.
12. DE BERTOLDI M., PERA A., VALLINI G. (1983). Principi del compostaggio. Proceedings of the international Symposium on "Biological reclamation and land utilization of urban waste". Naples 11-14 Oct., 1983. Ed. F. Zucconi, M. de Bertoldi and S. Coppola.
13. DE BERTOLDI M., VALLINI G., PERA A. (1983). The biology of composting: a review. Waste Management & Research, 1, 157-176.
14. DE BERTOLDI M., FRASSINETTI S., BIANCHIN L., PERA A. (1985). Sludge hygienization with different compost systems. Joint Seminar CEC-German Veterinary Medical Society: Inactivation of microorganisms in sewage sludge by stabilisation processes. Hohenheim, 8-10 Oct., 1984. Eds. D. Strauch, A.H. Havelaar and P. L'Hermite.

15. DELWICHE C.C., FINSTEIN M.S. (1965). Carbon and energy sources for the nitrifying autotroph Nitrobacter. J. Bacteriol. 90, 102-107.

16. DIAZ L.F., GOLUEKE C.G. (1983). Material recovery from Urban Solid wastes. Proceedings of the international Symposium on "Biological reclamation and land utilization of urban waste". Naples 11-14 Oct., 1983. Ed. F. Zucconi, M. de Bertoldi and S. Coppola.

17. DUDLEY D.J., GUENTZEL M.N., IBARRA M.J., MOORE B.E., SAGIK B.P. (1980). Enumeration of potentially pathogenic bacteria from sewage sludges. Applied Environm. Microbiol. 39, 118-126.

18. GIOVANNETTI M., MOSSE B. (1980). An evaluation of technique for measuring vesicular-arbuscular mycorrhizae infection in roots. New Phytol., 84, 489-500.

19. GIOVANNETTI M. (1985). Seasonal variations of vesicular-arbuscular mycorrhizae and Endogonaceous spores in a maritime sand dune. Trans. Br. Mycol. Soc. 84 (4), 679-684.

20. GOLUEKE C.G. (1977). Biological reclamation of solid wastes. Rodale Press, Emmaus, PA, USA.

21. IDA S., ALEXANDER M. (1965). Permeability of Nitrobacter agilis to organic compounds. J. Bacteriol. 90, 151-156.

22. KRUCKELMAN H.W. (1975). Effects of fertilizers, soils, soil tillage and plant species on the frequency of Endogone chlamydospores and mycorrhizal infection in arable soils. In "Endomycorrhizas". Proceedings of a Symposium held at the University of Leeds, 22-25 July, 1974. Eds. F.E. Sanders, B. Mosse, P.B. Tinker, Academic Press, London.

23. MATIN A. (1978). Organic nutrition of chemiolithotrophic bacteria. Ann. Rev. Microbiol. 32, 433-468.

24. MOSSE B., BOWEN G.D. (1968). The distribution of Endogone spores in some Australian and New Zealand soils, and in an experimental field soil at Rothamsted. Transactions of the British Mycological Society 72, 261-268.

25. MOSSEL D.A.A., BIJKER P.G.H., EELDERING J. (1978). Streptokokken der Lancefield-Gruppe D in Lebensmitteln und Trinkwasser – ihre Bedeutung, Erfassung. Arch. f. Lebensmittelhyg. 29, 121-127.

26. NICOLSON T.H., JOHNSTON C. (1979). Mycorrhiza in the Gramineae. III. Glomus fasciculatus as the endophyte of pioneer grasses in a maritime sand dune. Transactions of the British Mycological Society 72, 261-268.

27. PERA A., GIOVANNETTI M., VALLINI G., DE BERTOLDI M. (1981). Land application of sludge: effects on soil microflora. In "The influence of sewage sludge application on physical and biological properties of soil". Proceedings of a Seminar organized jointly by the Commission of the European Communities held in Munich, 23-24 June, 1981. D. Reidel Publishing Company.

28. PERA A., VALLINI G., SIRENO I., BIANCHIN L., DE BERTOLDI M. (1983). Effect of organic matter on rhyzosphere microorganisms and root development of Sorghum plants in two different soils. Plant and Soil 74, 3-18.

29. PEREIRA-NETO J.T., STENTIFORD E.I., MARA D.D., SMITH D.V. (at press). Survival of fecal indicator microorganisms in refuse/sludge composting using the aerated static pile system. Proceedings of the international Symposium on "Compost: production, quality and use". Udine 17-19 Apr. 1986.

30. PHILLIPS J.M., HAYMAN D.S. (1970). Improved procedure for clearing roots and staining parasitic and vesicular-arbuscular mycorrhizae fungi for rapid assessment of infection. Trans. Br. Mycol. Soc. 55, 158-161.

31. POCHON J., TARDIEUX P. (1962). Techniques d'analyse en Microbiologie du sol. Ed. La Tourelle, Paris.

32. REUTER G. (1978). Selektive Kultivierung von "Enterokokken" aus Lebensmitteln tierisher Herkunft. Arch. f. Lebensmittelhyg., 29, 128-131.

33. SMITH A.J., HOARE D.S. (1968). Acetate assimilation by Nitrobacter agilis in relation to its obligate autotrophy. J. Bacteriol. 95, 844-855.

34. STEINMüLLER W., BOCK E. (1976). Growth of Nitrobacter in presence of organic matter. I Mixotrophic growth. Arch. Microbiol. 108, 299-304.

35. STRAUCH D. (at press). Microbial specifications of disinfected compost. Proceedings of the international Symposium on "Compost: production, quality and use". Udine 17-19 Apr., 1986.

36. STRAUCH D., DE BERTOLDI M. (at press). Microbiological specifications of disinfected sewage sludge. Proceedings of the 4th international Symposium on "Processing and use of organic sludge and liquid agricultural wastes". Rome, 8-11 Oct., 1985.

37. SUTTON J.C., BARRON G.L. (1972). Population dynamics of Endogone spores in soil. Canadian Journal of Botany 50, 1909-1914.

38. TINKER P.B. (1984). The role of microorganisms in mediating and facilitating the uptake of plant nutrients from soil. Plant and Soil 76, 77-91.

39. WINOGRADSKY M.S. (1891). Récherches sur les organismes de la nitrification. Ann. Inst. Pasteur 5, 577.

40. WINOGRADSKY M.S., OMELIANSKY V. (1899). über den Einfluss der organischen Substanzen auf die Arbeit der nitrifizierenden Mikrobien. I. Zentr. Bakteriol. Parasitenk. Abt. II 5, 329-343.

41. WINOGRADSKY M.S., OMELIANSKY V. (1899). über den Einfluss der organischen Substanzen auf die Arbeit der nitrifizierenden Mikrobien. II. Sentr. Bakteriol. Parasitenk. Abt. II 5, 377-387.

42. WINOGRADSKY M.S., OMELIANSKY V. (1899). über den Einfluss der organischen Substanzen auf die Arbeit der nitrifizierenden Mikrobien. III. Zentr. Bakteriol. Parasitenk. Abt. II 5, 429-440.

43. ZUCCONI F., FORTE M., MONACO A., DE BERTOLDI M. (1981). Biological evaluation of compost maturity. Biocycle 22 (4), 27-29.

44. ZUCCONI F., PERA A., FORTE M., DE BERTOLDI M. (1981). Evaluating toxicity of immature compost. Biocycle 22 (2), 54-57.

45. ZUCCONI F. (1983). Processi di biostabilizzazione della sostanza organica durante il compostaggio. Proceedings of the international Symposium on "Biological reclamation and land utilization of urban waste". Naples, 11-14 Oct., 1983. Ed. F. Zucconi, M. de Bertoldi and S. Coppola.

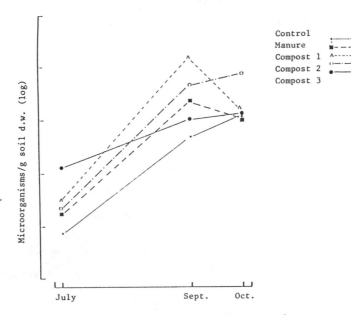

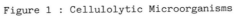

Figure 1 : Cellulolytic Microorganisms

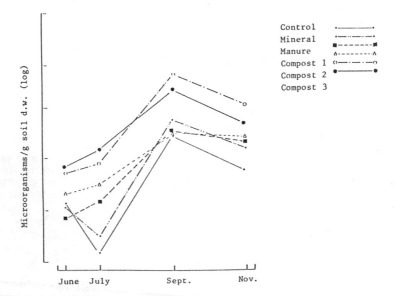

Figure 2 : Cellulolytic Microorganisms

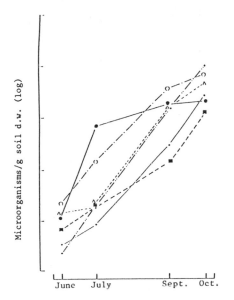

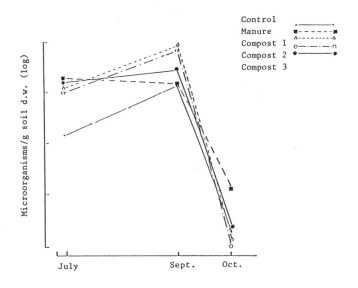

Figure 3 : Cellulolytic Microorganisms

Figure 4 : Autotrophic Nitrifiers

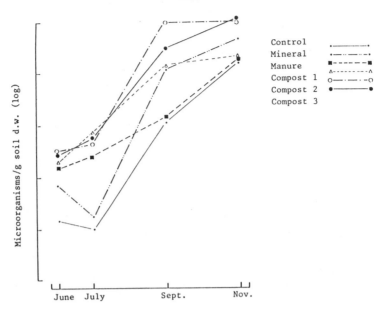

Figure 5 : Autotrophic Nitrifiers

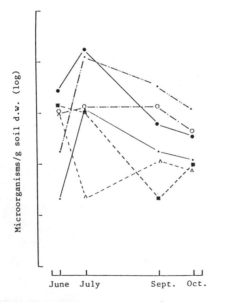

Figure 6 : Autotrophic Nitrifiers

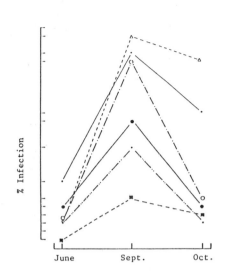

Figure 7 : Vesicular arbuscular mycorhizal infection

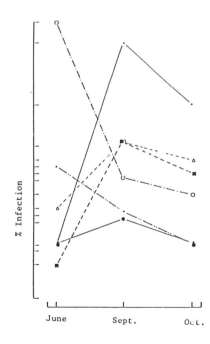

Figure 8 : Vesicular arbuscular mycorhizal infection

TABLE I: Types of fertilizers compared in open field trials

Treatment	No. Replications/ Fertilizer	N-assimilable (units)
Control (Cc)	4	-
Mineral fertilizer (Mf)	4	200
Manure (Mn)	4	200
Compost 1 (C1)	4	100
Compost 2 (C2)	4	200
Compost 3 (C3)	4	300

TABLE II: Number of cellulolytic microorganisms per g dry matter at the various sampling times in 1983

Treatment	Sampling time		
	July	September	October
Control	7.8×10^1 a	9.4×10^3 a	2.5×10^4 a
Manure	3.1×10^2 a	4.5×10^4 a	1.0×10^4 a
Compost 1	4.2×10^2 a	2.0×10^5 bc	3.1×10^4 a
Compost 2	3.2×10^2 a	5.1×10^4 ac	7.6×10^4 ab
Compost 3	1.2×10^3 b	1.7×10^4 ac	2.7×10^4 a

Results in columns followed by the same letter are not significantly different from each other (P = 0.05).

TABLE III: Number of cellulolytic microorganisms per g dry matter at the various sampling times in 1984

Treatment	Sampling time			
	June	July	September	November
Control	1.8×10^2 a	1.8×10^1 a	2.3×10^3 a	9.0×10^2 a
Mineral	1.5×10^2 a	3.6×10^1 a	6.9×10^3 a	2.0×10^3 a
Manure	9.5×10 a	2.5×10^2 b	4.5×10^3 a	3.0×10^3 a
Compost 1	2.8×10^2 ab	5.8×10^2 c	3.8×10^3 a	3.9×10^3 a
Compost 2	6.6×10^2 bc	8.4×10^2 d	8.7×10^4 c	6.3×10^3 a
Compost 3	8.5×10^2 c	1.2×10^3 e	5.2×10^4 b	2.3×10^4 b

Results in columns followed by the same letter are not significantly different from each other (P = 0.05).

TABLE IV: Number of cellulolytic microorganisms per g dry matter at the various sampling times in 1985

Treatment	Sampling time			
	June	July	September	October
Control	6.7×10^2 a	9.9×10^2 a	5.9×10^4 a	6.7×10^5 a
Mineral	5.8×10^2 a	3.3×10^3 a	1.5×10^5 a	1.1×10^6 b
Manure	1.9×10^3 b	2.5×10^3 a	2.8×10^4 a	3.1×10^5 c
Compost 1	8.7×10^2 a	2.9×10^3 a	1.4×10^5 a	8.3×10^5 ad
Compost 2	2.0×10^3 b	2.0×10^4 a	7.1×10^5 b	8.7×10^5 d
Compost 3	1.4×10^3 ab	7.8×10^4 a	1.0×10^5 a	5.2×10^5 ac

Results in columns followed by the same letter are not significantly different from each other (P = 0.05).

TABLE V: Number of autotrophic nitrifying bacteria per g dry matter at the various sampling times in 1983

Treatment	Sampling time		
	July	September	October
Control [*]	3.4×10^3 a	2.3×10^4 a	4.0×10 a
Manure	3.4×10^4 b	2.4×10^4 a	1.6×10^2 b
Compost 1	1.3×10^4 ac	5.8×10^4 a	3.5×10 a
Compost 2	1.0×10^4 ac	5.3×10^4 a	3.4×10 a
Compost 3	2.4×10^4 bc	2.8×10^4 a	4.1×10 a

Results in columns followed by the same letter are not significantly different from each other (P = 0.05).

TABLE VI: Number of autotrophic nitrifying bacteria per g dry matter at the various sampling times in 1984

Treatment	Sampling time			
	June	July	September	November
Control	5.8×10^3 a	3.9×10^3 a	1.8×10^5 a	1.4×10^6 a
Mineral	8.4×10^3 a	5.5×10^3 a	1.1×10^6 a	8.9×10^6 a
Manure	1.1×10^4 a	2.9×10^4 ab	6.5×10^5 a	1.5×10^6 a
Compost 1	1.8×10^4 ab	4.0×10^4 b	1.2×10^6 a	2.3×10^6 a
Compost 2	2.7×10^4 b	3.6×10^4 b	1.0×10^7 b	2.1×10^7 ab
Compost 3	2.6×10^4 b	3.7×10^4 b	8.2×10^6 b	3.6×10^7 b

Results in columns followed by the same letter are not significantly different from each other (P = 0.05).

631

TABLE VII: Number of autotrophic nitrifying bacteria per g dry
matter at the various sampling times in 1985

Treatment	Sampling time			
	June	July	September	October
Control	$4.3x10^{3}$ a	$1.1x10^{5}$ a	$3.3x10^{4}$ a	$1.7x10^{4}$ a
Mineral	$3.6x10^{4}$ a	$1.5x10^{6}$ a	$4.6x10^{5}$ a	$1.7x10^{5}$ b
Manure	$3.3x10^{5}$ a	$2.4x10^{5}$ a	$2.5x10^{3}$ a	$9.9x10^{3}$ a
Compost 1	$3.1x10^{5}$ a	$3.8x10^{3}$ a	$1.1x10^{4}$ a	$9.1x10^{3}$ a
Compost 2	$1.4x10^{5}$ a	$2.0x10^{5}$ a	$1.8x10^{5}$ a	$5.3x10^{4}$ a
Compost 3	$4.8x10^{5}$ a	$1.6x10^{6}$ a	$5.3x10^{4}$ a	$4.1x10^{4}$ a

Results in columns followed by the same letter are not significantly
different from each other (P = 0.05).

TABLE VIII: Total percentage infection in maize roots from six
different fertilizing trials, at three different
sampling times in 1984

Treatment	Sampling time		
	June	September	October
Control	7 c	22 b	15 b
Mineral	2 a	11 ab	2 a
Manure	0 a	5 a	3 a
Compost 1	2 a	24 b	21 b
Compost 2	2 a	21 b	5 a
Compost 3	4 a	14 ab	4 a

Results in columns followed by the same letter are not significantly
different from each other (P = 0.05).

TABLE IX: Total percentage infection in maize roots from six different
fertilizing trials, at three different sampling times in 1985

Treatment	Sampling time		
	June	September	October
Control	7.5 a	37.0 a	24.0 a
Mineral	19.0 a	12.5 b	6.0 b
Manure	5.0 a	22.5 ac	7.5 b
Compost 1	13.0 a	22.5 ac	16.0 a
Compost 2	40.0 a	17.5 bc	17.5 a
Compost 3	8.0 a	11.2 bc	9.3 b

Results in columns followed by the same letter are not significantly
different from each other (P = 0.05).

TABLE X: Number of colonies of pathogenic microorganisms per g of
compost (d.w.) in 1983, 1984, 1985

Microorganisms	1983	1984	1985
Salmonella sp	absent	absent	absent
Total Coliforms	$3 \times 10_2$	$1.2 \times 10_2$	$2.5 \times 10_2$
Faecal Streptococchi	$8 \times 10_2$	$8.2 \times 10_2$	$5.1 \times 10_3$

CONTROL OF A COMPOSTING PROCESS IN BIOREACTOR BY MONITORING CHEMICAL AND MICROBIAL PARAMETERS

B. CITTERIO, M. CIVILINI, A. RUTILI, A. PERA
and M. DE BERTOLDI
Istituto di Microbiologia Agraria, Università di Pisa and Centro Studio per la Microbiologia del Suolo, C.N.R., Pisa, Italy.

Summary

The aim of this research was to obtain a means by which composting in closed bioreactor could be checked on through chemical, physical and biological parameters. Colorimetric analysis and gas chromatography were used uninterruptedly to detect changes in the levels of oxygen, carbon dioxide, nitrogen, ammonium, hydrogen sulphide and water vapour in the internal atmosphere of the mass. Results indicated that only oxygen is a reliable indicator of the correct evolution of the process of composting.

1.1 Introduction

One of the most difficult technical problems to resolve in composting is monitoring the process (8,18,11,15,16). Spontaneously it evolves unevenly and does not give a standardized end-product (6,3), which gives a curing gradient varying according to the depth of the substrate.

One of the main causes for this gradient is inefficient oxygenation of the mass (6). The microorganisms involved in composting are aerobic and therefore consume oxygen. For this reason, this gas reaches very low levels (below 1%) in the lower layers of the mass after only two hours. In the upper layers contact with the external atmosphere guarantees a higher oxygen concentration (Fig. 1). The aerobic microorganisms involved in composting, require high levels of oxygen for their oxidative metabolism (3,4,5,10). So that a lack of oxygen does not limit the process, its level must not fall below 5% (11).

For this reason the practice of periodically turning the piles or of forced ventilation of windrows (by suction or blowing) has been adopted (4), but although this does ensure good oxygenation of the mass it has certain drawbacks which are impossible to eliminate without changing the aeration method (6,5). Simple periodical turning does not provide sufficient oxygen since anaerobic conditions arise inside the mass after only two or three hours (6).

This research was a contribution to the Research Project "Progetto Finalizzato: Energetica 2 sub-project: Biomass in Agriculture", Sottotema E.R. B.2.

For correct oxygenation the whole mass would have to be turned every two or three hours. This is impossible in practice partly because of high running costs and partly because of the disadvantages consequent on cooling the mass and its excessive dehydration.

On the other hand, forced ventilation – whether by blowing or suction through the bottom of the pile – creates curing gradients which cause enormous problems in obtaining a standardized and stabilized end-product. When air is blown through the bottom of the pile several things happen: there is swift dehydration and cooling of the lowest layers, but the all important factor for correct composting (oxygen supply, good moisture level and the right temperature) are created within the pile. Moisture level and temperature increase in the external layers of the pile (6,19). The effects of suction from the base are exactly the opposite: dehydration and rapid cooling of the outer layers with an increase in moisture and temperature in the lower layers (Fig. 2). This is revealed by transversal sectioning of a pile at the end of processing and analysing the section. Stratifications due to uneven curing are evident. The main consequence of this uneven processing is low quality and poorly sanitized compost, since pathogens are not eliminated where temperatures cannot reach a minimum of 55-60°C, and the product is not fit for farming purposes (7,14,18,19).

This research was planned to find by experiment those chemical, physical and biological parameters which would enable the process to be monitored in order to avoid the negative effects discussed here.

1.2 Materials and methods

It was chosen to use the organic fraction of solid urban waste as the raw material for composting. Pre-selection was carried out by a DANO plant (built at Pistoia, Italy). Table I gives the chemical and physical composition of the substrate.

A bioreactor with the following components was used:

1. MAIN COMPONENT: The bioreactor consists of two cylinders of 2 m³ each, constructed in fibreglass, a material which isolates from heat loss. The two cylinders, lying horizontally, can be opened at one end for charging and have a smaller opening on one side to allow sampling. Even distribution of air blown from the pumps is provided by a zinc grating placed 20 cm above the lowest part of the reactor.

One of these cylinders was used for gas chromatography and colorimetry analysis during the process; the lateral opening was kept tightly closed during the whole process while matter for sampling was taken from the second cylinder (Fig. 3 and 4).

2. COMPONENTS FOR GASEOUS ANALYSIS:

A) Gaschromatograph: An analytical gas-chromatograph AGC 111 with filament or thermistor thermal conductibility detector was used. These systems are interchangeable, the thermistor being used below 70°C and the filaments above this temperature. The apparatus has three columns:

    column 1 contains 80% poropak N + 20% poropak Q

    column 2 contains a 5 A molecular seive, and

    column 3 contains a second 5 A molecular seive.

It has two valves which govern in what order the gas passes through the columns. Continuous sampling is guaranteed by a microcomputer timer which can be programmed for 99 automatic analyses and by the attachment of instruments for registering data at required intervals.

B) <u>Colorimeter</u>: The TGH 555 can be used to measure the concentration of any particular gas - in the present case NH_3 - by reading the change in colour in the indicator. The flow of gas to be analyzed is regulated at a constant level by a vacuum pump. It passes through a reading-chamber. The intensity of colour is directly proportional to the concentration of the chosen gas and generates an electric signal amplified on a digital display screen and expressed as a percentage of the chosen range of values. The range chosen in the present case was from 0 to 100 ppm.

C) <u>Recorders</u>: Two dual channel recorders, BD 41, were attached to the colorimeter and gaschromatograph to obtain the graphs of the readings from the instruments.

3. AERATION: Oxygenation was carried out by blowing and suction through a perforated plastic tube running the length of the bioreactors inside the base. The fans had capacity of 0.1 m^3/min/metric Tonnes, enough to satisfy the requirements in oxygen. These fans are controlled by a timer which can be programmed for the various intervals of oxygenation required in different phases.

A tap on the pumps enables the direction of flow to be inverted when necessary.

4. TEMPERATURE CONTROL: This is carried out by three thermal couples placed at 10, 35 and 50 cm depth in the pile. These couples were connected to a recorder which gave instant readings and line graphs of temperatures during composting. When temperature differences between the highest and the lowest couples in the pile exceeded 15°C, flow was automatically inverted.

Gas samples were taken from perforated copper containers with a filter, placed at the same depth as the thermocouples. They were connected to a gaschromatograph by copper piping with taps to permit analyses in order of depth (Fig. 5). The gasses investigated during the 30 days of testing were: O_2, CO_2, N_2, H_2S, NH_3, H_2S, H_2O. Before charging the cylinders, moisture content in the raw material was 45% (see Table I). It was raised to 57% to improve composting conditions. The quantity of matter in each bioreactor was 10 qtls.

1.3 <u>Results</u>

The following are the analyses of data obtained from continuous monitoring of gasses present in the internal atmosphere of the composting mass.

<u>H_2O</u>: The percentage of water present within the mass is not proportional to the moisture of the composting mass itself. Generally, within certain limits, the internal atmosphere is almost saturated with water vapour; since saturation point depends on air temperature, water vapour content is unsuitable as a parameter for monitoring the process.

<u>NH_3/H_2S</u>: These products are abundantly present during the early stages of the process but tend to disappear as bio-oxidation of the mass by the microorganisms progresses. In the early stages ammonium is produced by hydrolysis of quaternary compounds. It partially volatilizes and is partially oxidised biologically by the nitrifying bacteria present in the mass [1,2]. Hydrogen sulphide undergoes a similar fate. It is produced by hydrolysis of proteins and sulphur compounds and is then oxidized by some of the sulphur bacteria (Fig. 6). For this reason these parameters would be more useful for measuring the stage reached in curing than for checking on the process. It must not be overlooked, however, that their

absolute levels in the internal atmosphere of the mass depend on the chemical composition of raw material at the outset. They can only be used as indicators for the degree of curing when the whole arc of the process is taken into consideration.

N_2:   This is the gas present in the greatest amount inside the mass. Percentage variations during the process are directly related to percentage variations of other gasses, in particular CO_2 and O_2. It is evident that molecular nitrogen is consumed by free nitrogen-fixers during composting but in such low amounts as to be irrelevant (2,3,4). For this reason analysis of this gas is not suitable for checking on the process.

CO_2:   Percentage varies with variations in microbial activity, this gas being the end or intermediate product of microbial metabolism. When aeration during composting is insufficient the CO_2 gradient may exceed 17-18%. Since carbon dioxide is produced by aerobic and anaerobic respiration as well as fermentation, its presence and variations in level within the internal atmosphere of the mass cannot be considered as a reliable indicator for good processing, that is, of exclusively oxidative processes which involve aerobic respiration.

O_2:   In microbial metabolism, oxygen is consumed only during aerobic respiration and therefore during all processes which involve oxidation of organic matter. There is in fact a precise stechiometric relationship betweem oxygen consumption and oxidized organic matter (13,14). This, therefore, is the most suitable parameter of all those considered here for checking on the process.

When the use of this parameter is applied to monitoring and controlling the process of composting from beginning to end, results are highly satisfying. When continuous readings of the level of this gas in the internal atmosphere of the mass are fed into a computer, a curve results which graphically expresses the concentration of oxygen in the sample analyzed. In theory this curve should tend to become a straight line with an angular coefficient equal to zero when composting evolves correctly. The observation of negative or positive variations in this angular coefficient could be used for modifying the air flow, so restoring correct values. If air is blown or suctioned constantly, anomalous values for oxygen and carbon dioxide would be registered, according to the metabolic stage of the process. In other words, during lively microbial activity oxygenation would be too low and the carbon dioxide level would increase (Fig. 7).

1.4   Conclusions

An efficient check on the process of composting can be obtained by continuously reading the oxygen level in the internal atmosphere of the mass during composting, in association with constant temperature readings, continuous gas analyses and by feeding data into a calculator (Fig. 8). This enables the fans to be manoeuvered in such a way that the whole process from beginning to end has ventilation required for each stage, with oxygen levels between 5 and 15%. Temperature readings at several levels inside the mass, which govern a change in the direction of air flow when differences exceed 15°C, guarantee standardized curing throughout the mass since they eliminate the drawbacks of oxygen, moisture and temperature gradients. The advantages of using this method are as follows:

1)   The best possible evolution of the process of composting, which also means time-saving as well as a high-quality end-product;

2) Guaranteed sanitization of the mass thanks to even distribution of oxygen, which then ensures an evenly-distributed temperature throughout the mass;
3) Considerable saving in terms of energy, since the fans only blow or suck as much air as is needed and no more at each stage in the process.

BIBLIOGRAPHY

1. BISHOP P.L., GODFREY C. (1983). Nitrogen transformations during sludge composting. BioCycle, 4, 34-39.
2. DE BERTOLDI M., VALLINI G., PERA A., ZUCCONI F. (1982). Comparison of three windrow compost system. BioCycle, 23 (2)45-50.
3. DE BERTOLDI M., VALLINI G., PERA A. (1982). Ecologia microbica del compostaggio. Ann. Microbiol. 32, 121-135.
4. DE BERTOLDI M., VALLINI G., PERA A. (1983). The biology of composting: a review. Waste Management and Research 1 (8), 157-176.
5. DE BERTOLDI M., PERA A., VALLINI G. (1983). The principles of composting. Proceedings of the international Symposium on "Biological reclamation and land utilization of urban waste". Naples 11-14 Oct., 1983. Ed. F. Zucconi, M. de Bertol, di, S. Coppola.
6. DE BERTOLDI M., VALLINI G., PERA A., ZUCCONI F. (1984). Technological aspects of composting including modelling and microbiology. In R&D Programme recycling of urban and industrial waste. Seminar on composting agricultural and other wastes, Oxford, 20-22 March, 1984.
7. DE BERTOLDI M., FRASSINETTI S., BIANCHIN L., PERA A. (1985). Sludge Hygienization with different compost systems. Joint Seminar CEC-German Veterinary Medical Society: inactivation of Microorganisms in Sewage Sludge by Stabilisation Processes. Hohenheim 8-10 Oct., 1984. Eds. D. Strauch. A.H. Havelaar and P. L'Hermite.
8. FINSTEIN M.S., CIRELLO J., MACGREGOR S.T., MILLER F.C., PSARIANOS K.M. (1980). "Sludge composting and utilization; rational approach to process control. Final Report to USEPA, NJ DEP, CC MUA, Rutgers University, New Brunswick, NJ, USA.
9. FINSTEIN M.S., MILLER F.C. (1984). Principle of composting leading to maximization of decomposition rate, odour control and cost effectiveness. Seminar on composting agricultural and other wastes, Oxford, 20-22 March, 1984.
10. FINSTEIN M.S., MORRIS M.L. (1975). Microbiology of municipal solid waste composting. Adv. Appl. Microbiol. 19, 113.11.
11. FINSTEIN M.S., MILLER F.C., STROM P.F., MACGREGOR S.T., PSARIANOS K.M. (1983). Composting ecosystem management for waste treatment. Bio/Technology 1, 347.
12. GOLUEKE C.G. (1977). Biological reclamation of solid wastes. Rodale Press Emmaus PA, USA.
13. HAUG R.T. (1979). Engineering principles of sludge composting. J. Water Poll. Contr. Fed. 51, 2189-2195.
14. HAUG R.T. (1980). Compost engineering: principle and practice. Ann. Arbor. Science, Ann Arbor, Michigan, USA.
15. MACGREGOR S.T., MILLER F.C., PSARIANOS K.M., FINSTEIN M.S. (1981). Composting process control based on interaction between microbial

heat output and temperature. Applied Environm. Microbiol. 41, 1321–1330.

16. MILLER F.C., FINSTEIN M.S. (1983). Equipment for control and monitoring of high rate composting. Proceedings of the international Symposium on "Biological reclamation and land utilization of urban waste". Naples 11-14 Oct., 1983. Ed. F. Zucconi, M. de Bertoldi, S. Coppola.

17. PEREIRA-NETO J.T., STENTIFORD E.I., MARA D.D., SMITH D.V. (at press). Survival of fecal indicator microorganisms in refuse/sludge composting using the aerated static pile system. Proceedings of the international Symposium on "Compost: production, quality and use". Udine 17-19 Apr., 1986.

18. STRAUCH D. (at press). Microbial specifications of disinfected compost. Proceedings of the international Symposium on "Compost: production, quality and use". Udine 17-19 Apr., 1986.

19. STRAUCH D., DE BERTOLDI M. (at press). Microbiological specifications of disinfected sewage sludge. Proceedings of the 4th international Symposium on "Processing and use of organic sludge and liquid agricultural wastes". Rome 8-11 Oct., 1985.

TABLE I: Physical and chemical characteristics of the biodegradable reaction of solid urban waste (S.U.W.) used for experimentation in bioreactor (% dry matter).

Moisture	45.0	%
pH	8.4	%
Ash	36.0	%
Organic matter	64.1	%
Organic carbon	37.3	%
Total nitrogen	1.1	%
C/N ratio	33.9	%
P_2O_5	0.2	%
K_2O	0.7	%
Cu	188.7	mg/Kg
Zn	169.8	mg/Kg
Pb	235.0	mg/Kg
Ni	11.0	mg/Kg
Cr	112.1	mg/Kg

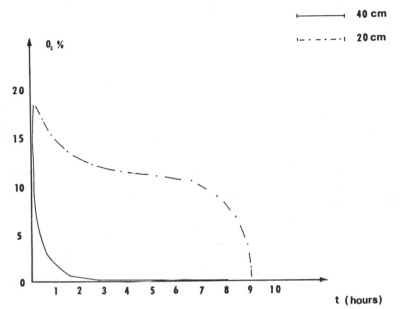

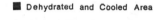

Figure 1 : Variation in Oxygen content in the internal atmosphere of the mass, without areation, at two different levels

■ Dehydrated and Cooled Area

□ Favourable Conditions

▦ Moisture and Temperature Excess Area

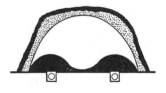

BLOWING

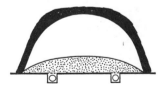

SUCTION

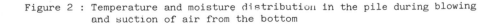

Figure 2 : Temperature and moisture distribution in the pile during blowing and suction of air from the bottom

Figure 3 : Bio-reactor in fiberglass

Figure 4 : Main opening of cylinder for charging

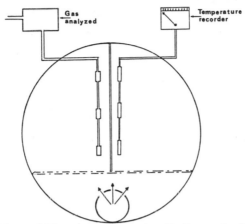

Figure 5 : Section of Bio-reactor showing instruments for measuring temperature and gas detection

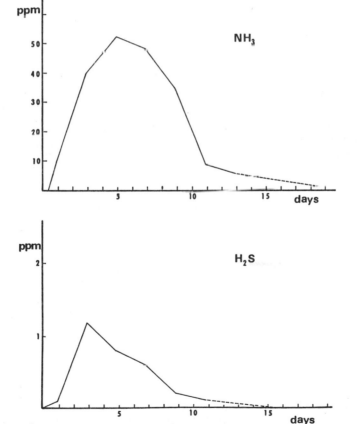

Figure 6 : Developments in the production of NH_3 and H_2S during composting

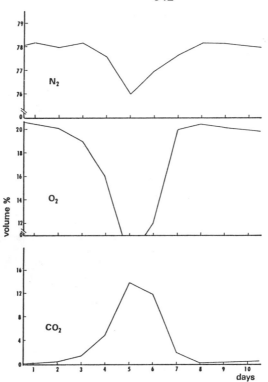

Figure 7 : Anomalous conditions ausing during composting with continuous areation

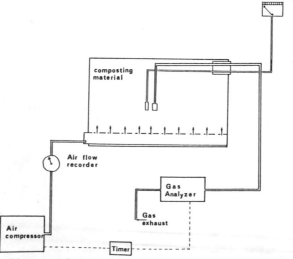

Figure 8 : Diagram of composting plant with instrumentation

FERTILIZING VALUE AND HEAVY METAL LOAD OF SOME COMPOSTS FROM URBAN REFUSE

P. Paris[1], A. Robotti[2], C. Gavazzi[1]

[1] Istituto di Agronomia, Botanica e Genetica Vegetale, Facoltà di Agraria, Università Cattolica del S. Cuore - Piacenza (Italy)
[2] Azienda Agraria Sperimentale "V. Tadini" - Podenzano, Piacenza

Summary

As part of two research programmes on compost production and evaluation - supported by C.N.R., Progetto Finalizzato Energetica, and, separately, by Regione Emilia Romagna - several field experiments have been carried out on maize, durum wheat, Italian ryegrass and sorghum, at four sites in Northern Italy, between 1978 and 1985. This paper is a concise account of the main results obtained. The kinds of compost tested have shown only minor differences with regard to their ability in supplying N to crops. They have usually proved to increase yields over the control soil between 10 and 25 %. Within the first year from application, the crops have shown a rather low N recovery - 2 to 9 % of the total N ploughed in - from compost rates ranging from 6 to 15 and up to 40 Mg/ha yr of OM. The overall ratio between compost and FYM as regards their N supplying power is fairly close to 1, with local soil factors for single season interacting sometimes in favour of one of the two.
After the addition of compost, the soil shows consistent improvement of its pH, as well as of its OM and total N content.
Even after 3 year application of compost, plants seem to remain unaffected by the HM added to the soil. Statistically significant differences are very rarely found between control and treated plants. In the soil, HM tend to accumulate in the "total" pool ($HNO_3/HClO_4$ extr.), with some effects even on the DTPA-extractable values.

1. Introductory remarks.

A research unit on compost production and evaluation was organized at the section of General Agronomy, Faculty of Agriculture, U.C.S.C., Piacenza, in 1977. The grouping was prompted by C.R.P.A. (Centro Ricerche Produzioni Animali - Reggio Emilia). It was aimed to carry out experiments on several aspects of compost production from urban refuse - on a pilot plant made available by Secit (MI) - as well as to test the agronomical value of such composts, both as organic manures for field crops and as physical amendments for soils.

With the financial support of the Progetto Finalizzato Energetica (C.N.R.) an initial programme was developed in three main steps : a) experimental production of composts and their physical and chemical characterization; b) preliminary greenhouse tests on crops (perennial ryegrass) during winter and spring; c) field experiments on maize, under repeated annual applications. The first research period ended in 1981. A final report was issued by C.N.R. as a "Libro bianco", in 1982 (4).

A second programme - again supported by C.N.R. and ENEA through the 2nd Progetto Finalizzato Energetica - was started in 1984 and is now undergoing its 3rd year activity. It is mainly centred in the study of the fate of HM added to the soil, though not disregarding the basic positive action of compost, i.e. its effects on yield, N supply to crops and soil improvement.

In the meantime, between 1982 and 1984, other field trials were carried out on the same topics, as part of a programme set up by Regione Emilia Romagna.

In this paper we will only review field experiment work, leaving aside all the matters concerning compost production and greenhouse testing. Moreover, data will be only referred to as by way of example, rather than as a full report, owing to scanty space available. Such data have been choosen among 13 'site-year-crop' combinations.

The rationale of the whole programme is a thorough comparison between compost from urban refuse and FYM (farmyard manure), in order to assess up to which extent the first can be used as a substitute for the disappearing FYM, in intensive arable agriculture where soils are being more and more deprived of their humus supply.

2. Materials and methods

The experimental work carried out so far may be divided into three groups.
Group 1 - From 1977 to 1980, three kinds of compost were yearly prepared on the Inka-Secit plant : the basic one - which we will refer to as the "C" type - made from straight sorted refuse, was always present in our experiments. The other two kinds were prepared by enrichment of the same "C" material with : a) waste cardboard and paper; b) effluents from piggery. Since no relevant differences have ever been detected among the three materials tested, at the end of the 4 year period, we will only consider the "C" compost in comparison with FYM taken as the standard organic manure.

The three experimental sites - Croara, Verano and Gariga - were all just around Piacenza, on alluvial loam to silty loam soils of very weak structure. Their main characters are shown below.

		Croara	Verano	Gariga
pH (H$_2$O)		7.75	6.50	6.59
(0.1 M KCl)		7.15	5.75	5.86
OM	%	1.98	1.70	1.80
Total N	%	0.135	0.117	0.125
Total P	%	0.065	0.052	(n.d.)
Available P (Olsen)	ppm	9	23	57
Total K	%	0.76	1.03	(n.d.)
Exchangeable K	ppm	97	155	81
Total CaCO$_3$	%	16.4	nil	nil

Compost and FYM were annually incorporated into the soil for three (Croara and Verano) or two (Gariga) subsequent years. The experiments were designed in a randomized complete block layout, with four replications, and split-plotting was superimposed to ensure the possibility of evaluating both cumulated and single carry-over effects of several applications. Maize was always grown, except in the 4th year in Verano (1981) when durum wheat was taken for residual effects to be controlled. In all three fields, other treatments were added, based on commercial N,P and K fertilizers given alone or in combination with organic manure. In the field experiment at Gariga (1980-1981), two other commercial kinds of compost from urban refuse were added to the three from our pilot plant : a Dano compost from Pistoia (marked as PT), and a Daneco compost from Udine (marked as UD). Comparison was based on a same rate of OM added, rather than on N. For Croara and Verano the applied amount was 11.4 Mg/ha yr, while for Gariga the rate was 6 Mg/ha yr. The average chemical composition of 4 kinds of organic manures is shown on Table 1, section I. Since outstanding differences among the composts tested were never detected, yields of crops and their N uptake are listed in Tables 2 and 3 only for the "C" and FYM treatments.

Group 2 - During 1983 and 1984, for field tests on maize, batches of the "C" compost were processed on the Inka-Secit plant mentioned above. In the mean time, the sorting and shredding operations of raw refuse had been modified and the quality of compost - as far as volatile solids are concerned - was clearly improved as shown by figures in Table 1, section II. The field site was at the Azienda Agraria Sperimentale "V. Tadini", in Gariga (PC) and the soil was very close to the one already described (see Gariga site, on previ ous page), both being from the same farm. The experimental design was a rand omized complete block with four replications. Several rates of the "C" compost were tested against control and FYM, as well as N,P,K treatments with commer cial fertilizers. In this paper, we will consider only "C" and FYM treatments at the same OM rate (10 Mg/ha yr).

Group 3 - Agronomical field tests of this last programme were established on the same farm, at the Azienda Agraria Sperimentale in Gariga, as per Group 2. Together with the control soil, five treatments are compared, with the follow ing specifications : FYM, C 1, C 2, PT and UD.The rate of compost and FYM tested is 15 Mg/ha yr of OM, except for C 2, which is at 40 Mg/ha yr. C, as well as PT and UD, composts have the same origin as stated above. The main purpose of this research is to trace the fate of HM added to the soil with composts, while positive effects on crop yield and soil characters are comple mentary targets. The experimental design is a randomized complete block of six treatments with four replications, without any arrangement to account for carry-over effects.

At the outset, in autumn 1983, the soil was sampled at two depths (0-30 and 30-50 cm) and analyzed at plot scale. Values for its physical and chemical characters are given below as means of 24 analyses (no significant variation has been detected) : texture : sand 49.2 %; silt 31.1 %; clay 19.7 %; pH (0.01 M CaCl$_2$) 6.16; OM (Walkley and Black) 1.54 %; total N (Kjeldahl) 0.098 %; C.E.C. (BaCl$_2$, pH 8.1) 17.2 meq/100 g. In 1983, the organic manures were incorporated to the soil by mean of a mouldboard plough (30 cm) and in 1984 by a rotary digger (20 cm). The first year crop was Italian ryegrass, v. Tiara while the second year crop was sorghum (NK 180).

Referring to initial HM content of the soil, analyses were taken from the two depth samples of each plot, following three extractions : 1 M KNO$_3$, for the 'soluble and exchangeable' amounts; 0.005 M DTPA, for the 'available' amounts and HNO$_3$/HClO$_4$ (conc.; 1:1 ratio) for the 'total' contents. At harvest, forage samples from all treatments and replications were analyzed for N,P,K, Ca and for total Cd, Cr, Cu, Fe, Mn, Mo, Ni, Pb, Zn. Soil is re-sampled after the crop, and HM analyses are repeated in order to ascertain possible varia tions in the three concentrations.

As far as yield effects are concerned, we will refer only to C and FYM treatments, since the three composts tested haven't displayed any differen tial behaviour, so far. As for HM, it seems interesting to report on the findings from all the four compost treatments, leaving aside FYM which obvious ly is of no relevance to the subject.

3. Results and discussion

3.1 Yield effects of compost

As a rule, compost gives usually rise to small yield increments, at least under our experimental conditions. From time to time, in single field trials differences between control and C treatments were unsignificant, mostly when the OM rate applied was below 10 Mg/ha yr, but sometimes even under heavier applications.

Repeated manuring in field experiments that last two or more years should bring about progressively superior performances of the compost treatment,this being due to increasing decline of fertility in the control soil deprived of any maintenance supply. Anyway, this trend can be very rarely observed, since season factors frequently overwhelm the effect of this faint decline, masking the depletion of soil fertility.

Table 2 gives some of the results we obtained, comparing control, C and FYM yields. When field trials were based on repeated annual manuring, yield figures have been corrected by the following procedure, in order to isolate and discard the superimposed carry-over effects :

$$Y_j = Y_0 + Y_{jn} - Y_{j(n-1)}$$

where :

Y_j = yield of the j treatment (compost or FYM) due to the last annual rate;

Y_0 = control yield;

Y_{jn} = observed yield of the j treatment in the n year, including all the carry-over effects;

$Y_{j(n-1)}$ = yield of the carry-over effect subtreatment.

To allow quick comparisons between treatments, percentage increments of yield due to C and FYM are shown in the same table. The C/FYM ratio is usually close to 1, with some scattering for single trials. The mean ratio is 0.98. It can thus be stated that compost from urban refuse and FYM are very similar in their ability to sustain the yield of crops.

This similarity, however, is mainly due to the low nutrient release from FYM rather than to the good performance of compost. The experimental layout of Croara (1978-1980), Verano (1978-1981) and Gariga (1980-1981) included a treatment with commercial fertilizers given in amounts corresponding to the N, P and K availability rates assumed for FYM by Cooke (1 ; see on page 95), that is : 1/3 of the total N in FYM, 1/2 of the total P and 100 % of total K. The yields offered by this treatment were always largely higher than those by FYM. Furthermore, the addition of 150 kg/ha of N from chemical fertilizers to organic manures - in Gariga field - resulted in a fading of the yield effects by the latters.

3.2 Availability of N from compost

The small yield response of the crops commented above is basically due to the low mineralization of the OM added to the soil with compost and to the consequent scanty amount of N supplied to the plants during the first year.

Table 3 enables a rough estimate of the availability of total N content of compost to be made. When necessary, these figures were corrected in a way similar to that for yields, to account for carry-over effects. Obviously, total N uptake data were put in the formula, to substitute for the yield data.

The nine 'year-site' pairs of data for which the C/FYM ratio may be worked out, give a general mean of 0.90. Once again, a substantial similarity between compost and FYM does exist, even in this respect.

If C/FYM ratios were calculated using the total N uptake figures, or the extra N quantities found in the C and FYM treatments (i.e., using data of columns 6 and 7, or 8 and 9, respectively) - instead of the percentage values of apparent N recovery (columns 10 and 11) - the mean ratios for the ten pairs of data come out to be closer to 1, in actual fact 0.997 and 0.994. This parity between the two organic manures undoubtedly springs from the FYM having low mineralization coefficients. The mean N recovery is 5.26 % for compost and 5.62 % for FYM, the last one being definitively lower than the figures suggested by Cooke (1).

In the years after application, the availability of N present in the compost ploughed under becomes smaller and smaller. On Verano experimental site, cumulated N recovery in crops at the end of the experimental period (1978-1981 : 3 years of maize and 1 year of durum wheat) totalled only 17 and 20 % from initial compost amounts equivalent to 302 and 604 kg/ha of N.

3.3 The soil as affected by compost

As compost and FYM contributions to N nutrition of the crops have come out to be so small, a consistent effect of these organic manures onto some properties of the soil - such as OM and total N content - was to be expected.

The analyses carried out on soil samples of two out of the four experimental sites have confirmed this suggestion. Introductory data of soil analyses for Verano soil are presented in table 4, section I. There is clear evidence of the role played by compost in restoring low OM and total N content of soil, as well as in improving soil pH. Even with regard to these aspects, compost and FYM reveal a very similar behaviour. Estimates of the OM amounts recovered in final soil samples give an approximate figure of 50 % of the total ploughed in, under the assumption that total volatile solids in the compost are 90 % true decomposable OM.

In the field trials now in progress (Gariga 1984-1985), the subject is receiving great attention. All plots are sampled and analyses are being runned for all treatments, at the harvest of the year crop. Table 4, section II, shows present trends. The agreement with the previous findings is very good for the three characters tested. While control soil is undergoing increasing acidification of the top layer, all the composts and FYM develop a strong counteracting effect, capable of rising soil pH towards neutral values. Two out of the three compost, namely C 1 and UD, are statistically more effective than FYM. Considering the same kind of compost, the pH increase is proportional to the amount applied (C 1 and C 2), while when different kinds of organic manures are compared on the same OM amount basis, the effect is neater where non-volatile solids in the DM are higher (UD > C 1 > FYM).

Composts and FYM, anyway, affect OM and total N content of soil in a no less consistent way. While the control soil seems to rest in a steady state (higher values found in 1985 samples are to be considered as erratic), OM and N rates annually applied and left in the soil lead to large statistical differences among the treatments tested. C 2, with its remarkably higher amounts applied each year, shows the highest increases which are statistically significant over all the remaining treatments. Here again, the extra OM found by soil analyses accounts for 45 % of the total OM given in two years.

3.4 The load of heavy metals in compost and the crop response

HM presence in compost and the hazard of their possible mobility from soil to crop (or to groundwater) has to be regarded as the main drawback for the agricultural disposal of urban refuse. This subject had just been sounded in field trials of the Group 1, while it is fully investigated in the experiments that are being runned at present (Gariga 1984-1985).

Table 5 shows a broad outline of HM concentrations in the batches of compost we have used. The elements checked vary in a relatively low degree with the kind of compost. In the Dano batches (PT) lower values for Fe, Mn and Ni are commonly found, while Cr is higher than in C compost from Inka-Secit plant.

A few differences may be found between the "C" experimental compost prepared and tested in the first years (1978-1981), and those of the last period (1983-1985). Such differences are explained by the already mentioned changes in sorting and shredding of the raw refuse. Tabulated data for all composts, anyway, compare well to those given in the literature (see, for instance, summarized values from several sources in Tab. 1.2, pg 33, refer. 4).It should be underlined that - as a general rule - Cd shows rather low concentrations.

Plant samples from the crops grown during 1978-1980 were systematically analyzed only for Cu, Mn and Zn. The concentrations found in Control, FYM and "C" plants are shown in table 6, section I. NS indication for F test is drawn from a wider layout including some other treatments which haven't been consi dered here. No increase in HM content due to compost application was ever det ected. Data from the 3rd year crop were choosen,to demonstrate that even those from the previous crops were unaffected by the applied amounts. The only case where statistical significance was found,is to be considered occas ional, as it is just one out of six 'site-year' combinations checked (Verano, grain Zn; C = FYM but C > Control).

Plants seem to be essentially insensitive to HM added to the soil, at least when annual rates of compost are not too heavy. Such a view is largely confirmed by data shown in Table 6, section II, and referring to Italian rye grass and sorghum. Fe and Mo were left aside as they are very unlike to deter mine toxicity symptoms in crops. No one of the HM tested increased its concen tration in plant tissues, neither in the first year nor in the second one. Statistical differences for Cd and Zn take place only from lower FYM values.

3.5 Heavy metals in the soil

What happens to the HM put into the soil and not taken up by plants : this is the problem which we first considered in the last two years and the one we are now dealing with (Gariga 1984-1985). Soil from all plots has been sampled each year and extracted by the three solutions specified above.

Table 7 presents a concise summary of the results we have obtained for the DTPA- and strong acid-extractable concentrations of the five more relev ant HM. Fe was left aside as it never changed the original high content of the soil (over 3 %). As for Cd, DTPA and strong acid concentrations in init ial soil samples - as well as those for total values in the samples taken after the first crop - were frequently below the sensitivity threshold of the AA spectrophotometer. For this reason, we only have complete sets of data for total Cd in samples taken after the second crop (1985) and for the DTPA- -extractable concentrations of the last two sampling occasions (1984 and 1985). While the total figures do not show any appreciable variation among treatments, the last DTPA extractions gave the following picture (ppm) :

Control	C 1	C 2	PT	UD
0.04 A	0.06 A	0.10 B	0.06 A	0.06 A

It can be seen that all composts start setting up small differences with respect to control soil, C 2 treatment being the only one statistically signi ficant.

DTPA extractions for Cr never gave instrumental readings, while the total values remained unchanged through the treatments. Total Mo in this soil is very low (around 1.5 ppm) and does not reveal any variation owing to the compost application; it has been discarded in the second year work.

The whole available results concerning the five remaining HM entitle the following comments. Two year applications of compost - even in large rates - have not modified the detectable concentrations of Mn and Ni, in neither kind of extracting solution. Only after the second application, Cu and Zn started a build-up process resulting both in higher DTPA and in higher total concentrations. On the contrary, Pb had a prompt reply, with both extractions showing clear increases, already after the first application of compost.

At present, KNO$_3$-extractable concentrations are of no relevance. Only

very weak values for Mn, Ni and Zn were recorded so far. They do not show
any hint of an increase, but rather suggest a non-mobility condition among
the chemical forms considered. Whenever statistical differences have been
found, the highest values are those of the control soil, as if the extra
yield afforded by compost were to bring about a shortage in the readily avai
lable pool of these metals.

The search for possible reasons for the increase in Cu, Pb and Zn values
brings to set up an approximate balance sheet of the metals we are considering,
in order to estimate the percentage by which the applied compost has increa
sed the starting content of the soil. The figures below show that Cu, Pb and

At start 1983 †	HM added with compost (two year applications)				% increment due to compost			
	C 1 †	C 2 †	PT †	UD †	C 1	C 2	PT	UD
Cd 1.44	0.30	0.82	0.30	0.41	21	57	21	28
Cr 170	6.6	17.7	6.6	6.4	4	10	4	4
Cu 117	14.6	39.1	13.4	17.5	12	33	11	15
Mn 3370	30.1	80.5	13.9	57.6	0.9	2.4	0.4	0.2
Ni 493	7.0	18.8	2.2	3.0	1.4	3.8	0.4	0.6
Pb 53	39.9	106.6	22.4	26.4	75	201	42	50
Zn 300	38.5	103.0	28.9	77.8	13	34	10	26

† kg/ha in the top 30 cm

Zn are three of the four HM for which the soil was greatly enriched.

The mobility and the risk of dangerous build up of HM content in the
soil seem to be tightly related both to the extent of the change occurred
in the size of the DTPA and total pools due to applications, on one hand,
and to the individual dynamic properties of the chemistry of the single
metal. Up to now, Cd exhibited only small increases probably because of its
low initial content and the relatively small amounts annually added.

4. Conclusions

Summing up 8 years' results of field experiments designed to test the
agricultural value of compost from urban refuse, we can consider that its
use in arable agriculture can give rise to moderate yield increases, through
small amounts of N released to the crop, during the first year from applica
tion. In our trials, N recovered by plants never exceeded 9 % of the total
amount applied, and this figure is near to, or a bit lower than, those repor
ted by Pauli (5).

Quite larger effects are likely to be brought about on some important
characters such as pH, OM and total N content of soils.

Under our experimental conditions, compost and FYM have very often proved
to be equal in their crop fertilizing and soil amending efficiencies, by way
of a low mineralization of FYM organic matter rather than of a high mineral
ization from compost.

Such an equivalency might well disappear in soils of poor K status or
under highly K-demanding crops, since the outstanding difference between
compost and FYM is that FYM supplies much more K.

The amending properties of compost which appear in the improvement of
soil pH seem to be a quite appreciable point in favour of its use for agricul
tural purposes. As it can rise soil pH from sub-acidic towards neutral values,

it ensures a low mobility status to the HM it brings into the soil, and in this way chemical pollution of the crop is prevented (2, 3).

In the first two or three years of repeated application, HM delivered to the soil through compost do not create serious problems to the plants, if the amounts used are large enough - up to 40 Mg/ha yr of OM equivalent - without being too high. They anyway tend to build up enrichments in the total and DTPA-extractable concentrations. Pb, followed by Cu and Zn, is the first metal to develop this trend, because of both its relatively small presence in the soil and of the high concentrations found in compost. In the mid-term, prolonged yearly application may result in a critical overloading of the soil C.E.C.

REFERENCES

1. COOKE,G.W. (1982). Fertilizing for Maximum Yield. Granada, London (3rd ed.)
2. COTTENIE, A. (1982). Assimilation Power of Soils for Industrial Waste Products : Possibilities and Limitations. Intern. Conference on Application and Recycling of Resources in Agriculture, Milan.
3. LEEPER, G.W. (1978). Managing the Heavy Metals on the Land. Dekker, New York.
4. PARIS, P., ROBOTTI, A. and GAVAZZI C., (1982). Prove agronomiche di compost da rifiuti solidi urbani. CNR - PFE - Libro Bianco 7, Roma.
5. PAULI, F.W. (1967). Soil Fertility. A Biodynamical Approach. Hilger, London.

TABLE 1. Analyses of organic manures used.

I - 3 year mean values and SEM, 1978-1980 - (Group 1)

		FYM	"C"	PT	UD
pH		8.4 ± 0.3	7.8 ± 0.1	7.4 ± 0.8	8.3 ± 0.6
DM	%	23.2 ± 2.6	63.1 ± 5.4	55.4 ± 13.3	60.7 ± 7.9
			on DM basis		
Vol. solids[†]	%	56.5 ± 0.4	23.2 ± 0.5	67.5 ± 7.6	22.7 ± 0.9
Total N	%	2.10 ± 0.19	0.94 ± 0.12	1.42 ± 0.11	0.76 ± 0.04
Total P	%	0.87 ± 0.35	0.24 ± 0.03	0.26 ± 0.02	0.29 ± 0.02
Total K	%	3.03 ± 0.91	0.32 ± 0.15	0.64 ± 0.09	0.27 ± 0.06
approx. C/N		15	14	27	18

II - Values of one batch per year.

		1983		1984	
		FYM	"C"	FYM	"C"
DM	%	28.9	49.3	29.0	87.4
			on DM basis		
Vol. solids[†]	%	55.3	33.5	60.2	42.9
Total N	%	1.49	1.14	2.00	1.38
Total P	%	0.15	0.26	0.66	0.27
Total K	%	1.75	0.51	2.49	0.66
approx. C/N		20	16	17	17

III - Values of one batch per year.

		1984				1985			
		FYM	C [††]	PT	UD	FYM	C [††]	PT	UD
pH		8.7	8.1	7.5	7.4	8.3	7.6	7.6	8.0
DM	%	27.8	85.5	60.1	60.7	34.2	81.7	73.2	69.8
					on DM basis				
Vol. solids[†]	%	70.5	46.7	68.4	23.3	73.2	40.5	59.0	28.0
Total N	%	2.17	1.41	1.24	0.59	2.23	1.35	1.17	0.65
Total P	%	0.84	0.27	0.21	0.35	0.65	0.30	0.28	0.22
Total K	%	2.66	0.70	0.54	0.31	1.42	0.67	0.54	0.25
approx. C/N		18	19	31	22	18	17	29	26

[†] By ignition at 600 °C.
[††] C applies for C 1 and C 2 in next tables.

TABLE 2. Yields of different crops as affected by "C" and FYM treatments. (Mg/ha; total above-ground DM, unless otherwise stated).

Site and year	Crop	OM rate	Yield			% yield increment of C over control	Ratio C/FYM
			Control	"C"	FYM		
V - 1979 (2nd)	Maize	11.4 a	9.71	11.08	10.66	+ 14	1.04
V - 1980 (3rd)	Maize	11.4 a	9.72	12.33	10.88	+ 27	1.13
V - 1981 (4th)	Durum wheat	- b	3.65	5.81	5.76	+ 59	1.01
C - 1979 (2nd)	Maize	11.4 a	13.42	12.87	14.60	(- 4)	0.88
C - 1980 (3rd)	Maize	11.4 a	8.55	10.14	11.90	+ 19	0.85
G - 1980 (1st)	Maize	6.0 c	22.14	22.53	23.42	+ 2	0.96
G - 1981 (2nd)	Maize	6.0 c	16.71	18.27	19.07	+ 9	0.96
G - 1983 (1st)	Maize	10.0 c†	8.84	9.54	9.35	+ 8	1.02
G - 1984 (2nd)	Maize	10.0 d†	13.37	15.81	15.68	+ 18	1.01
G - 1984 (1st)	Ryegrass	15.0 c	5.20	6.55	6.97	+ 26	0.94
G - 1985 (2nd)	Sorghum	15.0 d	6.88	7.73	8.10	+ 12	0.95

V = Verano; C = Croara; G = Gariga.

a "C" and FYM values are yields from single year application (adjusted, see text).

b Carry-over effect after 3 year applications.

c "C" and FYM yields are from single applications.

d "C" and FYM yields are from 2 repeated applications.

† Grain yield as DM

TABLE 3. N uptake by crops and percentage of apparent N recovery from compost and FYM. (kg/ha, unless otherwise stated).

| Site and year | Crop | N added with treatment | | N recovered in crop | | | N uptake over control | | % apparent recovery | | C/FYM |
		"C"	FYM	Control	"C"	FYM	"C"	FYM	"C"	FYM	(on % values)
V - 1979	Maize	398	416	69	86†	83†	17	14	4.3	3.4	1.26
V - 1980	Maize	533	465	67	95†	71†	28	4	5.3	0.9	5.88
C - 1979	Maize	398	416	102	99†	115†	(- 3)	13	-	7.2	-
C - 1930	Maize	533	465	59	74†	89†	15	30	2.8	6.5	0.43
G - 1980	Maize	280	247	193	210	206	17	13	6.9	6.7	1.03
G - 1981	Maize	240	205	120	141	143	21	23	8.8	11.2	0.79
G - 1983	Maize	340	271	164	181	180	17	16	5.0	5.9	0.85
G - 1984	Maize	323	334	102	128††	125††	26††	23††	8.0§	6.9§	1.16
G - 1984	Ryegrass	451	462	55	67	71	12	16	2.7§	3.5	0.77
G - 1985	Sorghum	516	471	83	101††	102††	18††	19††	3.5§	4.0§	0.88

† Corrected for carry-over effects (see text).
†† Carry-over effects included.
§ Based on N present in the year's amount of manures.

TABLE 4. The influence of compost and FYM on some soil properties.

I – VERANO

		At start	After 3 year manuring (1980)		
		1978	Control	"C" – 11.4	FYM – 11.4
pH (H₂O)		6.5	6.5	7.3	7.3
OM	%	1.84	1.76	2.18	2.23
Total N	%	0.117	0.108	0.137	0.139

II – GARIGA

Treatment and OM annual rate (Mg/ha)		pH (0.01 M CaCl2)			OM %			Total N %		
		1983	1984	1985	1983	1984	1985	1983	1984	1985
Control	nil	6.15	6.04 A	5.87 A	1.46	1.45 A	1.46 A	0.094	0.096 A	0.108 A
FYM	15	6.14	6.21 AB	6.42 B	1.59	1.63 AB	1.84 B	0.097	0.107 A	0.125 B
C 1	15	6.10	6.25 BC	6.78 C	1.52	1.71 AC	1.86 B	0.102	0.108 A	0.132 B
C 2	40	6.16	6.58 D	7.06 D	1.58	1.89 C	2.48 C	0.099	0.125 B	0.176 C
PT	15	6.15	6.15 AB	6.58 BC	1.54	1.70 AC	1.92 B	0.098	0.106 A	0.130 B
UD	15	6.25	6.44 CD	7.09 D	1.55	1.78 BC	2.06 B	0.097	0.106 A	0.132 B

(SN under 1983 in each section)

TABLE 5. Heavy metal concentrations in some composts tested (ppm on DM
       basis).

I - Means and SEM for 3 years' samples (1978-1980).

	"C"	PT	UD[†]
Cr	67 ± 5	182 ± 28	85 ± 51
Cu	405 ± 162	392 ± 35	151 ± 77
Fe	16,973 ± 2,326	12,217 ± 3,656	15,520 ± 1,245
Mn	412 ± 59	280 ± 70	570 ± 114
Pb	693 ± 414	613 ± 88	460[††]
Zn	803 ± 15	772 ± 93	790 ± 71

[†] Only 2 year means.
[††] One sample only.

II - One sample values.

	1984			1985		
	C	PT	UD	C	PT	UD
Cd	3.5	5.6	2.6	5.2	7.1	4.5
Cr	79	85	64	110	183	44
Cu	176	190	184	243	361	104
Fe	20,860	13,550	16,770	14,500	19,080	20,430
Mn	369	257	513	494	322	457
Mo	4.8	3.6	3.0	5.2	3.9	0.9
Ni	81	44	31	119	49	19
Pb	629	369	292	533	562	142
Zn	606	512	793	516	693	498

TABLE 6. Heavy metal concentrations in plant organs or total dry matter (ppm on DM basis).

656

VERANO - MAIZE - 3rd year (1980)

Treatments and OM rate (Mg/ha)	Cu grain	Cu leaves +stalk	Mn grain	Mn leaves +stalk	Zn grain	Zn leaves +stalk
Control nil	2.0	5.8	4.5	71	24	72
FYM 11.4	1.9	7.3	4.5	61	25	71
"C" 11.4	2.0	12.5	4.4	63	28	107
Statistical significance	NS	NS	NS	NS	0.01	NS

CROARA - MAIZE - 3rd year (1980)

Treatments and OM rate (Mg/ha)	Cu grain	Cu leaves +stalk	Mn grain	Mn leaves +stalk	Zn grain	Zn leaves +stalk
Control nil	1.9	6.0	4.9	81	23	55
FYM 11.4	1.9	9.6	4.2	60	23	56
"C" 11.4	1.9	8.4	4.2	68	25	76
Statistical significance	NS	NS	NS	NS	NS	NS

GARIGA - ITALIAN RYEGRASS - (1984[†]; 1st cut)

Treatments and OM rate (Mg/ha)	Cd	Cr	Cu	Mn	Ni	Pb	Zn
Control nil	0.04	0.38	2.3	40	2.1	0.81	18
FYM 15	0.04	0.33	2.5	30	2.0	0.83	19
C 1 15	0.04	0.34	2.1	27	1.8	0.79	20
C 2 40	0.04	0.36	2.6	26	1.8	0.99	34
PT 15	0.04	0.39	2.2	29	1.9	0.71	24
UD 15	0.05	0.77	2.7	27	2.4	0.95	40
Statistical significance	NS	NS	NS	NS	NS	NS	NS

GARIGA - SORGHUM - (1985)[†]

Treatments and OM rate (Mg/ha)	Cd	Cr	Cu	Mn	Ni	Pb	Zn
Control nil	0.25	0.73	2.7	33	1.3	0.50	41
FYM 15	0.13	0.58	2.2	28	1.3	0.61	36
C 1 15	0.19	0.56	3.4	29	1.2	0.77	53
C 2 40	0.28	0.68	4.0	27	1.3	0.90	50
PT 15	0.23	0.52	3.1	26	1.6	0.81	45
UD 15	0.17	0.58	2.8	26	1.1	1.00	39
Statistical significance	0.05	NS	NS	NS	NS	NS	0.05

† 1st and 2nd year of organic manuring.

TABLE 7. Heavy metal concentrations in soils of the GARIGA experiment.
Three sampling occasions : at start (1983) and at the end of
the first and the second year (1984 and 1985).

	Extr.	Year	Control		C 1 15 †		C 2 40 †		PT 15 †		UD 15 †		Stat. sign.
Cu	DTPA	1983	3.4		3.6		3.3		3.1		3.3		NS
		1984	2.3		2.4		2.5		2.2		2.6		NS
		1985	2.3	A	2.9	AB	4.7	C	2.8	A	3.5	B	×××
	TOTAL	1983	34		34		31		31		32		NS
		1984	31		32		32		31		33		NS
		1985	33	A	37	B	44	C	35	AB	39	B	×××
Mn	DTPA	1983	37		35		32		36		39		NS
		1984	20		20		15		18		15		NS
		1985	26	B	17	A	12	A	17	A	13	A	×××
	TOTAL	1983	1009		1000		879		912		957		NS
		1984	1036		1019		920		923		970		NS
		1985	1149		1098		1010		1033		1129		NS
Ni	DTPA	1983	2.6		2.7		2.4		2.4		2.2		NS
		1984	2.2	B	1.8	AB	1.5	A	1.8	AB	1.4	A	×
		1985	2.1	B	1.2	A	1.2	A	1.4	A	1.1	A	×××
	TOTAL	1983	152		149		126		136		137		NS
		1984	153		133		116		127		127		NS
		1985	94		100		86		86		89		NS
Pb	DTPA	1983	1.2		1.0		1.2		1.3		1.3		NS
		1984	0.9	A	1.6	A	3.0	B	1.2	A	1.4	A	×××
		1985	1.3	AB	3.2	C	9.4	D	2.8	DC	2.8	BC	×××
	TOTAL	1983	15		15		15		15		14		NS
		1984	14	A	17	AB	23	B	14	A	17	AB	×××
		1985	16	A	28	C	58	D	19	AB	23	BC	×××
Zn	DTPA	1983	5.5		5.7		5.1		4.5		9.0		NS
		1984	7.9		12.4		10.0		5.4		8.3		NS
		1985	2.0	A	4.3	B	8.4	C	3.2	AB	8.5	C	×××
	TOTAL	1983	85		83		79		80		90		NS
		1984	95		102		93		81		103		NS
		1985	72	A	83	B	103	C	76	AB	95	C	×××

† Mg/ha of OM added.
Cd and Cr have been disregarded as they have never shown significant
variations among treatments.

EVALUATION OF HEAVY METALS BIOAVAILABILITY IN COMPOST
TRATED SOILS

Gianniantonio Petruzzelli and Lamberto Lubrano
Institute of Soil Chemistry, C.N.R.
Via Corridoni 78, 56100 Pisa (Italy)

Summary

Utilization of compost in agriculture is an essential
disposal method as a supplementary organic matter resource
for crop production. The risk of the possible pollution of
crops by heavy metals, makes necessary the use of guidelines
for its utilization. Generally, adopted legislations refer
to the total amounts of heavy metals in compost and in soil,
nevertheless, much of experimentation concerning these
elements is actually engaged to determine the real availability of heavy metals to plants in relation to the chemical
forms of heavy metals in soil. This paper emphasized the
extractability of metals by a sequential extraction procedure in relation to soil chemistry and a plant uptake assay as
important diagnostic tools for metals bioavailability. Both
experimental procedures point out that only a small quantity
of the total amount of heavy metals in compost, once
incorporated into the soil, is in a mobile form and involved
in the nutritional process of plants and confirm the
hypothesis that the consideration of only the total content
of metal in compost as an index of possible environmental
hazard could be excessively cautious.

1 Introduction

Disposal of municipal refuse is a problem of increasing
importance in Italy. Untill now land filling and incineration are the most widely used methods, but growing
difficulties arise in finding suitable landfill sites, while
on the other hand incineration may be a serious source of
atmosferic pollution.
Composting process is a possible management alternative
compost being a supplementary humus resource for crop
production, which can counteract the decrease of organic
matter of intensively cultivated soils.
The large spectrum of municipal waste materials, the
different treatment processes, and treatment plant operations produce composts which varies widely in their
composition. Particularly, concentration of heavy metals in
compost is very variable, and benefits from compost
utilization in soil have to be weighed against the possible

hazards associated with these metals.

The risk of the possible pollution of crops by heavy metals, makes necessary the use of guidelines for the utilization of waste materials on agricultural land. Generally, adopted legislations refer to the total amounts of heavy metals in compost and in soil, nevertheless, much of experimentation concerning these elements is actually enganged to determine the real availability of heavy metals to plants (Lake et al. 1984) in relation to the chemical forms of heavy metals in soil.

The objective of this experiment was to evaluate the possible use of a sequential extraction procedure of heavy metals in compost-soil mixtures, and a plant uptake assay to provide reliable information about their bioavailability.

2 Materials and Methods

Compost - The used compost derived from the organic part of municipal refuse composted aerobically in a Dano plant (Pistoia). Some characteristics of the compost are reported in table I. The high levels of some heavy metals are ascribed to the large spectrum of municipal waste materials which contain significant quantities of these metals.

Soil - Surface soil samples, 20 cm in depth, were collected from two soils. The first located at San Cataldo (Pisa), according to the F.A.O. classification was an Entisol which contained on a dry weight basis 1.6% organic matter, 39.4% sand 92.8% silt and 27.8% clay. Cation exchange capacity was 17.5 meq $100g^{-1}$ of soil; the pH was 8.1. The second, was an Histosol, located at Orentano (Pisa) and contained 21.6% organic matter, 59.6% clay, 27.7% silt, and 12.7% sand. Cation exchange capacity was 57.7 meq/100g of soil and the pH was 8.1.

Extraction procedure - Soil and compost samples were air dried, ground to pass a 2 mm sieve, combined and thoroughly mixed, and then transferred to 50 ml polythene centrifuge tubes, where deionized water was added (2 g of compost, 10 g soil and 30 g water). Samples were maintained at a constant temperature of 18°C and shaken lengthwise on a mechanical shaker for 12 hours each day. After the selected period of incubation, one month, samples were subjected to a sequential extraction procedure with H_2O, 1M KNO_3 and DTPA, (30 g of each extractant were used), in order to estimate the different chemical forms of heavy metals (1). Samples were centrifuged at 12000xg for 10 minutes to obtain the H_2O fraction. The residuate was treated with 1M KNO_3 for 16 hours, and finally after centrifugation the last residue was shaken for 8 hours with DTPA. Three replicates of incubated samples were used at each extraction step. In all extracts from the sequential extraction procedure heavy metals were determined by atomic adsorption spectroscopy (Perkin Elmer mod 403, equipped with the background corrector). Total heavy metals content of the soil-compost mixtures was determine by HNO_3-HClO_4 digestion.

Pot experiment - 50 g of soil with different percentage of compost (0,10%, 20% w/w) was mixed with 150 g of pure siliceous sand in glass vessels, then 50 wheat seeds were sown uniformely for each vessel (2). Vessels, were placed in a climatic cell and arranged in a completely randomized design, five replicates were carried out for each soil-compost combination. Adequate moisture was mantained by means of a small glass tube inserted in the soil mixture through addition of distilled water. Temperature and humidity were kept at 20°C and 70% respectively. Seedlings were grown under fluorescent lighting, (Silvania Gro-lux 18000). After 18 days, plant height was measured and recorded, then plants were harvested and separated into tops and roots. Plant material was oven dried at 70°C and dry weights recorded. Heavy metals content in seedlings were determined after acid digestion (HNO_3-HClO_4), through the use of a Perkin Elmer 403 atomic absorption spectrophotometer, equipped with the back ground corrector.

3 Results and Discussion

Heavy metals extracted from the soil compost mixtures by the adopted sequential procedure are reported in table II. In the water extracts, of S. Cataldo soil only Copper and Zinc were recovered. Extraction by KNO_3 always solubilized, greater quantities of heavy metals than the one by H_2O. Nevertheless no extractable amounts of Cadmium were found.

The amount of heavy metals extractable by DTPA was very low for Cadmium and Chromium, while it was consistently higher in the case of Copper and Zinc. In Orentano soil, Lead and Cadmium were recovered neither in the water nor in the KNO_3 fractions, while also an appreciable quantity of Chromium was recovered in the water extraction together with Copper and Zinc. With nearly all of the investigated metals, extractability increased utilizing KNO_3 and DTPA, particularly for Copper and Zinc.

Taking into account the difference between the two soils in heavy metals extractability, the results show some specific trends. Zinc always was more extractable from samples of the Orentano soil. In both soils similar

concentrations were recovered in all extracts from the
sequential extraction for cadmium and, with the exception of
the water solubility, for chromium. With respect to Pb,
larger quantities were extracted by KNO_3 from the S. Cataldo
soil than from the Orentano soil. On the other hand, DTPA
extractability was greater from samples incubated with the
Orentano soil. Particularly remarkable were the differences
in the case of Cu. It was more water-soluble and more
extractable by KNO_3 from the S. Cataldo soil. Greater
quantities were extracted by DTPA from the Orentano soil.
These differences could be ascribed to the action of organic
matter, which, as is known, forms relatively stable complexs
with Copper. Orentano soil has a very high concentration of
organic matter.

It must be stressed that these extractable quantities
are rather small with respect to the total content of heavy
metals in compost. The only exception is Cd, which is
probably in a very loose form in the added compost and is
therefore more likely to be easily released and solubilized.
The percentages of extractability are reported in table II.
Each percentage was calculated as the ratio of the sum of
the quantities of metal extracted by all the three solvents
with respect to the total content of the same metal in the
soil compost mixture.

As far as the pot experiments are concerned, in all
treatments seedlings showed no visible symptons of any
nutritional disorders. Significant increase of yield was
found in samples treated with compost in the respect to the
original soil, both for tops and roots.

The higher addition of compost, in spite of the
increase in nutrient supply, was ineffective on the yield
i.e. the experimental conditions were of such a kind that
seedlings growth occurred in the "adequate zone" (3). The
dry matter yields of wheat seedlings are presented in Table
III. Heavy metal concentration in wheat seedlings grown on
the compost treated soils are reported in tables IV and V.

Concerning S. Cataldo soil, it is worth of note that
the values of Cd were below the detection limit of the
instrument in all the experiments.

On the average seedlings exhibited significant increases in heavy metals content after compost addition at 10%,
nevertheless the values of uptake remained unaltered at the
higher dose treatment. Zinc content nearly doubled both in
tops and roots after compost addition at 10% rate then
remained the same in tops but decresed in roots at the 20%
compost addition rate. Similar trends were found for copper
chromium and nickel contents in wheat seedlings. The 10%
rate of compost application produced a relevant increase of

these heavy metals both in the above and below ground biomass. On the contrary Lead amounts rised similarly to the other metals in tops, but increased in roots also after the 20% compost addition rate. With the exception of Copper in the Orentano soil, heavy metal contents of wheat seedlings were increased by compost applications, but in general did not increase with the rates of addition. The contents of heavy metals were higher in the root portion than in the aerial part, and the greater variations following compost addition were found for Zinc, Nickel and Cadmium. Particularly remarkable is the presence of Cadmium in the seedlings grown in this soil. Differences in the concentrations of heavy metals, in wheat seedlings grown on the two soils, show that uptake of a certain metal is not only due to the level of this metal in soil or compost, but it is associated with ionic imbalance involving the other metals (6). Even if an increase in the amounts of heavy metals absorbed by seedlings occurred, these were very low in the respect to the total content of compost. As a matter of fact the increase in the uptake of heavy metals expressed as percentage of total content accounts at most for only 2.2 Copper, 5-7% Zinc, 0.6 Lead and 0.9 Chromium, for the 10% addition rate of compost. An exception to this trend, however, was Cadmium, the percentage of which was higher, nearly 18%.

Both experimental procedures point out that only a small share of the total amount of heavy metals in compost, once incorporated into the soil is in a mobile form and involved in the nutritional process of wheat seedlings.

Results, agree with other findings in soils treated with composted sewage sludge and digested liquid sludge (4,5) and confirm the hypothesis that the consideration of only the total quantity of metal in compost as an index of possible environmental hazard could be excessively cautious. The complexity of organic and inorganic surfaces in soil, able to involve heavy metals in adsorption, precipitation or complexation reactions precludes a definitive predictability "a priori" of heavy metals uptake by plants. However in compost amended soil, where the concern is with excessive accumulation of metals and these elements added to soil are generally retained by sorption processes, a sequential extraction procedure which reveals the chemical nature of the metal, may be an important diagnostic tool, even more when heavy metals availability is assesed using a plant uptake assay, which appears to provide reliable information in a reasonably short time.

ACKNOWLEDGEMENTS
Work supported by the Progetto Finalizzato Energetica 2
(SP Biomasse e Agricoltura ER.B/2), CNR in cooperation with
ENEA, grant CNR.

REFERENCES

1) PETRUZZELLI G., LUBRANO L. and GUIDI G. - Heavy metal
   extractability Biocycle, 26, 46 (1985)
2) PETRUZZELLI G., GUIDI G. and LUBRANO L. - Interactions
   among heavy metals and organic matter in soil. Int. Conf.
   Heavy Metal in the Environment, 686-690. Amsterdam 1981.
3) URLICH A. - Plant tissue analysis. In Reisenaner HM (ed).
   Soil and plant tissue testing in California Univ.
   California Div. Agr. Sci. Bull. 1879, 1-4 (1976).
4) EMMERICH W.E., L.J. LUND, A.L. PAGE and A.C. CHANG, 1982
   - Solid phase forms of heavy metals in sewage sludge-treated soils. J. Environ. Qual. 11, 178.
5) SPOSITO G., L.J. LUND and A.C. CHANG, 1982 - Trace metal
   chemistry in arid-zone field soils amended with sewage
   sludge: I. Fractionation of Ni, Cu, Zn, Cd and Pb in
   solis phases. Soil Sci. Soc. Am. J. 46, 260.
6) KROGBJERRE G. and SCHIERUP H. - Uptake of six heavy
   metals by oat as influenced by soil type and addition of
   cadmium, lead, zinc and copper. Pl. Soil 88, 57 (1985).

Table I - Some characteristics of the used compost.

Water	31.2%
Organic C	39.5% of D.M.
Total-N	1.78 % "
Total P	0.61% "
Total K	0.09% "
pH	7.7
Cu	422 mg/kg
Zn	857 mg/kg
Cd	8 mg/kg
Pb	605 mg/kg
Cr	215 mg/kg
Ni	279 mg/kg

	S. CATALDO				ORENTANO			
	H_2O	KNO_3	DTPA	Ex%	H_2O	KNO_3	DTPA	Ex%
COPPER	5.4	6.0	19.1	3.7	2.5	3.7	19.5	3.0
ZINC	1	4.5	33.1	1.6	1.5	3.5	49.8	2.1
LEAD	n.d.	12.0	12.2	4.1	n.d.	n.d.	9.6	1.6
CHROMIUM	n.d.	3.9	1.0	0.9	1.0	2.0	1.3	0.7
CADMIUM	n.d.	n.d.	0.9	4.7	n.d.	n.d.	0.8	11
NICKEL	n.d.	1.0	3.4	1.4	n.d.	1.8	7.0	2.7

Table II : Heavy metals extractability from the two investigated soils (mean values and percentage of extractability)

Treatment	S. Cataldo		Relative	Orentano		Relative
	Tops	Roots	yield	Tops	Roots	yield
Original soil	0.683[a]	0.462[a]	1	0.629[a]	0.395[a]	1
+ compost 10%	0.944[a]	0.625[a]	1.37	0.717[b]	0.513[b]	1.13
+ compost 20 %	0.937[b]	0.628[a]	1.36	0.721[c]	0.516[b]	1.16

In each column values followed by different letters are significantly different at the P 0.05 level, according to the new Duncan's multiple range test.

Table III : Dry matter yield (g) of wheat seedlings (mean values)

	ZINC		COPPER		CHROMIUM		LEAD		NICKEL	
	Tops	roots	Tops	roots	Tops	roots	Tops	roots	Tops	roots
Original Soil	38.6^a	55.1^a	12.2^a	22.7^a	n.d.	7.6^a	n.d.	6.1^a	4.3^a	13.2^a
Compost 10 %	46.8^b	88.5^c	24.2^b	37.4^b	2.2^a	11.0^b	7.2^a	16.3^b	6.8^b	17.4^b
Compost 20 %	46.2^b	79.3^b	22.1^b	36.5^b	2.9^a	10.4^b	7.2^a	22.3^c	6.5^b	17.6^b

Entries in each subcolumn that have the same letter are not significantly different at the 95 % level of confidence

Table IV : Heavy metals concentration in wheat seedlings from an S. Cataldo soil treated with compost ($\mu g/g$)

	COPPER		ZINC		CHROMIUM		NICKEL		CADMIUM	
	Tops	Roots	Tops	Roots	Tops	Roots	Tops	Roots	Tops	Roots
Untreated Soil	19.4^a	24.1^a	51.9^a	152^a	5.0^a	22.2^c	6.7^a	16.8^a	n.d.	n.d.
+ Compost 2 %	19.6^a	23.2^a	61.2^b	205^b	10.1^b	28.0^c	17.3^b	37.3^b	0.31	2.17
+ Compost 5 %	18.8^a	23.5^a	67.8^b	206^b	10.3^b	28.8^a	16.8^b	38.6^c	0.98	2.15

In each column values followed by different letters are significantly different at the P 0.05 level, according to the new Duncan's multiple range test.

Table V : Heavy metals concentration ($\mu g/g$) in wheat seedlings grown on Orentano soil treated with compost

OPTIMIZATION OF COMPOSTING PROCESS UTILIZING URBAN AND AGRICULTURAL WASTES

A. ROBOTTI (****), G. RAMONDA (***), A. NASSISI (**), A. RATTOTTI (*), A. BARILLI (*).

(*) Centro Ricerche Produzioni Animali (Animal Production Research Centre) - Reggio Emilia
(**) Amministrazione Provinciale di Piacenza - Laboratorio Analisi Terreni (Provincial Administration of Piacenza - Soil Analysis Lab)
(***) Azienda Municipalizzata di Nettezza Urbana - (City-owned Enterprise for Street Cleaning) - Piacenza
(****) Azienda Agraria Sperimentale "V. Tadini" - (Experimental Farm "V. Tadini") - Piacenza

SUMMARY

In a plant for the treatment of Municipal Solid Wastes, several tests were carried out, concerning combined composting of M.S.W. and solid parts of pig slurry.

Pig slurry, directly added in the reactor originated an excess of oxidation on the organic matter, emphasized by a strong rise in temperature.

Mixing slurry with the refined compost before maturation on the threshing-floor improved the production of organic matter, nitrogen and phosphorus but left substantially unchanged the composition of finished product.

INTRODUCTION

Amongst the sources of organic matter for land use, the M.S.W. Compost should hold particular interest, as its production permits, at the same time, to remarkably reduce the problems concerning Municipal Wastes' removal: we could therefore suppose a concurrence of agricultural and municipal interests.

The transfer of a certain quantity of M.S.W. to agriculture should however take place with a considerable saving, both for the Municipal Community and for agriculture itself: as far as this latter is concerned, quality standards have to be respected according to the different uses, in order to avoid any negative effect, both in the short and in the long run.

It is not easy to obtain a product able to meet at the same time any requirement; the process charges often prove to

---

Report performed in the context of the "Progetto Finalizzato Energetica", CNR - ENEA, contract ENEA Nr. 124 dated 9.7.1985.

be a limit, since this method shouldn't be more expensive than the traditional systems for removal of Municipal Wastes.

For this reason it is interesting to verify the efficiency and the cheapness of small-sized plants for treatment of wastes, planned for communities under 50.000 inhabitants, in order to lower transport charges and incidence.

At the same time, the evolution of husbandry systems and the diffusion of industrial processing methods of agricultural products have originated the accumulation of large amounts of wastes hard to be removed.

If sources of organic substances of any kind are available to a farm, substances which can't be exploited in any way but by landfill, it doesn't seem either logical or far-sighted trying to replace them with composts deriving from Municipal Wastes: in such situations it seems instead indispensable to evaluate the chances offered by a combined use of such substances.

The combined use of M.S.W. and agricultural-zootechnical wastes could permit to raise the content in organic matter and in nutritive elements of compost, limiting furthermore the rate of inert matters and heavy metals, and improving at the same time the manipulation possibility and fertilizing dynamics of agricultural-zootechnical wastes.

MATERIALS AND METHODS

In order to evaluate this possibility, different survey campaigns were performed on a composting facility, consisting of: a shredder, a horizontal bio-reactor (average retaining time equal to 12 days, oxigenation performed by suction from the bottom, handling through Archimedean screws); refining system consisting of a rotating sieve (25 mm. dia. holes) and of a 2-staged vibrating screen (15 mm. and 8 mm. dia. holes).

At present some composting tests are being performed concerning M.S.W. with addition of wastes of tomato and bean processing and of purification sewages originated by food processing industries.

This report presents the results of two series of composting essays on M.S.W. only, or on M.S.W. with addition of two different amounts of pig slurry.

Each production cycle was planning one stage for bio-reactor loading and setting, on an average 10 days long, and one stage of 3 weeks' operation.

Every day electrical consumption and temperatures in different spots of the bio-reactor and in the heaps were surveyed. Production and analytical data are related to the central running week, and gather at least five surveys. During the maturation stage, surveys were performed every week, until the 78th day.

Main analytical parameters were determined according to the methods here below specified:

DRY MATTER: determined on samples weighing about 2 Kg, by oven-drying (forced ventilation, 105°C), up to a constant weight.

pH: determined by potentiometer, after dispersion in water (dilution ratio: 2,5:1).

GRANULOMETRY: separation performed on a sample of material, previously dried, and weighing at least Kg 1,5, by sieving through square-meshed sieves.

MATERIAL COMPOSITION ANALYSIS: hand performed on particles obtained from the previous sieving (particles below 2 mm. are not included in this detection).

ORGANIC MATTER: determined by incineration and subsequent liming at 600° C for 3 hours, in a muffle oven.

NITROGEN: mineralization with phosphoric acid and distillation (Kjeldahl method).

PHOSPHORUS: determined by spectrophotometry, further to mineralization with nitro-perchlorate mixture (1:1) in Teflon autoclaves, at 160° C for 12 hours.

POTASSIUM, CALCIUM, MAGNESIUM, IRON, MANGANESE, COPPER AND ZINC: determined by atomic absorption, after mineralization with nitro-perchlorate mixture (1:1) in Teflon autoclaves, at 160° C for 12 hours.

NICKEL, LEAD, CADMIUM, AND CHROMIUM: determined by atomic absorption, in graphite oven, after mineralization with nitro-perchlorate mixture (1:1) in Teflon autoclaves, at 160° C for 12 hours.

C/N RATIO: conventionally fixed equal to the content in organic substance, devided by 1.8, related to Nitrogen by Kjeldahl method.

RESULTS AND DISCUSSION

In. M.S.W. composting, we have verified a thermic pattern of sigmoid type - at least as to the time interval we considered. This function was tending at a maximum (theoretical) value of about 63°C, while the maximum temperature taken was 61°C; the average process temperature was around 50°C, with a summation degrees-day of about 700.

This pattern is typical, as to the type of digester tested, and represents a condition very close to the optimum one, in order to achieve a better mass sanitary condition, without however causing an excess of loss in organic matter: the material remains for about 10 days at temperatures above 55°C, but never reaches 65°C.

During the first test carried out by adding pig slurry directly into the bio-reactor, we have recorded a remarkably different thermic pattern.

Even without a strongly modified degrees-day summation, which was however rising to 775 at an average temperature of about 65°C, a twisting in the thermic pattern was recorded: the estimated function resulted to be of multinomial type, with a maximum actual value of about 71°C.

The addition of an easily fermentable substance, particularly rich in microbic flora, caused sudden rise in temperature: after 4 days of permanence in bio-reactor - equal to a 8 meters distance from the feeding side, about one third of the bio-reactor as a whole - temperatures above 71°C could be reached.

Once achieved this stage, also because of possible self-sterilization effects, the temperatures were rapidly decreasing, up to values significantly lower than the standard ones.

M.S.W. with addition of pig slurry were remaining for about 12 days at temperatures above 55°C; for half of this period, about 6 days, the mass temperature resulted to be above 65°C: this situation could only be fed by an excess of oxidation of organic matter and the low yields of this fraction prove it.

In order to obviate this situation, during the second stage of the experimental program, there was an attempt to perform a better calibration of proceeding parameters, which could enable to achieve the best results, with the involvement of as few technological and managerial interventions as possible; in fact a limitation of oxidation of the organic matter and a reduction of losses in Nitrogen were observed.

A further test could however allowed some improvements (limitation of organic matter and Nitrogen losses), by modifying the main processing parameters (oxigenation and humidity).

In order to achieve this first objective, we have tried both to keep the mass humidity rate within optimum values - between 35% and 45% referred to the compostable material - and to avoid excesses of ventilation.

As to the second objective - i.e. reducing Nitrogen losses, limitation of temperature and, whenever necessary, an excess of ventilation were performed.

The loss of nitrogen compounds in fact is strictly related both to the oxidation rate of organic matter - exothermic process which tends to rise temperature - and to the thermic level, determined by the heat source (burning organic substance), by the mass "thermic characteristics" (in this specific case the humidity rate) and by the existing relations with the environment.

With these interventions thermic patterns rather similar, with or without addition of pig slurry, have taken place.

During the second semester, in fact, the average process temperature was around 60°C for both kinds of produced material, thermic patterns related to retention time were always of sigmoid type, with maximum (theoretical) values of 61,9°C, with M.S.W only, and 62,5°C after adding pig slurry.

Having mainly operated a mass cooling and not an effective limitation of oxidizing phenomena, we could verify scarce reductions in the oxidation ratio of the organic matter; but, on the other hand, losses in nitrogen compounds resulted to be extremely limited, in respect of those of the previous semester.

For the other nutritive elements as well, essentially phosphorus and potassium, drastic reductions in transformation efficiency consequent to use of pig slurry were recorded.

TABLE 1

YIELDS AND TEMPERATURES IN TWO DIFFERENT COMPOSTING TESTS WITH COMBINED M.S.W. AND PIG SLURRY.

PARAMETERS	M.S.W. (average)	M.S.W.+PIG SLURRY (1st test)	M.S.W.+PIG SLURRY (2nd test)
Dry matter	45%	33%	36%
Organic matter	58%	33%	35%
Nitrogen	54%	28%	39%
Max. temperature (°C)	62	71	63
Average temperature (°C)	60	65	60
Nr. of days at T 65°C	0	6	0
Nr. of days at T 55-65°C	11	6	11
Nr. of days at T 55°C	1	0	1
Sum degrees*day	714	775	718

Further to these results we have considered adequate to verify alternative methods for inserting pig slurry into the production cycle of Compost from M.S.W.

In order to compare the alternative mixing systems, three experimental theses were arranged:
1 – COMPOST A: obtained through combined mixing of M.S.W. and pig slurry.
2 – COMPOST B: obtained through mixing of refined compost, obtained from M.S.W. only and pig slurry.
3 – COMPOST C: refined compost, obtained from M.S.W. only.

TABLE II

MIXING RATIOS SURVEYED DURING TESTS
     (PRE-SELECTED M.S.W./PIG SLURRY)

TYPE OF COMPOST	COMPOST A	COMPOST B
MATERIAL TEL QUEL	3,9:1	5,7:1
DRY MATTER	8,6:1	10,0:1
ORGANIC MATTER	2,9:1	4,0:1
NITROGEN	3,1:1	5,2:1

The transformation efficiencies obtained are quoted in tables III and IV.

TABLE III

COMPOSTING EFFICIENCY
(% of raw material)

PROCESS STAGE	COMPOST A	COMPOST B	COMPOST C
Production	20	27	27
Maturation	81	60	56
Total yield (*)	16	20	15

(*) As to COMPOST B, the increase of efficiency is due to the addition of pig slurry operated in the middle of the production cycle.

TABLE IV:

TOTAL YIELD AT THE END OF MATURATION
(% of raw material)

COMPONENTS	COMPOST A	COMPOST A	COMPOST C
Dry matter	27	40	30
Organic matter	18	43	37
Nitrogen	31	49	35
Phosphorus	45	77	57
Potassium	33	41	52

The production phase and the subsequent maturation on the threshing-floor of these three different kinds of compost were followed through specific surveys.

The mixing ratios are quoted, both in terms of material "tel quel" and of dry matter, organic matter and Nitrogen, in table II; these values are however originated by the ratio between M.S.W. at the inlet of the bio-reactor - after pre-selection carried out by the shredder - and pig slurry.

The compost obtained by composting of M.S.W. with addition of pig slurry into the bior-reactor (type A) always shows efficiencies far below standard values (type C).

The addition of pig slurry to the refined compost (type B) allows, instead, to elevate the total process efficiency, sometimes even in a showy way and exception made for the Potassium case: quite positive effects have been verified in relation with the balance of organic matter, nitrogen and phosphorus.

Table 5 quotes the main analytical data detected at the end of the heap maturation stage.

It must be pointed out that, according to the analytical data, it is hardly definable how much the use of pig slurry can have modified the quality of the organic matter, above all related to its agronomical, fertilizing and amending effects.

TABLE V

COMPOSITION AT THE END OF MATURATION
(referred to dry matter)

PARAMETERS		COMPOST A	COMPOST B	COMPOST C
Organic matter	(%)	25,01	40,88	41,39
Nitrogen	(%)	0,83	1,08	0,96
P205	(%)	0,55	0,81	0,68
K20	(%)	0,56	0,60	1,01
Cadmium	(ppm)	2,2	2,7	3,1
Zinc	(ppm)	687	744	693
Manganese	(ppm)	617	560	537
Copper	(ppm)	324	321	329
Chromium	(ppm)	166	118	126
Lead	(ppm)	541	534	511
Nickel	(ppm)	112	81	79
C/N Ratio		16,6	21,1	24,5

According to the heap maturation period, particular care must be given to the amount of heavy metals which turn to be made soluble and subsequently lixiviated.

Starting from less favourable ponderal evaluations, that are those indicating the maximum losses in metallic elements, we can estimate the values quoted in Table VI.

TABLE VI

EVALUATION OF LIXIVIATED HEAVY METALS DURING HEAP MATURATION

ELEMENTS	LOSSES IN HEAVY METALS	
	g/ton of compost	g/m3 of compost
Zinc	140	91
Manganese	100	65
Copper	80	52
Lead	70	46
Chromium	30	20
Nickel	15	10
Cadmium	0,3	0,2

The characteristics of the composts produced during the first testing year, detected at the plant outlet and before storage for the maturation stage, are quoted in Table VII.

TABLE VII

PARAMETERS OF REFINED COMPOSTS AT THE PLANT OUTLET.
(Average values quoted on dry matter)

PARAMETERS AND MATTERS		COMPOST FROM M.S.W.	COMPOST FROM M.S.W. + PIG SLURRY
Organic matter	(%)	42,23	39,98
Nitrogen	(%)	1,01	0,93
P205	(%)	0,65	0,65
K20	(%)	0,87	0,80
CaO	(%)	5,04	5,27
MgO	(%)	1,60	1,70
Cadmium	(ppm)	2,50	1,67
Iron	(ppm)	30020	32065
Zinc	(ppm)	685	667
Manganese	(ppm)	496	517
Copper	(ppm)	306	328
Chromium	(ppm)	142	143
Lead	(ppm)	541	779
Nickel	(ppm)	93	109
C/N RATIO		23	24
Glass	(%)	2,77	2,85
Metals	(%)	0,02	0,08
Plastics	(%)	0,08	0,05
Further inert matters	(%)	5,55	4,81

During heap maturation, the temperatures of the three compared materials could be taken by inserting two thermic probes, connected with a thermorecorder, in the centre of the heaps.

The main parameters detected and the function coefficients obtained, are quoted in Table VIII.

TABLE VIII

TEMPERATURES TAKEN DURING MATURATION

Parameters	Compost A	Compost B	Compost C
Max. Temperature (°C)	44	51	56
Sum degrees*day	3026	3755	3476
Av.ge temperature(°C)	38	47	43
Nr.of days T > 50° C	0	16	36
Nr.of days T > 45° C	0	57	42
Nr.of days T < 35° C	21	0	25

Evaluated function $T = A - B \cdot d + C \cdot d^2 + D \cdot d^3$
T= Temperature (°C)　　　　d= days of maturation

Coefficients:			
A	28,498	35,030	27,681
B	0,063	0,863	2,314
C	0,007	-0,014	-0,054
D	$-7,4 \cdot 10^{-5}$	$5,7 \cdot 10^{-5}$	$3,2 \cdot 10^{-4}$
R2	0,883	0,967	0,957

The reported data, point out once again the sharp differentiation among the types of material.

The compost C, obtained from M.S.W. only, and the one stocked after addition of pig slurry, compost B, show similar thermic patterns, above all in terms of degrees*day and of average temperature: the compost B, owing to its higher content of easily fermentable matter, tends to keep temperatures above 35°C for longer, while the compost C, starting from the 60th day of maturation, tends to slow down the oxidizing processes, involving a subsequent thermic stagnation.

The compost obtained by combined treatment of M.S.W. and pig slurry, type A, shows a substantially diversified situation: the type of function evaluated shows a rising phase significantly less slanting, and after reaching the maximum value (42°C about) it suddenly decreases.

The summation degrees*day results to be remarkably below the standard and, furthermore, fact even more aberrant, we never detected temperatures above 45° C, and for 21 days, out of the 80 ones, we have been detecting temperatures below 35°C.

The compost of type A, owing to a series of strong oxidation processes during the treatment in bio-reactor, was obviously showing a reduced activity, after storage.

CONCLUSIONS

The strong losses in organic substances and nutritive elements, detected further to the use of pig slurry inside the bio-reactor, were avoided by using such substances mixed with the compost before storage.

The mixing of pig slurry with compost led to efficiencies, expressed both in terms of dry and organic matter, Nitrogen and Phosphorus, remarkably higher than the standard ones (obtained therefore by using M.S.W. only).

At the end of the heap maturation process, conventionally fixed on the 78th day, the material obtained by mixing was showing chemical and physical characteristics remarkably more favourable than the ones of Compost A (composting in bio-reactor with pig slurry).

Compared to the standard compost, the mixture with pig slurry allows to slightly improve Nitrogen and phosphorus content, while it has almost no influence on the reduction of heavy metal and inert matter content.

In case no contrary motivations of sanitary-healthy type exist, it's adviceable to use pig slurry only outside the bio-reactor, and mix it with the refined compost, before storage.

COMPOST PRODUCTION IN A LONG—RETENTION—TIME HORIZONTAL REACTOR
TECHNICAL SIDES

ZULIANI A., PRESCIMONE V., BARAZZETTA G.R.

Summary

The present work has been drawn up with reference to the research
contract for year 1983 agreed between the Company SECIT S.p.A. and
ENEA within the limits of PFE n. 2, sub-project "Biomasses and
Agriculture".
The main purpose of this work is an assessment of power inputs and
energy consumptions of the solid wastes composting plant of Podenzano
(PC) in order to evidence the possible intervention areas allowing a
reduction of the unitary process consumptions.
This plant is operating since 1981 and it is placed within the
experimental farm V. TADINI, operated by the waste collection service
(AMNU) of the city of Piacenza.
At the plant are carried our since long various multidisciplinary
researches concerning u.a. production and agricultural use of
compost.

DESCRIPTION OF THE PLANT

The composting plant at Podenzano can be subdivided into 4 sections
operating in series : the waste reception and loading pit, the selection
line, the reactor, the refining line.
The plant's capacity covers the disposal of wastes produced by a
community of 15.000 - 20.000 persons. The plant has been designed for the
treatment of solid urban refuse (SUR) and of different organic by-products
according to the following data :

- yearly amount of SUR disposed of   4.000 t/y
- working days per week   5
- daily working shift   6 h 40'
- daily amount of treated SUR   10-15 t/d
- daily amount of treated sludges   3 - 5 t/d
- sludges moisture contents   80 %
- total installed power   abt. 120 kW

A number of distinctive features of the plant are sketched in tables
n. 1, 2 and 3 and in graph 1 as well.
The plant is focused on a stabilization system characterized by
extended retention times and consisting of a rectangular tank containing
the compostable material.
The reactor is fitted with a traveling bridge carrying a two stirring
screws allowing progress and homogenization of the material. The actions of
the stirring screws and of the aeration system at the bottom ensure the
continuous exchange of the oxygen consumed by the biological oxydation
reactions and the elimination of CO_2 produced by them.

Each section includes some servicing facilities for operation of the machinery. The wastes arriving at the plant are dumped in the reception pit and then, by means of traveling crane and bucket, transported to the selection line.

The section named "SUR pit" includes the motors for hoisting the orange-peel bucket, for the cross travel, the movement of the traveling bridge and the opening and shutting of the bucket.

The selection is carried out by a revolving sieve with extended retention times with 75 x 80 mm. openings (SHREDDER) from which originate two flows : one reaching the reactor for the aerobic stabilization stage ; another, consisting of coarse aggregates, directed to the AMNU packer. The "Selection" selection includes the motors driving the slat-conveyor fed by the waste-bin filled by the bucket ; the belt conveyor feeding the shredder; the shredder itself ; the belt-conveyor feeding the packer ; the belt-conveyor transporting the compostable fraction into the reactor.

The reactor is a 24 x 2,4 m rectangular tank intended for a maximum depth of the compost of abt. 2 metres ; it is fitted with a traveling bridge with two stirring screws ; two aeration units (a suction fan with compost filter and a blowing fan) ; a tilting dumper with three screws for sludges'feeding of the reactor mixing and immediate. The compost is discharged by means of a vibrating batching conveyor installed at the end of the reactor. The "Reactor" section includes the motors operating the tilting dumper for sludges ; the three mixing and sludge-feeding screws ; the centrifugal suction fan ; the blowing-fan ; the two stirring screws ; the hydraulical screws-lifting unit ; the traveling bridge and the vibrating batching conveyor.

The output material from the reactor is conveyed to the refining line consisting at present of a revolving screener with 25 mm holes and of a vibrating double-stage screener with 15 mm and 8 mm holes. The three screener residues flows (one from the revolving screener, two from the vibrating screener) are loaded on a AMNU truck ; the compost is unloaded by a screw on a paved dumping pad.

The "Refining" section includes the motors driving the belt conveyor to the refining screener and the screener rotation ; the vibrator at the screener's outlet ; the belt conveyor to the vibrating screener, the vibrating batching feeder with electromagnetic control, the vibrating screener ; the belt conveyor of residues and the compost unloading screw.

Figures relevant to the installed power, divided by plant sections, are condensed in table 4 and annexed graph. It can be noted that from the point of view of installed power the selection section is the most involved (45 % of the total supply) but it must be considered that no less than 30 kW are required by the shredder alone. The reactor (34 % of the total) is the section presenting the highest number of annexed facilities and the refining section calls for the 13 % of the installed power only.

The Podenzano plant process 0,70 t/d of SUR in a single shift with an average output of compost of 25-30 %. Above data serve therefore to reference purposes for the calculation of specific and unitary consumptions.

ANALYSIS OF ABSORPTIONS AND ELECTRIC POWER CONSUMPTIONS

In order to obtain a possibly most analytical picture of the plant, consumptions have been established taking down the power absorbed by each motor and studying the standard operating cycle, by single facilities, in the course of a working day.

For the wastes reception section has been drawn up an operation scheme of the different motors of the traveling bridge conforming as much as possible to the actual operation conditions of this section ; measurements of the absorptions were carried out at various times averaging values corresponding to different working conditions. Figures relevant to the absorptions of each plant section are summarized in table 5 and annexed graph. The comparison between installed and absorbed power is indicative of the utilization rate of the different facilities. For instance : it has been noted that of the 30 kW installed for the shredder, less than 10 are actually absorbed ; that the suction is normally working always at full charge, having to overcome the resistance of the compost filter ; that the blowing fan absorbs a mere 65 % of the installed power.

Forty per cent of the total absorbed kWs applies to the reactor section ; follow the selection line with 32 % and, with analogous rates of abt. 14 %, the SUR pit and the refining line. It is thus evidenced that the selection section is on the whole less "charged" than the reactor section, while the SUR pit section works at full charge.

In table 6 and annexed graph, data referring to energy consumption are summarized by single sections. Analysis of these data clearly shows that the most involved section from the energetic point of view is the stabilization line ; in fact, the reactor absorbs 60 % of the total available power. A considerable part of these consumptions is a consequence of the two aeration units (abt. 60 %) functioning full 24 h, i.e. 5,30 h/d the suction and 18,30 h/d the blowing. It might also be observed that the first shows proportionally higher consumption than the latter.

The selection line consumes 30 % of the total power and the remaining part is taken up by the refining line and by the SUR pit.

The low consumption rate of the refining line is also interesting see the absorbed kW ; this is apparently an effect of the automatic devices that start the motors only during the discharge stage of the reactor. The effectiveness of a careful timing of the facilities is thus confirmed.

ASSESSMENTS

The theoretical total consumption of the plant amounts to 224 kWh/d. This figure refers to the 0,70 t/d of SUR treated at full rate and corresponds to abt. 32 kWh/t treated SUR and to 120 kWh/t of produced compost.

These data may be compared with those appearing on table n. 7 and resulting from the measurements carried out during preceding researches of the CRPA of Reggio Emilia.

In this respect the actual daily consumption appears rather higher because during said research the plant practically never worked at full rate. (For instance, during the trial with 28 days retention an average of 0,486 t/d of SUR had been treated and 0,60 t/d during the trial of Nov. 1982) ; it must also be noted that kWh/d consumptions show an extreme variability, corresponding to either 48 % more or less with respect to the average values. On the contrary, the values per ton of treated SUR (32 against an average of 34) and per ton of produced compost (120 against an average of 153) are more conform ; the latter parametre results the most stable as a comparison element, whereas the kWh/t of treated SUR may be more significant when making an economical assessment.

The consumptions distribution among the different treatment sections follows conventional data, confirming that the biostabilization stage is the most heavily involved in terms of consumptions, while the final refining of the product (imperative in order to comply with Italian mandatory rules) is but slightly engaged in the general context of the plant.

The daily consumptions per ton of treated SUR, are comprised within the range of values shown in bibliography and are probably overvalued in comparison with a similar plant working at maximum rate. It must be remembered that this is an experimental plant and it is placed at the lower limits of the potentiality rating.

It can also be noted that the plant operates on a single working shift and that doubling the potentiality would not mean doubling consumptions, but actually a less than proportional increase ; (for instance, the aeration system already works full time even on a single shift).

In this respect it has been remarked that the timing system of the suction fan implies a considerable economy (33 %) on the energy consumptions.

Supposing that for the control of the aeration system the timing of the suction should be adopted, the total consumptions should then sink to 179 kWh/d vs. 224, while the specific consumptions should adjust at 25 kWh/t treated SUR and 96 kWh/t produced compost.

Table 8 is a general summary of consumptions with timed air suction. The rates may more easily be adjusted to the average figures shown by the bibliography.

The aeration system thus appears as a crucial point, notorily for a correct course of the biological process but also as an important factor of possible energy-saving procedures in this sort of plants.

ACKNOWLEDGEMENTS

We are particularly grateful to Mr. A. VITALE for his appreciated cooperation in the operative management of the plant and for his decisive role in the data collection stage and our Company's Engineering Division (Mr. E. ROSSI and Mr. S. FRIGGI).

TABLE 1

RECEPTION AND SELECTION SECTION : SUMMARY OF TECHNICAL DATA

— Waste pit	mc	200
— Traveling bridge with bucket	mc	0,5
— Bags shredder		
— Screener of organic fraction :		
. length	m	8
. diametre	m	3,5
— Total power involved	kW	60

TABLE 2

STABILIZATION SECTION : SUMMARY OF TECHNICAL DATA

Container-tank

- reactor type	horizontal	
- length	m	24
- width	m	2,4
- average compost depth	m	2
- effective section	mq	5
- reactor's volume	mc	120

Traveling bridge

- progress speed	n/min	1
- stirring screws	n.	2
- screws' rotation speed	rpm	50

Aeration system

- suction fans	n.	1
- effective fans' delivery	mc/h	400
- total volume of exhaust air	mc/h	400

Air distribution system consisting of small canals covered by tiles connected with the fan.

Total power involved	kW	40

TABLE 3

REFINING SECTION : SUMMARY OF TECHNICAL DATE

- Revolving screener for separation of coarse aggregates

    . diametre of holes   mm   20

    . length   m   4

    . diametre   m   1,5

- Circular vibrating screener for separations of fine aggregates

    . diametre of Ist stage holes   mm   15

    . diametre IInd stage holes   mm   8

Total power involved   kW   10

TABLE 4

GENERAL SUMMARY OF INSTALLED POWER

SECTION	INSTALLED KW	%
SUR pit	9,50	8
Selection	52,35	45
Reactor	40,07	34
Refining	14,65	13
TOTAL	116,57	100

TABLE 5

GENERAL SUMMARY ABSORBED POWER

SECTION	INSTALLED kW	%
SUR pit	10,95	14
Selection	25,46	32
Reactor	32,00	40
Refining	11,13	14
TOTAL	79,54	100

TABLE 6

GENERAL SUMMARY UNITARY AVERAGE CONSUMPTIONS

SECTION	TOTAL kWh CONSUMPTION/DAY	%
SUR pit	2,3568	1
Selection	66,5749	30
Reactor	134,8758	60
Refining	20,4340	9
TOTAL kWh/d	224,2415	100
TOTAL kWh/t SUR	32	
TOTAL kWh/t COMPOST	120	

TABLE 7

AVERAGE AND UNITARY CONSUMPTIONS MEASURED DURING PRECEEDING TRIALS

PERIOD	NOVEMBER 82	MAY/JUNE 83	NOVEMBER 83	MAY/JUNE 84	AUG./SEPT. 84	AVERAGE	S.D.
TRIALS	RETENTION 12 DAYS	RETENTION 28 DAYS	RETENTION 12 DAYS	RETENTION 12 DAYS	RETENTION 12 DAYS SUR + SLUDGE		
kWh/d	284	1C8	96	126	183	159,4	77,23 ($\pm$ 48,5)
kWh/t SUR	46	24	35	22	45	34,4	11,28 ($\pm$ 32,8)
kWh/t COMPOST	184	162	158	125	139	153,6	22,61 ($\pm$ 14,7)

TABLE 8

GENERAL SUMMARY OF UNITARY AVERAGE CONSUMPTIONS WITH TIMED AIR SUCTION

SECTION	TOTAL kWh CONSUMPTION/DAY	%
SUR pit	2,3568	2
Selection	66,5749	37
Reactor	90,4700	50
Refining	20,4340	11
TOTAL kWh/d	179,83	100
TOTAL kWh/t SUR	25,69	
TOTAL kWh/t COMPOST	96,23	

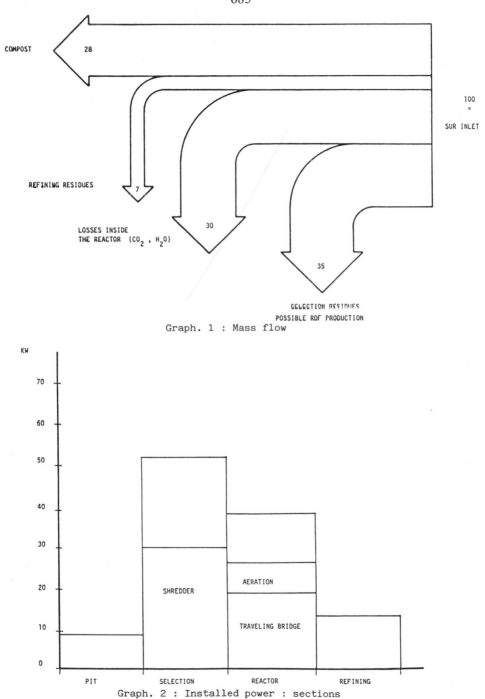

COMPOST

28

100
=
SUR INLET

REFINING RESIDUES

7

LOSSES INSIDE
THE REACTOR (CO_2 , H_2O)

30

35

SELECTION RESIDUES
POSSIBLE RDF PRODUCTION

Graph. 1 : Mass flow

KW

70

60

50

40

30

20

10

0

SHREDDER

AERATION

TRAVELING BRIDGE

PIT   SELECTION   REACTOR   REFINING

Graph. 2 : Installed power : sections

686

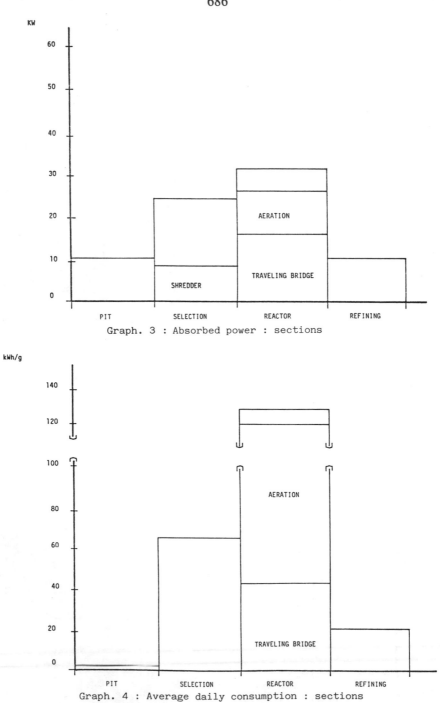

Graph. 3 : Absorbed power : sections

Graph. 4 : Average daily consumption : sections

SESSION : IV

C.N.R. and E.N.E.A. PANEL

Rapporteur : CAVAZZA L.

After the general context had been set by the reports given at the morning sitting on problems of producing compost and using it in agriculture, the afternoon sitting was devoted to papers given by the group of researchers working on the targeted project IPRA (improving the productivity of farm resources), subproject entitled "Factors intrinsic and extrinsic to the organism in production", problem area "Soil fertility", theme "Organic fertilizers from by-products and waste". The programme, which is now at an advanced stage, seeks to examine in depth certain aspects of this highly important and topical problem, which is of concern both to environmental management and to farming.

The papers presented supplied a wealth of data on particular aspects of the whole problem. Some were the initial results from multiannual trials still under way, and altogether they offered ample material for further discussion, comparisons and tentative conclusions.

Broadly speaking, the most striking thing to emerge was the immense diversity of the findings, stemming from the range and variety of almost every element involved : the origins of materials, the types of installation, their operating conditions and, coming to the results of practical application, the differences in soil types, crop rotation practices affecting soils, cultivation techniques and the species and varieties for which compost is to be used. Not the least cause of difficulties, to judge by the results of application, is the different and often very long periods needed to demonstrate the effects of compost on a large enough scale and in a manner which can be regarded as at least approximately stable and not merely transient.

These findings are demonstrated by the results - not always easy to interpret - of examining the physical properties of soils treated by different types of compost. The paper by Guidi and Poggio shows that no differences were found in calcareous soil examined, but differences were observed in the structural stability of non-calcareous soil, while in no case was it possible to establish differences of porousness. Seasonal variations were more important than the effects of treatment.

The most constant (and to some extent self-evident) finding reported was the increase in certain elements in soil generously treated with compost. These were the plant nutrients such as N, P and K in both total and assimilable content, and increases in organic materials (such as carbon: Del Zan et al.).

There was a greater admixture of heavy metals into the soil from compost than from manure, and greater still than from mineral fertilizers, which added virtually no heavy metals content (Genevini et al., Barbera et al.). These are quantities added in largely unavailable form, but their effect on absorption by cultivated plants was generally evident (Barbera ; Genevini et al.), especially in the early growing phases (e.g. for Lolium multiflorum, according to Genevini et al.). The results of determining the available fractions of these heavy metals (using strong acids such as EDTA, DTPA) were generally closely intercorrelated and were also correlated with the quantities absorbed by the plants (Barbera).

The results on production obtained by various authors on different crops (grain maize and silo maize, Italian rye-grass, beetroot, apples) after application of various types of compost, compared with manure and mineral fertilizers, varied widely. Generally, even after three years, mineral fertilizers had the greatest effect on production (Del Zan et al., Strabbioli et al.) ; composts often give results inferior to manure, and sometimes (usually composts not stabilized) actually have inhibiting effects on plant growth for reasons that have not yet been identified (Genevini et al., Strabbioli et al.). Some highly favourable results were obtained in sandy soils (Strabbioli et al.) with a combination of certain composts and mineral fertilizers (Del Zan et al.) ; in this last case the compost was derived from urban solid waste supplemented with sewage sludge, which (apart from the question of the accumulation of heavy metals) is of major practical interest.

The paper presented by Coppola et al. considered the problem of preparing compost, its stabilization and the sanitizing of sludge. The paper devoted particular attention to temperature changes in the fermenting mass and from gas exchanges, on which basis it was suggested that the process should be monitored.

As research continues and a more detailed critical and comparative examination is made of the results obtained, it will be possible to draw further conclusions on a firmer basis.

SESSION V : STRATEGIES, LEGISLATION AND MARKETING

Legislation for compost in the Netherlands
Part I
Part II

Compost marketing

Experimental work carried out by the Piedmont
(Italy) region with regard to the re-employment of
garbage in agriculture

Research on municipal solid-waste composting in
Greece

Review of the up-to-date technological trends
concerning compost production from solid domestic
wastes

Critical evaluations on the strategies used for
the municipal solid waste treatment

REPORT BY O. VERDONCK

LEGISLATION FOR COMPOST IN THE NETHERLANDS - PART I

J. OOSTHOEK - N.V. VAM

INTRODUCTION

The first part of this reading will deal with the history of the use of compost. This history clearly shows the useful function which compost has served in the past.

In earlier times, it was precisely the trace elements in the compost which were valuable. A large number of compost plants have disappeared since the 1960s, and the composting of household waste is currently only applied on a limited scale. Composting can receive greater attention in the future due to the high priority awarded to the re-use of waste materials within the Waste Act. The most important component of the household waste is the organic fraction.

Yet household waste contains not only beneficial elements for soil fertility, but harmful ones as well. The heavy metals factor is decisive in this regard.

The addition of heavy metals to the soil involves risks for the natural vegetation, as well as for food-crops. These risks apply both to the level of production and the quality of the products grown.

These problems are extremely present in densely populated areas and industrialised countries such as the Netherlands. A high load-level is already present in the form of emissions from industry and traffic.

There are large quantities of waste materials which contain heavy metals. Household waste, sewage sludge and sludge from harbours. The big rivers carry with them large quantities of metals to the harbours, where the sludge particles are deposited.

In the Netherlands, the contamination of waste materials by heavy metals has reached such a point that measurements must be taken to achieve regulations for the use of soil improvers made from waste materials.

Guidelines have already been established for compost made from household wastes.

In the short term, compost from existing separation installations is still permitted, in accordance with the levels of heavy metals contained. Only a limited quantity may be applied.

HISTORY

The use of the wastes from human society in agriculture is quite ancient. As long ago as the Middle Ages, waste materials were brought to the fields at specified times. There was even a livery trade in these waste materials. The product was actually considered so valuable that it was forbidden to export waste materials to Belgium. Not so very long ago, the Netherlands once again began exporting waste to Belgium, a fact with which the Netherlands and Belgium were actually not happy. In the long term, Belgium will definitively close its borders to these imports, and that is the other way around. Waste will have gone from valuable to worthless.

Yet after 1900, the introduction of artificial fertilisers changed the situation entirely. It became possible to bring in nutrients from outside. This made it possible to greatly increase productions levels. Even the poorer soils could now be cultivated.

During the first two decades of the 20th century, artificial fertilisers were used in such a one-sided manner that problems arose for certain soils in the Netherlands.

This problem was the most severe in the northeastern part of the Netherlands, where poor and sandy soils are common. We know now that these problems could largely be traced to deficiency-related diseases.

After the peat had been excavated (for use as fuel), these soils were cultivated with the use of city waste. Although production levels were not high, no problems arose. When artificial fertilisers conquered the market, however, the use of urban wastes was abandoned, and with bad results.

During the period 1920-1925, the farmers became aware of the problems caused by the lack of compost from urban waste. Farmers organisations called for compost from urban waste to once again be made available for use on their soil. These demands were heard most loudly in the province of Drenthe (northeastern Netherlands). During this same period, plans were being made in The Hague for the incineration of urban waste. These two factors have served to determine the history of the composting of household waste in the Netherlands.

The Dutch Ministry of Agriculture urged that the waste from the city of The Hague be used for arable farming. This resulted in the setting up of an organisation which was to provide the transport, upgrading and sales of these wastes.

In 1931, the VAM company was opened in the village of Wijster. The VAM (Waste-Disposal Company) is a limited liability company, all shares of which are in the hands of the Ministry of Agriculture.

The setting up of the VAM was actually the result of the fact that the soil in the northeastern Netherlands was lacking not only nutrients, but was particularly poor in trace elements as well. It was recognised at a later point that the good results obtained with the compost were due not only to the organic materials which they contained, but that the spectacular results were due primarily to the trace elements. A lack of copper was noted in particular.

What a tragedy therefore that it is now the heavy metals in particular, of which copper is certainly one of the problematic factors, which will serve to hem in the future sales of compost.

A great deal of renowed interest was shown in composting activities during the 1950s and the 1960s. In 1960, there were 15 compost plants in the Netherlands. The waste from some 2 million inhabitants was processed by these plants into compost.

Yet the composition of the waste changed greatly, and in a manner disadvantageous to composting. Although 80 % of the waste was converted into compost during the initial period, this percentage was reduced after 1960 to 30-40 %. For many municipalities, composting was no longer an interesting proposition for waste-treatment.

COMPOST PRODUCTION

Now only 80,000 tonnes of compost are produced each year. There are still five plants engaged in the production of compost from household waste. Yet a strong trend is being seen which would indicate that the production will be expanded in coming years. Dutch Waste Act has established the following priorities :
- limiting waste materials ;
- the re-use of waste materials.

In view of the fact that a large fraction of the waste is organic, consideration is being given within the context of re-use to the composting of this fraction.

In all of the concepts drafted until now, several of which are already at quite advanced stage, the central role is occupied by compost. As a result of this, the production of compost will be expanded. The main question therefore remains whether a market exists for this compost :
a. Is there a demand for compost ?
b. Can an acceptable quality be produced ?

It is difficult to ascertain the demand for compost. There exists, after all, a large surplus of manure (animals). This latter "product" contains relatively little organic matter and (too) many nutrients (phosphate and nitrate). In general, it can be stated that a market does exist for good compost, from the point of view of the organic matter, and particularly for clay soils.

A good compost is one which not only has a high level of organic matter, but also one which contains negligible levels of harmful substances. This primarily involves the quantity of heavy metals which are introduced into the soil via the compost.

HEAVY METALCONTENT OF THE SOIL AND ADMISSIBLE LEVELS

Studies have been carried out in the Netherlands into the levels of heavy metals contained in the soil (1). A study has also been carried out for the purpose of gathering information concerning admissible levels for the soil and for plants (2). Calculations have been made concerning the rate at which the metalcontent of the soil is increased with given qualities of compost and to determine the point at which the maximum admissible level is reached with given quantities.

The following is a calculation carried out for a number of metals in sandy soils. Premises :
- Topsoil weight 3×10^6 kg/ha ; tilling depth 25 cm ; mass in volume terms 1.2 kg per dm^3.
- Compost quality (average) ;

Zink	800	mg/kg	on dm
Lead	700	"	" "
Copper	270	"	" "
Nickel	35	"	" "
Cadmium	2.3	"	" "

- Compost dosage 3 tonnes d.m. per ha/yr.
  Every 4 years $\pm$ 20 tonnes of compost at 60 % d.m.
- In making the calculations, the normal dosage of artificial fertiliser has been assumed. No reductions have therefore been made in the dosage of artificial fertiliser for the nutrients given with the compost.

INFLUENCE OF COMPOST ON SOIL QUALITY

	Zn	Pb	Cu	Ni	Cd	Lit.
Dose in gr. per ha/yr.						
With : Compost	2400	2100	810	105	7.5	
Art. fert.	163	51	17	11	5.5	3, 4, 5, 6
Deposition	394	98	56	11	2.7	7
Total	2997	2249	883	127	15.7	
Discharge in gr. per ha/yr.						
With : Plantuptake	250	1.5	40	2.3	1.4	8
Leaching	88	4.0	75	25.0	1.3	9
Total	338	5.5	115	27.3	2.7	
Net amount in gr. per ha/yr.						
	2659	2243	768	100	13.0	
Increase in levels in soil per yr. in mg/kg/dm.						
	0.89	0.75	0.26	0.033	0.0043	
Normal levels in soil in mg/kg/dm.						
	44	31	11	5	0.3	1
Max. admissible in soil in mg/kg/dm.						
	100	100	50	20	1.0*	2
Years in which max. level is reached with annual dose						
	63	92	150	454	162	

* 0.5 mg/kg/dm is given for the most sensitive soils.

The above shows that zinc is the most critical element. With an annual dose of compost of the quality stated above, the maximum admissible level in the soil is reached after only 63 years. In other words, zinc is the element which limits the use of compost.

The use of compost of the quality stated above is less critical for the other elements. A point should be noted here, however, with regard to cadmium. Should the maximum admissible level in the soil be 0.5 mg/kg, the limit will be reached after only 47 years.

It would not be realistic, however, to suppose that compost will be applied consistently and regularly during these periods. Yet such calculations do show that levels harmful to crop yield or crop quality can be reached rather quickly.

It is for this reason that measurements must be taken, in order to achieve regulations for the use of compost from household waste materials.

LEVELS OF HEAVY METALS IN COMPOST

The raw materials for composting are household waste or fractions of household waste. A comparison has been made of a number of systems with the following processing methods :

A. Van Maanen composting : In this process, the mixed household waste is composted, with any preparation. This takes place in large heaps (8 metres in height) and the process takes about 12 months. After the composting, the compost is sieved out and inerts are removed.

B. The collected household waste is separated into two fractions. This takes place by the use of sieves. The fine material contains most of the easily degradable organic material. Following magnetic separation, the composting takes place. Between 2.5 and 5 months is needed for this process. After the composting process is completed, the inerts are removed or reduced by sieving and grinding.

C. The collected waste is shredded. Processing methods are then carried out which result in a fraction to be composted. This fraction is already free of inerts as glas, plastic. After the composting has taken place, no further processing is needed.

D. Separation at the source. The organic components are collected separately at the households. All necessary steps are taken to ensure that those components containing heavy metals do not enter the organic components.

Compost-quality rated according to the various processing systems and on the base of collection techniques.

System	A	B	C	D
level in mg/kg/dm				
Zinc	1700	800	520	230
Lead	800	700	420	160
Copper	600	270	100	50
Chrome	180	70	40	30
Nickel	110	35	25	10
Cadmium	7	2.5	1.8	1.0

It is clear that much depends on the processing system. The worst quality apparently occurs when the waste is composted in its entirety without any form of preparation (system A). Composting on high windrows for a period of 12 months has a negative effect on the quality.

The explanation is simple ; because everything passes through the composting process, including all those components containing metals, the chance that metals dissolve and enter the fine components is a real one. The composting period is very long, the leaching of metals is a process which takes place with time ; the longer the contact period, the more metals will dissolve.

Studies have shown that not only does leaching take place, but also that metal particles degrade into smaller particles. Lead capsules from wine bottles, for example, dissolve in powder form after several months in a compost heap (10).

If separation is carried out beforehand by means of sieves and magnets (system B), the quality appears to improve. Yet metal containing components will also be present in this fraction of the household waste. This assumption is supported by the results of studies which have shown that the composting period is an influencing factor. The same basic materials, when subjected to varying composting periods, display differing levels of heavy metals in the sieved compost. In both cases, a mature compost was produced with a C/N of less than 20.

The following levels were noted in mg/kg on dry matter.

Composting period	Zn	Pb	Cu	Cr	Ni	Cd
72 days	706	474	238	47	33	2.03
180 days	820	999	433	54	43	2.39

When inert materials were removed beforehand (system C), the quality with regard to heavy metals appeared to improve even further.

If household waste is collected in mixed form and later subjected to mechanical processing in order to extract components suitable for composting, the following recommendations are made :

a. If not all ballast materials are removed beforehand, a composting method should be applied which produces ripe compost in a short time.

b. The lowest levels of heavy metals are achieved if all ballast materials are removed beforehand.

The best possible quality with regard to heavy metals is achieved if care is taken to ensure that the organic components are kept separately in the households (system D).

The attempt has been made here above to indicate the possibilities to reach the best possible quality of compost from household waste or fractions of household waste.

LITERATURE

1. Driel, W. van and Smilde, K.W., 1981 : Heavy metal contents in Dutch arable soils. VDLUFA-Congres Trier. Landwirtschaftliche Forschung Sonder-heft 38 : 305-313

2. Landbouw-Advies-Commissie Milieukritische Stoffen, 1985: Signaalwaarden voor de gehalten van milieukritische stoffen in de grond met het oog op landbouwkundige gebruiksmogelijkheden van verontreinigde bodems. (voorlopige versie).

3. Maas, G., 1980 : Schatting van de hoeveelheid zware metalen, die door de toegediende scheikundige meststoffen op de Belgische landbouwgronden worden afgezet. Landbouwtijdschrift 33 : 326-332.

4. Henkens, Ch. H., 1983 : Beleid ten aanzien van de cadmiumaanvoer in de akkerbouw. De Buffer 29 (1) : 1-51.

5. Henkens, Ch. H., 1983 : Cadmium in meststoffen. Bedrijfsontwikkeling 14 (6) : 484-489.

6. Nog niet gepubliceerde IB-gegevens, 1985.

7. Meent, D. van de, Oosterwijk, J. van and Aldenberg, T., maart 198 RID-VEWIN Meetnet Regenwater 1978-1982. Deel 1 : Samenvatting en statistische bewerking van de meetresultaten. ECOWAD-84-01, RIVM.

8. Werkgroep Samenstellingseisen Meststoffen van de commissie van Deskundigen inzake het Meststoffenbesluit, 1983 : De zware-metaal-belasting van de grond door gebruik van meststoffen en afvalstoffen.

9. Haan, S. de, 1980 : Die chemische Zusammensetzung von Dränwassern und mit Klärschlamm oder Müllkompost behandelte Böden. Landwirtschaftliche Forschung 33 : 166-178.

10. Rosmalen, G.R.E.M., Lustenhouwer, J.W.A., Oosthoek, J., Senden, M.M.G.: Heavy metalsources and contamination mechanisms in compost production. MER-3 symposium, Antwerp, March 18-20, 1986.

LEGISLATION FOR COMPOST IN THE NETHERLANDS - PART II

J.P.N. SMIT, Ministry of Housing, Physical Planning and the Environment

Do we have in the Netherlands special legislation for compost only ? The answer must be : none ! It would be too easy to say to you : "That is all, thank you for your attention". But of course we have a lot of legislation that somehow does give rules concerning materials like compost (fig. 1)

FIG. 1

LEGISLATION FOR COMPOST ONLY ?

NONE, BUT

. FERTILISERS ACT
. SOIL PROTECTION ACT
. WASTES ACT

AND

. HINDRANCE ACT
. AIR POLLUTION ACT
. SURFACE WATERS POLLUTION ACT
. NOISE HINDRANCE ACT

SO :

YES, A LOT OF ACTS

We have the Fertilisers Act, the Soil Protection Act and the Wastes Act. These three acts can give straightforward rules for compost. There are a lot of acts that can give rules for the productionsite of compost, i.e. the Air Pollution Act, the Surfacewaters Pollution Act, the Noise Hindrance Act and the Hindrance Act. So I conclude : In the Netherlands there are a lot of acts concerning compost. We'll discuss the three first mentioned acts.

The Fertilisers Act was published in 1947, and gives rules concerning the prevention of falsifications and malversations with regard of (mainly) artificial fertilisers (fig. 2).

FIG. 2

FERTILISERS ACT

- SINCE 1947 PREVENTION OF FALSIFICATIONS AND MALVERSATIONS

- REVISION UNDER DISCUSSION IN PARLIAMANT

- RULES CONCERNING

  . TRADE OF FERT.
    ° QUALITY SPECIFICATIONS
    ° SOIL PROTECTION
  . REMOVAL OF ANIMAL MANURE

WHAT IS A FERTILISER,

1e SUPPLY FOR BETTER GROWTH
2e SUBSTRATE
3e NUTRIENT FOR PLANTS

COMPOST : 1 and/or 3.

     For animal manure as fertiliser the need for prevention of falsification was not high. The farmers used the manure produced in their own farms for their own arable land or grassland or sold it to their neighbours.

     But at the moment the situation in the Netherlands has changed dramatically compared with twenty years ago. Because of the fact that there is a socalled "bio-industry" that produces about a hundred million ton of animal manure each year, stringent rules are needed. Nowadays it is impossible to spread this enormous amount of manure all over the countryside without polluting the air, the soil, the groundwater and the surfacewaters.

     The revision of the Fertiliser Act is under discussion in the Parliament at the moment. The revision looks at rules concerning the trade of fertilisers, in concreto for the quality specifications as a fertiliser but also as a potential source for soil pollution and therefore for crop reduction.

     It also looks at rules for the trade, the quality and the quantity of animal manure, to be used as fertiliser. It is very important to realise what this act means by "fertiliser". A fertiliser can be :
1° a supply for a better growth for crops, plants and trees ;
2° a substrate to grow a crop on ;
3° a nutrient for plants and so on.

     Compost can be number one and/or number three, the organic content of compost improves the quality of the soil and the inorganic part of the compost can be the nutrient for the plant.

     The Soil Protection Act is alo under discussion in the Parliament (fig. 3).

FIG. 3

SOIL PROTECTION ACT

- UNDER DISCUSSION IN PARLIAMENT

- RULES CONCERNING THE PROTECTION OF THE SOIL AND THE GROUNDWATER

- ORDERS IN COUNCIL (DECREES) ABOUT

    . BRINGING SUBSTANCES ON OR IN THE SOIL
    . USING SUBSTANCES FOR IMPROVING THE SOIL
    . ETCETERA

TOP - ITEMS :

1e PRESERVATION GOOD QUALITY OF THE SOIL
2e NO DISTURBANCE BALANCES IN THE SOIL

It should not surprise you but this act is the "twin-brother" of the Fertilisers Act. These acts need each other very much. The Soil Protection Act gives rules about the protection of the soil and of the groundwater. In vast parts of the Netherlands groundwater is the only reliable source of drinkingwater. Decrees are prepared or will be prepared about bringing substances (i.e. different types of waste) on or in the soil and about using substances (i.e. compost, manure) for improving of fertilising the soil. The top-items anyway are :
1. the preservation of the good quality of the soil
2. no disturbance of the balances in the soil.
As a matter of fact these two items mean that all that has been brought in the soil (i.e. cadmium as impurity in artificial fertilisers) must be taken away by intake through the crop or disappear by natural processes (i.e. the organic compount of compost disappears by slow oxydation).
The Waste Act has been published in 1976 and gives rules concerning the protection of the environment against wastes (fig. 4).

FIG. 4

WASTES ACT

- RULES CONCERNING THE PROTECTION OF THE ENVIRONMENT AGAINST WASTES

- DECREES FOR CERTAIN WASTES IN RELATION TO PROVINCIAL PLANNING

- BY ORDER : REMOVAL OF HOUSEHOLD WASTE BY MUNICIPAL AUTHORITIES

- GUIDELINES BY NATIONAL GOVERNMENT

Very important instruments of this act are :
1. the possibility of ordering the Dutch Provinces to write plans for the handling of their wastes.
2. the duty that each municipality publishes an order about the removal of their household waste (and carries out this order).
3. the possibility that the central government writes guidelines about the removal of waste.

699

These instruments can be very important for compost. In concreto the provinces can dictate in their plans that the municipal authorities have to produce compost out of the household waste and other wastes. The municipal authorities can prescribe the citizens by their order to keep separated the organic fraction of their waste. After collection this organic waste has less impurities than the organic fraction out of waste-separation systems.

Last but (hopefully) not least the central government can give guidelines about the handling of organic waste, the processing (i.e. composting) of the waste and the use of the products.

Such a guideline has been written for the provincial plan for the removal of sewage sludge (February 1986) (fig. 5).

FIG. 5

GUIDELINES PROVINCIAL PLAN REMOVAL SEWAGE SLUDGE (7-2-1986)

- RECOMMENDATIONS FOR

. QUALITY OF COMPOST
. QUANTITY/YEAR. ACRE

DIVIDED IN COMPOST OF

I. PURE SEWAGE SLUDGE

II. MIX OF SLUDGE AND OTHER ORGANIC WASTES OR ONLY OTHER ORGANIC WASTES (i.e. HOUSEHOLD, BREWERIES, ETC.)

In it are written down recommendations for the quality of compost and for the quantities to use per acre per year.

The compost has been divided in two types. The firt type is compost, produced out of sewage sludge only. The second type is compost, produced out of a mix of sludge and other wastes or out of other wastes only (i.e. a mix of sludge and organic wastes of agrarian-industrial activities or the organic fraction of household waste).

Also the recommendations for the quality are divided in two sections.

Both recommendations are given the maximum level for seven heavy metals and for arsenic. The recommendations for type II are divided in short-term (i.e. the next five years) and the long term (i.e. from 1991 till 2000).

The recommendations for the quantities to be given are the result of both wishful and practical thinking. The wishful thinking gives the idea of preserving a good quality of the soil and the practical thinking comes out of the knowledge that in the Netherlands it is impossible with the normally used machinery to give less than 20 ton of substances like compost and dewatered manure pro hectare arable land.

The figures are given in fig. 6 and in the tables 1 till 4.

FIG. 6

	QUALITY			USE ON ARABLE LAND QUANTITY/HA
I	Hg	5	ppm dm	2 ton dm/1 year
	Cd	5	"	4 ton dm/2 year
	Cr	500	"	6 ton dm/3 year
	Ni	100	"	8 ton dm/4 year
	Pb	500	"	
	Cu	600	"	
	Zn	2000	"	
	As	10	"	

		Short	long	
II	Hg		1,5 ppm dm	3 ton dm/1 year
	Cd	3	1,5	6 ton dm/2 year
	Cr	300	100	9 ton dm/3 year
	Ni	60	50	12 ton dm/4 year
	Pb	300– 500	150	
	Cu	400	50	
	Zn	1300	250	
	As	10	10	

Till 1-1-1989

Pb :	750	ppm
Cu :	500	ppm

Because of the fact that it is impossible for the producers of compost out of the organic fractions of mechanical waste separation systems to conform to these recommendations for the quality of the compost, they have been given permission till January 1989 to produce a compost with maximal 750 ppm lead and maximal 500 ppm copper in the dry matter.

A last remark.

In my opinion a government who wishes to make rules, needs a good cooperation with the private enterprises who will be the target of those rules. Happily the VAM was very cooperative by giving a lot of figures about the quality of their different types of compost. On behalf of this cooperation it was possible to give the shown recommendations of the qualities and quantities of compost.

	indicative maximum contents
Hg	5 mg/kg ds
Cd	5 mg/kg ds
Cr	500 mg/kg ds
Ni	100 mg/kg ds
Pb	500 mg/kg ds
Cu	600 mg/kg ds
Zn	2000 mg/kg ds
As	10 mg/kg ds

Table 1 : Recommendations for the maximum contents in compost, produced out of sludge only.

	contents (100 % d.s.)
	arable land
per year	2 ton/ha
per 2 years	4 ton/ha
per 3 years	6 ton/ha
per 4 years	8 ton/ha

Table 2 : Dosage for compost, produced out of sludge only pro one or more years pro hectare arable land, based on 100 % dry matter.

	Short term	Long term
Hg	3 mg/kg ds	1,5 mg/kg ds
Cd	3 mg/kg ds	1,5 mg/kg ds
Cr	300 mg/kg ds	100 mg/kg ds
Ni	60 mg/kg ds	50 mg/kg ds
Pb	300 - 500 mg/kg ds	150 mg/kg ds
Cu	400 mg/kg ds	50 mg/kg ds
Zn	1300 mg/kg ds	250 mg/kg ds
As	10 mg/kg ds	10 mg/kg ds

Table 3 : Recommendations for the quality of compost out of a mix of sludge and other organic wastes or compost out of other organic wastes only.

	dosage (100 % d.s.) arable land
per year	3 ton/ha
per 2 years	6 ton/ha
per 3 years	9 ton/ha
per 4 years	12 ton/ha

Table 4 : Dosage of the compost of table 3.

COMPOST MARKETING

PROF. DR. U. FUNKE
Rhineland-Palatinate "Fachhochschule"*
Department Mainz II
- Economics -

Summary
This article deals with the marketing of municipal solid waste (MSW)
compost. It shows how to develop a marketing concept based on a
market survey.
Composting is a form of waste utilization which has its place
alongside recovery of materials such as paper and glass and
extraction of energy content. Consequently, compost is a typical
product of recycling with recycling defined as the sum of all
processes by which production or consumption wastes are returned to
the economic cycle as input factors.
The following remarks concern the marketing of MSW compost, i.e.
compost derived from household waste with or without the admixture of
sewage sludge ; the composting of garden wastes both of municipal and
household origin, mainly for own use, does not yet give rise to
marketing problems.

1. MSW COMPOST IN THE FEDERAL REPUBLIC OF GERMANY

Approximately 640,000 tonnes of waste and 50,000 tonnes of dewatered
sewage sludge were processed to about 250,000 - 300,000 tonnes of compost
in 17 composting plants in Germany in 1985 (figure 1). This is equivalent
to about 3 % of total domestic waste and less than 1 % of sewage sludge.

The main uses for compost are recultivation (35 %), viticulture
(25 %) and landscaping (25 %). However, finding outlets for MSW compost is
a constant problem. Only about 50-60 % of the production volume can
actually be sold, the rest is either given away free or cannot be disposed
of at all.

In the light of growing ecological awareness, it is becoming
increasingly difficult to market MSW compost, owing to the high level of
contamination. An order on MSW compost is in preparation in Germany,
containing comparatively low limit values for hazardous substances.

The key to compost marketing in future is therefore the quality of
the product. The following are the main measures taken with a view to
curtailing the content of hazardous substances in waste-derived compost :
- selection of relatively uncontaminated sewage sludge or exclusion of
  sludge admixture ;
- prior screening of the fine waste fraction ;
- separate collection of waste materials (paper, glass) and composting of
  residual refuse ;
- separate collection and composting of exclusively organic wastes (kitchen
  and garden wastes). This led to a sharp drop in heavy metal contamination
  (figure 2).

* equivalent to British Polytechnic

Figure I : Composting plants in Germany, 1985

In the light of the analysis data, the future of waste composting is considered to lie with the separate collection and composting of organic wastes.

Heavy metal	Means for MSW compost mg/kg DM (1)	Means from 'biocompost' pilot tests (mg/kg DM)				Limit values municipality of Tübingen mg/kg DM (6)
		Witzen-hausen (2)	Baienfurt (3)	Schorndorf (4)	Heidel-berg (5)	
Lead	513	189	50	38	40–140	150
Cadmium	5.5	0.7	0.5	0.5	0.6	3
Chromium	71.4	74	30	18	60	150
Copper	274	51	30	21	30	150
Nickel	44.9	36	20	18	12	25
Zinc	1,570	367	200	190	190	376

DM = day matter

Figure 2 : Analysis of heavy metals in MSW compost and compost from separately collected, exclusively organic wastes (biocompost) and limit values for the municipality of Tübingen (Land Baden-Württemberg).

2. MARKET ANALYSIS AS AN ESSENTIAL BASIS FOR A MARKETING CONCEPT

Before a compost marketing concept can be drawn up, both the structure of the market in question and emerging trends must be examined. The following aspects have proved to be significant for an analysis :

. demand analysis
  target groups
  structure of the marketing area
  competing soil conditioners
  attitude of the target groups to compost
  potential uses for compost
  quality requirements
  required degree of decomposition and particle size
  price acceptance
  preferred type of packaging, delivery and application
  readiness to accept long-term delivery contracts and to set up intermediate stores.

. analysis of the competition
  compost grades
  particle size, degree of decomposition
  production capacity and technology
  sales volume
  customer structure
  prices, terms

advertising
packaging
distribution organization
management quality

. <u>analysis of the relevant social, economic and technical developments</u>

. <u>sales estimates</u>

3. <u>COMPOST MARKETING CONCEPT</u>
    Basically the marketing concept for compost does not differ from that
for other products. It is derived from the business strategy and covers the
three major areas of marketing principles, marketing objectives and
marketing strategies and measures (figure 3).

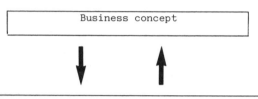

Business concept				
Marketing concept				
	Product	Market	Price	Communi-cation	Distri-bution
Principles	On which general guidelines is marketing to be based ?				
Objectives	What quantitative and qualitative results are to be achieved ?				
Strategies and measures	By means of which short-, medium- and long-term activities are these results to be achieved ?				

Figure 3 : Content of a marketing concept

3.1. <u>Marketing principles</u>
    The marketing principles contain general guidelines for compost
marketing, e.g. information on the target hierarchy in the waste-processing
industry, the desired compost quality including monitoring, geographical
extension of the market, cooperation with other composting plants, pricing
and logistics.

3.2. <u>Marketing objectives</u>
    When a composting plant is being planned, there are short-, medium-
and long-term marketing objectives in keeping with the three planning
stages of market preparation, launch phase and market
consolidation/expansion.
    The short-term objectives concern preparation of the market, which
should begin 2-3 years before the start of production. The aim is to create
the organizational and psychological conditions for a successful launching

of compost on the market, e.g. creation of the product image and of
confidence in the quality of the product on the part of the potential
buyer.

The medium-term objectives concern the launch phase, ie the first
three years of production. The aim is to sell a given volume of compost per
year. This involves recruiting as many first-time users as possible, with
particular emphasis on opinion-moulders.

Finally, the long-term objectives concern the phase of consolidation
and expansion of the market, during which first-time users are to be
converted to regular customers and new customer groups are to be recruited.

3.3. Marketing strategies and measures

While the marketing strategies stake out the framework for action,
the marketing measures determine the actual course of action with the aid
of the marketing mix. Thus, for example, the marketing strategy based on
the market analysis determines which target groups in which areas are to be
reached with which particle sizes, eg mature compost of the 20 mm fraction
for winegrowers within a radius of 25 km from the composting plant.

This is followed by the decision on the marketing mix to be adopted,
comprising the components product mix, contract mix, communication mix and
distribution mix (figure 4).

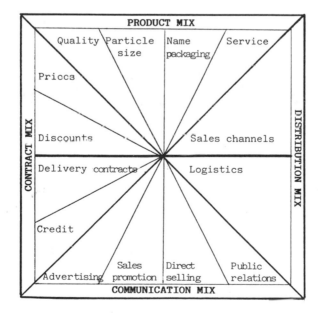

Figure 4 : Components of the compost marketing mix

The key to product mix is compost quality. Our market analyses revealed that most potential users, eg farmers and market gardeners, rejected compost derived from municipal waste/sludge owing to the high content of inerts and hazardous substances, and that there was heavy demand for compost derived from separately collected, exclusively organic wastes. As in the case of branded products, buyers expect maximum uniformity of quality, regularly monitored by an independent institute. Before compost is applied for the first time, a soil analysis should be made and repeated at regular intervals.

Generally speaking, mature compost is used in agriculture in Germany; raw compost is often used for organic filter construction and special compost consisting, for example, of a mixture of MSW compost, bark and peat in horticulture.

The compost price is the decisive factor in the contract mix. This ranges from 5 to 30 DM/t (without freight) in Germany for MSW compost, which is well below the production cost. Although we established that customers are prepared to pay more for better quality compost derived from separately collected, exclusively organic wastes, there are strict limits to price increases mainly as a result of the increase in green manuring, particularly in vineyards and orchards.

In view of inadequate knowledge of compost and reservations about its use, the communication mix is extremely important. There is a particular need to provide information about MSW composts which do not sell without promotion. In addition to practical advice, professional public relations activity is required in the form of information campaigns directed at specific target groups.

This is a possible area for supra-regional cooperation. In 1980, the three composting plants in North Rhine-Westphalia formed a compost marketing association with the following tasks :
- conducting of quality checks and monitoring in the three plants, with particular emphasis on compliance with hygiene standards and quality improvement ;
- development and testing of new compost products ;
- opening up of new outlets with the aid of application trials ;
- stepping up of practical advice services to potential customers in the form of information sessions and appointment of a sales officer for visits to clients ;
- expansion of the penetration of compost while simultaneously dismantling the negative image ;
- construction of a sales organization both for the public/commercial and the private sector.

The association considers the main advantages of its existence to be the following :
- regular exchange of experience ;
- continuous quality control using standard methods ;
- preparation of joint advertising and information material (compost film, compost handbook, brochures with practical tips) ;
- clearing house system for special requirements ;
- securing of supplies when one plant cannot deliver.

The following were the main problems :
- sluggish decision-making processes ;
- different composting methods and qualities ;
- mutual competition.

The distribution mix determines whether sales are made directly or through agents, e.g. agricultural cooperatives. It also concerns storage, construction of intermediate stores and transport media. Our market analyses revealed considerable regional differences regarding the preferred form of delivery and the willingness of clients to set up their own intermediate store.

4. FUTURE OUTLOOK

Quality is the key to the marketing of MSW composts. Increasing awareness of environmental issues and improved analytical methods are raising compost quality requirements. If relatively uncontaminated MSW compost can be produced in large quantities at an acceptable price, composting will become an increasingly important part of the waste-processing industry. The large number of small composting plants for green wastes which have been constructed in Germany in the last few years provide a clear indication of this.

COMMENTS

1. Guideline 10 "Quality criteria and recommended applications for MSW compost", Ministerial Gazette of the Rhineland-Palatinate Government, 1985.
2. Second interim report on the "Green waste bin" project in Witzenhausen, March 1985.
3. Baienfurt test report, 1984.
4. "Blue waste bin", Schorndorf, report for the City of Mainz, 1984.
5. Stuttgart University, March 1986.
6. W. Bidlingmaier/J. Folmer, Experience with composting moist wastes from the recyclable materials bin and the bio bin, in O. Tabasaran (ed.), Waste recycling options, Bielefeld 1985, p. 212.

EXPERIMENTAL WORK CARRIED OUT BY THE PIEDMONT (ITALY) REGION WITH REGARD TO THE RE-EMPLOYMENT OF GARBAGE IN AGRICULTURE

A. TROMBETTA

Assessorato per l'Ambiente e l'Energia della
Regione Piemonte (Italia)

Summary

Since 1982 the Environment Department of the Piedmont Region has been engaged on a primarily experimental five-year research study of the re-employment of urban and similar sludges in agriculture. As part of this research, a set of regulations has been drawn up to cover the application limits in relation to types of soil and cultivation,and the authorisation and checking criteria. The data collected with regard to sludge quality and quantity, types of treatment   plant and the forms of disposal envisaged have been automatically processed with reference to land capability maps; the constraints imposed by the programme and those arising from the nature of the territory. The actions described are preliminary steps towards planning, in particular with regard to assessing the possibility of using sludges as such, or the desirability of treating them, including composting, whenever certain factors relating to the quality of sludges, or local conditions, prevent their being employed without prior treatment. Similar studies have been launched for urban, industrial and agricultural wastes.

1.1. Introduction

The problems associated with the use of garbage in agriculture are highly complex. Investigation in depth from the scientific standpoint is needed to enable solutions that are correct in terms of recycling and re-employment to be identified.

With this in mind, the Piedmont Region has begun by facing the problems raised by the use in agriculture of sludges left over after the purification of urban waste water, in anticipation of the entry into operation of the purification plants contemplated in its Water Rehabilitation Plan.

A primarily experimental five-year research study was commenced for this purpose in 1982. The participants are two Turin University Departments (Agrarian Chemistry, Microbiology and Agrarian Industries), the Istituto per le Piante da Legno e l'Ambiente (Wood Plant and the Environment Institute - IPLA) and several public water purification consortia. The research is being coordinated by the Region's Environment Department.

Since that date, and in the light of technical and administrative experience acquired in the examination of authorisation applications within the meaning of D.P.R. n° 915/82 on garbage, showing that wastes are being actively employed in agriculture in Piedmont, the Region has extended the research to include urban, industrial and agricultural wastes.

The aims and modalities of the research, observations on its prelimina ry results and certain aspects of programming form the subject-matter of this paper.

1.2. Research aims

In the absence of a national and international reference standard, and in view of the variability and lack of uniformity of the data available, the research is much concerned with applications, though on strictly scientific bases.

The following aims are being pursued:
1) acquisition of data concerning the physical, chemical and biological of sludges and their agronomic effects;
2) determination of application limits and criteria in relation to sludges. soils, forms of cultivation and territorial constraints;
3) selection of application techniques
4) determination of authorisation and checking criteria and the technical tools required for rule-making and programming.

1.3. Research modalities

Determination of the quality and quantity of the sludges produced
A census has been made of the number, location and type of municipal wastewater treatment plants, the amount of sludge produced and the final disposal provisions contemplated (5-7). The quality aspect of this census has been put off to the next few years, since many of these plants are in the course of construction or at the start-up stage.

A total of 542 plants are to be found in 422 of the 1209 municipali- ties in Piedmont, some of which, of course, have more than one plant. In addition, there are 38 plants operated by consortia. No information is available with regard to 252 municipalities. These, however, all have less than 2000 inhabitants (80% have less than 1000).

Of these 542 plants, 65.9% are already in existence, while 32.3% are under construction or designed. As many as 447 (82.5%) serve populations of less than 5000, 63 cater for 5000 to 50,000 inhabitants, and only 13 serve more than 50,000.

An output of 74,393 tonnes of sludge (expressed as dry matter) is an- ticipated, 40% of which comes from the "Po-Sangone" (Turin) consortium, which has a plant serving 3 million inhabitants. 61.7% of the sludge will come from plants serving more than 50.000 inhabitants, 26.8% from plants serving 5000-50,000 and only 11.5% from those serving less than 5000.

Only 11% of these sludges are routed to land application. 65% is dumped. The way the remainder is disposed of is not known.

The data collected have been processed in map form to obtain information concerning the siting of these plants with reference to their potential, and in relation to land capability maps to determine the possible extent to which their output could be made accepted by land.

Analysis_of_sludges,_soils_and_types_of crops : choice_and_elaboration of_analytical methods - sludge_typing.
Parameters relating to the presence of toxic substances were chosen for the purpose of analysing the characteristics of sludges and establishing limits to their acceptability for land application, namely : a) permanent toxicity : total Cu, Zn, Pb, Ni, Cr, Cd, As, Hg, B, Se; b) Non-permanent toxicity (i.e. removable by simple treatments) : pH, salinity,S.A.R. (index), chlorides, sulphates, volatile phenols, surfactants; in relation to the amount of fertility features : total nitrogen, phosphorus and potassium, organic substance at 650°C (3-4) in relation to microbiological faecal contamination parameters and functional microbial groups conventionally determined in soils; in relation to biological parameters for the determination of phytotoxicity (germination and growth of test plants under controlled conditions in the laboratory and in the greenhouse) (2).

Analytical methods were devised and checked for these parameters.They were then used to analyse 8 sludges chosen as typical with respect to the waste water reaching the treatment plants, plant potential and type, and the sludge treatment line (7).

Four analysis were performed per year on each sludge to determine (in ter alia) their seasonal changes. The results (Table 1) are compared with the limits contained in the proposed EEC Directive (see Off. Gazz. C264/R of 8.10.82) as subsequently amended (Off.Gazz. C514/08 of 14.6.84).

Analytical methods were devised and checked for the following soil parameters : pH, texture (U.S.D.A.), cation exchange capacity extractable toxic element content (Cu, Zn, Pb, Ni, Cr, Cd, As, Hg, B, Se), and functional microbial parameters.

In the case of types of cultivation, methods were devised and checked solely for parameters regarded as indicators of permanent sludge toxicity.

Experimental_land application of_sludges
Numerous experimental applications were made on soils (1-7) mainly to assess : a) by field tests : the influence of sludges on the production of cereals (wheat, maize, rice) and trees (poplar); b) by greenhouse tests : the release into the soil of trace elements contained in the sludges and their absorption by test plants (Lolium italicum, Lactuca sativa), changes in sludges applied on soils over the course of time, and the effect of their application on the growing of vegetables (Tomatoes), flowers (Carnations, Tagetes, St. Paulia) and ornamental plants (Dieffenbachia and Dracaena).

As mentioned in the previous section, other greenhouse tests

Tab. 1 - Chemical composition of sludges.

| | Treatment Plant *) | | | | | | | | **) |
	BLL	BRA	COL	CAN	CSS	PIA	FOS	VER	ECC
pH	8.0	7.1	7.5	7.2	7.7	7.9	7.0	6.9	
Salinity	55	22	30	27	45	23	91	29	
					%				
Ashes	37.1	34.9	41.4	43.6	41.1	45.2	38.9	52.7	
Tot. C	34.9	36.2	32.9	31.3	32.6	30.8	34.0	26.9	
Tot. N	4.0	6.2	4.7	4.6	6.0	4.0	5.9	5.0	
Phosphorus	0.98	1.17	1.30	1.15	1.06	1.51	1.51	0.85	
Potassium	0.20	0.40	0.20	0.28	0.23	0.23	0.32	0.36	
					mg/kg				
Cu	292	351	684	240	296	796	415	277	1500
Zn	812	1723	3599	865	590	3225	2131	1287	3000
Pb	476	289	331	212	101	400	459	156	1000
Ni	80	67	236	62	49	481	69	125	400
Cr	100 0	130	900	69	55	2330	677	144	750
Cd	0.4	1.1	13	1.5	0.3	1.5	1.3	0.9	40
As	2.0	1.5	5.6	1.3	2.1	2.9	1.9	6.9	
Hg	3.1	1.1	3.4	2.3	1.6	1.2	4.6	0.9	16
Se	<0.1	<0.1	<0.1	<0.1	<0.1	<0.1	<0.1	<0.1	
B	86	59	88	52	55	89	68	75	
Surfactans	134	137	123	45	47	278	31	90	
Phenols vol.	6.4	1.8	0.9	1.6	2.5	1.4	3.2	1.0	

*) Treatment plant : BLL: Biella ; BRA : Bra; COLL : Collegno; CAN : Ca-
nelli; CAS : Cassano; PIA : Pianezza ; FOS : Fossano; VER : Verzuolo.

**) Imperative values of E.C.C.

were performed to devise methods for the evaluation of phytotoxicity.

Other organic substrates (composed sludges and municipal solid waste composts) were also used for some of the greenhouse tests, especially those concerned with phytotoxicity.

Lastly, the application techniques were tried out, primarily in relation to sludge humidity content.

1.4. Observations on the preliminary results

The sludges produced did not differ from each other in function of the plant from which they came. Despite their usually high levels of toxic elements and greatly varying composition, they also contained a large amount of organic substance and fertility elements, especially nitrogen. They were non-permanently toxic for crops. This was not due to their toxic content, but to the "non-stability" of their organic substances caused by incorrect treatment at the wastewater treatment plant.

The field and greenhouse trials showed that the crops tested had a production comparable with and occasionally higher than that of specimens amended with mineral fertiliser, and that the sludge had a positive residual effect. In the initial years of application, there were no substantial changes in the soil, nor was the absorption of heavy metals higher than in the untreated specimens. Phytotoxicity was apparent in both aerobically and anaerobically digested sludges, though not to the same extent. It was absent from sludges composted with lignocellulosic wastes.

In the light of these results, the study has been directed since its third year to the identification of parameters, the perfection of analytical methods and the establishment of limits for the "biological stability" of sludges and their content of physiologically active substances responsible for phytotoxicity. The heavy metals accumulation in soils and crops will also be evaluated.

1.5. Extention of the research study

Since experience acquired in the examination of authorisation applications within the meaning of D.P.R. n° 915/82 showed that some industrial and agricultural wastes were being traditionally and actively used by farmers, and in view of the fact that two plants for the treatment of municipal solid wastes and the production of compost forming part of the Regional Waste Disposal Plan had since come into operation, it was decided to extent the research study.

The wastes covered by this extension are primarily sludges and residues derived from operations in the agricultural food, paper, textile and pharmaceutical (extraction of active principles) industries and tanneries, and products derived from the treatment of the municipal solid and industrial wastes already mentioned.

It is expected that these wastes have a potential recovery value of

more than 70,000 tonnes of dry matter per year (i.e. the same as the amount
of sludges included in the census), giving a total of 140,000 of refuse in
the form of dry matter, plus at least 700,000 tonnes of garbage as such,e-
qual to about 15% of all the urban and industrial wastes produced in Piedmont.

The aims of this extension of the study are similar to those indicated
for urban sludges in section 2. They also concern the identification of
application limits, and technical criteria for the optimisation of processes and their economic soundness.

1.6. Regulations for land application of municipal sludges

The possibilities of using municipal sludges in agriculture that have
emerged from the study can only be put into practice on condition that the
provisions relating to their use are contained in specific technical standards, and that for each sludge specific authorisation on the part of the
proper authority is required.

These consideration also apply to other types of waste.

In this connection, the Piedmont Region has drawn up "Regulations for
land application of municipal sludges" (6). These contain:
   the general criteria for utilization on agricultural land in its various
   stages, from the production of sludge to its final utilisation;
- the limits of utilisation on the basis of the parameters analysed, in re
   lation to the time of application and the types of soil;
- the toxicity limits for soils and types of crop;
- the application rates;
- the criteria and procedures for authorisation and control.

With an eye to "utilisation" as opposed to "disposal", and in favour
of quality, the regulations lay down classes of sludge phytotoxicity in re
lation to toxic element content: less toxic sludges are subjected to smaller limitations on their use.

In the case of other types of garbage, rules differing with respect
to the type of sludge and its possible uses will be drawn up in the light
of the research results and what is produced in the Region.

1.7. Aspects of programming and conclusions

a) The use of garbage in agriculture is only possible through specific
rules governing its employment, careful checking of its quality and careful
management of its production, and examination of the extent to which the Re
gion can accept it.

b) Direct agricultural use is possible where the local conditions and
the quality of the garbage are favourable. In other words, land capable of
receiving garbage throughout the year must be available, the production of
garbage and the land must not be such as to require particular limitations,
and the quality of the garbage must make it possible to cut down the check-

ing of soils and crops. In Piedmont, for example, land application of muni
cipal sludges can be postulated for some small and medium-sized plants (up
to 50,000 inhabitants served), especially in some parts of the provinces
of Cuneo and Alessandria, provided the sludge characteristics fall within
the best toxicity classes laid down in the regulations.

c) Preference must be given to the composting of garbage, using simple
technologies wherever possible, in all cases where there are difficulties
in its direct use, especially where the treatments used are not sufficient
to ensure the stability of the organic substance, where controlled storage
of the garbage itself is impossible, and where special limits are placed
on its use on the land. For the purposes of composting, garbage must in
any event fall within the maximum limits laid down for the amount of toxic
elements and organic substance, so as to prevent hard-to-check dilutions
and avoidance of the technical rules.

d) Co-composting of municipal sludges with other good-quality industrial and agricultural residues (sludges or other garbage) is preferable to
ensure integrated treatments. In Piedmont at least three platforms with a
potential of more than 30,000 tonnes of refuse as such per year produced
in an area extending for a radius of 50 km can be postulated for the Torto
na (Alessandria) area, in the province of Novara and in the province of Cu
neo. Other platforms can be thought of as possible in the future in the
light of the indications of the qualitative census of the municipal wastes,
industrial residues and agricultural refuse produced.

e) A necessary first step to the provision of new municipal solid
waste composting plants is the trying out of the two recycling plants to
be brought into operation during 1986 according to the Region's waste disposal plan. The Region intends to check the quality of the compost, the
soundness of the technologies chosen, management questions, the economic
validity of the plants and the market for their products.

REFERENCES

1. CONSIGLIO, M., BARBERIS, R., PICCONE, G., DE LUCA, G. and TROMBETTA,
    A.,(1985). Productivity and quality of cereal crops grown on sludge
    treated soils, symposium on Processing and Use of Organic Sludge and
    liquid Agricultural Wastes E.C., Roma, 8-11 October 1985.
2. NAPPI, P., BARBERIS, R., CONSIGLIO, M., JODICE, R. and TROMBETTA A.,
    (1985). Biological evaluation of sludge phytotoxicity. Simposium on
    Processing and Use of Organic Sludge and Agricultural Wastes, E.C.,
    Roma, 8-11 October 1985.
3. PICCONE, G., SAPETTI, C., ORLANDO, P. and BARBIERI, D., (1982). Impie-
    go in agricoltura dei fanghi di depurazione. Controllo delle caratte-
    ristiche chimiche del fango prodotto nell'impianto consortile di Col-
    legno-Grugliasco-Rivoli (Torino). Ann. Fac. Sci. Agr., vol. VII, 513-
    523.
4. PICCONE, G., SAPETTI, C., BIASIOL, B., DE LUCA, G. and AJMONE MARSAN,
    F.A. (1985). Chemical properties of sewage sludges produced in the

Piedmontese area (italy). Symposium on Processing and Use of Organic
Sludge and liquid Agricultural Wastes, E.C., Roma, 8-11 October 1985.

5. Regione Piemonte, I.P.L.A. (1982). La capacità d'uso dei suoli del
    Piemonte ai fini agricoli e forestali. Published by Edizioni l'Equipe,
    Turin.

6. (1985) Regolamento per lo smaltimento in agricoltura dei fanghi resi-
    duati della depurazione delle acque. Proposta al Consiglio Regionale.
    D.G.R. n° 107÷42131 del 14 marzo 1985.

7. Regione Piemonte. Ricerca per l'utilizzo agricolo dei fanghi urbani.
    Stati di avanzamento della ricerca (1983-1984-1985).

RESEARCH ON MUNICIPAL SOLID-WASTE COMPOSTING IN GREECE

by
Evagelos KAPETANIOS
Unified Association of Municipalities and Communities of
Attica Compartment

Abstract
There are presently two research projects concerning municipal
solid-waste (MSW) composting in Greece. The Unified Association of
Municipalities and Communities of Attica Compartment (UAMCA) has
started a major research program for composting the fermentable
fraction of MSW which amounts to 59 % by weight. This program has two
main objectives. First, to experimentally produce compost and examine
its physical, chemical, and microbiological characteristics as well
as its effects on selected soil types and cultivations. Second, to
determine design parameters for constructing a compost production
plan based on available greek know-how. The results of this project
will be used in assessing the applicability of the composting process
in other regions of Greece.
In Heraklion, Crete a smaller research program is under way with the
objective of producing compost, determine its heavy metals content
and its effects on certain pot cultivations as well as assessing the
possibility of using this alternative for managing the fermentable
portion of the city's total solid waste stream.
The present paper describes in detail both of the above research
projects and gives certain results regarding the work performed thus
far.

INTRODUCTION
In Greece as in many other countries population increases in large
urban centers have resulted to problems such as unemployment, housing
scarcities, increase of criminality and others which have been of concern
to politicians, sociologists and psychologists. Concurrent increase in the
standard of living and growth of tourism have brought about radical changes
in the cultural life of the country. Consequently there have been
qualitative and quantitative changes in municipal solid-waste production in
Greece.
Greek cities were initially forced to organize themselves for
rudimentary collection of municipal solid-waste and its transport to
disposal sites which were rarely chosen based on environmental standards.
The impacts to the environment and the hazards to public health were
evident : pollution of surface and ground-waters, maladours, insects,
rodents and spontaneous ignition resulting in many cases to extensive
fires.
Similar situation is found in the countryside where uncontrolled
dumping of solid-waste has resulted in pollution of creeks, forests,
seashores, etc.
An urgent need for a solution to the above problem was sought

especially if one considers the highly touristic nature of Greece.

For this purpose there have been serious and continuous efforts in both urban centers and the countryside by Local Authorities responsible for solid waste management. These efforts have as objective the increase in collection and transport system efficiency as well as the improvement of utilized landfill construction and operation.

Lack of suitable sites for sanitary landfilling in the large urban centers such as Athens and Pireas in conjunction to a wider problematique have led to the investigation of other methods and systems with objective of minimizing environmental pollution and recovering useful materials and energy from solid-waste.

In line with the above, two research programs have been initiated in Greece. In Attica, a research program has been undertaken by the Unified Association of Municipalities and Communities of Attica (UAMCA) in collaboration with the Ministry of Agriculture, the Ministry of Environment, Physical Planning and Public Works, the Ministry of Interior and the National Technical University of Athens. A second research program has been initiated in Crete by the Municipality of Iraklion in collaboration with the Institute of Vine and Flower Culturing and the author's participation representing UAMCA.

The following discussion describes the above mentioned research programs.

THE ATTICA PROGRAM

As stated above this program has been undertaken by UAMCA in collaboration with other governmental and academic entities. UAMCA is an association of Local Authorities and its members include the majority of Municipalities and Communities of the Attica Compartment. From a population standpoint, the Compartment of Attica represents approximately 40 % of the entire Greek population. UAMCA is an agency for the protection of Public Health and the Environment with major responsability the sanitary landfilling of municipal solid-waste, the destruction of contaminated or spoiled raw materials and products and, under certain requirements, the disposal of excavation and earthworks materials as well as certain industrial wastes and sludges. The latter industrial wastes and sludges originate mainly from processing and transport of petroleum and petroleum products in the Compartment of Attica.

Parallel to its growth, the UAMCA has felt the need for performing applied research concerning the above mentioned problems so that its operations become more effective. Therefore, following a research program on the "Analysis of Household Refuse with Statistically Approved Methods in the Greater Athens Area" which resulted in determining the physical composition of this refuse with as much as 59 % (by weight) of fermentable materials in the waste stream, UAMCA directed its efforts towards two directions. First, the construction of an experimental system for recovering useful materials from household refuse with a capacity of 2 tonnes per hour separating the fermentable portion which in turn will be aerobically bio-stabilized. Second, the undertaking of the research program which will be described in detail below with the title "Research for the Use of Material Resulting from Household Refuse as Soil-Conditioner".

Program objectives

The Attica program takes into account the procedures followed by the program on the analysis of household refuse and has the following objectives :
1. To promote basic knowledge on the compost process with municipal solid-waste substrates.

2. To determine optimal methods and parameters for the production, control, and field-testing of compost from Attica's municipal solid-waste.
3. To investigate the feasibility of simple techniques in compost production.
4. To propose possible operational modifications concerning the pilot-plant for recycling and recovery of useful materials so that subsequent compost production is optimized.
5. To assess the following issues :
   a. If compost's heavy metal content can cause phyto-toxicity.
   b. If produced compost is an appropriate soil-conditioner and at what proportion it can be added to various soils in Attica.
   c. What types of soils are especially suited for compost application.
   d. What types of cultivations give the best results for compost application.
   e. How the compost compares with manures and other natural fertilizing materials.
   f. What are the effects of combining MSW compost with other natural fertilizing materials in various proportions so that results are optimized.

   The above research program is expected to have many benefits to the overall MSW management in Attica and the country in general. Some of these expected benefits include the investigation of compost production from greek MSW and its utilization under greek climatic conditions. These benefits are especially crucial in Greece where there are many areas with organically-poor, overcultivated, and destructed soils in urgent need of improvement.

Program tasks

1. Experimental compost production
   The method of natural maturing was chosen for the following reasons : (a) It is the simplest method ; (b) There is adequate space and appropriate know-how for this method within UAMCA ; and, (c) It is economical and avoids extensive capital investments in equipment. Regarding aeration of the compost piles the program follows three distinct phases : (a) Aeration through mixing of piles ; (b) Aeration by mechanically blowing air into the piles ; and (c) Aeration by mechanically withdrawing air from the pile. In more detail this task involves the following :
   a. Recovery of fermentable materials from household refuse using a specially-made bench equipped with a 40 x 40 mm screen. Hand-picking of organics that remain on top of the screen and removal of non-organic materials that pass the screen. The recovered fermentable materials are subsequently milled down to size 10 x 20 mm. This reduced-size material is placed in piles shaped as a pyramid approximately 2 m on the side and 1.5 m high where it is left to mature. The piles are placed both in open space as well as in spaces covered on top and open on the sides.
   b. Production of compost from fermentable material produced in the pilot-plant for the recovery of useful materials using the same kind of piles as those described above.

2. Measurement of productive and physical parameters
   a. Productive parameters
      (1) Date of pile construction
      (2) Weight and volume of pile
      (3) Pile mixing cycle (mixings per day)
      (4) Added water (kg per pile)
   b. Physical parameters

(1) Temperature at the center of the pile immediately following construction and after each mixing as well as on a routine basis three times per day
(2) Ambient temperature
(3) Precipitation

3. Determination of microbiological parameters

a. In its final sample of matured compost from every pile the following are determined :
(1) Total count of fungi
(2) Total count of spore-forming aerobic and anaerobic bacteria
b. In three piles and for each season weekly samples during the maturation process are analyzed for the following :
(1) Total bacterial count
(2) Total fungal count
(3) Total actinomycetal count
c. Upon completion of maturation a final sample is analyzed for the following :
(1) Total fungal count
(2) Total count for spore-forming aerobic and anaerobic bacteria.

4. Determination of chemical and physico-chemical parameters

Moisture, ash, total volatiles, pH, Free Air Space, specific conductance, carbonates, total nitrogen, ammonia-nitrogen, nitrate-nitrogen, nitrite-nitrogen, organic nitrogen, total phosphorus, organic phosphorus, water- and citrate-soluble phosphorus, Ca, Mg, Na, K, Fe, Ni, Mn, Zn, Cr, Cu, Pb, Cd, SAR, chlorides, borium, organic carbon, water- and organic solvent-soluble matter, 5 %-H_2SO_4-soluble matter, cellulosic and lignino-humic material, total humus, humic and fulvic acids, humus disaggregation through gel filtration, pile generated gases (O_2, CO_2, N_2).

5. Testing of compost in greenhouses and the fields

a. Greenhouse tests (compost-soils)
(1) In plastic pots 6-10 kg capacity
(2) Types of plants : Wheat, corn, spinach in rotation
(3) Soils : At least three (3) types representing typical Attica soils
(4) Watering : According to predetermined schedule given by soil physicists
(5) Fertilizer : Adequate for optimal crop production
(6) Compost-Soil Proportions : 0, 5, 12.5, 25, 50 and 100 %. Mixing is accomplished prior to introduction into the pots, watering for optimal moisture conditions and seeding after 15 days.
(7) Other : Observations on plant growth with emphasis on nutritional deficiences, height and size etc. Upon plant collection the weight of green and dry parts as well as their content in N, P, K, and heavy metals.
b. Tests on Attica representative soils
(1) No fertilizer - No compost
(2) No fertilizer - compost 6 tonnes/stremma
(3) No fertilizer - compost 12 tonnes/stremma
(4) Fertilizer A - No compost
(5) Fertilizer A - compost 6 tonnes/stremma
(6) Fertilizer A - compost 12 tonnes/stremma
(7) Fertilizer B - No compost
(8) Fertilizer B - compost 6 tonnes/stremma
(9) Fertilizer B - compost 12 tonnes/stremma
Based on the above test procedures there are two (2) experimental

fields of three year duration each with the following cultivations :
nitrogen-fixer, maize, oats. Field dimensions are 5 x 10 x 50 m. Possible
improvement of soil physical, chemical and microbiological properties by
the addition of compost are examined by representative soil sampling.

Program progress
The above outlined research program is under the scientific
responsability of the author and is expected to be completed in 3.5 to 4
years. Presently, the program has been under way for nine (9) months. A
large number of experimental data have been collected in this initial
period which will be given in subsequent papers. However, due to the
importance that heavy metal content has on the future applicability of any
produced compost it was considered essential to include here certain
preliminary results concerning these metals. These values are given below :

```
Cadmium               always <        2 ppm
Copper         max. 200 and min.     60 ppm
Nickel          "    65   "    "     30  "
Lead            "   180   "    "     90  "
Manganese       "   350   "    "     90  "
Zinc            "   900   "    "    400  "
```

THE PROGRAM IN HERAKLION, CRETE
The Municipality of Heraklion, Crete is seriously considering the
process of composting as the major MSW management option for the city's
refuse. For this reason it has undertaken a nine-month research program
with the following objectives.

Research objectives
1. To determine MSW physical composition with acceptable statistical
   methods.
2. To study the composting of fermentable materials under local climatic
   conditions.
3. To examine the physical and chemical characteristics of produced compost
   with emphasis given to its heavy metal content with a parallel
   investigation on major heavy metal sources within the city.
4. To assess the utility of the product compost to various cultivations and
   determine a probable price for its marketing.

Program tasks
Heraklion, a city with 120,000 inhabitants, was divided for refuse
sampling purposes into 6 sections. Each section included 4 to 5
neighbourhoods. Division criteria used were geographical location of
section and occupation of its inhabitants. The latter data were obtained
through questionnaires. The following tasks have been completed :

1. Sampling of MSW
The sampling period for each section lasted for a five-day week. The
volume of the collected sample was approximately 23 cubic meters. A sample
was obtained from each neighbourhood each working day. The volume of these
daily samples was determined based on the population contribution of the
particular neighbourhood to the total population of the section. Samples
were also collected within each section according to occupation of the
producing population. Since the overall objective was the production of
compost, sampling was not performed in the city's areas which were
suspected of producing undesirable wastes (industrial, hospital, laboratory
and other wastes).

2. Collection and transport of samples

Samples were collected in early morning prior to the regular routing of the city's collection trucks. The samples were loaded in a small truck by two workmen who subsequently analyze the collected samples upon their arrival to the laboratory.

3. Samples analysis

After the volume of each daily sample was determined it was weighed and hand-sorted into the following categories :
- Cardboard, paper
- Synthetic papers-plastics
- Non-magnetic metals
- Magnetic metals
- Glass
- Minerals, stones, sand, cloth, wood, leather, bones, rubber
- Fermentables

The fermentable portion was subsequently divided into three categories 100 mm, between 100 and 40 mm, and 40 mm with the aid of screens. This operation was done by hand. Each separated category and division was then weighed.

4. Biochemical stabilization of fermentables

The daily separated fermentable fragment is milled down to 2 mm size and then placed on a concrete platform. The fermentable portion of a week's collected refuse of a single section is placed in a single pile 2x2x1.5 m

The piles were aerated naturally by mixing them approximately once a week.

Ambient temperatures and temperatures in the center of the piles were measured three times a day.

Program progress

The following results have been obtained during the first three months of the program :
1. The fermentable portion of Heraklion's MSW is over 50 % by weight and approaches in some instances it exceeds 65 %.
2. The moisture content of the fermentable portion exceeds what is considered optimum for composting (60 %) and this was attributed to the fact that in this season (April-June) there is a high proportion of fruits and vegetables in the waste stream.
3. Pile temperatures in the examined period approached 70°C while it typically remained between 60 and 65°C throughout the said period of three months.
4. Initial visual observation of the first piles which are in their final maturation stage have shown a material of excellent microscopic appearance. Further laboratory analysis of compost samples will reveal its overall quality.
5. Preliminary results for heavy metal content have given the following values :

Cadmium	always <		2 ppm
Copper	max. 160	and min.	45 ppm
Nickel	" 50	" "	25 "
Lead	" 185	" "	80 "
Manganese	" 330	" "	25 "
Zinc	" 700	" "	180 "

REVIEW OF THE UP-TO-DATE TECHNOLOGICAL TRENDS
CONCERNING COMPOST PRODUCTION FROM SOLID DOMESTIC WASTES

F. Vastola - G. Pizzo
Intervento Straordinario nel Mezzogiorno
Rip. Unità di Ingegneria
Rip. Completamento Schemi Idrici

RIASSUNTO

Il lavoro evidenzia un quadro aggiornato delle tendenze tecnologiche in ma-
teria di impianti per la produzione di compost da rifiuti solidi urbani at-
traverso un esame analitico delle offerte presentate dalle Ditte concorrenti
(le maggiori tra quelle nel settore) nelle più recenti gare indette dalla
Cassa per il Mezzogiorno.
Viene preliminarmente proposta una "matrice logica" di lettura di progetti
per un razionale inquadramento funzionale delle varie componenti e sezioni
che costituiscono un impianto di compostaggio. Vengono analizzati gli schemi
proposti per "blocchi", "sezioni" e "componenti", rilevando alcuni significativi parametri tecnici delle singole macchine.
Viene soffermata l'attenzione sulle specifiche tecnologie di biostabilizzazione tra le quali figurano alcuni tra i più famosi brevetti di Ditte operan
ti a livello mondiale, acquisiti da Imprese Italiane.
Vengono rilevati dal complesso dei vari schemi tecnologici alcuni parametri
significativi del processo di compostaggio. Si è inoltre analizzato, per i
singoli processi, l'aspetto energetico, suddiviso in quattro quote significative: movimentazioni; frantumazioni ed omogeneizzazioni; insufflazioni d'a
ria; separazioni.
Il lavoro svolto può costituire utile riferimento per una più razionale ste-
sura di disciplinari di appalto-concorso, tanto più necessaria, di fronte
alla varietà delle tecnologie oggi proposte dal mercato.

SUMMARY

The Paper gives an up-to-date survey of technological trends in the design
of urban waste composting plants. The analysis is based on the comparison
on the projects presented by the Firms (the most important ones in this
field in Italy) which took part in the most recent competitions promoted by
the Cassa per il Mezzogiorno.
A logical grid "to read" the projects is devised in order to elaborate a
rational and functional arrangement of the many different elements of an
urban waste composting plant. Such elements are analized as part of
"sections", "steps" or "components", underlyning some significant technical
parameters of the single machines.
Attention is particularly paid to specific biological reactors, among which
some of the most relevant international patents which have been acquired by
italian Firms.
The values of relevant parameters of the composting process are identified
from the different technological schemes.
Furthmore, the energetic aspect is examined for each process and is subdivided into four significant sections: agitation, size reduction and homogeni-

zation, forced aeration, separation.

The results shown in this paper could be used to improve the specifications for a "contract-competition" bid that is even more necessary today being so various the technological proposal available.

1. INTRODUCTION

The assesment of many composting plants failures must persuade technicians and biologists to analyze the cause in order to remove the doubts and approximations which can already be seen in the planning phase of a plant and in its corresponding operating program. The problem should be tackled at its roots, that is in the pre-arrangement phase of tender-regulation since, up to present, the major part of the composting plants are realized by the public Administration through the above mentioned Istitute.

The "Cassa per il Mezzogiorno", with this in mind, has carried out since 1983, in a framework of a more general program of studies on composting in collaboration with Agricolture Faculties of Naples, Pisa and Sassari, a critical analysis of some of the most significant tender regulations used by different italian and foreign pubblic Administrations; pointing out the defi ciens and inaccuracies in order to direct the planning towards correct methods for a better reliability of composting.

This paper faces this problem from the point of view of the analysis of the projects realized on the basis of two tender regulations which in the above-mentioned review were considered among those having less defects. It was noted that, if, on one hand the above-mentioned tender regulations, which consented wide liberty of process choice, can appear lacking in a certain manner, on the other hand the planners, in general, don't seem to have contributed to fill these gaps with a sufficient rationality of proposals, and howevers, with a major coherence in those procedural details not indicated in the tender regulations.

2. METHOD OF ANALYSIS

The technological and procedural differences presented in the examined schemes have determined the necessity of a preliminary definition of a logical general framework of the operations which must be done on the waste to be transformed into compost.

Basingon the most recent specialized literature, on the analysis of the proj ects, and on the operational experiences in Italy and abroad, the composting plant leaving aside those process which are uninfluential to the process (storage, solid waste treatment, and in general the optional phases for the enhancement of the product etc.)should be articulated in 3 fundamental opera tional sections, each separated from the others but related to each other to the point where the deficiencies of one can cause the failure of the others. Each section is composed of several steps which in turn are carried out by means of one or more electromechanic components, as indicated in the scheme of Fig. 1.

The first section deals with pretreatment and includes all the operations aimed at the preparation of a homogeneous mass of suitable organic substance for an efficient and controlled development of the biochemical reactions.

The second section deals with the biological transformations and includes those operations which determine and favor the complete biological oxidation of the compost organic matter.

The third section includes the necessary final cleaning operations of the product of its use in agriculture also in conformity to present laws. This third section is to be kept distinct from the operations (refining, additive, manufacturing) of the product which are considered extra due to the particular requirement of business.

This "logical matrix" appears useful for a functional and conceptual framework of the various components and relative connections.

3. OUTLINE FRAMEWORK

The reference material for the analysis and evaluation which will follow consists of 12 projects selected on the basis of 2 tender regulations, having the same indications regarding: the type of solid waste to be treated : recovery and destination of solid waste (compost, residuals landfill of solid waste); capacity per hour (10 ton/hr for the first lot).

The total capacity of disposal requested in relation to the different seasonal fluctuations in consumption of the two project groups, is 62 ton/d and 100 ton/d; this fact reflects on the running times of the plants (about 6 hours in one case and 10 hours in the other) as well as the scaling of all the steps which must respect certain detention times. Figure 2 shows the single electromechanic component of each project in steps and sections in reference to the 12 examined schemes.

4.1. SECTION I - PRETREATMENT
4.1.1. Receiving - Feeding - Sack Lacerator
The components which characterize this step for all the proposed schemes are: the refuse receiving pit with recovery grab; the overhead transfer crane and grapple; the plat extractor; the sack lacerator. The size and the technical characteristic of the step components are quite uniform, and in particular: the refuse receiving pits are requested for production of 3 day heap; in general the expected volumes vary between 10-20 liter per inhabitant; the transfer crane grapple has a capacity which varies from 3 to 5 tons; the gauge varies from 7.5 and 8.8 m. The grapple capacity varies from 1.5 to 3 mc; a pressure plated feed belt is always inserted under the charging hopper and in many cases functions as sack dilacerator; it also acts as a capacity regulator of the waste to be processed since it can be set at different speeds. The width of this type of belt varies from 1.2 to 2 m; the power installed varies between 4 and 11 KW.

4.1.2. Magnetic Separation
All the examined schemes propose overband electromagnetic conveyors inserted on the line of the waste transportation. A great variety of situations is noted concerning the point of the process cycle where the electromagnet is inserted. This aspect has a particular importance in cases where the mechanical shredder is used for the obvious problems of mechanical wear. Among the schemes which propose hammer mills (which are 7 altogether) 3 provide

for the magnetic separation before passing into the shredder; the remaining schemes propose the magnetic separation after the size reduction. The two schemes A/1 and A/11 (the letter A denotes the same proponent) provides, in the presence of the same shredder, the use of the electromagnet once before the shredding and once after the shredding. Among the schemes which propose the size reduction/homogenization in rotating drums, 2 schemes (E/5 and E/10) put the electromagnet before the drum, also due to the presence of the sack dilacerator. The other schemes program the magnetic separation after the drum. The width of the belts proposed varies from 0.8 to 1.3 m; the most frequently used lenghts are between 2 and 3 m. The electric power given to the magnet ranges between 9 and 14 KW, the most frequent values are around 10 KW which seems to be considered as the reference value.

4.1.3. Size Reduction/Homogenization
This step can be defined as fundamental for a plant because it determines the complete success of the whole process; that is, both the reliability and regularity of the operation as well as its effects on the quality of the final product. Moreover as it will be pointed out further on in this report, the methodological diversification for the execution of this operation brings about a plant diversification which affects all the following steps. In order to obtain the necessary size of the organic matter, the waste must undergo mechanical steps which however causes the size reduction of the inor ganic matter that becomes more difficult to separate. In particular the size reduction with high rpm elements causes the pulverization of the inorganic matter (glass, ceramic etc.) whose separation becomes pratically impossible. Instead the low speed systems or the rubbing and rolling causes a more selec tive shredding which allows a major efficiency in the following separation operations. Among the proposed schemes two trends stand out: the schemes which use the size reduction/homogenization rotating drum with the starting of biological reactions; the schemes which use shredding.

4.1.3.1. Size Reduction/Homogenization by means of rotating drums
It's necessary to make the following observations on the use of rotating drums: generally they are cylinders with horizontal axis (fixed or variable to some degree) whose main technical characteristics can be summarized in the following table:

Scheme	Diameter (m)	Lenght (m)	Volume (mc)	Detenet. time (hrs)	Power Install. KW	Ventil. Capacity mc/h	Power Vent. KW
5/E;10/E	3,4	24	240	17	74	500	4
4/D;9/D	3,65	27,2	284	22	55	500	4
6/F	4,0	15	151	17	93	n.s.	3
G/7	2,4	9,8	74	8	45	---	-

proposed ventilation systems will have a capacity of 500 mc/h; the detention times, under the condition of maximum load covers a period between 8 and 22 hours; therefore all the cylinders present the common function of selective mincing of the organic component used for autogrinding due to reciprocal rubbing with the harder components, as well as the particular shape of the drum's internal surface; the aeration and the relative detention time favor a first of the biological reactions regarding the more soluable organic matter present; this also favors the breakaway from the inorganic matter which cannot be composted. With these characteristics the rototing drums are placed in the pretreatment section, in the size reduction/homogenization step. It must be pointed out also that while the schemes 6/F and G/7 attribute explicitly that function to the drums, in the reamining schemes, the function of rotating drums is presented aboveall as a biological reactor. This characteristic would be acceptable if the detention time was such to allow the completion of the termofila phase in the internal part of the cylinder (72-96 hours). With the detention times which have been used, the cylinder's function is limited to that of a component of the pre-selection called "mixed" (mechanical and biological). This type of pre-selection is more effi cient than the mechanical one because the first bacterial attack of the soluable organic matter (which also has a major density which becomes sensibly reduced and becomes different than that of inorganic matter which is not composted) contributes in making the air classification and inertial separation more efficient; moreover the breakaway of the organic matter from the other fraction is facilited with a two-fold advantage; a major yield in compost and a minor presence of rotting matter among the residuals. In relation to all this, the schemes which propose the cylinders can concentrate into one "step" the grading separation of organic matter operations which absorbs also the operation of a final cleaning of the compost with an evident semplification of the process and operative savings. On the other hand, with the indicated detention times, these schemes have no real "accelerated biological reactor".

4.1.3.2. Size reduction/homogenization by shredding
The shredding is introduced into those schemes in which the fixed bioreactor and the mechanical agitation of waste are present. Even if the marked proposes various kinds of shredders (tested however in incinerating plants or in only shredding of u.s.w.) all the schemes examined presented hammer mills. It must be pointed out that generally there is a certain deficiency in the description of machinary details. From the directions concerning electric power 3 categories semm to stand out: the low power shredder (6.25 KW per t/hr); medium power shredder (10 KW x t/hr); high power shredders (15.5 KW t/hr). Generally the low power shredders also have a low rotation speed. Fragmentary indications are given about the other elements of the machine in particular about the presence or absence of the passage grate, about the size of the grate's holes, the life of the hammers etc.. In conclusion one can claim that the mechanical shredding must still be streamlined not in the construction of the machine (itself on the market there are various types based on different principles) but above-all in the choice of the machine which best fits the characteristics of the urban solid waste and the goal of the compost production; therefore a shredder must offer which has functio nal reliability, low operating costs and the best possible results in redu-

cing the size distribution of the organic matter without excessively shredding the inorganic elements which must be separated.

4.1.4. Grading Separation of Organic Matter
The organic separation can be defined as a group of operations through which one obtains the first (and the most coarse) separation of organic matter to be passed on to the following process of biological transformation from the inorganic matter which is to be sent on to be treated with residuals. As it has already been pointed out, a basic difference existe between the schemes which propose rotating drums as shredders homogenizers and the schemes which propose a "mechanical" shredding. The former, since they also carry out in the homogenizing/shredding phase a first transformation of the organic matter with a subsequent improvement of the separation phase can concentrate into one step the grading separation of organic matter phase without having to finish the compost with a final cleaning. The schemes which propose shredding must instead provide a first phase of gradinf separation of organic matter after reduction; at this phase compost cleannes must follow after organic matter transformation. From methodological point of view, the operations performed immediately after the cylinder should be considered as "grading separation of organic matter". The step of organic separation is made up of one or both of the following electromagnetic components· air classification and inertial separation.

4.1.4.1. The Screening
It is the operation which permits the separation of the organic matter (presumably minced) from inorganic matter which is thicker than the first ones. The schemes that have been examined present the screening in the section on the separation of the matter. The kinds of screen presented are: trammel screen, and flat screen. The trammel screen's diameter varies from 200 cm. to 260 cm. (5 schemes out of 8). The lengths vary a great deal (from 4 m. to 10.5 m.) and the respective screening surfaces can be placed in three groups: 70-80 mq.; 45-55 mq.; 25-35 mq.; from which three surface indexes per t/hr are derived: 7, 4.5, 2.7 mq/t/hr; the flat screen's surface varies from 3.64 mq. to 8 mq. Finally for both trammel screens and (flat screens), the power varies from 7 to 15 KW, with the more frequent values included between 10-15 KW, with the only exception of scheme 12/H with 30 KW. The holes' diameter (the holes can vary during the operation) varies it is a primary screen following mechanical mincing or a screen placed after the shredding drum/homogenizer) which is unique. In the first case, there are hole diameters from 40 to 60 mm, for a less accurate classification; in the second there are diameters from 18 to 25 mm. The only exception is scheme 11/A which not only presents a screening of 20 mm before bioxidation but does not foresee a final cleaning, although it has the shredder inserted.

4.1.4. Air classificator and inertial separator
With fresh organic matter this operation has a low degree of efficiency due to the relative difference of density between the matters to separate and the organic matter itself. Only schemes 1/A and 11/A, which propose shred-

ding, are provided with air classification before the bioxidation. There are essentially two types of machines proposed for the said operation: inertial classificators; pneumatic classificators. The former is based on the different trajectory impressed on the particles which fall on it by a high speed rotor; the latter is based on the different deviations undergone by the particles hit by an air flow. The inertial classificators are very simple machines that use power ranging from 5 KW to 8.3 KW; the rotating drums have a diameter of 50 cm. Air classificators are geometrically made in variuos ways according to the type of machine. The only element of comparative reference is the maximum capacity of the ventilator and relation with the nominal capacity. The values found refer to the machines inserted below the cylinder (and therefore also used to clean the compost); the maximum capacity of the ventilator is 10,000 N.mc/hr per 6-8 t/hr corresponding to 1,250-1,600 mc/hr per t/hr. In the only case of pneumatic classificator following a shredder (scheme 11/A) there is a value of 21,000 N.mc/hr for a capacity of 11 t/hr e qual to about 2,000 N.mc/hr per t/hr. The electric power is very different; it goes from 11,2-18.5 KW for the classificator put after the cylinder to 51 KW for the classificators in scheme 11/A.

4.2. SECTION II - BIOLOGICAL TREATMENT

In Section II of the biological treatments are all the steps and the corresponding equipment which perform all the microbiological activities that transform the organic matter to be released into a stable and fito-consisten product, which in order to commercialized needs only proper final cleaning operations. The whole process is divided generally into two distinct phases: a) the initial phase characterized by the accelerated bioxidation; b) the final phase during which the transformation of more stable polymers occurs (maturation). Generally the two distinct phases are also separated physically: the first inside a reactor, the second on equiped floor. Among the schemes presented there are however some extreme cases in which the whole process develops or entirely in the "bioreactor" (scheme 2/B and 6/F) or on equiped floor (scheme 4/D, 5/E, 7/G, 9/D, 10/E); keeping in mind that the duration of the process can never be inferior, on the whole, to the time necessary for the primer, the growth, the evolution of the various bacterial and fungus specimen which determine the transformation and which usually is fixed in no less than 30 days.

4.2.1. Active Composting Phase

The first phase of the biological transformations, characterized by intense exothermic biological reaction, with strong absorption of oxigen and increase of temperature, takes place in appropriate reactors, inside of which the mass can be completely agistated with forced aeration system and in some cases automatically depending on the factors which control the development of microbial propulations (temperature, humidity, PH). In this way one obtains the active composting phase (with evident saving of both bioreactor volume and maturation equiped floor surface) and above all, one obtains the pathogen control of the product, since the mass, not only reaches the temperature which make all the patogens inoffensive; but the complete tumblings assure that all the points of the mass are affected by these temperatures. The step of the active composting phase is generally covered by an exclusive license or patent and the "composting system" characterize. The efficacy of this step mostly depend on the operations and on the machinary used in the steps before the preparation and in the following steps concerning the maturation and the cleaning of the product. Different "composting systems' exist on the market; the examined schemes are the major part of which are in the possession of Italian business.

4.2.2.1. Rotating Drums

In the paragraph 2.6. it was said that the schemes 4/D, 5/E, 9.D and 10/E which propose the rotating drum are to be considered without "accelerated bireactor". All this derives from the functional classification that has been attributed to rotating drum in consequence of limited detention times of the waste located inside. The 5th scheme proposes the drum explicitly used as shredder/homogenizer (6/F) and presents, for the active composting phase, a rectangular agitated solids bed system and therefore different from the previous ones where the entire composting actions must take place on the equiped floor.

4.2.1.2. Fixed cell-basin periodically tumbling

This system has to do with the patent SILODA - and is made up of 2 series of 4 concrete cells by passage separed one next to the other positioned; they are 4 m wide and with walls 1.6 m high with variable lenths and with a paddle wheelpassing through them (diamete 3.5 m-4 m wide) which during this movement, by means of rasps, collects the matter and moves it towards the center of the wheel itself from where, by means of a cocles, it is pushed upwards and in the direction of the next cell, causing with the entire passage, the complete transfer of the contents of one cell into the next. Each cell containe a day's production and is emptied every 2 days, for a total of 4 tumblings in 8 days of detention. The movement is fully automated, a complete cycle, as well as the displacement of the wheel from one cell to the next. Among the schemes which propose this patent (1/A, 11/A, 3/C, 8/C) there are rather significant difference as can be seen by the following table:

Scheme	Lenght (m)	Tot. Power Install. (KW)	Aerat. Capacity (Nmc/h	Ventil. Power (KW)
1/A	9	62,2	3600	36
11/A	10	32,3	–	--
3/C	15,5	68,5	2400	37
8/C	24,0	49,5	1200	18

4.2.1.3. Fixed basin periodically automatic tumbling

This is the method presented in scheme 6/F. It is made up of one dock called "biotunnel" and is furnished with a forced aeration system and an automatic tumbling system consisting of a special crane that is equiped with conveyor belts which allow the arrangement and agitation of the matter according to planned cycles. The pile's hieght is 3.5 m. The electric power for agitation is 18.5 KW, the aeration capacity is 126.000 mc/h with the head multiple augers mounted on a mobile bridge of mm 120 H_2O and the installed electric power is 42 KW. The aeration specific capacity is 88.8 mc/h per present ton or 53.2 mc/h per mq of the dock's surface. Detention time is 30 days, thus this scheme offers the development of the whols composting cycle in the same bioreactor and eliminates the distinction between maturation and active composting phases.

4.2.1.4. Fixed and unique basin with continous automatic tumbling

This is the method presented in schemes 2/B and 12/H that have the common characteristic of operating the mechanical agitation of solids inside a reactor with multiple augers mounted on a mobile bridge in the direction of the matter flow. The aeration system is present. The two schemes differ in volume and shape of the reactor; more precisely: the scheme 2/B has a rectangular reactor where the loading is from one of the short sides and the unloading is from the opposite side; the progress is provoqued by the movement in the direction of the bridge and is favoured by a proper slight inclination. The bed's size is 26 x 20 x 2.5 m and its volume is 1300 mc which allows a detention time of 30 days. The total installed electric power is 93 KW. Aeration capacity is 6500 Nmc/h; electric power for aeration is 37 KW; the following specific capacities come out: 12.5 Nmc/h per present ton, or 12.5 Nmc/h per mq of the basin. Like scheme 6/F, this scheme presents the whole composting cycle in the same bioreactor; the scheme 12/H has, instead, a circular reactor with multiple augers fixed on a radial mobile bridge crane. The organic mixture is placed along the exterior circumference and the unloading takes place in the center through cylindrical well; the overflow variable height in the well allows regulation of the flux. The basin diameter is 17 m, the useful height is 2.5 m, with a volume of 450 mc and detention time of 3.5 days. The total electric power is 90 KW, the specific aeration capacity is 29.6 Nmc/h per present ton, or 44.4 Nmc/h per mq of the basin.

4.2.2. Maturation

The conclusion of biological reaction generally takes place in a proper maturation equiped floor. In this phase the requirement of oxigen decreases, but the need to control humidity, temperature, and PH, to grant the regularity of the process is constant. This control may take place by means of more or less automated periodical tumblings, by means of forced aeration systems, or by means of both methods. With the exception of schemes 2/B and 6/F of which we have spoken, all other schemes have a proper maturation equiped floor which has very different characteristics for each scheme, as it is shown in tab. I. All the schemes, in which composting takes place completely in steady piles, have covered equiped floor with a forced aeration system. The values or surface vary from the minimum of 1000 sq.m. of scheme 4/D to the maximum of 2556 sq.m. of scheme 8/C. It must be pointed out that the

significative index, in this case, is the surface value related to daily
flux of the plant. For the same number of detention days (30), values range
from 10 mq per ton/day to 29 mq per ton/day. It must be taken into account
that schemes 4/D and 5/E have 2 m height piles, while all the others have
2.5 m height piles. Scheme 7/G should be considered separately with a value
of 41.2 mq sq.m. per ton/day since it has a detention time of 60 days; thus
the relative index is 20.6 mq ton/day if it is related to 30 days of detention. When composting active fase is present, the proposed surfaces vary
from 1728 sq.m. to 3000 sq.m.; the index per ton/day (homogenized in 30 days
of detention, on 2.5 m pile) ranges from 10 to 30.2 mq per ton/day. As far
as aeration is concerned, all schemes which do not have a proper biological
reaction upstream, have aeration in equiped-nut. Absolute values of installed power range from 10.000 to 22.000 Nmc/h; specific values, according to
surface and present tons, vary respectively from 6.1 to 15.23 Nmc/h per
sq.m. and from 5 to 21.8 Nmc/h per ton. Among the schemes which have biological reaction only two (1/A and 12/H) introduce aeration in equiped-nut
with specific power of 6 and 8.3 Nmc/h per sq.m. and about 10 Nmc/h per ton.

4.3. SECTION III – FINAL TREATMENTS

There can be two steps which make up this section: compost secondary shed-
ding; cleaning of the compost. The first step is seldom included in the process and is related to the need to obtain a reduced size final product. The
second step, instead, is always present (with the exception of scheme 11/A
whose process anomalies have been pointed out several times) and is made up
of the same elements of step "grading separation of organic matter", power
related to minimum quantity to be treated and to different density of the
matter after composting.

4.3.1. Secondary shredding

The shredding step is presented by one Firm only in schemes 3/C and 8/C with
the insertion of a hammer mill which is identical to that used for incoming
waste but with lower power (30 KW); it is supposable (even though it is not
pointed out) that the passage grate holes are about 10–12 mm. At the moment
there are contrasting evaluations about the need and opportunity of this
operation for the compost qualitative improvement.

4.3.2. Compost cleaning

The final compost cleaning is included only in those schemes which have a
purely mechanical size reduction and it consists of separation of undesirable inorganic particles from already mature compost. As for grading separation of organic matter, this goal is obtained by exploiting the different
size and density of the organic matter from the particles that are to be
separated; the operations the compost is to be submitted are: secondary size
classification; air classification and inertial separation.

4.3.2.1. Secondary size classification

Size classification in this phase follows the primary one which takes place
after size reduction/homogenization. Usually the same machinery that has

been employed for primary size classification is used also this time. There are the exception of scheme 2/B which has a secondary size classification which is geometrically different from the primary one and electric power is 50%, scheme 12/H which employes the same machinery but engine power is 25% of the primary one. The holes diameter is 10-12 mm; electric power varies from 7.5 to 15 KW.

4.3.2.2. Air classification and inertial separation

Air classification and inertial separation, for what has been said in paragraph 2.5.4.2, generally takes place after bioxidation or in any case after biological-mechanical size reduction/homogenization. The machines that are used are, as for grading separation of organic matter, the inertial separator and the pneumatic classifier. The first machines are very simple and require low power (from 2 to 5 KW); however, their efficiency is limited. The second machines are more sofisticated and their size varies according to the model; electric power and blowers maximum rate are the main comparison parameters. For decleared power per hour, electric power varies from 15 to 18.5 KW and the maximum rate varies from 10.000 to 13.000 Nmc/h; scheme 12/H has a classifier with power per hour equal to 10 t/hr with 26.000 Nmc/h and 37 KW which is superior to the plant's requirement.

5. ENERGETIC PARAMETERS

We can make some interesting consideration about electric consumption and its distribution in the several phases of the process. It must be pointed out that the elaborations come out from electric power data of the machinery and the mentioned working time. Values refer to the cycle essential machinery, thus excluding energy amount for general services, (hygienic purposes, lighting, and so on). The difference among the several "kinds" of energy which is "supplied" to waste along the working cycle according to a homogeneity criterion is the following one: energy for matter movimentation; energy for size reduction and homogenization; energy for separation; energy for forced aeration. The total electric amount distribution among the four kinds of energy is an useful indication of the kind of process (notwithstanding the particular patent). More or less breaking-down processes (size reduction amount) and more or less rationally distributed processe (agitation amount with more or less attention to the ventilation of matter). In

Scheme	Agitation	Size reduct. Homogeneiz.	Separat.	Air feeding	Power per unit KWH/tonn
A/1	31,0	40,0	9,0	20	36,0
B/2	19,0	26,7	10,6	43,7	30,1
C/3	19,7	45,8	9,5	25,0	39,1
D/4	20,0	39,3	8,4	32,3	37,9
E/5	14,1	45,6	8,2	32,1	26,4
C/8	19,5	44,4	6,3	29,8	30,6
D/9	12,4	45,7	6,1	35,8	21
E/10	12,3	45,1	6,2	36,4	24,1
A/11	25,6	50,8	23,6	----	15,8
H/12	18,6	23,0	13,0	46,0	32

the following prospectus; in the first four columns there is the per-cent distribution of the different electric forms which are employed; in the last column there is the synthetic total parameter of the electric amount per unity of the matter that is employed. The electric amount which is employed for agitation (which also includes, besides all conveyor belts, the bridge crane, the graffle, and so on) varies from 12 to 31%. The electric amount for size reduction/homogenization is always very high, both for purely mechanical shredder/homogenizer schemese and for rotating drum schemese, and is about 40-45%. There are remarkable lower values 23-26% in those schemes which have purely mechanical size reduction with low electric capacity. The electric amount for separation ranges from 6 to 10% of the total amount; the higher values are related to those schemes which have less size reduction. The electric amount for air provision varies from 32 to 46%, with the exception of those schemes which do not have aeration in equiped floor for maturation. As far as absolute total electric consumption is concerned (the last column of the prospectus) there are greater oscillations, from 20 to 40 KWh/ton; we must notice, however, that in this case the day and year different use if the plants influences values; in fact, higher values (30-40 KWh/ton) refer to those schemes which are characterized by a continuous functioning for 6 Hour/day, while lower values (20-30 KWh/ton) refer to plants which work up to 10 hour/day.

CONCLUSION

The plant articulation comparison of the same process, which has been interpreted in different ways in the 12 projects that have been examined, allows the following final considerations which, however, cannot be considered absolutely conclusive. This is due to the limited number of projects which have been examined, to the lack of other different technologies on the market and to the lack of an analytical check of data on a systematic operational observation. It has generally been noticed a vast availability on the international market of single methods and equipments which are highly valid and reliable but which are included in the project context in different ways (sometime by the same Firm in different projects too) with very different operative results. As a consequence, we can claim that, facing this vast availability, at the moment the business world of this field is going through a phase not only of technological evolution but mainly of "assimilation" of new established technologies for a rational connection of them with the complex biological phenomena which are the base of composting. The review has pointed out the following fundamental points about the process: pretreatment for grading separation of organic matter, operated by the so called "mixed" (biological-mechanical) system by means of short detention biotermical drums with size reduction and homogenization of waste mass, causes a clear difference of the following operations as compared to "mechanical" systems using shredders; so that while the former ones allow grading separation of organic matter only once before biological reaction (this for the already mentioned reasons about the limited presence of inorganic particles) the latter, besides a rough separation after size reduction necessarily require a final cleaning following biological reaction. It is likely

that, due to the drums'considerable cost, the first method is more convenient for low-medium power plants (as for the cases which have been examined where 6 Firms out of 12 have such a drum), while for a higher power the
second method is mere suitable; except in one case, aeration is always present at least in one or in both biological reaction steps and is associated
with periodical ot continuous tumbling (or agitation): this shows that every
body agrees on this need and that simple natural aeration with periodical
tumbling is not a completely reliable method. On the other hand, it is impor
tant to point out the following points of doubt which have come out from the
review: "size reduction" appeared as one of the most complex steps as
regards to the type of machinery, as we pointed out before. They are mainly
machines whose function is to reduce waste for other goals and have not
found and adequate place in composting plants; no Firm has clearly expressed
itself about the complex and fundamental balance between size distribution
of the matter that has to be separated, and quantity and size of inorganic
particles that have to be transferred by means of biological reaction, and
that have to be separated afterwards, in order to reach an optimum composting efficiency, related to energetic optimisation; in no project it is possible to find a definition of criteria an calculations of aeration potentiality dimension during biological reaction. One has the impression that every
body employed potentiality and methods according to exclusively empirical
criteria (which derive more or less from his own practical experience) whit-
hout any possibility to check them against anyone of the parameters which
characterize the process. By the way, one must notice that not even the speci
fic literature of this matter allows a synthesis of practical value range
of aeration potentiality to be supplied during the whole biological reaction, like air required to control temperature, humidity, PH, and so on.
These two problems are at the heart of composting process and are still to
be solved since a correct solution of them influence the product's quality
and working costs. This report only points out the need to define a rational
method to read a composting project in order to find out the type of machinery and optimal dimensions which derive from conceptual clarity about the
process which can lead to technological simplifications that are related to
a plant potentiality. These observations, which are not conclusive at all,
are intended to solicit those who are interested in the problem to give some
contribution, correction, or criticism, in order to get to a clear definition of some still dubious aspects of the process and, consequently, some
clear indication that the buyer must be able to supply for the correct reali
zation of this king of plant.

SECTIONS	STEPS		ELECTROMECHANICAL FRACTIONS	INITIALS
PRETREATMENTS	Receiving and feeding	1	Refuse storage pit – bridge crane grapple	FCB
			Feeder – conveyor with plattes	EDP
			Bag opener	DLS
	Magnetic separation	2	Magnetic separator	SMG
	Size reduction homogenization	3	Rotating drum	CLF
			Shredder	TRT
	Grading separation of organic matter	4	Primary screen	VRP
			Primary flat screen	VPP
			Primary pneumatic separator	SPP
			Primary inertial separator	SBP
	Mixing	5	Mixer	MDC
BIOLOGICAL TREATMENTS	Accelerated biological reaction	1	Biological reactor	BRT
	Maturation	2	Equiped floor	MTR
FINAL TREATMENTS	Secondary size reduction	1	Secondary shredder	FRS
	Compost cleaning	2	Secondary trammel	VRS
			Secondary flat screen	VPS
			Secondary pneumatic separator	SPS
			Secondary inertial separator	SBS

Fig.1

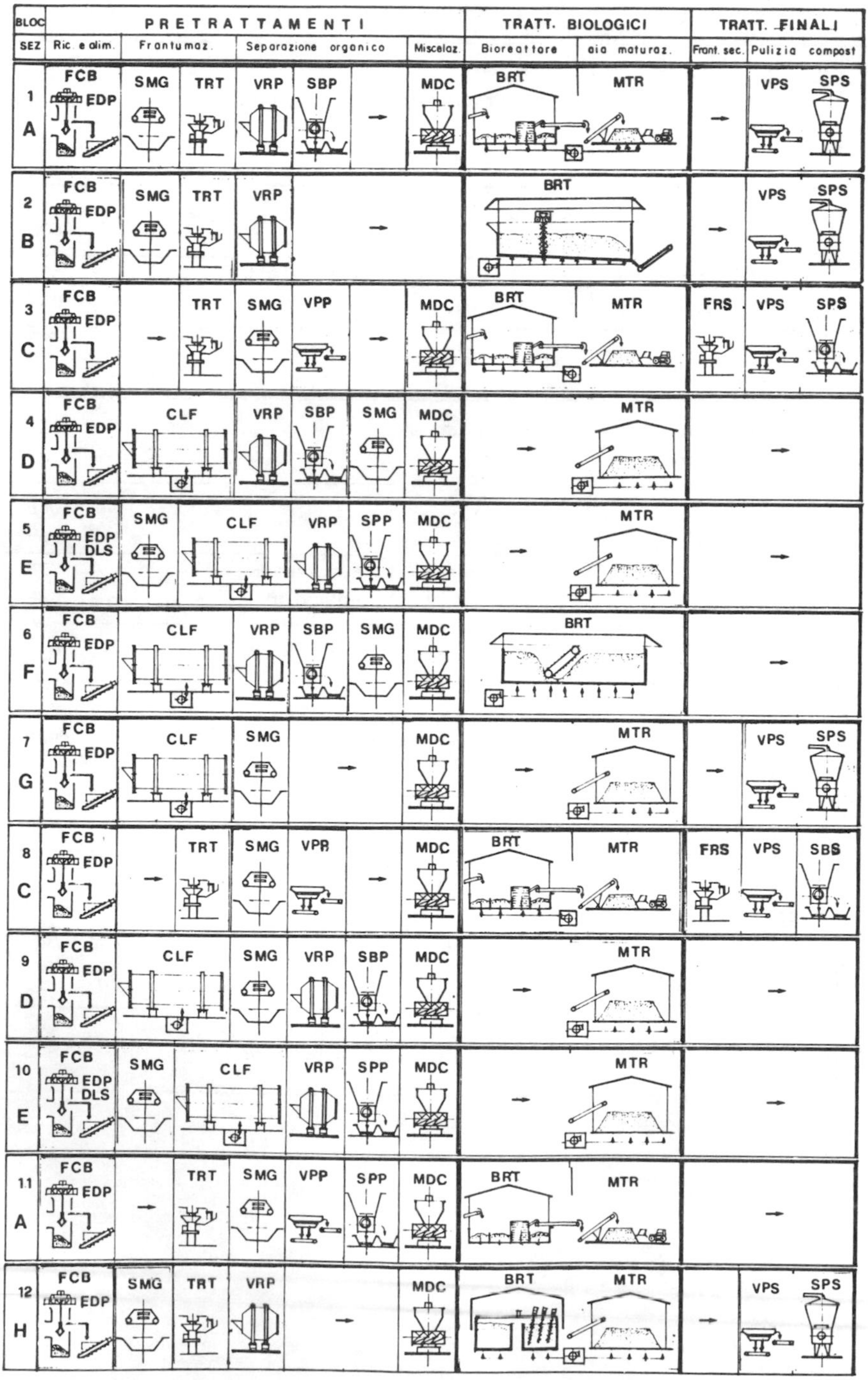

738

BLOC	PRETRATTAMENTI							TRATT. BIOLOGICI		TRATT. FINALI		
SEZ	Ric. e alim.	Frantumaz.		Separazione organico			Miscelaz.	Bioreattore	aia maturaz.	Front. sec.	Pulizia compost	
1 / A	FCB EDP	SMG	TRT	VRP	SBP		→	MDC	BRT	MTR	→	VPS	SPS
2 / B	FCB EDP	SMG	TRT	VRP			→		BRT		→	VPS	SPS
3 / C	FCB EDP	→	TRT	SMG	VPP		→	MDC	BRT	MTR	FRS	VPS	SPS
4 / D	FCB EDP	CLF		VRP	SBP	SMG		MDC	MTR		→	→	
5 / E	FCB EDP DLS	SMG	CLF		VRP	SPP		MDC	MTR		→	→	
6 / F	FCB EDP	CLF		VRP	SBP	SMG		MDC	BRT		→		
7 / G	FCB EDP	CLF		SMG		→		MDC	MTR		→	VPS	SPS
8 / C	FCB EDP	→	TRT	SMG	VPP		→	MDC	BRT	MTR	FRS	VPS	SBS
9 / D	FCB EDP	CLF		SMG	VRP	SBP		MDC	MTR		→	→	
10 / E	FCB EDP DLS	SMG	CLF		VRP	SPP		MDC	MTR		→	→	
11 / A	FCB EDP	→	TRT	SMG	VPP	SPP		MDC	BRT	MTR	→	→	
12 / H	FCB EDP	SMG	TRT	VRP			→	MDC	BRT	MTR	→	VPS	SPS

Fig. 2

MATURATION ON EQUIPED FLOOR

Scheme	Preceded by reactor	covered	matter in maturation (T)	SURFACE tot. (mq)	SURFACE spec. (mq/txg)	pile height (m)	maturation time (gg)	automatic spreading on the floor	tumbling	AERATION aeration (mc/h)	AERATION rate per surface unit (mc/hxmq)	AERATION specific rate (mq/hxT)	AERATION power (KW)	followed by fina
1/A	YES	YES	1100	1875	30,2	2,5	30	—	YES	11250	6,0	10,20	30,0	YES
2/B	YES	NO	complete biological reaction inside a reactor							complete biological reaction inside a reactor				YES
3/C	YES	YES	3900	2400	38,7	3,25	84	YES	—	22000	12,2	21,80	30,0	YES
4/D	NO	YES	1010	1800	25,0	2,0	30	—	YES	8050	6,1	7,0	28,0	NO
5/E	NO	YES	complete biological reaction inside a reactor							complete biological reaction inside a reactor				NO
6/F	YES	YES	1150	1320	21,3	2,0	30	YES	—	39000	15,3	16,13	67,5	YES
7/G	NO	NO	2418	2556	41,2	2,5	60	YES	—	—	—	—	—	YES
8/C	YES	YES	3000	3000	30,0	2,5	30	—	YES	10000	10,0	5,00	27,5	YES
9/D	NO	YES	2000	1000	10,0	(..) 2,5	30	—	YES	10000	7,0	5,40	34,0	NO
10/E	NO	YES	1850	1440	14,4	(::) 2,5	30	—	YES	—	—	—	—	NO
11/A	YES	NO	2205	1728	17,3	2,5	30	—	—	—	—	—	—	NO
12/A	YES	YES	1620	2160	21,6	2,0	30	YES	YES	18000	8,33	11,1	4,5	YES

(..) Potentiality required for all projects 10 t/h
For projects from 1 to 7: r.s.u. + slodge (6 days out of 7) max 62 t/d of working 6 h/d
"   "   "   8 " 12 " + " (6 " " 7) " 100 " " " 10 "
(::) Piles are isolated with a compost layer

Tab. I

CRITICAL EVALUATIONS ON THE STRATEGIES USED FOR THE
MUNICIPAL SOLID WASTE TREATMENT

by A. DANIELI
DANECO S.p.A.
S. Giovanni al Nat.
I - UDINE

Foreword

The following considerations begin with a simple, but necessary review on the aspects characterizing the object of our activity : the Municipal Solid Wastes (M.S.W.).
In fact we believe that the problem must be approached with a good deal of humility, spirit of responsability, clearness !
In conclusion, with good sense and concreteness.

1. WHAT ARE MUNICIPAL SOLID WASTES ?

Let's individuate their specific characteristics in order to ponder on :
- Non-hygienic
- Unpleasant (sight, smell)
- Non-homogeneous
- Bulky
- They do anyway have a "value" determined by the cost for their treatment (negative value).
  Example : M.S.W. 42000 Lit/ton
  M.S.W. 30000 Lit/ton
  M.S.W. zero Lit/ton

Inside this range of values it is therefore necessary to have the competence for being able to fix the right "value" for the waste treatment.

1.1. Since when do they represent a problem ? (or, even better) since when do they have a value ?

As a matter of fact they did not represent a problem until they did not have a value but were disposed of at zero lire.
The wastes begin to have a "value" in the societies that have reached a welfare, for which "the waste must disappear".
Furthermore we must remember that the production of waste is directly proportional to the welfare of a country (in New York for example the waste produced per person is higher than in Cairo), whereas the solutions for its treatment are inversely proportional.

1.2. What are the prior solutions to the problem ?

First of all we must distinguish between two different realities :
A) Industrial and welfare societies
For these societies prior is the treatment and/or disposal of the waste at the right price safeguarding the environmental impact.

B) Poor/third-world societies

For these societies prior is the waste recovery at the lowest cost under the form of hygienic humus.

1.3. For whom do they represent a problem ?

In societies like ours, that is industrial societies :
- public administrations, responsable by law for the M.S.W. and I.S.W. treatment ;
- private industries ;
- population/public opinion, producer and victim of the M.S.W.

1.4. Who must solve it ?

A) The public administration, being responsable for the destination of the Municipal Solid Wastes, must choose a technical solution.

B) The private and public industry must provide for a technical/plant and process solution for the Municipal Solid Waste treatment.

Aware that the above is real, let's enter the specific matter of this report.

2. DOES A CORRECT STRATEGY FOR THE MUNICIPAL SOLID WASTES TREATMENT EXIST ?

Firstly we put to ourselves this question :

Does a clear strategy that has given or gives concrete replies to the problem pointed out above exist, or has it ever existed in Italy ?

Unfortunately for us the answer is NO. We are in fact more in the presence of fashion than of strategies.

We must therefore speak about the absence of strategies more than about the critical evaluations of real strategies.

In fact, from our experience supported by researches made by national public organisms, since the problem manifested itself (towards the end of the 60's) the public administration, here in Italy, has operated in total absence of strategies, filling this deficiency from time to time, with isolated interventions that have not even been able to take to a datum-point, a model to follow as an example.

This deficiency has therefore fed the manifestation and development of fashions, whose course has been influenced by events that often did not have any technical basis, i.e. :
- the strong incineration of the first 70's, with misfortune towards the end of the 70's and being recuperated only lately ;
- the recycling ;
- the biogas, today.

Fashions that have been banners through which the public opinion has sustained ideological battles with the result of not having improved the situation in the slightest way.

Fashions that have influenced and conditioned the method of "who has to choose" on how to face and solve the problem, with the result that many plants, born at the sign of an idea in fashion, at the moment of rendering of accounts have not been able to realize what was promised.

Today therefore the hope that a plant works must be substituted by the certainty that the kind of treatment adopted gives sufficient guarantees of reliability and cheapness.

Let's not forget that the time factor is very important in this sector.

With regard to this subject, let's analyze some facts :
A) Health Ministry source
- Italy 1973 existing and running plants 125
- Italy 1980 existing and running plants 96

Note : In 1973 the plants had an average age of 3.6 years.
B) Daneco source
Tenders for the construction of new plants for the M.S.W. treatment
1980-1985.
From where we deduce that, out of the 24 tenders, only 2 reached the
objects of the effective construction of the plant.
- How many useless programs
- How much lost time
- How many wasted illusions
- How little positive material to work on and improve. We are still in
  the world of ideas and hopes and, let's be honest, also of lies.

In six years we have concluded very little, above all our major
activity has been a technical and theoretical practice on the writing out
of offers in which ideas on ideas were developed and maybe also lies on
lies.

It is like the famous story of the "Naked King", that by telling many
lies one can self-convince of their truth until someone or, in our case,
something, obliges us to see the plain truth of the facts.

3. <u>WHAT WE PROPOSE</u> ?
Not wanting to be considered as those that "play the wiseacre", we
must dare and propose those we think to be the correct ways to proceed.

In view of the actual Italian situation (confusion between who has to
manage the problem, interferences between ministries and public
administrations at a regional level, presence of only a few plants that
have been effectively running for many years with an acceptable index of
efficiency and productivity) speaking of a global strategy to solve the
problem can bring us again in an unreal and useless dimension.

Today we therefore prefer speaking of a method and solve the M.S.W.
treatment in a positive way (technical and economical).

Above all demand and offer must have the courage to sit around a
table and face the matter with constructive spirit based on an open - clear
- honest comparison - without shame of one's own experience.

But let's speak of demand and offer, if they really have something to
say each other, that is, that they have a 10 years' experience in
management at least.

The sources here above mentioned show that :
A) The plants work at an average of 60 % - 65 % of their potentiality. This
   means that in this sector there is a lack of productivity and typical
   efficiency mentality, which is present in all the other sectors. This is
   not justified, because if we said that the waste has a value (even if it
   is calculated in a negative way) it must be treated like any other raw
   material.
B) The treatment costs are always a mystery which confirms the existence of
   a wrong, non-productive mentality in this sector. The mysteries hide
   confusion, uncertainty, fundamental ignorance on a problem. Nothing can
   be built on mysteries.

Demand and offer must therefore face this problem together with a new
spirit and, above all, with a new productive and competitive mentality.

They must in this way propose a model of plant able to respect three
primary functions, which are the following :
1) Hygienize a non-hygienic product at the lowest possible cost of
   investment and management.
   (Attention : in our opinion the investment costs are directly
   proportional to the costs of management).

2) Recover and sell the hygienic material with the aim of treating it and not of making a business out of it.

3) Respect the environment.

In conclusion, with the risk to repeat ourselves until boredom, today in Italy more than big plans we require concrete, reliable and a few "demodé" (that is, "out of fashion") solutions.

Solutions that in fact solve the problem with humility and above all in silence.

A qualified service is "noted" for its silent efficiency.

It works but it cannot be seen.

SESSION:4

STRATEGIES, LEGISLATION AND MARKETING

Rapporteur: VERDONCK O.

There is one red line which is going through all these papers saying that the quality of the compost must be ameliorated through a better separation of the different materials and through separate collection of these materials.

This all will help to minimize the heavy matal content and to lower amounts in the future.

Then we will have the possibility to use much longer compost on our fields before the maximum levels of heavy metals are reached. From several papers we have seen that Zn and Cd are the main limiting elements for the use of compost in the future.

The quality is also the main factor at hand for the amelioration of the marketing.

Once we have a good product, then we can build a market based on a constant product because our growers like to use compost not only once but many times.

A few papers were dealing on how to solve the problems of recycling therefore we must certainly study in advance:
- what product we like to deliver;
- where we like to use the compost;
- where to do the regular control which is necessary for having a constant product so that advizers can be certain of the composition.

All efforts have to be done to bring the image of compost to a higher level so that everybody will think that it is a good product with which no difficulties will occur.

CONCLUSIONS OF THE SYMPOSIUM

CONCLUSIONS OF THE SYMPOSIUM

M. DE BERTOLDI, G-L. FERRERO, P. L'HERMITE and F. ZUCCONI

PREMISE
The more general themes dealt with in the Symposium have allowed for several conclusions to be reached, some of which are implicit in the papers presented and others which were stimulated during discussions and contacts both inside and outside the conference rooms. The areas of greatest interest concerned : the input materials ; improving the stabilization processes ; the quality of the products and relative hygienic problems ; the use of the compost ; and the problem of establishing standards and norms.

INPUT MATERIALS
We recognize different approaches to the recovery of waste depending upon the materials being processed. The greatest problems with municipal waste consist in the separation of the organic fraction. In the following stages this fraction appears easy to compost, however, favouring rapid processes and quality products.
The situation is reversed when dealing with agricultural or industrial wastes. Generally these wastes are found in a pure organic condition needing no separation. Nonetheless, they frequently tend to undergo a slow stabilization and often require pre-conditioning in order to achieve efficient composting.

SEPARATION OF THE ORGANIC FRACTION
This is a complex process which involves the largest and most complex part of the composting installations treating municipal solid waste. Analysis and separation of the fractions is necessary to :
- promote an evaluation of the installation requirement, comparing different technologies ;
- explore the potential of plants to be reduced in size in order to serve communities having less than 50,000 inhabitants which are the majority of settlements. This, of course, requires process simplifications rather than scaling down the actual plants ;
- explore the impact of a separate collection of waste on simplifying the retrievability of the various fractions and reducing processing costs.

OPTIMIZING THE PROCESSES OF STABILIZATION
It is necessary to optimize the factors in the biooxidative process and suggest specific solutions in respect of the different products to be stabilized.
There is a need to increase efficiency in the composting process, reduce processing times and achieve better quality products. In this sense, the ease with which the organic fraction of M.S.W. can be properly composted nullifies any attempt to justify today's badly conducted, excessively lengthy processes. These reveal an endemic inattention to the process control. They lead to inferior products, drawing unnecessary criticisms of the validity of choosing composting in the industrial treatment of wastes.
The process of composting requires more specific care when dealing with agricultural or industrial wastes, where the unique origin of the

materials postpones the humification process. Specific recipes capable of balancing the composition of these materials and compensating for their anomalous metabolic tendencies must be devised for each substrate, avoiding a simple transposition of processes perfected for municipal waste.

In any case, the impact of perfecting the chemical composition of the substrata is still a relatively unexplored field and, beyond a general awareness of the C/N ratio, we lack sufficient knowledge on the impact of phosphorous, calcium and other mineral elements.

It is necessary to analyze the economical interest of recovering other forms of energy from the organic waste previous to composting. In relation to the anaerobic treatment and production of methane, in particular, the potentiality and economy of a dual process must be defined as well as the impact of the anaerobic processes on the successive biooxidative stabilization phases.

Analogous considerations are necessary for worm-composting ; a process which must demonstrate its capability to operate in reduced time frames. Moreover, marketing of the worms themselves, in addition to the compost, could attract a greatest interest to the process.

QUALITY OF THE PRODUCT

Problems concerning the product must be viewed in relation to minimum requirements necessary to guarantee standard quality and diversified products to suit different utilizations.

It is necessary to reach a stabilization which allows storage of compost and its direct use in agriculture in an advantageous manner for the plants. An exception could exist for fresh compost. In this case the requirement is limited to the thermophilic phase to warrant hygienic conditions.

The need for cured compost with an advanced degree of mineralization must be analyzed in relation to its demand in nurseries, floriculture, protected cultivation and, moreover, in relation to the costs associated with the organic soil conditioners available on the market (peat, natural humus, etc.).

Presence of inerts and above all of glass and plastics must be thoroughly avoided for the negative connotation these materials give to the compost. Degradation of the organic substance favours its separability from inerts which remain unaltered by the process. Absence of inerts imparts a quality connotation to the process, and determines the value of the product.

Heavy metals – at present still increasing in waste – pose considerable problems regarding the use of compost in agriculture.

Nonetheless, means for reducing the impact of heavy metals are available. They include the separate collection of the organic fraction – certainly a most promising approach – or an early separation from inerts in the composting plant, or to the composting itself. Attention must be paid to the addition of sludges in the preparation of compost for agricultural purposes.

PROBLEMS OF HYGENIC

It is essential to develop a better understanding and agreement as to the limits of an eventual presence of pathogens as well as on methods required to evaluate compost safety.

Sanitation directly depends on characteristics of the thermophilic phase of composting and this, in turn, a function of oxygenation and humidity control. Accurate control of the biooxidative process is essential to warrant product safety as well as the economy of sanitation.

It is also imperative that operative conditions in composting installations are warranted which may safeguard the health of the operators.

USE OF COMPOSTS

Composts confront us with different problems depending on the specific use that is made of them. The most relevant aspects are compatibility of crops with the product in question, soil improvement and quality and safety of the compost.

The sensibility of crops to organic fertilization is a direct function of contact with the roots. This is maximized when transplanting in substrata prepared with compost. Cured compost, in this case, can guarantee compatability and chemical fertility in direct relation to the degree of stabilization achieved.

A different situation exists in the field use of compost where there exists no direct or diffuse contact with the roots. In this case mature products would guarantee a greater humus production with a direct energetic advantage for the soil resource. When employed between cultivations, in winter or for the recovery of degraded soil, fresh composts would allow the greatest energy contribution from the organic substance to the soil and its fertility.

With reference to these choices it appears necessary to promote a thorough study, in rigorously energy and economic terms, concerning the benefits of organic fertilization with regards to :
- the improvement of chemical and physical balance in the soil ;
- the increase of soil volumes explored by the roots and the consequent intensification of cultivation ;
- the curtailment of root diseases and, in general, improvement of the plant health and of the products value ;
- the reduction of rotation and, even more important, of fumigation - the latter representing an extremely dangerous operation to the soil ;
- the reduction of today's use of intensive cultivation methods with the advantage of reducing production costs and allowing better conservation of soil resources.

THE PROBLEM OF STANDARDS

The problem of compost standards and specifications should be faced from a less defensive and conservative stand than is current today, which tends to perpetuate a waste management approach that is dangerous in environmental and hygienic terms, and to subtain one of the most retrograde systems among all that have accompanied the development of our society in this century.

The interest in biological recovery of organic waste - whatever its origin - directly depends on the existence of standards which limit their disposal by dumping, burning, etc. A further factor is the demand for organic substances by agriculture as well as the continuing increase in the costs of natural organic fertilizers available on the market.

Reclamation of organic refuse requires a preliminary definition of "waste" and its differentiation from polluting and contaminating matters which may spoil them. It is also important that heavy metals as well as other harmful materials, are analyzed in relation to the problem of total quantities released in the environment. Today's short-sighted reliance on concentration requirements appears dangerous in as much as it would promote dilution of products having high concentrations with safe ones, contaminating all and contributing to dispersal, instead of controlling, the problem.

The possibility of separate disposal of heavy metals is in direct relation with their concentration. Separate management of waste and pollutants should therefore be encouraged.

Any action in this direction may only stem from a cooperative effort; the time is ripe for a thorough debate on problems connected with present waste management - as well as the advantages of adopting more advanced strategies.

GENERAL STRATEGIC ECONOMIC EVALUATION

The problems examined in the Symposium reveal the need for the development of more efficient technologies in the recovery of organic waste. The target to aim at is the planning of new plants with the dual capability of optimizating chemical, and biological balances with perfecting the mechanical requirements in the process of separation and stabilization.

Strategies for advanced processes and plants suffer both from a lack of sufficient understanding and from a clear separation of goals, creating inefficiency and mal-functioning. A more comprehensive effort should be made to understand the existing problem, with a united approach to the strategies of planning.

A new generation of plants should take the place of the present ones - capable of greater efficiency and lower costs. The recent decrease of energy costs suggests the requirement for a more accurate evaluation of the economic aspects of the process. Demonstrative actions carried-out at many levels should be foreseen for the development of advanced and competitive technologies in terms of lower energy consumption and production costs, and higher quality of the products.

POSTER SESSSION

Microbial biomass for fertilizer use from the photo-anaerobic treatment of pig wastes

Comparison between different air supply systems in composting

Enhanced direct composting of sludge in a vertical bioreactor

Urban solid waste processed by means of composting and incineration with energy recovery

Management and economic aspects of waste composting

Changes undergone by some characteristics of organic wastes during the composting process

Yield responses of four different crops to compost application

Spent mushroom compost, a possible growing medium ingredient ?

Vermistabilisation of sewage sludge in the UK

Effect of composts made from municipal and industrial wastes on the yields vegetables and the content of mincral elements in them

The siloda, a reactor composting technology combining forced aeration and turning action

Environmental impact of organic municipal refuse composting

A few additional parameters for a better determination of the compost quality

Earthworm compost versus classic compost in horticultural substrates

Vermicomposting of different organic wastes

Thermodynamics of refuse sludge composting

Combined solid and liquid domestic wastes treatment in the frame of economy and rationality

MICROBIAL BIOMASS FOR FERTILIZER USE FROM THE
PHOTO-ANAEROBIC TREATMENT OF PIG WASTES.

W.BALLONI, P.CARLOZZI, S.VENTURA and A.SACCHI
Istituto di Microbiologia Agraria e Tecnica e Centro di
Studio dei Microrganismi Autotrofi - CNR Firenze (Italy)

Summary
A new photosynthetic biotechnology based on the ability of purple non-
-sulphur bacteria to photometabolize organic compounds under anaerobic conditions, has been applied to the treatment of piggery wastewaters. The preliminary results of a pilot plant experiment with a photobioreactor of 120 litres capacity installed outdoor, are reported.

1. Introduction
    The use of photosynthetic bacteria (species of genera Rhodopseudo-
monas and Chromatium) in the reclamation of high BOD_5 wastewaters with
the concomitant production of microbial biomass has been recently considered (Kobayashi, 1977; Ensign, 1977; Sawada and Rogers, 1977; Balloni
et al., 1980; Vrati and Verma, 1983; Vrati, 1984).
    Previous works, carried out in our Institute, have led to the deve-
lopment of a two-phase process for the complete treatment of wastewaters.
This method is suitable for various types of effluents. The first stage
is carried out photoanaerobically with selected sulphur and non-sulphur
purple bacteria. The second stage in the reclamation process is carried
out by filamentous cyanobacteria growing in open ponds on the effluent
from the anaerobic photoreactors after the separation of the bacterial
biomass.
    We have tested our method on a pilot scale with sugar refinery ef-
fluent (Balloni et al., 1983). The results obtained, along with physiological and biochemical basis of this new photosynthetic biotechnology have
been reported in a monographic study (Balloni et al., 1982).
    In this communication we report results concerning the performance
of a single (anaerobic) stage photosynthetic process in the reclamation
of pig effluent and for the production of bacterial biomass for biofertilizer purpose.
    This single stage method fits well to pig and cattle wastewaters
when the resulting effluent is spread on the field, because in this case a complete reclamation is not required.
    We propose two alternate types of agricultural utilization of the
photosynthetic biomass grown on animal wastewaters: the pretreated wastewaters, along with the photosynthetic bacteria grown on them, can direc-

tly employed for field irrigation or, alternatively, the biomass is harvested and subsequently utilized as biofertilizer. In the former case the fertilizing value of the waste is increased while the decontamination from colibacteria is obtained (Balloni et al., 1981).

2. Pig-farm effluent treatment experiments and results obtained

We have tested the efficiency of an home-built photobioreactor for the depuration of the wastewater in a pig-farm (Azienda Zootecnica Rocchetta-Verona) during a period of 4 months (May-August 1985).

The photobioreactor (Fig. 1) was built with 2 coupled plexiglass tubes (internal volume 0.12 m^3, lightened surface 1 m^2) equipped with a mixing device that removes the bacterial cells sticking to the illuminated surface as a consequence of their phototactic response. Thermoregulation was achieved by immersing the tubes in a water bath.

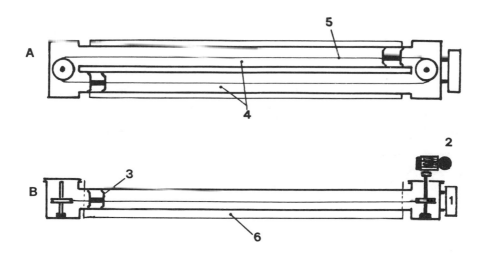

Figure 1 - Diagramatic representation of the photobioreactor described in the text. A) Plan view - B) Frontal view.
Legend: 1 = power swichboard; 2 = motor; 3 = cleaning device; 4 = plexiglass pipes; 5 = dragging wire; 6 = water bath.

The inoculum was composed of an association of selected strains of Chromatium minutissimum, Rhodobacter capsulatus, Rhodocyclus gelatinosus Rhodospirillum rubrum, Rhodopseudomonas palustris and Rhodomicrobium sp. isolated from enrichment liquid cultures, inoculated with sample of pig--waste.

Various parameters of the process in relation to the production of fertilizing biomass were evaluated: composition of the effluent (see

Table I) determined according to the Standard Methods (APHA, 1975), retention time, γBOD_5 (i.e. the ratio of the amount of produced biomass to the amount of eliminated BOD).

The biomass concentration in the waste was determined as optical density at 660 nm or as dry weight of the biomass.

The harvesting of the photosynthetic biomass was carried out by flocculation with the addition of 60 ppm of a cationic polyelectrolyte (Prodefloc C/4).

In Table I the main results are shown.

Table I - Biomass production and nutrient removal during the treatment of pig-farm wastewater in a single stage photobioreactor (average data obtained in the period May-August 1985).

PARAMETERS		A*	B		B+ 30% A	
			I**	II	I	II
COD	mg/l	13.500	1.750	365	4.170	985
BOD_5	"	5.850	920	80(-90%)	2.210	450 (-80%)
Total N	"	870	550	410	625	515
NH_4-N	"	520	480	380	515	400
NO_3-N	"	45	15	10	20	15
Total P	"	68	50	42	55	38
pH		7,8	7,5	7,4	7,4	7,2
Biomass yield:						
$g\ l^{-1}day^{-1}$		--		0,325		0,235
$g\ m^{-2}day^{-1}$				40		35
γBOD_5				0,7		0,7
Retention times:						
days			2		4,5	

* A - Non-digested wastewater;
 B - Partially digested wastewater;
**I - Initial composition of the effluent;
 II - Composition of the effluent after the treatment in the photobioreactor

As shown in Table I, after a 2-days treatment in the photobioreactor, a 90% removal of the BOD_5 from the pre-digested effluent was attained. The amount of photosynthetic biomass (dry matter) produced was 650 g per m^3 of effluent, with a $\gamma BOD_5 = 0,7$.

The results obtained with a mixture of 70% B (partially digested wastewater) and 30% A (raw wastewater) are particularly interesting: with a retention time of 4-5 days, 1.2-1.5 Kg of photosynthetic biomass (dry weight) per m^3 of waste mixture with a initial BOD$_5$ of 2200 ppm were obtained.

As regards the influence of the chemical composition of the effluent on the production of photosynthetic biomass the following points are vorthy of consideration:

a - the raw effluent (type A in Table I), even if clarified with allumine has very high COD and BOD values (5-10.000 ppm) and contains factors limiting the efficiency of the conversion of organic matter into photosynthetic biomass;

b - the partially digested effluent (type B in Table I) fits well to the photosynthetic treatment because it is more transparent and, above all, because during the previous digestion scototrophic anaerobic microorganisms have produced simple organic compounds (acids, aminoacids, alcohols, etc.) more easily photometabolized by anoxigenic photosynthetic bacteria.

In Table II a chemical and microbiological partial characterization of the photosynthetic bacterial biomass produced on pig-farm wastewaters is reported.

The sun-dried product has a red-brownish colour and an humidity of about 7%. The most important chemical features are the high content of easy degradable organic matter (C/N = 5), and of organic nitrogen, that reaches 8% of the dry weight, and the well balanced N/P ratio (8:1).

Table II - Chemical composition of the photosynthetic bacterial biomass, grown on pig-wastes.

Umidity	7,5%	
Organic matter	84,5%	d.w.
Ashes	15,5%	"
Total C	40,8%	"
Total N	8,1%	"
NH$_4$-NO$_3$-N	1,0%	"
P$_2$O$_5$	1,5%	"
Protein (Nx6,25)	50,6%	
Carbohydrates	12%	
Lipids	22,5%	
C/N	5%	

The microbiological safety of the product is attested by the absence of pathogenic microorganisms like Salmonella and Streptococcus faecalis. Moreover a 90% reduction of the E.coli content in the reclamed waters has been reached. This fact confirms the colicinogenic activity of anoxygenic photosynthetic bacteria (Guest, 1974; Kaspari and Klemme, 1977) and their important role in the hygienic improvement of wastewaters devolved fertilization by irrigation.

3. Conclusion

The results reported here attest the potential interest of the photoanaerobic system for pig-farm wastewater treatment whose efficiency could be prevedible improved by an appropriate biotecnological approach.

The scaling-up foresee the realization in the same pig-farm, of a pilot plant to increase from 1 to 5 m^3 day^{-1} the volume of reclaimed wastewater.

References

- APHA - American Public Health Association (1975): "Standard Methods for examination of water and wastewater", 14th edition, APHA, N.Y.
- BALLONI W., FILPI C., FLORENZANO G. (1980) - Recent trends in the research on wastewater reclamation by photosynthetic bacterial and algal system. In: Algal Biomass (Shelef G. and Soeder C. Eds.) Elsevier-North-Holland Biomedical Press. p. 217.
- BALLONI W., MATERASSI R., FLORENZANO G. (1981) - I sistemi di trattamento a batteri fotosintetici delle acque di scarico per l'utilizzazione diretta in agricoltura delle biomasse. - Conv.Inter.sulla Fitodepurazione ed impieghi delle biomasse prodotte. Parma 15-16 Maggio.
- BALLONI W., MATERASSI R., FILPI C., SILI C., VINCENZINI M., ENA A., e FLORENZANO G. (1982) - Il metodo di trattamento a batteri fotosintetici delle acque di scarico. Collana P.F.Promozione della Qualità dell'Ambiente. AQ/2/21.
- BALLONI W., FLORENZANO G. and FILPI C. (1983) - Pilot plant experiments on the photoanaerobic treatment of sugar refinery wastewater. Proc. Symp.: Anaerobic wastewater treatment. Noordwijkerhout. The Hague. p.601.
- ENSIGN J.C. (1977) - Biomass production from animal wastes by photosynthetic bacteria. In: Microbial energy conversion. Schlegel H.G., Barnea J. (Eds). Pergamon Press, Oxford pp. 455-482.
- GUEST J.R. (1974) - Bacteriocinogeny in the Athiorhodaceae. J.Gen.Microbiol. 81, 513.
- KASPARI H. and KLEMME J.H. (1977) - Characterization of antibiotic activities produced by Rhodopseudomonas sphaeroides. FEMS Microbiol.Lett., 1, 59.
- KOBAYASHI M. (1977) - Utilization and disposal of wastes by photosynthetic bacteria. In: Microbiol energy conversion. Schlegel H.G., Barnea J. (Eds). Pargamon Press, Oxford pp. 443-453.
- SAWADA H. and ROGERS P.L. (1977) - Photosynthetic bacteria in waste treatment.J.Ferment.Technol., 55, 311.
- VRATI S. and VERMA J. (1983) - Production of molecular hydrogen and sigle cell protein by Rhodopseudomonas capsulata from cow dung.J.Ferment. Technol., 61, 157.
- VRATI S. (1984) - Sigle cell protein production by photosynthetic bacteria grown on the clarified effluents of biogas plant.Appl.Microbiol.Biotechnol., 19, 199.

COMPARISON BETWEEN DIFFERENT AIR SUPPLY SYSTEMS IN COMPOSTING

G.M.BARUCHELLO (*), G.FISCON (**), G.JACOVELLINI (*), M.T.LUCARELLI (*)

*   SOGEIN S.p.A. - Roma
**   ACEA   - Roma

Summary

In composting of solid urban wastes, the availability of oxygene
is one of the main factors favouring microbic procreation. Accordingly,
aeration of the garbage mass during processing, and particularly during
the maturing phase, has been of utmost importance for the passage from
the so-called "first generation" technologies to those of the "second
generation".
In fact, elder techniques generally provide for aeration during
maturing by mechanical turning over, which results in significant losses
in heat and humidity of the treated mass, causing drastic reductions
in microbiological kinetics.
Otherwise the newer methods, which provide constant and controlled
forced air supply right into the mass of wastes.
Therefore, to avoid excessive cooling and dehydration, such plants
require constant and accurately controlled air supply per unit in time
and volume.
The present paper is intended to present the results of a
theoretical/experimental investigation performed at the SO.GE.IN. plants
in Rome, which was aimed to obtain comparative data on various air
immission systems into compost piles, considering both technological
and bio-chemical aspects, with reference to a not aerated pile.

0. OBJECTS

The present study was aimed to perform a series of experiments
by using existing facilities (Dano biostabilyzers) while maintaining
the usual hold-up time (48 hours) in order to obtain reliable information
allowing to guarantee not only the complete elimination of all
pathogenous microorganisms in the waste mass, but also to reach and
to maintain the correct process temperature of 55°C, as well as to
accellerate significantly the maturing phase.
These experiments were executed by adopting on the threshing floor
various aeration methods to a series of waste piles, while measuring

the respectively resulting thermal arrays within the piles, as well as the correlated chemical and physical parameters.

1. ARRANGEMENT OF EXPERIMENTS

1.1 Process description

Experiments were carried out at the composting plant of the Ponte Malnome facility, where at present approximately 700 Tons/day of urban solid wastes are processed and converted into approx. 200 tons/day of compost.

Presently, maturing is performed on the threshing floor, after balistic separation of glas and other inert materials, by keeping the mass in unaerated static piles for a hold-up time of approx. 90 days.

1.2 Description of experiments

For the purpose of the present investigation, a series of compost piles, having a height of ca. 2 metres and a base section of ca. 10 m^2, were prepared by taking the mass from the bio-reactor outlet. These piles were then treated in different ways as follows:

1) Pile aerated by compressor and mechanical turning-over;
2) Pile aerated by compressor
3) Pile aerated by aspiration
4) Pile aerated by mechanical turning (shovel)
5) Not aerated pile.

Piles Nr. 1-2-3 were supplied with 10 $Nm^3/h \times m^2$ of air.
Figure 1 illustrates schematically the compressor and aspiration systems adopted, with particular emphasis on the air injection system of self-cleaning type, arranged within a concrete base, and equipped with a drain system for percolation.

1.3 Process control

1.3.1 Temperature measurements

Two campaigns were carried out in the field, each of these lasting for one month, which is to be considered the "minimum" time interval necessary to obtain significant results in the maturing process of the compost.

During this period, the temperature array within the piles was measured every 5 days by means of thermocouples.

Temperatures were measured in each pile at different depths (20-50-120 cm) at a height of approximately 70 cm from the floor (which may be considered as the heart of the pile), according to the four orthogonal directions.

The figures 2 and 3 respectively show the mean values of the temperatures measured in the various piles.

1.3.2 Sampling method

During each experimental two-week campaign, all piles were subjected to analytic samplings (as foreseen by the DPR 915) in order to determine at the beginning the proprieties of the compost used, and in the following to check the behaviour of the degradation process undergone by the organic mass, as it developed along with the process temperature, being this parameter of particular bacteriological interest.

2. RESULTS

The analyses performed during the two testing periods according to the methods described above, as well as macroscopic checks of the piles, yielded the following results:

- Within the pile subjected to aeration and mechanical turning-over, humidity was reduced so far that, following turning-over, kinetics of enzymatic reactions came to a halt, even though only momentarily. This phenomenon makes us believe that aeration combined with mechanical turning-over does not yield benefits (due to thermal shock) in the accelleration of the mineralization process undergone by organic substances; on the contrary, in seems to act in the opposite direction, even though not significantly.

- The statically aerated pile (No. 2) showed a decrease both in temperature and in humidity of constant behavior in time, resulting therefore in improved mineralization and humidification of the waste mass, which was confirmed macroscopically by its brown and crumbly appearance and its typical earthy smell.

- Even though during the first days, the pile subjected to aeration by aspiration (No. 3) yielded positive results both in temperature and in humidity, later on it showed a behavior very similar to that of the static pile, which is probably due to not optimal air passages and internal recycling caused by obstruction of injection nozzles.

- The static pile, which was aerated mechanically every 10 days (No. 4) yielded appreciable results, but in no way comparable to the temperature behavior and the degree of mineralization obtained by pile No. 2. In fact it did not have to suffer thermal shocks like those of pile No. 1.

- Last not least, the static pile (No. 5), intended to serve as reference term, showed the typical behavior described already many times in literature: in fact, after 7 days it reached thermofile temperature within the mass, followed then by a stabile drop-rate in temperature, which was more pronounced during the second testing period.

No need to say that, neither in the beginning nor later-on, there were found samples showing the presence of salmonellae or other pathogenous microorganisms.

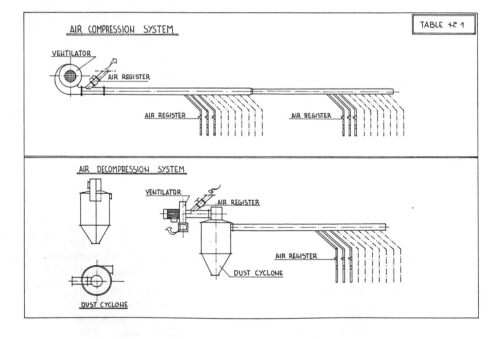

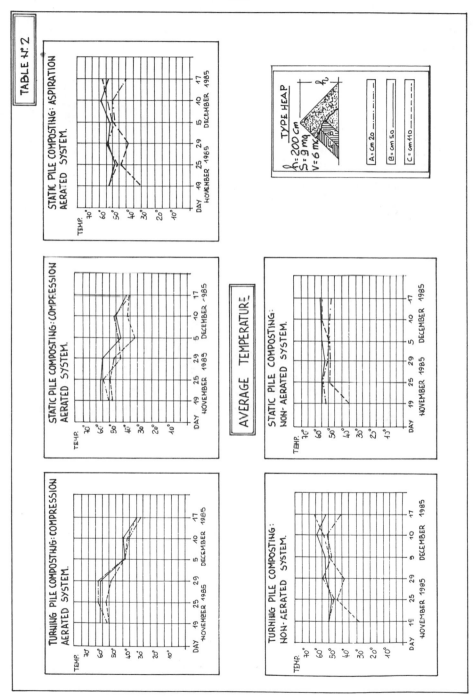

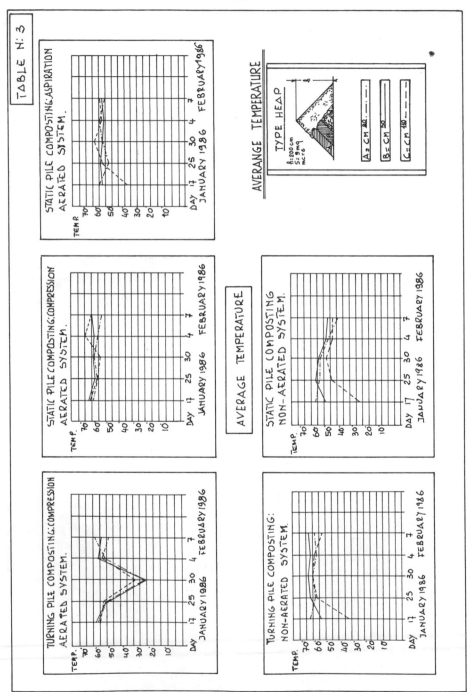

TABLE Nº 3

ENHANCED DIRECT COMPOSTING OF SLUDGE IN A VERTICAL BIOREACTOR

G.B. Benetti and A. Farneti
Snamprogetti - Ecology Division
Engineering, Research and Contracting Company
ENI Group - Italy

Summary

A typical plant scheme for biological stabilization and hygienic agricultural use of sludge which has been separated in the various phases of urban or similar waste-water treatment includes: the mechanical dewatering (by centrifuge or filter press, etc.) of fresh or predigested sludge, the mixing of sludge with high carbon content materials (usually sawdust or straw, chips, etc.); the initial forced aeration for the oxygenation of the whole mass under automatically controlled oxygen and temperature conditions in a vertical bioreactor.

During the composting process a part of the mass is recycled for a massive innoculation. After two weeks of biological stabilization, the material removed from the bioreactor is automatically conveyed and arranged in piles in a sheltered maturation yard for about six to eight weeks before use of the final product in agriculture. Windrow system or aerated piles can be provided for the maturation phase. Aerobic or anaerobic digestion of liquid sludge is thus unnecessary. The compost produced by the proposed scheme could easily be stored, with lower humidity and reduced volume, and would be free of unpleasant odours, pathogens and parasites, harmful weeds, phytotoxic or undesired substances. Moreover, the physico-chemical and biological characteristics of the soil and of the plants are favourably affected when the compost is used in agriculture.

DIRECT COMPOSTING OF SLUDGE FROM URBAN-SEWAGE AND SIMILAR TREATMENT PLANTS

A typical plant scheme comprises mechanical dewatering of the fresh or predigested sludge, mixing with by-products or waste products with a high carbon content, aerobic stabilization in a vertical bioreactor for about two weeks with air injection and partial recycling of compost to promote massive innoculation, and finally maturation of the fresh compost in a covered yard by direct action of the air on the heaps or by the use of a forced-aeration system.

The mature compost is a stable product that is easily stored (it takes up less space than the sludge and has a lower moisture content), is free of unpleasant odours, pathogenic organisms, parasites, harmful weeds or other phytotoxic or undesirable substances, and can improve the properties of the soil and of the plants grown in it. In practice it is a hygienic and stable organic product that is easily stocked and kept for long periods and is rich in humus which is essential to its complementary action when used in conjunction with chemical fertilizers. From the strictly agronomic point of view this type of product is an ideal soil conditioner and accelerates the exchange of nutrients between the roots and the soil, its porosity favours land drainage and it is particularly recommended as a substitute for manure and peat in floriculture, in nurseries, viticulture, fruit growing and specialized agriculture in general, where it can be used before ploughing or harrowing in doses varying between 5 and 25 tonnes per hectare on average.

1. Choice of treatment system

Sewage treatment produces substantial quantities of sludge. Besides substances worth recovering, it generally also contains toxic substances and pathogens. If high concentrations of toxic substances are present (heavy metals, pesticides) it is possible to digest or incinerate the discharged sludge. Both of these systems are too costly if the sludge contains no toxic substances (negative energy balance, rising costs, ash that has to be digested in any case). Proper re-use of liquid or semi-solid sludge directly in agriculture is possible only at certain times of the year, and the organic matter must be stabilized and, for certain crops, sanitized, to eliminate unpleasant odours, phytotoxic substances and the risk of infection.

Among the treatment systems in current use, mesophilic or thermophilic aerobic digestion stabilizes the organic fraction but cannot completely remove the pathogens contained; mesophilic or thermophilic anaerobic digestion allows stabilization and recovery of biogas, but provides good sanitation only if the temperature of the reactor remains within a thermophilic range; treatment with lime or chlorine stops biodegradation for a limited period only and is moreover an inefficient sanitation method; pasteurization and irradiation require a digestion phase upstream or downstream and present serious reinfection problems; thermal drying provides at high cost a product that can be stored for long periods, but which is not biodegraded and can be recontaminated as soon as there is a slight rise in humidity; aerobic composting, on the other hand, provides a stable product, of low volume, free of pathogens, parasites or harmful weeds, and rich in humus and microflora which improve soil fertility.

2. The biological aerobic composting process

The excess sludge from sewage treatment plants and other organic waste arising from human, stockfarming and industrial activities, besides having a high moisture content, contains a certain quantity of organic matter part of which is quickly biodegradable (resulting in unpleasant odours), a number of pathogens and parasites, and seeds of harmful weeds, all of which rule out direct use in agriculture. In order to make this possible it is necessary to use a biodegradation process consisting of a thermophilic phase to produce partial mineralization and natural drying.

Aerobic bioconversion of organic substances is a fairly complex dynamic natural process involving the combined activity of colonies of micro-organisms which appear and alternate or predominate in rapid succession in the various phases. These are bacteria, fungi and actinomycetes, each of which is adapted to a specific environment limited in time and space and each of which is active in the decomposition of a particular substrate. In order to grow and reproduce, aerobic micro-organisms need oxygen and moisture and also a source of carbon (organic waste or by-products), macronutrients, such as nitrogen, phosphorus (and potassium) and certain trace elements. The energy obtained by biological oxidation of a fraction of the organic carbon in the waste and sludge is partly used in the metabolism and the remainder is dissipated as heat and raises the temperature of the mass. The maximum temperature and its duration, and the speed and efficiency of the reaction, depend on certain predetermined variables (composition of the substrates) and certain others which may be altered (humidity, availability of nutrients, aeration, granulometry and microbe population). The rate of decomposition during the process can thus be increased and the quality of the products improved by optimizing these parameters.

The system proposed here for the aerobic biological treatment of organic sludge and waste makes use of this natural process and it is proposed to speed it up essentially in the initial stages of decomposition of the organic substances by forced aeration and recycling of decomposing materials containing a mixed and selected microbe population.

The initial mesophilic stage and the thermophilic stage, comprising the sanitation phase and an initial cooling stage, take place under controlled conditions inside a vertical bioreactor and last for about two weeks, while the fresh compost, no longer dangerous to operators and free of unpleasant odours, requires a final maturation stage of another six to eight weeks in total: during this stage, without any turning operation, complex condensation and polymerization reactions take place which give rise to humic compounds useful in agriculture.

3. Treatment section

The proposed plant scheme is outlined in the diagram and comprises six sections designed to perform the following functions: (1) dewatering of the sludge, (2) storage, (3) mixing, (4) removal and transport, (5) composting and aerobic stabilization in a vertical reactor with an aeration and control system, (6) maturation in heaps.

(1) In most cases the sludge comes in liquid form from sewage treatment plants and is dewatered with conventional equipment such as centrifuges, vacuum filters, filter presses and belt presses.

(2) A storage silo is filled with the sludge, substances with a low moisture content and containing organic carbon (sawdust, straw, wood chips, bark or splinters) and other products to be used in the process.

(3) The mixing phase is designed to homogenize the various products involved so as to attain the optimum humidity, porosity and composition of the mass (carbon/nitrogen ratio – C/N).

(4) The materials are transported and transferred by bucket and belt conveyors.

(5) Aerobic composting takes place in a vertical reactor consisting of a cylindrical structure which can be insulated, especially in colder climates, so as to retain the heat generated during the conversion process. Probes for determining CO_2 and O_2 levels and thermocouples for measuring the temperature are inserted at various heights to monitor and control the process, principally by regulating the compressed-air flow.

(6) The product can be matured in either covered or open yards in heaps 1.5–2 m high, without turning over, for six to eight weeks. Higher heaps and shorter maturation times are possible if the technique of oxygen injection by forced aeration is used.

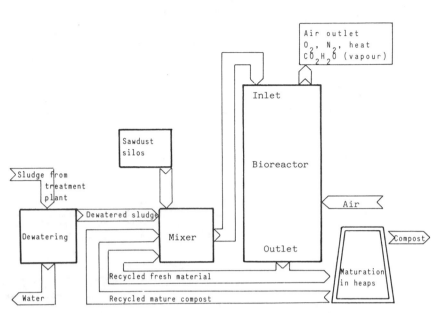

4. <u>Operating scheme of a typical plant</u>

For the composting of biological sludge produced by urban-sewage and similar treatment plants, the operation of the plant can be summarized as follows:
- the sludge is dewatered, generally to about 70-80% humidity, in the dewatering section;
- in the mixing section, sludge, substrate, fresh (and/or mature) compost are mixed and homogenized until the optimum values for carbon/nitrogen ratio (25-30), humidity (60 + 5%) and porosity are attained. Additives can take the form of sawdust, chippings, bark, solid organic waste, straw, etc.;
- the mixed and homogenized material is carried by bucket conveyor to the top of the reactor and distributed uniformly by means of an equalizer;
- as the process material moves down it meets a continuous countercurrent air flow (normally at a rate of 2.5-3 $Nm^3/h.m^3$). It remains in the reactor for about 14 days. During this time it is attacked by aerobic micro-organisms whose metabolism raises the temperature of the mass up to 55-60°C for at least three days during the thermophilic phase; this is controlled by regulating the air flow;
- the fresh compost is extracted every day from the bottom of the reactor by means of a silage cutter and arranged in the yard in trapezoidal-section heaps, where it takes an average of six to eight weeks to mature completely.
- during the loading and unloading of the reactor (which generally takes three to five hours a day), forced aeration is shut off.

**TYPICAL CHARACTERISTICS OF THE COMPOST OBTAINED FROM SLUDGE
WITH ADDED SAWDUST (URBAN SEWAGE)**

– appearance	fine soil, dark brown
– odour	damp earth
– humidity	40–50%
– pH	7–7.5
– organic matter	60–70% on dry matter
– organic carbon	25–35% on dry matter
– total nitrogen	1.5–3% on dry matter
– phosphorus pentoxide	1–2% on dry matter
– potassium oxide	0.5–1% on dry matter
– C/N (carbon/nitrogen ratio)	15–25
– heavy metals	within limits (Italian legislation)
– inert substances (glass, ferrous metals, plastics)	none
– pathogens and parasites	none
– seeds of harmful weeds	killed
– phytotoxicity	zero

URBAN SOLID WASTE PROCESSED BY MEANS OF COMPOSTING AND INCINERATION WITH ENERGY RECOVERY

G.B. BENETTI and A. FARNETI
Snamprogetti - Ecology Division
Engineering, Research and Contracting Company
ENI Group - ITALY

Summary

The proposed plant scheme includes two processes : composting for the organic fraction of solid waste, and incineration of the rejects with energy recovery. The solid waste contained in a storage bunker is usually loaded through a charging hopper and processed in a rotary bioreactor, which acts in three different ways : mixing of components, fragmentation of materials, oxygenation of the whole mass for aerobic process enhancing and spreading. Upper sections for refuse crushing and ferrous materials recovery may be provided when greater effective power is required for the bioreactor. The organic fraction involved is selected from the rejects (overriddles) by a rotary screen and from the ferrous and inorganic impurities by the magnetic and ballistic separators, and then automatically conveyed to the accelerated composting section, carried out in windrow system or in aerated piles arranged in sheltered yard (waste water sludge mixing is allowed). Composting of the organic fraction of refuse is completed in the open maturation yard. Any inert residual particles are removed in a special refining section. The process, performed in hygienic conditions and without unpleasant odours, yields in a reasonable time a good quality product containing humus, fit for agricultural use. The combustible materials (overriddles) having higher heat content are supplied to the incineration system completed with flue gas purification, heat recovery and electrical power generation units.

URBAN SOLID WASTE PROCESSED WITH COMPOSTING AND ENERGY RECOVERY

A mixed disposal plant normally comprises two sections : a section for composting the organic fraction of the waste, and a section for incinerating the remaining fraction with higher calorific value (overrriddles) with flue gas purification, heat recovery and steam and electricity generation.

1. COMPOSTING SECTION

1.1. Initial sorting

The waste is lifted from the storage bunker by a bridge crane with an hydraulic grab and either fed directly into an aerobic biostabilizer or first fed into a hammer mill so that the larger components are broken up and the mass is well mixed (to increase the effective power of the biostabilizer) and then through the recovery of larger ferrous items before the composting process is started.

1.2. Aerobic biostabilizing in a rotary-drum bioreactor

The waste, whether or not crushed, is fed through a charging hopper into a rotary-drum biostabilizer, where it remains for about two days. During that time an aerobic maturing process begins which starts the composting of the organic fraction proper (excluding inert components and pollutants), and facilitates the separation of the inert components.

The biostabilizer acts on all the waste to be treated and carries out three separate functions : homogenization of the components by the rotation of the drum, fragmentation as the materials impact against each other and against the walls of the drum, and oxygenation of the entire mass by circulation of air drawn in from outside. These phases of initial sorting and start-up of the aerobic biological process also attack the seeds of noxious plants and destroy pests and pathogenic bacteria.

COMPOSTING SECTION — FLOW SCHEME

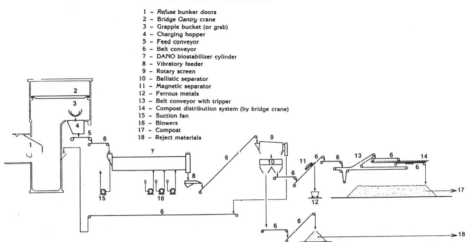

1 – Refuse bunker doors
2 – Bridge Gantry crane
3 – Grapple bucket (or grab)
4 – Charging hopper
5 – Feed conveyor
6 – Belt conveyor
7 – DANO biostabilizer cylinder
8 – Vibratory feeder
9 – Rotary screen
10 – Ballistic separator
11 – Magnetic separator
12 – Ferrous metals
13 – Belt conveyor with tripper
14 – Compost distribution system (by bridge crane)
15 – Suction fan
16 – Blowers
17 – Compost
18 – Reject materials

1.3. Fraction separation

After the biostabilizer phase the materials are sorted by size by means of a rotary screen : the primarily organic fraction, which is now in particles of a different size from the rest, is thus separated out from the fraction with a higher calorific value, which is conveyed to the incineration section for heat recovery and energy generation.

In the next phase the mainly organic fraction is conveyed first to a ballistic separator, which eliminates some of the impurities present (glass, stone, various inert substances), and then to a magnetic separator, which traps the fine ferrous particles.

1.4. Controlled stabilization in heaps

The organic fraction thus separated and still maturing is then brought to a sheltered yard where a bridge crane automatically spreads it in heaps. Dewatered sludge may be added at this point, and the controlled stabilization process continues : either by direct action of air on the heaps as they are turned at intervals or through a system of forced aeration.

1.5. Final maturation

After about a month the material is transferred mechanically to the open final maturation yard, where it may need to be turned from time to time. It remains there for about two months, the period varying with the method selected for the first stabilization stage, the size of the heaps and weather conditions.

2. MATURATION TECHNIQUES AND AGRICULTURAL USE OF THE COMPOST

The fresh compost may be taken straight from the stabilization yard to the farm and applied to hotbeds of particular crops. When enough time elapses between the yard-spreading of the compost and its use on crops, it can complete the humification process directly in the soil.

Where it is to be used for intensive culture with the need for immediate availability of the organic content, the final maturation process must first be completed : during this period the mass of material will be periodically turned or the heaps, without being turned, will be subjected to forced ventilation. By using this technique it is possible to combine the composting of the organic fraction contained in the waste with the composting of dewatered sludge from urban and similar sewage, provided (if the heaps are not to be turned) that is has previously been mixed in.

For the aeration of the heaps the ventilators are controlled by programmable time switches and thermostats set to maintain the temperature of the heaps (covered with mature compost) below 60ºC by aeration. The process is thus rendered hygienically safe without interfering with the activity of the microorganisms causing the accelerated stabilization of the organic content.

In every case the compost, of largely organic content is a useful product to complement chemical fertilizers in agriculture. It can cut the concentrations required, reduce elutriation and modify the structure of the soil, making it more friable and porous, without introducing any foreign substances such as plastic or glass provided it has gone through the refined separation stages. The product obtained from this process presents the agronomic characteristics required within the statutory limits of acceptability.

INCINERATION VERTICAL SECTION AND FLUE GAS PURIFICATION LINE

1 – Waste storage bunker
2 – Bridge crane with grab
3 – Incinerator
4 – Post-combustion chamber
5 – Halogenated acids salification column
6 – Lime-wash slurry equipment
7 – Electrostatic filter
8 – Chimney
9 – Clinkered ashes extractor
10 – Primary air fan

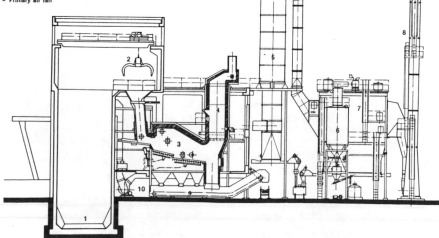

3. INCINERATION SECTION WITH ENERGY GENERATION

3.1. Incineration and secondary combustion

The waste fraction with the higher calorific value (overriddles), separated from the organic fraction by the rotary screen, returns to the waste storage bunker. From there it is taken by the same bridge crane with the hydraulic grab, transferred to the charging hopper and burnt in the incinerator.

To improve combustion conditions the flue gases pass from the furnace to a post-combustion chamber. The combustion temperature is maintained at high levels ranging between 1000°C and 1100°C. The residence times of the gases in the post-combustion chamber should be fairly long (more than 2 seconds) and they should be subjected to turbulence to guarantee the complete blending of all the gaseous mass so that there is negligible formation and emission into the atmosphere of noxious pollutants, particularly organochlorinated substances.

3.2. Heat recovery and energy generation

From the post-combustion chamber the flue gases are channelled to a recovery boiler, where through heat exchange they heat up water, generating steam. The steam is superheated and is conveyed to a turbo-alternator for electricity generation. The steam then passes at low pressure into an air condenser, which completes the thermal cycle together with a degasifier, feed pumps, condensate extraction tank and pumps and demineralization unit.

The alternator operates in parallel with the ENEL national grid and can therefore supply for outside use any electricity which is surplus to the requirements of the plant.

3.3. Salification of halogenated acids and flue gas purification

The flue gas purification system is essentially designed to remove dust, heavy metals and gaseous pollutants with particular reference to hydrochloric acid. The cleansing phases are carried out in two separate units : the first consists of a vertical column into which lime-wash slurry is sprayed and injected with resulting salification of the halogenated acids. The second comprises an electrostatic filter which traps any dusts and salts settling at the bottom of the column. A ventilator and a chimney evacuate the combustion gases to the atmosphere.

Emissions to the atmosphere are systematically analysed to monitor the efficiency of the flue gas purifications system. In ordinary operation plants running on this type of process and technology achieve linearly uniform operation conditions and maintain stable and satisfactory safety conditions.

MANAGEMENT AND ECONOMIC ASPECTS OF WASTE COMPOSTING

M. DE NARDO
B.E.A. s.a.s. - Bologna
A. BOTTAI
Termomeccanica Italiana S.p.A. - La Spezia

Summary
If waste is to be turned into a resource, it must be considered like
any raw material in a factory that must produce - and sell - useful
goods that attract demand.
This paper describes the example of a private composting plant, first
established as a fertilizer factory, which has been producing and
selling its entire output since 1974.

1. Introduction
    Waste is a basic by-product of every activity in so far as there are
no processes or cycles whether natural or industrial which do not give rise
to waste.
    In recent years, as both output and consumption have dramatically
increased, so waste arisings have also grown ; in addition   their
composition has changed.
    With the staggering increase in new consumption habits, goods are
replaced much more frequently and their useful life is ever shorter.

2. Management and economic aspects of waste recovery
    The growing appetite for consumption means an ever-increasing demand
for raw materials and energy, which can only continue to be met if every
effort is made to recover waste materials or at least their energy content.
    Resource recovery from   waste is   also necessary   to   prevent
environmental pollution and improve the economic viability of productive
processes.
    Yet if waste recovery is agreed to be a necessary adjunct to our
system, it clearly must also be understood to be feasible under genuinely
advantageous conditions and to yield products that are genuinely useful,
attractive and harmless to use.
    As things now stand it cannot be claimed that all waste, of whatever
source, can be recovered, yet it must be accepted that all waste ought to
be properly managed.
    To calculate the management and economic benefits of any particular
recovery process, a study must be made of total pollution, energy
consumption and the costs of the process itself, and these data must be
compared with the same calculations for producing the same products with
new raw materials plus the pollution, consumption and costs of disposing of
the waste arising.
    If the first total is greater than the second, the recovery process
is neither useful nor advantageous (unless there are other reasons for
using it).

Waste recovery presents a series of problems which are not only technical and economic but also to do with organization, regulatory standards, management and marketing. These problems cannot easily be resolved by the local authorities responsible for waste disposal.

For a recycling plant must operate to the standards of a normal productive activity, i.e. efficiency, operating economy and good business management are essential.

The difference between an ordinary factory and a recovery plant is simply that the raw materials used in the latter represent receipts, not costs.

This should mean a considerable economic advantage for the production of recycled goods. Production costs should be carried as disposal costs, while receipts from the sale of new products or recovered raw materials should constitute the plant's income.

But up to now the picture has been completely different : composting plants have generally failed either to produce compost of good quality or to market it. They have usually converted solid urban waste into other waste, very often to be dumped.

As a result, the disposal disposal of waste has hitherto been studied almost only from the public health and sanitary angle, which comprises the whole problem only for the planning of a tip or destruction plant.

The design of a recycling plant (while giving due importance to sanitary and health considerations) must lay greatest stress on the productive and economic aspects, because the waste will be genuinely disposed of only to the extent that the products obtained find a ready market.

For composting, it is worth remembering that there is quite a flourishing market in organic or mixed fertilizers and soil conditioners, not only in Italy, and that the marketing possibilities for compost are reasonable, provided that it is of good and consistent quality and that there is a marketing network to display and supply the goods, provide technical advice and make equipment available for using the fertilizers.

Since this commercial and productive activity is hardly a task for government departments, it should preferably be managed by private companies with solid experience in the sector.

3. Example of a factory producing fertilizers from waste

Our waste-processing experience began many years ago when we sought to prepare organic fertilizers of good quality and at low cost, in response to the growing need for organic substances in a farming industry which was turning away from livestock, crop rotation and many other techniques for maintaining the fertility of the land.

Much of the waste first used for composting came from arable and livestock farming and from associated processing industries. It was not until 1974-75 that we began using urban solid waste in ever-increasing proportions in the composting mix.

These changes in the proportions of raw materials prompted us to design and construct units for recovering non-combustible materials such as metals and glass and to produce alternative fuels.

The result was a system which uses uncomplicated machinery, involves low management costs and produces finished or semi-finished goods or recovered materials whose quality characteristics make them marketable at high prices.

This plant started production in 1974, operated by a private company which had already been producing organic fertilizers from waste for several years.

In 1977-78 the plant was radically modified to operate mainly with solid urban waste and double its productive capacity.

The company has an agreement with the municipalities supplying the waste (15 in 1985) under which each local authority undertakes to supply all its urban waste and the company undertakes to process it in accordance with current regulations for an agreed disposal price, at present LIT 26,987/t.

The plant has a capacity of about 1.000 quintals/day of solid urban waste and a further capacity (not precisely quantified) of about 200 quintals per day of organic residues from other sources, which include poultry and other farmyard manure, slaughterhouse waste, fruit-tree trimmings, apple peel, sewage sludge, distillery residues such as distillers' wash, grape stalks and marc, waste from saw mills, staff canteens, bone-processing, some pharmaceutical industries, drug manufacture and generally any natural organic residues.

All the processes were designed from the outset to produce consistently top-quality fertilizer all the year round, and to recover as much as possible of the non-compostible components in the solid urban waste.

The plant comprises four waste-processing units and a fifth is shortly to be built. The first unit is for the recovery of glass, metals and organic components. The second unit comprises machinery for separating the organic components from any extraneous material still present. This unit was built to a size to match the capacity of the packaging unit.

The third unit packages, bales, palletizes and load the fertilizers.

The fourth unit pellets part of the fertilizers produced by the plant.

The fifth unit will produce fuel.

For many years the plant's entire output of fertilizers has been marketed through a distribution network.

The present factory-gate selling prices for standard compost is LIT 5,500 per quintal sold in bulk and LIT 7,000 per quintal in 50 kg sacks.

Pelleted and enriched fertilizers are sold at various prices depending on specific characteristics.

The marketing network also offers technical advice to farmers, and besides advice on use and farming operation it makes available machinery for powder-spreading the compost.

It is almost always forgotten when speaking of compost that modern farms are fully mechanized and can use compost only if the spreading machinery is available.

For this reason specially designed compost-spreaders are made available to farms, both for field spreading and for crops under glass and also for special uses like covered vine growing, which is common in some southern italian regions.

4. Conclusions

Waste materials recovery is not only desirable but necessary, and composting is the simplest way of making use of organic waste.

But it is essential that every composting plant should be designed, equipped and organized like a proper factory and managed along business lines. It will then be an attractive proposition for private enterprise.

The use together with solid urban waste of all recoverable organic residues speeds up the maturation process, improves the quality of the finished product and reduces the proportion of heavy metals in the compost.

There is certainly a need for organic soil conditioners in agriculture, and there are market openings, provided that they are of good quality and are supported by an adequate technical and commercial structure.

Only in this way can waste become a useful and attractive resource and warrant proper processing, not only for sanitary public health and environmental reasons but also for sound economic reasons.

Otherwise we shall have squandered ideas, money and energy to turn waste into other waste.

REFERENCES

1. DE NARDO, M. (1982). La Planète – déchets. Ed. Fondations S.I. Patino (GE).

CHANGES UNDERGONE BY SOME CHARACTERISTICS OF ORGANIC WASTES DURING THE COMPOSTING PROCESS

J. CEGARRA, A. VAZQUEZ, F. COSTA, A. LAX and E. MORGAN
CSIC. Centro de Edafología y Biología Aplicada del Segura.
P.O. Box 195. 30003-Murcia. Spain

Summary

Six different samples including mixtures of household refuse, sewage sludge, animal manure, woodchips and grape residue were composted and matured for a total of 230 days. They were homogenized three times and the tempe-ature monitores. Samples were taken on the first day, after each homogenization and after maturity to assess the pH values and quantities of organic and inorganic nitrogen, oxidizable carbon (C_{ox}), extractable carbon (C_{ex}), hydrosoluble carbon (C_h), and humic and fulvic acid carbons. Over the first weeks a considerable degradation of the organic matter was noted, especially in the household refuse samples where C_{ox} fell to 30 % of their original values. C_{ex} and C_h behaved similarly. Important quantities of ammonia were evolved as indicated later by ammonium nitrogen analysis. This disappeared during maturation. Correlations between the different forms of organic carbon and with pH were found. Also the molecular weight distribution of the hydrosoluble fractions were determined by gel chromatography.

1. INTRODUCTION

Composting is a bioxidative process of organic waste material by a mixed microbial population in a moist and warm aerobic environment. It includes mineralization and partial humification of organic substances, leading to a stabilized organic product which may be used directly to amend soil and improve fertility. Some studies on the soluble fractions of the organic matter, and in particular the hydrosoluble fraction, have been carried out (1). In this work some of these fractions are studied during the composting and maturation of various organic wastes.

2. MATERIALS AND METHODS

The materials used were fresh household refuse (R), aerobic sewage sludge (S), fresh animal manure (M), grape residue (G) and woodchips (W) (table I). Starting with these materials four different mixtures were made R+W, R+W+S, M+W and G+W+S plus R and M apart. Details of the composition of the six samples are given in table II. They were homogenized in a concrete mixer, deposited in containers of 200 l. and composted under relatively isothermic conditions. The materials were rehomogenized and aerated on the 11th, 25th and 47th days of the composting process. Samples were taken on the first day, after each homogenization and at the end of the period of maturity (230th day) to assess the quantities of NH4-N, NO3-N, organic-N, oxidizable carbon (C_{ox}), carbon extractable by 0.1M Na4P2O7 (C_{ex}), water extract carbon (C_h), and humic and fulvic acid carbons, (C_{ha}) and (C_{fa}). The materials were analysed for nitrogen while wet and for carbon after drying. Organic-N was determined by Kjeldahl digestion, NH4-N by extraction with 2M KCl and NO3-N by further reduction with Devarda's alloy, C_{ox} analysis by the Walkley-Black method and other forms of carbon using a Beckman Organic Carbon Analyzer. Gel Chromatography of water extracts was carried out with

Sephadex G-15 (1), and K_{av} values calculated according to Fischer (3).

3. TEMPERATURE FLUCTUATIONS

Temperature rised from the first day in most of the samples (fig. 1), although the G+W+S sample rarely reached temperatures higher than 30°C and can hardly be considered as composted. The household refuse group (R-group) reached temperatures higher than the samples containing manure in which the thermophilic stage (temperature > 40°C) was prolonged until day 15, whereas it lasted a few days longer in the R-group. For the rest of the experiment all the materials remained in the mesophilic stage.

4. CHANGES IN THE ORGANIC WASTE CHARACTERISTICS

4.1. Overall nitrogen levels and amounts of organic carbon in the fractions

A general decrease in C_{ox} was found, especially important up to the 25th day. It continued less notably until the end of maturation (fig. 2). This decrease was greater in the R-group, and also for R and M individually than in their mixtures with W and S. In the R-group R and R+W mineralized most, in that after maturation approximately 30 % of the original C_{ox} remained, in comparison to the 50 % retained by R+W+S. These figures corresponded to 10 and 17 % respectively of the compost dry weight. Figure 3 (C_h, C_{ex} and C_{ha} contents expressed as % C_{ox}) shows that there were important losses of C_h in the R-group until the 47th day which decreased later. In M and M+W the C_h contents increased initially, although they also decreased later, reaching levels similar to those present at the beginning. The G+W+S sample had the smallest C_h values and its variations were inappreciable. Also the decreases in the slopes of the C_{ox} degradation curves of the R-group on the 25th day (fig. 2) coincided with C_h levels approximately equivalent to 50% of their original values (fig. 3). After maturation these decreased to 20%. In the R-group, the initial experimental values of C_h (fig. 3) were 95% for R, 87 % for R+W and 66 % for R+W+S of those calculated from tables I and II. This suggests that there were difficulties in extracting the hydrosoluble fractions during the early stages and was probably due to hydrophobic components such as fatty acids in S and R, and waxes in W. Later more hydrosoluble substances may have passed to the aqueous phase, where microbial metabolism occurs, caused by decreases in the fatty acid levels during composting (1) and by the succesive homogenizations. These contributed not only to the oxygenisation of the samples but also to an increased moistening as indicated by the four peaks in fig. 1. The other forms of carbon behaved similarly. In the R-group, the C_{ha} levels were generally higher than C_h although the opposite was found in the samples containing manure. In G+W+S the levels of both variables were similar and lowest of all the samples. After maturation, the C_{fa} contents (difference between C_{ex} and C_{ha}, fig. 3) in the R-group were similar to the C_{ha} contents although higher in the other samples. Total-N contents in the R-group decreased in the order R > R+W > R+W+S (table III). The NH_4-N contents were close to 0.3 % on the 11th day, increased to 0.4 % on the 25th day and almost disappeared after maturation. NH_4-N level in this group decreased in the opposite direction to total-N. In the other samples total-N increased and NH_4-N was almost undetectable. Only small amounts of NO_3-N were found during the latter stages, agreeing with other results (2). The C/N ratios generally decreased and were smaller in R and M than when mixed with W and S (table III). The N losses through NH_3 volatilization were related to the changes in the C/N ratios; being lowest when the losses were highest. However, other factors such as pH could also have led to increased losses. Sample R followed by R+W had the highest pH values. There were no N losses in samples M, M+W and G+W+S, and the initial values of C/N and its variations were similar to those of the R-group.

Therefore other characteristics such as the chemical nature of the nitrogen should be considered.

4.2. Relationships between the fractions of organic carbon and with pH.

The correlation coefficients between the carbon contents during the experiment (from fig. 3), combining the data from all the samples, were always positive (table IV). The correlation between C_{ex} and C_h was very significant on the first day but decreased later. This probably indicates a progressive differentiation between the compounds in the two fractions as a result of the extractants 0.1M Na P_2O_7 and water acting selectively. The correlation coefficients between C_{fa} and C_h, and those of C_{fa} and C_{ha} were significant during composting, becoming non-significant during maturation as above. C_{ha} and C_h were highly correlated in the early stages but were uncorrelated in the last two stages and would seem to indicate that the hydro soluble fraction shared some common components with the fulvic acids but less with the humics. The decreases in the similarities may have been the consequence of the later transformations.

The correlations between the forms of carbon and pH in the R-group samples were always negative and significant (table V), the most significant being those between C_{fa} and pH, and C_h and pH, indicating a relationship between the contents of the soluble fractions and pH since the pH increased when the carbon contents decreased. The higher correlation between C_{fa} and pH agrees with the current opinion of greater solubility and acidity of the fulvic acids with respect to the humic acids. However, the increases in pH may not only be due to increases in the soluble organic fractions but also to other factors such as the production of ammonia. In the other three samples the pH values varied only slightly.

4.3. Gel chromatography.

The chromatograms of the products obtained after maturation show increases in the excluded fractions and decreases in those of the included in comparison to those of the raw materials (fig. 4). Th K_{av} values of the included fractions decreased when the samples had composted. In the R-group one or two peaks were lost as an effect of composting and maturation. Taking this into account, and considering the results of other authors (1), a relative enrichment of certain hydrosoluble substances such as polysaccharides and peptides, and impoverishment of certain components, such as simple sugars and free amino acids, probably occurred.

5. CONCLUSIONS

Organic raw materials composted differently according to their proportion in the mixtures and their chemical natures. The samples containing household refuse, which is rich in easily assimilable hydrosoluble components, evolved intensily, whereas in those containing manure, a product of animal metabolism, the process was milder. The presence of hydrophobic components and different quantities of hydrosoluble compounds influenced the progress of the transformations. This was especially noticeable in the grape residue mixture.

REFERENCES

(1) CHANYASAK, V., YOSHIDA, T. and KUBOTA, H. (1980). Chemical Components in Gel Chromatographic Fractionation of Water Extract from Sewage Sludge Compost. Journal of Fermentation Technology. 58,(6), 533-539.
(2) DE BERTOLDI, M., VALLINI, G. and PERA, A. (1983). The Biology of Composting: a Review. Waste Management & Research. 1, 157-176.
(3) FISCHER, L. (1969). An Introduction to Gel Chromatography. North-Holland Publishing Company. Amsterdam.

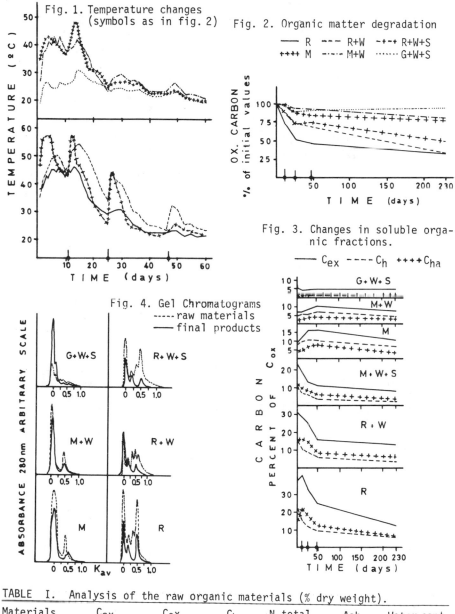

Fig. 1. Temperature changes (symbols as in fig. 2)

Fig. 2. Organic matter degradation

Fig. 3. Changes in soluble organic fractions.

Fig. 4. Gel Chromatograms
----- raw materials
—— final products

TABLE I. Analysis of the raw organic materials (% dry weight).

Materials	C_{ox}	C_{ex}	C_h	N total	Ash	Water cont.
G	35.7	2.09	0.64	2.00	6.6	20.4
S	23.2	3.91	1.78	3.86	42.2	79.3
W	46.8	2.07	1.20	0.11	1.1	7.0
R	29.1	11.39	7.09	1.87	34.5	58.0
M	35.4	3.28	2.68	3.07	19.3	65.6

TABLE II. Composition of the samples and the contributions of carbon and nitrogen in the original materials to each of these (%).

Samples	GRAPE R.			WOODCHIPS			SLUDGE			MANURE			REFUSE			Water content
	Comp.	C	N	Comp.	C	N	Comp.	C	N	Comp.	C	N	Comp.	C	N	
G+W+S	28.4	67.2	86.6	9.6	29.8	1.6	2.0	3.0	11.8	--	--	--	--	--	--	59.3
M+W	--	--	--	18.2	52.5	2.7	--	--	--	21.8	47.5	97.3	--	--	--	60.6
M	--	--	--	--	--	--	--	--	--	34.5	100	100	--	--	--	65.5
R+W+S	--	--	--	10.3	35.9	1.8	1.8	3.1	11.4	--	--	--	28.2	61.0	86.8	57.8
R+W	--	--	--	8.5	30.1	1.5	--	--	--	--	--	--	31.8	69.9	98.5	58.0
R	--	--	--	--	--	--	--	--	--	--	--	--	42.0	100	100	58.0

TABLE III. Total and ammonium nitrogen contents (%) and C/N values during the composting process.

Time days	R			R+W			R+W+S			M			M+W			G+W+S		
	N			N			N			N			N			N		
	NH4	Total	C/N	NH4	Total	C/N	NH4	Total	C/N	NH4	Total	C/N	NH4	Total	C/N	NH4	Total	C/N
1	0.02	1.97	15.5	0.04	1.64	18.4	0.03	1.33	26.4	0.01	2.32	15.3	0.01	1.65	24.3	0.05	1.71	22.0
11	0.28	1.92	11.7	0.29	1.67	16.2	0.30	1.80	17.4	0.03	2.64	13.1	0.04	1.66	23.9	0.01	1.63	22.2
25	0.39	1.66	9.5	0.42	1.62	13.7	0.34	1.59	16.0	0.06	2.54	12.2	0.02	1.65	22.7	0.00	1.90	17.7
47	0.30	1.52	9.3	0.20	1.45	14.4	0.05	1.29	20.3	0.01	2.65	11.3	0.01	1.78	20.9	0.00	1.89	18.2
230	0.03	1.13	8.6	0.01	1.16	8.7	0.01	1.17	14.7	0.01	2.96	9.2	0.01	1.93	16.7	0.02	2.24	15.8

TABLE IV. Correlation coefficients between the different forms of carbon at the various stages of the experiment combining the data from all the samples.

Time (days)	Cex v. Ch	Cfa v. Ch	Cha v. Ch	Cfa v. Cha
1	0.9599***	0.9699***	0.8996***	0.9048**
11	0.9069***	0.9423***	0.8754***	0.9772****
25	0.8693*	0.9269**	0.8184*	0.9643***
47	0.8217*	0.8942**	0.7238NS	0.9052**
230	0.6177NS	0.7099NS	0.3365NS	0.3698NS

TABLE V. Correlation coefficients between pH values and different forms of carbon in the household refuse group combining the data from the various stages of the experiment.

Samples	Cex v. pH	Ch v. pH	Cfa v. pH	Cha v. pH
R	-0.8287*	-0.9860***	-0.9789***	-0.5377NS
R+W	-0.9330**	-0.9905***	-0.9627***	-0.8529**
R+W+S	-0.9755***	-0.9795***	-0.9976****	-0.9291**

*, **, ***, ****: Level of significance greater than 0.1, 0.05, 0.01 and 0.001 respectively.
NS: Not significant.

YIELD RESPONSES OF FOUR DIFFERENT CROPS TO COMPOST APPLICATION

F. Del Zan,L. Baruzzini,M. Candotti,P.L. Nassimbeni,G. Murgut,I. Tonetti

Centro Regionale per la Sperimentazione Agraria per il
Friuli - Venezia Giulia
Pozzuolo del Friuli (Italy)

Short-term results from a fertilization trial are presented in which composts of different origin, at various rates of application, in comparison with mineral fertilizers and farmyard manure have been applied annually on the same site for three years. Four crops, of different botanical species and edible parts, were grown every year: maize, leaf beet, potato, dry bean.

MAIZE: organic dressings allowed to obtain higher yields than the untreated test, but lower with respect to the application of only mineral fertilizers. Combined applications of the two forms gave the best results. Among the organic fertilizers, the best results were attained by farmyard manure and by compost obtained mixing municipal solid wastes with sewage sludge. Lower results were achieved with immature or refined composts.

LEAF BEET: this plant exploited compost better than the other crops: yield response to increasing rates of m.s.w. + s.s. compost was linear. Moreover, yields higher than with only mineral fertilizers were obtained with maximum compost dressings. This crop, howewer, appeared very sensible to inhibitory effects of immature m.s.w. compost.

POTATO: yield response to compost dressings was moderate, lower than that obtained with only mineral fertilizers. Higher yields were obtained using fym in comparison with m.s.w. + s.s. compost application.

DRY BEAN: the different kinds of fertilizers had little influence on dry bean yields. Organic fertilizers generally showed a negative trend, lowering yields in comparison with only mineral fertilizers.

Tab. 1 – Fertilizers employed in the experimentation: description and quantities applied.

Treatment	Description	Quantities q x ha^{-1} x yr^{-1} supplied		
		1983	1984	1985
1	Control	–	–	–
2	Ammonium nitrate (26-27)	3.84	3.84	3.84
	Superphosphate (19-21)	3.74	3.74	3.74
	Potassium sulphate (50-52)	3.00	3.00	3.00
3	Ammonium nitrate (26-27)	7.69	7.69	7.69
	Superphosphate (19-21)	7.48	7.48	7.48
	Potassium sulphate (50-52)	6.00	6.00	6.00
4	m.s.w. compost	1483	1480	1639
5	Immature m.s.w. compost	1607	1111	1742
6	Refined m.s.w. compost	1481	1222	1404
7	Fym	1754	1296	1373
8	m.s.w. + s.s. compost	816	1037	1077
9	m.s.w. + s.s. compost	1633	2074	2155
10	m.s.w. + s.s. compost	2450	3111	3233
11	Treatment 8 + 2	816+(3.84+3.74+3.00)	1037+(3.84+3.74+3.00)	1077+(3.84+3.74+3.00)
12	Treatment 8 + 3	816+(7.69+7.48+6.00)	1037+(7.69+7.48+6.00)	1077+(7.69+7.48+6.00)

(m.s.w. = municipal solid wastes; s.s. = sewage sludge; fym = farmyard manure).

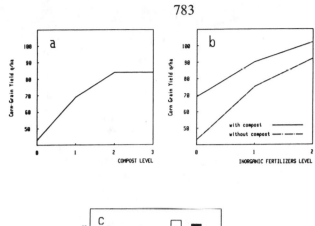

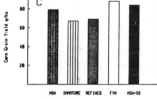

Figure I : Corn yield responses to : compost levels (a); compost + inorganic
dressings (b); different types of compost (c).

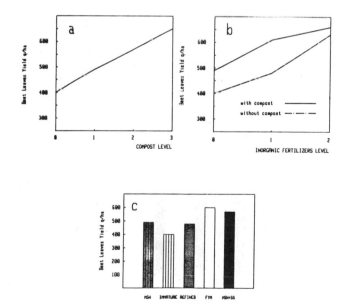

Figure II : Leaf beet yield responses to : compost levels (a); compost
+ inorganic dressings (b); different types of compost (c).

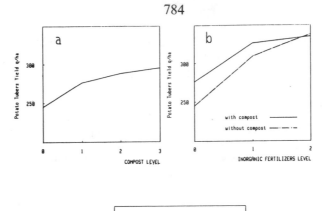

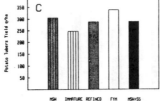

Figure III : Potato yield responses to : compost levels (a); compost + inorganic dressings (b); different types of compost (c).

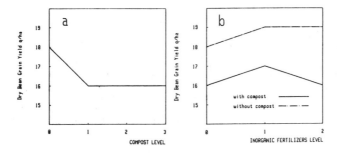

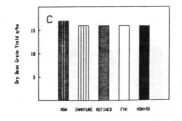

Figure IV : Dry bean yield responses to : compost levels (a); compost + inorganic dressings (b); different types of compost (c).

SPENT MUSHROOM COMPOST, A POSSIBLE GROWING MEDIUM INGREDIENT?

V.G. Devonald
Bath College of Higher Education
Newton Park
Bath, Avon
United Kingdom

Summary

Spent mushroom compost was sampled from four commercial sources on two occasions. Analysis showed that except for calcium, boron, copper and zinc, coefficients of variability were less than 25%. Conductivity and pH were consistently high.
A bulked sample of spent mushroom compost was used as an ingredient in growing media with peat or bark and sand. Different formulations were compared with GCRI potting compost I in short-term trials.

1.1 Introduction

The south west region of the United Kingdom is a centre of mushroom production. Twenty enterprises, one of which is the largest in the country occur in the area.
Mushroom production is based on the use of stacked composted material which is inoculated with mushroom 'spawn' and acts as a medium for the saprophytic growth of the mushroom mycelium. Traditionally growers have utilised mixtures of horse manure and wheat straw for composting. In view of the scarcity of horse manure and the large demands of the industry, chicken manure is frequently added as a nitrogen supplement. 'Synthetic' formulations are also used, the term being applied to mixtures in which the prime ingredient is not horse manure but organic substitutes such as turkey manure, poultry manure, sugar beet pulp etc. (Wuest, Duffy and Royse 1981). Whether traditional or synthetic, the compost receives significant additions of gypsum ($CaSO_4.2H_2O$) which cuts the 'greasiness' of the compost (Tunney 1977) and improves its aeration. Nitrogen supplements and water are also added during stacking.
Fermentation in the stack causes the stack temperature to rise to 54–60°C when pasteurisation occurs killing harmful pests and competitor fungi. The high temperature also encourages the removal of ammonia generated in the fermentation. After cooling to 24°C the compost is spread on trays or shelves and spawned using inoculated grain. Finally the compost is 'cased' ie covered with a layer of peat and lime to conserve moisture. Production soon begins and a 7–10 day harvesting cycle is instituted for about six weeks by which time yield declines. The compost and trays are then 'cooked out' i.e. steam pasteurised and the production trays cleared. The waste material is stacked and bagged for retail sale as an organic fertilizer and soil conditioner.
The present paper reports analytical results relating to the residual nutrient content of the waste compost and pilot experiments on its possible use as an ingredient in a bagged growing medium for retail marketing.

1.2 Methods and materials

Bagged samples of spent mushroom compost were obtained from four local sources on two different occasions (except for source D) in order to assess how consistent a production source was and how much variation occurred between sources.

The following physical and chemical characteristics were determined:- bulk density, % water content, % loss on ignition, % ash content, electrical conductivity, pH, total nitrogen, and the contents of available K, P, Mg, Ca, B, Cu and Zn.

In view of the generally excessively high nutrient levels in the spent mushroom compost samples (Table 2) it was decided not to use it on its own in growth trials. Instead, an initial trial was carried out in 1984 using a bulked sample from all four sources as an ingredient in three compost mixes, the three mixes being compared to GCRI potting compost I as a control. The mixes were assessed against the growth of five quick-growing plants, namely Antirrhinum cv. Orange Glow, Chinese cabbage cv. Pe Tsai, French marigold cv. Orange Boy, Nicotiana cv. Domino and Tagetes cv. Lemon Jem. Seeds were germinated in GCRI seed compost and pricked out into seed trays containing the following compost mixes:-

1. GRCI potting compost I   75% peat/25% sand.
   Added nutrients (Bunt 1976).
2. 75% spent mushroom compost/25% sand.
   No added nutrients.
3. 37.5% spent mushroom compost/37.5% shagnum peat/25% sand.
   No added nutrients.
4. As in (3) but with a nitrogen supplement of Nitram (NH_4NO_3) at the rate of 0.4 kg/m³.

All %s are by volume. Each tray was replicated three times. It was calculated that the mixes would have the nutrient levels shown in Table 1.

It can be seen that mix (2) would have a content of available phosphorus 3.32 times the recommended added phosphorus in GCRI potting compost I, a potassium content 7.6 times greater and a magnesium content 1.39 greater while in mixes (3) and (4) the respective quotients would be halved.

Harvesting occurred in April - May 1984 when the plants in the best treatment had reached marketable size. The mean fresh weight of single complete plants was determined.

In 1985-86 trials, the 75% spent mushroom compost/25% sand mix has been discarded and a new ingredient, bark, has been included. The bark used was coarse grade Cambark.

The mixes compared are:-

1. GCRI potting compost I 75% peat/25% sand.
   Added nutrients.
2. 37.5% spent mushroom compost/37.5% sphagnum peat/25% sand.
3. 37.5% spent mushroom compost/37.5% coarse bark/25% sand.
4. as in (3) but with a nitrogen supplement of Nitram (NH_4NO_3) at the rate of 0.4 kg/m³.

A selection of quick-growing and longer term containerised subjects are being assessed in these mixes and the results for two of them lettuce cv. Winter Density and Cineraria cv. Spring Glory are reported here.

1.3 Results

Analyses (Table 2) show some degree of consistency in physicochemical characters such as bulk density, % water content, % loss on ignition, % ash and conductivity (coefficients of variability < 20%) and a consistently high pH. Values of pH in the range 7.01 - 8.04 and of conductivity in the range 2000 – 4000 microsiemen would be unacceptably high if the spent compost were to be used directly as a growing medium.

Values for major nutrients are also fairly consistent, generally lying above the 'normal' range for soils and growing media. Inconsistency for calcium might be expected in view of the incomplete incorporation of gypsum and lime evident in most samples.

In the case of the micronutrients analysed, boron levels are satisfactory, neither toxicity nor deficiency being expected if the compost were directly used as a growing medium. The copper levels are also satisfactory though the level for sample A2 lies above the normal range for soils. The zinc levels are all high but toxicity would only be a danger in samples B2 and then only if the pH fell somewhat and zinc-sensitive crops were being grown.

In the 1984 trial (Table 3) generally seedlings survived in all the treatments except Nicotiana in 75% spent mushroom compost/25% sand in which there was 85% mortality. Deficiency symptoms were not apparent though significant differences in growth occurred. Generally none of the spent mushroom composts mixes produced results as good as the control, GCRI potting compost I except in the case of Nicotiana in which growth in mix (3) and (4) were significantly better than control.

In the case of the 1985-86 trials on lettuce (table 4) the plants were harvested at planting-out size. There were no mortalities and only slight differences in foliage colour. The mean fresh weight of whole plants was greatest in the control but the difference between it and that in mix 2 and 3 was not significant. Only in mix 4 was the mean dry weight of the plant significantly low.

In Cineraria, the plants were harvested at the flower bud stage. There were no mortalities and no apparent deficiency or toxicity symptoms. The greatest whole plant fresh weight occurred in the control but these values were not significantly different from those achieved in mix 3 and mix 4 (3/3/2 mushroom compost/bark/sand without and with N respectively). This was also true of the dry weights.

1.4 Discussion

Little analytical data is available on spent mushroom compost for comparison though Stokes (1976) reporting trials of it using nursery stock in containers refers to its high and variable conductivity. There is also the possibility of particular nutrients being present at dangerously high concentrations. It has been reported that too much phosphate, for instance can be damaging to container nursery stock (Scott 1981).

The present investigation suggests that incorporating the spent compost in a 3/1 mix with sand is not an acceptable growing medium though when half the mushroom compost is replaced with peat or bark, a level of growth can be achieved which approaches (Antirrhinum, Cineraria) or may, in vigorous subjects (Nicotiana), surpass it. Obviously, as the proportion of mushroom compost in the mix is lowered the case for its use as a cheap growing medium ingredient is weakened as its role approaches that of an unstandardised organic fertilizer.

The 1985-86 results suggest that the textural character of the mushroom/peat/sand mixes are not favourable since the more open bark composts sometimes produce significantly better growth (Cineraria). The Cineraria results also suggest that where the subject is containerised for a longer period in a mushroom/bark/sand mix nitrogen supplementation might be necessary.

Many more problems may be envisaged before any final recommendations can be arrived at. Experimentation is necessary on the homogenisation of the material before incorporation into the growing medium since the spent compost as disposed of is distinctly heterogeneous. There is also the possibility of prolonged stacking before use as a means of reducing conductivity and nutrient levels and thus allowing greater proportions of the spent compost to be used in growing medium formulations.

REFERENCES

1. BUNT, A.C., (1976). Modern Potting Composts. George Allen and Unwin, London.
2. SCOTT, M.A., (1981). The role of phosphate in the production of quality container-grown nursery stock. Leaflet No.2, Efford experimental Horticulture Station.
3. STOKES, D.A., (1976). Spent mushroom compost for nursery stock growing in containers. Lee Valley Experimental Horticultural Station. Report LV: 117.
4. TUNNEY, J., (1977). Practical considerations in the preparation of synthetic compost - compost without horse manure. In: Hayes, W.A. (Ed) (1977). Composting. Proc. 2nd. Seminar in Mushroom Science, Mushroom Growers Association.
5. WUEST, P.J., DUFFY, M.D. and ROYSE, D.J., (1981). Six steps to mushroom farming. Penns. State Uni., College of Agri. Special circular 268.

ACKNOWLEDGEMENTS

The author wishes to acknowledge the technical help of Mr N. Swain and Mr D. Watts.

Table 1 - 1984 trial: Contents of nitrogen, phosphorus, potassium and magnesium in four compost mixes. Values for mix (1) are mg of added nutrient/1 (Bunt 1976). Values for P, K and Mg in mixes (2), (3) and (4) are mg of available nutrient/1 derived from analytical data in the present paper. No data is available for nitrate- or ammonium-nitrogen in mixes (2), (3) and (4). The value for nitrogen in mix (4) is mg added nitrogen (as Nitram) /1.

Mix	N	P	K	Mg
(1)	230	120	290	270
(2)	-	399	2208	376.5
(3)	-	198.5	1104	188.2
(4)	117	198.5	1104	188.2

Table 2 – Analysis of seven samples of waste mushroom compost from four sources

	A		B		C		D	mean	range	coefficient of variability
Source	A		B		C		D			
Sample	1	2	1	2	1	2	1			
bulk density	0.17	0.15	0.19	0.17	0.23	0.24	0.19	0.19	0.15–0.24	17.3%
% water content	59	61	50	52	57	58	59	56.6	50–61	7.1%
% loss of ignition	79.0	76.1	72.6	68.3	63.7	64.9	69.8	70.6	63.7–79.0	7.8%
% ash	21.0	23.9	27.4	31.7	36.3	35.1	30.2	29.4	21.0–36.3	19.2%
conductivity	4000	3900	3250	3300	3900	3000	2900	3464	2900–4000	13.3%
pH	7.01	7.95	7.26	7.33	8.02	8.04	7.18	7.54	7.01–8.04	5.9%
total N	1.93	2.12	1.57	1.26	1.61	1.36	1.34	1.59	1.34–2.12	20.1%
available P	0.28	0.26	0.26	0.39	0.21	0.30	0.20	0.20	0.21–0.39	10.8%
available K	2.16	1.92	1.39	1.44	1.35	1.44	1.21	1.55	1.21–2.16	21.7%
available Ca	1.09	1.49	2.82	3.06	3.00	2.45	3.06	2.42	1.09–3.06	33.5%
Mg	2250	2625	2000	3500	2375	3500	2250	2642	2000–3500	23.2%
B	–	2.78	–	1.56	–	1.86	2.38	2.14	1.56–2.78	25.3%
Cu	–	19.0	–	3.2	–	3.4	2.8	7.1	2.8–19.0	111.0%
Zn	52	53	–	150	–	24	26	61	24–150	84.6%

Each sample datum derived from duplicate sub-samples.

Conductivity microsiemen, determined by shaking 20cm^3 of air-dried compost in 50cm^3 of saturated cal ium sulphate for 20 mins and filtering.

pH determined by shaking
20cm^3 of air-dried compost shaken in 50cm^3 distilled water for 20 mins.

Total nitrogen
w/w % of air-dried compost, Kjeldahl determination.

P, K, Ca, Mg, B, Cu, Zn. The data is for available nutrient determined using various extracting solutions.
P, K and Ca are w/w % of air-dried compost.
Mg is w/w ppm of air-dried compost.
B, Cu and Zn are mg/1 of air-dried compost.

ADDENDUM to Table 2. NH_4^+ and NO_3^- content, ppm.

	A		B		C		D		mean	range	coeff.
	1	2	1	2	1	2	1	2			varia.
NH_4^+	252	188	259	231	70	84	140	168	174	70 - 259	41.7
NO_3^-	105	39	0	42	21	35	42	28	39	0 - 105	77.3

Table 3 - 1984 trial, mean fresh weight of single plants, g. N = 30.
Significant differences, Student t test; *p = 0.05; **p = 0.01; NS = not
significant.

Subject	Compost mix			
	Mix 1 (JCRI potting compost I)	Mix 2 (3/1 mushroom compost/sand)	Mix 3 (3/3/2 mushroom compost/peat/ sand)	Mix 4 (as 3 + N)
Antirrhinum	3.00	0.70	2.41	2.50
Chinese cabbage	3.00	0.97	2.26	2.29
French marigold	4.75	0.60	3.67	2.75
Nicotiana	3.56	1.76	5.81	8.42
Tagetes	3.30	0.20	1.28	2.28

Tests of significance:

	1	2	3	4
1				
2	**			
3	*	**		
4	NS	**	NS	

Antirrhinum

	1	2	3	4
1				
2	**			
3	*	**		
4	*	NS	NS	

Chinese cabbage

	1	2	3	4
1				
2	**			
3	*	**		
4	**	**	*	

French marigold

	1	2	3	4
1				
2	NS			
3	*	*		
4	*	**	*	

Nicotiana

	1	2	3	4
1				
2	**			
3	**	**		
4	*	**	**	

Tagetes

Table 4 - Mean fresh and dry weights of single plants, shoot and root systems in different compost mixes, g. N = 10.
Significant differences, Student t test; *p = 0.5; **p = 0.01; NS = not significant

Subject	Compost mix			
	Mix 1 (GCRI potting compost I)	Mix 2 (3/3/2 mush- room compost/ peat/sand)	Mix 3 (3/3/2 mush- room compost/ bark/sand)	Mix 4 (as 3+N)
Lettuce:				
fresh weight, shoot	2.92	1.61	2.33	1.64
fresh weight, root	0.59	1.15	0.83	0.65
fresh weight, total	3.51	2.76	3.16	2.29
dry weight, shoot	0.16	0.11	0.13	0.08
dry weight, root	0.03	0.08	0.07	0.04
dry weight, total	0.19	0.19	0.20	0.12
Cineraria:				
fresh weight, shoot	29.76	17.41	23.71	28.24
fresh weight, root	15.67	13.75	14.17	12.37
fresh weight, total	45.43	31.16	37.88	40.61
dry weight, shoot	3.02	1.50	2.00	2.33
dry weight, root	2.44	1.98	2.35	2.41
dry weight, total	5.46	3.48	4.35	4.75

Test of significance.

```
             1   2   3   4     1   2   3   4     1   2   3   4     1   2   3   4
          1                 1                 1                 1
          2 **              2 **              2 NS              2 *
lettuce   3 NS  NS          3 *   NS          3 NS  NS          3 NS  NS
          4 **  NS  NS      4 NS  **  NS      4 **  NS  NS      4 **  NS  *

             1   2   3   4     1   2   3   4     1   2   3   4     1   2   3   4
          1                 1                 1                 1
          2 **              2 NS              2 **              2 **
cineraria 3 NS  **          3 NS  NS          3 NS  *           3 **  **
          4 NS  **  NS      4 NS  NS  NS      4 NS  *   NS      4 NS  **  NS
          shoot fr. w.        root fr. w.       total fr. w.      shoot DW.

             1   2   3   4     1   2   3   4
          1                 1
          2 NS              2 NS
lettuce   3 NS  NS          3 NS  NS
          4 *   *   *       4 *   *   *
             1   2   3   4     1   2   3   4
          1                 1
          2 NS              2 **
cineraria 3 NS  NS          3 NS  NS
          4 NS  NS  NS      4 NS  NS  NS
          root DW             total DW
```

VERMISTABILISATION OF SEWAGE SLUDGE IN THE UK

J E Hall*, R Bland** and E Neale***

*Water Research centre, Medmenham Laboratory, Marlow, Buckinghamshire
**Biggleswade Sewage Treatment Works, Anglian Water, Bedfordshire
*** British Earthworm Technology Ltd, St Ives, Cambridgeshire

Summary

The sewage treatment authorities in the UK are continually looking for more economic and effective means of stabilising sewage sludges. Potentially, earthworms offer a means of sludge stabilisation which not only reduces odour but produces a compost-like material that, if marketed successfully, may make vermistabilisation an attractive sludge treatment option for some sewage treatment works. With the development of commercial worm farming equipment by British Earthworm Technology, for treating livestock manures and other organic wastes, laboratory and pilot scale trials are being conducted by the Water Research centre and Anglian Water to assess the efficiency and costs of sludge stabilisation by Eisenia foetida. The research programme also includes plant growth trials and a market survey to estimate the potential size and value of the market for a plant growth media based on worm-worked sewage sludge. Results so far indicate that, although E. foetida will grow well in belt pressed and centrifuged dewatered unstabilised sludges, the hard physical nature of some plate pressed sludges appears to be difficult for the worms to work efficiently. Heavy metals do not appear to pose a problem except in sludges with very high industrial inputs of cadium and nickel. When dry enough, the vermicompost readily blends with other horticultural materials to produce an attractive plant growth media.

1. INTRODUCTION

The value of earthworms in comminuting and incorporating organic material into soils has been recognised since the work of Charles Darwin in the late nineteenth century. Scientists at Rothamsted Experimental Station continued the research on this subject and discovered that the application of animal manures to soils increased the earthworm population (1). In 1979, following some work in the United States, the researchers at Rothamsted began experiments on the utilisation of earthworms to break down manures (2). Not only did this render the waste innocuous but the resulting material had high levels of plant-available nutrients and the commercial potential of such a process was realised.

British Technology Group (BTG) had, at that time, the role of commercialising government-sponsored research. They took out patents on some of the processes and pieces of machinery which had been designed for this technique called "vermiculture". They encouraged the formation of a company which was registered in 1983 under the name British Earthworm Technology Ltd (BET). This company worked together with both Rothamsted and the National Institute of Agricultural Engineering (NIAE) to refine the process and to design suitable machinery for large-scale waste processing. BET is licensed to BTG to allow them to use the machinery and to gain access to the research carried out by Rothamsted and NIAE. BET also developed a range of organic horticultural plant growth media which have been tested in extensive trials at Rothamsted and others at Ministry of Agriculture, Fisheries and Food Experimental Horticulture Stations.

The Water Research centre (WRc) and the water authorities are continually seeking cheaper and more effective means of treating sewage sludge, with storage, handling and odour being particularly important issues. To this end Anglian Water (AW), WRc and BET are currently collaborating to assess the operational and marketing potential of vermistabilisation of dewatered unstabilised sewage sludges.

2. EARTHWORM CULTURE AND EQUIPMENT DESIGN

The most commonly used worm is Eisenia foetida, which lives naturally in organic wastes, including animal manures and sewage filter beds. It grows rapidly, consuming large quantities of food, and reproduces profusely. It can tolerate wide ranges of both temperature (2° - 30°C) and pH (4.5 - 9.5) and will ingest most wastes of a largely vegetable or microbial origin. Although in the United States and southern Europe, vermiculture is conducted outdoors successfully at ambient temperatures, under UK conditions in order to increase throughput, double skinned insulated polythene tunnels and soil warming cables (winter only) are used.

The traditional design of worm beds which are in contact with the floor causes problems with some wastes because of waterlogging, anaerobicity and overheating due to composting in the bed. The worms are disturbed at every harvest by digging out and restocking. The continuous-flow bed designed by NIAE has solved all of these problems. It has a mesh floor raised off the ground and an automatic gantry feed hopper which runs along the bed discharging a thin layer of waste. The worms work up into the fresh waste, remaining in the top few inches of the bed and the worked material is removed from the bottom of the bed. Thus there are no drainage problems and the bed does not need to be disturbed except to reduce the worm population. The waste is harvested in a two-stage process. A bar pulled along the mesh causes a thin layer of waste to fall to the ground and this is mechanically transferred to the end of the bed where it is removed for sterilising and blending to produce a compost.

NIAE have also designed a harvester to remove the worms from the waste. The machine has hundreds of spikes along its length which comb through the waste and extract the worms. With a suitable material, the machine can extract 90% of the worms. Whilst worms are high in good quality protein (60 - 70% dm), the production and processing costs make worm protein uneconomical at the moment in comparison to other protein sources.

3. CURRENT RESEARCH

3.1 Laboratory trials

Whilst the effects of temperature and moisture content on rate of worm working of organic wastes are fairly well known (3,4), there is no information on cake sludges dewatered by different methods (belt or plate press, centrifuge) which may pose physical difficulties to worms. Furthermore, it is now well recognised from worms analysed from fields treated with sludge (5,6,7) and from experiments with metal salts (6,8) that earthworms concentrate cadmium and zinc but there is very little information on the effect of worm working on metal levels in treated sludge itself. As worms may reduce the volume of waste by up to 50%, it is likely this will concentrate the metals although it appears that the passage of sludge through worms does not affect metal extractability (6).

For these reasons a series of worm (E. foetida) trials are currently being conducted by WRc with 20 different unstabilised cake sludges in 5 and 25 litre containers. Details of the sludges are given in Table 1. This shows that dewatering by plate press not only produces a drier sludge (30%) than belt press (22%) but it is also physically harder and generally retains the plate-like structure characteristic of plate presses. In the preliminary results, it appears that the plate press sludges are not as easily worked by worms, compared with the belt press sludges, due to their adverse physical nature. All sludges are maintained at about 80% moisture but the discrete lumps of plate press sludge prove more difficult to rewet.

Initial heavy metal and ammonia concentrations show wide variations between the different sludge sources reflecting the high industrial inputs to some sewage treatment works (eg sludges 1,5,7) and the effect sludge treatment (eg sludges 16 and 18 have high ammonia concentrations through storage after dewatering). Trials with metals salts (8) suggest that worm reproduction may be affected by some of the concentrations shown in Table 1 although the form and availability of metals will be different in the sludge. Furthermore ammonia is toxic to worms and has been shown to be killed by a concentration of 0.1% NH_4 acetate (10) although work at Rothamsted has shown that ammonia concentrations have to exceed 1-2 mg/g (fresh wt) to be toxic. In the trials in Table 1, it can be seen that concentrations of ammonia ranged from 0.06 - 3.46 mg/g but the only adverse effect that may be attributable to a high ammonia concentration was sludge 18 at 3.46 mg/g; worms in sludge 16 had the second highest concentration of 2.13 mg/g but grew quite satisfactorily.

Malecki et al (8) found critical concentrations for Cd, Cu, Pb, Ni and Zn salts which adversely affected worm growth and reproduction. Only sludge 5 and 7 exceeded the critical concentrations of 50 and 200 mg/kg for Cd and Ni respectively. Observations on worm growth to date would confirm Malecki's results as sludges 5 and 7 are markedly less attractive to worms. The high Cr concentration in sludge 1 of 8480 mg/kg has not had any adverse effect of rate of worm growth.

3.2 Production-scale trial

Biggleswade STW, operated by Anglian Water, receives sewage from 12,000 population plus industrial effluents from brewing and metal finishing. The purification process comprises primary sedimentation followed by biological filtration and secondary settlement. Humus sludge and other works liquors are returned to the works inlet so that the primary tanks produce about 20 m³/day of co-settled sludge at about 5% dry solids. Similar sludges are tankered in from nearby village STWs. The sludge is dewatered by filter belt presses, with polyelectrolyte conditioning, to produce a cake of about 30% dry solids (see Table 1 for analysis). All the sludge is currently spread on local arable land at no cost to the farmer.

Whilst the sludge can be spread directly from the presses during autumn and winter, it has to be stockpiled during the periods when land is unavailable due to growing crops. The unpleasant odours arising from spreading stockpiled sludge were the primary reason for assessing the value of vermistabilisation since the process may offer a low-cost reliable method of avoiding such odour problems. Furthermore, the resulting vermicompost could be sold to offset any additional production costs.

Initial trials in 1984 showed the E. foetida could survive in Biggleswade sludge cake. An open air pilot-scale bed (~4.5m x 2.5m in area) was innoculated with worms in October and operated for nine months

TABLE 1. Analyses of sludges currently being tested for suitability for vermistabilisation

Sewage Treatment Works	Chemical conditioning	Dewatering process	Hardness Hard 1 Soft 5	Structure Plate-like 1 Amorphous 5	DS %	NH$_3$ mg/g	Heavy Metals mg/kg (from Reference 9) (except *)					
							Zn	Cu	Cr	Pb	Ni	Cd
1. Abingdon	Poly.	Belt	4	4	25.6	0.06	715	470	8480	210	33	8.7
2. Appleton	Lime+iron	plate	4	2	24.6	0.08	655	325	20	110	24	3.7
3. Banbury	Poly.	Centrifuge	5	5	21.8	0.21	606	269	30	136	23	11.0
4. Biggleswade	Poly+Lime	Belt	4	2	30.2	0.51	1367	351	88	141	63	10.1*
5. Blackburn Meadows	Lime+iron	Plate	4	5	20.8	1.58	2665	795	2765	710	1385	52.0
6. Bloxham	Poly.	Belt	4	5	21.1	0.46	761	408	24	130	15	3.5
7. Bradley	Lime+iron	Plate	3	5	37.8	0.30	3211	674	1911	765	220	13.0
8. Byfield	Poly.	Belt	4	5	17.9	0.41	661	392	27	130	21	2.6
9. Chinnor	Lime+iron	Plate	1	1	40.7	0.06	408	159	18	103	41	1.9
10. Chipping Norton	Poly.	Belt	4	5	14.9	0.60	686	289	21	119	12	3.2
11. Farnham	Poly.	Plate	3	1	28.0	0.69	766	309	139	956	70	10.0
12. Godalming	Poly.	Plate	2	1	29.4	0.63	481	463	87	227	81	20.0
13. Guildford	Poly.	Plate	3	1	28.0	1.15	1534	436	1192	232	23	7.7
14. Kidlington	Poly.	Belt	5	5	16.5	0.41	1095	315	34	110	24	3.6
15. Lt.Marlow Fresh }	Lime+iron	Plate	{3	1	24.8	0.63	845	886	94	142	85	3.4*
16. Lt.Marlow Stored}			{4	5	26.0	2.13	822	839	112	141	187	4.7*
17. Sandford	Poly.	Belt	3	2	31.3	0.70	1865	508	133	572	56	4.4
18. Swindon	Poly.	Belt	4	5	23.5	3.46	629	245	29	233	52	4.0
19. Tring	Poly.	Belt	4	5	13.7	0.88	-	-	-	-	-	-
20. Wargrave	Poly.	Plate	2	1	33.5	0.36	918	554	102	112	34	7.2*
Cattle Waste	-	-	5	4	17.3	0.40						
MEANS (n):	Belt(5)		4.1	4.2	21.6	0.83						
	Plate(9)		2.7	2.0	29.6	0.81						
	Centrifuge(1)		5.0	5.0	21.8	0.21						

* mean analyses of sludge fed to worms

during which it was demonstrated that not only did the worms survive cold winter conditions and reproduce successfully if kept sufficiently moist and they converted the sludge cake into a friable compost with only a faint but pleasant earthy odour.

On the basis of this qualitative success, Anglian Water are funding a research project in co-operation with BET with the aims of:

(i) identifying optimum operating conditions and production rates.

(ii) providing costs for additional labour and power requirements.

(iii) assessing the potential uses and market for the compost.

Construction of a small production-scale vermicomposting bed and insulating tunnel was commenced in autumn 1985 and the initial layer of sludge cake was innoculated with worms in January 1986. Only when worm numbers and depth of sludge have increased sufficiently for a regular pattern of sludge feeding and compost removal to be established can production costs be assessed.

3.3 Market assessment

Successful marketing will have to offset any additional costs but it remains to be seen whether a sludge-based worm-worked compost will command the premium that worm-worked livestock waste does. A market survey conducted by WRc revealed that volume outlets such as landscaping and tree planting would be the most suitable both in terms of quantity and low specification required (11). Trials to test this will be conducted this year but initial growth trials in comparison with commercial multi-purpose compost have been very encouraging.

ACKNOWLEDGEMENTS

R Bland wishes to express gratitude to the Director of Operations and the management team of Cambridge Division, Anglian Water for permission to publish. Any views expressed are those of the authors and not AW, WRc or BET. Thanks are due to staff at Rothamsted and to A P Daw, WRc, Little Marlow for conducting laboratory trials.

REFERENCES

(1) EDWARDS, C.A., and LOFTY, J.R., (1977) Biology of earthworms. Bookworm Publishing Co. London.

(2) EDWARDS, C.A., BURROWS, I., FLETCHER, K.E. and JONES, B.A. (1985). The use of earthworms for composting farm wastes. In Composting of agricultural and other wastes. Proceedings of CEC seminar, Oxford, UK. 19-20 March 1984.

(3) TSUKAMOTO, J. and WATANABE, H. (1977). Influence of temperature on hatching and growth of Eisenia foetida. Pedobiologia. 17, 338-342.

(4) LOEHR, R.C., NEUHAUSER, E.F. and MALECKI, M.R. (1985). Factors affecting the vermistabilisation process. Water Res. 19(10), 1311-1317.

(5) BEYER, W.N., CHANEY, R.L. and MULLHERN, B.M. (1982). Heavy metal concentrations in earthworms from soil amended with sewage sludge. J. Environ. Qual., 11(3), 381-385.

(6) HARTENSTEIN, R., NEUHAUSER, E.F., and COLLIER, J. (1980). Accumulation of heavy metals in the earthworm Eisenia foetida. J. Environ. Qual., 9(1), 23-30.

(7) DIERCXSENS, P., DE WECK, D., BORSINGER, N., ROSSET, B. and TARRADELLAS, J. (1985). Earthworm contamination by PCBs and heavy metals. Chemosphere, 14(5), 511-522.

(8) MALECKI, M.R., NEUHAUSER, E.F. and LOEHR, R.C. (1982). The effect of metals on the growth and reproduction of <u>Eisenia foetida</u>. Pedobiologia, <u>24</u>, 129-137.

(9) DEPARTMENT OF THE ENVIRONMENT/NATIONAL WATER COUNCIL (1983). Sewage sludge survey 1980 data. DOE/NWC.

(10) KAPLAN, D.L., HARTENSTEIN, R., NEUHAUSER, E.F. and MALECKI, M.R. (1980). Physiochemical requirements in the environment of the earthworm <u>Eisenia foetida</u>. Soil Biol. Biochem. <u>12</u>, 347-352.

(11) HILL, P. (1985). A review of the market potential for a sewage sludge-based soil conditioner. Water Research centre report 1117-M.

EFFECT OF COMPOSTS MADE FROM MUNICIPAL AND INDUSTRIAL WASTES ON THE YIELDS VEGETABLES AND THE CONTENT OF MINERAL ELEMENTS IN THEM

A. KROPISZ
Department of Soil Management and Fertilization of Horticulture Plants
Warsaw Agricultural University, Poland

Summary

Field experiments with cabbage of the Amager variety, onion of the Wolska variety and spinach of the Matador variety were carried out on 10 objects in 5 replications by the method of random blocks.
Compost rates were calculated on the basis of the organic matter content in them, amounting to 25 t in conversion to 1 hectare and they were applied only in the first year of the 3-year crop rotation, for cabbage.
Mineral fertilizers (NPK) were applied every year reducing the NPK content in the upper (0-20 cm) soil layer to the standard level for every plant species.
The experiment results have proved that fertilization with composts of different kinds and with farmyard manure connected with mineral fertilization (NPK) led to significant yield increments of the vegetables tested, to increase in most cases of the content in them of macro- and microelements and to decrease of the nitrate nitrogen content.

1.1 Introduction

Vegetable crops constitute the most intensive branch of the plant production. A further intensification based exclusively on high rates of mineral, particularly nitrogen, phosphorus and potassium fertilizers, can lead to a disturbance of the equilibrium between mineral elements in soil and result in occurrence of symptoms of deficiency or excess of some of them in the yields of vegetables, what can considerably reduce their biological value.

In this connection it is necessary to apply in fertilization of vegetable crops, beside mineral, also organic fertilizers. Therefore much attention was paid recently to the question of using for fertilizing purposes the compost of municipal wastes produced by the biothermic method of Dane as well as to composts made from pine bark and wood sawdust. The fertilizing value of the composts of municipal wastes produced by the biothermic Dane method and the composts made from pine bark and wood sawdust has been positively evaluated by Brown and Pokorny (1975), Cappert, Verdonck and De Boodt (1975), Kropisz (1970), Kropisz and Russel (1979), Kropisz and Kalińska (1983).

The present work is a continuation of the above mentioned research works. Its aim was to investigate the effect of various kinds of composts and farmyard manure connected with mineral fertilization (NPK) on the yields of cabbage heads, onion and spinach and on the content of mineral macro- and microelements in them.

1.2 Description

Prior to the establishment of field experiments pine bark and wood sawdust composts were prepared. Pine bark and wood sawdust were composted in heaps both alone and with an addition of nitrogen (1 and 2%) in relation to their weight. Nitrogen was applied in the form of ammonium nitrate. Composting lasted 6 months.

Composts of municipal wastes were produced by the biothermic Dane method. This method consists in mechanical treatment of municipal wastes in a special implement (biostabilizer) with subsequent ripening of the treated mass in heaps in open air.

Table I. Chemical composition of the organic fertilizers

Kind of fertilizer	pH (H₂O)	Organic matter	Total N	N-NH₄+ +N-NO₃	P	K
		in % d.m.		in mg dm⁻³ d.m.		
Fresh compost Dano	8.1	44.8	0.87	157	143	784
Ripe compost Dano	7.7	51.7	1.23	286	196	962
Compost made from pine bark	5.6	92.3	0.39	74	61	173
Compost: pine bark + 1% N	5.4	94.2	0.78	328	86	280
Compost: pine bark + 2% N	5.2	91.8	1.12	640	118	305
Compost made from pine sawdust	5.0	90.8	0.33	64	59	149
Compost: pine sawdust + 1% N	4.8	86.9	0.74	296	76	176
Compost: pine sawdust + 2% N	4.7	91.2	0.97	582	121	214
Manure	6.8	85.3	2.53	1128	984	3120

Prior to the establishment of field experiments chemical analyses of composts and farmyard manure were performed (Table I), which proved that by the lowest pH value wood sawdust composts and by the highest one - the composts of municipal wastes were characterized. The chemical analyses proved also that pine bark and wood sawdust composts contained the highest amounts of organic matter and the lowest amounts of all mineral elements, whereas farmyard manure contained the highest amounts of all mineral elements.

The experiments were carried out at an Experiment Station on podzol soil (light leamy sand on loose sand). They comprised 10 objects in 5 replications and were established by the method of random blocks (Table II). The compost and farmyard manure rates were calculated on the basis of the organic matter content in them, at application of 25 t in conversion to 1 hectare and were used only in the first year of the 3-year crop rotation. Mineral fertilizers (NPK) were applied every year while reducing the nitrogen, phosphorus and potassium content in the upper (0-20 cm) soil layer to the standard level for every vegetable species.

In the growing season observations of plants and necessary agrotechnical and phytosanitary measures were carried out.

In the harvest of vegetables by 1.0 kg of fresh matter were taken from a mixed sample, then dried up to the air-dry state and ground. The materials prepared in such a way were used in chemical analyses for the content of mineral macro- and microelements.

The data of experiments for the fresh matter yields (cabbage heads, onion and spinach) were elaborated statistically. Chemical analyses of composts and farmyard manure as well as of yields of plants were performed at application of methods generally used in chemical laboratories in Poland.

The analysis of variability (Table II) proved that all the composts and farmyard manure led to increment of yields (cabbage heads, onion and spinach) as compared with the sole mineral (NPK) fertilization.

Chemical analyses of yields of the vegetables tested for the content of mineral elements proved that the organic fertilization connected with mineral fertilizers (NPK) led in most cases to an increase of mineral elements and to a decrease of the nitrate nitrogen. Data of Table III show that the fertilization with composts and farmyard manure resulted in an increase of the content of microelements (Fe, Mh, Zn, Cu), the composts of municipal wastes being most effective.

The investigations performed prove that the composts of municipal wastes produced by the Dano method contain more mineral elements than those made from pine bark and from wood sawdust and less organic matter, whereas farmyard manure contains the highest amounts of mineral elements among all the organic fertilizers tested. Moreover, it follows from these investigations that all the composts and farmyard manure led to a significant increase of yield of the vegetables tested and in most cases to increase of mineral macro- and microelements, except for nitrate nitrogen. Moreover, the data obtained in the experiment have proved that increased of composts with mineral fertilization led to an increase of organic matter and mineral elements in soil.

REFERENCES

1. BROWN, E. F. and POKORNY, F. A. (1975). Physical and chemical properties of media composed of milled pine bark and sand. J. Amer. Soc. Hort. Sci. 100: 119-121
2. CAPPEART, J., VERDONCK, O. and DE BOODT, M. (1975). Composting of hardwood bark. Compost Sci. 16: 12-15
3. KROPISZ, A. (1970). Komposty ze śmieci i odpadków miejskich jako nawóz organiczny w uprawie roślin warzywnych (Compost made of garbage and municipal wastes as organic fertilizers in vegetable crops growing). Zesz. nauk. SGGW, Warszawa, Rozpr. nauk. z. 3: 5-85
4. KROPISZ, A. and RUSSEL, S. (1979). Wpływ nawożenia kompostem Dano piasku gliniastego lekkiego na mikroflorę gleby oraz na plon i skłac chemiczny sałaty i szpinaku (Effect of fertilization of light soil with Dano compost on microflora as well as on yields and chemical composition of lettuce and spinach). Roczn. Nauk. roln. 103, 2: 19-37
5. KROPISZ, A. and KALIŃSKA, D. (1983). The effect of fertilization with composts from municipal and industry wastes on the yield of grass mixtures and the content of mineral elements. Pol. ecol. Stud. 9, 1-2: 143-154

Table II. Mean yields (t/ha) of cabbage heads, onions and spinach leaves, on the content of mineral elements (in a.d.m.)

Fertilization treatments	Crop[1]	Yields	N	P	K	Mg	N-NO$_3$
			in %				in ppm
NPK	C	41.7	2.84	0.41	3.45	0.25	920
	O	24.3	1.92	0.29	1.96	0.18	629
	S	10.8	3.94	0.45	3.54	0.26	2145
NPK + fresh compost Dano	C	48.4	3.08	0.43	3.62	0.29	732
	O	29.7	1.96	0.32	2.14	0.21	486
	S	12.9	3.88	0.47	3.70	0.30	1658
NPK + ripe compost Dano	C	50.5	3.20	0.42	3.70	0.30	683
	O	30.9	1.87	0.34	2.21	0.24	473
	S	13.6	3.94	0.49	3.72	0.31	1527
NPK + compost made from pine bark	C	47.2	3.18	0.38	3.42	0.23	483
	O	28.9	1.80	0.27	1.96	0.16	320
	S	12.2	3.79	0.43	3.45	0.24	942
NPK + compost: pine bark + + 1% N	C	50.1	3.02	0.44	3.56	0.21	686
	O	30.4	1.95	0.29	1.95	0.18	680
	S	13.5	3.96	0.42	3.47	0.26	1125
NPK + compost: pine bark + + 2% N	C	52.4	3.35	0.45	3.68	0.25	748
	O	32.6	1.97	0.31	2.03	0.17	732
	S	14.2	3.82	0,45	3.50	0.25	1284
NPK + compost made from pine sawdust	C	47.0	2.90	0.37	3.40	0.22	420
	O	28.2	1.80	0.28	1.89	0.17	283
	S	12.3	3.74	0.44	3.42	0.19	748
NPK + compost: pine sawdust + + 1% N	C	48.4	2.95	0.40	3.64	0.23	538
	O	30.2	1.93	0.31	1.92	0.19	634
	S	13.2	3.82	0.45	3.50	0.20	986
NPK + compost: pine sawdust + + 2% N	C	49.7	3.07	0.42	3.67	0.25	654
	O	33.0	1.92	0.27	1.96	0.17	688
	S	13.8	3.96	0.43	3.56	0.18	1054
NPK + manure	C	50.8	3.25	0.45	3.80	0.32	642
	O	33.5	1.98	0.32	2.21	0.23	454
	S	14.5	3.82	0.47	3.84	0.27	1245
LSd - α = 0,05	C	5.2					
	O	3.5					
	S	1.2					

[1] C - cabbage, O - onion, S - spinach

Table III. Content of mikroelements in air-dry matter of cabbage heads,
onions and spinach leaves (in ppm)

Fertilization treatments	Crop[1]	Fe	Mn	Zn	Cu
NPK	C	102	34	42	4.2
	O	78	21	25	3.4
	S	592	68	96	6.7
NPK + fresh compost Dano	C	198	75	89	7.8
	O	122	12	58	5.3
	S	1184	123	182	9.6
NPK + ripe compost Dano	C	182	68	94	8.2
	O	115	47	56	5.6
	S	1212	107	190	9.4
NPK + compost made from pine bark	C	115	42	51	7.1
	O	83	27	28	4.2
	S	680	76	104	7.3
NPK + compost: pune bark + 1% N	C	121	38	56	7.3
	O	87	25	32	4.5
	S	845	89	108	7.6
NPK + compost: pine bark + 2% N	C	118	44	48	7.0
	O	82	28	30	4.3
	S	872	96	118	7.9
NPK + compost made from pine sawdust	C	132	39	58	6.8
	O	79	24	27	4.1
	S	863	87	104	7.5
NPK + compost: pine sawdust + 1% N	C	127	47	50	6.6
	O	88	29	32	4.7
	S	896	96	112	7.4
NPK + compost: pine sawdust + 2% N	C	122	49	55	7.0
	O	92	34	34	4.5
	S	905	108	102	7.8
NPK + manure	C	134	53	52	6.7
	O	97	39	41	4.6
	S	845	92	118	7.4

[1] C - cabbage, O - onion, S - spinach

THE SILODA, A REACTOR COMPOSTING TECHNOLOGY COMBINING FORCED AERATION AND TURNING ACTION

P. MOUSTY[1], and JP. LEVASSEUR[2]

(1) ANJOU RECHERCHE, 52 Rue d'Anjou 75008 PARIS

(2) OTV, Le Doublon 11 Avenue Dubonnet 92407 COURBEVOIE

SUMMARY

Faced with problems posed by wastes removal, the Compagnie Générale des Eaux Group taking advantage of 20 years composting experience has selected treatment lines combining high quality composts production and low treatment costs. The combined need for new energy sources and better waste disposal techniques has conducted to the development of an efficient energy and soil improver recovery system. The Envermeu Plant (France) is a household refuse treatment line, combining the SILODA process to produce compost through both forced aeration and windrowing principles and the SILORCO process to produce RDF (Refuse Derived Fuel) in the form of pellets. This facility is described with emphasis on the technical principles and main caracteristics of the composts obtained.

1. INTRODUCTION

Once the refuse has been collected, there still remain the problem of disposing of it under conditions which are technically acceptable and cost-effective, all the while respecting the environment. Over the last 20 years, much technological progress has been achieved in the field of composting in Europe. France, for example, has an output of over 800,000 tons of composts each year and close to 100 composting plants. However the trends we have observed in the various factors involved, and which include costs, regulations and the need to prolonge the lifetime of land-fills, as well as to better protect the environment, have made it necessary to develop new techniques whose utilization is flexible enough to adapt to the gradual changes in refuse content and which are able to meet local demand for high quality composts.

Specialized firms in this particular field have, therefore, progressively worked out techniques for transforming household waste in such a way as to recycle the reclaimable fractions either for agricultural applications or for the production of energy.

This combined need for new energy sources and better waste disposal techniques has culminated in the development of an energy and soil improver recovery system called the SILORCO-SILODA system which has been designed by OTV to produce refuse derived fuels in the form of pellets and a wide variety of composts for commercialization.

The "Envermeu" Plant, a household refuse treatment facility located near Dieppe (France) and using the SILORCO-SILODA system will be described with emphasis on the composting equipment used, keeping in mind that this treatment line can be adapted for producing more or less of each by product, depending of the local situation.

2. COMPOSTING A WASTE DISPOSAL ALTERNATIVE

Composting is a way of treating wastes by recycling them as an organic soil conditioner. Composting of household refuse for agricultural use is faced with a certain number of obstacles, such as the appearance of the product, detrimental side effects (smells, plant tolerance) and handling and storage problems, all of which restrict the possibility of direct application. Composting techniques must be designed to overcome the restrictions. This means choosing the right process for the product to be treated in each case and an operating procedure to ensure that everything is done to create the physico-chemical environment conducive to the development of the aerobic microorganisms that induce fermentation. Aerobic composting is a biological conversion operated mainly by bacteria that, in the presence of suitable amounts of air and moisture and through exothermal oxidization reactions, stabilise, demoisturize and sanitize organic waste which can be recycled as soil conditioner. The composting of refuse should, in itself, be a mean of over-coming almost all the difficulties connected with its utilization, i.e.
- harmfull effects as instability of the product and obnoxious smells are normally eliminated through the thorough degradation of the fermentiscible matter ;
- storage and use in an easily handled form is achieved by an alteration in the physical properties of the feedstock and a decrease in the moisture content ;
- a high quality soil conditioner is produced, rich in organic matter, with the structural quality and good chemical balance required and, above all, sufficiently matured for its bulk use to be possible without creating unpleasant side effects or damage to vegetation.

3. A GREAT VARIETY OF COMPOSTING SYSTEMS

Several techniques can be used to classify composting systems. One element taken into account is that oxygen availability is the main limiting factor to the rate of composting and that the design of composting systems is centred on providing aeration. The first systems rely on agitation to periodically renew the porosity of the material to be composted. The second group of systems uses air injection to provide aerobic microorganisms with oxygen. Air injection may be accomplished by blowing or sucking air through a static pile. There are many conditions under which the static pile or the open windrow process are not suited for composting because of constraints such as land requirements, operating costs, odor problems or heavy rains. This is reason why the SILODA has been designed. This is a mechanical process combining the two modes of aeration and which has many of the advantages of the other composting processes without the drawbacks.

4. MANUFACTURE OF COMPOST THROUGH THE SILODA SYSTEM (see Fig.1)

Composting of household refuse has given rise to numerous processes suitable for dealing with a very heterogeneous feedstock. These involve a combination of physical treatments to remove the undesirable and inerts elements, leaving only the organic matter suitable for composting. In the Envermeu plant, the remaining fraction with a high percentage of combustible matter is conditionned in pellets.

4.1. The physical pre-treatment

Household refuse being of a very heterogeneous nature, the production of by-products goes first through a serie of mechanical treatments. Household refuse consists of three main constituents : inert matter

805

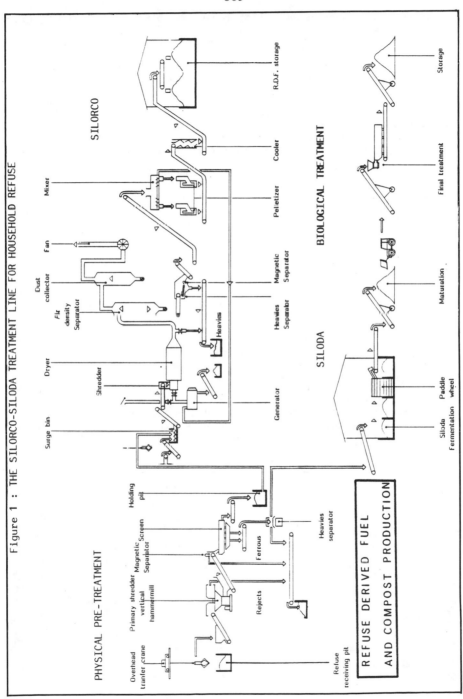

Figure 1 : THE SILORCO-SILODA TREATMENT LINE FOR HOUSEHOLD REFUSE

like glass, metal scraps or ashes, fermentiscible organics with a high
moisture content, papers, textiles and plastic materials.
The last of these fractions is attractive as a source of potential energy
and mainly when recycled in the form of stockable fuel. The organic
fraction, of little interest as regards energy, can be composted, and,
transformed into an organic soil improver for agricultural use.
The purposes of the physical pre-treatment are :
. to select through a shredding and a screening action a fraction with
a high percentage of non compostable matter (plastics) which will be
recycled as fuel after further conditioning.
. to give the remaining fraction a texture conducting to fermentation
and a finished product with a granulometry suitable for agricultural
use.
. to eliminate the ferrous scraps and the non desirable materials (glass,
ashes).
The reduction in the size of waste is achieved by the use of a vertical
shaft pulveriser, which has been especially designed for the treatment
of household refuse. This pulveriser has the added advantage of doing
the ballistic removal of heavy particles which would be unsuitable for
composting.

4.2. The biological treatement

After the physical pre-treatment (shredding, screening, inerts
and ferrous removal) takes place the biological treatment which is the
most important stage on which depends the quality of the compost as
regards health standards and agricultural efficiency.
Compared with fermentation in windrows, accelerated fermentation offers
the advantage of being easier to conduct (better follow-up of process,
easier to operate) and gives very regular quality compost. Moreover,
the two most important parameters in composting i.e. the degree of moisture and aeration, are more easily controlled. The SILODA process, is
a simple accelerated fermentation technique designed to produce a high-
quality finished product through an easy-to operate plant and machinery
with a minimum of maintenance. Fermentation occurs in longitudinal
silos placed side by side in a roofed structure. These silos are open
at both ends to allow the passage of a horizontal-shaft paddle-wheel,
travelling on top of the partition walls separating the silos (see
Fig.2).

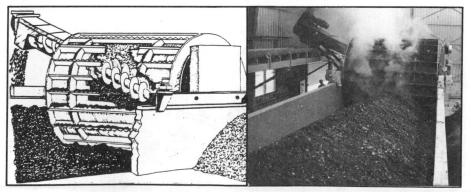

Fig.2. Paddle-wheel of the SILODA process with the double archimedean
screw.

This travel continues throughout the composting stage and is the essential part of the SILODA process. The number and the length of the silos varies according to the quality and the characteristics of the product to be treated each day and the results one desires to achieve. In Envermeu, four silos, 20 meters long, 4 meters wide are used for composting the organic fraction issued of the pre-treatment line processing 60 tons a day. In larger facilities as in Beyruth (500 tons a day) the length of the silos is adapted to the amount of matter to be treated. After mechanical tratment, the refuse is left for 48 hours in each of the silos into which air is blown through the bottom. The refuse is turned over every two days by the paddle-wheel, consisting of blades mounted on a fixed revolving cylinder, open at the top. The blades slice the product from bottom to top and discharge it, by gravity, from the uppermost point into a double archimedean screw installed in the shaft of the paddle-wheel assembly. The archimedean screw then projects the aerated, homogenized product into the next silo. As it reaches the end of the silo, the wheel automatically resumes its initial position on a crab that transfers it to the following silo. After 8 to 10 days, the compost is stacked outside for the maturing stage (4-6 weeks). The treatment line is completed with an extra refining unit designed to improve the physical quality of the product in consideration of the final use expected (mushrooms growing - vineyards - farm applications), keeping in mind that depending on the local demand more or less both by-products can be obtained by acting on the technical components of the treatment line.

CONCLUSION

Because of new disposal regulations and due to increasing costs of energy the choice of acceptable management alternatives is decreasing while at the same time the amount of waste generated is increasing. Until recently the main concerns in treating household wastes consisted in dumping or incineration. However, sound natural resources management and a concern for financial means and environment quality, have shown that it is necessary whenever possible to substitute recovery technologies for dumping or incineration systems.

The complexity of upstream constraints (wastes contents, collection organization) and those found downstream (agricultural and energy utilization possibilities) calls for specific organizations and appropriate technologies. During recent years, the combined efforts of researchers and plant operators have made it possible to design and engineer the SILORCO-SILODA process, an efficient technology able to convert the light fraction of the refuse in the form of pellets and using the organic fraction to produce high quality composts. However, the development of those methods is tied to the possibility of finding a market and necessity of meeting user's demands. That is why we had to design treatment lines that are sufficiently flexible to produce more or less of each by product depending of local needs.

These considerations were the basis for using various screening meshes depending of the compost utilization (mushrooms, vineyards, land application), for mixing sewage sludges and household wastes for complementation and to establish a nation-wide marketing structure for soil improvers.

ENVIRONMENTAL IMPACT OF ORGANIC MUNICIPAL REFUSE COMPOSTING

W. Obrist, Swiss Federal Institute for Water Resources and Water Pollution Control, EAWAG, CH-8600 Dübendorf, Switzerland

Organic (i.e. garden and kitchen) refuse is now collected separately in several swiss communities. Normally the organic waste materials are processed by wood shredders and composted in windrows (1 to 2 m high) in a municipal or regional plant.

Compared to municipal solid waste composting, leachate concentrations are similar (Table 1).

Table 1. Concentrations of compost leachates

	municipal solid waste	garden and kitchen refuse	regulatory maximum for sewers
pH	7.0 - 8.4	7.0 - 8.4	6.5 - 8.5
Lead μg/L	70 - 90	60 - 80	500
Cadmium μg/L	2.6 - 3.0	2.4 - 3.0	100
Copper μg/L	250 - 500	280 - 330	500
Mercury μg/L	2.0 - 3.0	2.0 - 3.0	10
Zinc μg/L	600 - 750	400 - 550	2000

Total Nitrogen reaches values up to 150 mg/L, Phosphorus 40 mg/L.

Matured organic composts show a lower heavy metal content and can thus meet environmental regulatory standards (Table 2).

Table 2. Heavy metal content of refuse composts

	concentration in g/t dry matter		
	solid waste	garden/kitchen	limit
Zinc	2'200	270	500
Copper	720	50	150
Lead	1'500	100	150
Cadmium	12	2	3
Mercury	7	1	3

Processing requires inexpensive equipment but well-trained employees and good monitaoring. The matured compost (9 months) is sieved at 10 mm diam. and used as soil conditioner.

A FEW ADDITIONAL PARAMETERS FOR A BETTER DETERMINATION
OF THE COMPOST QUALITY

R. PENNINCK and O. VERDONCK
Laboratory of Soil Physics, Soil Conditioning
and Horticultural Soil Science
Faculty of Agricultural Sciences, State University Ghent, Belgium.

SUMMARY

Up to now there has been done only little research of the effect of
composting on the more fundamental characteristics of organic matter.
The common analyses carried out in our laboratory are:
1. The maximum and total oxygen consumption during the composting
   process
2. The physico-chemical properties
3. The phytotoxicity
With these results one can judge of the quality of the compost and
find out whether the crop will grow or not.
To have an idea of the real changes in the compost itself, more fundamental analyses must be worked out. The physical characterization can
be improved with the determination of the particle size distribution,
the specific area and the contact-angle. The organo-chemical composition of the compost can be examined through appropriate analysis
methods. The evolution of the cellulose-compound and the lignin are
the more interesting parameters. An important biological parameter
is the ATP-content. This gives an idea of the microbiological life
present in the product. This paper gives a survey the difficulties
and the results of this research.

1. INTRODUCTION
    This research is applied fundamentally where we are looking for new
parameters which can be used for controlling the composting process.
    If we can determine parameters which are easy to check, then we have
more in hand to know better the composting process and to control the
maturity of the compost.
    The new parameters on which we will look are the following:
1. Soil physical parameters:
    - Particle size distribution: as we are working with very fine and very
      coarse materials we will determine 7 different fractions: 0-1 mm,
      1-2 mm, 2-3 mm, 3-5 mm, 5-10 mm, 10-20 mm and > 20 mm. To have our
      figure we calculate the total sum of the mean weightpercentage multi-
      plied by the mean size of the different fractions. Such a sum is very
      big for a coarse material and very small for a fine material. During
      the composting process we have a degradation of the material so that
      we easily can follow this particle size distribution sum
    - Specific surface: during the composting process the particles become
      finer so that normally we could suspect that the specific surface is
      increasing during the degradation process.

- Contact angle: this parameter gives us an idea about the hydrophobicity of the material which change during degradation

2. Organo-chemical parameters

Because of that the degradation of organic waste which are existing of easily degradable and difficult degradable products, we must find a good relationship between the cellulose and lignin content before and after composting. Therefore we will determine:
- extractable substances
- lignin
- holocellulose
- α, β and γ cellulose

3. Biological parameters

The ATP content (adenosine triphosphate) of a compost is a measure to the quantity of microbiological life and activity. In the beginning of the composting process there is enough easily degradable material so that high microbiological activity is present which must be represented by a high ATP content. During and at the end of a composting process the activity is much lower, which means a low ATP content.

All these new parameters will be compared with the normally used, as:
- maximum and total oxygen consumption
- physico-chemical parameters as pH, conductivity, nitrogen level and C/N ratio
- germination tests with cress

2. MATERIAL, METHODS AND RESULTS

We have carried out several trials in order to compare the different parameters. In this paper we will discuss the composting experiments with pine bark from 4 replicates. In table 1 we give the oxygen consumption of the 4 different composting experiments.

Table 1. Oxygen consumption of bark

Number	% organic matter	Air flux in l/h/kg dry material	% moisture content	Maximum O_2 consumption in mg O_2/g organic matter/h	Total O_2 consumption in mg O_2/g organic matter
1	95.55	7.97	63.46	0.5396	131.03
2	93.75	10,01	64.38	1.1141	164.98
3	94.77	8.04	57.70	0.8160	166.86
4	95.39	8.01	61.60	0.5745	115.67
mean	94.87	8.51	61.79	0.7611	144.64

From this results we see that there is a great variability in activity of bark depending on the time of composting after debarking and after harvesting of the trees.

From these composting experiments we have determined the different factors before and after composting.

The results are given in table 2, 3 and 4.

From these results we calculated the relations between the different parameters which are given in table 5.

Table 2. Particle size distribution sum, specific surface and contact angle of 4 composting experiments with bark.

Number	Particle size distribution sum			Specific surface in m²/g		Contact angle	
	Before composting	After composting	Decrease	Before composting	After composting	Before composting	After composting
1	510.7	363.1	147.6	1.16	1.21	78-79	95-96
2	425.9	374.8	51.1	1.02	1.05	89-90	89-90
3	488.9	427.5	61.4	1.30	1.16	81-82	94-95
4	723.9	605.6	118.3	0.55	0.78	82-83	87-88

Table 3. The organo-chemical parameters of pine bark before and after composting.

Number	Extractable compounds in %		Cellulose in % Before				Cellulose in % After				Lignin in %		Sum cellulose + lignin (%)	
	Before	After	Holo	α	β	γ	Holo	α	β	γ	Before	After	Before	After
1	8.74	11.91	64.96	43.07	7.11	14.78	54.58	38.47	5.78	10.33	34.51	39.22	99.47	93.80
2	7.46	6.92	60.36	41.31	9.65	9.39	62.11	44.12	4.73	13.26	38.90	46.10	99.26	108.21
3	8.34	5.57	61.10	41.00	7.55	12.54	59.93	44.97	5.26	9.70	35.28	43.32	96.38	103.25
4	6.32	5.85	73.17	48.66	10.04	14.46	71.40	55.94	3.92	11.54	37.42	38.86	110.59	110.26
mean	7.72	7.56	64.90	43.51	8.59	12.79	62.01	45.88	4.92	11.21	36.53	41.88	101.43	103.88

Table 4. ATP-values of pine bark before and after composting.

Number	ATP-content before composting	ATP-content after composting (in µg ATP/kg compost)	Difference in ATP-content
1	35 791.15	3 739.67	32 051.48
2	4 093.04	5 858.22	- 1 765.18
3	12 708.80	6 247.76	6 461.04
4	24 541.10	7 869.80	16 671.30
mean	19 283.52	5 928.86	13 354.66

Table 5. Relation between different parameters during the composting process of bark.

Parameters	Linear regression	Correlation coefficient
1. Oxygen consumption (Y) and particle size distribution sum (X)	Y = 234.2 - 0.167 X	0.85
2. Oxygen consumption (Y) and decrease of the particle size distribution sum (X)	Y = 186.6 - 0.476 X	0.86
3. Specific surface (Y) and particle size distribution sum (X)		
before composting	Y = 2.13 - 0.002 X	0.83
after composting	Y = 1.73 - 0.0015 X	0.90
4. Contact angle (Y) and particle size distribution sum (X)		
before composting	Y = 89.68 - 0.012 X	0.35
after composting	Y = 102.08 - 0.023 X	0.68
5. Oxygen consumption (Y) and contact angle (X)	Y = 148.95 - 0.49 X	0.15
6. Oxygen consumption (Y) and ATP (X) before composting	Y = 172.58 - 0.0014 X	0.79
7. Oxygen consumption (Y) and the decrease in ATP (X) during composting	Y = 161.65 - 0.0013 X	0.73

3. CONCLUSIONS
    From the obtained results we can say that:
- The particle size distribution sum gives a very good relaton with the
  total oxygen consumption. That means that the particle size distribution
  is a good factor for the determination of the activity of pine bark.
  Also the decrease in particle size during the composting is a good
  measure for the oxygen consumption. The determination of the particle
  size is much easier and needs less sofisticated equipment than the oxygen
  consumption. Therefore this can be a good parameter for determining the
  activity of the composting of pine bark.
- The specific surface which is normally influenced with the particle size
  distribution gives also a good correlation with the particle size
  distribution sum.
- The contact angle is not a good factor for following the composting
  process because there is not a good correlation with oxygen consumption
  and particle size distribution.

- The ATP-content seems to be also a good parameter for the determination
of the activity of pine bark. Also the decrease in ATP-content during
composting gives a good relation with the total oxygen consumption.

This research has confirmed that also other factors can be used for
the following up of a composting process. We also have stated that each
organic material react on a different way on all the composting parameters
so that they have to be determined before starting composting of an
unknown material.

This study is only the beginning of a new approach in following the
composting process, but more research is still necessary to clearify the
influence of the different parameters.

4. LITERATURE
- VERDONCK, O., DE VLEESCHAUWER, D., PENNINCK, R. and DE BOODT, M. (1982).
The determination of optimal parameters for the composting of solid
wastes. Seminar "Composting of organic wastes", Denmark, pp. 1-25.

EARTHWORM COMPOST VERSUS CLASSIC COMPOST IN HORTICULTURAL SUBSTRATES

R. PENNINCK and O. VERDONCK
Laboratory of Soil Physics, Soil Conditioning
and Horticultural Soil Science
Faculty of Agricultural Sciences, State University Ghent, Belgium.

SUMMARY

Many earthworm breeders claim that the produced earthworm compost has
magnificent properties. A trial was set up to check the truth of this
allegation. Twelve different peat-based substrates were composed.
The raw materials which were used were earthworm compost (based on
horse manure), ripe compost (a mixture of tree bark and soy scrap
sludge), old tree bark (which was not composted) and perlite.
Physical and also chemical and physico-chemical analysis were carried
out. We found that the physical and chemical characteristics of the
substrates were much more important for the growth of Ficus bejamini
than the would-be fytohormones that are supposed to be produced in
earthworm compost.

1. INTRODUCTION
    The most important aim was to test the vermicompost and mixtures with
peat against other already used growing media for ornamental plants. The
last five years the production of vermicompost is tremendously increased,
but the problem is to find enough possible uses for this compost, and more
the higher prices of this compost must be justified with better results.

2. PHYSICAL AND PHYSICO-CHEMICAL PROPERTIES OF THE USED SUBSTRATES.
    In our trial, we tested following growing media:
    1. peat
    2. 75 % peat + 25 % vermicompost
    3. 50 % peat + 50 % vermicompost
    4. composted bark and soy scrap (Skorso)
    5. 75 % peat + 25 % Skorso
    6. 50 % peat + 50 % Skorso
    7. old sieved pine bark (minimum 10 years old)
    8. 75 % peat + 25 % sieved bark
    9. 50 % peat + 50 % sieved bark
   10. 90 % peat + 10 % perlite
   11. 75 % peat + 25 % perlite
   12. 50 % peat + 50 % perlite
The physico-chemical properties are given in table 1.
    The results in table 1 indicate that:
- the pH is ideal for the ornamental plants except number 3, which is too
  high
- the saltcontent is low enough so that the fertilisers (1 kg/m^3) necessary
  for the growth can be added without having difficulties for the plants
- the other parameters (% organic material, % $CaCO_3$ and total nitrogen)
  do not affect very much the fertility of the growing media

Table 1. Most important physico-chemical properties of tested substrates.

Number substrate	pH H_2O	Ec µS/cm	% organic material	% $CaCO_3$	Tot N mg/100 g
1	5,22	240	95,91	0	1099
2	6,63	371	65,79	3,22	1321
3	7,10	330	55,40	5,20	1273
4	6,40	372	59,46	2,72	1624
5	5,41	291	80,19	0,25	1309
6	5,85	324	75,73	1,49	1463
7	6,57	235	78,54	2,23	857
8	5,50	223	90,17	0	956
9	5,88	202	82,32	0,74	886
10	5,53	222	88,26	0	994
11	5,38	194	81,32	0	880
12	5,41	203	46,83	0,25	560

The physical parameters are more important for plantgrowth because the water/air relationship will determine the quality of the substrates. These parameters are given in table 2.

From the results given in table 2 we can conclude the following:
- all the used substrates have enough air capacity for optimal growth (normally between 20 and 30 %),
- the easily available water must be also between 20 and 30 %. Only substrates nrs 1, 2, 5 and 6 have the ideal easily available water. The substrates based on pure bark have extremely low available water. These substrates must be irrigated more frequently with lower amounts of water,
- concerning the maximum watercapacity we can say that the substrates based on peat have a high watercapacity. Those where the amount of peat is lower and replaced by bark, vermicompost or perlite have much lower watercapacity. The irrigation must be adapted as we have said for the easily available water.

3. Growing experiments

In the 12 substrates we have grown Ficus benjamini from the end of 1984 to the beginning of 1986. The substrates are fertilised in the beginning of 1985 with 1 kg/m^3 of a slow-release fertiliser 20-10-15-6. In April 1985 we determined the quality of the plants and we measured the height of the plants and the number of end-shoots of minimum 10-15 cm length. These results are shown in table 3.

These results indicate that peat, peat with vermicompost and peat with Skorso (barkcompost + soy scrap) give the same quality of plants. Here out we can decide that good composted material can be used as a substitute of peat and that vermicompost doesn't give better results. The old bark, which is more than 10 years old, has still problems of phytotoxicity and/or nitrogen immobilization.

The substrates aerated with perlite have propable too much drainage pores so that fertilisers are easily leached out, which we found back in the height of the plant and the number of endshoots.

Table 2. Physical parameters of used substrates

Number substrate	Bulk density (kg/dm³)	Total pore space %	Volume % moisture content at a suction of			Volume % air	Volume easily available water	Volume water buffering capacity	Maximum water-capacity in g/100 g dry material	Volume % after shrinkage
			10 cm	50 cm	100 cm					
1	0.085	94.17	63.14	34.41	27.84	31.03	28.73	6.57	755.81	72.38
2	0.136	90.62	64.60	41.56	35.25	26.02	23.05	6.30	490.71	62.54
3	0.183	87.40	56.28	40.76	35.51	31.12	17.52	5.24	332.17	58.83
4	0.260	82.05	42.99	34.52	32.05	39.06	8.48	2.47	220.50	-
5	0.132	90.88	55.53	34.78	29.23	35.35	20.75	5.55	482.11	73.62
6	0.176	87.88	60.24	38.03	32.53	27.64	22.21	5.50	374.06	73.74
7	0.184	87.30	45.31	38.63	37.12	41.99	6.67	1.52	294.02	77.17
8	0.113	92.20	56.09	40.80	34.16	36.11	15.30	6.63	577.96	-
9	0.136	90.65	52.68	42.33	36.66	37.98	10.34	5.68	466.40	70.99
10	0.103	93.22	56.34	37.28	27.67	36.88	19.06	9.61	644.49	68.97
11	0.102	93.70	51.69	33.59	25.25	42.00	18.11	8.34	643.10	71.66
12	0.107	94.03	43.33	30.39	22.49	50.70	12.94	7.90	550.30	80.99

817

Table 3. Growth results of Ficus benjamini.

Substrates	Height of the plants in cm					Number of total endshoots of minimum 10-15 cm length					
1	74,50	a b				43,00	a b				
2	77,44	a				45,44	a b				
3	71,72	a b c				41,89	a b				
4	72,72	a b				38,67		b c			
5	73,22	a b				43,11	a b				
6	71,22	a b c				48,44	a				
7	47,44				f	11,22					f
8	64,44		c d e			29,33			d e		
9	57,44		e			23,33			e		
10	65,17	c d				38,00		b c			
11	69,28	b c				38,56		b c			
12	61,50	d e				32,56		c d			

4. CONCLUSION

The composted bark and soy scrap and the vermicompost was found to be a suitable material as growing medium. These composts can substitute peat as a primary component in substrates for ornamental plants. Growth in mixture with peat as observed with Ficus benjamini was as good as in the pure peat substrates. The vermicompost seems to be not better than a normal prepared compost.

5. LITERATURE

- ANONYMUS (1984). Het commerciëel kweken van regenwormen en het onderzoek daarnaar. Nationale Raad voor Landbouwkundig Onderzoek, 's Gravenhage, Nederland, pp. 1-47.
- ANRED (1983). Le lombricompostage. Compost Information nr 11, 1ière semester 1983.
- VERDONCK, O. and PENNINCK, R. (1985). The composting of bark with soy scrap sludge. Acta Horticulturae, nr 172, pp. 183-190.

VERMICOMPOSTING OF DIFFERENT ORGANIC WASTES

G. PICCONE, B. BIASIOL, G. DE LUCA, L. MINELLI
Istituto di Chimica Agraria - Università di Torino (Italy)
I. CURRADO
Istituto di Entomologia Agraria - Università di Torino (Italy)

SUMMARY

A new vermicomposting tecnique for different materials is verified.
Periodical samplings were made for about one year in order to
evaluate the variability of biological and chemical parameters.
It seems convenient to decrease the period of vermicomposting and
subdue the materials to a real composting treatment.

1. INTRODUCTION

Vermiculture, which began in the United States in the 1930s,
developed in Italy only from the second half of the 1970s. In this period
fertilizing properties of vermicompost were extremely emphasized by
producers who determined very high prices.

At present this phenomenon is decreasing and few but big vermicomposting plants are diffusing and mainly treat different organic wastes
coming from agricultural and industrial activities. This gives rise to
various problems of new technologies and of the use of sufficiently
transformable materials that cause pollution in soil and plants.

This work aims to verify a new vermicomposting technique for
different materials: pharmaceutical industry sewage sludges, paper and
food manufacturing wastes and their mixtures.

2. MATERIALS AND METHODS

Earthworms of the species **Eisenia foetida** were reared following the
Airfoical system of the Società Agricola e Zootecnica in Pontesuero, Asti
(Italy). This new technique differs from traditional breeding system
because it uses plastic cylinders (120 x 100 cm).

The mechanized and gradual filling of the cylinders with undecomposed
organic wastes lasts for one year, after which the product is
mechanically collected. In this way the transformed material, that is
deposed at bottom of the cylinder, is separated from the undecomposed
superficial layer that contains almost all the worms. These worms are used
to prepare new cylinders.

Periodical samplings were made on the materials for about one year in
order to evaluate the variability of biological and chemicals parameters.
Temperature variations inside the cilynders and worm population densities
were checked and mesures of pH, moisture, ashes, total C and N, were
carried out. Also the contents of other fertilizing elements and of some
heavy metals were determined.

Table no. 1 - Mean values and standard deviation of pH, ashes, total C and N

Organic Wastes		pH	Ashes %	C tot %	N tot %	C/N
A		7,68	60,19	22,07	3,10	13,67
	sd	0,24	10,60	6,02	3,96	2,06
B		7,76	49,78	27,92	1,10	41,44
	sd	0,23	9,12	5,11	0,53	49,77
C		7,60	58,13	21,87	1,21	18,74
	sd	0,21	5,71	2,69	0,20	4,55
A x B		7,82	60,34	21,99	1,26	17,45
	sd	0,13	6,06	3,32	0,13	1,64
B x C		7,74	66,06	18,85	1,11	17,00
	sd	0,02	3,42	1,90	0,07	0,95

A = pharmaceutical industry sewage sludges;

B = paper manufacturing waste;

C = food manufacturing waste;

A x B and B x C = mixtures.

Table no. 2 - Mean values of contents of total elements

Organic Wastes	P %	K %	Na %	Ca %	Mg %	Fe %
A	0,82	0,26	0,19	8,80	0,54	0,99
B	0,57	0,29	0,09	8,02	0,53	1,00
C	0,98	0,26	0,18	12,23	0,60	1,08
A x B	0,77	0,31	0,12	10,12	0,51	1,14
B x C	0,80	0,22	0,16	12,20	0,61	1,19

Organic Wastes	Co ppm	Cr ppm	Cu ppm	Mn ppm	Ni ppm	Zn ppm
A	12	46	112	240	44	433
B	10	50	236	282	42	1015
C	14	89	74	200	66	495
A x B	10	63	168	248	58	762
B x C	14	77	148	255	52	770

A = Pharmaceutical industry sewage sludges;

B = Paper manufacturing waste;

C = Food manufacturing waste;

A x B and B x C = Mixtures.

RESULTS AND CONCLUSIONS

The poster shows the variability of some parameters such as temperature, number of worms and C/N. In tables no.1 and 2 synthetize the results of the chemical analyses. The obtained values take to the following conclusions:

a) validity of the Airfoical technique;
b) good development of worms in different materials; the best results came from paper and food manufacturing wastes;
c) quick transformation of the organic matter in the first mounths, slower in the successive period.

In conclusion, it seems convenient to decrease the period of transformation in cilynders and subdue the materials to a real composting treatment for a better stabilization and humification.

REFERENCES

(1) BOUCHE', M.B., (1984). Un méthode de mesure du débit d'elements dans un sol non pertubé:azote et carbone des lombriciens (Lumbricidae, Annelida). Pedobiologia. Vol.27, 197-206.

(2) BOUCHE', M.B., (1972). Lombriciens de France. Ecologie et Sistematique. Institut National de la Récherche Agronomique. Paris, pubbl. 72/2.

(3) DI DONNA, A., and GANAPINI, W., (1985). Limiti e possibilità di applicazione del vermicomposting al trattamento di rifiuti solidi e fanghi. Acqua aria. Vol.1,33-41.

(4) SYERS, J.K., and SPRINGETT, J.A., (1984). Earthworms and soil fertility. Plant and soil. Vol. 76, 93-104.

THERMODYNAMICS OF REFUSE/SLUDGE COMPOSTING

V. Stahlschmidt chem. eng.   DTH
DANO - V. Stahlschmidt
CH-6924 Sorengo, Switzerland.

Summary

The composting process, defined as an aerobic microbial digestion and transformation of mixed organic solid matter, is exotherm. Methods for the determination
of quantity heat produced and rate of heat production
during the process are described. The heat produced by
the composting process has a low temperature and in general terms a low value.
The heat can however be used with high efficiency and
with very low costs to evaporate moisture in the material being composted as for example in mixtures of refuse and sludge.

1. Introduction

Refuse being a mixture of all kind of material must be
treated before it can be used for composting and for quantitative study of the composting process. Usually the refuse
is treated by grinding, mixing, mixing with sludge and screening. The non compostables are separated and the rest, a finer more homogenous product can now be composted in windrows,
towers or various aerated spaces and the composting process
can be followed analytically.
Many composting studies have been made just by inserting
thermometers in more or less well defined windrows or chambers.
Temperature and heat production are however by no means proportional and it is the heat production which indicates the
progress of the process. By low temperature the heat production can grow exponentially with the temperature, then a
maximum is reached and thereafter the heat production is falling off quickly with rising temperature. This is characteristic for a biological process, A biological process si also dependent on the presence of moisture in correct quantity. No
biologic activity is possible with too low moisture content
and in the case of composting a too high moisture content fills
the pores of the material and reduces the acces of air.

2. Thermodynamics of composting

Thermodynamic is concerned with the quantities of material transformed and the heat developed in the process. Neither quantity can be measured in the normal process of composting in windrows or in chambers.

The simple procedure is to determine weight, composition and calorific value in the same material at start and at the end of the process, whereby only heat, water vapor and carbondioxyde have left the material and oxygen entered.

It is more convenient in a smaller scale and the following determinations refer to 23 kg raw material produced of refuse from a swiss town in a rotating drum with the addition of 35% centrifugated sewage sludge, placed in a rectangular plast container at an ambient temperature of 20°C. The relatively small mass does not permit the temperature in the material to rise over 45°C. Results:

		start	18 days	diff.
total weight	kg	23.0	15.0	- 8.0
moisture	"	13.0	7.0	- 6.0
organics (loss by ignit.)	"	6.4	4.0	- 2.4
inert	"	3.6	4.0	⊢ 0.4
cal.val of dry matter	Kal/kg	2.545	1.930	
total cal. value	Kal.	25.450	15.400	-10.050

The heat developed by aerobic fermentation of one kg of organic matter = 4.200 Kal., as to be expected, because the main part of the organic matter in the refuse are carbohydrates with calorific values of 3.900-4.100 Kal/kg and mainly a content in the refuse of fat increase this value.

In such a smallscale experiment only less than the half of the produced heat (10.050 Kal.) has been used for evaporation, the rest is lost from the container walls and the surface. In large windrows or fermentation chambers the heat loss is much smaller and the produced heat can escape only or mainly as water vapor. This requires two conditions, one that sufficient moisture is available and the other that sufficient air is available to transport this water vapor.

Keeping in mind, that the ingoing air is ambient air with its temperature and moisture content and that the outgoing air can not be much warmer than 40-50°C and not more than saturated, then it can be calculated from the properties of air and water vapor mixtures, that the evaporation of 1 kg of water needs 720(50° sat.) -780(40° sat.) Kalories and further that 1 kg of dry air can transport 32.5 Kal.(40°sat.) and 57.5 Kal. (50°sat.).

Now the necessary water evaporation and air quantity for disposal of the heat produced by the fermentation of 1 kg of organic matter = 4.200 Kal. can be calculated. Taking the average between 720-780 Kal/kg water = 750 Kal, then 5.6 kg water must be evaporated. Hereof the o.6 kg is the water produced by fermentation of 1 kg organic whereas the rest 5 kg of the moisture content of the original matter must be evaporated.

The air quantity necessary for transportation the produced 4.200 Kal/kg digested org. matter is 73 kg dry air (50° sat) and 130 kg kg dry air (40°C saturation).

These are large quantities compared with the air necessary for oxygen supply. 1 kg organic matter needs ca. 1 kg of oxygen or less than 5 kg air, or with the necessary surplus less than 20 kg air.

Another type of experiment, illustrated below, confirm the calculations. The moisture content in the first batches was 47, 51 and 56% at start (ca. 60% organic in dry matter) and in all these batches the material was completely dried out and fermentation stopped in a few days. A final batch 58% moisture did very well and in less than a week at 55-60°C the weight loss was 50% and 5 kg moisture was evaporated for each kg of organic matter digested.

Fig. I.

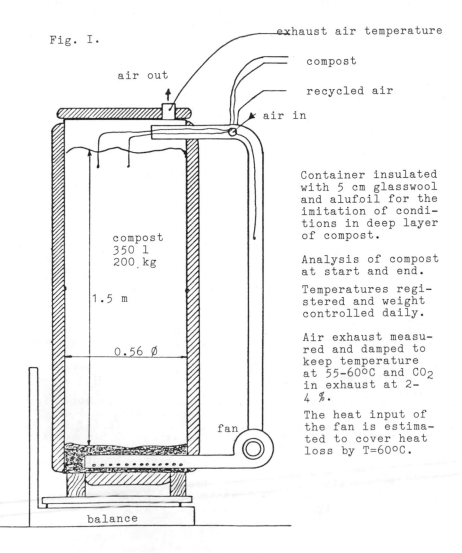

exhaust air temperature

compost

recycled air

air out

air in

compost
350 l
200 kg

1.5 m

0.56 ∅

fan

balance

Container insulated with 5 cm glasswool and alufoil for the imitation of conditions in deep layer of compost.

Analysis of compost at start and end.

Temperatures registered and weight controlled daily.

Air exhaust measured and damped to keep temperature at 55-60°C and CO_2 in exhaust at 2-4 %.

The heat input of the fan is estimated to cover heat loss by T=60°C.

3. Degree of fermentation

The fraction of the original organic matter in the raw compost which can be digested easily depends on the composition of the organic matter. Due to the prevalence of carbohydrates the ratio of carben to nitrogen C/N in raw compost is usually 30 or higher. In mature compost it must be below 20 and this can be achieved only by loss of carbon as carbondioxyde. This means that 40-50% of the original organic matter must be digested. A great part of the remaining organic matter is at the same time transformed to more stable products.

By the grinding and mixing of refuse in the much used rotating drums a certain prefermentation and selfheating is performed. Consequently the resulting raw compost can be matured in the average after the loss of 40% of the original organic matter. This has been confirmed by many batch experiments and also in many operating refuse/sludge composting plants.

This paper is concerned with the heat development during maturation, but it must be added that other aspects of maturation are important: the acidity in raw compost caused by production of organic acids, mainly acetic, must be reduced or in other words pH must change from 6.0-6.5 to over 7.0 at the end and the reducing state in raw compost (sol. carbohydrates and ammonia) must be changed to an oxydized state characterized through the presence of nitrate. Both changes result in a lower water solubility in the mature compost.

4. Content of organic matter in raw compost

The content of organic matter determines simply as loss by ignition in the dry matter can be from:
A) 50% found in european refuse 30-40 years ago and now in poor countries,
B) 60% found in european refuse 20 years ago and now in countries with medium standard of living and
C) 70% todays average composition in Europe and USA.

After maturation, defined here as a loss of 40% of organic matter the compositions will bo: A) 37.5%, B) 47.5% and C) 58.5% of organic in dry matter.

5. Moisture content in raw compost and mature compost

The moisture content in raw compost can be anywhere from 30-65%. In mature compost it is desirable to end up with 20-40% moisture. Somehow arbitrary 30% moisture is chosen in the following calculation, but the simple calculation can be made both with 20 and 40% moisture.

The calculation is aiming at the determination of the moisture content necessary in a raw compost in order to arrive at 30% moisture in the mature compost after having fermented 40% of the organic matter and evaporated 5 times as much by weight of moisture as organics digested (see before 2 & 3).

Starting with raw compost type A) the calculation is:

	moisture	organic	inert	total
raw compost	x	50	50	x + 100
fermentation loss	100	20	0	- 120
mature compost	34(30%)	30	50	114

x = 134 or moisture content 57.5% moisture/organic 2.68

The same calculations for other compositions:

	Raw compost composition organ. in dry matter	moisture	Ratio moisture/organic	weight loss
A)	50%	57.5%	2.68	51.4%
B)	60%	60.5%	2.54	57.0%
C)	70%	63.0%	2.44	62.0%

When the raw compost contains the indicated amount of moisture then no moisture in form of water or sludge can be added.

When the raw compost contains more moisture than indicated then it is not possible to produce mature compost with only 30% moisture.

When however the raw compost contains less moisture than indicated then it is not possible to produce mature compost without rehumidification, which means that a capacity for sludge drying is present.

The latter is the case in Europe and USA where it is normal to find refuse composition as follows: 30% moisture and 49% organic and 21% of inert.

How much concentrated sewage sludge with 80% moisture, 10% organic and 10% inert can be added to the above refuse and produce a compost with 30% moisture? About 130-140 tons of refuse is necessary for the production of 100 tons of raw compost and starting from these 100 tons, simple arithmetic, but too long to be quoted, yields the following result:

	total	moisture	organic	inert in tons
raw compost	100	30	49	21
sludge	165	132	16.5	16.5
mixture	265	162	65.5	37.5
fermentation loss	156	130	26	
mature compost	109	32	39.5	37.5

with 29.3 % moisture.

This means that one part of dry paper rich refuse can absorb and dry a little more than one part of concentrated sewage sludge and deliver less than one part of dried matured compost.

This is at the same time a substantial weight and volume reduction and a transformation of the unsympatic raw products into an inoffensive humus fertilizer or if so desired cover soil.

It is confirmed from large scale operation that equal parts of dry refuse can be composted with equal parts of concentrated sewage sludge. It must however be kept in mind, that the composition of the refuse can vary from season to season and not all refuse can absorb so much sludge.

6. Conclusion

It has been demonstrated how it is possible on the basis of a given composition of refuse and sludge to calculate the drying and transformation potential of the refuse.

COMBINED SOLID AND LIQUID DOMESTIC WASTES TREATMENT IN THE FRAME OF ECONOMY AND RATIONALITY

Francesco Vastola - Giovanni Grimaldi
Intervento Straordinario nel Mezzogiorno (Funds for Southern Italy)
Dep. Engeneering Unit - Dep. Completion Water Schemes.
Piazzale Kennedy, 20 - Roma - Italy

Summary
The paper describes the design and the "status" of realisation (now in progress, financed by "Cassa per il Mezzogiorno" (Funds for the South) Italian Government Organisation) of the Cosenza-Rende "integrated" solid and liquid domestic wastes treatment plant, serving, a large part of River Crati Walley (49 Municipalities with 300.000 inhabitants at the maximum of its potentiality).

Comparing the main cost parameters of this plant with the corresponding costs of that plants, in the same area, treating separately solid and liquid wastes the paper highlights the optimisation reached with the adopted scheme.

The plant will treat the maximum flow of 1 c.m./day of wastewater and 300 ton./day of domestic solid wastes and sludge. The liquid effluent will be reused in agricolture. The plant will produce 35.000 t/year of compost, 1.500 t/year of iron metals, 13 GWh/year of electric energy (burning the refuse) of this amount only 8 GWh will be self consumed.

The experience carried out with the Cosenza-Rende plant (and the other ones in progres in Southern Italy) highlights the need of coordination between the studies and territorial plans concerning solid wastes disposal (task in charge of the Regions by D.P.R. 915/82) and the water's clean-up ones (act 319/76) as to obtain -where it is possible and convenient-the united and integrated operation of wastes treatment plan that will give a better environment protection, less treatment costs and enhance of the recovery products.

The paper concludes with the hope if a State act imposing the above mentioned coordination.

1 - INTRODUCTION

Into the wide and complex problems of territorial planning, the rational definition of localizing the so-called "ecological" infrastructures is undoubtedly important, meaning by that all the works concerning the invironment protection from pollution.

The Italian legislation until now has taken the discipline of the various fields about environment protection into account in different times. However this chronological diversity has caused such a differentiation in work and institution influencing irrationally the different types of interventions. It is enough to say that the Law n. 615 (antismog) dated 13.7.1966; the Law n. 319 (water protection from pollution) dated 10.5.1976 and DPR 915 (solid wastes disposal) dated 10.9.98 they concern the discipline of wastes treatment into the three physical states of aggregation. While the first of these rules technically concerns with the prevention and depuration of the aeriform emissions, (works are generally circumscribed within the limits of the preparations the same imissions produce) the other ones, on the contrary discipline the construction of important works whose localization and management provoke enormous problems to the environment (hygienia, economic political, psychological).

The "sectoriality" of these rules (prevalently adopted carrying aut communitary directions) has already caused a dramatic repercussion in some actual cases, sometimes until the nonsense. Some works, whose purpose was to protect Environment, as regards, for example, the waste-water depuration, present negative changes in environment concerning disposal of the produced sludges; and that's happening for the non-coordination of planning and realization of the two different types of nifrastructures. The only point of contact between L. 319/76 and DPR 915/82 is the quasi-identity of composition of the Interministerial Commitees provided rispectively for Artt. 3 and 5 integrated with the Minister of Ecology by law 27.2.1984 n. 18.

We register numerous operative efforts of rationalization of the interventions because to face this situation, but they are restricted on episodic initiatives because of an organic unity of general direction locks.

We are going to mention now the following interventions alredy started, or in progress, in Southern Italy, whose "integrated plant" has become much more possible through programmatic arrangements than through an institution direction.

They are the integrated plants from:

- Cosenza-Rende (CS): now under construction serving the first lot, 200.000 nihabitants for s.d.w. and for water depuration (that may be lifted to 300.000 when plant is completed).
- Lamezia Terme (CS): finished , but not yed in operation, serving about 150.000 inhabitants for s.d.w. and 80.000 for liquid domestic depuration in addition to industrial wastes.
- Tempio Pausania (SS): now under bid (with the system of the so-called contract-competition); serving a first lot of 45.000 inhabitants for s.d.w. and 31.000 for liquid domestic depuration (that may be lifted respectively to 65.000 and 36.000 when plant is completed) in addition to industrial wastes.
- Villacidro (CA): planned; for the use of 150.000 inhabitants for s.d.w. and 110.000 inhabitants for liquid domestic depuration in addition to industrial wastes.
- Depuration in the Neapolitan area, in the frame of the Gulf of Naples clean-up Special Project; such a general plan concerns with the integrated plant of water depuration and treatment of s.d.w. for about 6 millions of inhabitants residents.

Among these interventions, we take the experience made for Cosenza-Rende plant into account. We are going to examine how this work has been realized, showing the technical and the most significant economic aspects until its actual realisation. That's necessary to talk about the problem of the integrated plant, at least as regards the whole territory of the Southern

Italy where an organic intervention about solid wastes disposal has to be still projected.

2 - Cosenza-Rende Plant

2.1.- Territorial localization of intervention

The "Cassa per il Mezzogiorno", had to carry out the following projects in Crati Wally Basin (Prov. Cosenza).
- waste-water depuration of the Cosenza-Rende great area, reaching afterwards others 13 municipalities and whose target was to re-use the depurated water according to the purposes of the Special Plan "Water Schemes of Calabria";
- Solid domestic wastes disposal in the same great area, likewise arranged in a very large basin of wastes including 49 municipalities.

This coincidence has permitted, after preliminary orographic controls and optimisation of solid and liquid wastes, the unification of intervention into a single integrated plant for treatment of solid and liquid domestic wastes with electric power production from combustion of residuals.

2.1.1- Water: Liquid domestic depuration besides solving the hygienic-sanitary problem, brings many other well-watered resources serving 800 ha of lands in the Crati walley.
Costs for collecting canalisation and centralized treatment are undoubtedly cheaper than single Municipalities treatments besides bringing about a considerable concentrated water source, otherwhise scattered.

2.1.2- Solid domestic wastes: (s.d.w.) Studies about technical-economic possibilities, enlarged to the whole region, have taken Crati Wally basin as the best district for picking, carriage and s.d.w. disposal, with afflux centre coincident to one of liquid treatment.
The biological plant necessities exalt sludge value into the qualitative and quantiative compost production, while the thermo-energetic ones induce the receiving of high calorific power wastes as well (agroforestal, industrial, etc.). The "Cassa per il Mezzogiorno" has managed a preliminary quali-quantiative analysis about s.d.w. of the place as starting point of designed developments.
On this basis a contract-competition has been carried out and the chosen project has been given out by contract in 1983.

2.2.- Potentiality and plant data: Taken into account the different coefficients of afflux concerning all the wastes, the equivalent inhabitants served for both services in 1995, respectively for 700 lt/sec. and 150 t/d about s.d.w., have been estimated at 200.000, while in 2015 (finishing) 300.000 eq. inh. served respectively for 1.200 lt/sec. and 250 t/d.

2.2.1 -Lquid line: Mixed water flow - Rain flow rate wholly treated mechanically. Pullings down BOD 13.125 kg/g; (248 mg/lt); N. Tot. 243 kg/g (40 mg/lt); W. 750 kg/g (14,2 mg/lt);S.S. 11.250 kg/g (212 mg/lt).

Treatment phases

- pretreatments:screening (coarse and fine), sand removal, grease
separationand preaeration, mc. 460 (mc. 900 finish);
- primary sedimentation: mc. 600 (1200), circular settling tanks with
seraping bridge. Pullings down BOD 5,35%, S.S. 90%;
- biological: mc. 9.600 (14.400), rectangular tanks N. 4 (6) fine bubbles
aeration. Pulling down BOD 35%,re-cycle sludges - Nitrification by max
pulling down of ammoniacal N. N. Total removed 70%, remaining 25 mg/lt;
- final sedimentation: mc. 8.000 (15.000) circular praisers n. 4 (4);
- disinfection: by sodium hypocholorite.

2.2.2- **Sludge line**: n. 2 (3) densifiers for primary and secondary sludges
for 470 mc (700) concentration in going out 5% of S.S.;subsequent partial
aeration tank: 1000 mc (1500) for 24 h by superficial turbines to avoid
risks of anaerobic matter until the composting phase; dehydration by **band-
presse** at 30% of S.S.

2.2.3- **Solid wastes line**: Potentiality 150 t/d (250) of s.d.w. + 50 b/d of
sludges; 20 t/h; operation 6 days/7, it is formed by the following steps:

- Weighing, pit, 5(3) d. pile mc 3600; ristarting with bridge crane grab and
slab puller;
- Pretreatments: bagopener,magnetic separation, pre-size reduction,
classification by rotating drum, refining organic material. The organic
fraction of s.d.w. , equivalent to 105 t/d (175) added to 50 t/d (73) of
sludges, is introduced ot the composting phose;residuals (40%) to the
combustion;
- Composting phase carried out into 1(2) drumming basins 31 m. in diameter
supplied with rotating bridge crane carryng a battery of 18 screws for
mixing. Holding time 4-5 days. Service gallery below for forced aeration
and automatic paraments control (ptt, H2O, temp.), material is transferred
to the final stage (20/30 days) - Subsequent storage for 3 months.
- Residuals treatment inorganic particles into landfill; combustible
material into 1 (2) grate Kilns 65 t/d by post-combustion chamber;pulling
dowm at moist of fumes with water of plant. Bailer with water-pipe:
production vapour at 38 atm, 400C, 7,5 t/h, turbo-alternator 1500 Kw, 6000
V. Electric connected parallely with Enel System.

2.2.4- **Additional works:** offices, workshop, laboratory and landfill for
inorganic and slags.

2.2.5- **Recoveries**:

- energy: 9,5 millions kWh (13 millions), of this amount 6,5 (8) will be
self consumed, all that remains to Enel;
- composto: 31.000 t/year;
- iron materials: 1,320 t/year.

2.3.- Present state of realisation

Works of plant construction have presently (March 1986) reached at advancement of the 50% about and have presented at first particular trouble, during the realisation of foundations, in consequence of a remarkable presence of underground waters. It is possible, however, to show some steps already realized, among them the final stage of compost, solid wastes receiving, works of liquid linking and graving, the primary sedimentation various services, outside arrongements such as the road of approach, containment works and so on.

2.4.- The "integrated plant"

The characteristics of integration may be synthesized into the following aspects:

2.4.1- Plant:

- management works unified (services, various arrangements, inclosure, centralization controls, etc.);
- direct and immediate contribution of fresh sludges to the composting (saving the relative stabilization and disposal);
- water available for all the necessitas of the cycle combustion production of energy and for other services, with recycle on the purified plant (saving the special plant);
- sufficient energy, used also for depuration plant, otherwise exigent, all or in part, of outside electric power;
- environment factors (physical and psychological) reduced from two to one;
- managing economy.

2.4.2- Functional

The solution of the hygienic-sanitary problem integrates important needs in agricolture; they permit an increasing income in the areas helped either by irriguous water or use of compost.

2.4.3- Economic

As regards costs, already determined by contracts, compared calculations have been made. Two solutions have been taken into account, that one adopted and that one equivalent divided in two plants having the same potentiality as for inhabitants served.

All the components that distinguish quantiatively and processistically the two solutions have been considered exluding combustion of residuals and recovery of energy; that's to point out the processistics espect of the co-composting of sludges and solid wastes ad essential element of "integration".

Distinct plants solution requires, in any case, the complete stabilization of sludges that, for plants of this capacity, risults suitable through anaerobic digestion, while as regards the destination of the same sludges, the following techniques, until now recognized practicable, have been examined:

a)natural drying up in aerated static composting (only suitable for small plants);
b)landfill of sludges;
c)landfill mixed to solid wastes;
d)incineration connected to the depuration plant;
e)carriage to the composting plant, at a reosonable distance;
f)composting sludges, connected to the depuration plant;
g)direct agricultural use of sludges.

Sludges that have not undergone any thermophil phase present still great hygienic-sanitary risks and, therefore, under this aspect, a), b), c), e) and g) hypothesis result remarkably problematical; the latter, in particular, hasn't had practice and generalization yet, in spite of the numerous experiments and studies that have taken place in various centres.
As regards the use, there is no doubt the only way to give lands effective increase of organic matter of any origin, is that one of composting and therefore c) and f) hypothesis are preferred.
As regards disposal costs, these ones result particularly high, in decreasing order, for d), f), b) and a) hypothesis.
e) (carriage to the composting plant) and c) (landfill mixed to solid domestic wastes) hypothesis are the most economic (for investment and management).
On the ground of these considerations an analysis of costs has taken place conforming, for homogeneity of valuations, to the prices of all works which attend the comparison, showed by the some firm into the offer of project. As regards the distinet plants, for example, we have considered that sludges could be destined half to the composting plant and half to landfill mixed to solid domestic wastes.
We are going to show now, omitting an analytical description, the following meaningful-results of the comparison, with up-to-date values of 1986, including all the emolument fees of Administration (included the probable future revisional costs)

	INVESTMENT COSTS L/inhab.	OPERATING COSTS L/inhab. yearly
"Integrated"plant		
- Liquid section and sludges	58.220	
- Composting section	95.200	10.740
Amount	135.420	
Distinct plants		
- Liquid plant and sludge	94.140	9.500
- Composting plant	113.040	6.400
Amount	207.180	15.900

You notice that the difference between the two solutions is about 26% concerning investment costs and 32% operation (excluded amortizations and deducted recoveries for compost and iron; these ones for an amount of L. 1600 /inhab. about). It is evident that the difference concerning operation results much more marked because of the managing unification sees drastically reduced staff employment which constitutes a heavy item in the same operation.

It is also important to notice that the greatest economic profit of investment into the unification, is given to the depuration plant with 38% against 16% of composting plant.

2.4.4- Processsistical :the processistical more delicate component of integration is undoubtedly the immediate use of primary and secondary sludges, which represents the "fulcrum" of the plant activity.

This action, not sufficiently proved yet in any plant knoun until to day, consist of a partial aerobic stabilization done before of dehydration and agitation together with the organic matter for the following phase composting. It has been foreseen, in fact, an aeration basin with a volume and capacity of oxidization equivalent to 25% about than one relative to a complete stabilization of sludges; more over this volume acts as lung in liquid phase excluding any storage of sludges during dehydrated phase in order to avoid risks of anaerobic matter. This expedient wants to constitute a prudence to check carefully during operation; it should recognize, practically, the must suitable point of technical-economic balance between the degree of stabilization of sludges and their pathogen control moving from a step to the other.

3 - The "integration" in an Institution Plan

The analysis of the actual case discussed, is the starting point for presenting the problem of Southern Italy because here-more than elsewhere. The organization of the services for liquid and solid wastes disposal is still at the beginning. However, this extrapolation, even if rough, tries to give meaningful suggestions in order that the problem con be discussed in the appropriate decision-marking centres.

3.1- Comparison of COSTS: The population of Southern and Insular Italy is 20 millions about of inhabitants residents with a pro-capite production of solid domestic wastes of 0.6835 kg/inh. per day; daily production 13.900 t. and yearly production 5.000.000 t. (CNR data Project Energy Aim 1980.)

Examining the various regional situations (orography, road conditions,distribution of pupulation, etc.) it is possible to say that the mumber of inhabitants served by integrated plants (including the initiatives already started) is not less than 50%.

If we apply the above-mentioned economv to this rate of inhabitants the probable saving as regards investment costs would be about 573 billions Italian Lire; likewise, as regards management, this economy would be about 52,6 billions lire per year, which saved at the moment (15 years 7%) would give an amount of 480 billions.

The total economy, therefore, would be not less than 1000 billions only in Southern Italy.

3.2.- <u>Considerations:</u>   the importance of the rationalization of liquid and solid treatments passes over the purely economic aspect,   certainly not to neglect, and deals with the following important points:

- it is well-known the management problem of depuration plants, usually " pulverized " over the territory and prevalently relied on local Organizations (Comunes) lacking in suitable technical economic structures. On the contrary, when such a plant will be included in a structure techonologically more important, the whole monagement could not present the same lacks because of the non-function would risult so macrospic to effect the public opinion and provoke the necessary attentions and cares;
- sludges would constitute no more the most problematical and expensive part of the single depuration plant, but a mealth for composting, either qualitative (increase of phosphorus and lowering of the relation C/N) or quantiative (1 of dehydrated sludge provedes 400 kg abcut of compost);
- who has a direct experience about construction of "ecological" plants, will knows the difficulties of localizing the work in front of oppositions (sometimes derived from emotional reasons and not information) so that when it is possible to reduce the two cases of socio-environment nature to one, a remarkable step towards the realization of work has been done.

4 - <u>Conclusion</u>

As already mentioned in the introduction, the achievement of the objective is not possibile in a rational and effective way over the whole territory if the present rules concerning Environment, in general, and the states of wastes aggregation, in particular, are not connected eiher in the directive part or in operating and managing structures.

However, we can say that our State has already got until today single and modern rules lined up with those ones of the most advanced Nations, but the foreseen results have some difficulty in appearing also for complained non -connection.

The most immediate necessity concerns with directions from Interministerial Committees Instituted respectively by law 319/76 and DPR 915/82, in order that the "Regional Plans of water's clean-up" and the "Regional Plans of wastes disposal" are coordinated and integrated by suitable rules, in all those parts that concern the problem here discussed.

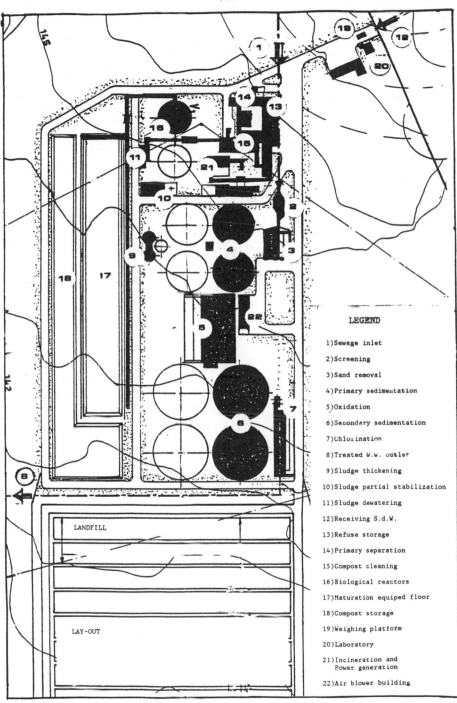

LEGEND

1) Sewage inlet
2) Screening
3) Sand removal
4) Primary sedimentation
5) Oxidation
6) Secondary sedimentation
7) Chlorination
8) Treated w.w. outlet
9) Sludge thickening
10) Sludge partial stabilization
11) Sludge dewatering
12) Receiving S.d.W.
13) Refuse storage
14) Primary separation
15) Compost cleaning
16) Biological reactors
17) Maturation equiped floor
18) Compost storage
19) Weighing platform
20) Laboratory
21) Incineration and
    Power generation
22) Air blower building

LANDFILL

LAY-OUT

LIST OF PARTICIPANTS

ADAMS, W.
Univ. College of Wales
Dept. Biochemistry
UK – ABERYSTWYTH (WALES)

AGUILA SANCHO, J.
Faculty of Biology
Univ. Barcelona
V. Augusta 275-2°
E – 08021 BARCELONA

ALLIEVI, L.
Dip. Scienze e Tecnologie Alim.
e Microbiologiche
V. Celoria 2
I – MILANO

ANGELI, A.
Soc. Agricola e Forestale Azienda
"Il Terzo" Roselle
I – GROSSETO

ANOLFO, M.
Consorzio C.S.R. Bassa Friulana
I – S. GIORGIO DI NOGARO (UD)

ANNUNZIATA, A.
Enichemfibre
Via Passatelli 61
I – MATERA

ARIIS, A.
Assessore all'Ecologia
Comune di Udine
I – UDINE

ARRIGONI, R.
De Bartolomei SpA
V. Settembrini 7
I – 20124 MILANO

AVNIMELECH, Y.
Israel Inst. of Technology
Technion City
IL – 32000 HAIFA

BABOS, L.
Risorse s.r.l.
Via Roma 163
I – S. GIOVANNI AL NATISONE (UD)

BALLONI, W.
Ist. Microbiologia Agraria
V. delle Cascine 27
I – FIRENZE

BARBERA, A.
Fertimont Spa
V. dell'Azoto 15
I – 30175 P.TO MARGHERA (VE)

BARBERIS, R.
Ist. Piante da Legno e Ambiente
C.so Casale 476
I – 10132 TORINO

BARBINA, G.
Villaggio Primavera
I – BASALDELLA DI CAMPOFORMIDO (UD)

BARGAGNI, M.
Confcoltivatori
V. Giovanni XXIII
I – 84014 NOCERA INFERIORE (SALERNO)

BOUFELDJA, B.
Pavillon Paul-Comtois
Univ. Laval
Bureau 1316
CDN – SAINTE-FOY, QC G1K 7P4

BARAZZETTA, R.
Secit
V. C. Farini 81
I – 20159 MILANO

BARILLI, A.
Centro Ricerche Produzioni Animali
V. Crispi 3
I – 42100 REGGIO EMILIA

BARRILLA', D.
SO.GE.IN.
Via del Giorgione 63
I – 00100 ROMA

BARUZZINI, L.
C.R.S.A.
Via Sabbatini 5
I – 33050 POZZUOLO DEL FR. (UD)

BAUDUIN, M.
Fac. Sciences Agronomiques
de l'Etat
av. de la Faculté 20
B - 5800 GEMBLOUX

BENETTI, G.
Snamprogetti - Div. Ecologia
V. Toniolo 1
I - 61032 FANO (PS)

BERNARDI, D.
Comune di S. Quirino
P.zza Roma 1
I - 33080 S.QUIRINO (PN)

BESSEGA, G.
Assessore LL.PP.
Comune di Caneva
I - 33070 CANEVA (PN)

BIASIOL, B.
Ist. Chimica Agraria
V. P. Giuria 15
I - 10126 TORINO

BIDLINGMAIER, W.
Inst. für Siedlingswasserbau
und Abfallwirtschaft Univ.
Bandtäle 1
D - 7000 STUTTGART 80

BIZZARRI, P.
Saceccav Depurazioni Sacede
V. S. Marta 19
I - 20123 MILANO

BLOCK, C.
Grodan Div. of Rockwoll
Lapinus BV
Industrieweg 15
NL - 6040 KD ROERMOND

BONETTI, M.
E.N.E.A.
V. Anguillarese 301
I - 00060 ROMA

BOTTAI, A.
Termomeccanica It.
V. del Molo 1
I - 19100 LA SPEZIA

BOTTER, R.
Assoc. Comuni Comprensorio
Basso Piave
P.zza Indipendenza 19
I - 30027 S. DONA DI PIAVE (VE)

BOUTIN, P.
C.E.M.A.G.R.E.F.
Groupement de Bordeaux
av. de Verdun 50, B.P. 3
F - GAZINET 33610 CESTAS PRINCIPAL

BOVE, L.
Assessorato Agricoltura
Regione Calabria
I - 88100 CATANZARO

BRAVAR, L.
Risorse s.r.l.
Via Roma 163
I - S. GIOVANNI AL NATISONE (UD)

BRECCIA, W.
Snamprogetti
Div. Ecologia
V. Toniolo 1
I - 61032 FANO (PS)

BURES, S.
Bures SA
Badal 19-21
E - 08014 BARCELONA

CARLOZZI, P.
Centro di Studio dei
Microorganismi Autotrofi
P.zzale delle Cascine 27
I - FIRENZE

CARLESI, F.
De Bartolomei SpA
V. Settembrini 7
I - 20124 MILANO

CASSARINO, C.
Cassarino Environmental
Services Inc.
Crooked S. Road - Box 261
USA - LYNDEBORO N.H. 03082

CAVAZZA, L.
Ist. Agronomia
Via Filippo Re
I - 40100 BOLOGNA

CAYROL, F.
Valsrga SA
ZI Vessdargnes
Atelier selais n. 2
rue H
F - 34740 VESSDARGNES

CEGARRA ROSIQUE, J.
Centro de Edafologia y Biologia
Aplicada del Segura
Apdo. 195
E - 30003 MURCIA

CEQUIEL SOLE, R.M.
Fac. de Farmacia Univ. Barcelona
Nucleo Univ. de Pedralbes
E - 08028 BARCELONA

CHEN, Y.
Hebrew Univ. of Jerusalem
Fac. of Agriculture
PO Box 12
IL - 76-100 REHOVÔT

CHIESA, G.
Castagnetti Spa
V. Acqui 86
I - 10090 CASCINE VICA
   (RIVOLI) (TO)

CIANCIOLO, G.
CCID
Castello 5620
I - 30122 SAN LIO (VE)

CHIOZZI, C.
c/o Peabody Stranich
Palazzo Verrocchio
Centro Direzionale
Milano 2 - Segrate
I - 20090 MILANO

CIRIANI, G.
Presidente V Commissione
Regione Autonoma
Friuli-V. Giulia
Casella Postale 523
I - 34100 TRIESTE

CIRILLO G.
CasMez
V. Cinzia
I - NAPOLI

CISCATO, P.
V. S. Lucano 4
I - 32100 BELLUNO

COCCHI, G.
De Bartolomei Spa
V. Settembrini 7
I - 20124 MILANO

COMOLLI, P.
A.M.S.A.
V. Olgettina 25
I - 20132 MILANO

CONA, D.
c/o CIVIT
Comune di Verona
V.le Palladio 10
I - 37138 VERONA

COPPOLA, S.
Ist. Microbiologia Agraria
v. dell'Università 100
I - 80055 NAPOLI PORTICI

COROMINAS ROIG, E.
Consejeria de Agricultura
C.R.I.D.A.C.
Apdo. 60 La Laguna
E - TENERIFE

CORTELLINO, R.
Regione Friuli-V. Giulia
Ufficio Affari Comunitari
Rapporti Esterni
V. S. Francesco 41
I - 34100 TRIESTE

CRUANAS TARRADAS, R.
Fac. Farmacia Univ. Barcelona
Zona Univ. Pedralbes
E - 08028 BARCELONA

CURZEL, G.
V. del Capitel 28
I - 38040 MARTIGNANO (TN)

D'ANGELO, U.
CasMez
Via Cinzia
I - NAPOLI

D'ANGELO, G.
Centro Lombardo Incremento
Floro-Orto-Frutticoltura
V.le Raimondi 48
I - 22070 MINOPRIO (CO)

DANIELI, A.
Daneco SpA
S. Giovanni al Nat.
I - UDINE

DAUDIN, D.
Chambre d'Agriculture de
Vaucluse
Bld. St. Michel 40
F - 84000 AVIGNON

DAVIES, S.
President Royer Fondry &
Machine Co.
Pringle Street 158
P.O. Box 1232
USA - KINGSTON PA 18704

DE BAERE, L.
ARBIOS Société Anonyme
av. P. Pastur 361
B - 6100 MONT-SUR-MARCHIENNE

DE BERTOLDI
Istituto di Microbiologia
Agraria
Universita di Pisa
Via del Borghetto 80
I - 56100 PISA

DE BLIGNIERES, F.-X.
A.N.R.E.D.
Square la Fayette 2
B.P. 406
F - 49004 ANGERS CEDEX

DEGANO, E.
Presidente Comunità Montana
Valli del Torre
V. Frangipane
I - 33017 TARCENTO (UD)

DE JAMBLINNE, E.
L.C.M. Belgium N.V.
Turnhoutsebaan 131
B - 2230 SCHILDE

DELLA CASA, A.
Termomeccanica Italiana SpA
V. del Molo 1
I - 19100 LA SPEZIA

DEL MAZO SUARES, V.
av. Henry Ford 2040
BRASIL - 03109 SAO PAULO

DENARO, G.
Assessorato Agricoltura
Prov. di Milano
Settore Servizi Tecnologici
C.so di Porta Vittoria 27
I - 20100 MILANO

DE NOBILI, M.
Ist. Produzione Vegetale
Univ. di Udine
P.zzale Kolbe
I - 33100 UDINE

DE SILGUY, C.
Assemblée Permanente des
Chambres d'Agriculture
av. George V. 9
F - 75008 PARIS

DESERTI, G.
SUFER SpA
C.so Giovecca 81
I - 44100 FERRARA

DEL ZAN, F.
C.R.S.A.
Via Sabbatini 5
I - 33050 POZZUOLO DEL FR. (UD)

DE VITTOR GIAN SANTE
V. Bortolotti 55
I - 33034 FAGAGNA (UD)

DEVONALD VIVIAN, G.
Bath College of
Higher Education
Newton Park
UK - BATH BA2 9BN

DIACOLI, P.
V. Patriarcato 2
I - 33043 CIVIDALE DEL FRIULI (UD)

DIAZ, L.
Cal Recovery Systems
160 Broadway Suite 200
USA - RICHMOND CA 94804

DI TOMMASO, D.
Tecnitalia
P.zza S. Francesco di Paola 7
I - FIRENZE

DUCATI, F.
Assess. Tutela Ambiente
Prov. Autonoma Bolzano
V. C. Battisti 21
I - 39100 BOLZANO

EROSS, I.
Agricultural College of
Kaposvar
7401 PO Box 16
H - KAPOSVAR

ESTRADA, J.
Marquesa Caldas de Montbui 4
E - 08032 BARCELONA

FAGGIOTTO, M.
Unione Cooperative
V. Battuti Rossi 6/A
I - 47100 FORLI

FARNETI, A.
Snamprogetti
Div. Ecologia
V. Toniolo 1
I - 61032 FANO (PS)

FERRANDI, L.
E.N.E.A.
V. Anguillarese 301
I - 00060 ROMA

FERRANDO, B.
Italimpianti
V. 12 Ottobre 2
I - 16121 GENOVA

FERRARI, G.
Ecobancatecnologica
V. S. Felice 21
I - 40122 BOLOGNA

FERRERO, G. L.
Commission of the Europ. Comm.
rue de la Loi 200
B - 1049 BRUXELLES

FERRERO, G.
Officine Meccaniche Ferrero
V. Privata Trento 4
I - 17047 VADO LIGURE

FOLETTO, B.
E.S.A.V.
S. Croce 1187
I - 30125 VENEZIA

FORTI, D.
Ist. Agrario Prov.le
I - 38010 S. MICHELE ALL'ADIGE (TN)

FUNKE, U.
Fachhochschule Rheinland-Pfalz
Abt. Mainz II
An der Bruchspitze 50
D - 6500 MAINZ

FUSTINONI
Politec
V. Pasubio 16
I - 20063 CERNUSCO (MI)

GALLI, E.
IREV-CNR
Area della Ricerca di Roma
V. Salaria km 29,300
ROMA
I - 00016 MONTEROTONDO SCALO

GANAPINI, W.
IPRA 2
V. Ceradini
I - 20100 MILANO

GASSER, J.
Laverstock Park West 9
LAVERSTOCK
UK - SALISBURY WILTS SP1 1QL

GAVAZZI, C.
Ist. Agronomia Generale
Univ. Cattolica S. Cuore
I - 29100 PIACENZA

GENEVINI, P.
Ist. Chimica Agraria
V. Celoria 2
I - 20133 MILANO

GERRITS, J.
Mushroom Experim. Station
P.O. Box 6042
NL - 5960 AA HORST

GIACOMELLI, G.
Greenland Recupero Ambientale
V. Roma 47
I - 33040 PRADAMANO (UD)

GIORDANO, M.V.
Regione Toscana
V. di Novoli 26
I - 50100 FIRENZE

GIOVANNOZZI SERMANNI, G.
Ist. Chimica Agraria
Univ. della Tuscia
V. S.C. de Lellis
I - 01100 VITERBO

GODDEN, B.
Lab. de Microbiologie
Univ. Libre de Bruxelles
av. E. Gryson 1
B - 1070 BRUXELLES

GOMEZ-RAYA, R.
Cons. Europeo Abono Organico
V. Augusta 128
E - 08006 BARCELONA

GRIMALDI, G.
V. T. Salvini 2/A
I - 00100 ROMA

GUIDI, G.
Ist. Chim. del Terreno del CNR
V. Corridoni 78
I - 56100 PISA

HADAR, Y.
Dept. Microbiology
and Plant Pathology
P.O. Box 12
IL - 76-100 REHOVOT

HALL, J.
Water Research Centre
Henley Road
Medmenham
P.O. Box 16
MARLOW
UK - BUCKINGHAMSHIRE SL7 2HD

HANSSENS, W.
Commission des C.E
rue de la Loi 200
B - 1049 BRUXELLES

HIDDING, A.
Advisory Service for Soils
and Fertilizing
Min. of Agriculture
P.O. Box 55
NL - 6700 AB WAGENINGEN

HOITINK, H.
Dept. Plant Pathology
O.A.R.D.C.
USA - WOOSTER OH 44691

HOOGHOUDT, H.O.
Min. of Housing, Physical
Planning and Environment
Dokter Van der Stamstraat 2
P.O. Box 450
NL - 2260 MB LEIDSCHENDAM

HOVSENIUS, G.
Tunavägen 32
S - 19451 UPPL. WÄSBY

IADEROSA, V.
C.C.I.D.
Castello 5620
I - 30122 SAN LIO (VE)

INGHILESI, E.
E.N.E.A.
V. Anguillarese 301
I - 00060 ROMA

JACOVELLINI, G.
Via Passo Lombardo 322
I - 00137 ROMA

JADOT, F.
S.A. Engrais Rosier
rue du Berceau 1
B - 7592 MOUSTIER (HT)

JODICE, R.
Ist. Piante da Legno e Ambiente
C.so Casale 476
I - 10132 TORINO

JUSTE, C.
I.N.R.A.
Centre de Recherche de Bordeaux
P.B. 131
F - 33140 PONT-DE-LA-MAYE

KAPETANIOS, E.
Unified Assoc. Municipalities
of Attica
Panepistimion 56
GR - ATHENS

KARELLIS, M.
Mayor of Heraklion City
GR - HERAKLION

843

KARPATI, I.
"Vermicultura" Ltd.
PO Box 2
H - 8641 FONYOD

KRAUSS, P.
Inst. für Organische Chemie
auf der Morgenstelle 18
D - 7400 TUBINGEN

KRESSE, E.
Coop. Extension Assoc.
Oneida County R.I.
Box 136, 2nd. St.
USA - ORISKANY N.Y. 13323

KUBOTA, H.
Tokyo Inst. Technol.
Research Lab. Resources Util.
4259 Nagatsuta
Midori-ku
JAPAN - 227 YOKOHAMA

KUHNEN, O.
Postfach 156
A - 1091 WIEN

LANTIERI ODOARDO, H.A.
av. Henry Ford 2040
BRASIL - 03109 SAO PAULO

LANTIERI ODOARDO, J.F.
av. Henry Ford 2040
BRASIL - 03109 SAO PAULO

LE BOZEC, A.
CEMAGREF
Div. "Genie Rural"
av. de Cucillé 17
B.P. 1312
F - 35016 REBBEN CEDEX

LECHNER, P.
Technische univ.
Inst. Wassergüte und
Landschaftswasserbau
Karlsplatz 13
A - 1040 WIEN

LEVASSEUR, J.P.
O.T.V. Le Doublon
av. Dubonnet 11
F - 92400 COURBEVOIE

LEVI MINZI, R.
Ist. Chimica Agraria
V. S. Michele 2
I - 56100 PISA

L'HERMITE, P.
Commission des C.E
rue de la Loi 200
B - 1049 BRUXELLES

LOPEZ REAL, J.
Univ. of London
Biological Sciences Dept.
Wye College
Wye, Ashford
UK - KENT

LUCIANER, A.
Ist. Agrario Prov.le
I - 38010 S. MICHELE ALL'ADIGE (TN)

LUCARELLI, M.T.
V. Carlo Dossi 15
I - 00137 ROMA

LYNCH, J.
Plant Pathology and Mic. Dept.
Glasshouse Crops Res. Inst.
Littlehampton
UK - WEST SUSSEX BN17 6LP

MACKERLE, S.
c/o Studio FDL
V. Locchi 8
I - 37124 VERONA

MANIOS, V.
Inst. Viticulture, Vegetable
Crops and Floriculture
GR - 711 10 HERAKLION CRETE

MARANGONI, W.
Consorzio Comunità Collinare
del Friuli
V. Mazzini 7
I - S. DANIELE (UD)

MARESCOTTI, F.
Saceccav Depurazioni sacede
V. S. Marta 19
I - 20123 MILANO

MARTINELLI, P.
Italimpianti
V. 12 Ottobre 2
I - 16121 GENOVA

MASHALI, A.
B-709 AGLS F.A.O.
V. delle Terme di Caracalla
I - 00100 ROMA

MATTIONI, R.
Risorse s.r.l.
V. Roma 163
I - S. GIOVANNI AL NATISONE (UD)

MEZZANOTTE, V.
Ist. Ingegneria Sanitaria
Redazione
Politecnico di Milano
V. F.lli Gorlini 1
I - 20151 MILANO

MILLI, D.
C.M.C. Ravenna
V. Trieste 76
I - RAVENNA

MINGUZZI R.
V. Romea Sud 270
I - 48100 RAVENNA

MONACO, A.
Ist. Colt. Arboree
V. dell'Università
I - 80100 NAPOLI

MONTORI, U.
Edilter
V. della Cooperazione 21
I - 40129 BOLOGNA

MORI, A.
Via dei Cilli 54
I - 19100 LA SPEZIA

MORRISETIE, D.
Pavillon Paul-Comtois
Bureau 1316
CDN - SAINTE-FOY, QC G1K 7P4

MOUSTY, P.
Anjou-Recherche
rue d'Anjou 52
F - 75008 PARIS

MOZZANICA, E.
Laboratorio REI
V. Dante Spaggiari 10
I - PARMA

MULLER, K.
National Agency of
Environmental Protection
Strandgade 29
DK - 1401 COPENHAGEN

NASSISI, A.
Ripartizione Rete
Agrometeorologica 29027
Gariga di Podenzano
I - PIACENZA

NYNS, E.-J.
Unité de Génie Biologique
Univ. Catholique de Louvain
Place Croix du Sud 1/9
B - 1348 LOUVAIN-LA-NEUVE

ONGARO, D.
Degremont Italia SpA
V. Crocefisso 27
I - MILANO

OOSTHOEK, J.
N.V. VAM
Staringgebouw
NL - 6703 BC WAGENINGEN

ORRICO, B.
CasMez
V. Cinzia
I - NAPOLI

PALAZZO, S.
Sotenco Equipamentos
Rua da Joaquina Ramalho 1048
BRASIL - 02065 SAO PAULO

PARLADE', P.
Consorcio de Abono Organico
V. Augusta 128
E - 08006 BARCELONA

PARIS, P.
Fac. Agraria
Univ. Cattolica S. Cuore
I - 29100 PIACENZA

PASCOLINI, G.
Direzione Regionale Agricoltura
V. C. Percoto
I - 33100 UDINE

PASELLA, M.
I - 07023 CALANGINUS (SASSARI)

PEASE, M.
The World Bank
Emena Region
H Street N.W. 1818
USA - WASHINGTON DC

PELTEKIAN, A.
idem c.s.

PENNINCKX, M.
Lab. de Microbiologie de
l'Univ. Libre de Bruxelles
av. E. Gryson 1
B - 1070 BRUXELLES

PEREIRA NETO, J.T.
Dept. of Civil Engineering
Univ. of Leeds
UK - LEEDS LS2 9JT

PEREZ DIAZ, M.L.
Consejeria de Agric. CRIDAC
Apdo. 60
La Laguna
Islas Canarias
E - TENERIFE

PETRUZZELLI, G.
Ist. Chim. del Terreno del CNR
V. Corridoni 78
I - 56100 PISA

PEZZONI, R.
Passavant Impianti
V. D. Chiesa 80
I - 20026 NOVATE MILANESE (MI)

PICCONE, G.
Ist. Chim. Agraria Università
I - 10100 TORINO

PIGNATELLI, A.
V. Galeazza 49
I - 40132 BOLOGNA

PIPPO, E.
Comune di Pordenone
Uff. Tutela Acque
Rip. LL.PP.
I - 33170 PORDENONE

PITTALUGA, F.
Regione Toscana
V. di Novoli 26
I - 50100 FIRENZE

PIZZO, G.
CasMez
Interv. Straordinario
Mezzogiorno
Rip. I - Div. II
P.zza Kennedy 20
I - 00144 ROMA

PLANELLS, F.
Ayuntamiento Valencia
c/ Guillém de Castro 12
E - 46001 VALENCIA

POIRAUD, G.
A.N.R.E.D.
rue Victor Lagrange 8
F - 69007 LYON

POL, C.
Soc. Promover
B.P. 135
Labege
F - 31318 INOPOLE

POTVIN, D.
La Tourbe du Saint-Laurent
C.P. 238 Rg St-Jean-Baptiste,
St. Henri
CDN - CTE LEVIS, QC GOR 3EO

PRESCIMONE, V.
SECIT SpA
V. C. Farini 81
I - 20159 MILANO

PUDELSKI, T.
Academy of Agriculture
Vegetable Dept.
ul. Dabrowskiego 159
PL - 60-594 POZNAN

QUATANNENS, T.
PVBA Quatannens
Kalsijdebrug 12
B - 8245 GISTEL/SNAASKERKE (WV)

RAMONDA, G.
c/o AMNU
V. Boselli 84
I - PIACENZA

RATTOTTI, A.
C.R.P.A.
V. Crispi 3
I - 42100 REGGIO EMILIA

RAVIV, M.
Agric. Research Organization
Newe-Yaar Experiment Station
P.O. Haifa 31999
ISRAEL

RENAGRI
V. dei Redentoristi 6
I - 00186 ROMA

RICCHIERI, E.
V. Riva di Reno 58/4
c/o AMIU
I - 40100 BOLOGNA

RIDHA, H.
C.S.T.E.
Inst. Nat. Recherche Scient.
et Technique
Bordj Cedria B.P. 95
TUNISIA - HAMMAN-LIF

RIFFALDI, R.
Ist. Chimica Agraria
V. S. Michele degli Scalzi 2
I - 56100 PISA

RIVARA, V.
Italimpianti
P.zza Piccapietra 9
I - 16121 GENOVA

ROBOGIANAKIS, E.
Leof. Dimokratias 47
GR - 71306 HERAKLION CRETE

ROBOTTI, A.
Az. Agr. Sperimentale
'V. Tadini'
loc. Gariga
Podenzano
I - 29027 PIACENZA

ROMANO, N.
c/o Comunità Montana Carnia
I - TOLMEZZO (UD)

ROMITI, R.
Ist. Zootecnica e Alimentaz.
Animale
Univ. di Bologna
V. S. Giacomo 11
I - 40100 BOLOGNA

ROSSELLI, A.
Comitato Regionale Conf
Coltivatori
C.so Meridionale 18
I - 80100 NAPOLI

ROVERANO, V.
AGIP GIZA
V. Schwerin 4
I - 42100 REGGIO EMILIA

SAETTI, G.
UNIECO s.r.l.
V. Puccini 17
I - 42100 REGGIO EMILIA

SALEM, N.
Fac. Agriculture
Univ. of Gent
Coupure Links 653
B - 9000 GENT

SANA VILASECA, J.
Escola d'Agric. de Barcelona
Urgell 187
E - 08036 BARCELONA

SANTARATO, B.
Direttore AMNU
P.zza V. Emanuele II 1
I - 45100 ROVIGO

SANTI, E.
Degremont Italia
V. Crocefisso 27
I - 20122 MILANO

SANTORI, M.
IRSA - CNR
I - 00100 ROMA

SASSAROLI, G.
GE.SE.N.U. SpA
V. della Molinella 7
I - 06100 PERUGIA

SAVIOZZI, A.
Ist. Chimica Agraria
V. S. Michele degli Scalzi 2
I - 56100 PISA

SAYAG, D.
Lab. de Pédologie
Physico-Chimie du Sol
Ecole Nat. Sup. Agronomique
av. de Muret 145
F - 31076 TOULOUSE CEDEX

SCHEFFOLD, K.
Wambrechiesstrasse 5
D - 4152 KEMPEN 1

SCHELTINGA, H.
Ministry VROM-NL
P.O. Box 9013
NL - 6800 DR ARNHEM

SILVESTRO, G.
A.M.R.R.
V. Germagnano 50
I - 10156 TORINO

SINDICI A.

SMIT J.P.N.
Vuil Afvoer Maatschappij
Staringgebouw
NL - 6703 BC WAGENINGEN

SOGNI, S.
V. B. Sestini 241
I - 51030 PONTENUOVO (PISTOIA)

SOINI, L.

SOLIVA TORRENTO', M.
Escola d'Agric. de Barcelona
Urgell 187
E - 08036 BARCELONA

SOTTANI, N.
Az. Industriali Municipalizzate
V. S. Biagio 76
I - 36100 VICENZA

SPAGGIARI, G.C.
Az. Gas Acqua Consorziale
V. Gastinelli 12
I - 42100 REGGIO EMILIA

SPIGONI G.

SPINOSA, L.
CNR - IRSA
V. F. de Blasio 5
I - 70123 BARI

STAHLSCHMIDT, V.
DANO S.A.
V. delle Dobbie 2
CH - 6924 SORENGO

STELLU, V.
Ministero Agricoltura
Direz. Prot. Ambiente
Aharnon Str. 2
GR - 10176 ATHENS

STENTIFORD, E.
Univ. of Leeds
Dept. of Civil Engineering
UK - LEEDS LS2 9JT

STICCHI, F.

STRABBIOLI, G.
Ist. Sperim. per la Fruttic.
V. Fioranello 52
Ciampino Aeroporto
I - 00040 ROMA

STRAUCH, D.
Ins. für Tiermedizin und
Tierhygiene
Univ. Hohenheim 460
Postfach 700562
D - 7000 STUTTGART

TARARAN, S.

TAWTIC ISMAIL, M.
Cleansing & Beautification
Authority
Abbasia Square bild. 3
EGYPT - CAIRO

TEIXEIRA, E.
L.C.M. Belgium N.V.
Turnhoutsebaan 131
B - 2230 SCHILDE

TENTI, R.
AMIU
V. Rotta 67
I - 48100 RAVENNA

THALMANN, K.
ORFA
Rütistrasse 2
CH - 5400 BADEN

THIELLA, R.
Lanerossi SpA
V. Pasubio 149
I - 36015 SCHIO (VI)

THOSTRUP, P.
Crone and Koch
Jernbanegade 22
DK - 8800 VIBORG

TITONE, P.
Centro Lombardo Incremento
Flor-Orto-Frutticoltura
V.le Raimondi 48
I - 22070 MINOPRIO (CO)

TOMATI, U.
IREV-CNR
Area della Ricerca di Roma
V. Salaria km. 29,300
I - 00016 MONTEROTONDO SCALO

TONIOLO, A.
c/o Cons. Smaltimento Rifiuti
Comune di Schio
V. Pasini 33
I - 36015 SCHIO (VI)

TORBEN H.
Gendan Ltd.
Holbergsgade 26
DK - 1057 COPENHAGEN K

TRASINO, G.
Assess. Agricoltura Regiona
Autonoma
Valle d'Aosta
P.zza Deffeyes 1
I - 11100 AOSTA

TRILLAS GAY M., I.
Dep. Fisiologia Vegetal
Univ. Barcelona
Avda. Diagona 637-647
E - 08028 BARCELONA

TUIS, I.
Assoc. Comuni Comprensorio
Basso Piave
P.zza Indipendenza 19
I - 30027 S. DONA DI PIAVE (VE)

TUNNEY, H.
Agricultural Institute
Johnstown Castle Res. Centre
IRL - WEXFORD

TURELLO, A.
Predium Ecologica s.r.l.
V. Roma 47
I - PRADAMANO (UD)

TUSNADI, L.
"Vermicultura" Ltd.
P.O. Box 2
H - 8641 FONYOD

VACCHINA, E.
Lombardia Risorse SpA
V. Dante 12
I - 20100 MILANO

VAN USSEL, G.
AGROFINO Products N.V.
Moerenstraat Brug IV
B - 2370 ARENDONK

VASSELLI, G.

VASTOLA, F.
CasMez
Interv. Straord. Mezzogiorno
Rip. I - Div. II
P.zza Kennedy 20
I - 00144 ROMA

VEKEMNAS, X.
Lab. de Microbiologie de
l'Univ. Libre de Bruxelles
av. E. Gryson 1
B - 1070 BRUXELLES

VERDONCK, O.
Lab. of Soil Physics
Fac. of Agriculture
Coupure Links 635
B - 9000 GENT

VIEL, M.
E.N.S.A.T.
av. de Muret 145
F - 31076 TOULOUSE CEDEX

VOLPE, G.

VON DER MEDE, K.
Bennogasse 8/19
A - 1080 WIEN

WALLER, P.
FISONS plc
Horticulture Division
Levington Research Station
Ipswich
UK - 1P10 ONG. SUFFOLK

WEJDLING, E.
Alehusvej 18
DK - 4160 HERLUFMAGLE

WITTER, E.
Wye College
Wye,Ashford
UK - KENT TN27 5AH

YOLDI LOPEZ, B.
Equipo Lorea
C/ Mercaderes 21 - 2'
Pamplona
E - 31001 NAVARRA

ZANCHI, L.
AGIP GIZA
V. Schwerin 4
I - 42100 REGGIO EMILIA

ZELARI, A.
V. Pratese 504
I - CHIAZZANO (PISTOIA)

ZORZI, G.
Ist. Agrario Prov.le
I - 38010 S. MICHELE ALL'ADIGE (TN)

ZUCCONI, F.
I.C.A. Università
I - 80055 NAPOLI

INDEX OF AUTHORS